THE AMERICAN PAGEANT

THE
AMERICAN PAGEANT

A History of the American People

FIFTEENTH EDITION

VOLUME 2: SINCE 1865

David M. Kennedy
Stanford University

Lizabeth Cohen
Harvard University

WADSWORTH
CENGAGE Learning

Australia • Brazil • Japan • Korea • Mexico • Singapore • Spain • United Kingdom • United States

The American Pageant, 15e
Volume 2: Since 1865
Kennedy/Cohen/Bailey

Senior Publisher: Suzanne Jeans

Senior Sponsoring Editor: Ann West

Senior Development Editor: Margaret McAndrew Beasley

Assistant Editor: Megan Chrisman

Editorial Assistant: Patrick Roach

Managing Media Editor: Lisa Ciccola

Marketing Communications Manager: Glenn McGibbon

Marketing Program Manager: Caitlin Green

Marketing Coordinator: Lorreen R. Towle

Senior Content Project Manager: Carol Newman

Senior Art Director: Cate Rickard Barr

Senior Print Buyer: Sandee Milewski

Senior Rights Acquisition Specialist: Jennifer Meyer Dare

Production Service/Compositor: Lachina Publishing Services

Photo Research: Pembroke Herbert and Sandi Rygiel, Picture Research Consultants & Archives, Inc.

Text Designer: Diane Beasley

Cover Designer: Connal Hughs, Cabbage Design

Cover Image: Flag made of wood and stars, Montana/©Sue Smith/Shutterstock

For product information and technology assistance, contact us at
Cengage Learning Customer & Sales Support, 1-800-354-9706

For permission to use material from this text or product,
submit all requests online at **www.cengage.com/permissions**.
Further permissions questions can be e-mailed to
permissionrequest@cengage.com.

Library of Congress Control Number: 2011939008

Student Edition:

ISBN-13: 978-1-111-83143-1

ISBN-10: 1-111-83143-2

Wadsworth
20 Channel Center St
Boston, MA 02210-1202
USA

Cengage Learning is a leading provider of customized learning solutions with office locations around the globe, including Singapore, the United Kingdom, Australia, Mexico, Brazil and Japan. Locate your local office at **international.cengage.com/region**

Cengage Learning products are represented in Canada by Nelson Education, Ltd.

For your course and learning solutions, visit **www.cengage.com**. Purchase any of our products at your local college store or at our preferred online store **www.cengagebrain.com**.

Instructors: Please visit **login.cengage.com** and log in to access instructor-specific resources.

Printed in the United States of America
1 2 3 4 5 6 7 15 14 13 12 11

ABOUT THE AUTHORS

David M. Kennedy is the Donald J. McLachlan Professor of History Emeritus and Co-Director of The Bill Lane Center for the Study of the North American West at Stanford University, where he has taught for four decades. Born and raised in Seattle, he received his undergraduate education at Stanford and did his graduate training at Yale in American Studies, com-

bining the fields of history, economics, and literature. His first book, *Birth Control in America: The Career of Margaret Sanger* (1970), was honored with both the Bancroft Prize and the John Gilmary Shea Prize. His study of the World War I era, *Over Here: The First World War and American Society* (1980; rev. ed., 2005), was a Pulitzer Prize finalist. In 1999 he published *Freedom from Fear: The American People in Depression and War, 1929–1945*, which won the Pulitzer Prize for History, as well as the Francis Parkman Prize, the English-Speaking Union's Ambassador's Prize, and the Commonwealth Club of California's Gold Medal for Literature. At Stanford he teaches both undergraduate and graduate courses in American political, diplomatic, intellectual, and social history, as well as in American literature. He has received several teaching awards, including the Dean's Award for Distinguished Teaching and the Hoagland Prize for Excellence in Undergraduate Teaching. He has been a visiting professor at the University of Florence, Italy, and in 1995–1996 served as the Harmsworth Professor of American History at Oxford University. He has also served on the Advisory Board for the PBS television series, *The American Experience*, and as a consultant to several documentary films, including *The Great War*, *Cadillac Desert*, and *Woodrow Wilson*. From 1990 to 1995 he chaired the Test Development Committee for the Advanced Placement United States History examination. He is an elected Fellow of the American Academy of Arts and Sciences and of the American Philosophical Society and served from 2002 to 2011 on the board of the Pulitzer Prizes. Married and the father of two sons and a daughter, in his leisure time he enjoys hiking, bicycling, river-rafting, flying, sea-kayaking, and fly-fishing. He is currently writing a book on the American national character.

Lizabeth Cohen is the Howard Mumford Jones Professor of American Studies in the history department of Harvard University. In 2007–2008 she was the Harmsworth Professor of American History at Oxford University. Previously she taught at New York University (1992–1997) and Carnegie Mellon University (1986–1992). Born and raised in the New York metropolitan area,

she received her A.B. from Princeton University and her M.A. and Ph.D. from the University of California at Berkeley. Her first book, *Making a New Deal: Industrial Workers in Chicago, 1919–1939* (1990), won the Bancroft Prize in American History and the Philip Taft Labor History Award, and was a finalist for the Pulitzer Prize. In 2008 it was reissued in a second edition with a new introduction. Her article "Encountering Mass Culture at the Grassroots: The Experience of Chicago Workers in the 1920s" (1989) was awarded the Constance Roarke Prize of the American Studies Association. Her most recent book, *A Consumers' Republic: The Politics of Mass Consumption in Postwar America* (2003), explored how an economy and culture built around mass consumption shaped social life and politics in post–World War II America. An article related to this book, "From Town Center to Shopping Center: The Reconfiguration of Community Marketplaces in Postwar America" (1996), was honored as the best article in urban history by the Urban History Association and received the ABC-CLIO, America: History and Life Award for the journal article that most advances previously unconsidered topics. She is currently writing a book, *Saving America's Cities: Ed Logue and the Struggle to Renew Urban America in the Suburban Age*, on urban renewal in American cities after World War II. At Harvard, she teaches courses in twentieth-century American history, with particular attention to the intersection of social and cultural life and politics, and in 2011 she was named the Interim Dean of the Radcliffe Institute for Advanced Study. Before attending graduate school, she taught history at the secondary level and worked in history and art museums. She continues to help develop public history programs for general audiences through museums and documentary films. She is married to an historian of modern France, with whom she has two daughters. For leisure, she enjoys swimming and bicycling with her family, watching films, and reading fiction.

Thomas A. Bailey (1903–1983) was the original author of *The American Pageant* and saw it through its first seven editions. He taught history for nearly forty years at Stanford University, his alma mater. Long regarded as one of the nation's leading historians of American diplomacy, he was honored by his colleagues in 1968 with election to the presidencies of both the Organization of American Historians and the Society for Historians of American Foreign Relations. He was the author, editor, or co-editor of some twenty books, but the work in which he took most pride was *The American Pageant*, through which, he liked to say, he had taught American history to several million students.

BRIEF CONTENTS

Maps xix
Figures xxi
Tables xxiii
Preface xxv

22 The Ordeal of Reconstruction 1865–1877 465

Part Four

Forging an Industrial Society

1865–1909

23 Political Paralysis in the Gilded Age 1869–1896 488

24 Industry Comes of Age 1865–1900 512

25 America Moves to the City 1865–1900 539

26 The Great West and the Agricultural Revolution 1865–1896 575

27 Empire and Expansion 1890–1909 608

Part Five

Struggling for Justice at Home and Abroad

1901–1945

28 Progressivism and the Republican Roosevelt 1901–1912 638

29 Wilsonian Progressivism at Home and Abroad 1912–1916 661

30 The War to End War 1917–1918 678

31 American Life in the "Roaring Twenties" 1919–1929 700

32 The Politics of Boom and Bust 1920–1932 728

33 The Great Depression and the New Deal 1933–1939 751

34 Franklin D. Roosevelt and the Shadow of War 1933–1941 778

35 America in World War II 1941–1945 798

Part Six

Making Modern America

1945 TO THE PRESENT

36 The Cold War Begins 1945–1952 830

37 The Eisenhower Era 1952–1960 860

38 The Stormy Sixties 1960–1968 889

39 The Stalemated Seventies 1968–1980 916

40 The Resurgence of Conservatism 1980–1992 942

41 America Confronts the Post–Cold War Era 1992–2011 965

42 The American People Face a New Century 990

APPENDIX

Documents A1
    Declaration of Independence
    Constitution of the United States of America
    Presidential Elections
    Presidents and Vice Presidents
    Admission of States
    Estimates of Total Costs and Number of Battle Deaths of
       Major U.S. Wars

Glossary of Key Terms A27

Index I1

CONTENTS

Maps   xix
Figures   xxi
Tables   xxiii
Preface   xxv

22   The Ordeal of Reconstruction   1865–1877   465

The defeated South • The freed slaves • President Andrew Johnson's
Reconstruction policies • The Black Codes • Congressional Reconstruction
policies • Johnson clashes with Congress • Military Reconstruction, 1867–
1877 • Freed people enter politics • "Black Reconstruction" and the Ku Klux
Klan • The impeachment of Andrew Johnson • The legacy of Reconstruction

CHRONOLOGY / KEY TERMS / PEOPLE TO KNOW / TO LEARN MORE   484–485

✴ EXAMINING THE EVIDENCE   Letter from a Freedman to His Old Master, 1865   468

✴ VARYING VIEWPOINTS   How Radical Was Reconstruction?   483

Part Four

Forging an Industrial Society
1865–1909
486

23   Political Paralysis in the Gilded Age   1869–1896   488

Ulysses S. Grant, soldier-president • Corruption and reform in the post-Civil
War era • The depression of the 1870s • Political parties and partisans • The
Compromise of 1877 and the end of Reconstruction • The emergence of Jim
Crow • Class conflict and ethnic clashes • Grover Cleveland and the tariff •
Benjamin Harrison and the "Billion Dollar Congress" • The Homestead Strike
• The Populists • Depression and Dissent

CHRONOLOGY / KEY TERMS / PEOPLE TO KNOW / TO LEARN MORE   510–511

✴ MAKERS OF AMERICA   The Chinese   500

✴ VARYING VIEWPOINTS   The Populists: Radicals or Reactionaries?   510

24 Industry Comes of Age 1865–1900 **512**

The railroad boom • Speculators and financiers • Early efforts at government regulation • The Rise of Mass Production • Lords of industry • The gospel of wealth • Reining in the Trusts • Industry in the South • The laboring classes • The rise of trade unions

CHRONOLOGY / KEY TERMS / PEOPLE TO KNOW / TO LEARN MORE 538
✳ EXAMINING THE EVIDENCE The Photography of Lewis W. Hine 531
✳ MAKERS OF AMERICA The Knights of Labor 534
✳ VARYING VIEWPOINTS Industrialization: Boon or Blight? 537

25 America Moves to the City 1865–1900 **539**

The rise of the city • The "New Immigrants" • Settlement houses and social workers • Nativists and immigration restriction • Churches in the city • Evolution and education • Booker T. Washington and W. E. B. Du Bois • Literary landmarks and intellectual achievements • The "New Woman" and the new morality • Realism reshapes American literature, art, and architecture • The commercialization of popular entertainment

CHRONOLOGY / KEY TERMS / PEOPLE TO KNOW / TO LEARN MORE 572–574
✳ MAKERS OF AMERICA The Italians 546
✳ EXAMINING THE EVIDENCE Manuscript Census Data, 1900 548
✳ MAKERS OF AMERICA Pioneering Pragmatists 560

26 The Great West and the Agricultural Revolution
1865–1896 **575**

The conquest of the Indians • The mining and cattle frontiers • Free lands and fraud • The fading frontier • The industrialization of agriculture • Farmers protest • The People's Party • Workers in revolt • Bryan versus McKinley, 1896

CHRONOLOGY / KEY TERMS / PEOPLE TO KNOW / TO LEARN MORE 606–607
✳ MAKERS OF AMERICA The Plains Indians 582
✳ EXAMINING THE EVIDENCE Robert Louis Stevenson's Transcontinental Journey, 1879 591
✳ THINKING GLOBALLY The Great Frontier 592
✳ VARYING VIEWPOINTS Was the West Really "Won"? 605

27   Empire and Expansion   1890–1909   608

The sources of American expansionism • The Hawaii Question • The Spanish-American War, 1898 • The invasion of Cuba • Acquiring Puerto Rico (1898) and the Philippines (1899) • Crushing the Filipino insurrection • The Open Door in China • Theodore Roosevelt becomes president, 1901 • The Panama Canal • Roosevelt on the World Stage

CHRONOLOGY / KEY TERMS / PEOPLE TO KNOW / TO LEARN MORE   634–635

✳ MAKERS OF AMERICA   The Puerto Ricans   618
✳ MAKERS OF AMERICA   The Filipinos   624
✳ THINKING GLOBALLY   The Age of Empire   632
✳ VARYING VIEWPOINTS   Why Did America Become a World Power?   634

Part Five

Struggling for Justice at Home and Abroad
1901–1945
636

28   Progressivism and the Republican Roosevelt   1901–1912   638

Campaigning against social injustice • The muckrakers • The politics of progressivism • Women battle for reforms and against the saloon • Roosevelt, labor, and the trusts • Consumer protection • Conservation • Roosevelt's legacy • The troubled presidency of William Howard Taft • Taft's "dollar diplomacy" • Roosevelt breaks with Taft

CHRONOLOGY / KEY TERMS / PEOPLE TO KNOW / TO LEARN MORE   659–660

✳ THINKING GLOBALLY   "Why Is There No Socialism in the United States?"   642
✳ EXAMINING THE EVIDENCE   *Muller v. Oregon*, 1908   648
✳ MAKERS OF AMERICA   The Environmentalists   652

29   Wilsonian Progressivism at Home and Abroad   1912–1916   **661**

The election of 1912: The New Freedom versus the New Nationalism • Wilson, the tariff, the banks, and the trusts • Wilson's diplomacy in Latin America • War in Europe and American neutrality • The reelection of Wilson, 1916

CHRONOLOGY / KEY TERMS / PEOPLE TO KNOW / TO LEARN MORE   676–677

✴ VARYING VIEWPOINTS   Who Were the Progressives?   675

30   The War to End War   1917–1918   **678**

America goes to war, 1917 • Wilsonian idealism and the Fourteen Points • Propaganda and civil liberties • Workers, blacks, and women on the home front • Drafting soldiers • The United States fights in France • Wilsonian peacemaking at Paris • The League of Nations • The Senate rejects the Versailles Treaty

CHRONOLOGY / KEY TERMS / PEOPLE TO KNOW / TO LEARN MORE   698–699

✴ EXAMINING THE EVIDENCE   "Mademoiselle from Armentières"   689

✴ VARYING VIEWPOINTS   Woodrow Wilson: Realist or Idealist?   697

31   American Life in the "Roaring Twenties"   1919–1929   **700**

The "red scare," 1919–1920 • The KKK returns • Immigration restriction, 1921–1924 • Prohibition and gangsterism • The Scopes trial • A mass-consumption economy • The automobile age • Radio and the movies • Modernism molds Jazz Age literature and culture • Economic boom and bust

CHRONOLOGY / KEY TERMS / PEOPLE TO KNOW / TO LEARN MORE   726–727

✴ MAKERS OF AMERICA   The Poles   706

✴ EXAMINING THE EVIDENCE   *The Jazz Singer*, 1927   717

✴ THINKING GLOBALLY   Modernism   722

32 **The Politics of Boom and Bust** 1920–1932 **728**

The Republicans return to power, 1921 • Disarmament and isolation • The Harding scandals • Calvin Coolidge's foreign policies • The international debt snarl • Herbert Hoover, cautious progressive • The great crash, 1929 • Hoover and the Great Depression • Hard Times • Aggression in Asia • "Good Neighbors" in Latin America

CHRONOLOGY / KEY TERMS / PEOPLE TO KNOW / TO LEARN MORE 749–750

✴ EXAMINING THE EVIDENCE Lampooning Hoover, 1932 745

33 **The Great Depression and the New Deal** 1933–1939 **751**

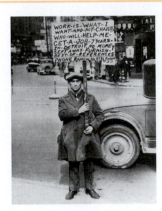

Franklin D. Roosevelt as president • The Hundred Days Congress, 1933 • Relief, Recovery, and Reform • Depression Demagogues • Women in public life • The National Recovery Administration • Aid for Agriculture • The dust bowl and the Tennessee Valley Authority • Housing and Social Security • A new deal for labor • The election of 1936 • The Supreme Court fight, 1937 • The New Deal assessed

CHRONOLOGY / KEY TERMS / PEOPLE TO KNOW / TO LEARN MORE 776–777

✴ VARYING VIEWPOINTS How Radical Was the New Deal? 775

34 **Franklin D. Roosevelt and the Shadow of War** 1933–1941 **778**

Roosevelt's early foreign policies • German, Japanese, and Italian aggression • The Neutrality Acts, 1935–1939 • The Spanish Civil War • Isolation and appeasement • The horrors of the Holocaust • France falls and Britian totters • FDR's historic third term • The Lend-Lease Act and the Atlantic Charter, 1941 • The Japanese attack on Pearl Harbor, December 7, 1941

CHRONOLOGY / KEY TERMS / PEOPLE TO KNOW / TO LEARN MORE 796–797

✴ EXAMINING THE EVIDENCE Public-Opinion Polling in the 1930s 787

35 America in World War II 1941–1945 798

The shock of war • The internment of Japanese Americans • Mobilizing the economy • Women in wartime • The war's effect on African Americans, Native Americans, and Mexican Americans • The economic impact of war • Turning the Japanese tide in the Pacific • Campaigns in North Africa (1942) and Italy (1943) • "D-Day" in Normandy (France), June 6, 1944 • Germany surrenders, May 1945 • The atomic bombing of Hiroshima and Nagasaki, August 1945 • V-J Day, August 15, 1945

CHRONOLOGY / KEY TERMS / PEOPLE TO KNOW / TO LEARN MORE   826–827

✶ MAKERS OF AMERICA   The Japanese   800

✶ EXAMINING THE EVIDENCE   Franklin Roosevelt at Teheran, 1943   817

✶ THINKING GLOBALLY   America and the World in Depression and War: A Study in Contrasts   822

✶ VARYING VIEWPOINTS   The Atomic Bombs: Were They Justified?   825

Part Six

Making Modern America
1945 to the Present
828

36 The Cold War Begins 1945–1952 830

Postwar prosperity • The "Sunbelt" and the suburbs • The postwar baby boom • Harry S Truman as president • Origins of the Cold War • The United Nations and the postwar world • Communism and containment • The Truman Doctrine, the Marshall Plan, and NATO • Anti-communism at home • The Korean War, 1950–1953

CHRONOLOGY / KEY TERMS / PEOPLE TO KNOW / TO LEARN MORE   858–859

✶ EXAMINING THE EVIDENCE   Advertising Prosperity, 1956   833

✶ MAKERS OF AMERICA   The Suburbanites   836

✶ THINKING GLOBALLY   The Era of Globalization   842

✶ VARYING VIEWPOINTS   Who Was to Blame for the Cold War?   857

37 The Eisenhower Era 1952–1960 860

Affluent America • Working women and feminism • Consumer culture in the 1950s • The election of Dwight D. Eisenhower • The menace of McCarthyism • Desegregating the South • *Brown* v. *Board of Education* (1954) and the civil rights revolution • Eisenhower Republicanism • Cold war crises • The space race and the arms race • The election of John F. Kennedy, 1960 • Postwar writers, painters, and architects

CHRONOLOGY / KEY TERMS / PEOPLE TO KNOW / TO LEARN 887–888

✷ MAKERS OF AMERICA   The Great African American Migration   870

✷ EXAMINING THE EVIDENCE   The Shopping Mall as New Town Square, 1960   881

✷ MAKERS OF AMERICA   The Beat Generation   884

38 The Stormy Sixties 1960–1968 889

The Kennedy spirit • Kennedy and the Cold War • The Vietnam quagmire • Bay of Pigs Invastion and the Cuban missile crisis • The struggle for civil rights • Kennedy assassinated, November 22, 1963 • Lyndon Baines Johnson and the "Great Society" • The civil rights revolution explodes • The Vietnam disaster • The election of Richard Nixon, 1968 • The cultural upheavals of the 1960s

CHRONOLOGY / KEY TERMS / PEOPLE TO KNOW / TO LEARN MORE   914–915

✷ EXAMINING THE EVIDENCE   Conflicting Press Accounts of the March on Washington, 1963   899

✷ VARYING VIEWPOINTS   The Sixties: Constructive or Destructive?   913

39 The Stalemated Seventies 1968–1980 916

Economic stagnation • Nixon and the Vietnam War • New policies toward China and the Soviet Union • Nixon and the Supreme Court • Nixon's domestic program • Nixon trounces McGovern, 1972 • Israelis, Arabs, and oil • The Watergate scandal • Nixon resigns and Ford takes over• Feminism • Desegregation and affirmative action • The election of Jimmy Carter, 1976 • The energy crisis and inflation • The Iranian hostage humiliation

CHRONOLOGY / KEY TERMS / PEOPLE TO KNOW / TO LEARN MORE   940–941

✷ EXAMINING THE EVIDENCE   The "Smoking Gun" Tape, June 23, 1972, 10:04–11:39 A.M.   927

✷ MAKERS OF AMERICA   The Vietnamese   930

✷ MAKERS OF AMERICA   The Feminists   934

40 The Resurgence of Conservatism 1980–1992 942

The "New Right" and Reagan's election, 1980 • Budget battles and tax cuts • Reagan and the Soviets • Mikhail Gorbachev, Ronald Reagan, and the thawing of the Cold War • The Iran-Contra scandal • Reagan's economic legacy • The religious right • Conservatism and the courts • The election of George Bush, 1988 • The end of the Cold War • The Persian Gulf War, 1991 • Bush's battles at home

CHRONOLOGY / KEY TERMS / PEOPLE TO KNOW / TO LEARN MORE   963–964

✷ VARYING VIEWPOINTS   Where Did Modern Conservatism Come From?   962

41 America Confronts the Post–Cold War Era 1992–2011 965

The election of Bill Clinton, 1992 • A false start for reform • The politics of distrust • Clinton as president • Post-Cold War foreign policy • The Clinton impeachment trial • The controversial 2000 election • George W. Bush as president • The terrorist attacks of September 11, 2001 • Wars in Iraq and Afghanistan • Grappling with the Great Recession • The Obama presidency • A polarized republic

CHRONOLOGY / KEY TERMS / PEOPLE TO KNOW / TO LEARN MORE   988–989

✷ THINKING GLOBALLY   America Through Foreign Eyes: Hyperpower or Hapless Power?   980

42 The American People Face a New Century 990

The high-tech economy • Widening inequality • The feminist revolution • The changing American family • Immigration and assimilation • Cities and suburbs • A multicultural society • Postmodern culture in the new century • The new media • The American prospect

TO LEARN MORE   1012

✷ MAKERS OF AMERICA   Scientists and Engineers   994

✷ MAKERS OF AMERICA   The Latinos   1002

APPENDIX

Documents A1

Declaration of Independence • Constitution of the United States of America • Presidential Elections • Presidents and Vice Presidents • Admission of States • Estimates of Total Costs and Number of Battle Deaths of Major U.S. Wars

Glossary of Key Terms A27

Index I1

You will find many additional text-wide resources, including a complete annotated **Suggested Readings** bibliography, a **Glossary of People to Know**, and **An American Profile: The United States and Its Peoples in Comparative Perspective,** on *The American Pageant* website found at www.cengagebrain.com

MAPS

22.1 Military Reconstruction, 1867 (five districts and commanding generals)   476
22.2 Alaska and the Lower Forty-eight States (a size comparison)   482

23.1 Hayes-Tilden Disputed Election of 1876 (with electoral vote by state)   494
23.2 A Southern Plantation, Before and After the Civil War   497
23.3 Presidential Election of 1892 (showing vote by county)   507

24.1 Federal Land Grants to Railroads   514
24.2 American Industry in 1900   529

25.1 Size of World Cities 1850–1900   540
25.2 Woman Suffrage Before the Nineteenth Amendment   563

26.1 Indian Wars, 1860–1890   578
26.2 Vanishing Lands   584
26.3 Cattle Trails   586
26.4 Average Annual Precipitation, with Major Agricultural Products, 1900   589
26.5 Myth and Reality in the West: Percentage of Federal Lands Within Each State, 2004   590
26.6 Presidential Election of 1896 (with electoral vote by state)   603

27.1 United States Expansion, 1857–1917   611
27.2 Dewey's Route in the Philippines, 1898   614
27.3 The Cuban Campaign, 1898   616
27.4 The Great Powers and Their Colonial Possessions, 1913   633

29.1 Presidential Election of 1912 (showing votes by county, with electoral vote by state)   663
29.2 The United States in the Caribbean, 1898–1941   668
29.3 British Military Area (declared November 3, 1914) and German Submarine War Zone (declared February 4, 1915)   672
29.4 Presidential Election of 1916 (with electoral vote by state)   675

30.1 Major U.S. Operations in France, 1918   688

32.1 Presidential Election of 1924 (showing popular vote by county)   736
32.2 Presidential Election of 1928 (with electoral vote by state)   739

33.1 The Extent of Erosion in the 1930s   765
33.2 TVA Area   766

34.1 Presidential Election of 1940 (with electoral vote by state)   791
34.2 Main Flow of Lend-Lease Aid (width of arrows indicates relative amount)   792

35.1 Internal Migration in the United States During World War II   805
35.2 Corregidor and Bataan   809
35.3 United States Thrusts in the Pacific, 1942–1945   811
35.4 World War II in Europe and North Africa, 1939–1945   815
35.5 Battle of the Bulge, 816

36.1 Distribution of Population Increase, 1950–2008   835
36.2 Postwar Partition of Germany   845

36.3 United States Foreign Aid, Military and Economic, 1945–1954   848
36.4 The Shifting Front in Korea   856

37.1 Presidential Election of 1952 (with electoral vote by state)   865
37.2 East and Southeast Asia, 1955–1956   875
37.3 Presidential Election of 1960 (with electoral vote by state)   880

38.1 Vietnam and Southeast Asia, 1954–1975   894
38.2 Presidential Election of 1964   901
38.3 Presidential Election of 1968 (with electoral vote by state)   910

40.1 Presidential Election of 1980 (with electoral vote by state)   944
40.2 The Middle East   948
40.3 Central America and the Caribbean   949
40.4 The End of the Cold War Changed the Map of Europe   957
40.5 Operation Desert Storm: The Ground War, February 23–27, 1991   960

41.1 Presidential Election of 1992 (with electoral vote by state)   966
41.2 Presidential Election of 1996 (with electoral vote by state)   968
41.3 Presidential Election of 2000 (with electoral vote by state)   972
41.4 America in Red and Blue   973
41.5 Iraq in Transition   977
41.6 Presidential Election of 2008   985
41.7 Demography Is (Political) Destiny   988

FIGURES

23.1 Civil-Service Employment   502

24.1 Railroads Worldwide, 1889   513
24.2 Cotton Manufacturing Moves South, 1880–1980   527
24.3 World Cotton Production, 1903   528

25.1 The Shift to the American City   540
25.2 Dumbbell Tenement   542
25.3 Annual Immigration, 1860–2010   543
25.4 Old and New Immigration (by decade, 1871–1920)   543

26.1 Homesteads from the Public Lands (acreage legally transferred to private ownership)   587

29.1 Organization of Holding Companies   666

30.1 Approximate Comparative Losses in World
  War I   690

31.1 Annual Immigration and the Quota Laws   704
31.2 The Cost of a Model T Ford, 1908–1924   712
31.3 International Comparison of Number of Automobiles   712

32.1 Limits Imposed by Washington Conference, 1921–1922   731
32.2 Aspects of the Financial Merry-go-round, 1921–1933   737
32.3 Index of Common Stock Prices
  (1926 = 100)   741

33.1 Bank Failures Before and After the Glass-Steagall Banking Reform Act of 1933   756
33.2 Occupied Households with Electric Service, 1900–1960   767
33.3 Labor Union Membership in Selected Countries, 1913–2007   769
33.4 Economic Impact of the Great Depression on the United States, the United Kingdom, and Germany,
  1929–1940   772

35.1 The National Debt, 1930–1950   808

36.1 National Defense Budget, 1940–2010   832

37.1 Women in the Labor Force, 1900–2008   862
37.2 Households with Television Sets, 946–1960   863

38.1 Poverty in the United States, 1960–2008   903

39.1 Median Household Income, 1970–2008   916
39.2 The History of the Consumer Price Index, 1967–2008   937

40.1 The National Debt, 1930–2009   952
40.2 Share of Income Received by Families, by Quintile, 1980–2009   953

41.1 Deficits into Surpluses and Back Again   974
41.2 The Great Recession Takes Hold   984

42.1 How the United States Measures Up   993

42.2 Demographic Profile of Women, Minorities, and the Foreign-Born in Nonacademic Science and Engineering Occupations, 1980–2000   995

42.3 Women in the Work Force Globally, 2008   996

42.4 Government Expenditures for Social Welfare, 1930–2009   999

42.5 Recent Legal Immigration by Area of Origin, 1961–2009   1000

42.6 Sources of Latino Population in the United States, 2008   1003

42.7 Percent of Total Population Living in Metropolitan Areas and in Their Central Cities and Suburbs, 1910–2000   1005

TABLES

22.1 Principal Reconstruction Proposals and Plans   471
22.2 Southern Reconstruction by State   477

23.1 Composition of the Electoral Commission, 1877   495
23.2 Persons in United States Lynched (by race), 1882–2005   497
23.3 Population of Chinese Ancestry in the United States, 1850–2008   501

25.1 Educational Levels, 1870–2010   556
25.2 Marriages and Divorces, 1890–2008   562

29.1 Principal Foreign Elements in the United States, Census of 1910   671
29.2 U.S. Exports to Belligerents, 1914–1916   671

30.1 A Chronology of Women's Right to Vote in National Elections in Selected Nations   684

33.1 Principal New Deal Acts During the Hundred Days Congress, 1933 (items in parentheses indicate secondary purposes)   755
33.2 Later Major New Deal Measures, 1933–1939 (items in parentheses indicate secondary purposes)   758

35.1 The Comparative Costs of World War II   823

36.1 International Trade, 1948–2008   843

37.1 Occupational Distribution of Workingwomen, 1900–2000   861

41.1 World Public Opinion of the United States   981

42.1 Widening Income Inequality   992
42.2 Who Pays Federal Income Taxes? (share of U.S. income tax, by income percentile)   993
42.3 Working Women: Labor Force Participation Rates for Wives and Mothers, 1950–2007   996

A.1 Presidential Elections   A21
A.2 Presidents and Vice Presidents   A24
A.3 Admission of States   A26
A.4 Estimates of Total Costs and Number of Battle Deaths of Major U.S. Wars   A26

PREFACE

This fifteenth edition of *The American Pageant* reflects our continuing collaboration to bring the most recent scholarship about American history to the broadest possible student audience, while preserving the readability that has long been the *Pageant*'s hallmark. We are often told that the *Pageant* stands out as the only American history text with a distinctive personality. We define its leading characteristics as clarity, concreteness, a strong emphasis on major themes, integration of a broad range of historical topics into a coherent and clutter-free narrative, attention to a variety of interpretive perspectives, and a colorful writing style leavened, as appropriate, with wit. That personality, we strongly believe, is what has made the *Pageant* both appealing and useful to countless students for more than five decades.

Our collaboration on the *Pageant* reflects our respective scholarly interests, which are complementary to a remarkable degree. David Kennedy is primarily a political and economic historian, while Lizabeth Cohen's work emphasizes social and cultural history. Together, we have once again revised the *Pageant* chapter by chapter, even paragraph by paragraph, guided by our shared commitment to tell the story of the American past as vividly and clearly as possible, without sacrificing a sense of the often sobering seriousness of history and of its sometimes challenging complexity.

Goals of *The American Pageant*

Like its predecessors, this edition of *The American Pageant* seeks to cultivate in its readers the capacity for balanced judgment and informed understanding about American society by holding up to the present the mirror and measuring rod that is the past. The division of the book into six parts, each with an introductory essay, encourages students to understand that the study of history is not just a matter of piling up mountains of facts, but is principally concerned with discovering complex patterns of change over time and organizing seemingly disparate events, actions, and ideas into meaningful chains of cause and consequence.

While the narrative propels the story, we bring in voices from the past to encourage critical thinking. Boxed quotes throughout help students hear the language of real people who experienced historical events. In addition, "Examining the Evidence" features give students an opportunity to deepen their understanding of the historical craft by conveying how historians develop interpretations of the past through research in many different kinds of primary sources. Here students learn to probe a wide range of historical documents and artifacts: correspondence between Abigail and John Adams in 1776, and what it reveals about women's place in the American Revolution; the Gettysburg Address and the light it sheds not only on President Lincoln's brilliant oratory but also on his vision of the American nation; a letter from a black freedman to his former master in 1865 that illuminates his family's experience in slavery as well as their hopes for a new life; the manuscript census of 1900 and what it teaches us about immigrant households on the Lower East Side of New York at the dawn of the twentieth century; and a new kind of architectural structure—the shopping mall—and how it changed both consumers' behavior and politicians' campaign tactics after World War II.

Thus, the book's goal is not to teach the art of prophecy but the much subtler and more difficult arts of seeing things in context, of understanding the roots and direction and pace of change, and of distinguishing what is truly new under the sun from what is not. The study of history, it has been rightly said, does not make one smart for the next time, but wise forever.

We hope that the *Pageant* will help to develop the art of critical thinking in its readers, and that those who use the book will take from it both a fresh appreciation of what has gone before and a seasoned perspective on what is to come. We hope, too, that readers will take as much pleasure in reading *The American Pageant* as we have had in writing it.

Changes in the Fifteenth Edition

As in past revisions, we have updated and streamlined the text narrative, with some reorganization of content and expansion of the discussion of social and economic history.

Cultural History

This edition also offers markedly deeper explorations of the cultural innovations, artistic movements, and intellectual doctrines that have engaged and inspired Americans and shaped the course of American history. We believe that works of the imagination are an organic part of the larger historical picture, and that they both reflect and mold the society that gives rise to them. Readers will accordingly find substantially enhanced treatment of transcendentalism in Chapter 15, post–Civil War literature and art in Chapter 25, the transnational spread of artistic "modernism" in Chapter 31, and late-twentieth-century letters, art, and architecture in Chapters 37 and 42. We have also added a new "Thinking Globally" essay on twentieth-century modernism and a new "Makers of America" feature on the "Beat Generation" of the 1950s. In all cases we have closely tied the discussion of these cultural and intellectual developments to the broader social and political contexts of which they were integral parts.

Global Context

We have also further expanded the *Pageant*'s treatment of the global context of American history. Today, political leaders, capital investment, consumer products, rock bands, the Internet, and much else constantly traverse the globe. But even before sophisticated technology and mass communication, complex exchanges among peoples and nations around the world deeply shaped the course of American history. Students will frequently encounter in these pages the people, ideas, and events that crossed national borders to influence the experience of the United States. They will also be invited to compare salient aspects of American history with developments elsewhere in the world. We believe that a full understanding of what makes America exceptional requires knowing about other societies, and knowing when and why America's path followed or departed from that taken by other nations.

Within each chapter, both text and graphics help students compare American developments to developments around the world. Railroad building, cotton production, city size and urban reform strategies, immigration, automobile ownership, the economic effects of the Great Depression, women's participation in voting and the work force, the cultural and artistic phenomena of modernism and postmodernism, and much more should now be understood as part of world trends, not just as isolated American experiences. New boxed quotes bring more international voices to the events chronicled in the *Pageant*'s historical narrative. Updated "Varying Viewpoints" essays reflect new interpretations of significant trends and events, emphasizing, when appropriate, their global contexts.

We have revised and expanded the "Thinking Globally" essays. Two such essays within each of the *Pageant*'s six parts present different aspects of the American experience contextualized within world history. Readers learn how developments in North America were part of worldwide phenomena, be it the challenge to empire in the eighteenth century, the rise of socialist ideology in the nineteenth century, or the globalization that followed World War II. Students also see how key aspects of American history—such as participating in the slave trade and its abolition, making a revolution for independence, creating a more united modern state in the mid-nineteenth century, and struggling to survive the Great Depression and World War II—were encountered by other nations but resolved in distinctive ways according to each country's history, cultural traditions, and political and economic structures.

This edition also gives renewed attention to teaching strategies and pedagogical materials aimed at helping students deepen their comprehension of American history. New visual materials—documentary images, graphs, and tables—illuminate complex and important historical ideas. Readers will also find redesigned maps with topographical detail and clear labeling to better communicate the text's analytical points. Key terms are printed in bold in each chapter and defined in a glossary at the end of the book. Every chapter concludes with an expanded chronology and a list of readable books to consult in order "To Learn More." (A fuller, chapter-by-chapter annotated bibliography suitable for deeper research is provided on the student Web site.) In addition, a list of the chapter key terms and a list of "People to Know"—created to help students focus on the most significant people introduced in that chapter—appear at the end of each chapter to help students review chapter highlights. Both lists are also included on the student Web site with expanded definitions for the "People to Know." A revised Appendix contains annotated copies of the Declaration of Independence and Constitution and key historical events and dates such as admission of the states and presidential elections. On the Web site, students will also find an extensive visual profile of the United States with charts and graphs illustrating many aspects of the American historical experience as well as comparisons to other nations.

At the end of each chapter we remind students to take advantage of the many interactive study materials found on the *American Pageant* Web site (located at www.cengagebrain.com). See the Supplements section below for a complete description of the many materials found there. It is our hope that readers will view our Web site as an exploratory laboratory enhancing *The American Pageant*'s text.

Notes on Content Revisions

Chapter 4: Expanded Thinking Globally essay on "Atlantic Slave Trade, 1500–1860"

Chapter 7: New material on women's role in the Revolutionary War

Chapter 8: New material in Varying Viewpoints "Whose Revolution?"

Chapter 9: New material in Varying Viewpoints "The Constitution: Revolutionary or Counterrevolutionary?"

Chapter 10: New material on conflicts over government powers

Chapter 13: Updating of voter turnout data

Chapter 15: New material on art and architecture in "Artistic Achievements" section; new material on romanticism and Margaret Fuller; new boxed quote from Washington Irving in "Blossoming of a National Literature" section

Chapter 16: Expanded Thinking Globally essay on "The Struggle to Abolish Slavery"

Chapter 19: New material in Varying Viewpoints "The Civil War: Repressible or Irrepressible?"

Chapter 21: New material in Varying Viewpoints "What Were the Consequences of the Civil War?"

Chapter 25: New material on realism, naturalism, and regionalism, including Henry James, Edith Wharton, Theodore Dreiser, Kate Chopin, and Henry Adams in "Literary Landmarks" section; under "Artistic Triumphs" new brief discussions of Thomas Eakins, Winslow Homer, and Frederick Law Olmsted

Chapter 31: New material on Hemingway, Gertrude Stein, T. S. Eliot, Ezra Pound, Robert Frost, Carl Sandburg, Sinclair Lewis, Faulkner, and Eugene O'Neill; new boxed quotes from Mencken and Henry van Dyck and Faulkner; new Thinking Globally essay on "Modernism"

Chapter 37: New material in "A Cultural Renaissance" section on abstract expressionism, Frank Lloyd Wright, Louis Kahn, John Updike, John Cheever, Gore Vidal, J. D. Salinger, Richard Wright, Harper Lee, Ralph Ellison, Robert Penn Warren, and Flannery O'Connor; new boxed quotes from Allen Ginsburg and Arthur Miller; new Makers of America essay on "The Beat Generation"

Chapter 41: New discussion of the Great Recession, the election of 2010, and the troubled Obama presidency

Chapter 42: New material on postmodernist thought, architecture, music, visual arts, literature, and film; new boxed quote from Twyla Tharp; new image of senior female military officer

Supplements Available with *The American Pageant, Fifteenth Edition*

Instructor Resources

Everything you need to teach the U.S. History survey course with *The American Pageant* can be found on a single Web site, using one single sign-on (SSO). Register at http://login.cengage.com and add *The American Pageant* 15e to your bookshelf to get instant access to most of the resources described below.

Instructor Companion Site The protected teaching materials in the instructor Web site include the Instructor's Resource Manual, customizable Microsoft® PowerPoint® slides of both lecture outlines and images from the text; and JoinIn® PowerPoint® slides with clicker content. The companion Web site also provides instructors with access to HistoryFinder and to the Wadsworth American History Resource Center.

Instructor's Resource Manual Prepared by Warren Hierl of the Career Center, Winston-Salem, N.C., this manual contains a variety of instructor tools, including focus questions, chapter themes, chapter summaries, suggested lecture and discussion topics, additional class topics, character sketches, questions for class discussion, and more. Available on the Instructor Companion site.

PowerLecture DVD with ExamView® and JoinIn® This dual-platform, all-in-one multimedia resource includes the Instructor's Resource Manual; a Test Bank written by Debra Michals of Merrimack College that includes short answer, multiple-choice, and essay questions; Microsoft® PowerPoint® slides of both lecture outlines and images and maps from the text that can be used as offered or customized by importing personal lecture slides or other material; and *JoinIn*® PowerPoint® slides with clicker content. Also included is ExamView, an easy-to-use assessment and tutorial system that allows instructors to create, deliver, and customize tests in minutes. Instructors can build tests with as many as 250 questions using up to 12 question types, and using ExamView's complete word-processing capabilities, they can enter an unlimited number of new questions or edit existing ones.

***WebTutor*™ *on Blackboard*® *and WebTutor*™ *on WebCT*®** With WebTutor's text-specific, preformatted content and total flexibility, instructors can easily create and manage their own custom course Web site. WebTutor's course management tool gives instructors the ability to provide virtual office hours, post syllabi, set up threaded discussions, track student progress with the quizzing material, and much more. For students, WebTutor offers real-time access to a full array of study tools, including animations and videos that bring the book's topics to life, plus chapter summaries, glossary flashcards, practice quizzes, and Web links.

CourseMate Cengage Learning's CourseMate for Kennedy's *The American Pageant*, 15e provides interactive learning, study, and exam preparation tools that support the printed textbook. The CourseMate site includes an integrated ebook, quizzes authored by Jason Ripper of Everett Community College, flashcards, videos, and EngagementTracker, a first-of-its-kind tool that monitors student engagement in the course. Learn more at www.cengagebrain.com.

Aplia Aplia™ is an online interactive learning solution that improves comprehension and outcomes by increasing student effort and engagement. Founded by a professor to enhance his own courses, Aplia provides automatically graded assignments with detailed, immediate explanations and innovative teaching materials. Chapter assignments developed specifically for *The American Pageant* include map- and content-based questions for each chapter, as well as primary source activities grouped around important topics. A course management system allows instructors to post announcements, upload course materials, host student discussions, e-mail students, and manage the gradebook. Instructors receive personalized support from a knowledgeable and friendly support team, who also offer assistance in customizing assignments to instructor course schedules. To learn more, visit www.aplia.com.

Custom Options Cengage Learning offers custom solutions for your course—whether it's making a small modification to *The American Pageant* to match your syllabus or combining multiple sources to create something truly unique. You can pick and choose chapters, include your own material, and add additional map exercises along with the *Rand McNally Atlas* to create a text that fits the way you teach. Ensure that your students get the most out of their textbook dollar by giving them exactly what they need. Contact your Cengage Learning representative to explore custom solutions for your course.

Print Reader Program Cengage Learning publishes a number of readers, some containing exclusively primary sources, others a combination of primary and secondary sources, and some designed to guide students through the process of historical inquiry. *The American Spirit* Volumes I and II are print, primary source readers compiled and edited by David M. Kennedy and designed specifically to accompany *The American Pageant*. Visit Cengage.com/history for a complete list of readers.

CourseReader for U.S. History CourseReader offers a way for instructors to build customized online readers for their courses. By selecting documents from a rich database of primary and secondary sources, including many from the Gale collections, instructors can create their own reader to match the specific needs of their course. An Editor's Choice developed for *The American Pageant* provides a useful starting point. Go to Cengage.com/coursereader for more information.

Student Resources

Cengagebrain.com Students can go to www.cengagebrain.com to find a choice of formats and savings on materials that will give them a better chance to succeed in class. *Cengagebrain.com*, Cengage Learning's online store, is a single destination for more than 10,000 new textbooks, etextbooks, echapters, study tools, and audio supplements. Students have the freedom to purchase a-la-carte exactly what they need when they need it. Students can save 50 percent on the electronic textbook and can pay as little as $1.99 for an individual echapter.

CourseMate For students, CourseMate provides an additional source of interactive learning, study, and exam preparation outside the classroom. Students will find an integrated ebook for *The American Pageant*, multiple quizzes, primary source assignments, zoomable maps, flashcards, videos, and more. Available at www.cengagebrain.com.

Book Companion Site *The American Pageant* Web site features a collection of free resources to help students master the text content. The Web site includes chapter outlines, glossaries of key terms and key people, crossword puzzles, chapter quizzes, Web links, and annotated bibliographies. Available at www.cengagebrain.com.

CL eBook This interactive multimedia ebook links out to rich media assets such as video and MP3 chapter summaries. Through this ebook, students can also access self-test quizzes, chronology exercises, primary source documents with critical thinking questions, and interactive (zoomable) maps. Available at www.cengagebrain.com.

Wadsworth American History Resource Center Wadsworth's American History Resource Center gives students access to a "virtual reader" with hundreds of primary sources, including speeches, letters, legal documents and transcripts, poems, maps, simulations, timelines, and additional images that bring history to life, along with interactive assignable exercises. The American History Resource Center can be bundled with any text.

Rand McNally Atlas of American History, 2e This comprehensive atlas features more than 80 maps, with new content covering global perspectives, including events in the Middle East from 1945 to 2005, as well as population trends in the United States and around the world. Additional maps document voyages of discovery; the settling of the colonies; major U.S. military engagements, including the American Revolution and World Wars I and II; and sources of immigrations, ethnic populations, and patterns of economic change. Can be bundled with *The American Pageant*.

Acknowledgments

Many people have contributed to this revision of *The American Pageant*. Foremost among them are the countless students and teachers who have written unsolicited letters of comment or inquiry. We have learned from every one of them and encourage all readers to offer us suggestions for improving future editions. In particular, we wish to thank the following reviewers who gave us important feedback about the features in the book, including especially the new emphasis on America in a global context.

Reviewers for the Fifteenth Edition

Jose Garcia, *University of Central Florida*
David Price, *Santa Fe Community College*
John Rawlins, *Bowling Green State University*
Lorna Rinear, *Regis College*
Jim Rogers, *Louisiana State University at Alexandria*
Kevin Sims, *Cedarville University*
Phyllis Soybel, *College of Lake County*
Joseph Zelasko, *Mount Union College*

We would also like to thank reviewers of the previous edition:

David Barber, *University of Tennessee at Martin*
Robert Berta, *Northern Kentucky University*
Timothy Buckner, *Troy University*
Cynthia Clark, *University of Texas at Arlington*
Matt Cone, *Plano Senior High School, Plano, Texas*
Will Corprew, *Broome Community College*
Charles Cox, *Bridgewater State College*
Chris Drake, *Houston Community College*
David Fitzpatrick, *Washtenaw Community College*
Christine Flood, *University of North Carolina at Greensboro*
Nancy Gentile Ford, *Bloomsburg University*
Ray Gunn, *University of Utah*
Neil Hamilton, *Spring Hill College*
Marc Horger, *Ohio State University*
Ronald Huetter, *Suffolk County Community College*
Gary Huey, *Ferris State University*
Don Jacobson, *Oakton Community College*

Jon Timothy Kelly, *West Valley College*
Paul Kelton, *University of Kansas*
Nonie Kouneski, *Southwest High School, Minneapolis, Minnesota*
Stacy Kowtko, *Spokane Community College*
Tim Lehman, *Rocky Mountain College*
Scott Lingenfelter, *Roosevelt University*
Robert Mayer, *Kean University*
Kenneth Millen-Penn, *Fairmont State University*
Sharon Musher, *Richard Stockton College of New Jersey*
Michael Namorato, *University of Mississippi*
Bridget Nimmer, *Wauwatosa West High School, Wauwatosa, Wisconsin*
Deanne Nuwer, *University of Southern Mississippi*
Jane O'Steen, *Leesburg High School, Leesburg, Florida*
Keith Pomakoy, *Adirondack Community College*
David Rayson, *Normandale Community College*
Lewie Reece, *Anderson University*
Marc Rodriguez, *University of Notre Dame*
Clyde Root, *Bethel College*
Horacio Salinas, *Laredo Community College*
Aldorigo Scopino, *Central Connecticut State University*
Karen J. Smith, *Columbia Southern University*
Robert St. Clair, *Central Virginia Community College*

Several people deserve special mention for their assistance:

Bob Burns, *Valley Christian High School*
Annika Christensen, *Barnard College*
Adrian Finucane, *University of Kansas*
Maria Ponomarenko, *Stanford University*
Scott Spillman, *Stanford University*
Daniel C. Wewers, *Yale Law School*

Our warm thanks to each of them.

David M. Kennedy
Lizabeth Cohen

Sail, sail thy best, ship of Democracy,
Of value is thy freight, 'tis not the Present only,
The Past is also stored in thee,
Thou holdest not the venture of thyself alone, not of
*   the Western continent alone,*
Earth's résumé entire floats on thy keel, O ship, is
*   steadied by thy spars,*
With thee Time voyages in trust, the antecedent
*   nations sink or swim with thee,*
With all their ancient struggles, martyrs, heroes, epics,
*   wars, thou bear'st the other continents,*
Theirs, theirs as much as thine, the destination-port
*   triumphant. . . .*

Walt Whitman
Thou Mother with Thy Equal Brood, 1872

Chapter 22

The Ordeal of Reconstruction

1865–1877

With malice toward none, with charity for all, with firmness in the right as God gives us to see the right, let us strive on to finish the work we are in, to bind up the nation's wounds, to care for him who shall have borne the battle and for his widow and orphan, to do all which may achieve and cherish a just and lasting peace among ourselves and with all nations.

ABRAHAM LINCOLN, SECOND INAUGURAL, MARCH 4, 1865

The battle was done, the buglers silent. Bone-weary and bloodied, the American people, North and South, now faced the staggering challenges of peace. Four questions loomed large. How would the South, physically devastated by war and socially revolutionized by emancipation, be rebuilt? How would liberated blacks fare as free men and women? How would the Southern states be reintegrated into the Union? And who would direct the process of Reconstruction—the Southern states themselves, the president, or Congress?

★ The Problems of Peace

Other questions also clamored for answers. What should be done with the captured Confederate ringleaders, all of whom were liable to charges of treason? During the war a popular Northern song had been "Hang Jeff Davis to a Sour Apple Tree," and even innocent children had lisped it. Davis was temporarily clapped into irons during the early days of his two-year imprisonment. But he and his fellow "conspirators" were finally released, partly because the odds were that no Virginia jury would convict them. All rebel leaders were finally pardoned by President Johnson as a sort of Christmas present in 1868. But Congress did not remove all remaining civil disabilities until thirty years later and only posthumously restored Davis's citizenship more than a century later.

Dismal indeed was the picture presented by the war-racked South when the rattle of musketry faded.

Not only had an age perished, but a civilization had collapsed, in both its economic and its social structure. The moonlight-and-magnolia Old South, largely imaginary in any case, had forever gone with the wind.

Handsome cities of yesteryear, such as Charleston and Richmond, were rubble-strewn and weed-choked. An Atlantan returned to his once-fair hometown and remarked, "Hell has laid her egg, and right here it hatched."

Economic life had creaked to a halt. Banks and businesses had locked their doors, ruined by runaway inflation. Factories were smokeless, silent, dismantled. The transportation system had broken down completely. Before the war five different railroad lines had converged on Columbia, South Carolina; now the nearest connected track was twenty-nine miles away. Efforts to untwist the rails corkscrewed by Sherman's soldiers proved bumpily unsatisfactory.

Agriculture—the economic lifeblood of the South—was almost hopelessly crippled. Once-white-carpeted cotton fields now yielded a lush harvest of nothing but green weeds. The slave-labor system had collapsed, seed was scarce, and livestock had been driven off by plundering Yankees. Pathetic instances were reported of men hitching themselves to plows, while women and children gripped the handles. Not until 1870 did the seceded states produce as large a cotton crop as that of the fateful year 1860, and much of that yield came from new acreage in the Southwest.

The princely planter aristocrats were humbled by the war—at least temporarily. Reduced to proud poverty, they faced charred and gutted mansions, lost investments, and almost worthless land. Their investments of more than $2 billion in slaves, their primary form of wealth, had evaporated with emancipation.

Beaten but unbent, many high-spirited white Southerners remained dangerously defiant. They cursed the "damnyankees" and spoke of "your government" in Washington instead of "our government." One Southern bishop refused to pray for President Andrew Johnson, though Johnson proved to be in sore need of divine guidance. Conscious of no crime, these former Confederates continued to believe that their view of secession was correct and that the "lost cause" was still a just war. One popular anti-Union song ran,

> *I'm glad I fought agin her, I only wish we'd won,*
> *And I ain't axed any pardon for anything I've done.*

Such attitudes boded ill for the prospects of painlessly binding up the Republic's wounds.

✶ Freedmen Define Freedom

Confusion abounded in the still-smoldering South about the precise meaning of "freedom" for blacks. Emancipation took effect haltingly and unevenly in different parts of the conquered Confederacy. As Union armies marched in and out of various localities, many blacks found themselves emancipated and then re-enslaved. A North Carolina slave estimated that he had celebrated freedom about twelve times. Blacks from one Texas county fleeing to the free soil of the liberated county next door were attacked by slaveowners as they swam across the river that marked the county line. The next day trees along the riverbank were bent with swinging corpses—a grisly warning to others dreaming of liberty. Other planters resisted emancipation more legalistically, stubbornly protesting that slavery was lawful until state legislatures or the Supreme Court declared otherwise. For many slaves the shackles of bondage were not struck off in a single mighty blow; long-suffering blacks often had to wrench free of their chains link by link.

The variety of responses to emancipation, by whites as well as blacks, illustrated the sometimes startling complexity of the master-slave relationship. Loyalty to the plantation master prompted some slaves to resist the liberating Union armies, while other slaves' pent-up bitterness burst forth violently on the day of liberation. Many newly emancipated slaves, for example, joined Union troops in pillaging their masters' possessions. In one instance a group of Virginia slaves laid twenty lashes on the back of their former master—a painful dose of his own favorite medicine.

Prodded by the bayonets of Yankee armies of occupation, all masters were eventually forced to recognize their slaves' permanent freedom. The once-commanding planter would assemble his former human chattels in front of the porch of the "big house" and announce their liberty. Though some blacks initially responded to news of their emancipation with suspicion and uncertainty, they soon celebrated their newfound freedom. Many took new names in place of the ones given by their masters and demanded that whites formally address them as "Mr." or "Mrs." Others abandoned the coarse cottons that had been their only clothing as slaves and sought

Charleston, South Carolina, in Ruins, April 1865 Rebel troops evacuating Charleston blew up military supplies to deny them to General William Tecumseh Sherman's forces. The explosions ignited fires that all but destroyed the city.

Library of Congress

Tuskegee University Archives

Educating Young Freedmen and Freedwomen, 1870s Freed slaves in the South regarded schooling as the key to improving their children's lives and the fulfillment of a long-sought right that had been denied blacks in slavery. These well-dressed school-children are lined up outside their rural, one-room schoolhouse alongside their teachers, both black and white.

silks, satins, and other finery. Though many whites perceived such behavior as insubordinate, they were forced to recognize the realities of emancipation. "Never before had I a word of impudence from any of our black folk," wrote one white Southerner, "but they are not ours any longer."

Tens of thousands of emancipated blacks took to the roads, some to test their freedom, others to search for long-lost spouses, parents, and children. Emancipation thus strengthened the black family, and many newly freed men and women formalized "slave marriages" for personal and pragmatic reasons, including the desire to make their children legal heirs. Other blacks left their former masters to work in towns and cities, where existing black communities provided protection and mutual assistance. Whole communities sometimes moved together in search of opportunity. From 1878 to 1880, some twenty-five thousand blacks from Louisiana, Texas, and Mississippi surged in a mass exodus to Kansas. The westward flood of these "Exodusters" was stemmed only when steamboat captains refused to transport more black migrants across the Mississippi River.

The church became the focus of black community life in the years following emancipation. As slaves, blacks had worshiped alongside whites, but now they formed their own churches pastored by their own ministers. Black churches grew robustly. The 150,000-member

Houston H. Holloway, age twenty at the time of his emancipation, recalled his feelings upon hearing of his freedom:

"I felt like a bird out of a cage. Amen. Amen. Amen. I could hardly ask to feel any better than I did that day. . . . The week passed off in a blaze of glory.**"**

The reunion of long-lost relatives also inspired joy; one Union officer wrote home,

"Men are taking their wives and children, families which had been for a long time broken up are united and oh! such happiness. I am glad I am here.**"**

Letter from a Freedman to His Old Master, 1865

What was it like to experience the transition from slavery to freedom? Four million Southern blacks faced this exhilarating and formidable prospect with the end of the war. For historians, recovering the African American perspective on emancipation is challenging. Unlike their white masters, freed blacks left few written records. But one former slave captured in a letter to his "Old Master" (whose surname he bore) the heroic determination of many blacks to build new independent and dignified lives for themselves and their families.

During the war Jourdon Anderson escaped slavery in Tennessee with his wife and two daughters. After relocating to the relative safety of Ohio, he received a communication from his former owner asking him to return. In his bold reply, reportedly "dictated by the old servant" himself, Anderson expressed his family's new expectations for life as free people and an uneasiness about his former master's intentions. He made reference to his "comfortable home," his daughters' schooling, the church that he and his wife were free to attend regularly, and the peace of mind that came with knowing that "my girls [would not be] brought to shame by the violence and wickedness of their young masters." To test the white man's sincerity, Anderson and his wife asked for the astronomical figure of $11,680 in back wages from decades as slaves. He closed by reiterating that "the great desire of my life is to give my children an education and have them form virtuous habits." This rare letter demonstrates that many black correspondents may have been illiterate, but they were hardly inarticulate. And they asserted themselves as parents, workers, and citizens not only from the distance of a former free state like Ohio but also deep within the former slave states of the South. Was the tone of Anderson's letter (and postscript) serious or tongue-in-cheek? What did "freedom" mean for Anderson and other blacks in the months following emancipation? How did the eventual accomplishments of Reconstruction correspond with the initial expectations of people like Anderson and his former owner?

Letter from a Freedman to his Old Master.

The following is a genuine document. It was *dictated* by the old servant, and contains his ideas and forms of expression. [Cincinnati Commercial.

DAYTON, Ohio, August 7, 1865.

To my Old Master, Col. P. H. ANDERSON, Big Spring, Tennessee.

SIR: I got your letter and was glad to find that you had not forgotten Jordan, and that you wanted me to come back and live with you again, promising to do better for me than anybody else can. I have often felt uneasy about you. I thought the Yankees would have hung you long before this for harboring Rebs they found at your house. I suppose they never heard about your going to Col. Martin's to kill the Union soldier that was left by his company in their stable. Although you shot at me twice before I left you, I did not want to hear of your being hurt, and am glad you are still living. It would do me good to go back to the dear old home again and see Miss Mary and Miss Martha and Allen, Esther, Green and Lee. Give my love to them all, and tell them I hope we will meet in the better world, if not in this. I would have gone back to see you all when I was working in the Nashville Hospital, but one of the neighbors told me Henry intended to shoot me if he ever got a chance.

I want to know particularly what the good chance is you propose to give me. I am doing tolerably well here; I get $25 a month, with victuals and clothing; have a comfortable home for Mandy (the folks here call her Mrs. Anderson), and the children, Milly Jane and Grundy, go to school and are learning well; the teacher says Grundy has a head for a preacher. They go to Sunday-School, and Mandy and me attend church regularly. We are kindly treated; sometimes we over-

As to my freedom, which you say I can have, there is nothing to be gained on that score, as I got my free-papers in 1864 from the Provost-Marshal-General of the Department at Nashville. Mandy says she would be afraid to go back without some proof that you are sincerely disposed to treat us justly and kindly—and we have concluded to test your sincerity by asking you to send us our wages for the time we served you. This will make us forget and forgive old sores, and rely on your justice and friendship in the future. I served you faithfully for thirty-two years, and Mandy twenty years, at $25 a month for me, and $2 a week for Mandy. Our earnings would amount to $11,680. Add to this the interest for the time our wages has been kept back and deduct what you paid for our clothing and three doctor's visits to me, and pulling a tooth for Mandy, and the balance will show what we are in justice entitled to. Please send the money by Adams Express, in care of V. Winters, esq., Dayton, Ohio. If you fail to pay us for faithful labors in the past we can have little faith in your promises in the future.

P. S.—Say howdy to George Carter, and thank him for taking the pistol from you when you were shooting at me.

New York Tribune, Tuesday, August 22, 1965

black Baptist Church of 1850 reached 500,000 by 1870, while the African Methodist Episcopal Church quadrupled in size from 100,000 to 400,000 in the first decade after emancipation. These churches formed the bedrock of black community life, and they soon gave rise to other benevolent, fraternal, and mutual aid societies. All these organizations helped blacks protect their newly won freedom.

Emancipation also meant education for many blacks. Learning to read and write had been a privilege generally denied to them under slavery. Freedmen wasted no time establishing societies for self-improvement, which undertook to raise funds to purchase land, build schoolhouses, and hire teachers. One member of a North Carolina education society asserted that "a schoolhouse would be the first proof of their *independence*." Southern blacks soon found, however, that the demand outstripped the supply of qualified black teachers. They accepted the aid of Northern white women sent by the American Missionary Association, who volunteered their services as teachers. They also turned to the federal government for help. The freed blacks were going to need all the friends—and power—they could muster in Washington.

✬ The Freedmen's Bureau

Abolitionists had long preached that slavery was a degrading institution. Now the emancipators were faced with the brutal reality that the freedmen were overwhelmingly unskilled, unlettered, without property or money, and with scant knowledge of how to survive as free people. To cope with this problem throughout the conquered South, Congress created the **Freedmen's Bureau** on March 3, 1865.

On paper at least, the bureau was intended to be a kind of primitive welfare agency. It was to provide food, clothing, medical care, and education both to freedmen and to white refugees. Heading the bureau was a warmly sympathetic friend of blacks, Union general Oliver O. Howard, who later founded and served as president of Howard University in Washington, D.C.

Women from the North enthusiastically embraced the opportunity to go south and teach in Freedmen's Bureau schools for emancipated blacks. One volunteer explained her motives:

❝I thought I must do something, not having money at my command, what could I do but give myself to the work. . . . I would go to them, and give them my life if necessary.**❞**

The bureau achieved its greatest successes in education. It taught an estimated 200,000 blacks how to read. Many former slaves had a passion for learning, partly because they wanted to close the gap between themselves and whites and partly because they longed to read the Word of God. In one elementary class in North Carolina sat four generations of the same family, ranging from a six-year-old child to a seventy-five-year-old grandmother.

But in other areas, the bureau's accomplishments were meager—or even mischievous. Although the bureau was authorized to settle former slaves on forty-acre tracts confiscated from the Confederates, little land actually made it into blacks' hands. Instead local administrators often collaborated with planters in expelling blacks from towns and cajoling them into signing labor contracts to work for their former masters. Still, the white South resented the bureau as a meddlesome federal interloper that threatened to upset white racial dominance. President Andrew Johnson, who shared the white supremacist views of most white Southerners, repeatedly tried to kill it, and it expired in 1872.

✬ Johnson: The Tailor President

Few presidents have ever been faced with a more perplexing sea of troubles than that confronting Andrew Johnson. What manner of man was this medium-built, dark-eyed, black-haired Tennessean, now chief executive by virtue of the bullet that killed Lincoln?

No citizen, not even Lincoln, has ever reached the White House from humbler beginnings. Born to impoverished parents in North Carolina and orphaned early, Johnson never attended school but was apprenticed to a tailor at age ten. Ambitious to get ahead, he taught himself to read, and later his wife taught him to write and do simple arithmetic. Like many another self-made man, he was inclined to overpraise his maker.

Johnson early became active in politics in Tennessee, where he had moved when seventeen years old. He shone as an impassioned champion of poor whites against the planter aristocrats, although he himself ultimately owned a few slaves. He excelled as a two-fisted stump speaker before angry and heckling crowds, who on occasion greeted his political oratory with cocked pistols, not just cocked ears. Elected to Congress, he attracted much favorable attention in the North (but not the South) when he refused to secede with his own state. After Tennessee was partially "redeemed" by Union armies, he was appointed war governor and served courageously in an atmosphere of danger.

Political exigency next thrust Johnson into the vice presidency. Lincoln's Union party in 1864 needed to

Crushed by the Constitution
President Andrew Johnson revered the U.S. Constitution but eventually felt its awesome weight in his impeachment trial.

Granger Collection

attract support from the War Democrats and other pro-Southern elements, and Johnson, a Democrat, seemed to be the ideal man. Unfortunately, he appeared at the vice-presidential inaugural ceremonies the following March in a scandalous condition. He had recently been afflicted with typhoid fever, and although not known as a heavy drinker, he was urged by his friends to take a stiff bracer of whiskey. This he did—with unfortunate results.

"Old Andy" Johnson was no doubt a man of parts—unpolished parts. He was intelligent, able, forceful, and gifted with homespun honesty. Steadfastly devoted to duty and to the people, he was a dogmatic champion of states' rights and the Constitution. He would often present a copy of the document to visitors, and he was buried with one as a pillow.

Yet the man who had raised himself from the tailor's bench to the president's chair was a misfit. A Southerner who did not understand the North, a Tennessean who had earned the distrust of the South, a Democrat who had never been accepted by the Republicans, a president who had never been elected to the office, he was not at home in a Republican White House. Hotheaded, contentious, and stubborn, he was the wrong man in the wrong place at the wrong time. A Reconstruction policy devised by angels might well have failed in his tactless hands.

⭐ Presidential Reconstruction

Even before the shooting war had ended, the political war over Reconstruction had begun. Abraham Lincoln believed that the Southern states had never legally withdrawn from the Union. Their formal restoration to the Union would therefore be relatively simple. Accordingly, Lincoln in 1863 proclaimed his **"10 percent" Reconstruction plan**. It decreed that a state could be reintegrated into the Union when 10 percent of its voters in the presidential election of 1860 had taken an oath of allegiance to the United States and pledged to abide by emancipation. The next step would be formal erection of a state government. Lincoln would then recognize the purified regime.

Lincoln's proclamation provoked a sharp reaction in Congress, where Republicans feared the restoration of the planter aristocracy to power and the possible re-enslavement of blacks. Republicans therefore rammed through Congress in 1864 the **Wade-Davis Bill**. The bill required that 50 percent of a state's voters take the oath of allegiance and demanded stronger safeguards for emancipation than Lincoln's as the price of readmission to the Union. Lincoln "pocket-vetoed" this bill by refusing to sign it after Congress had adjourned. Republicans were outraged. They refused to seat delegates from Louisiana after that state had reorganized its government in accordance with Lincoln's 10 percent plan in 1864.

The controversy surrounding the Wade-Davis Bill had revealed deep differences between the president and Congress. Unlike Lincoln, many in Congress insisted that the seceders had indeed left the Union—had "committed suicide" as republican states—and had therefore forfeited all their rights. They could be readmitted only as "conquered provinces" on such conditions as Congress should decree.

TABLE 22.1 Principal Reconstruction Proposals and Plans

Year	Proposal or Plan
1864–1865	Lincoln's 10 percent proposal
1865–1866	Johnson's version of Lincoln's proposal
1866–1867	Congressional plan: 10 percent plan with Fourteenth Amendment
1867–1877	Congressional plan of military Reconstruction: Fourteenth Amendment plus black suffrage, later established nationwide by Fifteenth Amendment

This episode further revealed differences among Republicans. Two factions were emerging. The majority moderate group tended to agree with Lincoln that the seceded states should be restored to the Union as simply and swiftly as reasonable—though on Congress's terms, not the president's. The minority radical group believed that the South should atone more painfully for its sins. Before the South should be restored, the radicals wanted its social structure uprooted, the haughty planters punished, and the newly emancipated blacks protected by federal power.

Some of the radicals were secretly pleased when the assassin's bullet felled Lincoln, for the martyred president had shown tenderness toward the South. Spiteful "Andy" Johnson, who shared their hatred for the planter aristocrats, would presumably also share their desire to reconstruct the South with a rod of iron.

Johnson soon disillusioned them. He agreed with Lincoln that the seceded states had never legally been outside the Union. Thus he quickly recognized several of Lincoln's 10 percent governments, and on May 29, 1865, he issued his own Reconstruction proclamation (see Table 22.1). It disfranchised certain leading Confederates, including those with taxable property worth more than $20,000, though they might petition him for personal pardons. It called for special state conventions, which were required to repeal the ordinances of secession, repudiate all Confederate debts, and ratify the slave-freeing Thirteenth Amendment. States that complied with these conditions, Johnson declared, would be swiftly readmitted to the Union.

Johnson, savoring his dominance over the high-toned aristocrats who now begged his favor, granted pardons in abundance. Bolstered by the political resurrection of the planter elite, the recently rebellious states moved rapidly in the second half of 1865 to organize governments. But as the pattern of the new governments became clear, Republicans of all stripes grew furious.

⭐ The Baleful Black Codes

Among the first acts of the new Southern regimes sanctioned by Johnson was the passage of the iron-toothed **Black Codes**. These laws were designed to regulate the affairs of the emancipated blacks, much as the slave statutes had done in pre–Civil War days. Mississippi passed the first such law in November 1865, and other Southern states soon followed suit. The Black Codes varied in severity from state to state (Mississippi's was the harshest and Georgia's the most lenient), but they had much in common. The Black Codes aimed, first of all, to ensure a stable and subservient labor force. The crushed Cotton Kingdom could not rise from its weeds until the fields were once again put under hoe and plow—and many whites wanted to make sure that they retained the tight control they had exercised over black field hands and plow drivers in the days of slavery.

Dire penalties were therefore imposed by the codes on blacks who "jumped" their labor contracts, which usually committed them to work for the same employer for one year, and generally at pittance wages. Violators could be made to forfeit back wages or could be forcibly dragged back to work by a paid "Negro-catcher." In Mississippi the captured freedmen could be fined and then hired out to pay their fines—an arrangement that closely resembled slavery itself.

Before President Andrew Johnson (1808–1875) softened his Southern policy, his views were radical. Speaking on April 21, 1865, he declared,

❝It is not promulgating anything that I have not heretofore said to say that traitors must be made odious, that treason must be made odious, that traitors must be punished and impoverished. They must not only be punished, but their social power must be destroyed. If not, they will still maintain an ascendancy, and may again become numerous and powerful; for, in the words of a former Senator of the United States, 'When traitors become numerous enough, treason becomes respectable.'❞

Early in 1866 one congressman quoted a Georgian:

❝ The blacks eat, sleep, move, live, only by the tolerance of the whites, who hate them. The blacks own absolutely nothing but their bodies; their former masters own everything, and will sell them nothing. If a black man draws even a bucket of water from a well, he must first get the permission of a white man, his enemy. . . . If he asks for work to earn his living, he must ask it of a white man; and the whites are determined to give him no work, except on such terms as will make him a serf and impair his liberty.❞

The codes also sought to restore as nearly as possible the pre-emancipation system of race relations. Freedom was legally recognized, as were some other privileges, such as the right to marry. But all the codes forbade a black to serve on a jury; some even barred blacks from renting or leasing land. A black could be punished for "idleness" by being sentenced to work on a chain gang. Nowhere were blacks allowed to vote.

These oppressive laws mocked the ideal of freedom, so recently purchased by buckets of blood. The Black Codes imposed terrible burdens on the unfettered blacks, struggling against mistreatment and poverty to make their way as free people. The worst features of the Black Codes would eventually be repealed, but their revocation could not by itself lift the liberated blacks into economic independence. Lacking capital, and with little to offer but their labor, thousands of impoverished former slaves slipped into the status of sharecropper farmers, as did many landless whites. Luckless sharecroppers gradually sank into a morass of virtual peonage and remained there for generations. Formerly slaves to masters, countless blacks as well as poorer whites in effect became slaves to the soil and to their creditors. Yet the dethroned planter aristocracy resented even this pitiful concession to freedom. Sharecropping was the "wrong policy," said one planter. "It makes the laborer too independent; he becomes a partner, and has a right to be consulted."

The Black Codes made an ugly impression in the North. If the former slaves were being re-enslaved, people asked one another, had not the Boys in Blue spilled their blood in vain? Had the North really won the war?

✵ Congressional Reconstruction

These questions grew more insistent when the congressional delegations from the newly reconstituted Southern states presented themselves in the Capitol in December 1865. To the shock and disgust of the Republicans, many former Confederate leaders were on hand to claim their seats.

The appearance of these ex-rebels was a natural but costly blunder. Voters of the South, seeking able representatives, had turned instinctively to their experienced statesmen. But most of the Southern leaders were tainted by active association with the "lost cause." Among them were four former Confederate generals, five colonels, and various members of the Richmond cabinet and Congress. Worst of all, there was the shrimpy but brainy Alexander Stephens, ex–vice

Sharecroppers Picking Cotton
Although many freed slaves found themselves picking cotton on their former masters' plantations, they took comfort that they were at least paid wages and could work as a family unit. In time, however, they became ensnared in the web of debt that their planter bosses spun to keep a free labor force tightly bound to them.

National Archives

president of the Confederacy, still under indictment for treason.

The presence of these "whitewashed rebels" infuriated the Republicans in Congress. The war had been fought to restore the Union, but not on these kinds of terms. The Republicans were in no hurry to embrace their former enemies—virtually all of them Democrats—in the chambers of the Capitol. While the South had been "out" from 1861 to 1865, the Republicans in Congress had enjoyed a relatively free hand. They had passed much legislation that favored the North, such as the Morrill Tariff, the **Pacific Railroad Act**, and the Homestead Act. Now many Republicans balked at giving up this political advantage. On the first day of the congressional session, December 4, 1865, they banged shut the door in the face of the newly elected Southern delegations.

Looking to the future, the Republicans were alarmed to realize that a restored South would be stronger than ever in national politics. Before the war a black slave had counted as three-fifths of a person in apportioning congressional representation. Now the slave was five-fifths of a person. Eleven Southern states had seceded and been subdued by force of arms. But now, owing to full counting of free blacks, the rebel states were entitled to twelve more votes in Congress, and twelve more presidential electoral votes, than they had previously enjoyed. Again, angry voices in the North raised the cry, Who won the war?

Republicans had good reason to fear that ultimately they might be elbowed aside. Southerners might join hands with Democrats in the North and win control of Congress or maybe even the White House. If this happened, they could perpetuate the Black Codes, virtually re-enslaving blacks. They could dismantle the economic program of the Republican party by lowering tariffs, rerouting the transcontinental railroad, repealing the free-farm Homestead Act, and possibly even repudiating the national debt. President Johnson thus deeply disturbed the congressional Republicans when he announced on December 6, 1865, that the recently rebellious states had satisfied his conditions and that in his view the Union was now restored.

✴ Johnson Clashes with Congress

A clash between president and Congress was now inevitable. It exploded into the open in February 1866, when the president vetoed a bill (later repassed) extending the life of the controversial Freedmen's Bureau.

Aroused, the Republicans swiftly struck back. In March 1866 they passed the **Civil Rights Bill**, which conferred on blacks the privilege of American citizenship and struck at the Black Codes. President Johnson

resolutely vetoed this forward-looking measure on constitutional grounds, but in April congressmen steamrollered it over his veto—something they repeatedly did henceforth. The hapless president, dubbed "Sir Veto" and "Andy Veto," had his presidential wings clipped, as Congress increasingly assumed the dominant role in running the government. One critic called Johnson "the dead dog of the White House."

Republicans now feared that the Southerners might one day win control of Congress and repeal the hated civil rights law. So the lawmakers undertook to rivet the principles of the Civil Rights Bill into the Constitution as the **Fourteenth Amendment**. The proposed amendment, approved by Congress and sent to the states in June 1866 and ratified in 1868, was among the most sweeping amendments ever passed, and proved to be a major pillar of constitutional law ever after. It

An Inflexible President, 1866 This Republican cartoon shows Johnson knocking blacks out of the Freedmen's Bureau by his veto. Library of Congress

(1) conferred civil rights, including citizenship but excluding the franchise, on the freedmen; (2) reduced proportionately the representation of a state in Congress and in the Electoral College if it denied blacks the ballot; (3) disqualified from federal and state office former Confederates who as federal officeholders had once sworn "to support the Constitution of the United States"; and (4) guaranteed the federal debt, while repudiating all Confederate debts. (See the text of the Fourteenth Amendment in the Appendix.)

The radical faction was disappointed that the Fourteenth Amendment did not grant the right to vote, but all Republicans were agreed that no state should be welcomed back into the Union fold without first ratifying the Fourteenth Amendment. Yet President Johnson advised the Southern states to reject it, and all of the "sinful eleven," except Tennessee, defiantly spurned the amendment. Their spirit was reflected in a Southern song:

> *And I don't want no pardon for what I was or am,*
> *I won't be reconstructed and I don't give a damn.*

✴ Swinging 'Round the Circle with Johnson

As 1866 lengthened, the battle grew between the Congress and the president. The root of the controversy was Johnson's "10 percent" governments that had passed the most stringent Black Codes. Congress had tried to temper the worst features of the codes by extending the life of the embattled Freedmen's Bureau and passing the Civil Rights Bill. Both measures Johnson had vetoed. Now the issue was Southern acceptance of the principles enshrined in the Fourteenth Amendment. The Republicans would settle for nothing less. Indeed, they soon insisted on even more.

The crucial congressional elections of 1866—more crucial than some presidential elections—were fast approaching. Johnson was naturally eager to escape from the clutch of Congress by securing a majority favorable to his soft-on-the-South policy. Invited to dedicate a Chicago monument to Stephen A. Douglas, he undertook to speak at various cities en route in support of his views.

Johnson's famous "swing 'round the circle," beginning in the late summer of 1866, was a seriocomedy of errors. The president delivered a series of "give 'em hell" speeches, in which he accused the radicals in Congress of having planned large-scale antiblack riots and murder in the South. As he spoke, hecklers hurled insults at him. Reverting to his stump-speaking days in Tennessee, he shouted back angry retorts, amid cries of "You be damned" and "Don't get mad, Andy." The dignity of his high office sank to a new low, as the old charges of drunkenness were revived.

As a vote-getter, Johnson was highly successful—for the opposition. His inept speechmaking heightened the cry "Stand by Congress" against the "Tailor of the Potomac." When the ballots were counted, the Republicans had rolled up more than a two-thirds majority in both houses of Congress.

✴ Republican Principles and Programs

The Republicans now had a veto-proof Congress and virtually unlimited control of Reconstruction policy. But moderates and radicals still disagreed over the best course to pursue in the South.

The radicals in the Senate were led by the courtly and principled idealist Charles Sumner, long since recovered from his prewar caning on the Senate floor, who tirelessly labored not only for black freedom but for racial equality. In the House the most powerful radical was Thaddeus Stevens, crusty and vindictive congressman from Pennsylvania. Seventy-four years old in 1866, he was a curious figure, with a protruding lower lip, a heavy black wig covering his bald head, and a deformed foot. An unswerving friend of blacks, he had defended runaway slaves in court without fee and, before dying, insisted on burial in a black cemetery. His affectionate devotion to blacks was matched by his vitriolic hatred of rebellious white Southerners. A masterly parliamentarian with a razor-sharp mind and withering wit, Stevens was a leading figure on the Joint (House-Senate) Committee on Reconstruction.

Still opposed to rapid restoration of the Southern states, the radicals wanted to keep them out as long as possible and apply federal power to bring about a drastic social and economic transformation in the South. But moderate Republicans, more attuned to the time-honored principles of states' rights and self-government, recoiled from the full implications of the radical program. They preferred policies that restrained the states from abridging citizens' rights, rather than policies that

---

Representative Thaddeus Stevens (1792–1868), in a congressional speech on January 3, 1867, urged the ballot for blacks out of concern for them and out of bitterness against Southern whites:

❝I am for Negro suffrage in every rebel state. If it be just, it should not be denied; if it be necessary, it should be adopted; if it be a punishment to traitors, they deserve it.**❞**

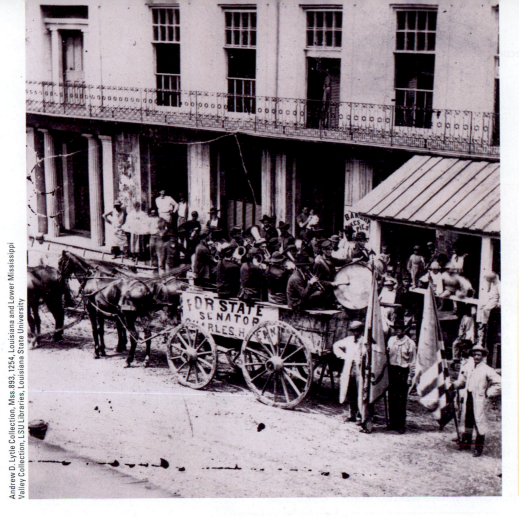

Republicans Campaigning in Baton Rouge, Louisiana, 1868 The soldiers' caps and regimental flags demonstrate the continuing federal military presence in the Reconstruction South. Radical Republican congressman Thaddeus Stevens said that Reconstruction must "revolutionize Southern institutions, habits, and manners. . . . The foundation of their institutions . . . must be broken up and relaid, or all our blood and treasure have been spent in vain."

directly involved the federal government in individual lives. The actual policies adopted by Congress showed the influence of both these schools of thought, though the moderates, as the majority faction, had the upper hand. And one thing both groups had come to agree on by 1867 was the necessity to enfranchise black voters, even if it took federal troops to do it.

✴ Reconstruction by the Sword

Against a backdrop of vicious and bloody race riots that had erupted in several Southern cities, Congress passed the **Reconstruction Act** on March 2, 1867 (see Map 22.1). Supplemented by later measures, this drastic legislation divided the South into five military districts, each commanded by a Union general and policed by blue-clad soldiers, about twenty thousand all told. The act also temporarily disfranchised tens of thousands of former Confederates.

Congress additionally laid down stringent conditions for the readmission of the seceded states. The wayward states were required to ratify the Fourteenth Amendment, giving the former slaves their rights as citizens. The bitterest pill of all to white Southerners was the stipulation that they guarantee in their state constitutions full suffrage for their former adult male slaves.

Yet the act, reflecting moderate sentiment, stopped short of giving the freedmen land or education at federal expense. The overriding purpose of the moderates was to create an electorate in Southern states that would vote those states back into the Union on acceptable terms and thus free the federal government from direct responsibility for the protection of black rights. As later events would demonstrate, this approach proved woefully inadequate to the cause of justice for blacks.

The radical Republicans were still worried. The danger loomed that once the unrepentant states were readmitted, they would amend their constitutions so as to withdraw the ballot from blacks. The only ironclad safeguard was to incorporate black suffrage in the federal Constitution. A pattern was emerging: just as the Fourteenth Amendment had constitutionalized the principles of the Civil Rights Bill, now Congress sought to provide constitutional protection for the suffrage provisions in the Reconstruction Act. This goal was finally achieved by the **Fifteenth Amendment**, passed by Congress in 1869 and ratified by the required number of states in 1870 (see the Appendix).

Military Reconstruction of the South not only usurped certain functions of the president as commander in chief but set up a martial regime of dubious legality. The Supreme Court had already ruled, in the case *Ex parte Milligan* (1866), that military tribunals

MAP 22.1 Military Reconstruction, 1867 (five districts and commanding generals) For many white Southerners, military Reconstruction amounted to turning the knife in the wound of defeat. An often-repeated story of later years had a Southerner remark, "I was sixteen years old before I discovered that damnyankee was two words." © Cengage Learning

could not try civilians, even during wartime, in areas where the civil courts were open. Peacetime military rule seemed starkly contrary to the spirit of the Constitution. But the circumstances were extraordinary in the Republic's history, and for the time being the Supreme Court avoided offending the Republican Congress.

Prodded into line by federal bayonets, the Southern states got on with the task of constitution making. By 1870 all of them had reorganized their governments

At a constitutional convention in Alabama, freed people affirmed their rights in the following declaration:

"We claim exactly the same rights, privileges and immunities as are enjoyed by white men— we ask nothing more and will be content with nothing less. . . . The law no longer knows white nor black, but simply men, and consequently we are entitled to ride in public conveyances, hold office, sit on juries and do everything else which we have in the past been prevented from doing solely on the ground of color.**"**

and had been accorded full rights (see Table 22.2). The hated "bluebellies" remained until the new Republican regimes—usually called "radical" regimes—appeared to be firmly entrenched. Yet when the federal troops finally left a state, its government swiftly passed back into the hands of white **Redeemers**, or "Home Rule" regimes, which were inevitably Democratic. Finally, in 1877, the last federal muskets were removed from state politics, and the "solid" Democratic South congealed.

✷ No Women Voters

The passage of the three Reconstruction-era Amendments—the Thirteenth, Fourteenth, and Fifteenth— delighted former abolitionists but deeply disappointed advocates of women's rights. Women had played a prominent part in the prewar abolitionist movement and had often pointed out that both women and blacks lacked basic civil rights, especially the crucial right to vote. The struggle for black freedom and the crusade for women's rights, therefore, were one and the same in the eyes of many women. Yet during the war, feminist leaders such as Elizabeth Cady Stanton and Susan B. Anthony had temporarily suspended their own demands and worked wholeheartedly for the cause of

TABLE 22.2 Southern Reconstruction by State

State	Readmitted to Representation in Congress	Home Rule (Democratic or "Redeemer" Regime) Reestablished	Comments
Tennessee	July 24, 1866		Ratified Fourteenth Amendment in 1866 and hence avoided military Reconstruction*
Arkansas	June 22, 1868	1874	
North Carolina	June 25, 1868	1870	
Alabama	June 25, 1868	1874	
Florida	June 25, 1868	1877	Federal troops restationed in 1877, as result of Hayes-Tilden electoral bargain
Louisiana	June 25, 1868	1877	Same as Florida
South Carolina	June 25, 1868	1877	Same as Florida
Virginia	January 26, 1870	1869	
Mississippi	February 23, 1870	1876	
Texas	March 30, 1870	1874	
Georgia	[June 25, 1868] July 15, 1870	1872	Readmitted June 25, 1868, but returned to military control after expulsion of blacks from legislature

*For many years Tennessee was the only state of the secession to observe Lincoln's birthday as a legal holiday. Many states in the South still observe the birthdays of Jefferson Davis and Robert E. Lee.

black emancipation. The **Woman's Loyal League** had gathered nearly 400,000 signatures on petitions asking Congress to pass a constitutional amendment prohibiting slavery.

Now, with the war ended and the Thirteenth Amendment passed, feminist leaders believed that their time had come. They reeled with shock, however, when the wording of the Fourteenth Amendment, which defined equal national citizenship, for the first time inserted the word *male* into the Constitution in referring to a citizen's right to vote. Both Stanton and Anthony campaigned actively against the Fourteenth Amendment despite the pleas of Frederick Douglass, who had long supported woman suffrage but believed that this was "the Negro's hour." When the Fifteenth Amendment proposed to prohibit denial of the vote on the basis of "race, color, or previous condition of servitude," Stanton and Anthony wanted the word *sex* added to the list. They lost this battle, too. Fifty years would pass before the Constitution granted women the right to vote.

✦ The Realities of Radical Reconstruction in the South

Blacks now had freedom, of a sort. Their friends in Congress had only haltingly and somewhat belatedly secured the franchise for them. Both Presidents Lincoln and Johnson had proposed to give the ballot gradually to selected blacks who qualified for it through education, property ownership, or military service. Moderate Republicans and even many radicals at first hesitated to bestow suffrage on the freedmen. The Fourteenth Amendment, in many ways the heart of the Republican program for Reconstruction, had fallen short of guaranteeing the right to vote. (It envisioned for blacks the same status as that of women—citizenship without

The prominent suffragist and abolitionist Susan B. Anthony (1820–1906) was outraged over the proposed exclusion of women from the Fourteenth Amendment. In a conversation with her former male allies Wendell Phillips and Theodore Tilton, she reportedly held out her arm and declared,

❝Look at this, all of you. And hear me swear that I will cut off this right arm of mine before I will ever work for or demand the ballot for the negro and not the woman.❞

Freedmen Voting, Richmond, Virginia, 1871 The exercise of democratic rights by former slaves constituted a political and social revolution in the South and was bitterly resented by whites.

Granger Collection

voting rights.) But by 1867 hesitation had given way to a hard determination to enfranchise the former slaves wholesale and immediately, while thousands of white Southerners were being denied the vote. By glaring contrast, most of the Northern states, before ratification of the Fifteenth Amendment in 1870, withheld the ballot from their tiny black minorities. White Southerners naturally concluded that the Republicans were hypocritical in insisting that blacks in the South be allowed to vote.

Having gained their right to suffrage, Southern black men seized the initiative and began to organize politically. Their primary vehicle became the **Union League**, originally a pro-Union organization based in the North. Assisted by Northern blacks, freedmen turned the League into a network of political clubs that educated members in their civic duties and campaigned for Republican candidates. The league's mission soon expanded to include building black churches and schools, representing black grievances before local employers and government, and recruiting militias to protect black communities from white retaliation.

Though African American women did not obtain the right to vote, they too assumed new political roles. Black women faithfully attended the parades and rallies common in black communities during the early years of Reconstruction and helped assemble mass meetings in the newly constructed black churches. They even showed up at the constitutional conventions held throughout the South in 1867, monitoring the proceedings and participating in informal votes outside the convention halls.

But black men elected as delegates to the state constitutional conventions held the greater political authority. They formed the backbone of the black political community. At the conventions, they sat down with whites to hammer out new state constitutions, which most importantly provided for universal male suffrage. Though the subsequent elections produced no black governors or majorities in state senates, black political participation expanded exponentially during Reconstruction. Between 1868 and 1876, fourteen black congressmen and two black senators, Hiram Revels and Blanche K. Bruce, both of Mississippi, served in Washington, D.C. Blacks also served in state governments as lieutenant governors and representatives, and in local governments as mayors, magistrates, sheriffs, and justices of the peace.

The sight of former slaves holding office deeply offended their onetime masters, who lashed out with particular fury at the freedmen's white allies, labeling them **scalawags** and **carpetbaggers**. The so-called scalawags were Southerners, often former Unionists and Whigs. The former Confederates accused them, often with wild exaggeration, of plundering the treasuries of the Southern states through their political influence in the radical governments. The carpetbaggers, on the other hand, were supposedly sleazy Northerners who had packed all their worldly goods into a carpetbag suitcase at war's end and had come south to seek personal power and profit. In fact, most were former Union soldiers and Northern businessmen and professionals who wanted to play a role in modernizing the "New South."

How well or badly did the radical regimes rule? The radical legislatures passed much desirable legislation and introduced many sorely needed reforms. For the first time in Southern history, steps were taken toward establishing adequate public schools. Tax systems were streamlined; public works were launched; and property rights were guaranteed to women. Many welcome reforms were retained by the all-white "Redeemer" governments that later returned to power.

Despite these achievements, graft ran rampant in many "radical" governments. This was especially true in South Carolina and Louisiana, where conscienceless promoters and other pocket-padders used politically inexperienced blacks as pawns. The worst "black-and-white" legislatures purchased, as "legislative supplies," such "stationery" as hams, perfumes, suspenders, bonnets, corsets, champagne, and a coffin. One "thrifty" carpetbag governor in a single year "saved" $100,000 from a salary of $8,000. Yet this sort of corruption was by no means confined to the South in these postwar years. The crimes of the Reconstruction governments were no more outrageous than the scams and felonies being perpetrated in the North at the same time, especially in Boss Tweed's New York.

✯ The Ku Klux Klan

Deeply embittered, some Southern whites resorted to savage measures against "radical" rule. Many whites resented the success and ability of black legislators as much as they resented alleged "corruption." A number of secret organizations mushroomed forth, the most notorious of which was the "Invisible Empire of the South," or **Ku Klux Klan**, founded in Tennessee in 1866. Besheeted nightriders, their horses' hooves muffled, would approach the cabin of an "upstart"

Collection of Thomas H. Gandy & Joan W. Gandy

Congressman John R. Lynch of Mississippi   After John Lynch was freed by the Union Army, he got an education at a freedmen's school in Natchez, Mississippi. At age twenty-four, he became speaker of the Mississippi House. In 1872, Lynch joined six other African Americans in Congress, where he made his greatest mark in the long debate over the Civil Rights Act of 1875, barring discrimination in public accommodations. Lynch drew on his own humiliating experiences as a black man in the South to argue for a law prohibiting discrimination on public transportation like trains and at places like inns, restaurants, and theaters. The law passed but was not enforced. It was ruled unconstitutional in 1883.

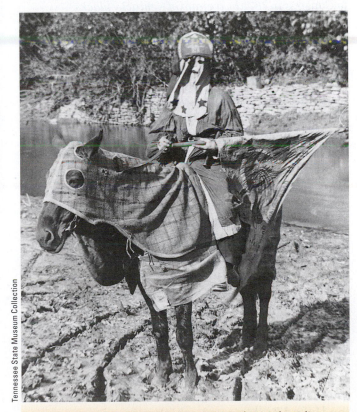

Tennessee State Museum Collection

The Ku Klux Klan, Tennessee, 1868   This night-riding terrorist has even masked the identity of his horse.

black and hammer on the door. In ghoulish tones one thirsty horseman would demand a bucket of water. Then, under pretense of drinking, he would pour it into a rubber attachment concealed beneath his mask and gown, smack his lips, and declare that this was the first water he had tasted since he was killed at the Battle of Shiloh. If fright did not produce the desired effect, force was employed.

Such tomfoolery and terror proved partially effective. Many ex-bondsmen and white "carpetbaggers," quick to take a hint, shunned the polls. Those stubborn souls who persisted in their "upstart" ways were flogged, mutilated, or even murdered. In one Louisiana parish in 1868, whites in two days killed or wounded two hundred victims; a pile of twenty-five bodies was found half-buried in the woods. By such atrocious practices were blacks "kept in their place"—that is, down. The Klan became a refuge for numerous bandits and cutthroats. Any scoundrel could don a sheet.

Congress, outraged by this night-riding lawlessness, passed the harsh **Force Acts** of 1870 and 1871. Federal troops were able to stamp out much of the "lash law," but by this time the Invisible Empire had already done its work of intimidation. Many of the outlawed groups

The following excerpt is part of a heartrending appeal to Congress in 1871 by a group of Kentucky blacks:

"We believe you are not familiar with the description of the Ku Klux Klans riding nightly over the country, going from county to county, and in the county towns, spreading terror wherever they go by robbing, whipping, ravishing, and killing our people without provocation, compelling colored people to break the ice and bathe in the chilly waters of the Kentucky River.

"The [state] legislature has adjourned. They refused to enact any laws to suppress Ku-Klux disorder. We regard them [the Ku-Kluxers] as now being licensed to continue their dark and bloody deeds under cover of the dark night. They refuse to allow us to testify in the state courts where a white man is concerned. We find their deeds are perpetrated only upon colored men and white Republicans. We also find that for our services to the government and our race we have become the special object of hatred and persecution at the hands of the Democratic Party. Our people are driven from their homes in great numbers, having no redress only [except] the United States court, which is in many cases unable to reach them."

A black leader protested to whites in 1868,

"It is extraordinary that a race such as yours, professing gallantry, chivalry, education, and superiority, living in a land where ringing chimes call child and sire to the Gospel of God—that with all these advantages on your side, you can make war upon the poor defenseless black man."

continued their tactics in the guise of "dancing clubs," "missionary societies," and "rifle clubs."

White resistance undermined attempts to empower blacks politically. The white South, for many decades, openly flouted the Fourteenth and Fifteenth Amendments. Wholesale disfranchisement of blacks, starting conspicuously about 1890, was achieved by intimidation, fraud, and trickery. Among various underhanded schemes were literacy tests, unfairly administered by whites to the advantage of illiterate whites. In the eyes of white Southerners, the goal of white supremacy fully justified these dishonorable devices.

✦ Johnson Walks the Impeachment Plank

Radicals meanwhile had been sharpening their hatchets for President Johnson. Annoyed by the obstruction of the "drunken tailor" in the White House, they falsely accused him of maintaining there a harem of "dissolute women." Not content with curbing his authority, they decided to remove him altogether by constitutional processes.*

As an initial step, Congress in 1867 passed the **Tenure of Office Act**—as usual, over Johnson's veto. Contrary to precedent, the new law required the president to secure the consent of the Senate before he could remove his appointees once they had been approved by that body. One purpose was to freeze into the cabinet the secretary of war, Edwin M. Stanton, a holdover from the Lincoln administration. Although outwardly loyal to Johnson, he was secretly serving as a spy and informer for the radicals.

Johnson provided the radicals with a pretext to begin impeachment proceedings when he abruptly dismissed Stanton early in 1868. The House of Representatives immediately voted 126 to 47 to impeach Johnson

---

*For impeachment, see Art. I, Sec. II, para. 5; Art. I, Sec. III, paras. 6, 7; Art. II, Sec. IV, in the Appendix.

Granger Collection

for "high crimes and misdemeanors," as required by the Constitution, charging him with various violations of the Tenure of Office Act. Two additional articles related to Johnson's verbal assaults on the Congress, involving "disgrace, ridicule, hatred, contempt, and reproach."

⭐ A Not-Guilty Verdict for Johnson

With evident zeal the radical-led Senate now sat as a court to try Johnson on the dubious impeachment charges. The House conducted the prosecution. The trial aroused intense public interest and, with one thousand tickets printed, proved to be the biggest show of 1868. Johnson kept his dignity and sobriety and maintained a discreet silence. His battery of attorneys argued that the president, convinced that the Tenure of Office Act was unconstitutional, had fired Stanton merely to put a test case before the Supreme Court. (That slow-moving tribunal finally ruled indirectly in Johnson's favor fifty-eight years later.) House prosecutors, including oily-tongued Benjamin F. Butler and embittered Thaddeus Stevens, had a harder time building a compelling case for impeachment.

On May 16, 1868, the day for the first voting in the Senate, the tension was electric, and heavy breathing could be heard in the galleries. By a margin of only one vote, the radicals failed to muster the two-thirds majority for Johnson's removal. Seven independent-minded Republican senators, courageously putting country above party, voted "not guilty."

Several factors shaped the outcome. Fears of creating a destabilizing precedent played a role, as did principled opposition to abusing the constitutional mechanism of checks and balances. Political considerations also figured conspicuously. As the vice presidency remained vacant under Johnson, his successor would have been radical Republican Benjamin Wade, the president pro tempore of the Senate. Wade was disliked by many members of the business community for his high-tariff, soft-money, pro-labor views and was distrusted by moderate Republicans. Meanwhile, Johnson indicated through his attorney that he would stop obstructing Republican policies in return for remaining in office.

Diehard radicals were infuriated by their failure to muster a two-thirds majority for Johnson's removal. "The Country is going to the Devil!" cried the crippled Stevens as he was carried from the hall. But the nation, though violently aroused, accepted the verdict with a good temper that did credit to its political maturity. In a less stable republic, an armed uprising might have erupted against the president.

The nation thus narrowly avoided a dangerous precedent that would have gravely weakened one of the three branches of the federal government. Johnson was clearly guilty of bad speeches, bad judgment, and bad temper, but not of "high crimes and misdemeanors." From the standpoint of the radicals, his greatest crime had been to stand inflexibly in their path.

⭐ The Purchase of Alaska

Johnson's administration, though enfeebled at home, achieved its most enduring success in the field of foreign relations.

The Russians by 1867 were in a mood to sell the vast and chilly expanse of land now known as Alaska. They had already overextended themselves in North America,

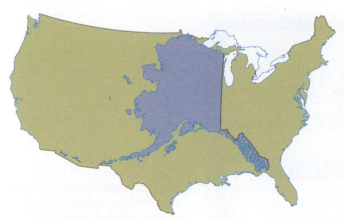

MAP 22.2 Alaska and the Lower Forty-eight States (a size comparison) © Cengage Learning

Harper's Weekly, September 2, 1876

Is This a Republican Form of Government? by Thomas Nast, Harper's Weekly, 1876 The nation's most prominent political cartoonist expressed his despair at the tragic way that Reconstruction had ended—with few real gains for the former slaves.

and they saw that in the likely event of another war with Britain, they probably would lose their defenseless northern province to the sea-dominant British. Alaska, moreover, had been ruthlessly "furred out" and was a growing economic liability. The Russians were therefore quite eager to unload their "frozen asset" on the Americans, and they put out seductive feelers in Washington. They preferred the United States to any other purchaser, primarily because they wanted to strengthen the American Republic as a barrier against their ancient enemy, Britain.

In 1867 Secretary of State William Seward, an ardent expansionist, signed a treaty with Russia that transferred Alaska to the United States for the bargain price of $7.2 million (see Map 22.2). But Seward's enthusiasm for these frigid wastes was not shared by his ignorant or uninformed countrymen, who jeered at **Seward's Folly**, "Seward's Icebox," "Frigidia," and "Walrussia."

Then why did Congress and the American public sanction the purchase? For one thing Russia, alone among the powers, had been conspicuously friendly to the North during the recent Civil War. Americans did not feel that they could offend their great and good friend, the tsar, by hurling his walrus-covered icebergs back into his face. Besides, the territory was rumored to be teeming with furs, fish, and gold, and it might yet "pan out" profitably—as it later did with natural resources, including oil and gas. So Congress and the country accepted "Seward's Polar Bear Garden," somewhat derisively but nevertheless hopefully.

✦ The Heritage of Reconstruction

Many white Southerners regarded Reconstruction as a more grievous wound than the war itself. It left a festering scar that would take generations to heal. They resented the upending of their social and racial system, the political empowerment of blacks, and the insult of federal intervention in their local affairs. Yet few rebellions have ended with the victors sitting down to a love feast with the vanquished. Given the explosiveness of the issues that had caused the war, and the bitterness of the fighting, the wonder is that Reconstruction was not far harsher than it was. The fact is that Lincoln, Johnson, and most Republicans had no clear picture at war's end of what federal policy toward the South should be. Policymakers groped for the right policies, influenced as much by Southern responses to defeat and emancipation as by any plans of their own to impose a specific program on the South.

The Republicans acted from a mixture of idealism and political expediency. They wanted both to protect the freed slaves and to promote the fortunes of the Republican party. In the end their efforts backfired badly. Reconstruction conferred only fleeting benefits on blacks and virtually extinguished the Republican party in the South for nearly one hundred years.

Moderate Republicans never fully appreciated the extensive effort necessary to make the freed slaves completely independent citizens, nor the lengths to which Southern whites would go to preserve their system of racial dominance. Had Thaddeus Stevens's radical program of drastic economic reforms and heftier protection of political rights been enacted, things might well have been different. But deep-seated racism, ingrained American resistance to tampering with property rights, and rigid loyalty to the principle of local self-government, combined with spreading indifference in the North to the plight of blacks, formed too formidable an obstacle. Despite good intentions by Republicans, the Old South was in many ways more resurrected than reconstructed, which spelled continuing woe for generations of southern blacks.

The remarkable ex-slave Frederick Douglass (1817?–1895) wrote in 1882,

❝ Though slavery was abolished, the wrongs of my people were not ended. Though they were not slaves, they were not yet quite free. No man can be truly free whose liberty is dependent upon the thought, feeling, and action of others, and who has himself no means in his own hands for guarding, protecting, defending, and maintaining that liberty. Yet the Negro after his emancipation was precisely in this state of destitution. . . . He was free from the individual master, but the slave of society. He had neither money, property, nor friends. He was free from the old plantation, but he had nothing but the dusty road under his feet. He was free from the old quarter that once gave him shelter, but a slave to the rains of summer and the frosts of winter. He was, in a word, literally turned loose, naked, hungry, and destitute, to the open sky.**❞**

Varying Viewpoints
How Radical Was Reconstruction?

Few topics have triggered as much intellectual warfare as the "dark and bloody ground" of Reconstruction. The period provoked questions—sectional, racial, and constitutional—about which people felt deeply and remain deeply divided even today. Scholarly argument goes back conspicuously to a Columbia University historian, William A. Dunning, whose students in the early 1900s published a series of histories of the Reconstruction South. Dunning and his disciples were influenced by the turn-of-the-century spirit of sectional conciliation as well as by current theories about black racial inferiority. Sympathizing with the white South, they wrote about the Reconstruction period as a kind of national disgrace, foisted upon a prostrate region by vindictive and self-seeking radical Republican politicians. If the South had wronged the North by seceding, the North had wronged the South by reconstructing.

A second cycle of scholarship in the 1920s was impelled by a widespread suspicion that the Civil War itself had been a tragic and unnecessary blunder. Attention now shifted to Northern politicians. Scholars like Howard Beale further questioned the motives of the radical Republicans. To Beale and others, the radicals had masked a ruthless desire to exploit Southern labor and resources behind a false front of "concern" for the freed slaves. Moreover, Northern advocacy of black voting rights was merely a calculated attempt to ensure a Republican political presence in the defeated South. The unfortunate Andrew Johnson, in this view, had valiantly tried to uphold constitutional principles in the face of this cynical Northern onslaught.

Although ignored by his contemporaries, scholar, black nationalist, and founder of the National Association for the Advancement of Colored People W. E. B. Du Bois wrote a sympathetic history of Reconstruction in 1935 that became the basis for historians' interpretations ever since. Following World War II, Kenneth Stampp and others, influenced by the modern civil rights movement, built on Du Bois's argument and claimed that Reconstruction had been a noble though ultimately failed attempt to extend American principles of equity and justice. The radical Republicans and the carpetbaggers were now heroes, whereas Andrew Johnson was castigated for his obstinate racism. By the early 1970s, this view had become orthodoxy, and it generally holds sway today. Yet some scholars, such as Michael Benedict and Leon Litwack, disillusioned with the inability to achieve full racial justice in the 1960s and 1970s, began once more to scrutinize the motives of Northern politicians immediately after the Civil War. They claimed to discover that Reconstruction had never been very radical and that the Freedmen's Bureau and other agencies had merely allowed white planters to maintain their dominance over local politics as well as over the local economy.

More recently, Eric Foner has powerfully reasserted the argument that Reconstruction was a truly radical and noble attempt to establish an interracial democracy. Drawing upon the work of Du Bois, Foner has emphasized the comparative approach to American Reconstruction. Clearly, Foner has admitted, Reconstruction did not create full equality, but it did allow blacks to form political organizations and churches, to vote, and to establish some measure of economic independence. In South Africa, the Caribbean, and other areas once marked by slavery, these opportunities were much harder to come by. Many of the benefits of Reconstruction were erased by whites in the South during the Gilded Age, but in the twentieth century, the constitutional principles and organizations developed during Reconstruction provided the focus and foundation for the post–World War II civil rights movement—which some have called the second Reconstruction. Steven Hahn's *A Nation Under Our Feet: Black Political Struggles in the Rural South from Slavery to the Great Migration* (2003) is the latest contribution to the literature on Reconstruction. Hahn emphasizes the assertiveness and ingenuity of African Americans in creating new political opportunities for themselves after emancipation.

Chapter Review

KEY TERMS

Freedmen's Bureau (469)

"10 percent" Reconstruction plan (470)

Wade-Davis Bill (470)

Black Codes (471)

Pacific Railroad Act (473)

Civil Rights Bill (473)

Fourteenth Amendment (473)

Reconstruction Act (475)

Fifteenth Amendment (475)

Ex parte Milligan (475)

Redeemers (476)

Woman's Loyal League (477)

Union League (478)

scalawags (478)

carpetbaggers (478)

Ku Klux Klan (479)

Force Acts (480)

Tenure of Office Act (480)

Seward's Folly (482)

PEOPLE TO KNOW

Oliver O. Howard

Andrew Johnson

Thaddeus Stevens

Hiram Revels

Edwin M. Stanton

Benjamin Wade

William Seward

TO LEARN MORE

Richard N. Current, *Those Terrible Carpetbaggers* (1988)

Eric Foner, *Reconstruction: America's Unfinished Revolution, 1863–1877* (1988)

———, *Forever Free: The Story of Emancipation and Reconstruction* (2005)

Steven Hahn, *A Nation Under Our Feet: Black Political Struggles in the Rural South from Slavery to the Great Migration* (2003)

James M. McPherson, *Ordeal by Fire: The Civil War and Reconstruction* (1981)

Peggy Pascoe, *What Comes Naturally: Miscegenation Law and the Making of Race in America* (2009)

Michael Perman, *Emancipation and Reconstruction* (rev. ed., 2003)

Lawrence Powell, *New Masters: Northern Planters During the Civil War and Reconstruction* (1980)

Julie Saville, *The Work of Reconstruction* (1994)

David O. Stewart, *The Trial of President Andrew Johnson and the Fight for Lincoln's Legacy* (2009)

Booker T. Washington, *Up from Slavery* (1901)

Heather Andrea Williams, *Self-Taught: African American Education in Slavery and Freedom* (2005)

A complete, annotated bibliography for this chapter—along with brief descriptions of the People to Know—may be found on the American Pageant website. The Key Terms are defined in a Glossary at the end of the text.

CHRONOLOGY

1863	Lincoln announces "10 percent" Reconstruction plan
1864	Lincoln vetoes Wade-Davis Bill
1865	Lincoln assassinated
	Johnson issues Reconstruction proclamation
	Congress refuses to seat Southern congressmen
	Freedmen's Bureau established
	Southern states pass Black Codes
1866	Congress passes Civil Rights Bill over Johnson's veto
	Congress passes Fourteenth Amendment
	Johnson-backed candidates lose congressional election
	Ex parte Milligan case
	Ku Klux Klan founded
1867	Reconstruction Act
	Tenure of Office Act
	United States purchases Alaska from Russia
1868	Johnson impeached and acquitted
	Johnson pardons Confederate leaders
1870	Fifteenth Amendment ratified
1870–1871	Force Acts
1872	Freedmen's Bureau ended
1877	Reconstruction ends

Part Four

Forging an Industrial Society

1865–1909

 nation of farmers fought the Civil War in the 1860s. By the time the Spanish-American War broke out in 1898, America was an industrial nation. For generations Americans had plunged into the wilderness and plowed their fields. Now they settled in cities and toiled in factories. Between the Civil War and the century's end, economic and technological change came so swiftly and massively that it seemed to many Americans that a whole new civilization had emerged.

In some ways it had. The sheer scale of the new industrial society was dazzling. Transcontinental railroads knit the country together from sea to sea. New industries like oil and steel grew to staggering size—and made megamillionaires out of entrepreneurs like oilman John D. Rockefeller and steel maker Andrew Carnegie.

Drawn by the allure of industrial employment, Americans moved to the city, much like their counterparts in industrializing Europe, Russia, and Japan. In 1860 only about 20 percent of the population were city dwellers. By 1900 that proportion doubled, as rural Americans and European immigrants alike flocked to mill town and metropolis in search of steady jobs.

These sweeping changes challenged the spirit of individualism that Americans had celebrated since the seventeenth century. Even on the western frontier, that historic bastion of rugged loners, the hand of government was increasingly felt, as large armies were dispatched to subdue the Plains Indians and federal authority was invoked to regulate the use of natural resources. The rise of powerful monopolies called into question the government's traditional hands-off policy toward business, and a growing band of reformers increasingly clamored for government regulation of private enterprise. The mushrooming cities, with their need for transport systems, schools, hospitals, sanitation, and fire and police protection, required bigger governments and budgets than an earlier generation could have imagined. As never before, Americans struggled to adapt old ideals of private autonomy to the new realities of industrial civilization.

With economic change came social and political turmoil. Labor violence brought bloodshed to places such as Chicago and Homestead, Pennsylvania. Small farmers, squeezed by debt and foreign competition, rallied behind the People's, or "Populist," party, a radical movement of the 1880s and 1890s

Factory Workers, with Railroad Spikes, Harrisburg, Pennsylvania, 1898
Immigrant and native-born workers alike bent their backs to build industrial America. William B. Becker Collection/American Museum of Photography

that attacked the power of Wall Street, big business, and the banks. Anti-immigrant sentiment swelled. Bitter disputes over tariffs and monetary policy deeply divided the country, setting debtors against lenders, farmers against manufacturers, the West and South against the Northeast. And in this unfamiliar era of big money and expanding government, corruption flourished, from town hall to Congress, fueling loud cries for political reform.

The bloodiest conflict of all pitted Plains Indians against the relentless push of westward expansion. As railroads drove their iron arrows through the heart of the West, the Indians lost their land and life-sustaining buffalo herds. By the 1890s, after three decades of fierce fighting with the U.S. Army, the Indians who had once roamed across the vast rolling prairies were struggling to preserve their shattered cultures within the confinement of reservations.

The South remained the one region largely untouched by the Industrial Revolution sweeping the rest of America. A few sleepy southern hamlets did become boomtowns, but for the most part, the South's rural way of life remained unperturbed. The post-emancipation era inflicted new forms of racial injustice on African Americans, the vast majority of whom continued to live in the Old South. State legislatures systematically deprived black Americans of their political rights, including the right to vote. Segregation of schools, housing, and all kinds of public facilities made a mockery of African Americans' Reconstruction-era hopes for equality before the law.

The new wealth and power of industrial America nurtured a growing sense of national self-confidence. Literature flowered, and a golden age of philanthropy dawned. The reform spirit spread. So did a restless appetite for overseas expansion. In a brief war against Spain in 1898, the United States, born in a revolutionary war of independence and long the champion of national self-determination, seized control of the Philippines and itself became an imperial power. Uncle Sam's venture into empire touched off a bitter national debate about America's role in the world and ushered in a long period of argument over the responsibilities, at home as well as abroad, of a modern industrial state.

Curt Teich Postcard Archives, Lake County Museum

Dearborn Street, Chicago Loop, Around 1900 "America is energetic, but Chicago is in a fever," marveled a visiting Englishman about turn-of-the-century Chicago. Street scenes like this were common in America's booming new cities, especially in the "Lord of the Midwest."

Chapter 23

Political Paralysis in the Gilded Age

1869–1896

Grant . . . had no right to exist. He should have been extinct for ages. . . . That, two thousand years after Alexander the Great and Julius Caesar, a man like Grant should be called—and should actually and truly be—the highest product of the most advanced evolution, made evolution ludicrous. . . . The progress of evolution, from President Washington to President Grant, was alone evidence enough to upset Darwin. . . . Grant . . . should have lived in a cave and worn skins.

HENRY ADAMS, THE EDUCATION OF HENRY ADAMS, 1907

The population of the post–Civil War Republic continued to vault upward by vigorous leaps, despite the awful bloodletting in both Union and Confederate ranks. Census takers reported over 39 million people in 1870, a gain of 26.6 percent over the preceding decade, as the immigrant tide surged again. The United States was now the third-largest nation in the Western world, ranking behind Russia and France.

But the civic health of the United States did not keep pace with its physical growth. The Civil War and its aftermath spawned waste, extravagance, speculation, and graft. Disillusionment ran deep among idealistic Americans in the postwar era. They had spilled their blood for the Union, emancipation, and Abraham Lincoln, who had promised "a new birth of freedom." Instead they got a bitter dose of corruption and political stalemate—beginning with Ulysses S. Grant, a great soldier but an utterly inept politician.

✦ The "Bloody Shirt" Elects Grant

Wrangling between Congress and President Andrew Johnson had soured the people on professional politicians in the Reconstruction era, and the notion still prevailed that a good general would make a good president. Stubbly-bearded General Grant was by far the most popular northern hero to emerge from the war. Grateful citizens of Philadelphia, Washington, and his hometown of Galena, Illinois, passed the hat and in each place presented him with a house. New Yorkers tendered him a check for $105,000. The general, silently puffing on his cigar, unapologetically accepted these gifts as his just deserts for having rescued the Union.

Grant was a hapless greenhorn in the political arena. His one presidential vote had been cast for the Democratic ticket in 1856. A better judge of horseflesh than of humans, his cultural background was breathtakingly narrow. He once reportedly remarked that Venice (Italy) would be a fine city if only it were drained.

The Republicans, freed from the Union party coalition of war days, enthusiastically nominated Grant for the presidency in 1868. The party's platform sounded a clarion call for continued Reconstruction of the South under the glinting steel of federal bayonets. Yet Grant, always a man of few words, struck a highly popular note in his letter of acceptance when he said, "Let us have peace." This noble sentiment became a leading campaign slogan and was later engraved on his tomb beside the Hudson River.

Expectant Democrats, meeting in their own nominating convention, denounced military Reconstruction but could agree on little else. Wealthy eastern delegates demanded a plank promising that federal war bonds be redeemed in gold—even though many of the bonds had been purchased with badly depreciated paper greenbacks. Poorer midwestern delegates answered with the "Ohio Idea," which called for redemption in greenbacks. Debt-burdened agrarian Democrats thus hoped to keep more money in circulation and keep interest rates lower. This dispute introduced a bitter contest over monetary policy that continued to convulse the Republic until the century's end.

Midwestern delegates got the platform but not the candidate. The nominee, former New York governor Horatio Seymour, scuttled the Democrats' faint hope for success by repudiating the Ohio Idea. Republicans whipped up enthusiasm for Grant by energetically **"waving the bloody shirt"**—that is, reviving gory memories of the Civil War—which became for the first time a prominent feature of a presidential campaign.* "Vote as You Shot" was a powerful Republican slogan aimed at Union army veterans.

Grant won, with 214 electoral votes to 80 for Seymour. But the former general scored a majority of only 300,000 in the popular vote (3,013,421 to 2,706,829). Most white voters apparently supported Seymour, and the ballots of three still-unreconstructed southern states (Mississippi, Texas, and Virginia) were not counted at all. An estimated 500,000 former slaves gave Grant his margin of victory. To remain in power, the Republican party somehow had to continue to control the South—and to keep the ballot in the hands of the grateful freedmen. Republicans could not take future victories "for Granted."

⭐ The Era of Good Stealings

A few skunks can pollute a large area. Although the great majority of businesspeople and government officials continued to conduct their affairs with decency and honor, the whole postwar atmosphere stunk of corruption. The Man in the Moon, it was said, had to hold his nose when passing over America. Freewheeling railroad promoters sometimes left gullible bond buyers with only "two streaks of rust and a right of way." Unethical stock-market manipulators were a cinder in the public eye. Too many judges and legislators put

---

*The expression is said to have derived from a speech by Representative Benjamin F. Butler of Massachusetts, who allegedly waved before the House the bloodstained nightshirt of a Klan-flogged carpetbagger.

their power up for hire. Cynics defined an honest politician as one who, when bought, would stay bought.

Notorious in the financial world were two millionaire partners, "Jubilee Jim" Fisk and Jay Gould. The corpulent and unscrupulous Fisk provided the "brass," while the undersized and cunning Gould provided the brains. The crafty pair concocted a plot in 1869 to corner the gold market. Their slippery game would work only if the federal Treasury refrained from selling gold. The conspirators worked on President Grant directly and also through his brother-in-law, who received $25,000 for his complicity. For weeks Fisk and Gould

In a famous series of newspaper interviews in 1905, George Washington Plunkitt (1842–1924), a political "boss" in the same Tammany Hall Democratic political "machine" that had spawned William Marcy ("Boss") Tweed, candidly described his ethical and political principles:

"Everybody is talkin' these days about Tammany men growin' rich on graft, but nobody thinks of drawin' the distinction between honest graft and dishonest graft. There's all the difference in the world between the two. Yes, many of our men have grown rich in politics. I have myself. I've made a big fortune out of the game, and I'm gettin' richer every day, but I've not gone in for dishonest graft—blackmailin' gamblers, saloonkeepers, disorderly people, etc.—and neither has any of the men who have made big fortunes in politics.

"There's an honest graft, and I'm an example of how it works. I might sum up the whole thing by sayin': 'I seen my opportunities and I took 'em.'

"Just let me explain by examples. My party's in power in the city, and it's goin' to undertake a lot of public improvements. Well, I'm tipped off, say, that they're going to lay out a new park at a certain place.

"I see my opportunity and I take it. I go to that place and I buy up all the land I can in the neighborhood. Then the board of this or that makes its plan public, and there is a rush to get my land, which nobody cared particular for before.

"Ain't it perfectly honest to charge a good price and make a profit on my investment and foresight? Of course, it is. Well, that's honest graft."

Can the Law Reach Him? 1872 Cartoonist Thomas Nast attacked "Boss" Tweed in a series of cartoons like this one that appeared in *Harper's Weekly* in 1872. Here Nast depicts the corrupt Tweed as a powerful giant, towering over a puny law force. © Bettmann/Corbis

madly bid the price of gold skyward, so they could later profit from its heightened value. But on "Black Friday" (September 24, 1869), the bubble broke when the Treasury, contrary to Grant's supposed assurances, was compelled to release gold. The price of gold plunged, and scores of honest businesspeople were driven to the wall. A congressional probe concluded that Grant had done nothing crooked, though he had acted stupidly and indiscreetly.

The infamous **Tweed Ring** in New York City vividly displayed the ethics (or lack of ethics) typical of the age. Burly "Boss" Tweed—240 pounds of rascality—employed bribery, graft, and fraudulent elections to milk the metropolis of as much as $200 million. Honest citizens were cowed into silence. Protesters found their tax assessments raised.

Tweed's luck finally ran out. The *New York Times* secured damning evidence in 1871 and courageously published it, though offered $5 million not to do so. Gifted cartoonist Thomas Nast pilloried Tweed mercilessly, after spurning a heavy bribe to desist. The portly thief reportedly complained that his illiterate followers could not help seeing "them damn pictures." New York attorney Samuel J. Tilden headed the prosecution, gaining fame that later paved the path to his presidential nomination. Unbailed and unwept, Tweed died behind bars.

✴ A Carnival of Corruption

More serious than Boss Tweed's peccadilloes were the misdeeds of the federal government. President Grant's cabinet was a rodent's nest of grafters and incompetents. Favor seekers haunted the White House, plying Grant himself with cigars, wines, and horses. His election was a godsend to his in-laws of the Dent family, several dozen of whom attached themselves to the public payroll.

The easygoing Grant was first tarred by the **Crédit Mobilier scandal**, which erupted in 1872. Union Pacific Railroad insiders had formed the Crédit Mobilier construction company and then cleverly hired themselves at inflated prices to build the railroad line, earning dividends as high as 348 percent. Fearing that Congress might blow the whistle, the company furtively distributed shares of its valuable stock to key congressmen. A newspaper exposé and congressional investigation of the scandal led to the formal censure of two congressmen and the revelation that the vice president of the United States had accepted payments from Crédit Mobilier.

The breath of scandal in Washington also reeked of alcohol. In 1874–1875 the sprawling Whiskey Ring robbed the Treasury of millions in excise-tax revenues. "Let no guilty man escape," declared President Grant. But when his own private secretary turned up among the culprits, he volunteered a written statement to the jury that helped exonerate the thief. Further rottenness in the Grant administration came to light in 1876, forcing Secretary of War William Belknap to resign after pocketing bribes from suppliers to the Indian reservations. Grant, ever loyal to his crooked cronies, accepted Belknap's resignation "with great regret."

✴ The Liberal Republican Revolt of 1872

By 1872 a powerful wave of disgust with Grantism was beginning to build up throughout the nation, even before some of the worst scandals had been exposed. Reform-minded citizens banded together to form the Liberal Republican party. Voicing the slogan "Turn the Rascals Out," they urged purification of the Washington administration as well as an end to military Reconstruction.

The Liberal Republicans muffed their chance when their Cincinnati nominating convention astounded the country by nominating the brilliant but erratic Horace Greeley for the presidency. Although Greeley was the fearless editor of the *New York Tribune*, he was dogmatic, emotional, petulant, and notoriously unsound in his political judgments.

More astonishing still was the action of the office-hungry Democrats, who foolishly proceeded to endorse Greeley's candidacy. In swallowing Greeley the Democrats "ate crow" in large gulps, for the eccentric editor had long blasted them as traitors, slave shippers, saloon keepers, horse thieves, and idiots. Yet Greeley pleased the Democrats, North and South, when he pleaded for clasping hands across "the bloody chasm." The Republicans dutifully renominated Grant. The voters were thus presented with a choice between two candidates who had made their careers in fields other than politics and who were both eminently unqualified, by temperament and lifelong training, for high political office.

In the mud-spattered campaign that followed, regular Republicans denounced Greeley as an atheist, a communist, a free-lover, a vegetarian, a brown-bread eater, and a cosigner of Jefferson Davis's bail bond. Democrats derided Grant as an ignoramus, a drunkard, and a swindler. But the regular Republicans, chanting "Grant us another term," pulled the president through. The count in the electoral column was 286 to 66, in the popular column 3,596,745 to 2,843,446.

Liberal Republican agitation frightened the regular Republicans into cleaning their own house before they were thrown out of it. The Republican Congress in 1872 passed a general amnesty act, removing political disabilities from all but some five hundred former Confederate leaders. Congress also moved to reduce high Civil War tariffs and to fumigate the Grant administration with mild civil-service reform. Like many American third parties, the Liberal Republicans left some enduring footprints, even in defeat.

✴ Depression, Deflation, and Inflation

Grant's woes deepened in the paralyzing economic **panic of 1873**. Bursting with startling rapidity, the crash was one of those periodic plummets that roller-coastered the economy in this age of unbridled capitalist expansion. Overreaching promoters had laid more railroad track, sunk more mines, erected more factories, and sowed more grainfields than existing markets could bear. Bankers, in turn, had made too many imprudent loans to finance those enterprises. When profits failed to materialize, loans went unpaid, and the whole credit-based house of cards fluttered down. The United States did not suffer alone. Nations worldwide underwent a similar economic collapse in 1873.

Boom times became gloom times as more than fifteen thousand American businesses went bankrupt. In New York City, an army of unemployed riotously battled police. Black Americans were hard hit. The Freedman's Savings and Trust Company had made unsecured loans to several companies that went under. Black depositors who had entrusted over $7 million to the bank lost their savings, and black economic development and black confidence in savings institutions went down with it.

Hard times inflicted the worst punishment on debtors, who intensified their clamor for inflationary policies. Proponents of inflation breathed new life into the issue of greenbacks. During the war $450 million of the "folding money" had been issued, but it had depreciated under a cloud of popular mistrust

Granger Collection

Can Greeley and the Democrats "Swallow" Each Other? 1872 This cartoon by Thomas Nast is a Republican gibe at the forced alliance between these former foes. General William Tecumseh Sherman wrote from Paris to his brother, "I feel amazed to see the turn things have taken. Grant who never was a Republican is your candidate; and Greeley who never was a Democrat, but quite the reverse, is the Democratic candidate."

and dubious legality.* By 1868 the Treasury had already withdrawn $100 million of the "battle-born currency" from circulation, and "hard-money" people everywhere looked forward to its complete disappearance. But now afflicted agrarian and debtor groups—"cheap-money" supporters—clamored for a reissuance of the greenbacks. With a crude but essentially accurate grasp of monetary theory, they reasoned that more money meant cheaper money and, hence, rising prices and easier-to-pay debts. Creditors, of course, reasoning from the same premises, advocated precisely the opposite policy. They had no desire to see the money they had loaned repaid in depreciated dollars. They wanted deflation, not inflation.

The "hard-money" advocates carried the day. In 1874 they persuaded a confused Grant to veto a bill to print more paper money. They scored another victory in the Resumption Act of 1875, which pledged the government to the further withdrawal of greenbacks from circulation and to the redemption of all paper currency in gold at face value, beginning in 1879.

Down but not out, debtors now looked for relief to another precious metal, silver. The "sacred white metal," they claimed, had received a raw deal. In the early 1870s, the Treasury stubbornly and unrealistically maintained that an ounce of silver was worth only one-sixteenth as much as an ounce of gold, though open-market prices for silver were higher. Silver miners thus stopped offering their shiny product for sale to the federal mints. With no silver flowing into the federal coffers, Congress formally dropped the coinage of silver dollars in 1873. Fate then played a sly joke when new silver discoveries later in the 1870s shot production up and forced silver prices down. Westerners from silver-mining states joined with debtors in assailing the "Crime of '73," demanding a return to the "Dollar of Our Daddies." Like the demand for more greenbacks, the demand for the coinage of more silver was nothing more nor less than another scheme to promote inflation.

Hard-money Republicans resisted this scheme and counted on Grant to hold the line against it. He did not disappoint them. The Treasury began to accumulate gold stocks against the appointed day for resumption of metallic-money payments. Coupled with the reduction of greenbacks, this policy was called "contraction." It had a noticeable deflationary effect—the amount of money per capita in circulation actually *decreased* between 1870 and 1880, from $19.42 to $19.37. Contraction probably

---

*The Supreme Court in 1870 declared the Civil War Legal Tender Act unconstitutional. With the concurrence of the Senate, Grant thereupon added to the bench two justices who could be counted on to help reverse that decision, which happened in 1871. This is how the Court grew to its current size of nine justices.

David A. Wells (1828–1898), a leading economist of the era, described the global dimensions of the depression that struck the United States in 1873:

"Its most noteworthy peculiarity has been its universality; affecting nations that have been involved in war as well as those which have maintained peace; those which have a stable currency, based on gold, and those which have an unstable currency, based on promises which have not been kept; those which live under systems of free exchange of commodities, and those whose exchanges are more or less restricted. It has been grievous in old communities like England and Germany, and equally so in Australia, South Africa, and California, which represent the new; it has been a calamity exceeding[ly] heavy to be borne, alike by the inhabitants of sterile Newfoundland and Labrador, and of the sunny, fruitful sugar-islands of the East and West Indies."

worsened the impact of the depression. But the new policy did restore the government's credit rating, and it brought the embattled greenbacks up to their full face value. When Redemption Day came in 1879, few greenback holders bothered to exchange the lighter and more convenient bills for gold.

Republican hard-money policy had a political backlash. It helped elect a Democratic House of Representatives in 1874, and in 1878 it spawned the Greenback Labor party, which polled over a million votes and elected fourteen members of Congress. The contest over monetary policy was far from over.

✴ Pallid Politics in the Gilded Age

The political seesaw was delicately balanced throughout most of the **Gilded Age** (a sarcastic name given to the three-decade-long post–Civil War era by Mark Twain in 1873). Even a slight nudge could tip the teeter-totter to the advantage of the opposition party. Every presidential election was a squeaker, and the majority party in the House of Representatives switched six times in the eleven sessions between 1869 and 1891. In only three sessions did the same party control the House, the Senate, and the White House. Wobbling in such shaky equilibrium, politicians tiptoed timidly, producing a political record that was often trivial and petty.

Few significant economic issues separated the major parties. Democrats and Republicans saw very nearly eye-to-eye on questions like the tariff and civil-service reform, and majorities in both parties substantially agreed even on the much-debated currency question. Yet despite their rough agreement on these national matters, the two parties were ferociously competitive with each other. They were tightly and efficiently organized, and they commanded fierce loyalty from their members. Voter turnouts reached heights unmatched before or since. Nearly 80 percent of eligible voters cast their ballots in presidential elections in the three decades after the Civil War. On election days droves of the party faithful tramped behind marching bands to the polling places, and "ticket splitting," or failing to vote the straight party line, was as rare as a silver dollar.

How can this apparent paradox of political consensus and partisan fervor be explained? The answer lies in the sharp ethnic and cultural differences in the membership of the two parties—in distinctions of style and tone, and especially of religious sentiment. Republican voters tended to adhere to those creeds that traced their lineage to Puritanism. They stressed strict codes of personal morality and believed that government should play a role in regulating both the economic and the moral affairs of society. Democrats, among whom immigrant Lutherans and Roman Catholics figured heavily, were more likely to adhere to faiths that took a less stern view of human weakness. Their religions professed toleration of differences in an imperfect world, and they spurned government efforts to impose a single moral standard on the entire society. These differences in temperament and religious values often produced raucous political contests at the local level, where issues like prohibition and education loomed large.

Democrats had a solid electoral base in the South and in the northern industrial cities, teeming with immigrants and controlled by well-oiled political machines. Republican strength lay largely in the Midwest and the rural and small-town Northeast. Grateful freedmen in the South continued to vote Republican in significant numbers. Another important bloc of Republican ballots came from the members of the Grand Army of the Republic (GAR)—a politically potent fraternal organization of several hundred thousand Union veterans of the Civil War.

The lifeblood of both parties was **patronage**—disbursing jobs by the bucketful in return for votes,

The Granger Collection/(inset photo) Collection of Janice L. and David J. Frent

The Political Legacy of the Civil War   Union veterans of the Civil War supported Republican candidate Rutherford B. Hayes in 1876. The Grand Army of the Republic (G.A.R.), the Union veterans' organization, voted heavily for the G.O.P. (Grand Old Party) in the post-civil war years.

kickbacks, and party service. Boisterous infighting over patronage beset the Republican party in the 1870s and 1880s. A "Stalwart" faction, led by the handsome and imperious Roscoe ("Lord Roscoe") Conkling, U.S. senator from New York, unblushingly embraced the time-honored system of swapping civil-service jobs for votes. Opposed to the Conklingites were the so-called Half-Breeds, who flirted coyly with civil-service reform, but whose real quarrel with the Stalwarts was over who should grasp the ladle that dished out the spoils. The champion of the Half-Breeds was James G. Blaine of Maine, a radiantly personable congressman with an elastic conscience. But despite the color of their personalities, Conkling and Blaine succeeded only in stalemating each other and deadlocking their party.

✦ The Hayes-Tilden Standoff, 1876

Hangers-on around Grant, like fleas urging their ailing dog to live, begged the "Old Man" to try for a third term in 1876. The general, blind to his own ineptitudes, showed a disquieting willingness. But the House, by a lopsided bipartisan vote of 233 to 18, derailed the third-term bandwagon. It passed a resolution that sternly reminded the country—and Grant—of the antidictator implications of the two-term tradition.

With Grant out of the running and with the Conklingites and Blaineites neutralizing each other, the Republicans turned to a compromise candidate, Rutherford B. Hayes, who was obscure enough to be dubbed "The Great Unknown." His foremost qualification was the fact that he hailed from the electorally doubtful but potent state of Ohio, where he had served three terms as governor. So crucial were the "swing" votes of Ohio in the cliffhanging presidential contests of the day that the state produced more than its share of presidential candidates. A political saying of the 1870s paraphrased Shakespeare:

> *Some are born great,*
> *Some achieve greatness,*
> *And some are born in Ohio.*

Pitted against the humdrum Hayes was the Democratic nominee, Samuel J. Tilden, who had risen to fame as the man who bagged Boss Tweed in New York. Campaigning against Republican scandal, Tilden racked up 184 electoral votes of the needed 185, with 20 votes in four states—three of them in the South—doubtful because of irregular returns (see Map 23.1). Surely Tilden could pick up at least one of these, especially in view of the fact that he had polled 247,448 more popular votes than Hayes, 4,284,020 to 4,036,572.

Both parties scurried to send "visiting statesmen" to the contested southern states of Louisiana, South Carolina, and Florida. All three disputed states submitted

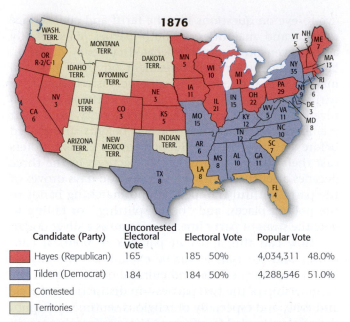

Candidate (Party)	Uncontested Electoral Vote	Electoral Vote		Popular Vote	
🟥 Hayes (Republican)	165	185	50%	4,034,311	48.0%
🟦 Tilden (Democrat)	184	184	50%	4,288,546	51.0%
🟧 Contested					
⬜ Territories					

MAP 23.1 Hayes-Tilden Disputed Election of 1876 (with electoral vote by state) Nineteen of the twenty disputed votes composed the total electoral count of Louisiana, South Carolina, and Florida. The twentieth was one of Oregon's three votes, cast by an elector who turned out to be ineligible because he was a federal officeholder (a postmaster), contrary to the Constitution (see Art. II, Sec. I, para. 2). © Cengage Learning

two sets of returns, one Democratic and one Republican. As the weeks drifted by, the paralysis tightened, generating a dramatic constitutional crisis. The Constitution merely specifies that the electoral returns from the states shall be sent to Congress, and in the presence of the House and Senate, they shall be opened by the president of the Senate (see the Twelfth Amendment in the Appendix). But who should count them? On this point the Constitution was silent. If counted by the president of the Senate (a Republican), the Republican returns would be selected. If counted by the Speaker of the House (a Democrat), the Democratic returns would be chosen. How could the impasse be resolved?

✦ The Compromise of 1877 and the End of Reconstruction

Clash or compromise was the stark choice. The danger loomed that there would be no president on Inauguration Day, March 4, 1877. "Tilden or Blood!" cried Democratic hotheads, and some of their "Minute Men" began to drill with arms. But behind the scenes, frantically laboring statesmen gradually hammered out an agreement in the Henry Clay tradition—the **Compromise of 1877**.

The election deadlock itself was to be broken by the Electoral Count Act, which Congress passed early

TABLE 23.1 Composition of the Electoral Commission, 1877		
Members	**Republicans**	**Democrats**
Senate (Republican majority)	3	2
House (Democratic majority)	2	3
Supreme Court	3	2
TOTAL	8	7

in 1877. It set up an electoral commission consisting of fifteen men selected from the Senate, the House, and the Supreme Court (see Table 23.1).

In February 1877, about a month before Inauguration Day, the Senate and House met together in an electric atmosphere to settle the dispute. The roll of the states was tolled off alphabetically. When Florida was reached—the first of the three southern states with two sets of returns—the disputed documents were referred to the electoral commission, which sat in a nearby chamber. After prolonged discussion the members agreed, by the partisan vote of eight Republicans to seven Democrats, to accept the Republican returns. Outraged Democrats in Congress, smelling defeat, undertook to launch a filibuster "until hell froze over."

Renewed deadlock was avoided by the rest of the complex Compromise of 1877, already partially concluded behind closed doors. The Democrats reluctantly agreed that Hayes might take office in return for his withdrawing intrusive federal troops from the two states in which they remained, Louisiana and South Carolina. Among various concessions, the Republicans assured the Democrats a place at the presidential patronage trough and support for a bill subsidizing the Texas and Pacific Railroad's construction of a southern transcontinental line. Not all of these promises were kept in later years, including the Texas and Pacific subsidy. But the deal held together long enough to break the dangerous electoral standoff. The Democrats permitted Hayes to receive the remainder of the disputed returns—all by the partisan vote of 8 to 7. So close was the margin of safety that the explosive issue was settled only three days before the new president was officially sworn into office. The nation breathed a collective sigh of relief.

The compromise bought peace at a price. Partisan violence was averted by sacrificing the civil rights of southern blacks. With the Hayes-Tilden deal, the Republican party quietly abandoned its commitment to racial equality. That commitment had been weakening in any case. Many Republicans had begun to question the worthiness of Reconstruction and were less willing to send dollars and enlisted sons to bolster southern state governments.

The **Civil Rights Act of 1875** was in a sense the last feeble gasp of the congressional radical Republicans. The act supposedly guaranteed equal accommodations in public places and prohibited racial discrimination in jury selection, but the law was born toothless and stayed that way for nearly a century. The Supreme Court pronounced much of the act unconstitutional in the *Civil Rights Cases* (1883). The Court

Library of Congress

THE "STRONG" GOVERNMENT 1869–1877.

THE "WEAK" GOVERNMENT 1877–1881.

The End of Reconstruction, 1877 President Hayes's "Let 'em Alone" policy replaces the carpetbags and bayonets of the Grant administration, signifying the end of federal efforts to promote racial equality in the South—until the "second Reconstruction" of the civil rights era nearly a century later.

declared that the Fourteenth Amendment prohibited only *government* violations of civil rights, not the denial of civil rights by *individuals*. When President Hayes withdrew the blue-clad federal troops that were propping up Reconstruction governments, the bayonet-backed Republican regimes collapsed.

The Birth of Jim Crow in the Post-Reconstruction South

The Democratic South speedily solidified and swiftly suppressed the now-friendless blacks. Reconstruction, for better or worse, was officially ended. Shamelessly relying on fraud and intimidation, white Democrats ("Redeemers") reassumed political power in the South and exercised it ruthlessly. Blacks who tried to assert their rights faced unemployment, eviction, and physical harm.

Many blacks (as well as poor whites) were forced into **sharecropping** and tenant farming. Former slaves often found themselves at the mercy of former masters who were now their landlords and creditors. Through the "crop-lien" system, storekeepers extended credit to small farmers for food and supplies and in return took a lien on their harvests. Shrewd merchants manipulated the system so that farmers remained perpetually in debt to them. For generations to come,

southern blacks were condemned to eke out a threadbare living under conditions scarcely better than slavery (see Map 23.2).

With white southerners back in the political saddle, daily discrimination against blacks grew increasingly oppressive. What had started as the informal separation of blacks and whites in the immediate postwar years developed by the 1890s into systematic state-level legal codes of segregation known as **Jim Crow** laws. Southern states also enacted literacy requirements, voter-registration laws, and poll taxes—and tolerated violent intimidation of black voters—to ensure full-scale disfranchisement of the South's freedmen. The Supreme Court validated the South's segregationist social order in the case of ***Plessy* v. *Ferguson*** (1896). It ruled that "separate but equal" facilities were constitutional under the "equal protection" clause of the Fourteenth Amendment. But in reality the quality of African American life was grotesquely unequal to that of whites. Segregated in inferior schools and separated from whites in virtually all public facilities, including railroad cars, theaters, and even restrooms, blacks were assaulted daily by galling reminders of their second-class citizenship. To ensure the stability of this political and economic "new order," southern whites dealt harshly with any black who dared to violate the South's racial code of conduct. A record number of blacks were lynched during the 1890s, most often for the "crime" of

Jim Crow Justice In 1893 a black man named Henry Smith was burned at the stake in Paris, Texas, for supposedly molesting a four-year-old white girl. Hundreds of gawkers poured into the city from the surrounding county to watch the gruesome spectacle. Public executions like this one, or the more common lynching of black men, were aimed at intimidating African Americans into accepting second-class status in the Jim Crow South.

MAP 23.2 A Southern Plantation, Before and After the Civil War The emancipated blacks moved out of the slave quarters and into humble cabins dispersed around the plantation. The master had now become the landlord and the employer, and the slaves had become tenant farmers and sharecroppers—but were they better off? © Cengage Learning

TABLE 23.2 Persons in United States Lynched (by race), 1882–2005*			
Year	**Whites**	**Blacks**	**Total**
1882	64	49	113
1885	110	74	184
1890	11	85	96
1895	66	113	179
1900	9	106	115
1905	5	57	62
1910	9	67	76
1915	13	56	69
1920	8	53	61
1925	0	17	17
1930	1	20	21
1935	2	18	20
1940	1	4	5
1945	0	1	1
1950	1	1	2
1965	0	0	0
1996	1	5	6
2000	5	3	8
2005	1	2	3

* Note the predominance of black lynchings after 1890. The worst year was 1892, when 161 blacks and 69 whites were lynched (total 230); the next worst was 1884, when 164 whites and 51 blacks were lynched (total 215). In 1992, the FBI began to collect statistics on hate crimes. From 1996 on, the numbers correspond to all hate crime murders, not limited to lynching.

(Sources: Tuskegee Institute Archives; Federal Bureau of Investigation Hate Crimes Report, relevant years.)

asserting themselves as equals (see Table 23.2). It would take a second Reconstruction, nearly a century later, to redress the racist imbalance of southern society.

✵ Class Conflicts and Ethnic Clashes

The year 1877 marked more than the end of Reconstruction. As the curtains officially closed on regional warfare, they opened on scenes of class struggle. The explosive atmosphere was largely a by-product of the long years of depression and deflation following the panic of 1873. Railroad workers faced particularly hard times, while they watched the railroads continue to rake in huge profits. When the presidents of the nation's four largest railroads collectively decided in 1877 to cut employees' wages by 10 percent, the workers struck back. President Hayes's decision to call in federal troops to quell the unrest brought the striking laborers an outpouring of working-class support. Work stoppages spread like wildfire in cities from Baltimore to St. Louis. When the battling between workers and soldiers ended after several weeks, over one hundred people were dead.

The failure of the great railroad strike exposed the weakness of the labor movement in the face of massive government intervention on the side of the railroads. The federal courts, United States Army, state militias, and local police all lent their muscle to keeping the engines of big business operating at full throttle, and the workers be damned. Meanwhile, racial and ethnic fissures among workers fractured labor unity. Divisions were particularly acute between the Irish and the Chinese in California (see "Makers of America: The Chinese," pp. 500–501). By 1880 the Golden State counted seventy-five thousand Asian newcomers, about 9 percent of its entire population. Mostly poor, uneducated, single males, they derived predominantly from the Taishan district of K'uang-t'ung (Guangdong) province in southern China. They had originally come to America to dig in the goldfields and to sledgehammer the tracks of the transcontinental railroads across the West. When the gold supply petered out and the tracks were laid, many—perhaps half of those who arrived before the 1880s—returned home to China with their meager savings.

Those who remained in America faced extraordinary hardships. They worked at the most menial jobs, often as cooks, laundrymen, or domestic servants. Without women or families, they were deprived of the children who in other immigrant communities eased their parents' assimilation through their exposure to the English language and American customs in school. The phrase "not a Chinaman's chance" emerged in this era to describe the daunting odds against which they struggled.

In San Francisco Irish-born demagogue Denis Kearney incited his followers to violent abuse of the hapless Chinese. The Kearneyites, many of whom were recently arrived immigrants from Europe, hotly resented the competition of cheap labor from the still more recently arrived Chinese. The beef-eater, they claimed, had no chance against the rice-eater in a life-and-death struggle for jobs and wages. The present tens of thousands of Chinese "coolies" were regarded as a menace, the prospective millions as a calamity. Taking to the streets, gangs of Kearneyites terrorized the Chinese by shearing off their precious pigtails. Some victims were murdered outright.

Congress slammed the door on Chinese immigrant laborers when it passed the **Chinese Exclusion Act** in 1882, prohibiting nearly all further immigration from China. The door stayed shut until 1943. Some exclusionists even tried to strip native-born Chinese Americans of their citizenship, but the Supreme Court ruled in *U.S.* v. *Wong Kim Ark* in 1898 that the Fourteenth Amendment guaranteed citizenship to all persons born in the United States. This doctrine of "birthright citizenship" (or *jus soli*, the "right of the soil," as contrasted with *jus sanguinis*, the "right of blood-tie," which based citizenship on the parents' nationality) provided important protections to Chinese Americans as well as to other immigrant communities.

The First Blow at the Chinese Question, 1877
Caucasian workers, seething with economic anxiety and ethnic prejudice, savagely mistreated the Chinese in California in the 1870s.

University of California at Berkeley, Bancroft Library

⭐ Garfield and Arthur

As the presidential campaign of 1880 approached, "Rutherfraud" Hayes was a man without a party, denounced and repudiated by the Republican Old Guard. The Republican party sought a new standard-bearer for 1880 and finally settled on a dark-horse candidate, James A. Garfield, from the electorally powerful state of Ohio. His vice-presidential running mate was a notorious Stalwart henchman, Chester A. Arthur of New York.

Energetically waving the bloody shirt, Garfield barely squeaked out a victory over the Democratic candidate and Civil War hero, Winfield Scott Hancock. He polled only 39,213 more votes than Hancock—4,453,295 to 4,414,082—but his margin in the electoral column was a comfortable 214 to 155.

The new president was energetic and able, but he was immediately ensnared in a political conflict between his secretary of state, James G. Blaine, and Blaine's Stalwart nemesis, Senator Roscoe Conkling. Then, as the Republican factions dueled, tragedy struck.

The Office Makes the Man, 1881 Besieged by his former New York cronies, Arthur tries to assert the dignity of his new presidential office.

system. The unlikely instrument of reform was Chester Arthur. Observers at first underestimated him. His record of cronyism and his fondness for fine wines and elegant clothing (including eighty pairs of trousers) suggested that he was little more than a foppish dandy. But Arthur surprised his critics by prosecuting several fraud cases and giving his former Stalwart pals the cold shoulder.

Disgust with Garfield's murder gave the Republican party itself a previously undetected taste for reform. The medicine finally applied to the long-suffering federal government was the **Pendleton Act** of 1883— the so-called Magna Carta of civil-service reform. It made compulsory campaign contributions from federal employees illegal, and it established the Civil Service Commission to make appointments to federal jobs on the basis of competitive examinations rather than "pull."

Although at first covering only about 10 percent of federal jobs, civil-service reform did rein in the most blatant abuses. Yet like many well-intentioned reforms, it bred unintended problems of its own. With the "plum" federal posts now beyond their reach, politicians were forced to look elsewhere for money, "the mother's milk of politics." Increasingly, they turned to the bulging coffers of the big corporations. A new breed of "boss" emerged—less skilled at mobilizing small armies of immigrants and other voters on election day, but more adept at milking dollars from manufacturers and lobbyists. The Pendleton Act partially divorced politics from patronage, but it helped drive politicians into "marriages of convenience" with big-business leaders (see Figure 23.1).

President Arthur's surprising display of integrity offended too many powerful Republicans. His

A disappointed and mentally deranged office seeker, Charles J. Guiteau, shot President Garfield in the back in a Washington railroad station. Garfield lingered in agony for eleven weeks and died on September 19, 1881. Guiteau, when seized, reportedly cried, "I am a Stalwart. Arthur is now President of the United States." The implication was that now the Conklingites would all get good jobs. Guiteau's attorneys argued that he was not guilty because of his incapacity to distinguish right from wrong—an early instance of the "insanity defense." The defendant himself demonstrated his weak grip on reality when he asked all those who had benefited politically from the assassination to contribute to his defense fund. These tactics availed little. Guiteau was found guilty of murder and hanged.

Garfield's death had one positive outcome: it shocked politicians into reforming the shameful spoils

Theodore Roosevelt (1858–1919), an ardent civil-service reformer, condemned the patronage system as

"tending to degrade American politics. . . . The men who are in office only for what they can make out of it are thoroughly unwholesome citizens, and their activity in politics is simply noxious. . . . Decent private citizens must inevitably be driven out of politics if it is suffered to become a mere selfish scramble for plunder, where victory rests with the most greedy, the most cunning, the most brazen. The whole patronage system is inimical to American institutions; it forms one of the gravest problems with which democratic and republican government has to grapple."

*B*etween 1800 and 1925, at least 3 million Chinese left their homeland to labor around the globe. The once-great Chinese Empire was disintegrating at the same time that its population was exploding, creating severe land shortages and opening up the unstable country to European imperial powers bent on unlocking the riches of a nation closed to outsiders for centuries. Chinese men, faced with economic hardship and political turmoil in their homeland and lured by labor shortages as far afield as Southeast Asia, Australia, and the Americas, migrated by the tens of thousands to work the plantations and dig the mines that fueled a burgeoning global economy. By 1900 more than 300,000 Chinese had entered the United States to contribute their muscle to building the West, wrenching minerals from stubborn rock and helping to lay the transcontinental railroads that stitched together the American nation (see Table 23.3).

A Chinese Railroad Worker Totes His Tools to Work

Picture Research Consultants & Archives

Although those who set off from China for destinations as diverse as Vietnam, Cuba, Peru, and the United States included a few merchants and artisans, most were unskilled country folk. In some cases families pooled their money to send out a son, but most travelers, desperately poor, obtained their passage through Chinese middlemen, who advanced them ship fare in return for their promise to work off their debts after they landed. This contracting sometimes led to conditions so cruel that the practice was ignominiously called "pig selling."

The first Chinese arrived in Spanish America as early as 1565, but few followed those earliest pioneers. Until the 1848 discovery of gold in California, there were fewer than 50 Chinese living in the United States. But by 1852 at least 25,000 Chinese had arrived in California, which they dubbed the "golden mountain." At that decade's end, Chinese workers made up nearly a quarter of the state's manual laborers, even though they were only a tenth of the population. Employers nationwide viewed the Chinese as cheap labor, recruiting them to cut sugar cane in the South and break strikes in New England shoe factories. A treaty negotiated with China in 1868 by the American diplomat Anson Burlingame guaranteed important civil rights to Chinese immigrants.

The Chinese America of the late nineteenth century was overwhelmingly a bachelor society. Women of good repute rarely made the passage. Of the very few Chinese women who ventured to California at this time, most became prostitutes. Many of them had been deceived by the false promise of honest jobs.

Although a stream of workers returned to their homeland, many Chinese stayed. "Chinatowns" sprang up wherever economic opportunities presented themselves—in railroad towns, farming villages, and cities. Chinese in these settlements spoke their own language, enjoyed the fellowship of their own compatriots, and sought safety from prejudice and violence, never rare in American society. Many immigrant clubs, American adaptations of Chinese traditions of loyalty to clan or region, were established in these communities. Rivaling such clubs and associations were the secret societies known as tongs. The word *tong*—literally, "meeting hall"—acquired a sinister reputation among non-Chinese, for the tongs counted the poorest and shadiest immigrants among their members. These were people without ties to a clan, those individuals most alienated from traditional Chinese organizations and from American society as well.

Mounting anti-Chinese agitation forced the repudiation of the Burlingame Treaty in 1880, and in 1882 the Chinese Exclusion Act barred nearly all Chinese from the United States for six decades. Slowly, however, those men and the few women who remained raised families and reared a new generation of Chinese Americans. They were joined by thousands more immigrants who made the journey illegally or took advantage of the few exceptions permissible under the Exclusion Act. But this second generation still suffered from discrimination, eking out their living in jobs despised by Caucasian laborers or taking daunting risks in small entrepreneurial ventures. Yet many hard-working Chinese did manage to open their own restaurants, laundries, and other small businesses. The enterprises formed a solid economic foundation for their small community and the much larger one that would emerge by the late twentieth century with a huge influx of new immigrants arriving from China.

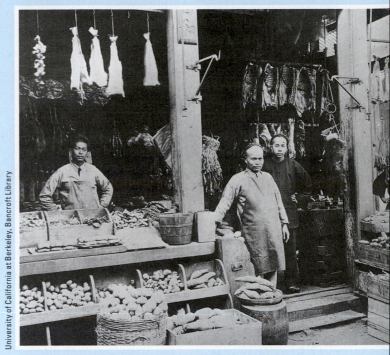

University of California at Berkeley, Bancroft Library

Chinese Butcher Shop, San Francisco, ca. 1890

TABLE 23.3 Population of Chinese Ancestry in the United States, 1850–2008

Year	Population	Males per One Female	Percentage U.S.-Born	Total Chinese Immigrants in Preceding Decade*
1850	4,018†	—	—	35
1860	34,933	19	—	41,397
1870	63,199	13	1	64,301
1880	105,465	21	1	123,201
1890	107,488	27	3	61,711
1900	89,863	19	10	14,799
1970††	435,062	N.A.	N.A.	34,764
1980	806,040	N.A.	N.A.	124,326
1990	1,645,472	N.A.	N.A.	346,747
2000	2,432,585	.94	29	419,114
2008	3,077,783	.90	31	631,476

*Includes Chinese immigrants in Hawaii after 1898; by 1970 Hawaii was a state.

†Estimated.

††The passage of the Chinese Exclusion Act in 1882 sharply reduced the Chinese population in the United States. Liberalization of American immigration laws and Chinese policies beginning in the 1970s, however, has led to a great increase in population of Chinese ancestry in the United States.

(Sources: U.S. Census Bureau, relevant years; U.S. Department of Homeland Security, *Statistical Yearbook of the Immigration and Naturalization Service*, 2000.)

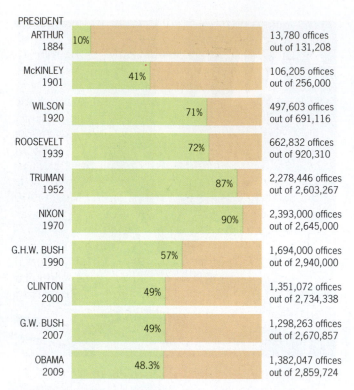

PRESIDENT ARTHUR 1884	10%	13,780 offices out of 131,208
McKINLEY 1901	41%	106,205 offices out of 256,000
WILSON 1920	71%	497,603 offices out of 691,116
ROOSEVELT 1939	72%	662,832 offices out of 920,310
TRUMAN 1952	87%	2,278,446 offices out of 2,603,267
NIXON 1970	90%	2,393,000 offices out of 2,645,000
G.H.W. BUSH 1990	57%	1,694,000 offices out of 2,940,000
CLINTON 2000	49%	1,351,072 offices out of 2,734,338
G.W. BUSH 2007	49%	1,298,263 offices out of 2,670,857
OBAMA 2009	48.3%	1,382,047 offices out of 2,859,724

FIGURE 23.1 Civil-Service Employment The proportion of federal jobs that are classified, or subject to rigid civil-service laws and competitive requirements, has greatly increased since Arthur's presidency. The total number of civil-service jobs has remained relatively stable since the 1950s, even as the government has expanded in size and budget. The decline in classified civil-service jobs in recent decades reflects the changes mandated by the Postal Reorganization Act of 1971, which moved U.S. Postal Service employees from competitive to excepted service. Excepted jobs are not subject to rigid civil-service laws passed by Congress. (Sources: U.S. Office of Personnel Management, *Federal Civilian Workforce Statistics—Employment and Trends*, http://www.opm.gov/feddata; and unpublished data.)

"I Want My Pa!" Malicious anti-Cleveland cartoon.

ungrateful party turned him out to pasture, and in 1886 he died of a cerebral hemorrhage.

✳ The Blaine-Cleveland Mudslingers of 1884

James G. Blaine's persistence in pursuit of his party's presidential nomination finally paid off in 1884. The dashing Maine politician, blessed with almost every political asset except a reputation for honesty, was the clear choice of the Republican convention in Chicago. But many reform-minded Republicans gagged on Blaine's candidacy. Blaine's enemies publicized the fishy-smelling "Mulligan letters," written by Blaine to a Boston businessman and linking the powerful politician to a corrupt deal involving federal favors to a

southern railroad. At least one of the damning documents ended with the furtive warning "Burn this letter." Some reformers, unable to swallow Blaine, bolted to the Democrats. They were sneeringly dubbed Mugwumps, a word of Indian derivation meant to suggest that they were "sanctimonious" or "holier-than-thou."*

Victory-starved Democrats turned enthusiastically to a noted reformer, Grover Cleveland. A burly bachelor with a soup-straining mustache and a taste for chewing tobacco, Cleveland was a solid but not brilliant lawyer of forty-seven. He had rocketed from the mayor's office in Buffalo to the governorship of New York and the presidential nomination in three short years. Known as "Grover the Good," he enjoyed a well-deserved reputation for probity in office.

But Cleveland's admirers soon got a shock. Resolute Republicans, digging for dirt in the past of bachelor Cleveland, unearthed the report that he had been involved in an amorous affair with a Buffalo widow. She had an illegitimate son, now eight years old, for whom Cleveland had made financial provision. Democratic elders were demoralized. They hurried to Cleveland and urged him to lie like a gentleman, but their ruggedly honest candidate insisted, "Tell the truth."

The campaign of 1884 sank to perhaps the lowest level in American experience, as the two parties grunted and shoved for the hog trough of office. Few fundamental differences separated them. Even

---

*Latter-day punsters gibed that the Mugwumps were priggish politicians who sat on the fence with their "mugs" on one side and their "wumps" on the other.

the bloody shirt had faded to a pale pink.* Personalities, not principles, claimed the headlines. Crowds of Democrats surged through city streets, chanting—to the rhythm of left, left, left, right, left—"Burn, burn, burn this letter!" Republicans taunted in return, "Ma, ma, where's my pa?" Defiant Democrats shouted back, "Gone to the White House, ha, ha, ha!"

The contest hinged on the state of New York, where Blaine blundered badly in the closing days of the campaign. A witless Republican clergyman damned the Democrats in a speech as the party of "Rum, Romanism, and Rebellion"—insulting with one swift stroke the culture, the faith, and the patriotism of New York's numerous Irish American voters. Blaine was present at the time but lacked the presence of mind to repudiate the statement immediately. The pungent phrase, shortened to "RRR," stung and stuck. Blaine's silence seemed to give assent, and the wavering Irishmen who deserted his camp helped account for Cleveland's paper-thin plurality of about a thousand votes in New York State, enough to give him the presidency. Cleveland swept the solid South and squeaked into office with 219 to 182 electoral votes and 4,879,507 to 4,850,293 popular votes.

✦ "Old Grover" Takes Over

Bull-necked Cleveland in 1885 was the first Democrat to take the oath of presidential office since Buchanan, twenty-eight years earlier. Huge question marks hung over his ample frame (5 feet 11 inches, 250 pounds). Could the "party of disunion" be trusted to govern the Union? Would desperate Democrats, ravenously hungry after twenty-four years of exile, trample the frail sprouts of civil-service reform in a stampede to the patronage trough? Could Cleveland restore a measure of respect and power to the maligned and enfeebled presidency?

Cleveland was a man of principles, most of them safely orthodox by the standards of his day. A staunch apostle of the hands-off creed of laissez-faire, the new president caused the hearts of business people and bankers to throb with contentment. He summed up his political philosophy in 1887 when he vetoed a bill to provide seeds for drought-ravaged Texas farmers. "Though the people support the government," he declared, "the government should not support the people." As tactless as

a mirror and as direct as a bulldozer, he was outspoken, unbending, and profanely hot-tempered.

At the outset Cleveland narrowed the North-South chasm by naming to his cabinet two former Confederates. As for the civil service, Cleveland was whipsawed between the demands of the Democratic faithful for jobs and the demands of the Mugwumps, who had helped elect him, for reform. Believing in the merit system, Cleveland at first favored the cause of the reformers, but he eventually caved in to the carpings of Democratic bosses and fired almost two-thirds of the 120,000 federal employees, including 40,000 incumbent (Republican) postmasters, to make room for "deserving Democrats."

Military pensions gave Cleveland some of his most painful political headaches. The politically powerful Grand Army of the Republic (GAR) routinely lobbied hundreds of private pension bills through a compliant

Battling over Lowering the Tariff in the 1880s
Advocates for both higher and lower tariffs claimed to be protecting American workers. In fact, workers were affected differently, depending on their jobs. Some U.S. manufacturing firms benefited from a protective tariff that shielded them from foreign competition, while others suffered from high duties on raw materials. Recognizing this tension, the American Federation of Labor declared neutrality on the tariff question in 1882.

---

*Neither candidate had served in the Civil War. Cleveland had hired a substitute to go in his stead while he supported his widowed mother and two sisters. Blaine was the only Republican presidential candidate from Grant through McKinley (1868 to 1900) who had not been a Civil War officer.

Congress. Benefits were granted to deserters, to bounty jumpers, to men who never served, and to former soldiers who in later years had incurred disabilities in no way connected with war service. A Democrat and a nonveteran, Cleveland was in an awkward position when it came to fighting the pension-grabbers. But the conscience-driven president read each bill carefully, vetoed several hundred of them, and then laboriously penned individual veto messages for Congress.

⭑ Cleveland Battles for a Lower Tariff

Cleveland also risked his political neck by prodding the hornet's nest of the tariff issue. During the Civil War, tariff schedules had been jacked up to new high levels, partly to raise revenues for the insatiable military machine. American industry, which was preponderantly in Republican hands, had profited from this protection and hated to see the sheltering benefits reduced in peacetime. But the high duties continued to pile up revenue at the customshouses, and by 1881 the Treasury was running an annual surplus amounting to an embarrassing $145 million. Most of the government's income, in those pre–income tax days, came from the tariff.

Congress could reduce the vexatious surplus in two ways. One was to squander it on pensions and "pork-barrel" bills and thus curry favor with veterans and other self-seeking groups. The other was to lower the tariff—something the big industrialists vehemently opposed. Grover Cleveland, the rustic Buffalo attorney, had known little and cared less about the tariff before entering the White House. But as he studied the subject, he was much impressed by the arguments for downward revision of the tariff schedules. Lower barriers would mean lower prices for consumers and less protection for monopolies. Most important, they would mean an end to the Treasury surplus, a standing mockery of Cleveland's professed belief in fiscal orthodoxy and small-government frugality. After much hesitation Cleveland saw his duty and overdid it.

With his characteristic bluntness, Cleveland tossed an appeal for lower tariffs like a bombshell into the lap of Congress in late 1887. The response was electric. Cleveland succeeded admirably in smoking the issue out into the open. Democrats were deeply frustrated by the obstinacy of their chief. Republicans rejoiced at his apparent recklessness, bellowing loudly that lower tariffs would mean higher taxes, lower wages, and increased unemployment. The old warrior Blaine gloated, "There's one more President for us in [tariff] protection." For the first time in years, a real issue divided the two parties as the 1888 presidential election loomed.

Dismayed Democrats, seeing no alternative, somewhat dejectedly renominated Grover Cleveland in their

Collection of Janice L. and David J. Frent

Weighing the Candidates, 1888 Novelties like this were widely distributed in late-nineteenth-century political campaigns. This miniature scale could be adjusted in either candidate's favor. Here the Republican Harrison rather improbably outweighs the corpulent Democratic candidate, Grover Cleveland.

St. Louis convention. Eager Republicans turned to Benjamin Harrison, whose grandfather was former president William Henry ("Tippecanoe") Harrison. The tariff was the prime issue. The two parties flooded the country with some 10 million pamphlets on the subject.

The specter of a lowered tariff spurred the Republicans to frantic action. In an impressive demonstration of the post–Pendleton Act politics of alliances with big business, they raised a war chest of some $3 million—the heftiest yet—largely by "frying the fat" out of nervous industrialists. The money was widely used to line up corrupt "voting cattle" known as "repeaters" and "floaters." In Indiana, always a crucial "swing" state, votes were shamelessly purchased for as much as $20 each.

On election day Harrison nosed out Cleveland, 233 to 168 electoral votes. A change of about 7,000 ballots in New York would have reversed the outcome. Cleveland actually polled more popular votes, 5,537,857 to 5,447,129, but he nevertheless became the first sitting president to be voted out of his chair since Martin Van Buren in 1840.

⭑ The Billion-Dollar Congress

After a four-year famine, the Republicans under Harrison licked their lips hungrily for the bounty of federal offices. They yearned to lavish upon the party faithful the fat surpluses produced by the high tariffs. But in the House of Representatives, they had only three more votes than the necessary quorum of 163 members, and the Democrats were preparing to obstruct all House business by refusing to answer roll calls, demanding roll calls to determine the presence of a quorum, and employing other delaying tactics.

Into this tense cockpit stepped the new Republican Speaker of the House, Thomas B. Reed of Maine. A hulking figure who towered six feet three inches, he was renowned as a master debater. He spoke with a harsh nasal drawl and wielded a verbal harpoon of sarcasm. To one congressman who quoted Henry Clay that he would "rather be right than be president," Reed caustically retorted that he "would never be either." Opponents cringed at the crack of his quip.

Reed soon bent the intimidated House to his imperious will. He counted as present Democrats who had

Library of Congress

Thomas B. Reed of Maine, Republican Speaker of the House, 1890 Sometimes referred to as "Czar" Reed, he served as Speaker for six years, dramatically increasing the power of the office in line with his dictum that "the best system is to have one party govern and the other party watch."

not answered the roll and who, rule book in hand, furiously denied that they were legally there. By such tactics "Czar" Reed utterly dominated the "Billion-Dollar" Congress—the first in history to appropriate that sum. Congress showered pensions on Civil War veterans and increased government purchases of silver. To keep the revenues flowing in—and to protect Republican industrialists from foreign competition—the Billion-Dollar Congress also passed the McKinley Tariff Act of 1890, boosting rates to their highest peacetime level ever (an average of 48.4 percent on dutiable goods).

Sponsored in the House by rising Republican star William McKinley of Ohio, the new tariff act brought fresh woes to farmers. Debt-burdened farmers had no choice but to buy manufactured goods from high-priced protected American industrialists, but were compelled to sell their own agricultural products into highly competitive, unprotected world markets. Mounting discontent against the McKinley Tariff caused many rural voters to rise in wrath. In the congressional elections of 1890, the Republicans lost their precarious majority and were reduced to just 88 seats, as compared with 235 Democrats. Even the much-touted McKinley went down to defeat. Ominously for conservatives, the new Congress also included nine members of the Farmers' Alliance, a militant organization of southern and western farmers.

✸ The Drumbeat of Discontent

Politics was no longer "as usual" in 1892, when the newly formed People's party, or "Populists," burst upon the scene. Rooted in the Farmers' Alliance of frustrated farmers in the great agricultural belts of the West and South, the Populists met in Omaha and adopted a scorching platform that denounced "the prolific womb of governmental injustice." They demanded inflation through free and unlimited coinage of silver at the rate of sixteen ounces of silver to one ounce of gold. They further called for a graduated income tax; government ownership of the railroads, telegraph, and telephone; the direct election of U.S. senators; a one-term limit on the presidency; the adoption of the initiative and referendum to allow citizens to shape legislation more directly; a shorter workday; and immigration restriction. As their presidential candidate, the Populists uproariously nominated the eloquent old Greenbacker, General James B. Weaver.

An epidemic of nationwide strikes in the summer of 1892 raised the prospect that the Populists could weld together a coalition of aggrieved workers and indebted farmers in a revolutionary joint assault on the capitalist order. At Andrew Carnegie's Homestead steel plant near Pittsburgh, company officials called in three

Minnesota Farmers Loading a Husker-Shredder, 1890s The purchase of technologically advanced farm equipment increased the productivity of farmers but also saddled them with debt. Many sought debt relief in the 1890s by clamoring for inflationary schemes, including the monetization of silver.

Wisconsin Historical Society

hundred armed Pinkerton detectives in July to crush the defiant **Homestead Strike** by steelworkers angry over pay cuts. Strikers, armed with rifles and dynamite, forced their assailants to surrender after a vicious battle that left ten people dead and some sixty wounded. Troops were eventually summoned, and both the strike and the union were broken. That same month, federal troops bloodily smashed a strike among silver miners in Idaho's fabled Coeur d'Alene district.

The Populists made a remarkable showing in the 1892 presidential election (see Map 23.3). Singing "Good-by, Party Bosses," they rolled up 1,029,846 popular votes and 22 electoral votes for General Weaver. They thus became one of the few third parties in U.S. history to break into the electoral column. But they fell far short of an electoral majority. Industrial laborers, especially in the urban East, did not rally to the Populist banner in appreciable numbers. Populist electoral votes came from only six midwestern and western states, four of which (Kansas, Colorado, Idaho, and Nevada) fell completely into the Populist basket.

The South, although a hotbed of agrarian agitation, proved especially unwilling to throw in its lot with the new party. Race was the reason. The more than 1 million southern black farmers organized in the Colored Farmers' National Alliance shared a host of complaints with poor white farmers, and for a time their common economic goals promised to overcome their racial differences. Recognizing the crucial edge that black votes could give them in the South, Populist leaders like Georgia's Tom Watson reached out to the black community. Watson was a wiry redhead who could "talk like the thrust of a Bowie knife." He declared, "There is no reason why the black man should not understand that the law that hurts me, as a farmer, hurts him, as a farmer." Many blacks were disillusioned enough with

© Bettmann/Corbis

The Homestead Strike, 1892 Three hundred armed Pinkerton detectives floated on barges down the Monongahela River to the site of the Carnegie steel plant at Homestead, Pennsylvania. Met by a defiant and disciplined force of strikers, they were compelled to surrender. Here the Pinkerton men are shown disembarking from their barges after their capitulation, while the jeering strikers ashore exult in their victory.

Kansas State Historical Society

The Kansas Legislature, 1893 Rifle-bearing Populists seized the Kansas capitol after the election of 1892 to make good their claim that they had won at the polls. Republicans disagreed and eventually prevailed when sergeants at arms, shown here, restored order.

the Republican party to respond. Alarmed, the conservative white "Bourbon" elite in the South played cynically upon historic racial antagonisms to counter the Populists' appeal for interracial solidarity and woo back poor whites.

Southern blacks were heavy losers. The Populist-inspired reminder of potential black political strength led to the near-total extinction of what little African American suffrage remained in the South. White southerners more aggressively than ever used literacy

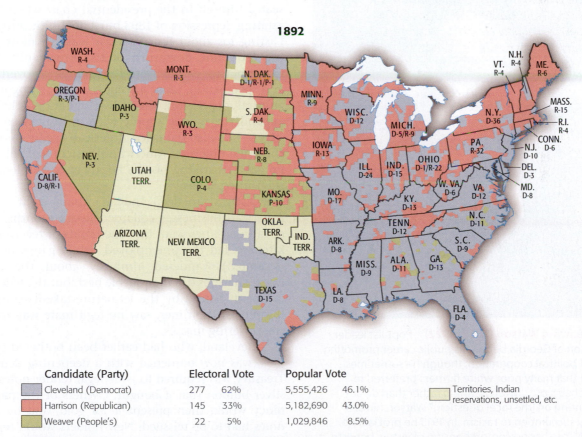

1892

Candidate (Party)	Electoral Vote		Popular Vote	
Cleveland (Democrat)	277	62%	5,555,426	46.1%
Harrison (Republican)	145	33%	5,182,690	43.0%
Weaver (People's)	22	5%	1,029,846	8.5%

Territories, Indian reservations, unsettled, etc.

MAP 23.3 Presidential Election of 1892 (showing vote by county) Note the concentration of Populist strength in the semiarid farming regions of the western half of the country. (Compare this with Map 26.4, showing average annual precipitation with major agricultural products as of 1900, on p. 589.) © Cengage Learning

A popular protest song of the 1890s among western farmers was titled "The Hayseed." One stanza ran,

"I once was a tool of oppression,
And as green as a sucker could be,
And monopolies banded together
To beat a poor hayseed like me."

tests and poll taxes to deny blacks the ballot. The notorious **grandfather clause** exempted from those requirements anyone whose forebear had voted in 1860—when, of course, black slaves had not voted at all. More than half a century would pass before southern blacks could again vote in considerable numbers. Accompanying this disfranchisement were more severe Jim Crow laws, designed to enforce racial segregation in public places, including hotels and restaurants, and backed up by atrocious lynchings and other forms of intimidation.

The conservative crusade to eliminate the black vote also had dire consequences for the Populist party itself. Even Tom Watson abandoned his interracial appeals and, in time, became a vociferous racist himself. After 1896 the Populist party lapsed increasingly into vile racism and staunchly advocated black disfranchisement. Such were the bitterly ironic fruits of the Populist campaign in the South.

✴ Cleveland and Depression

With the Populists divided and the Republicans discredited, Grover Cleveland took office once again in 1893, the only president ever reelected after defeat. He was the same old bull-necked and bullheaded Cleveland, with a little more weight, polish, conservatism, and self-assertiveness. But though it was the same old Cleveland, it was not the same old country. Debtors were up in arms, workers were restless, and the advance shadows of panic were falling. Hardly had Cleveland seated himself in the presidential chair when the devastating depression of 1893 burst about his burly frame. Lasting for about four years, it was the most punishing economic downturn of the nineteenth century. Contributing causes were the splurge of overbuilding and speculation, labor disorders, and the ongoing agricultural depression. Free-silver agitation—the cry to expand the money supply with unlimited coinage of silver—had also damaged American credit abroad, and the usual pinch on American finances had come when European banking houses began to call in loans from the United States.

Distress ran deep and far. About eight thousand American businesses collapsed in six months. Dozens of railroad lines went into the hands of receivers. Soup kitchens fed the unemployed, while gangs of hoboes ("tramps") wandered aimlessly about the country. Local charities did their feeble best, but the federal government, bound by the let-nature-take-its-course philosophy of the times, saw no legitimate way to relieve the suffering masses.

Cleveland, who had earlier been bothered by a surplus, was now burdened with a deepening deficit. The Treasury was required to issue legal tender notes for the silver bullion that it bought. Owners of the paper currency would then present it for gold, and by law the notes had to be reissued. New holders would repeat the process, thus draining away precious gold in an "endless-chain" operation.

Alarmingly, the gold reserve in the Treasury dropped below $100 million, which was popularly regarded as

Thomas Edward Watson (1865–1922) Populist leader Tom Watson of Georgia began his public career promoting interracial political cooperation, though he sometimes despaired that many poor white farmers preferred to "hug the chains of . . . wretchedness rather than do any experimenting on [the race] question." Watson himself eventually succumbed to racism. In 1913 he proclaimed that "the Negro has no comprehension of virtue, honesty, truth, gratitude, and principle. The South has to lynch him occasionally, and flog him, now and then, to keep him from blaspheming the Almighty by his conduct . . . and color."

Courtesy of Georgia Archives, Small Print Collection, spc07-038a the safe minimum for supporting about $350 million in outstanding paper money. Cleveland saw no alternative but to halt the bleeding away of gold by engineering a repeal of the Sherman Silver Purchase Act of 1890. For this purpose he summoned Congress into an extra session in the summer of 1893.

Unknown to the country, complications threatened from another quarter. A malignant growth had developed on the roof of Cleveland's mouth, and it had to be removed on a private yacht with extreme secrecy. If the president had died under the surgeon's knife, his place would have been taken by the "soft-money" vice president, Adlai E. Stevenson—an eventuality that would have deepened the crisis.

In Congress the debate over the repeal of the silver act was meanwhile running its heated course. A silver-tongued young Democratic congressman from Nebraska, thirty-three-year-old William Jennings Bryan, held the galleries spellbound for three hours as he championed the cause of free silver. The friends of silver announced that "hell would freeze over" before Congress would pass the repeal measure. But an angered Cleveland used his job-granting power to break the filibuster in the Senate. He thus alienated the Democratic silverites like Bryan and disrupted his party at the very outset of his administration.

Repeal of the Sherman Silver Purchase Act only partially stopped the hemorrhaging of gold from the Treasury. In February 1894 the gold reserve sank to a dismaying $41 million. The United States was now in grave danger of going off the gold standard—a move that would render the nation's currency volatile and unreliable as a measure of value and that would also mortally cripple America's international trade. Cleveland floated two Treasury bond issues in 1894, totaling over $100 million, but the "endless-chain" operations continued relentlessly.

Early in 1895 Cleveland turned in desperation to J. P. Morgan, "the bankers' banker" and the head of a Wall Street syndicate. After tense negotiations at the White House, the bankers agreed to lend the government $65 million in gold. They were obviously in business for profit, so they charged a commission amounting to about $7 million. But they did make a significant concession when they agreed to obtain one-half of the gold abroad and take the necessary steps to dam it up in the leaky Treasury. The loan, at least temporarily, helped restore confidence in the nation's finances.

✴ Cleveland Breeds a Backlash

The bond deal stirred up a storm. The Wall Street ogre, especially in the eyes of the silverites and other debtors,

symbolized all that was wicked and grasping in American politics. President Cleveland's secretive dealings with the mighty "Jupiter" Morgan were savagely condemned as a "sellout" of the national government. But Cleveland was certain that he had done no wrong. Sarcastically denying that he was "Morgan's errand boy," Cleveland asserted, "Without shame and without repentance I confess my share of the guilt."

Cleveland suffered further embarrassment with the passage of the Wilson-Gorman Tariff in 1894. The Democrats had pledged to lower tariffs, but by the time their tariff bill made it through Congress, it had been so loaded with special-interest protection that it made scarcely a dent in the high McKinley Tariff rates. An outraged Cleveland grudgingly allowed the bill, which also contained a 2 percent tax on incomes over $4,000, to become law without his signature. When the Supreme Court struck down the income-tax provision in 1895,* the Populists and other disaffected groups found proof that the courts were only the tools of the plutocrats.

Democratic political fortunes naturally suffered in the face of these several setbacks. The tariff dynamite that had blasted the Republicans out of the House in 1890 now dislodged the Democrats, with a strong helping hand from the depression. The revitalized Republicans, singing "Times Are Mighty Hard," won the congressional elections of 1894 in a landslide—244 seats to 105 for the Democrats. The Republicans began to look forward to the presidential race of 1896 with unconcealed glee.

Despite his gruff integrity and occasional courage, Grover Cleveland failed utterly to cope with the serious economic crisis that befell the country in 1893. He was tied down in office by the same threads that held all the politicians of the day to Lilliputian levels. Grant, Hayes, Garfield, Arthur, Harrison, and Cleveland are often referred to as the "forgettable presidents." Bewhiskered and bland in person, they left mostly blanks—or blots—on the nation's political record, as issues like the tariff, the money question, and the rights of labor continued to fester. What little political vitality existed in Gilded Age America was to be found in local settings or in Congress, which overshadowed the White House for most of this period. But before the century ended, down-and-out debtors and disgruntled workers would make one last titanic effort to wring reform out of the political system—in the momentous election of 1896.

---

*It violated the "direct tax" clause. See Art. I, Sec. IX, para. 4 in the Appendix. The Sixteenth Amendment to the Constitution, adopted in 1913, permitted an income tax.

Varying Viewpoints

The Populists: Radicals or Reactionaries?

Taking their cue from contemporary satirical commentaries like Mark Twain and Charles Dudley Warner's *The Gilded Age* (1873), the first historians who wrote about the post–Civil War era judged it harshly. They condemned its politicians as petty and corrupt, lamented the emergence of a new plutocratic class, and railed against the arrogance of corporate power. Such a view is conspicuous in Charles and Mary Beard's *The Rise of American Civilization* (4 vols., 1927–1942), perhaps the most influential American history textbook ever written.

The Beards were leaders of the so-called progressive school of historical writing that flourished in the early years of the twentieth century. Progressive historians, many of whom grew up in the Gilded Age, shared in a widespread disillusionment that the Civil War had failed to generate a rebirth of American idealism. Their political sympathies were chillingly antibusiness and warmly pro-labor, pro-farmer, and pro-reform.

Historians of the progressive persuasion identified Populism as virtually the only organized opposition to the social, economic, and political order that took shape in the last decades of the nineteenth century. The Populists thus became heroes to several generations of writers who bemoaned that order and looked back longingly at Americans' agrarian past. John D. Hicks, *The Populist Revolt* (1931), is the classic portrayal of the Populists as embattled farmers hurling defiance at Wall Street and the robber barons in a last-ditch defense of their simple, honest way of life. Bowed but unbroken by the defeat of their great champion, William Jennings Bryan, in the presidential election of 1896, the Populists, Hicks claimed, left a reforming legacy that flourished again in the progressive era and the New Deal.

Hicks's point of view was the dominant one until the 1950s, when it was sharply criticized by Richard Hofstadter in *The Age of Reform* (1955). Hofstadter charged that the progressive historians had romanticized the Populists, who were best understood not as picturesque protesters, but as "harassed little country businessmen" bristling with provincial prejudices. The city-born-and-bred Hofstadter argued that the Populist revolt was aimed not just at big business and the money power but also somewhat irrationally at urbanism, immigrants, the East, and modernity itself. Hofstadter thus exposed a "dark side" of Populism, which contained elements of backwoods anti-intellectualism, paranoia, and even anti-Semitism.

In the 1960s several scholars, inspired by the work of C. Vann Woodward, as well as by sympathy with the protest movements of that turbulent decade, began to rehabilitate the Populists as authentic reformers with genuine grievances. Especially notable in this vein was Lawrence Goodwyn's *Democratic Promise: The Populist Movement in America* (1976). Goodwyn depicted the Populists as reasonable radicals who were justifiably resentful of their eclipse by urban industrialism and finance capitalism. He also portrayed Populism as the last gasp of popular political participation, a democratic "moment" in American history that expired with the Populists' absorption into the Democratic party.

Two subsequent works, Edward L. Ayers's *Promise of the New South* (1992) and Robert C. McMath's *American Populism* (1993), synthesized many of the older perspectives and presented a balanced view of the Populists as radical in many ways but also limited by their nostalgia for a lost agrarian past. Recently, Eric Rauchway's *Blessed Among Nations* (2006) argued that Populism was a reaction to America's increased reliance on foreign investment. Farmers in southern and western states resented control by foreign capitalists, particularly the British. Although Hofstadter made a similar point fifty years earlier, the impact of the international economy on domestic politics is reemerging as a direction for new research.

Chapter Review

KEY TERMS

"waving the bloody shirt" (489)

Tweed Ring (490)

Crédit Mobilier scandal (490)

panic of 1873 (491)

Gilded Age (492)

patronage (493)

Compromise of 1877 (494)

Civil Rights Act of 1875 (495)

sharecropping (496)

Jim Crow (496)

Plessy v. *Ferguson* (496)

Chinese Exclusion Act (498)

Pendleton Act (499)

Homestead Strike (506)

grandfather clause (508)

PEOPLE TO KNOW

Jay Gould

Horace Greeley

Rutherford B. Hayes

James A. Garfield

Chester Arthur

Grover Cleveland

Thomas B. Reed

Tom Watson

William Jennings Bryan

J. P. Morgan

CHRONOLOGY

1868	Grant defeats Seymour for presidency
1869	Fisk and Gould corner gold market
1871	Tweed scandal in New York
1872	Crédit Mobilier scandal exposed Liberal Republicans break with Grant Grant defeats Greeley for presidency
1873	Panic of 1873
1875	Whiskey Ring scandal Civil Rights Act of 1875 Resumption Act
1876	Hayes-Tilden election standoff and crisis
1877	Compromise of 1877 Reconstruction ends Railroad strikes paralyze nation
1880	Garfield defeats Hancock for presidency
1881	Garfield assassinated; Arthur assumes presidency
1882	Chinese Exclusion Act
1883	*Civil Rights Cases* Pendleton Act sets up Civil Service Commission
1884	Cleveland defeats Blaine for presidency
1888	Harrison defeats Cleveland for presidency
1890	"Billion-Dollar" Congress McKinley Tariff Act Sherman Silver Purchase Act (repealed 1893)
1892	Homestead steel strike Coeur d'Alene (Idaho) silver miners' strike People's party candidate James B. Weaver wins twenty-two electoral votes Cleveland defeats Harrison and Weaver to regain presidency
1893	Depression of 1893 begins Republicans regain House of Representatives
1895	J. P. Morgan's banking syndicate loans $65 million in gold to federal government
1896	*Plessy* v. *Ferguson* legitimizes "separate but equal" doctrine

TO LEARN MORE

Stephen Cresswell, *Rednecks, Redeemers, and Race: Mississippi after Reconstruction, 1877–1917* (2006)

William Gillette, *Retreat from Reconstruction, 1869–1879* (1979)

Steven Hahn, *A Nation Under Our Feet: Black Political Struggles in the Rural South from Slavery to the Great Migration* (2003)

Michael F. Holt, *By One Vote: The Disputed Presidential Election of 1876* (2008)

Paul Krause, *The Battle for Homestead, 1880–1892: Politics, Culture, and Steel* (1992)

Jackson Lears, *Rebirth of a Nation: The Making of Modern America, 1877–1920* (2009)

Charles Postel, *The Populist Vision* (2007)

Heather Cox Richardson, *The Death of Reconstruction: Race, Labor, and Politics in the Post–Civil War North, 1865–1901* (2001)

Mark W. Summers, *The Era of Good Stealings* (1993)

Alan Trachtenberg, *The Incorporation of America: Culture and Society in the Gilded Age* (1982)

C. Vann Woodward, *Origins of the New South, 1877–1913* (1951)

———, *The Strange Career of Jim Crow* (rev. ed., 1974)

A complete, annotated bibliography for this chapter—along with brief descriptions of the People to Know—may be found on the American Pageant website. The Key Terms are defined in a Glossary at the end of the text.

Go to the CourseMate website at **www.cengagebrain.com** for additional study tools and review materials—including audio and video clips—for this chapter.

Chapter 24

Industry Comes of Age

1865–1900

The wealthy class is becoming more wealthy; but the poorer class is becoming more dependent. The gulf between the employed and the employer is growing wider; social contrasts are becoming sharper; as liveried carriages appear; so do barefooted children.

HENRY GEORGE, 1879

As the nineteenth century drew to a close, observers were asking, "Why are the best men not in politics?" One answer was that they were being lured away from public life by the lusty attractions of the booming private economy. As America's Industrial Revolution slipped into high gear, talented men ached for profits, not the presidency. They dreamed of controlling corporations, not the Congress. What the nation lost in civic leadership, it gained in an astounding surge of economic growth. As late as 1870, agriculture remained the nation's biggest business. By 1900 it accounted for less than half of the national economy. Until the end of the Civil War, the United States imported more merchandise than it exported. By 1900 it annually delivered more than $600 million worth of manufactured goods to the world's marketplace. Americans did not achieve this economic transformation all by themselves. Foreign investment, labor, trade, and technology made it possible. Although in many ways still a political dwarf, the United States was about to stand up before the world as an industrial colossus—and the lives of millions of working Americans would be transformed in the process.

The Iron Colt Becomes an Iron Horse

The government-business entanglements that increasingly shaped politics after the Civil War also undergirded the industrial development of the nation. The unparalleled outburst of railroad construction was a crucial case. When Lincoln was shot in 1865, there were only 35,000 miles of steam railways in the United States, mostly east of the Mississippi. By 1900 the figure had spurted up to 192,556 miles, or more than that for all of Europe combined, and much of the new trackage ran west of the Mississippi (see Figure 24.1).

Transcontinental railroad building was so costly and risky as to require government subsidies, as it had in many other industrializing nations. Everywhere, the construction of railway systems promised greater national unity and economic growth. The extension of rails into thinly populated regions was unprofitable until the areas could be built up, and private promoters were unwilling to suffer heavy initial losses. Congress, impressed by arguments pleading military and postal needs, began to advance liberal loans to two favored cross-continent companies in 1862 and added enormous donations of acreage paralleling the tracks. All told, Washington rewarded the railroads with 155,504,994 acres, and the western states contributed 49 million more—a total area larger than Texas (see Map 24.1).

Grasping railroads tied up even more land than this for a number of years. Land grants to railroads were made in broad belts along the proposed route. Within these belts the railroads were allowed to choose *alternate* mile-square sections in checkerboard fashion. But until they determined the precise location of their tracks and decided which sections were the choicest selections, the railroads withheld *all* the land from other users. President Grover Cleveland put an end to this foot-dragging practice in 1887 and threw open to

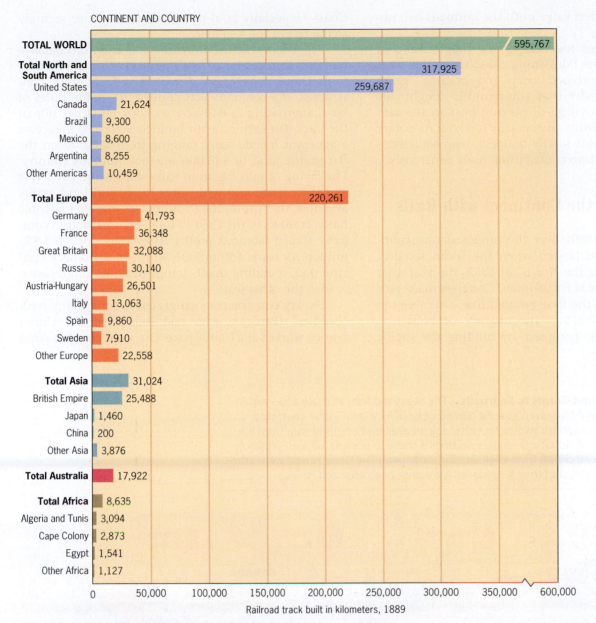

CONTINENT AND COUNTRY

TOTAL WORLD	595,767
Total North and South America	317,925
United States	259,687
Canada	21,624
Brazil	9,300
Mexico	8,600
Argentina	8,255
Other Americas	10,459
Total Europe	220,261
Germany	41,793
France	36,348
Great Britain	32,088
Russia	30,140
Austria-Hungary	26,501
Italy	13,063
Spain	9,860
Sweden	7,910
Other Europe	22,558
Total Asia	31,024
British Empire	25,488
Japan	1,460
China	200
Other Asia	3,876
Total Australia	17,922
Total Africa	8,635
Algeria and Tunis	3,094
Cape Colony	2,873
Egypt	1,541
Other Africa	1,127

Railroad track built in kilometers, 1889

FIGURE 24.1 Railroads Worldwide, 1889*

*Another calculation of railway track per 10,000 inhabitants in 1904 revealed that the United States was still far out in front, with 26.4 miles of track compared to 15.2 miles for the second-place country, Sweden. Much farther behind were the major western European nations of France (7.3), Germany (6.1), and Great Britain and Ireland (5.4).

(Sources: Henry Poor, *Poor's Manual of the Railroads of the United States for 1891* (1891); Slason Thompson, *Railway Statistics of the United States of America for the Year Ending June 30, 1906, Compared with the Official Reports of 1905 and Recent Statistics of Foreign Railways* (1907).)

settlement the still-unclaimed public portions of the land-grant areas.

Noisy criticism, especially in later years, was leveled at the "giveaway" of so valuable a birthright to greedy corporations. But the government did receive beneficial returns, including long-term preferential rates for postal service and military traffic. Granting land was

also a "cheap" way to subsidize a much-desired transportation system, because it avoided new taxes for direct cash grants. The railroads could turn the land into gold by using it as collateral for loans from private bankers or, later, by selling it. This they often did, at an average price of $3 an acre. Critics were also prone to overlook the fact that the land did not have even that relatively modest value until the railroads had ribboned it with steel.

Frontier villages touched by the magic wand of the iron rail became flourishing cities; those that were bypassed often withered away and became "ghost towns." Little wonder that communities fought one another for the privilege of playing host to the railroads. Ambitious towns customarily held out monetary and other attractions to the builders, who sometimes blackmailed them into contributing more generously.

✦ Spanning the Continent with Rails

Deadlock in the 1850s over the proposed transcontinental railroad was broken when the South seceded, leaving the field to the North. In 1862, the year after the guns first spoke at Fort Sumter, Congress made provision for starting the long-awaited line. One weighty argument for action was the urgency of bolstering the Union, already disrupted, by binding the Pacific Coast—especially gold-rich California—more securely to the rest of the Republic.

The Union Pacific Railroad—note the word *Union*—was thus commissioned by Congress to thrust westward from Omaha, Nebraska. For each mile of track constructed, the company was granted 20 square miles of land, alternating in 640-acre sections on either side of the track. For each mile the builders were also to receive a generous federal loan, ranging from $16,000 on the flat prairie land to $48,000 for mountainous country. The laying of rails began in earnest after the Civil War ended in 1865, and with juicy loans and land grants available, the "groundhog" promoters made all possible haste. Insiders of the Crédit Mobilier construction company reaped fabulous profits. They slyly pocketed $73 million for some $50 million worth of breakneck construction, spending small change to bribe congressmen to look the other way.

Sweaty construction gangs, containing many Irish "Paddies" (Patricks) who had fought in the Union armies, worked at a frantic pace. On one record-breaking

MAP 24.1 Federal Land Grants to Railroads   The heavy red lines indicate areas within which the railroads might be given specific parcels of land. As shown in the inset, land was reserved in belts of various widths on either side of a railroad's right of way. Until the railroad selected the individual mile-square sections it chose to possess, *all* such sections within the belt were withdrawn from eligibility for settlement. The "time zones" were introduced in 1883 (see p. 518), and their boundaries have since been adjusted. © Cengage Learning day, a sledge-and-shovel army of some five thousand men laid ten miles of track. A favorite song went like this:

Then drill, my Paddies, drill;
Drill, my heroes, drill;
Drill all day,
No sugar in your tay [tea]
Workin' on the U.P. Railway.

When hostile Indians attacked in futile efforts to protect what once rightfully had been their land, the laborers would drop their picks and seize their rifles. Scores of people—railroad workers and Indians—lost their lives as the rails stretched ever westward. At rail's end, workers tried their best to find relaxation and conviviality in their tented towns, known as "hells on wheels," often teeming with as many as ten thousand men and a sprinkling of painted prostitutes and performers.

Rail laying at the California end was undertaken by the Central Pacific Railroad. This line pushed boldly eastward from boomtown Sacramento, over and through the towering, snow-clogged Sierra Nevada. Four far-seeing men—the so-called Big Four—were the chief financial backers of the enterprise. The quartet included the heavyset, enterprising ex-governor Leland Stanford of California, who had useful political connections, and the burly, energetic Collis P. Huntington, an adept lobbyist. The Big Four cleverly operated through two construction companies, and although they walked away with tens of millions in profits, they kept their hands relatively clean by not becoming involved in the bribing of congressmen.

The Central Pacific, which was granted the same princely subsidies as the Union Pacific, had the same incentive to haste. Some ten thousand Chinese laborers, sweating from dawn to dusk under their basket hats, proved to be cheap, efficient, and expendable (hundreds lost their lives in premature explosions and other mishaps). The towering Sierra Nevada presented a formidable barrier, and the nerves of the Big Four were strained when their workers could chip only a few inches a day tunneling through solid rock, while the Union Pacific was sledgehammering westward across the open plains.

A "wedding of the rails" was finally consummated near Ogden, Utah, in 1869, as two locomotives—"facing on a single track, half a world behind each back"—gently kissed cowcatchers. The colorful ceremony included the breaking of champagne bottles and the driving of a last ceremonial (golden) spike, with ex-governor Stanford clumsily wielding a silver maul. In all, the Union Pacific built 1,086 miles, the Central Pacific 689 miles.

Completion of the transcontinental line—a magnificent engineering feat for that day—was one of America's most impressive peacetime undertakings. It welded the West Coast more firmly to the Union and facilitated a flourishing trade with Asia. It penetrated the arid barrier of the deserts, paving the way for the phenomenal growth of the Great West. Americans

Granger Collection

Snow Sheds on the Central Pacific Railroad in the Sierra Nevada Mountains, by Joseph H. Becker, ca. 1869 Formidable obstacles of climate and terrain confronted the builders of the Central Pacific Railroad in the mountainous heights of California. Note the Chinese laborers in the foreground.

Promoting the Union Pacific Railroad, 1869

Union Pacific Museum Collection

New Orleans to San Francisco and was consolidated in the same year.

The last spike of the last of the five transcontinental railroads of the nineteenth century was hammered home in 1893. The Great Northern, which ran from Duluth to Seattle north of the Northern Pacific, was the creation of a far-visioned Canadian American, James J. Hill, a bearlike man who was probably the greatest railroad builder of all. His enterprise was so soundly organized that it rode through later financial storms with flying colors.

Yet the romance of the rails was not without its sordid side. Pioneer builders were often guilty of gross overoptimism. Avidly seeking land bounties and pushing into areas that lacked enough potential population to support a railroad, they sometimes laid down rails that led "from nowhere to nothing." When prosperity failed to smile upon their coming, they went into bankruptcy, carrying down with them the savings of trusting investors. Many of the large railroads in the post–Civil War decades passed through seemingly endless bankruptcies, mergers, or reorganizations.

compared this electrifying achievement with the Declaration of Independence and the emancipation of the slaves; jubilant Philadelphians again rang the cracked bell of Independence Hall.

✶ Binding the Country with Railroad Ties

With the westward trail now blazed, four other transcontinental lines were completed before the century's end. None of them secured monetary loans from the federal government, as did the Union Pacific and the Central Pacific. But all of them except the Great Northern received generous grants of land.

The Northern Pacific Railroad, stretching from Lake Superior to Puget Sound, reached its terminus in 1883. The Atchison, Topeka and Santa Fe, stretching through the southwestern deserts to California, was completed in 1884. The Southern Pacific ribboned from

✶ Railroad Consolidation and Mechanization

The success of the western lines was facilitated by welding together and expanding the older eastern networks, notably the New York Central. The genius in this enterprise was "Commodore" Cornelius Vanderbilt—burly, boisterous, white-whiskered. Having made his millions in steamboating, he daringly turned, in his late sixties, to a new career in railroading. Though ill-educated, ungrammatical, coarse, and ruthless, he was clear-visioned. Offering superior railway service at lower rates, he amassed a fortune of $100 million. His name

The Union Pacific and the Central Pacific Link at Promontory Point, Utah, May 10, 1869 Railroad financiers, dignitaries, spectators, and Chinese (Central Pacific) and Irish (Union Pacific) work gangs witnessed the historic joining that created the nation's first transcontinental railroad. After the two locomotives chugged within a few feet of each other, Central Pacific chief and former California governor Leland Stanford tapped a golden spike into a prepared hole on the last tie with a silver-plated maul. The golden spike was whisked away to be preserved for posterity at the Stanford University Museum, but the iron one that replaced it was hardly ordinary. It was wired to a Union Pacific telegraph line, while a copper plate on the maul was connected to a Central Pacific wire. When they touched, they closed a telegraphic circuit that sent the news to cities all over the country.

is perhaps best remembered through his contribution of $1 million to the founding of Vanderbilt University in Tennessee.

Two significant new improvements proved a boon to the railroads. One was the steel rail, which Vanderbilt helped popularize when he replaced the old iron tracks of the New York Central with the tougher metal. Steel was safer and more economical because it could bear a heavier load. A standard gauge of track width likewise came into wide use during the postwar years, thus eliminating the expense and inconvenience of numerous changes from one line to another.

Other refinements played a vital role in railroading. The Westinghouse air brake, generally adopted in the 1870s, was a marvelous contribution to efficiency and safety. The Pullman Palace Cars, advertised as "gorgeous traveling hotels," were introduced on a considerable scale in the 1860s. Alarmists condemned them as "wheeled torture chambers" and potential funeral pyres, for the wooden cars were equipped with swaying kerosene lamps. Appalling accidents continued to be almost daily tragedies, despite safety devices like the telegraph ("talking wires"), double-tracking, and (later) the block signal.

✦ Revolution by Railways

The metallic fingers of the railroads intimately touched countless phases of American life. For the first time, a sprawling nation became united in a physical sense, bound with ribs of iron and steel. The railroads emerged as the nation's biggest business, employing more people than any other industry and gobbling up nearly 20 percent of investment dollars from foreign and domestic investors alike.

More than any other single factor, the railroad network spurred the amazing economic growth of the post–Civil War years. By stitching North America together from ocean to ocean, the puffing locomotives opened up the West with its wealth of resources. Trains hauled raw materials to factories and sped them back as finished goods for sale across the continent, making the United States the largest integrated national market in the world. The forging of the rails themselves generated the largest single source of orders for the adolescent steel industry.

The screeching iron horse especially stimulated mining and agriculture in the West. It took farmers out to their land, carried the fruits of their toil to market, and brought them their manufactured necessities. Clusters of farm settlements paralleled the railroads, just as earlier they had followed the rivers.

Railways were a boon for cities and played a leading role in the great cityward movement of the last decades of the century. The iron monsters could carry food to enormous concentrations of people and at the same time ensure them a livelihood by providing both raw materials and markets.

Railroad companies also stimulated the mighty stream of immigration. Seeking settlers to whom their land grants might be sold at a profit, they advertised seductively in Europe and sometimes offered to transport the newcomers free to their farms.

The land also felt the impact of the railroad—especially the broad, ecologically fragile midsection of the continent that Thomas Jefferson had purchased from France in 1803. Settlers following the railroads plowed up the tallgrass prairies of Iowa, Illinois, Kansas, and Nebraska and planted well-drained, rectangular cornfields. On the shortgrass prairies of the high plains in the Dakotas and Montana, range-fed cattle rapidly displaced the buffalo, which were hunted to near-extinction. The white pine forests of Michigan, Wisconsin, and Minnesota disappeared into lumber that was rushed by rail to prairie farmers, who used it to build houses and fences.

Time itself was bent to the railroads' needs. Until the 1880s every town in the United States had its own "local" time, dictated by the sun's position. When it was noon in Chicago, it was 11:50 a.m. in St. Louis and 12:18 p.m. in Detroit. For railroad operators worried about keeping schedules and avoiding wrecks, this patchwork of local times was a nightmare. Thus on November 18, 1883, the major rail lines decreed that the continent would henceforth be divided into four "time zones." Most communities quickly adopted railroad "standard" time.

Finally, the railroad, more than any other single factor, was the maker of millionaires. A raw new aristocracy, consisting of "lords of the rail," replaced the old southern "lords of the lash." The multiwebbed lines became the playthings of Wall Street, and colossal wealth was amassed by stock speculators and railroad wreckers.

★ Wrongdoing in Railroading

Corruption lurks nearby when fabulous fortunes can materialize overnight. The fleecings administered by the railroad construction companies, such as the Crédit Mobilier, were but the first of the bunco games that the railroad promoters learned to play. Methods soon became more refined, as fast-fingered financiers executed multimillion-dollar maneuvers beneath the noses of a bedazzled public. Jay Gould was the most adept of these ringmasters of rapacity. For nearly thirty years, he boomed and busted the stocks of the Erie, the Kansas Pacific, the Union Pacific, and the Texas and Pacific in an incredible circus of speculative skullduggery.

One of the favorite devices of the moguls of manipulation was "stock watering." The term originally referred to the practice of making cattle thirsty by feeding them salt and then having them bloat themselves with water before they were weighed in for sale. Using a variation of this technique, railroad stock promoters grossly inflated their claims about a given line's assets and profitability and sold stocks and bonds far in excess of the railroad's actual value. "Promoters' profits" were often the tail that wagged the iron horse itself. Railroad managers were forced to charge extortionate rates and wage ruthless competitive battles in order to pay off the

William H. Vanderbilt, Robber Baron This 1885 cartoon takes aim at Vanderbilt's notorious comment, "The public be damned!"

Library of Congress

exaggerated financial obligations with which they were saddled.

The public interest was frequently trampled underfoot as the railroad titans waged their brutal wars. Crusty old Cornelius Vanderbilt, when told that the law stood in his way, reportedly exclaimed, "Law! What do I care about the law? Hain't I got the power?" On another occasion he supposedly threatened some associates: "I won't sue you, for the law is too slow. I'll ruin you." His son, William H. Vanderbilt, when asked in 1883 about the discontinuance of a fast mail train, reportedly snorted, "The public be damned!"

While abusing the public, the railroaders blandly bought and sold people in public life. They bribed judges and legislatures, employed arm-twisting lobbyists, and elected their own "creatures" to high office. They showered free passes on journalists and politicians in profusion. One railroad man noted in 1885 that in the West "no man who has money, or official position, or influence thinks he ought to pay anything for riding on a railroad."

Railroad kings were, for a time, virtual industrial monarchs. As manipulators of a huge natural monopoly, they exercised more direct control over the lives of more people than did the president of the United States—and their terms were not limited to four years. They increasingly shunned the crude bloodletting of cutthroat competition and began to cooperate with one another to rule the railroad dominion. Sorely pressed to show at least some returns on their bloated investments, they entered into defensive alliances to protect precious profits.

The earliest form of combination was the "pool"—an agreement to divide the business in a given area and share the profits. Other rail barons granted secret rebates or kickbacks to powerful shippers in return for steady and assured traffic. Often they slashed their rates on competing lines, but they more than made up the difference on noncompeting ones, where they might actually charge more for a short haul than for a long one. As a result, small farmers usually paid the highest rates, while large customers got the best deals.

✬ Government Bridles the Iron Horse

It was neither healthy nor politically acceptable that so many people should be at the mercy of so few. Impoverished farmers, especially in the Midwest, began to wonder if the nation had not escaped from the slavery power only to fall into the hands of the money power, as represented by the railroad plutocracy.

But the American people, usually quick to respond to political injustice, were slow to combat economic injustice. Dedicated to free enterprise and to the principle that competition is the soul of trade, they cherished a traditionally keen pride in progress. They remembered that Jefferson's ideals were hostile to government interference with business. Above all, there shimmered the "American dream": the hope that in a catch-as-catch-can economic system, anyone might become a millionaire.

The depression of the 1870s goaded the farmers into protesting against being "railroaded" into bankruptcy. Under pressure from organized agrarian groups like the Grange (Patrons of Husbandry), many midwestern legislatures tried to regulate the railroad monopoly.

The scattered state efforts screeched to a halt in 1886. The Supreme Court, in the famed ***Wabash, St. Louis & Pacific Railroad Company*** v. ***Illinois*** case, decreed that individual states had no power to regulate *inter*state commerce. If the mechanical monster were to be corralled, the federal government would have to do the job.

Stiff-necked President Cleveland did not look kindly on effective regulation. But Congress ignored his grumbling indifference and passed the epochal **Interstate Commerce Act** in 1887. It prohibited rebates and pools and required the railroads to publish their rates openly. It also forbade unfair discrimination against shippers and outlawed charging more for a short haul than for a long one over the same line. Most important, it set up the Interstate Commerce Commission (ICC) to administer and enforce the new legislation.

Despite acclaim, the Interstate Commerce Act emphatically did not represent a popular victory over corporate wealth. One of the leading corporation lawyers of the day, Richard Olney, shrewdly noted that the new commission "can be made of great use to the railroads. It satisfies the popular clamor for a government supervision of railroads, at the same time that such supervision is almost entirely nominal. . . . The part of wisdom is not to destroy the Commission, but to utilize it."

What the new legislation did do was to provide an orderly forum where competing business interests could resolve their conflicts in peaceable ways. The country could now avoid ruinous rate wars among the railroads and outraged, "confiscatory" attacks on the lines by pitchfork-prodded state legislatures. This was a modest accomplishment but by no means an unimportant one. The Interstate Commerce Act tended to stabilize, not revolutionize, the existing business system.

Yet the act still ranks as a red-letter law. It was the first large-scale attempt by Washington to regulate business in the interest of society at large. It heralded the arrival of a series of independent regulatory commissions in the next century, which would irrevocably commit the government to the daunting task of monitoring and guiding the private economy. It foreshadowed the doom of freewheeling, buccaneering business practices and served full notice that there was a public interest in private enterprise that the government was bound to protect.

Miracles of Mechanization

Postwar industrial expansion, partly a result of the railroad network, rapidly began to assume mammoth proportions. When Lincoln was elected in 1860, the Republic ranked only fourth among the manufacturing nations of the world. By 1894 it had bounded into first place. Why the sudden upsurge?

Liquid capital, previously scarce, was now becoming abundant. The word *millionaire* had not been coined until the 1840s, and in 1861 only a handful of individuals were eligible for this class. But the Civil War, partly through profiteering, created immense fortunes, and these accumulations could now be combined with borrowings from foreign capitalists. Investors from abroad loaned more money to the United States in the postwar period than any country had previously received. Unlike in other countries, in America they mostly put the money into private hands, not public coffers. Investors primarily from Britain, but also from France, Germany, the Netherlands, and Switzerland, sometimes owned all or part of an American business. Other times they simply lent their money to the thousands of European companies set up to manage investment in U.S. industry. Either way, Europeans were usually content to let Americans run the business—until hard times hit and they demanded more say over company operations or government economic policies.

Innovations in transportation fueled growth, too, by bringing the nation's amazingly abundant natural resources—particularly coal, oil, and iron—to the factory door. A shipping system through the Great Lakes carried the rich iron deposits in the Mesabi Range of Minnesota to Chicago and Cleveland for refining. This priceless bonanza, where mountains of red-rusted ore could be scooped up by steam shovels, ultimately

Library of Congress

Thomas Alva Edison in His Lab, 1888 Edison was dubbed the "Wizard of Menlo Park," New Jersey, where he lived and established the first major industrial research laboratory. Edison was not only an ingenious inventor; he also figured out how to apply the principles of mass production to his inventions. Phonographs, telephones, telegraphs, incandescent electric lighting, fluoroscopes, kinetoscopes, and many more technological wonders spread throughout the world following their development in Edison's lab.

became a cornerstone of a vast steel empire. Copper, bauxite, and zinc made similar journeys from mine to manufacture.

The sheer size of the American market encouraged innovators to invent mass-production methods. With cheap transportation crisscrossing the nation and an ever-larger population able and eager to consume, anyone who could make an appealing new product available for a good price in large quantities—and figure out how to market it—thrived. Industrialists continued to refine the pre–Civil War "American System" of using specialized machinery to make interchangeable parts, culminating in 1913 with Henry Ford's fully developed moving assembly line for his Model T (see pp. 231–232 and 711–712).

The captains of industry had a major incentive to invent machines: they made it possible to replace expensive skilled labor with unskilled workers, now cheap and plentiful as a result of massive immigration. Steel, the keystone industry, was built largely on the

Regarding the exploitation of immigrant labor, Ralph Waldo Emerson (1803–1882) wrote in 1860,

" The German and Irish millions, like the Negro, have a great deal of guano in their destiny. They are ferried over the Atlantic, and carted over America, to ditch and to drudge, to make corn cheap, and then to lie down prematurely to make a spot of green grass on the prairie. **"**

sweat of low-priced immigrant labor from eastern and southern Europe, working in two 12-hour shifts, seven days a week.

Just as industry served as a hothouse of invention, brilliant ideas gave rise to whole new lines of business. Between 1860 and 1890, some 440,000 patents were issued. Business operations were facilitated by machines such as the cash register, the stock ticker, and the typewriter ("literary piano"), while the refrigerator car, the electric dynamo, and the electric railway speeded urbanization. One of the most ingenious inventions was the telephone, introduced by Alexander Graham Bell in 1876. America was suddenly turned into a nation of "telephoniacs," as a gigantic communications network was built on his invention. The social impact of the telephone further expanded when it lured "number please" women away from the stove to the switchboard. Telephone boys were at first employed as operators, but their profanity shocked patrons.

The most versatile inventor of all was Thomas Alva Edison (1847–1931), who as a boy had been considered so dull-witted that he was taken out of school. His severe deafness enabled him to concentrate without distraction. Edison was a gifted tinkerer and a tireless worker, not a pure scientist. "Genius," he said, "is one percent inspiration and ninety-nine percent perspiration." Wondrous devices poured out of his "invention factory" in New Jersey—the phonograph, the mimeograph, the dictaphone, and the moving picture. He is probably best known for his perfection in 1879 of the electric lightbulb, which turned night into day and transformed ancient human habits as well. People had previously slept an average of nine hours a night; now they slept just a bit more than seven.

✦ The Trust Titan Emerges

Despite pious protests to the contrary, competition was the bugbear of most business leaders of the day. Tycoons like Andrew Carnegie, the steel king; John D. Rockefeller, the oil baron; and J. Pierpont Morgan, the bankers' banker, exercised their genius in devising ways to circumvent competition. Carnegie integrated every phase of his steel-making operation. His miners scratched the ore from the earth in the Mesabi Range; Carnegie ships floated it across the Great Lakes; Carnegie railroads delivered it to the blast furnaces at Pittsburgh. When the molten metal finally poured from the glowing crucibles into the waiting ingot molds, no other hands but those in Carnegie's employ had touched the product. Carnegie thus pioneered the creative entrepreneurial tactic of **vertical integration**, combining into one organization all phases of manufacturing from mining to marketing. His goal was to improve efficiency by making supplies more reliable, controlling the quality of the product at all stages of production, and eliminating middlemen's fees.

Less justifiable on grounds of efficiency was the technique of **horizontal integration**, which simply meant allying with competitors to monopolize a given market. Rockefeller was a master of this stratagem. He perfected a device for controlling bothersome rivals—the **trust**. Stockholders in various smaller oil companies assigned their stock to the board of directors of his Standard Oil Company, formed in 1870. It then consolidated and concerted the operations of the previously competing enterprises. "Let us prey" was said to be Rockefeller's unwritten motto. Ruthlessly wielding vast power, Standard Oil soon cornered virtually the entire

The Octopus, 1904 This cartoon visually captures a feeling of widespread resentment against Standard Oil as a powerful, sprawling "octopus" whose tentacles controlled all branches of government.

world petroleum market. Weaker competitors, left out of the trust agreement, were forced to the wall. Rockefeller's stunning success inspired many imitators, and the word *trust* came to be generally used to describe any large-scale business combination.

The imperial Morgan devised still other schemes for eliminating "wasteful" competition. The depression of the 1890s drove into his welcoming arms many bleeding businesspeople, wounded by cutthroat competition. His prescribed remedy was to consolidate rival enterprises and to ensure future harmony by placing officers of his own banking syndicate on their various boards of directors. These came to be known as **interlocking directorates**.

The Supremacy of Steel

"Steel is king!" might well have been the exultant war cry of the new industrialized generation. The mighty metal ultimately held together the new steel civilization, from skyscrapers to coal scuttles, while providing it with food, shelter, and transportation. Steel making, notably rails for railroads, typified the dominance of "heavy industry," which concentrated on making "capital goods," as distinct from the production of "consumer goods" such as clothes and shoes.

Now taken for granted, steel was a scarce commodity in the wood-and-brick America of Abraham Lincoln. Considerable iron went into railroad rails and bridges, but steel was expensive and was used largely for products like cutlery. The early iron horse snorted exclusively (and dangerously) over iron rails. When in the 1870s "Commodore" Vanderbilt of the New York Central began to use steel rails, he was forced to import them from Britain.

Yet within an amazing twenty years, the United States had outdistanced all foreign competitors and was pouring out more than one-third of the world's supply of steel. By 1900 America was producing as much as Britain and Germany combined.

What wrought the transformation? Chiefly the invention in the 1850s of a method of making cheap steel—the Bessemer process. It was named after a derided British inventor, although an American had stumbled on it a few years earlier. William Kelly, a Kentucky manufacturer of iron kettles, discovered that cold air blown on red-hot iron caused the metal to become white-hot by igniting the carbon and thus eliminating impurities. He tried to apply the new "air boiling" technique to his own product, but his customers decried "Kelly's fool steel," and his business declined. Gradually the Bessemer-Kelly process won acceptance, and these two "crazy men" ultimately made possible the present steel civilization.

Carnegie and Other Sultans of Steel

Kingpin among steelmasters was Andrew Carnegie, an undersized, charming Scotsman. As a towheaded lad of thirteen, he was brought to America by his impoverished parents in 1848 and got a job as a bobbin boy at $1.20 a week. Mounting the ladder of success so fast that he was said to have scorched the rungs, he forged ahead by working hard, doing the extra chore, cheerfully assuming responsibility, and smoothly cultivating influential people.

After accumulating some capital, Carnegie entered the steel business in the Pittsburgh area. A gifted organizer and administrator, he succeeded by picking high-class associates and by eliminating many middlemen. Although inclined to be tough-fisted in business, he was not a monopolist and disliked monopolistic trusts. His remarkable organization was a partnership that involved, at its maximum, about forty "Pittsburgh millionaires." By 1900 he was producing one-fourth of the nation's Bessemer steel, and the partners in these pre–income tax days were dividing profits of $40 million a year as their take-home pay, with the "Napoleon of the Smokestacks" himself receiving a cool $25 million.

Into the picture now stepped the financial giant of the age, J. Pierpont Morgan. "Jupiter" Morgan had made a legendary reputation for himself and his Wall Street banking house by financing the reorganization of railroads, insurance companies, and banks. An impressive

J. P. Morgan (1837–1913) As the most influential banker of his day, Morgan symbolized to many people the power and arrogance of "finance capitalism." The chronic skin disorder on his nose inspired the taunt "Johnny Morgan's nasal organ has a purple hue."

Library of Congress

figure of a man, with massive shoulders, shaggy brows, piercing eyes, and a bulbous, acne-cursed red nose, he had established an enviable reputation for integrity. He did not believe that "money power" was dangerous, except when in dangerous hands—and he did not regard his own hands as dangerous.

The force of circumstances brought Morgan and Carnegie into collision. By 1900 the canny little Scotsman, weary of turning steel into gold, was eager to sell his holdings. Morgan had meanwhile plunged heavily into the manufacture of steel pipe tubing. Carnegie, cleverly threatening to invade the same business, was ready to ruin his rival if he did not receive his price. The steelmaster's agents haggled with the imperious Morgan for eight agonizing hours, and the financier finally agreed to buy out Carnegie for over $400 million. Fearing that he would die "disgraced" with so much wealth, Carnegie dedicated the remaining years of his life to giving away money for public libraries, pensions for professors, and other such philanthropic purposes—in all disposing of about $350 million.

Morgan moved rapidly to expand his new industrial empire. He took the Carnegie holdings, added others, "watered" the stock liberally, and in 1901 launched the enlarged United States Steel Corporation. Capitalized at $1.4 billion, it was America's first billion-dollar corporation—a larger sum than the total estimated wealth of the nation in 1800. The Industrial Revolution, with its hot Bessemer breath, had come into its own.

✦ Rockefeller Grows an American Beauty Rose

The sudden emergence of the oil industry was one of the most striking developments of the years during and after the Civil War. Traces of oil found on streams had earlier been bottled for back-rub and other patent medicines, but not until 1859 did the first well in Pennsylvania—"Drake's Folly"—pour out its liquid "black gold." Almost overnight an industry was born that was to take more wealth from the earth than all of the gold extracted by the forty-niners and their western successors. Kerosene, derived from petroleum, was the first major product of the infant oil industry. Burned from a cotton wick in a glass chimney lamp, kerosene produced a much brighter flame than whale oil. The oil business boomed; by the 1870s kerosene was America's fourth most valuable export. Whaling, in contrast, the lifeblood of ocean-roaming New Englanders since before the days of *Moby Dick*, swiftly became a sick industry.

But what technology gives, technology takes away. By 1885, 250,000 of Thomas Edison's electric lightbulbs were in use; fifteen years later, perhaps 15 million. The new electric industry rendered kerosene obsolete just

Library of Congress

Washington as Seen by the Trusts, 1900 "What a funny little government," John D. Rockefeller observes in this satirical cartoon. His own wealth and power are presumed to dwarf the resources of the federal government.

Robber Barons Cyrus Field, Jay Gould, Cornelius Vanderbilt, and Russell Sage Kept Afloat on the Broken Backs of America's Workingmen, 1883

as kerosene had rendered whale oil obsolete. Only in rural America and overseas did a market continue for oil-fired lamps.

Oil might thus have remained a modest, even a shrinking, industry but for yet another turn of the technological tide—the invention of the automobile. By 1900 the gasoline-burning internal combustion engine had clearly bested its rivals, steam and electricity, as the superior means of automobile propulsion. As the century of the automobile dawned, the oil business got a new, long-lasting, and hugely profitable lease on life.

John D. Rockefeller—lanky, shrewd, ambitious, abstemious (he neither drank, smoked, nor swore)—came to dominate the oil industry. Born to a family of precarious income, he became a successful businessman at age nineteen. One upward stride led to another, and in 1870 he organized the **Standard Oil Company** of Ohio, nucleus of the great trust formed in 1882. Locating his refineries in Cleveland, he sought to eliminate the middlemen and squeeze out competitors.

Pious and parsimonious, Rockefeller flourished in an era of completely free enterprise. So-called piratical practices were employed by "corsairs of finance," and business ethics were distressingly low. Rockefeller, operating "just to the windward of the law," pursued a policy of rule or ruin. "Sell all the oil that is sold in your district" was the hard-boiled order that went out to his local agents. By 1877 Rockefeller controlled 95 percent of all the oil refineries in the country.

Rockefeller—"Reckafellow," as Carnegie had once called him—showed little mercy. A kind of primitive

savagery prevailed in the jungle world of big business, where only the fittest survived. Or so Rockefeller believed. His son later explained that the giant American Beauty rose could be produced "only by sacrificing the early buds that grew up around it." His father pinched off the small buds with complete ruthlessness. Employing spies and extorting secret rebates from the railroads, he even forced the lines to pay him rebates on the freight bills of his competitors!

Rockefeller thought he was simply obeying a law of nature. "The time was ripe" for aggressive consolidation, he later reflected. "It had to come, though all we saw at the moment was the need to save ourselves from wasteful conditions. . . . The day of combination is here to stay. Individualism has gone, never to return."

On the other side of the ledger, Rockefeller's oil monopoly did turn out a superior product at a relatively cheap price. It achieved important economies, both at home and abroad, by its large-scale methods of production and distribution. This, in truth, was the tale of the other trusts as well. The efficient use of expensive machinery called for bigness, and consolidation proved more profitable than ruinous price wars.

Other trusts blossomed along with the American Beauty of oil. These included the sugar trust, the tobacco trust, the leather trust, and the harvester trust, which amalgamated some two hundred competitors. The meat industry arose on the backs of bawling western herds, and meat kings like Gustavus F. Swift and Philip Armour took their place among the new royalty. Wealth was coming to dominate the commonwealth.

These untrustworthy trusts, and the "pirates" who captained them, were disturbingly new. They eclipsed an older American aristocracy of modestly successful merchants and professionals. An arrogant class of "new rich" was now elbowing aside the patrician families in the mad scramble for power and prestige. Not surprisingly, the ranks of the antitrust crusaders were frequently spearheaded by the "best men"—genteel old-family do-gooders who were not radicals but conservative defenders of their own vanishing influence.

✦ The Gospel of Wealth

Monarchs of yore invoked the divine right of kings, and America's industrial plutocrats took a somewhat similar stance. Some candidly credited heavenly help. "Godliness is in league with riches," preached the Episcopal bishop of Massachusetts, and hardfisted John D. Rockefeller piously acknowledged that "the good Lord gave me my money." Steel baron Andrew Carnegie agreed that the wealthy, entrusted with society's riches, had to prove themselves morally responsible according to a "Gospel of Wealth." But most defenders of wide-open capitalism relied more heavily on the survival-of-the-fittest theories of English philosopher Herbert Spencer and Yale professor William Graham Sumner. Later mislabeled **Social Darwinists**, these theorists argued that individuals won their stations in life by competing on the basis of their natural talents. The wealthy and powerful had simply demonstrated greater abilities than the poor. Spencer and Sumner owed less to English evolutionary naturalist Charles Darwin, who stressed the adaptation of organisms, than to British laissez-faire economists David Ricardo and Thomas Malthus. In fact, Spencer, not Darwin, coined the phrase "survival of the fittest." "The millionaires are a product of natural selection," Sumner declared. In 1883 he asked, "What do social classes owe each other?" then answered his own question: nothing. Some Social Darwinists later applied this theory to explain why some nations were more powerful than others or had the right to dominate "lesser peoples," often defined by race.

Self-justification by the wealthy inevitably involved contempt for the poor. Many of the rich, especially the newly rich, had pulled themselves up by their own bootstraps; hence they concluded that those who stayed poor must be lazy and lacking in enterprise. The Reverend Russell Conwell of Philadelphia became rich by delivering his lecture "Acres of Diamonds" thousands of times. In it he charged, "There is not a poor person in the United States who was not made poor by his own shortcomings." Such attitudes were a formidable roadblock to social reform.

Plutocracy, like the earlier slavocracy, took its stand firmly on the Constitution. The clause that gave Congress sole jurisdiction over interstate commerce was a godsend to the monopolists; their high-priced lawyers used it time and again to thwart controls by the state legislatures. Giant trusts likewise sought refuge behind the Fourteenth Amendment, which had been originally designed to protect the rights of the ex-slaves as persons. The courts ingeniously interpreted a corporation to be a legal "person" and decreed that, as such, it could not be deprived of its property by a state without "due process of law" (see Amendment XIV, para. 1 in the Appendix). There is some questionable evidence that slippery corporation lawyers deliberately inserted this loophole when the Fourteenth Amendment was being fashioned in 1866.

Great industrialists likewise sought to incorporate in "easy states," like New Jersey, where the restrictions on big business were mild or nonexistent. For example, the Southern Pacific Railroad, with much of its trackage in California, was incorporated in Kentucky.

✦ Government Tackles the Trust Evil

At long last the masses of the people began to mobilize against monopoly. They first tried to control the trusts through state legislation, as they had earlier attempted to curb the railroads. Failing here, as before, they were forced to appeal to Congress. After prolonged pulling and hauling, the **Sherman Anti-Trust Act** of 1890 was finally signed into law.

The Sherman Act flatly forbade combinations in restraint of trade, without any distinction between "good" trusts and "bad" trusts. Bigness, not badness, was the sin. The law proved ineffective, largely because it had only baby teeth or no teeth at all, and because it contained legal loopholes through which clever corporation lawyers could wriggle. But it was unexpectedly effective in one respect. Contrary to its original intent, it was used to curb labor unions or labor combinations that were deemed to be restraining trade.

Industrial millionaires were condemned in the Populist platform of 1892:

❝ The fruits of the toil of millions are boldly stolen to build up colossal fortunes for a few . . . and the possessors of these, in turn despise the Republic and endanger liberty. From the same prolific womb of governmental injustice we breed the two great classes—tramps and millionaires.❞

The New Rich and the New Immigrants A well-to-do family plays chess at its parlor table (left), while a tenement family does "piecework" around its kitchen table— shelling nuts for commercial use (right). The young working girl seems to be "snitching" some nuts for herself. The apparently growing gulf between the rich and the poor deeply worried reformers in the late nineteenth century. They feared that democracy could not survive in the face of such gross inequality.

Early prosecutions of the trusts by the Justice Department under the Sherman Act of 1890, as it turned out, were neither vigorous nor successful. The decisions in seven of the first eight cases presented by the attorney general were adverse to the government. More new trusts were formed in the 1890s under President McKinley than during any other like period. Not until 1914 were the paper jaws of the Sherman Act fitted with reasonably sharp teeth. Until then, there was some question whether the government would control the trusts or the trusts the government.

But the iron grip of monopolistic corporations was being threatened. A revolutionary new principle had been written into the law books by the Sherman Anti-Trust Act of 1890, as well as by the Interstate Commerce Act of 1887. Private greed should henceforth be subordinated to public need.

★ The South in the Age of Industry

The industrial tidal wave that washed over the North after the Civil War caused only feeble ripples in the backwater of the South. As late as 1900, the South still produced a smaller percentage of the nation's manufactured goods than it had before the Civil War. The plantation system had degenerated into a pattern of absentee landownership. White and black sharecroppers now tilled the soil for a share of the crop, or they became tenants, in bondage to their landlords, who controlled needed credit and supplies.

Southern agriculture received a welcome boost in the 1880s, when machine-made cigarettes replaced the roll-your-own variety and tobacco consumption shot up. James Buchanan Duke took full advantage of the new technology to mass-produce the dainty "coffin nails." In 1890, in what was becoming a familiar pattern, he absorbed his main competitors into the American Tobacco Company. The cigarette czar later showed such generosity to Trinity College, near his birthplace

Henry W. Grady (1851–1889), editor of the Atlanta Constitution, *urged the new South to industrialize. In a Boston speech in 1889, he described the burial in Georgia of a Confederate veteran:*

❝ The South didn't furnish a thing on earth for that funeral but the corpse and the hole in the ground. . . . They buried him in a New York coat and a Boston pair of shoes and a pair of breeches from Chicago and a shirt from Cincinnati, leaving him nothing to carry into the next world with him to remind him of the country in which he lived, and for which he fought for four years, but the chill of blood in his veins and the marrow in his bones.❞

A Virginia Tobacco Factory, ca. 1880
The employment of women and children was a common practice in late-nineteenth-century American industry, north as well as south.

in Durham, North Carolina, that the trustees gratefully changed its name to Duke University.

Industrialists tried to coax the agricultural South out of the fields and into the factories, but with only modest success. The region remained overwhelmingly rural. Prominent among the boosters of a "new South" was silver-tongued Henry W. Grady, editor of the *Atlanta Constitution*. He tirelessly exhorted the ex-Confederates to become "Georgia Yankees" and outplay the North at the commercial and industrial game.

Yet formidable obstacles lay in the path of southern industrialization. One was the paper barrier of regional rate-setting systems imposed by the northern-dominated railroad interests. Railroads gave preferential rates to manufactured goods moving southward from the North, but in the opposite direction they discriminated in favor of southern raw materials. The net effect was to keep the South in a kind of servitude to the Northeast—as a supplier of raw materials to the manufacturing metropolis, unable to develop a substantial industrial base of its own.

A bitter example of this economic discrimination against the South was the "Pittsburgh plus" pricing system in the steel industry. Rich deposits of coal and iron ore near Birmingham, Alabama, worked by low-wage southern labor, should have given steel manufacturers there a competitive edge, especially in southern markets. But the steel lords of Pittsburgh brought pressure to bear on the compliant railroads. As a result, Birmingham steel, no matter where it was delivered, was charged a fictional fee, as if it had been shipped from Pittsburgh. This stunting of the South's natural economic advantages throttled the growth of the Birmingham steel industry.

In manufacturing cotton textiles, the South fared considerably better. Southerners had long resented shipping their fiber to New England, and now their cry was "Bring the mills to the cotton." Beginning about 1880, northern capitalists began to erect cotton mills in the South, largely in response to tax benefits and the prospect of cheap and nonunionized labor (see Figure 24.2 and Figure 24.3).

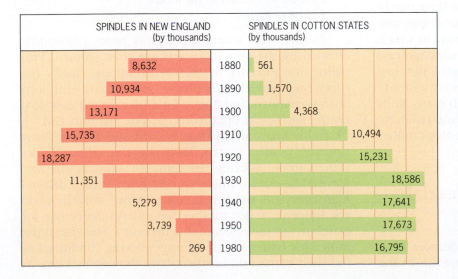

SPINDLES IN NEW ENGLAND (by thousands)		SPINDLES IN COTTON STATES (by thousands)
8,632	1880	561
10,934	1890	1,570
13,171	1900	4,368
15,735	1910	10,494
18,287	1920	15,231
11,351	1930	18,586
5,279	1940	17,641
3,739	1950	17,673
269	1980	16,795

FIGURE 24.2 Cotton Manufacturing Moves South, 1880–1980 Textile manufacturing usually looms large in the early stages of industrial development. In the later stages, it gives way to higher-technology businesses. This trend can be seen here, both in the migration of textile manufacturing to the southern United States and in the decline in the number of spindles in the United States as a whole since the 1930s, as developing Third World countries became major textile producers. (Source: *Historical Statistics of the United States* and *Statistical Abstract of the United States*, relevant years.)

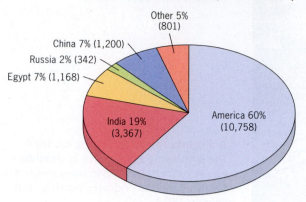

World cotton production, 1903
(Bales of approx. 500 lbs, in thousands)

Other 5% (801)
China 7% (1,200)
Russia 2% (342)
Egypt 7% (1,168)
India 19% (3,367)
America 60% (10,758)

Total: 17,636

FIGURE 24.3 World Cotton Production, 1903 Cotton manufacturing grew in the United States in the early twentieth century, and raw cotton production reached higher levels than anywhere else in the world. (Source: John A. Todd, *The World's Cotton Crops* (London: A. & C. Black, 1915), 395–396.)

The textile mills proved to be a mixed blessing to the economically blighted South. They slowly wove an industrial thread into the fabric of southern life, but at a considerable human cost. Cheap labor was the South's major attraction for potential investors, and keeping labor cheap became almost a religion among southern industrialists. The mills took root in the chronically depressed Piedmont region of southern Appalachia and came to dominate utterly the communities in which they were located.

Rural southerners—virtually all of them white, for blacks were excluded from all but the most menial jobs in the mills—poured out of the hills and hollows to seek employment in the hastily erected company mill towns. Entire families—often derided as "hillbillies" or "lintheads"—worked from dawn to dusk amid the whirring spindles. They were paid at half the rate of their northern counterparts and often received their compensation in the form of credit at a company store, to which they were habitually in debt. But despite their depressed working conditions and poor pay, many southerners saw employment in the mills as a salvation, the first steady jobs and wages they had ever known. With many mills anxious to tap the cheap labor of women and children, mill work often offered destitute farm-fugitive families their only chance to remain together.

✳ The Impact of the New Industrial Revolution on America

Economic miracles wrought during the decades after the Civil War enormously increased the wealth of the Republic. The standard of living rose sharply, and well-fed American workers enjoyed more physical comforts than their counterparts in any other industrial nation. Urban centers mushroomed as the insatiable factories demanded more American labor and as immigrants swarmed like honeybees to the new jobs (see Map 24.2 and "Makers of America: The Poles," pp. xxx–xxx).

Early Jeffersonian ideals were withering before the smudgy blasts from the smokestacks. As agriculture declined in relation to manufacturing, America could no longer aspire to be a nation of small freehold farms. Jefferson's concepts of free enterprise, with neither help nor hindrance from Washington, were being thrown out the factory window. Tariffs had already provided assistance, but the long arm of federal authority was now committed to decades of corporation curbing and "trust-busting."

Older ways of life also wilted in the heat of the factory furnaces. The very concept of time was revolutionized. Rural American migrants and peasant European immigrants, used to living by the languid clock of nature, now had to regiment their lives by the factory whistle. The seemingly arbitrary discipline of industrial labor did not come easily and sometimes had to be forcibly taught. One large corporation simultaneously instructed its Polish immigrant workers in the English language and in the obligations of factory work schedules:

I hear the whistle. I must hurry.
I hear the five-minute whistle.
It is time to go into the shop. . . .
I change my clothes and get ready to work.
The starting whistle blows.
I eat my lunch.
It is forbidden to eat until then. . . .
I work until the whistle blows to quit.
I leave my place nice and clean.
I put all my clothes in the locker.
I must go home.

Probably no single group was more profoundly affected by the new industrial age than women. Propelled into industry by recent inventions, chiefly the typewriter and the telephone switchboard, millions of stenographers and "hello girls" discovered new economic and social opportunities. The "Gibson Girl," a magazine image of an independent and athletic "new woman" created in the 1890s by the artist Charles Dana Gibson, became the romantic ideal of the age. For middle-class women, careers often meant delayed marriages and smaller families. Most women workers, however, toiled neither for independence nor for glamour, but out of economic necessity. They faced the same long hours and dangerous working conditions as did their mates and brothers, and they earned less, as

MAP 24.2 American Industry in 1900 By the end of the nineteenth century, once-rural America boasted the world's largest industrial output—a development with enormous consequences for politics, diplomacy, and family life. © Cengage Learning

wages for "women's jobs" were usually set below those for men's.

The clattering machine age likewise accentuated class division. "Industrial buccaneers" flaunted bloated fortunes, and their rags-to-riches spouses displayed glittering diamonds. Such extravagances evoked bitter criticism. Some of it was envious, but much of it rose from a small but increasingly vocal group of socialists and other radicals, many of whom were recent European immigrants. The existence of an oligarchy of money was amply demonstrated by the fact that in 1900 about one-tenth of the people owned nine-tenths of the nation's wealth.

Women Canning Shrimp, 1893 Long hours, low pay, and wretched working conditions were the common fate of women who labored not for "pin money," but to help support their families. The "family wage" for the workingman was more a hope than a reality.

Library of Congress

A nation of farmers and independent producers was becoming a nation of wage earners. In 1860 half of all workers were self-employed; by the century's end, two of every three working Americans depended on wages. Real wages were rising, and times were good for workers who were working. But with dependence on wages came vulnerability to the swings of the economy and the whims of the employer. The fear of unemployment was never distant. A breadwinner's illness could mean catastrophe for an entire family. Nothing more sharply defined the growing difference between working-class and middle-class conditions of life than the precariousness of the laborer's lot. Reformers struggled to introduce a measure of security—job and wage protection, and provision for temporary unemployment—into the lives of the working class.

Finally, strong pressures for foreign trade developed as the tireless industrial machine threatened to saturate the domestic market. Aided by developments like the laying of a transatlantic telegraph in 1866 and the opening of the Suez Canal in 1869, international trade became ever faster, cheaper, and easier. American products radiated out all over the world—notably the five-gallon kerosene can of the Standard Oil Company. The flag follows trade, and empire tends to follow the flag—a harsh lesson that America was soon to learn.

✦ In Unions There Is Strength

The sweat of the laborer lubricated the vast new industrial machine. Yet the wage workers did not share proportionately with their employers in the benefits of the age of big business.

The worker, suggestive of the Roman galley slave, was becoming a lever-puller in a giant mechanism. Individual originality and creativity were being stifled, and less value than ever before was being placed on manual skills. Before the Civil War, the worker might have toiled

Gibson Girl, 1899 Illustrator Charles Dana Gibson created a sensation with his drawings of healthy, athletic, young women. The image of the "Gibson Girl" inspired new standards of female fashion as the twentieth century opened, and came to symbolize women's growing independence and assertiveness. Granger Collection

Library of Congress

Breaker Boys at South Pittson, Pennsylvania, 1911 Photographer Lewis Hine captured the grimness of these mine helpers' lives. For hours they sat on benches above a moving belt, breathing coal dust deep into their lungs and kicking large pieces of coal with their feet, breaking the lumps to uniform size for shipment. Photographs like this one became icons of the reform crusade against child labor, a campaign that succeeded only with the passage of the Fair Labor Standards Act in 1938.

The Photography of Lewis W. Hine

The pell-mell onrush of industrialization after the Civil War spawned countless human abuses, few more objectionable than the employment of children, often in hazardous jobs. For decades reformers tried to arouse public outrage against child labor, and they made significant headway at last with the help of photography—especially the photographs of Lewis W. Hine (1874–1940). A native of Wisconsin, Hine in 1908 became the staff photographer for the National Child Labor Committee, an organization committed to ending child labor. This 1909 photo of young "doffers," whose job it was to remove fully wound bobbins from textile spinning machines, is typical of Hine's work. He shows the boys climbing dangerously on the whirling mechanism, and his own caption for the photo names the mill—"Bibb Mill No. 1, Macon, Georgia"—but not the boys, as if to underline the impersonal, dehumanizing nature of their work and the specific responsibilities of their employer. His other subjects included child workers on Colorado beet farms, in Pennsylvania coal mines and Gulf Coast fish canneries, and in the glass, tobacco, and garment trades. Hine's images contributed heavily to the eventual success of the campaign to end child labor in the New Deal era. He is also celebrated as one of the fathers of documentary photography. Why might Hine's graphic images have succeeded in stirring public opinion more powerfully than factual and statistical demonstrations of the evil

Library of Congress

of child labor? Given Hine's own reform objectives, can his photographs—or any so-called documentary images—be taken at face value as literal, accurate information about the past?

in a small plant whose owner hailed the employee in the morning by first name and inquired after the family's health. But now the factory hand was employed by a corporation—depersonalized, bodiless, soulless, and often conscienceless. The directors knew the worker not, and in fairness to their stockholders, they were not inclined to engage in large-scale private philanthropy.

New machines displaced employees, and though in the long run more jobs were created than destroyed, in the short run the manual worker was often hard hit. A glutted labor market, moreover, severely handicapped wage earners. Employers could take advantage of the vast new railroad network and bring in unemployed workers, from the four corners of the country and beyond, to beat down high wage levels. During the 1880s and 1890s, several hundred thousand unskilled workers a year poured into the country from Europe, creating a labor market more favorable to the boss than the worker.

Individual workers were powerless to battle single-handedly against giant industry. Forced to organize

and fight for basic rights, they found the dice heavily loaded against them. The corporation could dispense with the individual worker much more easily than the worker could dispense with the corporation. Employers could pool vast wealth through thousands of stockholders, retain high-priced lawyers, buy up the local press, and put pressure on the politicians. They could import strikebreakers ("scabs") and employ thugs to beat up labor organizers. In 1886 Jay Gould reputedly boasted, "I can hire one-half of the working class to kill the other half."

Corporations had still other weapons in their arsenals. They could call upon the federal courts—presided over by well-fed and conservative judges—to issue injunctions ordering the strikers to cease striking. If defiance and disorder ensued, the company could request the state and federal authorities to bring in troops. Employers could lock their doors against rebellious workers—a procedure called the "lockout"—and then starve them into submission. They could compel them to sign "ironclad oaths" or "yellow-dog contracts,"

The Strike, by Robert Koehler, 1886 Scenes like this were becoming more typical of American life in the late nineteenth century as industrialism advanced spectacularly and sometimes ruthlessly. Here Koehler (1850–1917) shows an entire community of men, women, and children—many of them apparently immigrant newcomers— challenging the power of the "boss." The scene is tense but orderly, though violence seems to be imminent as one striker reaches for a rock.

both of which were solemn agreements not to join a labor union. They could put the names of agitators on a "black list" and circulate it among fellow employers. A corporation might even own the "company town," with its high-priced grocery stores and "easy" credit. Often the worker sank into perpetual debt—a status that strongly resembled serfdom. Countless thousands of blackened coal miners were born in a company house, nurtured by a (high-priced) company store, and buried in a company graveyard—prematurely dead.

The middle-class public, annoyed by recurrent strikes, grew deaf to the outcry of the worker. American wages were perhaps the highest in the world, although a dollar a day for pick-and-shovel labor does not now seem excessive. Carnegie and Rockefeller had battled their way to the top, and the view was common that the laborer could do likewise. Somehow the strike seemed like a foreign importation—socialistic and hence unpatriotic. Big business might combine into trusts to raise prices, but the worker must not combine into unions to raise wages. Unemployment seemed to be an act of God, who somehow would take care of the laborer.

✷ Labor Limps Along

Labor unions, which had been few and disorganized in 1861, were given a strong boost by the Civil War. This bloody conflict, with its drain on human resources, put more of a premium on labor; and the mounting cost of living provided an urgent incentive to unionization. By 1872 there were several hundred thousand organized workers and thirty-two national unions, representing such crafts as bricklayers, typesetters, and shoemakers.

The **National Labor Union**, organized in 1866, represented a giant bootstride by workers. One of the earliest national-scale unions to organize in the Americas or Europe, it aimed to unify workers across locales and trades to challenge their ever more powerful bosses. The union lasted six years and attracted the impressive total of some 600,000 members, including the skilled, unskilled, and farmers, though in keeping with the times, it excluded the Chinese and made only nominal efforts to include women and blacks. Black workers organized their own Colored National Labor Union as an adjunct, but their support for the Republican party and the persistent racism of white unionists prevented the two national unions from working together. The National Labor Union agitated for the arbitration of industrial disputes and the eight-hour workday, winning the latter for government workers. But the devastating depression of the 1870s dealt it a knockout blow. Labor was generally rocked back on its heels during the tumultuous years of the depression, but it never completely toppled. Wage reductions in 1877 touched off such disruptive strikes on the railroads that nothing short of federal troops could restore order.

A new organization—the **Knights of Labor**—seized the torch dropped by the defunct National Labor Union (see "Makers of America: The Knights of Labor," pp. 534–535). Officially known as the Noble and Holy Order of the Knights of Labor, it began inauspiciously in 1869 as a secret society, with a private ritual, passwords, and a special handshake. Secrecy, which continued until 1881, would forestall possible reprisals by employers.

The Knights of Labor, like the National Labor Union, sought to include all workers in "one big union." Their slogan was "An injury to one is the concern of all." A welcome mat was rolled out for the skilled and unskilled, for men and women, for whites and blacks, some ninety thousand of whom joined. The Knights barred only "nonproducers"—liquor dealers, professional gamblers, lawyers, bankers, and stockbrokers.

Setting up broad goals, the embattled Knights refused to thrust their lance into politics. Instead they campaigned for economic and social reform, including producers' cooperatives and codes for safety and health. Voicing the war cry "Labor is the only creator of values and capital," they frowned upon industrial warfare while fostering industrial arbitration. The ordinary workday was then ten hours or more, and the Knights waged a determined campaign for the eight-hour stint. A favorite song of these years ran,

Hurrah, hurrah, for labor,
it is mustering all its powers,
And shall march along to victory
with the banner of eight hours.

Under the eloquent but often erratic leadership of Terence V. Powderly, an Irish American of nimble wit and fluent tongue, the Knights won a number of strikes for the eight-hour day. When the Knights staged a successful strike against Jay Gould's Wabash Railroad in 1885, membership mushroomed to about three-quarters of a million workers.

✴ Unhorsing the Knights of Labor

Despite their outward success, the Knights were riding for a fall. They became involved in a number of May Day strikes in 1886, about half of which failed. A focal point was Chicago, home to about eighty thousand Knights. The city was also honeycombed with a few hundred anarchists, many of them foreign-born, who were advocating a violent overthrow of the American government.

Tensions rapidly built up to the bloody **Haymarket Square** episode. Labor disorders had broken out, and on May 4, 1886, the Chicago police advanced on a meeting called to protest alleged brutalities by the authorities. Suddenly a dynamite bomb was thrown that killed or injured several dozen people, including police.

Hysteria swept the Windy City. Eight anarchists were rounded up, although nobody proved that they had anything to do directly with the bomb. But the judge and jury held that since they had preached incendiary doctrines, they could be charged with conspiracy. Five were sentenced to death, one of whom committed suicide, and the other three were given stiff prison terms.

Agitation for clemency mounted. In 1892, some six years later, John P. Altgeld, a German-born Democrat of strong liberal tendencies, was elected governor of Illinois. After studying the Haymarket case exhaustively, he pardoned the three survivors. Violent abuse was showered on him by conservatives, unstinted praise by those who thought the men innocent. He was defeated for reelection and died a few years later in relative obscurity, "The Eagle Forgotten." Whatever the merits of the case, Altgeld displayed courage in opposing what he regarded as a gross injustice.

The Haymarket Square bomb helped blow the props from under the Knights of Labor. They were associated in the public mind, though mistakenly, with the anarchists. The eight-hour movement suffered correspondingly, and subsequent strikes by the Knights met with scant success.

Another fatal handicap of the Knights was their inclusion of both skilled and unskilled workers. Unskilled labor could easily be replaced by strikebreaking "scabs." High-class craft unionists, who enjoyed a semimonopoly of skills, could not readily be supplanted and hence enjoyed a superior bargaining position. They finally wearied of sacrificing this advantage on the altar of solidarity with their unskilled coworkers and sought refuge in a federation of exclusively skilled craft unions—the American Federation of Labor. The desertion of the skilled craft unionists dealt the Knights a body blow. By the 1890s they had melted away to 100,000 members, and these gradually fused with other protest groups of that decade.

*J*t was 1875. The young worker was guided into a room, where his blindfold was removed. Surrounding him were a dozen men, their faces covered by hoods. One of the masked figures solemnly asked three questions: "Do you believe in God?" "Do you gain your bread by the sweat of your brow?" "Are you willing to take a solemn vow, binding you to secrecy, obedience, and mutual assistance?" Yes, came the reply. The men doffed their hoods and joined hands in a circle. Their leader, the Master Workman, declared, "On behalf of the toiling millions of earth, I welcome you to this Sanctuary, dedicated to the service of God, by serving humanity." Then the entire group burst into song:

> *Storm the fort, ye Knights of Labor,*
> *Battle for your cause;*
> *Equal rights for every neighbor,*
> *Down with tyrant laws!*

The carefully staged pageantry then drew to a close. The worker was now a full-fledged member of the Knights of Labor.

He had just joined a loose-knit organization of some 100,000 workingpeople, soon to swell to nearly a million after the Knights led several successful strikes in the 1880s. The first women Knights joined in 1881, when an all-female local was established in the shoe trade in Philadelphia, and one in ten members was a woman by 1885. Women were organizers, too. Fiery Mary Harris ("Mother") Jones got her start agitating for the Knights in the Illinois coalfields. The first all-black local was founded among coal miners in Ottumwa, Iowa. The Knights preached tolerance and the solidarity of all working men and women, and they meant it, but even their inclusionary spirit had its limits. Chinese workers were barred from joining, and the Knights vigorously supported the Chinese Exclusion Act of 1882. They also championed the Contract Labor Law of 1885, which aimed to restrain competition from low-wage immigrant workers—though immigrants, especially the Irish, were themselves disproportionately represented among the Knights' membership.

Terence V. Powderly, born to Irish immigrant parents in Carbondale, Pennsylvania, in 1849, became the Grand Master Workman of the Knights in 1879. Slightly built, with mild blue eyes behind glasses, he had dropped out of school at age thirteen to take a job guarding railroad track switches and rose to mayor of Scranton, Pennsylvania, in the 1870s. In 1894 he became a lawyer—despite the fact that the Knights excluded lawyers from membership. A complex, colorful, and sometimes cynical man, he denounced the "multimillionaires [for] laying the foundation for their colossal fortunes on the bodies and souls of living men." In the eyes of Powderly and his Knights, only the economic and political independence of American workers could preserve republican traditions and institutions from corruption by monopolists and other "parasites."

Powderly denounced "wage-slavery" and dedicated the Knights to achieving the "cooperative commonwealth." Shunning socialism, which advocated government ownership of the means of production, Powderly urged laborers to save enough from their wages to purchase mines, factories, railroads, and stores. They would thereby create a kind of toilers' utopia; because labor would own and operate those enterprises, workers themselves would be owner-producers, and the conflict between labor and capital would evaporate. The Knights actually did operate a few businesses, including coal mines in Indiana, but all eventually failed.

Powderly's vision of the cooperative commonwealth reflected the persistent dream of many nineteenth-century American workers that they would all one day

"Mother Jones"

Granger Collection

Granger Collection

Machinist Frank J. Ferrell, Black Delegate of District Assembly No. 49, Introducing General Master Workman Terence Powderly to the Tenth Annual Convention of the Knights of Labor, Held in Richmond, Virginia, 1886

become producers. As expectant capitalists, they lacked "class consciousness"—that is, a sense of themselves as a permanent working class that must organize to coax what benefits it could out of the capitalist system. Samuel Gompers, by contrast, accepted the framework of American capitalism, and his American Federation of Labor sought to work within that framework, not to overturn it. Gompers's conservative strategy, not Powderly's utopian dream, eventually carried the day. The swift decline of the Knights in the 1890s underscored the obsolescence of their unrealistic, even naive, view that a bygone age of independent producers could be restored. Yet the Knights' commitment to unifying all workers in one union—regardless of race, gender, ethnicity, or skill level—provided a blueprint for the eventual success of similarly committed unions like the Congress of Industrial Organizations in the 1930s.

© Bettmann/Corbis

Women Delegates to the 1886 Convention of the Knights of Labor

Brown Brothers

Samuel Gompers (1850–1924) Gompers (second from the right in the first row), shown here marching in a labor demonstration in Washington, D.C., in 1919, once declared, "Show me the country in which there are no strikes and I'll show you that country in which there is no liberty."

✵ The AF of L to the Fore

The elitist **American Federation of Labor**, born in 1886, was largely the brainchild of squat, square-jawed Samuel Gompers. This colorful Jewish cigar maker, born in a London tenement and removed from school at age ten, was brought to America when thirteen. Taking his turn at reading informative literature to fellow cigar makers in New York, he was pressed into overtime service because of his strong voice. Rising spectacularly in the labor ranks, he was elected president of the American Federation of Labor every year except one from 1886 to 1924.

Significantly, the American *Federation* of Labor was just what it called itself—a federation. It consisted of an association of self-governing national unions, each of which kept its independence, with the AF of L unifying overall strategy. No individual laborer could join the central organization.

Gompers adopted a down-to-earth approach, soft-pedaling attempts to engineer sweeping social reform. A bitter foe of socialism, he shunned politics for economic strategies and goals. Gompers had no quarrel with capitalism, but he demanded a fairer share for labor. All he wanted, he said, was "more." Promoting what he called a "pure and simple" unionism, he sought better wages, hours, and working conditions. Unlike the somewhat utopian Knights of Labor, he was not concerned with the sweet by-and-by, but with the bitter here and now. A major goal of Gompers was the "trade agreement" authorizing the **closed shop**—or all-union labor. His chief weapons were the walkout and the boycott, enforced by "We don't patronize" signs. The stronger craft unions of the federation, by pooling funds, were able to amass a war chest that would enable them to ride out prolonged strikes.

The AF of L thus established itself on solid but narrow foundations. Although attempting to speak for all workers, it fell far short of being representative of them. Composed of skilled craftsmen, like the carpenters and the bricklayers, it was willing to let unskilled laborers, including women and especially blacks, fend for themselves. Though hard-pressed by big industry, the federation was basically nonpolitical. But it did attempt to persuade members to reward friends and punish foes at the polls. The AF of L weathered the panic of 1893 reasonably well, and by 1900 it could boast a membership of 500,000. Critics referred to it, with questionable accuracy, as "the labor trust."

Labor disorders continued, peppering the years from 1881 to 1900 with a total of over 23,000 strikes. These disturbances involved 6,610,000 workers, with a total loss to both employers and employees of $450 million. The strikers lost about half their strikes and won or compromised the remainder. Perhaps the gravest weakness of organized labor was that it still embraced only a small minority of all workingpeople—about 3 percent in 1900.

But attitudes toward labor had begun to change perceptibly by 1900. The public was beginning to concede the right of workers to organize, to bargain collectively, and to strike. As a sign of the times, Labor Day was made a legal holiday by act of Congress in 1894. A few enlightened industrialists had come to perceive the wisdom of avoiding costly economic warfare by bargaining with the unions and signing agreements. But the vast majority of employers continued to fight organized labor, which achieved its grudging gains only after recurrent strikes and frequent reverses. Nothing was handed to it on a silver platter. Management still held the whip hand, and several trouble-fraught decades were to pass before labor was to gain a position of relative equality with capital. If the age of big business had dawned, the age of big labor was still some distance over the horizon.

Varying Viewpoints
Industrialization: Boon or Blight?

The capitalists who forged an industrial America in the late nineteenth century were once called captains of industry—a respectful title that bespoke the awe due their wondrous material accomplishments. But these economic innovators have never been universally admired. During the Great Depression of the 1930s, when the entire industrial order they had created seemed to have collapsed utterly, it was fashionable to speak of them as robber barons—a term implying scorn for their highhanded methods. This sneer often issued from the lips and pens of leftist critics like Matthew Josephson, who sympathized with the working classes that were allegedly brutalized by the factory system.

Criticism has also come from writers nostalgic for a preindustrial past. These critics believe that industrialization stripped away the traditions, values, and pride of native farmers and immigrant craftspeople. Conceding that economic development elevated the material standard of living for working Americans, this interpretation contends that the Industrial Revolution diminished their spiritual "quality of life." Accordingly, historians like Herbert Gutman and David Montgomery portray labor's struggle for control of the workplace as the central drama of industrial expansion.

Nevertheless, even these historians concede that class-based protest has never been as powerful a force in the United States as in certain European countries. Many historians believe that this is so because greater social mobility in America dampened class tensions. The French observer Alexis de Tocqueville noted in the 1830s that America had few huge inherited fortunes and that most of its wealthy men were self-made. For two centuries a majority of Americans have believed that greater opportunity distinguished the New World from the Old.

In the 1960s historians led by Stephan Thernstrom began to test this long-standing belief. Looking at such factors as occupation, wealth, and geographic mobility, they tried to gauge the nature and extent of social mobility in the United States. Most of these historians concluded that although relatively few Americans made rags-to-riches leaps like those heralded in the Horatio Alger stories, large numbers experienced small improvements in their economic and social status. Few sons of laborers became corporate tycoons, but many more became line bosses and white-collar clerks. These studies also have found that race and ethnicity often affected one's chances for success. For instance, the children and grandchildren of Jewish immigrants tended to rise faster in the professions than Americans of Italian and Irish descent. Throughout the nineteenth and early twentieth centuries, blacks lagged far behind other groups in almost every category.

In recent years such studies have been criticized by certain historians who point out the difficulties involved in defining social status. For instance, some white-collar clerical workers received lower wages than manual laborers did. Were they higher or lower on the social scale? Furthermore, James Henretta has pointed out that different groups defined success differently: whereas Jewish immigrants often struggled to give their sons professional educations, the Irish put more emphasis on acquiring land and the Italians on building small family-run businesses.

Meanwhile, leftist historians such as Michael Katz have argued that the degree of social mobility in America has been overrated. These historians argue that industrial capitalism created two classes: a working class that sold its labor, and a business class that controlled resources and bought labor. Although most Americans took small steps upward, they generally remained within the class in which they began. Thus, these historians argue, the inequality of a capitalistic class system persisted in America's seemingly fluid society.

Chapter Review

KEY TERMS

Wabash, St. Louis & Pacific Railroad Company v. *Illinois* (519)

Interstate Commerce Act (519)

vertical integration (521)

horizontal integration (521)

trust (521)

interlocking directorates (522)

Standard Oil Company (524)

Social Darwinists (525)

Sherman Anti-Trust Act (525)

National Labor Union (532)

Knights of Labor (533)

Haymarket Square (533)

American Federation of Labor (536)

closed shop (536)

PEOPLE TO KNOW

Cornelius Vanderbilt

Alexander Graham Bell

Thomas Alva Edison

Andrew Carnegie

John D. Rockefeller

Samuel Gompers

CHRONOLOGY

1862	Congress authorizes transcontinental railroad
1866	National Labor Union organized First working transatlantic telegraph cable
1869	Transcontinental railroad joined near Ogden, Utah Knights of Labor organized Suez Canal completed
1870	Standard Oil Company organized
1876	Bell invents telephone
1879	Edison invents electric light
1886	Haymarket Square bombing *Wabash* case American Federation of Labor formed
1887	Interstate Commerce Act
1890	Sherman Anti-Trust Act
1901	United States Steel Corporation formed

TO LEARN MORE

Edward L. Ayers, *The Promise of the New South: Life After Reconstruction* (1992)

David H. Bain, *Empire Express: Building the First Transcontinental Railroad* (1999)

Sven Beckert, *The Monied Metropolis: New York City and the Consolidation of the American Bourgeoisie, 1850–1896* (2001)

Alfred D. Chandler, Jr., *The Visible Hand: The Managerial Revolution in American Business* (1978)

James Green, *Death in the Haymarket: A Story of Chicago, the First Labor Movement, and the Bombing That Divided Gilded Age America* (2006)

Richard Hofstadter, *Social Darwinism in American Thought, 1860–1915* (rev. ed., 1955)

Tera W. Hunter, *To 'Joy My Freedom: Southern Black Women's Lives and Labors After the Civil War* (1997)

Alice Kessler Harris, *Out to Work: A History of Wage-Earning Women in the United States* (1982)

Maury Klein, *The Genesis of Industrial America, 1870–1920* (2007)

David Montgomery, *The Fall of the House of Labor: The Workplace, the State, and American Labor Activism, 1865–1925* (1987)

Daniel T. Rodgers, *The Work Ethic in Industrial America, 1850–1920* (1978)

Richard White, *Railroaded: The Transcontinentals and the Making of Modern America* (2011)

A complete, annotated bibliography for this chapter—along with brief descriptions of the People to Know—may be found on the American Pageant website. The Key Terms are defined in a Glossary at the end of the text.

 Go to the CourseMate website at **www.cengagebrain.com** for additional study tools and review materials—including audio and video clips—for this chapter.

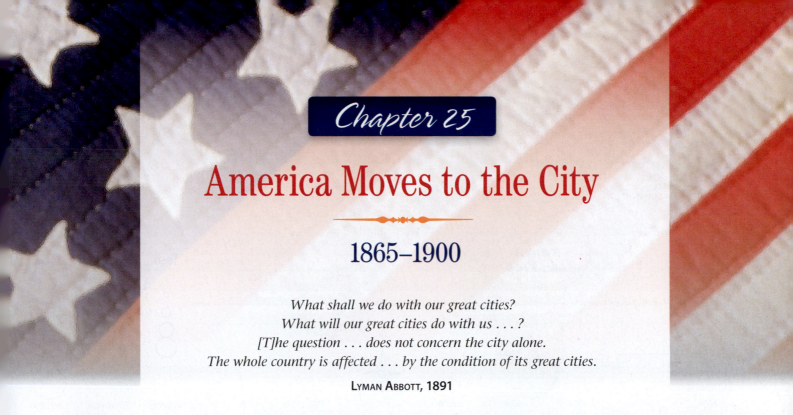

Chapter 25

America Moves to the City

1865–1900

What shall we do with our great cities?
What will our great cities do with us . . . ?
[T]he question . . . does not concern the city alone.
The whole country is affected . . . by the condition of its great cities.

LYMAN ABBOTT, 1891

Born in the country, America moved to the city in the decades following the Civil War. By the year 1900, the United States' upsurging population nearly doubled from its level of some 40 million souls enumerated in the census of 1870. Yet in the very same period, the population of American cities *tripled.* By the end of the nineteenth century, four out of ten Americans were city dwellers, in striking contrast to the rustic population of stagecoach days.

This cityward drift affected not only the United States but the entire industrializing world. European peasants, pushed off the land in part by competition from cheap American foodstuffs, were pulled into cities—in both Europe and America—by the new lure of industrial jobs. A revolution in American agriculture thus fed the industrial and urban revolutions in Europe, as well as in the United States.

✵ The Urban Frontier

The growth of American metropolises was spectacular. In 1860 no city in the United States could boast a million inhabitants; by 1890 New York, Chicago, and Philadelphia had vaulted past the million mark. By 1900 New York, with some 3.5 million people, was the second-largest city in the world, outranked only by London. Throughout the world, cities were exploding. London, Paris, Berlin, Tokyo, Moscow, Mexico City, Calcutta, and Shanghai all doubled or tripled in size between 1850 and 1900. The population of Buenos Aires multiplied by more than ten (see Map 25.1).

American cities grew both up and out. The cloud-brushing skyscraper allowed more people and workplaces to be packed onto a parcel of land. Appearing first as a ten-story building in Chicago in 1885, the skyscraper was made usable by the perfecting of the electric elevator. An opinionated Chicago architect, Louis Sullivan (1856–1924), contributed formidably to the further development of the skyscraper with his famous principle that "form follows function." Nesting loftily above city streets in the new steel-skeleton high-rises that Sullivan helped to make popular, many Americans were becoming modern cliff dwellers.

Americans were also becoming commuters, carted daily between home and job on the mass-transit lines that radiated out from central cities to surrounding suburbs. Electric trolleys, powered by wagging antennae from overhead wires, propelled city limits explosively outward. By the end of the century, the nation's first subway opened in Boston; London had led the way by building a subway as early as 1863. The compact and communal "walking city," its boundaries fixed by the limits of leg-power, gave way to the immense and impersonal megalopolis, carved into distinctly different districts for business, industry, and residential neighborhoods—which were in turn segregated by race, ethnicity, and social class.

Rural life could not compete with the siren song of the city (see Figure 25.1). Industrial jobs, above all, drew people off farms in America as well as abroad and into factory centers. But the urban lifestyle also held powerful attractions. The predawn milking of cows had little appeal when compared with the late-night glitter of

MAP 25.1 Size of World Cities 1850–1900   Sources: United Nations, "World Urbanization Prospects: The 2005 Revision"; Tertius Chandler and Gerald Fox, *3000 Years of Urban Growth* (New York: Academic Press, 1974); U.S. Census; Spencer H. Brown, "Public Health in Lagos, 1850–1900: Perceptions, Patterns, and Perspectives," *International Journal of African Historical Studies* 25, no. 2. (1992): 345; Josephine Olu Abiodun, "The Challenges of Growth and Development in Metropolitan Lagos," in *The Urban Challenge in Africa: Growth and Management of Its Large Cities*, ed. Carole Rakodi (New York: United Nations University Press, 1997), 193–195; United Nations Demographic Yearbook. © Cengage Learning

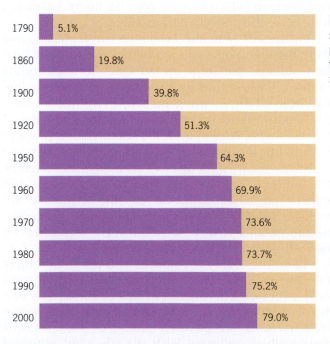

FIGURE 25.1 The Shift to the American City   This chart shows the percentage of total population living in locales with a population of twenty-five hundred or more. Note the slowing of the cityward trend from 1970 on. (Sources: *Historical Statistics of the United States*; U.S. Census Bureau.)

city lights, particularly alluring to young adults yearning for independence. Electricity, indoor plumbing, and telephones—whose numbers leapt from some 50,000 in 1880 to over 1 million in 1900—all made life in the big city more enticing. Engineering marvels like the skyscraper and New York's awesome Brooklyn Bridge, a harplike suspension span dedicated in 1883, further added to the seductive glamour of the gleaming cities.

Cavernous department stores such as Macy's in New York and Marshall Field's in Chicago attracted urban middle-class shoppers and provided urban working-class jobs, many of them for women. The bustling emporiums also heralded a dawning era of consumerism and accentuated widening class divisions. When Carrie Meeber, novelist Theodore Dreiser's fictional

Library of Congress

The Brooklyn Bridge   The Brooklyn Bridge opened on May 24, 1883. It had taken thirteen years to build and was the largest suspension bridge in the world, as well as the first made of steel wire. On opening day, an astonishing 1,800 vehicles and 150,300 people made the short but breathtaking trek between the New York City boroughs of Manhattan and Brooklyn. The first person to cross was Emily Warren Roebling, the daughter-in-law of the original designer, John Augustus Roebling, and the wife of his son, Washington Roebling, who had taken over the job when his father died suddenly in 1869. When Washington fell ill himself, Emily learned civil engineering and oversaw much of the remaining work on the bridge.

heroine in *Sister Carrie* (1900), escapes from rural boredom to Chicago just before the turn of the century, it is the spectacle of the city's dazzling department stores that awakens her fateful yearning for a richer, more elegant way of life—for entry into the privileged urban middle class, whose existence she had scarcely imagined in the rustic countryside.

The move to the city introduced Americans to new ways of living. Country dwellers produced little household waste. Domestic animals or scavenging pigs ate food scraps on the farm. Rural women mended and darned worn clothing rather than discard it. Household products were sold in bulk at the local store, without wrapping. Mail-order houses such as Sears and Montgomery Ward, which increasingly displaced the rural "general store" in the late nineteenth century, at first did not list trash barrels or garbage cans in their catalogues. In the city, however, goods came in throwaway

bottles, boxes, bags, and cans. Apartment houses had no adjoining barnyards where residents might toss garbage to the hogs. Cheap ready-to-wear clothing and swiftly changing fashions pushed old suits and dresses out of the closet and onto the trash heap. Waste disposal, in short, was an issue new to the urban age. And the mountains of waste that urbanites generated further testified to a cultural shift away from the virtues of thrift to the conveniences of consumerism.

The jagged skyline of America's perpendicular civilization could not fully conceal the canker sores of a feverish growth. Criminals flourished like lice in the teeming asphalt jungles. Sanitary facilities could not keep pace with the mushrooming population explosion. Impure water, uncollected garbage, unwashed bodies, and droppings from draft animals enveloped many cities in a satanic stench. Baltimore was described as smelling like a billion polecats.

FIGURE 25.2 Dumbbell Tenement
This was the standard architectural plan for the human warehouses on New York's Lower East Side. Despite the innovation of an air shaft to bring light and ventilation to the middle of the building, only one room in each of the apartments was directly exposed to sunlight and open air. All families on a floor shared the toilet ("W.C.") in the hallway.

The cities were monuments of contradiction. They represented "humanity compressed," remarked one observer, "the best and the worst combined, in a strangely composite community." They harbored merchant princes and miserable paupers, stately banks and sooty factories, green-grassed suburbs and treeless ghettos, towering skyscrapers and stinking tenements. The glaring contrasts that assaulted the eye in New York reminded one visitor of "a lady in ball costume, with diamonds in her ears, and her toes out at the boots."

Worst of all were the human pigsties known as slums. They seemed to grow ever more crowded, more filthy, and more rat-infested, especially after the perfection in 1879 of the "dumbbell" tenement (see Figure 25.2). So named because of the outline of its floor plan, the dumbbell was usually seven or eight stories high, with shallow, sunless, and ill-smelling air shafts providing minimal ventilation. Several families were sardined onto each floor of the barracks-like structures, and they shared a malodorous toilet in the hall. In these fetid warrens, conspicuously in New York's "Lung Block," hundreds of unfortunate urbanites coughed away their lives. "Flophouses" abounded where the half-starved and unemployed might sleep for a few cents on verminous mattresses. Small wonder that slum dwellers strove mightily to escape their wretched surroundings—as many of them did. The slums remained foul places, inhabited by successive waves of newcomers. To a remarkable degree, hard-working people moved up and out of them.

Cities were dangerous for everyone. In 1871 two-thirds of downtown Chicago burned in a raging fire that left ninety thousand people homeless and destroyed more than fifteen thousand buildings. Closely packed wooden structures fed the insatiable flames, prompting Chicago and other wary cities to require stone and iron buildings downtown. The wealthiest began to leave the risky cities behind and head for semirural suburbs. These leafy "bedroom communities" eventually ringed the brick-and-concrete cities with a greenbelt of affluence.

The New Immigration

The powerful pull of the American urban magnet was felt even in faraway Europe. A seemingly endless stream of immigrants continued to pour in from the old "mother continent." In each of the three decades from the 1850s through the 1870s, more than 2 million migrants had stepped onto America's shores. By the 1880s the stream had swelled to a rushing torrent, as more than 5 million cascaded into the country. A new high for a single year was reached in 1882, when 788,992 arrived—or more than 2,100 a day (see Figure 25.3).

Until the 1880s most immigrants had come from the British Isles and western Europe, chiefly Germany and Ireland. Also significant were the more than 300,000 Chinese immigrants. Many of these earlier immigrants had faced virulent nativism, especially the Irish and the Chinese. In fact, the latter were legally excluded in 1882 (see p. 498).

But by the last decades of the century, the "old" European immigrants had adjusted well to American

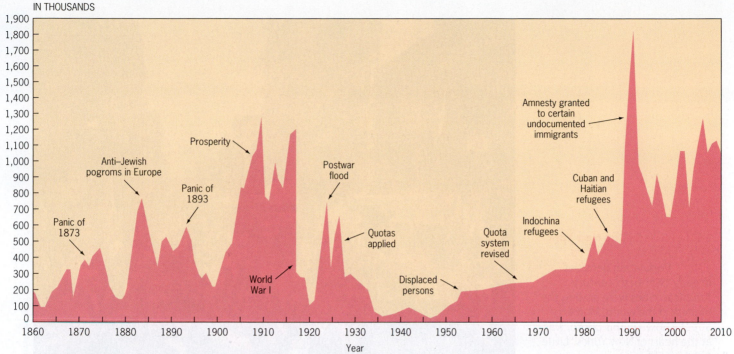

IN THOUSANDS

FIGURE 25.3 Annual Immigration, 1860–2010 After 1924 these numbers include only legal, documented immigrants. The 1989 total includes 478,814 people granted permanent residence status under the "amnesty" provisions of the 1986 Immigration Reform and Control Act. The 1990 total includes 880,372 people granted permanent residence under these provisions. The peak came in 1991, when 1,123,162 people were affected by amnesty. (Sources: *Statistical Abstract of the United States*, relevant years; Department of Homeland Security, *Yearbook of Immigration Statistics*, 2009.)

life by building supportive ethnic organizations and melding into established farm communities or urban craft unions. Although many still lived, worked, and worshiped among their own, they were largely accepted as "American" by the native-born.

In the 1880s the character of the immigrant stream changed drastically (see Figure 25.4). The so-called

New Immigrants came from southern and eastern Europe. Among them were Italians, Jews, Croats, Slovaks, Greeks, and Poles. They came from countries with little history of democratic government, where people had grown accustomed to cringing before despotism and where opportunities for advancement were few. These new peoples totaled only 19 percent of the

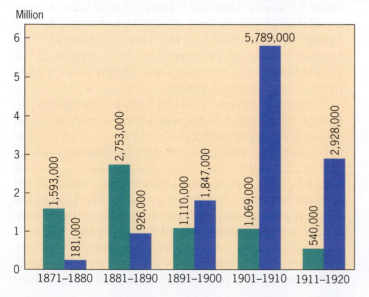

Million

FIGURE 25.4 Old and New Immigration (by decade, 1871–1920) In the 1880s the sources of immigration to the United States shifted from the British Isles and western Europe to southern and eastern Europe. A century later the old "mother continent" of Europe would account for only 10 percent of immigrants to America (see Figure 42.5 on p. 1000).

Leading nations of the Old Immigration: England, Ireland, Germany

Leading nations of the New Immigration: Italy, Austria– Hungary, Russia

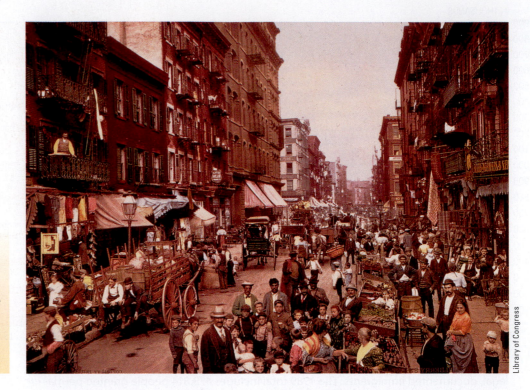

Mulberry Street on New York City's Lower East Side, ca. 1900 Population densities in early-twentieth-century American cities were among the highest in the world. Mulberry Street, shown in this photo, was at the heart of New York's "Little Italy" neighborhood.

Library of Congress

inpouring immigrants in the 1880s, but by the first decade of the twentieth century, they constituted an astonishing 66 percent of the total inflow. They hived together in cities like New York and Chicago, where the "Little Italys" and "Little Polands" soon claimed more inhabitants than many of the largest cities of the same nationality in the Old World (see "Makers of America: The Italians," pp. 546–547).

Largely illiterate and impoverished, many immigrants at first were content to live within these tightly bound communities based on native language and religion. There they worshiped in Orthodox or Roman Catholic churches or synagogues and in some cases nourished radical political ideas. There, too, they felt sheltered from Americans who revived old nativist fears that had plagued Old Immigrants in the 1840s and 1850s—fears that these New Immigrants would not, or could not, assimilate to life in their new land. The skeptics, who included some immigrants of the earlier wave, began asking whether the nation had become a melting pot or a dumping ground.

✦ Southern Europe Uprooted

Why were these bright-shawled and quaint-jacketed strangers hammering on the gates? In part they left their native countries because Europe seemed to have no room for them. The population of the Old World was growing vigorously. It nearly doubled in the century after 1800, thanks in part to abundant supplies of fish and grain from America and to the widespread cultivation in Europe of that humble New World transplant, the potato. American food imports and the galloping pace of European industrialization shook the peasantry loose from its ancient habitats and customary occupations, creating a vast, footloose army of the unemployed. Europeans by the millions drained out of the countryside and into European cities. Most stayed there, but some kept moving and left Europe altogether. About 60 million Europeans abandoned the Old Continent in the nineteenth and early twentieth centuries. More than half of them moved to the United States, while their compatriots spread out across the globe to South America, Canada, Africa, and Australia. Masses of people were already in motion in Europe before they felt the tug of the American magnet. This European diaspora, dominated by immigration to the United States, was, in many ways, simply a by-product of the urbanization of Europe.

"America fever" proved highly contagious in Europe. The United States was often painted as a land of fabulous opportunity in the "America letters" sent by friends and relatives already transplanted—letters that were soiled by the hands of many readers. "We eat here every day," wrote one jubilant Pole, "what we get only for Easter in our [native] country." The land of the free was also blessed with freedom from military conscription and institutionalized religious persecution.

Profit-seeking Americans trumpeted throughout Europe the attractions of the new promised land. Industrialists wanted low-wage labor, railroads wanted

The Italians

Mary Antin (1881–1949), who came to America from Russian Poland in 1894 when thirteen years of age, later wrote in The Promised Land *(1912),*

"So at last I was going to America! Really, really going, at last! The boundaries burst. The arch of heaven soared. A million suns shone out for every star. The winds rushed in from outer space, roaring in my ears, 'America! America!'**"**

buyers for their land grants, states wanted more population, and steamship lines wanted more human cargo for their holds. In fact, the ease and cheapness of steam-powered shipping greatly accelerated the transoceanic surge.

As the century lengthened, savage persecutions of minorities in Europe drove many shattered souls to American shores. In the 1880s the Russians turned violently upon their own Jews, chiefly in the Polish areas. Tens of thousands of these battered refugees, survivors of centuries of harassment as hated outcasts, fled their burning homes. They made their way to the seaboard cities of the Atlantic Coast, notably New York. Jews had experienced city life in Europe—a circumstance that made them virtually unique among the New Immigrants. Many of them brought their urban skills of tailoring or shopkeeping to American cities. Destitute and devout, eastern European Jews were frequently given a frosty reception not only by old-stock Americans but also by those German Jews who had arrived decades

earlier and prospered in the United States, some as garment manufacturers who now employed their coreligionists as cheap labor.

Many of the immigrants never intended to become Americans in any case. A large number of them were single men who worked in the United States for several months or years and then returned home with their hard-earned roll of American dollars. Some 25 percent of the nearly 20 million people who arrived between 1820 and 1900 were "birds of passage" who eventually returned to their country of origin. For them the attraction of the American magnet was never strong.

Even those who stayed in America struggled heroically to preserve their traditional culture. Catholics expanded their parochial-school systems, and Jews established Hebrew schools. Foreign-language newspapers abounded. Yiddish theaters, kosher-food stores, Polish parishes, Greek restaurants, and Italian social clubs all attested to the desire to keep old ways alive. Yet time took its toll on these efforts to conserve the customs of the Old World in the New. The children of the immigrants grew up speaking fluent English, sometimes mocking the broken grammar of their parents. They often rejected the Old Country manners of their mothers and fathers in their desire to plunge headlong into the mainstream of American life.

✴ Reactions to the New Immigration

America's government system, nurtured in wide-open spaces, was ill-suited to the cement forests of the great cities. Beyond minimal checking to weed out criminals

Brown Brothers

Jewish Women Working in a Sweatshop, ca. 1910 Countless immigrant women found their first American employment in shops like this.

Who were the "New Immigrants," these southern and eastern European birds of passage that flocked to the United States between 1880 and 1920? Prominent and typical among them were the Italians, some 4 million of whom sailed to the United States during the four decades of the New Immigration.

They came from the southern provinces of their native land, the heel and toe of the Italian boot. These areas had lagged economically behind the prosperous, industrial region of northern Italy. The north had been the seat of earlier Italian glory, as well as the fountainhead of the successful movement to unify the country in 1860. There industry had been planted and agriculture modernized. Unification raised hopes of similar progress in the downtrodden south, but it was slow in coming. Southern Italian peasants tilled their fields without fertilizer or machinery, using hand plows and rickety hoes that had been passed down for generations.

From such disappointed and demeaned conditions, southern Italians set out for the New World. Most came to the United States, but significant numbers headed for Argentina to work in agriculture. Almost all of them were young men who intended to spend only a few months, stuff their pockets with earnings, and return home. At least half of the Italian immigrants did indeed repatriate—as did comparable numbers of the other New Immigrants, with the conspicuous exception of the Jews, who had fled their native lands to escape religious persecution. Most of the Italian immigrants to the United States sailed through New York harbor, sighting the Statue of Liberty as they debarked from crowded ships. Many soon moved on to other large cities, but so many remained that in the early years of the twentieth century, more Italians resided in New York than in the Italian cities of Florence, Venice, and Genoa combined.

Since the immigrant Italians, with few exceptions, had been peasant farmers in the Old Country, the U.S. government encouraged them to practice their ancestral livelihood here, believing they would more

Italian Immigrants Arriving at Ellis Island, ca. 1910

Brown Brothers

Pietro Learning to Write on Jersey Street "The sons shall teach the fathers," the old saying goes. Many immigrants learned English from their children who attended American schools, like this youngster and parent in early-twentieth-century New Jersey.

Museum of the City of New York The Jacob A. Riis Collection, #160

and the insane, the federal government did virtually nothing to ease the assimilation of immigrants into American society. State governments, usually dominated by rural representatives, did even less. City governments, overwhelmed by the sheer scale of rampant urban growth, proved woefully inadequate to the task.

By default, the business of ministering to the immigrants' needs fell to the unofficial "governments" of the urban political machines, led by "bosses" like New York's notorious Boss Tweed.

Taking care of the immigrants was big business indeed. Trading jobs and services for votes, a powerful

Italian Immigrant Women Doing Piecework at Home in New York, ca. 1910 Culver Pictures

Italian Construction Workers, ca. 1910 Brown Brothers

rapidly assimilate in the countryside than in the ethnic enclaves of the cities. But almost all such ventures failed. The farmers lacked capital, and they were in any case more interested in earning quick money than in permanently sinking roots. Although they huddled in the cities, Italian immigrants did not abandon their rural upbringing entirely. Much to their neighbors' consternation, they often kept chickens in vacant lots and raised vegetables in small garden plots nestled between decaying tenement houses.

Those who bade a permanent farewell to Italy clustered in tightly knit communities that boasted opera clubs, Italian-language newspapers, and courts for playing bocci—a version of lawn bowling imported from the Old Country. Pizza emerged from the hot wood-burning ovens of these Little Italys, its aroma and flavor wafting into the hearts and stomachs of all Americans.

The Italians typically earned their daily bread as industrial laborers—most famously as longshoremen and construction workers. They owed their prominence in the building trades to the "padrone system." The *padrone*, or labor boss, met immigrants upon their arrival and secured jobs for them in New York, Chicago, the West, or wherever there was an immediate demand for labor. The padrone owed his power to his ability to meet the needs of both Italian newcomers and American bosses, and he often managed to manipulate both for his own gain.

Lacking education, the Italians, as a group, remained in blue-collar jobs longer than some of their fellow New Immigrants. Many Italians, valuing vocation over schooling, sent their children off to work as early in their young lives as possible. Before World War I, less than 1 percent of Italian children enrolled in high school. Over the next fifty years, Italian Americans and their offspring gradually prospered, moving out of the cities into the more affluent suburbs. Many served heroically in World War II and availed themselves of the GI Bill to finance the college educations and professional training their immigrant forebears had lacked.

boss might claim the loyalty of thousands of followers. In return for their support at the polls, the boss provided jobs on the city's payroll, found housing for new arrivals, tided over the needy with gifts of food and clothing, patched up minor scrapes with the law, and helped get schools, parks, and hospitals built in immigrant neighborhoods. Reformers gagged at this cynical exploitation of the immigrant vote, but the political boss gave valuable assistance that was forthcoming from no other source.

The nation's social conscience, slumbering since the antislavery crusade, gradually awakened to the plight

Manuscript Census Data, 1900

Article I of the Constitution requires that a census of the American people be taken every ten years, in order to provide a reliable basis for congressional apportionment. Early censuses gathered little more than basic population numbers, but over the years the census takers have collected information on other matters as well—including occupational categories, educational levels, and citizenship status—yielding copious raw data for historical analysis. The census of 1890 was the first to use punch cards and electric tabulating machines, which greatly expanded the range of data that could be assembled and correlated—though the basic information was still hand-recorded by individual canvassers who went door-to-door to question household members and fill out the census forms. Those handwritten forms, as much as the aggregate numbers printed in the final census tally, can furnish invaluable insights to the historian. Despite its apparent bureaucratic formality, the form shown here richly details the lives of the residents of a tenement house on New York's Lower East Side in 1900. See in particular the entries for the Goldberg family. In what ways does this document reflect the great demographic changes that swept late-nineteenth-century America? What light does it shed on the character of immigrant "ghettos"? What further use might historians make of information like this?

National Archives

Special Collections and University Archives,
The University of Illinois at Chicago

Hull House These immigrant children playing games at the settlement house that Jane Addams founded in Chicago were having some fun while also getting instruction from a settlement house worker in how to be a proper American.

of the cities, and especially their immigrant masses. Prominent in this awakening were several Protestant clergymen, who sought to apply the lessons of Christianity to the slums and factories. Noteworthy among them was Walter Rauschenbusch, who in 1886 became pastor of a German Baptist church in New York City. Also conspicuous was Washington Gladden, who took over a Congregational church in Columbus, Ohio, in 1882. Preaching the "social gospel," they both insisted that the churches tackle the burning social issues of the day. The Sermon on the Mount, they declared, was the science of society, and many social gospelers predicted that socialism would be the logical outcome of Christianity. These "Christian socialists" did much to prick callous middle-class consciences, thus preparing the path for the progressive reform movement after the turn of the century.

One middle-class woman who was deeply dedicated to uplifting the urban masses was Jane Addams (1860–1935). Born into a prosperous Illinois family, Addams was one of the first generation of college-educated women. Upon her graduation she sought other outlets for her large talents than could be found in teaching or charitable volunteer work, then the only permissible occupations for a young woman of her social class. Inspired by a visit to England, she acquired the decaying Hull mansion in Chicago in 1889. There she established Hull House, the most prominent (though not the first) American settlement house.

Soft-spoken but tenacious, Addams became a kind of urban American saint in the eyes of many admirers. The philosopher William James told her, "You utter instinctively the truth we others vainly seek." She was a broad-gauge reformer who courageously condemned war as well as poverty, and she eventually won the Nobel Peace Prize in 1931. But her pacifism

also earned her the enmity of some Americans, including the Daughters of the American Revolution, who choked on her antiwar views and expelled her from membership in their august organization.

Located in a poor immigrant neighborhood of Greeks, Italians, Russians, and Germans, Hull House offered instruction in English, counseling to help newcomers cope with American big-city life, child-care services for working mothers, and cultural activities for neighborhood residents. Following Jane Addams's lead, women founded **settlement houses** in other cities as well. Conspicuous among the houses was Lillian Wald's Henry Street Settlement in New York, which opened its doors in 1893.

The settlement houses became centers of women's activism and of social reform. The women of Hull House successfully lobbied in 1893 for an Illinois antisweatshop law that protected women workers and prohibited child labor. They were led in this case by the black-clad Florence Kelley, a guerrilla warrior in the urban jungle. Armed with the insights of socialism and endowed with the voice of an actress, Kelley was a lifelong battler for the welfare of women, children, blacks, and consumers. She later moved to the Henry Street Settlement in New York and served for three decades as general secretary of the National Consumers League. The pioneering work of Addams, Wald, and Kelley helped blaze the trail that many women—and some men—later followed into careers in urban reform and the new profession of social work. For these female reformers, and for many other women, the city offered a new kind of frontier opportunity.

More than a million women joined the work force in the single decade of the 1890s. Strict social codes prescribed which women might work and what jobs they might hold. Because employment for wives and mothers was considered taboo, the vast majority of working women were single. Their jobs depended on their race, ethnicity, and class. Black women had few opportunities beyond domestic service. White-collar jobs as social workers, secretaries, department store clerks, and telephone operators were largely reserved for native-born women. Immigrant women tended to cluster in particular industries, as Jewish women did in the garment trades. Although hours were often long, pay low, and advancement limited, a job still bought workingwomen some economic and social independence. After contributing a large share of their earnings to their families, many women still had enough money in their pocketbooks to enter a new urban world of sociability—excursions to amusement parks with friends on days off, Saturday night dances with the "fellas."

✴ Narrowing the Welcome Mat

Antiforeignism, or "nativism," earlier touched off by the Irish and German arrivals in the 1840s and 1850s, bared its ugly face in the 1880s with fresh ferocity. The New Immigrants had come for much the same reasons as the Old—to escape the poverty and squalor of Europe and to seek new opportunities in America. But "nativists" viewed the eastern and southern Europeans as culturally and religiously exotic hordes and often gave them a rude reception. The newest newcomers aroused widespread alarm. Their high birthrate, common among people with a low standard of living and sufficient youth and vigor to pull up stakes, raised worries that the original Anglo-Saxon stock would soon be outbred and outvoted. Still more horrifying was the

In response to nativists who condemned the New Immigrants as despicable human specimens threatening to drag down the American race, the Jewish immigrant playwright Israel Zangwill (1864–1926) celebrated the new superior American emerging out of what he called "the great melting pot" of European races:

❝America is God's crucible, the great melting pot, where all the races of Europe are melting and re-forming! . . . Germans and Frenchmen, Irishmen and Englishmen, Jews and Russians—into the Crucible with you all! God is making the American!❞

prospect that it would be mongrelized by a mixture of "inferior" southern European blood and that the fairer Anglo-Saxon types would disappear. One New England writer cried out in anguish,

O Liberty, white Goddess! is it well
To leave the gates unguarded?

Native-born Americans voiced additional fears. They blamed the immigrants for the degradation of urban government. Some trade unionists assailed the alien arrivals for their willingness to work for "starvation" wages that seemed to them like princely sums and for importing in their intellectual baggage such seemingly dangerous doctrines as socialism, communism, and anarchism. Many business leaders, who had welcomed the flood of cheap manual labor, began to fear that they had embraced a Frankenstein's monster.

Looking Backward Older immigrants, trying to keep their own humble arrival in America "in the shadows," sought to close the bridge that had carried them and their ancestors across the Atlantic.

"Looking Backward" by Joseph Keppler, 1893 Library of Congress

Antiforeign organizations, reminiscent of the "Know-Nothings" of antebellum days, were now revived in a different guise. Notorious among them was the American Protective Association (APA), which was created in 1887 and soon claimed a million members. In pursuing its nativist goals, the APA urged voting against Roman Catholic candidates for office and sponsored the publication of lustful fantasies about runaway nuns.

Organized labor was quick to throw its growing weight behind the move to choke off the rising tide of foreigners. Frequently used as strikebreakers, the wage-depressing immigrants were hard to unionize because of the language barrier. Labor leaders argued, not illogically, that if American industry was entitled to protection from foreign goods, American workers were entitled to protection from foreign laborers.

Congress finally nailed up partial bars against the inpouring immigrants. The first restrictive law, passed in 1882, banged the gate shut in the faces of paupers, criminals, and convicts, all of whom had to be returned at the expense of the greedy or careless shipper. Congress further responded to pained outcries

President Grover Cleveland (1837–1908) declared in 1897,

"It is said . . . that the quality of recent immigration is undesirable. The time is quite within recent memory when the same thing was said of immigrants who, with their descendants, are now numbered among our best citizens."

from organized labor when in 1885 it prohibited the importation of foreign workers under contract—usually for substandard wages.

In addition to the first federal restrictions on immigration, the year 1882 brought forth a law to bar completely one ethnic group—the Chinese. Hitherto America, at least officially, had embraced the oppressed and underprivileged of all races and creeds. Hereafter the gates would be padlocked against defective undesirables—plus the Chinese.

In later years other federal laws lengthened the list of undesirables to include the insane, polygamists, prostitutes, alcoholics, anarchists, and people carrying contagious diseases. A proposed literacy test, long a favorite of nativists because it favored the Old Immigrants over the New, met vigorous opposition. It was not enacted until 1917, after three presidents had vetoed it on the grounds that literacy was more a measure of opportunity than of intelligence.

In 1886 the Statue of Liberty arose in New York harbor, a gift from the people of France. On its base were inscribed the words of Emma Lazarus:

Give me your tired, your poor
Your huddled masses yearning to breathe free,
The wretched refuse of your teeming shore.

To many nativists, those noble words described only too accurately the "scum" washed up by the New Immigrant tides. Yet the uprooted immigrants, unlike "natives" lucky enough to have had parents who caught an earlier ship, became American citizens the hard way. They stepped off the boat, many of them full-grown and well muscled, ready to put their shoulders to the nation's industrial wheels. The Republic owes much to these latecomers—for their brawn, their brains, their courage, and the yeasty diversity they brought to American society.

Musee Carnavalet, Paris/Laurie Platt Winfrey, Inc.

Lady Liberty Being Readied for Travel A centennial "birthday present" from the French people, the Statue of Liberty arrived from France in 1886.

✺ Churches Confront the Urban Challenge

The swelling size and changing character of the urban population posed sharp challenges to American

Morning Service at Moody's Church, 1908 Thousands of Chicagoans found the gospel and a helping hand at evangelist Dwight Lyman Moody's church. Although Moody himself died in 1899, his successors continued to attract throngs of worshipers to his church, which could hold up to ten thousand people.

churches, which, like other national institutions, had grown up in the country. Protestant churches, in particular, suffered heavily from the shift to the city, where many of their traditional doctrines and pastoral approaches seemed irrelevant. Some of the larger houses of worship, with their stained-glass windows and thundering pipe organs, were tending to become merely sacred diversions or amusements. Reflecting the wealth of their prosperous parishioners, many of the old-line churches were distressingly slow to raise their voices against social and economic vices. John D. Rockefeller was a pillar of the Baptist Church, J. Pierpont Morgan of the Episcopal Church. Trinity Episcopal Church in New York actually owned some of the city's worst slum property. Cynics remarked that the Episcopal Church had become "the Republican party at prayer." Some religious leaders began to worry that in the age-old struggle between God and the Devil, the Wicked One was registering dismaying gains. The mounting emphasis was on materialism; too many devotees worshiped at the altar of avarice. Money was the accepted measure of achievement, and the new gospel of wealth proclaimed that God caused the righteous to prosper.

Into this spreading moral vacuum stepped a new generation of **liberal Protestants**. With roots in the Unitarian revolt against orthodox Calvinism, liberal ideas came into the mainstream of American Protestantism between 1875 and 1925, despite frequent and bitter controversies with fundamentalists. Entrenched in the leadership and seminaries of the dominant denominations, liberal Protestants adapted religious ideas to modern culture, attempting to reconcile Christianity with new scientific and economic doctrines. They rejected biblical literalism, urging Christians to

view biblical stories as models for Christian behavior rather than as dogma. They stressed the ethical teachings of the Bible and allied themselves with the reform-oriented "social gospel" movement and urban revivalists like Dwight Lyman Moody, a former shoe salesman who captivated audiences with his message of forgiveness. Their optimistic trust in community fellowship and their focus on earthly salvation and personal growth attracted many followers. They helped Protestant Americans reconcile their religious faith with modern, cosmopolitan ways of thinking.

Simultaneously, the Roman Catholic and Jewish faiths were gaining enormous strength from the New Immigration. By 1900 Roman Catholics had become the largest single denomination, numbering nearly 9 million communicants. Cardinal James Gibbons (1834–1921), an urban Catholic leader devoted to American unity, was immensely popular with Roman Catholics and Protestants alike. Acquainted with every president from Johnson to Harding, he employed his liberal sympathies to assist the American labor movement.

By 1890 the variety-loving Americans could choose from 150 religious denominations, 2 of them brand-new. One was the band-playing Salvation Army, whose soldiers without swords invaded America from England in 1879 and established a beachhead on the country's street corners. Appealing frankly to the down-and-outers, the boldly named Salvation Army did much practical good, especially with free soup.

The other important new faith was the Church of Christ, Scientist (Christian Science), founded by Mary Baker Eddy in 1879 after she had suffered much ill health. Preaching that the true practice of Christianity heals sickness, she set forth her views in a book entitled *Science and Health with Key to the Scriptures* (1875), which sold an amazing 400,000 copies before her death. A fertile field for converts was found in America's hurried, nerve-racked, and urbanized civilization, to which Eddy held out the hope of relief from discords and diseases through prayer as taught by Christian Science. By the time she died in 1910, she had founded an influential church that embraced several hundred thousand devoted worshipers.

Urbanites also participated in a new kind of religious-affiliated organization, the Young Men's and Women's Christian Associations. The YMCA and the YWCA, established in the United States before the Civil War, grew by leaps and bounds. Combining physical and other kinds of education with religious instruction, the "Y's" appeared in virtually every major American city by the end of the nineteenth century.

✳ Darwin Disrupts the Churches

The old-time religion received many blows from modern trends, including a booming sale of books on comparative religion and on historical criticism as applied to the Bible. Most unsettling of all were the writings of the English naturalist Charles Darwin. In lucid prose he set forth the sensational theory that higher forms of life had slowly evolved from lower forms, through a process of random biological mutation and adaptation.

Though not the first scientist to propose an evolutionary hypothesis, Darwin broke new ground with his idea of "natural selection." Nature, in his view, blindly selected organisms for survival or death based on random, inheritable variations that they happened to possess. Some traits conferred advantages in the struggle for life, and hence better odds of passing them along to offspring. By providing a material explanation for the evolutionary process, Darwin's theory explicitly rejected the "dogma of special creations," which ascribed the design of each fixed species to divine agency.

Darwin's radical ideas evoked the wrath of scientists and laymen alike. Many zoologists, like Harvard's Louis Agassiz, held fast to the old doctrine of "special creations." By 1875, however, the majority of scientists in America and elsewhere had embraced the theory of organic evolution, though not all endorsed natural selection as its agent. Many preferred an alternative mechanism proposed earlier by the French biologist Jean-Baptiste Lamarck, who argued that traits acquired during the course of an individual's life could shape the future genetic development of a species. Lamarckians briefly tamed the unsettling Darwinian view of chance mutation and competitive inheritance, but Darwin's version would become scientific orthodoxy by the 1920s.

Clergymen and theologians responded to Darwin's theory in several ways. At first most believers joined

> *As a student at Harvard Medical School, William James (1842–1910) was influenced by Darwinian science. He reviewed Darwin's theory in his first published article in 1865:*
>
> **"A doctrine like that of Transmutation of Species . . . cannot but be treated with some respect; and when we find that such naturalists, . . . many of whom but a few days ago were publicly opposing it, are now coming round, one by one, to espouse it, we may well doubt whether it may not be destined eventually to prevail."**

scientists in rejecting his ideas outright. After 1875, by which time most natural scientists had embraced evolution, the religious community split into two camps. A conservative minority stood firmly behind the Scripture as the infallible Word of God, and they condemned what they thought was the "bestial hypothesis" of the Darwinians. Their rejection of scientific consensus spawned a muscular view of biblical authority that eventually gave rise to fundamentalism in the twentieth century.

Most religious thinkers parted company with the conservatives and flatly refused to accept the Bible in its entirety as either history or science. These "accommodationists" feared that hostility toward evolution would alienate educated believers. Over time an increasing number of liberal thinkers were able to reconcile Darwinism with Christianity. They heralded the revolutionary theory as a newer and grander revelation of the ways of the Almighty. As one commentator observed,

> *Some call it Evolution,*
> *And others call it God.*

Darwinism undoubtedly did much to loosen religious moorings and to promote skepticism among the gospel-glutted. While the liberal efforts at compromise did succeed in keeping many Americans in the pews, those compromises also tended to relegate religious teaching to matters of personal faith, private conduct, and family life. As science began to explain more of the external world, commentators on nature and society increasingly refrained from adding religious perspectives to the discussion.

✳ The Lust for Learning

Public education continued its upward climb. The ideal of tax-supported elementary schools, adopted on a nationwide basis before the Civil War, was still gathering strength. Americans were accepting the truism that a free government cannot function successfully if the people are shackled by ignorance. Beginning about 1870, more and more states were making at least a grade-school education compulsory, and this gain, incidentally, helped check the frightful abuses of child labor.

Spectacular indeed was the spread of high schools, especially by the 1880s and 1890s. Before the Civil War, private academies at the secondary level were common, and tax-supported high schools were rare, numbering only a few hundred. But the concept that a high-school education, as well as a grade-school education, was the birthright of every citizen was now gaining impressive support. By 1900 there were some six thousand high schools. In addition, free textbooks were being provided in increasing quantities by the taxpayers of the states during the last two decades of the century.

Other trends were noteworthy. Teacher-training schools, then called "normal schools," experienced a striking expansion after the Civil War. In 1860 there were only twelve of them, in 1910 over three hundred. Kindergartens, earlier borrowed from Germany, also began to gain strong support. The New Immigration in the 1880s and 1890s brought vast new strength to private Catholic parochial schools, which were fast becoming a major pillar of the nation's educational structure.

Public schools, though showering benefits on children, excluded millions of adults. This deficiency was partially remedied by the Chautauqua movement, a successor to the lyceums, which was launched in 1874 on the shores of Lake Chautauqua, in New York. The organizers achieved gratifying success through nationwide public lectures, often held in tents and featuring well-known speakers, including the witty Mark Twain. In addition, there were extensive Chautauqua courses of home study, for which 100,000 people enrolled in 1892 alone.

Crowded cities, despite their cancers, generally provided better educational facilities than the old one-room, one-teacher red schoolhouse. The success of the public schools is confirmed by the falling of the illiteracy rate from 20 percent in 1870 to 10.7 percent in 1900. Americans were developing a profound faith, often misplaced, in formal education as the sovereign remedy for their ills.

✶ Booker T. Washington and Education for Black People

War-torn and impoverished, the South lagged far behind other regions in public education, and African Americans suffered most severely. A staggering 44

percent of nonwhites were illiterate in 1900. Some help came from northern philanthropists, but the foremost champion of black education was an ex-slave, Booker T. Washington. His classic autobiography, *Up from Slavery* (1900), tells how he slept under a board sidewalk to save pennies for his schooling. Called in 1881 to head the black normal and industrial school at Tuskegee, Alabama, he began with forty students in a tumbledown shanty. Undaunted, he taught black students useful trades so that they could gain self-respect and economic security. Washington's self-help approach to solving the nation's racial problems was labeled "accommodationist" because it stopped short of directly challenging white supremacy. Recognizing the depths of southern white racism, Washington avoided the issue of *social* equality. Instead he grudgingly acquiesced in segregation in return for the right to develop—however modestly and painstakingly—the economic and educational resources of the black community. Economic independence would ultimately be the ticket, Washington believed, to black political and civil rights.

Washington's commitment to training young blacks in agriculture and the trades guided the curriculum

Booker T. Washington (1856–1915) In a famous speech in New Orleans in 1895, Washington grudgingly acquiesced in social separateness for blacks. On that occasion, he told his largely white audience, "In all things that are purely social, we can be as separate as the fingers, yet one as the hand in all things essential to mutual progress."

Tuskegee University Archives

at **Tuskegee Institute** and made it an ideal place for slave-born George Washington Carver to teach and research. After Carver joined the faculty in 1896, he became an internationally famous agricultural chemist who provided a much-needed boost to the southern economy by discovering hundreds of new uses for the lowly peanut (shampoo, axle grease), sweet potato (vinegar), and soybean (paint).

Other black leaders, notably Dr. W. E. B. Du Bois, assailed Booker T. Washington as an "Uncle Tom" who was condemning their race to manual labor and perpetual inferiority. Born in Massachusetts, Du Bois was a mixture of African, French, Dutch, and Indian blood ("Thank God, no Anglo-Saxon," he would add). After a determined struggle, he earned a Ph.D. at Harvard, the first of his race to achieve that goal. ("The honor, I assure you, was Harvard's," he said.) He demanded complete equality for blacks, social as well as economic, and helped found the National Association for the Advancement of Colored People (NAACP) in 1909. Rejecting Washington's gradualism and separatism, he argued that the "talented tenth" of the black community should be given full and immediate access to the mainstream of American life. An exceptionally skilled historian, sociologist, and poet, he died as a self-exile in Africa in 1963,

W. E. B. Du Bois (1868–1963) wrote in his 1903 classic, The Souls of Black Folk,

❝It is a peculiar sensation, this double consciousness, this sense of always looking at one's self through the eyes of others, of measuring one's self through the eyes of others. . . . One ever feels his two-ness—an American, a Negro; two souls, two thoughts, two unreconciled strivings; two warring ideals in one dark body, whose dogged strength alone keeps it from being torn asunder.❞

at the age of ninety-five. Many of Du Bois's differences with Washington reflected the contrasting life experiences of southern and northern blacks.

✶ The Hallowed Halls of Ivy

Colleges and universities also shot up like lusty young saplings in the decades after the Civil War. A college education increasingly seemed indispensable in the scramble for the golden apple of success (see Table 25.1). Even women and African Americans were finding new opportunities for higher education. Women's colleges such as Vassar were gaining ground, and universities open to both genders were blossoming, notably in the Midwest. By 1880 every third college graduate was a woman. By the turn of the century, the black institutes and academies planted during Reconstruction had blossomed into a crop of southern black colleges. Howard University in Washington, D.C., Hampton Institute in Virginia, Atlanta University, and numerous others nurtured higher education for blacks until the civil rights movement of the 1960s made widespread attendance at white institutions possible.

The truly phenomenal growth of higher education owed much to the Morrill Act of 1862. This enlightened law provided a generous grant of public lands to the states for support of education. **Land-grant colleges**, most of which became state universities, in turn bound themselves to provide certain services, such as military training. The Hatch Act of 1887, extending the Morrill Act, provided federal funds for the establishment of agricultural experiment stations in connection with the land-grant colleges. These two pieces of legislation spawned over a hundred colleges and universities, including such institutions as the University of California (1868), the Ohio State University (1870), and Texas A&M (1876).

Private philanthropy richly supplemented government grants to higher education. Many of the new

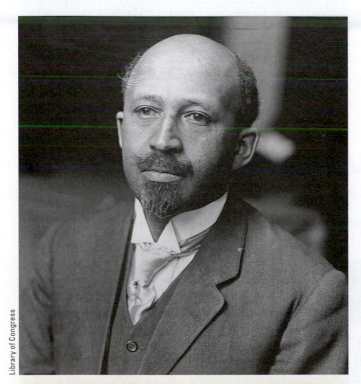

W. E. B. Du Bois (1868–1963) In 1961, at the end of a long lifetime of struggle for racial justice in the United States, Du Bois renounced his American citizenship at the age of ninety-three and took up residence in the newly independent African state of Ghana.

Library of Congress

TABLE 25.1 Educational Levels, 1870–2010

Year	Number Graduating from High School	Number Graduating from College	Median Number of School Years Completed*	High School Graduates as a Percentage of 17-Year-Old Population
1870	16,000	9,371		2.0%
1880	24,000	12,896		2.5%
1890	44,000	15,539		3.5%
1900	95,000	27,410		6.4%
1910	156,000	37,199	8.1†	8.8%
1920	311,000	48,622	8.2†	16.8%
1930	667,000	122,484	8.4†	29.0%
1940	1,221,000	186,500	8.6	50.8%
1950	1,199,700	432,058	9.3	59.0%
1960	1,858,000	392,440	10.5	69.5%
1970	2,889,000	792,316	12.2	76.9%
1980	3,043,000	929,417	12.5	71.4%
1990	2,574,000	1,051,344	12.7	73.4%
2000	2,833,000	1,237,875	NA	69.8%
2005	3,109,000	1,439,264	NA	79.5%
2010 (est.)	3,295,000	1,648,000	NA	82.4%

*People twenty-five years and over.

†1910–1930 based on retrogressions of 1940 data; 1940 was the first year measured. (Source: Folger and Nam, *Education of the American Population*, a 1960 Census Monograph.)

(Sources: *Digest of Education Statistics*, 1992, 2009, a publication of the National Center for Education Statistics; *Statistical Abstract of the United States*, relevant years.)

industrial millionaires, developing tender social consciences, donated immense fortunes to educational enterprises. A philanthropist was cynically described as "one who steals privately and gives publicly." In the twenty years from 1878 to 1898, these money barons gave away about $150 million. Noteworthy among the new private universities of high quality were Cornell (1865) and Leland Stanford Junior (1891), the latter founded in memory of the deceased fifteen-year-old only child of a builder of the Central Pacific Railroad.

Stanford University Under Construction, Late Nineteenth Century

Courtesy Stanford University Archives

The University of Chicago, opened in 1892, speedily forged into a front-rank position, owing largely to the lubricant of John D. Rockefeller's oil millions. Rockefeller died at ninety-seven, after having given some $550 million for philanthropic purposes.

Significant also was the sharp increase in professional and technical schools, where modern laboratories were replacing the solo experiments performed by instructors in front of their classes. Towering among the specialized institutions was Johns Hopkins University, opened in 1876, which maintained the nation's first high-grade graduate school. Several generations of American scholars, repelled by snobbish English cousins and attracted by painstaking Continental methods, had attended German universities. Johns Hopkins ably carried on the Germanic tradition of profusely footnoted tomes. Reputable scholars no longer had to go abroad for a gilt-edged graduate degree. Dr. Woodrow Wilson, among others, received his Ph.D. from Johns Hopkins.

✴ The March of the Mind

Homegrown influences shaped the modern American university as much as German models. Antebellum colleges had stressed the "unity of truth," or the idea that knowledge and morality existed in a single system. Religious instruction in moral philosophy and natural theology served as pillars of the old classical curriculum. In the wake of the Darwinian challenge, when religion and science seemed less compatible, university reformers struggled to reconcile scientific education and religion to preserve the unity of moral and intellectual purpose. When that effort faltered, university educators abandoned moral instruction and divorced "facts" from "values."

Other pressures also helped doom the traditional curriculum. The new industrialization brought insistent demands for "practical" courses and specialized vocational training in the sciences. The elective system, where students selected courses, was gaining popularity. Reformers also emphasized fields of concentration to prepare students for entry into a profession. Specialization, not synthesis, became the primary goal of a university education. The reform spirit received a powerful boost in the 1870s when Dr. Charles W. Eliot, a vigorous young chemist, became president of Harvard College and embarked upon a lengthy career of educational statesmanship. As a sign of the secularizing times, Eliot changed Harvard's motto from *Christo et Ecclesiae* (For Christ and Church) to *Veritas* (Truth).

Medical schools and medical science after the Civil War were prospering. Despite the enormous sale of patent medicines and so-called Indian remedies—"good for man or beast"—the new scientific gains were reflected in improved public health. Revolutionary discoveries abroad, such as those of the French scientist Louis Pasteur and the English physician Joseph Lister, left their imprint on America.* The popularity of heavy whiskers waned as the century ended; such hairy adornments were now coming to be regarded as germ traps. As a result of new health-promoting precautions, including campaigns against public spitting, life expectancy at birth was measurably increased.

One of America's most brilliant intellectuals, the slight and sickly William James (1842–1910), served for thirty-five years on the Harvard faculty. Through his numerous writings, he made a deep mark on many fields. His *Principles of Psychology* (1890) helped to establish the modern discipline of behavioral psychology. In *The Will to Believe* (1897) and *Varieties of Religious Experience* (1902), he explored the philosophy and psychology of religion. In his most famous work, *Pragmatism* (1907), he pronounced America's greatest contribution to the history of philosophy the concept of **pragmatism**—that the truth of an idea was to be tested, above all, by its practical consequences (see "Makers of America: Pioneering Pragmatists," pp. 560–561).

✴ The Appeal of the Press

Books continued to be a major source of edification and enjoyment, for both juveniles and adults. Best sellers of the 1880s were generally old favorites like *David Copperfield* and *Ivanhoe*.

Well-stocked public libraries—the poor person's university—were making encouraging progress, especially in Boston and New York. The magnificent Library of Congress building, which opened its doors in 1897, provided thirteen acres of floor space in the largest and costliest edifice of its kind in the world. A new era was inaugurated by the generous gifts of Andrew Carnegie. This openhanded Scotsman, book-starved in his youth, contributed $60 million for the construction of nearly 1,700 public libraries all over the country, with an additional 750 scattered around the English-speaking world from Great Britain to New Zealand. By 1900 there were about nine thousand free circulating libraries in America, each with at least three hundred books. Roaring newspaper presses, spurred by the invention of the Linotype in 1885, more than kept pace with the demands of a word-hungry public. But the heavy investment in machinery and plant was accompanied by a growing fear of offending advertisers and subscribers. Bare-knuckle editorials were, to an increasing

---

*From Pasteur came the word *pasteurize*; from Lister came *Listerine*.

The "Penny Press" The *Chicago Daily News* was but one of several cheap, mass-circulation newspapers that flourished in the new urban environment of Gilded Age America.

Chicago History Museum

degree, being supplanted by feature articles and non-controversial syndicated material. The day of slashing journalistic giants like Horace Greeley was passing.

Sensationalism, at the same time, was capturing the public taste. The semiliterate immigrants, combined with strap-hanging urban commuters, created a profitable market for news that was simply and punchily written. Sex, scandal, and other human-interest stories burst into the headlines, as a vulgarization of the press accompanied the growth of circulation. Critics now complained in vain of these "presstitutes."

Two new journalistic tycoons emerged. Joseph Pulitzer, Hungarian-born and near-blind, was a leader in the techniques of sensationalism through his ownership of the *St. Louis Post-Dispatch* and *New York World*. His use of colored comic supplements featuring the "Yellow Kid" gave the name **yellow journalism** to his lurid sheets. A close and ruthless competitor was the youthful William Randolph Hearst, who had been expelled from Harvard College for a crude prank. Able to draw on his California father's mining millions, he ultimately built a powerful chain of newspapers, beginning with the *San Francisco Examiner* in 1887.

Unfortunately, the overall influence of Pulitzer and Hearst was not altogether wholesome. Although both championed many worthy causes, both prostituted the press in their struggle for increased circulation; both "stooped, snooped, and scooped to conquer." Their flair for scandal and sensational rumor was happily somewhat offset by the introduction of syndicated material and by the strengthening of the news-gathering Associated Press, which had been founded in the 1840s.

✦ Apostles of Reform

Magazines partially satisfied the public appetite for good reading, notably old East Coast standbys like *Harper's*, the *Atlantic Monthly*, and *Scribner's Monthly* and new western entrants such as the California-based *Overland Monthly*. Possibly the most influential journal of all was the liberal and highly intellectual New York *Nation*, which was read largely by professors, preachers, and publicists as "the weekly Day of Judgment." Launched in 1865 by the Irish-born Edwin L. Godkin, a merciless critic, it crusaded militantly for civil-service reform, honesty in government, and a moderate tariff. The *Nation* attained only a modest circulation—about ten thousand in the nineteenth century—but Godkin believed that if he could reach the right ten thousand leaders, his ideas through them might reach tens of millions.

Another journalist-author, Henry George, was an original thinker who left an enduring mark. Poor in formal schooling, he was rich in idealism and in the milk of human kindness. After seeing poverty at its worst in India and land-grabbing at its greediest in California, he took pen in hand. His classic treatise *Progress and Poverty* undertook to solve "the great enigma of our times"—"the association of progress with poverty." According to George, the pressure of a growing population on a fixed supply of land unjustifiably pushed up property values, showering unearned profits on owners

Henry George (1839–1897) wrote in Progress and Poverty (1879),

"Our boasted freedom necessarily involves slavery, so long as we recognize private property in land. Until that is abolished, Declarations of Independence and Acts of Emancipation are in vain. So long as one man can claim the exclusive ownership of the land from which other men must live, slavery will exist, and as material progresses on, must grow and deepen!"

of land. A single 100 percent tax on those windfall profits would eliminate unfair inequalities and stimulate economic growth.

George soon became a most controversial figure. His single-tax idea was so horrifying to the propertied classes that his manuscript was rejected by numerous publishers. Finally brought out in 1879, the book gradually broke into the best-seller lists and ultimately sold some 3 million copies. George also lectured widely in America and Britain, where he left an indelible mark on English Fabian socialism. George's proposals resounded for decades. As late as 1903, a young female follower applied for a patent for "The Landlord's Game," which bore a striking resemblance to Parker Brothers' later Monopoly, released in 1935. In the earlier game, the point was not to amass property, but to expose the unfair advantage enjoyed by the landlord and to show "how the single tax would discourage speculation."

Edward Bellamy, a quiet Massachusetts Yankee, was another journalist-reformer of remarkable power. In 1888 he published a socialistic novel, *Looking Backward*, in which the hero, falling into a hypnotic sleep, awakens in the year 2000. He "looks backward" and finds that the social and economic injustices of 1887 have melted away under an idyllic government, which has nationalized big business to serve the public interest. To a nation already alarmed by the trust evil, the book had a magnetic appeal and sold over a million copies. Scores of Bellamy Clubs sprang up to discuss this mild utopian socialism, and they heavily influenced American reform movements near the end of the century.

✴ The New Morality

Like other radical reformers, Victoria Woodhull shook the pillars of conventional morality when she publicly proclaimed her belief in free love in 1871. Woodhull was a beautiful and eloquent divorcée, sometime stockbroker, and tireless feminist propagandist. Together with her sister, Tennessee Claflin, she published a far-out periodical, *Woodhull and Claflin's Weekly*. The sisters again shocked "respectable" society in 1872 when their journal struck a blow for the new morality by charging that Henry Ward Beecher, the most famous preacher of his day, had for years been carrying on an adulterous affair.

Pure-minded Americans sternly resisted these affronts to their moral principles. Their foremost champion was a portly crusader, Anthony Comstock, who made lifelong war on the "immoral." Armed after 1873 with a federal statute—the notorious "Comstock Law"—this self-appointed defender of sexual purity boasted that he had confiscated no fewer than 202,679 "obscene pictures and photos"; 4,185 "boxes of pills,

powders, etc., used by abortionists"; and 26 "obscene pictures, framed on walls of saloons." His proud claim was that he had driven at least fifteen people to suicide.

The antics of the Woodhull sisters and Comstock exposed to daylight the battle in late-nineteenth-century America over sexual attitudes and the place of women. Switchboards and typewriters in the booming cities became increasingly the tools of women's independence. Young workingwomen headed to dance halls and nightclubs when the day was done, enjoying a new sense of freedom in the cities. This "new morality" began to be reflected in soaring divorce rates, the spreading practice of birth control, and increasingly frank discussion of sexual topics. By 1913, said one popular magazine, the chimes had struck "sex o'clock in America."

The Granger Collection

"Get Thee Behind Me, (Mrs) Satan!" A colorful and charismatic figure, Victoria Claflin Woodhull was the first woman to run for the presidency, in 1872. That same year, noted cartoonist Thomas Nast viciously attacked her for advocating free love.

Nineteenth-century Americans, among them proper Bostonians of an intellectual bent, had a habit of joining clubs. Luminaries such as the philosopher Ralph Waldo Emerson, the novelist Nathaniel Hawthorne, and the natural scientist Louis Agassiz regularly met for sumptuous food and social conversation at the Saturday Club. Younger members of Boston's polite society mimicked their elders at a junior edition known simply as "The Club." In a world without academic conferences or professional forums, serious intellectual conversations in the United States tended to occur at private philosophical and literary societies, or simply at regular gatherings in a scholar's home study. One club, founded in Cambridge, Massachusetts, in January 1872, lasted only nine months, but its members left a lasting mark on American intellectual life.

"It was in the earliest Seventies that a knot of us young men in Old Cambridge, calling ourselves, half-ironically, half-defiantly, 'The Metaphysical Club,' . . . used to meet, sometimes in my study, sometimes in that of William James," recalled Charles Sanders Peirce in 1907. Peirce's Metaphysical Club was hardly a success by most conventional standards. It kept no records of its proceedings. Its members missed meetings and (except for Peirce) made no mention of its existence in their letters, diaries, or writings. Some of their relatives despised it. A young Henry James (novelist brother of William) griped, "It gives me a headache merely to know of it." But it did boast an impressive roster of members, including three young men in their early thirties who eventually became foundational figures in their respective fields: the logician and scientist Peirce; the medical doctor, psychologist, and philosopher William James; and the jurist and legal scholar Oliver Wendell Holmes, Jr. With their Harvard friend and fellow philosopher Chauncey Wright, they assembled frequently in their homes and, usually over a bottle of rum, argued over the meaning of life and the nature of the universe. Joined later by the philosophers John Dewey and George Herbert Mead, these thinkers gave earliest expression to a distinctive American philosophy known as "pragmatism."

Pragmatism sprouted in the fertile intellectual soil of the late-nineteenth-century Atlantic world. The ground had already been tilled by the naturalist Charles Darwin, whose revolutionary contributions to evolutionary science greatly influenced the early pragmatists. In place of fixed species, Darwin had posited a natural world of chance, change, and contingency. Thinkers like Peirce and James applied Darwin's insights from biology to fields such as philosophy, logic, and psychology. To them old ways of thinking that assumed absolute truths, sanctioned by religious teaching or idealist philosophy, no longer made sense in the Darwinian age. Instead they welcomed the provisional, fallible nature of experimental knowledge. As James put it, pragmatism "means the open air and possibilities of nature, as against dogma, artificiality,

William James (1842–1910), Physician, Psychologist, and Philosopher Granger Collection

Charles Sanders Peirce (1839–1914), Mathematician and Logician © Bettmann/Corbis

Oliver Wendell Holmes, Jr. (1841–1935), Supreme Court Justice and Scholar Granger Collection

John Dewey (1859–1952), Educator and Philosopher
Granger Collection

and the pretence of finality in truth." In short, they embraced uncertainty and developed an entire philosophical system around it. The true value of an idea, said the pragmatists, lay in its ability to solve problems.

While all the pragmatists were far-ranging in their intellectual pursuits, Dewey demonstrated his faith in the unity of theory and practice by becoming a public intellectual and social activist. He founded the Laboratory School at the University of Chicago in 1896 to experiment with an educational philosophy rooted in "learning by doing." He promoted an ethical vision of American society by linking arms with progressive reformers in the 1910s, and he championed democratic ideals by promoting third-party politics in the 1930s and anti-Stalinist agitation in the 1940s. Throughout a prolific career that spanned three generations, Dewey continually stressed the positive virtues of experience, cooperation, and democracy, and he urged philosophers to abandon futile debates about knowledge in favor of tackling the real "problems of men."

Holmes, as a justice on the Massachusetts Supreme Judicial Court for twenty years and on the U.S. Supreme Court for another three decades, similarly followed pragmatism's injunction to evaluate the effects of ideas rather than simply adopt prescriptions from the past. From his personal experience fighting in the Civil War (where he nearly died from his wounds), Holmes acquired a bleak skepticism toward jurisprudence.

While on the bench, he became renowned for his masterfully crafted dissents, most famously asserting the principle of "judicial deference" to legislatures in *Lochner* v. *New York* (1905) and protecting freedom of speech, even freedom for the "opinions that we loathe," in *Abrams* v. *United States* (1919).

Many commentators on pragmatism have considered it the quintessential expression of American practicality. To its critics pragmatism symbolizes the vulgar, can-do attitude and narrow anti-intellectualism of the American middle class. To its celebrants pragmatism offers a needed correction to conventional philosophy by accepting the uncertain and provisional nature of knowledge, reconciling science and culture, and promoting an ethical ideal of democracy. Pragmatism went out of fashion during the Cold War era (ca. 1945–1990), when Americans believed in moral certainties such as the superiority of the United States and the value-free empiricism of science. But it has enjoyed a striking renewal in recent years. As new kinds of uncertainty ranging from terrorist violence to scientific dilemmas raise fresh challenges in the twenty-first century, many modern American intellectuals are harking back to pragmatism. First formulated in the cozy confines of Cambridge's Metaphysical Club more than a century ago, pragmatism offers today's thinkers a philosophy of life built on experimentation, ethical commitment, and open-ended democratic debate.

✷ Families and Women in the City

The new urban environment was hard on families. Paradoxically, the crowded cities were emotionally isolating places. Urban families had to go it alone, separated from clan, kin, and village. As families increasingly became the virtually exclusive arena for intimate companionship and for emotional and psychological satisfaction, they were subjected to unprecedented stress. Many families cracked under the strain. The urban era launched the era of divorce. From the late nineteenth century dates the beginning of the "divorce revolution" that transformed the United States' social landscape in the twentieth century (see Table 25.2).

Urban life also dictated changes in work habits and even in family size. Not only fathers but mothers and even children as young as ten years old often worked, and usually in widely scattered locations. On the farm having many children meant having more hands to help with hoeing and harvesting; but in the city more children meant more mouths to feed, more crowding in sardine-tin tenements, and more human baggage to carry in the uphill struggle for social mobility. Not surprisingly, birthrates were still dropping and family size continued to shrink as the nineteenth century lengthened. Marriages were being delayed, and more couples learned the techniques of birth control. The decline in

In 1906 progressive reformer Jane Addams (1860–1935) argued that granting women the vote would improve the social and political condition of American cities:

"City housekeeping has failed partly because women, the traditional housekeepers, have not been consulted as to its multiform activities. The men have been carelessly indifferent to much of the civic housekeeping, as they have been indifferent to the details of the household. . . . City government demands the help of minds accustomed to detail and a variety of work, to a sense of obligation to the health and welfare of young children, and to a responsibility for the cleanliness and comfort of other people."

family size in fact affected rural Americans as well as urban dwellers, and old-stock "natives" as well as New Immigrants. Women were growing more independent in the urban environment, and in 1898 they heard the voice of a major feminist prophet, Charlotte Perkins Gilman. In that year the freethinking and original-minded Gilman published *Women and Economics*, a classic of feminist literature. A distant relative of Harriet Beecher Stowe and Catharine Beecher, Gilman displayed the restless temperament and reforming zeal characteristic of the remarkable Beecher clan. Strikingly handsome, she shunned traditional feminine frills and instead devoted herself to a vigorous regimen of physical exercise and philosophical meditation.

In her masterwork of 1898, Gilman called on women to abandon their dependent status and contribute to the larger life of the community through productive involvement in the economy. Rejecting all claims that biology gave women a fundamentally different character from men, she argued that "our highly specialized motherhood is not so advantageous as believed." She advocated centralized nurseries and cooperative kitchens to facilitate women's participation in the work force—anticipating by more than half a century the day-care centers and convenience-food services of a later day.

Fiery feminists also continued to insist on the ballot. They had been demanding the vote since before the Civil War, but many high-minded female reformers had temporarily shelved the cause of women to battle for the rights of blacks. In 1890 militant suffragists formed the **National American Woman Suffrage Association (NAWSA)**. Its founders included aging pioneers like Elizabeth Cady Stanton, who had helped

TABLE 25.2 Marriages and Divorces, 1890–2008*			
Year	Marriages	Divorces	Ratio of Divorces to Marriages
1890	570,000	33,461	1:17
1900	709,000	55,751	1:12
1910	948,166	83,045	1:11
1920	1,274,476	170,505	1:7
1930	1,126,856	195,961	1:5
1940	1,595,879	264,000	1:6
1950	1,667,231	385,144	1:4.3
1960	1,523,381	393,000	1:3.8
1970	2,159,000	708,000	1:3
1980	2,390,000	1,189,000	1:2
1990	2,443,000	1,182,000	1:2
2000	2,329,000	NA	NA
2008	2,017,000	NA	NA

*Divorce data have not been collected by the federal government since 1998.

(Sources: *Statistical Abstract of the United States*, relevant years; National Center for Health Statistics, *National Vital Statistics Report*, relevant years.)

SOUTHERN HORRORS.
LYNCH LAW
IN ALL
ITS PHASES

Miss IDA B. WELLS,

Price, - - - Fifteen Cents.

THE NEW YORK AGE PRINT,
1892.

Ida B. Wells (1862–1931) Ida B. Wells courageously and tirelessly crusaded against the lynching of African-Americans. Her sensational pamphlet of 1892 summoned blacks to defend themselves against white violence, declaring that "a Winchester rifle should have a place of honor in every black home."

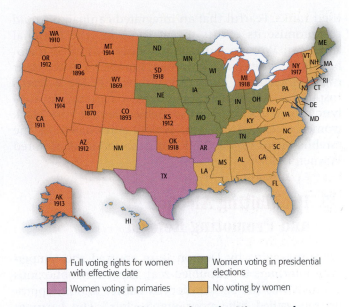

Full voting rights for women with effective date

Women voting in presidential elections

Women voting in primaries

No voting by women

MAP 25.2 Woman Suffrage Before the Nineteenth Amendment Dates show when a state or territory adopted woman suffrage. Note the concentration of woman-suffrage states in the West. © Cengage Learning

the vote if they were to continue to discharge their traditional duties as homemakers and mothers in the increasingly public world of the city. Women had special responsibility for the health of the family and the education of children, the argument ran. On the farm, women could discharge these responsibilities in the separate sphere of the isolated homestead. But in the city, they needed a voice on boards of public health, police commissions, and school boards.

By thus linking the ballot to a traditional definition of women's role, suffragists registered encouraging gains as the new century opened, despite continuing showers of rotten eggs and the jeers of male critics who insisted that women were made for loving, not for voting. Women were increasingly permitted to vote in local elections, particularly on issues related to the schools. Wyoming Territory—later called "the Equality State"—granted the first unrestricted suffrage to women in 1869. Many western states soon followed Wyoming's example (see Map 25.2). Paralleling these triumphs, most of the states by 1890 had passed laws to permit wives to own or control their property after marriage. City life also fostered the growth of a spate of women's organizations, including the General Federation of Women's Clubs, which counted some 200,000 members in 1900. Meanwhile, in 1893 New Zealand became the first nation to grant women equal suffrage rights, further inspiring American reformers.

The reborn suffrage movement and other women's organizations largely excluded black women from

organize the first women's rights convention in 1848, and her long-time comrade Susan B. Anthony, the radical Quaker spitfire who had courted jail by trying to cast a ballot in the 1872 presidential election.

By 1900 a new generation of women had taken command of the suffrage battle. Their most effective leader was Carrie Chapman Catt, a pragmatic and businesslike reformer of relentless dedication. Significantly, under Catt the suffragists deemphasized the argument that women deserved the vote as a matter of right, because they were in all respects the equals of men. Instead Catt stressed the desirability of giving women their ranks. Fearful that an integrated campaign would compromise its efforts to get the vote, the National American Woman Suffrage Association limited membership to whites. Black women, however, created their own associations. Journalist and teacher Ida B. Wells inspired black women to mount a nationwide anti-lynching crusade. She also helped launch the black women's club movement, which culminated in the establishment of the National Association of Colored Women in 1896.

✸ Prohibiting Alcohol and Promoting Reform

Alarming gains by Demon Rum spurred the temperance reformers to redoubled zeal. Especially obnoxious to them was the shutter-doored corner saloon, appropriately called "the poor man's club." The barroom helped keep both him and his family poor. Liquor consumption had increased during the nerve-racking days of the Civil War, and immigrant groups, accustomed to alcohol in the Old Country, were hostile to restraints. Whiskey-loving foreigners in Boston would rudely hiss temperance lecturers. Many tipplers charged, with some accuracy, that temperance reform amounted to a middle-class assault on working-class lifestyles.

The National Prohibition party, organized in 1869, polled a sprinkling of votes in some of the ensuing presidential elections. Among the favorite songs of these sober souls were "I'll Marry No Man If He Drinks," "Vote Down the Vile Traffic," and "The Drunkard's Doom." Typical was this:

> Now, all young men, a warning take,
> And shun the poisoned bowl;
> 'Twill lead you down to hell's dark gate,
> And ruin your own soul.

Militant women entered the alcoholic arena, notably when the **Woman's Christian Temperance Union (WCTU)** was organized in 1874. The white ribbon was its symbol of purity; the saintly Frances E. Willard—also a champion of planned parenthood—was its leading spirit. Less saintly was the muscular and mentally deranged "Kansas Cyclone," Carrie A. Nation, whose first husband had died of alcoholism. With her hatchet she boldly smashed saloon bottles and bars, and her "hatchetations" brought considerable disrepute to the prohibition movement because of the violence of her one-woman crusade.

But rum was now on the run. The potent Anti-Saloon League was formed in 1893, with its members singing "The Saloon Must Go" and "Vote for Cold Water, Boys." Female supporters sang "The Lips That Touch Liquor Must Never Touch Mine." Statewide prohibition,

Kansas State Historical Society

Carrie Nation Advertised as a Lecturer Nation took her antidrink crusade to several universities, including Harvard and Yale, which she denounced as "hellholes." Predictably, the students greeted her with wild burlesque. "All Nations Welcome but Carrie" became a standard saying in saloons throughout the land.

which had made surprising gains in Maine and elsewhere before the Civil War, was sweeping new states into the "dry" column. The great triumph—but only a temporary one—came in 1919, when the national prohibition amendment (Eighteenth) was attached to the Constitution.

Banners of other social crusaders were aloft. The American Society for the Prevention of Cruelty to Animals (ASPCA) was created in 1866 after its founder had witnessed brutality to horses in Russia. The American Red Cross was launched in 1881, with the dynamic and

Anoka County Historical Society

Doused for the Cause, Minnesota, 1878 These umbrella-toting temperance crusaders stood their ground, despite the water poured on them by the indignant wife of the billiard-hall owner.

diminutive five-foot-tall Clara Barton, the "angel" of Civil War battlefields, at the helm.

Postwar Popular Fiction

Not all social activity proved so serious. Post–Civil War Americans devoured millions of "dime novels," usually depicting the wilds of the woolly West. Paint-bedaubed Indians and quick-triggered gunmen like "Deadwood Dick" shot off vast quantities of powder, and virtue invariably triumphed. These lurid "paperbacks" were frowned upon by parents, but goggle-eyed youths read them in haylofts or in schools behind the broad covers of geography books. The king of the dime novelists was Harlan P. Halsey, who made a fortune by dashing off about 650 potboilers, often one in a day.

General Lew Wallace—lawyer, soldier, and author—was a colorful figure. Having fought with distinction in the Civil War, he sought to combat the prevailing wave of Darwinian skepticism with his novel *Ben-Hur: A Tale of the Christ* (1880). A phenomenal success, the book sold an estimated 2 million copies in many languages, including Arabic and Chinese, and later appeared on stage and screen. It was the *Uncle Tom's Cabin* of the anti-Darwinists, who found in it support for the Holy Scriptures.

An even more popular writer was Horatio Alger, a Puritan-reared New Englander, who in 1866 forsook the pulpit for the pen. "Holy Horatio" wrote more than a hundred volumes of juvenile fiction that sold over 17 million copies. His stock formula depicted a poor boy new to the city, who, through a combination of virtue, hard work, and bravery, achieved success, honor, and middle-class respectability—a kind of survival of the purest, especially nonsmokers, nondrinkers, nonswearers, and nonliars. Although accusations of sexual impropriety haunted Alger throughout his life, he implanted in his readers moral lessons and the conviction that there is always room at the top (especially if one is lucky enough to save the life of the boss's daughter and marry her).

Literary Landmarks

Literature and the arts were not immune to the era's sweeping changes. Confronted by new cities and industries, American writers and artists forsook the romantic sentimentality of an earlier age and generated three interrelated currents in the arts: realism, naturalism, and regionalism. Instead of depicting life as it ought to be lived or had supposedly existed in times gone by, realism sought to document contemporary life and society as it actually was, in all its raw and raucous and sometimes even scandalous detail. Naturalism took this fascination with modern life one step further, examining the determinative influence of heredity and social environments in shaping human character. Meanwhile, regionalism aspired to capture the peculiarity, or "local color," of a particular region, before national standardization bleached its variety away. All three movements responded to the Gilded Age's urban, industrial transformation.

Realism quickly came to dominate post–Civil War American literature. Foregoing romantic pageantry and supernatural melodrama, American authors increasingly found their subjects in the coarse human comedy and material drama of the world around them. William Dean Howells (1837–1920), the celebrated "father of American realism," emerged as the era's preeminent advocate of unsentimental literature. A printer's son from Ohio, Howells had scant schoolhouse education, but his busy pen carried him high into the literary circles of the East. In 1871 he became the editor in chief of the prestigious Boston-based *Atlantic Monthly*, where he championed the careers of several young American writers. In no less than thirty-six novels and nearly two hundred books, he wrote about ordinary men and women in familiar surroundings and about contemporary and sometimes controversial social themes. His most famous novel, *The Rise of Silas Lapham* (1885), describes the moral trials of a newly rich paint manufacturer caught up in the caste system of Brahmin Boston. Other well-known works dealt with the once-taboo subject of divorce and the reformers, strikers, and socialists of Gilded Age New York.

Two recipients of Howells's patronage and friendship—Mark Twain and Henry James—carried literary realism to new heights. With his meager formal schooling in frontier Missouri, the mustachioed Twain (1835–1910) typified a new breed of American authors in revolt against the elegant refinements of the old New England school of writing. Christened Samuel Langhorne Clemens, he had served for a time as a Mississippi riverboat pilot and later took his pen name, Mark Twain, from the boatman's cry that meant "two fathoms." After a two-week stint in the local Confederate militia, Twain journeyed westward to Nevada and California, a trip he described, with a mixture of truth and tall tales, in *Roughing It* (1872). One year later, he teamed up with Charles Dudley Warner to write *The Gilded Age*. An acid satire on post–Civil War political corruption and speculative greed, the book gave a name to an era.

Many other books flowed from Twain's busy pen. *The Adventures of Tom Sawyer* (1876) preceded *The Adventures of Huckleberry Finn* (1884), an American masterpiece that defied Twain's own definition of a classic as "a book which people praise and don't read." Over the decades, countless readers have been captivated by Huck's and Jim's search for freedom and friendship across the colorful (and often racist) backdrop of the antebellum Mississippi River valley. Twain's later years

> *In 1935 Ernest Hemingway (1899–1961) wrote,*
>
> **"All modern American literature comes from one book by Mark Twain called *Huckleberry Finn*. . . . All American writing comes from that. There was nothing before. There has been nothing as good since."**

were soured by bankruptcy growing out of unwise investments, and he was forced to take to the lecture platform and amuse what he called "the damned human race." Journalist, humorist, satirist, and foe of social injustice, he made his most enduring contribution in capturing frontier realism and colloquial humor in the authentic American dialect.

Twain's homegrown vernacular met its match in Henry James's elegantly filigreed prose. Brother of

Collection of the Mark Twain Archives, Elmira College, N.Y.

Mark Twain (1835–1910) Born Samuel Langhorne Clemens, he was not only America's most popular author but also a renowned platform lecturer. This photograph was taken at his house at Quarry Farm, near Elmira, New York, where he wrote major portions of both *The Adventures of Tom Sawyer* and *The Adventures of Huckleberry Finn*.

Harvard philosopher William James, Henry James (1843–1916) was a New Yorker who turned from law to literature and spent most of his life in Europe. Taking as his dominant theme the confrontation of innocent Americans with subtle Europeans, James penned a remarkable number of brilliant realist novels, including *The Portrait of a Lady* (1881) and *The Wings of the Dove* (1902). His book *The Bostonians* (1886) was one of the first novels about the rising feminist movement. James's fiction experimented with point of view and interior monologue, and he frequently made women his central characters, exploring their inner reactions to complex situations with a deftness that marked him as a master of "psychological realism." Long resident in England, he became a British subject shortly before his death.

Like her friend James, Edith Wharton (1862–1937) took a magnifying glass to the inner psychological turmoil and moral shortcomings of post–Civil War high society. Born into money, Wharton spent her years in the blue-blooded social circles of New York, Newport, and Paris. In 1885 she married well but not happily and increasingly turned her energies to writing. Wharton's many novels, including *The House of Mirth* (1905) and *The Age of Innocence* (1920), exposed the futile struggles and interior costs of striving characters stuck on the social ladder.

Wharton's portrayal of upper-crust social strife verged on **naturalism**, a more intense literary response than mainstream realism to the social dislocations and scientific tumult of late-nineteenth-century America. Naturalistic writers sought to apply detached scientific objectivity to the study of human beings—or "human beasts," in French novelist Émile Zola's famous phrase. While realist authors often treated middle- and upper-class characters in everyday settings, naturalistic novelists placed lower-class, marginal characters in extreme or sordid environments, including the urban jungle, where they were subject to the cruel operations of brute instinct, degenerate heredity, and pessimistic determinism.

Stephen Crane (1871–1900), the fourteenth child of a Methodist minister, exemplified this naturalistic urge in his writing. His *Maggie: A Girl of the Streets* (1893), a brutal tale about a poor prostitute driven to suicide, exposed the seamy underside of life in urban, industrial America. The novel proved too grim to find a publisher, so Crane had it printed privately. He rose quickly to prominence with *The Red Badge of Courage* (1895), the stirring story of a bloodied young Civil War recruit ("fresh fish") under the extreme stress of fire. Crane himself had never seen a battle and wrote entirely from printed Civil War records. Sharing the misfortune of his many characters, he died of tuberculosis in 1900, when only twenty-eight.

> In "The Art of Fiction" (1884), Henry James (1843–1916) articulated the technical goals of realist literature:
>
> **"**[T]he air of reality . . . seems to me to be the supreme virtue of a novel. . . . [I]t is here that he [the novelist] competes with his brother the painter in *his* attempt to render the look of things, the look that conveys their meaning, to catch the colour, the relief, the expression, the surface, the substance of the human spectacle.**"**

Candid, naturalistic portrayals of contemporary life and social problems were the literary order of the day by the turn of the century. Jack London (1876–1916), famous as a nature writer in such books as *The Call of the Wild* (1903), depicted a future fascistic revolution in *The Iron Heel* (1907), a book that displayed London's socialist leanings. Frank Norris (1870–1902), like London a Californian, wrote *The Octopus* (1901), an earthy saga of the stranglehold in which railroad and corrupt politicians held California wheat ranchers. A sequel, *The Pit* (1903), dealt with the making and breaking of speculators on the Chicago wheat exchange.

Conspicuous among the new naturalistic "social novelists" rising in the literary firmament was Theodore Dreiser (1871–1945), a homely, gangling writer from Indiana. He burst upon the literary scene in 1900 with *Sister Carrie*, a graphic narrative of a poor working girl adapting to urban life in Chicago and New York. She becomes one man's mistress, then elopes with another, and finally strikes out on her own to make a career on the stage. The fictional Carrie's disregard for prevailing moral standards so offended Dreiser's publisher that the book was soon withdrawn from circulation, though it later reemerged as an acclaimed American classic.

Sharing a common documentary impulse with realist and naturalistic fiction, **regionalism** as a movement sought to chronicle the peculiarities of local ways of life before the coming wave of industrial standardization. By the end of the nineteenth century, practically every region of the country had its share of "local colorists." At first blush, these regionalist writers accentuated the differences among still-distant American locales and indulged in a bit of provincial nostalgia. At the same time, however, their work also served to demystify (to some extent) regional differences, especially among national audiences bent on postwar reunification.

Twain, London, and Bret Harte, among other western writers, popularized (and often debunked) the lusty legends of the Old West. A foppishly dressed New Yorker,

Harte (1836–1902) struck it rich in California with gold-rush stories, especially "The Luck of Roaring Camp" (1868) and "The Outcasts of Poker Flat" (1869). Catapulted suddenly into notoriety by those short stories, he never again matched their excellence or their popularity.

Interest in local-color writing about the South also revived in the aftermath of Reconstruction. Two black writers, Paul Laurence Dunbar (1872–1906) and Charles W. Chesnutt (1858–1932), brought their distinctive voices to late-nineteenth-century literature. Dunbar's poetry—particularly his acclaimed *Lyrics of Lowly Life* (1896)—and Chesnutt's fiction—short stories in Howells's *Atlantic Monthly* and *The Conjure Woman* (1899)—embraced the use of black dialect and folklore, previously shunned by black authors, to capture the spontaneity and richness of southern black culture.

Pioneering women also contributed to the post–Civil War southern literary scene. Drawing from her experiences as a young bride and businesswoman in Louisiana, the daring feminist author Kate Chopin (1851–1904) wrote candidly about adultery, suicide, and women's ambitions in *The Awakening* (1899). Largely ignored after her death, Chopin was rediscovered by later readers, who cited her work as suggestive of the feminist yearnings that stirred beneath the surface of "respectability" in the Gilded Age.

Some important authors, of course, defied categorization. The gifted Henry Adams (1838–1918)—son of Charles Francis Adams, grandson of John Quincy Adams, and great-grandson of John Adams—turned unrivaled family connections into a prolific career as a historian, novelist, and critic. In his nine-volume *History of the United States During the Administrations of Jefferson and Madison* (1889–1891), Adams defended his patrician heritage from posthumous attack. Alarmed by modern trends, Adams penned a paean to the bygone beauty and spiritual unity of the High Middle Ages in *Mont-Saint-Michel and Chartres* (1905). Similar anxieties about modernity resurfaced in his best-known work, *The Education of Henry Adams* (1907), an autobiographical account of his own failure to come to grips with the chaotic forces of turn-of-the-century life.

✦ Artistic Triumphs

Realism and regionalism (more so than naturalism) also energized the American art world, much as they did the literary sphere. Philadelphia's native son Thomas Eakins (1844–1916) created a veritable artistic catalogue of his hometown's social, scientific, and sporting life at the end of the nineteenth century. Boston-born Winslow Homer (1836–1910), who as a youth had secretly drawn sketches in school, brought a similar mastery to the pastoral farms and swelling seas of the Northeast. Earthily American and largely resistant to foreign influences, he reveled in rugged realism and boldness of conception. His oil canvases of the sea and its fisherfolk were striking; probably no American artist has excelled him in portraying the awesome power of the ocean.

Following in the footsteps of the expatriate writers Henry James and Edith Wharton, prominent American painters working in the realist style made their living abroad. James Whistler (1834–1903) did much of his work, including the celebrated portrait of his mother, in England. This eccentric and quarrelsome Massachusetts Yankee had earlier dropped out of West Point after failing chemistry. "Had silicon been a gas," he later jested, "I would have been a major general." Another gifted portrait painter, likewise self-exiled in England, was John Singer Sargent (1856–1925). His flattering but somewhat superficial likenesses of the British nobility and America's nouveau riche were highly prized. Mary Cassatt, an American in exile in Paris, painted sensitive portrayals of modern women and children that earned her a place in the pantheon of the French impressionist painters, whose work revolutionized the European art world after their 1874 debut.

The most gifted sculptor yet produced by America was Augustus Saint-Gaudens (1848–1907). Born in Ireland of an Irish mother and a French father, he became an adopted American. The national urge to commemorate the Civil War brought him a number of famous commissions, including the stirring Robert Gould Shaw Memorial, erected on Boston Common in 1897. It depicts Colonel Shaw, a young white "Boston Brahmin" officer, leading his black troops into battle in the Civil War (see p. 443).

Music, too, was gaining popularity. America of the 1880s and 1890s was assembling high-quality symphony orchestras, notably in Boston, Chicago, and Philadelphia. The famed Metropolitan Opera House of New York was erected in 1883. In its fabled "Diamond Horseshoe," the newly rich, often under the pretense of enjoying the imported singers, would flaunt their jewels, gowns, and furs. While symphonies and operas were devoted to bringing European music to elite American audiences, new strains of homegrown American music were sprouting in the South, another outgrowth of the regionalist trend. Black folk traditions like spirituals and "ragged music" were evolving into the blues, ragtime, and jazz, which would transform American popular music in the twentieth century.

A marvelous invention was the reproduction of music by mechanical means. The phonograph, though a squeakily imperfect instrument when invented by the deaf Edison, had by 1900 reached over 150,000 homes. Americans were rapidly being dosed with "canned

Image copyright © The Metropolitan Museum of Art/Art Resource, NY

Winslow Homer, Snap the Whip (1872)   Among Homer's most famous and controversial paintings, it has been interpreted both as an homage to the innocence of youth and the simplicity of rural life and as a somber allegory about the fragility of human relationships.

music," as the "sitting room" piano increasingly gathered dust.

Wrenching changes to the nation's cities inspired a new generation of architects and planners to reshape American urban space with the **City Beautiful movement**. Its proponents wanted the new American city not just to look beautiful but also to convey a confident sense of harmony, order, and monumentality. To achieve these effects, they copied European styles of beaux arts classicism and planning ideas from the master builder of Paris, Baron Georges-Eugène Haussmann, who in the 1860s had recast the City of Light with grand boulevards, parks, and public buildings. Aiming to assert America's prominence among the greatest urban cultures of the Western world, architects constructed grandiose urban landmarks such as New York's Grand Central Terminal (1913). City planners like Daniel Burnham redesigned Chicago and Washington, D.C., in the belief they could make them perfect progressive cities, inspiring civic virtue in their inhabitants. To this end, they joined contemporary landscape architects and park builders like Frederick Law Olmsted, who sought to foster virtue and egalitarian values with his designs for New York's Central Park (1873) and Boston's "Emerald Necklace" (1896), as well as the campus of Stanford University, which opened in 1891.

Burnham's first major project, which came to symbolize the City Beautiful movement, was his design for the great **World's Columbian Exposition**, held in Chicago in 1893. His imposing landscape of pavilions and fountains honored the four hundredth anniversary

Hamlin Garland (1860–1940), the well-known midwestern novelist and writer of short stories, was immensely impressed by the cultural value of Chicago's Columbian Exposition. He wrote to his aged parents on their Dakota farm,

"Sell the cook stove if necessary and come. You must see this fair.**"**

World's Columbian Exposition, Chicago, 1893 Lagoons helped make the exposition's main buildings, dubbed the "White City," shimmer as the "City Beautiful," in stark contrast to the blocks of dull gray buildings that dominated the real Chicago.

of Columbus's first voyage. This so-called dream of loveliness was visited by 27 million people (roughly equivalent to two-fifths of the nation's population). The Chicago exposition did much to raise American artistic standards and promote city planning, although many fairgoers proved more interested in the contortions of a hootchy-kootchy dancer named "Little Egypt."

✴ The Business of Amusement

Fun and frolic were not neglected by the workaday American. The pursuit of happiness, heralded in the Declaration of Independence, had by century's end become a frenzied scramble. People sought their pleasures fiercely, as they had overrun their continent and built their cities fiercely. And now they had more time to play.

Varied diversions beckoned. The legitimate stage still flourished, as appreciative audiences responded to the lure of the footlights. Vaudeville, with its coarse jokes and graceful acrobats, continued to be immensely popular during the 1880s and 1890s, as were minstrel shows in the South, now performed by black singers and dancers rather than by whites wearing blackface as in the North before the Civil War.

The circus—high-tented and multiringed—finally emerged full-blown. Phineas T. Barnum, the master showman who had early discovered that "the public likes to be humbugged," joined hands with James A. Bailey in 1881 to stage the "Greatest Show on Earth."*

Colorful "Wild West" shows, first performed in 1883, were even more distinctively American. Headed by the knightly, goateed, and free-drinking William F. ("Buffalo Bill") Cody, the troupe included war-whooping Indians, live buffalo, and deadeye marksmen. Among them was the girlish Annie Oakley. Rifle in hand, she could at thirty paces perforate a tossed-up card half a dozen times before it fluttered to the ground (hence the term *Annie Oakley* for a punched ticket and later for a free pass).

Baseball, already widely played before the Civil War, was clearly emerging as the national pastime, if not a national mania. A league of professional players was formed in the 1870s, and in 1888 an all-star

---

*Now Ringling Bros. and Barnum & Bailey Circus.

baseball team toured the world, using the pyramids as a backstop while in Egypt. Basketball was invented in 1891 by James Naismith, a YMCA instructor in Springfield, Massachusetts. Designed as an active indoor sport that could be played during the winter months, it spread rapidly and enjoyed enormous popularity in the next century.

A gladiatorial trend toward spectator sports, rather than participative sports, was exemplified by football. This rugged game, with its dangerous flying wedge, had become popular well before 1889, when Yale man Walter C. Camp chose his first "All American" team. The Yale-Princeton game of 1893 drew fifty thousand cheering fans, while foreigners jeered that the nation was getting sports "on the brain."

Even pugilism, with its long background of bare-knuckle brutality, gained a new and gloved respectability in 1892. Agile "Gentleman Jim" Corbett, a scientific boxer, wrestled the world championship from the aging and alcoholic John L. Sullivan, the fabulous "Boston Strong Boy."

Two crazes swept the country in the closing decades of the century. First, croquet became all the rage, though condemned by moralists of the "naughty nineties" because it exposed feminine ankles and promoted flirtation. Second, the low-framed "safety" bicycle came to replace the high-seated model. By 1893 a million bicycles were in use, and thousands of young women, jokesters remarked, were turning to this new "spinning wheel," one that offered freedom, not tedium.

Buffalo Bill Historical Center, Wyoming, Gift of the Coe Foundation

Buffalo Bill's Wild West Show, ca. 1907 By the late 1800s, the "Wild West" was already passing into the realm of myth—and popular entertainment. Famed frontiersman William F. ("Buffalo Bill") Cody (1846–1917) made his fortune showing off his tame cowboys and Indians to enthusiastic urban audiences in Europe as well as the United States. Buffalo Bill's "Wild West"—an extravaganza featuring skilled horsemen from around the globe, including Turks, South American gauchos, Arabs, and Cossacks—was even more motley than the real one.

Courtesy of the California History Room, California State Library, Sacramento, California

Cyclists on the Monterey Peninsula, California, 1888   Men and women alike took to the roads on the newfangled "two-wheelers." Bicycling especially appealed to young women eager to escape nineteenth-century strictures against female exercise and bodily exposure.

The land of the skyscraper was plainly becoming more standardized, owing largely to the new industrialization. Although race and ethnicity assigned urban Americans to distinctive neighborhoods and workplaces, to an increasing degree they shared a common popular culture—playing, reading, shopping, and talking alike. As the century drew to a close, the explosion of cities paradoxically made Americans more diverse and more similar at the same time.

Chapter Review

KEY TERMS

New Immigrants (543)

settlement houses (549)

liberal Protestants (552)

Tuskegee Institute (555)

land-grant colleges (555)

pragmatism (557)

yellow journalism (558)

National American Woman
  Suffrage Association
  (NAWSA) (562)

Woman's Christian Temper-
  ance Union (WCTU) (564)

realism (566)

naturalism (567)

regionalism (567)

City Beautiful
  movement (569)

World's Columbian
  Exposition (569)

PEOPLE TO KNOW

Jane Addams

Charles Darwin

Booker T. Washington

W. E. B. Du Bois

Joseph Pulitzer

William Randolph Hearst

John Dewey

Carrie Chapman Catt

Horatio Alger

Mark Twain

Henry James

Winslow Homer

Augustus Saint-Gaudens

Frederick Law Olmsted

CHRONOLOGY

1859 Charles Darwin publishes *On the Origin of Species*

1862 Morrill Act provides public land for higher education

1863 World's first subway system opens in London

1866 American Society for the Prevention of Cruelty to Animals (ASPCA) created

1869 Wyoming Territory grants women right to vote

1871 *Woodhull and Claflin's Weekly* published

1872 Metaphysical Club meets in Cambridge, Massachusetts

1873 Comstock Law
Construction of New York's Central Park officially completed

1874 Woman's Christian Temperance Union (WCTU) organized
Chautauqua education movement launched
Impressionist artists debut in Paris

1876 Johns Hopkins University graduate school established

1879 Henry George publishes *Progress and Poverty*
Dumbbell tenement introduced
Mary Baker Eddy establishes Christian Science
Salvation Army begins work in America

1881 Booker T. Washington becomes head of Tuskegee Institute
American Red Cross founded
Henry James publishes *The Portrait of a Lady*
Barnum and Bailey first join to stage "Greatest Show on Earth"

1882 First immigration-restriction laws passed

1883 Brooklyn Bridge completed
Metropolitan Opera House built in New York

1884 Mark Twain publishes *The Adventures of Huckleberry Finn*

1885 Louis Sullivan builds first skyscraper, in Chicago
Linotype invented

1886 Statue of Liberty erected in New York harbor

1887 American Protective Association (APA) formed
Hatch Act supplements Morrill Act

1888 Edward Bellamy publishes *Looking Backward*
American all-star baseball team tours world

1889 Jane Addams founds Hull House in Chicago

1890 William James publishes *The Principles of Psychology*
National American Woman Suffrage Association (NAWSA) formed

1891 Basketball invented
Stanford University opens

1893 Lillian Wald opens Henry Street Settlement in New York
Anti-Saloon League formed
World's Columbian Exposition held in Chicago
New Zealand grants women right to vote

1895 Stephen Crane publishes *The Red Badge of Courage*

1897 Library of Congress opens
Robert Gould Shaw Memorial erected on Boston Common

1898 Charlotte Perkins Gilman publishes *Women and Economics*

1899 Kate Chopin publishes *The Awakening*

1900 Theodore Dreiser publishes *Sister Carrie*

1907 Henry Adams privately publishes *The Education of Henry Adams*

1910 National Association for the Advancement of Colored People (NAACP) founded

TO LEARN MORE

John Bodnar, *The Transplanted: A History of Immigrants in Urban America* (1985)

Irving Howe, *World of Our Fathers* (1976)

Kenneth T. Jackson, *Crabgrass Frontier: The Suburbanization of America* (1985)

David Levering Lewis, *W. E. B. Du Bois: Biography of a Race, 1868–1919* (1993)

————, *W. E. B. Du Bois: The Fight for Equality and the American Century, 1919–1963* (2000)

Louis Menand, *The Metaphysical Club: A Story of Ideas in America* (2001)

Kathy Peiss, *Cheap Amusements: Working Women and Leisure in Turn-of-the-Century New York* (1986)

Jacob Riis, *How the Other Half Lives* (1890)

Daniel Rodgers, *Atlantic Crossings: Social Politics in a Progressive Age* (1998)

Roy Rosenzweig and Elizabeth Blackmar, *The Park and the People: A History of Central Park* (1992)

Carroll Smith-Rosenberg, *Disorderly Conduct: Visions of Gender in Victorian America* (1985)

Ronald Takaki, *Strangers from a Different Shore: A History of Asian Americans* (1989)

Alan Trachtenberg, *The Incorporation of America: Culture and Society in the Gilded Age* (1982)

A complete, annotated bibliography for this chapter—along with brief descriptions of the People to Know—may be found on the American Pageant website. The Key Terms are defined in a Glossary at the end of the text.

Go to the CourseMate website at **www.cengagebrain.com** for additional study tools and review materials—including audio and video clips—for this chapter.

Chapter 26

The Great West and the Agricultural Revolution

1865–1896

Up to our own day American history has been in a large degree the history of the colonization of the Great West. The existence of an area of free land, its continuous recession, and the advance of American settlement westward, explain American development.

FREDERICK JACKSON TURNER, 1893

The White Man, who possesses this whole vast country from sea to sea, who roams over it at pleasure, and lives where he likes, cannot know the cramp we feel in this little spot, with the undying remembrance of the fact, which you know as well as we, that every foot of what you proudly call America, not very long ago belonged to the red man.

WASHAKIE (SHOSHONE INDIAN), 1878

*W*hen *the Civil War crashed* to a close, the frontier line was still wavering westward toward the fabled "100th Meridian," which defines the eastern boundary of the West, America's most arid region (see Map 26.4). A long fringe of settlement, bulging outward here and there, ran roughly north through central Texas and on to the Canadian border. Between this jagged line and the settled areas on the Pacific slope, there were virtually no white people. The few exceptions were the islands of Mormons in Utah, occasional trading posts and gold camps, and several scattered Spanish Mexican settlements throughout the Southwest.

Sprawling in expanse, the Great West was a rough square that measured about a thousand miles on each side. Embracing mountains, plateaus, deserts, and plains, it was the largely parched habitat of the Indian, the buffalo, the wild horse, the prairie dog, and the coyote. Twenty-five years later—that is, by 1890—the entire domain had been carved into states and the four territories of Utah, Arizona, New Mexico, and "Indian

Territory," or Oklahoma. Pioneers flung themselves greedily on this enormous prize, as if to ravish it. Probably never before in human experience had so huge an area been transformed so rapidly.

⭐ The Clash of Cultures on the Plains

Native Americans numbered about 360,000 in 1860, many of them scattered about the vast grasslands of the trans-Missouri West. But to their eternal misfortune, the Indians stood in the path of the advancing white pioneers. An inevitable clash loomed between an acquisitive, industrializing nation and the Indians' lifeways, highly evolved over centuries to adapt to the demanding environment of the sparsely watered western plains.

Migration and conflict—and sometimes dramatic cultural change—were no strangers in the arid West, even before the whites began to arrive. The Comanches had driven the Apaches off the central plains into

The Buffalo Hunt, by Frederic Remington, 1890 A New Yorker who first went west at the age of nineteen as a cowboy and ranch cook, Remington (1861–1909) became the foremost artist of the vanishing way of life of the old Far West. Once a common sight on the high plains, the kind of buffalo kill that Remington records here was a great rarity by the time he painted this scene in 1890. The once-vast herds of bison had long since been reduced to a pitiful few by the white man's rifles and the increasingly concentrated use of the land by ever more constricted Indians.

Buffalo Bill Historical Center, Cody, Wyoming; Gift of William E. Weiss; 23.62

the upper Rio Grande valley in the eighteenth century. Harried by the Mandans and Chippewas, the Cheyenne had abandoned their villages along the upper reaches of the Mississippi and Missouri Rivers in the century before the Civil War. The Sioux, displaced from the Great Lakes woodlands in the late eighteenth century, emerged onto the plains to prey upon the Crows, Kiowas, and Pawnees. Mounted on Spanish-introduced horses, peoples like the Cheyenne and the Sioux transformed themselves within just a few generations from foot-traveling, crop-growing villagers to wide-ranging nomadic traders and deadly efficient buffalo hunters—so deadly that they threatened to extinguish the vast bison herds that had lured them onto the plains in the first place.

When white soldiers and settlers edged onto the plains in the decades just before the Civil War, they accelerated a fateful cycle that exacerbated already fierce enmities among the Indians and ultimately undermined the foundations of Native American culture. White intruders unwittingly spread cholera, typhoid, and smallpox among the native peoples of the plains, with devastating results. Equally harmful, whites put further pressure on the steadily shrinking bison population by hunting and by grazing their own livestock on the prairie grasses. As the once-mammoth buffalo herds dwindled, warfare intensified among the Plains tribes for ever-scarcer hunting grounds. "I am traveling all over this country, and am cutting the trees of my brothers," an Arikara Indian told a U.S. Army officer along the Platte River in 1835. "I am killing their buffalo before my friends arrive so that when they come up, they can find no buffalo."

The federal government tried to pacify the Plains Indians by signing treaties with the "chiefs" of various "tribes" at Fort Laramie in 1851 and at Fort Atkinson in 1853. The treaties marked the beginnings of the **reservation system** in the West. They established

As early as the Coronado expedition in 1541, Spanish explorers marveled at the Plains Indians' reliance on the buffalo:

❝With the skins [the Indians] build their houses; with the skins they clothe and shoe themselves; from the skins they make ropes and also obtain wool. From the sinews they make thread, with which they sew their clothing and likewise their tents. From the bones they shape awls, and the dung they use for firewood, since there is no fuel in all that land. The bladders serve as jugs and drinking vessels. They sustain themselves on the flesh of the animals, eating it slightly roasted and sometimes uncooked. Taking it in their teeth, they pull with one hand; with the other they hold a large flint knife and cut off mouthfuls, swallowing it half chewed, like birds. They eat raw fat, without warming it.❞

One disheartened Indian complained to the white Sioux Commission created by Congress,

❝ Tell your people that since the Great Father promised that we should never be removed we have been moved five times. . . . I think you had better put the Indians on wheels and you can run them about wherever you wish. **❞**

boundaries for the territory of each tribe and attempted to separate the Indians into two great "colonies" to the north and south of a corridor of intended white settlement.

But the white treaty makers misunderstood both Indian government and Indian society. "Tribes" and "chiefs" were often fictions of the white imagination, which could not grasp the fact that many Native Americans, living in scattered bands, recognized only the authority of their immediate families or perhaps a band elder. And the nomadic culture of the Plains Indians was utterly alien to the concept of living out one's life in the confinement of a defined territory.

In the 1860s the federal government intensified this policy and herded the Indians into still-smaller confines, principally the "Great Sioux reservation" in Dakota Territory and Indian Territory in present-day Oklahoma, into which dozens of southern Plains tribes were forced.

The Indians surrendered their ancestral lands only when they had received solemn promises from Washington that they would be left alone and provided with food, clothing, and other supplies. Regrettably, the federal Indian agents were often corrupt. They palmed off moth-eaten blankets, spoiled beef, and other defective provisions on the friendless Indians. One of these cheating officials, on an annual salary of $1,500, returned home after four years with an estimated "savings" of $50,000.

For more than a decade after the Civil War, fierce warfare between Indians and the U.S. Army raged in various parts of the West (see Map 26.1). Army troops, many of them recent immigrants who had, ironically, fled Europe to avoid military service, met formidable adversaries in the Plains Indians, whose superb horsemanship gave them baffling mobility. Fully one-fifth of all U.S. Army personnel on the frontier were African American—dubbed "Buffalo Soldiers" by the Indians, supposedly because of the resemblance of their hair to the bison's furry coat.

✦ Receding Native Population

The Indian wars in the West were often savage clashes. Aggressive whites sometimes shot peaceful Indians on sight, just to make sure they would give no trouble. At Sand Creek, Colorado, in 1864, Colonel J. M. Chivington's militia massacred in cold blood some four hundred Indians who apparently thought they had been promised immunity. Women were shot praying for mercy, children had their brains dashed out, and braves were tortured, scalped, and unspeakably mutilated.

Courtesy Palace of the Governors (MNM/DCA) Neg. #58632

Pawnee Indians in Front of Their Lodge, ca. 1868 The Pawnees of central Nebraska never made war on the United States, which they regarded as an ally in their own struggles against the marauding Sioux.

Cruelty begot cruelty. In 1866 a Sioux war party attempting to block construction of the Bozeman Trail to the Montana goldfields ambushed Captain William J. Fetterman's command of eighty-one soldiers and civilians in Wyoming's Bighorn Mountains. The Indians left not a single survivor and grotesquely mutilated the corpses. One trooper's face was spitted with 105 arrows. George Armstrong Custer, the buckskinclad "boy general" of Civil War fame, now demoted to colonel and turned Indian fighter, wrote that Fetterman's annihilation "awakened a bitter feeling toward the savage perpetrators." The cycle of ferocious warfare intensified.

The Fetterman massacre led to one of the few—though short-lived—Indian triumphs in the plains wars, the **Battle of the Little Bighorn**. In another Treaty of Fort Laramie, signed in 1868, the government abandoned the Bozeman Trail. The sprawling "Great Sioux reservation" was guaranteed to the Sioux tribes. But in 1874 a new round of warfare with the Plains Indians began when Custer led a "scientific" expedition into the Black Hills of South Dakota (part of the Sioux reservation) and announced that he had discovered gold.

> *A young lieutenant told Colonel Chivington that to attack the Indians would be a violation of pledges:*
>
> **"**His reply was, bringing his fist down close to my face, 'Damn any man who sympathizes with Indians.' I told him what pledges were given the Indians. He replied that he 'had come to kill Indians, and believed it to be honorable to kill Indians under any and all circumstances.'**"**

MAP 26.1 Indian Wars, 1860–1890 Surrendering in 1877, Chief Joseph of the Nez Perce declared, "Our chiefs are killed. . . . The old men are all dead. . . . The little children are freezing to death. . . . I want to have time to look for my children. . . . Hear me, my chiefs. My heart is sick and sad. From where the sun now stands I will fight no more forever."

© Cengage Learning

Battle of the Little Big Horn, by Amos Bad Heart Bull   This depiction of the battle by an Oglala Sioux tribal historian and artist shows Crazy Horse (in spotted war paint, center) firing on a trooper of Custer's 7th Cavalry. The ground is littered with the bodies of dead soldiers.

Hordes of greedy gold-seekers swarmed into the Sioux lands. The aggrieved Sioux, aided by the Cheyenne and Arapaho Indians, took to the warpath, inspired by the influential and wily Sitting Bull.

Colonel Custer's 7th Cavalry, nearly half of them immigrants, set out to suppress the Indians and to return them to the reservation. Attacking what turned out to be a superior force of some 2,500 well-armed warriors camped along the Little Bighorn River in present-day Montana, the "White Chief with Yellow Hair" and about 250 officers and men were completely wiped out in 1876 when two supporting columns failed to come to their rescue. The Indians' victory was short-lived. In a series of battles across the northern plains in the ensuing months, the U.S. Army relentlessly hunted down the Indians who had humiliated Custer.

One band of Nez Percé Indians in northeastern Oregon were goaded into daring flight in 1877 when U.S. authorities tried to herd them onto a reservation. Chief Joseph finally surrendered his breakaway band of some seven hundred Indians after a tortuous, seventeen-hundred-mile, three-month trek across the Continental Divide toward Canada. There Joseph hoped to rendezvous with Sitting Bull, who had taken refuge north of the border after the Battle of the Little Bighorn. Betrayed into believing they would be returned to their ancestral lands in Idaho, the Nez Percés instead were sent to a dusty reservation in Kansas, where 40 percent of them perished from disease. The survivors were eventually allowed to return to Idaho.

Fierce Apache tribes of Arizona and New Mexico were the most difficult to subdue. Led by Geronimo, whose eyes blazed hatred of the whites, they were pursued into Mexico by federal troops using the sun-flashing heliograph, a communication device that impressed the Indians as "big medicine." Scattered remnants of the warriors were finally persuaded to surrender after the Apache women had been exiled to Florida. The Apaches ultimately became successful farmers in Oklahoma.

This relentless fire-and-sword policy of the whites at last shattered the spirit of the Indians. The vanquished Native Americans were finally ghettoized on reservations, where they could theoretically preserve their cultural autonomy but were in fact compelled to eke out a sullen existence as wards of the government. Their white masters had at last discovered that the Indians were much cheaper to feed than to fight. Even so, for many decades they were almost ignored to death.

The "taming" of the Indians was engineered by a number of factors. Of cardinal importance was the federal government's willingness to back its land claims with military force. Almost as critical was the railroad, which shot an iron arrow through the heart of the

Geronimo (ca. 1823–1909), Also Known by His Apache Name, Goyahkla (One Who Yawns) In 1851 Mexican troops killed Geronimo's mother and wife and three of his children, initiating his lifelong hatred of Mexicans. Ironically, in later life, when he repeatedly fled the intolerable confinement of reservations in the United States, he sought refuge—and freedom—in Mexico. Persuaded at last to surrender to American authorities in 1886, he spent the remainder of his life on reservations in Florida, Alabama, and Oklahoma.

© Bettmann/Corbis

West. Locomotives could bring out unlimited numbers of troops, farmers, cattlemen, sheepherders, and settlers. The Indians were also ravaged by the white people's diseases, to which they showed little resistance, and by their firewater, which they could resist even less. Above all, the virtual extermination of the buffalo doomed the Plains Indians' nomadic way of life.

Bellowing Herds of Bison

Tens of millions of buffalo—described by early Spaniards as "hunchback cows"—blackened the western prairies when white Americans first arrived. These shaggy, lumbering animals were the staff of life for Native Americans (see "Makers of America: The Plains Indians," pp. 582–583). Their flesh provided food; their dried dung provided fuel ("buffalo chips"); their hides provided clothing, lariats, and harnesses.

When the Civil War closed, some 15 million of these meaty beasts were still grazing on the western plains. In 1868 a Kansas Pacific locomotive had to wait eight hours for a herd to amble across the tracks. Much of the food supply of the railroad construction gangs came from leathery buffalo steaks. William "Buffalo Bill" Cody—sinewy, telescope-eyed, and a crack shot—killed over 4,000 animals in eighteen months while employed by the Kansas Pacific.

With the building of the railroad, the massacre of the herds began in deadly earnest. The creatures were slain for their hides, for their tongues or a few other choice cuts, or for sheer amusement. "Sportsmen" on lurching railroad trains would lean out the windows and blaze away at the animals to satisfy their lust for slaughter or excitement. Such wholesale butchery left fewer than a thousand buffalo alive by 1885, and the once-numerous beasts were in danger of complete extinction. The whole story is a shocking example of the greed and waste that accompanied the conquest of the continent.

The End of the Trail

By the 1880s the national conscience began to stir uneasily over the plight of the Indians. Helen Hunt Jackson, a Massachusetts writer of children's literature, pricked the moral sense of Americans in 1881 when she published *A Century of Dishonor*. The book chronicled the sorry record of government ruthlessness and chicanery in dealing with the Indians. Her later novel *Ramona* (1884), a love story about discrimination against California Indians, sold some 600,000 copies and further inspired sympathy for the Indians.

Debate seesawed. Humanitarians wanted to treat the Indians kindly and persuade them thereby to "walk the white man's road." Yet hard-liners insisted on the current policy of forced containment and brutal punishment. Neither side showed much respect for Native American culture. Christian reformers, who often administered educational facilities on the reservations, sometimes withheld food to force the Indians to give up their tribal religions and assimilate to white society. In 1884 these zealous white souls joined with military

Civil War veteran and long-time Indian fighter General Philip Sheridan (1831–1888) reflected on the wars against the Indians:

❝We took away their country and their means of support, broke up their mode of living, their habits of life, introduced disease and decay among them, and it was for this and against this they made war. Could anyone expect less?**❞**

men in successfully persuading the federal government to outlaw the sacred Sun Dance. When the "Ghost Dance" cult later spread to the Dakota Sioux, the army bloodily stamped it out in 1890 at the so-called **Battle of Wounded Knee**. In the fighting thus provoked, an estimated two hundred Indian men, women, and children were killed, as well as twenty-nine invading soldiers.

The misbegotten offspring of the movement to reform Indian policy was the **Dawes Severalty Act** of 1887. Reflecting the forced-civilization views of the reformers, the act dissolved many tribes as legal entities, wiped out tribal ownership of land, and set up individual Indian family heads with 160 free acres. If the Indians behaved themselves like "good white settlers," they would get full title to their holdings, as well as citizenship, in twenty-five years. The probationary period was later extended, but full citizenship was granted to all Indians in 1924.

Former reservation land not allotted to the Indians under the Dawes Act was to be sold to railroads and white settlers, with the proceeds used by the federal government to educate and "civilize" the native peoples. In 1879 the government had already funded the Carlisle Indian School in Pennsylvania, where Native American children, separated from their tribes, were taught English and inculcated with white values and customs. "Kill the Indian and save the man" was the school founder's motto. In the 1890s the government expanded its network of Indian boarding schools and sent "field matrons" to the reservations to teach Native American women the art of sewing and to preach the virtues of chastity and hygiene.

The Dawes Act struck directly at tribal organization and tried to make rugged individualists out of the Indians. This legislation ignored the inherent reliance of traditional Indian culture on tribally held land, literally pulling the land out from under them. By 1900 Indians had lost 50 percent of the 156 million acres

The Indian spokesman Plenty Coups (1848–1932) said in 1909,

❝I see no longer the curling smoke rising from our lodge poles. I hear no longer the songs of the women as they prepare the meal. The antelope have gone; the buffalo wallows are empty. Only the wail of the coyote is heard. The white man's medicine is stronger than ours. . . . We are like birds with a broken wing.**❞**

National Anthropological Archives, Smithsonian Institution, Washington, D.C.

Lakotas Receiving Rations at Standing Rock Reservation, ca. 1881 Once the scourge of the plains, the Lakota (part of the Sioux tribes) were reduced by the 1890s to the humiliation of living on government handouts.

The last of the native peoples of North America to bow before the military might of the whites, the Indians of the northern Great Plains long defended their lands and their ways of life against the American cavalry. After the end of the Indian wars, toward the close of the nineteenth century, the Plains tribes struggled on, jealously guarding their communities against white encroachment. Crowded onto reservations, subject to ever-changing federal Indian policies, assailed by corrupt settlers and Indian agents, the Plains Indians have nonetheless preserved much of their ancestral culture to this day.

Before Europeans first appeared in North America in the sixteenth century, the vast plains from northern Texas to Saskatchewan were home to some thirty different tribes. There was no typical Plains Indian; each tribe spoke a distinct language, practiced its own religion, and formed its own government. When members of different bands met on the prairies, communication depended on a special sign language.

Indians had first trod the arid plains to pursue sprawling herds of antelope, elk, and especially buffalo—all important sources of protein. But these early peoples of the plains were not exclusively hunters: the women were expert farmers, coaxing lush gardens of pumpkins, squash, corn, and beans from the dry but fertile soil. Still, the shaggy pelt and heavy flesh of the buffalo constituted the staff of life on the plains. Hunted by men, the great bison were butchered by women, who used every part of the beast. They fashioned horns and hooves into spoons, and intestines into containers. They stretched sinews into strong bowstrings and wove buffalo hair into ropes. Meat not immediately eaten was pounded into pemmican—thin strips of smoked or sun-dried buffalo flesh mixed with berries and stuffed into rawhide bags.

The nomadic Plains Indians sought what shelter they could in small bands throughout the winter, gathering together in summer for religious ceremonies, socializing, and communal buffalo hunts. At first these seasonal migrations required arduous loading and carting. The Indians carried all their possessions or heaped them on wheelless carts called travois, which were dragged by dogs—their only beasts of burden.

A Comanche Village, by George Catlin, 1834

Smithsonian American Art Museum, Washington, DC/Art Resource, NY

(above) A Sioux Carving Horses were essential to the culture of the Plains Indians, and they often carved likenesses of horses killed in battle. Note the red-stained holes depicting this horse's wounds. **(right) A Cheyenne Cradleboard for Carrying a Baby** © Smithsonian Institution/Corbis

Chan-Chä-Uiá-Teüin, Teton Sioux Woman, by Karl Bodmer, ca. 1830s Bodmer, a German artist, painted this woman's portrait during an expedition to the Great Plains. Her name means "Woman of the Crow Nation," which seems to suggest that she was taken captive from the Sioux's mortal enemies, the Crows.

Then in the sixteenth century, the mounted Spanish *conquistadores* ventured into the New World. Their steeds—some of them escaping to become mustangs, the wild horses of the American West, and others acquired by the Indians in trade—quickly spread over the plains. The horse revolutionized Indian societies, for a time turning the Plains tribes into efficient hunting machines that promised to banish hunger from the prairies. But horse-mounted hunters turned out to be too efficient: overhunting made buffalo ever harder to find. The plains pony also ignited a furious competition for grazing lands, for trade goods, and for ever more horses, so that wars of aggression and of revenge became increasingly bitter and frequent.

The European invasion soon eclipsed the short-lived era of the horse. After many battles the Plains Indians found themselves crammed together on tiny reservations, clinging with tired but determined fingers to their traditions. Although much of Plains Indian culture persists to this day, the Indians' free-ranging way of life has passed into memory. As Black Elk, an Oglala Sioux, put it, "Once we were happy in our own country and we were seldom hungry, for then the two-leggeds and the four-leggeds lived together like relatives, and there was plenty for them and for us. But then the Wasichus [white people] came, and they made little islands for us . . . and always these islands are becoming smaller, for around them surges the gnawing flood of Wasichus."

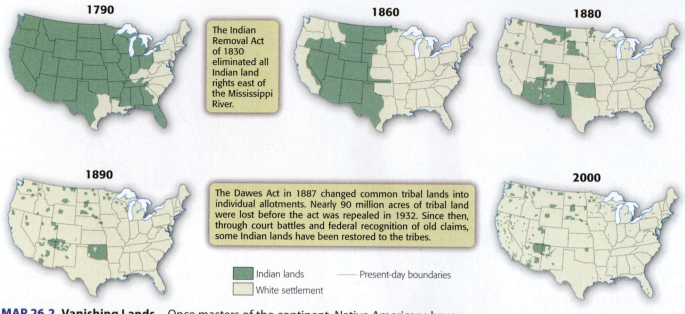

MAP 26.2 Vanishing Lands Once masters of the continent, Native Americans have been squeezed into just 2 percent of U.S. territory. (Source: Copyright © 2000 by *The New York Times*. Reprinted by permission.)

they had held just two decades earlier (see Map 26.2). The forced-assimilation doctrine of the Dawes Act remained the cornerstone of the government's official Indian policy for nearly half a century, until the Indian Reorganization Act (the "Indian New Deal") of 1934 partially reversed the individualistic approach and belatedly tried to restore the tribal basis of Indian life (see p. 765).

Under these new federal policies, defective though they were, the Indian population started to mount slowly. The total number had been reduced by 1887 to about 243,000—the result of bullets, bottles, and bacteria—but the census of 2000 counted more than 1.5 million Native Americans, urban and rural.

✸ Mining: From Dishpan to Ore Breaker

The conquest of the Indians and the coming of the railroad were life-giving boons to the mining frontier. The golden gravel of California continued to yield "pay dirt," and in 1858 an electrifying discovery convulsed Colorado. Avid "fifty-niners" or "Pikes Peakers" rushed west to rip at the ramparts of the Rockies. But there were more miners than minerals, and many gold-grubbers, with "Pikes Peak or Bust" inscribed on the canvas of their covered wagons, creaked wearily back with the added inscription, "Busted, by Gosh." Yet countless bearded fortune-seekers stayed on, some to strip away

the silver deposits, others to extract nonmetallic wealth from the earth in the form of golden grain.

"Fifty-niners" also poured feverishly into Nevada in 1859, after the fabulous Comstock Lode had been uncovered. A fantastic amount of gold and silver, worth more than $340 million, was mined by the "Kings of the Comstock" from 1860 to 1890. The scantily populated state of Nevada, "child of the Comstock Lode," was prematurely railroaded into the Union in 1864, partly to provide three electoral votes for President Lincoln.

Smaller "lucky strikes" drew frantic gold- and silver-seekers into Montana, Idaho, and other western states. Boomtowns, known as "Helldorados," sprouted from the desert sands like magic. Every third cabin was a saloon, where sweat-stained miners drank adulterated liquor ("rotgut") in the company of accommodating women. Lynch law and hempen vigilante justice, as in early California, preserved a crude semblance of order in the towns. And when the "diggings" petered out, the gold-seekers decamped, leaving eerily picturesque "ghost towns," such as Virginia City, Nevada, silhouetted in the desert. Begun with a boom, these towns ended with a whimper.

Once the loose surface gold was gobbled up, ore-breaking machinery was imported to smash the gold-bearing quartz. This operation was so expensive that it could ordinarily be undertaken only by corporations pooling the wealth of stockholders. Gradually the age of big business came to the **mining industry**. Dusty,

Library of Congress

Hydraulic Mining, Nevada, 1866 Once miners had panned and dredged the most accessible gold from streambeds, they ripped open the earth itself in search of other deposits. High-pressure streams of water, delivered through huge nozzles called "monitors," washed away entire hillsides and created the nightmarish, debris-strewn landscapes that still scar western mountains and foothills.

bewhiskered miners, dishpans in hand, were replaced by impersonal corporations, with their costly machinery and trained engineers. The once-independent gold-washer became just another day laborer.

Yet the mining frontier had played a vital role in conquering the continent. Magnetlike, it attracted population and wealth, while advertising the wonders of the Wild West. Women as well as men found opportunity, running boardinghouses or working as prostitutes. They won a kind of equality on the rough frontier that earned them the vote in Wyoming (1869), Utah (1870), Colorado (1893), and Idaho (1896) long before their sisters in the East could cast a ballot.

The amassing of precious metals helped finance the Civil War, facilitated the building of railroads, and intensified the already bitter conflict between whites and Indians. The outpouring of silver and gold enabled the Treasury to resume specie payments in 1879 and injected the silver issue into American politics. "Silver Senators," representing the thinly peopled "acreage states" of the West, used their disproportionate influence to promote the interests of the silver miners. Finally, the mining frontier added to American folklore and literature, as the writings of Bret Harte and Mark Twain so colorfully attest.

✴ Beef Bonanzas and the Long Drive

When the Civil War ended, the grassy plains of Texas supported several million tough, long-horned cattle.

These scrawny beasts, whose horn spreads sometimes reached eight feet, were killed primarily for their hides. There was no way of getting their meat profitably to market.

The problem of marketing was neatly solved when the transcontinental railroads thrust their iron fingers into the West. Cattle could now be shipped alive to the stockyards, and under "beef barons" like the Swifts and Armours, the highly industrialized meatpacking

© Bettmann/Corbis

Dressed to Kill Cowboys came in all varieties and sizes in the wild and woolly frontier West—and in all kinds of garb as well.

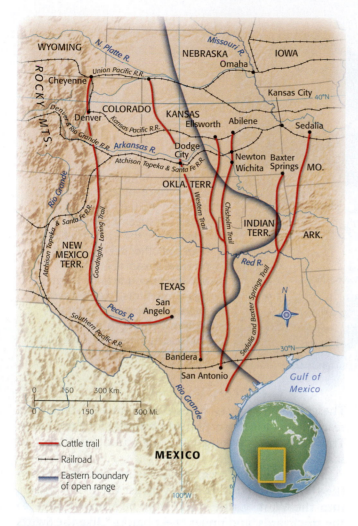

MAP 26.3 Cattle Trails © Cengage Learning

The steer was king in a Cattle Kingdom richly carpeted with grass. As long as lush grass was available, the Long Drive proved profitable—that is, to the luckier cattlemen who escaped Indians, stampedes, cattle fever, and other hazards. From 1866 to 1888, bellowing herds, totaling over 4 million steers, were driven northward from the beef bowl of Texas. The steer was king in a Cattle Kingdom richly carpeted with grass.

What the Lord giveth, the Lord also can taketh away. The railroad made the Long Drive, and the railroad unmade the Long Drive, primarily because the locomotives ran both ways. The same rails that bore the cattle from the open range to the kitchen range brought out the homesteader and the sheepherder. Both of these intruders, sometimes amid flying bullets, built barbed-wire fences that were too numerous to be cut down by the cowboys. Furthermore, the terrible winter of 1886–1887, with blinding blizzards reaching 68 degrees below zero, left thousands of dazed cattle starving and freezing. Overexpansion and overgrazing likewise took their toll, as the cowboys slowly gave way to plowboys.

The only escape for the stockmen was to make cattle-raising a big business and avoid the perils of overproduction. Breeders learned to fence their ranches, lay in winter feed, import blooded bulls, and produce fewer and meatier animals. They also learned to organize. The Wyoming Stock-Growers' Association, especially in the 1880s, virtually controlled the state and its legislature.

This was the heyday of the cowboy. The equipment of the cowhand—from "shooting irons" and ten-gallon hat to chaps and spurs—served a useful, not an ornamental, function. A "genuwine" gun-toting cowpuncher, riding where men were men and smelled like horses, could justifiably boast of his toughness.

These bowlegged Knights of the Saddle, with their colorful trappings and cattle-lulling songs, became part of American folklore. Many of them, perhaps five thousand, were blacks, who especially enjoyed the newfound freedom of the open range.

✴ The Farmers' Frontier

Miners and cattlemen created the romantic legend of the West, but it was the sober sodbuster who wrote the final chapter of frontier history. A fresh day dawned for western farmers with the **Homestead Act** of 1862. The new law allowed a settler to acquire as much as 160 acres of land (a quarter-section) by living on it for five years, improving it, and paying a nominal fee of about $30.

The Homestead Act marked a drastic departure from previous policy. Before the act, public land had been sold primarily for revenue; now it was to be given away to

business sprang into existence as a main pillar of the economy. Drawing upon the gigantic stockyards at Kansas City and Chicago, the meatpackers could ship their fresh products to the East Coast in the newly perfected refrigerator cars.

A spectacular feeder of the new slaughterhouses was the "Long Drive" (see Map 26.3). Texas cowboys—black, white, and Mexican—drove herds numbering from one thousand to ten thousand head slowly over the unfenced and unpeopled plains until they reached a railroad terminal. The bawling beasts grazed en route on the free government grass. Favorite terminal points were flyspecked "cow towns" like Dodge City—"the Bibulous Babylon of the Frontier"—and Abilene (Kansas), Ogallala (Nebraska), and Cheyenne (Wyoming). At Abilene order was maintained by Marshal James B. ("Wild Bill") Hickok, a fabulous gunman who reputedly killed only in self-defense or in the line of duty and who was fatally shot in the back in 1876 while playing poker.

Acres

FIGURE 26.1 **Homesteads from the Public Lands (acreage legally transferred to private ownership)** See related Map 26.5 on p. 590.

encourage a rapid filling of empty spaces and to provide a stimulus to the family farm—"the backbone of democracy." The new law was a godsend to a host of farmers who could not afford to buy large holdings. During the forty years after its passage, about half a million families took advantage of the Homestead Act to carve out new homes in the vast open stretches. Yet five times that many families *purchased* their land from the railroads, the land companies, or the states (see Figure 26.1).

The Homestead Act often turned out to be a cruel hoax. The standard 160 acres, quite adequate in the well-watered Mississippi basin, frequently proved pitifully inadequate on the rain-scarce Great Plains. Thousands of homesteaders, perhaps two out of three, were forced to give up the one-sided struggle against drought. Uncle Sam, it was said, bet 160 acres against ten dollars that the settlers could not live on their homesteads for five years. One of these unsuccessful gambles in Greer County, western Oklahoma, inspired a folk song:

> *Hurrah for Greer County! The land of the free,*
> *The land of the bedbug, grasshopper, and flea;*
> *I'll sing of its praises, I'll tell of its fame,*
> *While starving to death on my government claim.*

Naked fraud was spawned by the Homestead Act and similar laws. Perhaps ten times more of the public domain wound up in the clutches of land-grabbing promoters than in the hands of bona fide farmers. Unscrupulous corporations would use "dummy" homesteaders—often their employees or aliens bribed with cash or a bottle of beer—to grab the best properties containing timber, minerals, and oil. Settlers would later swear that they had "improved" the property by erecting a "twelve by fourteen" dwelling, which turned out to measure twelve by fourteen *inches*.

The railways also played a major role in developing the agricultural West, largely through the profitable marketing of crops. Some railroad companies induced Americans and European immigrants to buy the cheap land earlier granted to the railroads by the government. The Northern Pacific Railroad at one time had nearly a thousand paid agents in Europe distributing roseate leaflets in various languages.

Shattering the myth of the Great American Desert opened the gateways to the agricultural West even wider. The windswept prairies were for the most part treeless, and the tough sod had been pounded solid by millions of buffalo hooves. Pioneer explorers and trappers had assumed that the soil must be sterile, simply because it was not heavily watered and did not support immense forests. But once the prairie sod was broken with heavy iron plows pulled by four yokes of oxen—the "plow that broke the plains"—the earth proved astonishingly fruitful. "Sodbusters" poured onto the prairies. Lacking trees for lumber and fuel, they built

In making the arduous journey across the western prairies, many women settlers discovered new confidence in their abilities. Early on in her trek, Mary Richardson Walker (1811–1897) confided in her diary that

"my circumstances are rather trying. So much danger attends me on every hand. A long journey before me, going I know not whither, without mother or sister to attend me, can I expect to survive it all?**"**

Only a month later, she recorded that

"in the afternoon we rode thirty-five miles without stopping. Pretty well tired out, all of us. Stood it pretty well myself.**"**

homes from the very sod they dug from the ground and burned corncobs for warmth.

Lured by higher wheat prices resulting from crop failures elsewhere in the world, settlers in the 1870s rashly pushed still farther west, onto the poor, marginal lands beyond the 100th meridian. That imaginary line, running north to south from the Dakotas through west Texas, separated two climatological regions—a well-watered area to the east, and a semiarid area to the west (see Map 26.4). Bewhiskered and one-armed geologist John Wesley Powell, explorer of the Colorado River's Grand Canyon and director of the U.S. Geological Survey, warned in 1874 that beyond the 100th meridian so little rain fell that agriculture was impossible without massive irrigation.

Ignoring Powell's advice, farmers heedlessly chewed up the crusty earth in western Kansas, eastern Colorado, and Montana. They quickly went broke as a six-year drought in the 1880s further desiccated the already dusty region. Western Kansas lost half its population between 1888 and 1892. "There is no God west of Salina," one hapless homesteader declared.

In the wake of the devastating drought, the new technique of "dry farming" took root on the plains. Its methods of frequent shallow cultivation supposedly were adapted to the arid western environment, but over time "dry farming" created a finely pulverized surface soil that contributed to the notorious "Dust Bowl" several decades later (see p. 764).

Other adaptations to the western environment were more successful. Tough strains of wheat, resistant to cold and drought, were imported from Russia and blossomed into billowing yellow carpets. Wise farmers abandoned corn in favor of sorghum and other drought-resistant grains. Barbed wire, perfected by Joseph F. Glidden in 1874, solved the problem of how to build fences on the treeless prairies.

Eventually federally financed irrigation projects—on a colossal scale, beyond even what John Wesley Powell had dreamed—caused the Great American Desert to bloom. A century after Powell's predictions, arching dams had tamed the Missouri and Columbia Rivers and had so penned up and diverted the canyon-gnawing Colorado that its mouth in the Gulf of California was dry. More than 45 million acres were irrigated in seventeen western states. In the long run, the hydraulic engineers had more to do with shaping the modern West than all the trappers, miners, cavalrymen, and cowboys ever did (see Map 26.5). As one engineer boasted, "We enjoy pushing rivers around."

✦ The Far West Comes of Age

The Great West experienced a fantastic surge in migration from the 1870s to the 1890s. A parade of new western states proudly joined the Union. Boomtown Colorado, offspring of the Pikes Peak gold rush, was

The Homesteader's Wife, by Harvey Dunn   Women as well as men toiled without shade or respite on the sun-scorched and wind-parched Great Plains.

The South Dakota Art Museum

MAP 26.4 Average Annual Precipitation, with Major Agricultural Products, 1900
Northern Hemisphere storms typically circle the globe in a west-to-east direction. Much of the life-nourishing water in these storms is dumped as rainfall on the western slopes of the Pacific coastal ranges and the Rocky Mountains, casting huge "rain shadows" in the Great Basin and in the western Great Plains, up to the line of the 100th meridian. Westward-faring pioneers had to learn new agricultural techniques when they pushed settlement into the drought-prone regions west of the 100th meridian, as reflected in the patterns of crop distribution by 1900. © Cengage Learning

greeted in 1876 as "the Centennial State." In 1889–1890 a Republican Congress, eagerly seeking more Republican electoral and congressional votes, admitted in a wholesale lot six new states: North Dakota, South Dakota, Montana, Washington, Idaho, and Wyoming. The Mormon Church formally—and belatedly, in many Americans' eyes—banned polygamy in 1890, but not until 1896 was Utah deemed worthy of admission. Only Oklahoma, New Mexico, and Arizona remained to be lifted into statehood from contiguous territory on the mainland of North America.

In a last gaudy fling, the federal government made available to settlers vast stretches of fertile plains formerly occupied by the Indians in the district of Oklahoma ("the Beautiful Land"). Scores of overeager and well-armed "sooners," illegally jumping the gun, had entered Oklahoma Territory. They had to be evicted repeatedly by federal troops, who on occasion would shoot the intruders' horses. On April 22, 1889, all was in readiness for the legal opening, and some 50,000 "boomers" were poised expectantly on the boundary line. At high noon the bugle shrilled, and a horde of "eighty-niners" poured in on lathered horses or careening vehicles. That night a lonely spot on the prairie had mushroomed into the tent city of Guthrie, with over 10,000 people. By the end of the year, Oklahoma boasted 60,000 inhabitants, and Congress made it a territory. In 1907 it became the "Sooner State."

✴ The Fading Frontier

In 1890—a watershed date—the superintendent of the census announced that for the first time in America's experience, a frontier line was no longer discernible. All the unsettled areas were now broken into by isolated

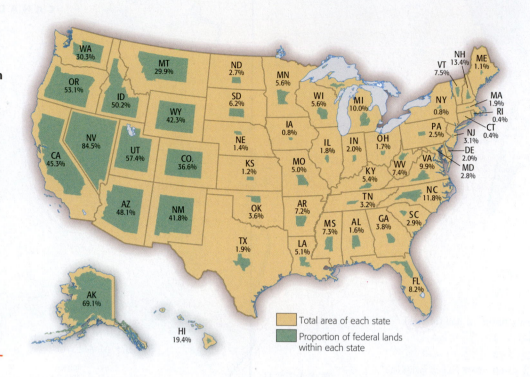

MAP 26.5 Myth and Reality in the West: Percentage of Federal Lands Within Each State, 2004 American folklore pictures the western United States as a land of rugged individualists who tamed the wild region with grit and brawn. The reality is that the federal government has long been by far the West's largest landowner—and that federal projects, especially dam building, have done more to shape the region than all the cowboys and sodbusters there ever were. (Source: Bill Lane Center for the American West, Stanford University.)

© Cengage Learning

Total area of each state

Proportion of federal lands within each state

bodies of American settlement. The "closing" of the frontier inspired one of the most influential essays ever written about American history—Frederick Jackson Turner's "The Significance of the Frontier in American History" in 1893 (see "Thinking Globally: The Great Frontier," pp. 592–593).

As the nineteenth century neared its sunset, the westward-tramping American people were disturbed to find that their fabled free land was going or had gone. The secretary of war had prophesied in 1827 that five hundred years would be needed to fill the West. But as the nation finally recognized that its land was not inexhaustible, seeds were planted to preserve the vanishing resource. The government set aside land for national parks—first Yellowstone in 1872, followed by Yosemite and Sequoia in 1890.

But the frontier was more than a place; it was also a state of mind and a symbol of opportunity. Its passing ended a romantic phase of the nation's internal development and created new economic and psychological problems.

Traditionally footloose, Americans have been notorious for their mobility. The nation's farmers, unlike the peasants of Europe, have seldom remained rooted to their soil. The land, sold for a profit as settlement closed in, was often the settler's most profitable crop.

Much has been said about the frontier as a "safety valve." The theory is that when hard times came, the unemployed who cluttered the city pavements merely moved west, took up farming, and prospered.

In truth, relatively few city dwellers, at least in the populous eastern centers, migrated to the frontier during depressions. Most of them did not know how to farm; few of them could raise enough money to transport themselves west and then pay for livestock and expensive machinery.

But the safety-valve theory does have some validity. Free acreage did lure to the West a host of immigrant farmers who otherwise might have remained in the eastern cities to clog the job markets and to crowd the festering and already overpopulated slums. And the very *possibility* of westward migration may have induced urban employers to maintain wage rates high enough to discourage workers from leaving. But the real safety valve by the late nineteenth century was in western cities like Chicago, Denver, and San Francisco, where failed farmers, busted miners, and displaced easterners found ways to seek their fortunes. Indeed, after about 1880 the area from the Rocky Mountains to the Pacific Coast was the most urbanized region in America, measured by the percentage of people living in cities.

U.S. history cannot be properly understood unless it is viewed in light of the westward-moving experience. As Frederick Jackson Turner wrote, "American history has been in a large degree the history of the colonization of the Great West." The story of settling and taming the trans-Mississippi West in the late nineteenth century was but the last chapter in the saga of colonizing various American "wests" since Columbus's

Robert Louis Stevenson's Transcontinental Journey, 1879

The celebrated Scottish writer Robert Louis Stevenson, author of such enduring classics as *Treasure Island*, *Kidnapped*, and *The Strange Case of Dr. Jekyll and Mr. Hyde*, journeyed from Scotland to California in 1879 to rendezvous with his American fiancée, Frances Osbourne. Between New York and San Francisco, Stevenson traveled on the transcontinental railroad line completed just ten years earlier, and he dutifully recorded his impressions of America, the West in particular, as he made his way toward California. Stevenson's account of his trip provides an unusually gifted writer's vivid portrait of the trans-Mississippi West at the close of the era of the Indian wars. Like all travelogues, Stevenson's colorful tale may reveal as much about the traveler as it does about the things he saw. Yet historians frequently make use of such documents to reconstruct the original appearance and texture of places that were once the exotic destinations of adventurous travelers, before they were transformed by the onrush of modernity. In the passages reproduced here, inspired by the view as Stevenson's train passed through Nebraska and Wyoming, what features of the landscape does the author find most remarkable? How does he portray the railroad?

Source: Robert Louis Stevenson, *Across the Plains* (New York: Charles Scribner's Sons, 1897).

THE PLAINS OF NEBRASKA

. . . We were at sea—there is no other adequate expression—on the plains of Nebraska. . . . It was a world almost without a feature; an empty sky, an empty earth; front and back, the line of railway stretched from horizon to horizon, like a cue across a billiard-board; on either hand, the green plain ran till it touched the skirts of heaven. . . . [G]razing beasts were seen upon the prairie at all degrees of distance and diminution; and now and again we might perceive a few dots beside the railroad which grew more and more distinct as we drew nearer till they turned into wooden cabins, and then dwindled and dwindled in our wake until they melted into their surroundings, and we were once more alone upon the billiard-board. The train toiled over this infinity like a snail; and being the one thing moving, it was wonderful what huge proportions it began to assume in our regard. . . .

[That] evening we left Laramie [Wyoming]. . . . And yet when day came, it was to shine upon the same broken and unsightly quarter of the world. Mile upon mile, and not a tree, a bird, or a river. Only down the long, sterile cañons, the train shot hooting and awoke the resting echo. That train was the one piece of life in all the deadly land; it was the one actor, the one spectacle fit to be observed in this paralysis of man and nature. And when I think how the railroad has been pushed through this unwatered wilderness and haunt of savage tribes, and now will bear an emigrant for some £12 from the Atlantic to the Golden Gates; how at each stage of the construction, roaring, impromptu cities, full of gold and lust and death, sprang up and then died away again, and are now but wayside stations in the desert; how in these uncouth places pig-tailed Chinese pirates worked side by side with border ruffians and broken men from Europe, talking together in a mixed dialect, mostly oaths, gambling, drinking, quarrelling and murdering like wolves; how the plumed hereditary lord of all America heard, in this last fastness, the scream of the 'bad medicine waggon' charioting his foes; and then when I go on to remember that all this epical turmoil was conducted by gentlemen in frock coats, and with a view to nothing more extraordinary than a fortune and a subsequent visit to Paris, it seems to me, I own, as if this railway were the one typical achievement of the age in which we live, as if it brought together into one plot all the ends of the world and all the degrees of social rank, and offered to some great writer the busiest, the most extended, and the most varied subject for an enduring literary work. . . .

The Great Frontier

The American pioneers who surged westward in the nineteenth century were part of a great global land grab that changed lives and landscapes on several continents. From the Australian Outback to the Canadian prairies, from the Argentine pampas to the Russian steppes and the African savannas, millions of mostly white settlers poured into vast new territories and claimed them as their own.

Everywhere, the settlers encountered indigenous peoples who had lived on those lands since time immemorial. With their superiority in weaponry, transportation, and political organization, everywhere the newcomers prevailed. By the century's close, they had displaced or destroyed countless native peoples and extended their dominion over parts of the planet once considered too remote or rugged to be habitable.

The American frontier soon became the stuff of legend, and even the subject of a scholarly explanation of American uniqueness—Frederick Jackson Turner's fabled "frontier thesis," which hailed the gumption and moxie of the pioneers and commended them as the agents of civilization and democracy. Yet far from being unique, those westering Americans had much in common with settlers in sister societies abroad. Argentina had its cowboys (gauchos), and Australia had its colorful backcountry outlaws, such as Ned Kelly, whose exploits rivaled those of Billy the Kid. The Russians and South Africans had their own versions of "Manifest Destiny," and like the Americans they often cloaked them in the language of racial superiority.

The world's various frontiers also reflected the particularities of geography and history. Australians soon conceded that much of their continent—the world's driest—was too arid for traditional farming. Most of the Outback proved suitable only for enormous "sheep stations," sometimes measuring tens of thousands of acres. Consequently, small-farm homesteading of the American and Canadian type never took root, nor did cities of any consequence emerge in the parched Australian interior.

Canada's westward movement came later than that in the United States and proceeded more peaceably. Only after

Royal Canadian Mounted Police

North-West Mounted Police, ca. 1890   Empowered by an act of Parliament in 1873 to establish Canadian authority and order in the Northwest Territories, this force made frontier settlement somewhat more peaceful in Canada than in the United States. In 1920 the North-West Mounted Police absorbed the Dominion Police and became the famed Royal Canadian Mounted Police, or "Mounties."

Russian Peasants in Siberia, 1910

the Ottawa government promised in 1871 to build a transcontinental railroad connecting eastern Canada to its western provinces did settlement begin in earnest. And unlike in America, where restless pioneers typically struck out on their own and made much mischief among themselves and with the Indians they encountered, in Canada settlers were generally preceded by government authorities—usually the red-jacketed North-West Mounted Police, or "Mounties"—who established at least a semblance of order before large numbers of pioneers appeared on the scene. As a result, Canada's frontier was markedly less violent than America's. Canada, then and now a more law-abiding society than the United States, never had a "Wild West" like that of its southern neighbor.

In Argentina and Russia, inherited patterns of landholding and politics shaped their nineteenth-century frontiers. When Argentina's General Julio Roca vanquished the native Araucanians in 1879, he flung open the horizonless pampas to white settlement. But he also retained the venerable custom, handed down from Spanish colonial times, of apportioning the land in gigantic *estancias* (ranches) to a few favored fellow soldiers and friends. These lordly landowners then employed wage workers, mostly Italian immigrants, who turned the fertile Argentine interior into a beef bowl and breadbasket to the world. The immigrants themselves, however, had little hope of ever possessing land of their own.

Russia's frontier lay to the east and long felt the heavy hand of the tsar. For centuries autocratic rulers had strong-armed landowning nobles to move their serfs onto the "virgin lands" beyond the settled edge of European Russia. By the nineteenth century, imperial Russia had pushed its frontier onto the rolling steppes of central Asia, home to Tartars, Kalmyks, Kazakhs, and myriad other indigenous peoples. Only military conquest and a strengthened state bureaucracy made possible European settlement in those regions. Between 1867 and 1897, more than a million of the tsar's subjects left for the hinterland. As elsewhere, the railroad proved essential to the growth of the tsarist empire, especially after the government began construction of the Trans-Siberian line in 1891.

The Dutch-descended Afrikaners, or Boers, in southern Africa found their frontier to the north, and unlike their American counterparts, they made scant claim to be spreading democracy. Rather, they sought to escape British rule in the Cape Colony—in particular, to escape from the threat of racial equality for blacks after Britain abolished slavery in the 1830s. The Afrikaners' "Great Trek" took them into the land of the Zulus, who ferociously resisted the oncoming Boers but eventually, like indigenous peoples everywhere, were forced to submit to white rule.

In the Americas, Australia, Asia, and Africa, the great frontier of the nineteenth century was the companion of conquest. The frontier brought opportunity to some and oppression to others. In many places it nurtured democracy; elsewhere it invigorated autocracy. And everywhere it expanded the domains of European civilization—for better or worse.

day—from the West Indies to the Chesapeake shore, from the valleys of the Hudson and Connecticut Rivers to the valleys of the Tennessee and Ohio Rivers.

And yet the trans-Mississippi West formed a distinct chapter in that saga and retains even to this day much of its uniqueness. There the Native American peoples waged their last and most desperate struggle against colonization, and there most Native Americans live today. There "Anglo" culture collided most directly with Hispanic culture—the historic rival of the Anglo-Americans for dominance in the New World—and the Southwest remains the most Hispanicized region in America. There America faced across the Pacific to Asia, and there most Asian Americans dwell today. There the scale and severity of the environment posed their largest challenges to human ambitions, and there the environment, with its aridity and still-magical emptiness, continues to mold social and political life, and the American imagination, as in no other part of the nation. And in no other region has the federal government, with its vast landholdings, its subsidies to the railroads, and its massive irrigation projects, played so conspicuous a role in economic and social development.

The westward-moving pioneers and the country they confronted have assumed mythic proportions in the American mind. They have been immortalized by such writers as Bret Harte, Mark Twain, Helen Hunt Jackson, and Francis Parkman, and by such painters as George Catlin, Frederic Remington, and Albert Bierstadt. For better or worse, those pioneers planted the seeds of American civilization in the immense western wilderness. The life we live, they dreamed of; the life they lived, we can only dream.

✦ The Farm Becomes a Factory

The situation of American farmers, once jacks-and-jills-of-all-trades, was rapidly changing. They had raised their own food, fashioned their own clothing, and bartered for other necessities with neighbors. Now high prices persuaded farmers to concentrate on growing single "cash" crops, such as wheat or corn, and use their profits to buy foodstuffs at the general store and manufactured goods in town or by mail order. The Chicago firm of Aaron Montgomery Ward sent out its first catalogue—a single sheet—in 1872. Farmers were becoming both consumers and producers in the world economy, as their crops journeyed by rail and ship to distant parts of the globe.

Large-scale farmers, especially in the immense grain-producing areas of the Mississippi Valley, were now both specialists and businesspeople. As cogs in the vast industrial machine, these farmers were intimately tied to banking, railroading, and manufacturing. They had to buy expensive machinery in order to plant and harvest their crops. A powerful steam engine could drag behind it simultaneously the plow, seeder, and harrow. The speed of harvesting wheat was dramatically increased in the 1870s by the invention of the twine binder and then in the 1880s by the "combine"—the combined reaper-thresher, which was drawn by twenty to forty horses and which both reaped and bagged the grain. Widespread use of such costly equipment naturally called for first-class management. But the farmers, often unskilled as businesspeople, were inclined to blame the banks and railroads or the volatility of the global marketplace, rather than their own shortcomings, for their losses.

This amazing **mechanization of agriculture** in the postwar years was almost as striking as the mechanization of industry. In fact, agricultural modernization drove many marginal farmers off the land, thus swelling the ranks of the new industrial work force. As the

Picture Research Consultants & Archives

Grain Harvesting in Washington State Humans, horses, and machines join forces in this turn-of-the-century scene.

rural population steadily decreased, those farmers who remained achieved miracles of production, making America the world's breadbasket and butcher shop. The farm was attaining the status of a factory—an outdoor grain factory. Bonanza wheat farms of the Minnesota–North Dakota area, for example, were enormous. By 1890 at least a half-dozen of them were larger than fifteen thousand acres, with communication by telephone from one part to another. These bonanza farms foreshadowed the gigantic agribusinesses of the next century.

Agriculture was a big business from its earliest days in California's phenomenally productive (and phenomenally irrigated) Central Valley. California farms, carved out of giant Spanish Mexican land grants and the railroads' huge holdings, were from the outset more than three times larger than the national average. The reformer Henry George in 1871 described the Golden State as "not a country of farms but a country of plantations and estates." With the advent of the railroad refrigerator car in the 1880s, California fruit and vegetable crops, raised on sprawling tracts by ill-paid migrant Mexican and Chinese farmhands, sold at a handsome profit in the rich urban markets of the East.

✴ Deflation Dooms the Debtor

Once the farmers became chained to a one-crop economy—wheat or corn—they were in the same leaky boat with the southern cotton growers. As long as prices stayed high, all went well. But when they skidded in the 1880s, bankruptcy fell like a blight on the farm belts.

The grain farmers were no longer the masters of their own destinies. They were engaged in one of the most fiercely competitive of businesses, for the price of their product was determined in a world market by the world output. If the wheat fields of Argentina, Russia, and other foreign countries flourished, the price of the farmers' grain would fall and American sodbusters would face ruin, as they did in the 1880s and 1890s.

Low prices and a deflated currency were the chief worries of the frustrated farmers—North, South, and West. If a family had borrowed $1,000 in 1855, when wheat was worth about a dollar a bushel, they expected to pay back the equivalent of one thousand bushels, plus interest, when the mortgage fell due. But if they let their debt run to 1890, when wheat had fallen to about fifty cents a bushel, they would have to pay back the price of two thousand bushels for the $1,000 they had borrowed, plus interest. This unexpected burden struck them as unjust, though their steely-eyed creditors often branded the complaining farmers as slippery and dishonest rascals.

The deflationary pinch on the debtor flowed partly from the static money supply. There were simply not

enough dollars to go around, and as a result, prices were forced down. In 1870 the currency in circulation for each person was $19.42; in 1890 it was only $22.67. Yet during these twenty years, business and industrial activity, increasing manyfold, had intensified the scramble for available currency.

The forgotten farmers were caught on a treadmill. Despite unremitting toil, they operated year after year at a loss and lived off their fat as best they could. In a vicious circle, their farm machinery increased their output of grain, lowered the price, and drove them even deeper into debt. Mortgages engulfed homesteads at an alarming rate; by 1890 Nebraska alone reported more than 100,000 farms blanketed with mortgages. The repeated crash of the sheriff-auctioneer's hammer kept announcing to the world that another sturdy American farmer had become landless in a landed nation.

Ruinous rates of interest, running from 8 to 40 percent, were charged on mortgages, largely by agents of eastern loan companies. The windburned sons and daughters of the sod, who felt that they deserved praise for developing the country, cried out in despair against the loan sharks and the Wall Street octopus.

Farm tenancy rather than farm ownership was spreading like stinkweed. The trend was especially marked in the sharecropping South, where cotton prices also sank dismayingly. By 1880 one-fourth of all American farms were operated by tenants. The United States was ready to feed the world, but under the new industrial feudalism, the farmers were about to sink into a status suggesting Old World serfdom.

✴ Unhappy Farmers

Even Mother Nature ceased smiling, as her powerful forces conspired against agriculture. Mile-wide clouds of grasshoppers, leaving "nothing but the mortgage," periodically ravaged prairie farms. The terrible cotton-boll weevil was also wreaking havoc in the South by the early 1890s.

The good earth was going sour. Floods added to the waste of erosion, which had already washed the topsoil off millions of once-lush southern acres. Expensive fertilizers were urgently needed. A long succession of

Nebraska Homesteaders in Front of Their Sod House, 1887 These two brothers and their families had escaped to Canada from the slave South during the Civil War. Returning to the United States in the 1880s, they took advantage of the Homestead Act to stake out farms in Custer County, Nebraska.

droughts seared the trans-Mississippi West, beginning in the summer of 1887. Whole towns were abandoned. "Going home to the wife's folks" and "In God we trusted, in Kansas we busted" were typical laments of many impoverished farmers, as they fled their weather-beaten shacks and sun-baked sod houses. One irate "poet" snarled,

> Fifty miles to water,
> A hundred miles to wood,
> To hell with this damned country,
> I'm going home for good.

To add to their miseries, the soil-tillers were gouged by their government—local, state, and national. Their land was overassessed, and they paid painful local taxes, whereas wealthy easterners could conceal their stocks and bonds in safe-deposit boxes. High protective tariffs in these years poured profits into the pockets of manufacturers. Farmers, on the other hand, had no choice but to sell their low-priced products in a fiercely competitive, unprotected world market, while buying high-priced manufactured goods in a protected home market.

The farmers were also "farmed" by the corporations and processors. They were at the mercy of the harvester trust, the barbed-wire trust, and the fertilizer trust, all of which could control output and raise prices to extortionate levels. Middlemen took a juicy "cut" from the selling price of the goods that the farmers bought, while operators pushed storage rates to the ceiling at grain warehouses and elevators.

In addition, the railroad octopus had the grain growers in its grip. Freight rates could be so high that the farmers sometimes lost less if they burned their corn for fuel than if they shipped it. If they raised their voices in protest, the ruthless railroad operators might let their grain spoil in damp places or refuse to provide them with cars when needed.

Farmers still made up nearly one-half the population in 1890, but they were hopelessly disorganized. The manufacturers and the railroad barons knew how to combine to promote their interests, and so, increasingly, did industrial workers. But the farmers were by nature independent and individualistic—dead set against consolidation or regimentation. No really effective Carnegie or Gompers arose among them to preach the gospel of economic integration and concentration. They never did organize successfully to restrict production until forced to by the federal government nearly half a century later, in Franklin Roosevelt's New Deal days. What they did manage to organize was a monumental political uprising.

★ The Farmers Take Their Stand

Agrarian unrest had flared forth earlier, in the Greenback movement shortly after the Civil War. Prices sagged in 1868, and a host of farmers unsuccessfully sought relief from low prices and high indebtedness by demanding an inflation of the currency with paper money.

The National Grange of the Patrons of Husbandry—better known as the Grange—was organized in 1867. Its leading spirit was Oliver H. Kelley, a shrewd and energetic Minnesota farmer then working as a clerk in Washington. Kelley's first objective was to enhance the lives of isolated farmers through social, educational, and fraternal activities. Farm men and women, cursed with loneliness in widely separated farmhouses, found the Grange's picnics, concerts, and lectures a godsend. Kelley, a Mason, even found farmers receptive to his mumbo-jumbo of passwords and secret rituals, as well as his four-ply hierarchy, ranging (for men) from Laborer to Husbandman and (for women) from Maid to

Matron. The Grange spread like an old-time prairie fire and by 1875 claimed 800,000 members, chiefly in the Midwest and South. Buzzing with gossip, these calicoed and callous folk often met in red schoolhouses around potbellied stoves.

The Grangers gradually raised their goals from individual self-improvement to improvement of the farmers' collective plight. In a determined effort to escape the clutches of the trusts, they established cooperatively owned stores for consumers and cooperatively owned grain elevators and warehouses for producers. Their most ambitious experiment was an attempt to manufacture harvesting machinery, but this venture, partly as a result of mismanagement, ended in financial disaster.

Embattled Grangers also went into politics, enjoying their most gratifying success in the grain-growing regions of the upper Mississippi Valley, chiefly in Illinois, Wisconsin, Iowa, and Minnesota. There, through state legislation, they strove to regulate railway rates and the storage fees charged by railroads and by the operators of warehouses and grain elevators. Many of the state courts, notably in Illinois, were disposed to recognize the principle of public control of private business for the general welfare. A number of the so-called Granger Laws, however, were badly drawn, and they were bitterly fought through the high courts by the well-paid lawyers of the "interests." Following judicial reverses, most severely at the hands of the Supreme Court in the famous *Wabash* decision of 1886 (see p. 519), the Grangers' influence faded. But their organization has lived on as a vocal champion of farm interests, while brightening rural life with social activities.

Farmers' grievances likewise found a vent in the Greenback Labor party, which combined the inflationary appeal of the earlier Greenbackers with a program for improving the lot of labor. In 1878, the high-water mark of the movement, the Greenback Laborites polled

Granger Collection

The Farmers' Grievances   This poster from 1875 expresses one of the agrarian radicals' fundamental premises: that all other walks of life were dependent—or even parasitic—on the indispensable work of farmers. In his famous "Cross of Gold" speech in 1896 (see p. 601), Populist presidential candidate William Jennings Bryan put it this way: "Burn down your cities and leave our farms, and your cities will spring up again as if by magic; but destroy our farms and the grass will grow in the streets of every city in the country."

over a million votes and elected fourteen members of Congress. In the presidential election of 1880, the Greenbackers ran General James B. Weaver, an old Granger who was a favorite of Civil War veterans and who possessed a remarkable voice and bearing. He spoke to perhaps half a million citizens in a hundred or so speeches but polled only 3 percent of the total popular vote.

⭐ Prelude to Populism

A striking manifestation of rural discontent came through the Farmers' Alliance, founded in Texas in the late 1870s (see p. 505). Farmers came together in the Alliance to socialize, but more importantly to break the strangling grip of the railroads and manufacturers through cooperative buying and selling. Local chapters spread throughout the South and the Great Plains during the 1880s, until by 1890 members numbered more than a million hard-bitten souls.

Unfortunately, the Alliance weakened itself by ignoring the plight of landless tenant farmers, sharecroppers, and farmworkers. Even more debilitating was the Alliance's exclusion of blacks, who counted for nearly half the agricultural population of the South. In the 1880s a separate Colored Farmers' National Alliance emerged to attract black farmers, and by 1890 membership numbered more than 250,000. The long history of racial division in the South, however, made it difficult for white and black farmers to work together in the same organization.

Out of the Farmers' Alliances a new political party emerged in the early 1890s—the People's party. Better known as the **Populists**, these frustrated farmers attacked Wall Street and the "money trust." They called for nationalizing the railroads, telephone, and telegraph; instituting a graduated income tax; and creating a new federal "subtreasury"—a scheme to provide farmers with loans for crops stored in government-owned warehouses, where they could be held until market prices rose. They also wanted the free and unlimited coinage of silver—yet another of the debtors' demands for inflation that echoed continuously throughout the Gilded Age.

Numerous fiery prophets leapt forward to trumpet the Populist cause. The free coinage of silver struck many Populists as a cure-all, especially after the circulation of an enormously popular pamphlet titled *Coin's Financial School* (1894). Written by William Hope Harvey, it was illustrated by clever woodcuts, one of which depicted the gold ogre beheading the beautiful silver maiden. In fiction parading as fact, the booklet showed how the "little professor"—"Coin" Harvey—overwhelmed the bankers and professors of economics with his brilliant arguments on behalf of free silver. Another notorious spellbinder was red-haired Ignatius Donnelly of Minnesota, three times elected to Congress. The queen of the Populist "calamity howlers" was Mary Elizabeth ("Mary Yellin'") Lease, a tall, athletic woman known as the "Kansas Pythoness." She reportedly demanded that Kansans should raise "less corn and more hell." The big-city *New York Evening Post* snarled, "We don't want any more states until we can civilize Kansas." To many easterners, complaint, not corn, was rural America's staple crop.

Yet the Populists, despite their oddities, were not to be laughed away. They were leading a deadly earnest and impassioned campaign to relieve the farmers' many miseries. Smiles faded from Republican and Democratic faces alike as countless thousands of Populists began to sing "Good-bye, My Party, Good-bye." In 1892 the Populists had jolted the traditional parties by winning several congressional seats and polling more than 1 million votes for their presidential candidate, James B. Weaver. Racial divisions continued to hobble the Populists in the South, but in the West their ranks were swelling. Could the People's party now reach beyond its regional bases in agrarian America, join hands with

Kansas State Historical Society

Mary E. Lease (1853–1933)   She was so eloquent as to be called the "Patrick Henry in Petticoats."

urban workers, and mount a successful attack on the northeastern citadels of power?

⭐ Coxey's Army and the Pullman Strike

The panic of 1893 and the severe ensuing depression strengthened the Populists' argument that farmers and laborers alike were being victimized by an oppressive economic and political system. Ragged armies of the unemployed began marching to protest their plight. In the growing hordes of displaced industrial toilers, the Populists saw potential political allies.

The most famous marcher was "General" Jacob S. Coxey, a wealthy Ohio quarry owner. He set out for Washington in 1894 with a few score of supporters and a swarm of newspaper reporters. His platform included a demand that the government relieve unemployment by an inflationary public works program, supported by some $500 million in legal tender notes to be issued by the Treasury. Coxey himself rode in a carriage with his wife and infant son, appropriately named Legal Tender Coxey, while his tiny "army" tramped along behind, singing,

> We're coming, Grover Cleveland,
> 500,000 strong,
> We're marching on to Washington
> to right the nation's wrong.

The "Commonweal Army" of Coxeyites finally straggled into the nation's capital, but the invasion took on the aspects of a comic opera when "General" Coxey and his "lieutenants" were arrested for walking on the grass.

Elsewhere, violent flare-ups accompanied labor protests, notably in Chicago. Most dramatic was the crippling **Pullman strike** of 1894. Eugene V. Debs, a charismatic labor leader, had helped organize the American Railway Union of about 150,000 members. The Pullman Palace Car Company, which maintained a model town near Chicago for its employees, was hit hard by the depression and cut wages by about one-third, while holding the line on rent for the company houses. The workers finally struck—in some places overturning Pullman cars—and paralyzed railway traffic from Chicago to the Pacific coast. The American Federation of Labor conspicuously declined to support the Pullman strikers, thus enhancing the AF of L's reputation for "respectability" even while weakening labor's cause by driving a large wedge into the workers' ranks.

The turmoil in Chicago was serious but not yet completely out of hand. At least this was the judgment of Governor John Peter Altgeld of Illinois, a friend of the downtrodden, who had pardoned the Haymarket

After the Pullman strike collapsed, Eugene Debs (1855–1926) said,

❝No strike has ever been lost.❞

In 1897 he declared,

❝The issue is Socialism versus Capitalism. I am for Socialism because I am for humanity.❞

Square anarchists the year before (see p. 533). But U.S. attorney general Richard Olney, an archconservative and an ex–railroad attorney, urged the dispatch of federal troops. His legal grounds were that the strikers were interfering with the transit of the U.S. mail. President Cleveland supported Olney with the ringing declaration, "If it takes the entire army and navy to deliver a postal card in Chicago, that card will be delivered."

To the delight of conservatives, federal troops, bayonets fixed, crushed the Pullman strike. Debs was sentenced to six months' imprisonment for contempt

William B. Becker Collection/American Museum of Photography

Coxey's Army on the March, 1894   This photograph shows two of the banners that Coxey's Army carried. The one in the foreground says "Death to Interest on Bonds," the usual debtors' protest against creditors. The larger one in the background reads "Pittsburg & Allegheny. Work for Americans. More Money, Less Misery, Good Roads," a reference to Coxey's plan to end the depression by employing the jobless to build public works and paying them with greenbacks.

The Pullman Strike, 1894
Illinois National Guardsmen fire on Pullman Company strikers on July 7, 1894. Police clubs and U.S. Army rifles and bayonets finally broke the back of the strike, which halted railroads throughout the country.

Granger Collection

of court because he had defied a federal court injunction to cease striking. Ironically, the lean labor agitator spent much of his enforced leisure reading radical literature, which led to his later leadership of the socialist movement in America.

Embittered cries of "government by injunction" now burst from organized labor. This was the first time that such a legal weapon had been used conspicuously by Washington to break a strike, and it was all the more distasteful because defiant workers who were held in contempt could be imprisoned without a jury trial. Signs multiplied that employers were striving to smash labor unions by court action. Nonlabor elements of the country, including the Populists and other debtors, were likewise incensed. They saw in the brutal Pullman episode further proof of an unholy alliance between business and the courts.

✶ Golden McKinley and Silver Bryan

The smoldering grievances of the long-suffering farmers and the depression-plagued laborers gave ominous significance to the election of 1896. Conservatives of all stripes feared an impending upheaval, while down-and-out husbandmen and discontented workers cast about desperately for political salvation. Increasingly, monetary policy—whether to maintain the gold standard or inflate the currency by monetizing silver—loomed as the issue on which the election would turn.

The leading candidate for the Republican presidential nomination in 1896 was former congressman William McKinley of Ohio, sponsor of the ill-starred tariff bill of 1890 (see p. 601). He had established a creditable Civil War record, having risen to the rank of major; he hailed from the electorally potent state of Ohio; and he could point to long years of honorable service in Congress, where he had made many friends with his kindly and conciliatory manner.

As a presidential candidate, McKinley was largely the creature of a fellow Ohioan, Marcus Alonzo Hanna, who had made his fortune in the iron business and now coveted the role of president maker. "I love McKinley," he once said. As a wholehearted Hamiltonian, Hanna believed that a prime function of government was to aid business. Honest, earnest, tough, and direct, he became the personification of big industry in politics. He was often caricatured in cartoons, quite unfairly, as a bloated bully in a loud checkered suit with a dollar sign in each square. He believed that in some measure prosperity "trickled down" to the laborer, whose dinner pail was full when business flourished. Critics assailed this idea as equivalent to feeding the horses in order to feed the sparrows.

The hardheaded Hanna, although something of a novice in politics, organized his preconvention campaign for McKinley with consummate skill and with a liberal outpouring of his own money. The convention steamroller, well lubricated with Hanna's dollars, nominated McKinley on the first ballot in St. Louis in June 1896. The Republican platform cleverly straddled the money question but leaned toward hard-money policies. It declared for the gold standard, even though McKinley's voting record in Congress had been embarrassingly friendly to silver. The platform also condemned hard times and Democratic incapacity, while pouring praise on the protective tariff.

Dissension riddled the Democratic camp. Cleveland no longer led his party. The depression had driven the last nail into his political coffin. Dubbed "the Stuffed Prophet," he was undeniably the most unpopular man in the country. Labor-debtor groups remembered too vividly his intervention in the Pullman strike, the backstairs Morgan bond deal, and especially his stubborn hard-money policies. Ultraconservative in finance, Cleveland now looked more like a Republican than a Democrat on the money issue.

Rudderless, the Democratic convention met in Chicago in July 1896, with the silverites lusting for victory.

Crying for Protection, 1896 Uncle Sam is called on in this cartoon to nurse so-called infant industries—some of which had in fact long since grown into vigorous adulthood.

McKinley Campaign Headquarters, Chicago, 1896 Those few black Americans who could exercise their right to vote in the 1890s still remained faithful to "the party of Lincoln."

Shouting insults at the absent Cleveland, the delegates refused, by a suicidal vote of 564 to 357, to endorse their own administration. They had the enthusiasm and the numbers; all they lacked was a leader.

A new Moses suddenly appeared in the person of William Jennings Bryan of Nebraska. Then only thirty-six years of age and known as "the Boy Orator of the Platte,"* he stepped confidently onto the platform before fifteen thousand people. His masterful presence was set off by a peninsular jaw and raven-black hair. He radiated honesty, sincerity, and energy.

The convention-hall setting was made to order for a magnificent oratorical effort. A hush fell over the delegates as Bryan stood before them. With an organlike voice that rolled into the outer corners of the huge hall, he delivered a fervent plea for silver. Rising to supreme heights of eloquence, he thundered, "We will answer their demands for a gold standard by saying to them: 'You shall not press down upon the brow of labor this crown of thorns, you shall not crucify mankind upon a cross of gold.'"

---

*One contemporary sneered that Bryan, like the Platte River in his home state of Nebraska, was "six inches deep and six miles wide at the mouth."

The Cross of Gold speech was a sensation. Swept off its feet in a tumultuous scene, the Democratic convention nominated Bryan the next day on the fifth ballot. The platform demanded inflation through the unlimited coinage of silver at the ratio of 16 ounces of silver to 1 of gold, though the market ratio was about 32 to 1. This meant that the silver in a dollar would be worth about fifty cents.

Democratic "Gold Bugs," unable to swallow Bryan, bolted their party over the silver issue. A conservative senator from New York, when asked if he was a Democrat still, reportedly replied, "Yes, I am a Democrat still—very still." The Democratic minority, including Cleveland, charged that the Populist-silverites had stolen both the name and the clothes of their party. They nominated a lost-cause ticket of their own, and many of them, including Cleveland, not too secretly hoped for a McKinley victory.

The Populists now faced a dilemma, because the Democratic majority had appropriated their main plank—"16 to 1," that "heaven-born ratio." The bulk of the Populists, fearing a hard-money McKinley victory, endorsed both "fusion" with the Democrats and Bryan for president, sacrificing their identity in the mix. Singing "The Jolly Silver Dollar of the Dads," they became in effect the "Demo-Pop" party, though a handful of the original Populists refused to support Bryan and went down with their colors nailed to the mast.

★ Class Conflict: Plowholders Versus Bondholders

Mark Hanna smugly assumed that he could make the tariff the focus of the campaign. But Bryan, a dynamo of energy, forced the free-trade issue into the backseat when he took to the stump in behalf of free silver. Sweeping through 27 states and traveling 18,000 miles, he made nearly 600 speeches—36 in one day—and even invaded the East, "the enemy's country." Vachel Lindsay caught the spirit of his oratorical orgy:

Prairie avenger, mountain lion,
Bryan, Bryan, Bryan, Bryan,
Gigantic troubadour, speaking like a siege gun,
Smashing Plymouth Rock with his boulders
*from the West.**

Free silver became almost as much a religious as a financial issue. Hordes of fanatical free-silverites hailed Bryan as the messiah to lead them out of the wilderness

---

*Reprinted with the permission of Scribner, a division of Simon & Schuster, Inc., from *The Collected Poems of Vachel Lindsay*, Revised Edition by Vachel Lindsay, New York: Macmillan, 1948.

of debt. They sang, "We'll All Have Our Pockets Lined with Silver" and "No Crown of Thorns, No Cross of Gold."

Bryan created panic among eastern conservatives with his threat of converting their holdings overnight into fifty-cent dollars. The "Gold Bugs" responded with their own free and unlimited coinage of verbiage. They vented their alarm in abusive epithets, ranging from "fanatic" and "madman" to "traitor" and "murderer." "In God We Trust, with Bryan We Bust," the Republicans sneered, while one eastern clergyman cried, "That platform was made in Hell." Widespread fear of Bryan and the "silver lunacy" enabled "Dollar Mark" Hanna, now chairman of the Republican National Committee, to shine as a money-raiser. He "shook down" the trusts and plutocrats and piled up an enormous "slush fund" for a "campaign of education"—or of propaganda, depending on one's point of view. Reminding the voters of Cleveland's "Democratic panic," Republicans appealed to the "belly vote" with their prize slogan, "McKinley and the Full Dinner Pail." The McKinleyites amassed the most formidable political campaign chest thus far in American history. At all levels—national, state, and local—it amounted to about $16 million, as contrasted with about $1 million for the poorer Democrats (roughly "16 to 1"). With some justification, the Bryanites accused Hanna of buying the election and of floating McKinley into the White House on a tidal wave of mud and money.

Bryan's cyclonic campaign began to lose steam as the weeks passed. Fear was probably Hanna's strongest ally, as it was Bryan's worst enemy. Republican businesspeople placed contracts with manufacturers, contingent on the election of McKinley. A few factory owners, with thinly veiled intimidation, paid off their workers and told them not to come to work on Wednesday morning if Bryan won. Reports also circulated that employers were threatening to pay their employees in fifty-cent pieces, instead of in dollars, if Bryan triumphed. Such were some of the "dirty tricks" of the "Stop Bryan, Save America" crusade.

Hanna's campaign methods paid off. On election day McKinley triumphed decisively. The vote was 271 to 176 in the Electoral College and 7,102,246 to 6,492,559 in the popular election. Driven by fear and excitement, an unprecedented outpouring of voters flocked to the polls. McKinley ran strongly in the populous East, where he carried every county of New England, and in the upper Mississippi Valley. Bryan's states, concentrated in the debt-burdened South and the trans-Mississippi West, boasted more acreage than McKinley's but less population (see Map 26.6).

The free-silver election of 1896 was perhaps the most significant political turning point since Lincoln's victories in 1860 and 1864. Despite Bryan's strength in

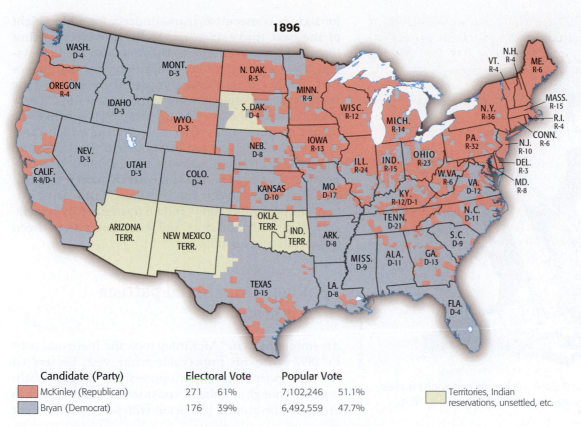

1896

Candidate (Party)	Electoral Vote		Popular Vote	
■ McKinley (Republican)	271	61%	7,102,246	51.1%
■ Bryan (Democrat)	176	39%	6,492,559	47.7%

□ Territories, Indian reservations, unsettled, etc.

MAP 26.6 Presidential Election of 1896 (with electoral vote by state) This election tolled the death knell of the Gilded Age political party system, with its razor-close elections, strong party loyalties, and high voter turnouts. Bryan's sweep of the southern states and strong showing in the West gave him only 176 electoral votes to McKinley's 271 from the more populous North and East. For years after 1896, Republicans predominated, and citizens showed a declining interest in joining parties and voting. © Cengage Learning

the South and West, the results vividly demonstrated his lack of appeal to the unmortgaged farmer and especially to the eastern urban laborer. Many wage earners in the East voted for their jobs and full dinner pails, threatened as they were by free silver, free trade, and fireless factories. Living precariously on a fixed wage, the factory workers had no reason to favor inflation, which was the heart of the Bryanites' program.

In gold-standard Britain, there was much relief over McKinley's victory. The London Standard *commented,*

❝ The hopelessly ignorant and savagely covetous waifs and strays of American civilization voted for Bryan, but the bulk of the solid sense, business integrity, and social stability sided with McKinley. The nation is to be heartily congratulated.❞

The Bryan-McKinley battle heralded the advent of a new era in American politics. At first glance the election seemed to be the age-old story of the underprivileged many against the privileged few, of the indebted backcountry against the wealthier seaboard, of the country against the city, of the agrarians against the industrialists, of Main Street against Wall Street, of the nobodies against the somebodies. Yet when Bryan made his evangelical appeal to all those supposed foes of the existing social order, not enough of them banded together to form a political majority.

The outcome was instead a resounding victory for big business, the big cities, middle-class values, and financial conservatism. Bryan's defeat marked the last serious effort to win the White House with mostly agrarian votes. The future of presidential politics lay not on the farms, with their dwindling population, but in the mushrooming cities, with their growing hordes of freshly arriving immigrants.

The Grand Old Party's smashing victory of 1896 also heralded a Republican grip on the White House

The Sacrilegious Candidate A hostile cartoonist makes sport of Bryan's notorious Cross of Gold speech in 1896.

Library of Congress

for sixteen consecutive years—indeed, for all but eight of the next thirty-six years. McKinley's election thus imparted a new character to the American political system. The long reign of Republican political dominance that it ushered in was accompanied by diminishing voter participation in elections, the weakening of party organizations, and the fading away of issues like the money question and civil-service reform, which came to be replaced by concern for industrial regulation and the welfare of labor. Scholars have dubbed this new political era the period of the **fourth party system**, signaling a break with the previous "third party system," in place since 1860 and characterized by remarkably high voter turnouts and close contests between Democrats and Republicans.

✴ Republican Stand-pattism Enthroned

An eminently "safe" McKinley took the inaugural oath in 1897. With his impeccable white vest, he seemed never to perspire, even in oppressively muggy Washington. Though a man of considerable ability, he was an ear-to-the-ground politician who seldom got far out

Campaign Gimcracks, 1896 These mechanical cards predicted Republican prosperity with McKinley and economic ruin with Bryan. Collection of Janice L. and David J. Frent

of line with majority opinion. His cautious, conservative nature caused him to shy away from the flaming banner of reform. Business was given a free rein, and the trusts, which had trusted him in 1896, were allowed to develop more mighty muscles without serious restraints.

Almost as soon as McKinley took office, the tariff issue, which had played second fiddle to silver in the "Battle of '96," quickly forced itself to the fore. The current Wilson-Gorman law was not raising enough revenue to cover the annual Treasury deficits, and the Republican trusts thought that they had purchased the right to additional tariff protection by their lush contributions to Hanna's war chest. In due course the Dingley Tariff Bill was jammed through the House in 1897, under the pounding gavel of the rethroned "Czar" Reed. The proposed new rates were high, but not high enough to satisfy the paunchy lobbyists, who once again descended upon the Senate. Over 850 amendments were tacked onto the overburdened bill. The resulting piece of patchwork finally established the average rates at 46.5 percent, substantially higher than the Democratic Wilson-Gorman Act of 1894 and in some categories even higher than the McKinley Act of 1890. (See the chart in the Appendix.)

Prosperity, long lurking around the corner, began to return with a rush in 1897, the first year of McKinley's term. The depression of 1893 had run its course, and farm prices rose. Paint-thirsty midwestern barns blossomed in new colors, and the wheels of industry resumed their hum. Republican politicians, like crowing roosters believing they caused the sun to rise, claimed credit for attracting the sunlight of prosperity.

With the return of prosperity, the money issue that had overshadowed politics since the Civil War gradually faded away. The **Gold Standard Act** of 1900, passed over last-ditch silverite opposition, provided that the paper currency be redeemed freely in gold. Nature and science gradually provided an inflation that the "Gold Bug" East had fought so frantically to prevent. Electrifying discoveries of new gold deposits in Canada's fabled Klondike, as well as in Alaska, South Africa, and Australia, brought huge quantities of gold onto world markets, as did the perfecting of the cheap cyanide process for extracting gold from low-grade ore. Moderate inflation thus took care of the currency needs of an explosively expanding nation, as its circulatory system greatly improved. The tide of "silver heresy" rapidly receded, and the "Popocratic" fish were left gasping high and dry on a golden-sanded beach.

Varying Viewpoints
Was the West Really "Won"?

For more than half a century, the Turner thesis dominated historical writing about the West. In his famous essay of 1893, "The Significance of the Frontier in American History," historian Frederick Jackson Turner argued that the frontier experience molded both region and nation. Not only the West, Turner insisted, but the national character had been uniquely shaped by the westward movement. Pioneers had brought the raw West into the embrace of civilization. And the struggle to overcome the hazards of the western wilderness—including distance, deserts, drought, and Indians—had transformed *Europeans* into tough, inventive, and self-reliant *Americans*.

Turner's thesis raised a question that Americans found especially intriguing in 1893. Just three years earlier, the superintendent of the census declared that the frontier, defined as the boundary of a zone with little or no settled population, had closed forever. What new forces, Turner asked, would shape a distinctive American national character, now that the testing ground of the frontier had been plowed and tamed?

Turner's hypothesis that the American character was forged in the western wilderness is surely among the most provocative statements ever made about the formative influences on the nation's development. But as the frontier era recedes ever further into the past, scholars are less persuaded that Turner's thesis adequately explains the national character. American society is still conspicuously different from European and other cultures, even though Turner's frontier disappeared more than a century ago.

Modern scholars charge that Turner based his thesis on several questionable assumptions. Historian David J. Weber, for example, suggests that the line of the frontier did not define the quavering edge of "civilization," but marked the boundary between diverse cultures, each with its own claims to legitimacy and, indeed, to legitimate possession of the land. The frontier should therefore be understood not as the place where "civilization" triumphed over "savagery," but as the principal site of interaction between those cultures.

Several so-called New Western historians take this argument still further. Scholars such as Patricia Nelson Limerick, Richard White, and Donald Worster suggest that the cultural and ecological damage inflicted by advancing "civilization" must be reckoned with in any final accounting of what the pioneers accomplished. These same scholars insist that the West did not lose its regional identity after the frontier line was no longer recognizable in 1890. The West, they argue, is still a unique part of the national mosaic, a region whose history, culture, and identity remain every bit as distinctive as those of New England or the Old South.

But where Turner saw the frontier as the principal shaper of the region's character, the New Western historians emphasize the effects of ethnic and racial confrontation, topography, climate, and the roles of government and big business as the factors that have made the modern West. The New Western historians thus reject Turner's emphasis on the triumphal civilizing of the wilderness. As they see the matter, European and American settlers did not tame the West, but rather conquered it, by suppressing the Native American and Hispanic peoples who had preceded them into the region. But those conquests were less than complete, so the argument goes, and the West therefore remains, uniquely among American regions, an unsettled arena of commingling and competition among those groups. Moreover, in these accounts the West's distinctively challenging climate and geography yielded to human habitation not through the efforts of heroic individual pioneers, but only through massive corporate—and especially federal government—investments in transportation systems (like the transcontinental railroad) and irrigation projects (like the watering of California's Central Valley). Such developments still give western life its special character today.

Chapter Review

KEY TERMS

reservation system (576)
Little Bighorn, Battle of the (578)
Wounded Knee, Battle of (581)
Dawes Severalty Act (581)
mining industry (584)
Homestead Act (586)
mechanization of agriculture (594)
Populists (598)
Pullman strike (599)
fourth party system (604)
Gold Standard Act (605)

PEOPLE TO KNOW

Frederick Jackson Turner
Jacob S. Coxey
William McKinley
Marcus Alonzo Hanna

TO LEARN MORE

Dee Brown, *Bury My Heart at Wounded Knee: An Indian History of the American West* (1970)

William Cronon, *Nature's Metropolis: Chicago and the Great West* (1991)

Jared Farmer, *On Zion's Mount: Mormons, Indians, and the American Landscape* (2008)

Steven Hahn, *The Roots of Southern Populism: Yeoman Farmers and the Transformation of the Georgia Upcountry, 1850–1890* (1983)

Robert V. Hine, *The American West: A New Interpretive History* (2nd ed., 1984)

Patricia Nelson Limerick, *Legacy of Conquest: The Unbroken Past of the American West* (1987)

Charles Postel, *The Populist Vision* (2007)

Frederick Jackson Turner, "The Significance of the Frontier in American History" (1893)

Louis S. Warren, *Buffalo Bill's America: William Cody and the Wild West Show* (2006)

Elliott West, *The Contested Plains: Indians, Goldseekers, and the Rush to Colorado* (1998)

Richard White, *"It's Your Misfortune and None of My Own": A New History of the American West* (1991)

R. Hal Williams, *Realigning America: McKinley, Bryan, and the Remarkable Election of 1896* (2010)

A complete, annotated bibliography for this chapter—along with brief descriptions of the People to Know—may be found on the American Pageant website. The Key Terms are defined in a Glossary at the end of the text.

CHRONOLOGY

ca. 1700–1800	New Indian peoples move onto Great Plains
1858	Pikes Peak gold rush
1859	Nevada Comstock Lode discovered
1862	Homestead Act
1864	Sand Creek massacre Nevada admitted to Union
1867	National Grange organized
1876	Battle of the Little Bighorn Colorado admitted to Union
1877	Nez Perce war
1881	Helen Hunt Jackson publishes *A Century of Dishonor*
1884	Federal government outlaws Indian Sun Dance
1885	Canadian Pacific Railway, first transcontinental rail line, completed across Canada
1885–1890	Local chapters of Farmers' Alliance formed
1887	Dawes Severalty Act
1889	Oklahoma opened to U.S. citizen settlement
1889–1890	North Dakota, South Dakota, Montana, Washington, Idaho, and Wyoming admitted to Union
1890	Census Bureau declares frontier line ended Emergence of People's party (Populists)
1891	Battle of Wounded Knee Construction of Trans-Siberian Railroad begins
1892	Populist party candidate James B. Weaver polls more than 1 million votes in presidential election
1893	Frederick Jackson Turner publishes "The Significance of the Frontier in American History"
1894	"Coxey's Army" marches on Washington Pullman strike
1896	Utah admitted to Union McKinley defeats Bryan for presidency
1897	Dingley Tariff Act
1900	Gold Standard Act
1907	Oklahoma admitted to Union
1924	Indians granted U.S. citizenship
1934	Indian Reorganization Act

Go to the CourseMate website at **www.cengagebrain.com** for additional study tools and review materials—including audio and video clips—for this chapter.

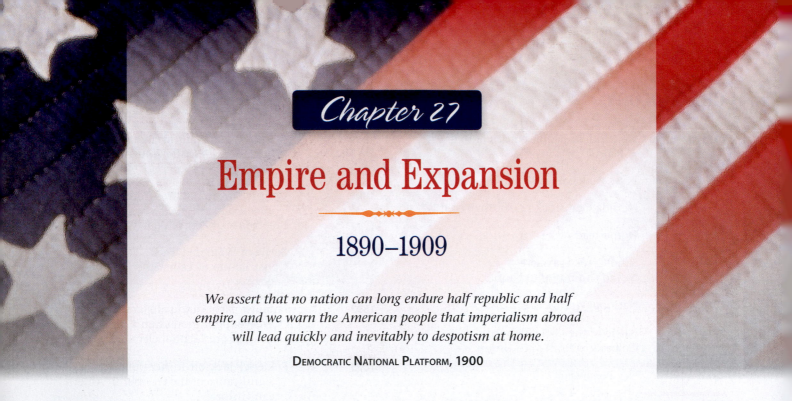

Chapter 27

Empire and Expansion

1890–1909

We assert that no nation can long endure half republic and half empire, and we warn the American people that imperialism abroad will lead quickly and inevitably to despotism at home.

DEMOCRATIC NATIONAL PLATFORM, 1900

*I*n the years immediately following the Civil War, Americans remained astonishingly indifferent to the outside world. Enmeshed in struggles over Reconstruction and absorbed in efforts to heal the wounds of civil war, build an industrial economy, make their cities habitable, and settle the sprawling West, most citizens took little interest in international affairs. But the sunset decades of the nineteenth century witnessed a momentous shift in U.S. foreign policy. America's new diplomacy reflected the far-reaching changes that were reshaping agriculture, industry, and the social structure. American statesmen also responded to the intensifying scramble of several other nations for international advantage in the dawning "age of empire." By the beginning of the twentieth century, America had acquired its own empire, an astonishing departure from its venerable anticolonial traditions. The world now had to reckon with a new great power, potentially powerful but with diplomatic ambitions and principles that remained to be defined.

★ America Turns Outward

Many developments fed the nation's ambition for overseas expansion. Both farmers and factory owners began to look for markets beyond American shores as agricultural and industrial production boomed. Many Americans believed that the United States had to expand or explode. Their country was bursting with a new sense of power generated by the robust growth in population, wealth, and productive capacity—and it was trembling from the hammer blows of labor violence and agrarian unrest. Overseas markets might provide a safety valve to relieve those pressures.

Other forces also whetted the popular appetite for overseas involvement. The lurid "yellow press" of Joseph Pulitzer and William Randolph Hearst described foreign exploits as manly adventures, the kind of dashing derring-do that was the stuff of young boys' dreams. Pious missionaries, inspired by books like the Reverend Josiah Strong's *Our Country: Its Possible Future and Its Present Crisis*, looked overseas for new souls to harvest. Strong trumpeted the superiority of Anglo-Saxon civilization and summoned Americans to spread their religion and their values to the "backward" peoples. He cast his seed on fertile ground. At the same time,

In 1896 the Washington Post *editorialized,*

"A new consciousness seems to have come upon us—the consciousness of strength—and with it a new appetite, the yearning to show our strength. . . . Ambition, interest, land hunger, pride, the mere joy of fighting, whatever it may be, we are animated by a new sensation. We are face to face with a strange destiny. The taste of Empire is in the mouth of the people even as the taste of blood is in the jungle. It means an Imperial policy, the Republic, renascent, taking her place with the armed nations.**"**

WELL, I HARDLY KNOW WHICH TO TAKE FIRST!

Granger Collection

The Imperial Menu A pleased Uncle Sam gets ready to place his order with headwaiter William McKinley. Swallowing some of these possessions eventually produced political indigestion.

aggressive Americans like Theodore Roosevelt and Congressman (later Senator) Henry Cabot Lodge were interpreting Darwinism to mean that the earth belonged to the strong and the fit—that is, to Uncle Sam. This view was strengthened as latecomers to the colonial scramble scooped up leavings from the banquet table of earlier diners. Africa, previously unexplored and mysterious, was partitioned by the Europeans in the 1880s in a pell-mell rush of colonial conquest. In the 1890s Japan, Germany, and Russia all extorted concessions from the anemic Chinese Empire. If America was to survive in the competition of modern nation-states, perhaps it, too, would have to become an imperial power.

The development of a new steel navy also focused attention overseas. Captain Alfred Thayer Mahan's book of 1890, *The Influence of Sea Power upon History, 1660–1783*, argued that control of the sea was the key to world dominance. Mahan helped stimulate the naval race among the great powers that gained momentum around the turn of the century. Red-blooded Americans joined in the demands for a mightier navy and for an American-built isthmian canal between the Atlantic and the Pacific.

America's new international interest manifested itself in several ways. Two-time secretary of state James G. Blaine pushed his **Big Sister policy**, aimed at rallying the Latin American nations behind Uncle Sam's leadership and opening Latin American markets to Yankee traders. Blaine's efforts bore some fruit in 1889,

when he presided over the first Pan-American Conference, held in Washington, D.C., the modest beginnings of an increasingly important series of inter-American assemblages.

A number of diplomatic crises or near-wars also marked the path of American diplomacy in the late 1880s and early 1890s. The American and German navies nearly came to blows in 1889 over the faraway Samoan Islands in the South Pacific, which were formally divided between the two nations in 1899. (German Samoa eventually became an independent republic; American Samoa remains an American possession.) The lynching of eleven Italians in New Orleans in 1891 brought America and Italy to the brink of war, until the United States agreed to pay compensation. In the ugliest affair, American demands on Chile after the deaths of two American sailors in the port of Valparaiso in 1892 made hostilities between the two countries seem inevitable. The threat of attack by Chile's modern navy spread alarm on the Pacific Coast, until the Chileans finally agreed to pay an indemnity. A simmering argument between the United States and Canada over seal hunting near the Pribilof Islands off the coast of Alaska was resolved by arbitration in 1893. The willingness of Americans to risk war over such distant and minor disputes demonstrated the aggressive new national mood.

America's new belligerence combined with old-time anti-British feeling to generate a serious crisis between the United States and Britain in 1895–1896.

The undiplomatic note to Britain by Secretary of State Richard Olney (1835–1917) read,

" To-day the United States is practically sovereign on this continent, and its fiat is law upon the subjects to which it confines its interposition. . . . Its infinite resources combined with its isolated position render it master of the situation and practically invulnerable as against any or all other powers. **"**

The jungle boundary between British Guiana and Venezuela had long been in dispute, but the discovery of gold in the contested area brought the conflict between Britain and Venezuela to a head.

President Cleveland and his pugnacious secretary of state, Richard Olney, waded into the affair with a combative note to Britain invoking the Monroe Doctrine. Not content to stop there, Olney haughtily informed the world's number one naval power that the United States was now calling the tune in the Western Hemisphere.

Unimpressed British officials shrugged off Olney's salvo as just another twist of the lion's tail and replied that the affair was none of Uncle Sam's business. President Cleveland—"mad clear through," as he put it—sent a bristling special message to Congress. He urged an appropriation for a commission of experts, who would run the line where it ought to go. If the British would not accept this rightful boundary, he implied, the United States would fight for it.

The entire country, irrespective of political party, was swept off its feet in an outburst of hysteria. War seemed inevitable. Fortunately, sober second thoughts prevailed on both sides of the Atlantic. A rising challenge from Kaiser Wilhelm's Germany, as well as a looming war with the Dutch-descended Boers in South Africa, left Britain in no mood for war with America. London backed off and consented to arbitration.

The chastened British, their eyes fully opened to the European peril, were now determined to cultivate Yankee friendship. The British inaugurated an era of "patting the eagle's head," which replaced a century or so of America's "twisting the lion's tail." Sometimes called the **Great Rapprochement**—or reconciliation—between the United States and Britain, the new Anglo-American cordiality became a cornerstone of both nations' foreign policies as the twentieth century opened.

✦ Spurning the Hawaiian Pear

Enchanted Hawaii had early attracted the attention of Americans. In the morning years of the nineteenth century, the breeze-brushed islands were a way station and provisioning point for Yankee shippers, sailors, and whalers. In 1820 the first New England missionaries arrived, preaching the twin blessings of Protestant Christianity and protective calico. They came to do good—and did well, as Hawaii became an increasingly important center for sugar production.

Americans gradually came to regard the Hawaiian Islands as a virtual extension of their own coastline. The State Department, beginning in the 1840s, sternly warned other powers to keep their grasping hands off. America's grip was further tightened in 1887 by a treaty with the native government guaranteeing priceless naval-base rights at spacious Pearl Harbor.

But trouble was brewing in the insular paradise. Old World pathogens had scythed the indigenous Hawaiian

Granger Collection

They Can't Fight Britain and America waged a war of words during the Venezuelan boundary dispute, but cooler heads prevailed. A new era of diplomatic cooperation between the two former foes dawned, as they saw themselves bound together by ties of language, culture, and mutual economic interest. As the German chancellor Otto von Bismarck reportedly remarked, "The supreme geopolitical fact of the modern era is that the Americans speak English."

MAP 27.1 United States Expansion, 1857–1917 With the annexation of the Philippines, Hawaii, and Puerto Rico in 1898, the United States became an imperial power.

© Cengage Learning

population down to one-sixth of its size at the time of the first contact with Europeans, leading the American sugar lords to import large numbers of Asian laborers to work the canefields and sugar mills. By century's end, Chinese and Japanese immigrants outnumbered both whites and native Hawaiians, amid mounting worries that Tokyo might be tempted to intervene on behalf of its often-abused nationals. Then sugar markets went sour in 1890 when the **McKinley Tariff** raised barriers against the Hawaiian product. White American planters thereupon renewed their efforts to secure the annexation of Hawaii to the United States. They were blocked by the strong-willed Queen Liliuokalani, who insisted that native Hawaiians should control the islands. Desperate whites, though only a tiny minority, organized a successful revolt early in 1893, openly assisted by American troops, who landed under the unauthorized orders of the expansionist American

minister in Honolulu. "The Hawaiian pear is now fully ripe," he wrote exultantly to his superiors in Washington, "and this is the golden hour for the United States to pluck it."

A treaty of annexation was rushed to Washington, but before it could be railroaded through the Senate, Republican president Harrison's term expired and Democratic president Cleveland came in. Suspecting that his powerful nation had gravely wronged the deposed Queen Liliuokalani and her people, "Old Grover" abruptly withdrew the treaty. A subsequent investigation determined that a majority of the Hawaiian natives opposed annexation. Although Queen Liliuokalani could not be reinstated, the sugarcoated move for annexation had to be temporarily abandoned. The Hawaiian pear continued to ripen until the fateful year of 1898, when the United States acquired its overseas empire (see Map 27.1).

Granger Collection

Queen Liliuokalani (1838–1917) Liliuokalani was the last reigning queen of Hawaii, whose defense of native Hawaiian self-rule led to a revolt by white settlers and to her dethronement. She wrote many songs, the most famous of which was "Aloha Oe," or "Farewell to Thee," played countless times by Hawaiian bands for departing tourists.

✹ Cubans Rise in Revolt

Cuba's masses, frightfully misgoverned, again rose against their Spanish oppressors in 1895. The roots of their revolt were partly economic. Sugar production—the backbone of the island's prosperity—was crippled when the American tariff of 1894 restored high duties on the toothsome product. The desperate insurgents now sought to drive out their Spanish overlords by adopting a scorched-earth policy. The *insurrectos* torched canefields and sugar mills and dynamited passenger trains. Their destructive tactics also menaced American interests on the island.

American sympathies went out to the Cuban underdogs. Sentiment aside, American business had an investment stake of about $50 million in Cuba and an annual trade stake of about $100 million, all of it put at risk by revolutionary upheaval. Moreover, as the calculating Senator Lodge put it, Cuba lay "right athwart the line" that led to the much-anticipated Panama Canal. Whoever controlled Cuba, said Lodge, "controls the Gulf [of Mexico]." Much was riding on the outcome of events in troubled Cuba.

Fuel was added to the Cuban conflagration in 1896 with the arrival of the Spanish general "Butcher" Weyler. He undertook to crush the rebellion by herding many civilians into barbed-wire reconcentration camps, where they could not give assistance to the armed *insurrectos*. Lacking proper sanitation, these enclosures turned into deadly pestholes; the victims died like dogs.

Atrocities in Cuba were red meat for the sensational new "yellow journalism" of William Randolph Hearst and Joseph Pulitzer. Engaged in a titanic duel for circulation, each attempted to outdo the other with screeching headlines and hair-raising "scoops." Where atrocity stories did not exist, they were invented. Hearst sent the gifted artist Frederic Remington to Cuba to draw sketches, allegedly with the pointed admonition "You furnish the pictures and I'll furnish the war." Among other outrages, Remington depicted Spanish customs officials brutally disrobing and searching an American woman. Most readers of Hearst's *Journal*, their indignation soaring, had no way of knowing that such tasks were performed by female attendants. Hearst also sensationally publicized a private letter from the Spanish minister in Washington, Dupuy de Lôme. The indiscreet epistle, stolen from the mails, described President McKinley in decidedly unflattering terms. The resulting uproar forced Dupuy de Lôme's resignation and further infuriated the American public.

Then early in 1898, Washington sent the battleship *Maine* to Cuba, ostensibly for a "friendly visit" but actually to protect and evacuate Americans if a dangerous flare-up should occur and to demonstrate Washington's concern for the island's stability. Tragedy struck on February 15, 1898, when the **Maine** mysteriously blew up in Havana harbor, with a loss of 260 sailors.

Many Spaniards felt that accusations about their blowing up the Maine *reflected on Spanish honor. One Madrid newspaper spoke up:*

❝ The American jingoes . . . imagine us capable of the most foul villainies and cowardly actions. Scoundrels by nature, the American jingoes believe that all men are made like themselves. What do they know about noble and generous feelings? . . . We should not in any way heed the jingoes: they are not even worth our contempt, or the saliva with which we might honor them in spitting at their faces.**❞**

Chicago History Museum

The Explosion of the Maine, February 15, 1898 Encouraged and amplified by the "yellow press," the outcry over the tragedy of the *Maine* helped drive the country into an impulsive war against Spain.

Two investigations of the iron coffin ensued, one by U.S. naval officers and the other by Spanish officials. The Spaniards concluded that the explosion had been internal and presumably accidental; the Americans argued that the blast had been caused by a submarine mine. Not until 1976 did U.S. Navy admiral H. G. Rickover confirm the original Spanish finding with overwhelming evidence that the initial explosion had resulted from spontaneous combustion in one of the coal bunkers adjacent to a powder magazine.

But Americans in 1898, now mad for war, blindly embraced the less likely explanation. Lashed to fury by the yellow press, they leapt to the inaccurate conclusion that the Spanish government had been guilty of intolerable treachery. The battle cry of the hour became

Remember the Maine!
To hell with Spain!

Nothing would do but to hurl the "dirty" Spanish flag from the hemisphere.

The national war fever burned ever higher, even though American diplomats had already gained Madrid's agreement to Washington's two basic demands: an end to the reconcentration camps and an armistice with Cuban rebels. The cautious McKinley found himself in a jam. He did not want hostilities, but neither did he want Spain to remain in possession of Cuba. Nor, for that matter, did he want a fully independent Cuba, over which the United States could exercise no control. More impetuous souls denounced the circumspect president as "Wobbly Willie" McKinley. Fight-hungry Theodore Roosevelt reportedly snarled that the "white-livered" occupant of the White House did not have "the backbone of a chocolate éclair." The president, whose shaken nerves required sleeping pills, was even being hanged in effigy.

McKinley, recognizing the inevitable, eventually yielded and gave the people what they wanted. But public pressure did not fully explain McKinley's course. He had little faith in Spain's oft-broken promises. He worried about Democratic reprisals in the upcoming presidential election of 1900 if he continued to appear indecisive in a time of crisis. He also acknowledged America's commercial and strategic interests in Cuba.

On April 11, 1898, McKinley sent his war message to Congress, urging armed intervention to free the oppressed Cubans. The legislators responded uproariously with what was essentially a declaration of war. In a burst of self-righteousness, they likewise adopted the hand-tying **Teller Amendment**. This proviso proclaimed to the world that when the United States had overthrown Spanish misrule, it would give the Cubans their freedom—a declaration that caused imperialistic Europeans to smile skeptically.

Dewey's May Day Victory at Manila

The American people plunged into the war lightheartedly, like schoolchildren off to a picnic. Bands blared incessantly "There'll Be a Hot Time in the Old Town Tonight" and "Hail, Hail, the Gang's All Here," leading some foreigners to believe that those were national anthems.

The war got off to a giddy start for American forces. Even before the declaration of war, on February 25, 1898, while Navy Secretary John D. Long was away from the office, his hot-blooded assistant secretary Theodore Roosevelt took matters into his own hands. Roosevelt cabled Commodore George Dewey, commanding the American Asiatic Squadron at Hong Kong, to descend upon Spain's Philippines in the event of war. "The very devil seemed to possess him," Long later wrote of Roosevelt's actions. But President McKinley subsequently confirmed Roosevelt's instructions, even though an attack in the distant Far East seemed like a strange way to free nearby Cuba.

Dewey carried out his orders magnificently on May 1, 1898 (see Map 27.2). Sailing boldly with his six warships at night into the fortified harbor of Manila, he trained his guns the next morning on the moldy tenship Spanish fleet. The entire collection of antiquated and overmatched vessels was quickly destroyed, with a loss of nearly four hundred Spaniards killed and wounded, and without the loss of a single American life.

Taciturn George Dewey became a national hero overnight. An amateur poet blossomed forth with this:

Oh, dewy was the morning
Upon the first of May,
And Dewey was the Admiral,
Down in Manila Bay.
And dewy were the Spaniards' eyes,
Them orbs of black and blue;
And dew we feel discouraged?
I dew not think we dew!

Yet Dewey was in a perilous position. He had destroyed the enemy fleet, but he could not storm the forts of Manila with his sailors. His nerves frayed, he was forced to wait in the sweltering bay while troop reinforcements were slowly assembled in America. The appearance of German warships in Manila harbor deepened the tension.

Long-awaited American troops, finally arriving in force, captured Manila on August 13, 1898, in collaboration with Filipino insurgents commanded by their well-educated, part-Chinese leader, Emilio Aguinaldo. Dewey, to his later regret, had brought this shrewd and magnetic revolutionary from exile in Asia so that he might weaken Spanish resistance.

These thrilling events in the Philippines had meanwhile focused attention on Hawaii. An impression spread that America needed the archipelago as a coaling and provisioning way station, in order to send supplies and reinforcements to Dewey. McKinley also worried that Japan might grab the Hawaiian Islands while America was distracted elsewhere. A joint resolution of annexation was rushed through Congress and approved by McKinley on July 7, 1898. It granted Hawaiian residents U.S. citizenship; Hawaii received full territorial status in 1900.

The Confused Invasion of Cuba

Shortly after the outbreak of war, the Spanish government ordered a fleet of decrepit warships to Cuba. Panic seized the eastern seaboard of the United States. American vacationers abandoned their seashore cottages, while nervous investors moved their securities

MAP 27.2 Dewey's Route in the Philippines, 1898 © Cengage Learning

Emilio Aguinaldo (ca. 1869–1964) and Followers, 1900 Aguinaldo had a colorfully checkered career. Exiled from the Philippines by the Spanish in 1897, he was brought back in 1898 to assist the American invasion. A year later he led the Filipino insurrection against the new American rulers. Captured in 1901, he declared his loyalty to the United States. During World War II, he collaborated with the Japanese when they occupied the Philippines. After a lifetime of political intrigue and armed struggle, Aguinaldo died peacefully in Manila in 1964 in his ninety-fifth year.

to inland depositories. The Spanish "armada" eventually wheezed into bottle-shaped Santiago harbor, Cuba, where it was easily blockaded by the much more powerful American fleet.

Sound strategy seemed to dictate that an American army be sent in from the rear to drive out the Spanish ships. Leading the invading force was the grossly overweight General William R. Shafter, a would-be warrior so blubbery and gout-stricken that he had to be carried about on a door. His troops were woefully unequipped for war in the tropics; they had been amply provided with heavy woolen underwear and uniforms designed for subzero operations against the Indians.

The **Rough Riders**, a part of the invading army, now charged onto the stage of history. This colorful regiment of volunteers, short on discipline but long on dash, consisted largely of western cowboys and other hardy characters, with a sprinkling of ex–polo players and ex-convicts. Commanded by Colonel Leonard Wood, the group was organized principally by the glory-chasing Theodore Roosevelt, who had resigned from the Navy Department to serve as lieutenant colonel. He was so nearsighted that as a safeguard he took along a dozen pairs of spectacles, cached in handy spots on his person or nearby.

About the middle of June, a bewildered American army of seventeen thousand men finally embarked at congested Tampa, Florida, amid scenes of indescribable confusion. Shafter's landing near Santiago, thanks to the diversionary tactics of Cuban *insurrectos*, met little opposition. Brisk fighting broke out on July 1 at El Caney and Kettle Hill, up which Colonel Roosevelt and his horseless Rough Riders charged, with strong support from two crack black regiments. They suffered heavy casualties, but the colorful colonel, having the time of his life, shot a Spaniard with his revolver and rejoiced to see his victim double up like a jackrabbit. He later wrote a book on his exploits, which the famed satirist Finley Peter Dunne's character "Mr. Dooley" remarked ought to have been entitled *Alone in Cubia* [sic].

The American army, fast closing in on Santiago, spelled doom for the badly outgunned Spanish fleet. On July 3 the Spaniards dutifully steamed out of the harbor and into the teeth of the waiting American warships. "Don't cheer, men," Captain Philip of the *Texas* admonished his seamen. "The poor devils are dying." Shortly thereafter Santiago surrendered (see Map 27.3).

With a mixture of modesty and immodesty, Colonel Theodore Roosevelt (1858–1919) wrote privately in 1903 of his "Rough Riders,"

❝In my regiment nine-tenths of the men were better horsemen than I was, and probably two-thirds of them better shots than I was, while on the average they were certainly hardier and more enduring. Yet after I had had them a very short while they all knew, and I knew too, that nobody else could command them as I could.❞

Colonel Theodore Roosevelt with Some of the "Rough Riders"
Roosevelt later described his first encounter with the Spanish enemy: "Soon we came to the brink of a deep valley. There was a good deal of cracking of rifles way off in front of us, but as they used smokeless powder we had no idea as to exactly where they were, or who they were shooting at. Then it dawned on us that we were the target. The bullets began to come overhead, making a sound like the ripping of a silk dress, with sometimes a kind of pop. . . . We advanced, firing at them, and drove them off."

Granger Collection

MAP 27.3 The Cuban Campaign, 1898 © Cengage Learning

Hasty preparations were now made for a descent upon Puerto Rico before the war should end. There the American army met even less resistance than in Cuba.

By this time Spain had satisfied its honor. On August 12, 1898, it signed an armistice.

If the Spaniards had held out a few months longer in Cuba, the American army might have melted away. The inroads of malaria, typhoid fever, dysentery, and yellow fever became so severe that hundreds were incapacitated—"an army of convalescents." Others suffered from malodorous canned meat known as "embalmed beef." All told, nearly four hundred men lost their lives to bullets; over five thousand succumbed to bacteria and other causes.

✦ America's Course (Curse?) of Empire

Late in 1898 Spanish and American negotiators met in Paris. War-racked Cuba, as expected, was freed from its Spanish overlords. The Americans had little difficulty in securing the remote Pacific island of Guam, which they had captured early in the conflict from the astonished Spaniards, who, lacking a cable, had not known that a war was on. Spain also ceded Puerto Rico to the United States as payment for war costs. Ironically, the last remnant of Spain's vast New World empire thus became the first territory ever annexed to the United States without the express promise of eventual statehood. In the decades to come, American investment in the island and Puerto Rican immigration to the United States would make this acquisition one of the weightier consequences of this somewhat carefree war (see "Makers of America: The Puerto Ricans," pp. 618–619).

Uncle Sam and People from His Colonies, Postcard, ca. 1900 The acquisition of Puerto Rico, the Philippines, Hawaii, and other Pacific islands brought millions of people of color under the American flag and, as depicted here, the paternal watch of "Uncle Sam." Whether they would eventually become citizens or remain colonial subjects was hotly debated in the United States. Many anti-imperialists opposed colonial expansion precisely because they regarded the exotic new peoples as "unassimilable."

Knottiest of all was the problem of the Philippines, a veritable apple of discord. These lush islands not only embraced an area larger than the British Isles but also contained an ethnically diverse population of some 7 million souls. McKinley was confronted with a devil's dilemma. He did not feel that America could honorably give the islands back to Spanish misrule, especially after it had fought a war to free Cuba. And America would be turning its back upon its responsibilities in a cowardly fashion, he believed, if it simply pulled up anchor and sailed away.

McKinley viewed virtually all the choices open to him as trouble-fraught. The Filipinos, if left to govern themselves, might fall into anarchy. One of the major powers, possibly aggressive Germany or Japan, might then try to seize them. The result could be a major war into which the United States would be sucked. Seemingly the least of the evils consistent with national honor and safety was to acquire all the Philippines and then perhaps give the Filipinos their freedom later.

President McKinley, ever sensitive to public opinion, kept a carefully attuned ear to the ground. The rumble that he heard seemed to call for the entire group of islands. Zealous Protestant missionaries were eager for new converts from Spanish Catholicism,* and the invalid Mrs. McKinley, to whom her husband was devoted, expressed deep concern about the welfare of the Filipinos. Wall Street had generally opposed the war, but awakened by the booming of Dewey's guns, it was clamoring for profits in the Philippines.

A tormented McKinley later claimed that he went down on his knees seeking divine guidance and heard an inner voice telling him to take all the Philippines and Christianize and civilize them. Accordingly, he decided for outright annexation of the islands. Manila remained a sticking point with the Spaniards because it had been captured the day *after* the armistice was signed, and the city could not therefore properly be claimed among the spoils of war. But the Americans broke the deadlock by agreeing to pay Spain $20 million for the Philippine Islands—the last great Spanish haul from the New World.

The signing of the pact of Paris touched off one of the most impassioned foreign-policy debates in American history. The issue of what to do with the Philippines confronted Americans with fundamental questions about their national identity. Except for glacial Alaska, coral-reefed Hawaii, and a handful of Pacific atolls acquired mostly for whaling stations and guano fertilizer needed

*The Philippines had been substantially Christianized by Catholics before the founding of Jamestown in 1607.

President William McKinley (1843–1901) later described his decision to annex the Philippines:

"When next I realized that the Philippines had dropped into our laps, I confess I did not know what to do with them. . . . I went down on my knees and prayed Almighty God for light and guidance. . . . And one night late it came to me this way. . . . That there was nothing left for us to do but to take them all, and to educate the Filipinos, and uplift and civilize and Christianize them and by God's grace do the very best we could by them, as our fellow men, for whom Christ also died. And then I went to bed and went to sleep, and slept soundly."

At dawn on July 26, 1898, the U.S. warship *Gloucester* steamed into Puerto Rico's Guánica harbor, fired at the Spanish blockhouse, and landed some thirty-three hundred troops. Within days the Americans had taken possession of the militarily strategic Caribbean island a thousand miles southeast of Florida. In so doing they set in motion changes on the island that ultimately brought a new wave of immigrants to U.S. shores.

Puerto Rico had been a Spanish possession since Christopher Columbus claimed it for Castile in 1493. The Spaniards enslaved many of the island's forty thousand Taino Indians and set them to work on farms and in mines. Many Tainos died of exhaustion and disease, and in 1511 the Indians rebelled. The Spaniards crushed the uprising, killed thousands of Indians, and began importing African slaves—thus establishing the basis for Puerto Rico's multiracial society.

The first Puerto Rican immigrants to the United States arrived as political exiles in the nineteenth century. From their haven in America, they agitated for the island's independence from Spain. In 1897 Spain finally granted the island local autonomy; ironically, however, the Spanish-American War the following year placed it in American hands. Puerto Rican political émigrés in the United States returned home, but they were soon replaced by poor islanders looking for work.

Changing conditions in Puerto Rico after the U.S. takeover had driven these new immigrants north. Although slow to grant Puerto Ricans U.S. citizenship, the Americans quickly improved health and sanitation on the island, triggering a population surge in the early twentieth century. At the same time, growing monopoly control of Puerto Rico's sugar cane plantations undermined the island's subsistence economy, and a series of hurricanes devastated the coffee plantations that had employed large numbers of people. With almost no industry to provide wage labor, Puerto Rico's unemployment rate soared.

Thus when Congress finally granted Puerto Ricans U.S. citizenship in 1917, thereby eliminating immigration hurdles, many islanders hurried north to find jobs. Over the ensuing decades, Puerto Ricans went to work in Arizona cotton fields, New Jersey soup factories, and

The First Puerto Ricans   The Spanish *conquistadores* treated the native Taino people in Puerto Rico with extreme cruelty, and the Indians were virtually extinct by the mid-1500s.

Utah mines. The majority, however, clustered in New York City and found work in the city's cigar factories, shipyards, and garment industry. Migration slowed somewhat after the 1920s as the Great Depression shrank the job market on the mainland and as World War II made travel hazardous.

When World War II ended in 1945, the sudden advent of cheap air travel sparked an immigration explosion (and set the stage for Leonard Bernstein's great musical production, *West Side Story*, which adapted the story of Romeo and Juliet to the clash of white and Puerto Rican gangs in New York City). As late as the 1930s, the tab for a boat trip to the mainland exceeded the average Puerto Rican's yearly earnings. But with an airplane surplus after World War II, the six-hour flight from Puerto Rico to New York cost under fifty dollars. The Puerto Rican population on the mainland quadrupled between 1940 and 1950 and tripled again by 1960. In 1970, 1.5 million Puerto Ricans lived in the United States, one-third of the island's total population.

U.S. citizenship and affordable air travel made it easy for Puerto Ricans to return home. Thus to a far greater degree than most immigrant groups, Puerto Ricans kept one foot in the United States and the other on their native island. By some estimates 2 million people a year journeyed to and from the island during the postwar period. Puerto Rico's gubernatorial candidates sometimes campaigned in New York for the thousands of voters who were expected to return to the island in time for the election.

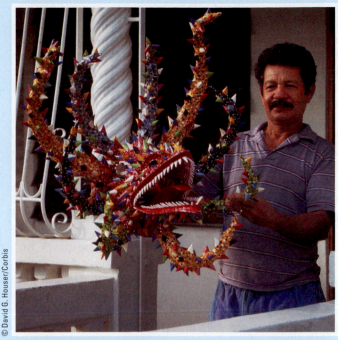

© David G. Houser/Corbis

Preparing for Carnaval (Carnival)   This mask-maker displays an elaborate *máscara de carton* (paper maché mask) made for the annual Puerto Rican festival. Masked figures at *Carnaval* have been part of Puerto Rican culture for more than two hundred years.

This transience worked to keep Puerto Ricans' educational attainment and English proficiency far below the national average. At the same time, the immigrants encountered a deep-seated racism in America unlike anything on their multiracial island. Throughout the postwar years, Puerto Ricans remained one of the poorest groups in the United States, with a median family income below that of African Americans and Mexican Americans.

Still, Puerto Ricans have fared better economically in the United States than on the island, where, in 1970, 60 percent of all inhabitants lived below the poverty line. In recent years Puerto Ricans have attained more schooling, and many have attended college. Invigorated by the civil rights movement of the 1960s, Puerto Ricans also became more politically active, electing growing numbers of congressmen and state and city officials.

AP Photo/Tina Fineberg

Protesting in New York   Puerto Ricans demonstrate in April 2001 against U.S. Navy bombing exercises on the Puerto Rican island of Vieques.

to replenish southern soil exhausted by overcultivation, the Republic had hitherto absorbed only contiguous territory on the continent. All previous accessions had been thinly peopled and eligible for ultimate statehood. But in the Philippines, the nation had on its hands a distant tropical area, thickly populated by Asians of a different culture, tongue, and government institutions.

Opponents of annexation argued that such a step would dishonor and ultimately destroy America's venerable commitments to self-determination and anti-colonialism. "Goddamn the United States for its vile conduct in the Philippine Isles!" burst out the usually mild-mannered Professor William James. The Harvard philosopher could not believe that the United States could "puke up its ancient soul in five minutes without a wink of squeamishness." Speaker of the House Thomas "Czar" Reed resigned in protest against America's new imperial adventure. Proponents countered that Philippine annexation would simply continue a glorious history of expansion that had pushed American civilization to the Pacific and now beyond. If Americans were "morally bound to abandon the Philippines," thundered Theodore Roosevelt, "we were also morally bound to abandon Arizona to the Apaches." The **Anti-Imperialist League** sprang into being to fight the McKinley administration's expansionist moves. The organization counted among its members some of the most prominent people in the United States, including the presidents of Stanford and Harvard Universities and the novelist Mark Twain. The anti-imperialist blanket even stretched over such strange bedfellows as the labor leader Samuel Gompers and the steel titan Andrew Carnegie.

Anti-imperialists raised many objections. The Filipinos thirsted for freedom; to annex them would violate the "consent of the governed" philosophy in the Declaration of Independence and the Constitution. Despotism abroad might well beget despotism at home. Imperialism was costly and unlikely ever to turn a profit. Finally, annexation would propel the United States into the political and military cauldron of East Asia.

Yet the expansionists or imperialists could sing a seductive song. They appealed to patriotism, invoked America's "civilizing mission," and played up possible trade profits. Manila, they claimed, might become another Hong Kong. Rudyard Kipling, the British poet laureate of imperialism, urged America down the slippery path with a quotable poem that he had circulated before publication to Theodore Roosevelt and Henry Cabot Lodge (Roosevelt found it "good sense" but "poor poetry"):

> Take up the White Man's burden—
> Ye dare not stoop to less—
> Nor call too loud on Freedom
> To cloak your weariness.

In short, the wealthy Americans must help to uplift (and exploit) the underprivileged, underfed, and underclad of the world.

Over heated protests, the Senate approved the treaty with Spain with just one vote to spare on February 6, 1899. America was now officially an empire.

⭐ Perplexities in Puerto Rico and Cuba

From the outset, the status of Puerto Rico was anomalous—neither a state nor a territory, and with little prospect of eventual independence. The **Foraker Act** of 1900 accorded the Puerto Ricans a limited degree of popular government (and outlawed cockfighting, a favorite island pastime). Congress granted U.S. citizenship to Puerto Ricans in 1917 but withheld full self-rule. Although the American regime worked wondrous improvements in education, sanitation, and transportation, many of the inhabitants still aspired to independence. Great numbers of Puerto Ricans ultimately moved to New York City, where they added to the complexity of the melting pot.

The annexation of Puerto Rico (and the Philippines) posed a thorny legal problem: Did the Constitution follow the flag? Did American laws, including tariff laws and the Bill of Rights, apply with full force to the newly acquired possessions? "Who are we?" a group of Puerto Rican petitioners asked Congress in 1900. "Are we citizens or are we subjects?" Beginning in 1901 with

The contest over American imperialism took place on the Senate floor as well as around the globe. In 1900 Senator Albert J. Beveridge (1862–1927), Republican from Indiana, returned from an investigative trip to the Philippines to defend its annexation:

❝ The Philippines are ours forever. . . . And just beyond the Philippines are China's illimitable markets. We will not retreat from either. We will not abandon our opportunity in the Orient. We will not renounce our part in the mission of our race: trustee, under God, of the civilization of the world.❞

Two years later Senator George F. Hoar (1826–1904), Republican from Massachusetts, broke with his party to denounce American annexation of the Philippines and other territories:

❝You cannot maintain despotism in Asia and a republic in America. If you try to deprive even a savage or a barbarian of his just rights you can never do it without becoming a savage or a barbarian yourself.❞

the ***Insular Cases***, a badly divided Supreme Court decreed, in effect, that the flag did outrun the Constitution, and that the outdistanced document did not necessarily extend with full force to the new windfall. Puerto Ricans (and Filipinos) might be subject to American rule, but they did not enjoy all American rights.

Cuba, scorched and chaotic, presented another headache. An American military government, set up under the administrative genius of General Leonard Wood of Rough Rider fame, wrought miracles in government, finance, education, agriculture, and public health. Under his leadership and that of Colonel William C. Gorgas, a frontal attack was launched on yellow fever. Spectacular experiments were performed by Dr. Walter Reed and others upon American soldiers, who volunteered as human guinea pigs, and the stegomyia mosquito was proved to be the lethal carrier. Cleaning up breeding places for mosquitoes wiped out yellow fever in Havana, while dampening the fear of recurrent epidemics in cities of the South and Atlantic seaboard.

The United States, honoring its self-denying Teller Amendment of 1898, withdrew from Cuba in 1902. Old World imperialists could scarcely believe their eyes. But the Washington government could not turn this rich and strategic island completely loose on the international sea; a grasping power like Germany might secure dangerous lodgment near America's soft underbelly. The Cubans were therefore forced to write into their own constitution of 1901 the so-called **Platt Amendment**.

The Cubans loathed the amendment, which served McKinley's ultimate purpose of bringing Cuba under American control. ("Plattism" survives as a colloquial term of derision even in modern-day Cuba.) The newly "liberated" Cubans were forced to agree not to conclude treaties that might compromise their independence (as Uncle Sam saw it) and not to take on debt beyond their resources (as Uncle Sam measured them). They further agreed that the United States might intervene with troops to restore order when it saw fit. Finally, the Cubans promised to sell or lease needed coaling or naval stations, ultimately two and then only one (Guantánamo), to their powerful "benefactor." The United States finally abrogated the amendment in 1934, although Uncle Sam still occupies a twenty-eight-thousand-acre Cuban beachhead at Guantánamo under an agreement that can be revoked only by the consent of both parties (see pp. 779–780).

✦ New Horizons in Two Hemispheres

In essence, the Spanish-American War was a kind of colossal coming-out party. Dewey's thundering guns merely advertised the fact that the nation was already a world power. The war itself was short (113 days), low in casualties, and theatrically successful—despite the

Three years after the Spanish-American War ended, a foreign diplomat in Washington remarked,

"I have seen two Americas, the America before the Spanish American War and the America since."

bungling. Secretary of State John Hay called it a "splendid little war." American prestige rose sharply, and the Europeans grudgingly accorded the Republic more respect. Britain, France, Russia, and other great powers pointedly upgraded their legations in Washington, D.C., which had previously been regarded as a diplomatic backwater.

An exhilarating new martial spirit thrilled America, buoyed along by the newly popular military marching-band music of John Philip Sousa. Most Americans did not start the war with consciously imperialistic motives, but after falling through the cellar door of imperialism in a drunken fit of idealism, they wound up with imperialistic and colonial fruits in their grasp. Captain Mahan's

Granger Collection

The New Jingoism An enthusiastic Uncle Sam cheers the U.S. Navy in the "splendid little war" of 1898. Many Americans, however, were less than enthused about America's new imperial adventure.

big-navyism seemed vindicated, energizing popular support for more and better battleships. A masterly organizer, Secretary of War Elihu Root established a general staff for the army and founded the War College in Washington.

One of the most beneficial results of the conflict was the further closing of the "bloody chasm" between North and South. Thousands of patriotic southerners had flocked to the Stars and Stripes, and the gray-bearded General Joseph ("Fighting Joe") Wheeler—a Confederate cavalry hero of about a thousand Civil War skirmishes and battles—was given a command in Cuba. He allegedly cried, in the heat of battle, "To hell with the Yankees! Dammit, I mean the Spaniards."

Even so, the newly imperial nation was not yet prepared to pay the full bill for its new status. By taking on the Philippine Islands, the United States became a full-fledged Far Eastern power. But the distant islands eventually became a "heel of Achilles"—a kind of indefensible hostage given to Japan, as events proved in World War II. Here and elsewhere, the Americans had shortsightedly assumed burdensome commitments that they proved unwilling to defend with appropriate naval and military outlays.

✪ "Little Brown Brothers" in the Philippines

The liberty-loving Filipinos assumed that they, like the Cubans, would be granted their freedom after the Spanish-American War. They were tragically deceived. Washington excluded them from the peace negotiations with Spain and made clear its intention to stay in the Philippines indefinitely. Bitterness toward the occupying American troops erupted into open insurrection on February 4, 1899, under Emilio Aguinaldo. Having plunged into war with Spain to free Cuba, the United States was now forced to deploy some 126,000 troops ten thousand miles away to rivet shackles onto a people who asked for nothing but freedom—in the American tradition.

The poorly equipped Filipino rebels soon melted into the jungle to wage vicious guerrilla warfare. Months earlier, American soldiers thought they were rescuing innocent victims of Spanish tyranny. Now they viewed the Filipinos as dangerous enemies of the United States. This shift contributed to a mounting "race war" in which both sides perpetrated sordid atrocities. Uncle Sam's soldiers adopted the "water cure"—forcing water down victims' throats until they yielded information or died. American-built reconcentration camps rivaled those of "Butcher" Weyler in Cuba. Having begun the Spanish war with noble ideals, America now dirtied its hands. One New York newspaper published a reply to Rudyard Kipling's famous poem:

We've taken up the white man's burden
Of ebony and brown;
Now will you kindly tell us, Rudyard,
How we may put it down?

American Soldier Interrogates Filipino Civilians For three years after its annexation of the Philippine Islands in 1898, the United States fought a savage war to suppress a Filipino rebellion against American rule. More than 200,000 Filipinos perished. There was bitter irony in this clash, as the Americans had claimed to be "liberating" the Filipinos from their oppressive Spanish masters; but the Yankee liberators were sometimes no less oppressive than the Spaniards they had ousted.

Keystone-Mast Collection, UCR/Califronia Museum of Photograph, University of California, Riverside

The Americans broke the back of the Filipino insurrection in 1901, when they cleverly infiltrated a guerrilla camp and captured Aguinaldo. But sporadic fighting dragged on for many dreary months, eventually claiming the lives of 4,234 Americans and as many as 600,000 Filipinos.

Future president William H. Taft, an able and amiable Ohioan who weighed some 350 pounds, became civil governor of the Philippines in 1901. Forming a strong attachment to the Filipinos, he called them his "little brown brothers" and danced light-footedly with the Filipino women. But McKinley's "benevolent assimilation" of the Philippines proceeded with painful slowness. Washington poured millions of dollars into the islands to improve roads, sanitation, and public health. Important economic ties, including trade in sugar, developed between the two peoples. American teachers set up an unusually good school system and helped make English a second language. But all this vast expenditure, which profited America little, was ill-received. The Filipinos hated compulsory Americanization and pined for liberty. They finally got their freedom on the Fourth of July, 1946. In the meantime, thousands of Filipinos emigrated to the United States (see "Makers of America: The Filipinos," pp. 624–625).

✦ Hinging the Open Door in China

Ominous events had meanwhile been brewing in faraway and enfeebled China. After its defeat by Japan in 1894–1895, the imperialistic European powers, notably Russia and Germany, moved in. Like vultures descending upon a wounded animal, they began to tear away valuable leaseholds and economic spheres of influence from the Manchu government.

A growing group of Americans viewed the vivisection of China with alarm. Churches worried about their missionary strongholds. Merchants feared that Europeans would monopolize Chinese markets. An alarmed American public, openly prodded by the press and slyly nudged by certain free-trade Britons, demanded that Washington do something. Secretary of State John Hay, a quiet but witty poet-novelist-diplomat with a flair for capturing the popular imagination, finally decided upon a dramatic move.

In the summer of 1899, Hay dispatched to all the great powers a communication soon known as the **Open Door note**. He urged them to announce that in their leaseholds or spheres of influence they would respect certain Chinese rights and the ideal of fair competition. Tellingly, Hay had not bothered to consult the Chinese themselves.

The phrase *Open Door* quickly caught the American public's fancy. But Hay's proposal caused much squirming in the leading capitals of the world, though all the great powers save Russia, with covetous designs on Manchuria, eventually agreed to it.

Open Door or not, patriotic Chinese did not care to be used as a doormat by the Western powers. In 1900 a superpatriotic group, known as the "Boxers" for their training in the martial arts, broke loose with the cry "Kill Foreign Devils." In what became known as the **Boxer Rebellion**, they murdered more than two hundred foreigners and thousands of Chinese Christians and besieged the foreign diplomatic community in the capital, Beijing (Peking).

By permission of the Houghton Library, Harvard University, ACB 78.1

American Missionary Grace Roberts Teaching in China, 1903 By the turn of the twentieth century, thousands of American men and women had established Christian missions in faraway places such as Hawaii, China, Africa, and Turkey. Missionaries' educational and religious work helped build sentimental, political, and economic ties between Americans and distant nations. At times, however, these close connections led to violent confrontations, such as when the nationalist Boxer rebels attacked missionaries in China in 1900 as symbols of foreign encroachment. Protestant women justified their missionary activities as a logical extension of their traditional female duty to nurture and uplift, but in reality these foreign assignments often propelled them to undertake responsibilities that their stateside mothers and sisters rarely encountered.

At the beginning of the twentieth century, the United States, its imperial muscles just flexed in the war with Spain, found itself in possession of the Philippines. Uncertain of how to manage this empire, which seethed resentfully against its new masters, the United States promised to build democracy in the Philippines and to ready the islanders for home rule. Almost immediately after annexation, the American governor of the archipelago sent a corps of Filipino students to the United States, hoping to forge future leaders steeped in American ways who would someday govern an independent Philippines. Yet this small student group found little favor in their adopted country, although in their native land many went on to become respected citizens and leaders.

Most Filipino immigrants to the United States in these years, however, came not to study but to toil. With Chinese immigration banned, Hawaii and the Pacific Coast states turned to the Philippines for cheap agricultural labor. Beginning in 1906 the Hawaiian Sugar Planters Association aggressively recruited Filipino workers. Enlistments grew slowly at first, but by the 1920s thousands of young Filipino men had reached the Hawaiian Islands and been assigned to sugar plantations or pineapple fields.

Typically a young Filipino wishing to emigrate first made his way to Manila, where he signed a contract with the growers that promised three years' labor in return for transportation to Hawaii, wages, free housing and fuel, and return passage at the end of the contract. Not all of the emigrants returned; there remain in Hawaii today some former field workers still theoretically eligible for free transport back to their native land.

Those Filipinos venturing as far as the American mainland found work less arduous but also less certain than did their countrymen on Hawaiian plantations. Many mainlanders worked seasonally—in winter as domestic servants, busboys, or bellhops; in summer journeying to the fields to harvest lettuce, strawberries, sugar beets, and potatoes. Eventually Filipinos, along with Mexican immigrants, shared the dubious honor of making up California's agricultural work force.

A mobile society, Filipino Americans also were overwhelmingly male; there was only one Filipino woman for every fourteen Filipino men in California in 1930. Thus the issue of intermarriage became acutely sensitive. California and many other states prohibited the marriage of Asians and Caucasians in demeaning laws that remained on the books until 1948. And if a Filipino so much as approached a Caucasian woman, he

Hawaii State Archives

Filipino Laborers at Work on a Hawaiian Pineapple Plantation, 1930s

Hawaii State Archives

Filipino Workers Arriving in Honolulu, 1940s Tags around their necks indicated the plantations to which they had been assigned.

could expect reprisals—sometimes violent. For example, white vigilante groups roamed the Yakima Valley in Washington and the San Joaquin and Salinas Valleys in California, intimidating and even attacking Filipinos whom they accused of improperly accosting white women. In 1930 one Filipino was murdered and others wounded after they invited some Caucasian women to a dance. Undeterred, the Filipinos challenged the restrictive state laws and the hooligans who found in them an excuse for mayhem. But Filipinos, who did not become eligible for American citizenship until 1946, long lacked political leverage.

After World War II, Filipino immigration accelerated. Between 1950 and 1970, the number of Filipinos in the United States nearly doubled, with women and men stepping aboard the new transpacific airliners in roughly equal numbers. Many of these recent arrivals sprang from sturdy middle-class stock and sought in America a better life for their children than the Philippines seemed able to offer. Today the war-torn and perpetually depressed archipelago sends more immigrants to American shores than does any other Asian nation.

© Dan Habib/The Concord Monitor/Corbis

Filipino Nurses The nursing shortage in the United States has created many job opportunities for Filipino nurses, who are trained to high medical standards and speak English. A nurse in the United States today can earn more than a physician in the Philippines.

Library of Congress

Columbia's Easter Bonnet Many Americans felt a surge of pride as the United States became an imperial power at the dawn of the twentieth century. But then and later, America's world role proved hotly controversial, at home as well as abroad.

A multinational rescue force of some eighteen thousand soldiers arrived in the nick of time and quelled the rebellion. They included several thousand American troops dispatched from the Philippines to protect U.S. rights under the 1844 Treaty of Wanghia (see p. 390) and to keep the Open Door propped open.

The victorious allied invaders acted angrily and vindictively. They assessed prostrate China an excessive

The commercial interests of Britain and America were imperiled by the power grabs in China, and a close concert between the two powers would have helped both. Yet as Secretary of State John Hay (1838–1905) wrote privately in June 1900,

"Every Senator I see says, 'For God's sake, don't let it appear we have any understanding with England.' How can I make bricks without straw? That we should be compelled to refuse the assistance of the greatest power in the world [Britain], in carrying out our own policy, because all Irishmen are Democrats and some [American] Germans are fools—is enough to drive a man mad.**"**

indemnity of $333 million, of which America's share was to be $24.5 million. When Washington discovered that this sum was much more than enough to pay damages and expenses, it remitted about $18 million, to be used for the education of a selected group of Chinese students in the United States—a not-so-subtle initiative to further the westernization of Asia.

Secretary Hay let fly another paper broadside in 1900, announcing that henceforth the Open Door would embrace the territorial integrity of China, in addition to its commercial integrity. Those principles helped spare China from possible partition in those troubled years and were formally incorporated into the Nine-Power Treaty of 1922, only to be callously violated by Japan's takeover of Manchuria a decade later (see pp. 731 and 747).

✦ Imperialism or Bryanism in 1900?

President McKinley's renomination by the Republicans in 1900 was a foregone conclusion. He had won a war and acquired rich, though burdensome, real estate; he had safeguarded the gold standard; and he had brought the promised prosperity of the full dinner pail. An irresistible vice-presidential boom developed for Theodore ("Teddy") Roosevelt (TR), the cowboy-hero of the Cuban campaign. Capitalizing on his war-born popularity, he had been elected governor of New York, where the local political bosses had found him headstrong and difficult to manage. They therefore devised a scheme to kick the colorful colonel upstairs into the vice presidency.

This plot to railroad Roosevelt worked beautifully. Gesticulating wildly, he sported a western-style cowboy hat that made him stand out like a white crow at the Republican convention. To cries of "We want Teddy!" he was handily nominated. A wary Mark Hanna reportedly moaned that there would now be only one heartbeat between "that damned cowboy" and the presidency of the United States.

William Jennings Bryan was the odds-on choice of the Democrats, meeting at Kansas City. Their platform proclaimed that the paramount issue was Republican overseas imperialism.

McKinley, the soul of dignity, once again campaigned safely from his front porch. Bryan again took to the stump in a cyclonic campaign. Lincoln, he charged, had abolished slavery for 3.5 million Africans; McKinley had reestablished it for 7 million Filipinos. Roosevelt out-Bryaned Bryan, touring the country with revolver-shooting cowboys. Flashing his monumental teeth and pounding his fist into his palm, Roosevelt denounced all dastards who would haul down Old Glory.

McKinley handily triumphed by a much wider margin than in 1896: 7,218,491 to 6,356,734 popular votes, and 292 to 155 electoral votes. But victory for the Republicans was not a mandate for or against imperialism. If there was any mandate at all it was for the two *P*s: prosperity and protectionism. Meanwhile, the New York bosses gleefully looked forward to watching the nettlesome Roosevelt "take the veil" as vice president.

✴ TR: Brandisher of the Big Stick

Kindly William McKinley had scarcely served another six months when, in September 1901, he was murdered by a deranged anarchist in Buffalo, New York. Roosevelt rode a buckboard out of his campsite in the Adirondacks to take the oath of office, becoming, at age forty-two, the youngest president thus far in American history.

Born into a wealthy and distinguished New York family, Roosevelt, a red-blooded blue blood, had fiercely built up his spindly, asthmatic body by a stern and self-imposed routine of exercise. Educated partly in Europe, he graduated from Harvard with Phi Beta Kappa honors and published, at the age of twenty-four,

© Bettmann/Corbis

Theodore Roosevelt Roosevelt gives a speech with both voice and body language in North Carolina in 1902.

the first of some thirty volumes of muscular prose. He worked as a ranch owner and cowboy in the Dakotas before pursuing his political career full-time. Barrel-chested, bespectacled, and five feet ten inches tall, with mulelike molars, squinty eyes, droopy mustache, and piercing voice, he was ever the delight of cartoonists.

The Rough Rider's high-voltage energy was electrifying. Believing that it was better to wear out than to rust out, he would shake the hands of some six thousand people at one stretch or ride horseback many miles in a day as an example for portly cavalry officers. Incurably boyish and bellicose, Roosevelt ceaselessly preached the virile virtues and denounced pacifistic "flubdubs" and "mollycoddles." An ardent champion of military and naval preparedness, he adopted as his pet proverb, "Speak softly and carry a big stick, [and] you will go far."

His outsized ego caused it to be said of him that he wanted to be the bride at every wedding and the corpse at every funeral. He loved people and mingled with those of all ranks, from Catholic cardinals to professional prizefighters, one of whom blinded a Rooseveltian eye in a White House bout. "TR" commanded an idolatrous personal following. After visiting him, a journalist wrote, "You go home and wring the personality out of your clothes."

Above all, TR believed that the president should lead, boldly. He had no real respect for the delicate checks and balances among the three branches of the government. The president, he felt, may take any action in the general interest that is not specifically forbidden by the laws of the Constitution.

✴ Building the Panama Canal

Roosevelt soon applied his bullish energy to foreign affairs. The Spanish-American War had reinvigorated interest in the long-talked-about canal across the Central American isthmus, through which only printer's ink had ever flowed. Americans had learned a sobering lesson when the battleship *Oregon*, stationed on the Pacific Coast at the outbreak of war in 1898, took weeks to steam all the way around South America to join the U.S. fleet in Cuban waters. An isthmian canal would plainly augment the strength of the navy by increasing its mobility. Such a waterway would also make easier the defense of such recent acquisitions as Puerto Rico, Hawaii, and the Philippines, while facilitating the operations of the U.S. merchant marine.

Initial obstacles in the path of the canal builders were legal rather than geographical. By the terms of the ancient Clayton-Bulwer Treaty, concluded with Britain in 1850, the United States could not secure exclusive control over an isthmian route. But by 1901 America's

Cutting Through the Continental Divide in Panama The Culebra Cut, the southeastern section of the Panama Canal that extends through the Continental Divide, was later renamed the Gaillard Cut in honor of the U.S. Army Corps of Engineers officer who oversaw this excavation but died shortly before the canal opened in 1914. The cut was one of the greatest engineering feats of its time. Hundreds of drills prepared holes for tons of dynamite, which twice daily blasted the rock so that it could be excavated by steam shovels. Dirt trains, shown in the foreground, then hauled loads of debris to dumps twelve miles away. The summit of Culebra Mountain, through which the cut was made, was lowered from 193 feet to 40 feet above sea level and widened considerably. Library of Congress

British cousins were willing to yield ground. Confronted with an unfriendly Europe and bogged down in the South African Boer War, they consented to the **Hay-Pauncefote Treaty** in 1901. It not only gave the United States a free hand to build the canal but conceded the right to fortify it as well.

But where exactly should the canal be dug? Many American experts favored a route across Nicaragua, but agents of the old French Canal Company were eager to salvage something from their costly failure at S-shaped Panama. Represented by a young, energetic, and unscrupulous engineer, Philippe Bunau-Varilla, the New Panama Canal Company suddenly dropped the price of its holdings from $109 million to the fire-sale price of $40 million.

Congress in June 1902 finally decided on the Panama route. The scene now shifted to Colombia, of which Panama was a restive part. The Colombian senate rejected an American offer of $10 million and annual payment of $250,000 for a six-mile-wide zone across Panama. Roosevelt railed against "those dagoes" who were frustrating his ambitions. Meanwhile, impatient Panamanians, who had rebelled numerous times, were ripe for another revolt. They had counted on a wave of prosperity to follow construction of the canal, and they feared that the United States would now turn to the Nicaraguan route. Scheming Bunau-Varilla was no less disturbed by the prospect of losing the company's $40 million. Working hand in glove with the revolutionists, he helped incite a rebellion on November 3, 1903. U.S. naval forces prevented Colombian troops from crossing the isthmus to quell the uprising.

Roosevelt moved rapidly to make steamy Panama a virtual outpost of the United States. Just three days after the insurrection, he hastily extended the right hand of recognition. Fifteen days later, Bunau-Varilla, who was now the Panamanian minister despite his French citizenship, signed the Hay–Bunau-Varilla Treaty in Washington. The price of the canal strip was left the same, but the zone was widened from six to ten miles. The French company gladly pocketed its $40 million from the U.S. Treasury.

Roosevelt, it seems clear, did not actively plot to tear Panama from the side of Colombia. But the conspirators knew of his angrily expressed views, and they counted on his using the big stick to hold Colombia at

Theodore Roosevelt wrote to a correspondent in February 1904,

❝I have been hoping and praying for three months that the Santo Domingans would behave so that I would not have to act in any way. I want to do nothing but what a policeman has to do. . . . As for annexing the island, I have about the same desire to annex it as a gorged boa-constrictor might have to swallow a porcupine wrong-end-to.**❞**

bay. The Rough Rider became so indiscreetly involved in the Panama affair as to create the impression that he had been a secret party to the intrigue, and the so-called rape of Panama marked an ugly downward lurch in U.S. relations with Latin America.

Canal construction began in 1904, in the face of daunting difficulties ranging from labor troubles to landslides and lethal tropical diseases. Colonel William C. Gorgas, the quiet and determined exterminator of yellow fever in Havana, ultimately made the Canal Zone "as safe as a health resort." At a cost of some $400 million, an autocratic West Point engineer, Colonel George Washington Goethals, ultimately brought the project to completion in 1914, just as World War I was breaking out.

✦ TR's Perversion of Monroe's Doctrine

Latin American debt defaults prompted further Rooseveltian involvement in affairs south of the border. Nations such as Venezuela and the Dominican Republic were chronically in arrears in their payments to European creditors. Germany actually bombarded a town in delinquent Venezuela in 1903.

Granger Collection

Theodore Roosevelt and His Big Stick in the Caribbean, 1904 Roosevelt's policies seemed to be turning the Caribbean into a Yankee pond.

Roosevelt feared that if the Germans or British got their foot in the door as bill collectors, they might remain in Latin America, in flagrant violation of the Monroe Doctrine. He therefore declared a brazen policy of "preventive intervention," better known as the **Roosevelt Corollary** to the Monroe Doctrine. He announced that in the event of future financial malfeasance by the Latin American nations, the United States itself would intervene, take over the customshouses, pay off the debts, and keep the troublesome Europeans on the other side of the Atlantic. In short, no outsiders could push around the Latin nations except Uncle Sam, Policeman of the Caribbean. This new brandishing of the big stick in the Caribbean became effective in 1905, when the United States took over the management of tariff collections in the Dominican Republic, an arrangement formalized in a treaty with the Dominicans two years later.

TR's rewriting of the Monroe Doctrine probably did more than any other single step to promote the "Bad Neighbor" policy begun in these years. As time wore on, the new corollary was used to justify wholesale interventions and repeated landings of the marines, all of which helped turn the Caribbean into a "Yankee lake." To Latin Americans it seemed as though the revised Monroe Doctrine, far from providing a shield, was a cloak behind which the United States sought to strangle them.

The shadow of the big stick likewise fell again on Cuba in 1906. Revolutionary disorders brought an appeal from the Cuban president, and "necessity being the mother of intervention," U.S. Marines landed. These police forces were withdrawn temporarily in 1909, but in Latin American eyes the episode was but another example of the creeping power of the Colossus of the North.

✦ Roosevelt on the World Stage

Booted and spurred, Roosevelt charged into international affairs far beyond Latin America. The outbreak of war between Russia and Japan in 1904 gave him a chance to perform as a global statesman. The Russian bear, having lumbered across Asia, was seeking to bathe its frostbitten paws in the ice-free ports of China's Manchuria, particularly Port Arthur. In Japanese eyes, Manchuria and Korea in tsarist hands were pistols pointed at Japan's strategic heart. The Japanese responded in 1904 with a devastating surprise pounce on the Russian fleet at Port Arthur. They proceeded to administer a humiliating series of beatings to the inept Russians—the first serious military setback to a major European power by a non-European force since the Turkish invasions of

the sixteenth century. But as the war dragged on, Japan began to run short of men and yen—a weakness it did not want to betray to the enemy. Tokyo officials therefore approached Roosevelt in the deepest secrecy and asked him to help sponsor peace negotiations.

Roosevelt was happy to oblige, as he wanted to avoid a complete Russian collapse so that the tsar's empire could remain a counterweight to Japan's growing power. At Portsmouth, New Hampshire, in 1905, TR guided the warring parties to a settlement that satisfied neither side and left the Japanese, who felt they had won the war, especially resentful. Japan was forced to drop its demands for a cash indemnity and Russian evacuation of Sakhalin Island, though it received some compensation in the form of effective control over Korea, which it formally annexed in 1910.

For achieving this agreement, as well as for helping arrange an international conference at Algeciras, Spain, in 1906 to mediate North African disputes, TR received the Nobel Peace Prize in 1906. But the price of his diplomatic glory was high for U.S. foreign relations. Two historic friendships withered on the windswept plains of Manchuria. U.S. relations with Russia, once friendly, soured as the Russians implausibly accused Roosevelt of robbing them of military victory. Revelations about savage massacres of Russian Jews further poisoned American feeling against Russia. Japan, once America's protégé, felt cheated out of its due compensation. Both newly powerful, Japan and America now became rivals in Asia, as fear and jealousy between them grew. "A subjick race is on'y funny whin it's raaly subjek," said Finley Peter Dunne's Mr. Dooley (see "Thinking Globally: The Age of Empire," pp. 632–633). "About three years ago I stopped laughin' at Japanese jokes."

✦ Japanese Laborers in California

America's Pacific Coast soon felt the effects of the Russo-Japanese War. A new restlessness swept over the rice paddies of Japan, occasioned by the recent conflict's dislocations and tax burdens. A new wave of Japanese immigrants began pouring into the spacious valleys of California. Although Japanese residents never amounted to more than 3 percent of the state's population, white Californians ranted about a new "yellow peril" and feared being drowned in an Asian sea.

A showdown on the influx came in 1906, when San Francisco's school board, coping with the aftermath of a frightful earthquake and fire, ordered the segregation of Chinese, Japanese, and Korean students in a special school to free more space for whites. Instantly the incident boiled into an international crisis. The people of Japan, understandably sensitive on questions of race,

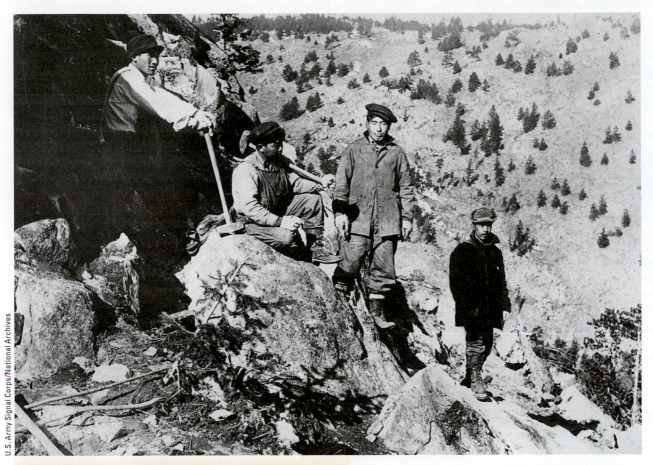

U.S. Army Signal Corps/National Archives

Japanese Workers Building a Road in California, ca. 1910

regarded this discrimination as an insult to them and their beloved children. On both sides of the Pacific, irresponsible war talk sizzled in the yellow press—the real "yellow peril." Roosevelt, who as a Rough Rider had relished shooting, was less happy over the prospect that California might stir up a war that all the other states would have to wage. He therefore invited the entire San Francisco Board of Education, headed by a bassoon-playing mayor under indictment for graft, to come to the White House.

TR finally broke the deadlock, but not until he had brandished his big stick and bared his big teeth. The Californians were induced to repeal the offensive school order and to accept what came to be known as the "Gentlemen's Agreement." By this secret understanding, worked out during 1907–1908, Tokyo agreed to stop the flow of laborers to the American mainland by withholding passports.

Worried that his intercession might be interpreted in Tokyo as prompted by fear, Roosevelt hit upon a dramatic scheme to impress the Japanese with the heft of his big stick. He daringly decided to send the entire battleship fleet on a highly visible voyage around the world. Late in 1907 sixteen sparkling-white, smoke-belching battleships started from Virginia waters. Their commander pointedly declared that he was ready for "a feast, a frolic, or a fight." The Great White Fleet—saluted by cannonading champagne corks—received tumultuous welcomes in Latin America, Hawaii, New Zealand, and Australia (though it ended up having to borrow coal from the British to complete the voyage).

As events turned out, an overwhelming reception in Japan was the high point of the trip. Tens of thousands of kimonoed schoolchildren, trained to wave tiny American flags, movingly sang "The Star-Spangled Banner." In the warm diplomatic atmosphere created by the visit of the fleet, the U.S. signed the **Root-Takahira agreement** with Japan in 1908. It pledged both powers to respect each other's territorial possessions in the Pacific and to uphold the Open Door in China. For the moment, at least, the two rising rival powers had found a means to maintain the peace.

Thinking Globally

The Age of Empire

The closing years of the nineteenth century witnessed an unprecedented explosion of imperialism, roughly defined as the forcible imposition of one country's rule on the unwilling inhabitants of another. Between 1870 and the outbreak of World War I in 1914, a handful of European states extended their sway over nearly one-quarter of the earth's surface. Other countries followed suit, notably Japan and eventually the United States.

All the imperial powers had in common a heritage of nationalism and a high degree of industrialization. They commanded the elaborate administrative apparatus of large unified states, along with quantities of wealth, technology, and murderous firepower utterly beyond the capacity of the so-called backward peoples they sought to dominate. As a result, imperialism was, from the start, a lopsided game. As one English wit mordantly noted in 1898,

> Whatever happens, we have got
> The Maxim gun, and they have not.

Yet ultimately, even with their enormously disproportionate advantages, the imperial states were unable to sustain the age of imperialism for much more than a century.

In many ways, modern imperialism resembled eighteenth-century mercantilism, as economically advanced states backed away from the free-trade doctrines that had energized the early stages of the Industrial Revolution and sought instead to create what one British imperialist called "a great self-sustaining and self-protecting empire." The new imperialism also differed from older colonialism in that the imperial powers sought not merely to exploit but also to transform, modernize, and "westernize" the "backward" societies under their control.

Imperialists often justified their dominion over less developed societies with high-toned slogans. The British professed to be nobly shouldering "the white man's burden." The French piously invoked their *mission civilisatrice* (civilizing mission). The Germans touted the benefits of spreading their vaunted *Kultur* (culture). The Americans prated about the superiority of the Anglo-Saxons, as the Japanese did about their own "Yamato" race.

These protestations may have been sincere, but other motives more powerfully propelled the imperial enterprise. Prominent among them was the quest for new markets, as maturing industrial economies appeared to be exhausting the possibilities for economic growth at home. The need for reliable sources of products such as cotton, sugar, copper, coffee, and tea also figured conspicuously. An even more compelling incentive was the need to protect the huge investments of capital that built the railroads, highways, bridges, ports, mills, foundries, mines, smelters, and telegraphs of the developing world. By the eve of the First World War, fully one-quarter of Britain's accumulated wealth was invested overseas.

But perhaps the most important factor driving the imperialist venture was simply the competitive nature of the international system itself. In an unstable, unpredictable world inhabited by ambitious and wary powers, no state thought it could afford to cede an advantage, however ill-defined, to any real or imagined rival. Indeed, quite independently of their hard economic value, colonies came to be considered the necessary symbols of great-power status. This perverse logic proved to be a powerful dynamic: once the imperial

A Young Ho Chi Minh   Ho Chi Minh (1890–1969) attended the Congress of the Socialist Party in Tours, France, where the French Communist party was created in late December 1920.

MAP 27.4 The Great Powers and Their Colonial Possessions, 1913 © Cengage Learning

The colonial powers and their possessions

- Germany
- France
- Great Britain
- Belgium
- Netherlands
- Portugal
- Italy
- Spain
- Russia
- United States
- Japan

race began, it was difficult to stop. As Cecil Rhodes, the fabled British colonizer in southern Africa, once said, "I would annex the planets, if I could. I often think of that."

So when Belgium's King Leopold took an interest in Africa's Congo basin in the 1870s, he touched off a mad imperial scramble that eventually involved Belgium, Britain, Germany, France, Italy, and Portugal. Less than two decades later, with the exceptions of Ethiopia and Liberia, the entire continent, much of it unexplored and of dubious economic value, lay under European domination (see Map 27.4).

In Asia, Germany annexed part of New Guinea in 1884. France completed its annexation of Indochina (present-day Vietnam, Laos, and Cambodia) that same year. Britain acquired Burma (now Myanmar) in 1885 and parts of Borneo and the Malay Peninsula soon after. Japan closed its grip on Okinawa in 1872, Formosa (Taiwan) in 1895, Port Arthur in 1905, and Korea in 1910. All those powers, in addition to Russia, also had designs on China, which despite its venerable history seemed a poor match for the energetic "nations on the make." In the Open Door notes of 1899 and 1900 (see pp. 623), the United States tried to temper the imperialists' appetites for Chinese territory and concessions, while at the same time America was becoming an imperial power itself with the takeover of the Philippines and Puerto Rico.

The imperialists brought not only their might and their majesty, their capital and their Maxim guns. They also brought their ideas, including concepts of nationalism, self-determination, and democracy. In 1919 a young Vietnamese nationalist named Nguyen Sinh Cung unsuccessfully petitioned the post–World War I peacemakers at Versailles for his country's right to self-determination. A little more than half a century later, under the name Ho Chi Minh, he secured Vietnam's independence by prevailing in a war first against the French and then against the Americans. By that time the United States had long since voluntarily relinquished the Philippines (in 1946, though Puerto Rico remains an American possession), and virtually all of Africa and Asia had been decolonized. With the handover of Hong Kong (1997) and Macao (1999) to the People's Republic of China, the age of empire effectively ended.

Varying Viewpoints

Why Did America Become a World Power?

American imperialism has long been an embarrassing topic for students of American history, who remember the Republic's own revolutionary origins and anticolonial tradition. Perhaps for that reason, many historians have tried to explain the dramatic overseas expansionism of the 1890s as some kind of aberration—a sudden, singular, and short-lived departure from time-honored American principles and practices. Various explanations have been offered to account for this spasmodic lapse. Scholars such as Julius Pratt pointed to the irresponsible behavior of the yellow press. Richard Hofstadter ascribed America's imperial fling as the "psychic crisis of the 1890s," a crisis brought on, he argued, by the strains of the decade's economic depression and the Populist upheaval. Howard K. Beale emphasized the contagious scramble for imperial possessions by the European powers, as well as Japan, in these years.

In Beale's argument, the United States—and Theodore Roosevelt in particular—succumbed to a kind of international peer pressure: if other countries were expanding their international roles and even establishing colonies around the globe, could the United States safely refrain from doing the same? In Beale's view, Theodore Roosevelt was no simpleminded imperial swashbuckler, but a coolly calculating diplomatic realist who perceived that if the United States did not hold its own against other powers, it would soon risk being pushed around, even in its own hemisphere, despite the Monroe Doctrine.

More recent scholarship by Paul Kramer and others has stressed the degree to which American imperialists turned to European precedents for guidance and inspiration. U.S. colonial officials in the Philippines and Puerto Rico circulated widely in the British colonial world, selectively adapting elements of British imperial policy.

Perhaps the most controversial interpretation of American imperialism has come from a so-called New Left school of writers, inspired by William Appleman Williams (and before him by V. I. Lenin's 1916 book *Imperialism: The Highest Stage of Capitalism*). Historians such as Williams and Walter LaFeber argue that the explanation for political and military expansion abroad is to be found in economic expansion at home. Increasing industrial output, so the argument goes, required ever more raw materials and, especially, overseas markets. To meet those needs, the nation adopted a strategy of "informal empire," shunning formal territorial possessions (with the conspicuous exceptions of Puerto Rico and the Philippines), but seeking economic dominance over foreign markets, materials, and investment outlets. That "revisionist" interpretation, in turn, has been sharply criticized by scholars who point out that foreign trade accounted for only a tiny share of American output and that the diplomacy of this period was far too complex to be reduced to "economic need."

Most recently, historians have highlighted the importance of race and gender in the march toward empire. Roosevelt and other imperialists perceived their world in gendered terms. American society, many feared, was losing touch with the manly virtues. It had grown soft and "feminine" since the closing of the frontier. Imperialists also saw the nations of the world in a strict racial hierarchy, with "primitive" blacks and Indians at the bottom and "civilized" Anglo-Saxons at the top. In this world-view the conquest of "inferior" peoples seemed natural—a tropical tonic to restore the nation's masculine virility. Scholars who emphasize these explanations of imperialism are less likely to see the expansionism of the 1890s as an aberration in American history. Instead, they argue, these overseas adventures were part of a long tradition of race-fueled militarism, from the nation's earliest Indian wars to Cold War engagements in Korea and Vietnam.

Chapter Review

KEY TERMS

Big Sister policy (609)
Great Rapprochement (610)
McKinley Tariff (611)
insurrectos (612)
Maine (612)
Teller Amendment (614)
Rough Riders (615)
Anti-Imperialist League (620)

Foraker Act (620)
Insular Cases (621)
Platt Amendment (621)
Open Door note (623)
Boxer Rebellion (623)
Hay-Pauncefote Treaty (628)
Roosevelt Corollary (630)
Root-Takahira agreement (631)

PEOPLE TO KNOW

Josiah Strong
Alfred Thayer Mahan
James G. Blaine
Richard Olney
Liliuokalani
"Butcher" Weyler
Dupuy de Lôme

George Dewey
Emilio Aguinaldo
William H. Taft
John Hay
Theodore ("Teddy") Roosevelt

CHRONOLOGY

1820	New England missionaries arrive in Hawaii
1889	Samoa crisis with Germany Pan-American Conference
1890	Mahan publishes *The Influence of Sea Power upon History*
1891	New Orleans crisis with Italy
1892	Valparaiso crisis with Chile
1893	Pribilof Islands dispute with Canada White planter revolt in Hawaii Cleveland refuses Hawaii annexation
1895	Cubans revolt against Spain
1895–1896	Venezuelan boundary crisis with Britain
1898	*Maine* explosion in Havana harbor Spanish-American War Teller Amendment Dewey's victory at Manila Bay Hawaii annexed
1899	Senate ratifies treaty acquiring Philippines Aguinaldo launches rebellion against United States in Philippines First American Open Door note
1900	Hawaii receives full territorial status Foraker Act for Puerto Rico Boxer Rebellion and U.S. military expedition to China Second Open Door note McKinley defeats Bryan for presidency

1901	Supreme Court *Insular Cases* Platt Amendment McKinley assassinated; Roosevelt becomes president Filipino rebellion suppressed Hay-Pauncefote Treaty with Britain gives United States exclusive right to build Panama Canal
1902	U.S. troops leave Cuba Colombian senate rejects U.S. proposal for canal across Panama
1903	Panamanian revolution against Colombia Hay–Bunau-Varilla Treaty gives United States control of Canal Zone in newly independent Panama
1904	Roosevelt Corollary to Monroe Doctrine
1904–1914	Construction of Panama Canal
1905	United States takes over Dominican Republic customs service Roosevelt mediates Russo-Japanese peace treaty
1906	San Francisco Japanese education crisis Roosevelt arranges Algeciras Conference
1906–1909	U.S. Marines occupy Cuba
1907	Great White Fleet makes world voyage
1907–1908	"Gentlemen's Agreement" with Japan
1908	Root-Takahira agreement
1917	Puerto Ricans granted U.S. citizenship

TO LEARN MORE

Gail Bederman, *Manliness and Civilization: A Cultural History of Gender and Race in the United States, 1880–1917* (1995)

Robert L. Beisner, *Twelve Against Empire: The Anti-Imperialists, 1898–1900* (1968)

Julia Greene, *The Canal Builders: Making America's Empire at the Panama Canal* (2009)

George C. Herring, *From Colony to Superpower: U.S. Foreign Relations Since 1776* (2008)

Kristin L. Hoganson, *Consumers' Imperium: The Global Production of American Domesticity, 1865–1920* (2007)

William R. Hutchison, *Errand to the World: American Protestant Thought and Foreign Missions* (1987)

Matthew Frye Jacobson, *Barbarian Virtues: The United States Encounters Foreign Peoples at Home and Abroad, 1876–1917* (2000)

Paul A. Kramer, *The Blood of Government: Race, Empire, the United States, and the Philippines* (2006)

Walter LaFeber, *The Cambridge History of American Foreign Relations*, vol. 2: *The American Search for Opportunity, 1865–1913* (1993)

Ernest R. May, *Imperial Democracy: The Emergence of America as a Great Power* (1961)

Louis A. Perez, Jr., *The War of 1898: The United States and Cuba in History and Historiography* (1998)

Emily S. Rosenberg, *Spreading the American Dream: American Economic and Cultural Expansion, 1890–1945* (1982)

Go to the CourseMate website at **www.cengagebrain.com** for additional study tools and review materials—including audio and video clips—for this chapter.

A complete, annotated bibliography for this chapter—along with brief descriptions of the People to Know—may be found on the American Pageant website. The Key Terms are defined in a Glossary at the end of the text.

Part Five

Struggling for Justice at Home and Abroad

1901–1945

The new century brought astonishing changes to the United States. Victory in the Spanish-American War made it clear that the United States was now a world power. Industrialization ushered in giant corporations, sprawling factories, sweatshop labor, and the ubiquitous automobile. A huge wave of immigration was altering the face of the nation, especially the cities, where a majority of Americans lived by 1920. With bigger cities came bigger fears—of crime, vice, poverty, and disease.

Changes of such magnitude raised vexing questions. What role should the United States play in the world? How could the enormous power of industry be controlled? How would the millions of new immigrants make their way in America? What should the country do about poverty, disease, and the continuing plague of racial inequality? All these issues turned on a fundamental point: should government remain narrowly limited in its powers, or did the times require a more potent

government that would actively shape society and secure American interests abroad?

The progressive movement represented the first attempt to answer those questions. Reform-minded men and women from all walks of life and from both major parties shared in the progressive crusade for greater government activism. Buoyed by this outlook, Presidents Theodore Roosevelt, William Howard Taft, and Woodrow Wilson enlarged the capacity of government to fight graft, "bust" business trusts, regulate corporations, and promote fair labor practices, child welfare, conservation, and consumer protection. These progressive reformers, convinced that women would bring greater morality to politics, bolstered the decades-long struggle for female suffrage. Women finally secured the vote in 1920 with the ratification of the Nineteenth Amendment.

The progressive-era presidents also challenged America's tradition of isolationism in foreign

Marching for Suffrage   Prominent New York socialite Mrs. Herbert Carpenter, bearing an American flag, marches in a parade for women's suffrage on Manhattan's Fifth Avenue, 1912. © Bettmann/Corbis policy. They felt the country had a moral obligation to spread democracy and an economic opportunity to reap profits in foreign markets. Roosevelt and Taft launched diplomatic initiatives in the Caribbean, Central America, and East Asia. Wilson aspired to "make the world safe for democracy" by rallying support for American intervention in the First World War.

The progressive spirit waned, however, as the United States retreated during the 1920s into what President Harding called "normalcy." Isolationist sentiment revived with a vengeance. Blessed with a booming economy, Americans turned their gaze inward to baseball heroes, radio, jazz, movies, and the first mass-produced American automobile, the Model T Ford. Presidents Harding, Coolidge, and Hoover backed off from the economic regulatory zeal of their predecessors.

"Normalcy" also had a brutal side. Thousands of suspected radicals were jailed or deported in the red scare of 1919 and 1920. Anti-immigrant passions flared until immigration quotas in 1924 squeezed the flow of newcomers to a trickle. Race riots scorched several northern cities in the summer of 1919, a sign of how embittered race relations had become in the wake of the "great migration" of southern blacks to wartime jobs in northern industry. A reborn Ku Klux Klan staged a comeback, not just in the South but in the North and West as well.

"Normalcy" itself soon proved short-lived, a casualty of the stock-market crash of 1929 and the Great Depression that followed. As Americans watched banks fail, businesses collapse, and millions of people lose their jobs, they asked with renewed urgency what role the government should play in rescuing the nation. President Franklin D. Roosevelt's answer was the "New Deal"—an ambitious array of relief programs, public works, and economic regulations that failed to cure the depression but furnished an impressive legacy of social reforms.

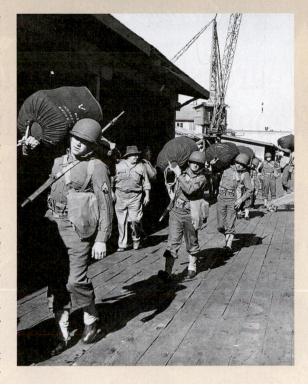

Bound for Guadalcanal, 1942 These troops were headed for one of the bloodiest battles of World War II, in the southwest Pacific's Solomon Islands. America threw some 15 million men and the full weight of its enormous economy into the struggle against German and Japanese aggression. National Archives

Most Americans came to accept an expanded federal government role at home under FDR's leadership in the 1930s, but they still clung stubbornly to isolationism. The United States did little in the 1930s to check the rising military aggression of Japan and Germany. By the early 1940s, events forced Americans to reconsider. Once Hitler's Germany had seized control of most of Europe, Roosevelt, who had long opposed the isolationists, found ways to aid a beleaguered Britain. When Japan attacked the American naval base at Pearl Harbor in December 1941, isolationists at last fell silent. Roosevelt led a stunned but determined nation into the Second World War, and victory in 1945 positioned the United States to assume a commanding position in the postwar world order.

The Great Depression and the Second World War brought to a head a half-century of debate over the role of government and the place of the United States in the world. In the name of a struggle for justice, Roosevelt established a new era of government activism at home and internationalism abroad. The New Deal's legacy set the terms of debate in American political life for the rest of the century.

Chapter 28

Progressivism and the Republican Roosevelt

1901–1912

*When I say I believe in a square deal I do not mean . . . to give every
man the best hand. If the cards do not come to any man, or if they
do come, and he has not got the power to play them, that is his affair.
All I mean is that there shall be no crookedness in the dealing.*

THEODORE ROOSEVELT, 1905

Nearly 76 million Americans greeted the new century in 1900. Almost one in seven of them was foreign-born. In the fourteen years of peace that remained before the Great War of 1914 engulfed the globe, 13 million more migrants would carry their bundles down the gangplanks to the land of promise.

Hardly had the twentieth century dawned on the ethnically and racially mixed American people than they were convulsed by a reform movement, the likes of which the nation had not seen since the 1840s. The new crusaders, who called themselves "progressives," waged war on many evils, notably monopoly, corruption, inefficiency, and social injustice. The progressive army was large, diverse, and widely deployed, but it had a single battle cry: "Strengthen the State." The "real heart of the movement," explained one of the progressive reformers, was "to use government as an agency of human welfare."

✵ Progressive Roots

The groundswell of the new reformist wave went far back—to the Greenback Labor party of the 1870s and the Populists of the 1890s, to the mounting unrest throughout the land as grasping industrialists concentrated more and more power in fewer and fewer hands. An outworn philosophy of hands-off individualism seemed increasingly out of place in the modern machine age. Social and economic problems were now too complex for the intentionally feeble Jeffersonian organs of government. Progressive theorists were insisting that society could no longer afford the luxury of a limitless "let-alone" (laissez-faire) policy. The people, through government, must substitute mastery for drift.

Well before 1900, perceptive politicians and writers had begun to pinpoint targets for the progressive attack. Bryan, Altgeld, and the Populists loudly branded the "bloated trusts" with the stigma of corruption and wrongdoing. In 1894 Henry Demarest Lloyd charged headlong into the Standard Oil Company with his book *Wealth Against Commonwealth*. Eccentric Thorstein Veblen assailed the new rich with his prickly pen in *The Theory of the Leisure Class* (1899), a savage attack on "predatory wealth" and "conspicuous consumption." In Veblen's view the parasitic leisure class engaged in wasteful "business" (or making money for money's sake) rather than productive "industry" (or making goods to satisfy real needs). He urged that social leadership pass from these superfluous titans to truly useful engineers.

Other pen-wielding knights likewise entered the fray. The keen-eyed and keen-nosed Danish immigrant Jacob A. Riis, a reporter for the *New York Sun*, shocked middle-class Americans in 1890 with *How the Other Half Lives*. His account was a damning indictment of the dirt, disease, vice, and misery of the rat-gnawed human rookeries known as New York slums. The book deeply

Melting Pot in P.S. 188, 1910   These immigrant children from the Lower East Side of New York are dressed in costumes from their native lands and surround their teacher, adorned as the Statue of Liberty. Schools like this one, flooded with immigrant children who could scarcely speak English, tried to respect their students' ancestral cultures while also cultivating loyalty to their adopted country by teaching American "civics" and appreciation for patriotic symbols and rituals.

influenced a future New York City police commissioner, Theodore Roosevelt. Novelist Theodore Dreiser used his blunt prose to batter promoters and profiteers in *The Financier* (1912) and *The Titan* (1914).

Caustic critics of social injustice issued from several other corners. Socialists, many of whom were European immigrants inspired by the strong movement for state socialism in the Old World, began to register appreciable strength at the ballot box (see "Thinking Globally: 'Why Is There No Socialism in the United States?'" pp. 642–643). High-minded messengers of the **social gospel** promoted a brand of progressivism based on Christian teachings. They used religious doctrine to demand better housing and living conditions for the urban poor. University-based economists urged new reforms modeled on European examples, importing policy ideas from Berlin to Baltimore. Feminists in multiplying numbers added social justice to suffrage on their list of needed reforms. With urban pioneers like Jane Addams in Chicago and Lillian Wald in New York

blazing the way, women entered the fight to improve the lot of families living and working in the festering cities.

✶ Raking Muck with the Muckrakers

Beginning about 1902 the exposing of evil became a flourishing industry among American publishers. A group of aggressive ten- and fifteen-cent popular magazines surged to the front, notably *McClure's, Cosmopolitan, Collier's,* and *Everybody's.* Waging fierce circulation wars, they dug deep for the dirt that the public loved to hate. Enterprising editors financed extensive research and encouraged pugnacious writing by their bright young reporters, whom President Roosevelt branded as **muckrakers** in 1906. Annoyed by their excess of zeal, he compared the mudslinging magazine dirt-diggers to the figure in Bunyan's *Pilgrim's Progress* who was so intent on raking manure that he could not see the celestial crown dangling overhead.

Room in a Tenement Flat, 1910 Tenement life on the Lower East Side of New York City was exposed by the camera of Jacob Riis, who compiled a large photographic archive of turn-of-the-century urban life. Many families counted themselves lucky to share a single room, no matter how squalid.

Despite presidential scolding, these muckrakers boomed circulation, and some of their most scandalous exposures were published as best-selling books. The reformer-writers ranged far, wide, and deep in their crusade to lay bare the muck of iniquity in American society. In 1902 a brilliant New York reporter, Lincoln Steffens, launched a series of articles in *McClure's* titled "The Shame of the Cities." He fearlessly unmasked the corrupt alliance between big business and municipal government. Steffens was followed in the same magazine by Ida M. Tarbell, a pioneering journalist who published a devastating but factual exposé of the Standard Oil Company. (Her father had been ruined by the oil interests.)

Plucky muckrakers fearlessly tilted their pen-lances at varied targets. They assailed the malpractices of life insurance companies and tariff lobbies. They roasted the beef trust, the "money trust," the railroad barons, and the corrupt amassing of American fortunes. Thomas W. Lawson, an erratic speculator who had himself made $50 million on the stock market, laid bare the practices of his accomplices in "Frenzied Finance," a series of articles that appeared in *Everybody's*. Lawson, by fouling his own nest, made many enemies among his rich associates, and he died a poor man.

David G. Phillips shocked an already startled nation by his series in *Cosmopolitan* titled "The Treason of the Senate" (1906). He boldly charged that seventy-five of the ninety senators did not represent the people at all but the railroads and trusts. This withering indictment, buttressed by facts, impressed President Roosevelt. Phillips continued his attacks through novels and was fatally shot in 1911 by a deranged young man whose family he had allegedly maligned.

Some of the most effective fire of the muckrakers was directed at social evils. The ugly list included the immoral "white slave" traffic in women, the rickety slums, and the appalling number of industrial accidents. The sorry subjugation of America's 9 million blacks—of whom 90 percent still lived in the South and one-third were illiterate—was spotlighted in Ray Stannard Baker's *Following the Color Line* (1908). The abuses of child labor were brought luridly to light by John Spargo's *The Bitter Cry of the Children* (1906).

Vendors of potent patent medicines (often heavily spiked with alcohol) likewise came in for bitter criticism. These conscienceless vultures sold incredible quantities of adulterated or habit-forming drugs, while "doping" the press with lavish advertising. Muckraking attacks in *Collier's* were ably reinforced by Dr. Harvey W. Wiley, chief chemist of the Department of Agriculture, who with his famous "Poison Squad" performed experiments on himself.

Full of sound and fury, the muckrakers signified much about the nature of the progressive reform movement. They were long on lamentation but stopped short of revolutionary remedies. To right social wrongs,

In his muckraker speech (1906), Theodore Roosevelt (1858–1919) said,

"Now, it is very necessary that we should not flinch from seeing what is vile and debasing. There is filth on the floor and it must be scraped up with the muck-rake; and there are times and places where this service is the most needed of all the services that can be performed. But the man who never does anything else, who never thinks or speaks or writes, save of his feats with the muck-rake, speedily becomes, not a help to society, not an incitement to good, but one of the most potent forces for evil."

© Bettmann/Corbis

Ida Tarbell (1857–1944) in Her Office Tarbell was the most eminent woman in the muckraking movement and one of the most respected business historians of her generation. In 1904 she earned a national reputation for publishing a scathing history of the Standard Oil Company, the "Mother of Trusts." Two years later she joined Ray Stannard Baker, William Allen White, and other muckrakers in purchasing the *American* magazine, which became a journalistic podium in their campaign for honest government and an end to business abuses.

they counted on publicity and an aroused public conscience, not drastic political change. They sought not to overthrow capitalism but to cleanse it. The cure for the ills of American democracy, they earnestly believed, was more democracy.

In his muckraking classic "The Shame of the Cities" (1904), Lincoln Steffens (1866–1936) decried the great threat posed by New York City's Tammany machine:

"Bribery is no ordinary felony, but treason; . . . 'corruption which breaks out here and there and now and then' is not an occasional offense, but a common practice, and . . . the effect of it is literally to change the form of our government from one that is representative of the people to an oligarchy, representative of special interests."

✳ Political Progressivism

The question "Who were the progressives?" evokes contradictory answers. Progressive reformers included militarists such as Theodore Roosevelt, who thrilled to the strenuous life, as well as pacifists such as Jane Addams, whose loftiest goals included the abolition of war. Female settlement workers hoping to "Americanize" recent immigrants mobilized alongside labor unionists and enlightened businessmen to strengthen the helping hand of government. In diverse ways, and sometimes with divergent aims, the progressives sought to modernize American institutions to achieve two chief goals: to use the state to curb monopoly power and to improve the common person's conditions of life and labor. Progressives emerged in both major parties, in all regions, and at all levels of government. The truth is that progressivism was less a monolithic minority movement and more a broadly dispersed majority mood. (See Varying Viewpoints, pp. 675–676.)

One of the first objectives of progressives was to regain the power that had slipped from the hands of the people into those of the "interests." These ardent reformers pushed for direct primary elections so as to undercut power-hungry party bosses. They favored the **initiative** so that voters could directly propose legislation themselves, thus bypassing the boss-bought state legislatures. Progressives also agitated for the **referendum**. This device would place laws on the ballot for final approval by the people, especially laws that had been railroaded through a compliant legislature by free-spending agents of big business. The **recall** would enable the voters to remove faithless elected officials, particularly those who had been bribed by bosses or lobbyists.

Rooting out graft also became a prime goal of earnest progressives. A number of the state legislatures passed corrupt-practices acts, which limited the amount of money that candidates could spend for their election. Such legislation also restricted huge gifts from corporations, for which the donors would expect special favors. The secret **Australian ballot** was likewise being introduced more widely in the states to counteract boss rule. Bribery was less feasible when bribers could not tell if they were getting their money's worth from the bribed.

Direct election of U.S. senators became a favorite goal of progressives, especially after the muckrakers had exposed the scandalous intimacy between greedy corporations and Congress. By 1900 the Senate had so many rich men that it was often sneered at as the "Millionaires' Club." Too many of these prosperous solons, elected as they then were by trust-dominated legislatures, heeded the voice of their "masters" rather than the voice of the masses.

"Why Is There No Socialism in the United States?"

The Industrial Revolution that began in Britain in the late eighteenth century had by 1900 utterly transformed life in the Western world and beyond. It also had spawned a powerful theory of history, grounded in the writings of Karl Marx. Marxists believed that history's driving engine was class conflict; that in the industrial era that conflict had been starkly reduced to the contest between capitalists and workers (the *bourgeoisie* and the *proletariat*); and that an inevitable socialist revolution would result in the triumph of the proletariat and the emergence of a classless society. Its organizing principle would be "From each according to his ability, to each according to his needs."

Improbable as it might seem today, many nineteenth-century Marxists expected the first socialist revolution to occur in the United States. Marx himself saw America as the country where capitalism had developed more "shamelessly" than elsewhere, thus setting the stage for the "final conflict" that would yield the socialist utopia. Violent labor upheavals like those at Homestead (see p. 506), Haymarket (see p. 533), and Pullman (see p. 599) seemed to confirm that analysis, and a chorus of European Marxists stepped up their prophecies. Marx's collaborator Friedrich Engels wrote in the aftermath of the Haymarket eruption in May 1886 that in Europe it had taken workers decades to evolve a common "class consciousness," but "on the more favored soil of America, where no medieval ruins bar the way . . . the working class" would do so "within 10 months."

But it was not to be. Twenty years later the head of the German Social Democratic party lamented that "we are waiting for you Americans to do something."

The Americans had done a little something, but amid all the ferment of reform in the progressive era, they remained a sore disappointment to European radicals. Eugene V. Debs organized the Socialist party in 1901 and won 6 percent of the vote in the presidential election of 1912. But the Socialist party remained a tiny, marginal group. It never posed a serious challenge to the major American parties and never remotely approached the stature of Old World working-class parties such as the French Socialists, the Italian Communists, the German Social Democrats, and the British Labour party. At one time or another, most of these European organizations became ruling parties that implemented socialist ideas such as national ownership of core industries, robust support for labor unions, and lavish welfare programs—developments that to this day have had only feeble if any counterparts in the United States.

The failure of Marx's predictions about America occasioned much soul-searching about the plausibility of his entire theory of history. In 1904 a young German scholar named Werner Sombart traveled to the United States—much as Alexis de Tocqueville had nearly seventy-five years earlier—to examine America's puzzling reality firsthand (see "Thinking Globally: Alexis de Tocqueville on Democracy in America and Europe," pp. 252–253). Two years later he published the notable book *Why Is There No Socialism in the United States?* "If Socialism follows as a necessary reaction to capitalism," he asked, why was there no socialist movement worthy of the name in "the country with the most advanced capitalist development, namely the United States?"

Sombart gave several answers:

1. The strikingly egalitarian manners of all Americans. "The bowing and scraping before the 'upper classes,'

The Prophet of the Class Struggle, Karl Marx (1818–1883)

© Michael Nicholson/Corbis

The IWW Seeks Subscribers, 1911 This poster aimed to attract subscribers to *Industrial Worker*, the newspaper of the Industrial Workers of the World (IWW). The IWW was a small but vocal radical labor union that hoped to unify American workers in "one big union," irrespective of their particular jobs, gender, or race. Its motto was "An injury to one is an injury to all." At its peak in 1923, the union claimed 100,000 members, commonly known as Wobblies, and could marshal the support of some 300,000 more, mostly workers on the docks and in mines, lumbering, and textiles.

which produces such an unpleasant impression in Europe, is completely unknown," he noted, reflecting the workers' refusal or inability to consider themselves a class apart.

2. The "safety valve" of the western frontier, which allowed workers to walk away from oppressive employers and strike out on their own. Sombart exaggerated the effects of the frontier (see p. 590), but he did call attention to the remarkable geographic mobility of American workers, which, together with their astonishing racial and ethnic diversity, worked to inhibit their sense of class permanence and class solidarity.

3. The American workers' remarkably high standard of living. "On roast beef and apple pie," he concluded in a famous sentence, "all socialist utopias have gone to pot."

4. An accident of historical timing. Sombart shared with Tocqueville a deep insight into the American experience. Unlike Europe, where the struggles for political and economic rights went forward in tandem, in America workers had largely achieved full political equality before the onset of America's own Industrial Revolution. They had a stake in the existing political order from the outset and little incentive to overturn it. As another German socialist put it, for the purposes of building class consciousness, "the *struggle* for freedom is very much superior to the effortless possession of a freedom that others have won before." That observation echoed

Tocqueville's celebrated dictum that because the United States never had a feudal phase, it was *born* free, instead of *becoming* so, and was "reaping the fruits of the democratic revolution without having had the revolution itself."

More than a century after Sombart's inquiry, and especially since the collapse of Soviet communism, Marxism stands largely discredited, and some western European societies are edging away from socialist ideas such as national ownership of industries. As one historian has suggested, "One might well ask not 'Why is there no socialism in the United States?' but 'Why has there been no socialist transformation in any advanced capitalist society?'"

Granger Collection

Jane Addams and Fellow Pacifists, 1915 Addams cofounded the Women's Peace Party in 1915. Its pacifist platform was said to represent the views of the "mother half of humanity." Although the party initially attracted twenty-five thousand members, America's entry into the war two years later eroded popular support, since pacifist internationalism became suspect as anti-American.

A constitutional amendment to bring about the popular election of senators had rough sledding in Congress, for the plutocratic members of the Senate were happy with existing methods. But a number of states established primary elections in which the voters expressed their preferences for the Senate. The local legislatures, when choosing senators, found it politically wise to heed the voice of the people. Partly as a result of such pressures, the Seventeenth Amendment to the Constitution, approved in 1913, established the direct election of U.S. senators (see the Appendix). But the expected improvement in caliber was slow in coming.

The suffrage campaign of the early twentieth century benefited from a new generation of women who considered themselves "feminists." At a mass meeting in New York in 1914, Marie Jenny Howe (1870–1934), a minister by training as well as a prominent early feminist, proclaimed,

"We intend simply to be ourselves, not just our little female selves, but our whole big human selves.**"**

Woman suffrage, the goal of female reformers for many decades, likewise received powerful new support from the progressives early in the 1900s. The political reformers believed that women's votes would elevate the political tone, and the foes of the saloon felt that they could count on the support of enfranchised females. The suffragists, with their cry of "Votes for Women" and "Equal Suffrage for Men and Women," protested bitterly against "Taxation Without Representation." Many of the states, especially the more liberal ones in the West, such as Washington, California, and Oregon, gradually extended the vote to women. But by 1910 nationwide female suffrage was still a decade away, and a suffragist could still be sneeringly defined as "one who has ceased to be a lady and has not yet become a gentleman."

✬ Progressivism in the Cities and States

Progressives scored some of their most impressive gains in the cities. Frustrated by the inefficiency and corruption of machine-oiled city government, many localities followed the pioneering example of Galveston, Texas. In 1901 it had appointed expert-staffed commissions to manage urban affairs. Other communities adopted the city-manager system, also designed to take politics out of municipal administration. Some of these "reforms" obviously valued efficiency more highly than democracy, as control of civic affairs was further removed from the people's hands.

Urban reformers likewise attacked "slumlords," juvenile delinquency, and wide-open prostitution (vice-at-a-price), which flourished in red-light districts unchallenged by bribed police. Public-spirited Americans looked to English and German cities for lessons on how to clean up their water supplies, light their streets, and run their trolley cars. The vogue of public ownership of utilities swept the nation as local governments tried to halt the corrupt sale of franchises.

Progressivism naturally bubbled up to the state level, notably in Wisconsin, which became a yeasty laboratory of reform. The governor of the state, pompadoured Robert M. ("Fighting Bob") La Follette, was an undersized but overbearing crusader who emerged as the most militant of the progressive Republican leaders. After a desperate fight with entrenched monopoly, he reached the governor's chair in 1901. Routing the lumber and railroad "interests," he wrested considerable control from the crooked corporations and returned it to the people. He also perfected a scheme for regulating public utilities, while laboring in close association with experts on the faculty of the state university at Madison.

Other states marched steadily toward the progressive camp, as they undertook to regulate railroads and trusts, chiefly through public utility commissions. Oregon was not far behind Wisconsin, and California made giant bootstrides under the stocky Hiram W. Johnson. Elected Republican governor in 1910, this dynamic prosecutor of grafters helped break the dominant grip of the Southern Pacific Railroad on California politics and then, like La Follette, set up a political machine of his own. Heavily whiskered Charles Evans Hughes, the able and audacious reformist Republican governor of New York, had earlier gained national fame as an investigator of malpractices by gas and insurance companies and by the coal trust.

✦ Progressive Women

Women proved themselves an indispensable part of the progressive army. A crucial focus for women's activism was the settlement house movement (see p. 549). At a time when women could neither vote nor hold political office, settlement houses offered a side door to public life. They exposed middle-class women to the problems plaguing America's cities, including poverty, political corruption, and intolerable working and living conditions. They also gave them the skills and confidence to attack those evils. The women's club movement provided an even broader civic entryway for many middle-class women. Literary clubs, where educated women met to improve themselves with poetry and prose, had existed for decades. But in the late nineteenth and early twentieth centuries, many of these clubs set aside Shakespeare and Henry James for social issues and current events. "Dante has been dead for several centuries," observed the president of the General Federation of Women's Clubs in 1904. "I think it is time that we dropped the study of his *Inferno* and turned our attention to our own."

Nineteenth-century notions of "separate spheres" dictated that a woman's place was in the home, so most female progressives defended their new activities as an extension—not a rejection—of the traditional roles of wife and mother. Thus they were often drawn to moral and "maternal" issues like keeping children out of smudgy mills and sweltering sweatshops, attacking the scourge of tuberculosis bred in airless tenements, winning pensions for mothers with dependent children, and ensuring that only safe food products found their way to the family table. Female activists agitated through organizations like the National Consumers League (1899) and the Women's Trade Union League (1903), as well as through two new federal agencies, the Children's Bureau (1912) and the Women's Bureau (1920), both in the Department of Labor. These wedges into the federal bureaucracy, however small, gave female reformers a national stage for social investigation and advocacy.

Campaigns for factory reform and temperance particularly attracted women foot soldiers. Unsafe and unsanitary sweatshops—factories where workers toiled long hours for low wages—were a public scandal in many cities. Florence Kelley, a former resident of Jane Addams's Hull House, became the State of Illinois's first chief factory inspector and one of the nation's leading advocates for improved factory conditions. In 1899 Kelley took control of the newly founded National Consumers League, which mobilized female consumers to pressure for laws safeguarding women and children in the workplace. In the landmark case ***Muller v. Oregon*** (1908), crusading attorney Louis D. Brandeis persuaded the Supreme Court to accept the constitutionality of laws protecting women workers by presenting evidence of the harmful effects of factory labor on women's weaker bodies. Although this argument calling for special protection for women seemed discriminatory by later standards and closed many "male" jobs to women, progressives at the time hailed Brandeis's achievement as a triumph over existing legal doctrine, which

The Wages of Negligence   Officials review the charred remains of some of the survivors of the catastrophic Triangle Shirtwaist Company fire in 1911. Outrage over this calamity galvanized a generation of reformers to fight for better workplace safety rules.

Hadwin Collection, Kheel Center, Cornell University

afforded employers total control over the workplace. The American welfare state that emerged from female activism focused more on protecting women and children than on granting benefits to everyone, as was the case in much of western Europe, with its stronger labor movements.

Crusaders for these humane measures did not always have smooth sailing. One dismaying setback came in 1905, when the Supreme Court, in *Lochner v. New York*, invalidated a New York law establishing a ten-hour day for bakers. Yet the reformist progressive wave finally washed up into the judiciary, and in 1917 the Court upheld a ten-hour law for factory workers.

Laws regulating factories were worthless if not enforced, a truth horribly demonstrated by a lethal fire in 1911 at the Triangle Shirtwaist Company in New York City. Locked doors and other flagrant violations of the fire code turned the factory into a death trap. One hundred forty-six workers, most of them young immigrant women, were incinerated or leapt from eighth- and ninth-story windows to their deaths. Lashed by the public outcry, including a massive strike by women in the needle trades, the New York legislature passed

much stronger laws regulating the hours and conditions of sweatshop toil. Other legislatures followed, and by 1917 thirty states had put workers' compensation laws on the books, providing insurance to workers injured in industrial accidents. Gradually the concept of the employer's responsibility to society was replacing the old dog-eat-dog philosophy of unregulated free enterprise.

Corner saloons, with their shutter doors, naturally attracted the ire and fire of progressives. Alcohol was intimately connected with prostitution in red-light districts, with the drunken voter, with crooked city officials dominated by "booze" interests, and with the blowsy "boss" who counted poker chips by night and miscounted ballots by day (including the "cemetery vote"). By 1900 cities like New York and San Francisco had one saloon for about every two hundred people.

Antiliquor campaigners received powerful support from several militant organizations, notably the **Woman's Christian Temperance Union (WCTU)**. Founder Frances E. Willard, who would fall to her knees in prayer on saloon floors, mobilized nearly 1 million women to "make the world homelike" and built the

Culver Pictures

Out of Work and the Reason Why, 1899 This temperance propaganda from an 1899 magazine illustrates the role of women in the temperance movement. Alcohol abuse threatened the stability of the family, still predominantly considered the "woman's sphere" in the late nineteenth century.

WCTU into the largest organization of women in the world. She found a vigorous ally in the Anti-Saloon League, which was aggressive, well organized, and well financed.

Caught up in the crusade, some states and numerous counties passed "dry" laws, which controlled, restricted, or abolished alcohol. The big cities were generally "wet," for they had a large immigrant vote accustomed in the Old Country to the free flow of wine and beer. When World War I erupted in 1914, nearly one-half of the population lived in "dry" territory, and nearly three-fourths of the total area had outlawed saloons. Demon Rum was groggy and about to be floored—temporarily—by the Eighteenth Amendment in 1919.

★ TR's Square Deal for Labor

Theodore Roosevelt, although something of an imperialistic busybody abroad, was touched by the progressive wave at home. Like other reformers, he feared that the "public interest" was being submerged in the drifting seas of indifference. Everybody's interest was nobody's interest. Roosevelt decided to make it his. His sportsman's instincts spurred him into demanding a "Square Deal" for capital, labor, and the public at large. Broadly speaking, the president's program embraced three C's: control of the corporations, consumer protection, and conservation of natural resources.

The Square Deal for labor received its acid test in 1902, when a crippling strike broke out in the anthracite coal mines of Pennsylvania. Some 140,000 besooted workers, many of them illiterate immigrants, had long been frightfully exploited and accident-plagued. They demanded, among other improvements, a 20 percent increase in pay and a reduction of the working day from ten to nine hours.

Unsympathetic mine owners, confident that a chilled public would react against the miners, refused to arbitrate or even negotiate. One of their spokesmen, multimillionaire George F. Baer, reflected the high-and-mighty attitude of certain ungenerous employers. Workers, he wrote, would be cared for "not by the labor agitators, but by the Christian men to whom God in His infinite wisdom has given the control of the property interests of this country."

As coal supplies dwindled, factories and schools were forced to shut down, and even hospitals felt the icy grip of winter. Desperately seeking a solution, Roosevelt summoned representatives of the striking miners and the mine owners to the White House. He was profoundly annoyed by the "extraordinary stupidity and bad temper" of the "wooden-headed gentry" who operated the mines. As he later confessed, if it had not been for the dignity of his high office, he would have taken one of them "by the seat of the breeches" and "chucked him out of the window."

Roosevelt finally resorted to his trusty big stick when he threatened to seize the mines and operate

Roosevelt was a charismatic figure who made a powerful impression on his contemporaries. The journalist William Allen White (1868–1944) later wrote of his first meeting with TR in 1897,

❝He sounded in my heart the first trumpet call of the new time that was to be. . . . I had never known such a man as he, and never shall again. He overcame me. And in the hour or two we spent that day at lunch, and in a walk down F Street, he poured into my heart such visions, such ideals, such hopes, such a new attitude toward life and patriotism and the meaning of things, as I had never dreamed men had. . . . After that I was his man.❞

Court records provide notably fruitful sources for historians. They not only tell often-colorful stories about the lives of ordinary men and women caught up in the legal system; they also by their very nature testify to the norms and values that lawyers employ to make their cases and that judges invoke to explain their decisions. The case of *Muller* v. *Oregon* (see p. 645) is especially instructive on both counts. The official Supreme Court records tell how on September 4, 1905, Joe Haselbock, a supervisor in Curt Muller's Grand Laundry in Portland, Oregon, asked an employee, Mrs. E. Gotcher, to remain after hours to do an extra load of laundry. That request violated Oregon's law prohibiting women from working more than ten hours per day. Mrs. Gotcher later complained to the authorities, and Muller was fined $10. Muller refused to pay and took his case all the way to the U.S. Supreme Court. In its landmark decision (below), the Court upheld the constitutionality of the Oregon statute, and Muller at last had to cough up his fine. On what grounds did the Court justify its ruling? What does Justice David J. Brewer's argument on behalf of the Court's decision suggest about the cultural identity and social role of women in early-twentieth-century American society?

(208 U.S. 412)
CURT MULLER, Plff. in Err.,
v.
STATE OF OREGON.

. . . That woman's physical structure and the performance of material functions place her at a disadvantage in the struggle for subsistence is obvious. This is especially true when the burdens of motherhood are upon her. . . . and as healthy mothers are essential to vigorous offspring, the physical well-being of woman becomes an object of public interest and care in order to preserve the strength and vigor of the race.

Still again, history discloses the fact that woman has always been dependent upon man. He established his control at the outset by superior physical strength, and this control in various forms, with diminishing intensity, has continued to the present. . . . It is still true that in the struggle for subsistence she is not an equal competitor with her brother. . . . Differentiated by these matters from the other sex, she is properly placed in a class by herself, and legislation designed for her protection may be sustained, even when like legislation is not necessary for men, and could not be sustained. It is impossible to close one's eyes to the fact that she still looks to her brother and depends upon him. . . . The two sexes differ in structure of body, in the functions to be performed by each, in the amount of physical strength, in the capacity for long continued labor, particularly when done standing, the influence of vigorous health upon the future well-being of the race, the self-reliance which enables one to assert full rights, and in the capacity to maintain the struggle for subsistence. This difference justifies a difference in legislation, and upholds that which is designed to compensate for some of the burdens which rest upon her.

We have not referred in this discussion to the denial of the elective franchise in the state of Oregon, for while that may disclose a lack of political equality in all things with her brother, that is not of itself decisive. The reason runs deeper, and rests in the inherent difference between the two sexes, and in the different functions in life which they perform. . . .

---

them with federal troops. Faced with this first-time-ever threat to use federal bayonets against capital, rather than labor, the owners grudgingly consented to arbitration. A compromise decision ultimately gave the miners a 10 percent pay boost and a working day of nine hours.

But their union was not officially recognized as a bargaining agent.

Keenly aware of the mounting antagonisms between capital and labor, Roosevelt urged Congress to create the new Department of Commerce and

Labor. This goal was achieved in 1903. (Ten years later the agency was split in two.) An important arm of the newborn cabinet body was the Bureau of Corporations, which was authorized to probe businesses engaged in interstate commerce. The bureau was highly useful in helping to break the stranglehold of monopoly and in clearing the road for the era of "trust-busting."

★ TR Corrals the Corporations

The sprawling railroad octopus sorely needed restraint. The Interstate Commerce Commission, created in 1887 as a feeble sop to the public, had proved woefully inadequate. Railroad barons could simply appeal the commission's decisions on rates to the federal courts—a process that might take ten years.

Spurred by the former-cowboy president, Congress passed effective railroad legislation, beginning with the **Elkins Act** of 1903. This curb was aimed primarily at the rebate evil. Heavy fines could now be imposed both on the railroads that gave rebates and on the shippers that accepted them.

Still more effective was the Hepburn Act of 1906. Free passes, with their hint of bribery, were severely restricted. The once-infantile Interstate Commerce Commission was expanded, and its reach was extended to include express companies, sleeping-car companies, and pipelines. For the first time, the commission was given real molars when it was authorized, on complaint of shippers, to nullify existing rates and stipulate maximum rates.

Railroads also provided Roosevelt with an opportunity to brandish his antitrust bludgeon. *Trusts* had come to be a fighting word in the progressive era. Roosevelt believed that these industrial behemoths, with their efficient means of production, had arrived to stay. He concluded that there were "good" trusts, with public consciences, and "bad" trusts, which lusted greedily for power. He was determined to respond to the popular outcry against the trusts but was also determined not to throw out the baby with the bathwater by indiscriminately smashing all large businesses.

Roosevelt as a trustbuster first burst into the headlines in 1902 with an attack on the Northern Securities Company, a railroad holding company organized by financial titan J. P. Morgan and empire builder James J. Hill. These Napoleonic moguls of money sought to achieve a virtual monopoly of the railroads in the Northwest. Roosevelt was therefore challenging the most regal potentates of the industrial aristocracy.

The railway promoters appealed to the Supreme Court, which in 1904 upheld Roosevelt's antitrust suit and ordered the Northern Securities Company to be dissolved. The *Northern Securities* decision jolted Wall

Library of Congress

Roosevelt Tames the Trusts   Legend to the contrary, Roosevelt did not attack all trusts indiscriminately. Rather, he pursued a few high-profile cases against a handful of corporate giants, in order to "tame" other businesses into accepting government regulation.

Street and angered big business but greatly enhanced Roosevelt's reputation as a trust smasher.

Roosevelt's big stick crashed down on other giant monopolies, as he initiated over forty legal proceedings against them. The Supreme Court in 1905 declared the beef trust illegal, and the heavy fist of justice fell upon monopolists controlling sugar, fertilizer, harvesters, and other key products.

Much mythology has inflated Roosevelt's reputation as a trustbuster. The Rough Rider understood the political popularity of monopoly-smashing, but he did not consider it sound economic policy. Combination and integration, he felt, were the hallmarks of the age, and to try to stem the tide of economic progress by political means he considered the rankest folly. Bigness was not necessarily badness, so why punish success? Roosevelt's real purpose in assaulting the Goliaths of industry was symbolic: to prove conclusively that the government, not private business, ruled the country. He believed in regulating, not fragmenting, the big business combines. The threat of dissolution, he felt, might make the sultans of the smokestacks more amenable to federal regulation—as it did.

In truth, Roosevelt never swung his trust-crushing stick with maximum force. In many ways the huge industrial behemoths were healthier—though perhaps more "tame"—at the end of Roosevelt's reign than they had been before. His successor, William Howard Taft, actually "busted" more trusts than TR did. In one celebrated instance in 1907, Roosevelt even gave his personal blessing to J. P. Morgan's plan to have U.S. Steel absorb the Tennessee Coal and Iron Company, without fear of antitrust reprisals. When Taft then launched a suit against U.S. Steel in 1911, the political reaction from TR was explosive.

Caring for the Consumer

Roosevelt backed a noteworthy measure in 1906 that benefited both corporations and consumers. Big meatpackers were being shut out of certain European markets because some American meat—from the small packinghouses, claimed the giants—had been found to be tainted. Foreign governments were even threatening to ban all American meat imports by throwing out the good beef with the bad botulism.

At the same time, American consumers hungered for safer canned products. Their appetite for reform was whetted by Upton Sinclair's sensational novel *The Jungle*, published in 1906. Sinclair, a dedicated Socialist, intended his revolting tract to focus attention on the plight of the workers in the big canning factories, but instead he appalled the public with his description of disgustingly unsanitary food products. (As he put it, he aimed for the nation's heart but hit its stomach.) The book described in noxious detail the filth, disease, and putrefaction in Chicago's damp, ill-ventilated slaughterhouses. Many readers, including Roosevelt, were so sickened that for a time they found meat unpalatable. The president was moved by

the loathsome mess in Chicago to appoint a special investigating commission, whose cold-blooded report almost outdid Sinclair's novel. It related how piles of poisoned rats, rope ends, splinters, and other debris were scooped up and canned as potted ham. A cynical jingle of the time ran,

> Mary had a little lamb,
> And when she saw it sicken,
> She shipped it off to Packingtown,
> And now it's labeled chicken.

Backed by a nauseated public, Roosevelt induced Congress to pass the **Meat Inspection Act** of 1906. It decreed that the preparation of meat shipped over state lines would be subject to federal inspection from corral to can. Although the largest packers resisted certain features of the act, they accepted it as an opportunity to drive their smaller, fly-by-night competitors out of business. At the same time, they could receive the government's seal of approval on their exports. As a companion to the Meat Inspection Act, the **Pure Food and Drug Act** of 1906 was designed to prevent the adulteration and mislabeling of foods and pharmaceuticals.

Earth Control

Wasteful Americans, assuming that their natural resources were inexhaustible, had looted and polluted their incomparable domain with unparalleled speed and greed. Western ranchers and timbermen were especially eager to accelerate the destructive process, for they panted to build up the country, and the environmental consequences be hanged. But even before the end of the nineteenth century, far-visioned leaders

Sausage Making, ca. 1906
White-jacketed inspectors like those on the right made some progress in cleaning up the septic slaughterhouses after the passage of the Meat Inspection Act in 1906.

Brown Brothers

saw that such a squandering of the nation's birthright would have to be halted, or America would sink from resource richness to despoiled dearth.

A first feeble step toward conservation had been taken with the Desert Land Act of 1877, under which the federal government sold arid land cheaply on the condition that the purchaser irrigate the thirsty soil within three years. More successful was the Forest Reserve Act of 1891, authorizing the president to set aside public forests as national parks and other reserves. Under this statute some 46 million acres of magnificent trees were rescued from the lumberman's saw in the 1890s and preserved for posterity. The Carey Act of 1894 distributed federal land to the states on the condition that it be irrigated and settled.

A new day in the history of conservation dawned with Roosevelt (see "Makers of America: The Environmentalists," pp. 652–653). Huntsman, naturalist, rancher, lover of the great outdoors, he was appalled by the pillaging of timber and mineral resources. Other dedicated conservationists, notably Gifford Pinchot, head of the federal Division of Forestry, had broken important ground before him. But Roosevelt seized the banner of leadership and charged into the fray with all the weight of his prestige, his energy, his firsthand knowledge, and his slashing invective.

The thirst of the desert still unslaked, Congress responded to the whip of the Rough Rider by passing the landmark Newlands Act of 1902. Washington was authorized to collect money from the sale of public lands in the sun-baked western states and then use these funds for the development of irrigation projects. Settlers repaid the cost of reclamation from their now-productive soil, and the money was put into a revolving fund to finance more such enterprises. The giant Roosevelt Dam, constructed on Arizona's Salt River, was appropriately dedicated by Roosevelt in 1911. Thanks to this epochal legislation, dozens of dams were thrown across virtually every major western river in the ensuing decades.

The Yosemite Museum, Yosemite National Park

High Point for Conservation Roosevelt and famed naturalist John Muir visit Glacier Point, on the rim of Yosemite Valley, California. In the distance is Yosemite Falls; a few feet behind Roosevelt is a sheer drop of 3,254 feet.

Roosevelt pined to preserve the nation's shrinking forests. By 1900 only about a quarter of the once-vast virgin timberlands remained standing. Lumbermen had already logged off most of the first-growth timber from Maine to Michigan, and the sharp thud of their axes was beginning to split the silence in the great fir forests of the Pacific slope. Roosevelt proceeded to set

In his annual message to Congress in 1907, Roosevelt declared prophetically,

"We are prone to speak of the resources of this country as inexhaustible; this is not so. The mineral wealth of the country, the coal, iron, oil, gas, and the like, does not reproduce itself, and therefore is certain to be exhausted ultimately; and wastefulness in dealing with it to-day means that our descendants will feel the exhaustion a generation or two before they otherwise would.**"**

Gifford Pinchot (1865–1946), a leading conservationist in the Roosevelt administration, wrote,

" The object of our forest policy is not to preserve the forests because they are refuges for the wild creatures of the wilderness, but the making of prosperous homes. Every other consideration comes as secondary. . . . The test of utility . . . implies that no lands will be permanently reserves which can serve the people better in any other way.**"**

Humans have long been awed by nature, but they have also yearned to be its masters. Native American peoples did what they could to shape the natural environment to serve their purposes—burning forests and grasslands, for example, to improve hunting habitats—but they lacked the tools to make Mother Earth bow deeply to their will. The earliest European colonists saw North America as a "howling wilderness" and toiled mightily with ax and plow to tame it. By the mid-nineteenth century, Americans commanded powerful new technologies like the railroad and steam-powered dredges, which promised unbridled dominion over the natural world. Only then did voices begin to be heard in defense of the wounded earth—the faint first stirrings of what would come to be called "environmentalism."

In a pattern that would often be repeated, nature's earliest defenders tended to be well-off townsfolk and city dwellers, like Henry David Thoreau and Ralph Waldo Emerson. The Americans most likely to appreciate the value of the pristine wilderness, it seemed, were those who had ceased to struggle against it. ("Cities, not log cabins, produce Sierra Clubbers," one historian noted.) For the loggers, miners, and farmers who continued to sweat their living out of nature's grudging embrace, concern for environmental niceties often seemed like the sanctimonious piety of a privileged elite.

By the dawn of the twentieth century, many genteel, urban Americans had come to romanticize their pioneer forebears. They reinvented hunting and fishing as sports for the well-to-do, not simply as ways to put food on the table. Preservationists like John Muir waxed lyrical about the mystic allure of unspoiled nature. Seizing the popular mood, Theodore Roosevelt deliberately constructed a public image of himself as a manly outdoorsman—raising cattle in the Dakotas, shooting lions in Africa, rafting down wild rivers in the Amazon basin—and as president he greatly expanded the system of national forests. But Roosevelt was also a pioneer of another sort—as a prominent promoter of the progressive-era "conservation" movement, composed of a loose coalition of scientists, bureaucrats, and businesspeople dependent on stable access to America's rich endowment of natural resources. Progressive conservationists believed that nature must be neither uncritically reverenced nor wastefully exploited, but must instead be efficiently utilized. Thus the same TR who admired the wonders of Yosemite Valley in the company of John Muir also supported the professional forester Gifford Pinchot, who declared that "the object of our forest policy is not to preserve the forests because they are refuges for the wild creatures of the wilderness, but the making of prosperous homes. . . . Use must be the test by which the forester tries himself."

Pinchot's "rational use" philosophy guided America's natural resource policy until the mid-twentieth century. It justified the systematic harvesting of millions of trees in the sprawling national forests whose boundaries Roosevelt had expanded, and the drowning of vast river valleys behind massive dams that Roosevelt's Reclamation Service helped to build. This attitude toward nature triumphed in the New Deal era of the 1930s, when the federal government initiated colossal projects that undertook nothing less than reengineering the face of the continent—including the Tennessee Valley Authority, the Soil Conservation Service, and the Shelterbelt tree-planting project on the Great Plains. The huge reach of these New Deal projects also introduced millions of Americans to the concept that nature had to be treated with respect, helping to stimulate the post–World War II grassroots environmental movement.

The rise of ecological science in the post–World War II era fundamentally changed the debate about the relation of nature to civilization. Ecologists charged that the apparent "rationality" of the earlier conservationists dangerously neglected the fateful intricacies of biological systems. They called attention to the stunningly complex webs of interrelationships that linked

Brown Brothers

Gifford Pinchot Going Trout Fishing   The father of the modern Forest Service, Pinchot championed the concept of "rational use" as the guiding principle of the federal government's natural resource management policies.

together seemingly unrelated organisms—and to the perils of tampering even slightly with the delicate biological fabrics that nature had taken millennia to weave. Rachel Carson helped to popularize the new outlook in her sensational 1962 exposé, *Silent Spring*, about the far-reaching effects of pesticides on birds, plants, and animals—including humans.

The advent of ecological studies coincided with a revival of preservationist sentiment, especially in the suburbs, where Americans increasingly dwelled. Hordes of affluent baby boomers took to America's trails, slopes, and waterways—often on public lands like Arizona's wondrous Grand Canyon National Park, or public waters like Utah's shimmering (and man-made) Lake Powell. Membership in environmental organizations such as the Sierra Club and the Audubon Society soared, as a generation infatuated with nature demanded a clean and green world. The first celebration of Earth Day, on April 22, 1970, marked the political maturation of modern-day environmentalism, which wedded scientific analysis with respect for nature's majesty. That same year saw the creation of the federal Environmental Protection Agency (EPA), soon followed by the Endangered Species Act and other legislation designed to regulate the relationship between humans and nature.

At the outset of the twenty-first century, developments like global warming served dramatic notice that planet earth was the biggest ecological system of them all—one that did not recognize national boundaries. Yet while Americans took pride in the efforts they had made to clean up their own turf, who were they, having long since consumed much of their own timberlands, to tell the Brazilians that they should not cut down the Amazon rain forest? Who were they, having tamed virtually all their own free-flowing waters, to tell the Chinese not to dam their rivers? For the peoples of the developing world, struggling to match America's standard of living, environmentalists often seemed like spoiled spoilers, preaching the same privileged pieties that had infuriated generations of working Americans.

Loggers in the State of Washington, 1912 It took the sweat and skill of many men to conquer a giant Douglas fir like this one. An ax-wielding "sniper" had rounded the edges of this log so that a team of oxen, driven by a "bullwhacker," could more easily drag it out of the woods along a "skid road." *Skid road* (sometimes corrupted as *skid row*) was also a name for the often-sleazy sections of logging towns, where loggers spent their time in the off-season.

aside in federal reserves some 125 million acres, or almost three times the acreage thus saved from the saw by his three predecessors. He similarly earmarked millions of acres of coal deposits, as well as water resources useful for irrigation and power. To set a shining example, in 1902 he banned Christmas trees from the White House.

Conservation, including reclamation, may have been Roosevelt's most enduring tangible achievement. He was buoyed in this effort by an upwelling national mood of concern about the disappearance of the frontier—believed to be the source of such national characteristics as individualism and democracy. An increasingly citified people worried that too much civilization might not be good for the national soul. City dwellers snapped up Jack London's *Call of the Wild* (1903) and other books about nature, and urban youngsters

made the outdoor-oriented Boy Scouts of America the country's largest youth organization. Middle-class clubwomen raised money for nature preserves and organized the Massachusetts—and later National—Audubon Society to save wild native birds by banning the use of plumes to ornament fashionable ladies' hats. The Sierra Club, founded in 1892, dedicated itself to preserving the wildness of the western landscape.

The preservationists lost a major battle in 1913 when the federal government allowed the city of San Francisco to build a dam for its municipal water supply in the spectacular, high-walled **Hetch Hetchy Valley** in Yosemite National Park. The Hetch Hetchy controversy laid bare a deep division between conservationists that persists to the present day. To the preservationists of the Sierra Club, including famed naturalist John Muir, Hetch Hetchy was a "temple" of nature that should

Flooding the Hetch Hetchy Valley to Quench San Francisco's Thirst
Preservationists led by John Muir battled for seven years—unsuccessfully—to prevent the building of a dam that would turn this spectacular glacial valley in Yosemite National Park into the Hetch Hetchy Reservoir, which would provide San Francisco with water. Muir observed, "Dam Hetch Hetchy! As well dam for water-tanks the people's cathedrals and churches, for no holier temple has ever been consecrated by the heart of man." Today environmentalists are campaigning to restore the Hetch Hetchy Valley by removing the dam.

North Wind Picture Archives

The Machine and Nature   These hardy sightseers at the Grand Canyon in 1911 ironically and probably unwittingly foreshadowed the mass tourism that arrived with the dawning automobile age. Soon millions of motorized Americans would regularly flee from the cities and suburbs to "get away from it all" in wilderness sites increasingly overrun by their fellow refugees from "civilization."

be held inviolable by the civilizing hand of humanity. But other conservationists, among them President Roosevelt's chief forester, Gifford Pinchot, believed that "wilderness was waste." Pinchot and Roosevelt wanted to *use* the nation's natural endowment intelligently. In their eyes they had to battle on two fronts: against greedy commercial interests that abused nature, as well as against romantic preservationists in thrall to simple "woodman-spare-that-tree" sentimentality.

Under Roosevelt professional foresters and engineers developed a policy of "multiple-use resource management." They sought to combine recreation, sustained-yield logging, watershed protection, and summer stock grazing on the same expanse of federal land.

At first many westerners resisted the federal management of natural resources, but they soon learned how to take advantage of new agencies like the Forest Service and especially the Bureau of Reclamation. The largest ranches and timber companies in particular figured out how to work hand in glove with federal conservation programs devoted to the rational, large-scale, and long-term use of natural resources. The one-man-and-a-mule logger or the one-man-and-a-dog sheepherder had little clout in the new resources bureaucracy. Single-person enterprises were shouldered aside, in the interest of efficiency, by the combined bulk of big business and big government.

✦ The "Roosevelt Panic" of 1907

Roosevelt was handily elected president "in his own right" in 1904 and entered his new term buoyed by his enormous personal popularity—the cuddly "teddy bear" honored one of his bear-hunting exploits (when he saved the life of a cub), and children piped vigorously on whistles modeled on his famous teeth. Yet the conservative Republican bosses considered him as dangerous and unpredictable as a rattlesnake. They grew increasingly restive as Roosevelt in his second term called ever more loudly for regulating corporations, taxing incomes, and protecting workers. Roosevelt, meanwhile, had partly defanged himself after his election in 1904 by announcing that under no circumstances would he be a candidate for a third term. This was a tactical blunder, for the power of the king wanes when the people know he will be dead in four years.

Roosevelt suffered a sharp setback in 1907, when a short but punishing panic descended on Wall Street. The financial flurry featured frightened "runs" on banks, suicides, and criminal indictments against speculators.

The financial world hastened to blame Roosevelt for the storm. It cried that this "quack" had unsettled industry with his boat-rocking tactics. Conservatives damned him as "Theodore the Meddler" and branded the current distress the "Roosevelt panic." The hot-tempered president angrily lashed back at his critics when he accused "certain malefactors of great wealth" of having deliberately engineered the monetary crisis to force the government to relax its assaults on trusts.

Fortunately, the panic of 1907 paved the way for long-overdue fiscal reforms. Precipitating a currency shortage, the flurry laid bare the need for a more elastic medium of exchange. In a crisis of this sort, the hard-pressed banks were unable to increase the volume of money in circulation, and those with ample reserves were reluctant to lend to their less fortunate competitors. Congress in 1908 responded by passing the

Aldrich-Vreeland Act, which authorized national banks to issue emergency currency backed by various kinds of collateral. The path was thus smoothed for the momentous Federal Reserve Act of 1913 (see p. 665).

✦ The Rough Rider Thunders Out

Still warmly popular in 1908, Roosevelt could easily have won a second presidential nomination and almost certainly the election. But he felt bound by his impulsive postelection promise after his victory in 1904.

The departing president thus naturally sought a successor who would carry out "my policies." The man of his choice was amiable, ample-girthed, and huge-framed William Howard Taft, secretary of war and a mild progressive. As an heir apparent, he had often been called upon in Roosevelt's absence to "sit on the lid"—all 350 pounds of him. At the Republican convention of 1908 in Chicago, Roosevelt used his control

Baby, Kiss Papa Good-bye Theodore Roosevelt leaves his baby, "My Policies," in the hands of his chosen successor, William Howard Taft. Friction between Taft and Roosevelt would soon erupt, however, prompting Roosevelt to return to politics and challenge Taft for the presidency.

Granger Collection

of the party machinery—the "steamroller"—to push through Taft's nomination on the first ballot. Three weeks later, in mile-high Denver, in the heart of silver country, the Democrats nominated twice-beaten William Jennings Bryan.

The dull campaign of 1908 featured the rotund Taft and the now-balding "Boy Orator" both trying to don the progressive Roosevelt mantle. The solid Judge Taft read cut-and-dried speeches, while Bryan griped that Roosevelt had stolen his policies from the Bryanite camp. A majority of voters chose stability with Roosevelt-endorsed Taft, who polled 321 electoral votes to 162 for Bryan. The victor's popular count was 7,675,320 to 6,412,294. The election's only surprise came from the Socialists, who amassed 420,793 votes for Eugene V. Debs, the hero of the Pullman strike of 1894 (see pp. 599–600).

Roosevelt, ever in the limelight, left soon after the election for a lion hunt in Africa. His numerous enemies clinked glasses while toasting "Health to the lions," and a few irreverently prayed that some big cat would "do its duty." But TR survived, still bursting with energy at the age of fifty-one in 1909.

Roosevelt was branded by his adversaries as a wild-eyed radical, but his reputation as an eater of errant industrialists now seems inflated. He fought many a sham battle, and the number of laws he inspired was certainly not in proportion to the amount of noise he emitted. He was often under attack from the reigning business lords, but the more enlightened of them knew that they had a friend in the White House. Roosevelt should be remembered first and foremost as the cowboy who started to tame the bucking bronco of adolescent capitalism, thus ensuring it a long adult life.

TR's enthusiasm and perpetual youthfulness, like an overgrown Boy Scout's, appealed to the young of all ages. "You must always remember," a British diplomat cautioned his colleagues, "that the president is about six." He served as a political lightning rod to protect capitalists against popular indignation—and against socialism, which Roosevelt regarded as "ominous." He strenuously sought the middle road between unbridled individualism and paternalistic collectivism. His conservation crusade, which tried to mediate between the romantic wilderness-preservationists and the rapacious resource-predators, was probably his most typical and his most lasting achievement.

Several other contributions of Roosevelt lasted beyond his presidency. First, he greatly enlarged the power and prestige of the presidential office—and masterfully developed the technique of using the big stick of publicity as a political bludgeon. Second, he helped shape the progressive movement and beyond it the liberal reform campaigns later in the century. His Square Deal, in a sense, was the grandfather of the New Deal later launched by his fifth cousin, Franklin D. Roosevelt. Finally, to a greater degree than any of his predecessors, TR opened the eyes of Americans to the fact that they shared the world with other nations. As a great power, they had fallen heir to responsibilities—and had been seized by ambitions—from which there was no escaping.

✳ Taft: A Round Peg in a Square Hole

William Howard Taft, with his ruddy complexion and upturned mustache, at first inspired widespread confidence. "Everybody loves a fat man," the saying goes, and the jovial Taft, with "mirthquakes" of laughter bubbling up from his abundant abdomen, was personally popular. He had graduated second in his class at Yale and had established an enviable reputation as a lawyer and judge, though he was widely regarded as hostile to labor unions. He had been a trusted administrator under Roosevelt—in the Philippines, at home, and in Cuba, where he had served capably as a troubleshooter.

But "good old Will" suffered from lethal political handicaps. Roosevelt had led the conflicting elements of the Republican party by the sheer force of his personality. Taft, in contrast, had none of the arts of a dashing political leader and none of Roosevelt's zest for the fray. Recoiling from the clamor of controversy, he generally adopted an attitude of passivity toward Congress. He was a poor judge of public opinion, and his candor made him a chronic victim of "foot-in-mouth" disease.

"Peaceful Bill" was no doubt a mild progressive, but at heart he was more wedded to the status quo than to change. Significantly, his cabinet did not contain a single representative of the party's "insurgent" wing, which was on fire for reform of current abuses, especially the tariff.

✳ The Dollar Goes Abroad as a Diplomat

Though ordinarily lethargic, Taft bestirred himself to use the lever of American investments to boost American political interests abroad, an approach to foreign policy that his critics denounced as **dollar diplomacy**. Washington warmly encouraged Wall Street bankers to sluice their surplus dollars into foreign areas of strategic concern to the United States, especially in the Far East and in the regions critical to the security of the Panama Canal. By preempting investors from rival powers, such as Germany, New York bankers would thus strengthen American defenses and foreign policies, while bringing further prosperity to their homeland—and to themselves. The almighty dollar thereby supplanted the big stick.

Granger Collection

Ex-President Theodore Roosevelt Watches President Taft Struggle with the Demands of Government, 1910

China's Manchuria was the object of Taft's most spectacular effort to inject the reluctant dollar into the Far Eastern theater. Newly ambitious Japan and imperialistic Russia, recent foes, controlled the railroads of this strategic province. President Taft saw in the Manchurian railway monopoly a possible strangulation of Chinese economic interests and a consequent slamming of the Open Door in the faces of U.S. merchants. In 1909 Secretary of State Philander C. Knox blunderingly proposed that a group of American and foreign bankers buy the Manchurian railroads and then turn them over to China under a self-liquidating arrangement. Both Japan and Russia, unwilling to be jockeyed out of their dominant position, bluntly rejected Knox's overtures. Taft was showered with ridicule.

Another dangerous new trouble spot was the revolution-riddled Caribbean—now virtually a Yankee lake. Hoping to head off trouble, Washington urged Wall Street bankers to pump dollars into the financial vacuums in Honduras and Haiti to keep out foreign funds. The United States, under the Monroe Doctrine, would not permit foreign nations to intervene, and consequently felt obligated to put its money where its mouth was to prevent economic and political instability.

Again necessity was the mother of armed Caribbean intervention. Sporadic disorders in palm-fronded Cuba, Honduras, and the Dominican Republic brought American forces to these countries to restore order and protect American investment. A revolutionary upheaval in Nicaragua, partly fomented by American interests, resulted in the landing of twenty-five hundred marines in 1912. The marines remained in Nicaragua for thirteen years (see Map 29.2 on p. 668).

✦ Taft the Trustbuster

Taft managed to gain some fame as a smasher of monopolies. The ironic truth is that the colorless Taft brought 90 suits against the trusts during his 4 years in office, as compared with some 44 for Roosevelt in 7½ years.

By fateful happenstance the most sensational judicial actions during the Taft regime came in 1911. In that year the Supreme Court ordered the dissolution of the mighty Standard Oil Company, which was judged to be a combination in restraint of trade in violation of the Sherman Anti-Trust Act of 1890. At the same time, the Court handed down its famous "rule of reason." This doctrine held that only those combinations that "unreasonably" restrained trade were illegal. This fine-print proviso ripped a huge hole in the government's antitrust net.

Even more explosively, in 1911 Taft decided to press an antitrust suit against the U.S. Steel Corporation. This initiative infuriated Roosevelt, who had personally been involved in one of the mergers that prompted the suit. Once Roosevelt's protégé, President Taft was increasingly taking on the role of his antagonist. The stage was being set for a bruising confrontation.

✦ Taft Splits the Republican Party

Lowering the barriers of the formidable protective tariff—the "Mother of Trusts"—was high on the agenda of the progressive members of the Republican party, and they at first thought they had a friend and ally in Taft. True to his campaign promises to reduce tariffs, Taft called Congress into special session in March 1909. The House proceeded to pass a moderately reductive bill, but senatorial reactionaries tacked on hundreds of upward tariff revisions. Only items such as hides, sea moss, and canary seed were left on the duty-free list. Much to the dismay of his supporters, Taft signed the **Payne-Aldrich Bill**, rubbing salt in their wounds by proclaiming it "the best bill that the Republican party ever passed."

Taft revealed a further knack for shooting himself in the foot in his handling of conservation. The portly president was a dedicated conservationist, and his contributions—like the establishment of the Bureau of Mines to control mineral resources—actually equaled or surpassed those of Roosevelt. But his praiseworthy accomplishments were largely erased in the public mind by the noisy Ballinger-Pinchot quarrel that erupted in 1910.

When Secretary of the Interior Richard Ballinger opened public lands in Wyoming, Montana, and Alaska to corporate development, he was sharply criticized by Gifford Pinchot, chief of the Agriculture Department's Division of Forestry and a stalwart Rooseveltian. When Taft dismissed Pinchot on the narrow grounds of insubordination, a storm of protest arose from conservationists and from Roosevelt's friends, who were legion. The whole unsavory episode further widened the growing rift between the president and the former president, onetime bosom political partners.

The reformist wing of the Republican party was now up in arms, while Taft was being pushed increasingly into the embrace of the stand-pat Old Guard. By the spring of 1910, the Grand Old Party was split wide-open, owing largely to the clumsiness of Taft. A suspicious Roosevelt returned triumphantly to New York in June 1910 and shortly thereafter stirred up a tempest. Unable to keep silent, he took to the stump at Osawatomie, Kansas, and shocked the Old Guard with a flaming speech. The doctrine that he proclaimed—popularly known as the "New Nationalism"—urged the national government to increase its power to remedy economic and social abuses.

Weakened by these internal divisions, the Republicans lost badly in the congressional elections of 1910. In a victory of landslide proportions, the Democrats emerged with 228 seats, leaving the once-dominant Republicans with only 161. In a further symptom of the reforming temper of the times, a Socialist representative, Austrian-born Victor L. Berger, was elected from Milwaukee.* The Republicans, by virtue of holdovers, retained the Senate, 51 to 41, but the insurgents in their midst were numerous enough to make that hold precarious.

★ The Taft-Roosevelt Rupture

The sputtering uprising in Republican ranks had now blossomed into a full-fledged revolt. Early in 1911 the National Progressive Republican League was formed, with the fiery, white-maned Senator La Follette of Wisconsin its leading candidate for the Republican presidential nomination. The assumption was that Roosevelt, an anti–third termer, would not permit himself to be "drafted."

But the restless Rough Rider began to change his views about third terms as he saw Taft, hand in glove with the hated Old Guard, discard "my policies." In

---

*He was eventually denied his seat in 1919, during a wave of anti-red hysteria.

February 1912 Roosevelt formally wrote to seven state governors that he was willing to accept the Republican nomination. His reasoning was that the third-term tradition applied to three *consecutive elective* terms. Exuberantly he cried, "My hat is in the ring!" and "The fight is on and I am stripped to the buff!"

Roosevelt forthwith seized the Progressive banner, while La Follette, who had served as a convenient pathbreaker, was protestingly elbowed aside. Girded for battle, the Rough Rider came clattering into the presidential primaries then being held in many states. He shouted through half-clenched teeth that the president had fallen under the thumb of the reactionary bosses and that although Taft "means well, he means well feebly." The once-genial Taft, now in a fighting mood, retorted by branding Roosevelt supporters "emotionalists and neurotics."

A Taft-Roosevelt explosion was near in June 1912, when the Republican convention met in Chicago. The Rooseveltites, who were about 100 delegates short of winning the nomination, challenged the right of some 250 Taft delegates to be seated. Most of these contests were arbitrarily settled in favor of Taft, whose supporters held the throttle of the convention steamroller. The Roosevelt adherents, crying "fraud" and "naked theft," in the end refused to vote, and Taft triumphed.

Roosevelt, the supposedly good sportsman, refused to quit the game. Having tasted for the first time the bitter cup of defeat, he was now on fire to lead a third-party crusade.

Chapter Review

KEY TERMS

social gospel (639)

muckrakers (639)

initiative (641)

referendum (641)

recall (641)

Australian ballot (641)

Muller v. *Oregon* (645)

Lochner v. *New York* (645)

Woman's Christian Temperance Union (WCTU) (646)

Elkins Act (649)

Meat Inspection Act (650)

Pure Food and Drug Act (650)

Hetch Hetchy Valley (654)

dollar diplomacy (657)

Payne-Aldrich Bill (658)

PEOPLE TO KNOW

Henry Demarest Lloyd

Thorstein Veblen

Jacob A. Riis

Robert M. ("Fighting Bob") La Follette

Hiram W. Johnson

Florence Kelley

Frances E. Willard

Gifford Pinchot

John Muir

CHRONOLOGY

1892	Sierra Club founded
1899	National Consumers League founded
1901	Commission system established in Galveston, Texas Progressive Robert La Follette elected governor of Wisconsin American Socialist party formed
1902	Lincoln Steffens and Ida Tarbell publish muckraking exposés Anthracite coal strike Newlands Act
1903	Department of Commerce and Labor established Elkins Act Women's Trade Union League founded
1904	*Northern Securities* case Roosevelt defeats Alton B. Parker for presidency
1905	*Lochner* v. *New York*
1906	Hepburn Act Upton Sinclair publishes *The Jungle* Meat Inspection Act Pure Food and Drug Act
1907	"Roosevelt panic"

1908	*Muller* v. *Oregon* Taft defeats Bryan for presidency Aldrich-Vreeland Act
1909	Payne-Aldrich Tariff
1910	Ballinger-Pinchot affair Washington State grants woman suffrage
1911	Triangle Shirtwaist Company fire Standard Oil antitrust case U.S. Steel Corporation antitrust suit California grants woman suffrage
1912	Taft wins Republican nomination over Roosevelt Arizona, Kansas, and Oregon grant woman suffrage Children's Bureau established in Department of Labor
1913	Seventeenth Amendment passed (direct election of U.S. senators) Federal Reserve Act San Francisco decides to build Hetch Hetchy Reservoir
1920	Women's Bureau established in Department of Labor

TO LEARN MORE

Peri E. Arnold, *Remaking the Presidency: Roosevelt, Taft, and Wilson, 1901–1916* (2009)

Nancy Cott, *The Grounding of Modern Feminism* (1987)

Alan Dawley, *Struggles for Justice: Social Responsibility and the Liberal State* (1991)

Glenda Gilmore, *Gender and Jim Crow: Women and the Politics of White Supremacy in North Carolina, 1896–1920* (1996)

Samuel P. Hays, *Conservation and the Gospel of Efficiency* (1959)

Richard Hofstadter, *The Age of Reform* (1955)

T. J. Jackson Lears, *No Place of Grace: Antimodernism and the Transformation of American Culture* (1981)

————, *Rebirth of a Nation: The Making of Modern America, 1877–1920* (2009)

Robyn Muncy, *Creating a Female Dominion in American Reform* (1991)

Kevin P. Murphy, *Political Manhood: Red Bloods, Mollycoddles, and the Politics of Progressive Era Reform* (2008)

Daniel T. Rodgers, *Atlantic Crossings: Social Politics in a Progressive Age* (1998)

Nick Salvatore, *Eugene V. Debs: Citizen and Socialist* (1982)

Kathryn Kish Sklar, *Florence Kelley and the Nation's Work* (1995)

A complete, annotated bibliography for this chapter—along with brief descriptions of the People to Know—may be found on the American Pageant website. The Key Terms are defined in a Glossary at the end of the text.

 Go to the CourseMate website at **www.cengagebrain.com** for additional study tools and review materials—including audio and video clips—for this chapter.

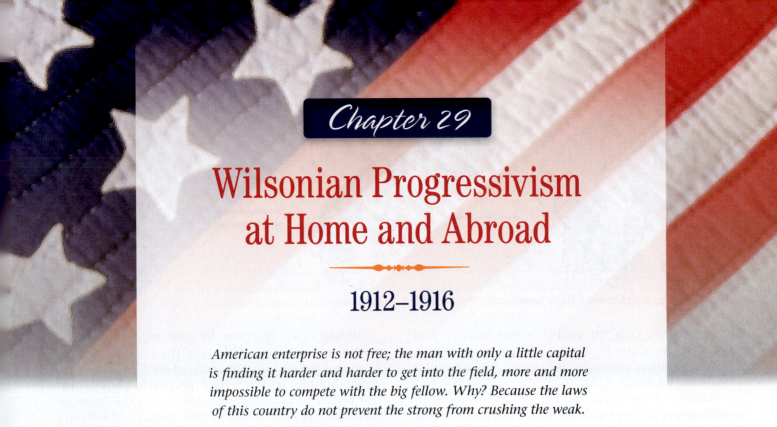

Chapter 29

Wilsonian Progressivism at Home and Abroad

1912–1916

American enterprise is not free; the man with only a little capital is finding it harder and harder to get into the field, more and more impossible to compete with the big fellow. Why? Because the laws of this country do not prevent the strong from crushing the weak.

WOODROW WILSON, THE NEW FREEDOM, 1913

Office-hungry Democrats—the "outs" since 1897—were jubilant over the disruptive Republican brawl at the convention in Chicago. If they could come up with an outstanding reformist leader, they had an excellent chance to win the White House. Such a leader appeared in Dr. Woodrow Wilson, once a mild conservative but now a militant progressive. Beginning professional life as a brilliant academic lecturer on government, he had risen in 1902 to the presidency of Princeton University, where he had achieved some sweeping educational reforms.

Wilson entered politics in 1910 when New Jersey bosses, needing a respectable "front" candidate for the governorship, offered him the nomination. They expected to lead the academic novice by the nose, but to their surprise, Wilson waged a passionate reform campaign in which he assailed the "predatory" trusts and promised to return state government to the people. Riding the crest of the progressive wave, the "Schoolmaster in Politics" was swept into office.

Once in the governor's chair, Wilson drove through the legislature a sheaf of forward-looking measures that made reactionary New Jersey one of the more liberal states. Filled with righteous indignation, Wilson revealed irresistible reforming zeal, burning eloquence, superb powers of leadership, and a refreshing habit of appealing over the heads of the scheming bosses to the sovereign people. Now a figure of national eminence, Wilson was being widely mentioned for the presidency.

⭐ The "Bull Moose" Campaign of 1912

When the Democrats met at Baltimore in 1912, Wilson was nominated on the forty-sixth ballot, aided by William Jennings Bryan's switch to his side. The Democrats gave Wilson a strong progressive platform to run on; dubbed the **New Freedom** program, it included calls for stronger antitrust legislation, banking reform, and tariff reductions.

Surging events had meanwhile been thrusting Roosevelt to the fore as a candidate for the presidency on a third-party Progressive Republican ticket. The fighting ex-cowboy, angered by his recent rebuff, was eager to lead the charge. A pro-Roosevelt Progressive convention, with about two thousand delegates from forty states, assembled in Chicago during August 1912. Dramatically symbolizing the rising political status of women, as well as Progressive support for the cause of social justice, settlement-house pioneer Jane Addams placed Roosevelt's name in nomination for the presidency. Roosevelt was applauded tumultuously as he cried in a vehement speech, "We stand at Armageddon, and we battle for the Lord!" The hosanna spirit of a religious revival meeting suffused the convention, as the

GOP Divided by Bull Moose Equals Democratic Victory, 1912 Library of Congress

hoarse delegates sang "Onward Christian Soldiers" and "Battle Hymn of the Republic." William Allen White, the caustic Kansas journalist, later wrote, "Roosevelt bit me and I went mad."

Fired-up Progressives entered the campaign with righteousness and enthusiasm. Roosevelt boasted that he felt "as strong as a bull moose," and the bull moose took its place with the donkey and the elephant in the American political zoo. As one poet whimsically put it,

> I want to be a Bull Moose,
> And with the Bull Moose stand
> With antlers on my forehead
> And a Big Stick in my hand.

Roosevelt and Taft were bound to slit each other's political throats; by dividing the Republican vote, they virtually guaranteed a Democratic victory. The two antagonists tore into each other as only former friends can. "Death alone can take me out now," cried the once-jovial Taft, as he branded Roosevelt a "dangerous egotist" and a "demagogue." Roosevelt, fighting mad, assailed Taft as a "fathead" with the brain of a "guinea pig."

Beyond the clashing personalities, the overshadowing question of the 1912 campaign was which of two varieties of progressivism would prevail—Roosevelt's **New Nationalism** or Wilson's New Freedom. Both men favored a more active government role in economic and social affairs, but they disagreed sharply over specific strategies. Roosevelt preached the theories spun out by the progressive thinker Herbert Croly in his book *The Promise of American Life* (1910). Croly and TR both favored continued consolidation of trusts and labor unions, paralleled by the growth of powerful regulatory agencies in Washington. Roosevelt and his "bull moosers" also campaigned for woman suffrage and a broad program of social welfare, including minimum wage laws and "socialistic" social insurance. Clearly, the bull moose Progressives looked forward to the kind of activist welfare state that Franklin Roosevelt's New Deal would one day make a reality.

Wilson's New Freedom, by contrast, favored small enterprise, entrepreneurship, and the free functioning of unregulated and unmonopolized markets. The Democrats shunned social-welfare proposals and pinned their economic faith on competition—on the "man on the make," as Wilson put it. The keynote of Wilson's campaign was not regulation but fragmentation of the big industrial combines, chiefly by means of vigorous enforcement of the antitrust laws. The election of 1912 thus offered the voters a choice not merely of policies but of political and economic philosophies—a rarity in U.S. history.

The heat of the campaign cooled a bit when, in Milwaukee, Roosevelt was shot in the chest by a fanatic. The Rough Rider suspended active campaigning for more than two weeks after delivering, with bull moose gameness and a bloody shirt, his scheduled speech.

✦ Woodrow Wilson: A Minority President

Former professor Wilson won handily, with 435 electoral votes and 6,296,547 popular votes. The "third-party" candidate, Roosevelt, finished second, receiving 88 electoral votes and 4,118,571 popular votes. Taft won only 8 electoral votes and 3,486,720 popular votes (see Map 29.1).

The election figures are fascinating. Wilson, with only 41 percent of the popular vote, was clearly a minority president, though his party won a majority in Congress. His popular total was actually smaller than Bryan had amassed in any of his three defeats, despite the increase in population. Taft and Roosevelt together polled over 1.25 million more votes than the Democrats. Progressivism rather than Wilson was the runaway winner. Although the Democratic total obviously included many conservatives in the solid South, the combined progressive vote for Wilson and Roosevelt, totaling 68 percent, far exceeded the tally of the

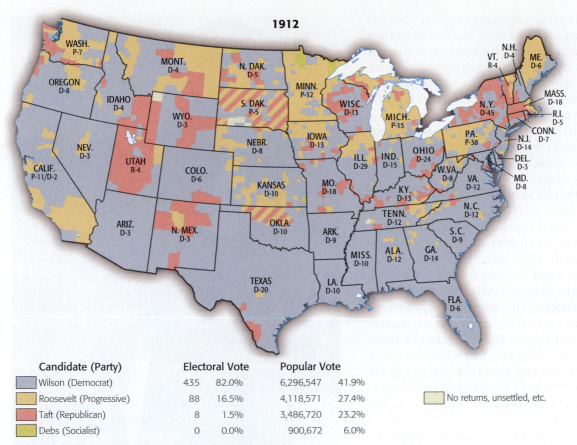

1912

Candidate (Party)	Electoral Vote		Popular Vote	
Wilson (Democrat)	435	82.0%	6,296,547	41.9%
Roosevelt (Progressive)	88	16.5%	4,118,571	27.4%
Taft (Republican)	8	1.5%	3,486,720	23.2%
Debs (Socialist)	0	0.0%	900,672	6.0%

No returns, unsettled, etc.

MAP 29.1 Presidential Election of 1912 (showing votes by county, with electoral vote by state)   The Republican split surely boosted Wilson to victory, as he failed to win a clear majority in any state outside the old Confederacy. The election gave the Democrats solid control of the White House and both houses of Congress for the first time since the Civil War. © Cengage Learning

more conservative Taft, who got only 23 percent. To the progressive tally must be added some support for the Socialist candidate, the persistent Eugene V. Debs, who rolled up 900,672 votes, 6 percent of the total cast, or more than twice as many as he had netted four years earlier. Starry-eyed Socialists dreamed of being in the White House within eight years.

Roosevelt's lone-wolf course was tragic both for himself and for his former Republican associates. Perhaps, to rephrase William Allen White, he had bitten himself and gone mad. The Progressive party, which was primarily a one-man show, had no future because it had elected few candidates to state and local offices; the Socialists, in contrast, elected more than a thousand. Without patronage plums to hand out to faithful workers, death by slow starvation was inevitable for the upstart party. Yet the Progressives made a tremendous showing for a hastily organized third party and helped spur the enactment of many of their pet reforms by the Wilsonian Democrats.

As for the Republicans, they were thrust into unaccustomed minority status in Congress for the next six years and were frozen out of the White House for eight years. Taft himself had a fruitful old age. He taught law for eight pleasant years at Yale University and in 1921 became chief justice of the Supreme Court—a job for which he was far more happily suited than the presidency.

★ Wilson: The Idealist in Politics

(Thomas) Woodrow Wilson, the second Democratic president since 1861, looked like the ascetic intellectual he was, with his clean-cut features, pinched-on eyeglasses, and trim figure. Born in Virginia shortly before the Civil War and reared in Georgia and the Carolinas, the professor-politician was the first man from one of the seceded southern states to reach the White House since Zachary Taylor, sixty-four years earlier.

The impact of Dixieland on young "Tommy" Wilson was profound. He sympathized with the Confederacy's gallant attempt to win its independence, a sentiment that partly inspired his ideal of self-determination for people of other countries. Steeped in the traditions of Jeffersonian democracy, he shared Jefferson's faith in the masses—if they were properly informed.

Son of a Presbyterian minister, Wilson was reared in an atmosphere of fervent piety. He later used the presidential pulpit to preach his inspirational political sermons. A moving orator, Wilson could rise on the wings of spiritual power to soaring eloquence. Skillfully using a persuasive voice, he relied not on arm-waving but on sincerity and moral appeal. As a lifelong student of finely chiseled words, he turned out to be a "phraseo-crat" who coined many noble epigrams. Someone has remarked that he was born halfway between the Bible and the dictionary and never strayed far from either.

A profound student of government, Wilson believed that the chief executive should play a dynamic role. He was convinced that Congress could not function properly unless the president, like a kind of prime minister, got out in front and provided leadership. He enjoyed dramatic success, both as governor and as president, in appealing over the heads of legislators to the sovereign people.

Splendid though Wilson's intellectual equipment was, he suffered from serious defects of personality. Though jovial and witty in private, he could be cold and standoffish in public. Incapable of unbending and acting the showman, like "Teddy" Roosevelt, he lacked the common touch. He loved humanity in the mass rather than the individual in person. His academic background caused him to feel most at home with scholars, although he had to work with politicians. An austere and somewhat arrogant intellectual, he looked down his nose through pince-nez glasses upon lesser minds, including journalists. He was especially intolerant of stupid senators, whose "bungalow" minds made him "sick."

Wilson's burning idealism—especially his desire to reform ever-present wickedness—drove him forward faster than lesser spirits were willing to go. His sense of moral righteousness was such that he often found compromise difficult; black was black, wrong was wrong, and one should never compromise with wrong. President Wilson's Scottish Presbyterian ancestors had passed on to him an inflexible stubbornness. When convinced that he was right, the principled Wilson would break before he would bend, unlike the pragmatic Roosevelt.

✦ Wilson Tackles the Tariff

Few presidents have arrived at the White House with a clearer program than Wilson's or one destined to be

Brown Brothers

Woodrow Wilson (1856–1924) at Princeton Commencement with Andrew Carnegie, 1906 Before his election to the presidency of the United States in 1912, Wilson (left) served as president of Princeton University (1902–1910) and governor of New Jersey (1910–1912). In all three offices, he undertook substantial reforms. Fighting desperately later for the League of Nations, at the cost of his health, Wilson said, "I would rather fail in a cause that I know some day will triumph than to win in a cause that I know some day will fail."

so completely achieved. The new president called for an all-out assault on what he called "the triple wall of privilege": the tariff, the banks, and the trusts.

He tackled the tariff first, summoning Congress into special session in early 1913. In a precedent-shattering move, he did not send his presidential message over to the Capitol to be read loudly by a bored clerk, as had been the custom since Jefferson's day. Instead he appeared in person before a joint session of Congress and presented his appeal with stunning eloquence and effectiveness.

Moved by Wilson's aggressive leadership, the House swiftly passed the **Underwood Tariff**, which provided for a substantial reduction of rates. When a swarm of lobbyists descended on the Senate seeking to disembowel the bill, Wilson promptly issued a combative message to the people, urging them to hold their elected representatives in line. The tactic worked. The force of public opinion, aroused by the president's oratory, secured late in 1913 final approval of the bill Wilson wanted.

The new Underwood Tariff substantially reduced import fees. It also was a landmark in tax legislation. Under authority granted by the recently ratified Sixteenth Amendment, Congress enacted a graduated income tax, beginning with a modest levy on incomes over $3,000 (then considerably higher than the average family's income). By 1917 revenue from the income tax shot ahead of receipts from the tariff. This gap has since been vastly widened.

✦ Wilson Battles the Bankers

A second bastion of the "triple wall of privilege" was the antiquated and inadequate banking and currency system, long since outgrown by the Republic's lusty economic expansion. The country's financial structure, still creaking along under the Civil War National Banking Act, revealed glaring defects. Its most serious shortcoming, as exposed by the panic of 1907, was the inelasticity of the currency. Banking reserves were heavily concentrated in New York and a handful of other large cities and could not be mobilized in times of financial stress into areas that were badly pinched.

In 1908 Congress had authorized an investigation headed by a mossback banker, Republican senator Aldrich. Three years later Aldrich's special commission recommended a gigantic bank with numerous branches—in effect, a third Bank of the United States.

For their part, Democratic banking reformers heeded the findings of a House committee chaired by Congressman Arsene Pujo, which traced the tentacles of the "money monster" into the hidden vaults of American banking and business. President Wilson's confidant, progressive-minded Massachusetts attorney Louis D. Brandeis, further fanned the flames of reform with his incendiary though scholarly book *Other People's Money and How the Bankers Use It* (1914).

In June 1913, in a second dramatic personal appearance before both houses of Congress, the president delivered a stirring plea for sweeping reform of the banking system. He ringingly endorsed Democratic proposals for a decentralized bank in government hands, as opposed to Republican demands for a huge private bank with fifteen branches.

Again appealing to the sovereign people, Wilson scored another triumph. In 1913 he signed the epochal **Federal Reserve Act**, the most important piece of economic legislation between the Civil War and the New Deal. The new Federal Reserve Board, appointed by the president, oversaw a nationwide system of twelve regional reserve districts, each with its own central bank. Although these regional banks were actually bankers' banks, owned by member financial institutions, the final authority of the Federal Reserve Board guaranteed a substantial measure of public control. The board was also empowered to issue paper money— "Federal Reserve Notes"—backed by commercial paper, such as promissory notes of businesspeople. Thus the amount of money in circulation could be swiftly increased as needed for the legitimate requirements of business.

The Federal Reserve Act was a red-letter achievement. It carried the nation with flying banners through the financial crises of the First World War of 1914–1918. Without it, the Republic's progress toward the modern economic age would have been seriously retarded.

Granger Collection

Reading the Death Warrant This cartoon appeared in a New York newspaper soon after Woodrow Wilson called for dramatic reform of the banking system before both houses of Congress. With the "money trust" of bankers and businessmen cowed, Wilson was able to win popular and congressional support for the Federal Reserve Act of 1913.

✴ The President Tames the Trusts

Without pausing for breath, Wilson pushed toward the last remaining rampart in the "triple wall of privilege"—the trusts. Early in 1914 he again went before Congress in a personal appearance that still carried drama.

Nine months and thousands of words later, Congress responded with the **Federal Trade Commission Act** of 1914. The new law empowered a presidentially appointed commission to turn a searchlight on industries engaged in interstate commerce, such as the meatpackers. The commissioners were expected to crush monopoly at the source by rooting out unfair trade practices, including unlawful competition, false advertising, mislabeling, adulteration, and bribery.

The knot of monopoly was further cut by the **Clayton Anti-Trust Act** of 1914. It lengthened the shopworn Sherman Act's list of business practices that were deemed objectionable, including price discrimination and interlocking directorates (whereby the same individuals served as directors of supposedly competing firms), an end often achieved through **holding companies** (see Figure 29.1).

The Clayton Act also conferred long-overdue benefits on labor. Conservative courts had unexpectedly been ruling that trade unions fell under the antimonopoly restraints of the Sherman Act. A classic case involved striking hatmakers in Danbury, Connecticut, who were assessed triple damages of more than $250,000, which resulted in the loss of their savings and homes. The Clayton Act therefore sought to exempt labor and agricultural organizations from antitrust prosecution, while explicitly legalizing strikes and peaceful picketing.

Union leader Samuel Gompers hailed the act as the Magna Carta of labor because it legally lifted human labor out of the category of "a commodity or article of commerce." But the rejoicing was premature, as conservative judges in later years continued to clip the wings of the union movement.

✴ Wilsonian Progressivism at High Tide

Energetically scaling the "triple wall of privilege," Woodrow Wilson had treated the nation to a dazzling demonstration of vigorous presidential leadership. He proved nearly irresistible in his first eighteen months in office. For once, a political creed was matched by deed, as the progressive reformers racked up victory after victory.

Standing at the peak of his powers at the head of the progressive forces, Wilson pressed ahead with further reforms. The Federal Farm Loan Act of 1916 made credit available to farmers at low rates of interest—as long demanded by the Populists. The Warehouse Act of 1916 authorized loans on the security of staple crops—another Populist idea. Other laws benefited rural America by providing for highway construction and the establishment of agricultural extension work in the state colleges.

Sweaty laborers also made gains as the progressive wave foamed forward. Sailors, treated brutally from cat-o'-nine-tails days onward, were given relief by the La Follette Seaman's Act of 1915. It required decent treatment and a living wage on American merchant ships. One unhappy result of this well-intentioned law was the crippling of America's merchant marine, as freight rates spiraled upward with the crew's wages.

Wilson further helped the workers with the **Workingmen's Compensation Act** of 1916, granting assistance to federal civil-service employees during periods of disability. In the same year, the president approved an act restricting child labor on products flowing into interstate commerce, though the stand-pat Supreme Court soon invalidated the law. Railroad workers, numbering about 1.7 million, were not sidetracked. The **Adamson Act** of 1916 established an eight-hour day for all employees on trains in interstate commerce, with extra pay for overtime.

Wilson earned the enmity of businesspeople and bigots but endeared himself to progressives when in 1916 he nominated for the Supreme Court the prominent reformer Louis D. Brandeis—the first Jew to be called to the high bench. Yet even Wilson's progressivism had its limits, and it clearly stopped short of better treatment for blacks. The southern-bred Wilson actually presided over accelerated segregation in the federal bureaucracy. When a delegation of black leaders personally protested to him, the schoolmasterish president virtually froze them out of his office.

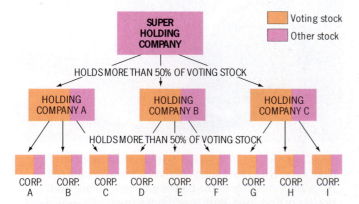

FIGURE 29.1 Organization of Holding Companies Keep in mind that the voting stock of a corporation is often only a fraction of the total stock.

Despite these limitations, Wilson knew that to be reelected in 1916, he needed to identify himself clearly as the candidate of progressivism. He appeased businesspeople by making conservative appointments to the Federal Reserve Board and the Federal Trade Commission, but he devoted most of his energy to cultivating progressive support. Wilson's election in 1912 had been something of a fluke, owing largely to the Taft-Roosevelt split in the Republican ranks. To remain in the White House, the president would have to woo the bull moose voters into the Democratic fold.

✦ New Directions in Foreign Policy

In one important area, Wilson chose not to answer the trumpet call of the bull moosers. In contrast to Roosevelt and even Taft, Wilson recoiled from an aggressive foreign policy. Hating imperialism, he was repelled by TR's big stickism. Suspicious of Wall Street, he detested the so-called dollar diplomacy of Taft.

In office only a week, Wilson declared war on dollar diplomacy. He proclaimed that the government would no longer offer special support to American investors in Latin America and China. Shivering from this Wilsonian bucket of cold water, American bankers pulled out of the Taft-engineered six-nation loan to China the next day.

In a similarly self-denying vein, Wilson persuaded Congress in early 1914 to repeal the Panama Canal Tolls Act of 1912, which had exempted American coastwise shipping from tolls and thereby provoked sharp protests from injured Britain. The president further chimed in with the anti-imperial song of Bryan and other Democrats when he signed the **Jones Act** in 1916. It granted to the Philippines the boon of territorial status and promised independence as soon as a "stable government" could be established. Wilson's racial prejudices, however, made it difficult for him to anticipate anything other than a long political tutelage for the Filipinos. Indeed, not until July 4, 1946—thirty years later—did the United States accept Philippine independence.

Wilson also partially defused a menacing crisis with Japan in 1913. The California legislature, still seeking to rid the Golden State of Japanese settlers, prohibited them from owning land. Tokyo, understandably irritated, lodged vigorous protests. At Fortress Corregidor, in the Philippines, American gunners were put on around-the-clock alert. But when Wilson dispatched Secretary of State William Jennings Bryan to plead with the California legislature to soften its stand, tensions eased somewhat.

Political turmoil in Haiti soon forced Wilson to eat some of his anti-imperialist words. The climax of the disorders came in 1914–1915, when an outraged populace literally tore to pieces the brutal Haitian president.

© Bettmann/Corbis

U.S. Marines in Haiti, 1919 The United States sent the marines to Haiti in 1915 to protect American economic interests. They remained for nineteen years.

In 1915 Wilson reluctantly dispatched marines to protect American lives and property. They remained for nineteen years, making Haiti an American protectorate. In 1916 he stole a page from Roosevelt's corollary to the Monroe Doctrine and concluded a treaty with Haiti providing for U.S. supervision of finances and the police. In the same year, he sent the leathernecked marines to quell riots in the Dominican Republic, and that debt-cursed land came under the shadow of the American eagle's wings for the next eight years. In 1917 Wilson purchased from Denmark the Virgin Islands, in the West Indies, tightening the grip of Uncle Sam in these shark-infested waters. Increasingly, the Caribbean Sea, with its vital approaches to the now-navigable Panama Canal, was taking on the earmarks of a Yankee preserve (see Map 29.2).

✹ Moralistic Diplomacy in Mexico

Rifle bullets whining across the southern border served as a constant reminder that all was not quiet in Mexico. For decades Mexico had been sorely exploited by foreign investors in oil, railroads, and mines. By 1913 American capitalists had sunk about a billion dollars into the underdeveloped but generously endowed country.

But if Mexico was rich, the Mexicans were poor. Fed up with their miserable lot, they at last revolted. Their revolution took an ugly turn in early 1913, when a conscienceless clique (with the support of President Taft's ambassador to Mexico) murdered the popular new revolutionary president and installed General Victoriano Huerta, an Indian, in the president's chair. All this chaos accelerated a massive migration of Mexicans to the United States. More than a million Spanish-speaking newcomers tramped across the southern border in the first three decades of the twentieth century. Settling mostly in Texas, New Mexico, Arizona, and California, they swung picks building highways and railroads or followed the fruit harvests as pickers. Though often segregated in Spanish-speaking enclaves, they helped to create a unique borderland culture that blended Mexican and American folkways.

MAP 29.2 The United States in the Caribbean, 1898–1941 This map explains why many Latin Americans accused the United States of turning the Caribbean Sea into a "Yankee lake." It also suggests that Uncle Sam was much less "isolationist" in his own backyard than he was in faraway Europe or Asia. © Cengage Learning

The revolutionary bloodshed also menaced American lives and property in Mexico. Cries for intervention burst from the lips of American jingoes. Prominent among those chanting for war was the influential chain newspaper publisher William Randolph Hearst, whose views presumably were colored by his ownership of a Mexican ranch larger than Rhode Island. Yet once again, President Wilson refused to practice the same old dollar diplomacy of his predecessors, deeming it "perilous" to determine foreign policy "in the terms of material interest."

Wilson strove as best he could to steer a moral course in Mexico. He sent his aggressive ambassador packing, imposed an arms embargo, and refused to recognize officially the murderous government of "that brute" Huerta, even though most foreign powers acknowledged Huerta's bloody-handed regime. "I am going to teach the South American republics to elect good men," the

In October 1913 President Woodrow Wilson (1856–1924) addressed the Southern Commercial Congress in Mobile, Alabama, and drew a connection between the battle against the trusts at home and the travails of countries south of the border:

"We have seen material interests threaten constitutional freedom in the United States. Therefore, we will now know how to sympathize with those in the rest of [Latin] America who have to contend with such powers, not only from within their borders but from outside their borders also.**"**

former professor declared. He put his munitions where his mouth was in 1914, when he allowed American arms to flow to Huerta's principal rivals, white-bearded Venustiano Carranza and the firebrand Francisco ("Pancho") Villa.

The Mexican volcano erupted at the Atlantic seaport of Tampico in April 1914, when a small party of American sailors was arrested. The Mexicans promptly released the captives and apologized, but they refused the affronted American admiral's demand for a salute of twenty-one guns. Wilson, heavy-hearted but stubbornly determined to eliminate Huerta, asked Congress for authority to use force against Mexico. Before Congress could act, Wilson ordered the navy to seize the Mexican port of Veracruz to thwart the arrival of a German steamer carrying Huerta-bound guns and ammunition. Huerta as well as Carranza hotly protested against this high-handed Yankee maneuver.

Just as a full-dress shooting conflict seemed inevitable, Wilson was rescued by an offer of mediation from the ABC Powers—Argentina, Brazil, and Chile. Huerta collapsed in July 1914 under pressure from within and without. He was succeeded by his archrival, Venustiano Carranza, still fiercely resentful of Wilson's military meddling. The whole sorry **Tampico Incident** did not augur well for the future of United States–Mexican relations.

"Pancho" Villa, a combination of bandit and Robin Hood, had meanwhile stolen the spotlight. He emerged as the chief rival to President Carranza, whom Wilson now reluctantly supported. Challenging Carranza's authority while also punishing the gringos, Villa's men ruthlessly hauled sixteen young American mining engineers off a train traveling through northern Mexico in January 1916 and killed them. A month later Villa and his followers, hoping to provoke a war between Wilson and Carranza, blazed across the border into Columbus, New Mexico, and murdered another nineteen Americans.

El Hijo del Ahuizote September 6, 1913

Wilson Confronts Huerta A Mexican view of the tense standoff between Wilson and the Mexican president, Victoriano Huerta. The artist's rendering seems to reflect the famous observation of long-time Mexican leader Porfirio Diaz: "Poor Mexico! So far from God, so close to the United States."

"Pancho" Villa with His Ragtag Army in Mexico, ca. 1916 His daring, impetuosity, and horsemanship made Villa a hero to the masses of northern Mexico. Yet he proved to be a violent and ineffective crusader against social abuses, and he was assassinated in 1923.

General John J. ("Black Jack")* Pershing, a grim-faced and ramrod-erect veteran of the Cuban and Philippine campaigns, was ordered to break up the bandit band. His hastily organized force of several thousand mounted troops penetrated deep into rugged Mexico with surprising speed. They clashed with Carranza's forces and mauled the Villistas but missed capturing Villa himself. As the threat of war with Germany loomed larger, the invading army was withdrawn in January 1917.

Thunder Across the Sea

Europe's powder magazine, long smoldering, blew up in the summer of 1914, when the flaming pistol of a Serb patriot killed the heir to the throne of Austria-Hungary in Sarajevo. An outraged Vienna government, backed by Germany, forthwith presented a stern ultimatum to neighboring Serbia.

An explosive chain reaction followed. Tiny Serbia, backed by its powerful Slav neighbor Russia, refused to bend the knee sufficiently. The Russian tsar began to mobilize his ponderous war machine, menacing Germany on the east, even as his ally, France, confronted Germany on the west. In alarm, the Germans struck suddenly at France through unoffending Belgium; their objective was to knock their ancient enemy out of action so that they would have two free hands to repel Russia. Great Britain, its coastline jeopardized by the assault on Belgium, was sucked into the conflagration on the side of France.

Almost overnight most of Europe was locked in a fight to the death. On one side were arrayed the **Central Powers**: Germany and Austria-Hungary, and later Turkey and Bulgaria. On the other side were the **Allies**:

principally France, Britain, and Russia, and later Japan and Italy.

Americans thanked God for the ocean moats and self-righteously congratulated themselves on having had ancestors wise enough to have abandoned the hell pits of Europe. America felt strong, snug, smug, and secure—but not for long.

A Precarious Neutrality

President Wilson's grief at the outbreak of war was compounded by the recent death of his wife. He sorrowfully issued the routine neutrality proclamation and called on Americans to be neutral in thought as well as deed. But such scrupulous evenhandedness proved difficult.

Both sides wooed the United States, the great neutral in the West. The British enjoyed the boon of close cultural, linguistic, and economic ties with America and had the added advantage of controlling most of the transatlantic cables. Their censors sheared away war stories harmful to the Allies and drenched the United States with tales of German bestiality.

The Germans and the Austro-Hungarians counted on the natural sympathies of their transplanted countrymen in America. Including persons with at least one foreign-born parent, people with blood ties to the Central Powers numbered some 11 million in 1914. Some of these recent immigrants expressed noisy sympathy for the fatherland, but most were simply grateful to be so distant from the fray (see Table 29.1).

Most Americans were anti-German from the outset. With his villainous upturned mustache, Kaiser Wilhelm II seemed the embodiment of arrogant autocracy, an impression strengthened by Germany's ruthless strike at neutral Belgium. German and Austrian agents further tarnished the image of the Central Powers in American eyes when they resorted to violence in American factories and ports. When a German operative in 1915 absentmindedly left his briefcase on a New York

---

*So called from his earlier service as an officer with the crack black 10th Cavalry.

TABLE 29.1 Principal Foreign Elements in the United States, Census of 1910

Country of Origin		Foreign-Born	Natives with Two Foreign-Born Parents	Natives with One Foreign-Born Parent	Total
Central Powers	Germany	2,501,181	3,911,847	1,869,590	8,282,61
	Austria-Hungary	1,670,524	900,129	131,133	2,701,786
Allied Powers	Great Britain	1,219,968	852,610	1,158,474	3,231,052
	(Ireland)*	1,352,155	2,141,577	1,010,628	4,504,360
	Russia	1,732,421	949,316	70,938	2,752,675
	Italy	1,343,070	695,187	60,103	2,098,360
TOTAL (for all foreign countries, including those not listed)		13,345,545	12,916,311	5,981,526	32,243,282
Percentage of total U.S. population (91,972,266)		14.5	14.0	6.5	35.0

*Ireland was not yet independent.

elevated car, its documents detailing plans for industrial sabotage were quickly discovered and publicized. American opinion, already ill-disposed, was further inflamed against the kaiser and Germany. Yet the great majority of Americans earnestly hoped to stay out of the horrible war.

✦ America Earns Blood Money

When Europe burst into flames in 1914, the United States was bogged down in a worrisome business recession. But as fate would have it, British and French war orders soon pulled American industry out of the morass of hard times and onto a peak of war-born prosperity (see Table 29.2). Part of this boom was financed by American bankers, notably the Wall Street firm of J. P. Morgan and Company, which eventually advanced to the Allies the enormous sum of $2.3 billion during the period of American neutrality. The Central Powers protested bitterly against the immense trade between America and the Allies, but this traffic did not in fact violate the international neutrality laws. Germany was technically free to trade with the United States. It was prevented from doing so not by American policy but by geography and the British navy. Trade between Germany and America had to move across the Atlantic; but the British controlled the sea-lanes, and they threw a noose-tight blockade of mines and ships across the North Sea,

The Fatherland, *the chief German-American propaganda newspaper in the United States, cried,*

"We [Americans] prattle about humanity while we manufacture poisoned shrapnel and picric acid for profit. Ten thousand German widows, ten thousand orphans, ten thousand graves bear the legend 'Made in America.'"

TABLE 29.2 U.S. Exports to Belligerents, 1914–1916

Belligerent	1914	1915	1916	1916 Figure as a Percentage of 1914 Figure
Britain	$594,271,863	$911,794,954	$1,526,685,102	257%
France	159,818,924	369,397,170	628,851,988	393
Italy*	74,235,012	184,819,688	269,246,105	363
Germany	344,794,276	28,863,354	288,899	0.08

*Italy joined the Allies in April 1915.

MAP 29.3 British Military Area (declared November 3, 1914) and German Submarine War Zone (declared February 4, 1915) © Cengage Learning

Map legend:
- British military area
- German submarine war zone
- Allied Powers
- Central Powers
- Neutral nations

Map labels: ICELAND, ATLANTIC OCEAN, NORWAY, SWEDEN, North Sea, Baltic Sea, UNITED KINGDOM, DENMARK, NETH., GERMANY, BELG., FRANCE, SWITZ., *Lusitania* torpedoed May 7, 1915

A German U-boat This deadly new weapon rendered useless existing rules of naval warfare, eventually pushing the United States to declare war against Germany in 1917.

© Bettmann/Corbis

gateway to German ports. Over the unavailing protests of American shippers, farmers, and manufacturers, the British began forcing American vessels off the high seas and into their ports. This harassment of American shipping proved highly effective, as trade between Germany and the United States virtually ceased.

Hard-pressed Germany did not tamely consent to being starved out. In retaliation for the British blockade, in February 1915 Berlin announced a submarine war area around the British Isles (see Map 29.3). The submarine was a weapon so new that existing international law could not be made to fit it. The old rule that a warship must stop and board a merchantman could hardly apply to submarines, which could easily be rammed or sunk if they surfaced.

The cigar-shaped marauders posed a dire threat to the United States—so long as Wilson insisted on maintaining America's neutral rights. Berlin officials declared that they would try not to sink *neutral* shipping, but they warned that mistakes would probably occur. Wilson now determined on a policy of calculated risk. He would continue to claim profitable neutral trading rights, while hoping that no high-seas incident would force his hand to grasp the sword of war. Setting his peninsular jaw, he emphatically warned Germany

that it would be held to "strict accountability" for any attacks on American vessels or citizens.

The German submarines (known as **U-boats**, from the German *Unterseeboot*, or "undersea boat") meanwhile began their deadly work. In the first months of 1915, they sank about ninety ships in the war zone. Then the submarine issue became acute when the British passenger liner ***Lusitania*** was torpedoed and sank off the coast of Ireland on May 7, 1915, with the loss of 1,198 lives, including 128 Americans.

The *Lusitania* was carrying forty-two hundred cases of small-arms ammunition, a fact the Germans used to justify the sinking. But Americans were swept by a wave of shock and anger at this act of "mass murder" and "piracy." The eastern United States, closer to the war, seethed with talk of fighting, but the rest of the country showed a strong distaste for hostilities. The peace-loving Wilson had no stomach for leading a disunited nation into war. He well remembered the mistake

Advertisement from the *New York Herald*, May 1, 1915 Six days later the *Lusitania* was sunk. Note the German warning.

in 1812 of his fellow Princetonian, James Madison. Instead, by a series of increasingly strong notes, Wilson attempted to bring the German warlords sharply to book. Even this measured approach was too much for Secretary of State Bryan, who resigned rather than sign a protestation that might spell shooting. But Wilson resolutely stood his ground. "There is such a thing," he declared, "as a man being too proud to fight." This kind of talk incensed the war-thirsty Theodore Roosevelt. The Rough Rider assailed the spineless simperers who heeded the "weasel words" of the pacifistic professor in the White House.

Yet Wilson, sticking to his verbal guns, made some diplomatic progress. After another British liner, the *Arabic*, was sunk in August 1915, with the loss of two American lives, Berlin reluctantly agreed not to sink unarmed and unresisting passenger ships *without warning*.

This pledge appeared to be violated in March 1916, when the Germans torpedoed a French passenger steamer, the *Sussex*. The infuriated Wilson informed the Germans that unless they renounced the inhuman practice of sinking merchant ships without warning,

"Here's Money for Your Americans. I May Drown Some More." Germany expressed "profound regret" for the deaths of 128 Americans aboard the torpedoed passenger liner *Lusitania* in 1915, but the incident helped feed a mounting anti-German sentiment in the United States.

he would break diplomatic relations—an almost certain prelude to war.

Germany reluctantly knuckled under to President Wilson's *Sussex* ultimatum, agreeing not to sink passenger ships and merchant vessels without giving warning. But the Germans attached a long string to their *Sussex* pledge: the United States would have to persuade the Allies to modify what Berlin regarded as their illegal blockade. This, obviously, was something that Washington could not do. Wilson promptly accepted the German pledge, without accepting the "string." He thus won a temporary but precarious diplomatic victory—precarious because Germany could pull the string whenever it chose, and the president might suddenly find himself tugged over the cliff of war.

Wilson Wins Reelection in 1916

Against this ominous backdrop, the presidential campaign of 1916 gathered speed. Both the bull moose Progressives and the Republicans met in Chicago. The Progressives uproariously renominated Theodore Roosevelt, but the Rough Rider, who loathed Wilson and all his works, had no stomach for splitting the Republicans again and ensuring the reelection of his hated rival. In refusing to run, he sounded the death knell of the Progressive party.

Roosevelt's Republican admirers also clamored for "Teddy," but the Old Guard detested the renegade who had ruptured the party in 1912. Instead they drafted Supreme Court justice Charles Evans Hughes, a cold intellectual who had achieved a solid liberal record when he was governor of New York. The Republican platform condemned the Democratic tariff, assaults on the trusts, and Wilson's wishy-washiness in dealing with Mexico and Germany.

The thick-whiskered Hughes ("an animated feather duster") left the bench for the campaign stump, where he was not at home. In anti-German areas of the country, he assailed Wilson for not standing up to the kaiser, whereas in isolationist areas he took a softer line. This fence-straddling operation led to the jeer "Charles Evasive Hughes."

Hughes was further plagued by Roosevelt, who was delivering a series of skin-'em-alive speeches against "that damned Presbyterian hypocrite Wilson." Frothing for war, TR privately scoffed at Hughes as a "whiskered Wilson"; the only difference between the two, he said, was "a shave."

Wilson, nominated by acclamation at the Democratic convention in St. Louis, ignored Hughes on the theory that one should not try to murder a man who is committing suicide. His campaign was built on the slogan "He Kept Us Out of War."

Theodore Roosevelt, War Hawk The former president clamored for American intervention in the European war, but the country preferred peace in 1916. Ironically, Roosevelt's archrival, Woodrow Wilson, would take the country into the war just months after the 1916 election. Library of Congress

Democratic orators warned that by electing Charles Evans Hughes, the nation would be electing a fight—with a certain frustrated Rough Rider leading the charge. A Democratic advertisement appealing to the American working people read,

> *You are Working;*
> *—Not Fighting!*
> *Alive and Happy;*
> *—Not Cannon Fodder!*
> *Wilson and Peace with Honor?*
> *or*
> *Hughes with Roosevelt and War?*

On election day Hughes swept the East and looked like a surefire winner. Wilson went to bed that night prepared to accept defeat, while the New York newspapers displayed huge portraits of "The President-Elect—Charles Evans Hughes."

But the rest of the country turned the tide. Midwesterners and westerners, attracted by Wilson's progressive reforms and antiwar policies, flocked to the polls for the president. The final result, in doubt for

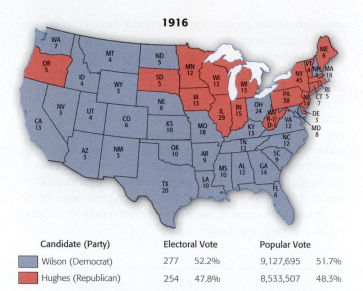

1916

Candidate (Party)	Electoral Vote		Popular Vote	
Wilson (Democrat)	277	52.2%	9,127,695	51.7%
Hughes (Republican)	254	47.8%	8,533,507	48.3%

MAP 29.4 Presidential Election of 1916 (with electoral vote by state) Wilson was so worried about being a lame duck president in a time of great international tensions that he drew up a plan whereby Hughes, if victorious, would be appointed secretary of state, Wilson and the vice president would resign, and Hughes would thus succeed immediately to the presidency. © Cengage Learning

During the 1916 campaign, J. A. O'Leary, the head of a pro-German and pro-Irish organization, sent a scorching telegram to Wilson condemning him for having been pro-British in approving war loans and ammunition traffic. Wilson shot back an answer:

❝Your telegram received. I would feel deeply mortified to have you or anybody like you vote for me. Since you have access to many disloyal Americans and I have not, I will ask you to convey this message to them.❞

President Wilson's devastating and somewhat insulting response probably won him more votes than it lost.

several days, hinged on California, which Wilson carried by some 3,800 votes out of about a million cast.

Wilson barely squeaked through, with a final vote of 277 to 254 in the Electoral College, and 9,127,695 to 8,533,507 in the popular column (see Map 29.4). The prolabor Wilson received strong support from the working class and from renegade bull moosers, whom Republicans failed to lure back into their camp. Wilson had not specifically promised to keep the country out of war, but probably enough voters relied on such implicit assurances to ensure his victory. Their hopeful expectations were soon rudely shattered.

Varying Viewpoints
Who Were the Progressives?

*D*ebate about progressivism has revolved mainly around a question that is simple to ask but devilishly difficult to answer: who were the progressives? It was once taken for granted that progressive reformers were simply the heirs of the Jeffersonian-Jacksonian-Populist reform crusades; they were the oppressed and downtrodden common folk who finally erupted in wrath and demanded their due.

But in his influential *Age of Reform* (1955), Richard Hofstadter astutely challenged that view. Progressive leaders, he argued, were not drawn from the ranks of society's poor and marginalized. Rather, they were middle-class people threatened from above by the emerging power of new corporate elites and from below by a restless working class. It was not economic deprivation, but "status anxiety," Hofstadter insisted, that prompted these people to become reformers. Their psychological motivation, Hofstadter concluded, rendered many of their reform efforts quirky and ineffectual.

By contrast, "New Left" historians, notably Gabriel Kolko, argued that progressivism was dominated by established business leaders who successfully directed "reform" to their own conservative ends. In this view government regulation (as embodied in new agencies like the Federal Reserve Board and the Federal Tariff Commission, and in legislation like the Meat Inspection Act) simply accomplished what two generations of private efforts had failed to do: dampen cutthroat competition, stabilize markets, and make America safe for monopoly capitalism.

Still other scholars, notably Robert H. Wiebe and Samuel P. Hays, argued that the progressives were neither the psychologically or economically disadvantaged nor the old capitalist elite, but were, rather, members of a rapidly emerging, self-confident social class possessed of the new techniques of scientific management, technological expertise, and organizational know-how. This "organizational school" of historians did not see progressivism as a struggle of the "people" against the "interests," as a confused and nostalgic campaign by status-threatened reformers, or as a conservative coup d'état. The progressive movement, in this view, was by and large an effort to rationalize and modernize many social institutions by introducing the wise and impartial hand of government regulation.

This view had much to recommend it. Yet despite its widespread acceptance among historians, it could not adequately account for the titanic political struggles of the progressive era over the very reforms that the "organizational school" regarded as simple adjustments to modernity. It also brushed over the deep philosophical differences that divided progressives themselves—such as between Roosevelt's New Nationalism and Wilson's New Freedom. In addition, the organizational approach did not account for the important role of women in advocating progressive reforms, as demonstrated by Robyn Muncy, Linda Gordon, and Theda Skocpol. Building the American welfare state in the early twentieth century, they have argued, was fundamentally a gendered activity inspired by a "female dominion" of social workers and "social feminists." Scholars such as Daniel T. Rodgers have added that essential inspiration also came from across the Atlantic. In European countries vibrant labor movements sought a welfare state to benefit the working class, whereas in the United States the strength of female reformers promoted welfare programs aimed at protecting women and children. All the same, American programs frequently were modeled after policies adopted in London, Paris, and Berlin.

Chapter Review

KEY TERMS

New Freedom (661)

New Nationalism (662)

Underwood Tariff (664)

Federal Reserve Act (665)

Federal Trade Commission Act (666)

Clayton Anti-Trust Act (666)

holding companies (666)

Workingmen's Compensation Act (666)

Adamson Act (666)

Jones Act (667)

Tampico Incident (669)

Central Powers (670)

Allies (670)

U-boats (672)

Lusitania (672)

PEOPLE TO KNOW

Herbert Croly

Louis D. Brandeis

Victoriano Huerta

Venustiano Carranza

Francisco ("Pancho") Villa

John ("Black Jack") Pershing

Charles Evans Hughes

CHRONOLOGY

1912	Wilson defeats Taft and Roosevelt for presidency
1913	Underwood Tariff Act Sixteenth Amendment (income tax) Federal Reserve Act Huerta takes power in Mexico
1914	Clayton Anti-Trust Act Federal Trade Commission established U.S. seizes port of Veracruz, Mexico World War I begins in Europe

1915	La Follette Seaman's Act
	Lusitania torpedoed and sunk by German
	  U-boat
	U.S. Marines sent to Haiti
	Germany declares submarine war area around
	  British Isles

1916	*Sussex* ultimatum and pledge U.S. exports to European belligerents skyrocket Workingmen's Compensation Act Federal Farm Loan Act Warehouse Act Adamson Act Pancho Villa raids New Mexico Brandeis appointed to Supreme Court Jones Act U.S. Marines sent to Dominican Republic Wilson defeats Hughes for presidency
1917	United States buys Virgin Islands from Denmark

TO LEARN MORE

Michael C. Adams, *The Great Adventure: Male Desire and the Coming of World War I* (1990)

John W. Chambers, *The Tyranny of Change: America in the Progressive Era, 1900–1917* (rev. ed., 2000)

John Milton Cooper, Jr., *Woodrow Wilson: A Biography* (2009)

————, *The Warrior and the Priest: Woodrow Wilson and Theodore Roosevelt* (1983)

Alexander L. George and Juliette L. George, *Woodrow Wilson and Colonel House* (1956)

Lewis L. Gould, *Four Hats in the Ring: The 1912 Election and the Birth of Modern Politics* (2008)

Henry May, *The End of American Innocence: A Study of the First Years of Our Time* (1959)

Frank A. Ninkovich, *The Wilsonian Century: U.S. Foreign Policy Since 1900* (1999)

Mary Renda, *Taking Haiti: Military Occupation and the Culture of U.S. Imperialism, 1915–1940* (2001)

Edward Stettner, *Shaping Modern Liberalism: Herbert Croly and Progressive Thought* (1993)

Philippa Strum, *Brandeis: Justice for the People* (1985)

Robert W. Tucker, *Woodrow Wilson and the Great War: Reconsidering America's Neutrality, 1914–1917* (2007)

Eileen Welsome, *The General and the Jaguar: Pershing's Hunt for Pancho Villa* (2006)

A complete, annotated bibliography for this chapter—along with brief descriptions of the People to Know—may be found on the American Pageant website. The Key Terms are defined in a Glossary at the end of the text.

Go to the CourseMate website at **www.cengagebrain.com** for additional study tools and review materials—including audio and video clips—for this chapter.

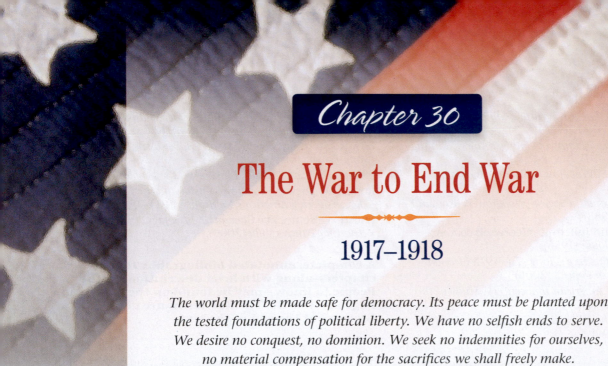

Chapter 30

The War to End War

1917–1918

The world must be made safe for democracy. Its peace must be planted upon the tested foundations of political liberty. We have no selfish ends to serve. We desire no conquest, no dominion. We seek no indemnities for ourselves, no material compensation for the sacrifices we shall freely make.

WOODROW WILSON, WAR MESSAGE, APRIL 2, 1917

Destiny dealt cruelly with Woodrow Wilson. The lover of peace, as fate would have it, was forced to lead a hesitant and peace-loving nation into war. As the last days of 1916 slipped through the hourglass, the president made one final, futile attempt to mediate between the embattled belligerents. On January 22, 1917, he delivered one of his most moving addresses, restating America's commitment to neutral rights and declaring that only a negotiated "peace without victory" would prove durable.

Germany's warlords responded with a blow of the mailed fist. On January 31, 1917, they announced to an astonished world their decision to wage *unrestricted* submarine warfare, sinking *all* ships, including America's, in the war zone.

Why this rash act? War with America was the last thing Germany wanted. But after three ghastly years in the trenches, Germany's leaders decided the distinction between combatants and noncombatants was a luxury they could no longer afford. Thus they jerked on the string they had attached to their *Sussex* pledge in 1916, desperately hoping to bring Britain to its knees before the United States entered the war. Wilson, his bluff called, broke diplomatic relations with Germany but refused to move closer to war unless the Germans undertook "overt" acts against American lives.

✦ War by Act of Germany

To defend American interests short of war, the president asked Congress for authority to arm American merchant ships. When a band of midwestern senators launched a filibuster to block the measure, Wilson denounced them as a "little group of willful men" who were rendering a great nation "helpless and contemptible." But their obstruction was a powerful reminder of the continuing strength of American isolationism.

Meanwhile, the sensational **Zimmermann note** was intercepted and published on March 1, 1917, infuriating Americans, especially westerners. German foreign secretary Arthur Zimmermann had secretly proposed a German-Mexican alliance, tempting anti-Yankee Mexico with veiled promises of recovering Texas, New Mexico, and Arizona.

On the heels of this provocation came the long-dreaded "overt" acts in the Atlantic, where German U-boats sank four unarmed American merchant vessels in the first two weeks of March. As one Philadelphia newspaper observed, "The difference between war and what we have now is that now we aren't fighting back." Simultaneously came the rousing news that a revolution in Russia had toppled the cruel regime of the tsars. America could now fight foursquare for democracy on the side of the Allies, without the black sheep of Russian despotism in the Allied fold.

Subdued and solemn, Wilson at last stood before a hushed joint session of Congress on the evening of April 2, 1917, and asked for a declaration of war. He had lost his gamble that America could pursue the profits of neutral trade without being sucked into the ghastly maelstrom. A myth developed in later years that America was dragged unwittingly into war by munitions makers and Wall Street bankers, desperate to protect their profits and loans. Yet the weapons merchants and financiers were already thriving, unhampered by

The New York Times.

"All the News That's Fit to Print."

THE WEATHER
Fair, colder today; tomorrow warmer, probably rain; wind northwest.

VOL. LXVI...NO. 21,619.   NEW YORK, TUESDAY, APRIL 3, 1917.—TWENTY-FOUR PAGES.   ONE CENT In New York City. | TWO CENTS New England and Middle States. | THREE CENTS Elsewhere.

PRESIDENT CALLS FOR WAR DECLARATION, STRONGER NAVY, NEW ARMY OF 500,000 MEN, FULL CO-OPERATION WITH GERMANY'S FOES

WAR! Attacks by German submarines finally forced Wilson's hand, and he asked Congress for a declaration of war on April 2, 1917. Four days later, after considerable debate and with fifty-six dissenting votes, Congress obliged the president.

wartime government restrictions and heavy taxation. Their slogan might well have been "Neutrality Forever." The simple truth is that British harassment of American commerce had been galling but endurable; Germany had resorted to the mass killing of civilians. The difference was like that between a gang of thieves and a gang of murderers. President Wilson had drawn a clear, if risky, line against the depredations of the submarine. The German high command, in a last desperate throw of the dice, chose to cross it. In a figurative sense, America's war declaration of April 6, 1917, bore the unambiguous trademark "Made in Germany."

✦ Wilsonian Idealism Enthroned

"It is a fearful thing to lead this great peaceful people into war," Wilson said in his war message. It was fearful indeed, not least of all because of the formidable challenge it posed to Wilson's leadership skills. Ironically, it fell to the scholarly Wilson, deeply respectful of American traditions, to shatter one of the most sacred of those traditions by entangling America in a distant European war.

How could the president arouse the American people to shoulder this unprecedented burden? For more than a century, they had prided themselves on their isolationism from the periodic outbursts of militarized violence that afflicted the Old World. Since 1914 their pride had been reinforced by the bountiful profits gained through neutrality. German U-boats had now roughly shoved a wavering America into the abyss, but ominously, no fewer than six senators and fifty representatives (including the first congresswoman, Jeannette Rankin of Montana) had voted against the war resolution. Wilson could whip up no enthusiasm, especially in the landlocked Midwest, by calling on the nation to fight to make the world safe from the submarine.

To galvanize the country, Wilson would have to proclaim more glorified aims. Radiating the spiritual fervor of his Presbyterian ancestors, he declared the supremely ambitious goal of a crusade "to make the world safe for democracy." Brandishing the sword of righteousness, Wilson virtually hypnotized the nation with his lofty ideals. He contrasted the selfish war aims of the other belligerents, Allied and enemy alike, with America's shining altruism. America, he preached, did not fight for the sake of riches or territorial conquest. The Republic sought only to shape an international order in which democracy could flourish without fear of power-crazed autocrats and militarists.

In Wilsonian idealism the personality of the president and the necessities of history were perfectly matched. The high-minded Wilson genuinely believed in the principles he so eloquently intoned—especially that the modern world could not afford the kind of hyper-destructive war that advanced industrial states were now capable of waging. In this, Wilson's vision was prophetic. In any case, probably no other appeal could have successfully converted the American people from their historic hostility to involvement in European squabbles. Americans, it seemed, could be either isolationists or crusaders, but nothing in between.

Wilson's appeal worked—perhaps too well. Holding aloft the torch of idealism, the president fired up the public mind to a fever pitch. "Force, force to the utmost, force without stint or limit," he cried, while the country responded less elegantly with "Hang the kaiser." Lost on the gale was Wilson's earlier plea for "peace without victory."

✦ Wilson's Fourteen Potent Points

Wilson quickly came to be recognized as the moral leader of the Allied cause. He scaled a summit of inspiring oratory on January 8, 1918, when he delivered his famed **Fourteen Points** Address to an enthusiastic Congress. Although one of his primary purposes was to keep reeling Russia in the war, Wilson's vision inspired all the drooping Allies to make mightier efforts and demoralized the enemy governments by holding out alluring promises to their dissatisfied minorities.

The first five of the Fourteen Points were broad in scope. (1) A proposal to abolish secret treaties pleased liberals of all countries. (2) Freedom of the seas appealed to the Germans, as well as to Americans who distrusted British sea power. (3) A removal of economic barriers among nations had long been the goal of liberal internationalists everywhere. (4) A reduction of armament burdens was gratifying to taxpayers in all countries. (5) An adjustment of colonial claims in the interests of both native peoples and the colonizers was reassuring to the anti-imperialists. Indeed Wilson's pronouncement about colonies was potentially revolutionary. It helped to delegitimize the old empires and opened the road to eventual national independence for millions of "subject peoples."

Other points among the fourteen proved to be no less seductive. They held out the hope of independence ("self-determination") to oppressed minority groups, such as the Poles, millions of whom lay under the heel of Germany and Austria-Hungary. The capstone point, number fourteen, foreshadowed the League of Nations—an international organization that Wilson dreamed would provide a system of collective security. Wilson earnestly prayed that this new scheme would effectively guarantee the political independence and territorial integrity of all countries, whether large or small.

Yet Wilson's appealing points, though raising hopes the world over, were not everywhere applauded. Certain leaders of the Allied nations, with an eye to territorial booty, were less than enthusiastic. Hard-nosed Republicans at home grumbled, and some of them openly mocked the "fourteen commandments" of "God Almighty Wilson."

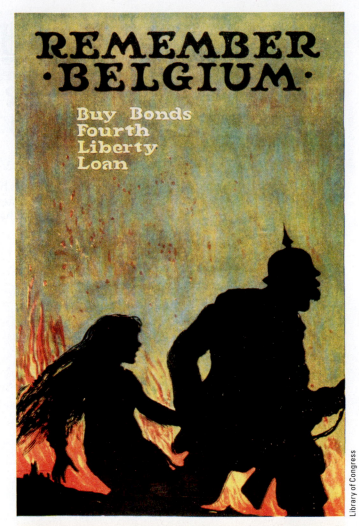

Library of Congress

Anti-German Propaganda   The government relied extensively on emotional appeals and hate propaganda to rally support for the First World War, which most Americans regarded as a distant "European" affair. This poster used gendered imagery to evoke the brutal German violation of Belgian neutrality in August 1914.

✴ Creel Manipulates Minds

Mobilizing people's minds for war, both in America and abroad, was an urgent task facing the Washington authorities. For this purpose the **Committee on Public Information** was created. It was headed by a youngish journalist, George Creel, who, though outspoken and tactless, was gifted with zeal and imagination. His job was to sell America on the war and sell the world on Wilsonian war aims.

The Creel organization, employing some 150,000 workers at home and overseas, proved that words were indeed weapons. It sent out an army of 75,000 "four-minute men"—often longer-winded than that—who

delivered countless speeches containing much "patriotic pep."

Creel's propaganda took varied forms. Posters were splashed on billboards in the "Battle of the Fences," as artists "rallied to the colors." Millions of leaflets and pamphlets, which contained the most pungent Wilsonisms, were showered like confetti upon the world. Propaganda booklets with red-white-and-blue covers were printed by the millions.

Hang-the-kaiser movies, carrying such titles as *The Kaiser, the Beast of Berlin* and *To Hell with the Kaiser,* revealed the helmeted "Hun" at his bloodiest. Arm-waving conductors by the thousands led huge audiences in songs that poured scorn on the enemy and glorified the "boys" in uniform.

ENLIST

LAURA BREY

On Which Side of the Window are YOU?

COPYRIGHTED 1917 GEO. F. GRIFFIN, CHICAGO, ILL.

NATIONAL PRINTING & ENG. CO. CHICAGO, U.S.A.

Library of Congress

Patriotic Persuasion   Worried about the public's enthusiasm for the war, the government employed all the arts of psychology and propaganda to sustain the martial spirit. The prewar song "I Didn't Raise My Boy to Be a Soldier" was changed to "I Didn't Raise My Boy to Be a Slacker," which in turn inspired the cruel parody "I Didn't Raise My Boy to Be a Sausage."

The entire nation, catching the frenzied spirit of a religious revival, burst into song. This was undoubtedly America's singingest war. Most memorable was George M. Cohan's spine-tingling "Over There":

Over there, over there
Send the word, send the word over there,
That the Yanks are coming, the Yanks are coming
The drums rum-tumming ev'rywhere.

Creel typified American war mobilization, which relied more on aroused passion and voluntary compliance than on formal laws. But he oversold the ideals of Wilson and led the world to expect too much. When the president proved to be a mortal and not a god, the resulting disillusionment both at home and abroad was disastrous.

✷ Enforcing Loyalty and Stifling Dissent

German Americans numbered over 8 million, counting those with at least one parent foreign-born, out of a total population of 100 million. On the whole they proved to be dependably loyal to the United States. Yet rumormongers were quick to spread tales of spying and sabotage; even trifling epidemics of diarrhea were blamed on German agents. A few German Americans were tarred, feathered, and beaten; in one extreme case a German Socialist in Illinois was lynched by a drunken mob.

As emotion mounted, hysterical hatred of Germans and things Germanic swept the nation. Orchestras found it unsafe to present German-composed music, like that of Wagner or Beethoven. German books were removed from library shelves, and German classes were canceled in high schools and colleges. Sauerkraut became "liberty cabbage," hamburger "liberty steak." Even beer became suspect, as patriotic Americans fretted over the loyalty of breweries with names like Schlitz and Pabst.

Both the **Espionage Act** of 1917 and the Sedition Act of 1918 reflected current fears about Germans and antiwar Americans. Especially visible among the nineteen hundred prosecutions pursued under these laws were antiwar Socialists and members of the radical Industrial Workers of the World (IWW). Kingpin Socialist Eugene V. Debs was convicted under the Espionage Act in 1918 and sentenced to ten years in a federal penitentiary. IWW leader William D. ("Big Bill") Haywood and ninety-nine associates were similarly convicted. Virtually any criticism of the government could be censored and punished. Some critics claimed the new laws were bending, if not breaking, the First Amendment. But in **Schenck v. United States** (1919), the Supreme Court affirmed their legality, arguing that freedom of speech could be revoked when such speech posed a "clear and present danger" to the nation.

These prosecutions form an ugly chapter in the history of American civil liberty. With the dawn of peace, presidential pardons were rather freely granted, including President Harding's to Eugene Debs in 1921. Yet a few victims lingered behind bars into the 1930s.

✷ The Nation's Factories Go to War

Victory was no foregone conclusion, especially since the Republic, despite ample warning, was caught flat-footedly unready for its leap into global war. The

Socialist Leader Eugene V. Debs Addresses an Antiwar Rally in 1918 For his denunciation of World War I, Debs was convicted under the Espionage Act of 1917 and sent to federal prison. In his courtroom speech defending himself against charges of disloyalty, he passionately declared, "While there is a lower class, I am in it; while there is a criminal element, I am of it; while there is a soul in prison, I am not free." He ran as a presidential candidate in 1920 while still incarcerated in his cell and received nearly a million votes.

pacifistic Wilson had only belatedly backed some mild preparedness measures beginning in 1915, including the creation of a civilian Council of National Defense to study problems of economic mobilization. He had also launched a shipbuilding program (as much to capture the belligerents' war-disrupted foreign trade as to anticipate America's possible entry into the war) and endorsed a modest beefing-up of the army, which with 100,000 regulars then ranked about fifteenth among the armies of the world, in the same category with Persia's. It would take a herculean effort to marshal America's daunting but disorganized resources and throw them into the field quickly enough to bolster the Allied war effort.

Towering obstacles confronted economic mobilizers. Sheer ignorance was among the biggest roadblocks. No one knew precisely how much steel or explosive powder the country was capable of producing. Old ideas also proved to be liabilities, as traditional fears of big government hamstrung efforts to orchestrate the economy from Washington. States' rights Democrats and businesspeople alike balked at federal economic controls, even though the embattled nation could ill afford the freewheeling, hit-or-miss chaos of the peacetime economy.

Late in the war, and after some bruising political battles, Wilson succeeded in imposing some order on this economic confusion. In March 1918 he appointed lone-eagle stock speculator Bernard Baruch to head the **War Industries Board**. Although the War Industries Board had only feeble formal powers, it set a precedent for the federal government to take a central role in economic planning in moments of crisis. It was disbanded just days after the armistice, and Americans returned to their preference for laissez-faire and a weak central government. But in the midst of the Great Depression of the 1930s, policymakers would look back to World War I agencies like this one as models.

✸ Workers in Wartime

Spurred by the slogan "Labor Will Win the War," American workers sweated their way to victory. In part they were driven by the War Department's "work or fight" rule of 1918, which threatened any unemployed male with being immediately drafted—a powerful

Suppressing the Steel Strike: Pittsburgh, 1919 The big steel producers ferociously resisted the unionization of their industry. In Pittsburgh compliant local officials bent to the steel makers' will and issued an order banning all outdoor meetings of strikers. This mounted policeman enforced the order with a flailing billy club. The steelworkers' strike eventually failed, leaving the steel industry un-unionized until the New Deal championed labor's cause in the depression decade of the 1930s.

discouragement to go on strike. But for the most part, government tried to treat labor fairly. The **National War Labor Board**, chaired by former president Taft, exerted itself to head off labor disputes that might hamper the war effort. While pressing employers to grant concessions to labor, including high wages and the eight-hour day, the board stopped short of supporting labor's most important demand: a government guarantee of the right to organize into unions.

Fortunately for the Allied cause, Samuel Gompers and his American Federation of Labor (AF of L) loyally supported the war, though some smaller and more radical labor organizations, including the **Industrial Workers of the World**, did not. The IWW, known as the "Wobblies" and sometimes derided as the "I Won't Works," engineered some of the most damaging industrial sabotage, and not without reason. As transient laborers in such industries as fruit and lumber, the Wobblies were victims of some of the shabbiest working conditions in the country. When they protested, many were viciously beaten, arrested, or run out of town.

Mainstream labor's loyalty was rewarded. At war's end, the AF of L had more than doubled its membership, to over 3 million, and in the most heavily unionized sectors—coal mining, manufacturing, and transporta-tion—real wages (after adjusting for inflation) had risen more than 20 percent over prewar levels. A new day seemed to be dawning for the long-struggling union movement.

Yet labor harbored grievances. Recognition of the right to organize still eluded labor's grasp. Wartime inflation—prices more than doubled between 1914 and 1920—threatened to eclipse wage gains. Not even the call of patriotism and Wilsonian idealism could defuse all labor disputes. Some six thousand strikes, several stained by blood, broke out in the war years. In 1919 the greatest strike in American history rocked the steel industry. More than a quarter of a million steelworkers walked off their jobs in a bid to force their employers to recognize their right to organize and bargain collectively. The steel companies resisted mercilessly. They refused to negotiate with union representatives and brought in thirty thousand African American strike-breakers to keep the mills running. After bitter confrontations that left more than a dozen workers dead, the steel strike collapsed, a grievous setback that crippled the union movement for more than a decade.

The black workers who entered the steel mills in 1919 were but a fraction of the tens of thousands of southern blacks drawn to the North in wartime by the magnet of war-industry employment. These migrants made up the small-scale beginnings of a great northward African American trek that would eventually grow to massive proportions. Their sudden appearance in previously all-white areas sometimes sparked inter-racial violence. An explosive riot in East St. Louis, Missouri, in July 1917 left nine whites and at least forty blacks dead. An equally gruesome race riot ripped through Chicago. The wartime Windy City was taut with racial tension as a growing black population expanded into white working-class neighborhoods and as African Americans found jobs as strikebreakers in meatpacking plants. Triggered by an incident at a bathing beach in July 1919, a reign of terror descended on the city for nearly two weeks. Black and white gangs roamed Chicago's streets, eventually killing fifteen whites and twenty-three blacks.

Chicago History Museum

Chicago Race Riot, 1919 The policeman apparently arrived too late to spare this victim from being pelted by stones from an angry mob.

✦ Suffering Until Suffrage

Women also heeded the call of patriotism and opportunity. Thousands of female workers flooded into factories and fields, taking up jobs vacated by men who left the assembly line for the frontline. But the war split the women's movement deeply. Many progressive-era feminists were pacifists, inclined to oppose the participation both of America in the war and women in the war effort. This group found a voice in the National Woman's party, led by Quaker activist Alice Paul, which

TABLE 30.1 A Chronology of Women's Right to Vote in National Elections in Selected Nations

Year	Nation
1893	New Zealand
1902	Australia (white women only until Aborigines included in 1962)
1906	Finland
1915	Denmark, Iceland
1918	Austria, Canada (women of British and French extraction only until 1950), Germany, Hungary, Poland, Russian Federation, United Kingdom (only women who were married, householders, or university graduates age 30 or over until 1928)
1919	Netherlands, Sweden
1920	United States, Czechoslovakia
1924	Mongolia
1930	South Africa (whites only until 1994), Turkey
1931	Spain (but women lost the vote under the dictator Francisco Franco, 1936–1976)
1934	Brazil, Cuba
1944	France
1945	Italy, Japan
1946	Yugoslavia
1947	Argentina, Mexico, Pakistan
1948	Israel, South Korea
1949	China, Syrian Arab Republic
1950	Haiti, India
1952	Greece, Lebanon
1956	Egypt
1963	Iran
1965	Afghanistan (revoked under Taliban rule, 1996–2001)
1971	Switzerland
1974	Jordan
2005	Kuwait

[Sources: Caroline Daley and Melanie Nolan, eds., *Suffrage and Beyond: International Feminist Perspectives* (1994); http://www.ipu.org/english/issues/wmndocs/suffrage.htm; About.com, Women's History, International Woman Suffrage Timeline, http://womenshistory.about.com/od/suffrage/a/intl timeline.htm.]

In an open address to Congress in 1917, suffragist Carrie Chapman Catt (1859–1947) capitalized on the idealism of the day and invoked the founding principles of American democracy in arguing the case for women's right to vote:

"How can our nation escape the logic it has never failed to follow, when its last unenfranchised class calls for the vote? Behold our Uncle Sam floating the banner with one hand, 'Taxation without representation is tyranny,' and with the other seizing the billions of dollars paid in taxes by women to whom he refuses 'representation.'. . . Is there a single man who can justify such inequality of treatment, such outrageous discrimination? Not one."

in shaping the peace. The fight for democracy abroad was women's best hope for winning true democracy at home.

War mobilization gave new momentum to the suffrage fight. Impressed by women's war work, President Wilson endorsed woman suffrage as "a vitally necessary war measure." In 1917 New York voted for suffrage at the state level; Michigan, Oklahoma, and South Dakota followed. The next year, governments in Great Britain, Austria, Hungary, and Germany extended the suffrage to women. Not long after, the United States followed suit. In 1920, more than seventy years after the first calls for suffrage at Seneca Falls, the **Nineteenth Amendment** was ratified, giving all American women the right to vote. (See the Appendix and Table 30.1.)

Despite political victory, women's wartime economic gains proved fleeting. Although a permanent Women's Bureau did emerge after the war in the Department of Labor to protect women in the workplace, most women workers soon gave up their war jobs. Meanwhile, Congress affirmed its support for women in their traditional role as mothers when it passed the **Sheppard-Towner Maternity Act** of 1921, providing federally financed instruction in maternal and infant health care. In doing so, it also expanded the responsibility of the federal government for family welfare.

Feminists continued to flex their political muscle in the postwar decade, pressing for more laws to protect women in the workplace and prohibit child labor. Complete success often eluded them in those crusades, but the developments of the World War I era nevertheless foreshadowed a future when women's wage-labor

demonstrated against "Kaiser Wilson" with marches and hunger strikes.

But the larger part of the suffrage movement, represented by the National American Woman Suffrage Association, supported Wilson's war. Leaders echoed Wilson's justification for fighting by arguing that women must take part in the war effort to earn a role

National Archives

Poster Collection, Hoover Institution Archives

In the Trenches and to the Polls   Wars often bring opportunities and innovations as well as danger and destruction. As U.S. Army nurses went into harm's way at the fighting front in France, the century-long struggle for women's suffrage intensified on the home front, culminating in the Nineteenth Amendment in 1920.

and political power would reshape the American way of life.

✦ Forging a War Economy

Mobilization relied as much on the heated emotions of patriotism as on the cool majesty of the laws. The largely voluntary character of economic war organization testified to ocean-insulated America's safe distance from the fighting—as well as to the still-modest scale of government powers in the progressive-era Republic. But as the war wore on, government took greater command of the nation's resources to secure an Allied victory.

As the larder of democracy, America had to feed itself and its allies. By a happy inspiration, the man chosen to head the Food Administration was the Quaker-humanitarian Herbert C. Hoover. He was already considered a hero because he had successfully led a massive charitable drive to feed the starving people of war-racked Belgium.

In common with other American war administrators, Hoover preferred to rely on voluntary compliance rather than on compulsory edicts. He deliberately rejected issuing ration cards, a practice used in Europe. Instead he waged a whirlwind propaganda campaign through posters, billboards, newspapers, pulpits, and movies. To save food for export, Hoover proclaimed wheatless Wednesdays and meatless Tuesdays—all on a voluntary basis. Even children, when eating apples, were urged to be "patriotic to the core."

The country soon broke out in a rash of vegetable "victory gardens," as perspiring patriots hoed their way to victory in backyards and vacant lots. Congress severely restricted the use of foodstuffs for manufacturing alcoholic beverages, and the war-spawned spirit of self-denial helped accelerate the wave of prohibition that was sweeping the country. Many leading brewers were German-descended, and this taint made the drive against alcohol all the more popular. The reformers' dream of a saloonless nation was finally achieved—temporarily—in 1919 with the passage of the Eighteenth Amendment, prohibiting all alcoholic drinks.

Thanks to the fervent patriotic wartime spirit, Hoover's voluntary approach worked. Farm production increased by one-fourth, and food exports to the Allies tripled in volume. Hoover's methods were widely imitated in other war agencies. The Fuel Administration exhorted Americans to save fuel with "heatless Mondays," "lightless nights," and "gasless Sundays." The Treasury Department sponsored huge parades and invoked slogans like "Halt the Hun" to promote four great Liberty Loan drives, followed by a Victory Loan campaign in 1919. Together these efforts netted the then-fantastic sum of about $21 billion, or two-thirds of the current cost of the war to the United States. The remainder was raised by increased taxes, which, unlike the loan subscriptions, were obligatory. (The ultimate bill, including interest and veterans' benefits, mounted to some $112 billion.)

Pressures of various kinds, patriotic and otherwise, were used to sell bonds. The unfortunate German American who could not display a Liberty Bond button might find his or her house bedaubed with yellow paint. A number of reluctant investors in war bonds were roughly handled. In at least one instance, a man signed for a bond with a rope around his neck.

Despite the Wilson administration's preference for voluntary means of mobilizing the economy, over the course of the war it expanded the federal government in size and power. The War Industries Board issued production quotas, allocated raw materials, and set prices for government purchases. Following indescribable traffic snarls in late 1917, Washington took over the railroads. Time itself came under Uncle Sam's control when the entire country was ordered to observe daylight saving time to extend the workday and save on fuel.

✦ Making Plowboys into Doughboys

Most citizens, at the outset, did not dream of sending a mighty force to France. As far as fighting went, America would use its navy to uphold freedom of the seas. It would continue to ship war materials to the Allies and supply them with loans, which finally totaled nearly $10 billion. But in April and May of 1917, the European associates laid their cards on the table. They confessed that they were scraping the bottom not only of their money chests but, more ominously, of their manpower barrels. A huge American army would have to be raised, trained, and transported, or the whole western front would collapse.

Conscription was the only answer to the need for raising an immense army with all possible speed. Wilson disliked a draft, as did many other Americans with Civil War memories, but he eventually accepted and eloquently supported conscription as a disagreeable and temporary necessity.

The proposed draft bill immediately ran into a barrage of criticism in Congress. A congressman from Missouri, deploring compulsion, cried out in protest that there was "precious little difference between a conscript

Food for Thought Wartime agencies flooded the country with posters like this in 1917–1918, exhorting women on the home front to "grow their own" and thus ease the pressure on food supplies.

Ignoring grisly tales of the agonies of trench warfare, many young American men saw an opportunity for adventure and seized it. Author John Dos Passos (1896–1970) recollected how he felt going off to war in 1917:

❝We had spent our boyhood in the afterglow of the peaceful nineteenth century. . . . What was war like? We wanted to see with our own eyes. We flocked into the volunteer services. I respected the conscientious objectors, and occasionally felt I should take that course myself, but hell, I wanted to see the show.❞

and a convict." Prophets of doom predicted that on draft-registration day, the streets would run red with blood. At length Congress—six weeks after declaring war—grudgingly got around to passing conscription.

The draft act required the registration of all males between the ages of eighteen and forty-five. No "draft dodger" could purchase his exemption or hire a substitute, as in the days of the Civil War, though the law exempted men in key industries, such as shipbuilding.

The draft machinery, on the whole, worked effectively. Registration day proved to be a day of patriotic pilgrimages to flag-draped registration centers, and the sign-up saw no shedding of blood, as some had gloomily predicted. Despite precautions, some 337,000 "slackers" escaped the draft, and about 4,000 conscientious objectors were excused.

Within a few frantic months, the army grew to over 4 million men. For the first time, women were admitted to the armed forces; some 11,000 to the navy and 269 to the marines. African Americans also served in the armed forces, though in strictly segregated units and usually under white officers. Reflecting racial attitudes of the time, military authorities hesitated to train black men for combat, and the majority of black soldiers were assigned to "construction battalions" or put to work unloading ships.

Recruits were supposed to receive six months of training in America and two more months overseas. But so great was the urgency that many doughboys were swept swiftly into battle scarcely knowing how to handle a rifle, much less a bayonet.

✴ Fighting in France—Belatedly

Russia's collapse underscored the need for haste. The communistic Bolsheviks, after seizing power late in 1917, ultimately withdrew their beaten country from the "capitalistic" war early in 1918. This sudden defection released hundreds of thousands of battle-tested Germans from the eastern front facing Russia for the western front in France, where, for the first time in the war, they were developing a dangerous superiority in manpower.

Berlin's calculations as to American tardiness were surprisingly accurate. Germany had counted on knocking out Britain six months after the declaration of unlimited submarine warfare, long before America

Miracles in Shipbuilding

Battling Venereal Disease   The American military waged a half-hearted war on rampant venereal disease.

could get into the struggle. No really effective American fighting force reached France until about a year after Congress declared war. Berlin had also reckoned on the inability of the Americans to transport their army, assuming that they were able to raise one. Here again the German predictions were not far from the mark, as shipping shortages plagued the Allies.

Nevertheless, France gradually began to bustle with American doughboys (see Map 30.1). The first trainees to reach the front were used as replacements in the Allied armies and were generally deployed in quiet sectors with the British and French. The newcomers soon made friends with the French girls—or tried to—and one of the most sung-about women in history was the fabled "Mademoiselle from Armentières." One of the printable stanzas ran,

> *She was true to me, she was true to you,*
> *She was true to the whole damn army, too.*

Not surprisingly, American soldiers suffered from high rates of venereal disease, which the army only contributed to by avoiding the subject.

American operations were not confined solely to France; small detachments fought in Belgium, Italy, and notably Russia. The United States, hoping to keep stores of munitions from falling into German hands when Bolshevik Russia quit fighting, contributed some 5,000 troops to an Allied invasion of northern Russia at Archangel. Wilson likewise sent nearly 10,000 troops to Siberia as part of an Allied expedition, which included more than 70,000 Japanese. Major American purposes were to prevent Japan from getting a stranglehold on Siberia, to rescue some 45,000 marooned Czechoslovak troops, and to snatch military supplies from Bolshevik control. Sharp fighting at Archangel and in Siberia involved casualties on both sides, including several hundred Americans. The Bolsheviks long resented these "capitalistic" interventions, which they regarded as high-handed efforts to suffocate their infant communist revolution in its cradle.

✵ America Helps Hammer the "Hun"

The dreaded German drive on the western front exploded in the spring of 1918. Spearheaded by about half a million troops, the enemy rolled forward with terrifying momentum. So dire was the peril that the Allied nations for the first time united under a supreme commander, the quiet French marshal Foch, whose axiom was "To make war is to attack." Until then the Allies had been fighting imperfectly coordinated actions.

At last the ill-trained "Yanks" were coming—and not a moment too soon. Late in May 1918, the German juggernaut, smashing to within forty miles of Paris,

MAP 30.1 Major U.S. Operations in France, 1918 One doughboy recorded in his diary his baptism of fire at St. Mihiel: "Hiked through dark woods. No lights allowed, guided by holding on the pack of the man ahead. Stumbled through underbrush for about half mile into an open field where we waited in soaking rain until about 10:00 P.M. We then started on our hike to the St. Mihiel front, arriving on the crest of a hill at 1:00 A.M. I saw a sight which I shall never forget. It was the zero hour and in one instant the entire front as far as the eye could reach in either direction was a sheet of flame, while the heavy artillery made the earth quake."

© Cengage Learning

Examining the Evidence

"Mademoiselle from Armentières"

Some familiar songs, such as Julia Ward Howe's stirring Civil War–era melody "Battle Hymn of the Republic," were penned by known composers and have well-established scores and lyrics. But many ballads have no specific author. Songwriters may fit new verses to known tunes, but the songs essentially grow out of the soil of popular culture and take on a life of their own. "Yankee Doodle Dandy," for example, originated during the seventeenth-century English Civil War, was adapted by the American revolutionaries more than a century later, and was parodied by Southerners during the American Civil War:

> Yankee Doodle had a mind
> To whip the Southern "traitors,"
> Because they didn't choose to live
> On codfish and potaters.

"Stagger Lee," or "Stagolee," a blues ballad supposedly based on a murder in Memphis in the 1930s, has been played in countless renditions, with its homicidal subject variously portrayed as a ruthless badman or a civil rights hero.

This process of accretion and adaptation can furnish valuable clues to historians about changing sentiments and sensibilities, just as the ballads themselves give expression to feelings not always evident in the official record. Folklorist Alan Lomax spent a lifetime tracking down American ballads, documenting layers of life and experience not usually excavated by traditional scholars. In the case of the First World War's most notorious song, "Mademoiselle from Armentières" (or "Hinky Dinky, Parley-Voo?"), he compiled from various sources more than six hundred soldier-authored stanzas, some of which are reproduced here (others he delicately described as "not mailable"). What fresh—and irreverent—perspectives do they reveal about the soldier's-eye view of military life?

> Mademoiselle from Armentières,
> She hadn't been kissed in forty years.

> She might have been young for all we knew,
> When Napoleon flopped at Waterloo. . . .

> You'll never get your Croix de Guerre,
> If you never wash your underwear. . . .

> The French, they are a funny race,
> They fight with their feet and save their face.

> The cootie [louse] is the national bug of France.
> The cootie's found all over France,
> No matter where you hang your pants. . . .

> Oh, the seventy-seventh went over the top,
> A sous lieutenant, a Jew, and a Wop. . . .

> The officers get all the steak,
> And all we get is the belly-ache.

> The general got a Croix de Guerre,
> The son-of-a-gun was never there. . . .

> There's many and many a married man,
> Wants to go back to France again.

> 'Twas a hell of a war as we recall,
> But still 'twas better than none at all.

Oh, land-lord, have you a daugh-ter fair, par-ley-voo? Oh, land-lord, have you a daughter fair, par-ley-voo? Oh, land-lord, have you a daughter fair, To wash a sol-dier's un-der-wear? Hin-ky-din-ky, par-ley-voo?

American Ballads and Folk Songs by John A. Lomax and Alan Lomax. The Macmillan Company, New York, 1935

Source: From John A. Lomax and Alan Lomax, *American Ballads and Folksongs*, pp. 558–560. Reprinted by permission of Odyssey Productions, Inc.

Gassed, by John Singer Sargent The noted artist captures the horror of trench warfare in World War I. The enemy was often distant and unseen, and death came impersonally from gas or artillery fire. American troops, entering the line only in the war's final days, were only briefly exposed to this kind of brutal fighting.

threatened to knock out France. Newly arrived American troops, numbering fewer than thirty thousand, were thrown into the breach at **Château-Thierry**, right in the teeth of the German advance. This was a historic moment—the first significant engagement of American troops in a European war. Battle-fatigued French soldiers watched incredulously as the roads filled with endless truckloads of American doughboys, singing New World songs at the top of their voices, a seemingly inexhaustible flood of fresh and gleaming youth. With their arrival it was clear that a new American giant had arisen in the West to replace the dying Russian titan in the East.

American weight in the scales was now being felt on both sides of the conflict (see Figure 30.1). By July 1918 the awesome German drive had spent its force, and keyed-up American men participated in a Foch counteroffensive in the Second Battle of the Marne.

This engagement marked the beginning of a German withdrawal that was never effectively reversed. In September 1918 nine American divisions (about 243,000 men) joined four French divisions to push the Germans from the St. Mihiel salient, a German dagger in France's flank.

The Americans, dissatisfied with merely bolstering the British and French, had meanwhile been demanding a separate army. General John J. ("Black Jack") Pershing was finally assigned a front of eighty-five miles, stretching northwestward from the Swiss border to meet the French lines.

As part of the last mighty Allied assault, involving several million men, Pershing's army undertook the **Meuse-Argonne offensive**, from September 26 to November 11, 1918. One objective was to cut the German railroad lines feeding the western front. This battle, the most gargantuan thus far in American history, lasted forty-seven days and engaged 1.2 million American troops. With especially heavy fighting in the rugged Argonne Forest, the killed and wounded mounted to 120,000, or 10 percent of the Americans involved. The slow progress and severe losses from machine guns resulted in part from inadequate training, in part from dashing open-field tactics, with the bayonet liberally employed. Tennessee-bred Alvin C. York, a member of an antiwar religious sect, became a hero when he single-handedly killed 20 Germans and captured 132 more. Victory was in sight—and fortunately so. The slowly advancing American armies in France were eating up their supplies so rapidly that they were in grave danger of running short. But the battered Germans were ready to stagger out of the trenches and cry *"Kamerad"* (Comrade). Their allies were deserting them, the

MEN KILLED IN BATTLE	
1,700,000	Russia
1,600,000	Germany
1,385,000	France
900,000	British Empire
800,000	Austria
462,000	Italy
53,000	United States

FIGURE 30.1 Approximate Comparative Losses in World War I

British blockade was causing critical food shortages, and the sledgehammer blows of the Allies pummeled them relentlessly. Propaganda leaflets, containing seductive Wilsonian promises, rained down upon their crumbling lines from balloons, shells, and rockets.

★ The Fourteen Points Disarm Germany

Berlin was now ready to hoist the white flag. Warned of imminent defeat by the generals, it turned to the presumably softhearted Wilson in October 1918, seeking a peace based on the Fourteen Points. In stern responses the president made it clear that the kaiser must be thrown overboard before an armistice could be negotiated. War-weary Germans, whom Wilson had been trying to turn against their "military masters," took the hint. The kaiser was forced to flee to Holland, where he lived out his remaining twenty-three years, "unwept, unhonored, and unhung."

The exhausted Germans were through. They laid down their arms at eleven o'clock on the eleventh day of the eleventh month of 1918, and an eerie, numbing silence fell over the western front. War-taut America burst into a delirium of around-the-clock rejoicing, as the war to end wars had ended. But the costs exceeded comprehension: nearly 9 million soldiers had died, and more than 20 million had suffered grievous wounds. To make matters worse, some 30 million people perished

Theodore Roosevelt (1858–1919) favored the Germans' unconditional surrender. Referring to Wilson's practice of drafting diplomatic notes on his own typewriter, Roosevelt telegraphed several senators (October 24, 1918),

❝Let us dictate peace by the hammering guns and not chat about peace to the accompaniment of clicking typewriters. The language of the fourteen points and the subsequent statements explaining or qualifying them are thoroughly mischievous.❞

in a worldwide influenza pandemic in 1918–1919. Over 550,000 Americans—more than ten times the number of U.S. combat casualties—died from the flu.

The United States' main contributions to the ultimate victory had been foodstuffs, munitions, credits, oil for this first mechanized war, and manpower—but

© Bettmann/Corbis

Home from the War, 1919 Most black troops in World War I were denied combat duty and served as laborers and stevedores, but this wounded veteran had seen some tough fighting—though in a segregated unit, the 369th Colored Infantry Regiment, also known as the "Hell-fighters of Harlem." Segregation followed black servicemen even into death. When Congress appropriated money in 1930 to send "Gold Star Mothers" to visit the graves of their slain soldier-sons in France, it provided for separate ships, hotels, and trains for African American women. Several black mothers, preferring "to remain at home and retain our honor and self-respect," reluctantly refused to make the trip.

VELL, IT DIDN'T PAY

NOT THIS TIME

German "Repentance," 1918 A prophetic reflection of the view that the failure to smash Germany completely would lead to another world war. Library of Congress not battlefield victories. The Yanks fought only two major battles, at St. Mihiel and the Meuse-Argonne, both in the last two months of the four-year war, and they were still grinding away in the Meuse-Argonne, well short of their objectives, when the war ended. It was the *prospect* of endless U.S. troop reserves, rather than America's actual military performance, that eventually demoralized the Germans.

Ironically enough, General Pershing in some ways depended more on the Allies than they depended on him. His army purchased more of its supplies in Europe than it shipped from the United States. Fewer than five hundred of Pershing's artillery pieces were of American manufacture. Virtually all of his aircraft were provided by the British and French. Britain and France transported a majority of the doughboys to Europe. The United States, in short, was no arsenal of democracy in this war; that role awaited it in the next global conflict, two decades later.

Wilson Steps Down from Olympus

Woodrow Wilson had helped to win the war. What part would he now play in shaping the peace? Expectations ran extravagantly high. As the fighting in Europe crashed to a close, the American president towered at the peak of his popularity and power. In lonely huts in the mountains of Italy, candles burned before poster-portraits of the revered American prophet. In Poland starry-eyed university students would meet in the streets, clasp hands, and utter only one word: "Wilson." No other man had ever occupied so dizzy a pinnacle as moral leader of the world. Wilson also had behind him the prestige of victory and the economic resources of the mightiest nation on earth. But at this fateful moment, his sureness of touch deserted him, and he began to make a series of tragic fumbles.

Under the slogan "Politics Is Adjourned," partisan political strife had been kept below the surface during the war crisis. Hoping to strengthen his hand at the Paris peace table, Wilson broke the truce by personally appealing for a Democratic victory in the congressional elections of November 1918. But the maneuver backfired when voters instead returned a narrow Republican majority to Congress. Having staked his reputation on the outcome, Wilson went to Paris as a diminished leader. Unlike all the parliamentary statesmen at the table, he did not command a legislative majority at home.

Wilson's decision to go in person to Paris to help make the peace infuriated Republicans. At that time no president had traveled to Europe, and Wilson's journey looked to his critics like flamboyant grandstanding. He further ruffled Republican feathers when he snubbed the Senate in assembling his peace delegation and neglected to include a single Republican senator in his official party. The logical choice was the new chairman of the Senate Committee on Foreign Relations, slender and aristocratically bewhiskered Henry Cabot Lodge of Massachusetts, a Harvard Ph.D. But including Lodge would have been problematic for the president. The senator's mind, quipped one critic, was like the soil of his native New England: "naturally barren but highly cultivated." Wilson loathed him, and the feeling was hotly reciprocated. An accomplished author, Lodge had been known as the "scholar in politics" until Wilson came on the scene. The two men were at daggers drawn, personally and politically.

An Idealist Amid the Imperialists

Woodrow Wilson, the great prophet arisen in the West, received tumultuous welcomes from the masses of France, England, and Italy late in 1918 and early in 1919. They saw in his idealism the promise of a better world. But the statesmen of France and Italy were careful to keep the new messiah at arm's length from worshipful crowds. He might so arouse the people as to prompt them to overthrow their leaders and upset finespun imperialistic plans.

The Paris Conference of great and small nations fell into the hands of an inner clique, known as the Big Four. Wilson, representing the richest and freshest great power, more or less occupied the driver's seat. He was joined by genial Premier Vittorio Orlando of Italy and brilliant Prime Minister David Lloyd George of Britain. Perhaps the most realistic of the quartet was cynical, hard-bitten Premier Georges Clemenceau of France, the seventy-eight-year-old "organizer of victory" known as "the Tiger."

Speed was urgent when the conference opened on January 18, 1919. Europe seemed to be slipping into anarchy; the red tide of communism was licking westward from Bolshevist Russia.

The English science fiction writer H. G. Wells (1866–1946), soon a strong proponent of the League of Nations, spoke for many Europeans when he praised Woodrow Wilson in 1917:

"In all the world there is no outstanding figure to which the world will listen, there is no man audible in all the world, in Japan as well as Germany and Rome as well as Boston—except the President of the United States."

Wilson in Dover, England, 1919 Hailed by many Europeans in early 1919 as the savior of the Western world, Wilson was a fallen idol only a few months later, when Americans repudiated the peace treaty he had helped to craft.

Wilson's ultimate goal was a world parliament to be known as the **League of Nations**, but he first bent his energies to preventing any vengeful parceling out of the former colonies and protectorates of the vanquished powers. (He was less attentive to the fate of colonies belonging to the victorious French and English.) Wilson tried to force through a compromise between naked imperialism and Wilsonian idealism. The victors would not take possession of the conquered territory outright, but would receive it as trustees of the League of Nations. Strategic Syria, for example, was awarded to France, and oil-rich Iraq went to Britain. In practice this half-loaf solution was little more than the old prewar colonialism, thinly disguised, although in the decades to come, anticolonial independence movements would wield the Wilsonian ideal of self-determination against their imperial occupiers.

Meanwhile, Wilson had been serving as midwife for the League of Nations, which he envisioned as containing an assembly with seats for all nations and a council to be controlled by the great powers. He gained a signal victory over the skeptical Old World diplomats in February 1919, when they agreed to make the League Covenant, Wilson's brainchild, an integral part of the final peace treaty. At one point he spoke with such ardor for his plan that even the hard-boiled newspaper reporters forgot to take notes.

⭐ Hammering Out the Treaty

Domestic duties now required Wilson to make a quick trip to America, where ugly storms were brewing in the Senate. Certain Republican senators, Lodge in the lead, were sharpening their knives for Wilson. To them the League was either a useless "sewing circle" or an overpotent "super-state." Their hard core was composed of a dozen or so militant isolationists, led by Senators

William Borah of Idaho and Hiram Johnson of California, who were known as **irreconcilables** or "the Battalion of Death."

Thirty-nine Republican senators or senators-elect—enough to defeat the treaty—proclaimed that the Senate would not approve the League of Nations in its existing imperfect form. These difficulties delighted

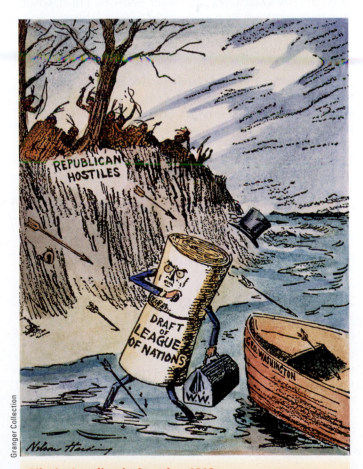

Pilgrim Landing in America, 1919

Wilson's Allied adversaries in Paris. They were now in a stronger bargaining position because Wilson would have to beg them for changes in the covenant that would safeguard the Monroe Doctrine and other American interests dear to the senators.

As soon as Wilson was back in Paris, the hardheaded Clemenceau pressed French demands for the German-inhabited Rhineland and the Saar Valley, a rich coal area. Faced with fierce Wilsonian opposition to this violation of self-determination, France settled for a compromise whereby the Saar basin would remain under the League of Nations for fifteen years, and then a popular vote would determine its fate.* In exchange for dropping its demands for the Rhineland, France got the Security Treaty, in which both Britain and America pledged to come to its aid in the event of another German invasion. The French later felt betrayed when this pact was quickly pigeonholed by the U.S. Senate, which shied away from all entangling alliances.

Wilson's next battle was with Italy over Fiume, a valuable seaport inhabited by both Italians and Yugoslavs. When Italy demanded Fiume, Wilson insisted that the seaport go to Yugoslavia and appealed over the heads of Italy's leaders to the country's masses. The maneuver fell flat. The Italian delegates went home in a huff, while the Italian masses turned savagely against Wilson.

Another crucial struggle was with Japan over China's Shandong (Shantung) Peninsula and the German islands in the Pacific, which the Japanese had seized during the war. Japan was conceded the strategic Pacific islands under a League of Nations mandate,† but Wilson staunchly opposed Japanese control of Shandong as a violation of self-determination for its 30 million Chinese residents. But when the Japanese threatened to walk out, Wilson reluctantly accepted a compromise whereby Japan kept Germany's economic holdings in Shandong and pledged to return the peninsula to China at a later date. The Chinese were outraged by this imperialistic solution, while Clemenceau jeered that Wilson "talked like Jesus Christ and acted like Lloyd George."

✴ The Peace Treaty That Bred a New War

A completed **Treaty of Versailles**, after more weeks of wrangling, was handed to the Germans in June 1919—almost literally on the point of a bayonet. Excluded from the settlement negotiations at Paris, Germany had capitulated in the hope that it would be granted a peace based on the Fourteen Points. A careful analysis of the treaty shows that only about four of the twenty-three original Wilsonian points and subsequent principles were fully honored. Vengeance, not reconciliation, was the treaty's dominant tone. Loud and bitter cries of betrayal burst from German throats—charges that Adolf Hitler would soon reiterate during his meteoric rise to power.

Wilson, of course, was guilty of no conscious betrayal. But the Allied powers were torn by conflicting aims, many of them sanctioned by secret treaties. There had to be compromise at Paris, or there would be no agreement. Faced with hard realities, Wilson was forced to compromise away some of his less cherished Fourteen Points in order to salvage the more precious League of Nations. He was much like the mother who had to throw her sickly younger children to the pursuing wolves to save her sturdy firstborn.

A troubled Wilson was not happy with the results. Greeted a few months earlier with frenzied acclaim in Europe, he was now a fallen idol, condemned alike by disillusioned liberals and frustrated imperialists. He was keenly aware of some of the injustices that had been forced into the treaty. But he was hoping that the League of Nations—a potent League with America as a leader—would iron out the inequities.

Yet the loudly condemned treaty had much to commend it. Not least among its merits was its liberation of millions of minority peoples, such as the Poles, from the yoke of imperial dynasties. Wilson's disappointments and his critics to the contrary, the settlement was almost certainly a fairer one because he had gone to Paris.

✴ The Domestic Parade of Prejudice

Returning for the second and final time to America, Wilson sailed straight into a political typhoon. Isolationists raised a whirlwind of protest against the treaty, especially against Wilson's commitment to usher the United States into his newfangled League of Nations. Invoking the revered advice of Washington and Jefferson, they wanted no part of any "entangling alliance."

Nor were the isolationists Wilson's only problem. Critics showered the Treaty of Versailles with abuse from all sides.

Rabid Hun-haters, regarding the pact as not harsh enough, voiced their discontent. Principled liberals, like the editors of the New York *Nation*, thought it too harsh—and a gross betrayal to boot. German Americans, Italian Americans, and others whom Wilson termed "hyphenated Americans" were aroused because the peace settlement was not sufficiently favorable to their native lands.

---

*The Saar population voted overwhelmingly to rejoin Germany in 1935.
†In due time the Japanese illegally fortified these islands—the Marshalls, Marianas, and Carolines—and used them as bases against the United States in World War II.

Contentious Nuptials Woodrow Wilson's visionary effort to end more than a century of American aloofness from world affairs met vigorous opposition from traditional isolationists, especially in the U.S. Senate. Senators eventually refused to ratify the Versailles Treaty, shattering Wilson's dream of making the United States a more engaged international actor.

Irish Americans, traditional twisters of the British lion's tail, also denounced the League. They felt that with the additional votes of the five overseas British dominions, it gave Britain undue influence, and they feared that it could be used to force the United States to crush any rising for Irish independence. Crowds of Irish American zealots hissed and booed Wilson's name.

✦ Wilson's Tour and Collapse (1919)

Despite mounting discontent, the president had reason to feel optimistic. When he brought home the treaty, with the "Wilson League" firmly riveted in as Part I, a strong majority of the people still seemed favorable. At this time—early July 1919—Senator Lodge had no real hope of defeating the Treaty of Versailles. His strategy was merely to amend it in such a way as to "Americanize," "Republicanize," or "senatorialize" it. The Republicans could then claim political credit for the changes.

Lodge effectively used delay to muddle and divide public opinion. He read the entire 264-page treaty aloud in the Senate Foreign Relations Committee and held protracted hearings in which people of various nationalities aired their grievances.

Wilson fretted increasingly as the hot summer of 1919 wore on. The bulky pact was bogged down in the Senate, while the nation was drifting into confusion and apathy. He therefore decided to take his case to the country in a spectacular speechmaking tour. He would appeal over the heads of the Senate to the sovereign people—as he often had in the past.

The strenuous barnstorming campaign was undertaken in the face of protests by physicians and friends. Wilson had never been robust; he had entered the White House nearly seven years before with a stomach pump and with headache pills for his neuritis. His frail body had begun to sag under the strain of partisan strife, a global war, and a stressful peace conference. But he declared that he was willing to die, like the soldiers he had sent into battle, for the sake of the new world order.

The presidential tour, begun in September 1919, got off to a rather lame start. The Midwest received Wilson lukewarmly, partly because of strong German American influence. Trailing after him like bloodhounds came two "irreconcilable" senators, Borah and Johnson, who spoke in the same cities a few days later. Hat-tossing crowds answered their attacks on Wilson, crying, "Impeach him, impeach him!"

But the reception was different in the Rocky Mountain region and on the Pacific Coast. These areas, which had elected Wilson in 1916, welcomed him with heartwarming outbursts. The high point—and the breaking point—of the return trip was at Pueblo, Colorado, September 25, 1919. Wilson, with tears coursing down his cheeks, pleaded for the League of Nations as the only real hope of preventing future wars. That night he collapsed from physical and nervous exhaustion.

Wilson was whisked back in the "funeral train" to Washington, where several days later a stroke paralyzed one side of his body. During the next few weeks, he lay in a darkened room in the White House, as much a victim of the war as the unknown soldier buried at Arlington. For more than seven months, he did not meet with his cabinet.

✦ Defeat Through Deadlock

Senator Lodge, coldly calculating, was now at the helm. After failing to amend the treaty outright, he finally came up with fourteen formal reservations to it—a sardonic slap at Wilson's Fourteen Points. These safeguards reserved the rights of the United States under the Monroe Doctrine and the Constitution and otherwise sought to protect American sovereignty. Senator Lodge and other critics were especially alarmed by Article X of the League because it *morally* bound the

United States to aid any member victimized by external aggression. A jealous Congress wanted to reserve for itself the constitutional war-declaring power.

Wilson, hating Lodge, saw red at the mere suggestion of the Lodge reservations. He was quite willing to accept somewhat similar reservations sponsored by his faithful Democratic followers, but he insisted that the Lodge reservations "emasculated" the entire pact.

Although too feeble to lead, Wilson was still strong enough to obstruct. When the day finally came for the voting in the Senate, he sent word to all true Democrats to vote *against* the treaty with the odious Lodge reservations attached. Wilson hoped that when these were cleared away, the path would be open for ratification without reservations or with only some mild Democratic ones.

Loyal Democrats in the Senate, on November 19, 1919, blindly did Wilson's bidding. Combining with the "irreconcilables," mostly Republicans, they rejected the treaty with the Lodge reservations appended, 55 to 39.

The nation was too deeply shocked to accept the verdict as final. About four-fifths of the senators professed to favor the treaty, with or without reservations, yet a simple majority could not agree on a single proposition. So strong was public indignation that the Senate was forced to act a second time. In March 1920 the treaty was brought up again, with the Lodge reservations tacked on.

There was only one possible path to success. Unless the Senate approved the pact with the reservations, the entire document would be rejected. But the sickly Wilson, still sheltered behind drawn curtains and blind to disagreeable realities, again sent word to all loyal Democrats to vote down the treaty with the obnoxious reservations. He thus signed the death warrant of the treaty as far as America was concerned. On March 19, 1920, the treaty netted a simple majority but failed to get the necessary two-thirds majority by a count of 49 yeas to 35 nays.

Who defeated the treaty? The Lodge-Wilson personal feud, traditionalism, isolationism, disillusionment, and partisanship all contributed to the confused picture. But Wilson himself must bear a substantial share of the responsibility. He asked for all or nothing—and got nothing. One Democratic senator angrily charged that the president had strangled his own brainchild with his own palsied hands rather than let the Senate straighten its crooked limbs.

★ The "Solemn Referendum" of 1920

Wilson had his own pet solution for the deadlock, and this partly explains why he refused to compromise on Lodge's terms. He proposed to settle the treaty issue in the forthcoming presidential campaign of 1920 by appealing to the people for a "solemn referendum." This was sheer folly, for a true mandate on the League in the noisy arena of politics was clearly an impossibility.

Jubilant Republicans gathered in Chicago in June 1920 with wayward bull moosers back in the corral (after Theodore Roosevelt's death in 1919) and the senatorial Old Guard back in the saddle. The convention devised a masterfully ambiguous platform that could appeal to both pro-League and anti-League sentiment in the party. The nominee would run on a teeter-totter rather than a platform.

As the leading presidential contestants jousted with one another, the political weathervane began to veer toward genial Senator Warren G. Harding of Ohio. A group of Senate bosses, meeting rather casually in the historic "smoke-filled" Room 404 of the Hotel Blackstone, informally decided on the affable and malleable Ohioan. Their fair-haired boy was a prosperous, back-slapping, small-town newspaper editor of the "folksy" type, quite the opposite of Wilson, who had earlier noted the senator's "disturbingly dull" mind. For vice president the party nominated frugal, grim-faced Governor Calvin ("Silent Cal") Coolidge of Massachusetts, who had attracted conservative support by breaking a police strike in Boston.

Meeting in San Francisco, Democrats nominated earnest Governor James M. Cox of Ohio, who strongly supported the League. His running mate was Assistant Navy Secretary Franklin D. Roosevelt, a young, handsome, vibrant New Yorker.

Democratic attempts to make the campaign a referendum on the League were thwarted by Senator Harding, who issued muddled and contradictory statements on the issue from his front porch. Pro-League and anti-League Republicans both claimed that Harding's election would advance their cause, while the candidate suggested that if elected he would work for a vague Association of Nations—*a* league but not *the* League.

With newly enfranchised women swelling the vote totals, Harding was swept into power with a prodigious plurality of over 7 million votes—16,143,407 to 9,130,328 for Cox, the largest victory margin to that date in a presidential election. The electoral count was 404 to 127. Eugene V. Debs, federal prisoner number 9653 at the Atlanta Penitentiary, rolled up the largest vote ever for the left-wing Socialist party—919,799.

Public desire for a change found vent in a resounding repudiation of "high-and-mighty" Wilsonism. People were tired of professional highbrowism, star-reaching idealism, bothersome do-goodism, moral overstrain, and constant self-sacrifice. Eager to lapse back into "normalcy," they were willing to accept a second-rate president—and they got a third-rate one.

Although the election could not be considered a true referendum, Republican isolationists successfully turned Harding's victory into a death sentence for the

League. Politicians increasingly shunned the League as they would a leper. When the legendary Wilson died in 1924, admirers knelt in the snow outside his Washington home. His "great vision" of a league for peace had perished long before.

✷ The Betrayal of Great Expectations

America's spurning of the League was tragically short-sighted. The Republic had helped to win a costly war, but it foolishly kicked the fruits of victory under the table. Whether a strong international organization would have averted World War II in 1939 will always be a matter of dispute. But there can be no doubt that the orphaned League of Nations was undercut at the start by the refusal of the mightiest power on the globe to join it. The Allies themselves were largely to blame for the new world conflagration that flared up in 1939, but they found a convenient justification for their own shortcomings by pointing an accusing finger at Uncle Sam.

The ultimate collapse of the Treaty of Versailles must be laid, at least in some degree, at America's doorstep. This complicated pact, tied in with the four other peace treaties through the League Covenant, was a top-heavy structure designed to rest on a four-legged table.

The fourth leg, the United States, was never put into place. This rickety structure teetered for over a decade and then crashed in ruins—a debacle that played into the hands of the German demagogue Adolf Hitler.

No less ominous events were set in motion when the Senate spurned the Security Treaty with France. The French, fearing that a new generation of Germans would follow in their fathers' goose steps, undertook to build up a powerful military force. Predictably resenting the presence of strong French armies, Germany began to rearm illegally. The seething cauldron of uncertainty and suspicion brewed an intoxicant that helped inflame the fanatical following of Hitler.

The United States, as the tragic sequel proved, hurt its own cause when it buried its head in the sand. Granted that the conduct of its Allies had been disillusioning, it had its own ends to serve by carrying through the Wilsonian program. It would have been well advised if it had forthrightly assumed its war-born responsibilities and had resolutely embraced the role of global leader proffered by the hand of destiny. In the interests of its own security, if for no other reason, the United States should have used its enormous strength to shape world-shaking events. Instead it permitted itself blithely to drift toward the abyss of a second and even more bloody international disaster.

Varying Viewpoints
Woodrow Wilson: Realist or Idealist?

As the first president to take the United States into a foreign war, Woodrow Wilson was obliged to make a systematic case to the American people to justify his unprecedented European intervention. His ideas have largely defined the character of American foreign policy ever since—for better or worse.

"Wilsonianism" comprised three closely related principles: (1) the era of American isolation from world affairs had irretrievably ended; (2) the United States must infuse its own founding political and economic ideas—including democracy, the rule of law, free trade, and national self-determination (or anticolonialism)—into the international order; and (3) American influence could eventually steer the world away from rivalry and warfare and toward a cooperative and peaceful international system, maintained by the League of Nations or, later, the United Nations.

Whether that Wilsonian vision constituted hard-nosed realism or starry-eyed idealism has excited scholarly debate for nearly a century. "Realists," such as George F. Kennan and Henry Kissinger, insist that Wilson was anything but a realist. They criticize the president as a naive, impractical dreamer who failed to understand that the international order was, and

always will be, an anarchic, unruly arena, outside the rule of law, where only military force can effectively protect the nation's security. In a sharp critique in his 1950 study, *American Diplomacy*, Kennan condemned Wilson's vision as "moralism-legalism." In this view Wilson dangerously threatened to sacrifice American self-interests on the altar of his admirable but ultimately unworkable ideas.

Wilson's defenders, including his biographers Arthur S. Link and Thomas J. Knock, argue that Wilson's idealism was in fact a kind of higher realism, recognizing as it did that armed conflict on the scale of World War I could never again be tolerated and that some framework of peaceful international relations simply had to be found. The development of nuclear weapons in a later generation gave this argument more force. This "liberal" defense of Wilsonianism derives from the centuries-old liberal faith that, given sufficient intelligence and willpower, the world can be made a better place. Realists reject this notion of moral and political progress as hopelessly innocent, especially as applied to international affairs.

Some leftist scholars, such as William Appleman Williams, have argued that Wilson was in fact a realist of another kind: a subtle and wily imperialist whose stirring rhetoric cloaked a grasping ambition to make the United States the world's dominant economic power. Sometimes called "the imperialism of free trade," this strategy allegedly sought not to decolonialize the world and open up international commerce for the good of peoples elsewhere, but to create a system in which American economic might would irresistibly prevail. Wilson's defenders, however, would claim that in a Wilsonian world, *all* parties would be better off because of free trade and international competition.

Still other scholars, especially John Milton Cooper, Jr., have emphasized the absence of economic factors in shaping Wilson's diplomacy. Isolationism, so this argument goes, held such sway over American thinking precisely because the United States had such a puny financial stake abroad—no hard American economic interests were mortally threatened in 1917, nor for a long time thereafter. In these circumstances

Wilson—and the Wilsonians who came after him, such as Franklin D. Roosevelt—had no choice but to appeal to abstract ideals and high principles. The "idealistic" Wilsonian strain in American diplomacy, in this view, may have been an unavoidable heritage of America's historically isolated situation. If so, it was Wilson's genius to make practical use of those ideas in his bid for popular support of his diplomacy.

Finally, a new generation of scholars has begun to explore the influence of Wilsonian ideals on social movements outside the United States and Europe. Erez Manela has argued that emerging anticolonial and nationalist movements appropriated Wilsonian ideals and adapted them to their own political ends, challenging forms of colonialism that Wilson himself failed to criticize. In this view the legacy of Wilsonian foreign policy may have been felt most strongly outside the United States.

Chapter Review

KEY TERMS

Zimmermann note (678)

Fourteen Points (680)

Committee on Public Information (680)

Espionage Act (681)

Schenck v. *United States* (681)

War Industries Board (682)

National War Labor Board (682)

Industrial Workers of the World (683)

Nineteenth Amendment (684)

Sheppard-Towner Maternity Act (684)

Château-Thierry, Battle of (690)

Meuse-Argonne offensive (690)

League of Nations (693)

irreconcilables (693)

Versailles, Treaty of (694)

PEOPLE TO KNOW

Arthur Zimmermann

George Creel

Eugene V. Debs

William D. ("Big Bill") Haywood

Bernard Baruch

Herbert C. Hoover

Henry Cabot Lodge

David Lloyd George

TO LEARN MORE

Christopher Capozzola, *Uncle Sam Wants You: World War I and the Making of the Modern American Citizen* (2008)

John W. Chambers, *To Raise an Army: The Draft Comes to Modern America* (1987)

Alan Dawley, *Changing the World: American Progressives in War and Revolution* (2003)

Ernest Freeberg, *Democracy's Prisoners: Eugene V. Debs, the Great War, and the Right to Dissent* (2008)

Paul Fussell, *The Great War and Modern Memory* (1975)

Maurine W. Greenwald, *Women, War, and Work* (1980)

Ellis Hawley, *The Great War and the Search for Modern Order* (rev. ed., 1997)

Jennifer Keene, *Doughboys, the Great War, and the Remaking of America* (2001)

David M. Kennedy, *Over Here: The First World War and American Society* (rev. ed., 2005)

Thomas J. Knock, *To End All Wars: Woodrow Wilson and the Quest for a New World Order* (1992)

Erez Manela, *The Wilsonian Moment: Self-Determination and the International Origins of Anticolonial Nationalism* (2007)

Paul L. Murphy, *World War I and the Origin of Civil Liberties in the United States* (1979)

A complete, annotated bibliography for this chapter—along with brief descriptions of the People to Know—may be found on the American Pageant website. The Key Terms are defined in a Glossary at the end of the text.

CHRONOLOGY

1915   Council of National Defense established

1917   Germany resumes unrestricted submarine warfare
Zimmermann note
Railroads placed under federal control
United States enters World War I
Espionage Act of 1917
Wilson calls for "peace without victory"
Bolshevik Revolution

1918   Wilson proposes Fourteen Points
Sedition Act of 1918
Battle of Château-Thierry
Second Battle of the Marne
Meuse-Argonne offensive

1918–1919   Armistice ends World War I
Worldwide influenza pandemic

1919   Paris Peace Conference and Treaty of Versailles
Wilson's pro-League tour and collapse
Eighteenth Amendment (prohibition of alcohol) passed
First Senate defeat of Versailles Treaty

1920   Final Senate defeat of Versailles Treaty after reconsideration
Nineteenth Amendment (woman suffrage) passed
Harding defeats Cox for presidency

Go to the CourseMate website at **www.cengagebrain.com** for additional study tools and review materials—including audio and video clips—for this chapter.

Chapter 31

American Life in the "Roaring Twenties"

1919–1929

America's present need is not heroics but healing; not nostrums but normalcy; not revolution but restoration; . . . not surgery but serenity.

WARREN G. HARDING, 1920

Bloodied by the war and disillusioned by the peace, Americans turned inward in the 1920s. Shunning diplomatic commitments to foreign countries, they also denounced "radical" foreign ideas, condemned "un-American" lifestyles, and clanged shut the immigration gates against foreign peoples. They partly sealed off the domestic economy from the rest of the world and plunged headlong into a dizzying decade of homegrown prosperity.

The boom of the golden twenties showered genuine benefits on Americans, as incomes and living standards rose for many. But there seemed to be something incredible about it all, even as people sang,

> My sister she works in the laundry,
> My father sells bootlegger gin,
> My mother she takes in the washing,
> My God! how the money rolls in!

New technologies, new consumer products, and new forms of leisure and entertainment made the twenties roar. Yet just beneath the surface lurked widespread anxieties about the future and fears that America was losing sight of its traditional ways.

⭐ Seeing Red

Hysterical fears of red Russia continued to color American thinking for several years after the Communists came to power in the **Bolshevik Revolution** of 1917, which spawned a tiny Communist party in America. Tensions were heightened by an epidemic of strikes that convulsed the Republic at war's end, many of them the result of high prices and frustrated union-organizing drives. Upstanding Americans jumped to the conclusion that labor troubles were fomented by bomb-and-whisker Bolsheviks. A general strike in Seattle in 1919, though modest in its demands and orderly in its methods, prompted a call from the mayor for federal troops to head off "the anarchy of Russia." Fire-and-brimstone evangelist Billy Sunday struck a responsive chord when he described a Bolshevik as "a guy with a face like a porcupine and a breath that would scare a pole cat. . . . If I had my way, I'd fill the jails so full of them that their feet would stick out the window."

The big **red scare** of 1919–1920 resulted in a nationwide crusade against left-wingers whose Americanism was suspect. Attorney General A. Mitchell Palmer, who "saw red" too easily, earned the title of the "Fighting Quaker" by his excess of zeal in rounding up suspects. They ultimately totaled about six thousand. This drive to root out radicals was redoubled in June 1919, when a bomb shattered both the nerves and the Washington home of Palmer. The "Fighting Quaker" was thereupon dubbed the "Quaking Fighter."

An author-soldier (Arthur Guy Empey, 1883–1963) applauded the "deportation delirium" when he wrote,

"I believe we should place them [the reds] all on a ship of stone, with sails of lead, and that their first stopping place should be hell."

Other events highlighted the red scare. Late in December 1919, a shipload of 249 alleged alien radicals was deported on the *Buford* (the "Soviet Ark") to the "workers' paradise" of Russia. One zealot cried, "My motto for the Reds is S.O.S.—ship or shoot." Hysteria was temporarily revived in September 1920, when a still-unexplained bomb blast on Wall Street killed thirty-eight people and wounded more than a hundred others.

Various states joined the pack in the outcry against radicals. In 1919–1920 a number of legislatures, reflecting the anxiety of "solid" citizens, passed **criminal syndicalism laws**. These anti-red statutes, some of which were born of the war, made unlawful the mere *advocacy* of violence to secure social change. Critics protested that mere words were not criminal deeds, that there was a great gulf between throwing fits and throwing bombs, and that "free screech" was for the nasty as well as the nice. Violence was done to traditional American concepts of free speech as IWW members and other radicals were vigorously prosecuted. The hysteria went so far that in 1920 five members of the New York legislature, all lawfully elected, were denied their seats simply because they were Socialists.

The red scare was a godsend to conservative businesspeople, who used it to break the backs of the fledgling unions. Labor's call for the "closed," or all-union, shop was denounced as "Sovietism in disguise." Employers, in turn, hailed their own antiunion campaign for the "open" shop as the **American plan**.

Anti-redism and antiforeignism were reflected in a notorious case regarded by liberals as a "judicial lynching." Nicola Sacco, a shoe-factory worker, and Bartolomeo Vanzetti, a fish peddler, were convicted in 1921 of the murder of a Massachusetts paymaster and his guard. The jury and judge were prejudiced in some degree against the defendants because they were Italians, atheists, anarchists, and draft dodgers.

Liberals and radicals the world over rallied to the defense of the two aliens doomed to die. The case dragged on for six years until 1927, when the condemned men were electrocuted. Communists and other radicals were thus presented with two martyrs in the "class struggle," while many American liberals hung their heads. The evidence against the accused, though damaging, betrayed serious weaknesses. If the trial had been held in an atmosphere less charged with anti-redism, the outcome might well have been only a prison term.

✦ Hooded Hoodlums of the KKK

A new **Ku Klux Klan**, spawned by the postwar reaction, mushroomed fearsomely in the early 1920s. Despite the familiar sheets and hoods, it more closely resembled the antiforeign "nativist" movements of the 1850s than the antiblack nightriders of the 1860s. It was antiforeign, anti-Catholic, antiblack, anti-Jewish,

Bomb Blast on Wall Street, September 1920 The target of this terrorist attack seemed to be the offices of the haughty financier J. P. Morgan, but no person or group claimed responsibility for the blast, and the victims were random financial district employees, not the moguls of Wall Street. The bombing fed the anti-radical, anti-immigrant mood of the day. Federal Hall, where George Washington was inaugurated, can be seen at the right.

National Archives

Klanswomen on Parade, 1928 Founded in the Reconstruction era, the Ku Klux Klan enjoyed a remarkable resurgence in the 1920s. Here women members, unmasked and unapologetic, march down Pennsylvania Avenue under the shadow of the Capitol dome.

Hiram Wesley Evans (1881–1966), imperial wizard of the Ku Klux Klan, in 1926 poignantly described the cultural grievances that fueled the Klan and lay behind much of the Fundamentalist revolt against "Modernism":

❝Nordic Americans for the last generation have found themselves increasingly uncomfortable and finally deeply distressed. . . . One by one all our traditional moral standards went by the boards, or were so disregarded that they ceased to be binding. The sacredness of our Sabbath, of our homes, of chastity, and finally even of our right to teach our own children in our own schools fundamental facts and truths were torn away from us. Those who maintained the old standards did so only in the face of constant ridicule. . . . We found our great cities and the control of much of our industry and commerce taken over by strangers. . . . We are a movement of the plain people, very weak in the matter of culture, intellectual support, and trained leadership. . . . This is undoubtedly a weakness. It lays us open to the charge of being 'hicks' and 'rubes' and 'drivers of second-hand Fords.'**❞**

antipacifist, anti-Communist, anti-internationalist, anti-evolutionist, antibootlegger, antigambling, antiadultery, and anti–birth control. It was also pro–Anglo-Saxon, pro–"native" American, and pro-Protestant. In short, the besheeted Klan betokened an extremist, ultraconservative uprising against many of the forces of diversity and modernity that were transforming American culture.

As reconstituted, the Klan spread with astonishing rapidity, especially in the Midwest and the **Bible Belt** South where Protestant Fundamentalism thrived. At its peak in the mid-1920s, it claimed about 5 million dues-paying members and wielded potent political influence. It capitalized on the typically American love of on-the-edge adventure and in-group camaraderie, to say nothing of the adolescent ardor for secret ritual. The "Knights of the Invisible Empire" included among their officials Imperial Wizards, Grand Goblins, King Kleagles, and other horrendous "kreatures." The most impressive displays were "konclaves" and huge flag-waving parades. The chief warning was the blazing cross. The principal weapon was the bloodied lash, supplemented by tar and feathers. Rallying songs were "The Fiery Cross on High," "One Hundred Percent American," and "The Ku Klux Klan and the Pope" (against kissing the Pope's toe). One brutal slogan was "Kill the Kikes, Koons, and Katholics."

This reign of hooded horror, so repulsive to the best American ideals, collapsed rather suddenly in the late 1920s. Decent people at last recoiled from the orgy of ribboned flesh and terrorism, while scandalous embezzling by Klan officials launched a congressional investigation. The bubble was punctured when the movement was exposed as a vicious racket based on a $10 initiation fee, $4 of which was kicked back to local organizers as an incentive to recruit. The KKK was an alarming manifestation of the intolerance and prejudice plaguing people anxious about the dizzying pace of social change in the 1920s. Despite the Klan's decline, civil rights activists fought in vain for legislation making lynching a federal crime, as lawmakers feared alienating southern white voters.

⭐ Stemming the Foreign Flood

Isolationist America of the 1920s, ingrown and provincial, had little use for the immigrants who began to flood into the country again as peace settled soothingly on the war-torn world. Some 800,000 stepped ashore in 1920–1921, about two-thirds of them from southern

The Granger Collection, New York

The Only Way to Handle It Isolationists and nativists succeeded in damming up the flow of immigrants to the United States in the early 1920s. The Immigration Act of 1924 placed strict quotas on European immigrants and completely shut out the Japanese.

and eastern Europe. The "one-hundred-percent Americans," recoiling at the sight of this resumed "New Immigration," once again cried that the famed poem at the base of the Statue of Liberty was all too literally true: they claimed that a sickly Europe was indeed vomiting on America "the wretched refuse of its teeming shore."

Congress temporarily plugged the breach with the Emergency Quota Act of 1921. Newcomers from Europe were restricted in any given year to a definite quota, which was set at 3 percent of the people of their nationality who had been living in the United States in 1910. This national-origins system was relatively favorable to the immigrants from southern and eastern Europe, for by 1910 immense numbers of them had already arrived.

This stopgap legislation of 1921 was replaced by the **Immigration Act of 1924**. Quotas for foreigners were cut from 3 percent to 2 percent. The national-origins base was shifted from the census of 1910 to that of 1890, by which time comparatively few southern Europeans had arrived.* Great Britain and Northern Ireland, for example, could send 65,721 a year as against 5,802 for Italy. Southern Europeans bitterly denounced the device as unfair and discriminatory—a triumph for the "nativist" belief that blue-eyed and fair-haired northern Europeans were of better blood. The purpose was clearly to freeze America's existing racial composition, which was largely northern European. A flagrantly discriminatory section of the Immigration Act of 1924 slammed the door absolutely against Japanese immigrants. Mass "Hate America" rallies erupted in Japan, and one Japanese superpatriot expressed his outrage by committing suicide near the American embassy in Tokyo. Exempt from the quota system were Canadians and Latin Americans, whose proximity made them easy to attract for jobs when times were good and just as easy to send back home when they were not.

The quota system effected a pivotal departure in American policy. It claimed that the nation was filling up and that a "No Vacancy" sign was needed. Immigration henceforth dwindled to a mere trickle. By 1931, probably for the first time in the American experience, more foreigners left than arrived. Quotas thus caused America to sacrifice something of its tradition of freedom and opportunity, as well as its future ethnic diversity (see Figure 31.1).

The Immigration Act of 1924 marked the end of an era—a period of virtually unrestricted immigration that in the preceding century had brought some 35

*Five years later the Immigration Act of 1929, using 1920 as the quota base, virtually cut immigration in half by limiting the total to 152,574 a year. In 1965 Congress abolished the national-origins quota system.

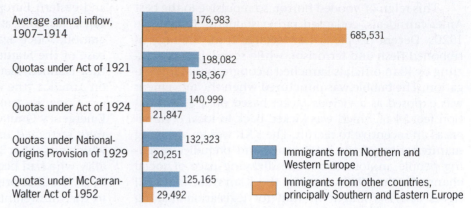

Average annual inflow, 1907–1914	176,983	685,531
Quotas under Act of 1921	198,082	158,367
Quotas under Act of 1924	140,999	21,847
Quotas under National-Origins Provision of 1929	132,323	20,251
Quotas under McCarran-Walter Act of 1952	125,165	29,492

Immigrants from Northern and Western Europe

Immigrants from other countries, principally Southern and Eastern Europe

FIGURE 31.1 Annual Immigration and the Quota Laws The national-origins quota system was abolished in 1965. Legislation in that year capped the level of immigration at 170,000 per year but made exceptions for children, spouses, and parents of persons already arrived. It also restricted immigration from any single country to 20,000 people per year. The immigration laws were again significantly revised in 1986, and changed twice more in 1990 and 1996. In the twenty-first century, immigration laws remain highly controversial. (See pp. 902 and 1000.)

million newcomers to the United States, mostly from Europe. The immigrant tide was now cut off, but it left on American shores by the 1920s a patchwork of ethnic communities separated from each other and from the larger society by language, religion, and customs. Many of the most recent arrivals, including the Italians, Jews, and Poles, lived in isolated enclaves with their own houses of worship, newspapers, and theaters (see "Makers of America: The Poles," pp. 706–707). Efforts to organize labor unions repeatedly foundered on the rocks of ethnic differences. Immigrant workers on the same shop floor might share a common interest in wages and working conditions, but they often had no common language with which to forge common cause. Indeed cynical employers often played upon ethnic rivalries to keep their workers divided and powerless. Ethnic variety thus undermined class and political solidarity. It was an old American story, but one that some reformers hoped would not go on forever.

Immigration restriction did not appeal to all reformers. Particularly opposed was the chorus of "cultural pluralists" who had long criticized the idea that an American "melting pot" would eliminate ethnic differences. Two intellectuals, the philosopher Horace Kallen and the critic Randolph Bourne, championed alternative conceptions of the immigrant role in American society. At a time when war hysteria demanded the "one-hundred-percent Americanization" of German and Austrian immigrants, Kallen defended the newcomers' right to practice their ancestral customs. In Kallen's vision the United States should provide a protective canopy for ethnic and racial groups to preserve their cultural

uniqueness. Like instruments in a symphony orchestra, each immigrant community would harmonize with the others while retaining its own singular identity.

If Kallen stressed the preservation of identity, Bourne advocated greater cross-fertilization among immigrants. Cosmopolitan interchange, Bourne believed, was destined to make America "not a nationality but a trans-nationality, a weaving back and forth, with the other lands, of many threads of all sizes and colors." In this view the United States should serve as the vanguard of a more international and multicultural age.

Kallen's pluralism and Bourne's cosmopolitanism attracted a handful of other intellectuals to the defense of ethnic diversity, including progressives like John Dewey, Jane Addams, and Louis Brandeis. Vastly outnumbered in the debate over immigration restriction in the 1920s, these early proponents of "cultural pluralism" planted the seeds for the blooming of "multiculturalism" in the last quarter of the twentieth century.

The Prohibition "Experiment"

One of the last peculiar spasms of the progressive reform movement was prohibition, loudly supported by crusading churches and by many women. The arid new order was authorized in 1919 by the **Eighteenth Amendment** (see the Appendix), as implemented by the **Volstead Act** passed by Congress later that year. Together these laws made the world "safe for hypocrisy."

The legal abolition of alcohol was especially popular in the South and West. Southern whites were eager

No More Moonshine   Federal agents gloat over a captured still in Dayton, Ohio, in 1930. "Moonshiners," or makers of illegal liquor, enjoyed a boom during prohibition, though zealous G-men (government agents) put the owner of this makeshift distillery out of business—at least temporarily.

to keep stimulants out of the hands of blacks, lest they burst out of "their place." In the West prohibition represented an attack on all the vices associated with the ubiquitous western saloon: public drunkenness, prostitution, corruption, and crime. But despite the overwhelming ratification of the "dry" amendment, strong opposition persisted in the larger eastern cities. For many "wet" foreign-born people, Old World styles of sociability were built around drinking in beer gardens and corner taverns. Yet most Americans now assumed that prohibition had come to stay. Everywhere carousers indulged in last wild flings, as the nation prepared to enter upon a permanent "alcoholiday."

But prohibitionists were naive in the extreme. They overlooked the tenacious American tradition of strong drink and of weak control by the central government, especially over private lives. They forgot that the federal authorities had never satisfactorily enforced a law where the majority of the people—or a strong minority—were hostile to it. They ignored the fact that one cannot make a crime overnight out of something that millions of people have never regarded as a crime. Lawmakers could not legislate away a thirst.

Peculiar conditions hampered the enforcement of prohibition. Profound disillusionment over the aftermath of the war raised serious questions as to the wisdom of further self-denial. Slaking thirst became a cherished personal liberty, and many ardent wets believed that the way to bring about repeal was to violate the law on a large enough scale. Hypocritical, hip-flasked legislators spoke or voted dry while privately drinking wet. ("Let us strike a blow for liberty" was an ironic toast.) Frustrated soldiers, returning from France, complained that prohibition had been "put over" on them while they were "over there." Grimy workers bemoaned the loss of their cheap beer, while pointing out that the idle rich could buy all the illicit alcohol they wanted. Flaming youth of the jazz age thought it "smart" to swill bootleg liquor—"liquid tonsillectomies." Millions of older citizens likewise found forbidden fruit fascinating, as they engaged in "bar hunts."

Prohibition might have started off on a better foot if there had been a larger army of enforcement officials.

Automaker Henry Ford (1863–1947), an ardent prohibitionist, posted this notice in his Detroit factory in 1922:

"From now on it will cost a man his job . . . to have the odor of beer, wine or liquor on his breath, or to have any of these intoxicants on his person or in his home. The Eighteenth Amendment is a part of the fundamental laws of this country. It was meant to be enforced. Politics has interfered with the enforcement of this law, but so far as our organization is concerned, it is going to be enforced to the letter."

The Poles were among the largest immigrant groups to respond to industrializing America's call for badly needed labor after the Civil War. Between 1870 and World War I, some 2 million Polish-speaking peasants boarded steamships bound for the United States. By the 1920s, when antiforeign feeling led to restrictive legislation that choked the immigrant stream to a trickle, Polish immigrants and their American-born children began to develop new identities as Polish Americans.

The first Poles to arrive in the New World had landed in Jamestown in 1608 and helped to develop that colony's timber industry. Over the ensuing two and a half centuries, scattered religious dissenters and revolutionary nationalists also made their way from Poland to America. During the Revolution about one hundred Poles, including two officers recruited by Benjamin Franklin, served in the Continental Army.

But the Polish hopefuls who poured into the United States in the late nineteenth century came primarily to stave off starvation and to earn money to buy land. Known in their homeland as *za chlebem* (for bread) emigrants, they belonged to the mass of central and eastern European peasants who had been forced off their farms by growing competition from the large-scale, mechanized agriculture of western Europe and the United States. An exceptionally high birthrate among the Catholic Poles compounded this economic pressure, creating an army of the land-poor and landless, who left their homes seasonally or permanently in search of work. In 1891 farmworkers and unskilled laborers in the United States earned about $1 a day, more than eight times as much as agricultural workers in the Polish province of Galicia. Such a magnet was irresistible.

These Polish-speaking newcomers emigrated not from a unified nation, but from a weakened country that had been partitioned in the eighteenth century by three great European powers: Prussia (later Germany), Austria-Hungary, and Russia. The Prussian Poles, driven from their homeland in part by the anti-Catholic policies that the German imperial government pursued in the 1870s, arrived in America first. Fleeing religious persecution as well as economic turmoil, many of these early immigrants came to the United States intending to stay. By contrast, most of those who came later from Austrian and Russian Poland simply hoped to earn enough American dollars to return home and buy land.

Some of the Polish peasants learned of America from propaganda spread throughout Europe by agents for U.S. railroad and steamship lines. But many more were lured by glowing letters from friends and relatives already living in the United States. The first wave of Polish immigrants had established a thriving network of self-help and fraternal associations organized around Polish Catholic parishes. Often Polish American entrepreneurs helped their European compatriots make travel arrangements or find jobs in the United States. One of the most successful of these, the energetic Chicago grocer Anton Schermann, is credited with "bringing over" 100,000 Poles and causing the Windy City to earn the nickname the "American Warsaw."

Most of the Poles arriving in the United States in the late nineteenth century headed for booming industrial cities such as Buffalo, Pittsburgh, Detroit, Milwaukee, and Chicago. In 1907 four-fifths of the men toiled as unskilled laborers in coal mines, meatpacking factories, textile and steel mills, oil refineries, and garment-making shops. Although married women usually stayed home and contributed to the family's earnings by taking in laundry and boarders, children and single girls often joined their fathers and brothers on the job.

Polish Coal Miners, ca. 1905   It was common practice in American mines to segregate mining crews by ethnicity and race.

Solidarity Still, 1981 Many Polish Americans continue to take a keen interest in the fate of their ancestral land. In the 1980s many of them supported a challenge to the communist government led by a renegade trade union federation called Solidarity. Thousands rallied in Chicago, the home of the largest Polish community in the United States, to protest against Polish prime minister General Wojciech Jaruzelski (mocked here leashed to Soviet leader Leonid Brezhnev), who had imposed martial law and ordered the mass arrest of Solidarity activists.

By putting the whole family to work, America's Polish immigrants saved tidy sums. By 1901 about one-third of all Poles in the United States owned real estate, and they sent so much money to relatives in Austria and Russia that American and European authorities fretted about the consequences: in 1907 a nativist U.S. immigration commission groused that the huge outflow of funds to eastern Europe was weakening the U.S. economy.

When an independent Poland was created after World War I, few Poles chose to return to their Old World homeland. Instead, like other immigrant groups in the 1920s, they redoubled their efforts to integrate into American society. Polish institutions like churches and fraternal organizations, which had served to perpetuate a distinctive Polish culture in the New World, now facilitated the transformation of Poles into Polish Americans. When Poland was absorbed into the communist bloc after World War II, Polish Americans clung still more tightly to their American identity, pushing for landmarks like Chicago's Pulaski Road to memorialize their culture in the New World.

© Bettmann/Corbis

But the state and federal agencies were understaffed, and their snoopers, susceptible to bribery, were underpaid. The public was increasingly distressed as scores of people, including innocent bystanders, were killed by quick-triggered dry agents.

Prohibition simply did not prohibit. The old-time "men only" corner saloons were replaced by thousands of "speakeasies," each with its tiny grilled window through which the thirsty spoke softly before the barred door was opened. Hard liquor, especially the cocktail, was drunk in staggering volume by both men and women. Largely because of the difficulties of transporting and concealing bottles, beverages of high alcoholic content were popular. Foreign rum-runners, often from the West Indies, had their inning, and countless cases of liquor leaked down from Canada. The zeal of American prohibition agents on occasion strained diplomatic relations with Uncle Sam's northern neighbor.

"Home brew" and "bathtub gin" became popular, as law-evading adults engaged in "alky cooking" with toy stills. The worst of the homemade "rotgut" produced blindness, even death. The affable bootlegger worked in silent partnership with the friendly undertaker.

Yet the "noble experiment" was not entirely a failure. Bank savings increased, and absenteeism in industry decreased, presumably because of the newly sober ways of formerly soused barflies. On the whole, probably less alcohol was consumed than in the days before prohibition, though strong drink continued to be available. As the legendary tippler remarked, prohibition was "a darn sight better than no liquor at all."

Brown Brothers

Gangster Al Capone Fishing in Florida Capone may have looked like any Chicago businessman on vacation, but his business was bigger and nastier than most, as he often eliminated his competition by murder. He was reported as saying, "Everybody calls me a racketeer. I call myself a businessman. When I sell liquor, it's bootlegging. When my patrons serve it on a silver tray on Lake Shore Drive, it's hospitality." He was finally jailed in 1932 for falsifying his income-tax returns.

✦ The Golden Age of Gangsterism

Prohibition spawned shocking crimes. The lush profits of illegal alcohol led to bribery of the police, many of whom were induced to see and smell no evil. Violent wars broke out in the big cities between rival gangs—often rooted in immigrant neighborhoods—who sought to corner the rich market in booze. Rival triggermen used their sawed-off shotguns and chattering "typewriters" (machine guns) to "erase" bootlegging competitors who were trying to "muscle in" on their "racket." In the gang wars of the 1920s in Chicago, about five hundred mobsters were murdered. Arrests were few and convictions were even fewer, as the button-lipped gangsters covered for one another with the underworld's code of silence.

Chicago was by far the most spectacular example of lawlessness. In 1925 "Scarface" Al Capone, a grasping and murderous booze distributor, began six years of gang warfare that netted him millions of blood-spattered dollars. He zoomed through the streets in an armor-plated car with bulletproof windows. A Brooklyn newspaper quipped,

> And the pistols' red glare,
> Bombs bursting in air
> Give proof through the night
> That Chicago's still there.

Capone, though branded "Public Enemy Number One," could not be convicted of the cold-blooded massacre, on St. Valentine's Day in 1929, of seven disarmed members of a rival gang. But after serving most of an eleven-year sentence in a federal penitentiary for income-tax evasion, he was released as a syphilitic wreck.

Gangsters rapidly moved into other profitable and illicit activities: prostitution, gambling, and narcotics. Honest merchants were forced to pay "protection money" to the organized thugs; otherwise their windows would be smashed, their trucks overturned, or their employees or themselves beaten up. **Racketeers** even invaded the ranks of local labor unions as organizers and promoters. Organized crime had come to be one of the nation's most gigantic businesses. By 1930 the annual "take" of the underworld was estimated to be from $12 billion to $18 billion—several times the income of the Washington government.

Criminal callousness sank to new depths in 1932 with the kidnapping for ransom, and eventual murder, of the infant son of aviator-hero Charles A. Lindbergh. The entire nation was inexpressibly shocked and saddened, causing Congress in 1932 to pass the so-called Lindbergh Law, making interstate abduction in certain circumstances a death-penalty offense.

✳ Monkey Business in Tennessee

Education in the 1920s continued to make giant bootstrides. More and more states were requiring young people to remain in school until age sixteen or eighteen, or until graduation from high school. The proportion of seventeen-year-olds who finished high school almost doubled in the 1920s, to more than one in four.

The most revolutionary contribution to educational theory during these yeasty years was made by mild-mannered Professor John Dewey, who served on the faculty of Columbia University from 1904 to 1930. By common consent one of America's few front-rank philosophers, he set forth the principles of "learning by doing" that formed the foundation of so-called progressive education, with its greater "permissiveness." He believed that the workbench was as essential as the blackboard, and that "education for life"

The bombastic Fundamentalist evangelist W. A. (Billy) Sunday (1862–1935) declared in 1925,

❝If a minister believes and teaches evolution, he is a stinking skunk, a hypocrite, and a liar.❞

should be a primary goal of the teacher. (For more on Dewey, see "Makers of America: Pioneering Pragmatists," pp. 560–561.)

Science also scored wondrous advances in these years. A massive public-health program, launched by the Rockefeller Foundation in the South in 1909, had virtually wiped out the ancient affliction of hookworm by the 1920s. Better nutrition and health care helped to increase the life expectancy of a newborn infant from fifty years in 1901 to fifty-nine years in 1929.

Yet both science and progressive education in the 1920s were subjected to unfriendly fire from the newly organized Fundamentalists. These devoted religionists charged that the teaching of Darwinian evolution was destroying faith in God and the Bible, while contributing to the moral breakdown of youth in the jazz age. Numerous attempts were made to secure laws prohibiting the teaching of evolution, "the bestial hypothesis," in the public schools, and three southern states adopted such shackling measures. The trio of states included Tennessee, in the heart of the so-called Bible Belt South, where the spirit of evangelical religion was still robust.

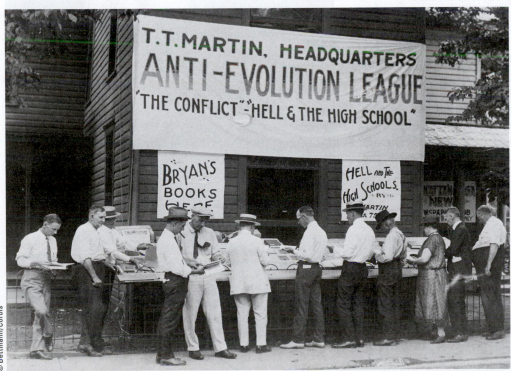

© Bettmann/Corbis

The Battle over Evolution Opponents of Darwin's theories set up shop at the opening of the famed "Monkey Trial" in Dayton, Tennessee, in 1925. The trial was an early battle in an American "culture war" that is still being waged more than seventy-five years later.

The stage was set for the memorable "Monkey Trial" at the hamlet of Dayton, in eastern Tennessee, in 1925. A likable high-school biology teacher, John T. Scopes, was indicted for teaching evolution. Batteries of newspaper reporters, armed with notebooks and cameras, descended upon the quiet town to witness the spectacle. Scopes was defended by nationally known attorneys, while former presidential candidate William Jennings Bryan, an ardent Presbyterian Fundamentalist, joined the prosecution. Taking the stand as an expert on the Bible, Bryan was made to appear foolish by the famed criminal lawyer Clarence Darrow. Five days after the trial was over, Bryan died of a stroke, no doubt brought on by the wilting heat and witness-stand strain.

This historic clash between theology and biology proved inconclusive. Scopes, the forgotten man of the drama, was found guilty and fined $100. But the supreme court of Tennessee, while upholding the law, set aside the fine on a technicality.* The Fundamentalists at best won only a hollow victory, for the absurdities of the trial cast ridicule on their cause. Yet even though increasing numbers of Christians were coming to reconcile the revelations of religion with the findings of modern science, **Fundamentalism**, with its emphasis on a literal reading of the Bible, remained a vibrant force in American spiritual life. It was especially strong in the Baptist Church and in the rapidly growing Churches of Christ, organized in 1906.

✸ The Mass-Consumption Economy

Prosperity—real, sustained, and widely shared—put much of the "roar" into the twenties. The economy kicked off its war harness in 1919, faltered a few steps in the recession of 1920–1921, and then sprinted forward for nearly seven years. Both the recent war and Treasury Secretary Andrew Mellon's tax policies favored the rapid expansion of capital investment. Ingenious machines, powered by relatively cheap energy from newly tapped oil fields, dramatically increased the productivity of the laborer. Assembly-line production reached such perfection in Henry Ford's famed Rouge River plant near Detroit that a finished automobile emerged every ten seconds.

Great new industries suddenly sprouted forth. Supplying electrical power for the humming new machines became a giant business in the 1920s. Above all, the automobile, once the horseless chariot of the rich, now became the carriage of the common citizen. By 1930 Americans owned almost 30 million cars.

The nation's deepening "love affair" with the automobile headlined a momentous shift in the character of the economy. American manufacturers seemed to have mastered the problems of production; their worries now focused on consumption. Could they find the mass markets for the goods they had contrived to spew forth in such profusion?

Responding to this need, a new arm of American commerce came into being: advertising. By persuasion and ploy, seduction and sexual suggestion, advertisers sought to make Americans chronically discontented with their paltry possessions and want more, more, more. A founder of this new "profession" was Bruce Barton, prominent New York partner in a Madison Avenue firm. In 1925 Barton published a best seller, *The Man Nobody Knows*, setting forth the provocative thesis that Jesus Christ was the greatest adman of all time. "Every advertising man ought to study the parables of Jesus," Barton preached. "They are marvelously condensed, as all good advertising should be." Barton even had a good word to say for Christ's executive ability:

Babe Ruth: The "Sultan of Swat"

Brown Brothers

---

*The Tennessee law was not formally repealed until 1967.

"He picked up twelve men from the bottom ranks of business and forged them into an organization that conquered the world."

Sports became big business in the consumer economy of the 1920s. Ballyhooed by the "image makers," home-run heroes like George H. ("Babe") Ruth were far better known than most statesmen. The fans bought tickets in such numbers that Babe's hometown park, Yankee Stadium, became known as "the house that Ruth built." In 1921 the slugging heavyweight champion, Jack Dempsey, knocked out the dapper French light heavyweight Georges Carpentier. The Jersey City crowd in attendance had paid more than a million dollars—the first in a series of million-dollar "gates" in the golden 1920s.

Buying on credit was another innovative feature of the postwar economy. "Possess today and pay tomorrow" was the message directed at buyers. Once-frugal descendants of Puritans went ever deeper into debt to own all kinds of newfangled marvels—refrigerators, vacuum cleaners, and especially cars and radios—*now*. Prosperity thus accumulated an overhanging cloud of debt, and the economy became increasingly vulnerable to disruptions of the credit structure.

✴ Putting America on Rubber Tires

A new industrial revolution slipped into high gear in America in the 1920s. Thrusting out steel tentacles, it changed the daily life of the people in unprecedented ways. Machinery was the new messiah—and the automobile was its principal prophet.

Of all the inventions of the era, the automobile cut the deepest track. It heralded an amazing new industrial system based on assembly-line methods and mass-production techniques.

Americans adapted rather than invented the gasoline engine; Europeans can claim the original honor. By the 1890s a few daring American inventors and promoters, including Henry Ford and Ransom E. Olds (Oldsmobile), were developing the infant automotive industry. By 1910 sixty-nine car companies rolled out a total annual production of 181,000 units. The early contraptions were neither speedy nor reliable. Many a stalled motorist, profanely cranking a balky automobile, had to endure the jeer "Get a horse" from the occupants of a passing dobbin-drawn carriage.

An enormous industry sprang into being, as Detroit became the motorcar capital of America. The mechanized colossus owed much to the stopwatch efficiency techniques of Frederick W. Taylor, a prominent inventor, engineer, and tennis player, who sought to eliminate wasted motion. His epitaph reads "Father of **Scientific Management**."

From the Collections of The Henry Ford

Henry Ford in His First Car, Built in 1896   Ford has been called the "Father of the Traffic Jam."

Best known of the new crop of industrial wizards was Henry Ford, who more than any other individual put America on rubber tires. His high and hideous Model T ("Tin Lizzie") was cheap, rugged, and reasonably reliable, though rough and clattering. The parts of Ford's "flivver" were highly standardized, but the behavior of this rattling good car was so eccentric that it became the butt of numberless jokes.

Lean and silent Henry Ford, who was said to have wheels in his head, erected an immense personal empire on the cornerstone of his mechanical genius, though his associates provided much of the organizational talent. Ill-educated, this multimillionaire mechanic was socially and culturally narrow. "History is bunk," he once testified. But he dedicated himself with one-track devotion to the gospel of standardization. After two early failures, he grasped and applied fully the technique of the moving assembly line—**Fordism**. He is

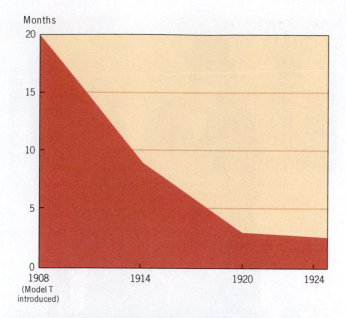

FIGURE 31.2 The Cost of a Model T Ford, 1908–1924
Henry Ford's mass-production techniques cut the costs of production dramatically and put the automobile within reach of the workingperson's purse. (Cost is shown in months of labor for an employee at the average national wage.)

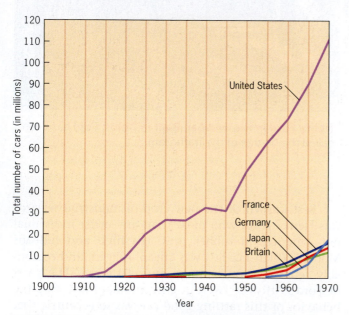

FIGURE 31.3 International Comparison of Number of Automobiles

supposed to have remarked that the purchaser could have his automobile in any color he desired—just as long as it was black. So economical were his methods that in the mid-1920s he was selling the Ford roadster for $260—well within the purse of a thrifty worker (see Figure 31.2). Before long, Fordism caught fire outside the United States. German engineers were particularly

enamored, though their workers resented those "American methods."

The flood of Fords was phenomenal. In 1914 the "Automobile Wizard" turned out his 500,000th Model T. By 1930 his total had risen to 20 million, or, on a bumper-to-bumper basis, more than enough to encircle the globe. A national newspaper and magazine poll conducted in 1923 revealed Ford to be the people's choice for the presidential nomination in 1924. By 1929, when the great bull market collapsed, 26 million motor vehicles were registered in the United States. This figure, averaging 1 for every 4.9 Americans, represented far more automobiles than existed in all the rest of the world (see Figure 31.3).

✦ The Advent of the Gasoline Age

The impact of the self-propelled carriage on various aspects of American life was tremendous. A gigantic new industry emerged, dependent on steel but displacing steel from its kingpin role. Employing directly or indirectly about 6 million people by 1930, it was a major wellspring of the nation's prosperity. Thousands of new jobs, moreover, were created by supporting industries. The lengthening list would include rubber, glass, and fabrics, to say nothing of highway construction and thousands of service stations and garages. America's standard of living, responding to this infectious vitality, rose to an enviable level.

New industries boomed lustily; older ones grew sickly. The petroleum business experienced an explosive development. Hundreds of oil derricks shot up in California, Texas, and Oklahoma, as these states expanded wondrously and the wilderness frontier became an industrial frontier. The once-feared railroad octopus, on the other hand, was hard hit by the competition of passenger cars, buses, and trucks. An age-old story was repeated: one industry's gains were another industry's pains.

Other effects were widely felt. Speedy marketing of perishable foodstuffs, such as fresh fruits, was accelerated. A new prosperity enriched outlying farms, as city dwellers were provided with produce at attractive prices. Countless new roads ribboned out to meet the demand of the American motorist for smoother and faster highways, often paid for by taxes on gasoline. The era of mud ended as the nation made haste to construct the finest network of hard-surfaced roadways in the world. Lured by sophisticated advertising, and encouraged by tempting installment-plan buying, countless Americans with shallow purses acquired the habit of riding as they paid.

Zooming motorcars were agents of social change. At first a luxury, they rapidly became a necessity. Essentially devices for needed transportation, they soon

Brown Brothers

Gas Station, 1923 Gas stations like this one began to appear about 1913. Before that the nation's handful of automobile owners bought fuel from their local oil companies and stored it in tanks in their own yards.

developed into a badge of freedom and equality—a necessary prop for self-respect. To some, ostentation seemed more important than transportation. Leisure hours could now be spent more pleasurably, as tens of thousands of cooped-up souls responded to the call of the open road on joyriding vacations. Women were further freed from clinging-vine dependence on men. Isolation among the sections was broken down, and the less attractive states lost population at an alarming rate. By the late 1920s, Americans owned more automobiles than bathtubs. "I can't go to town in a bathtub," one homemaker explained.

Other social by-products of the automobile were visible. Autobuses made possible the consolidation of schools and to some extent of churches. The sprawling suburbs spread out still farther from the urban core, as America became a nation of commuters.

The demon machine, on the other hand, exacted a terrible toll by catering to the American mania for speed. Citizens were becoming statistics. Not counting the hundreds of thousands of injured and crippled, the one millionth American had died in a motor vehicle accident by 1951—more than all those killed on all the battlefields of all the nation's wars to that date. "The public be rammed" seemed to be the motto of the new age.

Virtuous home life partially broke down as joyriders of all ages forsook the parlor for the highway. The morals of flaming youth sagged correspondingly—at least in the judgment of their elders. What might young people get up to in the privacy of a closed-top Model T? An Indiana juvenile court judge voiced parents' worst fears when he condemned the automobile as "a house of prostitution on wheels." Even the celebrated crime

Picture Research Consultants & Archives

The Modern Woman in the Driver's Seat As part of its effort to sell to a mass market, the Ford Motor Company used advertising to convey that driving an automobile was respectable for women. A woman who drove was not only modern, but she also better fulfilled her traditional duties as a household manager.

A lifelong resident of Muncie, Indiana, disguised as "Middletown" in Robert and Helen Lynd's exhaustive investigation of American life in a typical medium-size community during the 1920s, pooh-poohed their scientific sociological methods:

"Why on earth do you need to study what's changing this country? I can tell you what's happening in just four letters: A-U-T-O!"

waves of the 1920s and 1930s were aided and abetted by the motorcar, for gangsters could now make quick getaways.

Yet no sane American would plead for a return of the old horse and buggy, complete with fly-breeding manure. The automobile contributed notably to improved air and environmental quality, despite its later notoriety as a polluter. Life might be cut short on the highways, and smog might poison the air, but the automobile brought more convenience, pleasure, and excitement into more people's lives than almost any other single invention.

✴ Humans Develop Wings

Gasoline engines also provided the power that enabled humans to fulfill the age-old dream of sprouting wings. After near-successful experiments by others with heavier-than-air craft, the Wright brothers, Orville and Wilbur, performed "the miracle at Kitty Hawk," North Carolina.

On a historic day—December 17, 1903—Orville Wright took aloft a feebly engined plane that stayed airborne for 12 seconds and 120 feet. Thus the air age was launched by two obscure Ohio bicycle repairmen.

As aviation gradually got off the ground, the world slowly shrank. The public was made increasingly air-minded by unsung heroes—often martyrs—who appeared as stunt fliers at fairs and other public gatherings. Airplanes—"flying coffins"—were used with marked success for various purposes during the Great War of 1914–1918. Shortly thereafter private companies began to operate passenger lines with airmail contracts, which were in effect a subsidy from Washington. The first transcontinental airmail route was established from New York to San Francisco in 1920.

In 1927 modest and skillful Charles A. Lindbergh, the so-called Flyin' Fool, electrified the world with the first solo west-to-east conquest of the Atlantic. Seeking a prize of $25,000, the lanky stunt flier courageously piloted his single-engine plane, the *Spirit of St. Louis*, from New York to Paris in a grueling thirty-three hours and thirty-nine minutes.

Lindbergh's exploit swept Americans off their feet. Fed up with the cynicism and debunking of the jazz age, they found in this wholesome and handsome youth a genuine hero. They clasped the soaring "Lone Eagle" to their hearts much more warmly than the bashful young man desired. "Lucky Lindy" received an uproarious welcome in the "hero canyon" of lower Broadway, as eighteen hundred tons of ticker tape and other improvised confetti showered upon him. Lindbergh's achievement—it was more than a "stunt"—did

Lucky Lindy   Charles A. Lindbergh (1902–1974) stands in front of the aircraft that made him famous. The first person to fly solo across the Atlantic, Lindbergh became an acclaimed celebrity—perhaps the first media-made "hero" of the twentieth century. His shining reputation later lost some of its luster when he voiced anti-Semitic sentiments and opposed American entry into World War II, though he went on to fly several combat missions in the war against Japan.

Picture Research Consultants & Archives

much to dramatize and popularize flying, while giving a strong boost to the infant aviation industry.

The impact of the airship was tremendous. It provided the restless American spirit with yet another dimension. At the same time, it gave birth to a giant new industry. Unfortunately, the accident rate in the pioneer stages of aviation was high, though hardly more so than on the early railroads. But by the 1930s and 1940s, travel by air on regularly scheduled airlines was significantly safer than on many overcrowded highways.

Humanity's new wings also increased the tempo of an already breathless civilization. The floundering railroad received another setback through the loss of passengers and mail. A lethal new weapon was given to the gods of war, and with the coming of city-busting aerial bombs, people could well debate whether the conquest of the air was a blessing or a curse. The Atlantic Ocean was shriveling to about the size of the Aegean Sea in the days of Socrates, while isolation behind ocean moats was becoming a bygone dream.

✪ The Radio Revolution

The speed of the airplane was far eclipsed by the speed of radio waves. Guglielmo Marconi, an Italian, invented wireless telegraphy in the 1890s, and his brainchild was used for long-range communication during World War I.

© Bettmann/Corbis

Family "Listening In" to the Radio, 1922 The Lacambanne family of San Francisco gathered in their parlor to listen to a concert broadcast over the radio. In the early years, when only a handful of households could afford a radio, listening brought family and neighbors together to share a common experience.

Radio came in with a bang in the winter of 1921–1922. A San Francisco newspaper reported a discovery that countless citizens were making:

❝ There is radio music in the air, every night, everywhere. Anybody can hear it at home on a receiving set, which any boy can put up in an hour. ❞

Next came the voice-carrying radio, a triumph of many minds. A red-letter day was posted in November 1920, when the Pittsburgh radio station KDKA broadcast the news of the Harding landslide. Later miracles were achieved in transatlantic wireless phonographs, radiotelephones, and television. The earliest radio programs reached only local audiences. But by the late 1920s, technological improvements made long-distance broadcasting possible, and national commercial networks drowned out much local programming. Meanwhile, advertising "commercials" made radio another vehicle for American free enterprise, as contrasted with the government-owned systems of Europe.

While other marvels of the era—like the automobile—were luring Americans away from home, the radio was drawing them back. For much of the decade, family and neighbors gathered around a household's sole radio as they once had around the toasty hearth. Radio knitted the nation together. Various regions heard voices with standardized accents, and countless millions "tuned in" to perennial comedy favorites like "Amos 'n' Andy." Programs sponsored by manufacturers and distributors of brand-name products, like the "A&P Gypsies" and the "Eveready Hour," helped to make radio-touted labels household words and purchases.

Educationally and culturally, the radio made a significant contribution. Sports were further stimulated. Politicians had to adjust their speaking techniques to the new medium, and millions rather than thousands of voters heard their promises and pleas. A host of listeners swallowed the gospel of their favorite newscaster or were even ringside participants in world-shaking events. Finally, the music of famous artists and symphony orchestras was beamed into countless homes.

✪ Hollywood's Filmland Fantasies

The flickering movie was the fruit of numerous geniuses, including Thomas A. Edison. As early as the 1890s, this novel contraption, though still in crude form, had attained some popularity in the naughty peep-show penny arcades. The real birth of the movie came in 1903, when the first story sequence reached the screen. This breathless melodrama, *The Great Train Robbery*, was featured in the five-cent theaters, popularly called "nickelodeons." Spectacular among the first full-length classics was D. W. Griffith's *Birth of a Nation* (1915), which glorified the Ku Klux Klan of Reconstruction days and defamed both blacks and Northern carpetbaggers. White southerners reputedly fired guns at the screen during the attempted "rape" scene. African Americans were outraged at the film and angrily organized protest marches, petition campaigns, and public hearings.

A fascinating industry was thus launched. Hollywood, in southern California, quickly became the movie capital of the world, for it enjoyed a maximum of sunshine and other advantages. Early producers featured nudity and heavy-lidded female vampires ("vamps"), and an offended public forced the screen magnates to set up their own rigorous code of censorship. The motion picture really arrived during World War I, when it was used as an engine of anti-German propaganda. Specially prepared "hang the kaiser" films aided powerfully in selling war bonds and in boosting morale.

A new era began in 1927 with the success of the first "talkie"—*The Jazz Singer*, starring the white performer Al Jolson in blackface. The age of the "silents" was ushered out as theaters everywhere were "wired for sound." At about the same time, reasonably satisfactory color films were being produced.

Movies eclipsed all other new forms of amusement in the phenomenal growth of their popularity. Movie "stars" of the first pulchritude commanded much larger salaries than the president of the United States, in some cases as much as $100,000 for a single picture. Many actors and actresses were far more widely known than the nation's political leaders.

Critics bemoaned the vulgarization of popular tastes wrought by the new technologies of radio and motion pictures. But the effects of the new mass media were not all negative. The insularity of ethnic communities eroded as the immigrants' children, especially, forsook the neighborhood vaudeville theater for the downtown movie palace or turned away from Grandma's Yiddish storytelling to tune in "Amos 'n' Andy." If some of the rich diversity of the immigrants' Old Country cultures was lost, the standardization of tastes and of language hastened entry into the American mainstream—and set the stage for the emergence of a working-class political coalition that, for a time, would overcome the divisive ethnic differences of the past.

✴ The Dynamic Decade

Far-reaching changes in lifestyles and values paralleled the dramatic upsurge of the economy. The census of 1920 revealed that for the first time most Americans no longer lived in the countryside but in urban areas. Women continued to find opportunities for employment in the cities, though they tended to cluster in a few low-paying jobs (such as retail clerking and office typing) that became classified as "women's work." An organized birth-control movement, led by the fiery feminist Margaret Sanger, openly championed the

Margaret Sanger (1879–1966) in Boston, 1929 Forbidden to speak on the inflammatory topic of birth control, a defiant Sanger covered her mouth and "lectured" in Boston by writing on a blackboard. Since 1912 Sanger had devoted herself to promoting birth control and establishing contraceptive clinics throughout the United States.

© Bettmann/Corbis

Examining the Evidence

The Jazz Singer, 1927

The Jazz Singer was the first feature-length "talkie," a motion picture in which the characters actually spoke, and its arrival spelled the end for "silent" films, where the audience read subtitles with live or recorded music as background. Although moviegoers flocked to *The Jazz Singer* to hear recorded sound, when they got there they found a movie concerned with themes of great interest to the urban, first- or second-generation immigrant audiences who were Hollywood's major patrons. *The Jazz Singer* told the story of a poor, assimilating Jewish immigrant torn between following his father's wish that he train as an Orthodox cantor and his own ambition to make a success of himself as a jazz singer, performing in the popular blackface style. The movie's star, Al Jolson, was himself an immigrant Jew who had made his name as a blackface performer. White actors had gradually taken over the southern black minstrel show during the nineteenth century. By the early twentieth century, Jewish entertainers had entirely monopolized these roles. Jolson, like other Jewish blackface performers, used his ability to impersonate a black person to force his acceptance into mainstream white American society. This use of blackface seems ironic, since black Americans in the 1920s were struggling with their own real-life battles against Jim Crow–era segregation, a blatant form of exclusion from American society. Besides the novelty of being a "talkie," what may have made *The Jazz Singer* a box office hit in 1927? How might different types of viewers in the audience have responded to the story? What does the popularity of blackface reveal about racial attitudes at the time?

The Flapper New dance styles, like the "Charleston," flamboyantly displayed the new social freedom of the "flapper," whose dress and antics frequently flummoxed the guardians of respectability.

use of contraceptives. Alice Paul's National Woman's party began in 1923 to campaign for an Equal Rights Amendment to the Constitution. (The campaign was still stalled short of success nearly nine decades later.) To some defenders of traditional ways, it seemed that the world had suddenly gone mad.

Even the churches were affected. The Fundamentalist champions of the old-time religion lost ground to the Modernists, who liked to think that God was a "good guy" and the universe a pretty chummy place.

Some churches tried to fight the Devil with worldly weapons. Competing with joyriding automobiles and golf links, they turned to quality entertainment of their own, including wholesome moving pictures for young people. One uptown house of the Lord in New York advertised on a billboard, "Come to Church: Christian Worship Increases Your Efficiency."

Even before the war, one observer thought the chimes had "struck sex o'clock in America," and the 1920s witnessed what many old-timers regarded as a veritable erotic eruption. Advertisers exploited sexual allure to sell everything from soap to car tires. Once-modest maidens now proclaimed their new freedom as "flappers" in bobbed tresses and dresses. Young women appeared with hemlines elevated, stockings rolled, breasts taped flat, cheeks rouged, and lips a "crimson gash" that held a dangling cigarette. Thus did the "flapper" symbolize a yearned-for and devil-may-care independence (some said wild abandon) in some American women. Still more adventuresome females shocked their elders when they sported the new one-piece bathing suits.

Justification for this new sexual frankness could be found in the recently translated writings of Dr. Sigmund Freud. This Viennese physician appeared to argue that sexual repression was responsible for a variety of nervous and emotional ills. Thus not pleasure alone but also health demanded sexual gratification and liberation.

Many taboos flew out the window as sex-conscious Americans let themselves go. As unknowing Freudians, teenagers pioneered the sexual frontiers. Glued together in rhythmic embrace, they danced to jazz music squeaking from phonographs. In an earlier day, a kiss had been the equivalent of a proposal of marriage. But in the new era, exploratory young folk sat in darkened movie houses or took to the highways and byways in automobiles. There the youthful "neckers" and "petters" poached upon the forbidden territory of each other's bodies.

If the flapper was the goddess of the "era of wonderful nonsense," jazz was its sacred music. With its virtuoso wanderings and tricky syncopation, jazz moved

The Guardian of Morality Women's new one-piece bathing suits were a sensation in the 1920s. Here a check is carefully made to ensure that not too much leg is showing.

Not all Americans welcomed the rising popularity of jazz music. For some stuffy traditionalists, including clergyman and writer Henry van Dyck (1852–1933), jazz symbolized the excessive liberation and dangerous exuberance of modern society:

❝As I understand it, [jazz] is not music at all. It is merely an irritation of the nerves of hearing, a sensual teasing of the strings of physical passion. . . . '[J]azz' is an unmitigated cacophony, a combination of disagreeable sounds in complicated discords, a willful ugliness and a deliberate vulgarity.**❞**

up from New Orleans along with the migrating blacks during World War I. Tunes like W. C. Handy's "St. Louis Blues" (1914) became instant classics, as the wailing saxophone became the trumpet of the new era. Black performers such as Handy, "Jelly Roll" Morton, Louis Armstrong, and Joe "King" Oliver gave birth to jazz, but the entertainment industry soon spawned all-white bands—notably Paul Whiteman's. Caucasian impresarios cornered the profits, though not the creative soul, of America's most native music.

A new racial pride also blossomed in the northern black communities that burgeoned during and after the war. Harlem in New York City, counting some 150,000 African American residents in the 1920s, was one of the largest black communities in the world. Harlem sustained a vibrant, creative culture that nourished poets like Langston Hughes, whose first volume of verses, *The Weary Blues*, appeared in 1926. Harlem in the 1920s also spawned a charismatic political leader, Marcus Garvey. The Jamaican-born Garvey

Library of Congress

Marcus Garvey (1887–1940) In 1920 Garvey, the Jamaican-born founder of the United Negro Improvement Association, advocated a constitution to protect the rights of black Americans. By that year his nationalist self-help organization boasted eleven hundred branches in forty countries in the Americas and Africa. Most of those branches were located in the United States, his base of operations until 1927.

Stock Montage

King Oliver's Creole Jazz Band, Early 1920s Joe "King" Oliver arrived in Chicago from New Orleans in 1918. His band became the first important black jazz ensemble and made Chicago's Royal Garden Café a magnet for jazz lovers. Left to right: Honoré Dutrey, trombone; Baby Dodds, drums; "King" Oliver, cornet; Lil Hardin, piano; Bill Johnson, banjo; and Johnny Dodds, clarinet. Kneeling in the foreground is the young Louis Armstrong.

founded the **United Negro Improvement Association (UNIA)** to promote the resettlement of American blacks in their own "African homeland." Within the United States, the UNIA sponsored stores and other businesses, like the Black Star Line Steamship Company, to keep blacks' dollars in black pockets. Most of Garvey's enterprises failed financially, and Garvey himself was convicted in 1927 for alleged mail fraud and deported by a nervous U.S. government. But the race pride that Garvey inspired among the 4 million blacks who counted themselves UNIA followers at the movement's height helped these newcomers to northern cities gain self-confidence and self-reliance. And his example proved important to the later founding of the Nation of Islam (Black Muslim) movement.

✦ Cultural Liberation

Likewise in literature and the arts, an older era seemed to have ground to a halt with the recent war. By the dawn of the 1920s, most of the custodians of an aging genteel culture had died—Henry James in 1916, Henry Adams in 1918, and William Dean Howells ("the Dean of American literature") in 1920. A few novelists who had been popular in the previous decades continued to thrive, notably the well-to-do, cosmopolitan New Yorker Edith Wharton and the Virginia-born Willa Cather, esteemed for her stark but sympathetic portrayals of pioneering on the prairies.

But in the decade after the war, a new generation of writers and artists burst upon the scene. Many of them hailed from ethnic and regional backgrounds different from that of the Protestant New Englanders who traditionally had dominated American cultural life. The newcomers exhibited the energy of youth, the ambition of excluded outsiders, and in many cases the smoldering resentment of ideals betrayed. Animated by the spark of the international modernist movement (see "Thinking Globally: Modernism," pp. 722-723), they bestowed on American culture a new vitality, imaginativeness, and artistic daring.

Central to **modernism** was its questioning of social conventions and traditional authorities, considered outmoded by the accelerating changes of twentieth-century life. No one personified this iconoclasm better than H. L. Mencken, the "Bad Boy of Baltimore." As the era's most influential critic, Mencken promoted modernist causes in politics and literature. Little escaped his acidic wit. In his columns for the *Baltimore Sun*, he assailed marriage, patriotism, democracy, prohibition, Rotarians, and other sacred icons of the middle-class American "booboisie." The provincial South he contemptuously dismissed as "the Sahara of the Bozart" (a bastardization of *beaux arts*, French for

H. L. Mencken's (1880–1956) obituary of his old nemesis, William Jennings Bryan, seethed with contempt for the American heartland:

"Out where the grass grows high, and the horned cattle dream away the lazy days, and men still fear the powers and principalities of the air—out there between the corn-rows he held his old puissance to the end. There was no need of beaters to drive in his game. The news that he was coming was enough. For miles the flivver dust would choke the roads.**"**

the "fine arts"), and he scathingly attacked hypocritical do-gooders as "Puritans." Puritanism, he jibed, was "the haunting fear that someone, somewhere, might be happy."

The war had jolted many young writers out of their complacency about traditional values and literary standards. With their pens they probed for new codes of morals and understanding, as well as fresh forms of expression. F. Scott Fitzgerald, a handsome Minnesota-born Princetonian then only twenty-four years old, became an overnight celebrity when he published *This Side of Paradise* in 1920. The book became a kind of Bible for the young. It was eagerly devoured by aspiring flappers and their ardent wooers, many of whom affected an air of bewildered abandon toward life. Catching the spirit of the hour (often about 4 A.M.), Fitzgerald found "all gods dead, all wars fought, all faiths in man shaken." He followed this melancholy success with *The Great Gatsby* (1925), a brilliant commentary on the illusory American ideal of the self-made man. Midwesterner James Gatz reinvented himself as tycoon Jay Gatsby, only to be destroyed by the power of those with established wealth and social standing. Theodore Dreiser's masterpiece of 1925, *An American Tragedy*, similarly explored the pitfalls of social striving, as it dealt with the murder of a pregnant working girl by her socially ambitious young lover.

Ernest Hemingway, who had seen action on the Italian front in 1917, was among the writers most affected by the war. He responded to pernicious propaganda and the overblown appeal to patriotism by devising his own lean, word-sparing but word-perfect style. Hemingway wrote on the "iceberg" principle: "There is seven-eighths of it under water for every part that shows." His hard-boiled realism typified postwar writing. In *The Sun Also Rises* (1926), he told of disillusioned, spiritually numb American expatriates in Europe. In *A Farewell to Arms* (1929), he turned his own war story into one of the finest novels in any language about the war experience. Hemingway's literary successes and innovation. These "high modernists" experimented with the breakdown of traditional literary forms and exposed the losses associated with modernity. They wrote in a self-consciously internationalist mode, haughtily rejecting the parochialism they found at home. Pound, a brilliantly erratic Idahoan who permanently deserted America for Europe, rejected what he called "an old bitch civilization, gone in the teeth" and proclaimed his doctrine: "Make It New." Pound strongly influenced the Missouri-born and Harvard-educated Eliot, who took up residence (and eventual citizenship) in England. In *The Waste Land* (1922), Eliot produced one of the most impenetrable but influential poems of the century. Composed of discontinuous segments, multiple perspectives, and arcane allusions, the poem depicts the fragmentation and frightening desolation of postwar society. Much more accessible was the poetry of fellow Harvard graduate e.e. cummings, who relied on unorthodox diction and peculiar typesetting to produce startling poetical effects.

Not all literary efforts of the era proved so radical. Many American writers continued to employ a familiar regionalist style that was by turns celebratory and critical. Robert Frost, a San Francisco–born poet, wrote hauntingly about the nature and folkways of his adopted New England. Ever-popular Carl Sandburg extolled the working classes of Chicago in strong, simple cadences. Other regionalist writers caustically probed Middle American small-town life. Sherwood Anderson dissected various fictional personalities in *Winesburg, Ohio* (1919), finding them all in some way warped by their cramped psychological surroundings. Sinclair Lewis, a hotheaded, heavy-drinking journalist from Sauk Centre, Minnesota, sprang into prominence in 1920 with *Main Street*, the best-selling story of one woman's unsuccessful revolt against provincialism. In *Babbitt* (1922) he affectionately pilloried George F. Babbitt, a prosperous, vulgar, middle-class real estate broker who slavishly conforms to the respectable materialism of his group. The word *Babbittry* was quickly coined to describe his all-too-familiar lifestyle.

William Faulkner, a dark-eyed, pensive Mississippian, focused on the displacement of the agrarian Old South by a rising industrial order. His life's work offered a fictional chronicle of an imaginary, history-rich Deep

Stock Montage

F. Scott Fitzgerald and His Wife, Zelda The Fitzgeralds are shown here in the happy, early days of their stormy marriage.

flamboyant personal life made him one of the most famous writers in the world. He won the Nobel Prize in literature in 1954—and blew out his brains with a shotgun blast in 1961.

Hemingway, Fitzgerald, and many other American writers and painters formed an artistic **"Lost Generation"** as expatriates in postwar Europe. They found shelter and inspiration in the Paris salon of their brainy and eccentric countrywoman, Gertrude Stein. A literary innovator in her own right, Stein had studied at Radcliffe College at Harvard University under the famed philosopher William James; her early works apply his theory of "stream of consciousness" to literature. Hobnobbing in Paris with the iconoclastic artists Pablo Picasso and Henri Matisse, Stein wrote radically experimental poetry and prose, including *Three Lives* (1909), *Tender Buttons* (1914), and, most famously, *The Autobiography of Alice B. Toklas* (1933), named for her lifelong partner.

Stein joined fellow American poets Ezra Pound and T. S. Eliot in the vanguard of modernist literary

In a score of novels, William Faulkner (1897–1962) explored the collective psychology of his native South, where the pressures of historical memory continually reverberated in the present. As he wrote in Requiem for a Nun *(1951),*

❝ The past is never dead. It's not even past.❞

Modernism

"On or about" February 1913, to adapt a phrase from the British novelist Virginia Woolf, "the human character changed."* In that month, New York's 69th Regiment Armory hosted the International Exhibition of Modern Art. The event marked America's introduction to avant-garde European modernism and the arrival, so to speak, of a world-shattering cultural idiom. Nearly 1,250 works of art were displayed, including contributions by Vincent van Gogh, Edward Munch, Pablo Picasso, and some three hundred other European and American artists. Though scandalized critics considered many modernist works an affront to prim-and-proper Victorian values, captivated Americans visited the exhibition in droves. By the traveling show's end, upwards of half a million attendees had been exposed to modernist styles in New York, Chicago, and Boston.

Almost a full century after the Armory Show, modernism remains difficult to define. Not to be confused with modernization—that is, society's transformation from a traditional, agricultural basis to an urban, industrial, bureaucratic order—modernism can best be understood as an artistic or cultural response to the advent of modernity. Whether celebrating or criticizing twentieth-century life as new, complex, and demanding, all modernists revolted against nineteenth-century realism, formalism, and reverence for tradition. They sought to overthrow the smug Victorian mentality, with its comforting belief in abso-

*Woolf's original remark referred to December 1910, when a similar exhibition of postimpressionist art toured London.

lute "truth" in a stable, predictable, middle-class world. Modernists insisted instead on a radical, post-Darwinian appreciation of random chance, incessant change, contingency, uncertainty, and fragmentation. Having blasted the nineteenth-century intellectual order to pieces, modernists were in no rush to put the resulting fragments back together again. Instead, they turned inward, exploring the subconscious and humanity's supposedly animal nature in search of a more authentic, reintegrated self.

The 1913 New York exhibition symbolized two important facets of turn-of-the-century modernism: its global scope and its self-conscious sense of discontinuity with the past. Originating in the urban, bohemian circles of late-nineteenth-century Europe, especially Paris's Latin Quarter in the 1870s and 1880s, modernism soon colonized the globe. Many credited avant-garde European artists with leading this full-frontal assault on the tastes and values of the nineteenth-century bourgeoisie. Closer to home, American modernism claimed domestic roots, particularly in the pragmatic philosophy of William James and John Dewey (see "Makers of America: Pioneering Pragmatists," pp. 560-561). At its core, the modernist movement also emphasized a deep,

self-conscious break from history. Rejecting the authority of tradition, modernists extolled novel ways of thinking. They brought this iconoclastic fervor to art, music, literature, and architecture.

Of all modernism's cultural expressions, art was the most striking—and controversial. A vanguard of French symbolists, dadaists, and surrealists aimed to replace representation in art with pure abstraction. Picasso's cubist paintings, for instance, experimented with abstract multiperspectival techniques, setting up visual obstacles meant to disorient the viewer and isolate the individual's subjective consciousness. Marcel Duchamp's *Nude Descending a Staircase* (1912), the highlight of the Armory Show, offered a

The Philadelphia Museum of Art/Art Resource, NY

Nude Descending a Staircase No. 2, by Marcel Duchamp, 1912
This painting, now permanently displayed at the Philadelphia Museum of Art, caused a scandal both in Paris, where it was originally shown, and at the fabled New York Armory Show in 1913. Duchamp shattered convention by evoking motion with repeated superimposed images, and by rendering the human body with stark, angular lines.

The Darwin D. Martin House Buffalo, New York, by Frank Lloyd Wright Completed in 1905, the Martin House is one of Wright's masterworks and an outstanding example of the "prairie style." Architects of the Prairie School sought to create an indigenous American modern architectural form, free of inherited design ideas and based on simple, horizontal lines and native craftsmanship.

bewildering, ambulatory succession of superimposed images. One critic likened it to "an explosion in a shingle factory." Modernist music also proved riotous, quite literally in the case of the May 1913 Paris premiere of Igor Stravinsky's *Rite of Spring*, which provoked fistfights in the aisles. Stravinsky and Arnold Schoenberg introduced elements of dissonance and atonality in their music, often alienating listeners with their uncompromising technical experimentation.

Modernist literary pioneers adapted analogous experimental techniques to their own craft. Like their fellow artists, writers sought to debunk the notions of order, sequence, and unity and capture in words the fragmentary nature of modern life. Abandoning the omniscient third-person narrator, modernist writers often wrote in the first person, endowing their narrators with a less than complete (and not entirely trustworthy) vision of events. To add to the disorientation, authors like William Faulkner sometimes employed unsettling shifts in perspective among multiple narrators or across wide swaths of time. The overall effect served to focus attention on each character's unique individual consciousness. The new-fangled findings of psychological sci-

ence aided this pursuit. Some authors, including the flamboyantly idiosyncratic American Gertrude Stein, imported their "stream of consciousness" technique from the psychologist and philosopher William James (Stein's professor at Radcliffe). Others, including Eugene O'Neill, borrowed from the Viennese psychiatrist Sigmund Freud to explore their characters' subconscious and base motivations.

Architecture also reinvented itself as modern in the twentieth century. Here, American architects took the lead, especially Louis Sullivan and Frank Lloyd Wright operating in the nation's heartland. Sullivan coined the phrase "form follows function" (modernism's great credo) and practically invented the modern skyscraper in turn-of-the-century Chicago. Wright advanced the unorthodox theory that buildings should grow organically from their sites, incorporate indigenous materials, and not slavishly imitate classical and European importations. He designed open-plan "prairie-style" structures to fit the environment of the American Midwest. After 1918, an interwar European elite called for the rejection of architectural tradition, the elimination of ornament, and the outward expression of structure. German "Bauhaus"

(translated as "House of Building") architects Walter Gropius and Ludwig Mies van der Rohe joined the Swiss urbanist Le Corbusier in imagining the egalitarian possibilities of modernist buildings as "machines for living in." Around midcentury, fellow "international style" architects began to erect giant skyscrapers free of applied ornament. These steel-and-glass utopias, self-consciously engineered to promote global (rather than local) tastes and to signal a complete break from the past, symbolized for many the archetypal modernist structure.

The enduring presence of modernist buildings in American cities and towns suggests that modernism's impact on the American cultural landscape lasted considerably longer than the Armory Show's four-week run in 1913. Historians continue to debate the movement's full scope, timing, and legacy. At its most narrow, modernism can be seen as a small-scale movement confined to early-twentieth-century developments in literature and the arts. At its most broad, as Virginia Woolf claimed, modernism might represent nothing short of a complete cultural revolution, unfolding from its earliest stages into the dominant artistic and intellectual sensibility of the twentieth-century West.

South county he named "Yoknapatawpha." In powerful books like *The Sound and the Fury* (1929) and *As I Lay Dying* (1930), Faulkner peeled back layers of time and consciousness from the constricted souls of his ingrown southern characters. In contrast to Hemingway's spare prose, Faulkner experimented with multiple narrators, complex structure, and "stream of consciousness" techniques. His extended meditation on "the ragtag and bob-ends of old tales and talkings" culminated in what some readers consider his greatest work, *Absalom, Absalom!* (1936).

Though novelists and poets dominated modernist literary output in the 1920s, American composers and playwrights also made important contributions on the stage. Jerome Kern and Oscar Hammerstein's *Show Boat* debuted on Broadway in 1927 as the first true American "musical play." Eugene O'Neill, a restless Princeton dropout, emerged as America's first world-class playwright. In plays like *Strange Interlude* (1928), O'Neill laid bare Freudian notions of sex and the subconscious in a

Langston Hughes (1902–1967) celebrated Harlem's role in energizing a generation of artists and writers in his poem "Esthete in Harlem" (1930):

"Strange,
That in this nigger place
I should meet life face to face;
When, for years, I had been seeking
Life in places gentler-speaking,
Until I came to this vile street
And found Life stepping on my feet!"*

succession of dramatic soliloquies. A prodigious playwright, he authored more than a dozen productions in the 1920s and garnered the Nobel Prize in literature in 1936, six years after Sinclair Lewis had been named the first American winner .

O'Neill arose from New York's Greenwich Village, which before and after the war was a seething cauldron of writers, painters, musicians, actors, and other would-be artists. After the war a black cultural renaissance also took root uptown in Harlem, led by such gifted writers as Claude McKay, Langston Hughes, and Zora Neale Hurston, and by jazz artists like Louis Armstrong and Eubie Blake. In an outpouring of creative expression called the **Harlem Renaissance**, they proudly exulted in their black culture and argued for a "New Negro" who was a full citizen and a social equal to whites. Adopting modernist techniques, Hughes and Hurston captured the oral and improvisational traditions of contemporary blacks in dialect-filled poetry and prose.

✴ Wall Street's Big Bull Market

Signals abounded that the economic joyride might end in a crash; even in the best years of the 1920s, several hundred banks failed annually. This something-for-nothing craze was well illustrated by real estate speculation, especially the fantastic Florida boom that culminated in 1925. Numerous underwater lots were sold to eager purchasers for preposterous sums. The whole wildcat scheme collapsed when the peninsula was devastated by a West Indian hurricane, which belied advertisements of a "soothing tropical wind."

Granger Collection

Langston Hughes (1902–1967) Raised in the Midwest, Hughes arrived in New York City in 1921 to attend Columbia University. He spent most of his life in Harlem, making it so much the center of his prolific and versatile literary career that he was often introduced as "the Poet Laureate of Harlem."

---

*"Esthete in Harlem," from *The Collected Poems of Langston Hughes* by Langston Hughes, edited by Arnold Rampersad with David Roessel, Associate Editor. Copyright ©1994 by the Estate of Langston Hughes. Used by permission of Alfred A. Knopf, a division of Random House, Inc. and Harold Ober Associates Incorporated.

Calvin Coolidge Presides over the "Jazz Age" Coolidge's hands-off policies were sweet music to big business.

The stock exchange provided even greater sensations. Speculation ran wild, and an orgy of boom-or-bust trading pushed the market up to dizzy peaks. "Never sell America short" and "Be a bull on America" were favorite catchwords, as Wall Street bulls gored one another and fleeced greedy lambs. The stock market became a veritable gambling den.

As the 1920s lurched forward, everybody seemed to be buying stocks "on margin"—that is, with a small down payment. Barbers, stenographers, and elevator operators cashed in on "hot tips" picked up while on duty. One valet was reported to have parlayed his wages into a quarter of a million dollars. "The cash register crashed the social register," as rags-to-riches Americans reverently worshiped at the altar of the ticker-tape machine. So powerful was the intoxicant of quick profits that few heeded the warnings raised in certain quarters that this kind of tinsel prosperity could not last forever.

Little was done by Washington to curb money-mad speculators. In the wartime days of Wilson, the national debt had rocketed from the 1914 figure of $1,188,235,400 to the 1921 peak of $23,976,250,608. Conservative principles of money management pointed to a diversion of surplus funds to reduce this financial burden.

A businesslike move toward economic sanity was made in 1921, when a Republican Congress created the Bureau of the Budget. The bureau's director was to assist the president in preparing careful estimates of receipts and expenditures for submission to Congress as the annual budget. This new reform, long overdue, was designed in part to prevent haphazardly extravagant appropriations.

The burdensome taxes inherited from the war were especially distasteful to Secretary of the Treasury Mellon, as well as to his fellow millionaires. Their theory was that such high levies forced the rich to invest in tax-exempt securities rather than in the factories that provided prosperous payrolls. The Mellonites also argued, with considerable persuasiveness, that high taxes not only discouraged business but, in so doing, also brought a smaller net return to the Treasury than moderate taxes.

Seeking to succor the "poor" rich people, Mellon helped engineer a series of tax reductions from 1921 to 1926. Congress followed his lead by repealing the excess-profits tax, abolishing the gift tax, and reducing excise taxes, the surtax, the income tax, and estate taxes. In 1921 a wealthy person with an income of $1 million had paid $663,000 in income taxes; in 1926 the same person paid about $200,000. Secretary Mellon's spare-the-rich policies thus shifted much of the tax burden from the wealthy to the middle-income groups.

Mellon, lionized by conservatives as the "greatest secretary of the Treasury since Hamilton," remains a controversial figure. True, he reduced the national debt by $10 billion—from about $26 billion to $16 billion. But foes of the emaciated multimillionaire charged that he should have bitten an even larger chunk out of the debt, especially while the country was pulsating with prosperity. He was also accused of indirectly encouraging the bull market. If he had absorbed more of the national income in taxes, there would have been less money left for frenzied speculation. His refusal to do so typified the single-mindedly probusiness regime that dominated the political scene throughout the postwar decade.

Chapter Review

KEY TERMS

Bolshevik Revolution (700)

red scare (700)

criminal syndicalism laws (701)

American plan (701)

Ku Klux Klan (701)

Bible Belt (702)

Immigration Act of 1924 (703)

Eighteenth Amendment (704)

Volstead Act (704)

racketeers (708)

Fundamentalism (710)

Scientific Management (711)

Fordism (711)

United Negro Improvement Association (UNIA) (720)

modernism (720)

"Lost Generation" (721)

Harlem Renaissance (724)

PEOPLE TO KNOW

A. Mitchell Palmer

Nicola Sacco

Bartolomeo Vanzetti

Horace Kallen

Randolph Bourne

Al Capone

John T. Scopes

Frederick W. Taylor

Henry Ford

Charles A. Lindbergh

Sigmund Freud

H. L. Mencken

F. Scott Fitzgerald

Ernest Hemingway

T. S. Eliot

William Faulkner

Langston Hughes

TO LEARN MORE

Casey Nelson Blake, *Beloved Community: The Cultural Criticism of Randolph Bourne, Van Wyck Brooks, Waldo Frank, and Lewis Mumford* (1990)

Clare Corbould, *Becoming African Americans: Black Public Life in Harlem, 1919–1939* (2009)

Nancy Cott, *The Grounding of Modern Feminism* (1987)

John Higham, *Strangers in the Land: Patterns of American Nativism, 1860–1925* (1955)

Edward J. Larsen, *Summer for the Gods: The Scopes Trial and America's Continuing Debate over Science and Religion* (1997)

William Leuchtenburg, *The Perils of Prosperity, 1914–1932* (1958)

David Levering Lewis, *When Harlem Was in Vogue* (1981)

Michael Lienesch, *In the Beginning: Fundamentalism, the Scopes Trial, and the Making of the Antievolution Movement* (2007)

Nancy MacLean, *Behind the Mask of Chivalry: The Making of the Second Ku Klux Klan* (1993)

Roland Marchand, *Advertising the American Dream: Making Way for Modernity, 1920–1940* (1985)

Craig Monk, *Writing the Lost Generation: Expatriate Autobiography and American Modernism* (2008)

Mae M. Ngai, *Impossible Subjects: Illegal Aliens and the Making of Modern America* (2004)

Daniel Okrent, *Last Call: The Rise and Fall of Prohibition* (2010)

Christine Stansell, *American Moderns: Bohemian New York and the Creation of a New Century* (1999)

Jan Voogd, *Race Riots and Resistance: The Red Summer of 1919* (2008)

A complete, annotated bibliography for this chapter—along with brief descriptions of the People to Know—may be found on the American Pageant website. The Key Terms are defined in a Glossary at the end of the text.

CHRONOLOGY

1903 Wright brothers fly first airplane
First story-sequence motion picture

1908 Henry Ford introduces Model T

1914 W. C. Handy's "St. Louis Blues" debuts

1917 Bolshevik Revolution in Russia

1919 Eighteenth Amendment (prohibition)
Volstead Act
Seattle general strike
Anderson publishes *Winesburg, Ohio*

1919–1920 "Red scare"

1920 Radio broadcasting begins
Fitzgerald publishes *This Side of Paradise*
Lewis publishes *Main Street*

1921 Sacco-Vanzetti trial
Emergency Quota Act
Bureau of the Budget created

1922 Lewis publishes *Babbitt*
Eliot publishes *The Waste Land*

1923 Equal Rights Amendment (ERA) proposed

1924 Immigration Act of 1924

1925 Scopes trial
Florida real estate boom
Fitzgerald publishes *The Great Gatsby*
Dreiser publishes *An American Tragedy*

1926 Hughes publishes *The Weary Blues*
Hemingway publishes *The Sun Also Rises*

1927 Lindbergh flies solo across Atlantic
First talking motion picture, *The Jazz Singer*
Show Boat opens on Broadway
Sacco and Vanzetti executed

1928 Eugene O'Neill's *Strange Interlude* debuts on Broadway

1929 Faulkner publishes *The Sound and the Fury*
Hemingway publishes *A Farewell to Arms*

1932 Al Capone imprisoned

Go to the CourseMate website at **www.cengagebrain.com** for additional study tools and review materials—including audio and video clips—for this chapter.

Chapter 32

The Politics of Boom and Bust

1920–1932

*We in America today are nearer to the final triumph over poverty than
ever before in the history of any land. We have not yet reached
the goal—but . . . we shall soon, with the help of God, be in sight
of the day when poverty will be banished from this nation.*

HERBERT HOOVER, 1928

Three Republican presidents—Warren G. Harding, Calvin Coolidge, and Herbert Hoover— steered the nation on the roller-coaster ride of the 1920s, a thrilling ascent from the depths of post–World War I recession to breathtaking heights of prosperity, followed by a terrifying crash into the Great Depression. In a retreat from progressive reform, Republicans sought to serve the public good less by direct government action and more through cooperation with big business. Some corrupt officials served themselves as well, exploiting public resources for personal profit. Meanwhile, the United States retreated from its brief internationalist fling during World War I and resumed with a vengeance its traditional foreign policy of military unpreparedness and political isolationism.

★ The Republican "Old Guard" Returns

Warren G. Harding, inaugurated in 1921, *looked* presidential. With erect figure, broad shoulders, high forehead, bushy eyebrows, and graying hair, he was one of the best-liked men of his generation. An easygoing, warm-handed backslapper, he exuded graciousness and love of people. So kindly was his nature that he would brush off ants rather than crush them.

Yet the charming, smiling exterior concealed a weak, inept interior. With a mediocre mind, Harding quickly found himself beyond his depth in the presidency. "God! What a job!" was his anguished cry on one occasion.

Harding, like Grant, was unable to detect moral halitosis in his evil associates, and he was soon surrounded by his poker-playing, shirt-sleeved cronies of the "Ohio Gang." "A good guy," Harding was "one of the boys." He hated to hurt people's feelings, especially those of his friends, by saying no, and designing political leeches capitalized on this weakness. The difference between George Washington and Warren Harding, ran a current quip, was that while Washington could not tell a lie, Harding could not tell a liar. He "was not a bad man," said one Washington observer. "He was just a slob."

Candidate Harding, who admitted his scanty mental furnishings, had promised to gather about him the "best minds" of the party. Charles Evans Hughes—masterful, imperious, incisive, brilliant—brought to the position of secretary of state a dominating if somewhat conservative leadership. The new secretary of the Treasury was a lean and elderly Pittsburgh aluminum king, Andrew W. Mellon, multimillionaire collector of the paintings that are now displayed in Washington as his gift to the nation. Chubby-faced Herbert Hoover, famed feeder of the Belgians and wartime food administrator, became secretary of commerce. An energetic businessman and engineer, he raised his second-rate cabinet post to first-rate importance, especially in drumming up foreign trade for U.S. manufacturers.

But the "best minds" of the cabinet were largely offset by two of the worst. Senator Albert B. Fall of New Mexico, a scheming anticonservationist, was appointed secretary of the interior. As guardian of the nation's natural resources, he resembled the wolf hired to protect the sheep. Harry M. Daugherty, a small-town lawyer but a big-time crook in the "Ohio Gang," was supposed to prosecute wrongdoers as attorney general.

⭐ GOP Reaction at the Throttle

Well-intentioned but weak-willed, Harding was a perfect "front" for enterprising industrialists. A McKinley-style old order settled back into place with a heavy thud at war's end, crushing the reform seedlings that had sprouted in the progressive era. A nest-feathering crowd moved into Washington and proceeded to hoodwink Harding, whom many regarded as an "amiable boob."

This new Old Guard hoped to improve on the old business doctrine of laissez-faire. Their plea was not simply for government to keep its hands off business, but for government to help guide business along the path to profits. They subtly and effectively achieved their ends by putting the courts and the administrative bureaus into the safekeeping of fellow stand-patters for the duration of the decade.

The Supreme Court was a striking example of this trend. Harding lived less than three years as president, but he appointed four of the nine justices. Several of his choices were or became deep-dyed reactionaries, and they buttressed the dike against popular currents for nearly two decades. Harding's fortunate choice for chief justice was ex-president Taft, who not only performed his duties ably but surprisingly was more liberal than some of his cautious associates.

In the first years of the 1920s, the Supreme Court axed progressive legislation. It killed a federal child-labor law, stripped away many of labor's hard-won gains, and rigidly restricted government intervention in the economy. In the landmark case of **Adkins v. Children's Hospital** (1923), the Court reversed its

Justice Oliver Wendell Holmes (1841–1935), wryly dissenting in the Adkins *case, said,*

❝It would need more than the Nineteenth Amendment to convince me that there are no differences between men and women, or that legislation cannot take those differences into account.❞

own reasoning in *Muller* v. *Oregon* (see p. 645), which had declared women to be deserving of special protection in the workplace, and invalidated a minimum-wage law for women. Its strained ruling was that because women now had the vote (Nineteenth Amendment), they were the legal equals of men and could no longer be protected by special legislation. The contradictory premises of the *Muller* and *Adkins* cases framed a debate over gender differences that would continue for the rest of the century: were women sufficiently different from men that they merited special legal and social treatment, or were they effectively equal in the eyes of the law and therefore undeserving of special protections and preferences? (An analogous debate over racial differences haunted affirmative-action policies later in the century.)

Corporations, under Harding, could once more relax and expand. Antitrust laws were often ignored, circumvented, or feebly enforced by friendly prosecutors in the attorney general's office. The Interstate Commerce Commission, to single out one agency, came to be dominated by men who were personally sympathetic to the managers of the railroads. Harding reactionaries might well have boasted, "We care not what laws the Democrats pass as long as we are permitted to administer them."

Government for Sale This 1924 cartoon satirizing the corruption of the Harding administration shows the sale of the Capitol, the White House, and even the Washington Monument.

Big industrialists, striving to reduce the rigors of competition, now had a free hand to set up trade associations. Cement manufacturers, for example, would use these agencies to agree upon standardization of products, publicity campaigns, and a united front in dealing with the railroads and labor. Although many of these associations ran counter to the spirit of existing antitrust legislation, their formation was encouraged by Secretary Hoover. His sense of engineering efficiency led him to condemn the waste resulting from cutthroat competition, and his commitment to voluntary cooperation led him to urge businesses to regulate themselves rather than be regulated by big government.

✴ The Aftermath of War

Wartime government controls on the economy were swiftly dismantled. The War Industries Board disappeared with almost indecent haste. With its passing, progressive hopes for more government regulation of big business evaporated.

Washington likewise returned the railroads to private management in 1920. Reformers had hoped that wartime government operation of the lines might lead to their permanent nationalization. Instead Congress passed the Esch-Cummins Transportation Act of 1920, which encouraged private consolidation of the railroads and pledged the Interstate Commerce Commission to guarantee their profitability. The new philosophy was not to save the country from the railroads, as in the days of the Populists, but to save the railroads for the country.

The federal government also tried to pull up anchor and get out of the shipping business. The Merchant Marine Act of 1920 authorized the Shipping Board, which controlled about fifteen hundred vessels, to dispose of much of the hastily built wartime fleet at bargain-basement prices. The board operated the remaining vessels without conspicuous success. Under the La Follette Seaman's Act of 1915, American shipping could not thrive in competition with foreigners, who all too often provided their crews with wretched food and starvation wages.

Labor, suddenly deprived of its wartime crutch of friendly government support, limped along badly in the postwar decade. A bloody strike in the steel industry was ruthlessly broken in 1919, partly by exploiting ethnic and racial divisions among the steelworkers and partly by branding the strikers as dangerous "reds." The Railway Labor Board, a successor body to the wartime labor boards, ordered a wage cut of 12 percent in 1922, provoking a two-month strike. It ended when Attorney General Daugherty, who fully shared Harding's big-business bias, clamped on the strikers one of the most

sweeping injunctions in American history. Unions wilted in this hostile political environment, and membership shriveled by nearly 30 percent between 1920 and 1930.

Needy veterans were among the few nonbusiness groups to reap lasting gains from the war. Congress in 1921 generously created the Veterans Bureau, authorized to operate hospitals and provide vocational rehabilitation for the disabled.

Veterans quickly organized into pressure groups. The American Legion had been founded in Paris in 1919 by Colonel Theodore Roosevelt, Jr. Legionnaires met periodically to renew old hardships and let off steam in good-natured horseplay. The legion soon became distinguished for its militant patriotism, rock-ribbed conservatism, and zealous antiradicalism.

The legion also became notorious for its aggressive lobbying for veterans' benefits. The chief grievance of the former "doughboys" was monetary—they wanted their "dough." The former servicemen demanded "adjusted compensation" to make up for the wages they had "lost" when they turned in their factory overalls for military uniforms during the Great War.

Critics denounced this demand as a holdup "bonus," but the millions of veterans deployed heavy political artillery. They browbeat Congress into passing a bonus bill in 1922, which Harding promptly vetoed. Re-forming their lines, the repulsed veterans gathered for a final attack. In 1924 Congress again hoisted the white flag and passed the Adjusted Compensation Act. It gave every former soldier a paid-up insurance policy due in twenty years—adding about $3.5 billion to the total cost of the war. Penny-pinching Calvin Coolidge sternly vetoed the measure, but Congress overrode him, leaving the veterans with their loot.

✴ America Seeks Benefits Without Burdens

Making peace with the fallen foe was the most pressing problem left on Harding's doorstep. The United States, having rejected the Treaty of Versailles, was still technically at war with Germany, Austria, and Hungary nearly three years after the armistice. Peace was finally achieved by lone-wolf tactics. In July 1921 Congress passed a simple joint resolution that declared the war officially ended.

Isolation was enthroned in Washington. The Harding administration, with the Senate "irreconcilables" holding a hatchet over its head, continued to regard the League of Nations as a thing unclean. Harding at first refused even to support the League's world health program. But the new world body was much too important to be completely ignored. "Unofficial observers" were

"I Sympathize Deeply with You, Madam, but I Cannot Associate with You," 1923 President Harding's secretary of state, Charles Evans Hughes, broke the news to a desperate, war-tattered Europe that America was going, and staying, home.

sent to its seat in Geneva, Switzerland, to hang around like detectives shadowing a suspected criminal.

Harding could not completely turn his back on the outside world, especially the Middle East, where a sharp rivalry developed between America and Britain for oil-drilling concessions. Remembering that the Allies had floated to victory on a flood of oil, experts recognized that liquid "black gold" would be as necessary as blood in the battles of tomorrow. Secretary Hughes eventually secured for American oil companies the right to share in the exploitation of the sandy region's oil riches.

Disarmament was one international issue on which Harding, after much indecision, finally seized the initiative. He was prodded by businesspeople unwilling to dig deeper into their pockets for money to finance the ambitious naval building program started during the war. A deadly contest was shaping up with Britain and Japan, which watched with alarm as the oceans filled with American vessels. Britain still commanded the world's largest navy, but the clatter of American riveters proclaimed that the United States would soon overtake it.

Public agitation in America, fed by these worries, brought about the headline-making Washington "Disarmament" Conference in 1921–1922. Invitations went to all the major naval powers—except Bolshevik Russia, whose government the United States refused officially to recognize. The double agenda included naval disarmament and the situation in the Far East.

At the outset Secretary Hughes startled the delegates, who were expecting the usual diplomatic fence-straddling, with a comprehensive, concrete plan for declaring a ten-year "holiday" on the construction of battleships and even for scrapping some of the huge dreadnoughts already built. He proposed that the scaled-down navies of America and Britain should enjoy parity in battleships and aircraft carriers, with Japan on the small end of a 5:5:3 ratio. This arrangement sounded to the sensitive Japanese ambassador like "Rolls-Royce, Rolls-Royce, Ford."

Complex bargaining followed in the wake of Hughes's proposals. The Five-Power Naval Treaty of 1922 embodied Hughes's ideas on ship ratios, but only after face-saving compensation was offered to the insecure Japanese (see Figure 32.1). The British and Americans both conceded that they would refrain from fortifying their Far Eastern possessions, including the Philippines. The Japanese were not subjected to such restraints in their possessions. In addition, a Four-Power Treaty replaced the twenty-year-old Anglo-Japanese alliance. The new pact bound Britain, Japan, France, and the United States to preserve the status quo in the Pacific—another concession to the jumpy Japanese. Finally, the Washington Conference gave chaotic China—"the Sick Man of the Far East"—a shot in the arm with the **Nine-Power Treaty** of 1922, whose

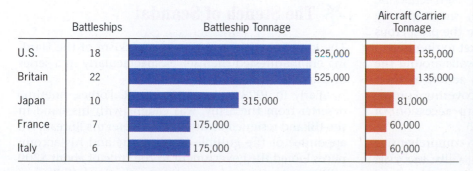

	Battleships	Battleship Tonnage	Aircraft Carrier Tonnage
U.S.	18	525,000	135,000
Britain	22	525,000	135,000
Japan	10	315,000	81,000
France	7	175,000	60,000
Italy	6	175,000	60,000

FIGURE 32.1 Limits Imposed by Washington Conference, 1921–1922 The pledge of the British and Americans to refrain from fortifying their Far Eastern possessions, while Japan was allowed to fortify its possessions, was the key to the naval-limitation treaty. The United States and Great Britain thus won a temporary victory but later paid a horrendous price when they had to dislodge the well-entrenched Japanese from the Pacific in World War II.

signatories agreed to nail wide-open the Open Door in China.

When the final gavel banged, the Hardingites boasted with much fanfare—and some justification—of their globe-shaking achievement in disarmament. But their satisfaction was somewhat illusory. No restrictions had been placed on small warships, and the other powers churned ahead with the construction of cruisers, destroyers, and submarines, while penny-pinching Uncle Sam lagged dangerously behind. Congress also pointedly declared that it was making no commitment to the use of armed force or any kind of joint action when it ratified the Four-Power Treaty. These reservations, in effect, rendered the treaty a dead letter. Ominously, the American people seemed content to rely for their security on words and wishful thinking rather than on weapons and hardheaded realism.

A similar sentimentalism welled up later in the decade, when Americans clamored for the "outlawry of war." The conviction spread that if quarreling nations would only take the pledge to foreswear war as an instrument of national policy, swords could be beaten into plowshares. Calvin Coolidge's secretary of state, Frank B. Kellogg, who later won the Nobel Peace Prize for his role, was lukewarm about the idea. But after petitions bearing more than 2 million signatures cascaded into Washington, he signed with the French foreign minister in 1928 the famed **Kellogg-Briand Pact**. Officially known as the Pact of Paris, it was ultimately ratified by sixty-two nations.

This new parchment peace was delusory in the extreme. Defensive wars were still permitted, and what scheming aggressor could not cook up an excuse of self-defense? Lacking both muscles and teeth, the pact was a diplomatic derelict—and virtually useless in a showdown. Yet it accurately—and dangerously—reflected the American mind in the 1920s, which was all too willing to be lulled into a false sense of security. This mood took even deeper hold in the ostrich-like neutralism of the 1930s.

✴ Hiking the Tariff Higher

A comparable lack of realism afflicted foreign economic policy in the 1920s. Businesspeople, shortsightedly obsessed with the dazzling prospects in the prosperous home market, sought to keep that market to themselves by flinging up insurmountable tariff walls around the United States. They were spurred into action by their fear of a flood of cheap goods from recovering Europe, especially during the brief but sharp recession of 1920–1921.

In 1922 Congress passed the comprehensive **Fordney-McCumber Tariff Law**. Glib lobbyists once more descended upon Washington and helped boost schedules from the average of 27 percent under Wilson's Underwood Tariff of 1913 to an average of 38.5 percent, which was almost as high as Taft's Payne-Aldrich Tariff of 1909. (See the Appendix.) Duties on farm produce were increased, and the principle was proclaimed that the general rates were designed to equalize the cost of American and foreign production. A promising degree of flexibility was introduced for the first time, when the president was authorized, with the advice of the fact-finding Tariff Commission, to reduce or increase duties by as much as 50 percent.

Presidents Harding and Coolidge, true to their big-industry sympathies, were far more friendly to tariff increases than to reductions. In six years they authorized thirty-two upward changes, including on their list vital commodities like dairy products, chemicals, and pig iron. During the same period, the White House ordered only five reductions. These included mill feed and such trifling items as bobwhite quail, paintbrush handles, phenol, and cresylic acid.

The high-tariff course thus charted by the Republican regimes set off an ominous chain reaction. European producers felt the squeeze, for the American tariff walls prolonged their postwar chaos. An impoverished Europe needed to sell its manufactured goods to the United States, particularly if it hoped to achieve economic recovery and to pay its huge war debt to Washington. America needed to give foreign nations a chance to make a profit from it so that they could buy its manufactured articles and repay debts. International trade, Americans were slow to learn, is a two-way street. In general, they could not sell to others in quantity unless they bought from them in quantity—or lent them more U.S. dollars.

Erecting tariff walls was a game that two could play. The American example spurred European nations, throughout the feverish 1920s, to pile up higher barriers themselves. These artificial obstacles were doubly bad: they hurt not only American-made goods but the products of European countries as well. The whole vicious circle further deepened the international economic distress, providing one more rung on the ladder by which Adolf Hitler scrambled to power.

✴ The Stench of Scandal

The loose morality and get-rich-quickism of the Harding era manifested themselves spectacularly in a series of scandals.

Early in 1923 Colonel Charles R. Forbes, onetime deserter from the army, was caught with his hand in the till and resigned as head of the Veterans Bureau. An appointee of the gullible Harding, he and his accomplices looted the government to the tune of about $200 million, chiefly in connection with the building of put a million dollars in jail" and "In America everyone is assumed guilty until proven rich."

Still more scandals erupted. Persistent reports as to the underhanded doings of Attorney General Daugherty prompted a Senate investigation in 1924 of the illegal sale of pardons and liquor permits. Forced to resign, the accused official was tried in 1927 but was released after a jury twice failed to agree. During the trial Daugherty hid behind the trousers of the now-dead Harding by implying that persistent probing might uncover crookedness in the White House.

Harding was mercifully spared the full revelation of these iniquities, though his worst suspicions were aroused. While news of the scandals was beginning to break, he embarked upon a speechmaking tour across the country all the way to Alaska. On the return trip, he died in San Francisco, on August 2, 1923, of pneumonia and thrombosis. His death may have been hastened by a broken heart resulting from the disloyalty of designing friends. Mourning millions, not yet fully aware of the graft in Washington, expressed genuine sorrow.

The brutal fact is that Harding was not a strong enough man for the presidency—as he himself privately admitted. Such was his weakness that he tolerated people and conditions that subjected the Republic to its worst disgrace since the days of President Grant.

✦ "Silent Cal" Coolidge

News of Harding's death was sped to Vice President Coolidge, then visiting at his father's New England farmhouse. By the light of two kerosene lamps, the elder Coolidge, a justice of the peace, used the old family Bible to administer the presidential oath to his son.

This homespun setting was symbolic of Coolidge. Quite unlike Harding, the stern-faced Vermonter, with his thin nose and tightly set lips, embodied the New England virtues of honesty, morality, industry, and frugality. As a youth, his father reported, he seemed to get more sap out of a maple tree than did any of the other boys. Practicing a rigid economy in both money and words, "Silent Cal" came to be known in Washington conversational circles for his brilliant flashes of silence. His dour, serious visage prompted the acid observation that he had been "weaned on a pickle."

Coolidge seemed to be a crystallization of the commonplace. Painfully shy, he was blessed with only mediocre powers of leadership. He would occasionally display a dry wit in private, but his speeches, delivered in a nasal New England twang, were invariably boring. A staunch apostle of the status quo, he was no knight in armor riding forth to tilt at wrongs. His only horse, in fact, was an electric-powered steed on which he took his exercise. True to Republican philosophy, he became

Washington Officials Trying to Outpace the Teapot Dome Scandal, ca. 1922

veterans' hospitals. He was sentenced to two years in a federal penitentiary.

Most shocking of all was the **Teapot Dome scandal**, an affair that involved priceless naval oil reserves at Teapot Dome (Wyoming) and Elk Hills (California). In 1921 the slippery secretary of the interior, Albert B. Fall, induced his careless colleague, the secretary of the navy, to transfer these valuable properties to the Interior Department. Harding indiscreetly signed the secret order. Fall then quietly leased the lands to oilmen Harry F. Sinclair and Edward L. Doheny, but not until he had received a bribe ("loan") of $100,000 from Doheny and about three times that amount in all from Sinclair.

Teapot Dome, no tempest in a teapot, finally came to a whistling boil. Details of the crooked transaction gradually began to leak out in March 1923, two years after Harding took office. Fall, Sinclair, and Doheny were indicted the next year, but the case dragged through the courts until 1929. Finally Fall was found guilty of taking a bribe and was sentenced to one year in jail. By a curious quirk of justice, the two bribe givers were acquitted while the bribe taker was convicted, although Sinclair served several months in jail for having "shadowed" jurors and for refusing to testify before a Senate committee.

The oily smudge from Teapot Dome polluted the prestige of the Washington government. Right-thinking citizens wondered what was going on when public officials could sell out the nation's vital resources, especially those reserved for the U.S. Navy. The acquittal of Sinclair and Doheny undermined faith in the courts, while giving further currency to the cynical sayings "You can't

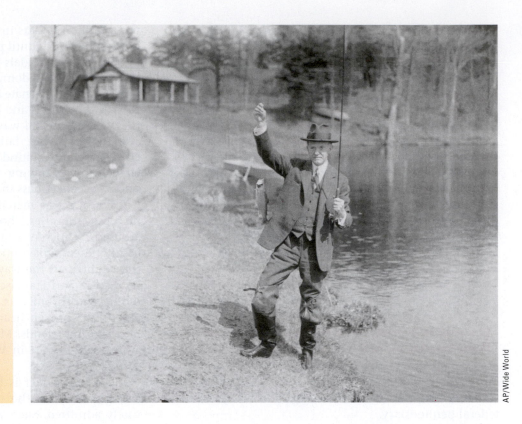

Calvin Coolidge, Gentleman Angler Coolidge "was a real conservative, a fundamentalist in religion, in the economic and social order, and in fishing," said his successor, Herbert Hoover, who had a fly fisherman's disdain for Coolidge's bait-fishing tactics—and for his predecessor's laissez-faire politics as well.

AP/Wide World

the "high priest of the great god Business." He believed that "the man who builds a factory builds a temple" and that "the man who works there worships there."

The hands-off temperament of "Cautious Cal" Coolidge suited the times perfectly. His thrifty nature caused him to sympathize fully with Secretary of the Treasury Mellon's efforts to reduce both taxes and debts. No foe of industrial bigness, he let business have its head. "Coolidge luck" held during his five and a half prosperity-blessed years.

Ever a profile in caution, Coolidge slowly gave the Harding regime a badly needed moral fumigation. Teapot Dome had scalded the Republican party badly, but so transparently honest was the vinegary Vermonter that the scandalous oil did not rub off on him. The public, though at first shocked by the scandal, quickly simmered down, and an alarming tendency developed in certain quarters to excuse some of the wrongdoers on the grounds that "they had gotten away with it." Some critics even condemned the government prosecutors for continuing to rock the boat. America's moral sensibility was evidently being dulled by prosperity.

✦ Frustrated Farmers

Sun-bronzed farmers were caught squarely in a boom-or-bust cycle in the postwar decade. While the fighting had raged, they had raked in money hand over gnarled

fist; by the spring of 1920, the price of wheat had shot up to an incredible $3 a bushel. But peace brought an end to government-guaranteed high prices and to massive purchases by other nations, as foreign production reentered the stream of world commerce.

Machines also threatened to plow the farmers under an avalanche of their own overabundant crops. The gasoline-engine tractor was working a revolution on American farms. This steel mule was to cultivation and sowing what the McCormick reaper was to harvesting. Blue-denimed farmers no longer had to plod after the horse-drawn plow with high-footed gait. They could sit erect on their chugging mechanized chariots and turn under and harrow many acres in a single day. They could grow bigger crops on larger areas, using fewer horses and hired hands. The wartime boom had encouraged them to bring vast new tracts under cultivation, especially in the "wheat belt" of the upper Midwest. But such improved efficiency and expanded agricultural acreage helped to pile up more price-dampening surpluses. A withering depression swept through agricultural districts in the 1920s, when one farm in four was sold for debt or taxes. As a plaintive song of the period ran,

No use talkin', any man's beat,
With 'leven-cent cotton and forty-cent meat.

Schemes abounded for bringing relief to the hard-pressed farmers. A bipartisan "farm bloc" from the

Have you placed a Sentimental Value on your Horses out of proportion to the work they are able to perform?

BAILOR MOTOR CULTIVATORS

Library of Congress

Mechanizing Agriculture Just as the automobile replaced the horse on city streets, so did the gas-engine tractor replace horses and mules on the nation's farms in the 1920s. American farmers owned ten times more tractors in 1930 than they did in 1920. The smoke-belching tractors bolstered productivity but also increased the farmers' debt burden, as the Great Depression made tragically clear.

agricultural states coalesced in Congress in 1921 and succeeded in driving through some helpful laws. Noteworthy was the Capper-Volstead Act, which exempted farmers' marketing cooperatives from antitrust prosecution. The farm bloc's favorite proposal was the **McNary-Haugen Bill**, pushed energetically from 1924 to 1928. It sought to keep agricultural prices high by authorizing the government to buy up surpluses and sell them abroad. Government losses were to be made up by a special tax on the farmers. Congress twice passed the bill, but frugal Coolidge twice vetoed it. Farm prices stayed down, and farmers' political temperatures stayed high, reaching a fever pitch in the election of 1924.

✴ A Three-Way Race for the White House in 1924

Self-satisfied Republicans, chanting "Keep Cool and Keep Coolidge," nominated "Silent Cal" for the presidency at their convention in Cleveland in the simmering summer of 1924. Squabbling Democrats had more difficulty choosing a candidate when they met in New York's sweltering Madison Square Garden. Reflecting many of the cultural tensions of the decade, the party was hopelessly split between "wets" and "drys," urbanites and farmers, Fundamentalists and Modernists, northern liberals and southern stand-patters, immigrants and old-stock Americans. In one symptomatic spasm of discord, the conventioneers failed by just one vote to pass a resolution condemning the Ku Klux Klan.

Deadlocked for an unprecedented 102 ballots, the convention at last turned wearily, sweatily, and unenthusiastically to John W. Davis. A wealthy corporation lawyer connected with the Wall Street banking house of J. P. Morgan and Company, the polished nominee was no less conservative than cautious Calvin Coolidge.

The field was now wide-open for a liberal candidate. The white-pompadoured Senator Robert ("Fighting Bob") La Follette from Wisconsin, perennial aspirant to the presidency and now sixty-nine years of age, sprang forward to lead a new Progressive party. He gained the endorsement of the American Federation of Labor and enjoyed the support of the shrinking Socialist party, but his major constituency was made up of the price-pinched farmers. La Follette's new Progressive party, fielding only a presidential ticket, with no candidates for local office, was a head without a body. It proved to be only a shadow of the robust Progressive coalition of prewar days. Its platform called for government ownership of railroads and relief for farmers, lashed out at monopoly and antilabor injunctions, and urged a constitutional amendment to limit the Supreme Court's power to invalidate laws passed by Congress.

La Follette turned in a respectable showing, polling nearly 5 million votes. But "Cautious Cal" and the oil-smeared Republicans slipped easily back into office, overwhelming Davis, 15,718,211 to 8,385,283. The electoral count stood at 382 for Coolidge, 136 for Davis, and 13 for La Follette, all from his home state of Wisconsin (see Map 32.1). As the so-called conscience of the callous 1920s, La Follette injected a badly needed liberal tonic into a decade drugged on prosperity. But

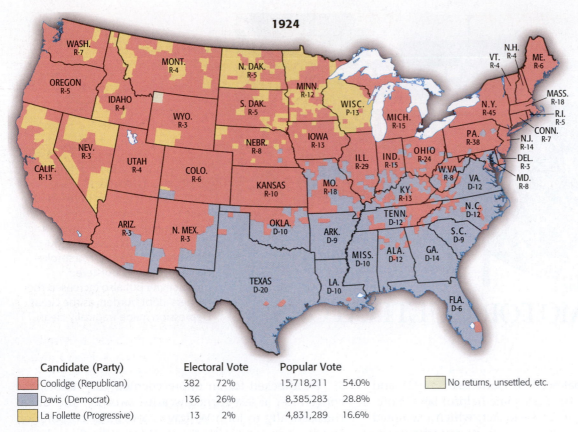

1924

Candidate (Party)	Electoral Vote		Popular Vote	
Coolidge (Republican)	382	72%	15,718,211	54.0%
Davis (Democrat)	136	26%	8,385,283	28.8%
La Follette (Progressive)	13	2%	4,831,289	16.6%

No returns, unsettled, etc.

MAP 32.1 Presidential Election of 1924 (showing popular vote by county) Note the concentration of La Follette's votes in the old Populist strongholds of the Midwest and the mountain states. His ticket did especially well in the grain-growing districts battered by the postwar slump in agricultural prices. © Cengage Learning

times were too good for too many for his reforming message to carry the day.

★ Foreign-Policy Flounderings

Isolation continued to reign in the Coolidge era. Despite presidential proddings, the Senate proved unwilling to allow America to adhere to the World Court—the judicial arm of the still-suspect League of Nations. Coolidge only halfheartedly—and unsuccessfully—pursued further naval disarmament after the loudly trumpeted agreements worked out at the Washington Conference in 1922.

A glaring exception to the United States' inward-looking indifference to the outside world was the armed interventionism in the Caribbean and Central America. American troops were withdrawn (after an eight-year stay) from the Dominican Republic in 1924, but they remained in Haiti from 1914 to 1934. President Coolidge in 1925 briefly removed American bayonets from troubled Nicaragua, where they had glinted

intermittently since 1909, but in 1926 he sent them back, five thousand strong, and they stayed until 1933. American oil companies clamored for a military expedition to Mexico in 1926 when the Mexican government began to assert its sovereignty over oil resources. Coolidge kept cool and defused the Mexican crisis with some skillful diplomatic negotiating. But his mailed-fist tactics elsewhere bred sore resentments south of the Rio Grande, where angry critics loudly assailed "*yanqui imperialism.*"

Overshadowing all other foreign-policy problems in the 1920s was the knotty issue of international debts, a complicated tangle of private loans, Allied war debts, and German reparations payments (see Figure 32.2). Almost overnight, World War I had reversed the international financial position of the United States. In 1914 America had been a debtor nation to the sum of about $4 billion; by 1922 it had become a creditor nation to the sum of about $16 billion. The almighty dollar rivaled the pound sterling as the financial giant of the world. American investors loaned some $10 billion to foreigners in the 1920s, though even this huge river

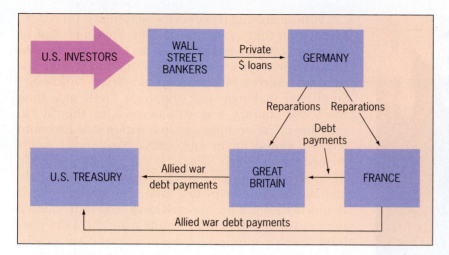

FIGURE 32.2 Aspects of the Financial Merry-go-round, 1921–1933 Great Britain, with a debt of over $4 billion owed to the U.S. Treasury, had a huge stake in proposals for inter-Allied debt cancellation, but France's stake was even larger. Less prosperous than Britain in the 1920s and more battered by the war, which had been fought on its soil, France owed nearly $3.5 billion to the United States and additional billions to Britain.

of money could not fully refloat the war-shelled world economy. Americans, bewitched by lucrative investment opportunities in their domestic economy, did not lend nearly so large a fraction of their national income overseas as had the British in the prewar period.

The key knot in the debt tangle was the $10 billion that the U.S. Treasury had loaned to the Allies during and immediately after the war. Uncle Sam held their IOUs—and he wanted to be paid. The Allies, in turn, protested that the demand for repayment was grossly unfair. The French and the British pointed out, with much justice, that they had held up a wall of flesh and bone against the common foe until America the Unready had finally entered the fray. America, they argued, should write off its loans as war costs, just as the Allies had been tragically forced to write off the lives of millions of young men. The debtors also complained that the real effect of their borrowed dollars had been to fuel the boom in the already roaring wartime economy in America, where nearly all their purchases had been made. And the final straw, protested the Europeans, was that America's postwar tariff walls made it almost impossible for them to sell their goods to earn the dollars to pay their debts.

✦ Unraveling the Debt Knot

America's tightfisted insistence on getting its money back helped to harden the hearts of the Allies against conquered Germany. The French and the British demanded that the Germans make enormous reparations payments, totaling some $32 billion, as compensation for war-inflicted damages. The Allies hoped to settle their debts to the United States with the money received from Germany. The French, seeking to extort lagging reparations payments, sent troops into Germany's industrialized Ruhr Valley in 1923.

Berlin responded by permitting its currency to inflate astronomically. At one point in October 1923, a loaf of bread cost 480 million marks, or about $120 million in preinflation money. German society teetered on the brink of mad anarchy, and the whole international house of financial cards threatened to flutter down in colossal chaos.

Sensible statesmen now urged that war debts and reparations alike be drastically scaled down or even canceled outright. But to Americans such proposals smacked of "welshing" on a debt. "We went across, but they won't come across," cried a prominent politician. Scroogelike, Calvin Coolidge turned aside suggestions of debt cancellation with a typically terse question: "They hired the money, didn't they?" The Washington administration proved especially unrealistic in its dogged insistence that there was no connection whatever between debts and reparations.

Reality finally dawned in the **Dawes Plan** of 1924. Negotiated largely by Charles Dawes, about to be nominated as Coolidge's running mate, it rescheduled German reparations payments and opened the way for further American private loans to Germany. The whole financial cycle now became still more complicated, as U.S. bankers loaned money to Germany, Germany paid reparations to France and Britain, and the former Allies paid war debts to the United States. Clearly the source of this monetary merry-go-round was the flowing well of American credit. When that well dried up after the great crash in 1929, the jungle of international finance quickly turned into a desert. President Herbert Hoover declared a one-year debt moratorium in 1931, and before long all the debtors had defaulted—except "honest little Finland," which struggled along making payments until the last of its debt was discharged in 1976.

The United States never did get its money, but it harvested a bumper crop of ill will. Irate French crowds on occasion attacked American tourists, and

A German Woman Burns Near-worthless Paper Currency for Cooking Fuel, 1923 The memory of the hyper-inflation of the 1920s haunted Germans well into the twenty-first century.

The Granger Collection, New York

throughout Europe Uncle Sam was caricatured as Uncle Shylock, greedily whetting his knife for the last pound of Allied flesh. The bad taste left in American mouths by the whole sorry episode contributed powerfully to the storm-cellar neutrality legislation passed by Congress in the 1930s.

✴ The Triumph of Herbert Hoover, 1928

Poker-faced Calvin Coolidge, the tight-lipped "Sphinx of the Potomac," bowed out of the 1928 presidential race when he announced, "I do not choose to run." His logical successor was super-Secretary (of Commerce) Herbert Hoover, unpopular with the political bosses but the much-admired darling of the masses, who asked, "Hoo but Hoover?" He was nominated on a platform that clucked contentedly over both prosperity and prohibition.

Still-squabbling Democrats nominated Alfred E. Smith, four-time governor of New York and one of the most colorful personalities in American politics. He was a wisecracking, glad-handing liberal who suffered from several fatal political handicaps. "Al(cohol)" Smith was soakingly and drippingly "wet" at a time when the country was still devoted to the "noble experiment" of prohibition. To a nation that had only recently moved to the city, native New Yorker Smith seemed too abrasively urban. He was a Roman Catholic in an overwhelmingly Protestant—and unfortunately prejudiced—land. Many dry, rural, and Fundamentalist Democrats gagged on his candidacy, and they saddled the wet Smith with a dry running mate and a dry platform. Jauntily sporting a brown derby and a big cigar, Smith, "the Happy Warrior," tried to carry alcohol on one shoulder and water on the other. But his effort was doomed from the start.

Radio figured prominently in this campaign for the first time, and it helped Hoover more than Smith. The New Yorker had more personal sparkle, but he could not project it through the radio (which in his Lower East Side twang he pronounced "radd-dee-o," grating on the ears of many listeners). Iowa-born Hoover, with his double-breasted dignity, came out of the microphone better than he went in. Decrying un-American "socialism" and preaching "rugged individualism," he sounded both grassrootish and statesmanlike.

Chubby-faced, ruddy-complexioned Herbert Hoover, with his painfully high starched collar, was a living example of the American success story and an intriguing mixture of two centuries. As a poor orphan boy who had worked his way through Stanford University, he had absorbed the nineteenth-century copybook maxims of industry, thrift, and self-reliance. As a fabulously successful mining engineer and a brilliant businessman, he had honed to a high degree the efficiency doctrines of the progressive era.

A small-town boy from Iowa and Oregon, he had traveled and worked abroad extensively. Long years of self-imposed exile had deepened his determination, abundantly supported by national tradition, to avoid foreign entanglements. His experiences abroad had further strengthened his faith in American individualism, free enterprise, and small government.

With his unshaken dignity and Quaker restraint, Hoover was a far cry from the typical backslapping politician. Though a citizen of the world and laden with international honors, he was quite shy, standoffish, and stiff. Personally colorless in public, he had been accustomed during much of his life to giving orders to subordinates and not to soliciting votes. Never before elected to public office, he was thin-skinned in the face of criticism, and he did not adapt readily to the necessary give-and-take of political accommodation.

His real power lay in his integrity, his humanitarianism, his passion for assembling the facts, his efficiency, his talents for administration, and his ability to inspire loyalty in close associates. They called him "the Chief."

As befitted America's newly mechanized civilization, Hoover was the ideal businessperson's candidate. A self-made millionaire, he recoiled from anything suggesting socialism, paternalism, or "planned economy." Yet as secretary of commerce, he had exhibited some progressive instincts. He endorsed labor unions and supported federal regulation of the new radio broadcasting industry. He even flirted for a time with the idea of government-owned radio, similar to the British Broadcasting Corporation (BBC).

As bands blared Smith's theme song, "The Sidewalks of New York," the campaign sank into the sewers beneath the sidewalks. Despite the best efforts of Hoover and Smith, below-the-belt tactics were employed to a disgusting degree by lower-level campaigners. Religious bigotry raised its hideous head over Smith's Catholicism. An irresponsible whispering campaign claimed that "A Vote for Al Smith Is a Vote for the Pope" and that the White House, under Smith, would become a branch of the Vatican—complete with "Rum, Romanism, and Ruin." Hoover's attempts to quash such rumors were in vain.

The proverbially solid South—"100 percent American" and a stronghold of Protestant Ku Klux Klanism—shied away from "city slicker" Al Smith. It might have accepted a Catholic, or a wet, or the descendant of Irish grandparents, or an urbanite. But a concoction of Catholicism, wettism, foreignism, and liberalism brewed on the sidewalks of New York was too bitter a dose for southern stomachs. Smith's theme song was a constant and rasping reminder that his upbringing had not been convincingly American.

Hoover triumphed in a landslide. He bagged 21,391,993 popular votes to 15,016,169 for his embittered opponent, while rolling up an electoral count of 444 to 87. A huge Republican majority was returned to the House of Representatives. Tens of thousands of dry southern Democrats—"Hoovercrats"—rebelled against Al Smith, and Hoover proved to be the first Republican candidate in fifty-two years, except for Harding's Tennessee victory in 1920, to carry a state that had seceded. He swept five states of the former Confederacy, as well as all of the Border States (see Map 32.2).

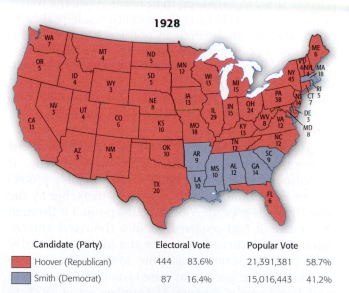

Herbert Hoover on the Road   "Whistle-stop" campaigns, with candidates speaking from the rear platforms of trains, were a standard feature of American politics before the advent of television. Herbert Hoover here greets a crowd in Newark, New Jersey, during the 1928 campaign.

© Bettmann/Corbis

1928

Candidate (Party)	Electoral Vote		Popular Vote	
Hoover (Republican)	444	83.6%	21,391,381	58.7%
Smith (Democrat)	87	16.4%	15,016,443	41.2%

MAP 32.2 Presidential Election of 1928 (with electoral vote by state)   Smith, despite his defeat, managed to poll almost as many votes as the victorious Coolidge had in 1924. By attracting to the party an immense urban or "sidewalk" vote, the breezy New Yorker foreshadowed Roosevelt's New Deal victory in 1932, when the Democrats patched together the solid South and the urban North. A cruel joke had the Catholic Smith cabling the Pope a single word after the election: "Unpack." © Cengage Learning

✦ President Hoover's First Moves

Prosperity in the late 1920s smiled broadly as the Hoover years began. Soaring stocks on the bull market continued to defy the laws of financial gravitation. But two immense groups of citizens were not getting their share of the riches flowing from the national cornucopia: the unorganized wage earners and especially the disorganized farmers.

Hoover's administration, in line with its philosophy of promoting self-help, responded to the outcry of the wounded farmers with legislative aspirin. The **Agricultural Marketing Act**, passed by Congress in June 1929, was designed to help the farmers help themselves, largely through producers' cooperatives. It set up the Federal Farm Board, with a revolving fund of half a billion dollars at its disposal. Money was lent generously to farm organizations seeking to buy, sell, and store agricultural surpluses.

In 1930 the Farm Board itself created both the Grain Stabilization Corporation and the Cotton Stabilization Corporation. The prime goal was to bolster sagging prices by buying up surpluses. But the two agencies were soon suffocated by an avalanche of farm produce, as wheat dropped to fifty-seven cents a bushel and cotton to five cents a pound.

Farmers had meanwhile clutched at the tariff as a possible straw to help keep their heads above the waters of financial ruin. During the recent presidential campaign, Hoover, an amateur in politics, had been stampeded into a politically unwise pledge. He had promised to call Congress into special session to consider agricultural relief and, specifically, to bring about "limited" changes in the tariff. These hope-giving assurances no doubt won many votes for Hoover in the midwestern farm belt.

The **Hawley-Smoot Tariff** of 1930 followed the well-worn pattern of Washington horse trading. It started out in the House as a fairly reasonable protective measure, designed to assist the farmers. But by the time the high-pressure lobbyists had pushed it through the Senate, it had acquired about a thousand amendments. It thus turned out to be the highest protective tariff in the nation's peacetime history. The average duty on nonfree goods was raised from 38.5 percent, as established by the Fordney-McCumber Act of 1922, to nearly 60 percent.

To angered foreigners, the Hawley-Smoot Tariff was a blow below the trade belt. It seemed like a declaration of economic warfare on the entire outside world. It reversed a promising worldwide trend toward reasonable tariffs and widened the yawning trade gaps. It plunged both America and other nations deeper into the terrible depression that had already begun. It increased international financial chaos and forced the United States further into the bog of economic isolationism. And economic isolationism, both at home and abroad, was playing directly into the hands of a hate-filled German demagogue, Adolf Hitler.

✦ The Great Crash Ends the Golden Twenties

When Herbert Hoover confidently took the presidential oath on March 4, 1929, there were few black clouds on the economic horizon. The "long boom" seemed endless, with the painful exception of the debt-blanketed farm belt. America's productive colossus—stimulated by the automobile, radio, movies, and other new industries—was roaring along at a dizzy speed that suggested a permanent plateau of prosperity. Few people sensed that it might smother its own fires by pouring out too much.

The speculative bubble was actually near the bursting point. Prices on the stock exchange continued to spiral upward and create a fool's paradise of paper profits, despite Hoover's early but fruitless efforts to curb speculation through the Federal Reserve Board. A few prophets of disaster were bold enough to sound warnings but were drowned out by the mad chatter of the ticker-tape machine.

A catastrophic crash came in October 1929. It was partially triggered by the British, who raised their interest rates in an effort to bring back capital lured abroad by American investments. Foreign investors and wary domestic speculators began to dump their "insecurities," and an orgy of selling followed. Tension built up to the panicky **Black Tuesday** of October 29, 1929, when 16,410,030 shares of stocks were sold in a save-who-may scramble. Wall Street became a wailing wall as gloom and doom replaced boom, and suicides increased alarmingly. A "sick joke" of the time had hotel room clerks ask registrants, "For sleeping or jumping?"

Losses, even in blue-chip securities, were unbelievable. By the end of 1929—two months after the initial crash—stockholders had lost $40 billion in paper values, or more than the total cost of World War I to the United States (see Figure 32.3).

The stock-market collapse heralded a business depression, at home and abroad, that was the most prolonged and prostrating in American or world experience. No other industrialized nation suffered so severe a setback. By the end of 1930, more than 4 million workers in the United States were jobless; two years later the figure had about tripled. Hungry and despairing workers pounded pavements in search of nonexistent jobs

Pride Goes Before a Fall   The great crash of 1929 humbled many a high-flying investor. The desperate curbside seller of this brand-new Chrysler Model 75 paid $1,550 for it just months before.

("We're firing, not hiring"). Where employees were not discharged, wages and salaries were often slashed. A current jingle ran,

> Mellon pulled the whistle,
> Hoover rang the bell
> Wall Street gave the signal
> And the country went to hell.

The misery and gloom were incalculable, as forests of dead chimneys stood stark against the sky. Over five thousand banks collapsed in the first three years of the depression, carrying down with them the life savings of tens of thousands of ordinary citizens. Countless thousands of honest, hard-working people lost their homes and farms to the forecloser's hammer. Breadlines formed, soup kitchens dispensed food, and apple sellers stood shivering on street corners trying to peddle their wares for five cents. Families felt the stress, as jobless fathers nursed their guilt and shame at not being able to provide for their households. Breadless breadwinners often blamed themselves for their plight, despite abundant evidence that the economic system, not individual initiative, had broken down. Mothers meanwhile nursed fewer babies, as hard times reached even into the nation's bedrooms, precipitating a decade-long dearth of births. As cash registers gathered cobwebs, the

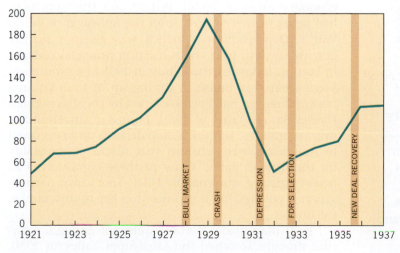

FIGURE 32.3 **Index of Common Stock Prices (1926 = 100)**

The Unemployed, by John Langley Howard, 1937 In this painting Howard soberly evokes the dispirited state of millions of unemployed Americans during the depression.

song "My God, How the Money Rolls In" was replaced with "Brother, Can You Spare a Dime?"

✵ Hooked on the Horn of Plenty

What caused the Great Depression? One basic explanation is overproduction by both farm and factory. Ironically, the depression of the 1930s was one of abundance, not want. It was the "great glut" or the "plague of plenty."

The nation's ability to produce goods had clearly outrun its capacity to consume or pay for them. Too

The Depression spectacle of want in the shadow of surplus moved an observer to write in Current History *(1932),*

❝We still pray to be given each day our daily bread. Yet there is too much bread, too much wheat and corn, meat and oil and almost every commodity required by man for his subsistence and material happiness. We are not able to purchase the abundance that modern methods of agriculture, mining and manufacture make available in such bountiful quantities. Why is mankind being asked to go hungry and cold and poverty stricken in the midst of plenty?**❞**

much money was going into the hands of a few wealthy people, who in turn invested it in factories and other agencies of production. Not enough was going into salaries and wages, where revitalizing purchasing power could be more quickly felt.

Other maladies were at work. Overexpansion of credit through installment-plan buying overstimulated production. Paying on so-called easy terms caused many consumers to dive in beyond their depth. Normal technological unemployment, resulting from new laborsaving machines, also added its burden to the abnormal unemployment of the "threadbare thirties."

This already bleak picture was further darkened by economic anemia abroad. Britain and the Continent had never fully recovered from the upheaval of World War I. Depression in America was given a further downward push by a chain-reaction financial collapse in Europe, following the failure in 1931 of a prominent Vienna banking house. A drying up of international trade, moreover, had been hastened by the shortsighted Hawley-Smoot Tariff of 1930. European uncertainties over reparations, war debts, and defaults on loans owed to America caused tensions that reacted unfavorably on the United States. Many of these conditions had been created or worsened by Uncle Sam's own narrow-visioned policies, but it was now too late to unscramble the omelet.

As if man-made disasters were not enough, a terrible drought scorched the Mississippi Valley in 1930.

© Bettmann/Corbis

"Hooverville" in Seattle, 1934
In the early years of the depression, desperate, homeless people constructed shacks out of scavenged materials. These shantytowns sprang up in cities across the country.

Thousands of farms were sold at auction for taxes, though in some cases kind neighbors would intimidate prospective buyers, bid one cent, and return the property to its original owner. Farm tenancy or rental—a species of peonage—was spreading at an alarming rate among both whites and blacks.

By 1930 the depression had become a national calamity. Through no fault of their own, a host of industrious citizens had lost everything. They wanted to work—but there was no work. The insidious effect of all this dazed despair on the nation's spirit was incalculable and long-lasting. America's "uniqueness" no longer seemed so unique or its Manifest Destiny so manifest. Hitherto the people had grappled with storms, trees, stones, and other physical obstacles. But the depression was a baffling wraith they could not grasp. Initiative and self-respect were stifled, as panhandlers begged for food or "charity soup." In extreme cases "ragged individualists" slept under "Hoover blankets" (old newspapers), fought over the contents of garbage cans, or cooked their findings in old oil drums in tin-and-paper shantytowns cynically named **Hoovervilles**. The very foundations of America's social and political structure trembled.

✦ Rugged Times for Rugged Individualists

Hoover's exalted reputation as a wonder-worker and efficiency engineer crashed about as dismally as the stock market. He doubtless would have shone in the prosperity-drenched Coolidge years, when he had foreseen the abolition of poverty and poor-houses. But damming the Great Depression proved to be a task beyond his engineering talents.

The perplexed president was impaled on the horns of a cruel dilemma. As a deservedly famed humanitarian, he was profoundly distressed by the widespread misery about him. Yet as a "rugged individualist," deeply rooted in an earlier era of free enterprise, he shrank from the heresy of government handouts. Convinced that industry, thrift, and self-reliance were the virtues that had made America great, President Hoover

Wall Streeter Martin Devries, observing President Herbert Hoover's struggle to keep his footing as the tidal wave of the Great Depression washed over him, decided he was a good man stuck in the wrong place, at the wrong time:

❝Hoover happened to be in a bad spot. The Depression came on, and there he was. If Jesus Christ had been there, he'd have had the same problem. It's too bad for poor old Herbie that he happened to be there. This was a world-wide Depression. It wasn't Hoover's fault. In 1932 . . . , a monkey could have been elected against him, no question about it.❞

Home Relief Station, by Louis Ribak, 1935–1936 Destitute and despairing, millions of hard-working Americans like these had to endure the degradation and humiliation of going on relief as the pall of depression descended over the land.

Whitney Museum of American Art

feared that a government doling out doles would weaken, perhaps destroy, the national fiber.

As the depression nightmare steadily worsened, relief by local government agencies broke down. Hoover was finally forced to turn reluctantly from his doctrine of log-cabin individualism and accept the proposition that the welfare of the people in a nationwide catastrophe is a direct concern of the national government.

The president at last worked out a compromise between the old hands-off philosophy and the "soul-destroying" direct dole then being used in England. He would assist the hard-pressed railroads, banks, and rural credit corporations, in the hope that if financial health were restored at the top of the economic pyramid, unemployment would be relieved at the bottom on a trickle-down basis.

Herbert Hoover (1874–1964) spoke approvingly in a campaign speech in 1928 of "the American system of Rugged Individualism." In 1930 he referred to Cleveland's 1887 veto of a bill to appropriate seed grain for the drought-stricken farmers of Texas:

"I do not believe that the power and duty of the General Government ought to be extended to the relief of individual suffering. . . . The lesson should be constantly enforced that though the people support the Government the Government should not support the people."

Partisan critics sneered at the "Great Humanitarian"—he who had fed the faraway Belgians but would not use federal funds to feed needy Americans. Hostile commentators remarked that he was willing to lend government money to the big bankers, who allegedly had plunged the country into the mess. He would likewise lend money to agricultural organizations to feed pigs—but not people. Pigs, the cynics of the time noted, had no character to undermine.

Much of this criticism was unfair. Although continued suffering seemed to mock the effectiveness of Hoover's measures, his efforts probably prevented a more serious collapse than did occur. And his expenditures for relief, revolutionary for that day, paved the path for the enormous federal outlays of his New Deal successor, Franklin Roosevelt. Hoover proved that the old bootstrap-pulling techniques would no longer work in a crisis of this magnitude, especially when people lacked boots.

★ Hoover Battles the Great Depression

President Hoover, in line with his "trickle-down" philosophy, at last recommended that Congress vote immense sums for useful public works. Though at heart an antispender, he secured from Congress appropriations totaling $2.25 billion for such projects.

Most imposing of the public enterprises was the gigantic Hoover Dam on the Colorado River. Voted by

Lampooning Hoover, 1932

The pages of *The American Pageant* are filled with political cartoons that provide pungent commentary on historical events. With one image rather than many words, a cartoonist can convey a point of view much the way an editorial writer does. This cartoon appeared in the *Washington Daily News* on July 25, 1932, three and a half months before Republican president Hoover lost the presidential election to his Democratic challenger, Franklin D. Roosevelt. The cartoonist foretells Hoover's defeat in November and departure from the White House the following March (not January, as at present) and expresses his support for the Home Loan Bank Bill. With this proposal Hoover sought to come to the aid of home mortgage lenders in order to forestall them from foreclosing on homeowners. The cartoonist jokes that Hoover supported this bill because he identified with homeowners about to lose their homes, but he also cleverly insinuates that Hoover's banking reform was motivated by electoral opportunism. Surely Hoover sought to win public support in return for his new banking program as he battled for reelection, but the Home Loan Bank Bill also reflected Hoover's growing recognition that the federal government had to take direct action to remedy flaws that had precipitated the crisis of the Great Depression. As Hoover later recorded in his memoirs, "All this seems dull economics, but the poignant American drama revolving around the loss of the old homestead had a million repetitions straight from life, not because of the designing villain but because of a fault in our financial system." How does the cartoonist use caricature to make his point? What accounts for the political cartoon's special power? Are there limitations to this genre? Find another cartoon in this book and subject it to similar analysis.

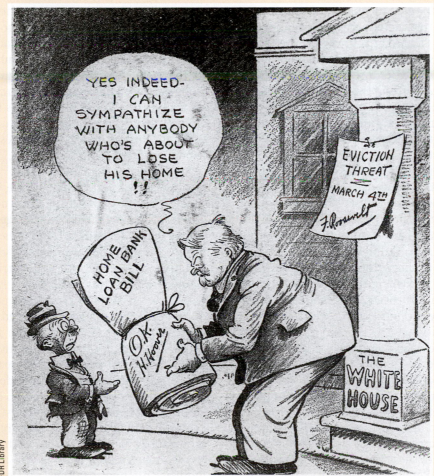

FDR Library

Congress in the days of Coolidge, it was begun in 1930 under Hoover and completed in 1936 under Roosevelt. It succeeded in creating a huge man-made lake for purposes of irrigation, flood control, and electric power.

But Hoover sternly fought all schemes that he regarded as "socialistic." Conspicuous among them was the Muscle Shoals Bill, designed to dam the Tennessee River and ultimately embraced by Franklin Roosevelt's Tennessee Valley Authority. Hoover emphatically vetoed this measure, primarily because he opposed the government's selling electricity in competition with its own citizens in private companies.

Early in 1932 Congress, responding to Hoover's belated appeal, established the **Reconstruction Finance Corporation (RFC)**. With an initial working capital of half a billion dollars, this agency became a government lending bank. It was designed to provide indirect relief by assisting insurance companies, banks, agricultural organizations, railroads, and even hard-pressed state and local governments. But to preserve individualism and character, there would be no loans to individuals from this "billion-dollar soup kitchen."

"Pump-priming" loans by the RFC were no doubt of widespread benefit, though the organization was established many months too late for maximum usefulness. Projects that it supported were largely self-liquidating, and the government as a banker actually profited to the tune of many millions of dollars. Giant corporations so obviously benefited from this assistance that the RFC was dubbed—rather unfairly—"the millionaires' dole." The irony is that the thrifty and individualistic Hoover had sponsored the project, though with initial reluctance. It actually had a strong New Dealish flavor.

Hoover's administration also provided some indirect benefits for labor. After stormy debate, Congress passed the **Norris–La Guardia Anti-Injunction Act** in 1932, and Hoover signed it. The measure outlawed "yellow-dog" (antiunion) contracts and forbade the federal courts to issue injunctions to restrain strikes, boycotts, and peaceful picketing.

The truth is that Herbert Hoover, despite criticism of his "heartlessness," did inaugurate a significant new policy. In previous panics the masses had been forced to "sweat it out." Slow though Hoover was to abandon this nineteenth-century bias, by the end of his term he had started down the road toward government assistance for needy citizens—a road that Franklin Roosevelt would travel much farther.

Hoover's woes were increased by a hostile Congress. At critical times during his first two years, the Republican majority proved highly uncooperative. Friction worsened during his last two years. A depression-cursed electorate, rebelling in the congressional elections of 1930, so reduced the Republican majority that Democrats controlled the new House and almost controlled the Senate. Insurgent Republicans could—and did—combine with opposition Democrats to harass Hoover. Some of the president's troubles were deliberately manufactured by Congress, which, in his words, "played politics with human misery."

✦ Routing the Bonus Army in Washington

Many veterans of World War I were numbered among the hard-hit victims of the depression. Industry had secured a "bonus"—though a dubious one—in the Hawley-Smoot Tariff. So the thoughts of the former soldiers naturally turned to what the government owed them for their services in 1917–1918, when they had "saved" democracy. A drive developed for the premature payment of the deferred bonus voted by Congress in 1924 and payable in 1945.

Thousands of impoverished veterans, both of war and of unemployment, were now prepared to move on Washington, there to demand of Congress the immediate payment of their *entire* bonus. The "Bonus Expeditionary Force" (BEF), which mustered about twenty thousand souls, converged on the capital in the summer of 1932. These supplicants promptly set up unsanitary public camps and erected shacks on vacant lots—a gigantic "Hooverville." They thus created a menace to the public health, while attempting to intimidate Congress by their presence in force. After the pending bonus bill had failed in Congress by a narrow margin, Hoover arranged to pay the return fare of about six thousand bonus marchers. The rest refused to decamp, though ordered to do so.

Following riots that cost two lives, Hoover responded to the demands of the Washington authorities by ordering the army to evacuate the unwanted guests. Although Hoover charged that the **Bonus Army** was led by riffraff and reds, in fact only a sprinkling of them were former convicts and communist agitators. The eviction was carried out by General Douglas MacArthur with bayonets and tear gas, and with far more severity than Hoover had planned. A few of the former soldiers were injured as the torch was put to their pathetic shanties in the inglorious "Battle of Anacostia Flats." An eleven-month-old "bonus baby" allegedly died from exposure to tear gas.

This brutal episode brought down additional abuse on the once-popular Hoover, who by now was the most loudly booed man in the country. The Democrats, not content with Hoover's vulnerable record, employed professional "smear" artists to drive him from office. Cynics sneered that the "Great Engineer" had in a few months "ditched, drained, and damned the country." The existing panic was unfairly branded "the Hoover

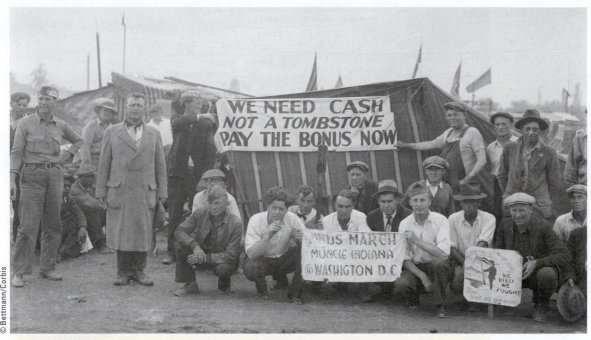

The Bonus Army in Washington, D.C., 1932 World War I veterans from Muncie, Indiana, were among many contingents to set up camp in the capital during the summer of 1932, determined to remain there until they received full payment of their promised bonuses.

depression." In truth, Hoover had been oversold as a wizard, and the public grumbled when his magician's wand failed to produce rabbits. The time was ripening for the Democratic party—and Franklin D. Roosevelt—to cash in on Hoover's calamities.

✦ Japanese Militarists Attack China

The Great Depression, which brewed enough distress at home, added immensely to difficulties abroad. Militaristic Japan stole the Far Eastern spotlight. In September 1931 the Japanese imperialists, noting that the Western world was badly mired in a depression, lunged into Manchuria. Alleging provocation, they rapidly overran the coveted Chinese province and proceeded to bolt shut the Open Door in the conquered area.

America had a strong sentimental stake in China but few significant economic interests. In fact, American commercial ties with Japan far outweighed those with China. Yet most Americans were stunned by this act of naked aggression. It flagrantly violated the League of Nations covenant, as well as various other international agreements solemnly signed by Tokyo, not to mention the American sense of fair play. Indignant Americans, though by no means a majority, urged strong measures ranging from boycotts to blockades. Possibly a tight blockade by the League,

backed by the United States, would have brought Japan sharply to book.

But the League was handicapped in taking two-fisted action by the nonmembership of the United States. Washington flatly rebuffed initial attempts in 1931 to secure American cooperation in applying economic pressure on Japan. Washington and Secretary of State Henry L. Stimson in the end decided to fire only paper bullets at the Japanese aggressors. The so-called Stimson doctrine, proclaimed in 1932, declared that the United States would not recognize any territorial acquisitions achieved by force. Righteous indignation—or a preach-and-run policy—would substitute for solid initiatives.

Hoover later wrote of his differences with Secretary of State Stimson over economic boycotts,

❝I was soon to realize that my able Secretary was at times more of a warrior than a diplomat. To him the phrase 'economic sanctions' was the magic wand of force by which all peace could be summoned from the vasty deep. . . . Ever since Versailles I had held that 'economic sanctions' meant war when applied to any large nation.**❞**

Japanese Aggression in Manchuria This American cartoon lambastes Japan for disregarding international treaty agreements when it seized Manchuria in 1931. The next year the Japanese would set up the puppet state of Manchukuo.

This verbal slap on the wrist from America did not deter the march of the Japanese militarists. Smarting under a Chinese boycott, they bombed Shanghai in 1932, with shocking losses to civilians. Outraged Americans launched informal boycotts of Japanese goods, chiefly dime-store knickknacks. But there was no real sentiment for armed intervention among a depression-ridden people, who remained strongly isolationist during the 1930s.

In a broad sense, collective security died and World War II was born in 1931 on the windswept plains of Manchuria. The League members had the economic and naval power to halt Japan but lacked the courage to act. One reason—though not the only one—was that they could not count on America's support. Even so, the Republic came closer to stepping into the chill waters of internationalism than American prophets would have dared to predict in the early 1920s.

✭ Hoover Pioneers the Good Neighbor Policy

Hoover's arrival in the White House brought a more hopeful turn to relations with America's southern neighbors. The new president was deeply interested in the often-troubled nations below the Rio Grande. Shortly after his election in 1928, he had undertaken a goodwill tour of Latin America—on a U.S. battleship.

World depression softened an age-old aggressive attitude in the United States toward weak Latin neighbors. Following the stock-market collapse of 1929, Americans had less money to invest abroad. As millions of dollars' worth of investments in Latin America went sour, many Yankees felt as though they were more preyed upon than preying. So-called economic imperialism became much less popular in the United States than it had been in the golden twenties.

As an advocate of international goodwill, Hoover strove to abandon the interventionist twist given to the Monroe Doctrine by Theodore Roosevelt. In 1932 he negotiated a new treaty with the French-speaking Republic of Haiti, and this pact, later supplanted by an executive agreement, provided for the complete withdrawal of American platoons by 1934. Further pleasing omens came early in 1933, when the last marine "leathernecks" sailed away from Nicaragua after an almost continuous stay of some twenty years.

Herbert Hoover, the engineer in politics, thus happily engineered the foundation stones of the Good Neighbor policy. Upon them rose an imposing edifice in the days of his successor, Franklin Roosevelt.

Chapter Review

KEY TERMS

Adkins v. *Children's Hospital* (729)

Nine-Power Treaty (731)

Kellogg-Briand Pact (732)

Fordney-McCumber Tariff Law (732)

Teapot Dome scandal (733)

McNary-Haugen Bill (735)

Dawes Plan (737)

Agricultural Marketing Act (740)

Hawley-Smoot Tariff (740)

Black Tuesday (740)

Hoovervilles (743)

Reconstruction Finance Corporation (RFC) (746)

Norris–La Guardia Anti-Injunction Act (746)

Bonus Army (746)

PEOPLE TO KNOW

Bonus Army

Warren G. Harding

Albert B. Fall

Calvin Coolidge

John W. Davis

Robert M. ("Fighting Bob") La Follette

Albert E. Smith

CHRONOLOGY

1919	American Legion founded
	Chicago race riot
1920	Esch-Cummins Transportation Act
	Merchant Marine Act
1921	Veterans Bureau created
	Capper-Volstead Act
1922	Five-Power Naval Treaty signed
	Four-Power and Nine-Power Treaties on the Far East
	Fordney-McCumber Tariff Law
1923	*Adkins* v. *Children's Hospital*
	Teapot Dome scandal
	Harding dies; Coolidge assumes presidency
1924	Adjusted Compensation Act for veterans
	Dawes Plan for international finance
	U.S. troops leave Dominican Republic
	Coolidge wins three-way presidential election

1926	U.S. troops occupy Nicaragua
1928	Kellogg-Briand Pact
	Hoover defeats Smith for presidency
	Hoover makes goodwill tour of Latin America
1929	Agricultural Marketing Act sets up Federal Farm Board
	Stock-market crash
1930	Hawley-Smoot Tariff
1931	Japanese invade Manchuria
1932	Reconstruction Finance Corporation (RFC) established
	Norris–La Guardia Anti-Injunction Act
	"Bonus Army" dispersed from Washington, D.C.

TO LEARN MORE

Liaquat Ahamed, *Lords of Finance: The Bankers Who Broke the World* (2009)

Michael A. Bernstein, *The Great Depression: Delayed Recovery and Economic Change in America, 1929–1939* (1987)

John D. Hicks, *Republican Ascendancy, 1921–1933* (1960)

Robert McElvaine, *The Great Depression: America, 1929–1941* (rev. ed., 1993)

Burl Noggle, *Into the Twenties: The United States from Armistice to Normalcy* (1974)

Emily Rosenberg, *Financial Missionaries to the World: The Politics and Culture of Dollar Diplomacy, 1900–1930* (1999)

Peter Temin, *Did Monetary Factors Cause the Great Depression?* (1976)

Joan Hoff Wilson, *American Business and Foreign Policy, 1920–1933* (1971)

———, *Herbert Hoover, Forgotten Progressive* (1975)

Robert H. Zieger, *American Workers, American Unions, 1920–1985* (1986)

A complete, annotated bibliography for this chapter—along with brief descriptions of the People to Know—may be found on the American Pageant website. The Key Terms are defined in a Glossary at the end of the text.

Go to the CourseMate website at **www.cengagebrain.com** for additional study tools and review materials—including audio and video clips—for this chapter.

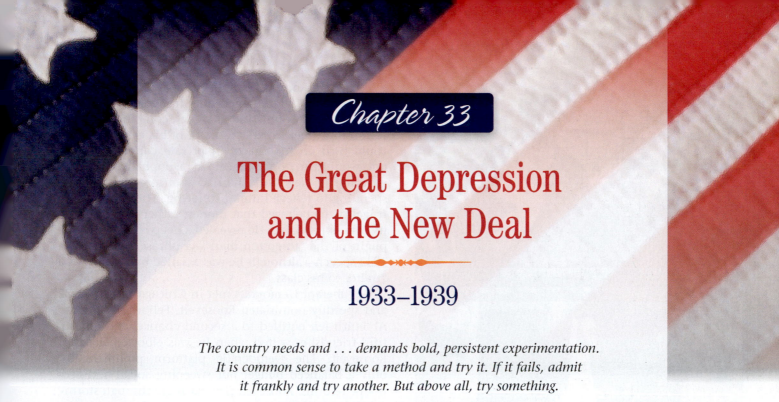

Chapter 33

The Great Depression and the New Deal

1933–1939

*The country needs and . . . demands bold, persistent experimentation.
It is common sense to take a method and try it. If it fails, admit
it frankly and try another. But above all, try something.*

FRANKLIN D. ROOSEVELT, CAMPAIGN SPEECH, 1932

*V*oters were in an ugly mood as the presidential campaign of 1932 neared. Countless factory chimneys remained ominously cold, while more than 11 million unemployed workers and their families sank ever deeper into the pit of poverty. Herbert Hoover may have won the 1928 election by promising "a chicken in every pot," but three years later that chicken seemed to have laid a discharge slip in every pay envelope.

Hoover, sick at heart, was renominated by the Republican convention in Chicago without great enthusiasm. The platform indulged in extravagant praise of Republican antidepression policies, while half-heartedly promising to repeal national prohibition and return control of liquor to the states.

The rising star of the Democratic firmament was Governor Franklin Delano Roosevelt of New York, a fifth cousin of Theodore Roosevelt. Like the Rough Rider, he had been born to a wealthy New York family, had graduated from Harvard, had been elected as a kid-gloved politician to the New York legislature, had served as governor of the Empire State, had been nominated for the vice presidency (though not elected), and had served capably as assistant secretary of the navy. Although both men were master politicians, adept with the colorful phrase, TR was pugnacious and confrontational, while FDR was suave and conciliatory—qualities that appealed strongly to a people traumatized by one of the greatest crises in American history.

✦ FDR: Politician in a Wheelchair

Infantile paralysis, while putting steel braces on Franklin Roosevelt's legs, put additional steel into his soul. Until 1921, when the dread disease struck, young Roosevelt—tall (six feet two inches), athletic, and handsome—impressed observers as charming and witty, yet at times as a superficial and arrogant "lightweight." But suffering humbled him to the level of common clay. In courageously fighting his way back from complete helplessness to a hobbling mobility, he schooled himself in patience, tolerance, compassion, and strength of will. He once remarked that after trying for two years to wiggle one big toe, all else seemed easy.

Another of Roosevelt's great personal and political assets was his wife, Eleanor. The niece of Theodore Roosevelt, she was Franklin Roosevelt's distant cousin as well as his spouse. Tall, ungainly, and toothy, she overcame the misery of an unhappy childhood and emerged as a champion of the dispossessed—and, ultimately, as the "conscience of the New Deal." FDR's political career was as much hers as it was his own. She traveled countless miles with him or on his behalf in all his campaigns, beginning with his run for the New York legislature before World War I, later considering herself "his legs." But Mrs. Roosevelt also marched to her own drummer. As a young woman she had worked in a New York settlement house, and later on she joined

AP Images

Eleanor Roosevelt (1884–1962) Roosevelt was America's most active First Lady and commanded enormous popularity and influence during FDR's presidency. Here she emerges, miner's cap in hand, from an Ohio coal mine.

the Women's Trade Union League (see p. 645) and the League of Women Voters. When she and Franklin moved into the White House, she brought an unprecedented number of women activists with her to Washington. This network of reformers helped make her the most active First Lady in history.

Through her lobbying of her husband, her speeches, and her syndicated newspaper column, Eleanor Roosevelt powerfully influenced the policies of the national government. Always she battled for the impoverished and the oppressed. At one meeting in Birmingham, Alabama, she confounded local authorities and flouted the segregation statutes by deliberately straddling the aisle separating the black and white seating sections. Sadly, her personal relationship with her husband was often rocky, due to his infidelities. Condemned by conservatives and loved by liberals, she was one of the most controversial—and consequential—public figures of the twentieth century.

Franklin Roosevelt's political appeal was amazing. His commanding presence and his golden speaking voice, despite a sophisticated accent, combined to make him the premier American orator of his generation. He could turn on his charm in private conversations as one would turn on a faucet. As a popular depression governor of New York, he had sponsored heavy state spending to relieve human suffering. Though favoring frugality, he believed that money, rather than humanity, was expendable. He revealed a deep concern for the plight of the "forgotten man"—a phrase he used in a 1932 speech—although he was assailed by the rich as a "traitor to his class."

Exuberant Democrats met in Chicago in June 1932 and speedily nominated Roosevelt. Fellow New Yorker Al Smith felt entitled to a second chance, and a beautiful friendship wilted when he was elbowed aside for Roosevelt. The Democratic platform promised not only a balanced budget but sweeping social and economic reforms. Roosevelt flew daringly through stormy weather to Chicago, where he smashed precedent by accepting the nomination in person. He electrified the delegates and the public with these words: "I pledge you, I pledge myself to a new deal for the American people."

★ Presidential Hopefuls of 1932

In the campaign that followed, Roosevelt seized the offensive with a slashing attack on the Republican Old Dealers. He was especially eager to prove that he was not an invalid ("Roosevelt Is Robust") and to display his magnificent torso and radiant personality to as many voters as possible.

Roosevelt consistently preached a New Deal for the "forgotten man," but he was annoyingly vague and somewhat contradictory. Many of his speeches were "ghostwritten" by the "Brains Trust" (popularly the **Brain Trust**), a small group of reform-minded intellectuals. They were predominantly youngish college professors who, as a kind of kitchen cabinet, later

In his successful campaign for the governorship of New York in 1928, Franklin Roosevelt (1882–1945) had played down alleged Democratic "socialism":

"We often hear it said that government operation of anything under the sun is socialistic. If that is so, our postal service is socialistic, so is the parcel post which has largely taken the place of the old express companies; so are the public highways which took the place of the toll roads."

authored much of the **New Deal** legislation. Roosevelt rashly promised a balanced budget and berated heavy Hooverian deficits, amid cries of "Throw the Spenders Out!" and "Out of the Red with Roosevelt." All of this was to make ironic reading in later months.

The high spirits of the Democrats found expression in the catchy air "Happy Days Are Here Again." This theme song fit FDR's indestructible smile, his jauntily angled cigarette holder, his breezy optimism, and his promises to do something, even at the risk of bold experimentation.

Grim-faced Herbert Hoover remained in the White House, conscientiously battling the depression through short lunches and long hours. Out on the firing line, his supporters halfheartedly assured half-listening voters, "The Worst Is Past," "It Might Have Been Worse,"

and "Prosperity Is Just Around the Corner." Hoover never ceased to insist that the uncertainty and fear produced by Roosevelt's impending victory plunged the nation deeper into the depression.

With the campaign going badly for the Republicans, a weary and despondent Hoover was persuaded to take to the stump. He stoutly reaffirmed his faith in American free enterprise and individual initiative, and gloomily predicted that if the Hawley-Smoot Tariff was repealed, grass would grow "in the streets of a hundred cities." Such down-at-the-mouthism contrasted sharply with Roosevelt's tooth-flashing optimism and sparkling promises.

✵ Hoover's Humiliation in 1932

Hoover had been swept into office on the rising tide of prosperity; he was swept out of office by the receding tide of depression. The flood of votes totaled 22,809,638 for Roosevelt and 15,758,901 for Hoover; the electoral count stood at 472 to 59. In all, the loser carried only six rock-ribbed Republican states.

One striking feature of the election was the beginning of a distinct shift of blacks, traditionally grateful to the Republican party of Lincoln, over to the Roosevelt camp. As the "last hired and first fired," black Americans had been among the worst sufferers from the depression. Beginning with the election of 1932, they became, notably in the great urban centers of the North, a vital element in the Democratic party.

Hard times unquestionably ruined the Republicans, for the electoral upheaval in 1932 was as much anti-Hoover as it was pro-Roosevelt. Democrats had only to harness the national grudge and let it pull them to victory. An overwhelming majority of Democrats appear to have voiced a demand for change: *a* new deal rather than *the* New Deal, for the latter was only a gleam in the eyes of its sponsors. Any upstanding Democratic candidate probably could have won.

The preinauguration lame duck period now ground slowly to an end. Hoover, though defeated and repudiated, continued to be president for four long months, until March 4, 1933. But he was helpless to embark upon any long-range policies without the cooperation of Roosevelt—and the victorious president-elect proved rather uncooperative. Hoover at length succeeded in arranging two meetings with him to discuss the war-debt muddle. But Roosevelt, who airily remarked to the press, "It's not my baby," fought shy of assuming responsibility without authority. As Hoover privately confessed, he was trying to bind his successor to an anti-inflationary policy that would have made impossible many of the later New Deal experiments. But in politics the winner, not the loser, calls the tune.

FDR Library

The Vanquished and the Victor   A dour Hoover and an ebullient Roosevelt ride to the inauguration ceremonies on March 4, 1933. This magazine cover was never published, presumably because of the editors' sensitivity about the attempted assassination of Roosevelt when he was riding in an open car in Florida on February 15, 1933, less than three weeks earlier. The attempt on Roosevelt's life ended in the death of Chicago mayor Anton J. Cermak.

With Washington deadlocked, the vast and vaunted American economic machine clanked to a virtual halt. One worker in four tramped the streets, feet weary and hands idle. Banks were locking their doors all over the nation, as people nervously stuffed paper money under their mattresses. Hooverites, then and later, accused Roosevelt of deliberately permitting the depression to worsen so that he could emerge the more spectacularly as a savior.

✴ FDR and the Three R's: Relief, Recovery, Reform

Great crises often call forth gifted leaders, and the hand of destiny tapped Roosevelt on the shoulder. On a dreary Inauguration Day, March 4, 1933, his vibrant voice, broadcast nationally from a bulletproof stand, provided the American people with inspirational new hope. He denounced the "money changers" who had brought on the calamity and declared that the government must wage war on the Great Depression as it would wage war on an armed foe. His clarion note was

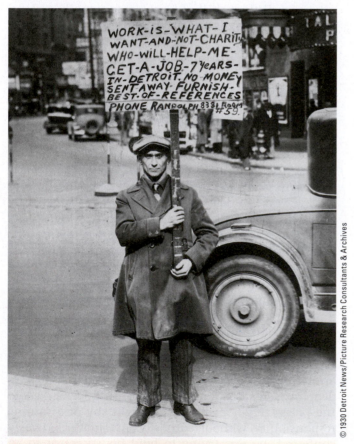

Unemployed and Frustrated Democratic candidate Franklin Roosevelt offered hope, if few concrete plans, to the millions struggling to cope with the Great Depression.

One Chinese observer of America, No-Yong Park (1899–1976), born in Manchuria and educated in the United States, remained optimistic about America even in the depths of the Great Depression. He wrote in An Oriental View of American Civilization *(1934),*

❝Of all the peoples of the world, Americans, to my mind, are the most progressive. They are the ones who live in the future tense. Their mind and soul are always bent for the future. They never move backward and always march forward.❞

"Let me assert my firm belief that the only thing we have to fear is fear itself."

Roosevelt moved decisively. Now that he had full responsibility, he boldly declared a nationwide banking holiday, March 6–10, as a prelude to opening the banks on a sounder basis. He then summoned the overwhelmingly Democratic Congress into special session to cope with the national emergency. For the so-called **Hundred Days** (March 9–June 16, 1933), members hastily cranked out an unprecedented basketful of remedial legislation (see Table 33.1). Some of it derived from earlier progressivism, but these new measures mostly sought to deal with a desperate emergency.

Roosevelt's New Deal programs aimed at three R's—relief, recovery, and reform. Short-range goals were relief and immediate recovery, especially in the first two years. Long-range goals were permanent recovery and reform of current abuses, particularly those that had produced the boom-or-bust catastrophe. The three-R objectives often overlapped and got in one another's way. But amid all the topsy-turvy haste, the gigantic New Deal program lurched forward.

Firmly ensconced in the driver's seat, President Roosevelt cracked the whip. A green Congress so fully shared the panicky feeling of the country that it was ready to rubber-stamp bills drafted by White House advisers—measures that Roosevelt called "must legislation." More than that, Congress gave the president extraordinary blank-check powers: some of the laws it passed expressly delegated legislative authority to the chief executive. One senator complained that if FDR asked Congress "to commit suicide tomorrow, they'd do it."

Roosevelt was delighted to exert executive leadership, and Congress responded to it, although he did not always know precisely where he was going. He was inclined to do things by intuition—off the cuff. He was like the quarterback, as he put it, whose next play depends on the outcome of the previous play. So desperate was the mood of an action-starved public that

TABLE 33.1 Principal New Deal Acts During the Hundred Days Congress, 1933* (items in parentheses indicate secondary purposes)

Recovery	Relief	Reform
FDR closes banks, March 6, 1933		
Emergency Banking Relief Act, March 9, 1933		
(Beer Act)	(Beer Act)	Beer and Wine Revenue Act, March 22, 1933
(CCC)	Unemployment Relief Act, March 31, 1933, creates Civilian Conservation Corps (CCC)	
FDR orders gold surrender, April 5, 1933		
FDR abandons gold standard, April 19, 1933		
(FERA)	Federal Emergency Relief Act, May 12, 1933, creates Federal Emergency Relief Administration (FERA)	
(AAA)	Agricultural Adjustment Act (AAA), May 12, 1933	
(TVA)	(TVA)	Tennessee Valley Authority Act (TVA), May 18, 1933
		Federal Securities Act, May 27, 1933
Gold-payment clause repealed, June 5, 1933		
(HOLC)	Home Owners' Refinancing Act, June 13, 1933, creates Home Owners' Loan Corporation (HOLC)	
National Industrial Recovery Act, June 16, 1933, creates National Recovery Administration (NRA), Public Works Administration (PWA)	(NRA, PWA)	(NRA)
(Glass-Steagall Act)	(Glass-Steagall Act)	Glass-Steagall Banking Reform Act, June 16, 1933, creates Federal Deposit Insurance Corporation

*For later New Deal measures, see p. 758.

any movement, even in the wrong direction, seemed better than no movement at all.

The frantic Hundred Days Congress passed many essentials of the New Deal "three R's," though important long-range measures were added in later sessions. These reforms owed much to the legacy of the pre–World War I progressive movement. Many of them were long overdue, sidetracked by the war in Europe and the Old Guard reaction of the 1920s. In an explosive burst of pent-up energy, New Dealers raided file cabinets full of old pamphlets on German social insurance, English housing and garden cities, Danish agricultural recovery, and American World War I collectivization. In time they embraced progressive ideas such as unemployment insurance, old-age insurance, minimum-wage regulations, the conservation and development of natural resources, and restrictions on child labor. They also invented some new schemes, such as the Tennessee Valley Authority (see p. 765). Soon depression-weary Europeans would come to the United States to marvel at the exciting din of reform activity under way. No longer would America look as backward in the realm of social welfare as it once had.

✴ Roosevelt Manages the Money

Banking chaos cried aloud for immediate action. Congress pulled itself together and in an incredible eight hours had the Emergency Banking Relief Act of 1933 ready for Roosevelt's busy pen. The new law invested the president with the power to regulate banking transactions and foreign exchange and to reopen solvent banks.

Roosevelt, the master showman, next turned to the radio to deliver the first of his thirty famous "fireside chats." As some 35 million people hung on his soothing

The Champ: FDR Chatting with Reporters Roosevelt mastered the press as few presidents before or since have been able to do. He was also ingenious in finding opportunities to converse with reporters in situations where he could conceal his physical limitations.

words, he gave assurances that it was now safer to keep money in a reopened bank than "under the mattress." Confidence returned with a gush, and the banks began to unlock their doors.

The Hundred Days, or Emergency, Congress buttressed public reliance on the banking system by enacting the memorable **Glass-Steagall Banking Reform Act**. This measure provided for the Federal Deposit Insurance Corporation, which insured individual deposits up to $5,000 (later raised). Thus ended the disgraceful epidemic of bank failures, which dated back to the "wildcat" days of Andrew Jackson (see Figure 33.1).*

Roosevelt moved swiftly elsewhere on the financial front, seeking to protect the melting gold reserves and to prevent panicky hoarding. He ordered all private holdings of gold to be surrendered to the Treasury in exchange for paper currency and then took the nation off the gold standard. The Emergency Congress responded to his recommendation by canceling the gold-payment clause in all contracts and authorizing repayment in paper money. A "managed currency" was well on its way.

*When FDR was inaugurated in 1933, not a single Canadian bank had failed.

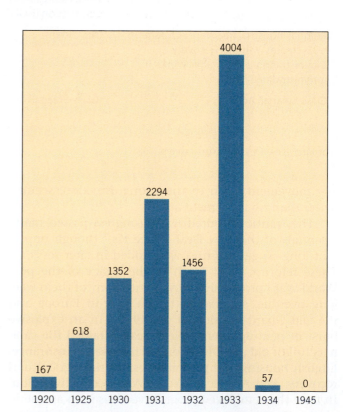

FIGURE 33.1 **Bank Failures Before and After the Glass-Steagall Banking Reform Act of 1933**

The goal of Roosevelt's "managed currency" was inflation, which he believed would relieve debtors' burdens and stimulate new production. Roosevelt's principal instrument for achieving inflation was gold buying. He instructed the Treasury to purchase gold at increasing prices, ratcheting the dollar price of gold up from $21 an ounce in 1933 to $35 an ounce in early 1934, a price that held for nearly four decades. This policy did increase the amount of dollars in circulation, as holders of gold cashed it in at the elevated prices. But this inflationary result also provoked the wrath of "sound-money" critics, who gagged on the "baloney dollar." The gold-buying scheme came to an end in February 1934, when FDR returned the nation to a limited gold standard for purposes of international trade only. Thereafter (until 1971—see p. 922), the United States pledged itself to pay foreign bills, if requested, in gold at the rate of one ounce of gold for every $35 due. But domestic circulation of gold continued to be prohibited, and gold coins became collectors' items.

✴ Creating Jobs for the Jobless

Overwhelming unemployment, even more than banking, clamored for prompt remedial action. One out of every four workers was jobless when FDR took his inaugural oath—the highest level of unemployment in the nation's history, before or since. Roosevelt had no hesitancy about using federal money to assist the unemployed and at the same time to "prime the pump" of industrial recovery. (A farmer has to pour a little water into a dry pump—that is, "prime it"—to start the flow.)

The Hundred Days Congress responded to Roosevelt's spurs when it created the **Civilian Conservation Corps (CCC)**, which proved to be perhaps the most popular of all the New Deal "alphabetical agencies." This law provided employment in fresh-air government camps for about 3 million uniformed young men, many of whom might otherwise have

© Bettmann/Corbis

CCC Workers in Alaska, 1939 These Tlingit carvers in Alaska's southeastern panhandle were part of a CCC project to restore totem poles. Here they stand with a pole carved in the likeness of Abraham Lincoln.

One desperate man wrote to a newspaper in 1932,

"I am forty-eight; married twenty-one years; four children, three in school. For the last eight years I was employed as a Pullman conductor. Since September, 1930, they have given me seven months part-time work. Today I am an object of charity. . . . My small, weak, and frail wife and two small children are suffering and I have come to that terrible place where I could easily resort to violence in my desperation.**"**

been driven by desperation into criminal habits. Their work was useful—including reforestation, firefighting (forty-seven lost their lives), flood control, and swamp drainage. The recruits were required to help their parents by sending home most of their pay. Both human resources and natural resources were thus conserved, though there were minor complaints of "militarizing" the nation's youth. Critics charged that CCC "soldiers" would later claim pensions for exposure to poison ivy.

The first major effort of the new Congress to grapple with the millions of adult unemployed was the Federal Emergency Relief Act. Its chief aim was immediate relief rather than long-range recovery. The resulting Federal Emergency Relief Administration (FERA) was handed over to zealous Harry L. Hopkins, a painfully thin, shabbily dressed, chain-smoking New York social worker who had earlier won Roosevelt's friendship and who became one of his most influential advisers. Hopkins's agency in all granted about $3 billion to the

TABLE 33.2 Later Major New Deal Measures, 1933–1939 (items in parentheses indicate secondary purposes)

Recovery	Relief	Reform
(CWA)	FDR establishes Civil Works Administration (CWA), November 9, 1933	
Gold Reserve Act, January 30, 1934, authorizes FDR's devaluation, January 31, 1934		
		Securities and Exchange Commission (SEC) authorized by Congress, June 6, 1934
(Reciprocal Trade Agreements Act)	(Reciprocal Trade Agreements Act)	Reciprocal Trade Agreements Act, June 12, 1934 (see p. 780)
		Indian Reorganization Act, June 18, 1934
(FHA)	National Housing Act, June 28, 1934, authorizes Federal Housing Administration (FHA)	(FHA)
(Frazier-Lemke Act)	Frazier-Lemke Farm Bankruptcy Act, June 28, 1934	
(Resettlement Administration)	FDR creates Resettlement Administration, April 30, 1935	
(WPA)	FDR creates Works Progress Administration (WPA), May 6, 1935, under act of April 8, 1935	
(Wagner Act)	(Wagner Act)	Wagner Act (National Labor Relations Act), July 5, 1935
		Social Security Act, August 14, 1935
		Public Utility Holding Company Act, August 26, 1935
(Soil Conservation Act)	Soil Conservation and Domestic Allotment Act, February 29, 1936	
(USHA)	(USHA)	United States Housing Authority (USHA) established by Congress, September 1, 1937
(Second AAA)	Second Agricultural Adjustment Act, February 16, 1938	
(Fair Labor Standards Act)	(Fair Labor Standards Act)	Fair Labor Standards Act (Wages and Hours Bill), June 25, 1938
		Reorganization Act, April 3, 1939
		Hatch Act, August 2, 1939

states for direct dole payments or preferably for wages on work projects.*

Immediate relief was also given to two large and hard-pressed special groups by the Hundred Days Congress. One section of the Agricultural Adjustment Act (AAA) made available many millions of dollars to help farmers meet their mortgages. Another law created the Home Owners' Loan Corporation (HOLC). Designed to refinance mortgages on nonfarm homes, it ultimately assisted about a million badly pinched households. The agency not only bailed out mortgage-holding banks, it also bolted the political loyalties of relieved middle-class homeowners securely to the Democratic party.

Harassed by the continuing plague of unemployment, FDR himself established the Civil Works Administration (CWA) late in 1933 (see Table 33.2). As a branch of the FERA, it also fell under the direction of

---

*A boast attributed to Hopkins in 1938 was "We will spend and spend, tax and tax, and elect and elect."

Hopkins. Designed to provide purely temporary jobs during the cruel winter emergency, it served a useful purpose. Tens of thousands of jobless were employed at leaf raking and other make-work tasks, which were dubbed "boondoggling." As this kind of labor put a premium on shovel-leaning slow motion, the scheme was widely criticized. "The only thing we have to fear," scoffers remarked, "is work itself."

✴ A Day for Every Demagogue

Direct relief from Washington to needy families helped pull the nation through the ghastly winter of 1933–1934. But the disheartening persistence of unemployment and suffering demonstrated that emergency relief measures had to be not only continued but supplemented. One danger signal was the appearance of various demagogues, notably a magnetic "microphone messiah," Father Charles Coughlin, a Catholic priest in Michigan who began broadcasting in 1930 and whose slogan was "Social Justice." His anti–New Deal harangues to some 40 million radio fans finally became so anti-Semitic, fascistic, and demagogic that he was silenced in 1942 by his ecclesiastical superiors.

Also notorious among the new brood of agitators were those who capitalized on popular discontent to make pie-in-the-sky promises. Most conspicuous

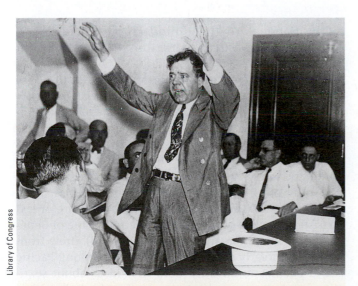

Library of Congress

Huey Long (1893–1935) Long pursued progressive policies as governor of Louisiana, even while he ruled the state with a dictatorial hand. A flamboyant and unpredictable populist, he set the orthodox political establishment on its ear, especially after he became a U.S. senator in 1930. Long's admirers called him the "Kingfish"; Franklin Roosevelt called him "one of the two most dangerous men in the country." (The other, said Roosevelt, was General Douglas MacArthur.)

In 1935 Father Charles Coughlin (1891–1979) single-handedly defeated President Roosevelt's effort to win Senate ratification of a treaty providing for American membership in the World Court, a judicial body of limited authority established by the League of Nations. What FDR saw as a symbolic embrace of international responsibility Coughlin convinced his radio listeners was a conspiracy of international moneyed interests against American sovereignty:

> **"**Our thanks are due to Almighty God in that America retains her sovereignty. Congratulations to the aroused people of the United States who, by more than 200,000 telegrams containing at least 1,000,000 names, demanded that the principles established by Washington and Jefferson shall keep us clear from foreign entanglements and European hatreds.**"**

of these individuals were Dr. Francis E. Townsend, a retired California physician who promised everyone over sixty $200 a month, and Senator Huey P. ("Kingfish") Long of Louisiana, who was said to have more brass than a government mule. He used his abundant rabble-rousing talents to publicize his "Share Our Wealth" program, which promised to make "Every Man a King." Every family was to receive $5,000, supposedly at the expense of the prosperous. H. L. Mencken called Long's chief lieutenant, former clergyman Gerald L. K. Smith, "the gutsiest, goriest, loudest and lustiest, the deadliest and damndest orator ever heard on this or any other earth, the champion boob-bumper of all time." Fear of Long's becoming a fascist dictator ended when he was shot by an assassin in the Louisiana state capitol in 1935.

Father Coughlin and Huey Long frightened many Americans because they raised troubling questions about the link between fascism and economic crisis. Danger seemed to be lurking ominously in many corners of the world. Authoritarian rule was strengthening in Japan, while Adolf Hitler was acquiring absolute authority in Germany. Some even worried that Franklin Roosevelt himself would turn into a dictator.

Partly to quiet the groundswell of unrest that might lead to a political explosion, Congress authorized the Works Progress Administration (WPA) in 1935. The objective was employment on useful projects. Launched under the supervision of the ailing but energetic Hopkins, this remarkable agency ultimately spent about $11 billion on thousands of public buildings, bridges, and hard-surfaced roads. Not every WPA project strengthened the infrastructure: for instance, one controlled crickets in Wyoming, while another

WPA Mural, by Victor Arnautoff (1896–1979), 1934 *The Pedestrian Scene*, painted on a wall of Coit Tower in San Francisco, was one of a series of murals commissioned by the federal government to employ artists during the Great Depression.

built a monkey pen in Oklahoma City. John Steinbeck, future Nobel Prize novelist, counted dogs in his California county. One of the most well-loved WPA programs was the Federal Art Project, which hired artists to create posters and murals—many still adorning post office walls. Critics sneered that WPA meant "We Provide Alms." But the fact is that over a period of eight years, nearly 9 million people were given jobs, not handouts. The WPA nourished much precious talent, preserved self-respect, and fostered the creation of more than a million pieces of art, many of them publicly displayed.

✸ New Visibility for Women

Just over a decade after the ratification of the Nineteenth Amendment, American women began to carve a larger space for themselves in the nation's political and intellectual life. First Lady Eleanor Roosevelt may have been the most visible woman in the Roosevelt White House, but she was hardly the only female voice. Secretary of Labor Frances Perkins (1880–1965) burst through the gender barrier when she became America's first woman cabinet member. Mary McLeod Bethune (1875–1955), director of the Office of Minority Affairs

in the National Youth Administration, served as the highest-ranking African American in the Roosevelt administration.

Women also made important contributions in the social sciences, especially in the relatively new and open field of anthropology. Ruth Benedict (1887–1948) carried on the work of her mentor, Franz Boas (1858–1942), by developing the "culture and personality movement" in the 1930s and 1940s. Benedict's landmark work, *Patterns of Culture* (1934), established the study of cultures as collective personalities. Each culture, like each individual, had its own "more or less consistent pattern of thought and action." One of Benedict's students, Margaret Mead (1901–1978), drew from her own scholarly studies of adolescence among Pacific island peoples to advance bold new ideas about sexuality, gender roles, and intergenerational relationships. With thirty-four books and a curatorship at the American Museum of Natural History in New York City to her credit, Mead helped popularize cultural anthropology and achieved a celebrity status rare among social scientists.

Pearl S. Buck (1892–1973) won similar acclaim as a novelist. Raised in China by Presbyterian missionary parents, Buck introduced American readers to Chinese

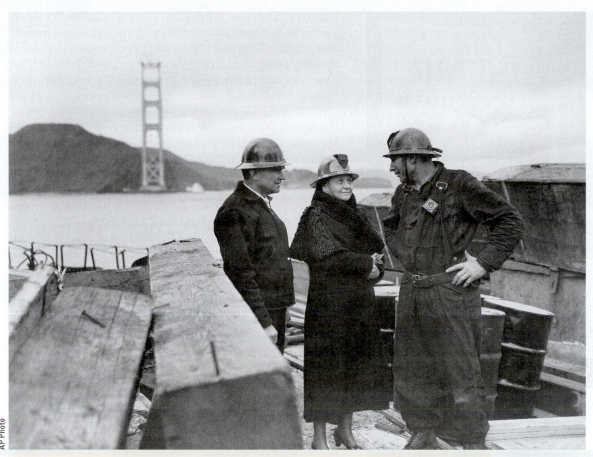

AP Photo

Frances Perkins (1880–1965) at the Site of the Golden Gate Bridge Project, 1935 The first woman cabinet member, Perkins served as secretary of labor under Roosevelt. She was subjected to much undeserved criticism from male businessmen, laborites, and politicians. They sneered that FDR "kept her in labor" for many years.

peasant society. Her best-selling novel, *The Good Earth* (1931), earned her the Nobel Prize for literature in 1938, making her the third American (after Sinclair Lewis and Eugene O'Neill) to win the award. A prolific author all her life, Buck also used her fame to advance humanitarian causes.

✴ Helping Industry and Labor

A daring attempt to stimulate a nationwide comeback was initiated when the Emergency Congress authorized the **National Recovery Administration (NRA)**. This ingenious scheme was by far the most complex and far-reaching effort by the New Dealers to combine immediate relief with long-range recovery and reform. Triple-barreled, it was designed to assist industry, labor, and the unemployed.

Individual industries—over two hundred in all—were to work out codes of "fair competition," under which hours of labor would be reduced so that

employment could be spread over more people. A ceiling was placed on the maximum hours of labor; a floor was placed under wages to establish minimum levels.

Labor, under the NRA, was granted additional benefits. Workers were formally guaranteed the right to organize and bargain collectively through representatives *of their own choosing*—not through handpicked agents of the company's choosing. The hated "yellow-dog," or antiunion, contract was expressly forbidden, and certain safeguarding restrictions were placed on the use of child labor.

Industrial recovery through the NRA's "fair competition" codes would at best be painful, for these called for self-denial by both management and labor. Patriotism was aroused by mass meetings and monster parades, which included 200,000 marchers on New York City's Fifth Avenue. A handsome blue eagle was designed as the symbol of the NRA, and merchants subscribing to a code displayed it in their windows with the slogan "We Do Our Part." A newly formed professional football team was christened the Philadelphia

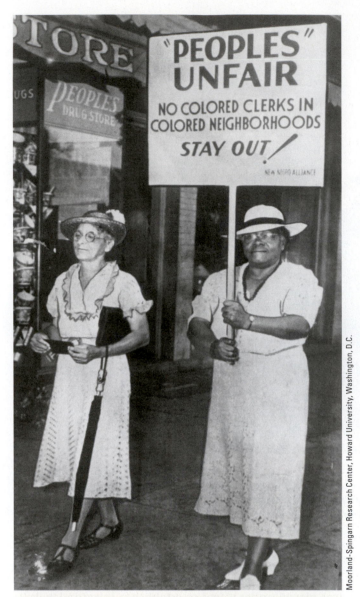

Mary McLeod Bethune (1875–1955) The daughter of ex-slaves and founder of a college in Florida, Bethune became the highest-ranking African American in the Roosevelt administration when she was appointed director of the Office of Minority Affairs in the National Youth Administration (NYA). From this base she organized the "Black Cabinet" to make sure blacks benefited from the New Deal programs along with whites. Here she is picketing against segregated hiring practices at the Peoples Drug Store chain, one of the earliest targets of the black civil rights movement.

Moorland-Spingarn Research Center, Howard University, Washington, D.C.

industry, and the public for such a scheme to work. Critics began to brand the NRA "National Run Around" and "Nuts Running America," symbolized by what Henry Ford called "that damn Roosevelt buzzard." A new "age of chiselry" dawned as certain unscrupulous businesspeople ("chiselers") publicly displayed the blue bird in their windows but secretly violated the codes. Complete collapse was imminent when, in 1935, the Supreme Court shot down the dying eagle in the famed *Schechter* "sick chicken" decision. The learned justices unanimously held that Congress could not "delegate legislative powers" to the executive. They further declared that congressional control of interstate commerce could not properly apply to a local fowl business, like that of the Schechter brothers in Brooklyn, New York. Roosevelt was incensed by this "horse and buggy" interpretation of the Constitution, but actually the Court helped him out of a bad jam.

The same act of Congress that hatched the NRA eagle also authorized the Public Works Administration (PWA), likewise intended both for industrial recovery and for unemployment relief. The agency was headed by the secretary of the interior, acid-tongued Harold L. Ickes, a free-swinging former bull mooser. Long-range recovery was the primary purpose of the new agency, and in time over $4 billion was spent on some thirty-four thousand projects, which included public buildings, highways, and parkways. One spectacular achievement was the Grand Coulee Dam on the Columbia River—the largest structure erected by humans since the Great Wall of China. In the depths of the depression, the grand dam seemed the height of folly. It made possible the irrigation of millions of acres of new farmland—at a time when the government was desperately trying to reduce farm surpluses. It created more electrical power than the entire Tennessee Valley Authority—in a region with little industry and virtually no market for additional power. But with the outbreak of World War II and then postwar prosperity, the dam would come to seem a stroke of genius, transforming the entire region with abundant water and power.

Special stimulants aided the recovery of one segment of business—the liquor industry. The imminent repeal of the prohibition amendment afforded an opportunity to raise needed federal revenue and at the same time to provide a measure of employment. Prodded by Roosevelt, the Hundred Days Congress, in one of its earliest acts, legalized light wine and beer with an alcoholic content (presumably nonintoxicating) not exceeding 3.2 percent by weight, and levied a tax of $5 on every barrel so manufactured. Disgruntled drys, unwilling to acknowledge the breakdown of law and order begotten by bootlegging, damned Roosevelt as "a 3.2 percent American." Prohibition was officially

Eagles. Such was the enthusiasm for the NRA that for a brief period, there was a marked upswing in business activity, although Roosevelt had warned, "We cannot ballyhoo our way to prosperity."

But the high-flying eagle gradually fluttered to earth. Too much self-sacrifice was expected of labor,

Grand Coulee Dam on the Columbia River, Washington State The Grand Coulee Dam was one of the most ambitious projects of the New Deal's Public Works Administration. It is one of the few man-made constructions visible from outer space, the largest concrete structure in the United States, and the central facility in the Columbia Basin Project, which generates electricity for the Pacific Northwest and provides irrigation for half a million acres of Columbia Valley farmland—services that have transformed the life of the region.

repealed by the Twenty-first Amendment late in 1933 (see the Appendix), and the saloon doors swung open.

✦ Paying Farmers Not to Farm

Ever since the war-boom days of 1918, farmers had suffered from low prices and overproduction, especially in grain. During the depression, conditions became desperate as innumerable mortgages were foreclosed, as corn was burned for fuel, and as embattled farmers tried to prevent the shipment of crops to glutted markets. In Iowa several volatile counties were placed under martial law.

A radical new approach to farm recovery was embraced when the Emergency Congress established the **Agricultural Adjustment Administration (AAA)**. Through "artificial scarcity" this agency was to establish "parity prices" for basic commodities. "Parity" was the price set for a product that gave it the same real value, in purchasing power, that it had enjoyed during the period from 1909 to 1914. The AAA would eliminate price-depressing surpluses by paying growers to reduce their crop acreage. The millions of dollars needed for these payments were to be raised by taxing processors of farm products, such as flour millers, who in turn would shift the burden to consumers.

Unhappily, the AAA got off to a wobbly start. It was begun after much of the cotton crop for 1933 had been planted, and balky mules, trained otherwise, were forced to plow under countless young plants. Several million squealing pigs were purchased and slaughtered. Much of their meat was distributed to people on relief, but some of it was used for fertilizer. This "sinful" destruction of food, at a time when thousands of citizens were hungry, increased condemnation of the American economic system by many left-leaning voices.

"Subsidized scarcity" did have the effect of raising farm income, but the whole confused enterprise met with acid criticism. Farmers, food processors, consumers, and taxpayers were all to some degree unhappy. Paying the farmers not to farm actually increased unemployment, at a time when other New Deal agencies were striving to decrease it. When the Supreme Court finally killed the AAA in 1936 by declaring its regulatory taxation provisions unconstitutional, foes of the plow-under program rejoiced loudly.

Quickly recovering from this blow, the New Deal Congress hastened to pass the Soil Conservation and Domestic Allotment Act of 1936. The withdrawal of acreage from production was now achieved by paying farmers to plant soil-conserving crops, like soybeans, or to let their land lie fallow. With the emphasis thus on conservation, the Supreme Court placed its stamp of approval on the revamped scheme.

The Second Agricultural Adjustment Act of 1938, passed two years later, was a more comprehensive substitute, although it continued conservation payments. If growers observed acreage restrictions on specified commodities like cotton and wheat, they would be eligible for parity payments. Other provisions of the new AAA were designed to give farmers not only a fairer price but a more substantial share of the national income. Both goals were partially achieved.

Novelist John Steinbeck (1902–1968) relates in his novel The Grapes of Wrath *(1939) that when the "Okies" and "Arkies" reached California, they found the big growers unwilling to pay more than twenty-five cents an hour for work in the fields. One owner mutters,*

"A Red is any son-of-a-bitch that wants thirty cents an hour when we're paying twenty-five!"

✶ Dust Bowls and Black Blizzards

Nature meanwhile had been providing some unplanned scarcity. Late in 1933 a prolonged drought struck the states of the trans-Mississippi Great Plains. Rainless weeks were followed by furious, whining winds, while the sun was darkened by millions of tons of powdery topsoil torn from homesteads in an area that stretched from eastern Colorado to western Missouri—soon to be dubbed the **Dust Bowl**. Despondent citizens sat on front porches with protective masks on their faces, watching their farms swirl by. A seven-year-old boy in Kansas suffocated. Overawed victims of the Dust Bowl disaster predicted the end of the world or the second coming of Christ.

Drought and wind triggered the dust storms, but they were not the only culprits. The human hand had also worked its mischief. High grain prices during World War I had enticed farmers to bring countless acres of marginal land under cultivation. Worse, dry-farming techniques and mechanization had revolutionized Great Plains agriculture. The steam tractor and the disk plow tore up infinitely more sod than a team of oxen ever could, leaving the powdery topsoil to be swept away at nature's whim (see Map 33.1).

Burned and blown out of the Dust Bowl, tens of thousands of refugees fled their ruined acres. In five years about 350,000 Oklahomans and Arkansans—"Okies" and "Arkies"—trekked to southern California in "junkyards on wheels." Undeterred by signs saying "KEEP OUT," many found a new home in the San Joaquin Valley, which shared much in common with the southern plains—arid climate, cotton growing, new-found oil deposits, and abundant land. Yet the transition was cruel. Food, shelter, and clothing were scarce; the winter months, without work and heat, proved nearly unendurable for the migrants. The dismal story of these human tumbleweeds was realistically portrayed in John Steinbeck's best-selling novel *The Grapes of Wrath* (1939), which proved to be the *Uncle Tom's Cabin* of the Dust Bowl.

Zealous New Dealers, sympathetic toward the soil-tillers, made various other efforts to relieve their burdens. The Frazier-Lemke Farm Bankruptcy Act, passed in 1934, made possible a suspension of mortgage foreclosures for five years, but it was voided the next year by the Supreme Court. A revised law, limiting the grace period to three years, was unanimously upheld. In 1935 the president set up the Resettlement Administration, charged with the task of removing near-farmless farmers to better land. And more than 200 million young trees were successfully planted on the bare prairies as windbreaks by the young men of the Civilian Conservation Corps, even though one governor jeered at trying to "grow hair on a bald head."

Native Americans also felt the far-reaching hand of New Deal reform. Commissioner of Indian Affairs John

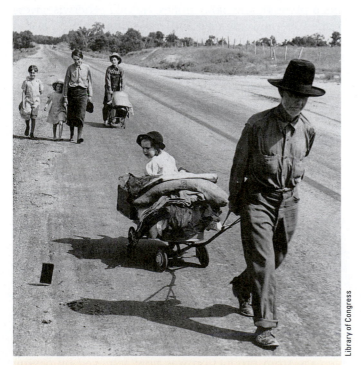

Library of Congress

An Okie Family Hits the Road in the 1930s to Escape the Dust Bowl

MAP 33.1 The Extent of Erosion in the 1930s Note the extensive wind erosion in the western Oklahoma panhandle region, which was dubbed the "Dust Bowl" in the 1930s. Mechanized farmers had "busted" the sod of the southern plains so thoroughly that they literally broke the back of the land. Tons of dust blew out of the Dust Bowl in the 1930s and blotted the sun from the skies as far away as New York. A Kansas newspaperman reported in 1935 that in his dust-darkened town, "Lady Godiva could ride through streets without even the horse seeing her." © Cengage Learning

Collier ardently sought to reverse the forced-assimilation policies in place since the Dawes Act of 1887 (see p. 581). Inspired by a sojourn among the Pueblo Indians in Taos, New Mexico, Collier promoted the Indian Reorganization Act of 1934 (the "Indian New Deal"). The new law encouraged tribes to establish local self-government and to preserve their native crafts and traditions. The act also helped to stop the loss of Indian lands and revived tribes' interest in their identity and culture. Yet not all Indians applauded it. Some denounced the legislation as a "back-to-the-blanket" measure that sought to make museum pieces out of Native Americans. Seventy-seven tribes refused to organize under its provisions, though nearly two hundred others did establish tribal governments.

✹ Battling Bankers and Big Business

Reformist New Dealers were determined from the outset to curb the "money changers" who had played fast and loose with gullible investors before the Wall Street crash of 1929. The Hundred Days Congress passed the "Truth in Securities Act" (Federal Securities Act), which required promoters to transmit to investors sworn information regarding the soundness of their stocks and bonds. An old saying was thus reversed to read "Let the seller beware," although the buyer might never read the fine print.

In 1934 Congress took further steps to protect the public against fraud, deception, and inside manipulation. It authorized the Securities and Exchange Commission (SEC), which was designed as a watchdog administrative agency. Stock markets henceforth were to operate more as trading marts and less as gambling casinos.

New Dealers likewise directed their fire at public utility holding companies, those supercorporations. Citizens had seen one of these incredible colossi collapse during the spring of 1932, when Chicagoan Samuel Insull's multibillion-dollar financial empire crashed. Possibilities of controlling, with a minimum of capital, a half-dozen or so pyramided layers of big business suggested to Roosevelt "a ninety-six-inch dog being wagged by a four-inch tail." The Public Utility Holding Company Act of 1935 finally delivered a "death sentence" to this type of bloated growth, except where it might be deemed economically needful.

✹ The TVA Harnesses the Tennessee

Inevitably, the sprawling electric-power industry attracted the fire of New Deal reformers. Within a few decades, it had risen from nothingness to a behemoth with an investment of $13 billion. As a public utility, it reached directly and regularly into the pocketbooks of millions of consumers for vitally needed services. Ardent New Dealers accused it of gouging the public with excessive rates, especially since it owed its success to having secured, often for a song, priceless water-power sites from the public domain.

The tempestuous Tennessee River provided New Dealers with a rare opportunity. With its tributaries, the river drained a badly eroded area about the size of

MAP 33.2 TVA Area More than twenty dams were constructed on the river's tributaries as part of a massive project to control flooding, generate hydroelectric power, and revitalize the Tennessee Valley region, while also creating jobs for the unemployed. The shaded area represents the area served by TVA electric power. © Cengage Learning

England, and one containing some 2.5 million of the most poverty-stricken people in America. The federal government already owned valuable properties at Muscle Shoals, where it had erected plants for needed nitrates in World War I. By developing the hydroelectric potential of the entire area, Washington could combine the immediate advantage of putting thousands of people to work and a long-term project for reforming the power monopoly.

An act creating the **Tennessee Valley Authority (TVA)** was passed in 1933 by the Hundred Days Congress. This far-ranging enterprise was largely a result of the steadfast vision and unflagging zeal of Senator George W. Norris of Nebraska, after whom one of the mighty dams was named. From the standpoint of "planned economy," the TVA was by far the most revolutionary of all the New Deal schemes.

This new agency was determined to discover precisely how much the production and distribution of electricity cost, so that a "yardstick" could be set up to test the fairness of rates charged by private companies. Utility corporations lashed back at this entering wedge of government control, charging that the low cost of TVA power was due to dishonest bookkeeping and the absence of taxes. Critics complained that the whole dream was "creeping socialism in concrete."

But the New Dealers, shrugging off such outcries, pointed a prideful finger at the amazing achievements of the TVA. The gigantic project brought to the area not only full employment and the blessings of cheap electric power (see Figure 33.2), but low-cost housing, abundant cheap nitrates, the restoration of eroded soil, reforestation, improved navigation, and flood control. Rivers ran blue instead of brown, and a once-poverty-cursed area was being transformed into one of the most flourishing regions in the United States.

Foreigners were greatly impressed with the possibilities of similar schemes in their own lands, and exulting New Dealers agitated for parallel enterprises in the valleys of the Columbia, Colorado, and Missouri Rivers. Federally built dams one day would span all those waterways, impounding more than 30 percent of the total annual runoff from the "roof of America" in the Rocky Mountains. Hydroelectric power from those dams would drive the growth of the urban West, and the waters they diverted would nurture agriculture in the previously bone-dry western deserts. But conservative reaction against the "socialistic" New Deal would confine the TVA's brand of federally guided resource management and comprehensive regional development to the Tennessee Valley (see Map 33.2).

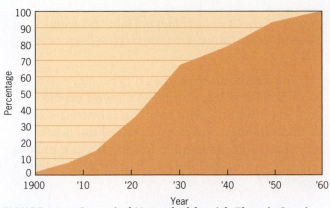

FIGURE 33.2 Occupied Households with Electric Service, 1900–1960 Well into the twentieth century, a majority of American households had no electrical service. The New Deal's Rural Electrification Agency and projects like the Tennessee Valley Authority (TVA) helped make electricity available to almost all Americans by 1960. African American leader Andrew Young later claimed that the TVA created the economic underpinnings of the civil rights movement: "It was the presence of the cheap electricity, lower interest rates, water projects, that laid the foundation for the New South."

✴ Housing and Social Security

The New Deal had meanwhile framed sturdy new policies for housing construction. To speed recovery and better homes, Roosevelt set up the Federal Housing Administration (FHA) as early as 1934. The building industry was to be stimulated by small loans to householders, both for improving their dwellings and for completing new ones. So popular did the FHA prove to be that it was one of the few "alphabetical agencies" to outlast the age of Roosevelt.

Congress bolstered the program in 1937 by authorizing the United States Housing Authority (USHA), an agency designed to lend money to states or communities for low-cost construction. Although units for about 650,000 low-income people were started, new building fell tragically short of needs. New Deal efforts to expand the project collided with brick-wall opposition from real estate promoters, builders, and landlords ("slumlords"), to say nothing of anti–New Dealers who attacked what they considered down-the-rathole spending. Nonetheless, for the first time in a century, the slum areas in America ceased growing and even shrank.

Incomparably more important was the success of New Dealers in the field of unemployment insurance and old-age pensions. Their greatest victory was the epochal **Social Security Act** of 1935—one of the

most complicated and far-reaching laws ever to pass Congress. To cushion future depressions, the measure provided for federal-state unemployment insurance. To provide security for old age, specified categories of retired workers were to receive regular payments from Washington. These payments ranged from $10 to $85 a month (raised periodically) and were financed by a payroll tax on both employers and employees. Provision was also made for the blind, the physically handicapped, delinquent children, and other dependents.

Republican opposition to the sweeping new legislation was bitter. "Social Security," insisted Hoover, "must be builded upon a cult of work, not a cult of leisure." The GOP national chairman falsely charged that every worker would have to wear a metal dog tag for life.

Social Security was largely inspired by the example of some of the more highly industrialized nations of Europe. In the agricultural America of an earlier day, there had always been farm chores for all ages, and the large family had cared for its own dependents. But in an urbanized economy, at the mercy of boom-or-bust cycles, the government was now recognizing its responsibility for the welfare of its citizens. By 1939 over 45 million people were eligible for Social Security benefits. In subsequent years further categories of workers were added, including, belatedly, farm and domestic workers. For decades millions of poor men and women were excluded from Social Security. In contrast to Europe, where welfare programs generally were universal, American workers had to be employed and in certain kinds of jobs to get coverage.

✴ A New Deal for Labor

The NRA blue eagles, with their call for collective bargaining, had been a godsend to organized labor. As New Deal expenditures brought some slackening of unemployment, labor began to feel more secure and hence more self-assertive. A rash of walkouts occurred in the summer of 1934, including a paralyzing general strike in San Francisco (following a "Bloody Thursday"), which was broken only when outraged citizens resorted to vigilante tactics.

When the Supreme Court axed the blue eagle, a Congress sympathetic to labor unions undertook to fill the vacuum. The fruit of its deliberations was the National Labor Relations Act of 1935, more commonly known as the **Wagner Act**, after its congressional sponsor, New York senator Robert F. Wagner. This trailblazing law created a powerful new National Labor Relations Board for administrative purposes and reasserted the right of labor to engage in self-organization and to bargain collectively through representatives of its own choice. Considered the Magna Carta of American labor, the Wagner Act proved to be a major milestone for American workers.

Under the encouragement of a highly sympathetic National Labor Relations Board, a host of unskilled workers began to organize themselves into effective unions. The leader of this drive was beetle-browed, domineering, and melodramatic John L. Lewis, boss of the United Mine Workers. In 1935 he succeeded in forming the Committee for Industrial Organization (CIO) within the ranks of the skilled-craft American Federation of Labor. But skilled workers, ever since the days of the ill-fated Knights of Labor in the 1880s, had shown only lukewarm sympathy for the cause of unskilled labor, especially blacks. In 1936, following inevitable friction with the CIO, the older federation suspended the upstart unions associated with the newer organization.

Undaunted, the rebellious CIO moved on a concerted scale into the huge automobile industry. Late in 1936 the workers resorted to a revolutionary technique (earlier used in both Europe and America) known as the sit-down strike: they refused to leave the factory building of General Motors at Flint, Michigan, and thus prevented the importation of strikebreakers. Conservative respecters of private property were scandalized. The CIO finally won a resounding victory when its union, after heated negotiations, was recognized by General Motors as the sole bargaining agency for its employees.

Unskilled workers now pressed their advantage. The United States Steel Company, hitherto an impossible

A worker at a Chevrolet plant in Flint, Michigan, wrote after the United Auto Workers–CIO victory in 1937,

❝ The inhuman high speed is *no more*. We now have a voice, and have slowed up the speed of the line. And [we] are now treated as human beings, and not as part of the machinery. The high pressure is taken off. . . . It proves clearly that united we stand, divided or alone we fall.**❞**

nut for labor to crack, averted a costly strike when it voluntarily granted rights of unionization to its CIO-organized employees. But the "little steel" companies fought back savagely. Citizens were shocked in 1937 by the Memorial Day massacre at the plant of the Republic Steel Company in South Chicago. In a bloody fracas, police fired upon pickets and workers, leaving the area strewn with several score dead and wounded.

A better deal for labor continued when Congress, in 1938, passed the memorable **Fair Labor Standards Act** (Wages and Hours Bill). Industries involved in interstate commerce were to set up minimum-wage and maximum-hour levels. The eventual goals were forty cents an hour (later raised) and a forty-hour week. Labor by children under sixteen (under eighteen if the occupation was dangerous) was forbidden. These

General Motors Sit-down Strikers, Flint, Michigan, 1937 Strikers like these sometimes kept their spirits up with the song "Sit Down":

*When the boss won't talk
Don't take a walk;
Sit down, sit down.*

© Bettmann/Corbis

Labor Triumphant After generations of struggle, organized labor made dramatic gains in membership and bargaining power during the New Deal years.

Granger Collection

FIGURE 33.3 **Labor Union Membership in Selected Countries, 1913–2007** In the United States, the percentage of the labor force that was unionized increased until 1954, when it began a long-term decline. In the 1990s it had a brief rise with the organization of service and government workers, only to decline again until it reached a low of 12 percent in 2006. In 2007 unionization grew by .1 percent, adding 311,000 workers, which brought total union membership to 15.7 million, the highest in many years. Note the different fortunes of organized labor in other countries in the face of the Great Depression, World War II, postwar prosperity, and deindustrialization.

Sources: James C. Docherty, *Historical Dictionary of Organized Labor*, 2nd ed., pp. 408–415 and 420–421. Copyright © 2004. Reprinted by permission of Scarecrow Press; Organisation for Economic Co-Operation and Development, online OECD Employment database.

reforms were bitterly though futilely opposed by many industrialists, especially by those southern textile manufacturers who had profited from low-wage labor. But the exclusion of agricultural, service, and domestic workers meant that blacks, Mexican Americans, and women—who were concentrated in these fields—did not benefit from the act.

In later New Deal days, labor unionization thrived (see Figure 33.3). "Roosevelt wants you to join a union" was the rallying cry of professional organizers. The president received valuable support at ballot-box time from labor leaders and many appreciative workingpeople. One mill worker remarked that Roosevelt was "the only man we ever had in the White House who would know that my boss is a s.o.b."

The CIO surged forward, breaking completely with the AF of L in 1938. On that occasion the *Committee for Industrial Organization* was formally reconstituted as the ***Congress of Industrial Organizations*** (the new **CIO**), under the visionary though high-handed presidency of John L. Lewis. By 1940 the CIO could claim about 4 million members in its constituent unions, including some 200,000 blacks. Nevertheless, bitter and annoying jurisdictional feuding involving strikes continued with the AF of L. At times labor seemed more bent on costly civil war than on its age-old war with management.

✦ Landon Challenges "the Champ"

As the presidential campaign of 1936 neared, the New Dealers were on top of the world. They had achieved considerable progress, and millions of "reliefers" were grateful to their bountiful government. The exultant Democrats renominated Roosevelt on a platform squarely endorsing the New Deal.

The Republicans were hard-pressed to find someone to feed to "the Champ." They finally settled on the colorless but homespun and honest governor of the Sunflower State of Kansas, Alfred M. Landon. Landon himself was a moderate who accepted some New Deal reforms, although not the popular Social Security Act. But the Republican platform vigorously condemned the New Deal of Franklin "Deficit" Roosevelt for its radicalism, experimentation, confusion, and "frightful waste." Backing Landon, ex-president Hoover called for a "holy crusade for liberty," echoing the cry of the American Liberty League, a group of wealthy conservatives who had organized in 1934 to fight "socialistic" New Deal schemes.

Roosevelt gave as good as he got. Angry enough to stretch sheet iron, the president took to the stump and denounced the "economic royalists" who sought to "hide behind the flag and the Constitution." "I welcome their hatred," he proclaimed.

A landslide overwhelmed Landon, as the demoralized Republicans carried only two states, Maine and Vermont. This dismal showing caused political wiseacres to make the old adage read, "As Maine goes, so goes Vermont."* The popular vote was 27,752,869 to 16,674,665; the electoral count was 523 to 8—the most lopsided in 116 years. A good-humored newspaper columnist quipped, "If Landon had given one more speech, Roosevelt would have carried Canada, too." Democratic majorities, riding in on Roosevelt's magic coattails, were again returned to Congress. Jubilant Democrats could now claim more than two-thirds of the seats in the House and a like proportion in the Senate.

The battle of 1936, perhaps the most bitter since Bryan's defeat in 1896, partially bore out Republican charges of class warfare. Even more than in 1932, the needy economic groups were lined up against the so-called greedy economic groups. CIO units contributed generously to FDR's campaign chest. Many left-wingers turned to Roosevelt, as the customary third-party protest vote sharply declined. Blacks, several million of whom had also appreciated welcome relief checks, had by now largely shaken off their traditional allegiance to the Republican party. To them, Lincoln was "finally dead."

FDR won primarily because he appealed to the "forgotten man," whom he never forgot. Some of the president's support was only pocketbook-deep: "reliefers" were not going to bite the hand that doled out the government checks. No one, as Al Smith remarked, "shoots at Santa Claus." But Roosevelt in fact had forged a powerful and enduring coalition of the South: blacks, urbanites, and the poor. He proved especially effective in marshaling the support of the multitudes of "New Immigrants"—mostly the Catholics and Jews who had swarmed into the great cities since the turn of

---

*Maine, which traditionally held its state elections in September, was long regarded as a political weathervane, hence the expression "As Maine goes, so goes the nation."

> *Three days before the 1936 election, Roosevelt took the moral high ground in his speech at New York's Madison Square Garden:*
>
> "I should like to have it said of my first Administration that in it the forces of selfishness and of lust for power met their match. I should like to have it said of my second Administration that in it these forces met their master."

the century. These once-scorned newcomers, with their now-numerous sons and daughters, had at last come politically of age. In the 1920s one out of every twenty-five federal judgeships went to a Catholic; Roosevelt appointed Catholics to one out of every four.

✷ Nine Old Men on the Bench

Bowing his head to the sleety blasts, Roosevelt took the presidential oath on January 20, 1937, instead of the traditional March 4. The Twentieth Amendment to the Constitution had been ratified in 1933. (See the Appendix.) It swept away the postelection lame duck session of Congress and shortened by six weeks the awkward period before inauguration.

Flushed with victory, Roosevelt interpreted his reelection as a mandate to continue New Deal reforms. But in his eyes, the cloistered old men on the supreme bench, like fossilized stumbling blocks, stood stubbornly in the pathway of progress. In nine major cases involving the New Deal, the Roosevelt administration had been thwarted seven times. The Court was ultraconservative, and six of the nine oldsters in black were over seventy. As luck would have it, not a single member had been appointed by FDR in his first term.

Roosevelt, his "Dutch up," viewed with mounting impatience what he regarded as the obstructive conservatism of the Court. Some of these Old Guard appointees were hanging on with a senile grip, partly because they felt it their patriotic duty to curb the "socialistic" tendencies of that radical in the White House. Roosevelt believed that the voters in three successive elections—the presidential elections of 1932 and 1936 and the midterm congressional elections of 1934—had returned a smashing verdict in favor of his program of reform. Democracy, in his view, meant rule by the people. If the American way of life was to be preserved, Roosevelt argued, the Supreme Court ought to get in line with the supreme court of public opinion.

Roosevelt finally hit upon a Court scheme that he regarded as "the answer to a maiden's prayer." In fact, it proved to be one of the most costly political misjudgments of his career. When he sprang his brainstorm on a shocked nation early in 1937, he caught the country and Congress completely by surprise. Roosevelt bluntly asked Congress for legislation to permit him to add a new justice to the Supreme Court for every member over seventy who would not retire. The maximum membership could then be fifteen. Roosevelt pointed to the necessity of injecting vigorous new blood, for the Court, he alleged, was far behind in its work. This charge, which turned out to be false, brought heated accusations of dishonesty. At best Roosevelt was headstrong and not fully aware of the fact that the Court, in popular thinking, had become something of a sacred cow.

✷ The Court Changes Course

Congress and the nation were promptly convulsed over Roosevelt's **Court-packing plan** to expand the Supreme Court. Franklin "Double-crossing" Roosevelt was vilified for attempting to break down the delicate checks and balances among the three branches of the government. He was accused of grooming himself as a dictator by trying to browbeat the judiciary. In the eyes of countless citizens, mostly Republicans but including many Democrats, basic liberties seemed to be in jeopardy. "God Bless the Supreme Court" was a fervent prayer.

The Court had meanwhile seen the ax hanging over its head. Whatever his motives, Justice Owen J. Roberts, formerly regarded as a conservative, began to vote on the side of his liberal colleagues. "A switch in time saves nine" was the classic witticism inspired by this ideological change. By a five-to-four decision, the Court, in March 1937, upheld the principle of a state minimum wage for women, thereby reversing its stand on a different case a year earlier. In succeeding decisions, a Court more sympathetic to the New Deal upheld the National Labor Relations Act (Wagner Act) and the Social Security Act. Roosevelt's "Court-packing" was further undermined when Congress voted full pay for justices over seventy who retired, whereupon one of the oldest conservative members resigned, to be replaced by a New Dealer, Justice Hugo Black.

Congress finally passed a court reform bill, but this watered-down version applied only to lower courts. Roosevelt, the master politician, thus suffered his first major legislative defeat at the hands of his own party in Congress. Americans have never viewed lightly a president's tampering with the Supreme Court, no matter how popular their chief executive may be. Yet in losing this battle, Roosevelt incidentally won his campaign. The Court, as he had hoped, became markedly more friendly to New Deal reforms. Furthermore, a succession of deaths and resignations enabled him in time to make nine appointments to the tribunal—more than any of his predecessors since George Washington. The clock "unpacked" the Court.

Granger Collection

The Response to Roosevelt's "Court-Packing" Plan, 1937
Even the Democratic donkey kicked up a storm in opposition to President Roosevelt's plan to expand the Supreme Court to as many as fifteen judges.

Yet in a sense, FDR lost both the Court battle and the war. He so aroused conservatives of both parties in Congress that few New Deal reforms were passed after 1937, the year of the fight to "pack" the bench. With this catastrophic miscalculation, he squandered much of the political goodwill that had carried him to such a resounding victory in the 1936 election.

✴ Twilight of the New Deal

Roosevelt's first term, from 1933 to 1937, did not banish the depression from the land. Unemployment stubbornly persisted in 1936 at about 15 percent, down from the grim 25 percent of 1933 but still miserably high (see Figure 33.4). Despite the inventiveness of New Deal programs and the billions of dollars in "pump priming," recovery had been dishearteningly modest, though the country seemed to be inching its way back to economic health.

Then, in 1937, the economy took another sharp downturn, a surprisingly severe depression-within-the-depression that the president's critics quickly dubbed

the "Roosevelt recession." In fact, government policies had caused the nosedive, as new Social Security taxes began to bite into payrolls and as the administration cut back on spending out of continuing reverence for the orthodox economic doctrine of the balanced budget.

Only at this late date did Roosevelt at last frankly and deliberately embrace the recommendations of the British economist John Maynard Keynes. The New Deal had run deficits for several years, but all of them had been rather small and none was intended. Now, in April 1937, Roosevelt announced a bold program to stimulate the economy by planned deficit spending. Although the deficits were still undersized for the herculean task of conquering the depression, this abrupt policy reversal marked a major turning point in the government's relation to the economy. **Keynesianism**—the use of government spending and fiscal policy to "prime the pump" of the economy and encourage consumer spending—became the new economic orthodoxy and remained so for decades.

Roosevelt had meanwhile been pushing the remaining reform measures of the New Deal. Early in 1937 he urged Congress—a Congress growing more

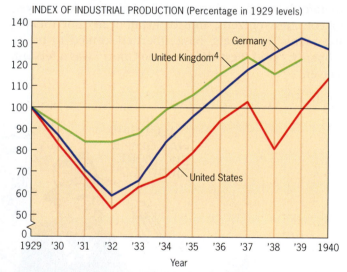

FIGURE 33.4 Economic Impact of the Great Depression on the United States, the United Kingdom, and Germany, 1929–1940

[1]Federal Emergency Relief Administration workers are counted as employed.

[2]Figure shows registered unemployment in Germany in 1929; industrial unemployment, as reported by unions, was 13.1 percent.

[3]Unemployment ceased to be an issue in Germany by 1939 with the mobilization for war. The labor force was actually augmented by the often-forced importation of foreign workers and the use of prison labor. Those who were unemployed suffered from a disability of some kind.

[4]This is an average of the industrial indexes in the United Kingdom for the first six months of 1939 only. Thereafter, no figures are available until 1946.

[Sources: *United States Historical Statistics*, vol. 2; *Statistical Yearbook of the League of Nations* (1938–1939 and 1941–1942); *International Historical Statistics, 1750–2005: Europe; State, Economy, and Society in Western Europe, 1815–1975*, vol. 2.]

A basic objective of the New Deal was featured in Roosevelt's second inaugural address (1937):

"I see one-third of a nation ill-housed, ill-clad, ill-nourished. . . . The test of our progress is not whether we add more to the abundance of those who have much; it is whether we provide enough for those who have too little.**"**

conservative—to authorize a sweeping reorganization of the national administration in the interests of streamlined efficiency. But the issue became tangled up with his presumed autocratic ambitions in regard to the Supreme Court, and he suffered another stinging defeat. Two years later, in 1939, Congress partially relented and in the Reorganization Act gave him limited powers for administrative reforms, including the key new Executive Office in the White House.

The New Dealers were accused of having the richest campaign chest in history, and in truth government relief checks had a curious habit of coming in bunches just before ballot time. To remedy such practices, Congress adopted the much-heralded Hatch Act of 1939. This act barred federal administrative officials, except the highest policy-making officers, from active political campaigning and soliciting. It also forbade the use of government funds for political purposes, as well as the collection of campaign contributions from people receiving relief payments. The Hatch Act was broadened in 1940 to place limits on campaign contributions and expenditures, but such clever ways of getting

around it were found that on the whole the legislation proved disappointing.

By 1938 the New Deal had clearly lost most of its early momentum. Magician Roosevelt could find few dazzling new reform rabbits to pull out of his tall silk hat. In the congressional elections of 1938, the Republicans, for the first time, cut heavily into the New Deal majorities in Congress, though failing to gain control of either house. The international crisis that came to a boil in 1938–1939 shifted public attention away from domestic reform and no doubt helped save the political hide of the Roosevelt "spendocracy." The New Deal, for all practical purposes, had shot its bolt.

✦ New Deal or Raw Deal?

Foes of the New Deal condemned its alleged waste, incompetence, confusion, contradictions, and cross-purposes, as well as the chiseling and graft in the alphabetical agencies—"alphabet soup," sneered Al Smith. Roosevelt had done nothing, cynics said, that an earthquake could not have done better. Critics deplored the employment of "crackpot" college professors, leftist "pinkos," and outright Communists. Such subversives, it was charged, were trying to make America over in the Bolshevik-Marxist image under "Rooseveltski." The Hearst newspapers lambasted,

> *The Red New Deal with a Soviet seal*
> *Endorsed by a Moscow hand,*
> *The strange result of an alien cult*
> *In a liberty-loving land.*

Whitney Museum of American Art

Employment Agency, by Isaac Soyer, 1937   Millions of jobless Americans felt the despair Soyer captured in this painting, as depression-era unemployment reached levels never seen before or since in American history.

Roosevelt was further accused by conservatives of being Jewish ("Rosenfield") and of tapping too many bright young Jewish leftists ("The Jew Deal") for his "Drain Trust."

Hardheaded businesspeople, who "had met a payroll," were shocked by the leap-before-you-look, try-anything-once spirit of Roosevelt, the jolly improviser. They accused him of confusing noise and movement with progress. Others appreciated the president's do-something approach. Humorist Will Rogers, the rope-twirling "poet lariat" of the era, remarked that if Roosevelt were to burn down the Capitol, people would say, "Well, we at least got a fire started, anyhow."

"Bureaucratic meddling" and "regimentation" were also bitter complaints of anti–New Dealers; in truth, bureaucracy did blossom. The federal government, with its hundreds of thousands of employees, became incomparably the largest single business in the country, as the states faded further into the background.

Promises of budget balancing, to say nothing of other promises, had flown out the window—so foes of the New Deal pointed out. The national debt had stood at the already enormous figure of $19,487,000,000 in 1932 and had skyrocketed to $40,440,000,000 by 1939. America was becoming, its critics charged, a "handout state" trying to squander itself into prosperity—*U.S.* stood for "unlimited spending." Such lavish benefactions were undermining the old virtues of thrift and initiative. Ordinary Americans, once self-reliant citizens, were getting a bad case of the "gimmies": their wishbones were becoming larger than their backbones. In the nineteenth century, hard-pressed workers went west; now they went on relief.

Business was bitter. Accusing the New Deal of fomenting class strife, conservatives insisted that the laborer and the farmer—especially the big operator—were being pampered. Why "soak the successful"? Countless businesspeople, especially Republicans, declared that they could pull themselves out of the depression if they could only get the federal government—an interventionist big government—off their backs. Private enterprise, they charged, was being stifled by "planned economy," "planned bankruptcy," "creeping socialism," and the philosophy "Washington can do it better," with a federal pill for every ill. States' rights were being ignored, while the government was competing in business with its own citizens, under a "dictatorship of do-gooders."

The aggressive leadership of Roosevelt—"one-man supergovernment"—also came in for denunciation. Heavy fire was especially directed at his attempts to browbeat the Supreme Court and to create a "dummy Congress." Roosevelt had even tried in the 1938 elections, with backfiring results, to "purge" members of Congress who would not march in lockstep with him.

The three senators whom he publicly opposed were all triumphantly reelected.

The most damning indictment of the New Deal was that it had failed to cure the depression. Afloat in a sea of red ink, some argued, it had merely administered aspirin, sedatives, and Band-Aids. Many economists came to believe that better results would have been achieved by much greater deficit spending. Despite some $20 billion poured out in six years of deficit spending and lending, of leaf raking and pump priming, the gap was not closed between production and consumption. There were even more mountainous farm surpluses under Roosevelt than under Hoover. Millions of dispirited men and women were still unemployed in 1939, after six years of drain, strain, and pain. Not until World War II blazed forth in Europe was the unemployment headache solved.

★ FDR's Balance Sheet

New Dealers staunchly defended their record. Admitting that there had been some waste, they pointed out that relief—not economy—had been the primary object of their multifront war on the depression. Conceding also that there had been some graft, they argued that it had been trivial in view of the immense sums spent and the obvious need for haste.

Apologists for Roosevelt further declared that the New Deal had relieved the worst of the crisis in 1933. It promoted the philosophy of "balancing the human budget" and accepted the principle that the federal government was morally bound to prevent mass hunger and starvation by "managing" the economy. The Washington regime was to be used, not feared. The collapse of America's economic system was averted, a fairer distribution of the national income was achieved, and the citizens were enabled to regain and retain their self-respect. "Nobody is going to starve" was Roosevelt's promise.

Though hated by business tycoons, FDR should have been their patron saint, so his admirers claimed. He deflected popular resentments against business and may have saved the American system of free enterprise. Roosevelt's quarrel was not with capitalism but with capitalists; he purged American capitalism of some of its worst abuses so that it might be saved from itself. He may even have headed off a more radical swing to the left by a mild dose of what was mistakenly reviled as "socialism." The head of the American Socialist party, when once asked if the New Deal had carried out the Socialist program, reportedly replied that it had indeed—on a stretcher. Nor, Roosevelt's defenders claimed, did the New Deal bankrupt the United States: the sensational increase in the national debt was caused

Our Skipper This pro-FDR cartoon depicts a confident Roosevelt ignoring his critics while heading cheerily toward economic recovery. In fact, FDR's New Deal brought neither the recovery he promised nor the ruin his detractors prophesied. The depression dragged on with only periodic improvement for nearly eight years under his leadership, until the cataclysmic emergency of World War II finally banished unemployment from the land.

by World War II, not the New Deal. The national debt was only $40 billion in 1939 but $258 billion in 1945.

Roosevelt, like Jefferson, provided bold reform without a bloody revolution—at a time in history when some foreign nations were suffering armed uprisings and when many Europeans were predicting either communism or fascism for America. He was upbraided by the left-wing radicals for not going far enough, by the right-wing radicals for going too far. Choosing the middle road, he has been called the greatest American conservative since Hamilton. He was in fact Hamiltonian in his espousal of big government, but Jeffersonian in his concern for the "forgotten man." Demonstrating anew the value of powerful presidential leadership, he exercised that power to relieve the erosion of the nation's greatest physical resource—its people. He helped preserve democracy in America in a time when democracies abroad were disappearing down the sinkhole of dictatorship. And in playing this role, he unwittingly girded the nation for its part in the titanic war that loomed on the horizon—a war in which democracy the world over would be at stake.

Varying Viewpoints
How Radical Was the New Deal?

The Great Depression was both a great calamity and a great opportunity. How effectively Franklin Roosevelt responded to the calamity and what use he made of the opportunity are the two great questions that have animated historical debate about the New Deal.

Some historians have actually denied that there was much of a connection between the depression and the New Deal. Arthur M. Schlesinger, Jr., for example, who believed in "cycles" of reform and reaction in American history, wrote that "there would very likely have been some sort of New Deal in the 1930s even without the Depression." But most of the first generation of historians who wrote about the New Deal (in the 1940s, 1950s, and early 1960s) agreed with Carl Degler's judgment that the New Deal was "a revolutionary response to a revolutionary situation." In this view, though Roosevelt never found a means short of war to bring about economic recovery,

he shrewdly utilized the stubborn economic crisis as a means to enact sweeping reforms.

Some leftist scholars writing in the 1960s, however, notably Barton J. Bernstein, charged that the New Deal did not reach far enough. This criticism echoed the socialist complaint in the 1930s that the depression represented the total collapse of American capitalism and that the New Deal had muffed the chance truly to remake American society. Roosevelt had the chance, these historians argued, to redistribute wealth, improve race relations, and bring the giant corporations to heel. Instead, said these critics, the New Deal simply represented a conservative holding action to shore up a sagging and corrupt capitalist order.

Those charges against the New Deal stimulated another generation of scholars in the 1970s, 1980s, and 1990s to look closely at the concrete institutional, attitudinal, and economic circumstances in which the New Deal unfolded. Historians such as James Patterson, Alan Brinkley, Kenneth Jackson, Harvard Sitkoff, and Lizabeth Cohen—sometimes loosely referred to as the "constraints school"—concluded that the New Deal offered just about as much reform as circumstances allowed and as the majority of Americans wanted. The findings of these historians are impressive: the system of checks and balances limited presidential power; the disproportionate influence of southern Democrats in Congress stalled attempts to move toward racial justice; the federal system, in fact, inhibited all efforts to initiate change from Washington.

Most important, a majority of the American people at the time wanted to reform capitalism, not overthrow it. Industrial workers, for example, were not hapless pawns upon whom the New Deal was foisted, frustrating their yearning for more radical change. Instead, as David Kennedy has argued, they sought security and self-determination in ways quite compatible with the New Deal's programs for unemployment insurance, old-age pensions, and guarantees of labor's right to organize.

Most recently, scholars such as Alice Kessler-Harris, Linda Gordon, and Suzanne Mettler have argued that the New Deal had a more radical effect on men than on women. Social Security, for example, was designed to assist male breadwinners, who were then expected to share their benefits with their dependent wives and children. In addition, married women were rarely favored for government jobs in agencies such as the WPA. As a result, many women found themselves cast ever more firmly in the traditional role of wife and mother. At the time, however, most people believed that these were fair, if unequal, solutions to the catastrophic Great Depression.

Perhaps William Leuchtenburg summed it up best when he described the New Deal as a "half-way revolution," neither radical nor conservative, but accurately reflecting the American people's needs and desires in the 1930s—and for a long time thereafter. The great "New Deal coalition" that dominated American politics for nearly four decades after Roosevelt's election in 1932 represented a broad consensus in American society about the opportunities and legitimate limits of government efforts to shape the social and economic order.

Chapter Review

KEY TERMS

Brain Trust (752)

New Deal (753)

Hundred Days (754)

Glass-Steagall Banking Reform Act (756)

Civilian Conservation Corps (CCC) (757)

National Recovery Administration (NRA) (761)

Agricultural Adjustment Administration (AAA) (763)

Dust Bowl (764)

Tennessee Valley Authority (TVA) (766)

Social Security Act (767)

Wagner Act (767)

Fair Labor Standards Act (768)

Congress of Industrial Organizations (CIO) (769)

Court-packing plan (771)

Keynesianism (772)

PEOPLE TO KNOW

Franklin Delano Roosevelt

Eleanor Roosevelt

Harry L. Hopkins

Father Charles Coughlin

Francis E. Townsend

Huey P. ("Kingfish") Long

Frances Perkins

Mary McLeod Bethune

Robert F. Wagner

CHRONOLOGY

1932	Roosevelt defeats Hoover for presidency
1933	Bank holiday
	Emergency Banking Relief Act
	Beer and Wine Revenue Act
	Hundred Days Congress enacts AAA, TVA, HOLC, NRA, and PWA
	Federal Securities Act
	Glass-Steagall Banking Reform Act
	CWA established
	Twentieth Amendment (changed calendar of congressional sessions and date of presidential inauguration)
	Twenty-first Amendment (prohibition repealed)
	Nazis legally come to power in Germany with passage of Enabling Act
1934	Gold Reserve Act
	Securities and Exchange Commission authorized
	Indian Reorganization Act
	FHA established
	Frazier-Lemke Farm Bankruptcy Act
1935	WPA established
	Wagner Act
	Resettlement Administration
	Social Security Act
	Public Utility Holding Company Act
	Schechter "sick chicken" case
	CIO organized
1936	Soil Conservation and Domestic Allotment Act
	Roosevelt defeats Landon for presidency
1937	USHA established
	Roosevelt announces "Court-packing" plan
1938	Second AAA
	Fair Labor Standards Act
1939	Reorganization Act
	Hatch Act

TO LEARN MORE

Alan Brinkley, *The End of Reform: New Deal Liberalism in Depression and War* (1995)

———, *Voices of Protest: Huey Long, Father Coughlin, and the Great Depression* (1982)

Lizabeth Cohen, *Making a New Deal: Industrial Workers in Chicago, 1919–1939* (rev. ed., 2008)

Blanche Wiesen Cook, *Eleanor Roosevelt: A Life* (1992).

Michael Denning, *The Cultural Front: The Laboring of American Culture in the Twentieth Century* (1996)

James N. Gregory, *American Exodus: The Dustbowl Migration and Okie Culture in California* (1989)

Robin D. G. Kelley, *Hammer and Hoe: Alabama Communists During the Great Depression* (1990)

David M. Kennedy, *Freedom from Fear: The American People in Depression and War* (1999)

Alice Kessler-Harris, *In Pursuit of Equity: Men, Women, and the Quest for Economic Citizenship in Twentieth-Century America* (2001)

Neil M. Maher, *Nature's New Deal: The Civilian Conservation Corps and the Roots of the American Environmental Movement* (2008)

Lois Scharf, *Eleanor Roosevelt: First Lady of American Liberalism* (1987)

Jeff Shesol, *Supreme Power: Franklin Roosevelt vs. the Supreme Court* (2010)

Nick Taylor, *American-Made: The Enduring Legacy of the WPA: When FDR Put the Nation to Work* (2008)

Studs Terkel, *Hard Times: An Oral History of the Great Depression* (1970)

Wendy Wall, *Inventing the "American Way": The Politics of Consensus from the New Deal to the Civil Rights Movement* (2008)

A complete, annotated bibliography for this chapter—along with brief descriptions of the People to Know—may be found on the American Pageant website. The Key Terms are defined in a Glossary at the end of the text.

Chapter 34

Franklin D. Roosevelt and the Shadow of War

1933–1941

The epidemic of world lawlessness is spreading. When an epidemic of physical disease starts to spread, the community approves and joins in a quarantine of the patients in order to protect the health of the community against the spread of the disease. . . . There must be positive endeavors to preserve peace.

FRANKLIN D. ROOSEVELT, CHICAGO "QUARANTINE SPEECH," 1937

Americans in the 1930s tried to turn their backs on the world's problems. Their president at first seemed to share these views. The only battle Roosevelt sought was against the depression. America had its own burdens to shoulder, and the costs of foreign involvement, whether in blood or treasure, simply seemed too great.

But as the clouds of war gathered over Europe, Roosevelt eventually concluded that the United States could no longer remain aloof. Events gradually brought the American people around to his thinking: no nation was safe in an era of international anarchy, and the world could not remain half-enchained and half-free.

★ The London Conference

The sixty-six-nation **London Economic Conference**, meeting in the summer of 1933, revealed how thoroughly Roosevelt's early foreign policy was subordinated to his strategy for domestic economic recovery. The delegates to the London Conference hoped to organize a coordinated international attack on the global depression. They were particularly eager to stabilize the values of the various nations' currencies and the rates at which they could be exchanged. Exchange-rate stabilization was essential to the revival of world trade, which had all but evaporated by 1933.

Roosevelt at first agreed to send an American delegation to the conference, including Secretary of State Cordell Hull. But the president soon began to have second thoughts about the conference's agenda. He wanted to pursue his gold-juggling and other inflationary policies at home as a means of stimulating American recovery. An international agreement to maintain the value of the dollar in terms of other currencies might tie his hands, and at bottom Roosevelt was unwilling to sacrifice the possibility of domestic recovery for the sake of international cooperation. While vacationing on a yacht along the New England coast, he dashed off a radio message to London, scolding the conference for attempting to stabilize currencies and essentially declaring America's withdrawal from the negotiations.

Roosevelt's bombshell announcement yanked the rug from under the London Conference. The delegates adjourned empty-handed, amid cries of American bad faith. Whether the conference could have arrested the worldwide economic slide is debatable, but Roosevelt's every-man-for-himself attitude plunged the planet even deeper into economic crisis. The collapse of the London Conference also strengthened the global trend toward extreme nationalism, making international cooperation ever more difficult as the dangerous decade of the 1930s unfolded. Reflecting the powerful persistence of American isolationism, Roosevelt's action played directly into the hands of the power-mad dictators who were determined to shatter the peace of the world. Americans themselves would eventually pay a high price for the narrow-minded belief that the United States could go it alone in the modern world.

✹ Freedom for (from?) the Filipinos and Recognition for the Russians

Roosevelt matched isolationism from Europe with withdrawal from Asia. The Great Depression burst the fragile bubble of President McKinley's imperialistic dream in the Far East. With the descent into hard times, American taxpayers were eager to throw overboard their expensive tropical liability in the Philippine Islands. Organized labor demanded the exclusion of low-wage Filipino workers, and American sugar producers clamored for the elimination of Philippine competition.

Remembering its earlier promises of freedom for the Philippines, Congress passed the Tydings-McDuffie Act in 1934. The act provided for the independence of the Philippines after a twelve-year period of economic and political tutelage—that is, by 1946. The United States agreed to relinquish its army bases, but naval bases were reserved for future discussion—and retention.

Jack Beers/The Dallas Morning News

Just Another Customer, 1933 The United States recognizes the Soviet Union.

In truth, the American people were not so much giving freedom to the Philippines as they were freeing themselves *from* the Philippines. With a selfish eye to their own welfare, and with apparent disregard for the political situation in Asia, they proposed to leave the Philippines to their fate, while imposing upon the Filipinos economic terms so ungenerous as to threaten the islands with economic prostration. Once again, American isolationists rejoiced. Yet in Tokyo, Japanese militarists were calculating that they had little to fear from an inward-looking America that was abandoning its principal possession in Asia.

At the same time, Roosevelt made at least one internationalist gesture when he formally recognized the Soviet Union in 1933. Over the noisy protests of anticommunist conservatives, as well as Roman Catholics offended by the Kremlin's antireligious policies, Roosevelt extended the hand of diplomatic recognition to the sixteen-year-old Bolshevik regime. He was motivated in part by the hope for trade with Soviet Russia, as well as by the desire to bolster the Soviet Union as a friendly counterweight to the possible threat of German power in Europe and Japanese power in Asia.

✹ Becoming a Good Neighbor

Closer to home, Roosevelt inaugurated a refreshing new era in relations with Latin America. He proclaimed in his inaugural address, "I would dedicate this nation to the policy of the Good Neighbor." Taken together, Roosevelt's noninvolvement in Europe and withdrawal from Asia, along with this brotherly embrace of his New World neighbors, suggested that the United States was giving up its ambition to be a world power and would content itself instead with being merely a regional power, its interests and activities confined exclusively to the Western Hemisphere.

Old-fashioned intervention by bayonet in the Caribbean had not paid off, except in an evil harvest of resentment, suspicion, and fear. The Great Depression had cooled off Yankee economic aggressiveness, as thousands of investors in Latin American securities became sackholders rather than stockholders. There were now fewer dollars to be protected by the rifles of the hated marines.

With war-thirsty dictators seizing power in Europe and Asia, Roosevelt was eager to line up the Latin Americans to help defend the Western Hemisphere. Embittered neighbors would be potential tools of transoceanic aggressors. President Roosevelt made clear at the outset that he was going to renounce armed intervention, particularly the vexatious corollary to the Monroe Doctrine devised by his cousin Theodore Roosevelt. Late in 1933, at the Seventh Pan-American

Conference in Montevideo, Uruguay, the U.S. delegation formally endorsed nonintervention.

Deeds followed words. The last marines departed from Haiti in 1934. The same year, after military strongman Fulgencio Batista had come to power, restive Cuba was released from the worst hobbles of the Platt Amendment, under which America had been free to intervene, although the United States retained its naval base at Guantánamo (see p. 621). The tiny country of Panama received a similar uplift in 1936, when Washington partially relaxed its grip on the isthmus nation.

The hope-inspiring **Good Neighbor policy**, with the accent on consultation and nonintervention, received its acid test in Mexico. When the Mexican government seized Yankee oil properties in 1938, American investors vehemently demanded armed intervention to repossess their confiscated businesses. But Roosevelt successfully resisted the badgering, and a settlement was finally threshed out in 1941, even though the oil companies lost much of their original stake.

Spectacular success crowned Roosevelt's Good Neighbor policy. His earnest attempts to usher in a new era of friendliness, though hurting some U.S. bondholders, paid rich dividends in goodwill among the peoples to the south. No other citizen of the United States has ever been held in such high esteem in Latin America during his lifetime. Roosevelt was cheered with tumultuous enthusiasm when, as a "traveling salesman for peace," he journeyed to the special Inter-American Conference at Buenos Aires, Argentina, in 1936. The Colossus of the North now seemed less a vulture and more an eagle.

✵ Secretary Hull's Reciprocal Trade Agreements

Intimately associated with Good Neighborism, and also popular in Latin America, was the reciprocal trade policy of the New Dealers. Its chief architect was idealistic Secretary of State Hull, a high-minded Tennessean of the low-tariff school. Like Roosevelt, he believed that trade was a two-way street, that a nation can sell abroad only as it buys abroad, that tariff barriers choke off foreign trade, and that trade wars beget shooting wars.

Responding to the Hull-Roosevelt leadership, Congress passed the **Reciprocal Trade Agreements Act** in 1934. Designed in part to lift American export trade from the depression doldrums, this enlightened measure was aimed at both relief and recovery. At the same time, it activated the low-tariff policies of the New Dealers. (See the tariff chart in the Appendix.)

The Reciprocal Trade Agreements Act avoided the dangerous uncertainties of a wholesale tariff revision; it merely whittled down the most objectionable schedules of the Hawley-Smoot law by amending them. Roosevelt was empowered to lower existing rates by as much as 50 percent, provided that the other country involved was willing to respond with similar reductions. The resulting pacts, moreover, were to become effective without the formal approval of the Senate. This novel feature not only ensured speedier action but sidestepped the twin evils of high-stakes logrolling and high-pressure lobbying in Congress.

Secretary Hull, whose zeal for reciprocity was unflagging, succeeded in negotiating pacts with twenty-one countries by the end of 1939. During these same years, U.S. foreign trade increased appreciably, presumably in part as a result of the Hull-Roosevelt policies. Trade agreements undoubtedly bettered economic and political relations with Latin America and proved to be an influence for peace in a war-bent world.

The Reciprocal Trade Agreements Act was a landmark piece of legislation. It reversed the traditional high-protective-tariff policy that had persisted almost unbroken since Civil War days and that had so damaged the American and international economies following World War I. It also paved the way for the American-led free-trade international economic system that took shape after World War II, a period that witnessed the most robust growth in the history of international trade.

✵ Storm-Cellar Isolationism

Post-1918 chaos in Europe, followed by the Great Depression, spawned the ominous spread of totalitarianism. The individual was nothing; the state was everything. The communist USSR led the way, with the crafty and ruthless Joseph Stalin finally emerging as dictator. In 1936 he began to purge his communist state of all suspected dissidents, ultimately executing hundreds of thousands and banishing millions to remote Siberian forced-labor camps. Blustery Benito Mussolini, a swaggering Fascist, seized the reins of power in Italy during 1922. And Adolf Hitler, a fanatic with a toothbrush mustache, plotted and harangued his way into control of Germany in 1933 with liberal use of the "big lie."

Hitler was the most dangerous of the dictators, because he combined tremendous power with impulsiveness. A frustrated Austrian painter, with hypnotic talents as an orator and a leader, he had secured control of the Nazi party by making political capital of the Treaty of Versailles and Germany's depression-spawned unemployment. He was thus a misbegotten child of the shortsighted postwar policies of the victorious Allies, including the United States. The desperate German people had fallen in behind the new Pied Piper, for they saw no other hope of escape from the plague of economic chaos and national disgrace. Hitler withdrew Germany from the League of Nations in 1933 and began clandestinely (and illegally) rearming. In 1936 the Nazi Hitler and the Fascist Mussolini allied themselves in the **Rome-Berlin Axis**.

International gangsterism was likewise spreading in the Far East, where imperial Japan was on the make. Like Germany and Italy, Japan was a so-called have-not power. Like them, it resented the ungenerous Treaty of Versailles. Like them, it demanded additional space for its teeming millions, cooped-up in their crowded island nation.

Japanese navalists were not to be denied. Determined to find a place in the Asiatic sun, Tokyo gave notice in 1934 of the termination of the twelve-year-old Washington Naval Treaty. A year later at London, the Japanese torpedoed all hope of effective naval disarmament. Upon being denied complete parity, they walked out of the multipower conference and accelerated their construction of giant battleships. By 1935 Japan, too, had quit the League of Nations. Five years later it joined arms with Germany and Italy in the Tripartite Pact.

Jut-jawed Mussolini, seeking both glory and empire in Africa, brutally attacked Ethiopia in 1935 with bombers and tanks. The brave defenders, armed with spears and ancient firearms, were speedily crushed. Members of the League of Nations could have caused Mussolini's war machine to creak to a halt—if they had only dared to embargo oil. But when the League quailed rather than risk global hostilities, it merely signed its own death warrant.

Isolationism, long festering in America, received a strong boost from these alarms abroad. Though disapproving of the dictators, Americans still believed that

Adolf Hitler Reviewing Troops, Berlin, 1939 Egging his people on with theatrical displays of pomp and ceremony, Hitler had created a vast military machine by 1939, when he started World War II with a brutal attack against Poland.

Hugo Jaeger/Time & Life Pictures/Getty Images

Page 792 in the Poster Collection, Hoover Institution Archives

The Wages of Despair Disillusioned and desperate, millions of Germans in the 1930s looked to Adolf Hitler as their savior from the harsh terms of the Treaty of Versailles, which had concluded World War I. This Nazi poster reads, "Our Last Hope: Hitler."

The thirst of Benito Mussolini (1883-1945) for national glory in Ethiopia is indicated by his remark in 1940:

" To make a people great it is necessary to send them to battle even if you have to kick them in the pants. **"** (The Italians were notoriously unwarlike.)

In 1934 Mussolini proclaimed in a public speech,

" We have buried the putrid corpse of liberty. **"**

their encircling seas conferred a kind of mystic immunity. They were continuing to suffer the disillusionment born of their participation in World War I, which they now regarded as a colossal blunder. They likewise nursed bitter memories of the ungrateful and defaulting debtors. As early as 1934, a spiteful Congress passed the **Johnson Debt Default Act**, which prevented debt-dodging nations from borrowing further in the United States. If attacked again by aggressors, these delinquents could "stew in their own juices."

Mired down in the Great Depression, Americans had no real appreciation of the revolutionary forces being harnessed by the dictators. The "have-not" powers were out to become "have" powers. Americans were not so much afraid that totalitarian aggression would cause trouble as they were fearful that they might be drawn into it. Strong nationwide sentiment welled up for a constitutional amendment to forbid a declaration of war by Congress—except in case of invasion—unless there was a favorable popular referendum. With a mixture of seriousness and frivolity, a group of Princeton University students began to agitate in 1936 for a bonus to be paid to the Veterans of Future Wars (VFW) while the prospective frontliners were still alive.

✦ Congress Legislates Neutrality

As the gloomy 1930s lengthened, an avalanche of lurid articles and books condemning the munitions manufacturers as war-fomenting "merchants of death" poured from American presses. A Senate committee, headed by Senator Gerald Nye of North Dakota, was appointed in 1934 to investigate the "blood business." By sensationalizing evidence regarding America's entry into World War I, the senatorial probers tended to shift the blame away from the German submarines onto the American bankers and arms manufacturers. Because the munitions makers had obviously made money out of the war, many a naive citizen leaped to the illogical conclusion that these soulless scavengers had *caused* the war in order to make money. This kind of reasoning

suggested that if the profits could only be removed from the arms traffic—"one hell of a business"—the country could steer clear of any world conflict that might erupt in the future.

Responding to overwhelming popular pressure, Congress made haste to legislate the nation out of war. Action was spurred by the danger that Mussolini's Ethiopian assault would plunge the world into a new bloodbath. The **Neutrality Acts of 1935, 1936, and 1937**, taken together, stipulated that *when the president proclaimed* the existence of a foreign war, certain restrictions would automatically go into effect. No American could legally sail on a belligerent ship, sell or transport munitions to a belligerent, or make loans to a belligerent.

This head-in-the-sand legislation in effect marked an abandonment of the traditional policy of freedom of the seas—a policy for which America had professedly fought two full-fledged wars and several undeclared wars. The Neutrality Acts were specifically tailored to keep the nation out of a conflict like World War I. If they had been in effect at that time, America probably would not have been sucked in—at least not in April 1917. Congress was one war too late with its legislation. What had seemed dishonorable to Wilson seemed honorable and desirable to a later disillusioned generation.

"The Only Way We Can Save Her," 1939 Even as war broke out in Europe, many Americans continued to insist on the morality of U.S. neutrality.

Storm-cellar neutrality proved to be tragically shortsighted. America falsely assumed that the decision for peace or war lay in its own hands, not in those of the satanic forces already unleashed in the world. Prisoner of its own fears, it failed to recognize that it might have used its enormous power to shape international events. Instead it remained at the mercy of events controlled by the dictators.

Statutory neutrality, though of undoubted legality, was of dubious morality. America served notice that it would make no distinction whatever between brutal aggressors and innocent victims. By striving to hold the scales even, it actually overbalanced them in favor of the dictators, who had armed themselves to the teeth. By declining to use its vast industrial strength to aid its democratic friends and defeat its totalitarian foes, it helped goad the aggressors along their blood-spattered path of conquest.

✦ America Dooms Loyalist Spain

The Spanish Civil War of 1936–1939—a proving ground and dress rehearsal in miniature for World War II—was a painful object lesson in the folly of neutrality-by-legislation. Spanish rebels, who rose against the left-leaning republican government in Madrid, were headed by fascistic General Francisco Franco. Generously aided by his fellow conspirators Hitler and Mussolini, he undertook to overthrow the established Loyalist regime, which in turn was assisted on a smaller scale by the Soviet Union. This pipeline from communist Moscow chilled the natural sympathies of many Americans, especially Roman Catholics, for the republican Loyalists. But other Americans burned with passion to defend the struggling republic against Franco's fascist coup. Some three thousand young men and women headed to Spain to fight as volunteers in the **Abraham Lincoln Brigade**.

Washington continued official relations with the Loyalist government. But Congress, with the encouragement of Roosevelt and with only one dissenting vote, amended the existing neutrality legislation so as to apply an arms embargo to both Loyalists and rebels. "Roosevelt," remarked the dictator Franco, "behaved in the manner of a true gentleman." FDR later regretted being so gentlemanly.

Uncle Sam thus sat on the sidelines while Franco, abundantly supplied with arms and men by his fellow dictators, strangled the republican government of Spain. The democracies, including the United States, were so determined to stay out of war that they helped to condemn a fellow democracy to death. In so doing they further encouraged the dictators to take the dangerous road that led over the precipice to World War II.

Canute Frankson (1890–194?), an African American member of the Abraham Lincoln Brigade, explained why he went to Spain to fight against the fascist Franco in 1937:

❝Since this is a war between whites who for centuries have held us in slavery, and have heaped every kind of insult and abuse upon us, segregated and Jim-crowed us; why [am] I, a Negro . . . in Spain today? Because we are no longer an isolated minority group fighting hopelessly against an immense giant. . . . Because if we crush Fascism here we'll save our people in America, and in other parts of the world from the vicious persecution, wholesale imprisonment, and slaughter which the Jewish people . . . are suffering under Hitler's Fascist heels. . . . We will build us a new society—a society of peace and plenty. There will be no color line, no jim-crow trains, no lynching. That is why, my dear, I'm here in Spain.❞

Such peace-at-any-price-ism was further cursed with illogic. Although determined to stay out of war, America declined to build up its armed forces to a point where it could deter the aggressors. In fact, it allowed its navy to decline in relative strength. It had been led to believe that huge fleets caused huge wars; it was also trying to spare the complaining taxpayer during the grim days of the Great Depression. When President Roosevelt repeatedly called for preparedness, he was branded a warmonger. Not until 1938, the year before World War II exploded, did Congress come to grips with the problem when it passed a billion-dollar naval construction act. The calamitous story was repeated of too little, too late.

America's policy toward Spain "had been a grave mistake," Franklin D. Roosevelt (1882–1945) told his cabinet in early 1939:

❝ The policy we should have adopted was to forbid the transportation of munitions of war in American bottoms [ships]. This could have been done and Loyalist Spain would still have been able to come to us for what she needed to fight for her life against Franco—to fight for her life and for the lives of some of the rest of us as well, as events will very likely prove.❞

✦ Appeasing Japan and Germany

Sulfurous war clouds had meanwhile been gathering in the tension-taut Far East. In 1937 the Japanese militarists, at the Marco Polo Bridge near Beijing (Peking), touched off the explosion that led to an all-out invasion of China. In a sense this attack was the curtain-raiser of World War II.

Roosevelt shrewdly declined to invoke the recently passed neutrality legislation by refusing to call the China incident an officially declared war. If he had put the existing restrictions into effect, he would have cut off the trickle of munitions on which the Chinese were desperately dependent. The Japanese, of course, could continue to buy mountains of war supplies in the United States.

In Chicago—unofficial isolationist "capital" of America—President Roosevelt delivered his sensational **Quarantine Speech** in the autumn of 1937. Alarmed by the recent aggressions of Italy and Japan, he called for "positive endeavors" to "quarantine" the aggressors—presumably by economic embargoes.

The speech triggered a cyclone of protest from isolationists and other foes of involvement; they feared that a moral quarantine would lead to a shooting quarantine. Startled by this angry response, Roosevelt retreated and sought less direct means to curb the dictators.

America's isolationist mood intensified, especially in regard to China. In December 1937 Japanese aviators bombed and sank an American gunboat, the *Panay*, in Chinese waters, with a loss of two killed and thirty wounded. In the days of 1898, when the *Maine* went down, this outrage might have provoked war. But after Tokyo hastened to make the necessary apologies and pay a proper indemnity, Americans breathed a deep sigh of relief. Japanese militarists were thus encouraged to vent their anger against the "superior" white race by subjecting American civilians in China, both male and female, to humiliating slappings and strippings.

Adolf Hitler meanwhile grew louder and bolder in Europe. In 1935 he had openly flouted the Treaty of Versailles by introducing compulsory military service in Germany. The next year he brazenly marched into the demilitarized German Rhineland, likewise contrary to the detested treaty, while France and Britain looked on in an agony of indecision. Lashing his following to a frenzy, Hitler undertook to persecute and then exterminate the Jewish population in the areas under his control. In the end he wiped out about 6 million innocent victims, mostly in gas chambers. Calling upon his people to sacrifice butter for guns, he whipped the new German air force and mechanized ground divisions into the most devastating military machine the world had yet seen.

Suddenly, in March 1938, Hitler bloodlessly occupied German-speaking Austria, his birthplace. The democratic powers, wringing their hands in despair, prayed that this last grab would satisfy his passion for conquest.

But like a drunken reveler calling for madder music and stronger wine, Hitler could not stop. Intoxicated by his recent gains, he began to make bullying demands for the German-inhabited Sudetenland of neighboring Czechoslovakia. The leaders of Britain and France, eager to appease Hitler, sought frantically to bring the dispute to the conference table. President Roosevelt, also deeply alarmed, kept the wires hot with personal messages to both Hitler and Mussolini urging a peaceful settlement.

A conference was finally held in Munich, Germany, in September 1938. The Western European democracies, badly unprepared for war, betrayed Czechoslovakia to Germany when they consented to the shearing away of the Sudetenland. They hoped—and these hopes were shared by the American people—that the concessions at the conference table would slake Hitler's thirst for power and bring "peace in our time." Indeed Hitler publicly promised that the Sudetenland "is the last territorial claim I have to make in Europe."

Appeasement of the dictators, symbolized by the ugly word *Munich*, turned out to be merely surrender on the installment plan. It was like giving a cannibal a finger in the hope of saving an arm. In March 1939, scarcely six months later, Hitler suddenly erased the rest of Czechoslovakia from the map, contrary to his solemn vows. The democratic world was again stunned.

✦ Hitler's Belligerency and U.S. Neutrality

Joseph Stalin, the sphinx of the Kremlin, was a key to the peace puzzle. In the summer of 1939, the British and French were busily negotiating with Moscow, hopeful of securing a mutual-defense treaty that would halt Hitler. But mutual suspicions proved insuperable. Then the Soviet Union astounded the world by signing, on August 23, 1939, a nonaggression treaty with the German dictator.

The notorious **Hitler-Stalin pact** meant that the Nazi German leader now had a green light to make war on Poland and the Western democracies, without fearing a stab in the back from the Soviet Union—his Communist arch-foe. Consternation struck those wishful thinkers in Western Europe who had fondly hoped that Hitler might be sicced upon Stalin so that the twin menaces would bleed each other to death. It was as plain as the mustache on Stalin's face that the wily Soviet dictator was plotting to turn his German

Poland Falls to the Nazi Juggernaut, 1939 After swallowing Austria and Czechoslovakia in 1938, Hitler launched all-out war on Poland in September 1939, and the Nazi war machine seemed unstoppable.

accomplice against the Western democracies. The two warring camps would then kill each other off—and leave Stalin bestriding Europe like a colossus.

With the signing of the Nazi-Soviet pact, World War II was only hours away. Hitler now demanded from neighboring Poland a return of the areas wrested from Germany after World War I. Failing to secure satisfaction, he sent his mechanized divisions crashing into Poland at dawn on September 1, 1939.

Britain and France, honoring their commitments to Poland, promptly declared war. At long last they

President Roosevelt was roused at 3 A.M. on September 1, 1939, by a telephone call from Ambassador William Bullitt (1891–1967) in Paris:

❝Mr. President, several German divisions are deep in Polish territory. . . . There are reports of bombers over the city of Warsaw.**❞**

FDR replied,

❝Well, Bill, it has come at last. God help us all.**❞**

perceived the folly of continued appeasement. But they were powerless to aid Poland, which succumbed in three weeks to Hitler's smashing strategy of terror. Stalin, as prearranged secretly in his fateful pact with Hitler, came in on the kill for his share of old Russian Poland. Long-dreaded World War II was now fully launched, and the long truce of 1919–1939 had come to an end.

President Roosevelt speedily issued the routine proclamations of neutrality. Americans were overwhelmingly anti-Nazi and anti-Hitler; they fervently hoped that the democracies would win; they fondly believed that the forces of righteousness would triumph, as in 1918. But they were desperately determined to stay out: they were not going to be "suckers" again.

Neutrality promptly became a heated issue in the United States. Ill-prepared Britain and France urgently needed American airplanes and other weapons, but the Neutrality Act of 1937 raised a sternly forbidding hand. Roosevelt summoned Congress in special session, shortly after the invasion of Poland, to consider lifting the arms embargo. After six hectic weeks of debate, a makeshift law emerged.

The **Neutrality Act of 1939** provided that henceforth the European democracies might buy American war materials, but only on a "cash-and-carry basis." This meant that they would have to transport the munitions in their own ships, after paying for them in cash. America would thus avoid loans, war debts, and the torpedoing of American arms-carriers. While Congress thus loosened former restrictions in response to interventionist cries, it added others in response to isolationist fears. Roosevelt was now also authorized to proclaim danger zones into which American merchant ships would be forbidden to enter.

This unneutral neutrality law unfortunately hurt China, which was effectively blockaded by the Imperial Japanese Navy. But despite its defects, it clearly favored the European democracies against the dictators. As the British and French navies controlled the Atlantic, the European aggressors could not send their ships to buy America's munitions. The United States not only improved its moral position but simultaneously helped its economic position. Overseas demand for war goods brought a sharp upswing from the recession of 1937–1938 and ultimately solved the decade-long unemployment crisis (see Figure 33.4 on p. 772).

✦ The Fall of France

The months following the collapse of Poland, while France and Britain marked time, were known as the "phony war." An ominous silence fell on Europe, as Hitler shifted his victorious divisions from Poland for a knockout blow at France. Inaction during this anxious period was relieved by the Soviets, who wantonly attacked neighboring Finland in an effort to secure strategic buffer territory. The debt-paying Finns, who had a host of admirers in America, were speedily granted $30 million by an isolationist Congress for *nonmilitary* supplies. But despite heroic resistance, Finland was finally flattened by the Soviet steamroller.

An abrupt end to the "phony war" came in April 1940 when Hitler, again without warning, overran his weaker neighbors Denmark and Norway. Hardly pausing for breath, the next month he attacked the Netherlands and Belgium, followed by a paralyzing blow at France. By late June France was forced to surrender, but not until Mussolini had pounced on its rear for a jackal's share of the loot. In a pell-mell but successful evacuation from the French port of Dunkirk, the British managed to salvage the bulk of their shattered and partially disarmed army. The crisis providentially brought forth an inspired leader in Prime Minister Winston Churchill, the bulldog-jawed orator who

Adolf Hitler (1889–1945) promised to win his fellow Germans Lebensraum, or "living space," and to win it by war if necessary. In his eyes, his nationalist and racist crusade justified every violent means at hand. As he told his commanders,

"When you start a war, what matters is not who is right, but who wins. Close your hearts to pity. Act with brutality. Eighty million Germans must get what is their due. Their existence must be made secure. The stronger man is in the right."

nerved his people to fight off the fearful air bombings of their cities.

France's sudden collapse shocked Americans out of their daydreams. Stouthearted Britons, singing "There'll Always Be an England," were all that stood between Hitler and the death of constitutional government in Europe. If Britain went under, Hitler would have at his disposal the workshops, shipyards, and slave labor of Western Europe. He might even have the powerful British fleet as well. This frightening possibility, which seemed to pose a dire threat to American security, steeled the American people to a tremendous effort.

Roosevelt moved with electrifying energy and dispatch. He called upon an already debt-burdened nation to build huge airfleets and a two-ocean navy, which could also check Japan. Congress, jarred out of its apathy toward preparedness, within a year appropriated

Hitler Swaggers into Paris, 1940 The fall of France to German forces in June 1940 was a galling blow to French pride and convinced many Americans that their country must mobilize to defeat the Nazi menace.

Hulton-Deutsch/Corbis

President Roosevelt made a compelling case against the isolationists in a speech at the University of Virginia on June 10, 1940:

"Some indeed still hold to the now somewhat obvious delusion that we of the United States can safely permit the United States to become a lone island, a lone island in a world dominated by the philosophy of force. Such an island may be the dream of those who still talk and vote as isolationists. Such an island represents to me and to the overwhelming majority of Americans today a helpless nightmare of a people without freedom—the nightmare of a people lodged in prison, handcuffed, hungry, and fed through the bars from day to day by the contemptuous, unpitying masters of other continents."

Public-Opinion Polling in the 1930s

In 1936 the prominent news publication *Literary Digest* made a monumental gaffe when it relied on public-opinion polling data to forecast a victory for the Republican candidate, Alf Landon, over the incumbent, Franklin D. Roosevelt. As it happened, Roosevelt racked up a monstrous majority, winning the electoral votes of all but two states. The *Digest*'s error had been to compile its polling lists from records of automobile registration and telephone directories—unwittingly skewing its sample toward relatively well-off voters in an era when fewer than half of American families owned either a car or a telephone. The *Digest*'s embarrassing mistake ended an era of informal polling techniques, as new, scientifically sophisticated polling organizations founded by George Gallup and Elmo Roper forged to the fore. From this date forward, polling became a standard tool for marketers and advertisers—as well as for political strategists and historians. Yet controversy has long clouded the relationship between pollsters and politicians, who are often accused of abdicating their roles as leaders and slavishly deferring to public opinion, rather than trying to shape it. Franklin Roosevelt confronted this issue in the 1930s, as polls seemed to confirm the stubborn isolationism of the American people, even as the president grew increasingly convinced that the United States must play a more active international role. What do the poll results below suggest about Roosevelt's handling of this issue? About the reliability of polling data? What are the legitimate political uses of public-opinion polls? How valuable are they to the historian?

[1.] (U.S. Oct 3 '39) Do you think the United States should do everything possible to help England and France win the war, except go to war ourselves? (AIPO)

Yes 62%   No 38%

[2.] (U.S. Oct 3 '39) If it appears that Germany is defeating England and France, should the United States declare war on Germany and send our army and navy to Europe to fight? (AIPO)

	Yes	No
National total	29%	71%
BY GEOGRAPHICAL SECTION		
New England	33%	67%
Middle Atlantic	27	73
East central	25	75
West central	26	74
South	47	53
West	28	72
(Jan 30 '40) National total	23%	77%

[3.] (U.S. May 29 '40) If the question of the United States going to war against Germany came up for a national vote to go to war (go into the war or stay out of the war)? (AIPO)

Yes 16%   No 84%
(June 11 '40) . . . . Go in 19%   Stay out 81%

[4.] (U.S. Aug 5 '41) Should the United States go to war now against Japan? (AIPO)

	Yes	No	No opinion
	22%	78% = 100%	11%
(Oct 22 '41)	13	74	13

[5.] (U.S. Sept 17 '41) Should the United States go into the war now and send an army to Europe to fight? (AIPO)

Yes 9%   No 87%   No opinion 4%

[6.] (U.S. Nov 5 '41) If, in trying to defeat Germany, it becomes necessary to send a large American army to Europe, would you favor this step? (AIPO)

Yes 47%   No 46%   No opinion 7%

Source: From Hadley Cantril, ed., *Public Opinion, 1935–1946* (Princeton, N.J.: Princeton University Press, 1951).

the astounding sum of $37 billion. This figure was more than the total cost of fighting World War I and about five times larger than any New Deal annual budget.

Congress also passed a conscription law, approved September 6, 1940. Under this measure—America's first peacetime draft—provision was made for training each year 1.2 million troops and 800,000 reserves. The act was later adapted to the requirements of a global war.

The Latin American bulwark likewise needed bracing. The Netherlands, Denmark, and France, all crushed under the German jackboot, had orphaned colonies in the New World. Would these fall into German hands?

At the Havana Conference of 1940, the United States agreed to share with its twenty New World neighbors the responsibility of upholding the Monroe Doctrine. This ancient dictum, hitherto unilateral, had been a bludgeon brandished only in the hated Yankee fist. Now multilateral, it was to be wielded by twenty-one pairs of American hands—at least in theory.

✴ Refugees from the Holocaust

Aroused by Adolf Hitler, the ancient demon of anti-Semitism brutally bared its fangs. During the late nineteenth century, Jewish communities in Eastern Europe were frequent victims of pogroms, mob attacks approved or condoned by local authorities. In modern Germany primeval violence reappeared with shocking efficiency on the night of November 9, 1938. Instigated by a speech by Nazi propagandist Joseph Goebbels, mobs ransacked more than seven thousand Jewish shops and almost all of the country's synagogues. At least ninety-one Jews lost their lives, and about thirty thousand were sent to concentration camps in the turbulent wake of **Kristallnacht**, the "night of broken glass."

Many Jews attempted to escape from Hitler's racist juggernaut. To take one poignant case, in May 1939, 937 passengers, almost all of them Jewish refugees, boarded the ship *St. Louis* in Hamburg and departed for Havana. When they reached Cuba, however, most were denied entry for lack of a valid Cuban visa. The *St. Louis* then sailed to Miami, which proved no more hospitable. President Roosevelt briefly showed some interest in accepting the beleaguered passengers, but restrictive immigration laws, together with opposition from southern Democrats and Secretary of State Cordell Hull, convinced him otherwise. After being turned away one last time in Canada, the *St. Louis* eventually deposited its passengers in England, France, Belgium, and the Netherlands, where many of them subsequently perished under the Nazi heel.

After reports of the Nazi genocide began to be verified in 1942, Roosevelt created the **War Refugee Board**, which saved thousands of Hungarian Jews from deportation to the notorious death camp at Auschwitz. But all told, only 150,000 Jews, mostly Germans and Austrians, found refuge in the United States. By the end of the war, some 6 million Jews had been murdered in the Holocaust.

Shattered Jewish Storefronts in Berlin This photo was taken after the attacks of Kristallnacht on November 9, 1938.

Bildarchiv Preussicher Kulterbesitz/Art Resource, NY

Albert Einstein Arriving in America, 1933 Sadly, the United States admitted only a trickle of Jewish refugees, while the Holocaust engulfed European Jewry.

Library of Congress

✦ Bolstering Britain

Before the fall of France in June 1940, Washington had generally observed a technical neutrality. But now, as Britain alone stood between Hitler and his dream of world domination, the wisdom of neutrality seemed increasingly questionable. Hitler launched air attacks against Britain in August 1940, preparatory to an invasion scheduled for September. For months the Battle of Britain raged in the air over the British Isles. The Royal Air Force's tenacious defense of its native islands eventually led Hitler to postpone his planned invasion indefinitely.

During the precarious months of the Battle of Britain, debate intensified in the United States over what foreign policy to embrace. Radio broadcasts from London brought the drama of the nightly German air raids directly into millions of American homes. Sympathy for Britain grew, but it was not yet sufficient to push the United States into war.

Roosevelt faced a historic decision: whether to hunker down in the Western Hemisphere, assume a "Fortress America" defensive posture, and let the rest of the world go it alone; or to bolster beleaguered Britain by all means short of war itself. Both sides had their advocates.

Supporters of aid to Britain formed propaganda groups, the most potent of which was the Committee to Defend America by Aiding the Allies. Its argument was double-barreled. To interventionists it could appeal for direct succor to the British by such slogans as "Britain Is Fighting Our Fight." To isolationists it could appeal for assistance to the democracies by "All Methods Short of War," so that the terrible conflict would be kept in faraway Europe.

The isolationists, both numerous and sincere, were by no means silent. Determined to avoid American bloodshed at all costs, they organized the America First

Committee and proclaimed, "England Will Fight to the Last American." They contended that America should concentrate what strength it had to defend its own shores, lest a victorious Hitler, after crushing Britain, plot a transoceanic assault. Their basic philosophy was "The Yanks Are Not Coming," and their most effective speechmaker was the famed aviator Colonel Charles A. Lindbergh, who, ironically, had narrowed the Atlantic in 1927.

Britain was in critical need of destroyers, for German submarines were again threatening to starve it out with attacks on shipping. Roosevelt moved boldly when, on September 2, 1940, he agreed to transfer to Great Britain fifty old-model, four-funnel destroyers left over from World War I. In return, the British promised to hand over to the United States eight valuable defensive base sites, stretching from Newfoundland to South America. These strategically located outposts

Imperial War Museum

Pro-British Propaganda This patriotic poster was put out by the Committee to Defend America by Aiding the Allies.

were to remain under the Stars and Stripes for ninety-nine years.

Transferring fifty destroyers to a foreign navy was a highly questionable disposal of government property, despite a strained interpretation of existing legislation. The exchange was achieved by a simple presidential agreement, without so much as a "by your leave" to Congress. Applause burst from the aid-to-Britain advocates, many of whom had been urging such a step. But condemnation arose from America Firsters and other isolationists, as well as from anti-administration Republicans. Some of them approved the transfer but decried Roosevelt's secretive and arbitrary methods. Yet so grave was the crisis that the president was unwilling to submit the scheme to the uncertainties and delays of a full-dress debate in the Congress.

Shifting warships from a neutral United States to a belligerent Britain was, beyond question, a flagrant violation of neutral obligations—at least neutral obligations that had existed before Hitler's barefaced aggressions rendered foolish such old-fashioned concepts of fair play. Public-opinion polls demonstrated that a majority of Americans were determined, even at the risk of armed hostilities, to provide the battered British with "all aid short of war."

✴ Shattering the Two-Term Tradition

A distracting presidential election, as fate decreed, came in the midst of this crisis. The two leading Republican aspirants were round-faced and flat-voiced Senator Robert A. Taft of Ohio, son of the ex-president, and the energetic boy wonder, lawyer-prosecutor Thomas E. Dewey of New York. But in one of the miracles of American political history, the Philadelphia convention was swept off its feet by a colorful latecomer, Wendell L. Willkie, a German-descended son of Hoosier Indiana. This dynamic lawyer—tousled-headed, long-lipped, broad-faced, and large-framed—had until recently been a Democrat and the head of a huge public utility corporation. A complete novice in politics, he had rocketed from political nothingness in a few short weeks. His great appeal lay in his personality, for he was magnetic, transparently trustful, and honest in a homespun, Lincolnesque way.

With the galleries in Philadelphia wildly chanting "We Want Willkie," the delegates finally accepted this political upstart as the only candidate who could possibly beat Roosevelt. The Republican platform condemned FDR's alleged dictatorship, as well as the costly and confusing zigzags of the New Deal. Willkie, an outspoken liberal, was opposed not so much to the New Deal as to its extravagances and inefficiencies. Democratic critics branded him "the rich man's Roosevelt" and "the simple barefoot Wall Street lawyer."

While the rumor pot boiled, Roosevelt delayed to the last minute the announcement of his decision to challenge the sacred two-term tradition. Despite what he described as his personal yearning for retirement, he avowed that in so grave a crisis he owed his experienced hand to the service of his country and humanity. The Democratic delegates in Chicago, realizing that only with "the Champ" could they defeat Willkie, drafted him by a technically unanimous vote. "Better a Third Term Than a Third-Rater" was the war cry of many Democrats.

Burning with sincerity and energy, Willkie launched out upon a whirlwind, Bryanesque campaign in which he delivered over five hundred speeches. At times his voice became a hoarse croak. The country was already badly split between interventionists and isolationists, and Willkie might have widened the breach dangerously by a violent attack on Roosevelt's aid-to-Britain policies. But seeing eye-to-eye with FDR on the necessity of bolstering the beleaguered democracies, he refrained from assailing the president's interventionism, though objecting to his methods.

In the realm of foreign affairs, there was not much to choose between the two candidates. Both promised to stay out of the war; both promised to strengthen the nation's defenses. Yet Willkie, with a mop of black hair in his eyes, hit hard at Rooseveltian "dictatorship" and the third term. His enthusiastic followers cried, "Win with Willkie," "No Fourth Term Either," and "There's No Indispensable Man."

Roosevelt, busy at his desk with mounting problems, made only a few speeches. Stung by taunts that he was leading the nation by the back door into the European slaughterhouse, he repeatedly denied any such intention. His most specific statement was at Boston, where he emphatically declared, "Your boys are not going to be sent into any foreign wars"—a pledge that later came back to plague him. He and his supporters vigorously defended the New Deal, as well as all-out preparations for the defense of America and aid to the Allies.

Roosevelt triumphed, although Willkie ran a strong race. The popular total was 27,307,819 to 22,321,018, and the electoral count was 449 to 82 (see Map 34.1). This contest was much less of a walkaway than in 1932 or 1936; Democratic majorities in Congress remained about the same.

Jubilant Democrats hailed their triumph as a mandate to abolish the two-term tradition. But the truth is that Roosevelt won in spite of the third-term handicap. Voters generally felt that should war come, the experienced hand of the tried leader was needed at the helm. Less appealing was the completely inexperienced hand of the well-intentioned Willkie, who had never held public office.

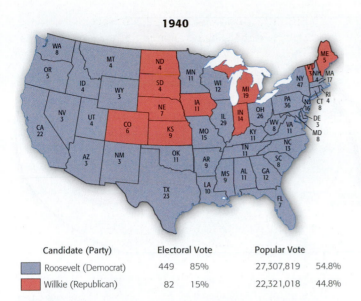

1940

Candidate (Party)	Electoral Vote		Popular Vote	
Roosevelt (Democrat)	449	85%	27,307,819	54.8%
Willkie (Republican)	82	15%	22,321,018	44.8%

MAP 34.1 Presidential Election of 1940 (with electoral vote by state) Willkie referred to Roosevelt only as "the third-term candidate." On election eve FDR hinted that communists and fascists were among Willkie's supporters. Despite these campaign conflicts, the two men respected each other. FDR later asked Willkie to serve as his emissary abroad and even suggested that they run together on a coalition ticket in 1944. © Cengage Learning

The time-honored argument that one should not change horses in the middle of a stream was strong, especially in an era of war-pumped prosperity. Roosevelt might not have won if there had not been a war crisis. On the other hand, he probably would not have run if foreign perils had not loomed so ominously. In a sense, his opponent was Adolf Hitler, not Willkie.

✯ A Landmark Lend-Lease Law

By late 1940 embattled Britain was nearing the end of its financial tether; its credits in America were being rapidly consumed by insatiable war orders. But Roosevelt, who had bitter memories of the wrangling over the Allied debts of World War I, was determined, as he put it, to eliminate "the silly, foolish, old dollar sign." He finally hit on the scheme of lending or leasing American arms to the reeling democracies. When the shooting was over, to use his comparison, the guns and tanks could be returned, just as one's next-door neighbor would return a garden hose when a threatening fire was put out. But isolationist Senator Taft (who was reputed to have the finest mind in Washington until he made it up) retorted that lending arms was like lending chewing gum: "You don't want it back." Who wants a chewed-up tank?

The **Lend-Lease Bill**, patriotically numbered 1776, was entitled "An Act Further to Promote the Defense of the United States." Sprung on the country after the election was safely over, it was praised by the administration as a device that would keep the nation out of the war rather than drag it in. The underlying concept was "Send guns, not sons" or "Billions, not bodies." America, so President Roosevelt promised, would be the "arsenal of democracy." It would send a limitless supply of arms to the victims of aggression, who in turn would finish the job and keep the war on

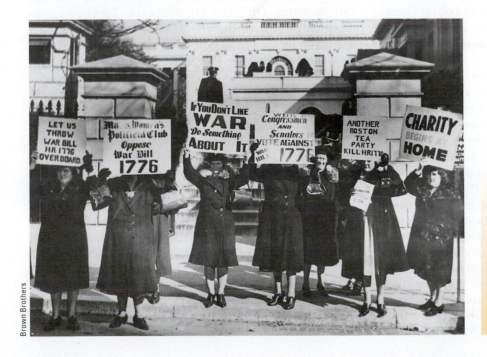

No to Lend-Lease Members of the Massachusetts Woman's Political Club presented President Roosevelt with a petition protesting adoption of the Lend-Lease Bill and picketed the White House. They feared that America's increasing involvement with the Allied cause would eventually draw their sons into battle—as it did, despite the president's assurances to the contrary.

Brown Brothers

MAP 34.2 Main Flow of Lend-Lease Aid (width of arrows indicates relative amount) The proud but desperate British prime minister, Winston Churchill, declared in early 1941, "Give us the tools and we will finish the job." Lend-lease eventually provided the British and other Allies with $50 billion worth of "tools." © Cengage Learning

their side of the Atlantic. Accounts would be settled by returning the used weapons or their equivalents to the United States when the war was ended.

Lend-lease was heatedly debated throughout the land and in Congress. Most of the opposition came, as might be expected, from isolationists and anti-Roosevelt Republicans. The scheme was assailed as "the blank-check bill" and, in the words of isolationist Senator Burton Wheeler, as "the new Triple-A [Agricultural Adjustment Act] bill"—a measure designed to "plow under every fourth American boy." Nevertheless, lend-lease was finally approved in March 1941 by sweeping majorities in both houses of Congress.

Lend-lease was one of the most momentous laws ever to pass Congress; it was a challenge hurled squarely into the teeth of the Axis dictators. America pledged itself, to the extent of its vast resources, to bolster those nations that were indirectly defending it by fighting aggression. When the gigantic operation ended in 1945, America had sent about $50 billion worth of arms and equipment—much more than the cost to the country of World War I—to those nations fighting aggressors (see Map 34.2). The passing of lend-lease was in effect an economic declaration of war; now a shooting declaration could not be very far around the corner.

By its very nature, the Lend-Lease Bill marked the abandonment of any pretense of neutrality. It was no destroyer deal arranged privately by President Roosevelt. The bill was universally debated, over drugstore counters and cracker barrels, from California all the way to Maine, and the sovereign citizen at last spoke through convincing majorities in Congress. Most people probably realized that they were tossing the old concepts of neutrality out the window. But they also recognized that they would play a suicidal game if they bound themselves by the oxcart rules of the nineteenth century—especially while the Axis aggressors

themselves openly spurned international obligations. Lend-lease would admittedly involve a grave risk of war, but most Americans were prepared to take that chance rather than see Britain collapse and then face the diabolical dictators alone.

Lend-lease had the somewhat incidental result of gearing U.S. factories for all-out war production. The enormously increased capacity thus achieved helped save America's own skin when, at long last, the shooting war burst around its head.

Hitler evidently recognized lend-lease as an unofficial declaration of war. Until then Germany had avoided attacking U.S. ships; memories of America's decisive intervention in 1917–1918 were still fresh in German minds. But after the passing of lend-lease, there was less point in trying to curry favor with the United States. On May 21, 1941, the *Robin Moor*, an unarmed American merchantman, was torpedoed and destroyed by a German submarine in the South Atlantic, outside a war zone. The sinkings had started, but on a limited scale.

✦ Charting a New World

Two globe-shaking events marked the course of World War II before the assault on Pearl Harbor in December 1941. One was the fall of France in June 1940; the other was Hitler's invasion of the Soviet Union, almost exactly one year later, in June 1941.

The scheming dictators Hitler and Stalin had been uneasy yoke-fellows under the ill-begotten Nazi-Soviet pact of 1939. As masters of the double cross, neither trusted the other. They engaged in prolonged dickering in a secret attempt to divide potential territorial spoils between them, but Stalin balked at dominant German control of the Balkans. Hitler thereupon decided to crush his coconspirator, seize the oil and other resources of the Soviet Union, and then have two free hands to snuff out Britain. He assumed that his invincible armies would subdue Stalin's "Mongol half-wits" in a few short weeks.

Out of a clear sky, on June 22, 1941, Hitler launched a devastating attack on his Soviet neighbor. This timely assault was an incredible stroke of good fortune for the democratic world—or so it seemed at the time. The two fiends could now slit each other's throats on the icy steppes of Russia. Or they would if the Soviets did not quickly collapse, as many military experts predicted.

Sound American strategy seemed to dictate speedy aid to Moscow while it was still afloat. Roosevelt immediately promised assistance and backed up his words by making some military supplies available. Several months later, interpreting the lend-lease law to mean that the defense of the USSR was now essential for the defense of the United States, he extended $1 billion in lend-lease—the first installment on an ultimate total of $11 billion. Meanwhile, the valor of the red army, combined with the white paralysis of an early Russian winter, had halted Hitler's invaders at the gates of Moscow.

With the surrender of the Soviet Union still a dread possibility, the drama-charged Atlantic Conference was held in August 1941. British prime minister Winston Churchill, with cigar embedded in his cherubic face,

Unexpected Guest, 1941 Stalin joins the democracies, Britain and America. Library of Congress

Senator (later president) Harry S Truman (1884–1972) expressed a common reaction to Hitler's invasion of the Soviet Union in 1941:

"If we see that Germany is winning, we ought to help Russia, and if we see Russia is winning, we ought to help Germany, and that way let them kill as many as possible."

secretly met with Roosevelt on a warship off the foggy coast of Newfoundland. This was the first of a series of history-making conferences between the two statesmen for the discussion of common problems, including the menace of Japan in the Far East.

The most memorable offspring of this get-together was the eight-point **Atlantic Charter**. It was formally accepted by Roosevelt and Churchill and endorsed by the Soviet Union later that year. Suggestive of Wilson's Fourteen Points, the new covenant outlined the aspirations of the democracies for a better world at war's end. Arguing for the rights of individuals rather than nations, the Atlantic Charter laid the groundwork for later advocacy on behalf of universal human rights.

Many were surprised by how specific the document was. Opposing imperialistic annexations, the charter promised that there would be no territorial changes contrary to the wishes of the inhabitants (self-determination). It further affirmed the right of a people to choose their own form of government and, in particular, to regain the governments abolished by the dictators. Among various other goals, the charter declared for disarmament and a peace of security, pending a "permanent system of general security" (a new League of Nations).

Liberals the world over took heart from the Atlantic Charter, as they had taken heart from Wilson's comparable Fourteen Points. It was especially gratifying to subject populations, like the Poles, who were then ground under the iron heel of a conqueror. But the agreement was roundly condemned in the United States by isolationists and others hostile to Roosevelt. What right, they charged, had "neutral" America to confer with belligerent Britain on common policies? Such critics missed the point: the nation was in fact no longer neutral.

★ U.S. Destroyers and Hitler's U-boats Clash

Lend-lease shipments of arms to Britain on British ships were bound to be sunk by German wolf-pack submarines. If the intent was to get the munitions to England, not to dump them into the ocean, the freighters would have to be escorted by U.S. warships. Britain simply did not have enough destroyers. The dangerous possibility of being "convoyed into war" had been mentioned in Congress during the lengthy debate on lend-lease, but administration spokespeople had brushed the idea aside. Their strategy was to make only one commitment at a time.

Roosevelt made the fateful decision to convoy in July 1941. By virtue of his authority as commander in chief of the armed forces, the president issued orders to the navy to escort lend-lease shipments as far as Iceland. The British would then shepherd them the rest of the way.

Inevitable clashes with submarines ensued on the Iceland run, even though Hitler's orders were to strike at American warships only in self-defense. In September 1941 the U.S. destroyer *Greer*, provocatively trailing a German U-boat, was attacked by the undersea craft, without damage to either side. Roosevelt then proclaimed a shoot-on-sight policy. On October 17 the escorting destroyer *Kearny*, while engaged in a battle with U-boats, lost eleven men when it was crippled but not sent to the bottom. Two weeks later the destroyer *Reuben James* was torpedoed and sunk off southwestern Iceland, with the loss of more than a hundred officers and enlisted men.

Neutrality was still inscribed on the statute books, but not in American hearts. Congress, responding to public pressures and confronted with a shooting war, voted in mid-November 1941 to pull the teeth from the now-useless Neutrality Act of 1939. Merchant ships could henceforth be legally armed, and they could enter the combat zones with munitions for Britain. Americans braced themselves for wholesale attacks by Hitler's submarines.

✦ Surprise Assault on Pearl Harbor

The blowup came not in the Atlantic, but in the faraway Pacific. This explosion should have surprised no close observer, for Japan, since September 1940, had been a formal military ally of Nazi Germany—America's shooting foe in the North Atlantic.

Japan's position in the Far East had grown more perilous by the hour. It was still mired down in the costly and exhausting "China incident," from which it could extract neither honor nor victory. Its war machine was fatally dependent on immense shipments of steel, scrap iron, oil, and aviation gasoline from the United States. Such assistance to the Japanese aggressor was highly unpopular in America. But Roosevelt had resolutely held off an embargo, lest he goad the

Tokyo warlords into a descent upon the oil-rich but defense-poor Dutch East Indies.

Washington, late in 1940, finally imposed the first of its embargoes on Japan-bound supplies. This blow was followed in mid-1941 by a freezing of Japanese assets in the United States and a cessation of all shipments of gasoline and other sinews of war. As the oil gauge dropped, the squeeze on Japan grew steadily more nerve-racking. Japanese leaders were faced with two painful alternatives. They could either knuckle under to the Americans or break out of the embargo ring by a desperate attack on the oil supplies and other riches of Southeast Asia.

Final tense negotiations with Japan took place in Washington during November and early December of 1941. The State Department insisted that the Japanese clear out of China, but to sweeten the pill offered to renew trade relations on a limited basis. Japanese imperialists, after waging a bitter war against the Chinese for more than four years, were unwilling to lose face by withdrawing at the behest of the United States. Faced with capitulation or continued conquest, they chose the sword.

Officials in Washington, having "cracked" the top-secret code of the Japanese, knew that Tokyo's decision was for war. But the United States, as a democracy committed to public debate and action by Congress, could not shoot first. Roosevelt, misled by Japanese ship movements in the Far East, evidently expected the blow to fall on British Malaya or on the Philippines. No one in high authority in Washington seems to have believed that the Japanese were either strong enough or foolhardy enough to strike Hawaii.

But the paralyzing blow struck **Pearl Harbor**, while Tokyo was deliberately prolonging negotiations in Washington. Japanese bombers, winging in from distant aircraft carriers, attacked without warning on the "Black Sunday" morning of December 7, 1941. It was a date, as Roosevelt told Congress, "which will live in infamy." About three thousand casualties were inflicted on American personnel, many aircraft were destroyed, the battleship fleet was virtually wiped out when all eight of the craft were sunk or otherwise

> *Roosevelt's war message to Congress began with these famous words:*
>
> **"Yesterday, December 7, 1941—a date which will live in infamy—the United States of America was suddenly and deliberately attacked by naval and air forces of the Empire of Japan."**

U.S. Army

The Battleship *West Virginia* The shocking Japanese attack on Pearl Harbor on December 7, 1941, propelled the United States into World War II. One of the first ships to be hit, the USS *West Virginia* quickly sank at its mooring, taking at least seventy sailors down with it. By September 1944 the *West Virginia* had been repaired and was back in service.

immobilized, and numerous small vessels were damaged or destroyed. Fortunately for America, the three priceless aircraft carriers happened to be outside the harbor.

An angered Congress the next day officially recognized the war that had been "thrust" upon the United States. The roll call in the Senate and House fell only one vote short of unanimity. Germany and Italy, allies of Japan, spared Congress the indecision of debate by declaring war on December 11, 1941. This challenge was formally accepted on the same day by a unanimous vote of both Senate and House. The unofficial war, already of many months' duration, was now official.

✴ America's Transformation from Bystander to Belligerent

Japan's hara-kiri gamble in Hawaii paid off only in the short run. True, the Pacific fleet was largely destroyed or immobilized, but the sneak attack aroused and united America as almost nothing else could have done. To the very day of the blowup, a strong majority of Americans still wanted to keep out of war. But the bombs that pulverized Pearl Harbor blasted the isolationists into silence. The only thing left to do, growled isolationist Senator Wheeler, was "to lick hell out of them."

But Pearl Harbor was not the full answer to the question of why the United States went to war. This treacherous attack was but the last explosion in a long chain reaction. Following the fall of France, Americans were confronted with a devil's dilemma. They desired above all to stay out of the conflict, yet they did not want Britain to be knocked out. They wished to halt Japan's conquests in the Far East—conquests that menaced not only American trade and security but international peace as well. To keep Britain from collapsing, the Roosevelt administration felt compelled to extend the unneutral aid that invited attacks from German submarines. To keep Japan from expanding, Washington undertook to cut off vital Japanese supplies with embargoes that invited possible retaliation. Rather than let democracy die and dictatorship rule supreme, most citizens were evidently determined to support a policy that might lead to war. It did.

Chapter Review

KEY TERMS

London Economic Conference (778)

Good Neighbor policy (780)

Reciprocal Trade Agreements Act (780)

Rome-Berlin Axis (781)

Johnson Debt Default Act (782)

Neutrality Acts of 1935, 1936, and 1937 (782)

Abraham Lincoln Brigade (783)

Quarantine Speech (784)

Appeasement (784)

Hitler-Stalin pact (784)

Neutrality Act of 1939 (785)

Kristallnacht (788)

War Refugee Board (788)

Lend-Lease Bill (791)

Atlantic Charter (793)

Pearl Harbor (794)

PEOPLE TO KNOW

Benito Mussolini

Adolf Hitler

Francisco Franco

Cordell Hull

Wendell L. Willkie

CHRONOLOGY

1933
FDR torpedoes London Economic Conference
United States recognizes Soviet Union
FDR declares Good Neighbor policy toward Latin America
Hitler becomes German chancellor
Germany quits League of Nations

1934
Tydings-McDuffie Act provides for Philippine independence on July 4, 1946
Reciprocal Trade Agreements Act
U.S. Marines vacate Haiti

1935
Nuremberg Laws implemented against German Jews
Mussolini invades Ethiopia
U.S. Neutrality Act of 1935
Japan quits League of Nations

1936
U.S. Neutrality Act of 1936
Mussolini and Hitler form Rome-Berlin Axis
Stalin begins Great Purge
German troops invade Rhineland

1936–1939 Spanish Civil War

1937
U.S. Neutrality Act of 1937
Panay incident
Japan invades China

1938
Hitler seizes Austria
Munich Conference
Kristallnacht in Germany

1939
Hitler seizes all of Czechoslovakia
Nazi-Soviet pact
World War II begins in Europe with Hitler's invasion of Poland
U.S. Neutrality Act of 1939

1940
Fall of France
Hitler invades Denmark, Norway, Netherlands, and Belgium
United States invokes first peacetime draft
Havana Conference
Battle of Britain
Bases-for-destroyers deal with Britain
FDR defeats Willkie for presidency

1941
Lend-Lease Act
Hitler attacks Soviet Union
Atlantic Charter
Japan attacks Pearl Harbor

TO LEARN MORE

Peter N. Carroll, *The Odyssey of the Abraham Lincoln Brigade: Americans in the Spanish Civil War* (1994)

Robert Dallek, *Franklin D. Roosevelt and American Foreign Policy, 1932–1945* (1995)

Justus D. Doenecke, *Storm on the Horizon: The Challenge to American Intervention, 1939–1941* (2000)

Irwin F. Gellman, *Good Neighbor Diplomacy: United States Policies in Latin America, 1933–1945* (1979)

Akira Iriye, *The Globalizing of America, 1913–1945* (1993)

Manfred Jonas, *Isolationism in America, 1935–1941* (1966)

Primo Levi, *Survival in Auschwitz: The Nazi Assault on Humanity* (1961)

B. J. C. McKercher, *Transition of Power: Britain's Loss of Global Pre-eminence to the United States, 1930–1945* (1999)

Edward S. Miller, *Bankrupting the Enemy: The U.S. Financial Siege of Japan Before Pearl Harbor* (2007)

Gordon W. Prange, *At Dawn We Slept: The Untold Story of Pearl Harbor* (1981)

David Reynolds, *From Munich to Pearl Harbor: Roosevelt's America and the Origins of the Second World War* (2001)

Dominic Tierney, *FDR and the Spanish Civil War: Neutrality and Commitment in the Struggle That Divided America* (2007)

A complete, annotated bibliography for this chapter—along with brief descriptions of the People to Know—may be found on the American Pageant website. The Key Terms are defined in a Glossary at the end of the text.

Go to the CourseMate website at **www.cengagebrain.com** for additional study tools and review materials—including audio and video clips—for this chapter.

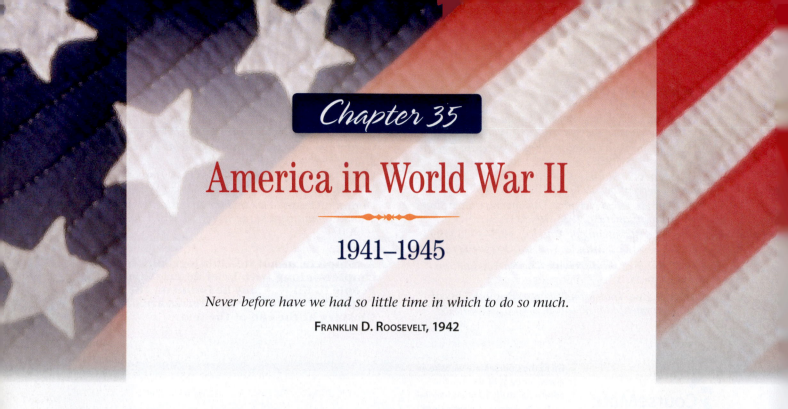

Chapter 35

America in World War II

1941–1945

Never before have we had so little time in which to do so much.

FRANKLIN D. ROOSEVELT, 1942

The United States was plunged into the inferno of World War II with the most stupefying and humiliating military defeat in its history. In the dismal months that ensued, the democratic world teetered on the edge of disaster.

Japan's fanatics forgot that whoever stabs a king must stab to kill. A wounded but still potent American giant pulled itself out of the mud of Pearl Harbor, grimly determined to avenge the bloody treachery. "Get Japan first" was the cry that rose from millions of infuriated Americans, especially on the Pacific Coast. These outraged souls regarded America's share in the global conflict as a private war of vengeance in the Pacific, with the European front a kind of holding operation.

But Washington, in the so-called **ABC-1 agreement** with the British, had earlier and wisely adopted the grand strategy of "getting Germany first." If America diverted its main strength to the Pacific, Hitler might crush both the Soviet Union and Britain and then emerge unconquerable in Fortress Europe. But if Germany was knocked out first, the combined Allied forces could be concentrated on Japan, and its daring game of conquest would be up. Meanwhile, just enough American strength would be sent to the Pacific to prevent Japan from digging in too deeply.

The get-Germany-first strategy was the solid foundation on which all American military strategy was built. But it encountered much ignorant criticism from two-fisted Americans who thirsted for revenge against Japan. Aggrieved protests were also registered by short-handed American commanders in the Pacific and by Chinese and Australian allies. But President Roosevelt, a competent strategist in his own right, wisely resisted these pressures.

★ The Allies Trade Space for Time

Given time, the Allies seemed bound to triumph. But would they be given time? True, they had on their side the great mass of the world's population, but the wolf is never intimidated by the number of the sheep. The United States was the mightiest military power on earth—potentially. But wars are won with bullets, not blueprints. Indeed America came perilously close to losing the war to the well-armed aggressors before it could begin to throw its full weight onto the scales.

Time, in a sense, was the most needed munition. Expense was no limitation. The overpowering problem confronting America was to retool itself for all-out war production, while praying that the dictators would not meanwhile crush their adversaries who still remained in the field—notably Britain and the Soviet Union. Haste was all the more imperative because the highly skilled German scientists might turn up with unbeatable secret weapons, including rocket bombs and perhaps even atomic arms.

America's task was far more complex and back-breaking than during World War I. It had to feed, clothe, and arm itself, as well as transport its forces to regions as far separated as Britain and Burma. More than that, it had to send a vast amount of food and munitions to its hard-pressed allies, who stretched all the way from the USSR to Australia. Could the American people, reputedly "gone soft," measure up to this herculean task? Was democracy "rotten" and "decadent," as the dictators sneeringly proclaimed?

✴ The Shock of War

National unity was no worry, thanks to the electrifying blow by the Japanese at Pearl Harbor. American Communists had denounced the Anglo-French "imperialist" war before Hitler attacked Stalin in 1941, but they now clamored for an unmitigated assault on the Axis powers. The handful of strutting pro-Hitlerites in the United States melted away, while millions of Italian Americans and German Americans loyally supported the nation's war program. In contrast to World War I, when the patriotism of millions of immigrants was hotly questioned, World War II actually speeded the assimilation of many ethnic groups into American society. Immigration had been choked off for almost two decades before 1941, and America's ethnic communities were now composed of well-settled members, whose votes were crucial to Franklin Roosevelt's

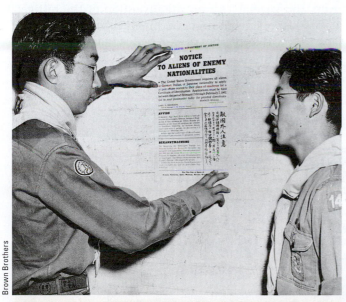

Brown Brothers

Enemy Aliens When the United States suddenly found itself at war with Germany, Italy, and Japan in December 1941, noncitizen German, Italian, and Japanese immigrants became "enemy aliens" and were required to register with the authorities. Several hundred resident Germans and Italians were detained in internment camps, but the harshest treatment was meted out to the Japanese, some 110,000 of whom, noncitizens and citizens alike, were eventually interned. Ironically, the two Japanese American Boy Scouts posting this notice in Los Angeles would soon be on their way to a government detention camp.

American song titles after Pearl Harbor combined nationalism with unabashed racism: "We Are the Sons of the Rising Guns," "Oh, You Little Son of an Oriental," "To Be Specific, It's Our Pacific," "The Sun Will Soon Be Setting on the Land of the Rising Sun," "The Japs Don't Stand a Chinaman's Chance," and "We're Gonna Find a Fellow Who Is Yellow and Beat Him Red, White, and Blue."

Monica Sone (b. 1919), a college-age Japanese American woman in Seattle, recorded the shock she and her brother felt when they learned of Executive Order No. 9066, which authorized the War Department to remove Japanese—aliens and citizens alike—from their homes:

❝In anger, Henry and I read and reread the Executive Order. Henry crumbled the newspaper in his hand and threw it against the wall. 'Doesn't my citizenship mean a single blessed thing to anyone? Why doesn't somebody make up my mind for me? First they want me in the army. Now they're going to slap an alien 4-C on me because of my ancestry. . . .' Once more I felt like a despised, pathetic two-headed freak, a Japanese and an American, neither of which seemed to be doing me any good.❞

Democratic party. Consequently, there was virtually no government witch-hunting of minority groups, as had happened in World War I.

A painful exception was the plight of some 110,000 Japanese Americans, concentrated on the Pacific Coast (see "Makers of America: The Japanese," pp. 800-801). The Washington top command, fearing that they might act as saboteurs for Japan in case of invasion, forcibly herded them together in concentration camps, though about two-thirds of them were American-born U.S. citizens. This brutal precaution, authorized under **Executive Order No. 9066**, was both unnecessary and unfair, as the loyalty and combat record of Japanese Americans proved to be admirable. But a wave of post–Pearl Harbor hysteria, backed by the long historical swell of anti-Japanese prejudice on the West Coast, temporarily robbed many Americans of their good sense—and their sense of justice. The internment camps deprived these uprooted Americans of dignity and basic rights; the internees also lost hundreds of millions of dollars in property and foregone earnings. The wartime Supreme Court in 1944 upheld the constitutionality of the Japanese relocation in *Korematsu* v. *U.S.* But more than four decades later, in 1988, the

In 1853 the American commodore Matthew Perry sailed four gunboats into Japan's Uraga Bay and demanded that the nation open itself to diplomatic and commercial exchange with the United States. Perry's arrival ended two centuries of Japan's self-imposed isolation and eventually led to the overthrow of the last Japanese shogun (military ruler) and the restoration of the emperor. Within two decades of Perry's arrival, Japan's new "Meiji" government had launched the nation on an ambitious program of industrialization and militarization designed to make it the economic and political equal of the Western powers.

As Japan rapidly modernized, its citizens increasingly took ship for America. A steep land tax imposed by the Meiji government to pay for its reforms drove more than 300,000 Japanese farmers off their land. In 1884 the Meiji government permitted Hawaiian planters to recruit contract laborers from among this displaced population. By the 1890s many Japanese were sailing beyond Hawaii to the ports of Long Beach, San Francisco, and Seattle.

Between 1885 and 1924, roughly 200,000 Japanese migrated to Hawaii, and around 180,000 more ventured to the U.S. mainland. They were a select group: because the Meiji government saw overseas Japanese as representatives of their homeland, it strictly regulated emigration. Thus Japanese immigrants to America arrived with more money than their European counterparts. Also, because of Japan's system of compulsory education, Japanese immigrants on average were better educated and more literate than European immigrants.

Women as well as men migrated. The Japanese government, wanting to avoid the problems of an itinerant bachelor society that it observed among the Chinese in the United States, actively promoted women's migration. Although most Japanese immigrants were young men in their twenties and thirties, thousands of women also ventured to Hawaii and the mainland as contract laborers or "picture brides," so called because their courtship had consisted exclusively of an exchange of photographs with their prospective husbands.

Like many Chinese and European immigrants, most Japanese who came to America expected to stay only temporarily. They planned to work hard for wages that were high by Japanese standards and then to return home and buy land. In Hawaii most Japanese labored on the vast sugar cane plantations. On the mainland they initially found migratory work on the railroads or in fish, fruit, or vegetable canneries. A separate Japanese economy of restaurants, stores, and boardinghouses soon sprang up in cities to serve the immigrants' needs.

From such humble beginnings, many Japanese—particularly those on the Pacific Coast—quickly moved into farming. In the late nineteenth century, the spread of irrigation shifted California agriculture from grain to fruits and vegetables, and the invention of the refrigerated railcar opened hungry new markets in the East. The Japanese, with centuries of experience in intensive farming, arrived just in time to take advantage of these developments. As early as 1910, Japanese farmers produced 70 percent of California's strawberries, and by 1940 they

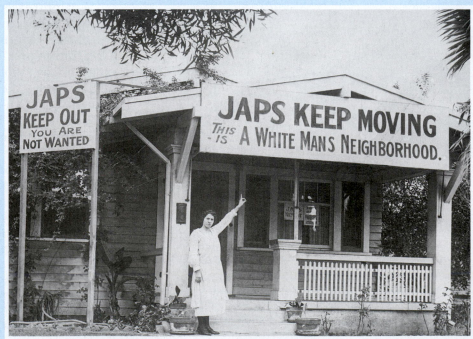

Campaign Against the Japanese, Hollywood, California, 1923 Long before Japanese Americans were interned during World War II as a security risk, they faced intense discrimination throughout the United States.

© Bettmann/Corbis

Japanese American Evacuees, 1942 After the U.S. Army's Western Defense Command ordered the forced evacuation of all Japanese and Japanese Americans living on the Pacific Coast, families had no choice but to pack up whatever they could carry and move to the "relocation centers" hastily erected farther inland.

grew 95 percent of the state's snap beans and more than half of its tomatoes. One Japanese farmer, known as the Potato King, sent his children to Harvard and Stanford and died in 1926 with an estate valued at $15 million.

But the very success of the Japanese proved a lightning rod for trouble. On the West Coast, Japanese immigrants had long endured racist barbs and social segregation. Increasingly, white workers and farmers, jealous of Japanese success, pushed for immigration restrictions. Bowing to this pressure, President Theodore Roosevelt in 1908 negotiated the "Gentlemen's Agreement," under which the Japanese government voluntarily agreed to limit emigration. In 1913 the California legislature denied Japanese immigrants already living in the United States the right to own land.

Legally barred from becoming citizens, Japanese immigrants (the "Issei," from the Japanese word for *first*) became more determined than ever that their American-born children (the "Nissei," from the Japanese word for *second*) would reap the full benefits of their birthright. Japanese parents encouraged their children to learn English, to excel in school, and to get a college education. Many Nissei grew up in two worlds, a fact they often recognized by Americanizing their Japanese names. Although education and acculturation did not protect the Nissei from the hysteria of World War II, those assets did give them a springboard to success in the postwar era.

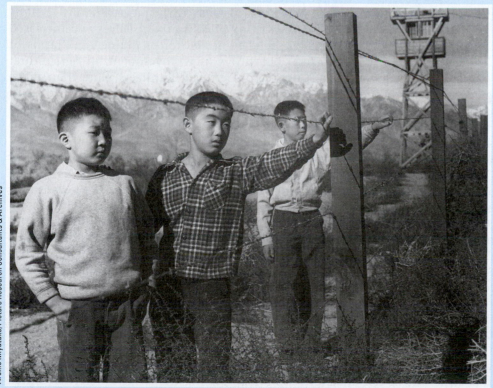

Three Boys at Manzanar, by Toyo Miyatake (1895–1979) Miyatake was an acclaimed Japanese American photographer with his own studio in Los Angeles before he and his family were evacuated to the Manzanar internment camp. He was determined to pursue his craft there, at first working secretly and then with the knowledge of the authorities. His pictures are the only photographic records of daily camp life taken by an internee. The guards allowed him to step outside the barbed-wire fence to take this photograph.

Image by © Swim Ink 2, LLC/Corbis

Anti-Japanese Poster, World War II Government propaganda during the war exploited racial stereotypes, often depicting Japanese people with big teeth and poor vision.

U.S. government officially apologized for its actions and approved the payment of reparations of $20,000 to each camp survivor.

The war prompted other changes in the American mood. Many programs of the once-popular New Deal—including the Civilian Conservation Corps, the Works Progress Administration, and the National Youth Administration—were wiped out by the conservative Congress elected in 1942. Roosevelt declared in 1943 that "Dr. New Deal" was going into retirement, to be replaced by "Dr. Win-the-War." His announcement acknowledged not only the urgency of the war effort but the power of the revitalized conservative forces in the country. The era of New Deal reform was over.

World War II was no idealistic crusade, as World War I had been. The Washington government did make some effort to propagandize at home and abroad with the Atlantic Charter, but the accent was on action. Opinion polls in 1942 revealed that nine out of ten

Americans could cite no provisions of the Atlantic Charter. A majority then, and a near-majority two years later, confessed to having "no clear idea what the war is about." All Americans knew was that they had a dirty job on their hands and that the only way out was forward. They went about their bloody task with astonishing efficiency.

✴ Building the War Machine

The war crisis caused the drooping American economy to snap to attention. Massive military orders—over $100 billion in 1942 alone—almost instantly soaked up the idle industrial capacity of the still-lingering Great Depression. Orchestrated by the **War Production Board (WPB)**, American factories poured forth an avalanche of weaponry: 40 billion bullets, 300,000 aircraft, 76,000 ships, 86,000 tanks, and 2.6 million machine guns. Miracle-man shipbuilder Henry J. Kaiser was dubbed "Sir Launchalot" for his prodigies of ship construction; one of his ships was fully assembled in fourteen days, complete with life jackets and coat hangers.

The War Production Board halted the manufacture of nonessential items such as passenger cars. It assigned priorities for transportation and access to raw materials. When the Japanese invasion of British Malaya and the Dutch East Indies snapped America's lifeline of natural rubber, the government imposed a national speed limit and gasoline rationing in order to conserve rubber and built fifty-one synthetic-rubber plants. By war's end they were far outproducing the prewar supply.

Farmers, too, rolled up their sleeves and increased their output. The armed forces drained the farms of workers, but heavy new investment in agricultural machinery and improved fertilizers more than made up the difference. In 1944 and 1945, blue-jeaned farmers hauled in record-breaking billion-bushel wheat harvests.

These wonders of production also brought economic strains. Full employment and scarce consumer goods fueled a sharp inflationary surge in 1942. The **Office of Price Administration (OPA)** eventually brought ascending prices under control with extensive regulations. Rationing held down the consumption of critical goods such as meat and butter, though some "black marketeers" and "meatleggers" cheated the system. The **National War Labor Board (NWLB)** imposed ceilings on wage increases.

Labor unions, whose membership grew from about 10 million to more than 13 million workers during the war, fiercely resented the government-dictated wage ceilings. Despite the no-strike pledges of most of the major unions, a rash of labor walkouts plagued the war effort. Prominent among the strikers were the United

Mine Workers, who several times were called off the job by their crusty and iron-willed chieftain, John L. Lewis.

Threats of lost production through strikes became so worrisome that Congress, in June 1943, passed the **Smith-Connally Anti-Strike Act**. This act authorized the federal government to seize and operate tied-up industries. Strikes against any government-operated industry were made a criminal offense. Under the act, Washington took over the coal mines and, for a brief period, the railroads. Yet work stoppages, although dangerous, actually accounted for less than 1 percent of the total working hours of the United States' wartime laboring force—a record better than blockaded Britain's. American workers, on the whole, were commendably committed to the war effort.

The Four Freedoms, by Norman Rockwell In his January 6, 1941, speech to Congress requesting lend-lease aid to the Allies, President Roosevelt spoke eloquently of the "four freedoms" then threatened by Nazi and Japanese aggression. They are here given pictorial representation by Norman Rockwell, probably the most popular and best-loved American artist of the time.

✦ Manpower and Womanpower

The armed services enlisted nearly 15 million men in World War II and some 216,000 women, who were employed for noncombat duties. Best known of these "women in arms" were the **WACs (Women's Army Corps)**, **WAVES (Women Accepted for Volunteer Emergency Service)** (navy), and **SPARs (U.S. Coast Guard Women's Reserve)**. As the draft net was tightened after Pearl Harbor, millions of young men were plucked from their homes and clothed in "GI" (government issue) outfits. As the arsenal of democracy, the United States exempted certain key categories of industrial and agricultural workers from the draft, in order to keep its mighty industrial and food-producing machines humming.

But even with these exemptions, the draft left the nation's farms and factories so short of personnel that new workers had to be found. An agreement with Mexico in 1942 brought thousands of Mexican agricultural workers, called *braceros*, across the border to harvest the fruit and grain crops of the West. The **Bracero program** outlived the war by some twenty years, becoming a fixed feature of the agricultural economy in many western states.

Even more dramatic was the march of women onto the factory floor. More than 6 million women took up jobs outside the home; over half of them had never before worked for wages. Many of them were mothers, and the government was obliged to set up some 3,000 day-care centers to care for "Rosie the Riveter's" children while she drilled the fuselage of a heavy bomber or joined the links of a tank track. When the war ended, Rosie and many of her sisters were in no hurry to put down their tools. They wanted to keep on working and often did. The war thus foreshadowed an eventual revolution in the roles of women in American society.

Yet the war's immediate impact on women's lives has frequently been exaggerated. The great majority of American women—especially those with husbands present in the home or with small children to care for—did not work for wages in the wartime economy but continued in their traditional roles. In both Britain and the Soviet Union, a far greater percentage of women, including mothers, were pressed into industrial employment

Poster appeals and slogans urging women to enlist in the WACs (Women's Army Corps) were "Speed Them Back, Join the WAC," "I'd Rather Be with Them—Than Waiting for Them," "Back the Attack, Be a WAC! For America Is Calling," and (a song throwback to World War I) "The WACs and WAVES Will Win the War, Parlez Vous."

National Archives

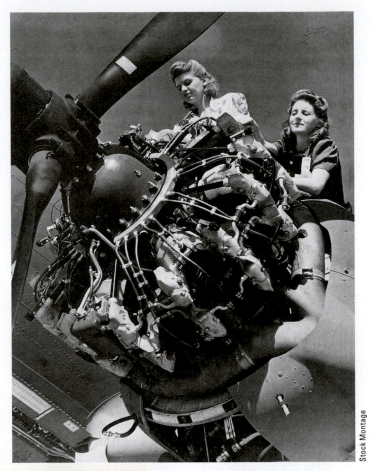

Stock Montage

War Workers More than 6 million women—more than 3 million of them homemakers who had never before worked for wages—entered the work force during World War II. In contrast to the experience of women workers in World War I, many of these newly employed women continued as wage workers after the war ended.

as the gods of war laid a much heavier hand on those societies than they did on the United States. A poll in 1943 revealed that a majority of American women would not take a job in a war plant if it were offered.

At war's end, two-thirds of women war workers left the labor force. Many of them were forced out of their jobs by employers and unions eager to reemploy returning servicemen. But half of them told census takers that they quit their jobs voluntarily because of family obligations. The immediate postwar period witnessed not a permanent widening of women's employment opportunities, but a widespread rush into suburban domesticity and the mothering of the "baby boomers," who were born by the tens of millions in the decade and a half after 1945. America was destined to experience a thoroughgoing revolution in women's status later in the postwar period, but that epochal change was only beginning to gather momentum in the war years.

✦ Wartime Migrations

The war also proved to be a demographic cauldron, churning and shifting the American population. Many of the 15 million men and women in uniform, having seen new sights and glimpsed new horizons, chose not to go home again at war's end. War industries sucked people into boomtowns like Los Angeles, Detroit, Seattle, and Baton Rouge. California's population grew by nearly 2 million. The South experienced especially dramatic changes. Franklin Roosevelt had called the South "the nation's number one economic problem" in 1938; when war came, he seized the opportunity to accelerate the region's economic development. The states of the old Confederacy received a disproportionate share of defense contracts, including nearly $6 billion of federally financed industrial facilities. Here were the seeds of the postwar blossoming of the "Sunbelt" (see Map 35.1).

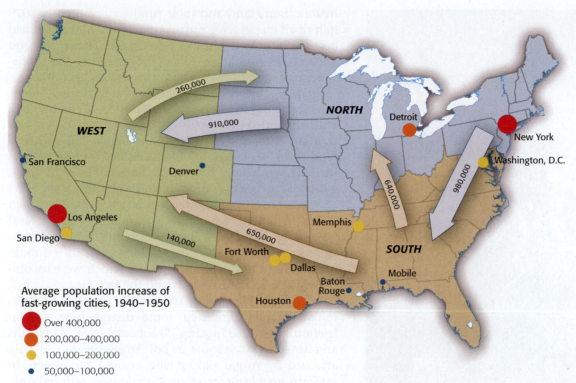

MAP 35.1 Internal Migration in the United States During World War II   Few events in American history have moved the American people about so massively as World War II. The West and the South boomed, and several war-industry cities grew explosively. A majority of migrants from the South were blacks; 1.6 million African Americans left the region in the 1940s. (Source: United States Department of Labor, Bureau of Labor Statistics.) © Cengage Learning

Despite this economic stimulus in the South, some 1.6 million blacks left the land of their ancient enslavement to seek jobs in the war plants of the West and North. Forever after, race relations constituted a national, not a regional, issue. Explosive tensions developed over employment, housing, and segregated facilities. Black leader A. Philip Randolph, head of the Brotherhood of Sleeping Car Porters, threatened a massive "Negro March on Washington" in 1941 to demand equal opportunities for blacks in war jobs and in the armed forces. Roosevelt's response was to issue an executive order forbidding discrimination in defense industries. In addition, the president established the **Fair Employment Practices Commission (FEPC)** to monitor compliance with his edict. Blacks were also drafted into the armed forces, though they were still generally assigned to service branches rather than combat units and subjected to petty degradations such as segregated blood banks for the wounded. But in general the war helped to embolden blacks in their long struggle for equality. They rallied behind the slogan "Double V"—victory over the dictators abroad and over

racism at home. Membership in the National Association for the Advancement of Colored People (NAACP) shot up almost to the half-million mark, and a new militant organization committed to nonviolent "direct

An African American soldier angrily complained about segregation in the armed forces during World War II:

❝Why is it we Negro soldiers who are as much a part of Uncle Sam's great military machine as any cannot be treated with equality and the respect due us? The same respect which white soldiers expect and demand from us? . . . There is great need for drastic change in this man's Army! How can we be trained to protect America, which is called a *free nation,* when all around us rears the ugly head of segregation?❞

Segregation in the Military A white officer reviews the 99th Pursuit Squadron, the famed "Tuskegee Airmen." They flew more than sixteen hundred fighter-support missions in North Africa and compiled an outstanding record, never losing a bomber to enemy aircraft. But these fliers were among the few African Americans who saw combat duty in World War II, when a still strictly segregated military assigned most blacks to construction, longshoreman, and mess-hall service.

action," the **Congress of Racial Equality (CORE)**, was founded in 1942.

The northward migration of African Americans accelerated after the war, thanks to the advent of the mechanical cotton picker—an invention whose impact rivaled that of Eli Whitney's cotton gin. Introduced in 1944, this new mechanical marvel did the work of fifty people at about one-eighth the cost. Overnight, the Cotton South's historic need for cheap labor disappeared. Their muscle no longer required in Dixie, some 5 million black tenant farmers and sharecroppers headed north in the three decades after the war. Theirs was one of the great migrations in American history, comparable in size to the immigrant floods from Ireland, Italy, and Poland. Within a single generation, a near-majority of African Americans gave up their

historic homeland and their rural way of life. By 1970 half of all blacks lived outside the South, and *urban* had become almost a synonym for *black*. The speed and scale of these changes jolted the migrants and sometimes convulsed the communities that received them.

The war also prompted an exodus of Native Americans from the reservations. Thousands of Indian men and women found war work in the major cities, and thousands more answered Uncle Sam's call to arms. More than 90 percent of Indians resided on reservations in 1940; six decades later more than half lived in cities, with a large concentration in southern California.

Some twenty-five thousand Native American men served in the armed forces. Comanches in Europe and Navajos in the Pacific made especially valuable contributions as "**code talkers**." They transmitted radio messages in their native languages, which were incomprehensible to the Germans and the Japanese.

The sudden rubbing against one another of unfamiliar peoples produced some distressingly violent friction. In 1943 young "zoot-suit"–clad Mexicans and Mexican Americans in Los Angeles were viciously attacked by Anglo sailors who cruised the streets in taxicabs searching for victims. Order was restored only after the Mexican ambassador made an emotional plea, pointing out that such outbreaks were grist for Nazi propaganda mills. At almost the same time, an even more brutal race riot that killed twenty-five blacks and nine whites erupted in Detroit.

Navajo Code Talkers, 1943 One of the best-kept secrets of World War II was the use of the Navajo language in a Marine Corps code designed to confuse the Japanese. Two marines in the leatherneck unit made up of Native Americans from Arizona and New Mexico transmitted in code during the battle for Bougainville Island in the South Pacific in 1943.

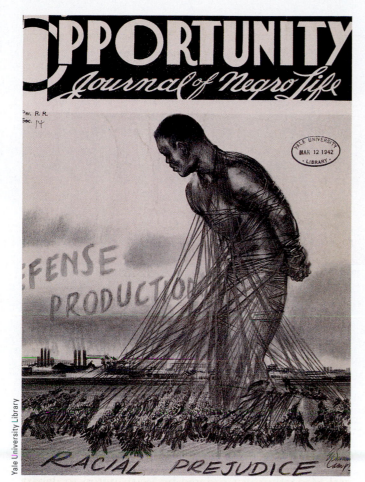

"Let John Henry Go" This image from the cover of the National Urban League's publication *Opportunity* reflects the rising militancy of African Americans in the World War II era. That militancy helped to energize the civil rights movement in the postwar years.

✦ Holding the Home Front

Despite these ugly episodes, Americans on the home front suffered little from the war, compared to the peoples of the other fighting nations. By war's end much of the planet was a smoking ruin. But in America the war invigorated the economy and lifted the country out of a decade-long depression. The gross national product vaulted from less than $100 billion in 1940 to more than $200 billion in 1945. Corporate profits rose from about $6 billion in 1940 to almost twice that amount four years later. ("If you are going to try to go to war in a capitalist country," said Secretary of War Henry Stimson, "you have to let business make money out of the process, or business won't work.") Despite wage ceilings, overtime pay fattened pay envelopes. Disposable personal income, even after payment of wartime taxes, more than doubled. On December 7, 1944, the third anniversary of Pearl Harbor, Macy's department store rang up the biggest sales day in its history. Americans had never had it so good—and they wanted it a lot better. When price controls were finally lifted in 1946, America's pent-up lust to consume pushed prices up 33 percent in less than two years. The rest of the world, meanwhile, was still clawing its way out from under the rubble of war.

The hand of government touched more American lives more intimately during the war than ever before. The war, perhaps even more than the New Deal, pointed the way to the post-1945 era of big-government interventionism. Every household felt the constraints of the rationing system. Millions of men and women worked for Uncle Sam in the armed forces. Millions more worked for him in the defense industries, where their employers and unions were monitored by the FEPC and the NWLB, and their personal needs were cared for by government-sponsored housing projects, day-care facilities, and health plans. The Office of Scientific Research and Development channeled hundreds of millions of dollars into university-based scientific research, establishing the partnership between the government and universities that underwrote America's technological and economic leadership in the postwar era.

The flood of war dollars—not the relatively modest rivulet of New Deal spending—at last swept the plague of unemployment from the land. War, not enlightened social policy, cured the depression. As the postwar economy continued to depend dangerously on military spending for its health, many observers looked back to the years 1941–1945 as the origins of a "warfare-welfare state."

The conflict was phenomenally expensive. The wartime bill amounted to more than $330 billion—ten times the direct cost of World War I and twice as much as *all* previous federal spending since 1776. Roosevelt would have preferred to follow a pay-as-you-go policy to finance the war, but the costs were simply too gigantic. The income-tax net was expanded to catch about four times as many people as before, and maximum tax rates rose as high as 90 percent. But despite such drastic measures, only about two-fifths of the war costs were paid from current revenues. The remainder was borrowed. The national debt skyrocketed from $49 billion in 1941 to $259 billion in 1945 (see Figure 35.1). When production finally slipped into high gear, the war was costing about $10 million an hour. This was the price of victory over such implacable enemies.

✦ The Rising Sun in the Pacific

Early successes of the efficient Japanese militarists were breathtaking: they realized that they would have to

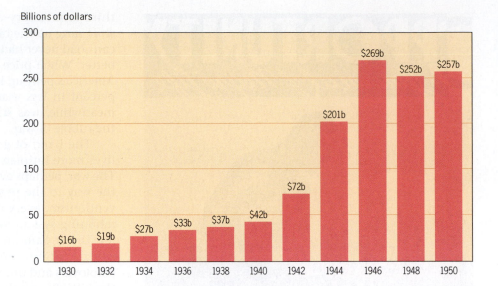

Billions of dollars

FIGURE 35.1 The National Debt, 1930–1950 Contrary to much popular mythology, it was World War II, not the New Deal, that first ballooned the national debt. The debt accumulated to still greater amounts in the 1980s and 1990s, and exploded with the onset of the "Great Recession" in 2008 (see Figure 40.1 on p. 952). (Source: *Historical Statistics of the United States*.)

win quickly or lose slowly. Seldom, if ever, has so much territory been conquered so rapidly with so little loss.

Simultaneously with the assault on Pearl Harbor, the Japanese launched widespread and uniformly successful attacks on various Far Eastern bastions. These included the American outposts of Guam, Wake, and the Philippines. In a dismayingly short time, the Japanese invader seized not only the British-Chinese port of Hong Kong but also British Malaya, with its critically important supplies of rubber and tin.

Nor did the Japanese tide stop there. The overambitious soldiers of the emperor, plunging into the snake-infested jungles of Burma, cut the famed Burma Road. This was the route over which the United States had been trucking a trickle of munitions to the armies of the Chinese generalissimo Jiang Jieshi (Chiang Kai-shek), who was still resisting the Japanese invader in China. Thereafter, intrepid American aviators were forced to fly a handful of war supplies to Jiang "over the hump" of the towering Himalaya mountains from the India-Burma theater. Meanwhile, the Japanese had lunged southward against the oil-rich Dutch East Indies. The jungle-matted islands speedily fell to the assailants after the combined British, Australian, Dutch, and American naval and air forces had been smashed at an early date by their numerically superior foe.

Better news came from the Philippines, which succeeded dramatically in slowing down the mikado's warriors for five months. The Japanese promptly landed a small but effective army, and General Douglas MacArthur, the eloquent and egotistical American commander, withdrew to a strong defensive position at Bataan, not far from Manila. There about twenty thousand American troops, supported by a much larger force of ill-trained Filipinos, held off violent Japanese attacks until April 9, 1942. The defenders, reduced to eating mules and monkeys, heroically traded their lives for time in the face of hopeless odds. They grimly joked while vainly hoping for reinforcements:

> *We're the battling bastards of Bataan;*
> *No Mamma, no Papa, no Uncle Sam.*

Before the inevitable American surrender, General MacArthur was ordered by Washington to depart secretly for Australia, there to head the resistance against the Japanese. Leaving by motorboat and airplane, he proclaimed, "I shall return." After the battered remnants of his army had hoisted the white flag, they were treated with vicious cruelty in the infamous eighty-mile Bataan Death March to prisoner-of-war camps—the first in a series of atrocities committed by both sides in the unusually savage Pacific war. The island fortress of Corregidor, in Manila harbor, held out until May 6, 1942, when it too surrendered and left Japanese forces in complete control of the Philippine archipelago (see Map 35.2).

★ Japan's High Tide at Midway

The aggressive warriors from Japan, making hay while the Rising Sun shone, pushed relentlessly southward. They invaded the turtle-shaped island of New Guinea, north of Australia, and landed on the Solomon Islands, from which they threatened Australia itself. Their onrush was finally checked by a crucial naval battle fought in the Coral Sea, in May 1942. An American carrier task force, with Australian support, inflicted heavy

MAP 35.2 Corregidor and Bataan © Cengage Learning

April, 1942 Route of Bataan Death March

San Fernando

Luzon

BATAAN PENINSULA

Manila Bay

Manila

15°N

119°E

Mariveles

Corregidor Island

Lamon Bay

14°N

120°E

0 15 30 Km.
0 15 30 Mi.

Philippine Is.

Mindoro

George Strock/Time & Life Pictures/Getty Images

Hell in the Pacific Assaulting Japanese island fortresses in the Pacific was a bloody, costly business. These American soldiers perished as they stepped ashore at Buna beach in New Guinea in 1942. Their damaged landing craft wallows in the surf behind them. Appearing in *Life* magazine on September 20, 1943, nearly two years after Pearl Harbor, this was the first photograph of dead GIs that the War Department allowed to be published.

losses on the victory-flushed Japanese. For the first time in history, the fighting was all done by carrier-based aircraft, and neither fleet saw or fired a shot directly at the other.

Japan next undertook to seize Midway Island, more than a thousand miles northwest of Honolulu. From this strategic base, it could launch devastating assaults on Pearl Harbor and perhaps force the weakened American Pacific fleet into destructive combat—possibly even compel the United States to negotiate a cease-fire in the Pacific. The epochal **Battle of Midway** was fought on June 3–6, 1942. Admiral Chester W. Nimitz, a high-grade naval strategist, directed a smaller but skillfully maneuvered carrier force, under Admiral Raymond A. Spruance, against the powerful invading fleet. The fighting was all done by aircraft, and the Japanese broke off action after losing four vitally important carriers.

Midway was a pivotal victory. Combined with the Battle of the Coral Sea, the U.S. success at Midway halted Japan's juggernaut. But the thrust of the Japanese into the eastern Pacific did net them America's fog-girt islands of Kiska and Attu, in the Aleutian archipelago, off Alaska. This easy conquest aroused fear of an invasion of the United States from the northwest. Much American strength was consequently diverted to the defense of Alaska, including the construction of the "Alcan" Highway through Canada.

Yet the Japanese imperialists, overextended in 1942, suffered from "victory disease." Their appetites were bigger than their stomachs. If they had only dug in and consolidated their gains, they would have been much more difficult to dislodge once the tide turned.

American Leapfrogging Toward Tokyo

Following the heartening victory at Midway, the United States for the first time was able to seize the initiative in the Pacific. In August 1942 American ground forces gained a toehold on Guadalcanal Island, in the Solomons, in an effort to protect the lifeline from America to Australia through the southwest Pacific. An early naval defeat inflicted by the Japanese shortened American supplies dangerously, and for weeks the U.S. troops held on to the malarial island by their fingernails. After several desperate sea battles for naval control, the Japanese troops evacuated Guadalcanal in February 1943. Japanese losses were 20,000, compared to 1,700 for the Americans. That casualty ratio of more than ten to one, Japanese to American, persisted throughout the Pacific war.

American and Australian forces, under General MacArthur, meanwhile had been hanging on courageously to the southeastern tip of New Guinea, the last buffer protecting Australia. The scales of war gradually began to tip as the American navy, including submarines, inflicted lethal losses on Japanese supply ships and troop carriers. Conquest of the north coast of New Guinea was completed by August 1944, after General MacArthur had fought his way westward through tropical jungle hells. This hard-won victory was the first leg of his long return journey to the Philippines.

The U.S. Navy, with marines and army divisions doing the meat-grinder fighting, had meanwhile been "leapfrogging" the Japanese-held islands in the Pacific. Old-fashioned strategy dictated that the American forces, as they drove toward Tokyo, should reduce the fortified Japanese outposts on their flank. This course would have taken many bloodstained months, for the holed-in defenders were prepared to die to the last man in their caves. The new strategy of island hopping called for bypassing some of the most heavily fortified Japanese posts, capturing nearby islands, setting up airfields on them, and then neutralizing the enemy bases through heavy bombing. Deprived of essential supplies from the homeland, Japan's outposts would slowly wither on the vine—as they did.

Brilliant success crowned the American attacks on the Japanese island strongholds in the Pacific, where Admiral Nimitz skillfully coordinated the efforts of naval, air, and ground units. In May and August of 1943, Attu and Kiska in the Aleutians were easily retaken. In November 1943 "bloody Tarawa" and Makin, both in the Gilbert Islands, fell after suicidal resistance. In January and February 1944, the key outposts of the Marshall Islands group succumbed after savage fighting.

Especially prized were the Marianas, including America's conquered Guam. From bases in the Marianas, the United States' new B-29 superbombers could carry out round-trip bombing raids on Japan's home islands. The assault on the Marianas opened on June 19, 1944, with what American pilots called the "Great Marianas Turkey Shoot." A combination of the combat superiority of the recently developed American "Hellcat" fighter plane and the new technology of the antiaircraft proximity fuse destroyed nearly 250 Japanese aircraft, with a loss of only 29 American planes. The following day, in the Battle of the Philippine Sea, U.S. naval forces sank several Japanese carriers. The

Japanese navy never recovered from these massive losses of planes, pilots, and ships.

After fanatical resistance, including a mass suicide leap of surviving Japanese soldiers and civilians from "Suicide Cliff" on Saipan, the major islands of the Marianas fell to the U.S. attackers in July and August 1944. With these unsinkable aircraft carriers now available, virtual round-the-clock bombing of Japan began in November 1944 (see Map 35.3).

✷ The Allied Halting of Hitler

Early setbacks for America in the Pacific were paralleled in the Atlantic. Hitler had entered the war with a formidable fleet of ultramodern submarines, which ultimately operated in "wolf packs" with frightful effect, especially in the North Atlantic, the Caribbean, and the Gulf of Mexico. During ten months of 1942 more than 500 merchant ships were reported lost—111 in June alone—as ship destruction far outran construction.

The tide of subsea battle turned with agonizing slowness. Old techniques, such as escorting convoys of merchant vessels and dropping depth bombs from destroyers, were strengthened by air patrol, the newly invented technology of radar, and the bombing of submarine bases. "Keep 'Em Sailing" was the motto of oil-begrimed merchant seamen, hundreds of whom perished as unsung heroes in icy seas. Eventually Allied antisubmarine tactics improved substantially, thanks especially to British code breakers, who had cracked the Germans' "Enigma" codes and could therefore pinpoint the locations of the U-boats lurking in the North Atlantic.

Not until the spring of 1943 did the Allies clearly have the upper hand against the U-boat. If they had not won the Battle of the Atlantic, Britain would have been forced under, and a second front could not have been launched from its island springboard. Victory over the undersea raiders was nerve-rackingly narrow. When the war ended, Hitler was about to mass-produce a fearsome new submarine—one that could remain underwater indefinitely and cruise at seventeen knots when submerged.

British prime minister Winston Churchill (1874–1965) observed in a speech in May 1943,

❝ The proud German Army has by its sudden collapse, sudden crumbling and breaking up . . . once again proved the truth of the saying, 'The Hun [German] is always either at your throat or at your feet.'❞

MAP 35.3 **United States Thrusts in the Pacific, 1942–1945**
American strategists had to choose among four proposed plans for waging the war against Japan:

1. Defeating the Japanese in China by funneling supplies over the Himalayan "hump" from India.
2. Carrying the war into Southeast Asia (a proposal much favored by the British, who could thus regain Singapore).
3. Heavy bombing of Japan from Chinese air bases.
4. "Island hopping" from the South Pacific to within striking distance of the Japanese home islands. This strategy, favored by General Douglas MacArthur, was the one finally emphasized. © Cengage Learning

Meanwhile, the turning point of the land-air war against Hitler had come late in 1942. The British had launched a thousand-plane raid on Cologne in May. In August 1942 they were joined by the American air force and were cascading bombs on German cities. The Germans under Marshal Erwin Rommel—the "Desert Fox"—had driven eastward across the hot sands of North Africa into Egypt, perilously close to the Suez Canal. A breakthrough would have spelled disaster for the Allies. But late in October 1942, British general Bernard Montgomery delivered a withering attack at El Alamein, west of Cairo. With the aid of several hundred hastily shipped American Sherman tanks, he speedily drove the enemy back to Tunisia, more than a thousand miles away.

On the Soviet front, the unexpected successes of the red army gave a new lift to the Allied cause. In September 1942 the Russians stalled the German steamroller at rubble-strewn Stalingrad, graveyard of Hitler's hopes. More than a score of invading divisions, caught in an icy noose, later surrendered or were "mopped up." In November 1942 the resilient Russians unleashed a crushing counteroffensive, which was never seriously reversed. A year later Stalin had regained about two-thirds of the blood-soaked Soviet motherland wrested from him by the German invader.

A Second Front from North Africa to Rome

Soviet losses were already staggering in 1942: millions of soldiers and civilians lay dead, and Hitler's armies had overrun most of the western USSR. Anglo-American losses at this time could be counted only in the thousands. By war's end, the grave had closed over some 20 million Soviets, and a great swath of their country, equivalent in the United States to the area from Chicago to the Atlantic seaboard, had been laid waste. Small wonder that Kremlin leaders clamored for a second front to divert the German strength westward.

Many Americans, including FDR, were eager to begin a diversionary invasion of France in 1942 or 1943. They feared that the Soviets, unable to hold out forever against Germany, might make a separate peace as they had in 1918 and leave the Western Allies to face Hitler's fury alone. Roosevelt rashly promised the Soviets in early 1942 that he would open a second front on the European continent by the end of the year—a promise that proved utterly impossible to keep.

British military planners, remembering their appalling losses in 1914–1918, were not enthusiastic about a frontal assault on German-held France. It might end in disaster. They preferred to attack Hitler's Fortress Europe through the "soft underbelly" of the Mediterranean. Faced with British boot-dragging and a woeful lack of resources, the Americans reluctantly agreed to postpone a massive invasion of Europe.

An assault on French-held North Africa was a compromise second front, and a far cry from what the badly battered Soviets were demanding. The highly secret attack, launched in November 1942, was headed by a gifted and easy-smiling American general, Dwight D. ("Ike") Eisenhower, a master of organization and conciliation. As a joint Allied operation ultimately involving some 400,000 men (British, Canadian, French, and chiefly American) and about 850 ships, the invasion was the mightiest waterborne effort up to that time in history. After savage fighting, the remnants of the German-Italian army were finally trapped in Tunisia and surrendered in May 1943.

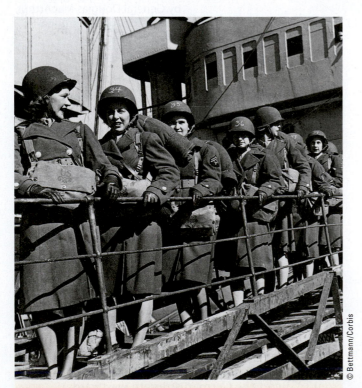

Women at War Members of the Women's Army Corps disembark in North Africa in 1944. (Note: "Auxiliary" was dropped from the name in 1943.)

© Bettmann/Corbis

New blows were now planned by the Allies. At Casablanca, in newly occupied French Morocco, President Roosevelt, who had boldly flown the Atlantic, met in a historic conference with Winston Churchill in January 1943. The Big Two agreed to step up the Pacific war, invade Sicily, increase pressure on Italy, and insist upon an "unconditional surrender" of the enemy, a phrase earlier popularized by General Ulysses S. Grant during the Civil War. Such an unyielding policy would presumably hearten the ultrasuspicious Soviets, who professed to fear separate Allied peace negotiations. It would also forestall charges of broken armistice terms, such as had come after 1918. Paradoxically, the tough-sounding unconditional surrender declaration was an admission of the weakness of the Western Allies. Still unable in 1943 to mount the kind of second front their Soviet partner desperately demanded, the British and the Americans had little but words to offer Stalin.

"Unconditional surrender" proved to be one of the most controversial moves of the war. The main criticism was that it steeled the enemy to fight to a last-bunker resistance, while discouraging antiwar groups in Germany from revolting. Although there was some truth in these charges, no one can prove that "unconditional surrender" either shortened or lengthened the war. But this is known: by helping to destroy the German government utterly, the harsh policy forced a thorough postwar reconstruction.

The Allied forces, victorious in Africa, now turned against the not-so-soft underbelly of Europe. Sicily fell in August 1943 after sporadic but sometimes bitter resistance. Shortly before the conquest of the island, Mussolini was deposed, and Italy surrendered unconditionally soon thereafter, in September 1943. President Roosevelt, referring to the three original Axis countries—Germany, Italy, and Japan—joked grimly that it was now one down and two to go.

But if Italy dropped out of the war, the Germans did not drop out of Italy. Hitler's well-trained troops stubbornly resisted the Allied invaders now pouring into the toe of the Italian boot. They also unleashed their fury against the Italians, who had turned their coats and declared war on Germany in October 1943. "Sunny Italy" proceeded to belie its name, for in the snow-covered and mud-caked mountains of its elongated peninsula occurred some of the filthiest, bloodiest, and most frustrating fighting of the war.

For many months Italy appeared to be a dead end, as the Allied advance was halted by a seemingly impregnable German defense centered on the ancient monastery of Monte Cassino. After a touch-and-go assault on the Anzio beachhead, Rome was finally taken on June 4, 1944. The tremendous cross-channel invasion of France begun two days later turned Italy into a kind of sideshow, but the Allies, limited in manpower,

The Big Two British Prime Minister Winston Churchill and U.S. President Franklin D. Roosevelt meet at the Casablanca conference in Morocco, January 1943. The two leaders had a remarkable personal relationship that shaped the outcome of World War II and the course of history. They met in person nine times over the course of the war. "It is fun to be in the same decade with you," FDR cabled to Churchill after one of their meetings. As for Churchill, who was desperate for American aid in the struggle against Hitler, he once commented that "No lover ever studied the whims of his mistress as I did those of Franklin Roosevelt."

continued to fight their way slowly and painfully into northern Italy. On May 2, 1945, only five days before Germany's official surrender, several hundred thousand Axis troops in Italy laid down their arms and became prisoners of war. While the Italian second front opened the Mediterranean and diverted some German divisions from the blazing Soviet and French battle lines, it also may have delayed the main Allied invasion of Europe, from England across the English Channel to France, by many months—allowing more time for the Soviet army to advance into Eastern Europe.

⭐ D-Day: June 6, 1944

The Soviets had never ceased their clamor for an all-out second front, and the time rapidly approached for Churchill, Roosevelt, and Stalin to meet in person to coordinate the promised effort. Marshal Joseph Stalin, with a careful eye on Soviet military operations, balked at leaving Moscow. President Roosevelt, who jauntily remarked in private, "I can handle that old buzzard," was eager to confer with him. The president seemed confident that Rooseveltian charm could woo the hardened conspirator of the Kremlin from his nasty communist ways.

Tehran, the capital of Iran (Persia), was finally chosen as the meeting place. To this ancient city Roosevelt riskily flew, after a stopover conference in Cairo with Britain's Churchill and China's Jiang Jieshi regarding the war against Japan. At Tehran the discussions among Stalin, Roosevelt, and Churchill—from November 28 to December 1, 1943—progressed smoothly. Perhaps the most important achievement was agreement on broad plans, especially those for launching Soviet attacks on Germany from the east simultaneously with the prospective Allied assault from the west.

Preparations for the cross-channel invasion of France were gigantic. Britain's fast-anchored isle virtually groaned with munitions, supplies, and troops, as nearly 3 million fighting men were readied. Because the United States was to provide most of the Allied warriors, the overall command was entrusted to an American, General Eisenhower. He had already distinguished himself in the North African and Mediterranean campaigns, not only for his military capacity but also for his gifts as a conciliator of clashing Allied interests.

French Normandy, less heavily defended than other parts of the European coast, was pinpointed for the invasion assault. On **D-Day**, June 6, 1944, the enormous operation, which involved some forty-six hundred vessels, unwound. Stiff resistance was encountered from the Germans, who had been misled by a feint into expecting the blow to fall farther north. The Allies had already achieved mastery of the air over France. They were thus able to block reinforcements by crippling the railroads, while worsening German fuel shortages by bombing gasoline-producing plants.

The Allied beachhead, at first clung to with fingertips, was gradually enlarged, consolidated, and reinforced. After desperate fighting, the invaders finally broke out of the German iron ring that enclosed the Normandy landing zone. Most spectacular were the lunges across France by American armored divisions, brilliantly commanded by blustery and profane General George S. ("Blood 'n' Guts") Patton. The retreat of the German defenders was hastened when an American-French force landed in August 1944 on the southern coast of France and swept northward. With the assistance of the French "underground," Paris was liberated in August 1944, amid exuberant manifestations of joy and gratitude.

Allied forces rolled irresistibly toward Germany, and many of the Americans encountered places, like

Allies Landing in Normandy, June 6, 1944   Nine-foot ocean swells on invasion day made loading the assault landing craft, such as the one pictured here, treacherous business. Many men were injured or tossed into the sea as the bathtublike amphibious vessels bobbed wildly up and down alongside the troop transports. As the vulnerable boats churned toward the beach, some officers led their tense, grim-faced troops in prayer. One major, recalling the remarkable Battle of Agincourt in 1415, quoted from Shakespeare's Henry V: "He that outlives this day, and comes safe home / Will stand a tip-toe when this day is named."

Château-Thierry, familiar to their fathers in 1918. "Lafayette, we are here again," quipped some of the American soldiers. The first important German city (Aachen) fell to the Americans in October 1944, and the days of Hitler's "thousand-year Reich" were numbered (see Map 35.4).

✵ FDR: The Fourth-Termite of 1944

The presidential campaign of 1944, which was bound to divert energy from the war program, came most awkwardly as the awful conflict roared to its climax. But the normal electoral processes continued to function, despite some loose talk of suspending them "for the duration."

Victory-starved Republicans met in Chicago with hopeful enthusiasm. They quickly nominated the short, mustachioed, and dapper Thomas E. Dewey, popular vote-getting governor of New York. Regarded as a liberal, he had already made a national reputation as a prosecutor of grafters and racketeers in New York City. His shortness and youth—he was only forty-two—had caused one veteran New Dealer to sneer that

the candidate had cast his diaper into the ring. To offset Dewey's mild internationalism, the convention nominated for the vice presidency a strong isolationist, handsome and white-maned Senator John W. Bricker of Ohio. Yet the platform called for an unstinted prosecution of the war and for the creation of a new international organization to maintain peace.

FDR, aging under the strain, was the "indispensable man" of the Democrats. No other major figure was available, and the war was apparently grinding to its finale. He was nominated at Chicago on the first ballot by acclamation. But in a sense he was the "forgotten man" of the convention, for in view of his age, an unusual amount of attention was focused on the vice presidency.

The scramble for the vice-presidential plum turned into something of a free-for-all. Henry A. Wallace, onetime "plow 'em under" secretary of agriculture, had served four years as vice president and desired a renomination. But conservative Democrats distrusted him as an ill-balanced and unpredictable liberal. A "ditch Wallace" move developed tremendous momentum, despite the popularity of Wallace with large numbers of voters and many of the delegates. With Roosevelt's

MAP 35.4 World War II in Europe and North Africa, 1939–1945 © Cengage Learning

blessing, the vice-presidential nomination finally went to smiling and self-assured Senator Harry S Truman of Missouri ("the new Missouri Compromise"). Hitherto inconspicuous, he had recently attained national visibility as the efficient chairman of a Senate committee conducting an investigation of wasteful war expenditures. Nobody had much against him or on him.

⭐ Roosevelt Defeats Dewey

A dynamic Dewey took the offensive, for Roosevelt was too consumed with directing the war to spare much time for speechmaking. The vigorous young "crime buster," with his beautiful baritone voice and polished diction, denounced the tired and quarrelsome "old men" in Washington. He proclaimed repeatedly that after "twelve long years" of New Dealism, it was "time for a change." As for the war, Dewey would not alter the basic strategy but would fight it better—a type of "me-tooism" ridiculed by the Democrats. The fourth-term issue did not figure prominently, now that the ice had been broken by Roosevelt's third term. But "Dewey-eyed" Republicans half-humorously professed to fear fifth and sixth terms by the "lifer" in the White House.

In the closing weeks of the campaign, Roosevelt left his desk for the stump. He was stung by certain Republican charges, including criticism that he had sent a U.S. Navy destroyer to retrieve his pet Scottie dog, Fala. He was also eager to show himself, even in chilling rains, to spike well-founded rumors of failing health.

Substantial assistance came from the new political action committee of the CIO, which was organized to get around the law banning the direct use of union funds for political purposes. Zealous CIO members, branded as communists by the Republicans, rang countless doorbells and asked, with pointed reference to the recent depression, "What were you doing in 1932?" At times Roosevelt seemed to be running again against Hoover. As in every one of his previous three campaigns, FDR was opposed by a majority of the newspapers, which were owned chiefly by Republicans.

Roosevelt, as customary, won a sweeping victory: 432 to 99 in the Electoral College; 25,606,585 to 22,014,745 in the popular vote. Elated, he quipped that "the first twelve years are the hardest."

Roosevelt won primarily because the war was going well. A winning pitcher is not ordinarily pulled from the game. Foreign policy was a decisive factor with untold thousands of voters, who concluded that Roosevelt's experienced hand was needed in fashioning a future organization for world peace. The dapper Dewey, cruelly dubbed "the little man on top of the wedding cake," had spoken smoothly of international cooperation, but his isolationist running mate, Bricker, had implanted serious doubts. The Republican party was still suffering from the taint of isolationism fastened on it by the Hardingites.

✦ The Last Days of Hitler

By mid-December 1944, the month after Roosevelt's fourth-term victory, Germany seemed to be wobbling on its last legs. The Soviet surge had penetrated eastern Germany. Allied aerial "blockbuster" bombs, making the "rubble bounce" with around-the-clock attacks, were falling like giant explosive hailstones on cities, factories, and transportation arteries. The German western front seemed about to buckle under the sledgehammer blows of the United States and its Allies.

MAP 35.5 Battle of the Bulge, December 1944–January 1945 © Cengage Learning

Hitler then staked everything on one last throw of his reserves. Secretly concentrating a powerful force, he hurled it, on December 16, 1944, against the thinly held American lines in the heavily befogged and snow-shrouded Ardennes Forest. His objective was the Belgian port of Antwerp, key to the Allied supply operation. Caught off guard, the outmanned Americans were driven back, creating a deep "bulge" in the Allied line. The ten-day penetration was finally halted after the 101st Airborne Division had stood firm at the vital bastion of Bastogne. The commander, Brigadier General A. C. McAuliffe, defiantly answered the German demand for surrender with one word: "Nuts." Reinforcements were rushed up, and the last-gasp Hitlerian offensive was at length bloodily stemmed in the Battle of the Bulge (see Map 35.5).

In March 1945, forward-driving American troops reached Germany's Rhine River, where, by incredibly good luck, they found one strategic bridge undemolished. Pressing their advantage, General Eisenhower's troops reached the Elbe River in April 1945. There, a short distance south of Berlin, American and Soviet advance guards dramatically clasped hands amid cries of *"Amerikanskie tovarishchi"* (American comrades). The conquering Americans were horrified to find blood-spattered and still-stinking concentration camps, where

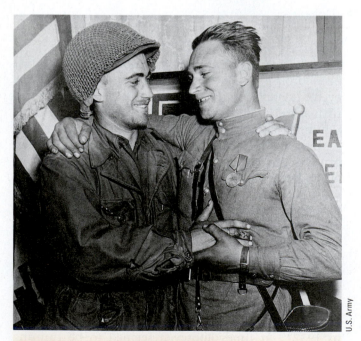

American and Soviet Soldiers Meet in Germany, 1945
Such friendly sights soon became rare as mutual suspicion deepened.

Franklin Roosevelt at Tehran, 1943

In late 1943 the "Big Three" wartime leaders—British prime minister Winston Churchill, American president Franklin Roosevelt, and Soviet leader Joseph Stalin—gathered together for the first time. They met amid growing Soviet frustration with the British and Americans for their failure thus far to open a "second front" against Germany in Western Europe, while the Soviets continued to suffer horrendous losses in the savage fighting in Eastern Europe. American military planners were eager to open a second front as soon as possible, but the British, who would necessarily have to supply most of the troops until America was fully mobilized, balked. Tension among the three leaders over the second-front plan—code-named OVERLORD, the operation that resulted in the Anglo-American invasion of Normandy on "D-Day," June 6, 1944—is evident in this report of their discussions in the Iranian city of Tehran on November 28, 1943. The excerpts printed here are actually taken from two separate accounts: one composed by the American diplomat and Roosevelt's official translator Charles Bohlen, the other written by a military officer on behalf of the United States Joint Chiefs of Staff. Both versions were published in *Foreign Relations of the United States*, a compilation of American diplomatic records since 1861. The Soviets and the British also kept their own records of the Tehran meetings, giving historians remarkably rich sources with which to reconstruct the crucial negotiations and decisions that shaped wartime diplomacy. Why might the history of diplomacy be so lavishly documented? At this meeting, what were the principal objectives that each leader pursued? How did each man address his task? In what ways was the future of the war—and the postwar world—here foreshadowed?

FIRST PLENARY MEETING, NOVEMBER 28, 1943, 4 P.M., CONFERENCE ROOM, SOVIET EMBASSY

Bohlen Minutes

SECRET

THE PRESIDENT said as the youngest of the three present he ventured to welcome his elders. He said he wished to welcome the new members to the family circle and tell them that meetings of this character were conducted as between friends with complete frankness on all sides with nothing that was said to be made public. . . .

Chief of Staff Minutes

MARSHAL STALIN asked who will be the commander in this Operation Overlord. (THE PRESIDENT and PRIME MINISTER interpolated this was not yet decided.) MARSHAL STALIN continued, "Then nothing will come out of these operations." . . .

THE PRESIDENT said we again come back to the problem of the timing for OVERLORD. It was believed that it would be good for OVERLORD to take place about 1 May, or certainly not later than 15 May or 20 May, if possible.

THE PRIME MINISTER said that he could not agree to that. . . .

. . . He said he (the Prime Minister) was going to do everything in the power of His Majesty's Government to begin OVERLORD at the earliest possible moment. However, he did not think that the many great possibilities in the Mediterranean should be ruthlessly cast aside as valueless merely on the question of a month's delay in OVERLORD.

MARSHAL STALIN said all the Mediterranean operations are diversions. . . .

THE PRESIDENT said he found that his staff places emphasis on OVERLORD. While on the other hand the Prime Minister and his staff also emphasize OVERLORD, nevertheless the United States does not feel that OVERLORD should be put off.

THE PRESIDENT questioned whether it would not be possible for the ad hoc committee to go ahead with their deliberations without any further directive and to produce an answer by tomorrow morning.

MARSHAL STALIN questioned, "What can such a committee do?" He said, "We Chiefs of State have more power and more authority than a committee. General Brooke cannot force our opinions and there are many questions which can be decided only by us." He said he would like to ask if the British are thinking seriously of OVERLORD only in order to satisfy the U.S.S.R.

THE PRIME MINISTER replied that if the conditions specified at Moscow regarding OVERLORD should exist, he firmly believed it would be England's duty to hurl every ounce of strength she had across the Channel at the Germans.

THE PRESIDENT observed that in an hour a very good dinner would be awaiting all and people would be very hungry. He suggested that the staffs should meet tomorrow morning and discuss the matter. . . .

Source: FDR Library

The Horror of the Holocaust Although the outside world had some knowledge of the Nazi death camps before the war's end, the full revelation of Hitler's atrocities as the Allies overran Germany in the spring of 1945 stunned and sickened the invading troops. At General Eisenhower's orders, German civilians were compelled to view the evidence of the Nazi regime's genocidal crimes—though these witnesses at Buchenwald tried to look the other way, as many had done during the war itself.

the German Nazis had engaged in the scientific mass murder of "undesirables," including an estimated 6 million Jews. The Washington government had long been informed about Hitler's campaign of genocide against the Jews and had been reprehensibly slow to take steps against it. Roosevelt's administration had bolted the door against large numbers of Jewish refugees, and his military commanders declined even to bomb the rail lines that carried the victims to the camps. But until the war's end, the full dimensions of the "Holocaust" had not been known. When the details were revealed, the whole world was aghast.

The vengeful Soviets, clawing their way forward from the east, reached Berlin in April 1945. After desperate house-to-house fighting, followed by an orgy of pillage and rape, they captured the bomb-shattered city. Adolf Hitler, after a hasty marriage to his mistress, committed suicide in an underground bunker on April 30, 1945.

Tragedy had meanwhile struck the United States. President Roosevelt, while relaxing at Warm Springs, Georgia, suddenly died from a massive cerebral hemorrhage on April 12, 1945. The crushing burden of twelve depression and war years in the White House had finally taken its toll. Knots of confused, leaderless citizens gathered to discuss the future anxiously, as a bewildered, unbriefed Vice President Truman took the helm.

On May 7, 1945, what was left of the German government surrendered unconditionally. May 8 was officially proclaimed **V-E (Victory in Europe) Day** and was greeted with frenzied rejoicing in the Allied countries.

✦ Japan Dies Hard

Japan's rickety bamboo empire meanwhile was tottering to its fall. American submarines—"the silent service"—were sending the Japanese merchant marine to the bottom so fast they were running out of prey. All told, these "undersea craft" destroyed 1,042 ships, or about 50 percent of Japan's entire life-sustaining merchant fleet.

Giant bomber attacks were more spectacular. Launched from Saipan and other captured Mariana Islands, they were reducing the enemy's fragile cities to cinders. The massive firebomb raid on Tokyo, March 9–10, 1945, was annihilating. It destroyed over 250,000 buildings, gutted a quarter of the city, and killed an estimated 83,000 people—a loss comparable to that later inflicted by the atomic bombs.

General MacArthur was also on the move. Completing the conquest of jungle-draped New Guinea, he headed northwest for the Philippines, en route to Japan, with 600 ships and 250,000 men. In a scene well staged for the photographers, he splashed ashore at Leyte Island on October 20, 1944, with the summons, "People of the Philippines, I have returned. . . . Rally to me."

Japan's navy—still menacing—now made one last-chance effort to destroy MacArthur by wiping out his transports and supply ships. A gigantic clash at Leyte Gulf, fought on the sea and in the air, was actually three battles (October 23–26, 1944). The Americans won all of them, though the crucial engagement was almost lost when Admiral William F. ("Bull") Halsey was decoyed away by a feint.

Japan was through as a sea power: it had lost about sixty ships in the greatest naval battle of all time. American fleets, numbering more than four thousand vessels, now commanded the western Pacific. Several battleships, raised from the mud of Pearl Harbor, were exacting belated but sweet revenge.

Overrunning Leyte, MacArthur next landed on the main Philippine island of Luzon in January 1945. Manila was his major objective; the ravaged city fell in March, but the Philippines were not conquered until July. Victory was purchased only after bitter fighting against holed-in Japanese, who took a toll of over sixty thousand American casualties.

America's steel vise was tightening mercilessly around Japan. The tiny island of Iwo Jima, needed as a haven for damaged American bombers returning from Japan, was captured in March 1945. This desperate twenty-five-day assault cost over four thousand American dead.

Okinawa, a well-defended Japanese island, was next on the list: it was needed for closer bases from which to blast and burn enemy cities and industries. Fighting dragged on from April to June of 1945. Japanese soldiers, fighting with incredible courage from their caves, finally sold Okinawa for fifty thousand American casualties, while suffering far heavier losses themselves.

The U.S. Navy, which covered the invasion of Okinawa, sustained severe damage. Japanese suicide pilots ("kamikazes") in an exhibition of mass hara-kiri for their god-emperor, crashed their bomb-laden planes onto the decks of the invading fleet. All told, the death squads sank over thirty ships and badly damaged scores more.

✴ The Atomic Bombs

Strategists in Washington were meanwhile planning an all-out invasion of the main islands of Japan—an invasion that presumably would cost hundreds of thousands of American (and even more Japanese) casualties. Tokyo, recognizing imminent defeat, had secretly sent peace feelers to Moscow, which had not yet entered the Far Eastern war. The Americans, having broken the secret Japanese radio codes, knew of these feelers. But bomb-scorched Japan still showed no outward willingness to surrender *unconditionally* to the Allies.

National Archives

The Flag Raising at Iwo Jima   Atop Mount Suribachi, press photographer Joe Rosenthal snapped this dramatic picture, probably the most famous of the war.

Hiroshima, Japan, August 1945 The almost incomprehensibly destructive power of history's first atomic bomb is vividly evident in this photograph. The single bomb killed an estimated 130,000 Japanese, many of whom succumbed months after the blast to agonizing deaths from exposure to radiation.

The **Potsdam conference**, held near Berlin in July 1945, sounded the death knell of the Japanese. There President Truman, still new on his job, met in a seventeen-day parley with Joseph Stalin and the British leaders. The conferees issued a stern ultimatum to Japan: surrender or be destroyed. American bombers showered the dire warning on Japan in tens of thousands of leaflets, but no encouraging response was forthcoming.

America had a fantastic ace up its sleeve. Early in 1940, after Hitler's wanton assault on Poland, Roosevelt was persuaded by American and exiled scientists, notably German-born Albert Einstein, to push ahead with preparations for unlocking the secret of an atomic bomb. Congress, at Roosevelt's blank-check request, blindly made available nearly $2 billion. Many military minds were skeptical of this "damned professor's nonsense," but fears that the Germans might first acquire such an awesome weapon provided a powerful spur to action. Ironically, Germany eventually abandoned its own atomic project as too costly. And as it happened, the war against Germany ended before the American weapon was ready. In a cruel twist of fate, Japan—not Germany, the original target—suffered the fate of being the first nation subjected to atomic bombardment.

What was called the **Manhattan Project** pushed feverishly forward, as American know-how and industrial power were combined with the most advanced scientific knowledge. Much technical skill was provided by British and refugee scientists, who had fled to America to escape the torture chambers of the dictators. Finally, in the desert near Alamogordo, New Mexico, on July 16, 1945, the experts detonated the first awesome and devastating atomic device.

With Japan still refusing to surrender, the Potsdam threat was fulfilled. On August 6, 1945, a lone American bomber dropped one atomic bomb on the city of Hiroshima, Japan. In a blinding flash of death, followed by a funnel-shaped cloud, about 180,000 people were left killed, wounded, or missing. Some 70,000 of them died instantaneously. Sixty thousand more soon perished from burns and radiation disease.

The scientific director of the Manhattan Project, J. Robert Oppenheimer (1904–1967), recalled his reaction as he witnessed the detonation of the first atomic bomb at the Trinity test site in Alamogordo, New Mexico, in July 1945. He was not only awed by the extraordinary force of this new weapon. He also feared the power to do harm that it gave to humans:

❝I remembered the line from the Hindu scripture, the Bhagavad-Gita: 'Now I am become Death, the destroyer of Worlds.'❞

Two days later, on August 8, Stalin entered the war against Japan, exactly on the deadline date previously agreed upon with his allies. Soviet armies speedily overran the depleted Japanese defenses in Manchuria and Korea in a six-day "victory parade" that involved several thousand Russian casualties. Stalin was evidently determined to be in on the kill, lest he lose a voice in the final division of Japan's holdings.

Fanatically resisting Japanese, though facing atomization, still did not surrender. American aviators, on August 9, dropped a second atomic bomb on the city of Nagasaki. The explosion took a horrible toll of about eighty thousand people killed or missing. (See "Varying Viewpoints," p. 825.) The Japanese nation could endure no more. On August 10, 1945, Tokyo sued for peace on one condition: that Hirohito, the bespectacled Son of Heaven, be allowed to remain on his ancestral throne as nominal emperor. Despite their "unconditional surrender" policy, the Allies accepted this condition on August 14, 1945. The Japanese, though losing face, were able to save both their exalted ruler and what was left of their native land.

The formal end came, with dramatic force, on September 2, 1945. Official surrender ceremonies were conducted by General MacArthur on the battleship *Missouri* in Tokyo Bay. At the same time, Americans at home hysterically celebrated **V-J (Victory in Japan) Day** after the most horrible war in history had ended in mushrooming atomic clouds.

✴ The Allies Triumphant

World War II proved to be terribly costly. American forces suffered some 1 million casualties, more than one-third of which were deaths. Compared with other wars, the proportion killed by wounds and disease was sharply reduced, owing in part to the use of blood

The Japanese Surrender   Representatives of the Japanese government arrived to sign the surrender document on the deck of the battleship *Missouri* in Tokyo harbor, September 2, 1945. General Douglas MacArthur then made a conciliatory address, expressing hope "that from this solemn occasion a better world shall emerge . . . a world founded on faith and understanding." A Japanese diplomat attending wondered "whether it would have been possible for us, had we been victorious, to embrace the vanquished with a similar magnanimity." Soon thereafter General MacArthur took up his duties as director of the U.S. occupation of Japan.

AP Photo

America and the World in Depression and War: A Study in Contrasts

The Great Depression of the 1930s was a monstrous, planetary-scale economic hurricane that wreaked havoc around the globe. All nations were walloped by its destructive force, but two were especially hard hit: the United States and Germany. In both countries production of goods declined by nearly 50 percent, and unemployment approached 25 percent. Also in both countries the depression discredited existing political regimes and created opportunities for new leadership to emerge. Fatefully, Germany got Adolf Hitler, while the United States got Franklin D. Roosevelt.

Roosevelt and Hitler were of the same generation, both born in the 1880s. They came to power within weeks of each other—Hitler as Germany's chancellor on January 30, 1933, and Roosevelt as U.S. president on March 4, 1933. Both achieved office through democratic elections, though democracy soon withered under one's hand and flourished under the other's.

Roosevelt's entire presidency unfolded under the looming threat, and eventually the armed challenge, of Hitler's Nazi regime. FDR's record, as well as the very character of American democracy in the mid-twentieth century, can only be properly understood in that larger context.

Consider: In the spring of 1933, Roosevelt was coaxing legislation out of the Hundred Days Congress, forging labor unions and sundry ethnic and racial minorities into a long-lasting Democratic party coalition, and making innovative use of the radio to outflank the hostile media magnates who controlled the nation's newspapers. In those same months, Hitler was dissolving German labor unions and ruthlessly censoring the German press. Soon he declared the Nazis the only legal political party in Germany and proceeded to impose on the German people a reign of terror cruelly enforced by the Gestapo, the Nazis' grimly efficient secret police.

A year later, while Roosevelt worried about a possible political challenge from the swashbuckling Louisiana senator Huey P. Long, Hitler dispatched with his main Nazi rival, Ernst Röhm, by ordering his execution.

The following year, 1935, Roosevelt shepherded his sweeping reform program through Congress, notably including the Social Security Act, which helped to usher millions of Americans into the mainstream of American life, especially members of the great immigrant communities that had arrived a generation or so earlier. "We are going to make a country," Roosevelt said, "in which no one is left out." That same year Hitler codified the Nazis' viciously anti-Semitic policies in the notorious Nuremberg Laws, stripping German Jews of their citizenship, barring them from the professions and military service, and prohibiting marriage between Jews and "Aryans" (defined by the Nazis as a master race of non-Jewish Caucasians, especially those having Nordic features)—all gruesome steps on the road to the genocidal war-time Holocaust, which would eventually murder some 6 million Jews.

Meanwhile, Hitler was relentlessly building his war machine, while FDR's America clung stubbornly to its traditional isolationism. And when the great conflict of World War II finally erupted, Hitler's Germany and Roosevelt's America fought decidedly different wars. Indeed the United States' experience in the war stands in vivid contrast to the experience of *all* other combatants, including not only Germany but also America's allies in the "Grand Alliance."

Hitler's vaunted "thousand-year Reich" lay in smoldering ruins at war's end, his people dazed, demoralized, and starving. The strutting Führer had brewed a catastrophe so vast that its conclusion seemed to sunder the web of time itself. Germans remember the moment of their surrender on May 7, 1945, as the *Stunde null*, or "zero hour," when history's clock came to a fearful halt. Elsewhere, even America's main wartime partners, Great Britain and the

Franklin Delano Roosevelt, Thirty-second President of the United States

FDR Library

TABLE 35.1 The Comparative Costs of World War II

Country	Military Deaths	Civilian Deaths	Government Expenditures	Damage to Civilian Property
China	2,000,000	7,750,000		
France	250,000	350,000		
Poland	123,000	6,000,000		
USSR	10,000,000	17,000,000	$192 billion	$128 billion
United Kingdom	300,000	60,600	$120 billion	$5 billion
United States	405,399	6*	$317 billion	
Germany (including Austria)	3,500,000	1,600,000	$272 billion	$50–$75 billion
Italy	242,000	60,000	$94 billion	
Japan	2,000,000	650,000		

*In the forty-eight states; additional civilian deaths occurred in Hawaii, Alaska, and the Philippines.

Sources: World War II casualty estimates vary widely. The figures here are largely taken from David M. Kennedy, ed., *The Library of Congress World War II Companion;* I. C. B. Dear, ed., *The Oxford Companion to the Second World War*; Louis L. Snyder, *Historical Guide to World War II*; and John Ellis, *World War II: A Statistical Survey.*

Soviet Union, had paid a far greater price in blood and treasure than the United States. Uniquely among all the belligerents in World War II—perhaps uniquely in the history of warfare—the United States had managed to grow its civilian economy even while waging a hugely costly war. In Germany, Britain, and the Soviet Union, the civilian standard of living had gone down by approximately one-third. In the United States, the civilian economy had actually expanded by 15 percent, preparing the way for phenomenal prosperity in the postwar decades.

And though 405,399 brave American service members died in World War II, proportionate to population American losses were about one-third those of Britain and about one-sixtieth those of the Soviet Union, where some 10 million soldiers and a staggering 17 million civilians perished (see Table 35.1). By glaring contrast, in the forty-eight continental American states that had a star on the flag in 1945, the U.S. civilian death toll due to enemy action was just six persons, all of them the victims of a crude Japanese balloon-borne firebomb that exploded in their faces near the hamlet of Bly, Oregon, on May 5, 1945.

For all the misery that depression and war visited upon the United States, Americans could count their blessings that fortune had spared them the enormous deprivations and horrors that were all too common elsewhere. Yet some observers worried that America was now assuming leadership in a world where the depths of other peoples' wounds and woes could scarcely be imagined.

U.S. Army Center of Military History

German Chancellor Adolf Hitler

D. Wigmore Fine Art Ltd

V-J Day: Crowds Cheering at Times Square, by Edward Dancig, 1947
Russian-born American artist Edward Dancig captured the feelings of triumph and relief that Americans felt at the end of World War II. His painting shows the V-J (Victory in Japan) Day celebration of August 15, 1945, in New York's Times Square.

This complex conflict was the best-fought war in America's history. Though unprepared for it at the outset, the nation was better prepared than for the others, partly because it had begun to buckle on its armor about a year and a half before the war officially began. It was actually fighting German submarines in the Atlantic months before the explosion in the Pacific at Pearl Harbor. In the end the United States showed itself to be resourceful, tough, adaptable—able to accommodate itself to the tactics of an enemy who was relentless and ruthless.

American military leadership proved to be of the highest order. A new crop of war heroes emerged in brilliant generals like Eisenhower, MacArthur, and Marshall (chief of staff) and in imaginative admirals like Nimitz and Spruance. President Roosevelt and Prime Minister Churchill, as kindred spirits, collaborated closely in planning strategy. "It is fun to be in the same decade with you," FDR once cabled Churchill.

Industrial leaders were no less skilled, for marvels of production were performed almost daily. Assembly lines proved as important as battle lines, and victory went again to the side with the most smokestacks. The enemy was almost literally smothered by bayonets, bullets, bazookas, and bombs. Hitler and his Axis co-conspirators had chosen to make war with machines, and the ingenious Yankees could ask for nothing better. They demonstrated again, as they had in World War I, that the American way of war was simply more—more men, more weapons, more machines, more technology, and more money than any enemy could hope to match. From 1940 to 1945, the output of American factories was simply phenomenal. As Winston Churchill remarked, "Nothing succeeds like excess."

Hermann Goering, a Nazi leader, had sneered, "The Americans can't build planes—only electric iceboxes and razor blades." Democracy had given its answer, as the dictators, despite long preparation, were overthrown and discredited. It is true that an unusual amount of direct control was exercised over the individual by the Washington authorities during the war emergency. But the American people preserved their precious liberties without serious impairment.

plasma and "miracle" drugs, notably penicillin. Yet heavy though American losses were, the Soviet allies suffered casualties many times greater—more than 25 million people killed. In grim testimony to the nature of modern warfare, World War II was the first war that killed more civilians than armed combatants (see "Thinking Globally: America and the World in Depression and War: A Study in Contrasts," pp. 822–823).

America was fortunate in emerging with its mainland virtually unscathed. Two Japanese submarines, using shells and bombers, had rather harmlessly attacked the California and Oregon coast, and a few Japanese fire-bomb balloons had drifted across the Pacific, killing six civilians in Oregon. But that was about all. Much of the rest of the world was utterly destroyed and destitute. America alone was untouched and healthy—oiled and muscled like a prize bull, standing astride the world's ruined landscape.

Varying Viewpoints

The Atomic Bombs: Were They Justified?

No episode of the World War II era has provoked sharper controversy than the atomic bombings of Japan in August 1945. Lingering moral misgivings about the nuclear incineration of Hiroshima and Nagasaki have long threatened to tarnish America's crown of military victory. Some critics have accused the United States of racist motives because the bombs were dropped on a nonwhite people. Other commentators note that the Japanese were already reeling on the verge of collapse by 1945, and therefore history's most awful weapons—especially the second bomb, on Nagasaki—were unnecessary to bring the war to a conclusion. Still other scholars, notably Gar Alperovitz, have further charged that the atomic attacks on Hiroshima and Nagasaki were not the last shots of World War II, but the first salvos in the emerging Cold War. Alperovitz argues that President Truman willfully ignored Tokyo's attempts to negotiate a surrender in the summer of 1945 and rejected all alternatives to dropping the bomb because he wanted to intimidate and isolate the Soviet Union. He unleashed his horrible new weapons, so this argument goes, not simply to defeat Japan, but to end the Far Eastern conflict before the Soviets could enter it, and thereby freeze them out of any role in formulating postwar reconstruction policy in Asia.

Each of these accusations has been vigorously rebutted. Richard Rhodes's exhaustive history of the making of the atomic bomb emphasizes that the Anglo-American atomic project began as a race against the Germans, who were known to be actively pursuing a nuclear weapons program. (Unknown to the Americans, Germany effectively terminated its effort in 1942, just as the Anglo-American project went into high gear.) From the outset both British and American planners believed that the bomb, if successful, would be not just another weapon, but *the* ultimate instrument of destruction that would decisively deliver victory into the hands of whoever possessed it. They consequently assumed that it would be used at the earliest possible moment. There is, therefore, no credible reason to conclude that German cities would not have suffered the fate of Hiroshima and Nagasaki if nuclear weapons had become available sooner or if the European phase of the war had lasted longer.

It is true that American intelligence sources in the early summer of 1945 reported that some Japanese statesmen were trying to enlist the still-neutral Russians' good offices to negotiate a surrender. But as R. J. C. Butow's fine-grained study of Japan's decision to surrender demonstrates, it was unclear whether those initiatives had the full backing of the Japanese government. Moreover, the Japanese clung to several unac-ceptable conditions, including protection for their imperial system of government, the right to disarm and repatriate their own troops, no military occupation of the home islands, no international trials of alleged war criminals, and possible retention of some of their conquered territories. All this flew squarely in the face of America's repeatedly declared intention to settle for nothing less than *unconditional* surrender. As for the Nagasaki bomb (dropped on August 9), Butow also notes that it conclusively dispelled the Japanese government's original assessment that the Hiroshima attack (on August 6) was a one-time-only stunt, with little likelihood of further nuclear strikes to follow. (Even then, some diehard military officers, refusing to acknowledge defeat, tried, on the night of August 14, to storm the Imperial Palace to seize the recording of the emperor's surrender announcement before it could be broadcast the following day.)

Could the use of the atomic bombs have been avoided? Studies by Martin J. Sherwin, Barton J. Bernstein, and McGeorge Bundy have shown that few policymakers at the time seriously asked that question. As Winston Churchill later wrote, "The decision whether or not to use the atomic bomb to compel the surrender of Japan was never even an issue. There was unanimous, automatic, unquestioned agreement around our table; nor did I ever hear the slightest suggestion that we should do otherwise." In fact, the "decision" to use the bomb was not made in 1945, but in 1942, when the United States committed itself to a crash program to build—and use—a nuclear weapon as swiftly as possible. Intimidating the Soviets might have been a "bonus" to using the bomb against Japan, but influencing Soviet behavior was never the *primary* reason for the fateful decision. American leaders wanted to end the war as soon as possible. To that end they had always assumed the atomic bomb would be dropped as soon as it was available. That moment came on August 6, 1945.

Doubt and remorse about the atomic conclusion of World War II have plagued the American conscience ever since. Less often remarked on are the deaths of four times more Japanese noncombatants than died at Hiroshima and Nagasaki in the so-called conventional firebombing of some five dozen Japanese cities in 1945. Those deaths suggest that the deeper moral question should perhaps be addressed not to the particular technology of nuclear weaponry and the fate of those two unfortunate Japanese cities, but to the quite deliberate decision, made by several combatants—including the Germans, the British, the Americans, and the Japanese themselves—to designate civilian populations as legitimate military targets.

Chapter Review

KEY TERMS

ABC-1 agreement (791)

Executive Order No. 9066 (792)

War Production Board (WPB) (802)

Office of Price Administration (OPA) (802)

National War Labor Board (NWLB) (802)

Smith-Connally Anti-Strike Act (803)

WACs (Women's Army Corps) (803)

WAVES (Women Accepted for Volunteer Emergency Service) (803)

SPARs (U.S. Coast Guard Women's Reserve) (803)

Bracero program (803)

Fair Employment Practices Commission (FEPC) (805)

Congress of Racial Equality (CORE) (806)

code talkers (806)

Midway, Battle of (809)

D-Day (813)

V-E (Victory in Europe) Day (818)

Potsdam conference (820)

Manhattan Project (820)

V-J (Victory in Japan) Day (821)

PEOPLE TO KNOW

Douglas MacArthur

Chester Nimitz

Dwight D. "Ike" Eisenhower

Harry S Truman

Albert Einstein

CHRONOLOGY

1941
United States declares war on Japan
Germany declares war on United States
Randolph plans black march on Washington
Fair Employment Practices Commission (FEPC) established
Roosevelt delivers "Four Freedoms" speech

1942
Japanese Americans sent to internment camps
Japan conquers the Philippines
Battle of the Coral Sea
Battle of Midway
United States invades North Africa
Congress of Racial Equality (CORE) founded

1943
Allies hold Casablanca conference
Allies invade Italy
Smith-Connally Anti-Strike Act
"Zoot-suit" riots in Los Angeles
Race riot in Detroit
Japanese driven from Guadalcanal
Tehran conference

1944
Korematsu v. U.S.
D-Day invasion of France
Battle of the Marianas
Roosevelt defeats Dewey for presidency

1944–1945 Battle of the Bulge

1945
Roosevelt dies; Truman assumes presidency
Germany surrenders
Battles of Iwo Jima and Okinawa
Potsdam conference
Atomic bombs dropped on Hiroshima and Nagasaki
Yalta conference
Japan surrenders

TO LEARN MORE

Kai Bird and Martin J. Sherwin, *American Prometheus: The Triumph and Tragedy of J. Robert Oppenheimer* (2005)

John M. Blum, *V Was for Victory: Politics and American Culture During World War II* (1976)

Roger Daniels, *Prisoners Without Trial: Japanese Americans in World War II* (1993)

Norman Davies, *No Simple Victory: World War II in Europe, 1939–1945* (2007)

John W. Dower, *War Without Mercy: Race and Power in the Pacific War* (1986)

Sherna Gluck, *Rosie the Riveter Revisited: Women, the War, and Social Change* (1988)

David M. Kennedy, *Freedom from Fear: The American People in Depression and War, 1929–1945* (1999)

Kevin Allen Leonard, *The Battle for Los Angeles: Racial Ideology and World War II* (2006)

Nelson Lichtenstein, *Labor's War at Home: The CIO in World War II* (1982)

Sean L. Malloy, *Atomic Tragedy: Henry L. Stimson and the Decision to Use the Bomb against Japan* (2008)

Richard Rhodes, *The Making of the Atomic Bomb* (1986)

Ronald H. Spector, *Eagle Against the Sun: The American War with Japan* (1985)

Ronald T. Takaki, *Double Victory: A Multicultural History of America in World War II* (2000)

Isabel Wilkerson, *The Warmth of Other Suns: The Epic Story of America's Great Migration* (2010)

A complete, annotated bibliography for this chapter—along with brief descriptions of the People to Know—may be found on the American Pageant website. The Key Terms are defined in a Glossary at the end of the text.

Go to the CourseMate website at **www.cengagebrain.com** for additional study tools and review materials—including audio and video clips—for this chapter.

Part Six

Making Modern America

1945 to the Present

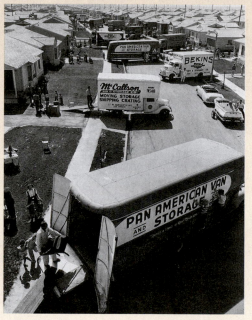

World War II broke the back of the Great Depression in the United States and also ended the century-and-a-half-old American tradition of isolationism in foreign affairs. Alone among the warring powers, the United States managed to emerge from the great conflict physically unscarred, economically healthy, and diplomatically strengthened. Yet if Americans faced a world full of promise at the war's end, it was also a world full of dangers, none more disconcerting than Soviet communism. These two themes of promise and menace mingled uneasily throughout the nearly five decades of the Cold War era, from the end of World War II in 1945 to the collapse of the Soviet Union in 1991.

At home unprecedented prosperity in the postwar quarter-century nourished a robust sense of national self-confidence and fed a revolution of rising expectations. Invigorated by the prospect of endlessly spreading affluence, Americans in the 1940s, 1950s, and 1960s had record numbers of babies, aspired to ever-higher standards of living, generously expanded the welfare state (especially for the elderly), widened opportunities for women,

welcomed immigrants, and even found the will to grapple at long last with the nation's grossest legacy of injustice, its treatment of African Americans. With the exception of Dwight Eisenhower's presidency in the 1950s, Americans elected liberal Democratic presidents (Harry Truman in 1948, John F. Kennedy in 1960, and Lyndon Johnson in 1964). The Democratic party, the party of the liberal New Deal at home and of an activist foreign policy abroad, comfortably remained the nation's majority party. Americans trusted their government and had faith in the American dream that their children would lead a richer life than their parents had done. Anything and everything seemed possible.

The rising curve of ascending expectations, propelled by exploding economic growth, bounded upward throughout the 1950s. It peaked in the 1960s, an exceptionally stormy decade during which faith in government, in the wisdom of American foreign policy, and in the American dream itself, began to sour. Lyndon Johnson's "Great Society" reforms, billed as the completion of the unfinished work of the New Deal, foundered on the rocks of fiscal limitations and stubborn racial

A Suburban Society In the phenomenally affluent post-WWII years, newly prosperous Americans flocked to spanking-new suburban housing developments. By the twentieth century's end, a majority of Americans were suburbanites. J. R. Eyerman/Time & Life Pictures/Getty Images resentments. Johnson, the most ambitious reformer in the White House since Franklin Roosevelt, eventually saw his presidency destroyed by the furies unleashed over the Vietnam War.

When economic growth flattened in the 1970s, the horizon of hopes for the future seemed to vanish as well. The nation entered a frustrating period of stalled expectations, increasingly rancorous racial tensions, disillusion with government, and political stalemate. Yet in one important arena progress continued. As "second-wave feminism" gathered steam, women burst through barriers that had long excluded them from traditional male domains from the factory floor and U.S. Army to the Ivy League.

Beginning in 1968, Americans stopped sending New Deal–style liberals to the White House, electing moderate Republicans (Richard Nixon in 1968 and 1972, succeeded by the unelected Gerald Ford after Watergate), moderate southern Democrats (Jimmy Carter in 1976 and Bill Clinton in 1992 and 1996), and conservative Republicans (Ronald Reagan in 1980 and 1984, George H. W. Bush in 1992, and George W. Bush in 2000 and 2004). Throughout these years, Democrats usually remained in control of both houses of Congress, until the "Republican revolution" of 1994 put a new generation of conservative legislators in power. Only with popular discontent over the Iraq War did the Democrats narrowly regain control of both houses in 2006, and the White House in 2008, with the election of the nation's first African American president, Barack Obama. Then in 2010 newly energized conservative Republicans once again won a majority of seats in the House, and political gridlock ensued. As the twenty-first century lengthened, the nation seemed increasingly polarized, unable to reconcile progressive ambitions for more social provision and economic and environmental regulation with conservative demands for lower taxes and smaller government.

Abroad the fierce competition with the Soviet Union, and after 1949 with communist China as well, colored almost every aspect of America's foreign relations and shaped domestic life, too. Unreasoning fear of communists at home unleashed the destructive force of McCarthyism in the 1950s—a modern-day witch hunt in which careers were capsized and lives ruined by reckless accusations of communist sympathizing. The FBI encroached on

The End of an Era? As surely as victory in World War II restored confidence and prosperity to a people demoralized by the Great Depression, the terrorist attacks of September 11, 2001, struck electric fear into the American people—and menaced their historical commitment to an open society and individual liberties. Photo by Spencer Platt/Getty Images

sacred American liberties in its zeal to uncover communist "subversives."

The Cold War remained cold, in the sense that no shooting conflict broke out between the great-power rivals. But the United States did fight two shooting wars in the Cold War era, in Korea in the 1950s and Vietnam in the 1960s. Vietnam, the only foreign war in which the United States has ever been defeated, cruelly convulsed American society, ending not only Lyndon Johnson's presidency but the thirty-five-year era of the Democratic party's political dominance as well. Vietnam also touched off the most vicious inflationary cycle in American history, and embittered and disillusioned an entire generation.

Uncle Sam in the Cold War era built a fearsome—and expensive—arsenal of nuclear weapons, great air and missile fleets to deliver them, a two-ocean navy, and, for a time, a large army raised by conscription. When the Cold War ended, Americans turned to the promise of an information age in a global economy. But terrorist attacks on American soil in 2001 shifted the country's attention back to national defense and international military strategy, launching two wars (in Iraq and Afghanistan) and fundamentally transforming both foreign and domestic politics. The "Great Recession" that walloped the global economy in 2008 and hit America with special force further intensified partisan divisions and perhaps spelled an end to an era of expanding personal opportunity, government-sponsored social provision, and American global hegemony.

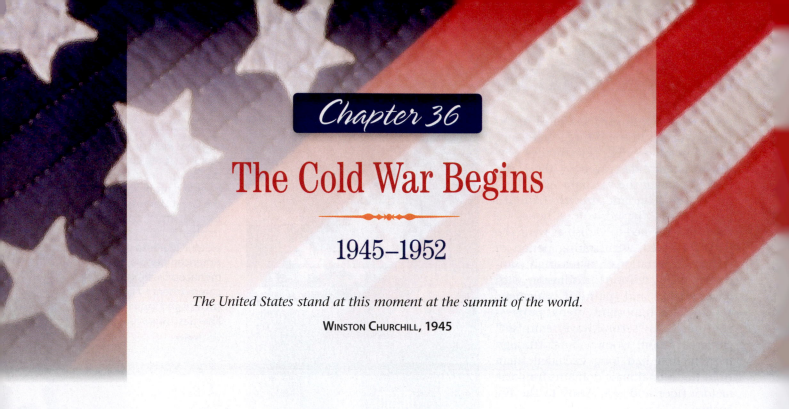

Chapter 36

The Cold War Begins

1945–1952

The United States stand at this moment at the summit of the world.

WINSTON CHURCHILL, 1945

The American people, 140 million strong, cheered their nation's victories in Europe and Asia at the conclusion of World War II. But before the shouting had even faded, many Americans began to worry about their future. Four fiery years of global war had not entirely driven from their minds the painful memories of twelve desperate years of the Great Depression. Still more ominously, victory celebrations had barely ended before America's crumbling relations with its wartime ally, the Soviet Union, threatened a new and even more terrible international conflict.

✴ Postwar Economic Anxieties

The decade of the 1930s had left deep scars. Joblessness and insecurity had pushed up the suicide rate and dampened the marriage rate. Babies went unborn as pinched budgets and sagging self-esteem wrought a sexual depression in American bedrooms. The war had banished the blight of depression, but would the respite last? Grim-faced observers were warning that the war had only temporarily lifted the pall of economic stagnation and that peace would bring the return of hard times. Homeward-bound GIs, so the gloomy predictions ran, would step out of the army's chow lines and back into the breadlines of the unemployed.

The faltering economy in the initial postwar years threatened to confirm the worst predictions of the doomsayers who foresaw another Great Depression. Real gross national product (GNP) slumped sickeningly in 1946 and 1947 from its wartime peak. With the removal of wartime price controls, prices giddily levitated by 33 percent in 1946–1947. An epidemic of strikes swept the country. During 1946 alone some 4.6 million laborers laid down their tools, fearful that soon they could barely afford the autos and other goods they were manufacturing.

The growing muscle of organized labor deeply annoyed many conservatives. They had their revenge against labor's New Deal gains in 1947, when a Republican-controlled Congress (the first in fourteen years) passed the **Taft-Hartley Act** over President Truman's vigorous veto. Labor leaders condemned the Taft-Hartley Act as a "slave-labor law." It outlawed the "closed" (all-union) shop, made unions liable for damages that resulted from jurisdictional disputes among themselves, and required union leaders to take a noncommunist oath.

Taft-Hartley was only one of several obstacles that slowed the growth of organized labor in the years after World War II. In the heady days of the New Deal, unions had spread swiftly in the industrialized Northeast, especially in huge manufacturing industries like steel and automobiles. But labor's postwar efforts to organize in the historically antiunion regions of the South and West proved frustrating. The CIO's **Operation Dixie**, aimed at unionizing southern textile workers and steelworkers, failed miserably in 1948 to overcome lingering fears of racial mixing. And workers in the rapidly growing service sector of the economy—many of them middle-aged women, often working only part-time in small shops, widely separated from one another—proved much more difficult to organize than the thousands of assembly-line workers who in the 1930s had poured into the auto and steel unions.

© Bettmann/Corbis

Going to College on the GI Bill Financed by the federal government, thousands of World War II veterans crowded into college classrooms in the late 1940s. Universities struggled to house these older students, many of whom already had families. Pennsylvania State College resorted to setting up hundreds of trailers.

Union membership would peak in the 1950s and then begin a long, unremitting decline.

The Democratic administration meanwhile took some steps of its own to forestall an economic downturn. It sold war factories and other government installations to private businesses at fire-sale prices. It secured passage of the **Employment Act of 1946**, making it government policy "to promote maximum employment, production, and purchasing power." The act created a three-member Council of Economic Advisers to provide the president with the data and the recommendations to make that policy a reality.

Most dramatic was the passage of the Servicemen's Readjustment Act of 1944—better known as the GI Bill of Rights, or the **GI Bill**. Enacted partly out of fear that the employment markets would never be able to absorb 15 million returning veterans at war's end, the GI Bill made generous provisions for sending the former soldiers to school. In the postwar decade, some 8 million veterans advanced their education at Uncle Sam's expense. The majority attended technical and vocational schools, but colleges and universities were crowded to the blackboards as more than 2 million ex-GIs stormed the halls of higher learning. The total eventually spent for education was some $14.5 billion in taxpayer dollars. The act also enabled the Veterans Administration (VA) to guarantee about $16 billion in loans for veterans to buy homes, farms, and small businesses. By raising educational levels and stimulating the construction industry, the GI Bill powerfully nurtured the robust and long-lived economic expansion that eventually took hold in the late 1940s and that profoundly shaped the entire history of the postwar era.

✦ The Long Economic Boom, 1950–1970

Gross national product began to climb haltingly in 1948. Then, beginning about 1950, the American economy surged onto a dazzling plateau of sustained growth that was to last virtually uninterrupted for two decades. America's economic performance became the envy of the world. National income nearly doubled in the 1950s and almost doubled again in the 1960s, shooting through the trillion-dollar mark in 1973. Americans, some 6 percent of the world's people, were enjoying about 40 percent of the planet's wealth.

Nothing loomed larger in the history of the post–World War II era than this fantastic eruption of affluence. It did not enrich all Americans, and it did not touch all people evenly, but it transformed the lives of a majority of citizens and molded the agenda of politics and society for at least two generations. Prosperity underwrote social mobility; it paved the way for the eventual success of the civil rights movement; it funded vast new welfare programs, like Medicare; and it gave Americans the confidence to exercise unprecedented international leadership in the Cold War era.

As the gusher of postwar prosperity poured forth its riches, Americans drank deeply from the gilded goblet. Millions of depression-pinched souls sought to make up for the sufferings of the 1930s. They determined to "get theirs" while the getting was good. A people who had once considered a chicken in every pot the standard of comfort and security now hungered for two cars in every garage, swimming pools in their backyards, vacation homes, and gas-guzzling recreational vehicles. The size of the "middle class," defined as households earning between $3,000 and $10,000 a year, doubled from pre–Great Depression days and included 60 percent of the American people by the mid-1950s. By the end of that decade, the vast majority of American families owned their own cars and washing machines, and nearly 90 percent owned a television set—a gadget invented in the 1920s but virtually unknown until the late 1940s. In another revolution of sweeping consequences, almost 60 percent of American families owned their own homes by 1960, compared with less than 40 percent in the 1920s.

Of all the beneficiaries of postwar prosperity, none reaped greater rewards than women. More than ever, urban offices and shops provided a bonanza of employment for female workers. The great majority of new jobs created in the postwar era went to women, as the service sector of the economy dramatically outgrew the old industrial and manufacturing sectors. Women accounted for a quarter of the American work force at the end of World War II and for nearly half the labor pool five decades later. Yet even as women continued their march into the workplace in the 1940s and 1950s, popular culture glorified the traditional feminine roles of homemaker and mother. The clash between the demands of suburban housewifery and the realities of employment eventually sparked a feminist revolt in the 1960s.

✵ The Roots of Postwar Prosperity

What propelled this unprecedented economic explosion? The Second World War itself provided a powerful stimulus. While other countries had been ravaged by years of fighting, the United States had used the war crisis to fire up its smokeless factories and rebuild its depression-plagued economy. Invigorated by battle, America had almost effortlessly come to dominate the ruined global landscape of the postwar period.

Ominously, much of the glittering prosperity of the 1950s and 1960s rested on the underpinnings of colossal military budgets, leading some critics to speak of a "permanent war economy" (see Figure 36.1). The economic upturn of 1950 was fueled by massive

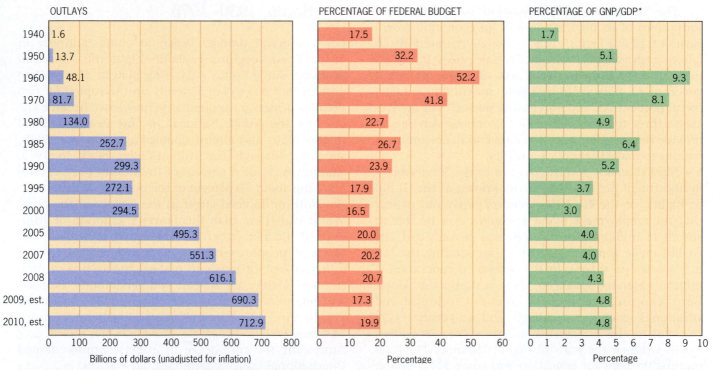

FIGURE 36.1* National Defense Budget, 1940–2010

*Gross *national* product (GNP) was used before 1960. It includes income from overseas investment and excludes profits generated in the United States but accruing to foreign accounts. Gross *domestic* product (GDP), used thereafter, excludes overseas profits owed to American accounts but includes the value of all items originating in the United States, regardless of the destination of the profits. Until recent years those factors made for negligible differences in the calculation of *national* and *domestic* product, but most economists now prefer the latter approach.

(Sources: *Statistical Abstract of the United States, 2010,* from US Office of Management and Budget (Congressional Budget Office), *Budget of the United States Government, Historical Tables,* annual. http://whitehouse.gov/omb/budget/fy2009/budget.html.)

Advertising Prosperity, 1956

This Ford advertisement in a popular magazine encouraged readers to buy a second car. By the mid-1950s, once manufacturers had met the demand for cars, homes, appliances, and other consumer goods that a decade and a half of depression and world war had pent up, they worried about how to keep expanding their markets. "Planned obsolescence"—changing design frequently enough to necessitate replacement purchasing—was one strategy. Altering expectations about what consumers needed was another. This advertisement suggests that the up-to-date family, living in its modern-style suburban home, had no choice but to own two cars, one for the male breadwinner's business, the other for the wife's "ferrying the family." What kinds of gender role prescriptions are reinforced in this advertisement? What assumptions has Ford made about prospective buyers of its cars? How much can mass advertising tell us about the actual values of Americans living at a particular time?

The only problem in posing this picture was getting the two Fords to stand still.

Seven good reasons for two FORDS

To free their family from one-car captivity the Bremers got two Fords: a Country Sedan and a Thunderbird—the car that inspired the styling and performance of all '56 Fords.

"We saw the need for a second car even before our first youngster arrived. If you're married you know why. The five children just made two Fords *more* necessary. I need a car for business. My wife needs one for ferrying the family.

"*Why are they Fords?* In the first place, you can't beat Ford's looks at *twice* the price. You get extra zip in a Ford V-8, too. That's why it's the world's best seller! It's a good investment, too. Nothing at the price keeps its value like a Ford. And, of course, you don't need children to appreciate the extra safety of Ford Lifeguard Design," says Mr. Bremer.

SEE YOUR LOCAL FORD DEALER

The Country Sedan, one of six Ford do-it-alls, has 4-doors, lots of room. And its 202-h.p. V-8 is the most powerful standard "8" in its field.

The Ford Thunderbird inspired the styling for all Fords. And you can have its own 225-h.p. Special V-8 in most of them.

Join the 300,000 TWO FORD families!

appropriations for the Korean War, and defense spending accounted for some 10 percent of the GNP throughout the ensuing decade. Pentagon dollars primed the pumps of high-technology industries such as aerospace, plastics, and electronics—areas in which the United States reigned supreme over all foreign competitors. The military budget also financed much scientific research and development ("R and D"—hence the name of one of the most famous "think tanks," the Rand Corporation). More than ever before, unlocking the secrets of nature was the key to unleashing economic growth.

Cheap energy also fed the economic boom. American and European companies controlled the flow of abundant petroleum from the sandy expanses of the Middle East, and they kept prices low. Americans doubled their consumption of inexpensive and seemingly inexhaustible oil in the quarter-century after the war. Anticipating a limitless future of low-cost fuels, they flung out endless ribbons of highways, installed air-conditioning in their homes, and engineered a sixfold increase in the country's electricity-generating capacity between 1945 and 1970. Spidery grids of electrical cables carried the pent-up power of oil, gas, coal, and falling water to activate the tools of workers on the factory floor.

With the forces of nature increasingly harnessed in their hands, workers chalked up spectacular gains in productivity—the amount of output per hour of work. In the two decades after the outbreak of the Korean War in 1950, productivity increased at an average rate of more than 3 percent per year. Gains in productivity were also enhanced by the rising educational level of the work force. By 1970 nearly 90 percent of the school-age population was enrolled in educational institutions—a dramatic contrast with the opening years of the century, when only half of this age group had attended school. Better educated and better equipped, American workers in 1970 could produce nearly twice as much in an hour's labor as they had in 1950. Productivity was the key to prosperity. Rising productivity in the 1950s and 1960s virtually doubled the average American's standard of living in the postwar quarter-century.

Also contributing to the vigor of the postwar economy were some momentous changes in the nation's basic economic structure. Conspicuous was the accelerating shift of the work force out of agriculture, which achieved productivity gains virtually unmatched by any other economic sector. The family farm nearly became an antique artifact as consolidation produced giant agribusinesses able to employ costly machinery. Thanks largely to mechanization and to rich new fertilizers—as well as to government subsidies and price supports—one farmworker by the century's end could produce food for over fifty people, compared with about fifteen people in the 1940s. Farmers whose

Agribusiness Expensive machinery of the sort shown here made most of American agriculture a capital-intensive, phenomenally productive big business by the twenty-first century—and sounded the death knell for many small-scale family farms.

forebears had busted sod with oxen or horses now plowed their fields in air-conditioned tractor cabs, listening on their stereophonic radios to weather forecasts or the latest Chicago commodities market quotations. Once the mighty backbone of the agricultural Republic, and still some 15 percent of the labor force at the end of World War II, farmers made up a slim 2 percent of working Americans by the turn of the twenty-first century—yet they fed much of the world.

⭐ The Smiling Sunbelt

The convulsive economic changes of the post-1945 period shook and shifted the American people, amplifying the population redistribution set in motion by World War II. As immigrants and westward-trekking pioneers, Americans had always been a people on the move, but they were astonishingly footloose in the postwar years. For some three decades after 1945, an average of 30 million people changed residences every year. Families especially felt the strain, as distance divided parents from children, and brothers and sisters from one another. One sign of this sort of stress was the phenomenal popularity of advice books on child-rearing, especially Dr. Benjamin Spock's *The Common Sense Book of Baby and Child Care*. First published in 1945, it instructed millions of parents during the ensuing decades in the kind of homely wisdom that was once transmitted naturally from grandparent to parent, and from parent to child. In fluid postwar neighborhoods, friendships were also hard to sustain. Mobility could exact a high human cost in loneliness and isolation.

Especially striking was the growth of the **Sunbelt**—a fifteen-state area stretching in a smiling crescent from Virginia through Florida and Texas to Arizona and California. This region increased its population at a rate nearly double that of the old industrial zones of the Northeast (the "Frostbelt"). In the 1950s California alone accounted for one-fifth of the entire nation's population growth and by 1963 had outdistanced New York as the most populous state—a position it still holds in the early years of the twenty-first century, with more than 36 million people, or more than one out of every eight Americans.

The South and Southwest were a new frontier for Americans after World War II. These modern pioneers came in search of jobs, a better climate, and lower taxes. Jobs they found in abundance, especially in the California electronics industry, in the aerospace complexes in Florida and Texas, and in the huge military installations that powerful southern congressional representatives secured for their districts (see Map 36.1).

A Niagara of federal dollars accounted for much of the Sunbelt's prosperity, though, ironically, southern and western politicians led the cry against government spending. By the early twenty-first century, states in the South and West were annually receiving some $444 billion more in federal funds than those in the Northeast and Midwest. A new economic war between the states seemed to be shaping up. Northeasterners and their allies from the hard-hit heavy-industry region of the Ohio Valley (the "Rustbelt") tried to rally political support with the sarcastic slogan "The North shall rise again."

These dramatic shifts of population and wealth further broke the historic grip of the North on the nation's political life. Every elected occupant of the White House from 1964 to 2008 hailed from the Sunbelt, and the region's congressional representation rose as its population grew.

✸ The Rush to the Suburbs

In all regions America's modern migrants—if they were white—fled from the cities to the burgeoning new suburbs (see "Makers of America: The Suburbanites," pp. 836–837). While other industrial countries struggled to rebuild their war-ravaged cities, government policies in the United States encouraged movement away from urban centers. Federal Housing Administration (FHA) and Veterans Administration (VA) home-loan guarantees made it more economically attractive to own a home in the suburbs than to rent an apartment in the city. Tax deductions for interest payments on home mortgages provided additional financial incentive. And government-built highways that sped commuters from suburban homes to city jobs further facilitated this mass migration. By 1960 one in every four Americans

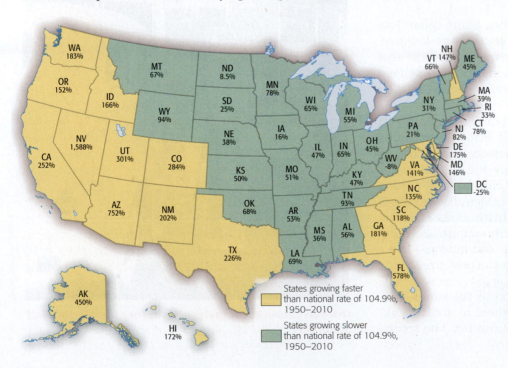

MAP 36.1 Distribution of Population Increase, 1950–2008 States with figures higher than 102 percent were growing faster than the national average between 1950 and 2008. Note that much of the growth was in the "Sunbelt," a loose geographical concept, as some Deep South states had very little population growth, whereas the mountain and Pacific states were booming. (Sources: *Statistical Abstract of the United States* and U.S. Census, relevant years.) © Cengage Learning

Few images evoke more vividly the prosperity of the postwar era than aerial photographs of sprawling suburbs. Neat rows of look-alike tract houses, each with a driveway and lawn and here and there a backyard swimming pool, came to symbolize the capacity of the economy to deliver the "American dream" to millions of families.

Suburbanization was hardly new. Well-off city dwellers had beaten paths to leafy outlying neighborhoods since the nineteenth century. But after 1945 the steady flow became a stampede. The baby boom, new highways, government guarantees for mortgage lending, and favorable tax policies all made suburbia blossom.

Who were the Americans racing to the new postwar suburbs? War veterans led the way in the late 1940s, aided by Veterans Administration mortgages that featured tiny down payments and low interest rates. The general public soon followed. The Federal Housing Administration (FHA) offered insured mortgages with low down payments and 2 to 3 percent interest rates on thirty-year loans. With deals like this, it was hardly surprising that American families flocked into "Levittowns," built by William and Alfred Levitt, and other similar suburban developments.

People of all kinds found their way to suburbia, heading for neighborhoods that varied from the posh to the plain. Yet for all this diversity, the overwhelming majority of suburbanites were white and middle-class. In 1967 sociologist Herbert Gans published *The Levittowners*, based on his own move to a Levitt-built community outside Philadelphia. He described suburban families in tract developments as predominantly third- or fourth-generation Americans with some college education and at least two children.

Men tended to work in either white-collar jobs or upper-level blue-collar positions such as foremen. Women usually worked in the home, so much so that suburbia came to symbolize the domestic confinement that feminists in the 1960s and 1970s decried in their campaign for women's rights.

The house itself became more important than ever as postwar suburbanites built their leisure lives around television, home improvement projects, and barbecues on the patio. The center of family life shifted to the fenced-in backyard, as neighborly city habits of visiting on the front stoop, gabbing on the sidewalk, and strolling to local stores disappeared. Institutions that had thrived as social centers in the city—churches, women's clubs, fraternal organizations, and taverns—had a tougher time attracting patrons in the privatized world of postwar suburbia.

Life in the suburbs was a boon to the automobile, as parents jumped behind the wheel to shuttle children, groceries, and golf clubs to and fro. The second car, once an unheard-of luxury, became a practical "necessity" for suburban families constantly "on the go." A car culture sprang up with new destinations, like drive-thru restaurants and drive-in movies. Roadside shopping centers edged out downtowns as places to shop. Meanwhile, the new interstate highway system enabled breadwinners to live farther and farther from their jobs and still commute to work daily.

Many suburbanites continued to depend on cities for jobs, though by the 1980s the suburbs themselves became important sites of employment. Wherever they worked, suburbanites turned their backs on the city and its problems. They fought to maintain their communities as secluded retreats, independent municipalities with their own taxes, schools, and zoning restrictions designed to keep out public housing and the poor. Even the naming of towns and streets reflected a pastoral ideal. Poplar Terrace and Mountainview Drive were popular street names; East Paterson, New Jersey, was renamed Elmwood Park in 1973. With a majority of Americans living in suburbs by the 1980s, cities lost their political clout. Bereft of state and federal aid, cit-

Drive-in Café in Los Angeles, the Mother and Model of All Suburbias

Slim Aarons/Getty Images

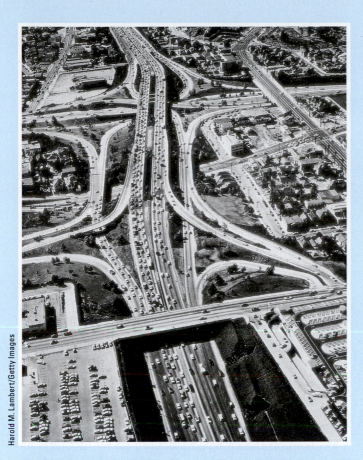

Aerial View of the On-ramps to a Typical New Interstate Highway, 1950s

ies festered with worsening social problems: poverty, drug addiction, and crime.

Middle-class African Americans began to move to the suburbs in substantial numbers by the 1980s, but even that migration failed to alter dramatically the racial divide of metropolitan America. Black suburbanites settled in towns like Rolling Oaks outside Miami or Brook Glen near Atlanta—black middle-class towns in white-majority counties. By the end of the twentieth century, suburbia as a whole was more racially diverse than at midcentury. But old patterns of urban "white flight" and residential segregation endured.

Buyers Line Up for a Levittown Home, 1951   Mass construction techniques and a New Deal-inspired revolution in home mortgage financing made first-time homeowners out of millions of Americans in the post-World War II years.

dwelt in suburbia, and a half-century later, more than half the nation's population did.

The construction industry boomed in the 1950s and 1960s to satisfy this demand. Pioneered by innovators like the Levitt brothers, whose first **Levittown** sprouted on New York's Long Island in the 1940s, builders revolutionized the techniques of home construction. Erecting hundreds or even thousands of dwellings in a single project, specialized crews working from standardized plans laid foundations, while others raised factory-assembled framing modules, put on roofs, strung wires, installed plumbing, and finished the walls in record time and with cost-cutting efficiency. Snooty critics wailed about the aesthetic monotony of the suburban "tract" developments, but eager home buyers nevertheless moved into them by the millions.

"White flight" to the leafy green suburbs left the inner cities—especially those in the Northeast and Midwest—black, brown, and broke. Migrating blacks from the South filled up the urban neighborhoods that were abandoned by the departing white middle class (see "Makers of America: The Great African American Migration," pp. 870–871). In effect, the incoming blacks imported the grinding poverty of the rural South into the inner cores of northern cities. Taxpaying businesses fled with their affluent customers from downtown shops to suburban shopping malls (another post–World War II invention).

Government policies sometimes aggravated this spreading pattern of residential segregation. FHA administrators, citing the "risk" of making loans to blacks and other "unharmonious racial or nationality groups," often refused them mortgages for private home purchases, thus limiting black mobility out of the inner cities and driving many minorities into public housing projects. Even public housing programs frequently followed a so-called neighborhood composition rule, which effectively built housing for blacks in neighborhoods that were already identified as predominantly black—thus solidifying racial separation.

The Postwar Baby Boom

Of all the upheavals in postwar America, none was more dramatic than the **baby boom**—the huge leap in the birthrate in the decade and a half after 1945. Confident young men and women tied the nuptial knot in record numbers at war's end, and they began immediately to fill the nation's empty cradles. They thus touched off a demographic explosion that added more than 50 million bawling babies to the nation's population by the end of the 1950s. The soaring birthrate finally crested in 1957 and was followed by a deepening birth dearth. By 1973 fertility rates had dropped below the point necessary to maintain existing population figures without further immigration.

This boom-or-bust cycle of births begot a bulging wave along the American population curve. As the oversize postwar generation grew to maturity, it was destined—like the fabled pig passing through the python—to strain and distort many aspects of American life. Elementary-school enrollments, for example, swelled to nearly 34 million pupils in 1970. Then began a steady decline, as the onward-marching age group left in its wake closed schools and unemployed teachers.

The maturing babies of the postwar boom sent economic shock waves undulating through the decades. As tykes and toddlers in the 1940s and 1950s, they made up a lucrative market for manufacturers of canned food and other baby products. As teenagers in the 1960s, the same youngsters spent an estimated $20 billion a year for clothes and recorded rock music—and their sheer numbers laid the basis of the much-ballyhooed "youth culture" of that tumultuous decade. In the 1970s the consumer tastes of the aging baby boomers changed again, and the most popular jeans maker began marketing pants with a fuller cut for those former "kids" who could no longer squeeze into their size-thirty Levi's. In the 1980s the horde of baby boomers bumped and jostled one another in the job market, struggling to get a foothold on the crowded ladder of social mobility. As the boomers entered middle age, a "secondary boom" of children peaked in the early 1990s—a faint demographic echo of the postwar population explosion. The impact of the huge postwar generation will continue to ripple through American society well into the twenty-first century, when its members pass eventually into retirement, placing enormous strains on the Social Security system.

Truman: The "Gutty" Man from Missouri

Presiding over the opening of the postwar period was an "accidental president"—Harry S Truman. "The moon, the stars, and all the planets" had fallen on him, he remarked when he was called upon to shoulder the dead Roosevelt's awesome burdens of leadership. Trim and owlishly bespectacled, with his graying hair and friendly, toothy grin, Truman was called "the average man's average man." Even his height—five feet eight inches—was average. The first president in many years without a college education, he had farmed, served as an artillery officer in France during World War I, and failed as a haberdasher. He then tried his hand at precinct-level Missouri politics, through which he rose from a judgeship to the U.S. Senate. Though a protégé of a notorious political machine in Kansas City, he had managed to keep his own hands clean.

The problems of the postwar period were staggering, and the suddenly burdened new president at first approached his tasks with humility. But gradually he evolved from a shrinking pipsqueak into a scrappy little cuss, gaining confidence to the point of cockiness. When the Soviet foreign minister complained, "I have never been talked to like that in my life," Truman shot back, "Carry out your agreements and you won't get talked to like that." Truman later boasted, "I gave him the one-two, right to the jaw."

A smallish man thrust suddenly into a giant job, Truman permitted designing old associates of the "Missouri gang" to gather around him and, like Grant, was stubbornly loyal to them when they were caught with cream on their whiskers. On occasion he would send critics hot-tempered and profane "s.o.b." letters. Most troubling, in trying to demonstrate to a skeptical public his decisiveness and power of command, he was inclined to go off half-cocked or stick mulishly to a wrongheaded notion. "To err is Truman," cynics jibed.

But if he was sometimes small in the small things, he was often big in the big things. He had down-home authenticity, few pretensions, rock-solid probity, and a lot of that old-fashioned character trait called moxie. Not one to dodge responsibility, he placed a sign on his White House desk that read, "The buck stops here." Among his favorite sayings was "If you can't stand the heat, get out of the kitchen."

✦ Yalta: Bargain or Betrayal?

Vast and silent, the Soviet Union continued to be the great enigma. The conference at Tehran in 1943, where Roosevelt first met Joseph Stalin man to man, had cleared the air somewhat, but much remained unresolved—especially questions about the postwar fates of Germany, Eastern Europe, and Asia.

The **Yalta conference**, the final fateful conference of the Big Three, took place in February 1945. At this former tsarist resort on the relatively warm shores of the Black Sea, Stalin, Churchill, and the fast-failing Roosevelt reached momentous agreements, after pledging their faith with vodka. Final plans were laid for smashing the buckling German lines and assigning occupation zones in Germany to the victorious powers. Stalin agreed that Poland, with revised boundaries, should have a representative government based on free elections—a pledge he soon broke. Bulgaria and Romania were likewise to have free elections—a promise also flouted. The Big Three further announced plans for fashioning a new international peacekeeping organization—the United Nations.

Of all the grave decisions at Yalta, the most controversial concerned the Far East. The atomic bomb had not yet been tested, and Washington strategists expected frightful American casualties in the projected assault on Japan. From Roosevelt's standpoint it seemed highly desirable that Stalin should enter the Asian war,

Granger Collection

The Big Three From left to right, Churchill, Roosevelt, and Stalin sit somberly at their fateful meeting at Yalta in February 1945. Roosevelt was only weeks away from death.

pin down Japanese troops in Manchuria and Korea, and lighten American losses. But Soviet casualties had already been enormous, and Moscow presumably needed inducements to bring it into the Far Eastern conflagration.

Horse trader Stalin was in a position at Yalta to exact a high price. He agreed to attack Japan within three months after the collapse of Germany, and he later redeemed this pledge in full. In return, the Soviets were promised the southern half of Sakhalin Island, lost by Russia to Japan in 1905, and Japan's Kurile Islands as well. The Soviet Union was also granted joint control over the railroads of China's Manchuria and special privileges in the two key seaports of that area, Dairen and Port Arthur. These concessions evidently would give Stalin control over vital industrial centers of America's weakening Chinese ally.

As it turned out, Moscow's muscle was not necessary to knock out Japan. Critics charged that Roosevelt had sold Jiang Jieshi (Chiang Kai-shek) down the river when he conceded control of Manchuria to Stalin. The consequent undermining of Chinese morale, so the accusation ran, contributed powerfully to Jiang's overthrow by the communists four years later. The critics also assailed the "sellout" of Poland and other Eastern European countries.

Roosevelt's defenders countered that Stalin, with his mighty red army, could have secured much more of China if he wished and that the Yalta conference really set limits on his ambitions. Apologists for Roosevelt also contended that if Stalin had kept his promise to support free elections in Poland and the liberated Balkans, the sorry sequel would have been different. Actually, Soviet troops had then occupied much of Eastern Europe, and a war to throw them out was unthinkable.

The fact is that the Big Three at Yalta were not drafting a comprehensive peace settlement; at most they were sketching general intentions and testing one another's reactions. Later critics who howled about broken promises overlooked that fundamental point. In the case of Poland, Roosevelt admitted that the Yalta agreement was "so elastic that the Russians can stretch it all the way from Yalta to Washington without ever technically breaking it." More specific understandings among the wartime allies—especially the two emerging superpowers, the United States and the Soviet Union—awaited the arrival of peace.

✸ The United States and the Soviet Union

History provided little hope that the United States and the Soviet Union would reach cordial understandings about the shape of the postwar world. Mutual suspicions were ancient, abundant, and abiding. Communism and capitalism were historically hostile social philosophies. The United States had refused officially to recognize the Bolshevik revolutionary government in Moscow until it was sixteen years old, in 1933. Soviet skepticism toward the West was nourished by the British and American delays in opening up a second front against Germany, while the Soviet army paid a grisly price to roll the Nazi invaders back across Russia and Eastern Europe. Britain and America had also frozen their Soviet "ally" out of the project to develop atomic weapons, further feeding Stalin's mistrust. The Washington government rubbed salt in Soviet wounds when it abruptly terminated vital lend-lease aid to a battered USSR in 1945 and spurned Moscow's plea for a $6 billion reconstruction loan—while approving a similar loan of $3.75 billion to Britain in 1946.

Different visions of the postwar world also separated the two superpowers. Stalin aimed above all to guarantee the security of the Soviet Union. The USSR had twice in the twentieth century been stabbed in its heartland by attacks across the windswept plains of Eastern Europe. Stalin made it clear from the outset of the war that he was determined to have friendly governments along the Soviet western border, especially in Poland. By maintaining an extensive Soviet sphere of influence in Eastern and Central Europe, the USSR could protect itself and consolidate its revolutionary base as the world's leading communist country.

To many Americans, that "sphere of influence" looked like an ill-gained "empire." Doubting that Soviet goals were purely defensive, they remembered the earlier Bolshevik call for world revolution. Stalin's emphasis on "spheres" also clashed with Franklin Roosevelt's Wilsonian dream of an "open world," decolonized, demilitarized, and democratized, with a strong international organization to oversee global peace.

Even the ways in which the United States and the Soviet Union resembled each other were troublesome. Both countries had been largely isolated from world affairs before World War II—the United States through choice, the Soviet Union through rejection by the other powers. Both nations also had a history of conducting a kind of "missionary" diplomacy—of trying to export to all the world the political doctrines precipitated out of their respective revolutionary origins.

Unaccustomed to their great-power roles, unfamiliar with or even antagonistic to each other, and each believing in the universal applicability of its own particular ideology, America and the USSR suddenly found themselves staring eyeball-to-eyeball over the prostrate body of a battered Europe—a Europe that had been the traditional center of international affairs. In these circumstances some sort of confrontation was virtually unavoidable. The wartime "Grand Alliance" of the United States, the Soviet Union, and Britain had been a misbegotten child of necessity, kept alive only until the

The Communist Menace First appearing in the *New York Daily News* on January 6, 1946, this map reflected Americans' rising anxiety after World War II that the Soviet Union was an aggressively expansionist power, relentlessly gobbling up territory and imposing its will across both Europe and Asia.

mutual enemy was crushed. When the hated Hitler fell, suspicion and rivalry between communistic, despotic Russia and capitalistic, democratic America were all but inevitable. In a fateful progression of events, marked often by misperceptions as well as by genuine conflicts of interest, the two powers provoked each other into a tense standoff known as the **Cold War**. Enduring four and a half decades, the Cold War not only shaped Soviet-American relations; it overshadowed the entire postwar international order in every corner of the globe. The Cold War also molded societies and economies and the lives of individual people all over the planet.

⭐ Shaping the Postwar World

Despite these obstacles, the United States did manage at war's end to erect some of the structures that would support Roosevelt's vision of an open world. At the **Bretton Woods Conference** in Bretton Woods, New Hampshire, in 1944, the Western Allies established the

International Monetary Fund (IMF) to encourage world trade by regulating currency exchange rates. They also founded the International Bank for Reconstruction and Development (World Bank) to promote economic growth in war-ravaged and underdeveloped areas. In contrast to its behavior after World War I, the United States took the lead in creating these important international bodies and supplied most of their funding. The stubborn Soviets declined to participate (see "Thinking Globally: The Era of Globalization," pp. 842–843).

As flags wept at half-mast, the United Nations Conference opened on schedule, April 25, 1945, despite Roosevelt's dismaying death thirteen days earlier. Unlike Woodrow Wilson, Roosevelt had shrewdly moved to establish the new international body before the war's conclusion, so as to capitalize on the wartime spirit of cooperation and insulate planning for the United Nations from the potentially divisive issue of the peace settlement. Meeting at the San Francisco War Memorial Opera House, representatives from fifty nations fashioned the United Nations Charter.

The Era of Globalization

Woodrow Wilson had envisioned a world order organized around the principles of self-determination and free trade—a world "made safe for democracy." But Wilson's dream perished in the turbulent aftermath of World War I. The United States retreated into a selfish and short-sighted isolationism: hiking tariffs to record levels, refusing to join the new League of Nations, and stoutly asserting its neutrality, even as the Great Depression plunged the planet into economic chaos and World War II eventually wreathed the globe in fire and destruction.

Franklin Roosevelt had served Wilson as assistant secretary of the navy. He had shared his chief's idealistic goals, as well as Wilson's bitter disappointment when they failed to be achieved. FDR also believed that many of the ills that beset the world in the post–World War I era could have been avoided if only the United States had played an international role commensurate with its power and its own highest ideals. He resolved not to squander another opportunity for American international leadership.

So on August 9, 1941, as much of Europe writhed under the Nazi jackboot, President Roosevelt rendezvoused with British prime minister Winston Churchill aboard two warships anchored off the coast of Newfoundland. After three days of talks, they publicly announced their vision of the postwar world. What came to be called the "Atlantic Charter" proclaimed for all nations the rights to self-determination and free access to trade. It also foresaw the creation of a new international organization to replace the defunct League of Nations. And it declared that a postwar peace must ensure "freedom from fear and want" for all individuals, everywhere—the first time global economic prosperity was formally declared to be an objective of any country's foreign policy. Roosevelt and

United Nations, 1947 by Henry Rowland Eveleigh

Great Hopes for World Peace with the United Nations, 1947 The achievements of the new international regime were dramatic. International trade doubled in the 1950s and again in the 1960s. By century's end, the volume of global commerce was ten times larger than in 1950 (see Table 36.1). Increased trade fueled postwar recovery in Europe and Japan and set several underdeveloped countries—notably Taiwan, Singapore, South Korea, India, and China—on the path to modernization and prosperity.

Churchill had drafted the charter for a new era in American diplomacy and for a new phase of world history as well.

After World War II, the United States, victorious and robust at the end of a conflict that had laid waste all the traditional great powers, was uniquely positioned to shape the world order

after World War II. To a remarkable degree, it followed the Wilsonian principles embodied in the Atlantic Charter. It gave birth to an array of multilateral institutions to promote trade and international investment, support the rule of law, and nurture democracy. They included the World Bank, to fund post-

TABLE 36.1 International Trade, 1948–2008

	1948	1953	1963	1973	1983	1993	2003	2008
Total volume of world trade (in billions of U.S. dollars)	59	84	157	579	1,838	3,676	7,377	15,717
Total volume of U.S. exports (in billions of U.S. dollars)	13	12	22	71	202	457	728	1,305
Share of world exports (%)								
United States	22	19	15	12	11	13	10	8
Europe	35	39	48	51	43	45	46	41
Africa	7	6	6	5	4	3	2	3
Middle East	2	3	3	4	7	4	4	7
Asia	14	13	12	15	19	26	26	28
GATT/WTO members	63	69	75	84	77	89	94	93

(Sources: All data except total volume of U.S. exports are from World Trade Organization, *International Trade Statistics*, 2009. U.S. export data for 1948–1993 are from *United States Historical Statistics of the United States*, vol. 5; data for 2003 and 2008 are from Foreign Exports Division, U.S. Census Bureau. Because different organizations rely on different methodologies for estimating total exports, WTO estimates used to compute the U.S. share of world exports differ slightly from those presented in this table.)

war reconstruction; the International Monetary Fund (IMF), to stabilize world currencies; and the General Agreement on Tariffs and Trade (GATT), to lower barriers to international commerce. In the ensuing decades, 102 nations, accounting for 80 percent of world trade, signed GATT (succeeded by the World Trade Organization, or WTO, in the 1990s). The United States also took the lead in founding and funding the United Nations (U.N.), which worked to arbitrate international disputes, improve standards of living worldwide, and encourage decolonization, particularly in Asia and Africa.

As Roosevelt and Churchill anticipated, the benefits of trade extended far beyond rising incomes. As goods flowed across borders, so too did advances in medicine and nutrition. Since 1950 the average life expectancy worldwide has increased by twenty years, with the biggest gains in the developing world.

Rising prosperity and improved standards of living also strengthened the middle classes in developing countries, with democracy often following in the footsteps of globalization. The number of electoral democracies increased from 44 in 1950 to 120 in 2000. Recent studies confirm that states with open trade policies are three times more likely to protect civil liberties than those without such policies.

For some four decades, the full effects of this liberalized world order were muffled by the Cold War. Eastern Europe and the Soviet Union in particular were conspicuous nonparticipants in the emerging global economy, and the United States often supported repressive, undemocratic regimes simply to keep them out of the Soviet camp. But the end of the Cold War and the dissolution of the Soviet bloc in the early 1990s unleashed the full force of globalization. International trade, investment, and migration exploded. More than fifty new electoral democracies, notably in Eastern Europe, Asia, and Latin America, emerged in the last decade of the twentieth century.

Global trade, already at record levels, doubled between 1990 and 2003.

Despite these gains, problems persist. Critics decry the job insecurity, exploitative labor practices, inflationary pressures, widening income disparities both within and between nations, and environmental degradation that have accompanied worldwide industrial growth. Many African nations have proved chronically unable to overcome political instability, systemic poverty, and devastating epidemics. Africa's woes, and those of many Middle Eastern states as well, demonstrate that many parts of the world are still very far from safe for democracy. Yet the liberalized world order that the United States took the lead in building after World War II left an impressive legacy of international stability, burgeoning prosperity, and freedom from fear and want for millions of human beings—a lasting testament to Wilson's vision and to Roosevelt's leadership.

In June 1946 Bernard Baruch (1870–1965), in presenting his plan for the control of atomic energy to the United Nations, said,

"We are here to make a choice between the quick and the dead. That is our business. Behind the black portent of the new atomic age lies a hope which, seized upon with faith, can work our salvation. If we fail, then we have damned every man to be the slave of fear. Let us not deceive ourselves; we must elect world peace or world destruction."

The **United Nations (U.N.)** was a successor to the old League of Nations, but it differed from its predecessor in significant ways. Born in a moment of idealism and designed to prevent another great-power war, the League had adopted rules denying the veto power to any party to a dispute. The U.N., by contrast, more realistically provided that no member of the Security Council, dominated by the Big Five powers (the United States, Britain, the USSR, France, and China), could have action taken against it without its consent. The League, in short, presumed great-power conflict; the U.N. presumed great-power cooperation. Both approaches had their liabilities. The U.N. also featured the General Assembly, which could be controlled by smaller countries. In contrast to the chilly American reception of the League in 1919, the Senate overwhelmingly approved the U.N. Charter on July 28, 1945, by a vote of 89 to 2—not least because it provided safeguards for American sovereignty and freedom of action.

The United Nations, setting up its permanent glass home in New York City, had some gratifying initial successes. It helped preserve peace in Iran, Kashmir, and other trouble spots. It played a large role in creating the new Jewish state of Israel. The U.N. Trusteeship Council guided former colonies to independence. Through such arms as UNESCO (United Nations Educational, Scientific, and Cultural Organization), FAO (Food and Agricultural Organization), and WHO (World Health Organization), the U.N. brought benefits to peoples the world over.

The fearsome new technology of the atom put to an early test the spirit of cooperation on which the U.N. had been founded. The new organization failed badly. U.S. delegate Bernard Baruch called in 1946 for a U.N. agency, free from the great-power veto, with worldwide authority over atomic energy, weapons, and research. The Soviet delegate countered that the possession of nuclear weapons should simply be outlawed by every nation. President Truman said that it would be folly to "throw away our gun until we are sure the rest of the world can't arm against us." The suspicious Soviets felt the same way and used their veto power to scuttle the proposals. A priceless opportunity to tame the nuclear monster in its infancy was lost. The atomic clock ticked ominously on for the next forty-five years, shadowing all relations between the Soviet Union and the United States and threatening the very future of the human race.

The Problem of Germany

Hitler's ruined Reich posed especially thorny problems for all the wartime Allies. They agreed only that the cancer of Nazism had to be cut out of the German

The Nuremberg War Crimes Trial, 1946 Of the Nazi defendants pictured here, from left to right in the first row, Hermann Goering committed suicide during the trial; Rudolf Hess was sentenced to life in prison and died of an apparent suicide in his cell in 1987; Joachim von Ribbentrop, Wilhelm Keitel, and Ernest Kaltenbrunner were executed; in the second row, Karl Doenitz was sentenced to ten years in prison; Erich Raeder was sentenced to life in prison but released in 1955; Baldur von Schirach was sentenced to twenty years in prison; and Fritz Sauckel was executed.

© Bettmann/Corbis

MAP 36.2 **Postwar Partition of Germany** Germany lost much of its territory in the east to Poland and the Soviet Union. The military occupation zones were the bases for the formation of two separate countries in 1949, when the British, French, and American zones became West Germany, and the Soviet zone became East Germany. (The two Germanys were reunited in 1990.) Berlin remained under joint four-power occupation from 1945 to 1990 and became a focus and symbol of Cold War tensions.

© Cengage Learning

body politic, which involved punishing Nazi leaders for war crimes. The Allies joined in trying twenty-two top culprits at the **Nuremberg war crimes trial** during 1945–1946. Accusations included committing crimes against the laws of war and humanity and plotting aggressions contrary to solemn treaty pledges.

Justice, Nuremberg-style, was harsh. Twelve of the accused Nazis swung from the gallows, and seven were sentenced to long jail terms. "Foxy Hermann" Goering, whose blubbery chest had once blazed with ribbons, cheated the hangman a few hours before his scheduled execution by swallowing a hidden cyanide capsule. The trials of several small-fry Nazis continued for years. Legal critics in America and elsewhere condemned these proceedings as judicial lynchings, because the victims were tried for offenses that had not been clear-cut crimes when the war began.

Beyond punishing the top Nazis, the Allies could agree on little about postwar Germany. Some American Hitler-haters, noting that an industrialized Germany had been a brutal aggressor, at first wanted to dismantle German factories and reduce the country to a potato patch. The Soviets, denied American economic assistance, were determined to rebuild their shattered land by extracting enormous reparations from the Germans. Both these desires clashed headlong with the reality that an industrial, healthy German economy

was indispensable to the recovery of Europe. The Americans soon came to appreciate that fact. But the Soviets, deeply fearful of another blitzkrieg, resisted all efforts to revitalize Germany.

Along with Austria, Germany had been divided at war's end into four military occupation zones, each assigned to one of the Big Four powers (France, Britain, America, and the USSR) (see Map 36.2). The Western Allies refused to allow Moscow to bleed their zones of the reparations that Stalin insisted he had been promised at Yalta. They also began to promote the idea of a reunited Germany. The communists responded by tightening their grip on their Eastern zone. Before long, it was apparent that Germany would remain indefinitely divided. West Germany eventually became an independent country, wedded to the West. East Germany, along with other Soviet-dominated Eastern European

Former British prime minister Winston Churchill (1874–1965), in a highly controversial speech at Fulton, Missouri (March 1946), warned of Soviet expansionism:

❝From Stettin in the Baltic to Trieste in the Adriatic an iron curtain has descended across the Continent.❞

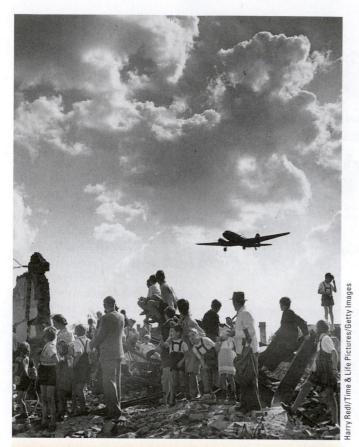

Berlin, 1948 Grateful city residents watch a U.S. airplane fly in much-needed supplies.

Harry Redl/Time & Life Pictures/Getty Images

some of the very aircraft that had recently dropped bombs on Berlin, American pilots ferried thousands of tons of supplies a day to the grateful Berliners, their former enemies. Western Europeans took heart from this vivid demonstration of America's determination to honor its commitments in Europe. The Soviets, their bluff dramatically called, finally lifted their blockade in May 1949. In the same year, the governments of the two Germanys, East and West, were formally established. The Cold War had icily congealed.

✦ The Cold War Congeals

A crafty Stalin also probed the West's resolve at other sensitive points, including oil-rich Iran. Seeking to secure oil concessions similar to those held by the British and Americans, Stalin in 1946 broke an agreement to remove his troops from Iran's northernmost province, which the USSR had occupied, with British and American approval, during World War II. Instead he used the troops to aid a rebel movement. Truman sent off a stinging protest, and the Soviet dictator backed down.

Moscow's hard-line policies in Germany, Eastern Europe, and the Middle East wrought a psychological Pearl Harbor. The eyes of Americans were jarred wide-open by the Kremlin's apparent unwillingness to continue the wartime partnership. Any remaining goodwill from the period of comradeship-in-arms evaporated in a cloud of dark distrust. "I'm tired of babying the Soviets," Truman remarked privately in 1946, as attitudes on both sides began to harden frostily.

Truman's piecemeal responses to various Soviet challenges took on intellectual coherence in 1947, with the formulation of the **containment doctrine**. Crafted by a brilliant young diplomat and Soviet specialist, George F. Kennan, this concept held that Russia, whether tsarist or communist, was relentlessly expansionary. But the Kremlin was also cautious, Kennan argued, and the flow of Soviet power into "every nook and cranny available to it" could be stemmed by "firm and vigilant containment."

Truman embraced Kennan's advice when he formally and publicly adopted a "get-tough-with-Russia" policy in 1947. His first dramatic move was triggered by word that heavily burdened Britain could no longer bear the financial and military load of defending Greece against communist pressures. If Greece fell, Turkey would presumably collapse, and the strategic eastern Mediterranean would pass into the Soviet orbit.

In a surprise appearance, the president went before Congress on March 12, 1947, and requested support for what came to be known as the **Truman Doctrine**. Specifically, he asked for $400 million to bolster Greece

countries, such as Poland and Hungary, became nominally independent "satellite" states, bound to the Soviet Union. Eastern Europe virtually disappeared from Western sight behind the "iron curtain" of secrecy and isolation that Stalin clanged down across Europe from the Baltic to the Adriatic. The division of Europe would endure for more than four decades.

With Germany now split in two, there remained the problem of the rubble heap known as Berlin. Lying deep within the Soviet zone, this beleaguered isle in a red sea had been broken, like Germany as a whole, into sectors occupied by troops of each of the four victorious powers. In 1948, following controversies over German currency reform and four-power control, the Soviets abruptly choked off all rail and highway access to Berlin. They evidently reasoned that the Allies would be starved out.

Berlin became a hugely symbolic issue for both sides. At stake was not only the fate of the city but a test of wills between Moscow and Washington. The Americans organized the gigantic **Berlin airlift** in the midst of hair-trigger tension. For nearly a year, flying and Turkey, which Congress quickly granted. More generally, he declared that "it must be the policy of the United States to support free peoples who are resisting attempted subjugation by armed minorities or by outside pressures"—a sweeping and open-ended commitment of vast and worrisome proportions. Critics then and later charged that Truman had overreacted by promising unlimited support to any tinhorn despot who claimed to be resisting "Communist aggression." Critics also complained that the Truman Doctrine needlessly polarized the world into pro-Soviet and pro-American camps and unwisely construed the Soviet threat as primarily military in nature. Apologists for Truman have explained that it was Truman's fear of a revived isolationism that led him to exaggerate the Soviet threat and to pitch his message in the charged language of a holy global war against godless communism—a description of the Cold War that straightjacketed future policymakers who would seek to tone down Soviet-American competition and animosity.

Truman found support for casting the Cold War as a battle between good and evil from theologians like the influential liberal Protestant clergyman Reinhold Niebuhr (1892–1971). For over five decades after World War I, Niebuhr crusaded against what he perceived as

In February 1946 Kremlin specialist George F. Kennan (1904–2005) sent his landmark "Long Telegram" to the State Department. In the eight-thousand-word, eighteen-page message, Kennan assessed the Soviet threat and called for a new kind of response, which would eventually become known as the "containment doctrine":

"In summary, we have here a political force [Stalin's regime] committed fanatically to the belief that with [the] US there can be no permanent *modus vivendi*, that it is desirable and necessary that the internal harmony of our society be disrupted, our traditional way of life be destroyed, the international authority of our state be broken, if Soviet power is to be secure."

the drift away from Christian foundations. A vocal enemy of fascism, pacifism, and communism in the 1940s and 1950s, Niebuhr divided the world into two polarized camps: the "children of light" and the "children of darkness." For Niebuhr, Christian justice, including force if necessary, required a "realist" response to "children of darkness" like Hitler and Stalin.

A threat of a different sort loomed in Western Europe—especially France, Italy, and Germany. These key nations were still suffering from the hunger and economic chaos spawned by war. They were in grave danger of being taken over from the inside by Communist parties that could exploit these hardships.

President Truman responded with a bold policy. In a commencement address at Harvard University on June 5, 1947, Secretary of State George C. Marshall invited the Europeans to get together and work out a *joint* plan for their economic recovery. If they did so, then the United States would provide substantial financial assistance. This forced cooperation constituted a powerful nudge on the road to the eventual creation of the European Community (EC).

The democratic nations of Europe rose enthusiastically to the life-giving bait of the so-called **Marshall Plan**. They met in Paris in July 1947 to thrash out the details. There Marshall offered the same aid to the Soviet Union and its allies, if they would make political reforms and accept certain outside controls. In fact, the Americans worried that the Russian bear might hug the Marshall Plan to death, and therefore made the terms deliberately difficult for the USSR to accept. Nobody was surprised when the Soviets walked out, denouncing the "Martial Plan" as one more capitalist trick.

Where To? 1947 As this satirical view of the Truman Doctrine shows, not all Americans were sure where the country's new foreign policy was taking them.

The Granger Collection, New York

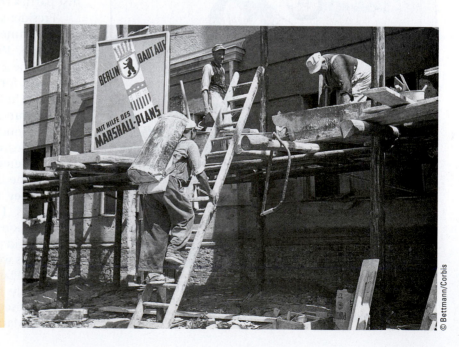

MAP 36.3 United States Foreign Aid, Military and Economic, 1945–1954 Marshall Plan aid swelled the outlay for Europe. Note the emphasis on the "developed" world, with relatively little aid going to "developing." © Cengage Learning

The Marshall Plan called for spending $12.5 billion over four years in sixteen cooperating countries (see Map 36.3). Congress at first balked at this mammoth sum. It looked even more huge when added to the nearly $2 billion the United States had already contributed to European relief through the United Nations Relief and Rehabilitation Administration (UNRRA) and the hefty American contributions to the United Nations, IMF, and World Bank. But a Soviet-sponsored communist coup in Czechoslovakia finally awakened the legislators to reality, and they voted the initial appropriations in April 1948. Congress evidently concluded that if Uncle Sam did not get the Europeans back on their feet, they would never get off his back.

Truman's Marshall Plan was a spectacular success. American dollars pumped reviving blood into the economic veins of the anemic Western European nations. Within a few years, most of them were exceeding their prewar outputs, as an "economic miracle" drenched Europe in prosperity. The Communist parties in Italy and France lost ground, and these two keystone countries were saved from the westward thrust of communism.

A resolute Truman made another fateful decision in 1948. Access to Middle Eastern oil was crucial to the European recovery program and, increasingly, to the health of the U.S. economy, given finite American oil reserves. Yet the Arab oil countries adamantly opposed the creation of the Jewish state of Israel in the British mandate territory of Palestine. Should Israel be born, a Saudi Arabian leader warned Truman, the Arabs "will lay siege to it until it dies of famine." Defying Arab wrath as well as the objections of his own State and Defense Departments and the European Allies, all of

The Marshall Plan Turns Enemies into Friends The poster in this 1950 photograph in Berlin reads, "Berlin Rebuilt with Help from the Marshall Plan."

American Motor of the Latest Type   In this Russian cartoon, the conquering Truman uses U.S. moneybags to induce dollar-hungry European nations to draw the American capitalistic chariot.

them afraid to antagonize the oil-endowed Arabs, Truman officially recognized the state of Israel on the day of its birth, May 14, 1948. Humanitarian sympathy for the Jewish survivors of the Holocaust ranked high among his reasons, as did his wishes to preempt Soviet influence in the Jewish state and to retain the support of American Jewish voters. Truman's policy of strong support for Israel would vastly complicate U.S. relations with the Arab world in the decades ahead.

✦ America Begins to Rearm

The Cold War, the struggle to contain Soviet communism, was not war, yet it was not peace. The standoff with the Kremlin banished the dreams of tax-fatigued Americans that tanks could be beaten into automobiles.

The Soviet menace spurred the unification of the armed services as well as the creation of a huge new national security apparatus. Congress in 1947 passed the National Security Act, creating the Department of Defense. The department was to be housed in the sprawling Pentagon building on the banks of the Potomac and to be headed by a new cabinet officer, the secretary of defense. Under the secretary, but now without cabinet status, were the civilian secretaries of the navy, the army (replacing the old secretary of war), and

the air force (a recognition of the rising importance of airpower). The uniformed heads of each service were brought together as the Joint Chiefs of Staff.

The National Security Act also established the National Security Council (NSC) to advise the president on security matters and the Central Intelligence Agency (CIA) to coordinate the government's foreign fact gathering. The "Voice of America," authorized by Congress in 1948, began beaming American radio broadcasts behind the iron curtain. In the same year, Congress resurrected the military draft, providing for the conscription of selected young men from nineteen to twenty-five years of age. The forbidding presence of the Selective Service System shaped millions of young people's educational, marital, and career plans in the following quarter-century. One shoe at a time, a war-weary America was reluctantly returning to a war footing.

The Soviet threat was also forcing the democracies of Western Europe into an unforeseen degree of unity. In 1948 Britain, France, Belgium, the Netherlands, and Luxembourg signed a path-breaking treaty of defensive alliance at Brussels. They then invited the United States to join them.

The proposal confronted the United States with a historic decision. America had traditionally avoided entangling alliances, especially in peacetime (if the Cold War could be considered peacetime). Yet American participation in the emerging coalition could serve many purposes: it would strengthen the policy of containing the Soviet Union; it would provide a framework for the reintegration of Germany into the European family; and it would reassure jittery Europeans that a traditionally isolationist Uncle Sam was not about to abandon them to the marauding Russian bear—or to a resurgent and domineering Germany.

The Truman administration decided to join the European pact, called the **North Atlantic Treaty Organization (NATO)** in recognition of its transatlantic character. With white-tie pageantry, the NATO treaty was signed in Washington on April 4, 1949. The twelve original signatories pledged to regard an attack on one as an attack on all and promised to respond with "armed force" if necessary. Despite last-ditch howls from immovable isolationists, the Senate approved the treaty on July 21, 1949, by a vote of 82 to 13. Membership was boosted to fourteen in 1952 by the inclusion of Greece and Turkey, to fifteen in 1955 by the addition of West Germany.

The NATO pact was epochal. It marked a dramatic departure from American diplomatic convention, a gigantic boost for European unification, and a significant step in the militarization of the Cold War. NATO became the cornerstone of all Cold War American policy toward Europe. With good reason pundits summed

Reaching Across the Atlantic in Peacetime, 1948
When the United States joined with the Western European powers in the North Atlantic Alliance, soon to be called the North Atlantic Treaty Organization, it overcame its historic isolationism in the wake of wars. By 1955 former enemy West Germany would be admitted to NATO to help defend Western Europe against Soviet aggression.

Granger Collection

up NATO's threefold purpose: "to keep the Russians out, the Germans down, and the Americans in."

✦ Reconstruction and Revolution in Asia

Reconstruction in Japan was simpler than in Germany, primarily because it was largely a one-man show. The occupying American army, under the supreme Allied commander, five-star general Douglas MacArthur, sat in the driver's seat. In the teeth of violent protests from Soviet officials, MacArthur went inflexibly ahead with his program for the democratization of Japan. Following the pattern in Germany, top Japanese "war criminals" were tried in Tokyo from 1946 to 1948. Eighteen of them were sentenced to prison terms, and seven were hanged.

General MacArthur, as a kind of Yankee mikado, enjoyed stunning success. The Japanese cooperated to an astonishing degree. They saw that good behavior and the adoption of democracy would speed the end of the occupation—as it did. A MacArthur-dictated constitution was adopted in 1946. It renounced militarism, provided for women's equality, and introduced Western-style democratic government—paving the way for a phenomenal economic recovery that within a few decades made Japan one of the world's mightiest industrial powers.

If Japan was a success story for American policymakers, the opposite was true in China, where a bitter civil war had raged for years between Nationalists and communists. Washington had halfheartedly supported the Nationalist government of Generalissimo Jiang Jieshi in his struggle with the communists under Mao Zedong (Mao Tse-tung). But ineptitude and corruption within the generalissimo's regime gradually began to corrode the confidence of his people. Communist armies swept south overwhelmingly, and late in 1949 Jiang was forced to flee with the remnants of his once-powerful force to the last-hope island of Formosa (Taiwan).

The collapse of Nationalist China was a depressing defeat for America and its allies in the Cold War—the

In August 1949 Secretary of State Dean Acheson (1893–1971) explained publicly why America had "dumped" Jiang Jieshi:

❝ The unfortunate but inescapable fact is that the ominous result of the civil war in China was beyond the control of the government of the United States. Nothing that this country did or could have done within the reasonable limits of its capabilities could have changed that result; nothing that was left undone by this country has contributed to it. It was the product of internal Chinese forces, forces which this country tried to influence but could not.❞

worst to date. At one fell swoop, nearly one-fourth of the world's population—some 500 million people—was swept into the communist camp. The so-called fall of China became a bitterly partisan issue in the United States. The Republicans, seeking "goats" who had "lost China," assailed President Truman and his bristly mustached, British-appearing secretary of state, Dean Acheson. They insisted that Democratic agencies, wormy with communists, had deliberately withheld aid from Jiang Jieshi so that he would fall. Democrats heatedly replied that when a regime has forfeited the support of its people, no amount of outside help will save it. Truman, the argument ran, did not "lose" China, because he never had China to lose. Jiang himself had never controlled all of China.

More bad news came in September 1949 when President Truman shocked the nation by announcing that the Soviets had exploded an atomic bomb—approximately three years earlier than many experts had thought possible. American strategists since 1945 had counted on keeping the Soviets in line by threats of a one-sided aerial attack with nuclear weapons. But atomic bombing was now a game that two could play.

To outpace the Soviets in nuclear weaponry, Truman ordered the development of the "H-bomb" (hydrogen bomb)—a city-smashing thermonuclear weapon that was a thousand times more powerful than the atomic bomb. J. Robert Oppenheimer, former scientific director of the Manhattan Project and current chair of the Atomic Energy Commission, led a group of scientists in opposition to the crash program to design thermonuclear weapons. The H-bomb, these scientists

Atomic scientist Edward Condon (1902–1974) warned as early as 1946—three years before the Soviets exploded their own atomic bomb—that Americans' confidence in their nuclear monopoly was a dangerous delusion that could unleash vicious accusations and scapegoating:

" The laws of nature, some seem to think, are ours exclusively. . . . Having created an air of suspicion and distrust, there will be persons among us who think our nations can know nothing except what is learned by espionage. So, when other countries make atom bombs, these persons will cry 'treason' at our scientists, for they will find it inconceivable that another country could make a bomb in any other way.**"**

warned, was so deadly that "it becomes a weapon which in practical effect is almost one of genocide." Famed physicist Albert Einstein, whose theories had helped give birth to the atomic age, declared that "annihilation of any life on earth has been brought within the range of technical possibilities."

But Einstein and Oppenheimer, the nation's two most famous scientists, could not persuade Truman, anxious over communist threats in East Asia. The United States exploded its first hydrogen device on a South Pacific atoll in 1952. Not to be outdone, the Soviets countered with their first H-bomb explosion in

The Hydrogen Bomb, 1954
This test blast at Bikini Atoll in the Marshall Islands was so powerful that one Japanese fisherman was killed and all twenty-two of his crewmates were seriously injured by radioactive ash that fell on their vessel some eighty miles away. Fishing boats a thousand miles from Bikini later brought in radioactively contaminated catches.

1953, and the nuclear arms race entered a perilously competitive cycle. Nuclear "superiority" became a dangerous and delusive dream, as each side tried to outdo the other in the scramble to build more destructive weapons. If the Cold War should ever blaze into a hot war, there might be no world left for the communists to communize or the democracies to democratize—a chilling thought that constrained both camps. Peace through mutual terror brought a shaky stability to the superpower standoff.

★ Ferreting Out Alleged Communists

One of the most active Cold War fronts was at home, where a new anti-red chase was in full cry. Many nervous citizens feared that communist spies, paid with Moscow gold, were undermining the government and treacherously misdirecting foreign policy. In 1947 Truman launched a massive "loyalty" program. The attorney general drew up a list of ninety supposedly disloyal

Richard Nixon, Red-hunter Congressman Nixon examines the microfilm that figured as important evidence in Alger Hiss's conviction for perjury in 1950.

© Bettmann/Corbis

organizations, none of which was given the opportunity to prove its innocence. The Loyalty Review Board investigated more than 3 million federal employees, some 3,000 of whom either resigned or were dismissed, none under formal indictment.

Individual states likewise became intensely security-conscious. Loyalty oaths in increasing numbers were demanded of employees, especially teachers. The gnawing question for many earnest Americans was, Could the nation continue to enjoy traditional freedoms—especially freedom of speech, freedom of thought, and the right of political dissent—in a Cold War climate?

In 1949 eleven communists were brought before a New York jury for violating the Smith Act of 1940, the first peacetime antisedition law since 1798. Convicted of advocating the overthrow of the American government by force, the defendants were sent to prison. The Supreme Court upheld their convictions in *Dennis* v. *United States* (1951).

The House of Representatives in 1938 had established the **House Un-American Activities Committee (HUAC)** to investigate "subversion." In 1948 committee member Richard M. Nixon, an ambitious red-catcher, led the chase after Alger Hiss, a prominent ex–New Dealer and a distinguished member of the "eastern establishment." Accused of being a communist agent in the 1930s, Hiss demanded the right to defend himself. He dramatically met his chief accuser before HUAC in August 1948. Hiss denied everything but was caught in embarrassing falsehoods, convicted of perjury in 1950, and sentenced to five years in prison.

Was America really riddled with Soviet spies? Soviet agents did infiltrate certain government agencies, though without severely damaging consequences, and espionage may have helped the Soviets to develop an atomic bomb somewhat sooner than they would have otherwise. Truman's loyalty program thus had a basis in reality. But for many ordinary Americans, the hunt for communists was not just about fending off the military threat of the Soviet Union. Unsettling dangers lurked closer to home. While men like Nixon and Senator Joseph McCarthy led the search for communists in Washington, conservative politicians at the state and local levels discovered that all manner of real or perceived social changes—including declining religious sentiment, increased sexual freedom, and agitation for civil rights—could be tarred with a red brush. Anticommunist crusaders ransacked school libraries for "subversive" textbooks and drove debtors, drinkers, and homosexuals, all alleged to be security risks, from their jobs.

Some Americans, including President Truman, realized that the red hunt was turning into a witch hunt. In 1950 Truman vetoed the McCarran Internal Security Bill, which among other provisions authorized the president to arrest and detain suspicious people during an "internal security emergency." Critics protested that the bill smacked of police-state, concentration-camp tactics. But the congressional guardians of the Republic's liberties enacted the bill over Truman's veto.

The stunning success of the Soviet scientists in developing an atomic bomb was attributed by many to the cleverness of communist spies in stealing American secrets. Notorious among those who had allegedly "leaked" atomic data to Moscow were two American citizens, Julius and Ethel Rosenberg. They were convicted in 1951 of espionage and went to the electric chair in 1953—the only people in American history ever executed in peacetime for espionage. Their sensational trial and electrocution, combined with sympathy for their two orphaned children, began to sour some sober citizens on the excesses of the red-hunters.

✦ Democratic Divisions in 1948

Attacking high prices and "High-Tax Harry" Truman, the Republicans had won control of Congress in the congressional elections of 1946. Their prospects had seldom looked rosier as they gathered in Philadelphia to choose their 1948 presidential candidate. They noisily renominated warmed-over New York governor Thomas E. Dewey, still as debonair as if he had stepped out of a bandbox.

Also gathering in Philadelphia, Democratic politicos looked without enthusiasm on their hand-me-down president and sang, "I'm Just Mild About Harry." But their "dump Truman" movement collapsed when war hero Dwight D. Eisenhower refused to be drafted. The peppery president, unwanted but undaunted, was then chosen in the face of vehement opposition by southern delegates, who had been alienated by his strong stand in favor of civil rights for blacks, especially his decision in 1948 to desegregate the military.

Truman's nomination split the party wide-open. Embittered southern Democrats from thirteen states, like their fire-eating forebears of 1860, next met in their own convention, in Birmingham, Alabama, with Confederate flags brashly in evidence. Amid scenes of heated defiance, these "Dixiecrats" nominated Governor J. Strom Thurmond of South Carolina on a States' Rights party ticket.

To add to the confusion within Democratic ranks, former vice president Henry A. Wallace threw his hat into the ring. Having parted company with the administration over its get-tough-with-Russia policy, he was nominated at Philadelphia by the new Progressive party—a bizarre collection of disgruntled former New

Harry S. Truman Library

The Harried Piano Player, 1948 Besieged by the left and right wings of his own party, and by a host of domestic and foreign problems, Truman was a long shot for reelection in 1948. But the scrappy president surprised his legions of critics by handily defeating his opponent, Thomas E. Dewey.

Dealers, starry-eyed pacifists, well-meaning liberals, and communist-fronters.

Wallace, a vigorous if misguided liberal, assailed Uncle Sam's "dollar imperialism" from the stump. This so-called Pied Piper of the Politburo took an apparently pro-Soviet line that earned him drenchings with rotten eggs in hostile cities. But to many Americans, Wallace raised the only hopeful voice in the deepening gloom of the Cold War.

With the Democrats ruptured three ways and the Republican congressional victory of 1946 just past, Dewey's victory seemed assured. Succumbing to overconfidence engendered by his massive lead in public-opinion polls, the cold, smug Dewey confined himself to dispensing soothing-syrup trivialities like "Our future lies before us."

The seemingly doomed Truman, with little money and few active supporters, had to rely on his "gut-fighter" instincts and folksy personality. Traveling the country by train to deliver some three hundred "give 'em hell" speeches, he lashed out at the Taft-Hartley "slave-labor" law and the "do-nothing" Republican Congress, while whipping up support for his program of civil rights, improved labor benefits, and health

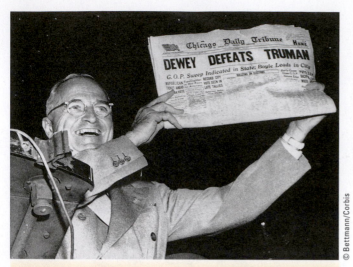

© Bettmann/Corbis

That Ain't the Way I Heard It! Truman wins.

insurance. "Pour it on 'em, Harry!" cried increasingly large and enthusiastic crowds, as the pugnacious president rained a barrage of verbal uppercuts on his opponent.

On election night the *Chicago Tribune* ran off an early edition with the headline "DEWEY DEFEATS TRUMAN." But in the morning, it turned out that "President" Dewey had embarrassingly snatched defeat from the jaws of victory. Truman had swept to a stunning triumph, to the complete bewilderment of politicians, pollsters, prophets, and pundits. Even though Thurmond took away 39 electoral votes in the South, Truman won 303 electoral votes, primarily from the South, Midwest, and West. Dewey's 189 electoral votes came principally from the East. The popular vote was 24,179,345 for Truman, 21,991,291 for Dewey, 1,176,125 for Thurmond, and 1,157,326 for Wallace. To make the victory sweeter, the Democrats regained control of Congress as well.

Truman's victory rested on farmers, workers, and blacks, all of whom were Republican-wary. Republican

In his inaugural address in January 1949, President Harry S Truman (1884–1972) said,

❝Communism is based on the belief that man is so weak and inadequate that he is unable to govern himself, and therefore requires the rule of strong masters. . . . Democracy is based on the conviction that man has the moral and intellectual capacity, as well as the inalienable right, to govern himself with reason and justice.❞

As Truman's Fair Deal was rebuffed by a hostile Congress, critics like the conservative New York Daily News *gloated that the odious New Deal was finally vanquished:*

❝ The New Deal is kaput like the Thirty Years' War or the Black Plague or other disasters. . . . [Its demise] is like coming out of the darkness into sunlight. Like feeling clean again after a long time in the muck.❞

overconfidence and Truman's lone-wolf, never-say-die campaign also won him the support of many Americans who admired his "guts." No one wanted him, someone remarked, except the people. Dewey, in contrast, struck many voters as arrogant, evasive, and wooden. When Dewey took the platform to give a speech, said one commentator, "he comes out like a man who has been mounted on casters and given a tremendous shove from behind."

Smiling and self-assured, Truman sounded a clarion note in the fourth point of his inaugural address, when he called for a "bold new program" (known thereafter as "Point Four"). The plan was to lend U.S. money and technical aid to underdeveloped lands to help them help themselves. Truman wanted to spend millions to keep underprivileged peoples from becoming communists rather than spend billions to shoot them after they had become communists. This farseeing program was officially launched in 1950, and it brought badly needed assistance to impoverished countries, notably in Latin America, Africa, the Near East, and the Far East.

At home Truman outlined a sweeping **Fair Deal** program in his 1949 message to Congress. It called for improved housing, full employment, a higher minimum wage, better farm price supports, new TVAs, and an extension of Social Security. But most of the Fair Deal fell victim to congressional opposition from Republicans and southern Democrats. The only major successes came in raising the minimum wage, providing for public housing in the Housing Act of 1949, and extending old-age insurance to many more beneficiaries in the Social Security Act of 1950.

✴ The Korean Volcano Erupts

Korea, the Land of the Morning Calm, heralded a new and more disturbing phase of the Cold War—a shooting phase—in June 1950. When Japan collapsed in

1945, Soviet troops had accepted the Japanese surrender north of the thirty-eighth parallel on the Korean peninsula, and American troops had done likewise south of that line. Both superpowers professed to want the reunification and independence of Korea, a Japanese colony since 1910. But, as in Germany, each helped to set up rival regimes above and below the parallel.

By 1949, when the Soviets and Americans had both withdrawn their forces, the entire peninsula was a bristling armed camp, with two hostile regimes eyeing each other suspiciously. Secretary of State Acheson seemed to wash his hands of the dispute early in 1950, when he declared in a memorable speech that Korea was outside the essential United States defense perimeter in the Pacific.

The explosion came on June 25, 1950. Spearheaded by Soviet-made tanks, North Korean army columns rumbled across the thirty-eighth parallel. Caught flat-footed, the South Korean forces were shoved back southward to a dangerously tiny defensive area around Pusan, their weary backs to the sea.

President Truman sprang quickly into the breach. The invasion seemed to provide devastating proof of a fundamental premise in the "containment doctrine" that shaped Washington's foreign policy: that even a slight relaxation of America's guard was an invitation to communist aggression somewhere.

The Korean invasion prompted a massive expansion of the American military. A few months before, Truman's National Security Council had issued its famous **National Security Council Memorandum Number 68 (NSC-68)**, recommending that the United States quadruple its defense spending. Ignored at first because it seemed politically impossible to implement, NSC-68 got a new lease on life from the Korean crisis. "Korea saved us," Secretary of State Acheson later commented. Truman now ordered a massive military buildup, well beyond what was necessary for Korea. Soon the United States had 3.5 million men under arms and was spending $50 billion per year on the defense budget—some 13 percent of the GNP.

NSC-68 was a key document of the Cold War period, not only because it marked a major step in the militarization of American foreign policy, but also because it vividly reflected the sense of almost limitless possibility that pervaded postwar American society. NSC-68 rested on the assumption that the enormous American economy could bear without strain the huge costs of a gigantic rearmament program. Said one NSC-68 planner, "There was practically nothing the country could not do if it wanted to do it."

Truman took full advantage of a temporary Soviet absence from the United Nations Security Council on June 25, 1950, to obtain a unanimous condemnation of North Korea as an aggressor. (Why the Soviets were absent remains controversial. Scholars once believed that the Soviets were just as surprised as the Americans by the attack. It now appears that Stalin had given his reluctant approval to North Korea's strike plan but believed that the fighting would be brief and that the United States would take little interest in it.) The Security Council also called upon all U.N. members, including the United States, to "render every assistance" to restore peace. Two days later, without consulting Congress, Truman ordered American air and naval units to support South Korea. Before the week was out, he also ordered General Douglas MacArthur's Japan-based occupation troops into action alongside the beleaguered South Koreans. So began the ill-fated **Korean War**.

Officially, the United States was simply participating in a United Nations "police action." But in fact, the United States made up the overwhelming bulk of the U.N. contingents, and General MacArthur, appointed U.N. commander of the entire operation, took his orders from Washington, not from the Security Council.

✦ The Military Seesaw in Korea

Rather than fight his way out of the southern Pusan perimeter, MacArthur launched a daring amphibious landing behind the enemy's lines at Inchon. This bold gamble on September 15, 1950, succeeded brilliantly; within two weeks the North Koreans had scrambled back behind the "sanctuary" of the thirty-eighth parallel. Truman's avowed intention was to restore South Korea to its former borders, but the pursuing South Koreans had already crossed the thirty-eighth parallel, and there seemed little point in permitting the North Koreans to regroup and come again. The U.N. General Assembly tacitly authorized a crossing by MacArthur, whom President Truman ordered northward, provided that there was no intervention in force by the Chinese or Soviets (see Map 36.4).

The Americans thus raised the stakes in Korea, and in so doing they quickened the fears of another potential player in this dangerous game. The Chinese communists had publicly warned that they would not sit idly by and watch hostile troops approach the strategic Yalu River boundary between Korea and China. But MacArthur pooh-poohed all predictions of an effective intervention by the Chinese and reportedly boasted that he would "have the boys home by Christmas."

MacArthur erred badly. In November 1950 tens of thousands of Chinese "volunteers" fell upon his rashly overextended lines and hurled the U.N. forces reeling

MAP 36.4 The Shifting Front in Korea © Cengage Learning

Territory held by South Korean forces
Territory held by North Korean forces
— Front

North Korean attack
MacArthur attack
Chinese counterattack
Armistice line

0 100 200 Km.
0 100 200 Mi.

Truman Takes the Heat

The Granger Collection, New York

back down the peninsula. The fighting now sank into a frostbitten stalemate on the icy terrain near the thirty-eighth parallel.

An imperious MacArthur, humiliated by this rout, pressed for drastic retaliation. He favored a blockade of the Chinese coast and bombardment of Chinese bases in Manchuria. He even suggested that the United States use nuclear weapons on the advancing Chinese and their supply lines. But Washington policymakers, with anxious eyes on Moscow, refused to enlarge the already costly conflict. The chairman of the Joint Chiefs of Staff declared that a wider clash in Asia would be "the wrong war, at the wrong place, at the wrong time, and with the wrong enemy." Europe, not Asia, was the administration's first concern; and the USSR, not China, loomed as the more sinister foe.

Two-fisted General MacArthur felt that he was being asked to fight with one hand tied behind his back. He sneered at the concept of a "limited war" and insisted that "there is no substitute for victory." Truman bravely resisted calls for nuclear escalation, a rare example of a military commander refusing to use the most powerful weapons at his disposal. When MacArthur began to criticize the president's policies publicly, Truman had no choice but to remove the insubordinate MacArthur from command on April 11, 1951. MacArthur, a legend in his own mind, returned to an uproarious welcome, whereas Truman was condemned as a "pig," an "imbecile," a "Judas," and an appeaser of "Communist Russia and Communist China." In July 1951 truce discussions began in a rude field tent near the firing line but were almost immediately snagged on the issue of prisoner exchange. Talks dragged on unproductively for nearly two years while men continued to die.

Varying Viewpoints
Who Was to Blame for the Cold War?

Whose fault was the Cold War? (And, for that matter, who should get credit for ending it?) For two decades after World War II, American historians generally agreed that the aggressive Soviets were solely responsible. This "orthodox" or "official" appraisal squared with the traditional view of the United States as a virtuous, innocent land with an idealistic foreign policy. This point of view also justified America's Cold War containment policy, which cast the Soviet Union as the aggressor that must be confined by an ever-vigilant United States. America supposedly had only defensive intentions, with no expansionary ambitions of its own.

In the 1960s a vigorous revisionist interpretation flowered, powerfully influenced by disillusion over U.S. involvement in Vietnam. The revisionists stood the orthodox view on its head. The Soviets, they argued, had only defensive intentions at the end of World War II; it was the Americans who had behaved provocatively by brandishing their new atomic weaponry. Some of these critics pointed an accusing finger at President Truman, alleging that he abandoned Roosevelt's conciliatory approach to the Soviets and adopted a bullying attitude, emboldened by the American atomic monopoly.

More radical revisionists like Gabriel and Joyce Kolko even claimed to have found the roots of Truman's alleged belligerence in long-standing American policies of economic imperialism—policies that eventually resulted in the tragedy of Vietnam (see pp. 874–875). In this view the Vietnam War followed logically from America's insatiable "need" for overseas markets and raw materials. Vietnam itself may have been economically unimportant, but, so the argument ran, a communist Vietnam represented an intolerable challenge to American hegemony. Revisionists cited their own version of the "domino theory," which war apologists used to defend America's military actions in Vietnam. According to the domino theory, if the United States declined to fight in Vietnam, other countries would lose their faith in America's will (or their fear of American power) and would tumble one after the other like "dominoes" into the Soviet camp. Revisionists stressed what they saw as the *economic necessity* behind the domino theory: losing in Vietnam, they claimed, would unravel the American economy.

In the 1970s a "postrevisionist" interpretation emerged that is widely agreed upon today. Historians such as John Lewis Gaddis and Melvyn Leffler pooh-pooh the economic determinism of the revisionists, while frankly acknowledging that the United States did have vital security interests at stake in the post–World War II era. The postrevisionists analyze the ways in which inherited ideas (like isolationism) and the contentious nature of postwar domestic politics, as well as miscalculations by American leaders, led a nation in search of security into seeking not simply a sufficiency but a "preponderance" of power. The American *overreaction* to its security needs, these scholars suggest, exacerbated U.S.-Soviet relations and precipitated the four-decade-long nuclear arms race that formed the centerpiece of the Cold War.

In the case of Vietnam, the postrevisionist historians focus not on economic necessity, but on a failure of political intelligence, induced by the stressful conditions of the Cold War, that made the dubious domino theory seem plausible. Misunderstanding Vietnamese intentions, exaggerating Soviet ambitions, and fearing to appear "soft on communism" in the eyes of their domestic political rivals, American leaders plunged into Vietnam, sadly misguided by their own Cold War obsessions.

Most postrevisionists, however, still lay the lion's share of the blame for the Cold War on the Soviet Union. By the same token, they credit the Soviets with ending the Cold War—a view hotly disputed by Ronald Reagan's champions, who claim that it was his anti-Soviet policies in the 1980s that brought the Russians to their knees (see pp. 946–947). The great unknown, of course, is the precise nature of Soviet thinking in the Cold War years. Were Soviet aims predominantly defensive, or did the Kremlin incessantly plot world conquest? Was there an opportunity for reconciliation with the West following Stalin's death in 1953? Should Mikhail Gorbachev or Ronald Reagan be remembered as the leader who ended the Cold War? With the opening of Soviet archives, scholars are eagerly pursuing answers to such questions.

Chapter Review

KEY TERMS

Taft-Hartley Act (830)
Operation Dixie (830)
Employment Act
  of 1946 (831)
GI Bill (831)
Sunbelt (835)
Levittown (838)
baby boom (838)
Yalta conference (839)
Cold War (841)
Bretton Woods
  Conference (841)
United Nations (U.N.) (844)
Nuremberg war crimes
  trial (845)

Berlin airlift (846)
containment doctrine (846)
Truman Doctrine (846)
Marshall Plan (847)
North Atlantic Treaty Orga-
  nization (NATO) (849)
House Un-American
  Activities Committee
  (HUAC) (852)
Fair Deal (854)
National Security Council
  Memorandum Number
  68 (NSC-68) (855)
Korean War (855)

PEOPLE TO KNOW

Benjamin Spock
Joseph Stalin
Jiang Jieshi

George F. Kennan
Reinhold Niebuhr
George C. Marshall

CHRONOLOGY

1944	Servicemen's Readjustment Act (GI Bill) Bretton Woods economic conference
1945	Spock publishes *The Common Sense Book of Baby and Child Care* Yalta conference United States ends lend-lease to USSR United Nations established
1945–1946	Nuremberg war crimes trial in Germany
1946	Employment Act creates Council of Economic Advisers Iran crisis Kennan's "Long Telegram" lays out "containment doctrine"
1946–1948	Tokyo war crimes trials
1947	Truman Doctrine Marshall Plan Taft-Hartley Act National Security Act creates Department of Defense, National Security Council (NSC), and Central Intelligence Agency (CIA)
1948	Israel founded; United States recognizes it "Voice of America" begins radio broadcasts behind iron curtain Alger Hiss case begins Truman defeats Dewey for presidency
1948–1949	Berlin blockade
1949	NATO established Communists defeat Nationalists in China Soviets explode their first atomic bomb
1950	American economy begins postwar growth McCarthy red hunt begins McCarran Internal Security Bill passed by Congress over Truman's veto
1950–1953	Korean War
1951	Truman fires MacArthur Rosenbergs convicted of treason
1952	United States explodes first hydrogen bomb
1957	Postwar peak of U.S. birthrate
1973	U.S. birthrate falls below replacement level

TO LEARN MORE

Dean Acheson, *Present at the Creation* (1969)

Lizabeth Cohen, *A Consumers' Republic: The Politics of Mass Consumption in Postwar America* (2003)

John Lewis Gaddis, *The Cold War: A New History* (2005)

Herbert J. Gans, *The Levittowners* (1967)

David Halberstam, *The Coldest Winter: America and the Korean War* (2007)

Kenneth T. Jackson, *Crabgrass Frontier: The Suburbanization of the United States* (1985)

Kevin Kruse and Thomas Sugrue, eds., *The New Suburban History* (2006)

Marvyn P. Leffler, *A Preponderance of Power: National Security, the Truman Administration, and the Cold War, 1945–1950* (1980)

Ellen Schrecker, *Many Are the Crimes* (1998)

Bruce Schulman, *From Cotton Belt to Sunbelt: Federal Policy, Economic Development, and the Transformation of the South* (1991)

A complete, annotated bibliography for this chapter—along with brief descriptions of the People to Know—may be found on the American Pageant website. The Key Terms are defined in a Glossary at the end of the text.

Go to the CourseMate website at **www.cengagebrain.com** for additional study tools and review materials—including audio and video clips—for this chapter.

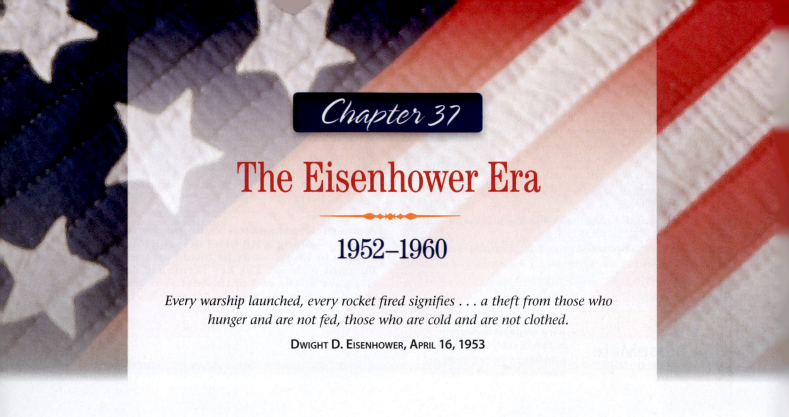

Chapter 37

The Eisenhower Era

1952–1960

Every warship launched, every rocket fired signifies . . . a theft from those who hunger and are not fed, those who are cold and are not clothed.

DWIGHT D. EISENHOWER, APRIL 16, 1953

In President Dwight D. Eisenhower, the man and the hour met. Americans yearned for a period of calm in which they could pursue without distraction their new visions of consumerist affluence. The nation sorely needed a respite from twenty years of depression and war. Yet the American people unexpectedly found themselves in the early 1950s dug into the frontlines of the Cold War abroad and dangerously divided at home over the explosive issues of communist subversion and civil rights. They longed for reassuring leadership. "Ike" seemed ready both to reassure and to lead.

✵ Affluence and Its Anxieties

The continuing post–World War II economic boom wrought wondrous changes in American society in the 1950s. Prosperity triggered a fabulous surge in home construction, as a nation of renters became a nation of homeowners. One of every four homes standing in America in 1960 had been built during the 1950s, and 83 percent of those new homes were in suburbia.

More than ever, science and technology drove economic growth. The invention of the transistor in 1948 sparked a revolution in electronics, and especially in computers. The first electronic computers assembled in the 1940s were massive machines with hundreds of miles of wiring and thousands of fickle cathode ray tubes. Transistors and, later, printed circuits on silicon wafers made possible dramatic miniaturization and phenomenal computational speed. Computer giant International Business Machines (IBM) expanded robustly, becoming the prototype of the "high-tech" corporation in the dawning "information age." Eventually personal computers and even inexpensive pocket calculators contained more computing power than room-size early models. Computers transformed age-old business practices like billing and inventory control and opened genuine new frontiers in areas like airline scheduling, high-speed printing, and telecommunications.

Aerospace industries also grew fantastically in the 1950s, thanks both to Eisenhower's aggressive buildup of the Strategic Air Command and to a robustly expanding passenger airline business—as well as to connections between military and civilian aircraft production. In 1957 the Seattle-based Boeing Company brought out the first large passenger jet, the "707." Its design owed much to the previous development of SAC's long-range strategic bomber, the B-52. Two years later Boeing delivered the first presidential jet, a specially modified 707, to its first user, Dwight D. Eisenhower. "Air Force One" dazzled him with its speed and comfort.

The nature of the work force was also changing. A quiet revolution was marked in 1956 when "white-collar" workers for the first time outnumbered "blue-collar" workers, signaling the passage from an industrial to a postindustrial, or service-based, economy. Keeping pace with that fundamental transformation, organized labor withered along with the smokestack industries that had been its sustenance. Union membership as a

An Early Computer, ca. 1950 Just a few decades later, technological improvements would bring the computing power of this bulky behemoth to the user's desktop.

World War II ended, many women, including those who had worked in war plants, returned to highly conventional female roles as wives and mothers—the remarkably prolific mothers of the huge "baby-boom" generation. A "cult of domesticity" emerged in popular culture to celebrate those eternal feminine functions. When 1950s television programs like "Ozzie and Harriet" or "Leave It to Beaver" depicted idyllic suburban families with a working husband, two children, and a wife who did not work outside the home, they did so without irony; much of white, middle-class America really did live that way. But as the 1950s progressed, another quiet revolution was gaining momentum that was destined to transform women's roles and even the character of the American family.

Of some 40 million new jobs created in the three decades after 1950, more than 30 million were in clerical and service work. Women filled the huge majority of these new positions. They were the principal employment beneficiaries of the postwar era, creating an extensive "pink-collar ghetto" of occupations that came to be dominated by women (see Figure 37.1).

Exploding employment opportunities for women in the 1950s unleashed a groundswell of social and psychological shocks that mounted to tidal-wave proportions in the decades that followed. From one perspective women's surge into the workplace was nothing new, only a return to the days when the United States was an agricultural nation, and men and women alike toiled on the family farm. But the urban age was not the agricultural age, and women's new dual role as *both* workers *and* homemakers raised urgent questions about family life and traditional definitions of gender differences.

Feminist Betty Friedan gave focus and fuel to women's feelings in 1963 when she published **The Feminine Mystique**, a runaway best seller and a classic of

percentage of the labor force peaked at about 35 percent in 1954 and then went into steady decline (see p. 769). Some observers concluded that the union movement had played out its historic role of empowering workers and ensuring economic justice, and that unions would eventually disappear altogether in the postindustrial era.

The surge in white-collar employment opened special opportunities for women (see Table 37.1). When

TABLE 37.1 Occupational Distribution of Workingwomen, 1900–2000*						
	1900	1920	1940	1960	1980	2000
Total white-collar workers†	17.8%	38.8%	44.9%	52.5%	65.6%	73.0%
Clerical workers	4.0	18.7	21.5	28.7	30.5	36.7
Manual workers	27.8	23.8	21.6	18.0	14.8	8.7
Farmworkers	18.9	13.5	4.0	1.8	1.0	0.3
Service workers‡	35.5	23.9	29.4	21.9	18.1	18.0

*Major categories; percentage of all women workers in each category, calculated at fourteen and older until 1970 and then sixteen and older.
†Includes clerical, sales, professional, and technical workers, managers, and officials.
‡Includes domestic servants.

(Sources: *Historical Statistics of the United States* and *Statistical Abstract of the United States*, relevant years.)

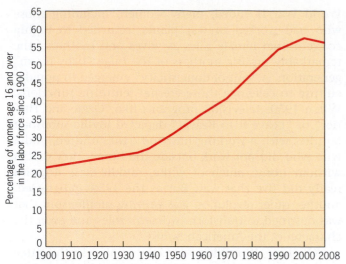

FIGURE 37.1 Women in the Labor Force, 1900–2008
(Sources: *Historical Statistics of the United States* and *Statistical Abstract of the United States*, relevant years.)

Consumer Culture in the Fifties

The 1950s witnessed a huge expansion of the middle class and the blossoming of a consumer culture. Diner's Club introduced the plastic credit card in 1949, just one year after the first "fast-food"–style McDonald's hamburger stand opened in San Bernardino, California. In 1955 Disneyland opened its doors in Anaheim, California. Easy credit, high-volume "fast-food" production, and new forms of leisure marked an emerging affluent lifestyle that soon moved beyond America's borders. Manufacturers, retailers, and advertisers spread American-style consumer capitalism throughout much of the noncommunist world.

Crucial to the development of that lifestyle was the rapid rise of the new technology of television. Only 6 TV stations were broadcasting in 1946; a decade later 442 stations were operating. TV sets were rich people's novelties in the 1940s, but 7 million sets were sold in 1951. By 1960 virtually every American home had one, in a stunning display of the speed with which new technologies can pervade and transform modern societies (see Figure 37.2).

Attendance at movies sank as the entertainment industry changed its focus from the silver screen to the picture tube. By the mid-1950s, advertisers annually spent $10 billion to hawk their wares on television, while critics fumed that the wildly popular new mass medium was degrading the public's aesthetic, social, moral, political, and educational standards. To the

feminist protest literature that launched the modern women's movement. Friedan spoke in rousing accents to millions of able, educated women who applauded her indictment of the stifling boredom of suburban housewifery. Many of those women were already working for wages, but they were also struggling against the guilt and frustration of leading an "unfeminine" life as defined by the postwar "cult of domesticity."

The Booming Service Sector
Services displaced manufacturing as the most dynamic area of the economy in the post–World War II era, and women made up a majority of new workers in the nation's offices and classrooms and on sales floors and hospital wards.

© Bettmann/Corbis

Courtesy McDonald Corporation

The Original Golden Arches, 1955 Maurice and Richard McDonald replaced their original drive-in hamburger stand in San Bernardino, California, with this double-arched design in 1953. McDonald's soon became one of the largest franchised restaurant chains in the world and a global symbol of American consumerism.

question "Why is television called a medium?" pundits replied, "Because it's never rare or well done."

Even religion capitalized on the powerful new electronic pulpit. "Televangelists" like the Baptist Billy Graham, the Pentecostal Holiness preacher Oral Roberts, and the Roman Catholic Fulton J. Sheen took to the airwaves to spread the Christian gospel. Television also catalyzed the commercialization of professional sports, as viewing audiences that once numbered in the stadium-capacity thousands could now be counted in the couch-potato millions.

Sports also reflected the shift in population toward the West and South. In 1958 baseball's New York Giants moved to San Francisco, and the Brooklyn Dodgers abandoned Flatbush for Los Angeles. Those moves touched off a new westward and southward movement of sports franchises. Shifting population and spreading affluence led eventually to substantial expansion of the major baseball leagues and the principal football and basketball leagues as well.

Popular music was dramatically transformed in the fifties. The chief revolutionary was Elvis Presley, a white singer born in 1935 in Tupelo, Mississippi. Fusing black rhythm and blues with white bluegrass and country styles, Elvis created a new musical idiom known forever after as **rock 'n' roll**. Rock was "crossover" music, carrying its heavy beat and driving rhythms across the cultural divide that separated black and white musical traditions. Listening and dancing to rock 'n' roll became a rite of passage for millions of young people around the world, from Japan to working-class Liverpool, England, where Elvis's music inspired teenagers John Lennon and Paul McCartney to form a band that would become the Beatles.

Traditionalists were repelled by Presley, and they found much more to upset them in the affluent fifties. Movie star Marilyn Monroe, with her ingenuous smile and mandolin-curved hips, helped to popularize—and commercialize—new standards of sensuous sexuality. So did *Playboy* magazine, whose first issue Monroe graced in 1953. As the decade closed, Americans were well on their way to becoming free-spending

FIGURE 37.2 Households with Television Sets, 1946–1960 Note the rapid adoption of this new device, a harbinger of the viral spread of technologies like cell phones and the Internet later in the century.

The King   With his fleshy face, pouting lips, and antic, sexually suggestive gyrations, Elvis Presley became the high priest of rock 'n' roll in the 1950s, to the chagrin of parents everywhere. Bloated by fame, fortune, and drugs, he died in 1977 at the age of forty-two.

consumers of mass-produced, standardized products, which were advertised on the electronic medium of television and often sold for their alleged sexual allure.

Many critics lamented the implications of this new consumerist lifestyle. Harvard sociologist David Riesman portrayed the postwar generation as a pack of conformists in *The Lonely Crowd* (1950), as did William H. Whyte, Jr., in *The Organization Man*. Novelist Sloan Wilson explored a similar theme in *The Man in the Gray Flannel Suit* (1955). Harvard economist John Kenneth Galbraith questioned the relation between private wealth and the public good in a series of books beginning with *The Affluent Society* (1958). The postwar explosion of prosperity, Galbraith claimed, had produced a troublesome combination of private opulence amid public squalor. Americans had televisions in their homes but garbage in their streets. They ate rich food but breathed foul air. But Galbraith's call for social spending to match private purchasing fell on mostly deaf ears in the giddily affluent 1950s.

✦ The Advent of Eisenhower

Democratic prospects in the presidential election of 1952 were blighted by the military deadlock in Korea, Truman's clash with MacArthur, war-bred inflation, and whiffs of scandal from the White House. Dispirited

Democrats nominated a reluctant Adlai E. Stevenson, the eloquent and idealistic governor of Illinois. Republicans enthusiastically chose war hero General Dwight D. Eisenhower on the first ballot. "Ike's" running mate was California senator Richard M. Nixon, who had gained notoriety as a relentless red-hunter.

Eisenhower was already the most popular American of his time, as "I Like Ike" buttons everywhere testified. Striking a grandfatherly, nonpartisan pose, Eisenhower left the rough campaigning to Nixon, who relished bare-knuckle political combat. The vice-presidential candidate lambasted his opponents with charges that they had cultivated corruption, caved in on Korea, and coddled communists. He particularly blasted the cerebral Stevenson as "Adlai the appeaser," with a "Ph.D. from [Secretary of State] Dean Acheson's College of Cowardly Communist Containment."

Nixon himself faltered late in the campaign amid accusations that he had accepted illegal donations. Responding with a self-pitying live address on television, Nixon denied the charges and solemnly declared that the only campaign gift he had ever received was the family cocker spaniel, Checkers. The shameless and mawkish **Checkers Speech** saved Nixon's spot on the ticket and spotlighted a fundamental change in American politics. Television was now a formidable political tool that, much more than radio, allowed candidates to bypass traditional party machinery and speak directly to voters.

The Republicans' Choice, 1952   Nominee Eisenhower and his vice-presidential running mate, Nixon, greet the delegates.

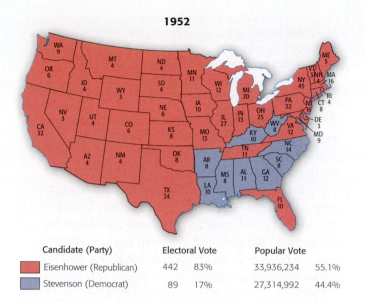

1952

Candidate (Party)	Electoral Vote		Popular Vote	
Eisenhower (Republican)	442	83%	33,936,234	55.1%
Stevenson (Democrat)	89	17%	27,314,992	44.4%

MAP 37.1 Presidential Election of 1952 (with electoral vote by state)   A Democrat quipped that "if the voters liked the Republicans the way they liked Ike, the two-party system would be in bad shape." Fortunately for Democrats, Eisenhower scored a personal, not a party, victory. Republicans won minuscule majorities in Congress, which disappeared in the congressional elections two years later. © Cengage Learning

Soon even Eisenhower was reluctantly appearing in short, tightly scripted televised "spots" that foreshadowed the future of political advertising. Devoid of substance, they vastly oversimplified complicated economic and social issues. They amounted, as one critic observed, to "selling the President like toothpaste." And given television's origins in entertainment and advertising, political messages would be increasingly tuned to the standards of show business and commercialism.

The outcome of the presidential election of 1952 was never really in doubt. Given an extra prod by Eisenhower's last-minute pledge to go personally to Korea to end the war, the voters overwhelmingly declared for Ike. He garnered 33,936,234 votes to Stevenson's 27,314,992, ringing up 442 electoral votes to 89 for his opponent (see Map 37.1). Ike also managed to pull enough Republican legislators into office on his military coattails to gain GOP control of the new Congress by a hairbreadth.

True to his campaign pledge, president-elect Eisenhower undertook a flying three-day visit to Korea in December 1952. But even a glamorous Ike could not immediately budge the peace negotiations off dead center. Seven long months later, after Eisenhower had hinted that he might use atomic weapons, an armistice was finally signed. (Subsequent inquiries suggested that Ike's hints were so artfully veiled that the Chinese

never understood them. They agreed to end the war for reasons of their own, especially its burdensome financial costs.)

The brutal and futile fighting had lasted three years. About fifty-four thousand Americans lay dead, joined by perhaps more than a million Chinese, North Koreans, and South Koreans. Tens of billions of American dollars had been poured down the Asian sinkhole. Yet this terrible toll in blood and treasure bought only a return to the conditions of 1950: Korea remained divided at the thirty-eighth parallel, Communist in the North, Western-looking in the South. Americans took what little comfort they could from the fact that communism had been "contained" and that the bloodletting had been "limited" to something less than full-scale global war. The shooting had ended, but the Cold War still remained frigidly frozen.

As a military commander, Eisenhower had cultivated a leadership style that self-consciously projected an image of sincerity, fairness, and optimism. He had been widely perceived during World War II as an "unmilitary" general, and in the White House he similarly struck the pose of an "unpolitical" president, serenely above the petty partisan fray. He also shrewdly knew that his greatest "asset" was his enjoyment of the "affection and respect of our citizenry," as he confided to his diary in 1949.

Ike thus seemed ideally suited to soothe the anxieties of troubled Americans, much as a distinguished and well-loved grandfather brings stability to his family.

U.S. Army Photograph

Korean War Scene   A grief-stricken American soldier whose buddy has been killed is being comforted, while a medical corpsman fills out casualty tags.

He played this role well as he presided over a decade of shaky peace and shining prosperity. Yet critics charged that he unwisely hoarded the "asset" of his immense popularity, rather than spend it for a good cause (especially civil rights), and that he cared more for social harmony than for social justice.

✵ The Rise and Fall of Joseph McCarthy

One of the first problems Eisenhower faced was the swelling popularity and swaggering power of an obstreperous anticommunist crusader, Wisconsin Republican senator Joseph R. McCarthy. Elected to the Senate on the basis of a trumped-up war-hero record, McCarthy had crashed into the limelight in February 1950 when he accused Secretary of State Dean Acheson of knowingly employing 205 Communist party members. Pressed to reveal the names, McCarthy later conceded that there were only 57 genuine communists and in the end failed to root out even one. Some of McCarthy's Republican colleagues nevertheless realized the partisan usefulness of this kind of attack on the Democratic administration. Ohio's Senator John Bricker reportedly said, "Joe, you're a dirty s.o.b., but there are

Senator McCarthy Extinguishes the Torch of Liberty
While preaching patriotism, McCarthy irresponsibly menaced American traditions of civil liberties.

In a moment of high drama during the Army-McCarthy hearings, attorney Joseph Welch (1890–1960) reproached McCarthy in front of a huge national television audience for threatening to slander a young lawyer on Welch's staff:

"Until this moment, Senator, I think I never really gauged your cruelty or your recklessness. Little did I dream you could be so cruel as to do an injury to that lad. . . . If it were in my power to forgive you for your reckless cruelty, I would do so. I like to think that I am a gentleman, but your forgiveness will have to come from someone other than me. . . . Have you no decency, sir, at long last? Have you left no sense of decency?**"**

times when you've got to have an s.o.b. around, and this is one of them."

McCarthy's rhetoric grew bolder and his accusations spread more wildly after the Republican victory in 1952. McCarthy saw the red hand of Moscow everywhere. The Democrats, he charged, "bent to whispered pleas from the lips of traitors." Incredibly, he even denounced General George Marshall, former army chief of staff and ex–secretary of state, as "part of a conspiracy so immense and an infamy so black as to dwarf any previous venture in the history of man."

McCarthy—and what became known as **McCarthyism**—flourished in the seething Cold War atmosphere of suspicion and fear. The senator was neither the first nor the most effective red-hunter, but he was surely the most ruthless, and he did the most damage to American traditions of fair play and free speech. The careers of countless officials, writers, and actors were ruined after "Low-Blow Joe" had "named" them, often unfairly, as communists or communist sympathizers. Politicians trembled in the face of such onslaughts, especially when opinion polls showed that a majority of the American people approved of McCarthy's crusade.

Eisenhower privately loathed McCarthy but publicly tried to stay out of his way, saying, "I will not get in the gutter with that guy." Trying to appease the brash demagogue from Wisconsin, Eisenhower allowed him, in effect, to control personnel policy at the State Department. One baleful result was severe damage to the morale and effectiveness of the professional foreign service. In particular, McCarthyite purges deprived the government of a number of Asian specialists who might have counseled a wiser course in Vietnam in the fateful decade that followed. McCarthy's extreme antics also damaged America's international reputation for fair and open democracy at a moment when it was important to keep Western Europe on the United States' side in an intensifying Cold War.

McCarthy finally bent the bow too far when he attacked the U.S. Army. The embattled military men fought back in thirty-five days of televised hearings in the spring of 1954. The political power of the new broadcast medium was again demonstrated by the **Army-McCarthy hearings**, as up to 20 million Americans at a time watched in fascination while a boorish, surly McCarthy publicly cut his own throat by parading his essential meanness and irresponsibility. A few months later, the Senate formally condemned him for "conduct unbecoming a member." Three years later, unwept and unsung, McCarthy died of chronic alcoholism. But "McCarthyism" has passed into the English language as a label for the dangerous forces of unfairness and fear that a democratic society can unleash only at its peril.

✦ Desegregating American Society

America counted some 15 million black citizens in 1950, two-thirds of whom still made their homes in the South. There they lived bound by the iron folkways of a segregated society. A rigid set of antiquated rules known as **Jim Crow** laws governed all aspects of their existence, from the schoolroom to the restroom. Every day of their lives, southern blacks dealt with a bizarre array of separate social arrangements that kept them insulated from whites, economically inferior, and politically powerless. Blacks in the South not only attended segregated schools but were compelled to use separate public toilets, drinking fountains, restaurants, and waiting

The New York Times Co./Getty Images

The Face of Segregation   These women in the segregated South of the 1950s were compelled to enter the movie theater through the "Colored Entrance." Once inside, they were restricted to a separate seating section, usually in the rear of the theater.

A black woman described the day-in, day-out humiliations of life in the Jim Crow South:

❝You could not go to a white restaurant; you sat in a special place at the movie house; and Lord knows, you sat in the back of the bus. It didn't make any difference if you were rich or poor, if you were black you were nothing. You might have a hundred dollars in your pocket, but if you went to the store you would wait at the side until all the clerks got through with all the white folks, no matter if they didn't have change for a dollar. Then the clerk would finally look at you and say, 'Oh, did you want something? I didn't see you there.'❞

rooms. Trains and buses had "whites only" and "colored only" seating. Only about 20 percent of eligible southern blacks were registered to vote, and fewer than 5 percent were registered in some Deep South states like Mississippi and Alabama. As late as 1960, white southern sensibilities about segregation were so tender that television networks blotted out black speakers at the national political conventions for fear of offending southern stations.

Where the law proved insufficient to enforce this regime, vigilante violence did the job. Six black war veterans, claiming the rights for which they had fought overseas, were murdered in the summer of 1946. A Mississippi mob lynched black fourteen-year-old Emmett Till in 1955 for allegedly leering at a white woman. It is small wonder that a black clergyman declared that "everywhere I go in the South the Negro is forced to choose between his hide and his soul."

Segregation tarnished America's international image, much as McCarthyism did. After the war African

American entertainers like Paul Robeson and Josephine Baker toured widely in Europe and Latin America, informing audiences about the horrors of Jim Crow and raising doubts about America's reputation as the beacon of freedom against Soviet communism. In response, the State Department confiscated Robeson's passport, but it had to find other ways to silence Baker, who had assumed French citizenship. Intellectuals poured on criticism as well. Swedish scholar Gunnar Myrdal published his landmark book, *An American Dilemma*, exposing the scandalous contradiction between "The American Creed"—allegiance to the values of "progress, liberty, equality, and humanitarianism"—and the nation's shameful treatment of black citizens.

International pressure combined with grassroots and legal activism to propel some racial progress in the North after World War II. In a growing number of northern cities and states, African Americans battled for—and won—equal access to public accommodations like restaurants, hotels, theaters, and beaches. Jackie Robinson cracked baseball's color barrier when the Brooklyn Dodgers signed him in 1947. The National Association for the Advancement of Colored People (NAACP) pushed the Supreme Court in 1950 to rule in *Sweatt* v. *Painter* that separate professional schools for blacks failed to meet the test of equality. The national conscience was slowly awakening from its centuries-long slumber, but black suffering still continued, especially in the South.

Increasingly, however, African Americans refused to suffer in silence (see "Makers of America: The Great African American Migration," pp. 870–871). On a chilly day in December 1955, Rosa Parks, a college-educated black seamstress, made history in Montgomery, Alabama. She boarded a bus, took a seat in the "whites only" section, and refused to give it up. Her arrest for violating the city's Jim Crow statutes sparked a year-long black boycott of city buses and served notice throughout the South that blacks would no longer submit meekly to the absurdities and indignities of segregation.

The **Montgomery bus boycott** also catapulted to prominence a young pastor at Montgomery's Dexter Avenue Baptist Church, the Reverend Martin Luther King, Jr. Barely twenty-seven years old, King seemed an unlikely champion of the downtrodden and disfranchised. Raised in a prosperous black family in Atlanta and educated partly in the North, he had for most of his life been sheltered from the grossest cruelties of segregation. But his oratorical skill, his passionate devotion to biblical and constitutional conceptions of justice, and his devotion to the nonviolent principles of India's Mohandas Gandhi were destined to thrust him to the forefront of the black revolution that would soon pulse across the South and the rest of the nation.

★ Seeds of the Civil Rights Revolution

When President Harry Truman heard about the lynching of black war veterans in 1946, he exclaimed, "My God! I had no idea it was as terrible as that." The horrified Truman responded by commissioning a report titled "To Secure These Rights." Following the report's recommendations, Truman in 1948 ended segregation in federal civil service and ordered "equality of treatment and opportunity" in the armed forces. Yet Congress stubbornly resisted passing civil rights legislation, and Truman's successor, Dwight Eisenhower, showed no real interest in racial issues. It was the Supreme Court that assumed political leadership in the civil rights struggle.

Chief Justice Earl Warren, former governor of California, shocked traditionalists with his active judicial intervention in previously taboo social issues. Publicly snubbed and privately scorned by President Eisenhower, Warren courageously led the Court to address urgent issues that Congress and the president preferred to avoid, as "Impeach Earl Warren" signs blossomed along the nation's highways.

The unanimous decision of the Warren Court in **Brown** v. **Board of Education of Topeka, Kansas** in May 1954 was epochal. In a forceful opinion, the learned justices ruled that segregation in the public schools was "inherently unequal" and thus unconstitutional. The uncompromising sweep of the decision startled conservatives like an exploding time bomb, for it reversed the Court's earlier declaration of 1896 in *Plessy* v. *Ferguson* (see p. 496) that "separate but equal" facilities were allowable under the Constitution. That

Joseph E. Lowery (b. 1921), a Methodist minister and civil rights activist in Mobile, Alabama, reflected on the powerful message of the 1955 Montgomery bus boycott for blacks:

❝You see, what the bus thing did was simply more than withholding patronage from the bus; it was restoring a sense of dignity to the patrons, as best expressed by an oft-quoted black woman in Montgomery who said, 'Since I've been walking, my feet are tired, but my soul's rested.' . . . [P]rior to the bus boycotts, the determination of our freedom rested with the courts. With the bus boycott, we determined it. . . . The court could say what it liked, we weren't gon' ride—in the back of the bus. We'd walk.❞

Integration in Little Rock, Arkansas, 1957 Fifteen-year-old Elizabeth Eckford endured scathing insults from white students and parents as she attempted to enter Little Rock's Central High School. The showdown at Little Rock was a replay of nineteenth-century confrontations over "states' rights," and forced a reluctant Eisenhower administration to assert the supremacy of federal power.

doctrine was now dead. Desegregation, the justices insisted, must go ahead with "all deliberate speed."

The Border States generally made reasonable efforts to comply with this ruling, but in the Deep South diehards organized "massive resistance" against the Court's annulment of the sacred principle of "separate but equal." More than a hundred southern congressional representatives and senators signed the "Declaration of Constitutional Principles" in 1956, pledging their unyielding resistance to desegregation. Several states diverted public funds to hastily created "private" schools, for there the integration order was more difficult to apply. Throughout the South white citizens' councils, sometimes with fire and hemp, thwarted attempts to make integration a reality. Ten years after the Court's momentous ruling, fewer than 2 percent of the eligible blacks in the Deep South were sitting in classrooms with whites.

President Eisenhower remained reluctant to promote integration. He shied away from employing his vast popularity and the prestige of his office to educate white Americans about the need for racial justice. His personal attitudes may have helped to restrain him. He had grown up in an all-white town, spent his career in a segregated army, and advised against integration of the armed forces in 1948. He complained that the Supreme Court's decision in *Brown* v. *Board of Education* had upset "the customs and convictions of at least two generations of Americans," and he steadfastly refused to issue a public statement endorsing the Court's conclusions. "I do not believe," he explained, "that prejudices, even palpably unjustifiable prejudices, will succumb to compulsion."

But in September 1957, Ike was forced to act. Orval Faubus, the governor of Arkansas, mobilized the National Guard to prevent nine black students from enrolling in Little Rock's Central High School. Confronted with a direct challenge to federal authority, Eisenhower sent troops to escort the children to their classes.

In the same year, Congress passed the first Civil Rights Act since Reconstruction days. Eisenhower characteristically reassured a southern senator that the legislation represented "the mildest civil rights bill possible." It set up a permanent Civil Rights Commission to investigate violations of civil rights and authorized federal injunctions to protect voting rights.

Blacks meanwhile continued to take the civil rights movement into their own hands. Martin Luther King, Jr., formed the Southern Christian Leadership Conference (SCLC) in 1957. It aimed to mobilize the vast power of the black churches on behalf of black rights. This was an exceptionally shrewd strategy, because the churches were the largest and best-organized black institutions that had been allowed to flourish in a segregated society.

More spontaneous was the "sit-in" movement launched on February 1, 1960, by four black college freshmen in Greensboro, North Carolina. Without a detailed plan or institutional support, they demanded service at a whites-only Woolworth's lunch counter. Observing that "fellows like you make our race look bad," the black waitress refused to serve them. But they kept their seats and returned the next day with nineteen classmates. The following day, eighty-five students joined in; by the end of the week, a thousand. The sit-in movement rolled swiftly across the South, swelling into a wave of wade-ins, lie-ins, and pray-ins to compel equal treatment in restaurants, transportation, employment, housing, and voter registration. In April 1960

The great social upheavals of World War II continued to transform America well after the guns had fallen silent in 1945. Among the groups most affected by the war were African Americans. Predominantly a rural, southern people before 1940, African Americans were propelled by the war into the cities of the North and West, and by 1970 a majority lived outside the states of the old Confederacy. The results of that massive demographic shift were momentous, for African Americans and for all of American society.

So many black southerners took to the roads during World War II that local officials lost track of their numbers. Black workers on the move crowded into boardinghouses, camped out in cars, and clustered in the juke joints of roadside America en route to their new lives.

Southern cotton fields and tobacco plantations had historically yielded slender sustenance to African American farmers, most of whom struggled to make ends meet as tenants or sharecroppers. The Great Depression dealt black southerners yet another blow, for when New Deal farm programs paid growers to leave their land fallow, many landlords simply pocketed the money and evicted their tenants—white as well as black—from their now-idle fields. As the Depression deepened, dispossessed former tenants and sharecroppers toiled as seasonal farmworkers or languished without jobs, without shelter, and without hope.

The spanking-new munitions plants and bustling shipyards of wartime America at first offered little solace to African Americans, particularly in the South. In 1940 and 1941, the labor-hungry war machine soaked up unemployed white workers but commonly denied jobs to blacks. When the army constructed a training camp near Petersburg, Virginia, it imported white carpenters from all parts of the United States, rather than employ the hundreds of skilled black carpenters who lived nearby. Fed up with such injustices, many African Americans headed for shipyards, factories, foundries, and fields on the Pacific Coast or north of the Mason-Dixon line, where their willing hands found more work awaiting them.

Angered by the racism that was depriving their people of a fair share of jobs, black leaders cajoled President Roosevelt into issuing an executive order in June 1941 declaring that "there shall be no discrimination in the

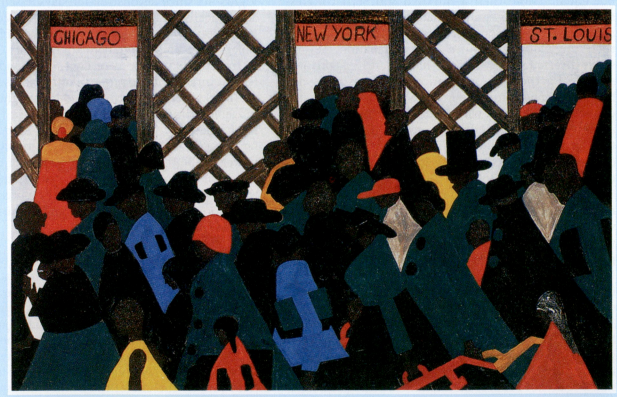

The Migration of the Negro, by Jacob Lawrence, 1940–1941   Artist Jacob Lawrence depicted the migration of southern blacks to the North during and after World War II in a series of paintings. The first panel of the series bears the description "During the World War there was a great migration north by southern Negroes."

New York Public Library, Schomberg Center for Research in Black Culture

The Home Front Though often confronted by prejudice and discrimination, many African American migrants from the rural South found their first industrial jobs in wartime defense plants during World War II.

AP Images

Detroit Race Riot, 1943 A black passenger is dragged from a streetcar.

employment of workers in defense industries or government because of race, creed, color, or national origin." Roosevelt's action was a tenuous, hesitant step. Yet in its way Executive Order 8802 amounted to a second Emancipation Proclamation, as the federal government for the first time since Reconstruction had committed itself to ensuring justice for African Americans.

The entire nation was now forced to face the evil of racism, as bloody wartime riots in Detroit, New York, Philadelphia, and other cities tragically demonstrated. But for the first time, large numbers of blacks secured a foothold in the industrial economy, and they were not about to give it up.

By war's end the great wartime exodus had scattered hundreds of thousands of African Americans to new regions and new ways of life—a second black diaspora comparable in its scale and consequence to the original black dispersal out of Africa. In the postwar decades, blacks continued to pour out of the South in

search of economic opportunity and political freedom. In western and northern cities, blacks now competed for housing and jobs, and they also voted—many of them for the first time in their lives.

As early as 1945, NAACP leader Walter White concluded that the war "immeasurably magnified the Negro's awareness of the disparity between the American profession and practice of democracy." After the war, he predicted, African Americans would be "convinced that whatever betterment of their lot is achieved must come largely from their own efforts." The wartime migration thus set the stage for the success of the civil rights movement that began to stir in the late 1940s and the 1950s. With their new political base outside the Old South, and with new support from the Democratic party, African Americans eventually forced an end to the hated segregationist practices that had kept them from enjoying full rights as citizens.

Martin Luther King, Jr., and His Wife, Coretta, Arrested King and his wife were arrested for the first time in Montgomery, Alabama, in 1955 while organizing the bus boycott.

© Bettmann/Corbis

southern black students formed the **Student Nonviolent Coordinating Committee** (**SNCC**, pronounced "snick") to give more focus and force to these efforts. Young and impassioned, SNCC members would eventually lose patience with the more stately tactics of the SCLC and the even more deliberate legalisms of the NAACP.

✵ Eisenhower Republicanism at Home

The balding, sixty-two-year-old General Eisenhower had entered the White House in 1953 pledging his administration to a philosophy of "dynamic conservatism." "In all those things which deal with people, be liberal, be human," he advised. But when it came to "people's money, or their economy, or their form of government, be conservative." This balanced, middle-of-the-road course harmonized with the depression-daunted and war-weary mood of the times. Some critics called Eisenhower's presidency a case of "the bland leading the bland."

Above all, Eisenhower strove to balance the federal budget and guard the Republic from what he called "creeping socialism." The former supreme Allied commander put the brakes on Truman's enormous military buildup, though defense spending still soaked up some 10 percent of the GNP. True to his small-government philosophy, Eisenhower supported the transfer of control over offshore oil fields from the federal government to the states. Ike also tried to curb the TVA (see p. 766) by encouraging a private power company to build a generating plant to compete with the massive public utility spawned by the New Deal. Eisenhower's secretary of health, education, and welfare condemned the free distribution of the Salk antipolio vaccine as "socialized medicine."

Eisenhower responded to the Mexican government's worries that illegal Mexican immigration to the United States would undercut the *bracero* program of legally imported farmworkers inaugurated during

Operation Wetback Thousands of illegal Mexican immigrants were forcibly repatriated to Mexico in the federal government's 1954 roundup operation, which was promoted in part by the Mexican government. The man in this photograph is being pulled across the border by a Mexican official, while an American spectator tries to pull him back into the United States.

© Bettmann/Corbis

J. R. Everman/Time & Life Pictures/Getty Images

Drive-in Movie Theater, Utah, 1958   Going to the movies became one more thing Americans could do in their cars in the 1950s. Here moviegoers watch Charlton Heston as Moses in the Academy Award–winning motion picture *The Ten Commandments*. It was the last film made by famed director Cecil B. DeMille.

World War II (see p. 803). In a massive roundup of illegal immigrants, dubbed **Operation Wetback** in reference to the migrants' watery route across the Rio Grande, as many as 1 million Mexicans were apprehended and returned to Mexico in 1954.

In yet another of the rude and arbitrary reversals that long have afflicted the government's relations with Native Americans, Eisenhower also sought to cancel the tribal preservation policies of the "Indian New Deal," in place since 1934 (see p. 765). He proposed to "terminate" the tribes as legal entities and to revert to the assimilationist goals of the Dawes Severalty Act of 1887 (see p. 581). Most Indians resisted termination, and the policy was abandoned in 1961.

Eisenhower obviously could not unscramble all the eggs that had been fried by New Dealers and Fair Dealers for twenty long years. He pragmatically accepted and thereby legitimated many New Dealish programs, stitching them permanently into the fabric of American society. As he told his brother, "Should

any political party attempt to abolish Social Security, unemployment insurance, and eliminate labor and farm programs, you would not hear of that party again in our political history."

In some ways Eisenhower even did the New Deal one better. In a public works project that dwarfed anything the New Dealers had ever dreamed of, Ike backed the **Federal Highway Act of 1956**, a $27 billion plan to build forty-two thousand miles of sleek, fast motorways. The former general believed that such roads were essential to national defense, allowing U.S. troops to mobilize anywhere in the country in the event of a Soviet invasion. Beyond being a defense strategy, laying down these modern, multilane roads created countless construction jobs and speeded the suburbanization of America. The Highway Act offered juicy benefits to the trucking, automobile, oil, and travel industries, while at the same time robbing the railroads, especially passenger trains, of business. The act also exacerbated problems of air quality and energy consumption, and it had especially disastrous consequences for cities, whose once-vibrant downtowns withered away while shopping malls and other sites of leisure and consumption flourished in the far-flung suburbs.

A "New Look" in Foreign Policy

The 1952 Republican platform called for a "new look" in foreign policy. It condemned mere "containment" of communism as "negative, futile, and immoral." Incoming secretary of state John Foster Dulles promised not merely to stem the red tide but to "roll back" its gains and "liberate captive peoples." At the same time, the new administration promised to balance the budget by cutting military spending.

How were these two contradictory goals to be reached? Dulles answered with a **policy of boldness**

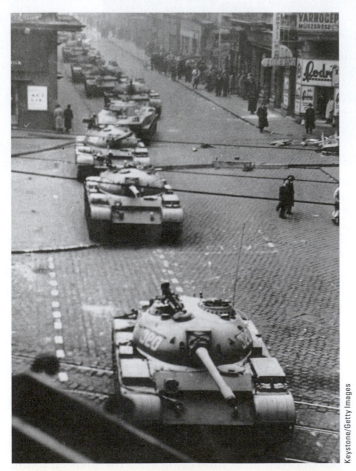

Hungarian Uprising, October 26, 1956 Soviet tanks rolled through the streets of Budapest to crush an anticommunist uprising against the Soviets, who had controlled Hungary since World War II. This demonstration of brute force against a grassroots democratic movement turned many communist sympathizers in the West definitively against the Soviet Union.

Keystone/Getty Images

in early 1954. Eisenhower would relegate the army and the navy to the backseat and build up an airfleet of superbombers (called the Strategic Air Command, or SAC) equipped with city-flattening nuclear bombs. These fearsome weapons would inflict "massive retaliation" on the Soviets or the Chinese if they got out of hand. The advantages of this new policy were thought to be its paralyzing nuclear impact and its cheaper price tag when compared with conventional forces—"more bang for the buck." At the same time, Eisenhower sought a thaw in the Cold War through negotiations with the new Soviet leaders who came to power after dictator Joseph Stalin's death in 1953.

In the end, the touted "new look" proved illusory. A new Soviet premier, the burly apparatchik Nikita Khrushchev, rudely rejected Ike's call in 1955 for an "open skies" mutual inspection program over both the Soviet Union and the United States. In 1956 the Hungarians rose up against their Soviet masters and felt badly betrayed when the United States turned a deaf ear to their desperate appeals for aid. The brutally crushed **Hungarian uprising** revealed the sobering truth that America's mighty nuclear sledgehammer was too heavy a weapon to wield in such a relatively minor crisis. The rigid futility of the "massive retaliation" doctrine was thus starkly exposed. To his dismay, Eisenhower also discovered that the aerial and atomic hardware necessary for "massive retaliation" was staggeringly expensive.

The Vietnam Nightmare

Western Europe, thanks to the Marshall Plan and NATO, seemed reasonably secure by the early 1950s, but Southeast Asia was a different can of worms. In Vietnam and elsewhere, nationalist movements had sought for years to throw off the yoke of French colonial rule. The legendary Vietnamese leader, goateed Ho Chi Minh, had tried to appeal personally to Woodrow Wilson in Paris as early as 1919 to support self-determination for the peoples of Southeast Asia. Franklin Roosevelt had likewise inspired hope among Asian nationalists.

But Cold War events dampened the dreams of anticolonial Asian peoples. Their leaders—including Ho Chi Minh—became increasingly communist while the United States became increasingly anticommunist. By 1954 American taxpayers were financing nearly 80 percent of the costs of a bottomless French colonial war in Indochina. The United States' share amounted to about $1 billion a year.

Despite this massive aid, French forces continued to crumble under pressure from Ho Chi Minh's nationalist guerrilla forces, called the Viet Minh. In March

MAP 37.2 East and Southeast Asia, 1955–1956 © Cengage Learning

The Americans had evidently backed a losing horse but could see no easy way to call off their bet.

✦ Cold War Crises in Europe and the Middle East

The United States had initially backed the French in Indochina in part to win French approval of a plan to rearm West Germany. Despite French fears, the Germans were finally welcomed into the NATO fold in 1955, with an expected contribution of half a million troops. In the same year, the Eastern European countries and the Soviets signed the Warsaw Pact, creating a red military counterweight to the newly bolstered NATO forces in the West.

Despite these hardening military lines, the Cold War seemed to be thawing a bit in 1955. In May the Soviets rather surprisingly agreed to end their occupation of Austria. A summit conference in Geneva in July produced little progress on the burning issues, but it bred a conciliatory "spirit of Geneva" that caused a modest blush of optimism to pass over the face of the Western world. Hopes rose further the following year when Soviet Communist party boss Khrushchev publicly denounced the bloody excesses of Joseph Stalin, the dictator dead since 1953.

Violent events late in 1956 ended the post-Geneva lull. When the liberty-loving Hungarians struck for their freedom, they were ruthlessly overpowered by Soviet tanks, while the Western world looked on in horror.

Fears of Soviet penetration into the oil-rich Middle East further heightened Cold War tensions. The government of Iran, supposedly influenced by the Kremlin, began to resist the power of the gigantic Western companies that controlled Iranian petroleum. In response, the American Central Intelligence Agency (CIA) helped to engineer a coup in 1953 that installed the youthful shah of Iran, Mohammed Reza Pahlevi, as a kind of dictator. Though successful in the short run in securing Iranian oil for the West, the American intervention left a bitter legacy of resentment among many Iranians. More than two decades later, they took their revenge on the shah and his American allies (see pp. 936–938).

The **Suez crisis** proved far messier than the swift stroke in Iran. President Nasser of Egypt, an ardent Arab nationalist, was seeking funds to build an immense dam on the upper Nile for urgently needed irrigation and power. America and Britain tentatively offered financial help, but when Nasser began to flirt openly with the communist camp, Secretary of State Dulles dramatically withdrew the dam offer. Nasser promptly regained face by nationalizing the Suez Canal, owned chiefly by British and French stockholders.

1954 a key French garrison was trapped hopelessly in the fortress of Dien Bien Phu in the northwestern corner of Vietnam. The new "policy of boldness" was now put to the test. Secretary Dulles, Vice President Nixon, and the chairman of the Joint Chiefs of Staff favored intervention with American bombers to help bail out the beleaguered French. But Eisenhower, wary about another war in Asia so soon after Korea and correctly fearing British nonsupport, held back.

The **Battle of Dien Bien Phu** proved a victory for the nationalists, and a multination conference in Geneva roughly halved Vietnam at the seventeenth parallel (see Map 37.2). The victorious Ho Chi Minh in the north consented to this arrangement on the assurance that Vietnam-wide elections would be held within two years. In the south a pro-Western government under Ngo Dinh Diem was soon entrenched at Saigon. The Vietnamese never held the promised elections, primarily because the communists seemed certain to win, and Vietnam remained a dangerously divided country.

The United States did not sign the Geneva accords, though Eisenhower promised economic and military aid to the autocratic Diem regime, provided that it undertook certain social reforms. Change came at a snail's pace, but American aid continued, as communist guerrillas heated up their campaign against Diem.

Egyptian President Gamal Abdel Nasser, 1954 Shown here greeting exuberant supporters after his election as the first president of the new Egyptian republic, Nasser was long a thorn in the flesh of American and European policymakers anxious to protect the precious oil resources of the Middle East. "Nassarism," his version of pan-Arabism, won a great following in the Arab world during the 1950s and 1960s.

AP Images

Nasser's action placed a razor's edge at the jugular vein of Western Europe's oil supply. America's jittery French and British allies, deliberately keeping Washington in the dark and coordinating their blow with one from Israel, staged a joint assault on Egypt late in October 1956.

For a breathless week, the world teetered on the edge of the abyss. The French and British, however, had made a fatal miscalculation—that the United States would supply them with oil while their Middle Eastern supplies were disrupted, as an oil-rich Uncle Sam had done in the two world wars. But to their unpleasant surprise, a furious President Eisenhower resolved to let them "boil in their own oil" and refused to release emergency supplies. The oilless allies resentfully withdrew their troops, and for the first time in history, a United Nations police force was sent to maintain order.

The Suez crisis also marked the last time in history that the United States could brandish its "oil weapon." As recently as 1940, the United States had produced two-thirds of the world's oil, while a scant 5 percent of the global supply flowed from the Middle East. But by 1948 the United States had become a net oil importer. Its days as an "oil power" clearly were numbered as the economic and strategic importance of the Middle East oil region grew dramatically.

The U.S. president and Congress proclaimed the Eisenhower Doctrine in 1957, pledging U.S. military and economic aid to Middle Eastern nations threatened by communist aggression. The real threat to U.S. interests in the Middle East, however, was not communism but nationalism, as Nasser's wild popularity among the masses of all Arab countries demonstrated. The poor, sandy sheikdoms increasingly resolved to reap for themselves the lion's share of the enormous oil wealth that Western companies pumped out of the scorching Middle Eastern deserts. In a portentous move, Saudi Arabia, Kuwait, Iraq, and Iran joined with Venezuela in 1960 to form the **Organization of Petroleum Exporting Countries (OPEC)**. In the next two decades, OPEC's stranglehold on the Western economies would tighten to a degree that even Nasser could not have imagined.

✦ Round Two for Ike

The election of 1956 was a replay of the 1952 contest, with President Eisenhower pitted once more against Adlai Stevenson. The Democrats were hard-pressed to find issues with which to attack the genial general in a time of prosperity and peace, and the voters made it clear that they still liked Ike. Eisenhower piled up an enormous majority of 35,590,472 popular votes to Stevenson's 26,022,752; in the Electoral College, the count was even more unbalanced at 457 for Republicans to 73 for Democrats. Eisenhower made deeper inroads into the traditional bastion of Democratic strength, the once-solid South, than he had in 1952. Louisiana went Republican for the first time since 1876, during

Reconstruction days. But the general's coattails were not so stiff or broad as in 1952. He failed to win for his party either house of Congress—the first time since Zachary Taylor's election in 1848 that a winning president had headed such a losing ticket.

In fragile health, Eisenhower began his second term as a part-time president. Critics charged that he kept his hands on his golf clubs, fly rod, and shotgun more often than on the levers of power. But in his last years in office, Ike rallied himself to do less golfing and more governing.

A key area in which the president bestirred himself was labor legislation. Congressional investigations produced scandalous revelations of gangsterism, fraud, and brass-knuckles tactics in many American unions, especially the Teamsters. The AF of L–CIO, born of a merger of the two giants in 1955, expelled the Teamsters in 1957 for choosing leaders like two-fisted James R. "Jimmy" Hoffa. Convicted of jury tampering, Hoffa served part of his sentence before disappearing without a trace—evidently the victim of gangsters he had

The Helicopter Era, 1957 President Eisenhower was routinely criticized by liberals, as in this Herblock cartoon in the *Washington Post,* for his apparent indifference to many seething social problems of the day. His failure to employ his vast prestige on behalf of civil rights was especially conspicuous. *The Helicopter Era. A 1957 Herblock Cartoon, copyright by The Herb Block Foundation*

crossed. To counter such corruption, Eisenhower persuaded Congress to pass the Landrum-Griffin Act in 1959. The act was designed to bring labor leaders to book for financial shenanigans and bullying tactics, but it also expanded some of the antilabor strictures of the earlier Taft-Hartley Act (see p. 830).

Soviet scientists astounded the world on October 4, 1957, by lofting into orbit around the globe a beep-beeping "baby moon" (*Sputnik I*) weighing 184 pounds. A month later they topped their own ace by sending aloft a larger satellite (*Sputnik II*) weighing 1,120 pounds and carrying a dog.

This amazing breakthrough rattled American self-confidence. It cast doubts on America's vaunted scientific superiority and raised some sobering military questions. If the Soviets could fire heavy objects into outer space, they certainly could reach America with intercontinental ballistic missiles (ICBMs).

"Rocket fever" swept the nation. Eisenhower established the National Aeronautics and Space Administration (NASA) and directed billions of dollars to missile development. After humiliating and well-advertised failures—notably the Vanguard missile, which blew up on national television just a few feet above the ground in 1957—in February 1958 the United States managed to put into orbit a grapefruit-sized satellite weighing 2.5 pounds. By the end of the decade, several satellites had been launched, and the United States had successfully tested its own ICBMs.

The **Sputnik** success led to a critical comparison of the American educational system, which was already under fire as too easygoing, with that of the Soviet Union. A strong move now developed in the United States to replace "frills" with solid subjects—to substitute square roots for square dancing. Congress rejected demands for federal scholarships, but late in 1958 the National Defense and Education Act (NDEA) authorized $887 million in loans to needy college students and in grants for the improvement of teaching the sciences and languages.

✦ The Continuing Cold War

The fantastic race toward nuclear annihilation continued unabated. Humanity-minded scientists urged that nuclear tests be stopped before the atmosphere became so polluted as to produce generations of deformed mutants. The Soviets, after completing an intensive series of exceptionally "dirty" tests, proclaimed a suspension in March 1958 and urged the Western world to follow. Beginning in October 1958, Washington did halt both underground and atmospheric testing. But attempts to regularize such suspensions by proper inspection sank on the reef of mutual mistrust.

Thermonuclear suicide seemed nearer in July 1958, when both Egyptian and communist plottings threatened to engulf Western-oriented Lebanon. After its president had called for aid under the Eisenhower Doctrine, the United States boldly landed several thousand troops and helped restore order without taking a single life.

The burly Khrushchev, seeking new propaganda laurels, was eager to meet with Eisenhower and pave the way for a "summit conference" with Western leaders. Despite grave misgivings as to any tangible results, the president invited him to America in 1959. Arriving in New York, Khrushchev appeared before the U.N. General Assembly and dramatically resurrected the ancient Soviet proposal of complete disarmament. But he offered no practical means of achieving this end.

A result of this tour was a meeting at Camp David, the presidential retreat in Maryland. Khrushchev emerged saying that his ultimatum for the evacuation of Berlin would be extended indefinitely. The relieved world gave prayerful but premature thanks for the "spirit of Camp David."

The Camp David spirit quickly evaporated when the follow-up Paris "summit conference," scheduled for May 1960, turned out to be an incredible fiasco. Both Moscow and Washington had taken a firm stand on the burning Berlin issue, and neither could risk backing down publicly. Then, on the eve of the conference, an American U-2 spy plane was shot down deep in the heart of Russia. After bungling bureaucratic denials in Washington, "honest Ike" took the unprecedented step of assuming personal responsibility. Khrushchev stormed into Paris filling the air with invective, and the conference collapsed before it could get off the ground. The concord of Camp David was replaced with the grapes of wrath.

� Cuba's Castroism Spells Communism

Latin Americans bitterly resented Uncle Sam's lavishing of billions of dollars on Europe, while doling out only millions to its poor relations to the south. They also chafed at Washington's continuing habit of intervening in Latin American affairs—as in a CIA-directed coup that ousted a leftist government in Guatemala in 1954. On the other hand, Washington continued to support—even decorate—bloody dictators who claimed to be combating communists.

Most ominous of all was the communist beachhead in Cuba. Iron-fisted dictator Fulgencio Batista, in power since the 1930s, had encouraged huge investments of American capital, and Washington in turn had given him some support. But early in 1959, black-bearded Fidel Castro engineered a revolution that ousted

Batista. Castro then denounced the Yankee imperialists and began to expropriate valuable American properties in pursuing a land-distribution program. Washington, finally losing patience, released Cuba from "imperialistic slavery" by cutting off the heavy U.S. imports of Cuban sugar. Castro retaliated with further wholesale confiscations of Yankee property and in effect made his left-wing dictatorship an economic and military satellite of Moscow, to the Kremlin's delighted surprise. An exodus of anti-Castro Cubans headed for the United States, especially Florida. Nearly 1 million arrived between 1960 and 2000. Washington broke diplomatic relations with Castro's government early in 1961 and imposed a strict embargo on trade with Cuba. Strengthened by the Helms-Burton Act in 1996, the embargo has remained in place, even since Castro's departure from power in 2008.

Americans talked seriously of invoking the Monroe Doctrine before the Soviets set up a communist base only ninety miles from their shores. Khrushchev angrily proclaimed that the Monroe Doctrine was dead and indicated that he would shower missiles upon the United States if it attacked his new friend Castro.

✶ Kennedy Challenges Nixon for the Presidency

Republicans approached the presidential campaign of 1960 with Vice President Nixon as their heir apparent. To many he was a gifted party leader, to others a ruthless opportunist. The "old" Nixon had been a no-holds-barred campaigner, adept at skewering Democrats and left-wingers. The "new" Nixon was represented as a mature, seasoned statesman. He had gained particular notice in a finger-pointing **kitchen debate** with Khrushchev in Moscow in 1959, where Nixon extolled the virtues of American consumerism over Soviet economic planning. The next year he handily won the Republican nomination. His running mate was patrician Henry Cabot Lodge, Jr., of Massachusetts (grandson of Woodrow Wilson's arch-foe).

By contrast, the Democratic race for the presidential nomination started as a free-for-all. John F. Kennedy—a youthful, dark-haired millionaire senator from Massachusetts—won impressive victories in the primaries. He then scored a first-ballot triumph in Los Angeles over his closest rival, Senator Lyndon B. Johnson, the Senate majority leader from Texas. A disappointed South was not completely appeased when Johnson accepted second place on the ticket in an eleventh-hour marriage of convenience. Kennedy's challenging acceptance speech called upon the American people for sacrifices to achieve their potential greatness, which he hailed as the New Frontier.

Bigotry inevitably showed its snarling face. Senator Kennedy was a Roman Catholic, the first to be nominated since Al Smith's ill-starred campaign in 1928. Smear artists revived the ancient charges about the Pope's controlling the White House. Kennedy pointed to his fourteen years of service in Congress, denied that he would be swayed by Rome, and asked if some 40 million Catholic Americans were to be condemned to second-class citizenship from birth.

Kennedy's Catholicism aroused misgivings in the Protestant, Bible Belt South, which was ordinarily Democratic. "I fear Catholicism more than I fear communism," declaimed one Baptist minister in North Carolina. But the religious issue largely canceled itself out. If many southern Democrats stayed away from the polls because of Kennedy's Catholicism, northern Democrats in unusually large numbers supported Kennedy because of the bitter attacks on their Catholic faith.

Kennedy charged that the Soviets, with their nuclear bombs and circling Sputniks, had gained on America in prestige and power. Nixon retorted that the nation's prestige had not slipped, although Kennedy was causing it to do so by his unpatriotic talk.

Television may well have tipped the scales. Nixon agreed to meet Kennedy in four so-called debates. The

> *Candidate John F. Kennedy (1917–1963), in a speech to a Houston group of Protestant ministers (September 12, 1960), declared,*
>
> **❝I believe in an America where the separation of church and state is absolute—where no Catholic prelate would tell the President, should he be a Catholic, how to act, and no Protestant minister would tell his parishioners for whom to vote . . . and where no man is denied public office because his religion differs from the President who might appoint him or the people who might elect him.❞**

contestants crossed words in millions of living rooms before audiences estimated at 60 million or more. Nobody "won" the debates. But Kennedy at least held his own and did not suffer by comparison with the more "experienced" Nixon. The debates once again demonstrated the importance of image over substance in the television age. Many viewers found Kennedy's glamour and vitality far more appealing than Nixon's tired and pallid appearance.

Kennedy squeezed through by the rather comfortable margin of 303 electoral votes to 219,* but with the breathtakingly close popular margin of only 118,574 votes out of over 68 million cast (see Map 37.3). He was the first Roman Catholic and the youngest person to date to be elected president. Like Franklin Roosevelt, Kennedy ran well in the large industrial centers, where he had strong support from workers, Catholics, and African Americans. (He had solicitously telephoned the pregnant Coretta King, whose husband, Martin Luther King, Jr., was then imprisoned in Georgia for a sit-in.) Although losing a few seats, the Democrats also swept both houses of Congress by wide margins.

✦ An Old General Fades Away

President Eisenhower continued to enjoy extraordinary popularity to the final curtain. Despite Democratic jibes about "eight years of golfing and goofing," of "putting and puttering," Eisenhower was universally admired and respected for his dignity, decency, sincerity, goodwill, and moderation.

Pessimists had predicted that Eisenhower would be a seriously crippled "lame duck" during his second

John F. Kennedy Campaigning for the Presidency, 1960 At right is his wife, Jacqueline Kennedy.

Cornell Capa/Magnum Photos

---

*Six Democratic electors in Alabama, all eight unpledged Democratic electors in Mississippi, and one Republican elector in Oklahoma voted for Senator Harry F. Byrd, who ran as an independent.

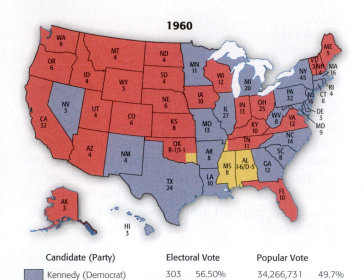

1960

Candidate (Party)	Electoral Vote		Popular Vote	
Kennedy (Democrat)	303	56.50%	34,266,731	49.7%
Nixon (Republican)	219	40.75%	34,108,157	49.5%
Byrd (Independent)	15	2.75%	501,643	0.7%

MAP 37.3 Presidential Election of 1960 (with electoral vote by state) Kennedy owed his hairbreadth triumph to his victories in twenty-six of the forty largest cities—and to Lyndon Johnson's strenuous campaigning in the South, where Kennedy's Catholicism may have been a hotter issue than his stand on civil rights. © Cengage Learning

term, owing to the barrier against reelection erected by the Twenty-second Amendment, ratified in 1951. (See the Appendix.) In truth, he displayed more vigor, more political know-how, and more aggressive leadership during his last two years as president than ever before. For an unprecedented six years, from 1955 to 1961, Congress remained in Democratic hands, yet Eisenhower exerted unusual control over the legislative branch. He wielded the veto 169 times, and only twice was his nay overridden by the required two-thirds vote.

America was fabulously prosperous in the Eisenhower years, despite pockets of poverty and unemployment, recurrent recessions, and perennial farm problems. To the north the vast St. Lawrence waterway project, constructed jointly with Canada and completed in 1959, had turned the cities of the Great Lakes into bustling ocean seaports. "Old Glory" could now proudly display fifty stars. Alaska attained statehood in 1959, as did Hawaii. Alaska, though gigantic, was thinly populated and noncontiguous, but these objections were overcome in a Democratic Congress that expected Alaska to vote Democratic. Hawaii had ample population (largely of Asian descent), advanced democratic institutions, and more acreage than the mainland states of Rhode Island, Delaware, or Connecticut. As the first noncontiguous states to join the Union, Alaska and Hawaii helped turn America's face toward the Pacific and East Asia.

After campaigning with promises to reduce the defense budget, President Dwight Eisenhower (1890–1969) presided over unprecedented increases in military spending. In his Farewell Address on January 17, 1961, he sagely but ironically warned against the menace his own policies had nurtured:

" This conjunction of an immense military establishment and a large arms industry is new in the American experience. . . . In the councils of government, we must guard against the acquisition of unwarranted influence, whether sought or unsought, by the military-industrial complex."

Though a crusading general, Eisenhower as president mounted no moral crusade for civil rights. This was perhaps his greatest failing. Yet he was no bigot, and he had done far more than grin away problems and tread water. As a Republican president, he had further woven the reforms of the Democratic New Deal and Fair Deal into the fabric of national life. As a former general, he had exercised wise restraint in his use of military power and had soberly guided foreign policy away from countless threats to peace. The old soldier left office crestfallen at his failure to end the arms race with the Soviets. Yet he had ended one war and avoided all others. As the decades lengthened, appreciation of him grew.

✦ A Cultural Renaissance

America's unprecedented global power in the heady post–World War II decades was matched by its new international ascendancy in the arts. Shedding the national inferiority complex that had vexed previous generations, American creative genius exerted a powerful worldwide influence in painting, architecture, and literature.

New York became the art capital of the world after World War II, as well-heeled Americans supported countless painters and sculptors. The open and tradition-free American environment seemed especially congenial to the experimental mood of much modern art. Jackson Pollock pioneered **abstract expressionism** in the 1940s and 1950s, flinging paint on huge flats stretched across his studio floor. Realistic representation went out the window, as artists like Pollock and Willem de Kooning strove to create spontaneous "action paintings" that expressed the painter's individuality and made the viewer a creative participant in defining the painting's meaning. Mark Rothko and his fellow "color field"

The Shopping Mall as New Town Square, 1960

In this photograph, Democratic presidential candidate John F. Kennedy is shown campaigning at the Bergen Mall in Paramus, New Jersey, in 1960. The Bergen Mall opened in 1957, at a time when similar shopping centers were popping up in suburbanizing metropolitan areas all over the United States. Real estate developers watched Americans flee cities for suburbs, and they followed the money, locating shopping centers strategically at new highway intersections or along the busiest thoroughfares. As suburbanites increasingly found branches of their favorite department and chain stores closer to home during the 1950s and 1960s, they found it less and less necessary to go downtown. Shopping centers for their part went out of their way to sell themselves as modern-style downtowns worthy of being the public core of new suburban communities, even though legally they were privately owned space. They provided the full range of shops and services once found in city centers, including restaurants, post offices, Laundromats, banks, and even chapels. They offered entertainment, from movie theaters and skating rinks to free open-air concerts, carnivals, and exhibitions. They made auditoriums available for community meetings. And they attracted public events like Kennedy on the stump. Just four years earlier, a regional shopping center would have been a rare campaign stop for a presidential candidate. Look closely at this photograph. What kind of audience greeted candidate Kennedy at the Bergen Mall? How different might the crowd have looked in a more socially diverse urban center like Manhattan or in nearby Newark, the largest city in New Jersey at the time? What did it mean for sites of consumption, such as privately owned shopping centers, to take on the roles and responsibilities previously associated with urban streets, squares, and parks? How might current struggles of downtown merchants against big-box chain stores like Wal-Mart be related to this history?

Courtesy of the Newark Public Library

881

Jackson Pollock Flinging Paint on a Canvas, 1950
Promoters of the avant-garde lauded Pollock's paintings, but some critics dismissed them as meaningless explosions of formless energy.

employed plain geometric forms and basic building materials like brick and concrete to make beautiful, simple buildings, such as the serene, seaside Salk Institute (1965) in La Jolla, California. Eero Saarinen, the son of a Finnish immigrant, contributed a number of imaginative structures, including the sleek TWA Flight Center (1962) at New York's JFK Airport and the lofty Gateway Arch (1965) in St. Louis. Chinese-born I. M. Pei designed numerous graceful buildings on several college campuses, as well as the dramatic East Wing of the National Gallery of Art (1978) in Washington and the angular John F. Kennedy Library (1979) in Boston.

Postwar America reaped its greatest cultural harvest in the field of literature. In fiction writing some of the prewar masters continued to ply their trade, notably Ernest Hemingway in *The Old Man and the Sea* (1952). A Nobel laureate in 1954, Hemingway was dead by his own duck gun in 1961. John Steinbeck, another prewar writer who persisted in graphic portrayals of American society, such as *East of Eden* (1952) and *Travels with Charley* (1962), received the Nobel Prize for literature in 1962, the seventh American to be so honored.

painters likewise dispatched with figurative representation, enveloping whole canvases with bold, shimmering swaths of color. Other artists creatively exploited more familiar forms. "Pop" (short for popular) artists in the 1960s, notably Andy Warhol, canonized on canvas mundane items of consumer culture like soup cans and soda bottles. Roy Lichtenstein parodied old-fashioned comic strips, and Claes Oldenburg surprised viewers with exotic versions of everyday objects, such as giant plastic sculptures of pillow-soft telephones.

American architecture also reached new heights in the postwar era. While a residential building boom erected vast tracts of look-alike, ranch-style houses across the suburban landscape, ultra-modern skyscrapers arose in the nation's urban centers. Conceived in the modernist or "**International Style**," these massive corporate high-rises were essentially giant steel boxes wrapped in glass. Classic examples of this "curtain-wall" design include the United Nations headquarters (1952) and the Seagram Building (1957) in New York City and, later, the Sears Tower (1974) in Chicago and the John Hancock Tower (1976) in Boston.

Other postwar architectural achievements transcended the stark steel-and-glass box. Old master Frank Lloyd Wright continued to produce strikingly original designs, conspicuously in the round-walled Guggenheim Museum (1959) in New York. Louis Kahn

Ernest Hemingway (1899–1961) Celebrated both for his writing and his colorful, swashbuckling lifestyle, Hemingway poses here with a dead leopard in 1953.

Curiously, World War II did not inspire the same kind of literary outpouring that World War I had. Searing realism, the trademark style of war writers in the 1920s, characterized the earliest novels that portrayed soldierly life in World War II, such as Norman Mailer's *The Naked and the Dead* (1948) and James Jones's *From Here to Eternity* (1951). But as time passed, realistic war writing fell from favor. Authors tended increasingly to write about the war in fantastic and even psychedelic prose. Joseph Heller's *Catch-22* (1961) dealt with the improbable antics and anguish of American airmen in the wartime Mediterranean. A savage satire, it made readers hurt when they laughed. The supercharged imagination of Kurt Vonnegut, Jr., poured forth works of puzzling complexity in sometimes impenetrably inventive prose, including the dark comedy war tale *Slaughterhouse Five* (1969).

More than the war itself, the fruits of victory at home captured America's literary imagination at mid-century. Postwar pens reacted to the nation's newly affluent, exuberantly consumerist society in two typical ways. One group of countercultural "Beat" writers rejected modern American life outright, seeking romantic self-expression in stridently nonconformist lifestyles (see "Makers of America: The Beat Generation," pp. 884–885).

A larger group of mainstream writers tackled the realities and dilemmas of postwar American society head on. Pennsylvania-born John Updike celebrated the feats and failings of ordinary, small-town America in sensual detail in his four-part "Rabbit" series, starting with *Rabbit, Run* (1960). Updike explicitly addressed suburban, middle-class infidelity in *Couples* (1968). Massachusetts-bred John Cheever, "the Chekhov of the exurbs," similarly chronicled suburban manners and morals in short stories such as "The Swimmer" (1964) and novels like *The Wapshot Chronicle* (1957). Gore Vidal penned a series of intriguing historical novels, as well as several impish and always iconoclastic works, including *Myra Breckinridge* (1968), about a reincarnated transsexual. Together these writers constituted the rear guard of an older, WASP (white Anglo-Saxon Protestant) elite that had long dominated American writing.

Poets were often highly critical, even deeply despairing, about the conformist character of midcentury American life. Older poets were still active, including cantankerous Ezra Pound, jailed after the war in a U.S. Army detention center near Pisa, Italy, for alleged collaboration with the Fascists. Connecticut insurance executive Wallace Stevens and New Jersey pediatrician William Carlos Williams continued after 1945 to pursue second careers as prolific poets of world-class stature.

But younger poets increasingly came to the fore during the postwar period. In short lyric meditations,

In his poem "A Supermarket in California" (1956), Allen Ginsburg (1926–1997) fantasized about meeting nineteenth-century American poet Walt Whitman amidst the lavish consumerism (and spiritual emptiness) of a postwar supermarket:

"I saw you, Walt Whitman, childless, lonely old grubber, poking among the meats in the refrigerator and eyeing the grocery boys.

I heard you asking questions of each: Who killed the pork chops? What price bananas? Are you my Angel?

I wandered in and out of the brilliant stacks of cans following you, and followed in my imagination by the store detective.

We strode down the open corridors together in our solitary fancy tasting artichokes, possessing every frozen delicacy, and never passing the cashier."

they experimented with a frank, "confessional" style, revealing personal experiences with sex, drugs, and madness. Inspired by the Beat poets, Robert Lowell helped inaugurate this trend with his psychologically intense *Life Studies* (1959). Descended from a long line of patrician New Englanders, Lowell sought to apply the wisdom of the Puritan past to the perplexing present in allegorical poems like *For the Union Dead* (1964). Troubled Sylvia Plath crafted the moving verses of *Ariel* (published posthumously in 1966) and a disturbing autobiographical novel, *The Bell Jar* (1963), but her career was cut short when she took her own life in 1963. Along with Plath, Anne Sexton attended Lowell's Boston poetry seminar. She produced brooding autobiographical poems, including *To Bedlam and Part Way Back* (1960), until her death by apparent suicide in 1974. Another brilliant poet of the period, John Berryman, ended his prolific career in 1972 by leaping from a Minneapolis bridge onto the frozen bank of the Mississippi River. Writing poetry seemed to be a dangerous pursuit in modern America. The life of the poet, it was said, began in sadness and ended in madness.

Playwrights were also acute observers of postwar American social mores. Tennessee Williams wrote a series of blistering dramas about psychological misfits struggling to hold themselves together amid the disintegrating forces of modern life. Noteworthy were *A Streetcar Named Desire* (1947) and *Cat on a Hot Tin Roof* (1955), each delivering powerful critiques of the contemporary restrictions placed on women's lives. Arthur Miller brought to the stage searching probes of

"I saw the best minds of my generation," Beat poet Allen Ginsberg (1926–1997) proclaimed, "destroyed by madness, starving hysterical naked, dragging themselves through the negro streets at dawn looking for an angry fix, angelheaded hipsters burning for the ancient heavenly connection to the starry dynamo in the machinery of night. . . ." Ginsberg's famous opening lines of "Howl" (1955) introduced the **Beat Generation** to the literary world. The poem's unruly verse and riotous content encapsulated the Beat Generation's contempt for the listless, middle-class suburban conformity they saw in World War II–weary America. Striving for liberation, these social drifters advocated free-form experimentation in life as well as literature: marching to one's own "beat." At once "beaten down" by the relentless, everyday pressures of bourgeois existence, these bohemian hedonists also deemed themselves capable of "beatitude," or blessedness.

Jack Kerouac (1922–1969) coined the term that defined this "generation" (more accurately, a small coterie) of alternative poets and personalities. Born Jean-Louis Lebris Kerouac to working-class, French-Canadian parents in Lowell, Massachusetts, he grew up speaking Quebecois French instead of English and hardly seemed the likely voice of a new literary generation. But a football scholarship to Columbia University sent him to New York City in the early 1940s, where he met the charismatic Neal Cassady, who introduced him to a shadowy underworld of hobos, jazz musicians, drug addicts, and petty criminals located around Times Square. Drifting in and out of school and employment, Kerouac eventually joined Cassady on a series of wild transcontinental road trips between 1947 and 1950.

These wanderings became the substance of Kerouac's landmark novel *On the Road* (1957), a sort of pocket bible for social rebels in the late 1950s. Legendarily written on a 120-foot roll of teletype paper over the course of only twenty days, the book recounted the impulsive, and ultimately disappointing, adventures of Kerouac and Cassady (fictionalized as Sal Paradise and Dean Moriarty) among the outcasts and eccentrics they encountered

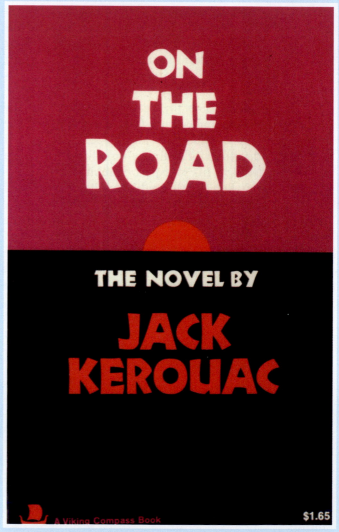

"Beat" Author Jack Kerouac at Work, 1950 A generation of "hipsters" and wannabe nonconformists took Kerouac's impulsive writings to be almost sacred texts and tried to conform their lifestyles to his errant ways.

Private Collection / Picture Research Consultants & Archives

The Cover of Kerouac's Celebrated Novel Hailed as an homage to unfettered spontaneity, *On the Road* was actually the product of several years of writing, revising, and editing.

Picture Research Consultants & Archives

A Gaggle of Beats From left to right, Bob Donlin, Neal Cassady, Allen Ginsberg, Robert LaVinge, and Lawrence Ferlinghetti stand outside Ferlinghetti's famed City Lights Bookstore in San Francisco, California, 1956.

along the way. Kerouac called his nonstop, drug-fueled writing technique "spontaneous prose" and conceptualized it as the literary equivalent of jazz improvisation or bebop. Though the book made him an instant literary celebrity, Kerouac's alcoholic lifestyle eventually killed him at the relatively young age of forty-seven.

Bearded and bespectacled Allen Ginsberg, the Beat Generation's most eloquent spokesman, lasted longer on the literary scene. Raised in New Jersey by a school teacher father and a Russian émigré mother who suffered from bouts of mental illness, Ginsberg made his way to nearby Columbia in the 1940s and fell in with the seedy Times Square circle, where he made friends with Kerouac, Cassady, and other Beat figures. After an eight-month confinement in a psychiatric institution, Ginsberg relocated to San Francisco's bohemian North Beach neighborhood. A 1955 public reading of Ginsberg's epic poem "Howl" launched a literary renaissance in the city, centered on Lawrence Ferlinghetti's City Lights Bookstore. Ginsberg's poem eulogized his peers. Its long, tumbling poetic line recalled Walt Whitman's exuberant voice and recounted the Beat poet's experiences with homosexual sex, psychedelic drugs, and spiritual illumination. Ferlinghetti's publication of *Howl and Other Poems* in 1956 led to a highly publicized San Francisco obscenity trial, which brought national media attention to Beat culture and scored a victory for First Amendment freedom of expression.

Tall and bleak William S. Burroughs (1914–1997), though a decade older than Kerouac and Ginsberg, contributed the third great work of Beat literature in *Naked Lunch* (1962). Scion of a wealthy St. Louis family, Burroughs developed an unhealthy penchant for guns and petty crime as a maladjusted youth. After graduating from Harvard, he landed in New York City and befriended Kerouac, Ginsberg, and other Beats. The circle of friends fell in trouble with the law when one of them slayed an unwanted sexual partner; Burroughs and Kerouac were material witnesses to the crime. Later, a drunken Burroughs shot dead his common-law wife in Mexico City. Drug addict, fugitive, and homosexual, he resettled in Morocco and wrote *Naked Lunch*, a disjointed tale of urban junkies and extreme sexual practices that satirized Cold War conformity, anxiety, and psychiatric science. *Newsweek* called Burroughs's work "a masterpiece, but a totally insane and anarchic one." Its controversial publication spurred an obscenity trial in Massachusetts and made Burroughs an early icon of postmodernism (see Chapter 42, pp. 1007–1010).

As the latest in America's tradition of "protest" cultures, the writers of the Beat Generation enjoyed their moment in the sun in the late 1950s. To literature, they contributed a new style of free-form narration. Beyond the page, they promoted interest in bebop jazz and eastern religious mysticism, particularly Zen Buddhism. By the early 1960s, much of their energy had dissipated. Later generations often remembered not the Beats' literary achievements or spiritual aspirations, but their ostentatious embrace of cool jazz, snapping fingers, goatees, berets, and bad coffeehouse poetry. (San Francisco columnist Herb Caen coined the sneering term *beatnik* in 1958, linking Cold War anxiety over the recent Sputnik launch with disapproval of the Beats' antisocial and delinquent tendencies.) Nonetheless, many features of the Beat spirit lived on in the countercultural "hippie" movement of the 1960s, including sexual liberation, alternative spirituality, experimentation with drugs, and an emphasis on spontaneity, authenticity, and extreme sensation. Long after hippies had passed out of fashion, youngsters in America and around the world continued to find inspiration in the writings of Kerouac, Ginsberg, Burroughs, and their fellow Beats.

Culver Pictures

Death of a Salesman   First performed in 1949, Arthur Miller's play probed the psychic costs of failure in a society that held out the promise of "success" to all. The play especially resonated with audiences in the booming 1950s and quickly took its place as an American classic. This scene from the original Broadway production shows Arthur Kennedy as Biff Loman (left) confronting his father, Willy, played by Lee J. Cobb (seated), while his brother, Happy, portrayed by Cameron Mitchell, looks on. Not shown here is Willy's compassionate wife, Linda, brilliantly acted by Mildred Dunnock.

American values, notably *Death of a Salesman* (1949), a tragic indictment of the American dream of material success, and *The Crucible* (1953), which treated the Salem witch trials as a dark parable warning against the dangers of McCarthyism. Lorraine Hansberry offered an affecting, realistic portrait of African American life in *A Raisin in the Sun* (1959). In the 1960s Edward Albee

Arthur Miller (1915–2005) challenged America's blind faith in postwar material success in his masterpiece Death of a Salesman *(1949). Early in the play, Miller's protagonist, Willy Loman, offers the era's customary advice on success in business to his son Biff:*

❝[T]he man who makes an appearance in the business world, the man who creates personal interest, is the man who gets ahead. Be liked and you will never want.❞

exposed the rapacious underside of middle-class life in *Who's Afraid of Virginia Woolf?* (1962).

Still, the realist novel remained the preferred genre for chroniclers of the postwar literary scene. With no shortage of ambition, a number of authors set out to produce "the great American novel." In the same mold as Mark Twain's *Adventures of Huckleberry Finn* and F. Scott Fitzgerald's *Great Gatsby*, many of these works took the form of a *Bildungsroman* (German for "formation novel"), or a tale chronicling the education and maturation of a young protagonist. New York novelist and infamous recluse J. D. Salinger painted an unforgettable portrait of adolescent angst, alienation, and rebellion in *The Catcher in the Rye* (1951). Ralph Ellison depicted the African American's often tortured quest for personal identity in *Invisible Man* (1952), a haunting novel narrated by a nameless black person who finds that none of his supposed supporters—white philanthropists, black nationalists, and Communist party members—can see him as a real man. Chicagoan Saul Bellow concocted a more readily recognizable Everyman in *The Adventures of Augie March* (1953), a coming-of-age tale about a young man buffeted by fate and struggling to make sense of the chaotic modern world. Alabama novelist Harper Lee drew from the Southern Gothic tradition to tell of racial injustice and the loss of youthful innocence in *To Kill a Mockingbird* (1960), one of the most widely read novels in all of American literature.

As these works attested, underrepresented groups gained new prominence in midcentury literary circles. Black authors built on the earlier achievements of the Harlem Renaissance. A decade before Ellison's emergence, Richard Wright had found literary acclaim with his chilling portrait of a black Chicago killer in *Native Son* (1940). The book made Wright the first African American best seller, and he followed its success with the semi-autobiographical and highly influential *Black Boy* (1945). Later, James Baldwin won plaudits as a novelist and essayist, particularly for his sensitive reflections on the racial question in *The Fire Next Time* (1963). Black nationalist LeRoi Jones, who changed his name to Imamu Amiri Baraka, crafted powerful plays like *Dutchman* (1964).

The South boasted its own literary renaissance, led by veteran Mississippi author William Faulkner, a Nobel recipient in 1950. Distancing themselves from an earlier "Lost Cause" literature that had glorified the antebellum South, **Southern Renaissance** writers brought a new critical appreciation to the region's burdens of history, racism, and conservatism. After taking his stand with fellow conservative "agrarian" writers in the 1930s, Tennessean Robert Penn Warren immortalized Louisiana politico Huey Long in *All the King's Men* (1946). Fellow Mississippians Walker Percy and Eudora Welty grasped the falling torch from the failing Faulkner, who died in 1962. Along with Georgian Flannery O'Connor, these later Southern Renaissance writers perceptively tracked the changes reshaping the postwar South, while also exploring universal themes of yearning, failure, success, and sorrow. Virginian William Styron confronted the harsh history of his home state in a controversial fictional representation of an 1831 slave rebellion, *The Confessions of Nat Turner* (1967).

Especially bountiful was the harvest of books by Jewish novelists. Some critics quipped that a knowledge of Yiddish was becoming necessary to understand much of the dialogue presented in modern American novels. Many Jewish writers found their favorite subject matter in the experience of lower- and middle-class Jewish immigrants. Bernard Malamud rendered a touching portrait of a family of New York Jewish storekeepers in *The Assistant* (1957). Malamud also explored the mythic qualities of the culture of baseball in *The Natural* (1952). Philip Roth wrote comically about young New Jersey suburbanites in *Goodbye, Columbus* (1959) and penned an uproarious account of a sexually obsessed middle-aged New Yorker in *Portnoy's Complaint* (1969). Saul Bellow contributed masterful sketches of Jewish urban and literary life, following the landmark achievement of *Augie March* with *Herzog* (1962). Bellow won the Nobel Prize for literature in 1976, becoming the eighth American so honored in the previous half-century.

Chapter Review

KEY TERMS

The Feminine Mystique (861)
rock 'n' roll (863)
Checkers Speech (864)
McCarthyism (866)
Army-McCarthy hearings (867)
Jim Crow (867)
Montgomery bus boycott (868)
Brown v. Board of Education of Topeka, Kansas (868)
Student Nonviolent Coordinating Committee (SNCC) (872)
Operation Wetback (873)
Federal Highway Act of 1956 (873)

policy of boldness (874)
Hungarian uprising (874)
Dien Bien Phu, Battle of (875)
Suez crisis (875)
Organization of Petroleum Exporting Countries (OPEC) (876)
Sputnik (877)
kitchen debate (878)
abstract expressionism (880)
International Style (882)
Beat Generation (884)
Southern Renaissance (886)

PEOPLE TO KNOW

Dwight D. ("Ike") Eisenhower
Richard M. Nixon
Betty Friedan
Elvis Presley
Joseph McCarthy
Rosa Parks
Martin Luther King, Jr.
Earl Warren
John Foster Dulles
Nikita Khrushchev
Ho Chi Minh

Gamal Abdel Nasser
Fidel Castro
John F. Kennedy
Lyndon B. Johnson
Jackson Pollock
Andy Warhol
Eero Saarinen
Jack Kerouac
Allen Ginsberg
Arthur Miller
Ralph Ellison

TO LEARN MORE

Glenn Altschuler, *All Shook Up: How Rock 'N' Roll Changed America* (2003)

Stephen Ambrose, *Eisenhower: The President* (1984)

Laura A. Belmonte, *Selling the American Way: U.S. Propaganda and the Cold War* (2010)

James Campbell, *This Is the Beat Generation: New York, San Francisco, Paris* (2001)

Lizabeth Cohen, *A Consumers' Republic: The Politics of Mass Consumption in Postwar America* (2003)

Mary Dudziak, *Cold War Civil Rights* (2000)

John Egerton, *Speak Now Against the Day: The Generation Before the Civil Rights Movement in the South* (1994)

Tom Engelhardt, *The End of Victory Culture* (1995)

Melvyn Leffler, *For the Soul of Mankind: The United States, the Soviet Union, and the Cold War* (2007)

Elaine May, *Homeward Bound: American Families in the Cold War Era* (1988)

David Nichols, *A Matter of Justice: Eisenhower and the Beginning of the Civil Rights Revolution* (2007)

Thomas Sugrue, *The Origins of the Urban Crisis: Race and Inequality in Postwar Detroit* (1996)

Theodore White, *Making of the President, 1960* (1961)

A complete, annotated bibliography for this chapter—along with brief descriptions of the People to Know—may be found on the American Pageant website. The Key Terms are defined in a Glossary at the end of the text.

CHRONOLOGY

1951   Salinger publishes *The Catcher in the Rye*

1952   Eisenhower defeats Stevenson for
            presidency
            Ellison publishes *Invisible Man*
            United Nations headquarters open in New
            York City

1953   CIA-engineered coup installs shah of Iran
            Joseph Stalin dies
            Miller's *The Crucible* debuts on Broadway
            Bellow publishes *The Adventures of Augie
            March*

1954   French defeated at Dien Bien Phu in
            Vietnam
            Army-McCarthy hearings
            Brown v. *Board of Education*
            Nasser becomes prime minister of Egypt
            CIA-sponsored coup in Guatemala

1955   Montgomery bus boycott by blacks begins;
            emergence of Martin Luther King, Jr.
            Geneva summit meeting on Vietnam
            Soviet Union withdraws troops from
            Austria
            Warsaw Pact signed
            AF of L merges with CIO
            Tennessee Williams's *Cat on a Hot Tin Roof*
            first performed

1956   Soviets crush Hungarian revolt
            Suez crisis
            Eisenhower defeats Stevenson for
            presidency
            Ginsberg publishes *Howl and Other Poems*

1957   Little Rock school desegregation crisis
            Civil Rights Act passed
            Southern Christian Leadership Conference
            (SCLC) formed
            Eisenhower Doctrine
            Soviet Union launches Sputnik satellites
            Kerouac publishes *On the Road*

1958   U.S. troops sent to Lebanon
            NDEA authorizes loans and grants for sci-
            ence and language education
            Galbraith publishes *The Affluent Society*

1958–1959   Berlin crisis

1959   Castro seizes power in Cuba
            Landrum-Griffin Act
            Alaska and Hawaii attain statehood
            Guggenheim Museum opens in New York
            City

1960   Sit-in movement for civil rights begins
            U-2 incident sabotages Paris summit
            OPEC formed
            Kennedy defeats Nixon for presidency
            Updike publishes *Rabbit, Run*
            Lee publishes *To Kill a Mockingbird*

1961   Heller publishes *Catch-22*

1962   TWA Flight Center opens in New York

1963   Plath publishes *The Bell Jar*

 CourseMate

Go to the CourseMate website at **www.cengagebrain.com** for additional study tools and review materials—including audio and video clips—for this chapter.

Chapter 38

The Stormy Sixties

1960–1968

Let the word go forth from this time and place, to friend and foe alike, that the torch has been passed to a new generation of Americans.

JOHN F. KENNEDY, INAUGURAL, 1961

Complacent and comfortable as the 1950s closed, Americans elected in 1960 a young, vigorous president who pledged "to get the country moving again." Neither the nation nor the new president had any inkling as the new decade opened just how action-packed it would be, both at home and abroad. The 1960s would bring a sexual revolution, a civil rights revolution, the emergence of a "youth culture," a devastating war in Vietnam, and the beginnings, at least, of a feminist revolution. By the end of the stormy sixties, many Americans would yearn nostalgically for the comparative calm of the fifties.

✴ Kennedy's "New Frontier" Spirit

Hatless and topcoatless in the twenty-two-degree chill, John F. Kennedy delivered a stirring inaugural address on January 20, 1961. Tall, elegantly handsome, speaking crisply and with staccato finger jabs at the air, Kennedy personified the glamour and vitality of the new administration. The youngest president ever elected, he assembled one of the youngest cabinets, including his thirty-five-year-old brother, Robert F. Kennedy, as attorney general. "Bobby," the president quipped, would find "some legal experience" useful when he began to practice law. The new attorney general set out, among other reforms, to recast the priorities of the FBI. The bureau deployed nearly a thousand agents on "internal security" work but targeted only a dozen against organized crime and gave virtually no attention to civil rights violations. Robert Kennedy's efforts were stoutly resisted by J. Edgar Hoover, who had served as

FBI director longer than the new attorney general had been alive. Business whiz Robert S. McNamara left the presidency of the Ford Motor Company to take over the Defense Department. Along with other youthful, talented advisers, these appointees made up an inner circle of "the best and the brightest" men around the president.

From the outset Kennedy inspired high expectations, especially among the young. His challenge of a **New Frontier** quickened patriotic pulses. He brought a warm heart to the Cold War when he proposed the **Peace Corps**, an army of idealistic and mostly youthful volunteers to bring American skills to underdeveloped countries. He summoned citizens to service with his clarion call to "ask not what your country can do for you: ask what you can do for your country."

Himself Harvard-educated, Kennedy and his Ivy League lieutenants (heavily from Harvard) radiated confidence in their abilities. The president's personal grace and wit won him the deep affection of many of his fellow citizens. A journalist called Kennedy "the most seductive man I've ever met. He exuded a sense of vibrant life and humor that seemed naturally to bubble

Richard Goodwin (b. 1931), a young Peace Corps staffer, eloquently summed up the buoyantly optimistic mood of the early 1960s:

❝For a moment, it seemed as if the entire country, the whole spinning globe, rested, malleable and receptive, in our beneficent hands.❞

President John F. Kennedy and His Wife, Jacqueline Bouvier Kennedy Shown here leaving the White House to attend a series of inaugural balls in January 1961, the young and vibrant first couple brought beauty, style, and grace to the presidency.

© Bettmann/Corbis

up out of him." In an unprecedented gesture, he invited white-maned poet Robert Frost to speak at his inaugural ceremonies. The old Yankee versifier shrewdly took stock of the situation. "You're something of Irish and I suppose something of Harvard," he told Kennedy—and advised him to be more Irish than Harvard.

The New Frontier at Home

Kennedy came into office with fragile Democratic majorities in Congress. Southern Democrats threatened to team up with Republicans and ax New Frontier proposals such as medical assistance for the aged and increased federal aid to education. Kennedy won a first round in his campaign for a more cooperative Congress when he forced an expansion of the all-important House Rules Committee, dominated by conservatives who could have bottled up his entire legislative program. Despite this victory, the New Frontier did not expand swiftly. Key medical and education bills remained stalled in Congress.

Another vexing problem was the economy. Kennedy had campaigned on the theme of revitalizing the economy after the recessions of the Eisenhower years. His administration helped negotiate a noninflationary wage agreement in the steel industry in early 1962. The assumption was that the companies, for their part, would keep the lid on prices. But almost immediately steel management announced significant price increases, thereby seemingly demonstrating bad faith. The president erupted in wrath. "My father always told me that all businessmen were sons of bitches," he said, "but I never believed him till now." He called the "big steel" men onto the Oval Office carpet and unleashed his Irish temper. Overawed, the steel operators backed down.

The steel episode provoked fiery attacks by big business on the New Frontier, but Kennedy soon appealed to believers in free enterprise when he announced his support of a general tax-cut bill. He rejected the advice of those who wished greater government spending and instead chose to stimulate the economy by slashing taxes and putting more money directly into private hands. When he announced his policy before a big business group, one observer called it "the most Republican speech since McKinley."

Kennedy's New Frontier vision also extended to the "final frontier." Early in his term, the president promoted a multibillion-dollar project dedicated, as he put it, to "landing a man on the Moon and returning him safely to earth." When skeptics objected that the money could be better spent elsewhere, Kennedy summoned stirring rhetoric of rising to challenges and expanding human possibilities. In reality, the moon shot was a calculated plan to restore America's prestige in the space race, severely damaged by the Soviet Sputnik successes (see p. 877). Twenty-four billion dollars later, in July 1969, two NASA astronauts triumphantly planted their footprints—and the American flag—on

NASA

NASA

On the Moon   This moon's-eye view of the earth greeted the first men to land on the lunar surface. (right) Astronaut Edwin ("Buzz") Aldrin descends from the spacecraft. As he stepped onto the moon's surface, his companion, Neil Armstrong, said, "That's one small step for man; one giant leap for mankind."

the moon's dusty surface. As people around the globe huddled around televisions to watch the **Apollo** mission live, the world had never seemed so small and interconnected, nor the United States so dominant.

✦ Rumblings in Europe

A few months after settling into the White House, the new president met Soviet premier Khrushchev at Vienna in June 1961. The tough-talking Soviet leader adopted a belligerent attitude, threatening to make a treaty with East Germany and cut off Western access to Berlin. Though visibly shaken, the president refused to be bullied.

The Soviets backed off from their most bellicose threats but suddenly began to construct the **Berlin Wall** in August 1961. A barbed-wire and concrete barrier, it was designed to plug the heavy population drain from East Germany to West Germany through the Berlin funnel. But to the free world, the "Wall of Shame" looked like a gigantic enclosure around a concentration camp. The wall stood for almost three decades as an ugly scar symbolizing the post–World War II division of Europe into two hostile camps.

Kennedy meanwhile turned his attention to Western Europe, now miraculously prospering after the tonic of Marshall Plan aid and the growth of the American-encouraged **European Economic Community (EEC)**, the free-trade area that later evolved into the European Union. He finally secured passage of the Trade Expansion Act in 1962, authorizing tariff cuts of up to 50 percent to promote trade with EEC countries. This act led to the so-called Kennedy Round of tariff negotiations, concluded in 1967, and to a significant expansion of European-American trade. These liberalized trade policies inaugurated a new era of such robustly invigorated international commerce that a new word was coined to describe it: *globalization*.

But not all of Kennedy's ambitious designs for Europe were realized. American policymakers were dedicated to an economically and militarily united "Atlantic Community," with the United States the dominant partner. But they found their way blocked by towering, stiff-backed Charles de Gaulle, president of France. With a haughty "*non*," de Gaulle vetoed the British application for Common Market membership in 1963, fearing that the British "special relationship" with the United States would make Britain a Trojan horse for deepening American control over European

The Berlin Wall, 1961–1989 The wall separating East and West Berlin stood for nearly thirty years as a hated symbol of the division of Europe into democratic and communist camps. (left) East German soldiers stand guard as the concrete wall is constructed, November 20, 1961. (right) Demonstrators celebrating the impending reunification of East and West Germany begin to tear down the wall in 1989.

affairs. De Gaulle deemed the Americans unreliable in a crisis, so he tried to preserve French freedom of action by developing his own small atomic force. Despite the perils of nuclear proliferation or Soviet domination, de Gaulle demanded an independent Europe, free of Yankee influence.

✷ Foreign Flare-ups and "Flexible Response"

Special problems for U.S. foreign policy emerged from the worldwide decolonization of European overseas possessions after World War II. Sparsely populated Laos, freed of its French colonial overlords in 1954, was festering dangerously by the time Kennedy came into office. The Eisenhower administration had drenched this jungle kingdom with dollars but failed to cleanse the country of an aggressive communist element. A red Laos, many observers feared, would be a river on which

the influence of Communist China would flood into all of Southeast Asia.

As the Laotian civil war raged, Kennedy's military advisers seriously considered sending in American troops. But the president found that he had insufficient forces to put out the fire in Asia and still honor his commitments in Europe. Kennedy thus sought a diplomatic escape hatch in the fourteen-power Geneva conference, which imposed a shaky peace on Laos in 1962.

These "brushfire wars" intensified the pressure for a shift away from Secretary Dulles's dubious doctrine of "massive retaliation." Kennedy felt hamstrung by the knowledge that in a crisis, he had the Devil's choice between humiliation and nuclear incineration. With Defense Secretary McNamara, he pushed the strategy of "flexible response"—that is, developing an array of military "options" that could be precisely matched to the gravity of the crisis at hand. To this end Kennedy increased spending on conventional military forces and bolstered the Special Forces (Green Berets). They were an elite antiguerrilla outfit trained to survive on snake meat and to kill with scientific finesse.

✴ Stepping into the Vietnam Quagmire

The doctrine of "flexible response" seemed sane enough, but it contained lethal logic. It potentially lowered the level at which diplomacy would give way to shooting. It also provided a mechanism for a progressive, and possibly endless, stepping-up of the use of force. Vietnam soon presented grisly proof of these pitfalls.

The corrupt, right-wing government of Ngo Dinh Diem in Saigon, despite a deluge of American dollars, had ruled shakily since the partition of Vietnam in 1954 (see p. 875). Anti-Diem agitators noisily threatened to topple the pro-American government from power. In a fateful decision late in 1961, Kennedy ordered a sharp increase in the number of "military advisers" (U.S. troops) in South Vietnam.

American forces allegedly entered Vietnam to foster political stability—to help protect Diem from the communists long enough to allow him to enact basic social reforms favored by the Americans. But the Kennedy administration eventually despaired of the reactionary Diem and encouraged a successful coup against him in November 1963. Ironically, the United States thus contributed to a long process of political disintegration that its original policy had meant to prevent. Kennedy still told the South Vietnamese that it was "their war," but he had made dangerously deep political commitments. By the time of his death, he had ordered more than fifteen thousand American men into the far-off Asian slaughter pen. A graceful pullout was becoming increasingly difficult (see Map 38.1).

"Modernization theory" provided the theoretical underpinnings for an activist U.S. foreign policy in the "underdeveloped" world. Its proponents believed that the traditional societies of Asia, Africa, and Latin America could develop into modern industrial and democratic nations by following the West's own path. Noted economic historian Walt Whitman Rostow, one of the most influential modernization theorists, charted the route from traditional society to "the age of high mass-consumption" in his book *The Stages of Economic Growth* (1960). Though it would later come under attack for its Eurocentric bias, modernization theory offered a powerful intellectual framework for policymakers ensnared in the Cold War. Rostow himself served as an influential adviser to the Kennedy and Johnson administrations.

✴ Cuban Confrontations

Although the United States regarded Latin America as its backyard, its southern neighbors feared and resented the powerful Colossus of the North. In 1961 Kennedy extended the hand of friendship with the Alliance for Progress (*Alianza para el Progreso*), hailed as a Marshall Plan for Latin America. A primary goal was to help the Good Neighbors close the gap between the callous rich and the wretched poor, and thus quiet communist agitation. But results were disappointing; there was little alliance and even less progress. American handouts had little positive impact on Latin America's immense social problems.

President Kennedy also struck below the border with the mailed fist. He had inherited from the Eisenhower administration a CIA-backed scheme to topple Fidel Castro from power by invading Cuba with anticommunist exiles. On April 17, 1961, some twelve hundred exiles landed at Cuba's Bay of Pigs. When the ill-starred **Bay of Pigs invasion** bogged down, Kennedy stood fast in his decision to keep hands off, and the bullet-riddled band of anti-Castroites surrendered. President Kennedy assumed full responsibility for the

Backbone The United States supports South Vietnam.
Wil-Jo Associates

MAP 38.1 Vietnam and Southeast Asia, 1954–1975   Le Ly Hayslip (b. 1949) was born in a peasant village in South Vietnam, just south of Da Nang. In her memoir, *When Heaven and Earth Changed Places*, she describes the trauma endured by ordinary Vietnamese as a result of America's fight against the Viet Cong: "In 1963—the year the Viet Cong came to my village—American warplanes bombed Man Quang. It was at noon, just when the children were getting out of school. My aunt Thu and her pregnant daughter-in-law were making lunch for her husband and four grandchildren when the air-raid signal blared. They all jumped under the wooden table and sheltered the pregnant woman with their bodies—even the little kids. A bomb fell in Aunt Thu's front yard. . . . Hot shrapnel tore through everyone except the pregnant woman. Aunt Thu and one of her grandchildren were killed. The passing fragment left only a weeping hole where her generous heart had been." © Cengage Learning

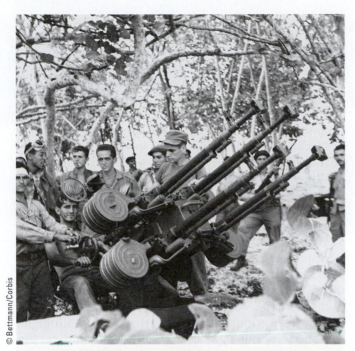

© Bettmann/Corbis

Failed Bay of Pigs Invasion, 1961 Cuban soldiers demonstrate a beach gun they used against a brigade of ex-Cubans who furtively invaded Cuba as agents of the United States. The debacle was one of several unsuccessful American attempts to overthrow Cuban leader Fidel Castro.

For an anxious week, Americans waited while Soviet ships approached the patrol line established by the U.S. Navy off the island of Cuba. Seizing or sinking a Soviet vessel on the high seas would unquestionably be regarded by the Kremlin as an act of war. The world teetered breathlessly on the brink of global atomization. Only in 1991 did the full dimensions of this nuclear peril become known, when the Russians revealed that their ground forces in Cuba already had operational nuclear weapons at their disposal and were authorized to launch them if attacked.

In this tense eyeball-to-eyeball confrontation, Khrushchev finally flinched. On October 28 he agreed to a partially face-saving compromise, by which he would pull the missiles out of Cuba. The United States in return agreed to end the quarantine and not invade the island. The American government also quietly signaled that it would remove from Turkey some of its own missiles targeted at the Soviet Union.

Fallout from the **Cuban missile crisis** was considerable. A disgraced Khrushchev was ultimately hounded out of the Kremlin and became an "unperson." Hardliners in Moscow, vowing never again to be humiliated in a nuclear face-off, launched an enormous program of military expansion. The Soviet buildup reached a crescendo in the next decade, stimulating, in turn, a vast American effort to "catch up with the Russians." The Democrats did better than expected in the midterm elections of November 1962—allegedly because the Republicans were "Cubanized." Kennedy, apparently sobered by the appalling risks he had just run, pushed harder for a nuclear test-ban treaty with the Soviet Union. After prolonged negotiations in Moscow, a pact prohibiting trial nuclear explosions in the atmosphere was signed in late 1963. Another barometer indicating a thaw in the Cold War was the installation (August 1963) of a Moscow-Washington "hot line," permitting immediate teletype communication in case of a crisis.

Most significant was Kennedy's speech at American University in Washington, D.C., in June 1963. The president urged Americans to abandon a view of the Soviet Union as a Devil-ridden land filled with fanatics and instead to deal with the world "as it is, not as it might have been had the history of the last eighteen years been different." Kennedy thus tried to lay the foundation for a realistic policy of peaceful coexistence with the Soviet Union. Here were the modest origins of the policy that later came to be known as "détente" (French for "relaxation of tension").

failure, remarking that "victory has a hundred fathers, and defeat is an orphan."

The Bay of Pigs blunder, along with continuing American covert efforts to assassinate Castro and overthrow his government, naturally pushed the Cuban leader even further into the Soviet embrace. Wily Chairman Khrushchev lost little time in taking full advantage of his Cuban comrade's position just ninety miles off Florida's coast. In October 1962 the aerial photographs of American spy planes revealed that the Soviets were secretly and speedily installing nuclear-tipped missiles in Cuba. The Soviets evidently intended to use these devastating weapons to shield Castro and to blackmail the United States into backing down in Berlin and other trouble spots.

Kennedy and Khrushchev now began a nerve-racking game of "nuclear chicken." The president flatly rejected air force proposals for a "surgical" bombing strike against the missile-launching sites. Instead, on October 22, 1962, he ordered a naval "quarantine" of Cuba and demanded immediate removal of the threatening weaponry. He also served notice on Khrushchev that any attack on the United States from Cuba would be regarded as coming from the Soviet Union and would trigger nuclear retaliation against the Russian heartland.

★ The Struggle for Civil Rights

Kennedy had campaigned with a strong appeal to black voters, but he proceeded gingerly to redeem his promises. Although he had pledged to eliminate racial discrimination in housing "with a stroke of the pen," it took him nearly two years to find the right pen. Civil rights groups meanwhile sent thousands of pens to the White House in an "Ink for Jack" protest against the president's slowness.

Political concerns stayed the president's hand on civil rights. Elected by a wafer-thin margin, and with shaky control over Congress, Kennedy needed the support of southern legislators to pass his economic and social legislation, especially his medical and educational bills. He believed, perhaps justifiably, that those measures would eventually benefit black Americans at least as much as specific legislation on civil rights. Bold moves for racial justice would have to wait.

But events soon scrambled these careful calculations. After the wave of sit-ins that surged across the South in 1960, groups of **Freedom Riders** fanned out to end segregation in facilities serving interstate bus passengers. A white mob torched a Freedom Ride bus near Anniston, Alabama, in May 1961, and Attorney General Robert Kennedy's personal representative was beaten unconscious in another anti–Freedom Ride riot in Montgomery. When southern officials proved unwilling or unable to stem the violence, Washington dispatched federal marshals to protect the Freedom Riders.

Reluctantly but fatefully, the Kennedy administration had now joined hands with the civil rights movement. Because of that partnership, the Kennedys proved ultrawary about the political associates of Martin Luther King, Jr. Fearful of embarrassing revelations that some of King's advisers had communist affiliations, Robert Kennedy ordered FBI director J. Edgar Hoover

to wiretap King's phone in late 1963. But for the most part, the relationship between King and the Kennedys was a fruitful one. Encouraged by Robert Kennedy, and with financial backing from Kennedy-prodded private foundations, SNCC and other civil rights groups inaugurated the **Voter Education Project** to register the South's historically disfranchised blacks. Because of his support for civil rights, President Kennedy told a group of black leaders in 1963, "I may lose the next election . . . I don't care."

Integrating southern universities threatened to provoke wholesale slaughter. Some desegregated painlessly, but the University of Mississippi ("Ole Miss") became a volcano. A twenty-nine-year-old air force veteran, James Meredith, encountered violent opposition when he attempted to register in October 1962. In the end President Kennedy was forced to send in four hundred federal marshals and three thousand troops to enroll Meredith in his first class—in colonial American history.

In the spring of 1963, Martin Luther King, Jr., launched a campaign against discrimination in Birmingham, Alabama, the most segregated big city in America. Although blacks constituted nearly half of the city's population, they made up fewer than 15 percent of the city's voters. Previous attempts to crack the city's rigid racial barriers had produced more than fifty cross burnings and eighteen bomb attacks since 1957. "Some of the people sitting here will not come back alive from this campaign," King advised his organizers. Events soon confirmed this grim prediction of violence. Watching developments on television screens, a horrified world saw peaceful civil rights marchers repeatedly repelled by police with attack dogs and electric cattle

Freedom Ride, 1961   Rampaging whites near Anniston, Alabama, burned this bus carrying an interracial group of Freedom Riders on May 14, 1961.

© Bettmann/Corbis

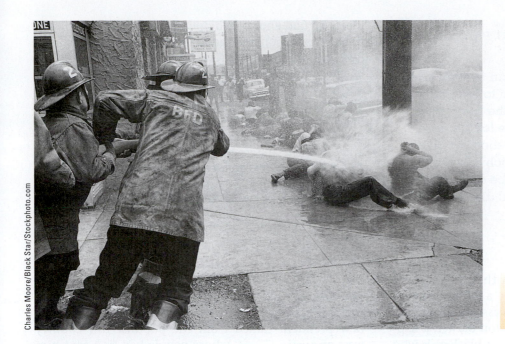

Charles Moore/Black Star/Stockphoto.com

prods. Most fearsome of all were the high-pressure water hoses directed at the civil rights demonstrators. They delivered water with enough force to knock bricks loose from buildings or strip bark from trees at a distance of one hundred feet. Water from the hoses bowled little children down the street like tumbleweeds.

Jolted by these vicious confrontations, President Kennedy delivered a memorable televised speech to the nation on June 11, 1963. In contrast to Eisenhower's cool aloofness from the racial question, Kennedy called the situation a "moral issue" and committed his personal and presidential prestige to finding a solution.

Drawing on the same spiritual traditions as Martin Luther King, Jr., Kennedy declared that the principle at stake "is as old as the Scriptures and is as clear as the American Constitution." He called for new civil rights legislation to protect black citizens. In August King led more than 200,000 black and white demonstrators on a peaceful **March on Washington** in support of the proposed legislation. In an electrifying speech from the Lincoln Memorial, King declared, "I have a dream that my four little children will one day live in a nation where they will not be judged by the color of their skin, but by the content of their character."

© Bettmann/Corbis

Martin Luther King, Jr., Addresses the March on Washington, August 1963 This was the occasion of King's famous "I Have a Dream" speech, in which he declared, "When the architects of our great republic wrote the magnificent words of the Constitution and the Declaration of Independence, they were signing a promissory note to which every American was to fall heir. This note was a promise that all men, yes, black men as well as white men, would be guaranteed the inalienable rights of life, liberty, and the pursuit of happiness."

In his civil rights address of June 11, 1963, President John F. Kennedy (1917–1963) said,

"If an American, because his skin is dark, cannot eat lunch in a restaurant open to the public; if he cannot send his children to the best public school available; if he cannot vote for the public officials who represent him; if, in short, he cannot enjoy the full and free life which all of us want, then who among us would be content to have the color of his skin changed and stand in his place?"

Still the violence continued. On the very night of Kennedy's stirring television address, a white gunman shot down Medgar Evers, a black Mississippi civil rights worker. In September 1963 an explosion blasted a Baptist church in Birmingham, killing four black girls who had just finished their lesson called "The Love That Forgives." By the time of Kennedy's death, his civil rights bill was making little headway, and frustrated blacks were growing increasingly impatient.

✯ The Killing of Kennedy

Violence haunted America in the mid-1960s, and it stalked onto center stage on November 22, 1963. While riding in an open limousine in downtown Dallas, Texas, President Kennedy was shot in the brain by a concealed rifleman and died within seconds. As a stunned nation grieved, the tragedy grew still more unbelievable. The alleged assassin, a furtive figure named Lee Harvey Oswald, was himself shot to death in front of television cameras by a self-appointed avenger, Jack Ruby. So bizarre were the events surrounding the two murders that even an elaborate official investigation conducted by Chief Justice Warren could not quiet all doubts and theories about what had really happened.

Vice President Johnson was promptly sworn in as president on a waiting airplane and flown back to Washington with Kennedy's body. Although he mistrusted "the Harvards," Johnson retained most of the bright Kennedy team. The new president managed a dignified and efficient transition, pledging continuity with his slain predecessor's policies.

For several days the nation was steeped in sorrow. Not until then did many Americans realize how fully their young, vibrant president and his captivating wife had cast a spell over them. Chopped down in his prime after only slightly more than a thousand days in the White House, Kennedy was acclaimed more for the ideals he had enunciated and the spirit he had kindled than for the concrete goals he had achieved. He had laid one myth to rest forever—that a Catholic could not be trusted with the presidency of the United States.

In later years revelations about Kennedy's womanizing and allegations about his involvement with organized crime figures tarnished his reputation. But despite those accusations, his apparent vigor, charisma, and idealism made him an inspirational figure for the generation of Americans who came of age in the 1960s—including Bill Clinton, who as a boy had briefly met President Kennedy and would himself be elected president in 1992.

✯ The LBJ Brand on the Presidency

The torch passed to craggy-faced Lyndon Baines Johnson, a Texan who towered six feet three inches. The new president hailed from the populist hill country west of Austin, Texas, whose people had first sent him to Washington as a twenty-nine-year-old congressman in 1937. Franklin D. Roosevelt was his political "Daddy," Johnson claimed, and he had supported New Deal measures down the line. But when LBJ lost a Senate race in 1941, he learned the sobering lesson that liberal political beliefs did not necessarily win elections in Texas. He trimmed his sails to the right and squeezed himself into a Senate seat in 1948 with a questionable eighty-seven-vote margin—hence the ironic nickname "Landslide Lyndon."

Entrenched in the Senate, Johnson developed into a masterful wheeler-dealer. He became the Democratic majority leader in 1954, wielding power second only to that of Eisenhower in the White House. He could move mountains or checkmate opponents as the occasion demanded, using what came to be known as the "Johnson treatment"—a flashing display of backslapping, flesh-pressing, and arm-twisting that overbore friend and foe alike. His ego and vanity were legendary. On a visit to the Pope, Johnson was presented with a precious fourteenth-century painting from the Vatican art collection; in return, LBJ gave the Pope a bust—of LBJ!

As president, Johnson quickly shed the conservative coloration of his Senate years to reveal the latent liberal underneath. "No memorial oration or eulogy," Johnson declared to Congress, "could more eloquently honor President Kennedy's memory than the earliest possible passage of the Civil Rights Bill for which he fought so long." After a lengthy conservative filibuster, Congress at last passed the landmark **Civil Rights Act of 1964**. The act banned racial discrimination in most private facilities open to the public, including theaters, hospitals, and restaurants. It strengthened the federal government's power to end segregation in

Examining the Evidence

Conflicting Press Accounts of the March on Washington, 1963

200,000 Join Orderly March in Capital for Civil Rights; Kennedy Sees Negro Gain

LEADERS OF RALLY URGE ACTION 'NOW'

Ask Laws Against Inequity —Picnic Air Prevails as Crowds Clap and Sing

Continued From Page 1, Col. 8

would speed the legislation, which faces a filibuster by Southerners.

Senator Everett McKinley Dirksen of Illinois, the Republican leader, said he thought the demonstration would be neither an advantage nor a disadvantage to the prospects for the civil rights bill.

The human tide that swept over the Mall between the shrines of Washington and Lincoln fell back faster than it came on. As soon as the ceremony broke up this afternoon, the exodus began. With astounding speed, the last buses and trains cleared the city by mid-evening.

At 9 P.M. the city was as calm as the waters of the Reflecting Pool between the two memorials.

At the Lincoln Memorial early in the afternoon, in the midst of a songfest before the addresses, Josephine Baker, the singer, who had flown from her home in Paris, said to the thousands stretching down both sides of the Reflecting Pool:

"You are on the eve of a complete victory. You can't go wrong. The world is behind

LEADERS MEET WITH KENNEDY: From left Whitney M. Young Jr., of National Urban League; the Rev. Dr. Martin Luther King Jr., Southern Christian Leadership Conference; John Lewis, partly hidden, Student Nonviolent Coordinating Committee; Rabbi Joachim Prinz, American Jewish Congress; the Rev. Dr. Eugene Carson Blake, United Presbyterian Church in U.S.A.; A. Philip Randolph, Negro American Labor President; Walter P. Reuther, the United Automobile Workers President Johnson, almost hidden, and Roy Wilkins, N.A... Kennedy and Mr. Johnson met with leaders of the civil at the White House after the ceremonies at the Lincoln...

President Meets March Chiefs; Urges Bipartisan Aid on Rights

Continued From Page 1, Col. 7

canapes and sandwiches by Filipino mess boys.

Several of the march leaders had not eaten during a long, exhausting day.

The leaders, a mixed Negro and white group for whom A. Philip Randolph served as spokesman, made it plain in a news conference after their meeting with the President that they were exhilarated and encouraged by the day's events.

Mr. Randolph, president of the Brotherhood of Sleeping Car Porters, called the march "one of the biggest, most creative and constructive demonstrations ever held in the history of our nation" and one of which "every American could be proud."

"We have witnessed today in Washington tens of thousands of Americans—both Negro and white —exercising their right to assemble peacefully and direct the widest possible attention to a great national issue," Kennedy said.

He added, "The gains of 1963 will never be reversed" in the field of Negro rights.

march," He said he hoped there need be no more all-Negro protest marches or demonstrations.

Mr. Randolph said the march also demonstrated "unity among leadership of the Negroes." But at the White House news conference there was what appeared to be some subtle jockeying for position among them.

Mr. Blake referred, for instance, to Dr. King as "clearly the religious leader of this demonstration."

Randolph Lauds Wilkins

Almost immediately, Mr. Randolph introduced Mr. Wilkins as "the acknowledged leader of the civil rights movement in America."

When it came time to introduce Dr. King, Mr. Randolph termed him "the moral leader...

March a Big Boost for Bill, Kennedy Tells 10 Leaders

Continued From Page 1

ministration "will continue its efforts to obtain increased employment and to eliminate discrimination in employment practices," two of the prime goals of the march.

The statement did not say specifically whether the President intends to alter his program by writing in a specific Fair Employment Practice Commission section which they demanded.

JUBILANT AT PEACE

The Negro leadership obviously was jubilant over the fact that no outbreak occurred at the program. "Today we had a peaceful demonstration, an orderly demonstration," said march leader A. Philip Randolph.

"An historic occasion was written today that will have its lasting effect on history," Randolph added.

The Rev. Martin Luther King Jr., called by Randolph, "the moral leader of our nation," said it was "one of the greatest days of America . . . it was one of the greatest — if not the greatest — march of all times."

That summation came following a full day of activity that began at 8 a.m. (Atlanta time) on Capitol Hill in a series of meetings with congressional leaders.

First the civil rights leaders walked into Senate majority leader Mike Mansfield's office about 10 minutes early, and emerged saying they had stressed the need for a Fair Employment Practices Act.

Mansfield said, however, that no promises were asked and none given during the 40-minute session.

The crucial visit—to Republican leaders Everett Dirksen and Charles Halleck in Dirksen's office—was a bit more brief.

DIRKSEN UNYIELDING

Wilkins said Dirksen told them he had not changed his mind about Title II of the President's bill, the public accommodations section. He opposes it. Dirksen added he supports the rest of the President's civil rights bill, Wilkins said.

As for Halleck, whose control of Republican House votes could make or break the bill, he was "very friendly" on civil rights, Wilkins said.

Again, however, there were no specific promises about either House or Senate passage, the Negro leaders said. Without sizable Republican support, the administration cannot override Southern Democratic objections.

ASSURED BY McCORMICK

On to House Speaker John McCormick's office went the marchers for a 50-minute session where

"he assured us that if FEPC and Title 3 [allowing the Justice department to institute civil rights suits] are put into the package, these two measures will get through the house."

Randolph, president of the AFL-CIO Brotherhood of Sleeping Car Porters and originator of the march, added that the meeting with McCormick was "very encouraging to the committee."

Randolph made his brief comment to newsmen on the House steps and then joined the other march leaders in a limousine parade back to the Washington Monument to lead the walk to the Lincoln Memorial.

PREDICTS PASSAGE

Inside the Capitol, McCormick admitted reporters and predicted "a bill will pass," although he did not know whether the controversial FEPC and public accommodations sections would be passed.

McCormick said United Auto Workers Union president Walter Reuther brought up a possible increase in the minimum wage from $1.25 to $2.

Asked whether the giant march would hurt or help in seeking passage of the civil rights bill, McCormick replied, "I think if the demonstration is done in an orderly way it will be helpful. They've got a serious task today" keeping the march orderly and peaceful.

SKIRT CAPITOL AREA

Somewhat to everyone's surprise, the marchers generally stayed away from the Capitol area. Most congressmen said they had not been approached for appointments, and the corridors were generally bare. Many Capitol workers took off for the day.

But precautions had been taken anyway. There was such a force

of uniformed officers on hand to cope with any possible trouble that one senator was prompted to comment: "It almost looks like we had a military coup d'etat during the night."

It was almost certain, however, that there would be post mortems for weeks of what effect the march had on Congress.

10-DAY RECESS

There will be plenty of time for assessment and reassessment of the march, since Congress has decided to take a 10-day Labor Day recess.

Rep. Emanuel Celler, D-NY, chairman of the House Judiciary Committee, said he had hoped to begin committee action on the bill this week but that it must be postponed until after the recess.

Celler joined McCormick in predicting passage of some sort of FEPC law—the one thing that most speakers at the giant rally stressed most.

Dr. King Names Ex-Red Cross Official as Aide

A former official of the American Red Cross has been appointed special assistant to Dr. Martin Luther King Jr., president of the Southern Christian Leadership Conference.

SCLC announced the appointment of Harry G. Boyte, 52, of Atlanta, who served 17 years with the Red Cross.

Boyte was born in Charlotte, N.C. He joined the Red Cross in 1942 and subsequently became administrative assistant chief of personnel.

Atlanta Constitution (vertical text, left side of right columns)

*T*he day after the March on Washington of August 28, 1963 (see p. 897), newspapers all over the country carried reports of this historic assembly of more than 200,000 people to demand civil rights and equal job opportunities for African Americans. Although the basic outlines of the story were the same in most papers, ancillary articles, photographs, and editorials revealed deep-seated biases in coverage. Shown here are continuations from the front-page stories in the *New York Times*, a bastion of northeastern liberalism (above), and the *Atlanta Constitution*, a major southern newspaper (right). While the *Times* called the march "orderly" in its headline, the *Constitution*'s story in its right columns highlighted the potential for violence and the precautions taken by police. The article read: "There was such a force of uniformed officers on hand to cope with any possible trouble that one senator was prompted to comment: 'It almost looks like we had a military coup d'état during the night.'" In addition to stressing the march's potential for disruption, the *Constitution* ran an advertisement right below the March on Washington story for a National Ku Klux Klan Rally two days hence, featuring prominent speakers and a cross burning. This comparison of newspaper coverage of a controversial event serves as a reminder that press reporting must always be scrutinized for biases when it is used as historical evidence. What other differences in coverage separated these two newspapers? What factors contribute to press biases?

(top) *New York Times;* **(above)** *Atlanta Constitution* schools and other public places. Title VII of the act barred employers from discriminating based on race or national origin in hiring and empowered the Equal Employment Opportunity Commission (EEOC, a body Kennedy had created in 1961) to enforce the law. When conservatives tried to derail the legislation by adding a prohibition on sexual, as well as racial, discrimination, the tactic backfired. The bill's opponents cynically calculated that liberals would not be able to support a bill that threatened to wipe out laws that singled out women for special protection because of their sex. But the act's Title VII passed with the sexual clause intact. It soon proved to be a powerful instrument of federally enforced gender equality, as well as racial equality. Johnson struck another blow for women and minorities in 1965 when he issued an executive order requiring all federal contractors to take **affirmative action** against discrimination.

Johnson also rammed Kennedy's stalled tax bill through Congress and added proposals of his own for a billion-dollar "War on Poverty." Johnson voiced special concern for Appalachia, where the sickness of the soft-coal industry had left tens of thousands of mountain folk on the human slag heap.

Johnson dubbed his domestic program the **Great Society**—a sweeping set of New Dealish economic and welfare measures aimed at transforming the American way of life. Public support for LBJ's antipoverty war was aroused by Michael Harrington's *The Other America* (1962), which revealed that in affluent America 20 percent of the population—and over 40 percent of the black population—suffered in poverty.

✵ Johnson Battles Goldwater in 1964

Johnson's nomination by the Democrats in 1964 was a foregone conclusion; he was chosen by acclamation in Atlantic City as his birthday present. Thanks to the tall Texan, the Democrats stood foursquare on their most liberal platform since Truman's Fair Deal days. The Republicans, convening in San Francisco's Cow Palace, nominated box-jawed Senator Barry Goldwater of Arizona, a bronzed and bespectacled champion of rock-ribbed conservatism. The American stage was thus set for a historic clash of political principles.

Goldwater's forces had galloped out of the Southwest to ride roughshod over the moderate Republican "eastern establishment." Insisting that the GOP offer "a choice not an echo," Goldwater attacked the federal income tax, the Social Security system, the Tennessee Valley Authority, civil rights legislation, the nuclear test-ban treaty, and, most loudly, the Great Society. His fiercely dedicated followers proclaimed, "In Your Heart You Know He's Right," which prompted the Democratic

Lyndon B. Johnson Presidential Library/Picture Research Consultants & Archives

Negative Campaigning This infamous "attack ad" was televised only once as a paid political advertisement, but it signaled the emergence of a newly noxious style of political campaigning. The ad showed a child dreamily pulling petals from a flower. Suddenly her voice gave way to that of a man reciting an ominous countdown, followed by an exploding nuclear bomb and a throaty voice warning "Vote for President Johnson on November 3. The stakes are too high for you to stay home." The ad implied that a Goldwater presidency would risk nuclear Armageddon. Controversy forced the ad's sponsors to take it off the air, but it was repeatedly reshown in news coverage of the controversy itself—raising serious questions about the very definition of "news."

1964

Candidate (Party)	Electoral Vote		Popular Vote	
■ Johnson (Democrat)	486	90.3%	43,129,566	61.1%
■ Goldwater (Republican)	52	9.7%	27,178,188	38.5%

MAP 38.2 Presidential Election of 1964 In the map on the left the size of each state is distorted according to its weight in the Electoral College. In New Orleans, toward the end of the campaign, a gutsy Johnson displayed his commitment to civil rights when he told a story about an old senator who once said of his Deep South constituents, "I would like to go back down there and make them just one more Democratic speech. . . . The poor old State, they haven't heard a Democratic speech in 30 years. All they hear at election time is Negro, Negro, Negro!" Johnson's open voicing of sentiments like this contributed heavily to his losses in the traditionally Democratic "solid South." © Cengage Learning

response, "In Your Guts You Know He's Nuts." Goldwater warmed right-wing hearts when he proclaimed that "extremism in the defense of liberty is no vice. And . . . moderation in the pursuit of justice is no virtue."

Democrats gleefully exploited the image of Goldwater as a trigger-happy cowboy who would "Barry us" in the debris of World War III. Johnson cultivated the contrasting image of a resolute statesman by seizing upon the Tonkin Gulf episode early in August 1964. Unbeknownst to the American public or Congress, U.S. Navy ships had been cooperating with South Vietnamese gunboats in provocative raids along the coast of North Vietnam. Two of these American destroyers were allegedly fired upon by the North Vietnamese on August 2 and 4, although exactly what happened still remains unclear. Later investigations strongly suggested that the North Vietnamese fired in self-defense on August 2 and that the "attack" of August 4 never happened. Johnson later reportedly wisecracked, "For all I know, the Navy was shooting at whales out there."

Johnson nevertheless promptly called the attack "unprovoked" and moved swiftly to make political hay out of this episode. He ordered a "limited" retaliatory air raid against the North Vietnamese bases, loudly proclaiming that he sought "no wider war"—thus implying that the truculent Goldwater did. Johnson also used the incident to spur congressional passage of the all-purpose Tonkin Gulf Resolution. With only two dissenting votes in both houses, the lawmakers virtually abdicated their war-declaring powers and handed the president a blank check to use further force in Southeast Asia. The Tonkin Gulf Resolution, Johnson boasted, was "like grandma's nightshirt—it covered everything."

The towering Texan rode to a spectacular victory in November 1964. The voters were herded into Johnson's column by fondness for the Kennedy legacy, faith in Great Society promises, and fear of Goldwater. A stampede of 43,129,566 Johnson votes trampled the Republican ticket with its 27,178,188 supporters. The tally in the Electoral College was 486 to 52 (see Map 38.2). Goldwater carried only his native Arizona and five other states—all of them, significantly, in the traditionally Democratic but now racially restless South. Johnson's record-breaking 61 percent of the popular vote swept lopsided Democratic majorities into both houses of Congress.

✦ The Great Society Congress

Johnson's huge victory temporarily smashed the conservative congressional coalition of southern Democrats and northern Republicans. A wide-open legislative road stretched before the Great Society programs, as the president skillfully ringmastered his two-to-one Democratic majorities. Congress poured out a flood of legislation, comparable only to the output of the New Dealers in the Hundred Days Congress of 1933. Johnson, confident that a growing economy gave him ample fiscal and political room for maneuver, delivered at last on long-deferred Democratic promises of social reform.

Escalating the War on Poverty, Congress doubled the appropriation of the Office of Economic Opportunity to $2 billion and granted more than $1 billion to redevelop the gutted hills and hollows of Appalachia. Johnson also prodded Congress into creating two new cabinet offices: the Department of Transportation and the Department of Housing and Urban Development (HUD), to which he named the first black cabinet secretary in the nation's history, respected economist Robert C. Weaver. Other noteworthy laws established the National Endowments for the Arts and the Humanities, designed to lift the level of American cultural life.

Even more impressive were the Big Four legislative achievements that crowned LBJ's Great Society program: aid to education, medical care for the elderly and indigent, immigration reform, and a new voting rights bill.

Johnson neatly avoided the thorny question of separation of church and state by channeling educational aid to students, not schools, thus allowing funds to flow to hard-pressed parochial institutions. (Catholic John F. Kennedy had not dared to touch this prickly issue.) With a keen eye for the dramatic, LBJ signed the education bill in the humble one-room Texas schoolhouse he had attended as a boy.

Medicare for the elderly, accompanied by Medicaid for the poor, became a reality in 1965. Like the New Deal's Social Security program, Medicare and Medicaid created "entitlements." That is, they conferred rights on certain categories of Americans virtually in perpetuity, without the need for repeated congressional approval. These programs were part of a spreading "rights revolution" that materially improved the lives of millions of Americans—but also eventually undermined the federal government's financial health.

Immigration reform was the third of Johnson's Big Four feats. The Immigration and Nationality Act of 1965 abolished at last the "national-origins" quota system that had been in place since 1921 (see p. 703). The act also doubled (to 290,000) the number of immigrants allowed to enter annually, while for the first time setting limits on immigrants from the Western Hemisphere (120,000). The new law further provided for the admission of close relatives of United States citizens, outside those numerical limits. To the surprise of many of the act's architects, more than 100,000 persons per year took advantage of its "family unification" provisions in the decades after 1965, and the immigrant stream swelled beyond expectations. Even more surprising to the act's sponsors, the sources of immigration soon shifted heavily from Europe to Latin America and Asia, dramatically changing the racial and ethnic composition of the American population.

Great Society programs came in for rancorous political attack in later years. Conservatives charged that the billions spent for "social engineering" had simply been flushed down the waste pipe. Yet the poverty rate declined measurably in the ensuing decade (see Figure

Giving Thanks for Medicare An elderly woman showed her gratitude to President Lyndon B. Johnson for his signing of the Medicare bill in April 1965, providing basic medical care for the aged. In tribute to former president Truman's unsuccessful effort to pass a national medical insurance program twenty years earlier, Johnson flew to Truman's Missouri home to sign the bill that he claimed would deliver "care for the sick and serenity for the fearful." No one acknowledged that Truman's earlier plan had been much more comprehensive or that Johnson, then a young Texas congressman, had opposed it.

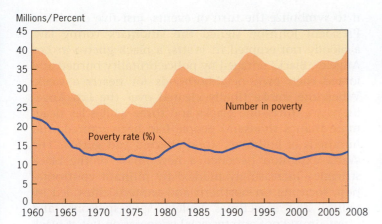

FIGURE 38.1 Poverty in the United States, 1960–2011
In 2000 the poverty rate fell to 11.3 percent, its lowest level since 1979. In the "Great Recession" of the early twenty-first century, it ticked upward again, to 15.1 percent in 2011. The absolute numbers refer to those people who live in families whose total income is lower than a set "poverty threshold," which is tied to the consumer price index, so it varies with inflation. The "poverty rate" means the percentage of all Americans living below that threshold. (Source: U.S. Bureau of the Census, http://www.census.gov/hhes/www/poverty/histpov/hstpov2.html.)

38.1). Medicare made especially dramatic reductions in the incidence of poverty among America's elderly. Other antipoverty programs, among them Project Head Start, sharply improved the educational performance of underprivileged youth. Infant mortality rates also fell in minority communities as general health conditions improved. Lyndon Johnson was not fully victorious in the war against poverty, but he did win several noteworthy battles.

✴ Battling for Black Rights

With the last of his Big Four reforms, the Voting Rights Act of 1965, Johnson made heartening headway against one of the most persistent American evils, racial discrimination. In Johnson's native South, the walls of segregation were crumbling, but not fast enough for long-suffering African Americans. The Civil Rights Act of 1964 gave the federal government more muscle to enforce school-desegregation orders and to prohibit racial discrimination in all kinds of public accommodations and employment. But the problem of voting rights remained. In Mississippi, which had the largest black minority of any state, only about 5 percent of eligible blacks were registered to vote. The lopsided pattern was similar throughout the South. Ballot-denying devices like the poll tax, literacy tests, and barefaced intimidation still barred black people from the political

process. Mississippi law required the names of prospective black registrants to be published for two weeks in local newspapers—a device that virtually guaranteed economic reprisals, or worse.

Beginning in 1964, opening up the polling booths became the chief goal of the black movement in the South. The Twenty-fourth Amendment, ratified in January 1964, abolished the poll tax in federal elections. (See the Appendix.) Blacks joined hands with white civil rights workers—many of them student volunteers from the North—in a massive voter-registration drive in Mississippi during the **Freedom Summer** of 1964. Singing "We Shall Overcome," they zealously set out to soothe generations of white anxieties and black fears.

But events soon blighted bright hopes. In late June 1964, one black and two white civil rights workers disappeared in Mississippi. Their badly beaten bodies were later found buried beneath an earthen dam. FBI investigators eventually arrested twenty-one white Mississippians, including the local sheriff, in connection with the killings. But white juries refused to convict the whites for these murders. In August an integrated **Mississippi Freedom Democratic party** delegation was denied its seat at the national Democratic convention. Only a handful of black Mississippians had succeeded in registering to vote.

Early in 1965 Martin Luther King, Jr., resumed the voter-registration campaign in Selma, Alabama, where blacks made up 50 percent of the population but only 1 percent of the voters. State troopers with tear gas and whips assaulted King's demonstrators as they marched peacefully to the state capital at Montgomery. A Boston Unitarian minister was killed, and a few days later a white Detroit woman was shotgunned to death by Klansmen on the highway near Selma.

As the nation recoiled in horror before these violent scenes, President Johnson, speaking in soft southern accents, delivered a compelling address on television. What happened in Selma, he insisted, concerned all Americans, "who must overcome the crippling legacy of bigotry and injustice." Then, in a stirring adaptation of the anthem of the civil rights movement, the president concluded, "And we shall overcome." Following words with deeds, Johnson speedily shepherded through Congress the landmark **Voting Rights Act of 1965**, signed into law on August 6. It outlawed literacy tests and sent federal voter registrars into several southern states.

The passage of the Voting Rights Act, exactly one hundred years after the conclusion of the Civil War, climaxed a century of awful abuse and robust resurgence for African Americans in the South. "Give us the ballot," said Martin Luther King, Jr., "and the South will never be the same again." He was right. The act did not end discrimination and oppression overnight, but

Charles Moore/Black Star/Stockphoto.com

Confrontation at the Edmund Pettus Bridge, Selma, Alabama, 1965 Named for a Confederate general, the Edmund Pettus Bridge became the scene of a violent clash in March, 1965. Moments after this photo was taken, Alabama state troopers, wielding billy clubs and lobbing tear gas canisters, assaulted peaceful civil rights demonstrators marching to the Alabama state capital in Montgomery. Dozens of demonstrators were hospitalized. Heavy media coverage of this and similar events helped stir the nation's conscience about civil rights and led to passage of the historic Voting Rights Act in 1965.

it placed an awesome lever for change in blacks' hands. Black southerners now had power and began to wield it without fear of reprisals. White southerners began to court black votes and business as never before. In the following decade, for the first time since emancipation, African Americans began to migrate *into* the South.

✦ Black Power

The Voting Rights Act of 1965 marked the end of an era in the history of the civil rights movement—the era of nonviolent demonstrations, focused on the South, led by peaceful moderates like Martin Luther King, Jr., and aimed at integrating blacks into American society. As

if to symbolize the turn of events, just five days after President Johnson signed the landmark voting law, a bloody riot erupted in Watts, a black ghetto in Los Angeles. Blacks enraged by police brutality burned and looted their own neighborhoods for nearly a week. When the smoke finally cleared over the Los Angeles basin, thirty-one blacks and three whites lay dead, more than a thousand people had been injured, and hundreds of buildings stood charred and gutted. The Watts explosion heralded a new phase of the black struggle—increasingly marked by militant confrontation, focusing on northern and western cities, led by radical and sometimes violent spokespersons, and often aiming not at interracial cooperation but at black separatism.

The pious Christian moderation of Martin Luther King, Jr., came under heavy fire from this second wave of younger black leaders, who privately mocked the dignified Dr. King as "de Lawd." Deepening division among black leaders was highlighted by the career of Malcolm X. Born Malcolm Little, he was at first inspired by the militant black nationalists in the Nation of Islam. Like

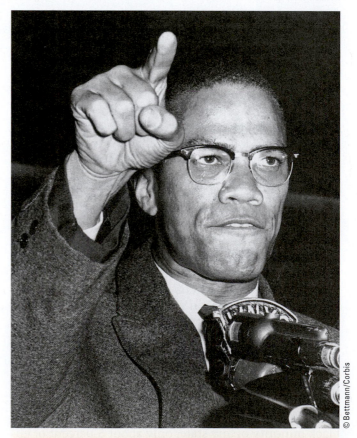

© Bettmann/Corbis

Malcolm X The charismatic black leader was a hypnotizing speaker who could rivet and arouse crowds with his call for black separatism. At the end of his life, Malcolm began to temper his separatist creed.

the Nation's founder, Elijah Muhammed (born Elijah Poole), Malcolm changed his surname to advertise his lost African identity in white America. A brilliant and charismatic preacher, Malcolm X trumpeted black separatism and inveighed against the "blue-eyed white devils." Eventually Malcolm distanced himself from Elijah Muhammed's separatist preachings and moved toward mainstream Islam. (By the 1990s Islam was among America's fastest-growing religions and counted some 2 million African American converts—or "reverts," as Muslims described it—in its ranks.) In early 1965 he was cut down by rival Nation of Islam gunmen while speaking to a large crowd in New York City.

The militant **Black Panther party** meanwhile brandished weapons in the streets of Oakland, California, even while it was establishing children's breakfast programs. Then in 1966 Trinidad-born Stokely Carmichael, a leader of the Student Nonviolent Coordinating Committee (SNCC), began to preach the doctrine

Dr. Martin Luther King, Jr. (1929–1968) and Malcolm X (1925–1965) not only differed in the goals they held out to their fellow African Americans—King urging racial integration and Malcolm X black separatism— but also in the means they advocated to achieve them. In his famous "I Have a Dream" speech during the interracial March on Washington on August 28, 1963, King proclaimed to a quarter of a million people assembled at the Lincoln Memorial,

"In the process of gaining our rightful place we must not be guilty of wrongful deeds. Let us not seek to satisfy our thirst for freedom by drinking from the cup of bitterness and hatred. . . . We must not allow our creative protest to degenerate into physical violence. Again and again we must rise to the majestic heights of meeting physical force with soul force.**"**

About three months later, Malcolm X angrily rejected King's "peaceful, turn-the-other-cheek revolution":

"Revolution is bloody, revolution is hostile, revolution knows no compromise, revolution overturns and destroys everything that gets in its way. And you, sitting around here like a knot on the wall, saying, 'I'm going to love these folks no matter how much they hate me,' . . . Whoever heard of a revolution where they lock arms . . . , singing 'We shall overcome?' You don't do that in a revolution. You don't do any singing, you're too busy swinging.**"**

of **Black Power**, which, he said, "will smash everything Western civilization has created." Some advocates of Black Power insisted that they simply intended the slogan to describe a broad-front effort to exercise the political and economic rights gained by the civil rights movement and to speed the integration of American society. But other African Americans, recollecting previous black nationalist movements like that of Marcus Garvey earlier in the century (see pp. 719–720), breathed a vibrant separatist meaning into the concept of Black Power. They emphasized African American distinctiveness, promoted "Afro" hairstyles and dress, shed their "white" names for new African identities, and demanded black studies programs in schools and universities.

Ironically, just as the civil rights movement had achieved its greatest legal and political triumphs, more city-shaking riots erupted in the black ghettos of several American cities. A bloody outburst in Newark, New Jersey, in the summer of 1967 took twenty-five lives. Federal troops restored order in Detroit, Michigan, after forty-three people died in the streets. As in Los Angeles, black rioters torched their own neighborhoods, attacking police officers and even firefighters, who had to battle both flames and mobs howling "Burn, baby, burn."

These riotous outbursts angered many white Americans, who threatened to retaliate with their own "backlash" against ghetto arsonists and killers. Inner-city anarchy baffled many northerners, who had considered racial problems a purely "southern" question. But black concerns had moved north—as had nearly half the nation's black people. In the North the Black Power movement now focused less on civil rights and more on economic demands. Black unemployment, for example, was nearly double that for whites. These oppressive new problems seemed even less likely to be solved peaceably than the struggle for voting rights in the South.

Despair deepened when the magnetic and moderate voice of Martin Luther King, Jr., was forever silenced by a sniper's bullet in Memphis, Tennessee, on April 4, 1968. A martyr for justice, he had bled and died against the peculiarly American thorn of race. The killing of King cruelly robbed the American people of one of the most inspirational leaders in their history—at a time when they could least afford to lose him. This outrage triggered a nationwide orgy of ghetto-gutting and violence that cost over forty lives.

Rioters noisily made news, but thousands of other blacks quietly made history. Their voter registration in the South shot upward, and by the late 1960s several hundred blacks held elected office in the Old South. Cleveland, Ohio, and Gary, Indiana, elected black mayors. By 1972 nearly half of southern black children sat in integrated classrooms. Actually, more schools in the South were integrated than in the North. About a third of black families had risen economically into the ranks of the middle class—though an equal proportion remained below the "poverty line." King left a shining legacy of racial progress, but he was cut down when the job was far from completed.

✦ Combating Communism in Two Hemispheres

Violence at home eclipsed Johnson's legislative triumphs, while foreign flare-ups threatened his political life. Discontented Dominicans rose in revolt against their military government in April 1965. Johnson speedily announced that the Dominican Republic was the target of a Castro-like coup by "Communist conspirators," and he dispatched American troops, ultimately some twenty-five thousand, to restore order. But the evidence of a communist takeover was fragmentary at best. Johnson was widely condemned, at home and in Latin America, for his temporary reversion to the officially abandoned "gunboat diplomacy."

At about the same time, Johnson was sinking deeper into the monsoon mud of Vietnam. Guerillas loyal to the North Vietnamese communists, called Viet Cong, attacked an American air base at Pleiku, South Vietnam, in February 1965. The president immediately ordered retaliatory bombing raids against military installations in North Vietnam and for the first time ordered attacking U.S. troops to land. By the middle of March 1965, the Americans had "Operation Rolling Thunder" in full swing—regular full-scale bombing

attacks against North Vietnam. Before 1965 ended, some 184,000 American troops were involved, most of them slogging through the jungles and rice paddies of South Vietnam searching for guerrillas.

Johnson had now taken the first fateful steps down a slippery path. He and his advisers believed that a fine-tuned, step-by-step "escalation" of American force would drive the enemy to defeat with a minimum loss of life on both sides. But the enemy matched every increase in American firepower with more men and more wiliness in the art of guerrilla warfare.

The South Vietnamese themselves were meanwhile becoming spectators in their own war, as the fighting became increasingly Americanized. Corrupt and collapsible governments succeeded each other in Saigon with bewildering rapidity. Yet American officials continued to talk of defending a faithful democratic ally. Washington spokespeople also defended America's action as a test of Uncle Sam's "commitment" and of the reliability of his numerous treaty pledges to resist communist encroachment. Persuaded by such panicky thinking, Johnson steadily raised the military stakes in Vietnam. By 1968 he had poured more than half a million troops into Southeast Asia, and the annual bill for the war was exceeding $30 billion. Yet the end was nowhere in sight.

✦ Vietnam Vexations

America could not defeat the enemy in Vietnam, but it seemed to be defeating itself. World opinion grew

The Mechanized War High technology and modern equipment, such as this helicopter, gave the Americans in Vietnam a huge military advantage. But unaccompanied by a clear political purpose and a national will to win, technological superiority was insufficient to achieve final victory.

AP Images

increasingly hostile; the blasting of an underdeveloped country by a mighty superpower struck many critics as obscene. Several nations expelled American Peace Corps volunteers. The ever-censorious Charles de Gaulle withdrew France from NATO in 1966 and ordered all American troops out of the country, reportedly prompting Johnson to ask if that included the thousands buried in Normandy.

Overcommitment in Southeast Asia also tied America's hands elsewhere. Attacked by Soviet-backed Egypt, Jordan, and Syria, a beleaguered Israel stunned the world with a military triumph in June 1967. When the smoke cleared after the **Six-Day War**, Israel expanded to control new territories in the Sinai Peninsula, the Golan Heights, the Gaza Strip, and the West Bank of the Jordan River, including Jerusalem (see Map 40.2 on p. 948). The Israeli victory brought some 1 million resentful Palestinian Arabs under direct Israeli control, while another 350,000 Palestinian refugees fled to neighboring Jordan. The Israelis eventually withdrew from the Sinai after signing a peace treaty with Egypt, but they refused to relinquish the other areas without a treaty and began moving Jewish settlers into the heavily Arab district of the West Bank. The Six-Day War markedly intensified the problems of the already volatile Middle East, leading to an intractable standoff between the Israelis and Palestinians, now led by Yasir Arafat (1929–2004), head of the Palestine Liberation Organization (PLO). For decades a return to the "pre-1967 boundaries" would be a key negotiating aim for Palestinians. The Middle East became an ever more dangerously packed powder keg that the war-plagued United States proved powerless to defuse.

Domestic discontent festered as the Vietnamese entanglement dragged on. Antiwar demonstrations had begun on a small scale with campus "teach-ins" in 1965, and gradually these protests mounted to tidal-wave proportions. As the long arm of the military draft dragged more and more young men off to the Southeast Asian slaughter pen, resistance stiffened. Thousands of draft registrants fled to Canada; others publicly burned their draft cards. Hundreds of thousands of marchers filled the streets of New York, San Francisco, and other cities, chanting, "Hell no, we won't go" and "Hey, hey, LBJ, how many kids did you kill today?" Many Americans felt pangs of conscience at the spectacle of their countrymen burning peasant huts and blistering civilians with ghastly napalm.

Opposition in Congress to the Vietnam involvement centered in the influential Senate Committee on Foreign Relations, headed by Senator William Fulbright of Arkansas. A constant thorn in the side of the president, he staged a series of widely viewed televised hearings in 1966 and 1967, during which prominent personages aired their views, largely antiwar. Gradually the public

The Vietnam Quagmire Marine PFC Phillip Mark Wilson of Wolfforth, Texas, carries a rocket launcher across a stream near the "demilitarized zone" (DMZ) that separated North and South Vietnam. Wilson was killed in action soon after this photo was taken, just five days after his 21st birthday.

came to feel that it had been deceived about the causes and "winnability" of the war. A yawning "credibility gap" opened between the government and the people. New flocks of antiwar "doves" were hatching daily.

Even within the administration, doubts were deepening about the wisdom of the war in Vietnam. When Defense Secretary McNamara expressed increasing discomfiture at the course of events, he was quietly eased out of the cabinet. (Years later McNamara wrote that "we were wrong, terribly wrong," about Vietnam.) By early 1968 the brutal and futile struggle had become the longest and most unpopular foreign war in the nation's history. The government had failed utterly to explain to the people what was supposed to be at stake in Vietnam. Many critics wondered if any objective could be worth the vast price, in blood and treasure, that America was paying. Casualties, killed and wounded, already exceeded 100,000. More bombs had been dropped on Vietnam than on all enemy territory in World War II.

The war was also ripping apart the fabric of American society and even threatening to shred the Constitution. In 1967 President Johnson ordered the CIA, in clear violation of its charter as a *foreign* intelligence agency, to spy on domestic antiwar activists. He also encouraged the FBI to turn its counterintelligence program, code-named "Cointelpro," against the peace movement. "Cointelpro" subverted leading "doves" with false accusations that they were communist sympathizers. These clandestine tactics made the FBI look like a totalitarian state's secret police rather than a guardian of American democracy.

As the war dragged on, evidence mounted that America had been entrapped in an Asian civil war, fighting against highly motivated rebels who were striving to overthrow an oppressive regime. Yet Johnson clung to his basic strategy of ratcheting up the pressure bit by bit. He stubbornly assured doubting Americans that he could see "the light at the end of the tunnel." But to growing numbers of Americans, it seemed that Johnson was bent on "saving" Vietnam by destroying it.

Vietnam Topples Johnson

Hawkish illusions that the struggle was about to be won were shattered by a blistering communist offensive launched in late January 1968, during Tet, the Vietnamese New Year. At a time when the Viet Cong were supposedly licking their wounds, they suddenly and simultaneously mounted savage attacks on twenty-seven key South Vietnamese cities, including the capital, Saigon. Although eventually beaten off with heavy losses, they demonstrated anew that victory could not be gained by Johnson's strategy of gradual escalation. The Tet offensive ended in a military defeat but a political victory for the Viet Cong. With an increasingly insistent voice, American public opinion demanded a speedy end to the war. Opposition grew so vehement that President Johnson could feel the very foundations of government shaking under his feet. He was also

President Lyndon Johnson Haunted by Specters of Vietnam, 1967

Paul Szep/Getty Images

suffering through hells of personal agony over American casualties. He wept as he signed letters of condolence and slipped off at night to pray with monks at a small Catholic church in Washington.

American military leaders responded to the Tet attacks with a request for 200,000 more troops. The size of the request staggered many policymakers. Former secretary of state Dean Acheson reportedly advised the president that "the Joint Chiefs of Staff don't know what they're talking about."

The president meanwhile was being sharply challenged from within his own party. Eugene McCarthy, a little-known Democratic senator from Minnesota, had emerged as a contender for the 1968 Democratic presidential nomination. The soft-spoken McCarthy, a sometime poet and devout Catholic, gathered a small army of antiwar college students as campaign workers. Going "clean for Gene," with shaven faces and shortened locks, they helped him gain an impressive 41.4 percent of the Democratic vote in the New Hampshire primary on March 12, 1968. Although still second to Johnson's 49.6 percent, McCarthy's showing was devastating for the president. Johnson's star fell further four days later when Senator Robert F. Kennedy, now a senator from New York and an outspoken dove on the war, threw his hat into the ring. The charismatic and handsome Kennedy, heir to his murdered brother's mantle of leadership, stirred a passionate response among workers, African Americans, Latinos, and young people.

These startling events abroad and at home were not lost on LBJ. In a bombshell address on March 31, 1968, he announced on nationwide television that he would freeze American troop levels and scale back the bombing. Then, in a dramatic plea to unify a dangerously divided nation, Johnson startled his vast audience by firmly declaring that he would not be a candidate for the presidency in 1968.

Johnson's "abdication" had the effect of preserving the military status quo. He had held the "hawks" in check, while offering himself as a sacrifice to the militant "doves." The United States could thus maintain the maximum *acceptable* level of military activity in Vietnam with one hand, while trying to negotiate a settlement with the other. North Vietnam shortly agreed to commence negotiations in Paris. But progress was glacially slow, as prolonged bickering developed over the very shape of the conference table.

The Presidential Sweepstakes of 1968

The summer of 1968 was one of the hottest political seasons in the nation's history. Johnson's heir apparent for the Democratic nomination was his liberal vice

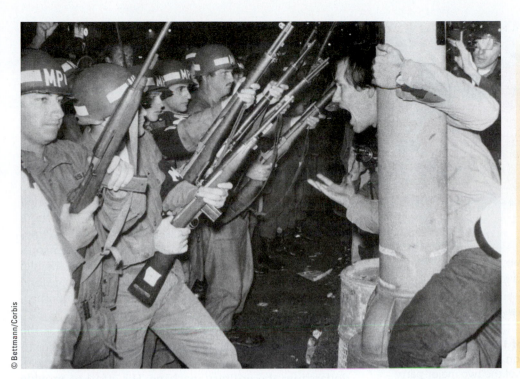

© Bettmann/Corbis

The Siege of Chicago, 1968
Antiwar protesters staged demonstrations in the streets of Chicago during the Democratic National Convention in August 1968. Some 2,500 members of the radical Youth International Party (known as the Yippies) planned a peaceful "festival of light" across the street from the convention hall, but instead found themselves drawn into a melee with the police and National Guardsmen. The confrontation in Chicago badly tarnished Democratic candidate Hubert Humphrey's presidential campaign. His Republican opponent, Richard Nixon, won the presidency with calls for an "honorable peace" in Vietnam and "law and order" at home.

president, Hubert H. Humphrey, a former pharmacist, college professor, mayor, and U.S. senator from Minnesota. Senators McCarthy and Kennedy meanwhile dueled in several state primaries, with Kennedy's bandwagon gathering ever-increasing speed. But on June 5, 1968, the night of an exciting victory in the California primary, Kennedy was shot to death by a young Arab immigrant resentful of the candidate's pro-Israel views.

Angry antiwar zealots, deprived by an assassin's bullet of their leading candidate, streamed menacingly into Chicago for the Democratic convention in August 1968. Mayor Richard Daley responded by arranging for barbed-wire barricades around the convention hall ("Fort Daley"), as well as thousands of police and National Guard reinforcements. Some militant demonstrators baited the officers in blue by calling them "pigs," chanting "Ho, Ho, Ho Chi Minh," shouting obscenities, and hurling bags and cans of excrement at the police lines. As people the world over watched on television, the exasperated "peace officers" broke into a "police riot," clubbing and manhandling innocent and guilty alike. Acrid tear gas fumes hung heavy over the city even as Humphrey steamrollered to the nomination on the first ballot.

The Humphrey forces blocked the McCarthyites' attempt to secure an antiwar platform plank and hammered into place their own declaration that armed force would be relentlessly applied until the enemy showed more willingness to negotiate.

Scenting victory over the badly divided Democrats, the Republicans convened in plush Miami Beach,

Florida, where former vice president Richard M. Nixon arose from his political grave to win the nomination. As a "hawk" on Vietnam and a right-leaning middle-of-the-roader on domestic policy, Nixon pleased the Goldwater conservatives and was acceptable to party moderates. He appealed to white southern voters and to the "law-and-order" element when he tapped as his vice-presidential running mate Maryland's Governor Spiro T. Agnew, noted for his tough stands against dissidents and black militants. The Republican platform called for victory in Vietnam and a strong anticrime policy.

Adding color and confusion to the campaign was a "spoiler" third-party ticket—the American Independent party—headed by a scrappy ex-pugilist, George C. Wallace, former governor of Alabama. In 1963 he had stood in the doorway to prevent two black students from entering the University of Alabama. "Segregation now! Segregation tomorrow! Segregation forever!" he shouted. Wallace jabbed repeatedly at "pointy-headed bureaucrats," and he taunted hecklers as "bums" in need of a bath. Speaking behind a bulletproof screen, he called for prodding the blacks into their place, with bayonets if necessary. He and his running mate, former air force general Curtis LeMay, also proposed smashing the North Vietnamese to smithereens by "bombing them back to the Stone Age."

Between the positions of the Republicans and the Democrats on Vietnam, there was little choice. Both candidates were committed to carrying on the war until the enemy settled for an "honorable peace," which

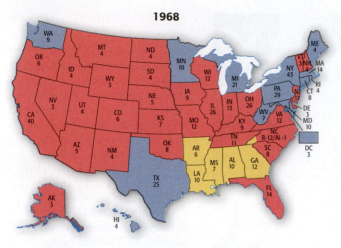

1968

Candidate (Party)	Electoral Vote		Popular Vote	
Nixon (Republican)	301	56.1%	31,785,480	43.4%
Humphrey (Democrat)	191	35.5%	31,275,166	42.7%
Wallace (American Independent)	46	8.4%	9,906,473	13.5%

MAP 38.3 Presidential Election of 1968 (with electoral vote by state) George Wallace won in five states, and he denied a clear majority to either of the two major-party candidates in twenty-five other states. A shift of some fifty thousand votes might well have thrown the election into the House of Representatives, giving Wallace the strategic bargaining position he sought. © Cengage Learning

seemed to mean an American victory. The millions of "doves" had no place to roost, and many refused to vote at all. Humphrey, scorched by the LBJ brand, went down to defeat as a loyal prisoner of his chief's policies.

Nixon, who had lost a cliffhanger to Kennedy in 1960, won one in 1968. He garnered 301 electoral votes, with 43.4 percent of the popular tally (31,785,480), as compared with 191 electoral votes and 42.7 percent of the popular votes (31,275,166) for Humphrey (see Map 38.3). Unlike most new presidents, Nixon faced congressional majorities of the opposing party in both houses. He carried not a single major city, thus attesting to the continuing urban strength of the Democrats, who also won about 95 percent of the black vote. Nixon had received no clear mandate to do anything. He was a minority president who owed his election to divisions over the war and protest against the unfair draft, crime, and rioting.

As for Wallace, he won an impressive 9,906,473 popular votes and 46 electoral votes, all from five states of the Deep South, four of which the Republican Goldwater had carried in 1964. Wallace remained a formidable force, for he had amassed the largest third-party popular vote in American history to that point and was the last third-party candidate to win any electoral votes. (In 1992 Ross Perot enjoyed a greater

popular-vote margin but won no states; see p. 996.) Wallace had also resoundingly demonstrated the continuing power of "populist" politics, which appealed to voters' fears and resentments rather than to the better angels of their nature. His candidacy foreshadowed a coarsening of American political life that would take deep root in the ensuing decades.

✶ The Obituary of Lyndon Johnson

Talented but tragedy-struck Lyndon Johnson returned to his Texas ranch in January 1969 and died there four years later. His party was defeated, and his "me-too" Hubert Humphrey was repudiated. Yet Johnson's legislative leadership for a time had been remarkable. No president since Lincoln had worked harder or done more for civil rights. None had shown more compassion for the poor, blacks, and the ill-educated.

But by 1966 Johnson was already sinking into the Vietnam quicksands. Great Society programs began to wither on the vine, as soaring war costs sucked tax dollars into the military machine. His effort to provide both guns and butter prevented him from delivering either in sufficient quantity. The War on Poverty met resistance that was as stubborn as the Viet Cong and eventually went down to defeat. Great want persisted alongside great wealth.

Johnson had crucified himself on the cross of Vietnam. The Southeast Asian quagmire engulfed his noblest intentions. Committed to some degree by his two predecessors, he had chosen to defend the American foothold and enlarge the conflict rather than be run out. He was evidently persuaded by his brightest advisers, both civilian and military, that massive aerial bombing and limited troop commitments would make a "cheap" victory possible. His decision not to escalate the fighting further offended the "hawks," and his refusal to back off altogether antagonized the "doves." Like the Calvinists of colonial days, luckless Lyndon Johnson was damned if he did and damned if he did not.

✶ The Cultural Upheaval of the 1960s

The struggles of the 1960s against racism, poverty, and the war in Vietnam had momentous cultural consequences. The decade came to be seen as a watershed dividing two distinct eras in terms of values, morals, and behavior.

Everywhere in 1960s America, a newly negative attitude toward all kinds of authority took hold. Disillusioned by the discovery that American society was not free of racism, sexism, imperialism, and oppression, many young people lost their traditional moral rudders. Neither families nor churches nor schools seemed to be able to define values and shape behavior with the certainty of shared purpose that many people believed had once existed. The nation's mainline Protestant denominations, which had dominated American religious life for centuries, lost their grip in the 1960s, as weekly churchgoing declined from 48 percent in the late 1950s to 41 percent in the early 1970s. The liberal Protestant churches suffered the most. They increasingly ceded religious authority to conservative evangelicals while surrendering cultural authority to secular professionals and academic social scientists. A new cultural divide began to take shape, as educated Americans became increasingly secular and the less educated became more religious. Religious upheaval even churned the tradition-bound Roman Catholic Church, among the world's oldest and most conservative institutions. Clerics abandoned their Roman collars and Latin lingo, folk songs replaced Gregorian chants, and meatless Fridays became ancient history. No matter what the topic, conventional wisdom and inherited ideas came under fire. "Trust no one over thirty" was a popular sneer of rebellious youth.

Skepticism about authority had deep historical roots in American culture, and it had even bloomed in the supposedly complacent and conformist 1950s. "Beat" poets like Allen Ginsberg and iconoclastic novelists like Jack Kerouac had voiced dark disillusion with the materialistic pursuits and "establishment" arrogance of the Eisenhower era. In movies like *Rebel Without a Cause* (1955), the attractive young actor James Dean expressed the restless frustration of many young people.

The disaffection of the young reached crisis proportions in the tumultuous 1960s. One of the first organized protests against established authority broke out at the University of California at Berkeley in 1964, in the aptly named Free Speech Movement. Students objected to an administrative ban on the use of campus space for political debate. During months of protest, they accused the Cold War "megaversity" of promoting corporate interests rather than humane values. But in only a few years, the clean-cut Berkeley activists and their sober-minded sit-ins would seem downright quaint. Fired by outrage against the war in Vietnam, some sons and daughters of the middle class became radical political rebels. Others turned to mind-bending drugs, tuned in to "acid rock," and dropped out of "straight" society. Still others "did their own thing" in communes or "alternative" institutions. Patriotism became a dirty word. Beflowered women in trousers and long-haired men with earrings heralded the rise of a self-conscious "counterculture" stridently opposed to traditional American ways.

Social upheaval in the 1960s was far from an American-only phenomenon. As people born in the wake of World War II came of age across the world, they questioned established authority everywhere. Waves of protests and calls for individual rights and political freedom spread like wildfire. The year 1968 was so stormy that it became synonymous with unrest in many languages. In May of that year, leftist French students organized city-crippling strikes against their country's antiquated university system. Joined by millions of workers, they nearly toppled the government. The global spirit of protest—against the Vietnam War, racial injustice, and the strictures of bourgeois society—spread from Berkeley, California, to Columbia University in New York, to West Berlin, and even to

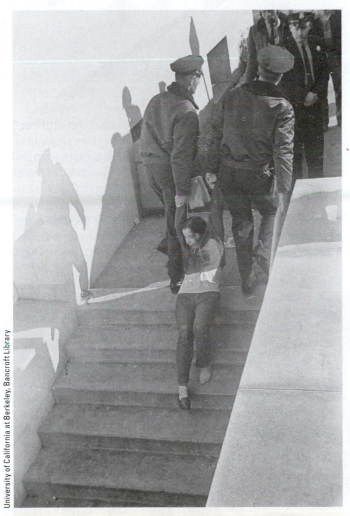

University of California at Berkeley, Bancroft Library

The Free Speech Movement, Berkeley, California, 1964
The Free Speech Movement on the campus of the University of California at Berkeley marked the first of the large-scale student mobilizations that rocked campuses across the country throughout the rest of the 1960s. Here a student schooled in passive resistance is dragged by police to a waiting bus.

Paris, 1968 Protests ripped through the world in 1968. In Paris student battles with campus authorities and police triggered a massive nationwide labor strike and nearly brought down the French government.

Bruno Barbey/Magnum Photos, Inc.

Communist China. In Czechoslovakia, deep within the Soviet bloc, Western-inspired reformers launched the liberating program that became known as the "Prague Spring" in January 1968. For eight months political freedom blossomed, until ruthlessly mowed down by Soviet tanks. Despite backlashes—by university presidents, conservative politicians, and communist leaders—the genie of cultural and political protest was out of the bottle.

The 1960s also witnessed a "sexual revolution," though its novelty and scale are often exaggerated. Without doubt, the introduction of the birth-control pill in 1960 made unwanted pregnancies much easier to avoid and sexual appetites easier to satisfy. The Mattachine Society, founded in Los Angeles in 1951, was a pioneering advocate for gay rights, as gay men and lesbians increasingly demanded sexual tolerance. A brutal attack on gay men by off-duty police officers at New

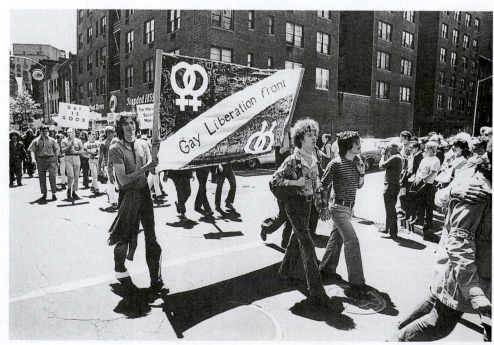

The First Gay Pride Parade, New York City, 1970 On the first anniversary of homosexuals' celebrated resistance to police harassment at the Stonewall Inn, on June 27, 1969, two hundred men and women marched from Greenwich Village to Central Park, initiating a tradition that now has spread to many other American cities and around the globe, attracting thousands of paraders, onlookers, and even prominent politicians.

Michael Evans/The New York Times/Redux

York's Stonewall Inn in 1969 proved a turning point, when the victims fought back in what became known as the **Stonewall Rebellion**. Widening worries in the 1980s about sexually transmitted diseases like genital herpes and AIDS (acquired immunodeficiency syndrome) finally slowed, but did not reverse, the sexual revolution.

Launched in youthful idealism, many of the cultural "revolutions" of the 1960s sputtered out in violence and cynicism. **Students for a Democratic Society (SDS)**, once at the forefront of the antipoverty and antiwar campaigns, had by decade's end spawned an underground terrorist group called the Weathermen. Peaceful civil rights demonstrations had given way to blockbusting urban riots. What started as apparently innocent experiments with drugs like marijuana and LSD had fried many youthful brains and spawned a loathsome underworld of drug lords and addicts.

Straight-laced guardians of respectability denounced the self-indulgent romanticism of the "flower children" as the beginning of the end of modern civilization. Sympathetic observers hailed the "greening" of America—the replacement of materialism and imperialism by a new consciousness of human values. The upheavals of the 1960s could be largely attributed to the three P's: the youthful population bulge, protest against racism and the Vietnam War, and the apparent permanence of prosperity. As the decade flowed into the 1970s, the flower children grew older and had children of their own, the civil rights movement fell silent, the war ended, and economic stagnation blighted the bloom of prosperity. Young people in the 1970s seemed more concerned with finding a job in the system than with tearing the system down. But if the "counterculture" had not managed fully to replace older values, it had weakened their grip, perhaps permanently.

Varying Viewpoints
The Sixties: Constructive or Destructive?

The 1960s were convulsed by controversy, and they have remained controversial ever since. Conflicts raged in that turbulent decade between social classes, races, sexes, and generations. More than three decades later, the shock waves from the 1960s still reverberate through American society. The "Contract with America" that swept conservative Republicans to power in 1994 amounted to nothing less than a wholesale repudiation of the government activism that marked the sixties and a resounding reaffirmation of the "traditional values" that sixties culture supposedly trashed. Liberal Democrats, on the other hand, continue to press affirmative action for women and minorities, protection for the environment, an expanded welfare state, and sexual tolerance—all legacies of the stormy sixties.

Four issues dominate historical discussion of the 1960s: the struggle for civil rights, the Great Society's "War on Poverty," the Vietnam War and the antiwar movement, and the emergence of the "counterculture."

Although most scholars praise the civil rights achievements of the 1960s, they disagree over the civil rights movement's turn away from nonviolence and its embrace of separatism and Black Power. The Freedom Riders and Martin Luther King, Jr., find much more approval in most history books than do Malcolm X and the Black Panther party. But some scholars, notably William L. Van Deburg in *New Day in Babylon: The Black Power Movement and American Culture, 1965–1975* (1992), argue that the "flank effect" of radical Black Power advocates like Stokely Carmichael actually enhanced the bargaining position of moderates like Dr. King. Deburg

also suggests that the enthusiasm of Black Power advocates for African American cultural uniqueness reshaped both black self-consciousness and the broader culture, as it provided a model for the feminist and multiculturalist movements of the 1970s and later.

Johnson's War on Poverty has found its liberal defenders in scholars like Allen Matusow (*The Unraveling of America*, 1984) and John Schwarz (*America's Hidden Success*, 1988). Schwarz demonstrates, for example, that Medicare and Social Security reforms virtually eliminated poverty among America's elderly. But the Great Society has also provoked strong criticism from writers such as Charles Murray (*Losing Ground*, 1984) and Lawrence Meade (*Beyond Entitlements*, 1986). As those conservative critics see the poverty issue, the Great Society was part of the problem, not part of the solution. In their view the War on Poverty did not simply fail to eradicate poverty among the so-called underclass; it actually deepened the dependency of the poor on the welfare state and even generated a multigenerational "cycle" of poverty. In this argument Johnson's Great Society stands indicted of creating in effect a permanent welfare class.

For many young people of the 1960s, the antiwar movement protesting America's policy in Vietnam provided their initiation into politics and their introduction to "movement culture," with its sense of community and shared purpose. But scholars disagree over the movement's real effectiveness in checking the war. Writers like John Lewis Gaddis (*Strategies of Containment*, 1982) explain America's eventual withdrawal from Vietnam essentially without reference to the protesters in the streets. Others, like Todd Gitlin (*The Sixties: Years of Hope, Days of Rage*, 1987), insist that mass protest was the force that finally pressed the war to a conclusion.

Debate over the counterculture not only pits liberals against conservatives but also pits liberals against radicals. A liberal historian like William O'Neill (*Coming Apart*, 1971) might sympathize with what he considers some of the worthy values pushed by student activists, such as racial justice, nonviolence, and the antiwar movement, but he also claims that much of the sixties "youth culture" degenerated into hedonism, arrogance, and social polarization. In contrast, younger historians such as Michael Kazin and Maurice Isserman argue that cultural radicalism and political radicalism were two sides of the same coin. Many young people in the sixties made little distinction between the personal and the political. As Sara Evans demonstrates in *Personal Politics* (1980), "the personal *was* the political" for many women. She finds the roots of modern feminism in the sexism women activists encountered in the civil rights and antiwar movements.

Although scholars rightly see the 1960s as a liberal decade, some have also started to focus on the other side of the political spectrum. Historians like Lisa McGirr (*Suburban Warriors*, 2001) argue that even though Barry Goldwater lost in a landslide in 1964, the conservative movement he kick-started laid the foundation for later successes by Ronald Reagan and both George Bushes. Rebecca Klatch shows in *A Generation Divided* (1999) how the New Right fed off the New Left, reshaping American politics in profound ways. Liberal policies toward minorities, women, and the poor fueled the fires of traditionalists who wanted a return to "the good old days." And the hedonistic counterculture sparked a religious revival that led to politically powerful groups like the Moral Majority by the 1970s.

While critics may argue over the "good" versus the "bad" sixties, there is no denying the degree to which that tumultuous time, for better or worse, shaped the world in which we now live.

Chapter Review

KEY TERMS

New Frontier (889)

Peace Corps (889)

Apollo (891)

Berlin Wall (891)

European Economic
  Community (EEC) (891)

Bay of Pigs invasion (893)

Cuban missile crisis (895)

Freedom Riders (896)

Voter Education
  Project (896)

March on Washington (897)

Civil Rights Act
  of 1964 (898)

affirmative action (900)

Great Society (900)

Freedom Summer (903)

Mississippi Freedom
  Democratic party (903)

Voting Rights Act
  of 1965 (903)

Black Panther party (905)

Black Power (905)

Six-Day War (907)

Stonewall Rebellion (913)

Students for a Democratic
  Society (SDS) (913)

PEOPLE TO KNOW

Robert F. Kennedy

Robert S. McNamara

Ngo Dinh Diem

James Meredith

Lee Harvey Oswald

Malcolm X

Eugene McCarthy

George C. Wallace

CHRONOLOGY

1957	European Economic Community (EEC, Common Market) created by Treaty of Rome
1961	Berlin Wall built Alliance for Progress Bay of Pigs invasion Kennedy sends "military advisers" to South Vietnam
1962	Pressure from Kennedy results in rollback of steel prices Trade Expansion Act Laos neutralized Cuban missile crisis
1963	France vetoes British membership in EEC Anti-Diem coup in South Vietnam Civil rights march in Washington, D.C. Kennedy assassinated; Johnson assumes presidency
1964	Twenty-fourth Amendment (abolishing poll tax in federal elections) ratified "Freedom Summer" voter registration in South Gulf of Tonkin Resolution Johnson defeats Goldwater for presidency War on Poverty begins Civil Rights Act
1965	Great Society legislation Voting Rights Act U.S. troops occupy Dominican Republic
1965–1968	Race riots in U.S. cities
1966	France withdraws from NATO
1967	Six-Day War between Israel and Egypt
1968	North Vietnamese army launches Tet offensive in South Vietnam Worldwide protests Martin Luther King, Jr., and Robert Kennedy assassinated Prague Spring crushed by Soviet army Nixon defeats Humphrey and Wallace for presidency
1969	Stonewall Inn riot in New York City Astronauts land on moon

TO LEARN MORE

Dan Carter, *The Politics of Rage: George Wallace, the Origins of the New Conservatism, and the Transformation of American Politics* (1995)

Robert Dallek, *An Unfinished Life: John F. Kennedy, 1917–1963* (2003)

Alex Haley, *The Autobiography of Malcolm X* (1966)

Maurice Isserman and Michael Kazin, *America Divided: The Civil War of the 1960s* (2000)

Robert F. Kennedy, *Thirteen Days* (1969)

G. Calvin Mackenzie and Robert Weisbrot, *The Liberal Hour: Washington and the Politics of Change in the 1960s* (2008)

Lisa McGirr, *Suburban Warriors: The Origins of the New American Right* (2001)

James Miller, *"Democracy Is in the Streets": From Port Huron to the Siege of Chicago* (1987)

Ann Moody, *Coming of Age in Mississippi* (1968)

Bruce Schulman, *Lyndon B. Johnson and American Liberalism* (1994)

Thomas J. Sugrue, *Sweet Land of Liberty: The Forgotten Struggle for Civil Rights in the North* (2008)

Jeremi Suri, *Power and Protest: Global Revolution and the Rise of Détente* (2003)

A complete, annotated bibliography for this chapter—along with brief descriptions of the People to Know—may be found on the American Pageant website. The Key Terms are defined in a Glossary at the end of the text.

Go to the CourseMate website at **www.cengagebrain.com** for additional study tools and review materials—including audio and video clips—for this chapter.

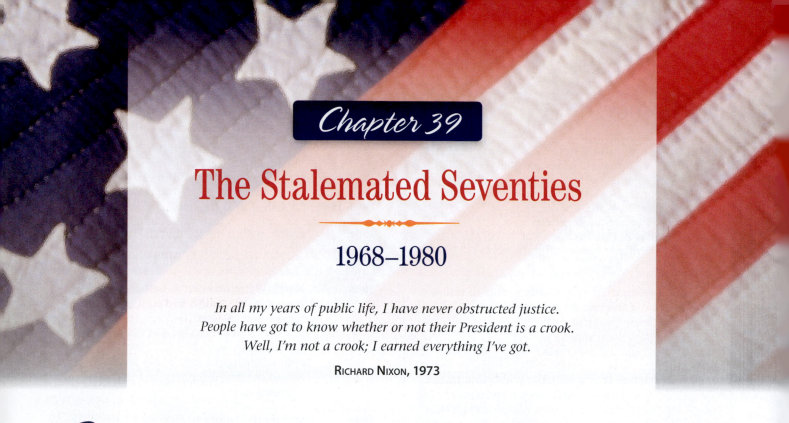

Chapter 39

The Stalemated Seventies

1968–1980

In all my years of public life, I have never obstructed justice.
People have got to know whether or not their President is a crook.
Well, I'm not a crook; I earned everything I've got.

RICHARD NIXON, 1973

As the 1960s lurched to a close, the fantastic quarter-century economic boom of the post–World War II era also showed signs of petering out. By increasing their productivity, American workers had doubled their average standard of living in the twenty-five years since the end of World War II. Now, fatefully, productivity gains slowed to the vanishing point. The entire decade of the 1970s did not witness a productivity advance equivalent to even one year's progress in the preceding two decades. At the new rate, it would take five hundred more years to bring about another doubling of the average worker's standard of living. The median income of the average American family stagnated in the two decades after 1970 and failed to decline only because of the addition of working wives' wages to the family income (see Figure 39.1). The rising baby-boom generation now faced the depressing prospect of a living standard that would be lower than that of their parents. As the postwar wave of robust economic growth crested by the early 1970s, at home and abroad the "can-do" American spirit gave way to an unaccustomed sense of limits.

★ Sources of Stagnation

What caused the sudden slump in productivity? Some observers cited the increasing presence in the work force of women and teenagers, who typically had fewer skills than adult male workers and were less likely to take the full-time, long-term jobs where skills might be developed. Other commentators blamed declining investment in new machinery, the heavy costs of compliance

with government-imposed safety and health regulations, and the general shift of the American economy from manufacturing to services, where productivity gains were allegedly more difficult to achieve and measure. Yet in the last analysis, much mystery attends the productivity slowdown, and economists have wrestled inconclusively with the puzzle.

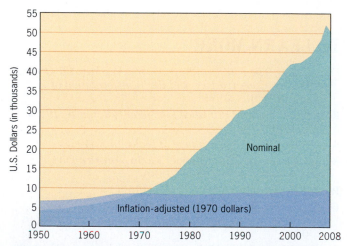

FIGURE 39.1 **Median Household Income, 1970–2008**
During the long post–World War II economic boom (from about 1950 to 1970), family incomes increased dramatically, but after 1970 "real," or inflation-adjusted, incomes stagnated. Prosperity in the late 1990s led to a slight upward trend, though adjusted median family income began to decline in the early years of the twenty-first century. (Sources: U.S. Census Bureau, Historical Income Tables—Households, 2007; U.S. Census Bureau *Consumer Income Report*, relevant years; *Statistical Abstract of the United States*, 2010.)

New York Daily World

THE NIXON WAVE

The Nixon Wave During Richard Nixon's presidency, Americans experienced the first serious inflation since the immediate post–World War II years. The inflationary surge grew to tidal-wave proportions by the late 1970s, when the consumer price index rose at an annual rate of more than 10 percent.

The Vietnam War also precipitated painful economic distortions. The disastrous conflict in Southeast Asia drained tax dollars from needed improvements in education, deflected scientific skill and manufacturing capacity from the civilian sector, and touched off a sickening spiral of inflation. Sharply rising oil prices in the 1970s also fed inflation, but its deepest roots lay in deficit spending in the 1960s—especially Lyndon Johnson's insistence on simultaneously fighting the war in Vietnam and funding Great Society programs at home, all without a tax increase to finance the added expenditures. Both military spending and welfare spending are inherently inflationary (in the absence of offsetting tax collections), because they put dollars into people's hands without adding to the supply of goods that those dollars can buy.

Whatever its cause, the effects of inflation were deeply felt. Prices increased astonishingly throughout the 1970s. The cost of living tripled in the dozen years after Richard Nixon's inauguration, in the longest and steepest inflationary cycle in American history.

Other weaknesses in the nation's economy were also laid bare by the abrupt reversal of America's financial fortunes in the 1970s. The competitive advantage of many major American businesses had been so enormous after World War II that they had small incentive to modernize plants and seek more efficient methods of production. The defeated German and Japanese people had meanwhile clawed their way out of the ruins of war and built wholly new factories with the most up-to-date technology and management techniques. By the 1970s their efforts paid handsome rewards, as they came to dominate industries like steel, automobiles, and consumer electronics—fields in which the United States had once been unchallengeable.

The poor economic performance of the 1970s hung over the decade like a pall. It frustrated both policymakers and citizens who keenly remembered the growth and optimism of the quarter-century since World War II. The overachieving postwar generation had never met a problem it could not solve. But now a stalemated, unpopular war and a stagnant, unresponsive economy heralded the end of the self-confident postwar era. With it ended the liberal dream, vivid since New Deal days, that an affluent society could spend its way to social justice.

✦ Nixon "Vietnamizes" the War

Inaugurated on January 20, 1969, Richard Nixon urged the American people, torn with dissension over Vietnam and race relations, to "stop shouting at one another." Yet the new president seemed an unlikely conciliator of the clashing forces that appeared to be ripping apart American society. Solitary and suspicious by nature, Nixon could be brittle and testy in the face of opposition. He also harbored bitter resentments against the "liberal establishment" that had cast him into the political darkness for much of the preceding decade. Yet Nixon brought one hugely valuable asset with him to the White House—his broad knowledge and thoughtful expertise in foreign affairs. With calculating shrewdness he applied himself to putting America's foreign-policy house in order.

The first burning need was to quiet the public uproar over Vietnam. President Nixon's announced policy, called **Vietnamization**, was to withdraw the 540,000 U.S. troops in South Vietnam over an extended period. The South Vietnamese—with American money, weapons, training, and advice—could then gradually take over the burden of fighting their own war.

The so-called **Nixon Doctrine** thus evolved. It proclaimed that the United States would honor its existing defense commitments but that in the future, Asians and others would have to fight their own wars without the support of large bodies of American ground troops.

Nixon sought not to end the war, but to win it by other means, without the further spilling of American blood. But even this much involvement was distasteful to the American "doves," many of whom demanded a withdrawal that was prompt, complete, unconditional, and irreversible. Antiwar protesters staged a massive national Vietnam moratorium in October 1969, as nearly 100,000 people jammed Boston Common and some 50,000 filed by the White House carrying lighted candles.

Undaunted, Nixon launched a counteroffensive by appealing to the **silent majority** who presumably supported the war. Though ostensibly conciliatory, Nixon's appeal was in fact deeply divisive. His intentions soon became clear when he unleashed tough-talking Vice President Agnew to attack the "nattering nabobs of negativism" who demanded a quick withdrawal from Vietnam. Nixon himself in 1970 sneered at the student antiwar demonstrators as "bums."

By January 1970 the Vietnam conflict had become the longest in American history and, with 40,000 killed and over 250,000 wounded, the third most costly foreign war in the nation's experience. It had also become grotesquely unpopular, even among troops in the field. Because draft policies largely exempted college students and men with critical civilian skills, the armed forces in Vietnam were largely composed of the least privileged young Americans. Especially in the war's early stages, African Americans were disproportionately represented in the army and accounted for a disproportionately high share of combat fatalities. Black and white soldiers alike fought not only against the Vietnamese enemy but also against the coiled fear of floundering through booby-trapped swamps and steaming jungles, often unable to distinguish friend from foe among the Vietnamese peasants. Drug abuse, mutiny, and sabotage dulled the army's fighting edge. Morale appeared

Vietnam Vets Protest the War, 1971 Public opinion gradually but inexorably turned against the war. In 1965 polls showed that only 15 percent of Americans favored withdrawal from Vietnam. But by 1969, 69 percent of those interviewed indicated that they considered the war a "mistake," and by 1970 a majority supported withdrawal of U.S. troops. In this demonstration on April 23, 1971, eight hundred veterans threw away their Purple Hearts, Bronze Stars, Silver Stars, and other military honors in front of the U.S. Capitol in protest against a war they no longer could support.

A Marine Corps officer expressed the disillusion that beset many American troops in Vietnam:

"For years we disposed of the enemy dead like so much garbage. We stuck cigarettes in the mouths of corpses, put *Playboy* magazines in their hands, cut off their ears to wear around our necks. We incinerated them with napalm, atomized them with B-52 strikes, shoved them out the doors of helicopters above the South China Sea. . . . All we did was count, count bodies. Count dead human beings. . . . That was our fundamental military strategy. Body count. And the count kept going up."

to have plummeted to rock bottom when rumors filtered out of Vietnam that soldiers were "fragging" their own officers—murdering them with fragmentation grenades.

Domestic disgust with the war was further deepened in 1970 by revelations of the **My Lai Massacre**, in which American troops had murdered innocent women and children in the village of My Lai two years earlier. Increasingly desperate for a quick end to the demoralizing conflict, Nixon widened the war in 1970 by ordering an attack on Vietnam's neighbor, Cambodia.

✦ Cambodianizing the Vietnam War

For several years the North Vietnamese and Viet Cong had been using Cambodia, bordering South Vietnam on the west, as a springboard for troops, weapons, and supplies. Suddenly, on April 29, 1970, without consulting Congress, Nixon ordered American forces to join with the South Vietnamese in cleaning out the enemy sanctuaries in officially neutral Cambodia.

Angry students nationwide responded to the Cambodian invasion with rock throwing, window smashing, and arson. At **Kent State University** in Ohio, jumpy members of the National Guard fired into a noisy crowd, killing four and wounding many more; at historically black Jackson State College in Mississippi, the highway patrol discharged volleys at a student dormitory, killing two students. The nation fell prey to turmoil as rioters and arsonists convulsed the land.

Nixon withdrew the American troops from Cambodia on June 29, 1970, after only two months. But in America the Cambodian invasion deepened the bitterness between "hawks" and "doves," as right-wing groups physically assaulted leftists. Disillusionment with "whitey's war" increased ominously among African Americans in the armed forces. The Senate (though not the House) overwhelmingly repealed the Gulf of Tonkin blank check that Congress had given Johnson in 1964 and sought ways to restrain Nixon. The youth of America, still aroused, were only slightly mollified when the government reduced draft calls and shortened the period of draftability, on a lottery basis, from eight years to one year. They were similarly pleased, though not

The War at Home, Spring 1970 President Nixon's order to invade Cambodia sparked angry protests on American campuses. At Kent State University in Ohio, the nation watched in horror as four student demonstrators were shot by jittery National Guardsmen.

John Filo

pacified, when the Twenty-sixth Amendment in 1971 lowered the voting age to eighteen (see the Appendix).

New combustibles fueled the fires of antiwar discontent in June 1971, when a former Pentagon official leaked to the *New York Times* the **Pentagon Papers**, a top-secret Pentagon study that documented the blunders and deceptions of the Kennedy and Johnson administrations, especially the provoking of the 1964 North Vietnamese attack in the Gulf of Tonkin.

✴ Nixon's Détente with Beijing (Peking) and Moscow

As the antiwar firestorm flared ever higher, Nixon concluded that the road out of Vietnam ran through Beijing and Moscow. The two great communist powers, the Soviet Union and China, were clashing bitterly over their rival interpretations of Marxism. In 1969 they had even fought several bloody skirmishes along the "inner border" that separated them in Asia. Nixon astutely perceived that the Chinese-Soviet tension afforded the United States an opportunity to play off one antagonist against the other and to enlist the aid of both in pressuring North Vietnam into peace.

Nixon's thinking was reinforced by his national security adviser, Dr. Henry A. Kissinger. Bespectacled and German-accented, Kissinger had reached America as a youth when his parents fled Hitler's anti-Jewish

Cold War? Not for Some Library of Congress

persecutions. In 1969 the former Harvard professor had begun meeting secretly on Nixon's behalf with North Vietnamese officials in Paris to negotiate an end to the war in Vietnam. He was meanwhile preparing the president's path to Beijing and Moscow.

Nixon, heretofore an uncompromising anticommunist, announced to a startled nation in July 1971 that he had accepted an invitation to visit Communist China the following year. He made his historic journey in February 1972, enjoying glass-clinking toasts and walks on the fabled Great Wall of China. He capped his visit with the Shanghai Communiqué, in which the two nations agreed to "normalize" their relationship. An important part of the accord was America's acceptance of a "one-China" policy, implying a lessened American commitment to the independence of Taiwan.

Nixon next traveled to Moscow in May 1972 to play his "China card" in a game of high-stakes diplomacy in the Kremlin. The Soviets, hungry for American foodstuffs and alarmed over the possibility of intensified rivalry with an American-backed China, were ready to deal. Nixon's visits ushered in an era of **détente**, or relaxed tension, with the two communist powers and produced several significant agreements in 1972,

including a three-year arrangement by which the food-rich United States agreed to sell the Soviets at least $750 million worth of wheat, corn, and other cereals.

More important, the United States and the USSR agreed to an anti–ballistic missile (ABM) treaty, which limited each nation to two clusters of defensive missiles, and to a series of arms-reduction negotiations known as SALT (Strategic Arms Limitation Talks), aimed at freezing the numbers of long-range nuclear missiles for five years. The ABM and SALT accords constituted long-overdue first steps toward slowing the arms race. Yet even though the ABM treaty forbade elaborate defensive systems, the United States forged ahead with the development of "MIRVs" (multiple independently targeted reentry vehicles), designed to overcome any defense by "saturating" it with large numbers of warheads, several to a rocket. Predictably, the Soviets proceeded to "MIRV" their own missiles, and the arms race ratcheted up to a still more perilous plateau, with over sixteen thousand nuclear warheads deployed by both sides by the end of the 1980s.

Nixon's détente diplomacy did, to some extent, deice the Cold War. Yet Nixon remained staunchly anticommunist when the occasion seemed to demand it. He strongly opposed the election of the outspoken Marxist Salvador Allende to the presidency of Chile in 1970. His administration slapped an embargo on the Allende regime, and the Central Intelligence Agency worked covertly to undermine the legitimately elected leftist president. When Allende died during a Chilean army attack on his headquarters in 1973, many observers smelled a Yankee rat—an impression that deepened when Washington warmly embraced Allende's successor, military dictator General Augusto Pinochet. Even so, by checkmating and coopting the two great communist powers, the president had cleverly set the stage for America's exit from Vietnam, although the concluding act in that wrenching tragedy remained to be played.

✶ A New Team on the Supreme Bench

Nixon had lashed out during the campaign at the "permissiveness" and "judicial activism" of the Supreme Court presided over by Chief Justice Earl Warren. Following his appointment in 1953, the jovial Warren had led the Court into a series of decisions that drastically affected sexual freedom, the rights of criminals, the practice of religion, civil rights, and the structure of political representation. The decisions of the Warren Court reflected its deep concern for the individual, no matter how lowly.

In *Griswold* v. *Connecticut* (1965), the Court struck down a state law that prohibited the use of contraceptives, even among married couples. The Court pro-

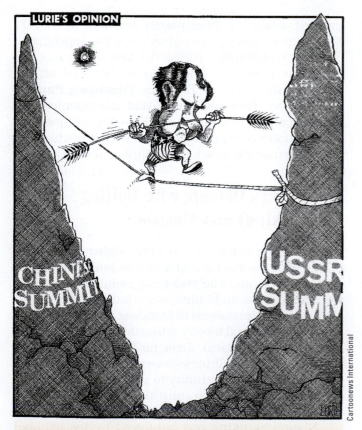

LURIE'S OPINION

CHINESE SUMMIT

USSR SUMMIT

Cartoonews International

Balancing Act Nixon treads delicately between the two communist superpowers in 1973, holding some of the wheat with which he enticed both into détente.

Picture Research Consultants & Archives

The Embattled Warren Court The United States Supreme Court, presided over by Chief Justice Earl Warren, made historic decisions in areas ranging from criminal justice to civil rights and political representation. Its achievements provoked often ferocious conservative backlash, as seen in this billboard advertisement calling for Warren's impeachment.

claimed (critics said "invented") a "right of privacy" that soon provided the basis for decisions protecting women's abortion rights.

In 1963 the Court held (*Gideon* v. *Wainwright*) that all criminal defendants were entitled to legal counsel, even if they were too poor to afford it. More controversial still were decisions in two cases—*Escobedo* (1964) and *Miranda* (1966)—that ensured the right of the accused to remain silent and enjoy other protections. The latter case gave rise to the **Miranda warning** that arresting police officers must read to suspects. These several court rulings sought to prevent abusive police tactics, but they appeared to conservatives to coddle criminals and subvert law and order.

Conservatives also objected to the Court's views on religion. In two stunning decisions, *Engel* v. *Vitale* (1962) and *School District of Abington Township* v. *Schempp* (1963), the justices argued that the First Amendment's separation of church and state meant that public schools could not require prayer or Bible reading. Social conservatives raised anew the battle cry "Impeach Earl Warren" (see p. 868).

From 1954 on, the Court came under relentless criticism, the bitterest since New Deal days. But for better or worse, the black-robed justices were grappling with stubborn social problems spawned by midcentury tensions, even—or especially—if duly elected legislatures failed to do so.

Fulfilling campaign promises, President Nixon undertook to change the Court's philosophical complexion. Taking advantage of several vacancies, he sought appointees who would strictly interpret the Constitution, cease "meddling" in social and political questions, and not coddle radicals or criminals. The Senate in 1969 speedily confirmed his nomination of white-maned Warren E. Burger of Minnesota to succeed the retiring Earl Warren as chief justice. Before the end of 1971, the Court counted four conservative Nixon appointments out of nine members.

Yet Nixon was to learn the ironic lesson that many presidents have learned about their Supreme Court appointees: once seated on the high bench, the justices are fully free to think and decide according to their own beliefs, not according to the president's expectations. The Burger Court that Nixon shaped proved reluctant to dismantle the "liberal" rulings of the Warren Court; it even produced the most controversial judicial opinion of modern times, the momentous *Roe* v. *Wade* decision in 1973, which legalized abortion (see p. 932).

✦ Nixon on the Home Front

Surprisingly, Nixon presided over significant expansion of the welfare programs that conservative Republicans routinely denounced. He approved increased appropriations for entitlements like Food Stamps, Medicaid, and Aid to Families with Dependent Children (AFDC), while adding a generous new program, Supplemental Security Income (SSI), to assist the indigent aged, blind, and disabled. He signed legislation in 1972 guaranteeing automatic Social Security cost-of-living increases to protect the elderly against the ravages of inflation when prices rose more than 3 percent in any year. Ironically, this "indexing" actually helped to fuel the inflationary fires that raged out of control later in the decade.

Amid much controversy, Nixon in 1969 implemented his so-called Philadelphia Plan, requiring construction-trade unions to establish "goals and timetables" for the hiring of black apprentices. Nixon may have been motivated in part by a desire to weaken the forces of liberalism by driving a wedge between blacks and trade unions. But whatever his reasoning, the president's new policy had far-reaching implications. Soon extended to all federal contracts, the **Philadelphia Plan** in effect required thousands of employers to meet hiring quotas or to establish "set-asides" for minority subcontractors.

Nixon's Philadelphia Plan drastically altered the meaning of "affirmative action." Lyndon Johnson had intended affirmative action to protect *individuals* against discrimination. Nixon now transformed and escalated affirmative action into a program that conferred privileges on certain *groups*. The Supreme Court went along with Nixon's approach. In *Griggs* v. *Duke Power Co.* (1971), the black-robed justices prohibited intelligence tests or other devices that had the effect of excluding minorities or women from certain jobs. The Court's ruling strongly suggested to employers that the only sure protection against charges of discrimination was to hire minority workers—or admit minority students—in proportion to their presence in the population.

Together the actions of Nixon and the Court opened broad employment and educational opportunities for minorities and women. They also opened a Pandora's box of protest from critics who assailed the new style of affirmative action as "reverse discrimination," imposed by executive order and judicial decision, not by democratically elected representatives. Yet

Author Rachel Carson (1907–1964) Some call her the mother of the modern conservation movement because of the impact of her 1962 book, *Silent Spring*.

what other remedy was there, defenders asked, to offset centuries of prejudice and opportunity denied?

Among Nixon's legacies was the creation in 1970 of the **Environmental Protection Agency (EPA)**, which climaxed two decades of mounting concern for the environment. Scientist and author Rachel Carson gave the environmental movement a huge boost in 1962 when she published *Silent Spring*, an enormously effective piece of latter-day muckraking that exposed the poisonous effects of pesticides. On April 22, 1970, millions of environmentalists around the world celebrated the first **Earth Day** to raise awareness and to encourage their leaders to act. In the wake of what became a yearly event, the U.S. Congress passed the Clean Air Act of 1970 and the Endangered Species Act of 1973. The EPA now stood on the frontline of the battle for ecological sanity and made notable progress in reducing automobile emissions and cleaning up befouled waterways and toxic waste sites.

The federal government also expanded its regulatory reach on behalf of workers and consumers. Late in 1970 Nixon signed the Occupational Safety and Health Administration (OSHA) into law, creating an agency dedicated to improving working conditions, preventing work-related accidents and deaths, and issuing safety standards. The Consumer Product Safety Commission (CPSC) followed two years later, holding companies to account for selling dangerous products. Together these three mega-agencies gave the federal government far more direct control over business operations than in years past, drawing the ire of many big companies, which chastised the overbearing "national nanny."

Worried about creeping inflation (then running at about 5 percent), Nixon overcame his distaste for economic controls and imposed a ninety-day wage and price freeze in 1971. To stimulate the nation's sagging exports, he next stunned the world by taking the United States off the gold standard and devaluing the dollar. These moves effectively ended the "Bretton Woods" system of international currency stabilization that had functioned for more that a quarter of a century after World War II (see p. 841).

Elected as a minority president, with only 43 percent of the vote in 1968, Nixon devised a clever but cynical plan—called the **southern strategy**—to achieve a solid majority in 1972. Appointing conservative Supreme Court justices, soft-pedaling civil rights, and opposing school busing to achieve racial balance were all parts of the strategy.

The Nixon Landslide of 1972

But as fate would have it, the southern strategy became superfluous as foreign policy dominated the

Alfred Eisenstadt/Time Life Pictures/Getty Images

Fritz Behrendt

presidential campaign of 1972. Vietnam continued to be the burning issue. Nearly four years had passed since Nixon had promised, as a presidential candidate, to end the war and "win" the peace. Yet in the spring of 1972, the fighting escalated anew to alarming levels when the North Vietnamese, heavily equipped with foreign tanks, burst through the demilitarized zone (DMZ) separating the two Vietnams. Nixon reacted promptly by launching massive bombing attacks on strategic centers in North Vietnam, including Hanoi, the capital. Gambling heavily on foreign forbearance, he also ordered the dropping of contact mines to blockade the principal harbors of North Vietnam. Either Moscow or Beijing, or both, could have responded explosively, but neither did, thanks to Nixon's shrewd diplomacy.

The continuing Vietnam conflict spurred the rise of South Dakota senator George McGovern to the 1972 Democratic nomination. McGovern's promise to pull the remaining American troops out of Vietnam in ninety days earned him the backing of the large antiwar element in the party. But his appeal to racial minorities, feminists, leftists, and youth alienated the traditional working-class backbone of his party. Moreover, the discovery shortly after the convention that McGovern's running mate, Missouri senator Thomas Eagleton, had undergone psychiatric care—including electroshock therapy—forced Eagleton's ouster from the ticket and virtually doomed the Democrats' hopes of recapturing the White House.

Nixon's campaign emphasized that he had wound down the "Democratic war" in Vietnam from some 540,000 troops to about 30,000. His candidacy received an added boost just twelve days before the election when the high-flying Dr. Kissinger announced that "peace is at hand" in Vietnam and that an agreement would be reached in a few days.

Nixon won the election in a landslide. His lopsided victory encompassed every state except Massachusetts and the nonstate District of Columbia (which was granted electoral votes by the Twenty-third Amendment in 1961—see Appendix). He piled up 520 electoral votes to 17 for McGovern and a popular majority of 47,169,911 to 29,170,383 votes. McGovern had counted on a large number of young people's votes, but less than half the 18–21 age group even bothered to register to vote.

The dove of peace, "at hand" in Vietnam just before the balloting, took flight after the election. Fighting on both sides escalated again, and Nixon launched a furious two-week bombing of North Vietnam in an iron-handed effort to force the North Vietnamese back to the conference table. This merciless pounding drove the North Vietnamese negotiators to agree to a cease-fire in the Treaty of Paris on January 23, 1973, nearly three months after peace was prematurely proclaimed.

Nixon hailed the face-saving cease-fire as "peace with honor," but the boast rang hollow. The United States was to withdraw its remaining 27,000 or so troops and could reclaim some 560 American prisoners of war. The North Vietnamese were allowed to keep some 145,000 troops in South Vietnam, where they still occupied about 30 percent of the country. The shaky "peace" was in reality little more than a thinly disguised American retreat.

The Secret Bombing of Cambodia and the War Powers Act

The constitutionality of Nixon's continued aerial battering of Cambodia had meanwhile been coming under increasing fire. In July 1973 America was shocked to learn that the U.S. Air Force had secretly conducted some thirty-five hundred bombing raids against North Vietnamese positions in Cambodia, beginning in March 1969 and continuing for some fourteen months prior to the open American incursion in May 1970. The most disturbing feature of these sky forays was that while they were going on, American officials, including the president, had sworn that Cambodian neutrality was being respected. Countless Americans began to wonder what kind of representative government they had if the United States had been fighting a war they knew nothing about.

Defiance followed secretiveness. After the Vietnam cease-fire in January 1973, Nixon brazenly continued large-scale bombing of communist forces in order to help the rightist Cambodian government, and he repeatedly vetoed congressional efforts to stop him. The years of bombing inflicted grisly wounds on Cambodia, blasting its people, shredding its economy, and revolutionizing its politics. The long-suffering Cambodians soon groaned under the sadistic heel of Pol Pot, a murderous tyrant who dispatched as many as 2 million of his people to their graves. He was forced from power, ironically enough, only by a full-dress Vietnamese invasion in 1978, followed by a military occupation that dragged on for a decade.

Congressional opposition to the expansion of presidential war-making powers by Johnson and Nixon led to the **War Powers Act** in November 1973. Passed over Nixon's veto, it required the president to report to Congress within forty-eight hours after committing

The *Washington Post* (*July 19, 1973*) *carried this news item:*

"American B-52 bombers dropped about 104,000 tons of explosives on Communist sanctuaries in neutralist Cambodia during a series of raids in 1969 and 1970. . . . The secret bombing was acknowledged by the Pentagon the Monday after a former Air Force major . . . described how he falsified reports on Cambodian air operations and destroyed records on the bombing missions actually flown."

troops to a foreign conflict or "substantially" enlarging American combat units in a foreign country. Such a limited authorization would have to end within sixty days unless Congress extended it for thirty more days.

The War Powers Act was but one manifestation of what came to be called the "New Isolationism," a mood of caution and restraint in the conduct of the nation's foreign affairs after the bloody and futile misadventure in Vietnam. Meanwhile, the draft ended in January 1973, although it was retained on a standby basis. Future members of the armed forces were to be volunteers, greatly easing anxieties among draft-age youth.

The Arab Oil Embargo and the Energy Crisis

The long-rumbling Middle East erupted anew in October 1973, when the rearmed Syrians and Egyptians unleashed surprise attacks on Israel in an attempt to regain the territory they had lost in the Six-Day War of 1967. With the Israelis in desperate retreat, Kissinger, who had become secretary of state in September, hastily flew to Moscow in an effort to restrain the Soviets, who were arming the attackers. Believing that the Kremlin was poised to fly combat troops to the Suez area, Nixon placed America's nuclear forces on alert and ordered a gigantic airlift of nearly $2 billion in war materials to the Israelis. This assistance helped save the day, as the Israelis aggressively turned the tide and threatened Cairo itself before American diplomacy brought about an uneasy cease-fire to what became known as the Yom Kippur War.

America's policy of backing Israel against its oil-rich neighbors exacted a heavy penalty. Late in October 1973, the OPEC nations announced an embargo on oil shipments to the United States and several European allies supporting Israel, especially the Netherlands. What was more, the oil-rich Arab states cut their oil production, further ratcheting up pressure on the entire West, whose citizens suffered a long winter of lowered thermostats and speedometers. Lines at gas stations grew longer as tempers grew shorter. The shortage triggered a major economic recession not just in America but also in France and Britain. Although the latter two countries had not supported Israel and had thus been exempted from the embargo, in an increasingly globalized, interconnected world, all nations soon felt the crunch.

The "energy crisis" suddenly energized a number of long-deferred projects. Congress approved a costly Alaska pipeline and a national speed limit of fifty-five miles per hour to conserve fuel. Agitation mounted for heavier use of coal and nuclear power, despite the environmental threat they posed.

The five months of the Arab "blackmail" embargo in 1974 clearly signaled the end of an era—the era of

Uncle Sam's Bed of Nails
The oil crises of the 1970s tortured the American economy.

cheap and abundant energy. A twenty-year surplus of world oil supplies had masked the fact that since 1948 the United States had been a net importer of oil. American oil production peaked in 1970 and then began an irreversible decline. Blissfully unaware of their dependence on foreign suppliers, Americans, like revelers on a binge, had more than tripled their oil consumption since the end of World War II. The number of automobiles increased 250 percent between 1949 and 1972, and Detroit's engineers gave nary a thought to building more fuel-efficient engines.

By 1974 America was oil-addicted and extremely vulnerable to any interruption in supplies. That stark fact would deeply color the diplomatic and economic history of the next three decades and beyond, as the

Middle East loomed ever larger on the map of America's strategic interests. OPEC approximately quadrupled its price for crude oil after lifting the embargo in 1974. Huge new oil bills wildly disrupted the U.S. balance of international trade and added further fuel to the already raging fires of inflation. The United States took the lead in forming the International Energy Agency in 1974 as a counterweight to OPEC, and various sectors of the economy, including Detroit's carmakers, began their slow, grudging adjustment to the rudely dawning age of energy dependency. But full reconciliation to that uncomfortable reality was a long time coming.

✶ Watergate and the Unmaking of a President

Nixon's electoral triumph in 1972 was almost immediately sullied—and eventually undone—by the so-called **Watergate** scandal. On June 17, 1972, five men were arrested in the Watergate apartment-office complex in Washington after a bungled effort to plant electronic "bugs" in the Democratic party's headquarters. They were soon revealed to be working for the Republican Committee to Re-Elect the President—popularly known as CREEP. The Watergate break-in turned out to be just one in a series of Nixon administration "dirty tricks" that included forging documents to discredit Democrats, using the Internal Revenue Service to harass innocent citizens named on a White House "enemies list," burglarizing the office of the psychiatrist who had treated the leaker of the Pentagon Papers, and perverting the FBI and the CIA to cover the tricksters' tracks.

Meanwhile, the moral stench hanging over the White House worsened when Vice President Agnew was forced to resign in October 1973 for taking bribes

Oil Shock When OPEC dramatically jacked up oil prices in the 1970s, many Americans—as represented by the Henry Kissinger figure in this cartoon—were slow to realize that an era of low energy prices had ended forever.

Nixon, the "Law-and-Order-Man" New York Newsday

about the Watergate affair in 1973–1974. Nixon indignantly denied any prior knowledge of the break-in and any involvement in the legal proceedings against the burglars. But John Dean III, a former White House lawyer with a remarkable memory, accused top White House officials, including the president, of obstructing justice by trying to cover up the Watergate break-in and silence its perpetrators. Then another former White House aide revealed that a secret taping system had recorded most of Nixon's Oval Office conversations. Now Dean's sensational testimony could be checked against the White House tapes, and the Senate committee could better determine who was telling the truth. But Nixon, stubbornly citing his "executive privilege," refused to hand over the tapes. Then, on October 20, 1973, he ordered the "Saturday Night Massacre," firing his own special prosecutor appointed to investigate the Watergate scandal, as well as his attorney general and deputy attorney general because they had refused to go along with firing the prosecutor.

Responding at last to the House Judiciary Committee's demand for the Watergate tapes, Nixon agreed in the spring of 1974 to the publication of "relevant" portions of the tapes, with many sections missing (including Nixon's frequent obscenities, which were excised with the phrase "expletive deleted"). But on July 24, 1974, the president suffered a disastrous setback when the Supreme Court unanimously ruled that "executive privilege" gave him no right to withhold evidence relevant to possible criminal activity. Skating on thin ice over hot water, Nixon reluctantly complied.

Seeking to soften the impact of inevitable disclosure, Nixon now made public three subpoenaed tapes of conversations with his chief aide on June 23, 1972. Fatally for his own case, one of them—the notorious **"smoking gun" tape** (see p. 927)—revealed the president giving orders, six days after the Watergate break-in, to

from Maryland contractors while governor and also as vice president. In the first use of the Twenty-fifth Amendment (see the Appendix), Nixon nominated and Congress confirmed Agnew's successor, a twelve-term congressman from Michigan, Gerald ("Jerry") Ford.

Amid a mood of growing national outrage, a select Senate committee conducted widely televised hearings

Smoking Pistol Exhibit A The tape-recorded conversations between President Nixon and his top aide on June 23, 1972, proved mortally damaging to Nixon's claim that he had played no role in the Watergate cover-up.

The "Smoking Gun" Tape, June 23, 1972, 10:04–11:39 A.M.

The technological capability to record Oval Office conversations combined with Richard Nixon's obsession with documenting his presidency to give the public—and the Senate committee investigating his role in the break-in of the Democratic National Committee headquarters in the Watergate Office Tower—rare access to personal conversations between the president and his closest advisers. This tape, which undeniably exposed Nixon's central role in constructing a "cover-up" of the Watergate break-in, was made on Nixon's first day back in Washington after the botched burglary of June 17, 1972. In this conversation with White House Chief of Staff H. R. Haldeman, Nixon devised a plan to block a widening FBI investigation by instructing the director of the CIA to deflect any further FBI snooping on the grounds that it would endanger sensitive CIA operations. Nixon refused to turn over this and other tapes to Senate investigators until so ordered by the Supreme Court on July 24, 1974. Within four days of its release on August 5, Nixon was forced to resign. After eighteen months of protesting his innocence of the crime and his ignorance of any effort to obstruct justice, Nixon was finally undone by the evidence in this incriminating "smoking gun" tape. While tapes documented two straight years of Nixon's Oval Office conversations, other presidents, such as Franklin Roosevelt, John F. Kennedy, and Lyndon Baines Johnson, recorded important meetings and crisis deliberations. Since Watergate, however, it is unlikely that any president has permitted extensive tape recording, depriving historians of a unique insight into the inner workings of the White House. Should taped White House discussions be part of the public record of a presidency, and if so, who should have access to them? What else might historians learn from a tape like this one, besides analyzing the Watergate cover-up?

Haldeman: . . . yesterday, they concluded it was not the White House, but are now convinced it is a CIA thing, so the CIA turn off would . . .

President: Well, not sure of their analysis, I'm not going to get that involved. I'm (unintelligible).

Haldeman: No, sir. We don't want you to.

President: You call them in

President: Good. Good deal! Play it tough. That's the way they play it and that's the way we are going to play it.

Haldeman: O.K. We'll do it.

President: Yeah, when I saw that news summary item, I of course knew it was a bunch of crap, but I thought ah, well it's good to have them off on this wild hair thing because when they start bugging us, which they have, we'll know our little boys will not know how to handle it. I hope they will though. You never know. Maybe, you think about it. Good!

President: When you get in these people when you . . . get these people in, say: "Look, the problem is that this will open the whole, the whole Bay of Pigs thing, and the President just feels that" ah, without going into the details . . . don't, don't lie to them to the extent to say there is no involvement, but just say this is sort of a comedy of errors, bizarre, without getting into it, "the President believes that it is going to open the whole Bay of Pigs thing up again. And, ah because these people are plugging for, for keeps and that they should call the FBI in and say that we wish for the country, don't go any further into this case," period!

Source: Nixon Presidential Materials Project, National Archives and Record Administration use the CIA to hold back an inquiry by the FBI. Nixon's own tape-recorded words convicted him of having been an active party to the attempted cover-up. The House Judiciary Committee proceeded to draw up articles of impeachment, based on obstruction of justice, abuse of the powers of the presidential office, and contempt of Congress.

The public's wrath proved to be overwhelming. Republican leaders in Congress concluded that the guilty and unpredictable Nixon was a loose cannon on the deck of the ship of state. They frankly informed the president that his impeachment by the full House and removal by the Senate were foregone conclusions and that he would do best to resign.

Left with no better choice, Nixon choked back his tears and announced his resignation in a dramatic television appearance on August 8, 1974. Few presidents had flown so high, and none had sunk so low. In his Farewell Address, Nixon admitted having made some "judgments" that "were wrong" but insisted that he had always acted "in what I believed at the time to be the best interests of the nation." Unconvinced, countless Americans would change the song "Hail to the Chief" to "Jail to the Chief."

The nation had survived a wrenching constitutional crisis, which proved that the impeachment machinery forged by the Founding Fathers could work when public opinion overwhelmingly demanded that it be implemented. The principles that no person is above the law and that presidents must be held to strict accountability for their acts were strengthened. The United States of America, on the eve of its two-hundredth birthday as a republic, had eventually cleaned its own sullied house, giving an impressive demonstration of self-discipline and self-government to the rest of the world.

✯ The First Unelected President

Gerald Rudolph Ford, the first man to be made president solely by a vote of Congress, entered the besmirched White House in August 1974 with serious handicaps. He was widely—and unfairly—suspected of being little more than a dim-witted former college football player. President Johnson had sneered that "Jerry" was so lacking in brainpower that he could not walk and chew gum at the same time. Worse, Ford had been selected, not elected, vice president, following Spiro Agnew's resignation in disgrace. The sour odor of illegitimacy hung about this president without precedent.

Then, out of a clear sky, Ford granted a complete pardon to Nixon for any crimes he may have committed as president, discovered or undiscovered. Democrats were outraged, and lingering suspicions about the circumstances of the pardon cast a dark shadow over Ford's prospects of being elected president in his own right in 1976.

Ford at first sought to enhance the so-called détente with the Soviet Union that Nixon had crafted. In July 1975 President Ford joined leaders from thirty-four other nations in Helsinki, Finland, to sign several sets of historic accords. One group of agreements officially wrote an end to World War II by finally legitimizing the Soviet-dictated boundaries of Poland and other Eastern European countries. In return, the Soviets signed a "third basket" of agreements, guaranteeing more liberal exchanges of people and information between East and West and protecting certain basic "human rights." The Helsinki accords kindled small dissident movements in Eastern Europe and even in the USSR itself, but the Soviets soon poured ice water on these sputtering flames of freedom.

Western Europeans, especially the West Germans, cheered the Helsinki conference as a milestone of détente. But in the United States, critics increasingly charged that détente was proving to be a one-way street. American grain and technology flowed across the Atlantic to the USSR, and little of comparable importance flowed back. Moscow also continued its human rights violations, including restrictions on Jewish emigration, which prompted Congress in 1974 to add punitive restrictions to a U.S. Soviet trade bill. Despite these difficulties, Ford at first clung stubbornly to détente. But the American public's fury over Moscow's double-dealing so steadily mounted that by the end of his term, the president was refusing even to pronounce the word *détente* in public. The thaw in the Cold War was threatening to prove chillingly brief.

✯ Defeat in Vietnam

Early in 1975 the North Vietnamese gave full throttle to their long-expected drive southward. President Ford urged Congress to vote still more weapons for Vietnam, but his plea was in vain, and without the crutch of massive American aid, the South Vietnamese quickly and ingloriously collapsed.

The dam burst so rapidly that the remaining Americans had to be frantically evacuated by helicopter, the last of them on April 29, 1975. Also rescued were about 140,000 South Vietnamese, most of them so dangerously identified with the Americans that they feared a bloodbath by the victorious communists. Ford compassionately admitted these people to the United States, where they added further seasoning to the melting pot. Eventually some 500,000 arrived (see "Makers of America: The Vietnamese," pp. 930–931).

America's longest, most frustrating war thus ended not with a bang but a whimper. In a technical sense, the Americans had not lost the war; their client nation had. The United States had fought the North Vietnamese to a standstill and had then withdrawn its troops in 1973, leaving the South Vietnamese to fight their own war, with generous shipments of costly American aircraft, tanks, and other munitions. The estimated cost to America was $118 billion in current outlays, together with some 56,000 dead and 300,000 wounded. The people of the United States had in fact provided just about everything, except the will to win—and that could not be injected by outsiders.

Technicalities aside, America had lost more than a war. It had lost face in the eyes of foreigners, lost its own self-esteem, lost confidence in its military prowess, and lost much of the economic muscle that had made possible its global leadership since World War II.

Americans reluctantly came to realize that their power as well as their pride had been deeply wounded in Vietnam and that recovery would be slow and painful.

✦ Feminist Victories and Defeats

As the army limped home from Vietnam, there was little rejoicing on the college campuses, where demonstrators had once braved tear gas and billy clubs to denounce the war. The antiwar movement, like many of the other protest movements that convulsed the country in the 1960s, had long since splintered and stalled. One major exception to this pattern stood out: American feminists, although they had their differences, showed vitality and momentum. They won legislative

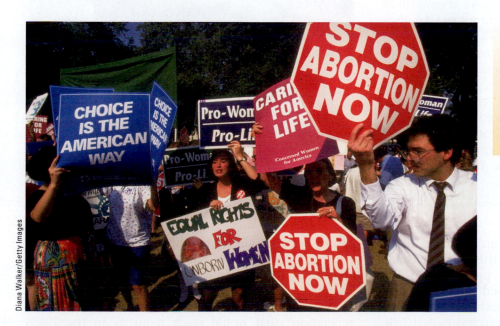

Diana Walker/Getty Images

At first glance the towns of Westminster and Fountain Valley, California, seem to resemble other California communities nearby. Tract homes line residential streets; shopping centers flank the busy thoroughfares. But these are no ordinary American suburbs. Instead they make up "Little Saigons," vibrant outposts of Vietnamese culture in the contemporary United States. Shops offer exotic Asian merchandise; restaurants serve such delicacies as lemongrass chicken. These neighborhoods, living reminders of America's anguish in Vietnam, are a rarely acknowledged consequence of that sorrowful conflict.

Before South Vietnam fell in 1975, few Vietnamese ventured across the Pacific. Indeed, throughout most of American history until the mid-twentieth century, the bulk of U.S. immigrants had come from Europe, with the notable exception of the Chinese and, to a lesser extent, the Japanese (see pp. 500–501 and pp. 800–801). This trend began to change in the 1960s, as people from South America and Asia began arriving in greater numbers. The war-weary Vietnamese were at the forefront of this new immigration, so much so that in 1966 the U.S. Immigration authorities designated "Vietnamese" as a separate category of newcomers. Most early immigrants were the wives and children of U.S. servicemen.

As the communists closed in on Saigon in the mid-1970s, many Vietnamese, particularly those who had worked closely with American or South Vietnamese authorities, feared for their lives. Gathering together as many of their extended-family members as they could, thousands of Vietnamese prepared to flee the country. In a few hectic days in 1975, some 140,000 Vietnamese escaped before the approaching communist gunfire, a few dramatically clinging to the bottoms of departing U.S. helicopters. From Saigon they were conveyed to military bases in Guam and the Philippines. Another 60,000 less fortunate Vietnamese escaped at the same time over land and sea to Hong Kong and Thailand, where they waited nervously for permission to move on.

To accommodate the refugees, the U.S. government set up camps across the United States. Arrivals were crowded into army barracks affording little room and less privacy. These were boot camps not for military service but for assimilation into American society.

A rigorous program trained the Vietnamese in English, forbade children from speaking their native language in the classroom, and even immersed them in American slang. Many resented this attempt to mold them, to strip them of their culture.

Their discontent boiled over when authorities prepared to release the refugees from camps and board them with families around the nation. The resettlement officials had decided to find a sponsor for each Vietnamese family—an American family that would provide food, shelter, and assistance for the refugees until they could fend for themselves. But the Vietnamese people cherish their traditional extended families—grandparents, uncles, aunts, and cousins living communally with parents and children. Few American sponsors would accommodate a large extended family; fewer Vietnamese families would willingly separate.

The refugees were dispersed to Iowa, Illinois, Pennsylvania, New York, Washington, and California. But

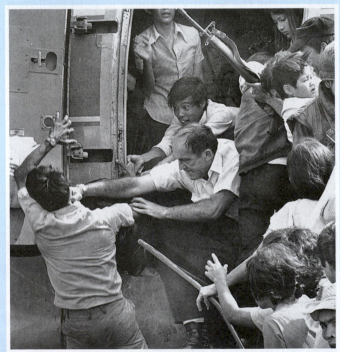

The Last Days of Saigon Violence often attended the frantic American evacuation from Vietnam in 1975.

© Bettmann/Corbis

and judicial victories and provoked an intense rethinking of gender roles. (On the roots of this movement, see "Makers of America: The Feminists," pp. 934–935.)

Thousands of women marched in the Women's Stride for Equality on the fiftieth anniversary of woman suffrage in 1970. In 1972 Congress passed Title IX of the Education Amendments, prohibiting sex discrimination in any federally assisted educational program or activity. Perhaps this act's biggest impact was to create opportunities for girls' and women's athletics at schools and colleges, giving birth to a new "Title IX generation" that would reach maturity in the 1980s

Lawrence Migdale

Preserving the Past A Vietnamese American boy learns classical calligraphy from his grandfather.

the settlement sites, many of them tucked away in rural districts, offered scant economic opportunities. The immigrants, who had held mainly skilled or white-collar positions in Vietnam, bristled as they were herded into menial labor. As soon as they could, they relocated, hastening to established Vietnamese enclaves around San Francisco, Los Angeles, and Dallas.

Soon a second throng of Vietnamese immigrants pushed into these Little Saigons. Fleeing from the ravages of poverty and from the oppressive communist government, these stragglers had crammed themselves and their few possessions into little boats, hoping to reach Hong Kong or get picked up by foreign ships. Eventually many of these "boat people" reached the United States. Usually less educated than the first arrivals and receiving far less resettlement aid from the U.S. government, they were, however, more willing to start at the bottom. Today these two groups total more than half a million people. Differing in experience and expectations, the Vietnamese share a new home in a strange land. Their uprooting is an immense, unreckoned consequence of America's longest war.

Christopher Morris/Black Star/Stockphoto.com

Boat People Vietnamese refugees flee to freedom.

and 1990s and help professionalize women's sports as well. The **Equal Rights Amendment (ERA)** to the Constitution won congressional approval in 1972. It declared, "Equality of rights under the law shall not be denied or abridged by the United States or by any State on account of sex." Twenty-eight of the necessary

thirty-eight states quickly ratified the amendment, first proposed by suffragists in 1923. Hopes rose that the ERA might soon become the law of the land.

Even the Supreme Court seemed to be on the movement's side. In *Reed* v. *Reed* (1971) and *Frontiero* v. *Richardson* (1973), the Court challenged sex discrimination in legislation and employment. And in the landmark case of ***Roe*** v. ***Wade*** (1973), the Court struck down laws prohibiting abortion, arguing that a woman's decision to terminate a pregnancy was protected by the constitutional right of privacy.

But the feminist movement soon faced a formidable backlash. In 1972 President Nixon vetoed a proposal to set up nationwide public day care, saying it would weaken the American family. Antifeminists blamed the women's movement for the rising divorce rate, which tripled between 1960 and 1976. And the Catholic Church and the religious right organized a powerful grassroots movement to oppose the legalization of abortion.

For many feminists the most bitter defeat was the death of the ERA. Antifeminists, led by conservative activist Phyllis Schlafly, argued that the ERA would remove traditional protections that women enjoyed by forcing the law to see them as men's equals. They

Antifeminist Phyllis Schlafly (b. 1924) Schlafly traveled the country promoting her "STOP ERA" campaign. She argued that ratification of the Equal Rights Amendment would undermine the American family by violating "the right of a wife to be supported by her husband," requiring women to serve in combat, and legalizing homosexual marriage.

Joan Roth/Getty Images

further believed that the amendment would threaten the basic family structure of American society. Schlafly charged that the ERA's advocates were just "bitter women seeking a constitutional cure for their personal problems." In 1979 Congress extended the deadline for ratification of the amendment, but opponents dug in their heels. The ERA died in 1982, three states short of success.

⬟ The Seventies in Black and White

Although the civil rights movement had fractured, race remained an explosive issue in the 1970s. The Supreme Court in *Milliken* v. *Bradley* (1974) blindsided school integrationists when it ruled that desegregation plans could not require students to move across school-district lines. The decision effectively exempted suburban districts from shouldering any part of the burden of desegregating inner-city schools, thereby reinforcing "white flight" from cities to suburbs. By the same token, the decision distilled all the problems of desegregation into the least prosperous districts, often pitting the poorest, most disadvantaged elements of the white and black communities against one another.

Affirmative-action programs also remained highly controversial. White workers who were denied advancement and white students who were refused college admission continued to raise the cry of "reverse discrimination," charging that their rights had been violated by employers and admissions officers who put more weight on racial or ethnic background than on ability or achievement.

One white Californian, Allan Bakke, made headlines in 1978 when the Supreme Court, by the narrowest of margins (five to four) upheld his claim that his application to medical school had been turned down because of an admissions program that favored minority applicants. In a tortured decision reflecting the troubling moral ambiguities and insoluble political complexities of this issue, the Court ordered the University of California at Davis medical school to admit Bakke and declared that preference in admissions could not be given to members of any group, minority or majority, on the basis of ethnic or racial identity alone. Yet at the same time, the Court said that racial factors might be taken into account in a school's overall admissions policy for purposes of assembling a diverse student body. Among the dissenters on the sharply divided bench was the Court's only black justice, Thurgood Marshall. He warned in an impassioned opinion that the denial of racial preferences might sweep away years of progress by the civil rights movement. But many conservatives cheered the decision as affirming the principle that justice is colorblind.

Stanley Forman, Pulitzer Prize 1976, www.stanleyformanphotos.com

A Sad Day for Old Glory   In 1976, America's bicentennial year, anti-busing demonstrators convulsed Boston, the historic "cradle of liberty." White disillusionment with the race-based policies that were a legacy of Lyndon Johnson's "Great Society" programs of the 1960s helped to feed the conservative, antigovernment movement that elected Ronald Reagan in 1980.

Inspired by the civil rights movement, Native Americans in the 1970s gained remarkable power through using the courts and well-planned acts of civil disobedience. But while blacks had fought against segregation, Indians used the tactics of the civil rights movement to assert their status as separate semi-sovereign peoples. Indian activists captured the nation's attention by seizing the island of Alcatraz in 1970 and the village of Wounded Knee, South Dakota, in 1972. A series of victories in the courts consolidated the decade's gains. In the case of *United States* v. *Wheeler* (1978), the Supreme Court declared that Indian tribes possessed a "unique and limited" sovereignty, subject to the will of Congress but not to individual states.

✷ The Bicentennial Campaign

America's two-hundredth birthday, in 1976, fell during a presidential election year—a fitting coincidence for a proud democracy. President Gerald Ford energetically sought the Republican nomination in his own right and defeated challenger Ronald Reagan, former actor and governor of California, who ran as a more conservative candidate.

The Democratic standard-bearer was fifty-one-year-old James Earl ("Jimmy") Carter, Jr., a dark-horse candidate who galloped out of obscurity during the long primary-election season. A peanut farmer and former Georgia governor who insisted on the humble "Jimmy" as his first name, this born-again Baptist touched many people with his down-home sincerity. He ran against the memory of Nixon and Watergate as much as he ran against Ford. His most effective campaign pitch was his promise "I'll never lie to you." Untainted by ties with a corrupt and cynical Washington, he attracted voters as an outsider who would clean the disorderly house of "big government."

Carter squeezed out a narrow victory on election day, with 51 percent of the popular vote. The electoral count stood at 297 to 240. The winner swept every state except Virginia in his native South. Especially important were the votes of African Americans, 97 percent of whom cast their ballots for Carter.

Carter enjoyed hefty Democratic majorities in both houses of Congress. Hopes ran high that the stalemate of the Nixon-Ford years between a Republican White House and a Democratic Capitol Hill would now be ended. At first Carter enjoyed notable success, as Congress granted his requests to create a new cabinet-level Department of Energy and to cut taxes. The new president's popularity remained exceptionally high during his first few months in office, even when he courted public disfavor by courageously keeping his campaign promise to pardon some ten thousand draft evaders of the Vietnam War era.

But Carter's honeymoon did not last long. An inexperienced outsider, he had campaigned against the Washington "establishment" and never quite made the transition to being an insider himself. He repeatedly rubbed congressional fur the wrong way, especially by failing to consult adequately with the leaders. Critics charged that he isolated himself in a shallow pool of fellow Georgians, whose ignorance of the ways of Washington compounded the problems of their greenhorn chief.

✷ Carter's Humanitarian Diplomacy

As a committed Christian, President Carter displayed from the outset an overriding concern for "human rights" as the guiding principle of his foreign policy. In the African nations of Rhodesia (later Zimbabwe) and South Africa, Carter and his eloquent U.N. ambassador, Andrew Young, championed the oppressed black majority.

The president's most spectacular foreign-policy achievement came in September 1978 when he invited President Anwar Sadat of Egypt and Prime Minister

A well-to-do housewife and mother of seven, Elizabeth Cady Stanton (1815–1902) was an unlikely revolutionary. Yet this founding mother of American feminism devoted seven decades of her life to the fight for women's rights.

Young Elizabeth Cady drew her inspiration from the fight against slavery. In 1840 she married fellow abolitionist Henry Stanton. Honeymooning in London, they attended the World Anti-Slavery Convention, where women were forced to sit in a screened-off balcony above the convention floor. This insult awakened Stanton to the cause that would occupy her life. With Lucretia Mott and other female abolitionists, Stanton went on to organize the Seneca Falls Convention in 1848. There she presented her Declaration of Sentiments, modeled on the Declaration of Independence and proclaiming that "all men *and women* are created equal." She demanded for women the right to own property, to enter the professions, and, most daring of all, to vote.

As visionaries of a radically different future for women, early feminists encountered a mountain of hostility and tasted bitter disappointment. Stanton failed in her struggle to have women included in the Fourteenth Amendment to the U.S. Constitution, which granted African Americans equal citizenship. She died before seeing her dream of woman suffrage realized in the Nineteenth Amendment (1920). Yet by imagining women's emancipation as an expansion of America's founding principles of citizenship, Stanton charted a path that other feminists would follow a century later.

Historians use the terms "first wave" and "second wave" to distinguish the women's movement of the nineteenth century from that of the late twentieth century. The woman most often credited with launching the "second wave" is Betty Friedan (1921–2006). Growing up in Peoria, Illinois, she had seen her mother grow bitter over sacrificing a journalism career to raise her family. Friedan, a suburban housewife, went on to write the 1963 best seller *The Feminine Mystique*, exposing the quiet desperation of millions of housewives trapped in the "comfortable concentration camp" of the suburban home. The book struck a resonant chord and catapulted its author onto the national stage. In 1966 Friedan cofounded the National Organization for Women (NOW), the chief political arm and more moderate wing of second-wave feminism.

Elizabeth Cady Stanton Trust/Picture Research Consultants & Archives

Elizabeth Cady Stanton (1815–1902) and Two of Her Sons, 1848 In the same year this photo was taken, Stanton delivered her Declaration of Sentiments to the first Woman's Rights Convention in Seneca Falls, New York.

Just as first-wave feminism grew out of abolitionism, the second wave drew ideas, leaders, and tactics from the civil rights movement of the 1960s. Civil rights workers and feminists alike focused on equal rights. NOW campaigned vigorously for the Equal Rights Amendment, which fell just three states short of ratification in 1982. But second-wave feminism knew no national boundaries. In the late 1960s, activists around the world resurrected the tradition of International Women's Day, which first-wave feminists had marked through the 1920s. March 8 became an

Menachem Begin of Israel to a summit conference at Camp David, the woodsy presidential retreat in the Maryland highlands. Skillfully serving as go-between, Carter persuaded the two visitors to sign an accord (September 17, 1978) that held considerable promise

of peace. Israel agreed in principle to withdraw from territory conquered in the 1967 war, and Egypt in return promised to respect Israel's borders. Both parties pledged themselves to sign a formal peace treaty within three months.

Steve Northrup/TimeLife Pictures/Getty Images

Marching for Women's Rights, 1977 A multiethnic and multiracial group of women, accompanied by noted "second-wave" feminists Bella Abzug (in hat) and Betty Friedan (far right), helped to carry a torch from Seneca Falls, New York, birthplace of the feminist movement, to Houston, Texas, site of the National Women's Conference.

international day of celebration and awareness of the continued inequality and violence that many women faced around the globe.

Second-wave feminism also had an avowedly radical wing, supported by younger women who were eager to challenge almost every traditional male and female gender role and to take the feminist cause to the streets. Among these women was Robin Morgan (b. 1941). As a college student in the 1960s, Morgan was active in civil rights organizations that provided her with a model for crusading against social injustice. They also exposed her to the same sexism that plagued society at large. Women in the movement who protested against gender discrimination met ridicule, as in SNCC leader Stokely Carmichael's famous retort, "The only position for women in SNCC is prone." Morgan went on to found WITCH (Women's International Terrorist Conspiracy from Hell), made famous by its protest at the 1968 Miss America pageant in Atlantic City, New Jersey. There demonstrators crowned a sheep Miss America and threw symbols of women's oppression—bras, girdles, and dishcloths—into trash cans. (Contrary to news stories, they did not burn the bras.)

As the contrast between WITCH and NOW suggests, second-wave feminism was a remarkably diverse movement. Feminists disagreed over many issues—from pornography and marriage to how much to expect from government, capitalism, and men. Some feminists placed a priority on gender equality—for example, full female service in the military. Others defended a feminism of gender difference—such as maternity leave and other special protections for women in the workplace.

Still, beyond these differences feminists had much in common. Most advocated a woman's right to choose in the battle over abortion rights. Most regarded the law as the key weapon against gender discrimination. By the early twenty-first century, radical and moderate feminists alike could take pride in a host of achievements that had changed the landscape of gender relations beyond what most people could have imagined at midcentury. Yet like Elizabeth Cady Stanton, second-wave feminists also shared the burden of understanding that the goals of genuine equality would take more than a lifetime to achieve.

The president crowned this diplomatic success by resuming full diplomatic relations with China in early 1979 after a nearly thirty-year interruption. Carter also successfully pushed through two treaties to turn over the Panama Canal to the Panamanians. Although these treaties were decried by conservatives such as Ronald Reagan—who stridently declared, "We bought it, we paid for it, we built it, and we intend to keep it!"—the United States gave up control of the canal on December 31, 1999.

Celebrating the Camp David Agreement, September 1978 Anwar Sadat of Egypt (left) and Menachem Begin of Israel (right) join U.S. president Jimmy Carter in confirming the historic accord that brought the hope of peace to the war-torn Middle East.

Black Star/Stockphoto.com

Despite these dramatic accomplishments, trouble stalked Carter's foreign policy. Overshadowing all international issues was the ominous reheating of the Cold War with the Soviet Union. Détente fell into disrepute as thousands of Cuban troops, assisted by Soviet advisers, appeared in Angola, Ethiopia, and elsewhere in Africa to support revolutionary factions. Arms-control negotiations with Moscow stalled in the face of this Soviet military meddling.

★ Economic and Energy Woes

Adding to Carter's mushrooming troubles was the failing health of the economy. A stinging recession during Ford's presidency had brought the inflation rate down slightly to just under 6 percent, but from the moment Carter took over, prices resumed their dizzying ascent, driving the inflation rate well above 13 percent by 1980 (see Figure 39.2). The soaring bill for imported oil plunged America's balance of payments deeply into the red (an unprecedented $40 billion in 1978).

The "oil shocks" of the 1970s taught Americans a painful but necessary lesson: that they could never again seriously consider a policy of economic isolation, as they had tried to do in the decades between the two world wars. For most of American history, foreign trade had accounted for no more than 10 percent of gross national product (GNP). But huge foreign-oil bills drove that figure steadily upward in the 1970s and thereafter. By century's end, some 27 percent of GNP depended on foreign trade. Unable to dominate international trade and finance as easily as they once had, Americans would have to master foreign languages and study foreign cultures if they wanted to prosper in the rapidly globalizing economy.

Historical Double Take Many Americans who looked back reverently to Theodore Roosevelt's "Rough Rider" diplomacy were outraged at the Panama "giveaway." But the Carter administration, looking to the future, argued persuasively that relinquishing control of the canal would be healthy for U.S.–Latin American relations. © Valtman/Rothco

FIGURE 39.2 The History of the Consumer Price Index, 1967–2008 This graph shows both the annual percentage rate of inflation and the cumulative shrinkage of the dollar's value since 1967. (By 2008 it took more than six dollars to buy what one dollar had purchased in 1967.) (Sources: Bureau of Labor Statistics and *Statistical Abstract of the United States*, relevant years.)

Yawning deficits in the federal budget, reaching nearly $60 billion in 1980, further aggravated the U.S. economy's inflationary ailments. The elderly and other Americans living on fixed incomes suffered from the shrinking dollar. People with money to lend pushed interest rates ever higher, hoping to protect themselves from being repaid in badly depreciated dollars. The "prime rate" (the rate of interest that banks charge their very best customers) vaulted to an unheard-of 20 percent in early 1980. The high cost of borrowing money shoved small businesses to the wall and strangled the construction industry, which was heavily dependent on loans to finance new housing and other projects.

Carter diagnosed America's economic disease as stemming primarily from the nation's costly dependence on foreign oil. Unfortunately, his legislative proposals for energy conservation in 1977 ignited a blaze of indifference among the American people, who had already forgotten the long gasoline lines of 1973.

Events in Iran jolted Americans out of their complacency about energy supplies in 1979. The imperious Mohammed Reza Pahlevi, installed as shah of Iran with help from America's CIA in 1953, had long ruled his oil-rich land with a will of steel. His repressive regime was finally overthrown in January 1979. Violent revolution was spearheaded in Iran by Muslim fundamentalists who fiercely resented the shah's campaign to westernize and secularize his country. Denouncing the United States as the "Great Satan" that had abetted the shah's efforts, these extremists engulfed Iran in chaos in the wake of his departure. The crippling upheavals soon spread to Iran's oil fields. As Iranian oil stopped flowing into the stream of world commerce, shortages appeared, and OPEC again seized the opportunity to hike petroleum prices. Americans once more found themselves waiting impatiently in long lines at gas stations or buying gasoline only on specified days.

As the oil crisis deepened, President Carter sensed the rising temperature of popular discontent. In July

President Jimmy Carter (b. 1924) delivered what became known as his "malaise speech" (although he never used the word) on television in 1979:

"In a nation that was proud of hard work, strong families, close-knit communities, and our faith in God, too many of us now tend to worship self-indulgence and consumption. Human identity is no longer defined by what one does, but by what one owns. But we've discovered that owning things and consuming things does not satisfy our longing for meaning. We've learned that piling up material goods cannot fill the emptiness of lives which have no confidence or purpose. . . . The symptoms of this crisis of the American spirit are all around us."

In time cultural conservatives would take up Carter's theme to support their call for a return to "traditional values."

1979 he retreated to the presidential mountain hideaway at Camp David, where he remained largely out of public view for ten days. Like a royal potentate of old, summoning the wise men of the realm for their counsel in a time of crisis, Carter called in over a hundred leaders from all walks of life to give him their views. Meanwhile, the nation waited anxiously for the results of these extraordinary deliberations.

When Carter came down from the mountaintop on July 15, 1979, he stunned a perplexed nation with his **malaise speech**, chiding his fellow citizens for falling into a "moral and spiritual crisis" and for being too concerned with "material goods." A few days later, in a bureaucratic massacre of almost unprecedented proportions, he fired four cabinet secretaries and circled the wagons of his Georgia advisers more tightly about the White House by reorganizing and expanding the power of his personal staff. Critics began to wonder aloud whether Carter, the professed man of the people, was losing touch with the popular mood of the country.

✺ Foreign Affairs and the Iranian Imbroglio

Hopes for a less dangerous world rose slightly in June 1979, when President Carter met with Soviet leader Leonid Brezhnev in Vienna to sign the long-stalled **SALT II** agreements, limiting the levels of lethal strategic weapons in the Soviet and American arsenals. But conservative critics of the president's defense policies, still regarding the Soviet Union as the Wicked Witch of the East, unsheathed their long knives to carve up the SALT II treaty when it came to the Senate for debate in the summer of 1979.

Political earthquakes in the petroleum-rich Persian Gulf region finally buried all hopes of ratifying the SALT II treaty. On November 4, 1979, a mob of rabidly anti-American Muslim militants stormed the United States embassy in Tehran, Iran, and took all of its occupants hostage. The captors then demanded that the American authorities ship back to Iran the exiled shah,

Europeans are Skeptical about US-USSR SALT II Talks As President Carter and Soviet leader Leonid Brezhnev prepared to meet for arms-reduction talks in Vienna in June 1979, a German newspaper cartoonist questioned the depth of their commitment to genuine disarmament.

Behrendt/Frankfurter Allgemeine Zeitung

who had arrived in the United States two weeks earlier for medical treatment.

World opinion hotly condemned the diplomatic felony in Iran, while Americans agonized over both the fate of the hostages and the stability of the entire Persian Gulf region, so dangerously close to the Soviet Union. The Soviet army then aroused the West's worst fears on December 27, 1979, when it blitzed into the mountainous nation of Afghanistan, next door to Iran, and appeared to be poised for a thrust at the oil jugular of the gulf.

President Carter reacted vigorously to these alarming events. He slapped an embargo on the export of grain and high-technology machinery to the USSR and called for a boycott of the upcoming Olympic Games in Moscow. He proposed the creation of a "Rapid Deployment Force" to respond to suddenly developing crises in faraway places and requested that young people (including women) be made to register for a possible military draft. The president proclaimed that the United States would "use any means necessary, including force," to protect the Persian Gulf against Soviet incursions. He grimly conceded that he had misjudged the Soviets, and the SALT II treaty became a dead letter in the Senate. Meanwhile, the Soviet army met unexpectedly stiff resistance in Afghanistan and bogged down in a nasty, decade-long guerrilla war that came to be called "Russia's Vietnam."

The **Iranian hostage crisis** was Carter's—and America's—bed of nails. The captured Americans languished in cruel captivity, while the nightly television news broadcasts in the United States showed humiliating scenes of Iranian mobs burning the American flag and spitting on effigies of Uncle Sam.

Carter at first tried to apply economic sanctions and the pressure of world public opinion against the Iranians, while waiting for the emergence of a stable government with which to negotiate. But the political turmoil in Iran rumbled on endlessly, and the president's frustration grew. Carter at last ordered a daring rescue mission. A highly trained commando team penetrated deep into Iran's sandy interior. Their plan required ticktock-perfect timing to succeed, and when equipment failures prevented some members of the team from reaching their destination, the mission had to be scrapped. As the commandos withdrew in the dark desert night, two of their aircraft collided, killing eight of the would-be rescuers.

This disastrous failure of the rescue raid proved anguishing for Americans. The episode seemed to underscore the nation's helplessness and even incompetence in the face of a mortifying insult to the national honor. The stalemate with Iran dragged on throughout the rest of Carter's term, providing an embarrassing backdrop to the embattled president's struggle for reelection.

Iranians Denounce President Jimmy Carter, November 1979 Scenes like this one appeared almost nightly on American television during the 444 days of the Iranian hostage crisis, humiliating Carter and angering American citizens.

Chapter Review

KEY TERMS

Vietnamization (917)

Nixon Doctrine (917)

silent majority (918)

My Lai Massacre (918)

Kent State University (919)

Pentagon Papers (919)

détente (920)

Miranda warning (921)

Philadelphia Plan (921)

Environmental Protection
  Agency (EPA) (922)

Earth Day (922)

southern strategy (922)

War Powers Act (924)

Watergate (925)

"smoking gun" tape (926)

Equal Rights Amendment
  (ERA) (931)

Roe v. *Wade* (932)

malaise speech (938)

SALT II (938)

Iranian hostage crisis (939)

PEOPLE TO KNOW

Henry A. Kissinger

Warren E. Burger

Rachel Carson

George McGovern

Gerald ("Jerry") Ford

John Dean III

James Earl ("Jimmy")
  Carter, Jr.

Leonid Brezhnev

CHRONOLOGY

1968 My Lai Massacre
WITCH protests Miss America pageant in
  Atlantic City, New Jersey

1970 Nixon orders invasion of Cambodia
Kent State and Jackson State incidents
Environmental Protection Agency (EPA)
  created
Clean Air Act

1971 Pentagon Papers published

1972 Twenty-sixth Amendment (lowering voting
  age to eighteen) passed
Nixon visits China and Soviet Union
Shanghai Communiqué begins "normaliza-
  tion" of U.S.-Chinese relations
ABM and SALT I treaties ratified
Nixon defeats McGovern for presidency
Equal Rights Amendment passes Congress
  (not ratified by states)
Title IX of Education Amendments passed

1973 Treaty of Paris enacts cease-fire in Vietnam
  and U.S. withdrawal
Agnew resigns; Ford appointed vice
  president
War Powers Act
Yom Kippur War
OPEC oil embargo
Endangered Species Act
Chilean president Salvador Allende killed in
  CIA-backed coup
Frontiero v. *Richardson*
Roe v. *Wade*

1973–1974 Watergate hearings and investigations

1974 Nixon resigns; Ford assumes presidency
OPEC ends embargo, increases oil prices
International Energy Agency formed
Milliken v. *Bradley*

1975 Helsinki accords
South Vietnam falls to communists

1976 Carter defeats Ford for presidency

1978 Camp David accords between Egypt and
  Israel
United States v. *Wheeler*

1979 Iranian revolution and oil crisis
SALT II agreements signed (never ratified by
  Senate)
Soviet Union invades Afghanistan

1979–1981 Iranian hostage crisis

1980 U.S. boycotts Summer Olympics in Moscow

TO LEARN MORE

Stephen Ambrose, *Nixon: The Triumph of a Politician, 1962–1972* (1989)

Carl Bernstein and Bob Woodward, *All the President's Men* (1974)

James Bill, *The Eagle and the Lion* (1987)

Robert Dallek, *Nixon and Kissinger: Partners in Power* (2007)

Alice Echols, *Daring to Be Bad: Radical Feminism in America, 1967–1975* (1989)

David Greenberg, *Nixon's Shadow: The History of an Image* (2003)

Linda Greenhouse, *Becoming Justice Blackmun: Harry Blackmun's Supreme Court Journey* (2005)

Walter LaFeber, *Inevitable Revolutions: The United States in Central America*, 2nd ed., (1993)

Matthew D. Lassiter, *The Silent Majority: Suburban Politics in the Sunbelt South* (2007)

Rick Perlstein, *Nixonland: The Rise of a President and the Fracturing of America* (2008)

Bruce Schulman, *The Seventies: The Great Shift in American Culture, Society, and Politics* (2001)

          , and Julian Zelizer, eds., *Rightward Bound: Making America Conservative in the 1970s* (2008)

Jeremi Suri, *Henry Kissinger and the American Century* (2007)

Bob Woodward and Scott Armstrong, *The Brethren: Inside the Supreme Court* (1979)

A complete, annotated bibliography for this chapter—along with brief descriptions of the People to Know—may be found on the American Pageant website. The Key Terms are defined in a Glossary at the end of the text.

Go to the CourseMate website at **www.cengagebrain.com** for additional study tools and review materials—including audio and video clips—for this chapter.

Chapter 40

The Resurgence of Conservatism

1980–1992

It will be my intention to curb the size and influence of the federal establishment and to demand recognition of the distinction between the powers granted to the federal government and those reserved to the states or to the people.

RONALD REAGAN, INAUGURAL, 1981

"*It's morning in America*" was the slogan of Republican candidate Ronald Reagan in his 1984 presidential campaign. Certainly the 1980s were a new day for America's conservative right. Census figures confirmed that the average American was older than in the stormy sixties and much more likely to live in the South or West, the traditional bastions of the "Old Right," where many residents harbored suspicions of federal power. The conservative cause drew added strength from the emergence of a "New Right" movement, partly in response to the countercultural protests of the 1960s. Spearheading the New Right were evangelical Christian groups such as the Moral Majority, dedicated believers who enjoyed startling success as political fund-raisers and organizers.

Many New Right activists were far less agitated about economic questions than about cultural concerns—the so-called social issues. They denounced abortion, pornography, homosexuality, feminism, and affirmative action. They championed prayer in the schools and tougher penalties for criminals. Together the Old and New Right added up to a powerful political combination, devoted to changing the very character of American society.

✦ The Election of Ronald Reagan, 1980

Ronald Reagan was well suited to lead the gathering conservative crusade. Reared in a generation whose values were formed well before the upheavals of the 1960s, he naturally sided with the New Right on social issues. In economic and social matters alike, he denounced the activist government and failed "social engineering" of the 1960s. Just as his early political hero, Franklin Roosevelt, had championed the "forgotten man" against big business, Reagan championed the "common man" against big government. He condemned federal intervention in local affairs, favoritism for minorities, and the elitism of arrogant bureaucrats. He aimed especially to win over from the Democratic column working-class and lower-middle-class white voters by implying that the Democratic party had become the party of big government and the exclusive tool of its minority constituents.

Though Reagan was no intellectual, he drew on the ideas of a small but influential group of thinkers known as "neoconservatives." Their ranks included Norman Podhoretz, editor of *Commentary* magazine, and Irving Kristol, editor of *The Public Interest*. Reacting against what they saw as the excesses of 1960s liberalism, the neoconservatives championed free-market capitalism liberated from government restraints, and they took tough, harshly anti-Soviet positions in foreign policy. They also questioned liberal welfare programs and affirmative-action policies and called for the reassertion of traditional values of individualism and the centrality of the family.

An actor-turned-politician, Reagan enjoyed enormous popularity with his crooked grin and aw-shucks manner. The son of a ne'er-do-well, impoverished Irish

President Ronald Reagan Older than any man previously elected to the presidency, Reagan displayed youthful vigor both on the campaign trail and in office.

American father with a fondness for the bottle, he had grown up in a small Illinois town. Reagan got his start in life in the depressed 1930s as a sports announcer for an Iowa radio station. Good looks and a way with words landed him acting jobs in Hollywood, where he became a B-grade star in the 1940s. He displayed a flair for politics as president of the Screen Actors Guild in the McCarthy era of the early 1950s, when he helped purge communists and other suspected "reds" from the film industry. In 1954 he became a spokesman for General Electric and began to abandon his New Deal-ish political views and increasingly to preach a conservative, antigovernment line. Reagan's growing skill at promoting the conservative cause inspired a group of wealthy California businessmen to help him launch his political career as governor of California from 1966 to 1974.

By 1980 the Republican party was ready to challenge the Democrats' hold on the White House. Bedeviled abroad and becalmed at home, Jimmy Carter's administration struck many Americans as bungling and befuddled. Carter's inability to control double-digit inflation was especially damaging. Frustrated critics bellyached loudly about the Georgian's alleged mismanagement of the nation's affairs.

Disaffection with Carter's apparent ineptitude ran deep even in his own Democratic party, where an "ABC" (Anybody but Carter) movement gathered steam. The liberal wing of the party found its champion in Senator Edward Kennedy of Massachusetts, the last survivor of the assassin-plagued Kennedy brothers. He and Carter slugged it out in a series of bruising primary elections, while delighted Republicans decorously proceeded to name Reagan their presidential nominee. In the end Kennedy's candidacy fell victim to the country's conservative mood and to lingering suspicions about a 1969 automobile accident on Chappaquiddick Island, Massachusetts, in which a young woman assistant was drowned when Kennedy's car plunged off a bridge. A badly battered Carter, his party divided and in disarray, was left to do battle with Reagan.

The Republican candidate proved to be a formidable campaigner. Using his professional acting skills to great advantage, Reagan attacked the incumbent's fumbling performance in foreign policy and blasted the "big-government" philosophy of the Democratic party (a philosophy that Carter did not fully embrace). Galloping inflation, sky-high interest rates, and a faltering economy also put the incumbent president on the defensive. Carter countered ineffectively with charges that Reagan was a trigger-happy cold warrior who might push the country into nuclear war.

Carter's spotty record in office was no defense against Reagan's popular appeal. On election day the Republican rang up a spectacular victory, bagging over 51 percent of the popular vote, while 41 percent went to Carter. Reflecting a small but vocal protest against both candidates, nearly 7 percent of the electorate voted for liberal Republican congressman John Anderson, who ran as an independent. The electoral count stood at 489 for Reagan and 49 for Carter, making him the first elected president to be unseated by voters since Herbert Hoover in 1932 (see Map 40.1). Equally startling, the Republicans gained control of the Senate for the first time in twenty-six years. Leading Democratic

In a speech to the National Association of Evangelicals on March 8, 1983, President Ronald Reagan (1911–2004) defined his stand on school prayer:

❝ The Declaration of Independence mentions the Supreme Being no less than four times. 'In God We Trust' is engraved on our coinage. The Supreme Court opens its proceedings with a religious invocation. And the Members of Congress open their sessions with a prayer. I just happen to believe the schoolchildren of the United States are entitled to the same privileges as Supreme Court Justices and Congressmen. ❞

1980

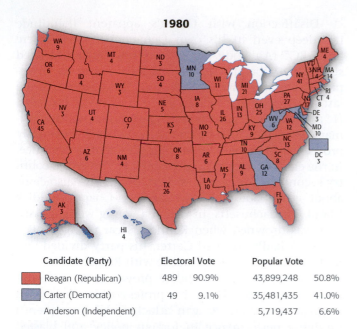

Candidate (Party)	Electoral Vote		Popular Vote	
Reagan (Republican)	489	90.9%	43,899,248	50.8%
Carter (Democrat)	49	9.1%	35,481,435	41.0%
Anderson (Independent)			5,719,437	6.6%

MAP 40.1 Presidential Election of 1980 (with electoral vote by state) This map graphically displays Reagan's landslide victory over both Carter and Anderson. © Cengage Learning

federal government. He sought nothing less than the dismantling of the welfare state and the reversal of the political evolution of the preceding half-century. Assembling a conservative cabinet of "the best and the rightest," he took dead aim at what he regarded as the bloated federal budget. "Government is not the solution to our problem," he declared. "Government is the problem." Years of New Deal–style tax-and-spend programs, Reagan jested, had created a federal government that reminded him of the definition of a baby as a creature who was all appetite at one end, with no sense of responsibility at the other.

On his conservative crusade for smaller government, less bureaucracy, and freer markets, Reagan found common cause with the new leader of America's oldest ally, Great Britain. Conservative Margaret Thatcher became Britain's first female prime minister in 1979. With a mandate to improve her nation's economy, which had suffered through the 1970s as the United States had, she embarked on a mission to reduce the power of labor unions and government involvement in business, two of Reagan's chief goals. The philosophic kinship between "Ronnie and Maggie," as the press dubbed the two heads of state, went beyond

liberals, including George McGovern, had been targeted for defeat by well-heeled New Right groups. They went down like dead timber in the conservative windstorm that swept the country.

Carter showed dignity in defeat, delivering a thoughtful Farewell Address that stressed his efforts to scale down the deadly arms race, to promote human rights, and to protect the environment. In one of his last acts in office, he signed a bill preserving some 100 million acres of Alaska land for national parks, forests, and wildlife refuges. An unusually intelligent, articulate, and well-meaning president, he had been hampered by his lack of managerial talent and had been badly buffeted by events beyond his control, such as the soaring price of oil, runaway inflation, and the galling insult of the hostages still held in Iran. Though unsuccessful in the White House, Carter earned much admiration in later years for his humanitarian and human rights activities. He received the Nobel Peace Prize in 2002.

✦ The Reagan Revolution

Reagan's arrival in Washington was triumphal. The Iranians contributed to the festive mood by releasing the hostages on Reagan's Inauguration Day, January 20, 1981, after 444 days of captivity.

The new president, a hale and hearty sixty-nine-year-old, was devoted to fiscal fitness and a leaner

Coming Home After more than a year in captivity in Iran, these hostages were released on the very day of Ronald Reagan's presidential inauguration.

© Bettmann/Corbis

economics. Emboldened by each other, they strengthened the Anglo-American alliance through muscular foreign policy against a number of foes, especially the Soviet bloc. Their common refrain was that free markets made free peoples and that shrinking government meant keeping their nations safer from communism.

By the early 1980s, this antigovernment message found a receptive audience in the United States. In the two decades since 1960, federal spending had risen from about 18 percent of gross national product to nearly 23 percent. At the same time, the composition of the federal budget had been shifting from defense to entitlement programs, including Social Security and Medicare (see the chart in the Appendix). In 1973 the budget of the Department of Health, Education, and Welfare surpassed that of the Department of Defense. Citizens increasingly balked at paying the bills for further extension of government "benefits." After four decades of advancing New Deal and Great Society programs, a strong countercurrent took hold. Californians staged a "tax revolt" in 1978 (known by its official ballot title of **Proposition 13**) that slashed property taxes and forced painful cuts in government services. The California "tax quake" jolted other state capitals and even rocked the pillars of Congress in faraway Washington, D.C. Ronald Reagan had ridden this political shock wave to presidential victory in 1980 and now proceeded to rattle the "welfare state" to its very foundations.

Reagan pursued his smaller-government policies with near-religious zeal and remarkable effectiveness.

The Triumph of the Right, 1980 Republican conservatives scored a double victory in 1980, winning control of both the White House and the Senate. Aided by conservative Democratic "boll weevils," they also dominated the House of Representatives, and a new era of conservatism dawned in the nation's capital. Jim Borgman. Reprinted with permission of Universal Press Syndicate. All rights reserved.

He proposed a new federal budget that necessitated cuts of some $35 billion, mostly in social programs like food stamps and federally funded job-training centers. Reagan worked naturally in harness with the Republican majority in the Senate, but to get his way in the Democratic House, he undertook some old-fashioned politicking. He enterprisingly wooed a group of mostly southern conservative Democrats (dubbed **boll weevils**), who abandoned their own party's leadership to follow the president. The new president seemed strong and motivated, all the more so after a failed assassination attempt in March 1981 brought an outpouring of sympathy and support.

✴ The Battle of the Budget

Swept along on a tide of presidential popularity, Congress swallowed Reagan's budget proposals. The new president's triumph amazed political observers, especially defeated Democrats. He had descended upon Washington like an avenging angel of conservatism, kicking up a blinding whirlwind of political change. His impressive performance demonstrated the power of the presidency with a skill not seen since Lyndon Johnson's day. Out the window went the textbooks that had concluded, largely on the basis of the stalemated 1970s, that the Oval Office had been eclipsed by a powerful, uncontrollable Congress.

Reagan hardly rested to savor the sweetness of his victory. The second part of his economic program called for substantial reductions in marginal tax rates over a period of three years. Many Democrats, the president quipped, had "never met a tax they didn't hike." Thanks largely to Reagan's skill as a television performer and the continued defection of the "boll weevils" from the Democratic camp, the president again had his way. In late 1981 Congress approved a set of far-reaching tax reforms that lowered individual tax rates, reduced federal estate taxes, and created new tax-free savings plans for small investors. Reagan's **supply-side economics** advisers assured him that the combination of budgetary discipline and tax reduction would stimulate new investment, boost productivity, foster dramatic economic growth, and eventually even reduce the federal deficit.

But at first "supply-side" economics seemed to be a beautiful theory mugged by a gang of brutal facts, as the economy slid into its deepest recession since the 1930s. Unemployment reached nearly 11 percent in 1982, businesses folded, and several bank failures jolted the nation's entire financial system. The automobile industry, once the brightest jewel in America's industrial crown, turned in its dimmest performance in history. Battling against Japanese imports, major automakers reported losses in the hundreds of millions of dollars. Fuming and frustrated Democrats angrily charged that the president's budget cuts slashed especially cruelly at the poor and the handicapped and that his tax cuts favored the well-to-do. In reality, the anti-inflationary "tight money" policies that led to the so-called "Reagan recession" of 1981–1982 had been launched by the Federal Reserve Board in 1979, on Carter's watch.

Ignoring the yawping pack of Democratic critics, President Reagan and his economic advisers serenely waited for their supply-side economic policies (**Reaganomics**) to produce the promised results. The supply-siders seemed to be vindicated when a healthy economic recovery finally got under way in 1983. Yet the economy of the 1980s was not uniformly sound. For the first time in the twentieth century, income gaps widened between the richest and the poorest Americans. The poor got poorer and the very rich grew fabulously richer, while middle-class incomes largely stagnated. Symbolic of the new income stratification was the emergence of "yuppies," or young, urban professionals. Sporting Rolex watches and BMW sports cars, they made a near-religion out of conspicuous consumption. Though something of a stereotype and numbering only about 1.5 million people, yuppies showcased the values of materialism and the pursuit of wealth that came to symbolize the high-rolling 1980s.

Some economists located the sources of the economic upturn neither in the president's budget cuts and tax reforms nor in the go-get-'em avarice of the yuppies. It was massive military expenditures, they argued, that constituted the real foundation of 1980s prosperity. Reagan cascaded nearly $2 trillion dollars onto the Pentagon in the 1980s, asserting the need to close a "window of vulnerability" in the armaments race with the Soviet Union. Ironically, this conservative president thereby plunged the government into a red-ink bath of deficit spending that made the New Deal look downright stingy. Federal budget deficits topped $100 billion in 1982, and the government's books were nearly $200 billion out of balance in every subsequent year of the 1980s. Massive government borrowing to cover those deficits kept interest rates high, and high interest rates in turn elevated the value of the dollar to record altitudes in the international money markets. The soaring dollar was good news for American tourists and buyers of foreign cars, but it dealt crippling blows to American exporters, as the American international trade deficit reached a record $152 billion in 1987. The masters of international commerce and finance for a generation after World War II, Americans suddenly became the world's heaviest borrowers in the global economy of the 1980s.

✴ Reagan Renews the Cold War

Hard as nails toward the Soviet Union in his campaign speeches, Reagan saw no reason to soften up after he checked in at the White House. He claimed that the Soviets were "prepared to commit any crime, to lie, to cheat," in pursuit of their goals of world conquest. He denounced the Soviet Union as the "focus of evil in the modern world."

Reagan believed in negotiating with the Soviets— but only from a position of overwhelming strength. Accordingly, his strategy for dealing with Moscow was simple: by enormously expanding U.S. military capabilities, he could threaten the Soviets with a fantastically expensive new round of the arms race. The American economy, theoretically, could better bear this new financial burden than could the creaking Soviet system. Desperate to avoid economic ruin, Kremlin leaders would come to the bargaining table and sing Reagan's tune.

This strategy resembled a riverboat gambler's ploy. It wagered the enormous sum of Reagan's defense budgets on the hope that the other side would not call Washington's bluff and initiate a new cycle of arms competition. Reagan played his trump card in this risky game in March 1983, when he announced his intention to pursue a high-technology missile-defense system called the **Strategic Defense Initiative (SDI)**, popularly known as Star Wars. The plan called for orbiting battle stations in space that could fire laser beams or other

Star Wars Fantasies President Reagan's Strategic Defense Initiative (popularly known as Star Wars) evoked extravagant hopes for an impermeable defensive shield, but its daunting physical and engineering requirements also occasioned much ridicule in the scientific community.

forms of concentrated energy to vaporize intercontinental missiles on liftoff. Reagan described SDI as offering potential salvation from the nuclear nightmare by throwing an "astrodome" defense shield over American cities. Most scientists considered this an impossible goal. But the deeper logic of SDI lay in its fit with Reagan's overall Soviet strategy. By pitching the arms contest onto a stratospheric plane of high technology and astronomical expense, it would further force the Kremlin's hand.

Relations with the Soviets further nosedived in late 1981, when the government of Poland, needled for over a year by a popular movement of workingpeople organized into a massive union called "Solidarity," clamped martial law on the troubled country. Reagan saw the heavy fist of the Kremlin inside this Polish iron glove, and he imposed economic sanctions on Poland and the USSR alike.

Dealing with the Soviet Union was additionally complicated by the inertia and ill health of the aging oligarchs in the Kremlin, three of whom died between late 1982 and early 1985. Relations grew even more tense when the Soviets, in September 1983, blasted from the skies a Korean passenger airliner that had inexplicably violated Soviet airspace. Hundreds of civilians, including many Americans, plummeted to their deaths in the frigid Sea of Okhotsk. By the end of 1983, all arms-control negotiations with the Soviets were broken off. The deepening chill of the Cold War was further felt in 1984, when USSR and Soviet-bloc athletes boycotted the Olympic Games in Los Angeles.

✮ Troubles Abroad

The volatile Middle Eastern pot continued to boil ominously. Israel badly strained its bonds of friendship with the United States by continuing to allow new settlements to be established in the occupied territory of the Jordan River's West Bank (see Map 40.2). Israel further raised the stakes in the Middle East in June 1982 when it invaded neighboring Lebanon, seeking to suppress once and for all the guerrilla bases from which Palestinian fighters harassed beleaguered Israel. The Palestinians were bloodily subdued, but Lebanon, already pulverized by years of episodic civil war, was plunged into armed chaos. President Reagan was obliged to send American troops to Lebanon in 1983 as part of an international peacekeeping force, but their presence did not bring peace. A suicide bomber crashed an explosives-laden truck into a United States Marine barracks on October 23, 1983, killing more than two hundred marines. President Reagan soon thereafter withdrew the remaining American troops, while

miraculously suffering no political damage from this horrifying and humiliating attack. His mystified Democratic opponents began to call him the "Teflon president," to whom nothing hurtful could stick.

Central America, in the United States' own backyard, also rumbled menacingly. A leftist revolution had deposed the long-time dictator of Nicaragua in 1979. President Carter had tried to ignore the hotly anti-American rhetoric of the revolutionaries, known as **Sandinistas**, and to establish good diplomatic relations with them. But cold warrior Reagan took their rhetoric at face value and hurled back at them some hot language of his own. He accused the Sandinistas of turning their country into a forward base for Soviet and Cuban military penetration of all of Central America. Brandishing photographs taken from high-flying spy planes, administration spokespeople claimed that Nicaraguan leftists were shipping weapons to revolutionary forces in tiny El Salvador, torn by violence since a coup in 1979.

Reagan sent military "advisers" to prop up the pro-American government of El Salvador. He also provided covert aid, including the CIA-engineered mining of harbors, to the rebel **contras** opposing the anti-American government of Nicaragua. Reagan flexed his military muscles elsewhere in the turbulent Caribbean. In a dramatic display of American might, in October 1983 he dispatched a heavy-firepower invasion force to the island of Grenada, where a military coup had killed the prime minister and brought Marxists to power. Swiftly overrunning the tiny island and ousting the insurgents, American troops vividly demonstrated Reagan's determination to assert the dominance of the United States in the Caribbean, just as Theodore Roosevelt had done (see Map 40.3).

✮ Round Two for Reagan

A confident Ronald Reagan, bolstered by a buoyant economy at home and by the popularity of his defiant posture abroad, met little opposition in his bid for a second White House term in 1984. His opponent was Democrat Walter Mondale, who made history by naming as his vice-presidential running mate Congresswoman Geraldine Ferraro of New York. She was the first woman ever to appear on a major-party presidential ticket. But even this dramatic gesture could not salvage Mondale's candidacy, which was fatally tainted by his service as vice president in the deeply discredited Carter administration. On election day Reagan walked away with 525 electoral votes to Mondale's 13, winning everywhere except in Mondale's home state of Minnesota and the District of Columbia. Reagan also over-

MAP 40.2 The Middle East A combination of political instability and precious petroleum resources has made the region from Egypt to Afghanistan an "arc of crisis." © Cengage Learning

Map labels and annotations:

GREECE — Athens
Crete
Mediterranean Sea
CYPRUS
TURKEY — Ankara
GEORGIA
ARMENIA
AZERBAIJAN
Caspian Sea
TURKMENISTAN
CHINA

Soviet occupation, 1979–1989
U.S. aid to rebels, 1980s
International and Northern Alliance forces defeat Taliban, 2001

U.S. troops, 1958, 1983–1984

SYRIA — Damascus
LEBANON
ISRAEL — Tel Aviv
Amman
JORDAN
Tikrit
Kirkuk
Fallujah
Baghdad
IRAQ
Tigris R.
Euphrates R.
Tehran
IRAN

Mazar e Sharif
Kabul
AFGHANISTAN — Herat
Islamabad
Kandahar
PAKISTAN
Quetta
Indus R.
INDIA

U.S. arms sales, 1955–1978: $20.8 billion
Shah overthrown, 1979
American hostages taken, 1979–1981

LIBYA
Cairo
EGYPT
Nile R.
Tropic of Cancer
Aswan Dam
Red Sea
SUDAN

Basra
Kuwait
KUWAIT
Persian Gulf
Manama
BAHRAIN
Doha
QATAR
Dubayy
Abu Dhabi
UNITED ARAB EMIRATES
Muscat
Strait of Hormuz
OMAN
Karachi
Arabian Sea

U.S. and allies launch First U.S.-Iraq War, 1991

U.S. arms sales, 1980s, during Iran-Iraq War
Iraq invades Kuwait, 1990
Second U.S.-Iraq War, 2003

Riyadh
SAUDI ARABIA

Partner in U.S. efforts to eradicate al-Qaeda, 2001–

Oil embargo, 1973
Source of 17% of U.S. oil imports in 1975
Largest buyer of U.S. arms, 1978

Mecca
YEMEN — Sana
Mukalla
Aden
Gulf of Aden
Socotra (Yemen)

ETHIOPIA
SOMALIA
Mogadishu

INDIAN OCEAN

U.S. troops assist in relief of famine, 1992–1993; U.S. troops withdrawn, 1994

Equator 0°

Members of the Organization of Petroleum Exporting Countries (OPEC)
Oil fields

0   250   500 Km.
0   250   500 Mi.

N

ARAB-ISRAELI CONFLICT (inset map)

Jewish state after UN partition of Palestine, 1947
Israel after War of 1948–1949
Area controlled by Israel after Six-Day War, 1967
Israeli-occupied area after Yom Kippur War, 1973

By Egyptian-Israeli agreements of 1975 and 1979, Israel withdrew from the Sinai in 1982. In 1981 Israel annexed the Golan Heights. Through negotiations between Israel and the PLO, Jericho and the Gaza Strip were placed under Palestinian self-rule, and Israeli troops were withdrawn in 1994. In 1994 Israel and Jordan signed an agreement opening their borders and normalizing their relations.

LEBANON — Beirut
Damascus
SYRIA
Haifa
GOLAN HEIGHTS
Sea of Galilee
Tel Aviv
WEST BANK
ISRAEL
Jerusalem
Gaza
Amman
Jordan R.
Dead Sea
JORDAN
Mediterranean Sea
Port Said
Suez Canal
EGYPT
Cairo
Suez
Nile R.
SINAI PENINSULA
Elath
Gulf of Suez
Gulf of Aqaba
SAUDI ARABIA
Sharm el-Sheikh
Red Sea

---

whelmed Mondale in the popular vote—52,609,797 to 36,450,613.

Shrinking the federal government and reducing taxes had been the main objectives of Reagan's first term; foreign-policy issues dominated the news in his second term. The president soon found himself contending for the world's attention with a charismatic new Soviet leader, Mikhail Gorbachev, installed as chairman of the Soviet Communist party in March 1985. Gorbachev was personable, energetic, imaginative, and committed to radical reforms in the Soviet Union. He announced two policies with remarkable, even revolutionary, implications. **Glasnost**, or "openness," aimed to ventilate the secretive, repressive stuffiness of Soviet society by introducing free speech and a measure of political liberty. **Perestroika**, or "restructuring," was intended to revive the moribund Soviet economy by adopting many of the free-market practices—such as the profit motive and an end to subsidized prices—of the capitalist West.

Both glasnost and perestroika required that the Soviet Union shrink the size of its enormous military machine and redirect its energies to the dismal civilian economy. That requirement, in turn, necessitated an end to the Cold War. Gorbachev accordingly made warm overtures to the West, including an announcement in April 1985 that the Soviet Union would cease to deploy intermediate-range nuclear forces (INF) targeted at Western Europe, pending an agreement on their complete elimination. He pushed this goal when he met with Ronald Reagan at the first of four summit meetings, in Geneva in November 1985. A second summit meeting, in Reykjavik, Iceland, in October 1986, broke down when a furious Reagan stormed out, convinced that Gorbachev had come to end plans for the beloved SDI. But at a third summit, in Washington, D.C., in December 1987, the two leaders at last signed the **Intermediate-Range Nuclear Forces (INF) Treaty**, banning all of these missiles from Europe. Reagan and Gorbachev capped their new friendship in May 1988 at a final summit in Moscow. There Reagan, who had entered office condemning the "evil empire" of Soviet communism, warmly praised Gorbachev. Reagan, the consummate cold warrior, had been flexible and savvy enough to seize a historic opportunity to join with the Soviet chief to bring the Cold War to a kind of conclusion. For this, history would give both leaders high marks.

Reagan made other decisive moves in foreign policy. His administration provided strong backing in February 1986 for Corazon Aquino's ouster of dictator Ferdinand Marcos in the Philippines. Reagan also ordered a lightning air raid against Libya in 1986, in retaliation for alleged Libyan sponsorship of terrorist attacks, including a bomb blast in a West Berlin discotheque that killed a U.S. serviceman.

MAP 40.3 Central America and the Caribbean This region, so important to the United States throughout its history, remained a hotbed of unrest through the last years of the Cold War and beyond. © Cengage Learning

East Meets West President Reagan greets Soviet leader Mikhail Gorbachev at a summit meeting in Moscow in May 1988.

★ The Iran-Contra Imbroglio

Two foreign-policy problems seemed insoluble to Reagan: the continuing captivity of a number of American hostages, seized by Muslim extremist groups in bleeding, battered Lebanon; and the continuing grip on power of the left-wing Sandinista government in Nicaragua. The president repeatedly requested that Congress provide military aid to the contra rebels fighting against the Sandinista regime. Congress repeatedly refused, and the administration grew increasingly frustrated, even obsessed, in its search for a means to help the contras.

Unknown to the American public, some Washington officials saw a possible linkage between the two thorny problems of the Middle Eastern hostages and the Central American Sandinistas. In 1985 American diplomats secretly arranged arms sales to Iran, which

was mired in a devastating territorial war with neighboring Iraq. In return, the Iranians helped obtain the release of at least one American hostage held by Middle Eastern terrorists. Meanwhile, the money Iran paid for the American weapons was diverted to the contras in Nicaragua. These actions brazenly violated a congressional ban on military aid to the Nicaraguan rebels—not to mention Reagan's repeated vow that he would never negotiate with terrorists. Washington also continued to support Iraqi dictator Saddam Hussein, to whom it sold weapons used against Iran.

News of these secret dealings broke in November 1986 and ignited a firestorm of controversy. President Reagan claimed he was innocent of wrongdoing and ignorant of his subordinates' activities. Reviving a refrain from the Watergate era, the public clamored to know "what the president knew and when he knew

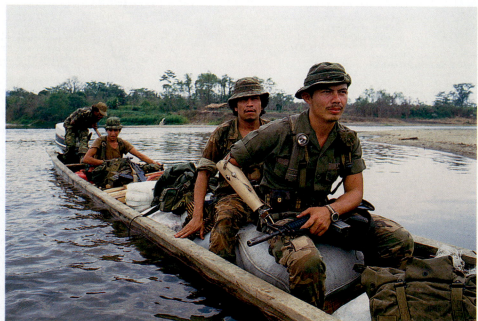

Contra Rebel Troops Head for Battle These rebels were long-seasoned and battle-scarred veterans of Nicaragua's civil war by the time this photograph was taken in 1987.

On March 4, 1987, President Ronald Reagan somewhat confusingly tried to explain his role (or lack of role) in the arms-for-hostages deal with Iran:

"A few months ago I told the American people I did not trade arms for hostages. My heart and my best intentions still tell me that is true, but the facts and the evidence tell me it is not."

it." Although Reagan was never found to have lied outright, a congressional committee condemned the "secrecy, deception, and disdain for the law" displayed by administration officials and concluded that "if the president did not know what his national security advisers were doing, he should have."

The **Iran-Contra affair** cast a dark shadow over the Reagan record on foreign policy, tending to obscure the president's outstanding achievement in establishing a new relationship with the Soviets. Out of the several Iran-Contra investigations, a picture emerged of Reagan as a lazy, perhaps even senile, president who napped through meetings and paid little or no attention to the details of policy. Reagan's critics pounced on this portrait as proof that the movie-star-turned-politician was a mental lightweight who had merely acted his way through the role of the presidency without really understanding the script. But despite these damaging revelations, Reagan remained among the most popular and beloved presidents in modern American history.

★ Reagan's Economic Legacy

Ronald Reagan had taken office vowing to invigorate the American economy by rolling back government regulations, lowering taxes, and balancing the budget. He did ease many regulatory rules, and he pushed major tax reform bills through Congress in 1981 and 1986. But a balanced budget remained grotesquely out of reach. Supply-side economic theory had promised that lower taxes would actually *increase* government revenue because they would stimulate the economy as a whole. But, in fact, the combination of tax reduction and huge increases in military spending opened a vast "revenue hole" of $200 billion annual deficits. In his eight years in office, President Reagan added nearly $2 trillion to the national debt—more than all of his predecessors combined, including those who had fought protracted global wars (see Figure 40.1).

The staggering deficits of the Reagan years assuredly constituted a great economic failure. And because

so much of the Reagan-era debt was financed by foreign lenders, especially the Japanese, the deficits virtually guaranteed that future generations of Americans would either have to work harder than their parents, lower their standard of living, or both to pay their foreign creditors when the bills came due.

But if the deficits represented an economic failure, they also constituted, strangely enough, a kind of political triumph. Among the paramount goals of Reagan's political life was his ambition to slow the growth of government, and especially to block or even repeal the social programs launched in the era of Lyndon Johnson's Great Society. By appearing to make new social spending both practically and politically impossible for the foreseeable future, the deficits served exactly that purpose. They achieved, in short, Reagan's highest political objective: the containment of the welfare state. Ronald Reagan thus ensured the long-term perpetuation of his dearest political values to a degree that few presidents have managed to achieve. For better or worse, the consequences of "Reaganomics" would be large and durable.

Yet another legacy of the 1980s was a sharp reversal of a long-term trend toward a more equitable distribution of income and an increasing squeeze on the middle class. In the early 1990s, median household income (in 1993 dollars) actually declined, from about $33,500 in 1989 to about $31,000 in 1993 (see Figure 40.2). Whether that disturbing trend should be attributed to Reagan's policies or to more deeply running economic currents remained controversial.

★ The Religious Right

Religion pervaded American politics in the 1980s. Especially conspicuous was a coalition of conservative, evangelical Christians known as the religious right. In 1979 the Reverend Jerry Falwell, an evangelical minister from Lynchburg, Virginia, founded a political organization called the **Moral Majority**. Falwell preached with great success against sexual permissiveness, abortion, feminism, and the spread of gay rights. In its first two years, the Moral Majority registered between 2 million and 3 million voters. Using radio, direct-mail marketing, and cable TV, "televangelists" reached huge audiences in the 1980s, collected millions of dollars, and became aggressive political advocates of conservative causes.

Members of the religious right were sometimes called "movement conservatives," a term that recalls the left-wing protest movements of the 1960s. In many ways the religious right of the 1980s was a reflection of, or answer to, sixties radicalism. Feminists in the 1960s declared that "the personal was political." The

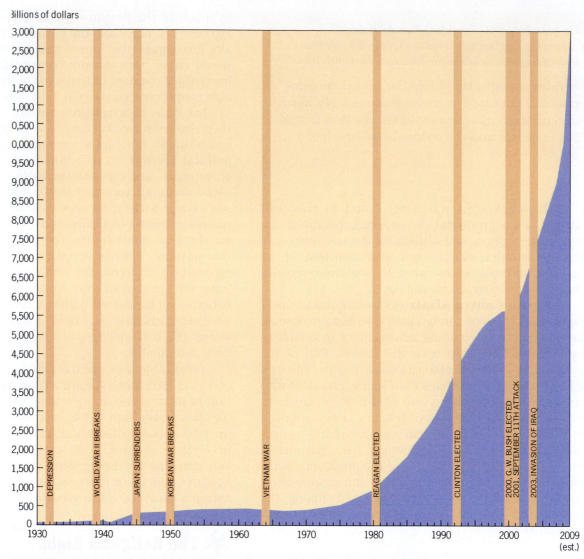

Billions of dollars

FIGURE 40.1 The National Debt, 1930–2009 World War II provided the first major boost to the national debt. The policies of the Reagan and George H. W. Bush administrations, 1981–1993, explosively expanded the debt to the $4 trillion level. By the 1990s, 14 percent of federal revenues went to interest payments on the debt. The budget surpluses created by the booming economy of the second Clinton administration (1997–2001) raised the prospect that the debt might be paid off. But the combination of the George W. Bush tax cuts and increased military spending sent the debt soaring again after 2001. Those tax cuts, combined with the revenue losses and stimulus expenditures occasioned by the "Great Recession" that began in 2008, kicked the debt up to unprecedented peacetime levels, approaching 100 percent of GDP. Real-time updates of the public debt are available from the Department of the Treasury's Bureau of the Public Debt, at http://www.publicdebt. treas.gov. (Sources: *Historical Statistics of the United States* and *Statistical Abstract of the United States*, relevant years; Office of Management and Budget Historical Tables.)

religious right did the same. What had in the past been personal matters—gender roles, homosexuality, and prayer—became the organizing ground for a powerful political movement. Like advocates of multiculturalism and affirmative action, the religious right practiced a form of "identity politics." But rather than defining

themselves as Latino voters or gay voters, they declared themselves Christian or pro-life voters. The New Right also mimicked the New Left in some of its tactics. If the left had consciousness-raising sessions, the right had prayer meetings. Adherents articulated their positions in a language of rights and entitlements, as in the

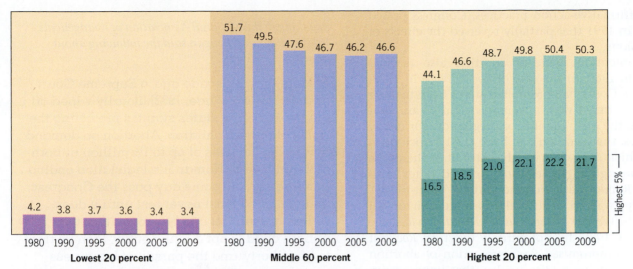

FIGURE 40.2 Share of Income Received by Families, by Quintile, 1980–2009   Since 1980 the incomes of the lowest 20 percent and the middle 60 percent have been shrinking, while the incomes of the highest 20 percent, and particularly the top 5 percent, have climbed steadily. (Source: *Statistical Abstract of the United States*, 2010; U.S. Census Bureau *Consumer Income Report*, relevant years.)

"right-to-life" (or anti-abortion) movement. They even mirrored the tactics of civil disobedience. Protesters in the 1960s blocked entrances to draft offices; protesters in the 1980s blocked entrances to abortion clinics.

Several leaders of the religious right fell from grace in the latter part of the decade. One tearfully admitted to repeated trysts with prostitutes. Another went to prison following revelations of his own financial and sexual misconduct. But such scandals would not shake the faith of America's conservative Christians or diminish the new political clout of activist, evangelical religionists.

✦ Conservatism in the Courts

If the budget was Reagan's chief weapon in the war against the welfare state, the courts became his principal instrument in the "cultural wars" demanded by the religious right. By the time he left office, Reagan had appointed a near-majority of all sitting judges. Equally important, he had named three conservative-minded justices to the U.S. Supreme Court. They included Sandra Day O'Connor, a brilliant, public-spirited Arizona judge. When she was sworn in on September 25, 1981, she became the first woman to ascend to the high bench in the Court's nearly two-hundred-year history.

Reaganism repudiated two great icons of the liberal political culture: affirmative action and abortion. The Court showed its newly conservative colors in 1984, when it decreed, in a case involving Memphis firefighters, that union rules about job seniority could outweigh affirmative-action concerns in guiding promotion policies in the city's fire department. In two cases in 1989 (*Ward's Cove Packing* v. *Antonia* and *Martin* v. *Wilks*), the Court made it more difficult to prove that an employer practiced racial discrimination in hiring and made it easier for white males to argue that they were the victims of reverse discrimination by employers who

Eve Arnold/Magnum Photos, Inc.

The Moral Majority, 1981   Television evangelist and religious leader the Reverend Jerry Falwell mobilized his national Moral Majority organization in support of Ronald Reagan's presidential campaign in 1980 and a conservative social agenda.

followed affirmative-action practices. Congress passed legislation in 1991 that partially reversed the effects of those decisions.

The contentious issue of abortion also reached the Court in 1989. In the case of *Roe* v. *Wade* in 1973, the Supreme Court had prohibited states from making laws that interfered with a woman's right to an abortion during the early months of pregnancy. For nearly two decades, that decision had been the bedrock principle on which "pro-choice" advocates built their case for abortion rights. It had also provoked bitter criticism from Roman Catholics and various "right-to-life" groups, who wanted a virtually absolute ban on all abortions. In *Webster* v. *Reproductive Health Services*, the Court in July 1989 did not entirely overturn *Roe*, but it seriously compromised *Roe*'s protection of abortion rights. By approving a Missouri law that imposed certain restrictions on abortion, the Court signaled that it was inviting the states to legislate in an area in which *Roe* had previously forbidden them to legislate. The Court renewed that invitation in *Planned Parenthood* v.

"WELL, IT'S ABOUT TIME"

The Justice Is a Lady, 1981 Herblock hails Sandra Day O'Connor's appointment to the Supreme Court. *The Justice Is a Lady, A 1981 Herblock Cartoon, copyright by The Herb Block Foundation*

Speaking to the National Association of Evangelicals, President Ronald Reagan said the following about abortion:

"More than a decade ago, a Supreme Court decision [*Roe* v. *Wade*, 1973] literally wiped off the books of fifty states statutes protecting the rights of unborn children. Abortion on demand now takes the lives of up to 1½ million unborn children a year. Human life legislation ending this tragedy will some day pass the Congress, and you and I must never rest until it does. Unless and until it can be proven that the unborn child is not a living entity, then its right to life, liberty, and the pursuit of happiness must be protected.**"**

Casey in 1992, when it ruled that states could restrict access to abortion as long as they did not place an "undue burden" on the woman. Using this standard, the Court held that Pennsylvania could not compel a wife to notify her husband about an abortion but could require a minor child to notify parents, as well as other restrictions.

Right-to-life advocates were at first delighted by the *Webster* decision. But the Court's ruling also galvanized pro-choice organizations into a new militancy. Bruising, divisive battles loomed as state legislatures across the land confronted abortion. This painful cultural conflict over the unborn was also part of the Reagan era's bequest to the future.

✶ Referendum on Reaganism in 1988

Republicans lost control of the Senate in the off-year elections of November 1986. Hopes rose among Democrats that the "Reagan Revolution" might be showing signs of political vulnerability at last. The newly Democratic majority in the Senate flexed its political muscles in 1987 when it rejected an ultraconservative nominee for the Supreme Court.

Democrats also relished the prospect of making political hay out of both the Iran-Contra affair and disquieting signs of economic trouble. The "double mountain" of deficits—the federal budget deficit and the international trade deficit—continued to grow ominously. Falling oil prices blighted the economy of the Southwest, slashing real estate values and undermining hundreds of savings and loan (S&L) institutions. The damage to the S&Ls was so massive that a federal rescue operation was eventually estimated to carry a price tag of well over $500 billion. Meanwhile, many American banks found themselves holding near-worthless loans they had unwisely foisted upon Third World countries, especially in Latin America. In 1984 it took federal assistance to save Continental Illinois Bank from a catastrophic failure. More banks and savings institutions were folding than at any time since the Great Depression of the 1930s. A wave of mergers, acquisitions, and leveraged buyouts washed over Wall Street, leaving many brokers and traders megarich and many companies saddled with megadebt. A cold spasm of fear struck the money markets on **Black Monday**, October 19, 1987, when the leading stock-market index plunged 508 points—the largest one-day decline in history to that point. This crash, said *Newsweek* magazine, heralded "the final collapse of the money culture . . . , the death knell of the 1980s." But as Mark Twain famously commented about his own obituary, this announcement proved premature.

Hoping to cash in on these ethical and economic anxieties, a pack of Democrats—dubbed the "Seven Dwarfs" by derisive Republicans—chased after their party's 1988 presidential nomination. The handsome and charismatic Democratic front-runner, former Colorado senator Gary Hart, was forced to drop out of the race in May 1987 after charges of sexual misconduct. African American candidate Jesse Jackson, a rousing speechmaker who hoped to forge a "rainbow coalition" of minorities and the disadvantaged, campaigned energetically. But the Democratic nomination in the end went to the coolly cerebral governor of Massachusetts, Michael Dukakis. Republicans nominated Reagan's vice president, George H. W. Bush, who ran largely on the Reagan record of tax cuts, strong defense policies, toughness on crime, opposition to abortion, and a long-running if hardly robust economic expansion. Dukakis made little headway exploiting the ethical and economic sore spots and came across to television viewers as almost supernaturally devoid of emotion. On election day the voters gave him just 41,016,429 votes to 47,946,422 for Bush. The Electoral College count was 111 to 426.

Hollywood director Oliver Stone's (b. 1946) film Wall Street *both romanticized and vilified the business culture of the 1980s. The character of Gordon Gekko, inspired by real-life corporate raider Ivan Boesky, captured the spirit of the times:*

"Ladies and gentlemen, greed is good. Greed works, greed is right. . . . Greed for life, money, love, knowledge, has marked the upward surge of mankind—and greed, mark my words, will save the malfunctioning corporation called the U.S.A.**"**

✦ George H. W. Bush and the End of the Cold War

George Herbert Walker Bush was born with a silver ladle in his mouth. His father had served as a U.S. senator from Connecticut, and young George had enjoyed a first-rate education at Yale. After service in World War II, he had amassed a modest fortune of his own in the oil business in Texas. His deepest commitment, however, was to public service; he left the business world to serve briefly as a congressman and then held various posts in several Republican administrations, including emissary to China, ambassador to the United Nations, director of the Central Intelligence Agency, and vice president. He capped this long political career when he was inaugurated president in January 1989, promising to work for "a kinder, gentler America."

In the first months of the Bush administration, the communist world commanded the planet's fascinated attention. Everywhere in the communist bloc, it seemed, the season of democracy had arrived.

In China hundreds of thousands of prodemocracy demonstrators thronged through Beijing's Tiananmen Square in the spring of 1989. They proudly flourished a thirty-foot-high "Goddess of Democracy," modeled on the Statue of Liberty, as a symbol of their aspirations.

But in June of that year, China's aging and autocratic rulers brutally crushed the prodemocracy movement. Tanks rolled over the crowds, and

George Herbert Walker Bush (b. 1924) Campaigning, October 1988 Bush soundly defeated Democratic candidate Michael Dukakis in the November 1988 election.

AP Images

Tiananmen Square, Beijing, China, June 1989 The Chinese communist state mobilized all its forces against students demonstrating for a more democratic China.

machine-gunners killed hundreds of protesters. World opinion roundly condemned the bloody suppression of the prodemocracy demonstrators. President Bush joined in the criticism. Yet despite angry demands in Congress for punitive restrictions on trade with China, the president insisted on maintaining normal relations with Beijing.

Stunning changes also shook Eastern Europe. Long oppressed by puppet regimes propped up by Soviet guns, the region was revolutionized in just a few startling months in 1989. The Solidarity movement in Poland led the way when it toppled Poland's communist government in August. With dizzying speed, communist regimes collapsed in Hungary, Czechoslovakia, East Germany, and even hyperrepressive Romania. In December 1989, jubilant Germans danced atop the hated Berlin Wall, symbol of the division of Germany and all of Europe into two armed and hostile camps. The wall itself soon came down, heralding the imminent end of the forty-five-year-long Cold War. Chunks of the wall's

Fallen Idol Romanians toppled this statue of Vladimir Lenin in 1990, symbolically marking the collapse of the Marxian dream that had agitated the world for more than a century.

MAP 40.4 The End of the Cold War Changed the Map of Europe © Cengage Learning

- Communist regimes overthrown since 1989
- Soviet Union, dissolved in 1991
- Yugoslavia, dissolved in civil war, 1991–1992
- Elections, 1989
- Berlin Wall opened, Nov. 1989 German reunification, 1990
- Czechoslovakia broke into Czech Republic and Slovakia in 1993
- Largest and most influential of the former Soviet republics after 1991
- Gorbachev in power, 1985–1991 Moscow coup fails; Boris Yeltsin declared president of Russia, 1990
- Chechnya declares independence 1991; Russia attacks, 1994
- NATO airwar against Serbia to protect Kosovo, 1994
- U.S. troops join NATO peacekeeping forces, Dec. 1995

concrete became instant collectors' items—gray souvenirs of a grim episode in Europe's history. With the approval of the victorious Allied powers of World War II, the two Germanys, divided since 1945, were at last reunited in October 1990.

Most startling of all were the changes that rolled over the heartland of world communism, the Soviet Union itself. Mikhail Gorbachev's policies of glasnost and perestroika had set in motion a groundswell that surged out of his control. Old-guard hard-liners, in a last-gasp effort to preserve the tottering communist system, attempted to dislodge Gorbachev with a military coup in August 1991. With the support of Boris Yeltsin, president of the Russian Republic (one of the several republics that composed the Union of Soviet Socialist Republics, or USSR), Gorbachev foiled the plotters. But his days were numbered. In December 1991 Gorbachev resigned as Soviet president. He had become a leader without a country as the Soviet Union dissolved into its component parts, some fifteen republics loosely confederated in the **Commonwealth of Independent States (CIS)**, with Russia the most powerful state and Yeltsin the dominant leader. To varying degrees, all the new governments in the CIS repudiated communism and embraced democratic reforms and a free-market economy (see Map 40.4).

These developments astonished the "experts," who had long preached that the steely vise-grip of communist rule never could be peacefully broken. Yet suddenly and almost miraculously, the totalitarian tonnage of communist oppression had been rendered politically weightless. Most spectacularly, the demise of the Soviet Union wrote a definitive finish to the Cold War era. More than four decades of nail-biting tension between two nuclear superpowers, the Soviet Union and the United States, evaporated when the USSR dismantled itself. With the Soviet Union swept into the dustbin of history and communism all but extinct, Bush spoke hopefully of a "new world order," where democracy would reign and diplomacy would supersede weaponry. Some observers even saw in these developments "the end of history," in the sense that democracy, victorious in its two-century-long struggle against foes on the left and right, had no ideological battles left to fight.

Exultant Americans joked that the USSR had become the "USS *were*." But the disintegration of the Soviet Union was no laughing matter. Rankling questions remained. For example, who would honor arms-control agreements with the United States? Which of the successor states of the former Soviet Union would take command of the formidable Soviet nuclear arsenal? (A partial answer was provided in early 1993, when

In his state of the union address on January 31, 1990, President George H. W. Bush (b. 1924) declared,

❝ The events of the year just ended, the revolution of '89, have been a chain reaction, changes so striking that it marks the beginning of a new era in the world's affairs.❞

Just six months later, speaking at Stanford University, Soviet president Mikhail Gorbachev (b. 1931) said,

❝ The Cold War is now behind us. Let us not wrangle over who won it. It is in the common interest of our two countries and nations not to fight this trend toward cooperation, but rather to promote it.❞

President Bush, in one of his last official acts, signed the START II accord with Russian president Boris Yeltsin, committing both powers to reduce their long-range nuclear arsenals by two-thirds within ten years.)

Throughout the former Soviet empire, waves of nationalistic fervor and long-suppressed ethnic and racial hatreds rolled across the vast land as communism's roots were wrenched out. A particularly nasty conflict erupted in the Russian Caucasus in 1991, when the Chechnyan minority tried to declare their independence from Russia, prompting President Yeltsin to send in Russian troops. Ethnic warfare flared in other disintegrating communist countries as well, notably in misery-drenched Yugoslavia, racked by vicious "ethnic cleansing" campaigns against various minorities.

The end of the Cold War also proved a mixed blessing for the United States. For nearly half a century, the containment of Soviet communism had been the paramount goal of U.S. foreign policy. Indeed the Cold War era had been the only lengthy period in American history when the United States had consistently pursued an internationalist foreign policy. With the Soviet threat now canceled, would the United States revert to its traditional isolationism? What principles would guide American diplomacy now that "anticommunism" had lost its relevance?

The Soviet-American rivalry, with its demands for high levels of military preparedness, had also deeply shaped and even invigorated the U.S. economy. Huge economic sectors such as aerospace were heavily sustained by military contracts. The economic cost of beating swords into plowshares became painfully apparent in 1991 when the Pentagon announced the closing of thirty-four military bases and canceled a $52 billion order for a navy attack plane. More closings and cancellations followed. Communities that had been drenched with Pentagon dollars now nearly dried up, especially in hard-hit southern California, where scores of defense plants shut their doors and unemployment soared. The problems of weaning the U.S. economy from its decades of dependence on defense spending tempered the euphoria of Americans as they welcomed the Cold War's long-awaited finale.

Elsewhere in the world, democracy marched triumphantly forward. The white regime in South Africa took a giant step toward liberating that troubled land from its racist past when in 1990 it freed African leader Nelson Mandela, who had served twenty-seven years

The Agony of Yugoslavia, 1992 These Bosnian refugees from the town of Jajce illustrate the plight of millions of Yugoslavians as their country slid into vicious interethnic battles in the wake of the Cold War's conclusion.

Black Star/Stockphoto.com

in prison for conspiring to overthrow the government. Four years later Mandela was elected South Africa's president. Free elections in Nicaragua in February 1990 removed the leftist Sandinistas from power. Two years later peace came at last to war-ravaged El Salvador.

✹ The Persian Gulf Crisis

Sadly, the end of the Cold War did not mean the end of all wars. President Bush flexed the United States' still-intimidating military muscles in tiny Panama in December 1989, when he sent airborne troops to capture dictator and drug lord Manuel Noriega.

Still more ominous events in the summer of 1990 severely tested Bush's dream of a democratic and peaceful new world order. On August 2 Saddam Hussein, the brutal and ambitious ruler of Iraq, sent his armies to overrun Kuwait, a tiny, oil-rich desert sheikdom on Iraq's southern frontier.

Oil fueled Saddam's aggression. Financially exhausted by its eight-year war with Iran, which had ended in a stalemate in 1988, Iraq needed Kuwait's oil to pay its huge war bills. Saddam's larger design was ironfisted control over the entire Persian Gulf region. With his hand thus firmly clutching the world's economic jugular vein, he dreamed of dictating the terms of oil supplies to the industrial nations, and perhaps of totally extinguishing the Arabs' enemy, Israel.

Ironically, the United States and its allies had helped supply Saddam with the tools of aggression. He was widely known to be a thug and assassin who intimidated his underlings by showing them the bodies of his executed adversaries hanging on meat hooks. But in the 1980s, American enmity for Islamic-fundamentalist Iran was intense, and Saddam was at war with Iran. Assuming that "the enemy of my enemy is my friend," American policymakers helped build Saddam's military machine into a formidable force.

On August 2, 1990, Saddam's army roared into Kuwait. The speed and audacity of the invasion was stunning, but the world responded just as swiftly. The United Nations Security Council unanimously condemned the invasion on August 3 and demanded the immediate and unconditional withdrawal of Iraq's troops. When an economic embargo failed to squeeze the Iraqis into compliance by November, the Security Council delivered an ultimatum to Saddam to leave Kuwait by January 15, 1991, or U.N. forces would "use all necessary means" to expel his troops. For perhaps the first time in the post–World War II era, the U.N. seemed to be fulfilling its founders' dreams that it could preserve international order by putting guns where its mouth was. It also put them where the world's critical oil supply was.

In a logistical operation of astonishing complexity, the United States spearheaded a massive international military deployment on the sandy Arabian Peninsula. As the January 15 deadline approached, some 539,000 U.S. soldiers, sailors, and pilots—many of them women and all of them members of the new, post-Vietnam, all-volunteer American military—swarmed into the Persian Gulf region. They were joined by nearly 270,000 troops, pilots, and sailors from twenty-eight other countries in the coalition opposed to Iraq. When all diplomatic efforts to resolve the crisis failed, the U.S. Congress voted regretfully on January 12 to approve the use of force. On January 16 the time bomb of war ticked off its last beats.

The United States and its U.N. allies unleashed a hellish air attack against Iraq. For thirty-seven days, warplanes pummeled targets in occupied Kuwait and in Iraq itself, in an awesome display of high-technology, precision-targeting modern warfare. Iraq responded to this pounding by launching several dozen "Scud" short-range ballistic missiles against military and civilian targets in Saudi Arabia and Israel. These missile attacks claimed several lives but did no significant military damage.

Yet if Iraq made but a feeble military response to the air campaign, the allied commander, the beefy and blunt American general Norman ("Stormin' Norman") Schwarzkopf, took nothing for granted. Saddam, who had threatened to wage "the mother of all battles," had the capacity to inflict awful damage. Iraq had stockpiled tons of chemical and biological weapons, including poison gas and the means to spread epidemics of anthrax. Saddam's tactics also included ecological warfare as he released a gigantic oil slick into the Persian Gulf to forestall amphibious assault and ignited hundreds of oil-well fires, whose smoky plumes shrouded the ground from aerial view. Faced with these horrifying tactics, Schwarzkopf's strategy was starkly simple: soften the Iraqis with relentless bombing, then suffocate them on the ground with a tidal-wave rush of troops and armor.

On February 23 the dreaded and long-awaited land war began. Dubbed **Operation Desert Storm**, it lasted only four days—the "hundred-hour war" (see Map 40.5). With lightning speed the U.N. forces penetrated deep into Iraq, outflanking the occupying forces in Kuwait and blocking the enemy's ability either to retreat or to reinforce. Allied casualties were amazingly light, whereas much of Iraq's remaining fighting force was quickly destroyed or captured. On February 27 Saddam accepted a cease-fire, and Kuwait was liberated.

Most Americans cheered the war's rapid and enormously successful conclusion. Many people echoed President Bush's sentiments when he declared, "By God,

The Highway of Death The allied coalition wreaked gruesome destruction on Iraqi forces fleeing back to Iraq after their defeat in Kuwait in 1991.

© Peter Turnley/Corbis

we've kicked the Vietnam Syndrome once and for all!" But when the smoke cleared, Saddam Hussein had survived to menace the world another day. America and its allies had agreed to the liberation of Kuwait, but Bush, fearing that a full assault on Baghdad would cost many lives and much public support, stopped well short of overthrowing the tyrant Saddam. The perpetually troubled Middle East knew scarcely less trouble after Desert Storm had ceased to thunder, and the United States, for better or worse, found itself even more deeply ensnared in the region's web of mortal hatreds and intractable conflicts.

MAP 40.5 Operation Desert Storm: The Ground War, February 23–27, 1991 © Cengage Learning

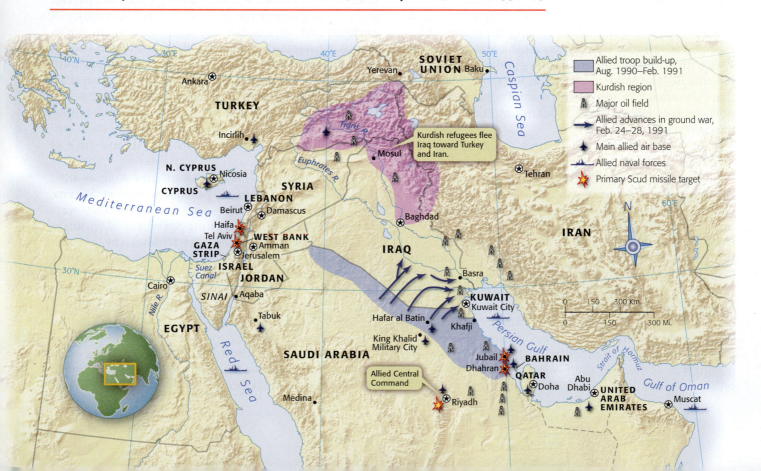

✦ Bush on the Home Front

George H. W. Bush partly redeemed his pledge to work for a "kinder, gentler America" when he signed the **Americans with Disabilities Act (ADA)** in 1990, a landmark law prohibiting discrimination against the 43 million U.S. citizens with physical or mental disabilities. The president also signed a major water projects bill in 1992 that fundamentally reformed the distribution of subsidized federal water in the West. The bill put the interests of the environment ahead of agriculture, especially in California's heavily irrigated Central Valley, and made much more water available to the West's thirsty cities.

The new president continued to aggravate the explosive "social issues" that had so divided Americans throughout the 1980s, especially the nettlesome questions of affirmative action and abortion. In 1990 Bush's Department of Education challenged the legality of college scholarships targeted for racial minorities. Bush repeatedly threatened to veto civil rights legislation that would make it easier for employees to prove discrimination in hiring and promotion practices. (He grudgingly accepted a watered-down civil rights bill in 1991.)

Most provocatively, in 1991 Bush nominated for the Supreme Court the conservative African American jurist Clarence Thomas, a stern critic of affirmative action. Thomas's nomination was loudly opposed by liberal groups, including organized labor, the National Association for the Advancement of Colored People (NAACP), and the National Organization for Women (NOW). Reflecting irreconcilable divisions over affirmative action and abortion, the Senate Judiciary Committee concluded its hearings on the nomination with a divided 7–7 vote and forwarded the matter to the full Senate without a recommendation.

Then, just days before the Senate was scheduled to vote in early October 1991, a press leak revealed that Anita Hill, a law professor at the University of Oklahoma, had accused Thomas of sexual harassment. The Senate Judiciary Committee was forced to reopen its hearings. For days a prurient American public sat glued to their television sets as Hill graphically detailed her charges of sexual improprieties and Thomas angrily responded. In the end, by a 52–48 vote, the Senate confirmed Thomas as the second African American ever to sit on the supreme bench (Thurgood Marshall was the first). While many Americans hailed Hill as a heroine for focusing the nation's attention on issues of sexual harassment, Thomas maintained that Hill's widely publicized, unproved allegations amounted to "a high-tech lynching for uppity blacks who in any way deign to think for themselves, to do for themselves."

The furor over Thomas's confirmation suggested that the social issues that had helped produce three Republican presidential victories in the 1980s were losing some of their electoral appeal. Many women, enraged by the all-male judiciary committee's behavior in the Thomas hearings, grew increasingly critical of the president's uncompromising stand on abortion. A "gender gap" opened between the two political parties, as pro-choice women grew increasingly cool toward the strong anti-abortion stand of the Republicans.

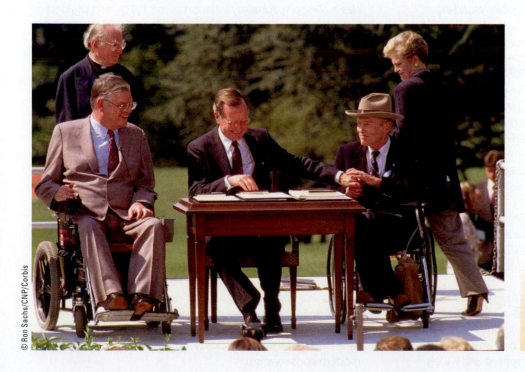

President George H. W. Bush Signs the Americans with Disabilities Act on the South Lawn of the White House, July 26, 1990

Still more damaging to President Bush's political health was the economy, which sputtered and stalled almost from the outset of his administration. By 1992 the unemployment rate exceeded 7 percent. It approached 10 percent in the key state of California, ravaged by defense cutbacks. The federal budget deficit continued to mushroom cancerously, topping $250 billion in each of Bush's years as president. In a desperate attempt to stop the hemorrhage of red ink, Bush agreed in 1990 to a budget increase that included $133 billion in new taxes.

Bush's 1990 tax and budget package added up to a political catastrophe. In his 1988 presidential campaign, Bush had belligerently declared, "Read my lips—no new taxes." Now he had flagrantly broken that campaign promise.

Varying Viewpoints
Where Did Modern Conservatism Come From?

Ronald Reagan's election surprised many historians. Reflecting a liberal political outlook that is common among academic scholars, they were long accustomed to understanding American history as an inexorable, almost evolutionary, unfolding of liberal principles, including the quests for economic equality, social justice, and active government. That point of view animated the enormously popular writings of the so-called progressive historians, such as Charles and Mary Beard, earlier in the century (see "Varying Viewpoints: The Populists: Radicals or Reactionaries?" on p. 510). For the Beards, "conservatives" were the rich, privileged elites bent on preserving their wealth and power and determined to keep government impotent, but doomed in the end to give way to the forces of liberal democracy.

Even the "New Left" revisionists of the 1960s, while critical of the celebratory tone of their progressive forebears, were convinced that the deepest currents of American history flowed leftward. But whether they were liberal or revisionist, most scholars writing in the first three post–World War II decades dismissed conservatism as an obsolete political creed. The revisionists were much more interested in decrying liberalism's deficiencies than in analyzing conservatism's strengths. Liberals and revisionists alike abandoned the Beards' image of powerful conservative elites and offered instead a contemptuous portrait of conservatives as fringe wackos—paranoid McCarthyites or racist demagogues who, in the words of the liberal critic Lionel Trilling, trafficked only in "irritable mental gestures which seem to resemble ideas." Such an outlook is conspicuous in books such as Daniel Bell's *The Radical Right* (1963) and Richard Hofstadter's *The Paranoid Style in American Politics* (1965).

Yet what flowed out of the turbulent decade of the 1960s was not a strengthened liberalism, but a revived conservatism. Ronald Reagan's huge political success compelled a thorough reexamination of the tradition of American conservatism and the sources of its modern resurgence.

Historians such as Leo Ribuffo and Alan Brinkley have argued that characters once dismissed as irrational crackpots or colorful irrelevancies—including religious fundamentalists and depression-era figures like Huey Long and Father Charles Coughlin—articulated values deeply rooted and widely shared in American culture. Those conservative spokespersons, whatever their peculiarities, offered a vision of free individuals, minimal government, and autonomous local communities that harked back to many of the themes of "civic republicanism" in the era of young nationhood.

But modern conservatism, however deep its roots, is also a product of the recent historical past. As scholars like Thomas Sugrue and Thomas Edsall have shown, the economic stagnation that set in after 1970 made many Americans insecure about their futures and receptive to new political doctrines. At the same time, as the commentator Kevin Phillips has stressed, "social issues," with little or no apparent economic content, became increasingly prominent, as movements for sexual liberation, legal abortion, and women's rights sharply challenged traditional beliefs. Perhaps most important, the success of the civil rights movement thrust the perpetually agonizing question of race relations to the very center of American political life. Finally, the failure of government policies in Vietnam, runaway inflation in the 1970s, and the disillusioning Watergate episode cast doubt on the legitimacy, the efficacy, and even the morality of "big government."

Many modern conservatives, including the pundit George Will, stress the deep historical roots of American conservatism. In their view, as Will once put it, it took sixteen years to count the ballots from the 1964 (Goldwater versus Johnson) election, and Goldwater won after all. But that argument is surely overstated. Goldwater ran against the legacy of the New Deal and was overwhelmingly defeated. Reagan ran against the consequences of the Great Society and won decisively. Many conservatives, in short, apparently acknowledge the legitimacy of the New Deal and the stake that many middle-class Americans feel they have in its programs of Social Security, home mortgage subsidies, farm price supports, and similar policies. But they reject the philosophy of the Great Society, with its more focused attack on urban poverty and its vigorous support of affirmative action. Modern conservatism springs less from a repudiation of government per se and more from a disapproval of the particular priorities and strategies of the Great Society. The different historical fates of the New Deal and the Great Society suggest the key to the rise of modern conservatism.

Chapter Review

KEY TERMS

Proposition 13 (945)

boll weevils (945)

supply-side economics (945)

Reaganomics (946)

Strategic Defense Initiative (SDI) (946)

Sandinistas (947)

contras (947)

glasnost (949)

perestroika (949)

Intermediate-Range Nuclear Forces (INF) Treaty (949)

Iran-Contra affair (951)

Moral Majority (951)

Black Monday (955)

Commonwealth of Independent States (CIS) (957)

Operation Desert Storm (959)

Americans with Disabilities Act (ADA) (961)

PEOPLE TO KNOW

Ronald Reagan

Margaret Thatcher

Mikhail Gorbachev

Saddam Hussein

Jerry Falwell

Sandra Day O'Connor

George H. W. Bush

Boris Yeltsin

Nelson Mandela

Manuel Noriega

Norman ("Stormin' Norman") Schwarzkopf

Clarence Thomas

CHRONOLOGY

1980	Reagan defeats Carter for presidency
1981	Iran releases American hostages
	"Reaganomics" spending and tax cuts passed
	Solidarity movement in Poland
	O'Connor appointed to Supreme Court (first woman justice)
1981–1991	United States aids anti-leftist forces in Central America
1982	Recession hits U.S. economy
	Israel invades Lebanon
1983	Reagan announces SDI plan (Star Wars)
	U.S. marines killed in Beirut, Lebanon
	U.S. invasion of Grenada
1984	Reagan defeats Mondale for presidency
	Soviet Union boycotts Summer Olympics in Los Angeles
1985	Gorbachev comes to power in Soviet Union, announces glasnost and perestroika
	First Reagan-Gorbachev summit meeting in Geneva
1986	Reagan administration backs Aquino in Philippines
	Iran-Contra affair revealed
	Second Reagan-Gorbachev summit meeting in Reykjavik, Iceland

1987	Stock market plunges 508 points
	Third Reagan-Gorbachev summit meeting in Washington, D.C.; INF treaty signed
1988	Fourth Reagan-Gorbachev summit meeting in Moscow
	Bush defeats Dukakis for presidency
1989	Chinese government suppresses prodemocracy demonstrators in Tiananmen Square
	Webster v. *Reproductive Health Services*
	Eastern European countries oust communist governments
	Berlin Wall torn down
1990	Iraq invades Kuwait
	East and West Germany unite
	Americans with Disabilities Act (ADA)
1991	Persian Gulf War
	Thomas appointed to Supreme Court
	Gorbachev survives coup attempt, resigns as Soviet president
	Soviet Union dissolves; republics form Commonwealth of Independent States
1992	Twenty-seventh Amendment (prohibiting congressional pay raises from taking effect until an election seats a new session of Congress) ratified
	Planned Parenthood v. *Casey*

TO LEARN MORE

Robert Collins, *Transforming America: Politics and Culture During the Reagan Years* (2007)

Donald T. Critchlow, *The Conservative Ascendancy: How the GOP Right Made Political History* (2007)

Barbara Ehrenreich, *The Worst Years of Our Lives: Irreverent Notes from a Decade of Greed* (1990)

Irving Kristol, *Reflections of a Neoconservative* (1983)

Walter LaFeber, *Inevitable Revolutions* (2nd ed., 1993)

Melvyn Leffler, *For the Soul of Mankind: The United States, the Soviet Union, and the Cold War* (2007)

William Martin, *With God on Our Side: The Rise of the Religious Right in America* (1996)

Richard L. Pacelle, Jr., *The Transformation of the Supreme Court's Agenda: From the New Deal to the Reagan Administration* (1991)

Kevin Phillips, *The Politics of Rich and Poor: Wealth and the American Electorate in the Reagan Aftermath* (1990)

Paul C. Roberts, *The Supply-Side Revolution* (1984)

Daniel T. Rodgers, *Age of Fracture* (2011)

Jonathan M. Schoenwald, *A Time for Choosing: The Rise of Modern American Conservatism* (2001)

John W. Sloan, *The Reagan Effect: Economics and Presidential Leadership* (1999)

David A. Stockman, *The Triumph of Politics: Why the Reagan Revolution Failed* (1986)

Gil Troy, *Morning in America: How Ronald Reagan Invented the 1980s* (2007)

Sean Wilentz, *The Age of Reagan: A History, 1974–2008* (2008)

A complete, annotated bibliography for this chapter—along with brief descriptions of the People to Know—may be found on the American Pageant website. The Key Terms are defined in a Glossary at the end of the text.

Go to the CourseMate website at **www.cengagebrain.com** for additional study tools and review materials—including audio and video clips—for this chapter.

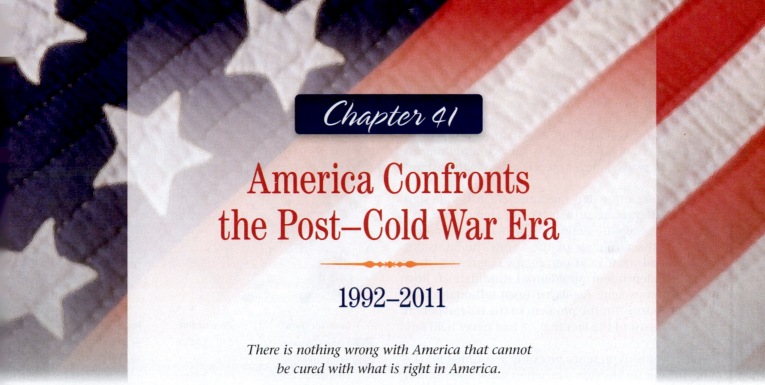

Chapter 41

America Confronts the Post–Cold War Era

1992–2011

There is nothing wrong with America that cannot be cured with what is right in America.

WILLIAM J. CLINTON, INAUGURAL, 1993

The collapse of the Soviet Union and the democratization of its client regimes in Eastern Europe ended the four-decade-old Cold War and left the United States the world's sole remaining superpower. Americans welcomed these changes but seemed unsure how to exercise their unprecedented economic and military might in this new international scenario. The culture wars that had started in the 1960s fed ferociously partisan political squabbles that distracted the nation from the urgent task of clearly defining its role in the dawning age of globalization. In 2000 George W. Bush won a bitterly contested presidential election that left the nation more rancorously divided than ever, until the spectacular terrorist attacks on September 11, 2001, called forth, at least temporarily, a resurgent sense of national unity. Bush responded to the 9/11 attacks by invading the terrorist haven of Afghanistan. Amidst roiling controversy over his claims that Iraq possessed **weapons of mass destruction (WMD)** and had ties to terrorists, Bush proceeded to invade Iraq as well. After the failure to find WMD and over four thousand American battle deaths in the prolonged Iraq War, a war-weary country, nostalgic for the prosperity and peace of the 1990s, made history by electing the first African American president, Barack Obama. The new president inherited a crushing economic crisis, soon dubbed "The Great Recession." Its scale was exceeded in modern times only by the Great Depression of the 1930s. And like Franklin Roosevelt in the depression era, Obama seized the occasion to pursue major reforms in health care and financial regulation. But unlike FDR, Obama triggered a powerful Republican backlash that erased the Democratic majority in

the House of Representatives in the congressional elections of 2010.

�֍ Bill Clinton: The First Baby-Boomer President

As the last decade of the twentieth century opened, the slumbering economy, the widening gender gap, and the rising anti-incumbent spirit spelled opportunity for Democrats, frozen out of the White House for all but four years since 1968. Governor William Jefferson ("Bill") Clinton of Arkansas weathered blistering accusations of womanizing and draft evasion to emerge as his party's standard-bearer. He selected a fellow forty-something southern white male Protestant moderate, Senator Albert Gore of Tennessee, as his vice-presidential running mate.

Clinton claimed to be a "new" Democrat, chastened by the party's long exile in the political wilderness. With other centrist Democrats, he had formed the **Democratic Leadership Council** to point the party away from its traditional antibusiness, dovish, champion-of-the-underdog orientation and toward pro-growth, strong defense, and anticrime policies. Clinton campaigned especially vigorously on promises to stimulate the economy, reform the welfare system, and overhaul the nation's health-care apparatus.

Trying to wring one more win out of the social issues that had underwritten two Reagan and one Bush presidential victories, the Republicans emphasized "family values" and, as expected, nominated George H. W. Bush and Vice President J. Danforth Quayle for a second

965

term. But Bush's listless campaign could not keep pace with the super-energetic and phenomenally articulate Clinton. Bush claimed credit for ending the Cold War and trumpeted his leadership role in the Persian Gulf War. But pocketbook problems as the economy dipped into recession swayed more voters than pride in past foreign policy.

At Clinton's campaign headquarters, a simple sign reminded staffers of his principal campaign theme: "It's the economy, stupid." Reflecting pervasive economic unease and the virulence of the throw-the-bums-out national mood, nearly 20 percent of voters cast their ballots for independent presidential candidate H. Ross Perot, a bantamweight, jug-eared Texas billionaire who harped incessantly on the problem of the federal deficit and made a boast of the fact that he had never held any public office.

Perot's colorful presence probably accounted for the record turnout on election day, when some 100 million voters—55 percent of those eligible—went to the polls. The final tally gave Clinton 44,909,889 popular votes and 370 votes in the Electoral College. He was the first baby boomer to ascend to the White House, a distinction reflecting the electoral profile of the population,

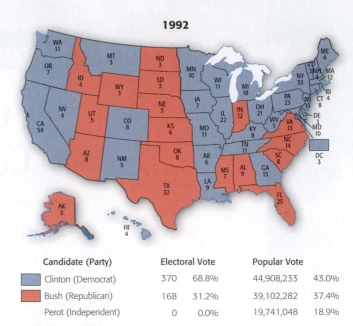

1992

Candidate (Party)	Electoral Vote		Popular Vote	
Clinton (Democrat)	370	68.8%	44,908,233	43.0%
Bush (Republican)	168	31.2%	39,102,282	37.4%
Perot (Independent)	0	0.0%	19,741,048	18.9%

MAP 41.1 Presidential Election of 1992 (with electoral vote by state) © Cengage Learning

70 percent of whom had been born after World War II. Bush polled some 39,104,545 popular votes and 168 electoral votes. Perot won no electoral votes but did gather 19,742,267 popular votes—the strongest showing for an independent or third-party candidate since Theodore Roosevelt ran on the Bull Moose ticket in 1912 (see Map 41.1). Democrats also racked up clear majorities in both houses of Congress, which seated near-record numbers of new members, including thirty-nine African Americans, nineteen Hispanic Americans, seven Asian Americans, one Native American, and forty-eight women, six of them in the Senate. Clinton also seized the opportunity in 1993 to nominate Ruth Bader Ginsburg to the Supreme Court, where she joined Sandra Day O'Connor to make a pair of women justices.

✯ A False Start for Reform

Badly overestimating his electoral mandate for liberal reform, the young president made a series of costly blunders upon entering the White House. He stirred a hornet's nest of controversy by advocating an end to the ban on gays and lesbians in the armed services. Confronted with fierce opposition, the president finally had to settle for a **"Don't Ask, Don't Tell"** policy that quietly accepted gay and lesbian soldiers and sailors without officially acknowledging their presence in the military. (Congress finally repealed the discriminatory policy in 2010.)

Even more damaging to Clinton's political standing, and to his hopes for lasting liberal achievement,

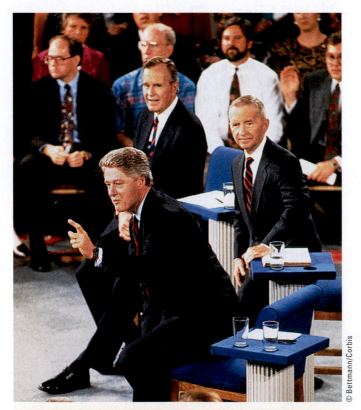

© Bettmann/Corbis

Presidential Campaign Debate, 1992 George Bush, Ross Perot, and Bill Clinton squared off at the University of Richmond (Virginia) on October 16, 1992. The telegenic Clinton handily dominated the televised debates, especially in the "talk-show" format used on this occasion.

was the fiasco of his attempt to reform the nation's health-care system. In a dramatic but personally and politically risky move, the president appointed his wife, nationally prominent lawyer and children's advocate Hillary Rodham Clinton, as the director of a task force charged with redesigning the medical-service industry. Their stupefyingly complicated plan was dead on arrival when it was presented to Congress in October 1993. The First Lady was doused with a torrent of abuse, although she eventually rehabilitated herself sufficiently to win election as a U.S. senator from New York in 2000—the first First Lady ever to hold elective office—and later became President Obama's secretary of state. President Clinton had better luck with a deficit-reduction bill in 1993, which combined with an increasingly buoyant economy by 1996 to shrink the federal deficit to its lowest level in more than a decade. By 1998 Clinton's policies seemed to have caged the ravenous deficit monster, as Congress argued over the unfamiliar question of how to manage federal budget *surpluses*.

Despite these successes, a sour antigovernment mood persisted. A huge explosion destroyed a federal office building in Oklahoma City in 1995, taking 168 lives, in retribution for a 1993 standoff in Waco, Texas, between federal agents and a fundamentalist sect known as the Branch Davidians. That showdown had ended in the destruction of the sect's compound and the deaths of many Branch Davidians, including women and children. Events like the **Oklahoma City bombing** brought to light a lurid and secretive underground of paramilitary private "militias" composed of alienated citizens armed to the teeth and ultrasuspicious of all government.

Even many law-abiding citizens shared to some degree in the antigovernment attitudes that drove the militia members to murderous extremes. Thanks largely to the disillusioning agony of the Vietnam War and the naked cynicism of Richard Nixon in the Watergate scandal, the confidence in government that had come naturally to the generation that had licked the Great Depression and won the Second World War was in short supply by century's end. Reflecting that pervasive disenchantment with politics and politicians, several states passed term-limit laws for elected officials, although the Supreme Court ruled in 1995 that the restrictions did not apply to federal officeholders.

AP Images

Bombing of Federal Building in Oklahoma City, 1995   A truck bomb killed 168 people in this federal office building in the worst act of terrorism in the United States until September 11, 2001. Convicted in 2001 for the attack, antigovernment militant Timothy McVeigh became the first person executed by the federal government in nearly forty years.

✦ The Politics of Distrust

Clinton's failed initiatives and widespread antigovernment sentiment afforded Republicans a golden opportunity in 1994, and they seized it aggressively. Led by outspoken Georgia Representative Newt Gingrich, Republicans offered voters a **Contract with America** that promised an all-out assault on budget deficits and radical reductions in welfare programs. Their campaign succeeded fabulously, as a conservative tornado roared across the land in the 1994 congressional elections. Republicans picked up eleven new governorships, eight seats in the Senate, and fifty-three seats in the House (where Gingrich became Speaker), giving them control of both chambers of the federal Congress for the first time in forty years.

But if President Clinton had overplayed his mandate for liberal reform in 1993, the congressional Republicans soon proceeded to overplay their mandate for conservative retrenchment. In 1996 the new Congress achieved a major conservative victory when it compelled a reluctant Clinton to sign the **Welfare Reform Bill**, which made deep cuts in welfare grants and required able-bodied welfare recipients to find employment. The new welfare law also tightly restricted welfare benefits for legal and illegal immigrants alike, reflecting a rising tide of anti-immigrant sentiment as the numbers of newcomers climbed toward an all-time high. Old-line liberal Democrats howled with pain at the president's alleged betrayal of his party's heritage. But Clinton's acceptance of the welfare reform package was part of his shrewd political strategy of accommodating the electorate's conservative mood by moving to his right.

Many Americans gradually came to feel that the Gingrich Republicans were bending their conservative bow too far, especially when the new Speaker advocated provocative ideas like sending the children of welfare families to orphanages. In a tense confrontation between the Democratic president and the Republican Congress, the federal government was actually forced to shut down for several days at the end of 1995 until a budget package was agreed upon. These outlandishly partisan antics bred a backlash that helped President Clinton rebound from his political near-death experience.

As the 1996 election approached, the Republicans chose Kansas senator Robert Dole as their presidential candidate. A decorated World War II veteran, Dole ran a lackluster campaign. Clinton, buoyed by a healthy economy and by his artful trimming to the conservative wind, breezed to an easy victory, with 47,401,898 popular votes to Dole's 39,198,482 (see Map 41.2). The Reform party's egomaniacal leader, Ross Perot, ran a sorry third, picking up less than half the votes he had garnered in 1992. Clinton won 379 electoral votes, Dole only 159. But Republicans remained in control of Congress.

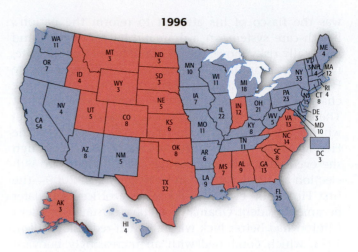

1996

Candidate (Party)	Electoral Vote		Popular Vote	
Clinton (Democrat)	379	70.4%	47,401,054	49.2%
Dole (Republican)	159	29.6%	39,197,350	40.7%
Perot (Independent)	0	0.0%	8,085,285	8.4%

MAP 41.2 Presidential Election of 1996 (with electoral vote by state) The "solid South," once a safe Democratic stronghold, had by century's end largely become Republican territory. © Cengage Learning

✦ Clinton Again

As Clinton began his second term—the first Democratic president since Franklin Delano Roosevelt to be reelected—the heady promises of far-reaching reform with which he had entered the White House four years earlier were no longer heard. Still facing Republican majorities in both houses of Congress, he proposed only modest legislative goals, even though soaring tax revenues generated by the prosperous economy produced in 1998 a balanced federal budget for the first time in three decades.

Clinton cleverly managed to put Republicans on the defensive by claiming the political middle ground. He now warmly embraced the landmark Welfare Reform Bill of 1996 that he had initially been slow to endorse. Juggling the political hot potato of affirmative action, Clinton pledged to "mend it, not end it." When voters in California in 1996 approved Proposition 209, prohibiting affirmative-action preferences in government and higher education, the number of minority students in the state's public universities temporarily plummeted. A federal appeals court decision, *Hopwood v. Texas*, had a similar effect in Texas. Clinton criticized these broad assaults on affirmative action but stopped short of trying to reverse them, aware that public support for affirmative action, especially among white Americans, had diminished since the 1970s.

Clinton's major political advantage continued to be the roaring economy, which by 2000 had sustained the

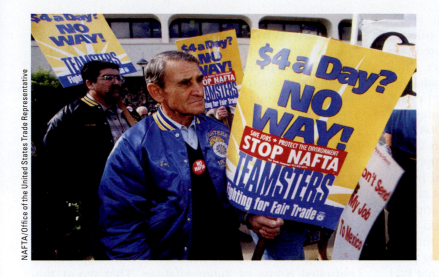

NAFTA/Office of the United States Trade Representative

Protesting NAFTA, 1993 These members of the Teamsters Union feared that the adoption of the North American Free Trade Agreement would mean the replacement of high-paying American jobs with low-wage, nonunion Mexican labor. More than a decade later, the treaty still rankled. Policymakers disagreed about whether NAFTA had been damaging to American workers. In the 2008 election, the Republicans endorsed it, while the Democrats attacked it.

longest period of growth in American history, driven by the Federal Reserve Board's low-interest, easy-money policies and by the explosive growth of new Internet ("dot-com") businesses. While unemployment crept down to 4 percent and employers scrambled madly for workers, inflationary pressure remained remarkably low.

Prosperity did not make Clinton immune to controversy over trade policy. During his first term, he had shown political courage by supporting the **North American Free Trade Agreement (NAFTA)**, creating in 1993 a free-trade zone encompassing Mexico, Canada, and the United States. In doing so, he bucked the opposition of protectionists in his own party, especially labor leaders fearful of losing jobs to low-wage Mexican workers. Clinton took another step in 1994 toward a global free-trade system when he vigorously promoted the creation of the **World Trade Organization (WTO)**, the successor to the General Agreement on Tariffs and Trade (GATT) and a cherished goal of free-trade advocates since the end of the Second World War.

Simmering discontent over trade policy boiled over in 1999 when Clinton hosted the meeting of the WTO in Seattle. The city's streets filled with protesters railing against what they viewed as the human and environmental costs of economic "globalization."

✴ Problems Abroad

The end of the Cold War dismantled the framework within which the United States had conducted foreign policy for nearly half a century. Clinton groped for a diplomatic formula to replace anticommunism as the basic premise of American diplomacy.

Absorbed by domestic issues, President Clinton at first seemed uncertain and even amateurish in his conduct of foreign policy. He followed his predecessor's lead in dispatching American troops as part of a peacekeeping mission to Somalia. But after Somali rebels

killed more than a dozen Americans, the president quietly withdrew the U.S. units in March 1994, without having accomplished any clearly defined goal. Burned in Somalia, Washington stood on the sidelines in 1994 when catastrophic ethnic violence in the central African country of Rwanda resulted in the deaths of half a million people.

Clinton also struggled to define a policy with respect to China, which was rapidly emerging as an economic and political powerhouse. Clinton soft-pedaled his earlier criticism of the Beijing regime on human rights issues and instead began seeking improved trade relations with that robustly industrializing country and potential market bonanza. By 2000 Clinton was crusading for a controversial China trade bill. Congress passed it in May 2000, making the Asian giant a full-fledged trading partner of the United States.

Other problems boiled up in the tormented Balkans in southeastern Europe. As vicious ethnic conflict raged through Bosnia, the Washington government dithered until finally deciding to commit American troops to a NATO peacekeeping contingent in late 1995. Yet NATO's expansion to include the new member states of Poland, Hungary, and the Czech Republic in 1997, and its continuing presence in Bosnia, failed to pacify the Balkans completely. When Serbian president Slobodan Milošević in 1999 unleashed a new round of "ethnic cleansing" in the region, this time against ethnic Albanians in the province of Kosovo, U.S.-led NATO forces launched an air war against Serbia. The bombing campaign eventually forced Milošević to accept a NATO peacekeeping force on the ground in Kosovo. Milošević was arrested in 2001 and put on trial before the International Criminal Court in The Hague, where he died in 2006 before the trial was completed.

The Middle East remained a major focus of American diplomacy right up to the end of Clinton's tenure. In 1993 Clinton presided over a historic meeting at the White House between Israeli premier Yitzhak Rabin and Palestine Liberation Organization (PLO) leader Yasir Arafat. They agreed in principle on self-rule for the Palestinians within Israel. But hopes flickered two years later when Rabin fell to an assassin's bullet. Clinton and his second-term secretary of state, Madeleine Albright, spent the rest of the 1990s struggling in vain to broker the permanent settlement that continued to elude Israelis and Palestinians. Arafat died in 2004 with his dream of creating a Palestinian state still unrealized.

In his final year as president, Clinton stepped up his efforts to leave a legacy as an international peacemaker. Along with his work in the Middle East, he sought to bring peace to Northern Ireland and the Korean peninsula, and he traveled to India and Pakistan in hopes of reducing the rivalry between the two nuclear powers of southern Asia. But the guiding principles of American foreign policy in the post–Cold War era remained ill-defined and elusive.

✦ Scandal and Impeachment

Scandal had dogged Bill Clinton from the beginning of his presidency. Critics brought charges of everything from philandering to illegal financial transactions.

Allegations of corruption stemming from a real estate deal called **Whitewater** while he was governor of Arkansas triggered an investigation by a special prosecutor, but no indictment ever materialized.

All the previous scandals were overshadowed by the revelation in January 1998 that Clinton had engaged in a sexual affair with a young White House intern, Monica Lewinsky, and then blatantly lied about it when testifying under oath in another woman's civil suit accusing him of sexual harassment. Caught in his bold lie, the president made a humiliating confession, but his political opponents smelled blood in the water. In September 1998 the special prosecutor investigating Whitewater, who had broad powers to investigate *any* evidence of presidential malfeasance, presented a stinging report, including lurid sexual details, to the Republican-controlled House of Representatives. That report presented eleven possible grounds for impeachment, all related to lying about the **Lewinsky affair**.

The House quickly cranked up the rusty machinery of impeachment. As an acrid partisan atmosphere enveloped the Capitol, House Republicans in December 1998 passed two articles of impeachment against the president: perjury before a grand jury and obstruction of justice. Crying foul, the Democratic minority

Intifada Against Israeli Control, 1994 Beginning in 1987, Palestinians living in the Israeli-controlled territories of the West Bank and Gaza rose up in protest. As the stalemate dragged on, the likelihood of Middle East peace receded, despite repeated international diplomatic efforts to reach a settlement. These young Palestinians in East Jerusalem wave Palestine Liberation Organization (PLO) flags outlawed by Israel.

© Bettmann/Corbis

Michael Dougan

The Legacy of Impeachment
Time magazine's cartoonist asked how future generations would judge the Clinton impeachment episode—and how it might be treated in history textbooks.

charged that, however deplorable Clinton's personal misconduct, sexual transgressions did not rise to the level of "high crimes and misdemeanors" prescribed in the Constitution (see Art. II, Sec. IV in the Appendix). The House Republican managers (prosecutors) of impeachment for the Senate trial replied that perjury and obstruction were grave public issues and that nothing less than the "rule of law" was at stake.

As cries of "honor the Constitution" and "sexual McCarthyism" filled the air, the nation debated whether the president's peccadilloes amounted to high crimes or low follies. Most Americans apparently leaned toward the latter view. In the 1998 midterm elections, voters reduced the House Republicans' majority, causing fiery House speaker Newt Gingrich to resign his post. Although Americans held a low opinion of Clinton's slipshod personal morals, most liked the president's political and economic policies and wanted him to stay in office.

In early 1999, for the first time in 130 years, the nation witnessed an impeachment proceeding in the U.S. Senate. Dusting off ancient precedents from Andrew Johnson's trial, the one hundred senators solemnly heard arguments in the case. With the facts widely known and the two parties' political positions firmly locked in, the trial's outcome was a foregone conclusion. On the key obstruction of justice charge, five northeastern Republicans joined all forty-five Democratic senators in voting not guilty. The fifty Republican votes for conviction fell far short of the constitutionally required two-thirds majority. The vote on the perjury charge was forty-five guilty, fifty-five not guilty.

Clinton's Legacy and the 2000 Election

Beyond the obvious stain of impeachment, Clinton's legacy was mixed. His sound economic policies encouraged growth and trade in a rapidly globalizing post–Cold War world. Yet as a "New Democrat" and avowed centrist, Clinton did more to consolidate than to reverse the Reagan-Bush revolution against New Deal liberalism that for half a century had provided the compass for the Democratic party and the nation. Further, by setting such a low standard in his personal conduct, he replenished the sad reservoir of public cynicism about politics that Vietnam and Watergate had created a generation before.

Nonetheless, as the end of the Clinton term and the beginning of the new millennium approached, the Democrats stayed on their political course and nominated loyal vice president Albert Gore for president. Gore faced the tricky challenge of linking himself to Clinton-era peace and prosperity while at the same time distancing himself from his boss's personal foibles. He chose as his running mate Connecticut senator Joseph Lieberman, an outspoken Clinton critic and the first Jew nominated to a major national ticket. Their Republican challenger, George W. Bush, won the nomination on the strength of his father's name and his years as governor of Texas. Bush surrounded himself with Washington insiders, including vice-presidential nominee Richard Cheney, and, in a clear jab at Clinton, promised to "restore dignity to the White House."

Rosy estimates that the federal budget would produce a surplus of some $2 trillion in the coming decade set the stage for the presidential contest. Echoing the Republican creed of smaller government, Bush argued for returning the budget surplus to "the people" through massive tax cuts and for promoting private-sector programs, such as school vouchers and a reliance on "faith-based" institutions to help the poor. Gore proposed smaller tax cuts, targeted at middle- and lower-class people, and strengthening Social Security. In an era of peace, foreign policy figured hardly at all in the campaign, although Bush struck a moderate note when he urged that America should act like "a humble nation."

Pollsters predicted a close election, but none foresaw the epochal cliffhanger that the election would become. On election day the country split nearly evenly between the two candidates, and it was soon clear that Florida's electoral votes would determine the winner. Television news programs announced that Bush had won the Sunshine State, and Al Gore called the Texas governor to concede defeat. Yet just an hour later, Gore's camp decided that Florida was too close to call, and the vice president—in perhaps the most awkward phone call in modern politics—phoned back to retract his concession.

What ensued was a five-week political standoff over how to count the votes in Florida. Democrats argued that some ballots were confusing or had been misread by machines and asked for recounts by hand in several counties. Republicans claimed that such recounts would amount to "changing the rules in the middle of

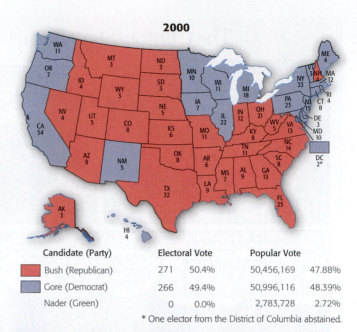

2000

Candidate (Party)	Electoral Vote		Popular Vote	
Bush (Republican)	271	50.4%	50,456,169	47.88%
Gore (Democrat)	266	49.4%	50,996,116	48.39%
Nader (Green)	0	0.0%	2,783,728	2.72%

* One elector from the District of Columbia abstained.

MAP 41.3 Presidential Election of 2000 (with electoral vote by state) Although Democrat Albert Gore won the popular election by half a million votes, George W. Bush's contested 537-vote advantage in Florida gave him a slight lead in the Electoral College. The 2.7 million popular votes won by Green party candidate and consumer activist Ralph Nader almost surely deprived Gore of victory, casting Nader in the role of spoiler. Bush's failure to win the popular vote inspired critics to protest at his inauguration with placards reading "Hail to the Thief." © Cengage Learning

the game" and thus thwart the rule of law. After weeks of legal bickering with the presidency in the balance, the Supreme Court finally intervened. By a five-to-four vote along partisan lines, the Court reasoned that since neither Florida's legislature nor its courts had established a uniform standard for evaluating disputed ballots, the hand counts amounted to an unconstitutional breach of the Fourteenth Amendment's equal protection clause.

That ruling gave Bush the White House but cast a dark shadow of illegitimacy over his presidency. Bush officially won Florida by 537 votes out of 6 million cast, and he squeaked by in the Electoral College, 271 to 266 (see Maps 41.3 and 41.4). The national popular vote went decisively to Gore, 50,999,897 to 50,456,002. For the first time since 1888, a candidate won the White House with fewer popular votes than his opponent. Calls to abolish the Electoral College, however, were few and muted (see Art. V of the Constitution).

✦ Bush Begins

As the son of the forty-first president ("41"), George W. Bush ("43") became the first presidential offspring

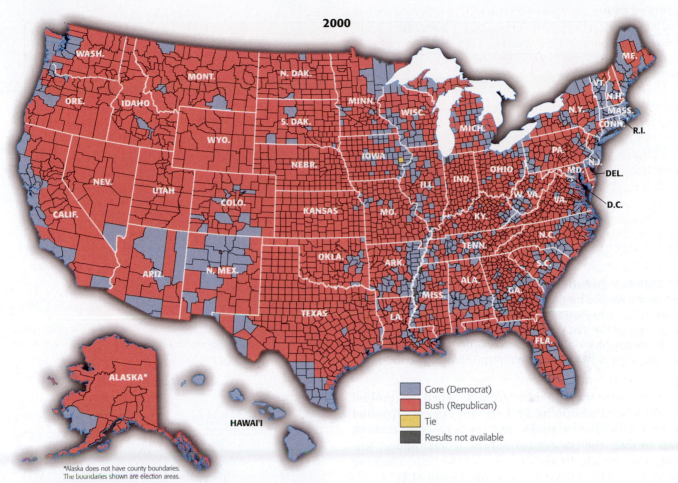

2000

Gore (Democrat)
Bush (Republican)
Tie
Results not available

*Alaska does not have county boundaries.
The boundaries shown are election areas.

MAP 41.4 America in Red and Blue This map showing the vote by county in the hotly contested 2000 presidential election vividly illustrates the geography of modern America's political divisions. Democratic candidate Albert Gore won a popular majority by carrying just 676 mostly urban counties, heavily populated by union members, minorities, and prosperous, educated white-collar workers. Republican George W. Bush won the election by taking 2,477 mostly rural counties, where feelings about "social issues" such as abortion and gun control ran high and shaped solid conservative constituencies. (Source: Adapted from VNS Graphic by Stanford Kay-Newsweek.) © Cengage Learning

since John Quincy Adams to reach the White House. Raised largely in Texas, the younger Bush publicly distanced himself from his family's privileged New England heritage and affected the chummy manner of a self-made good ol' boy—though he held degrees from Yale and Harvard. (His adversaries sniped that he had been born on third base and claimed to have hit a triple.) He promised to bring to Washington the conciliatory skills he had honed as the Republican governor of Texas, where he had worked well with the Democratic majority in the state's legislature.

But as president, Bush soon proved to be more of a divider than a uniter, less a "compassionate conservative" than a crusading ideologue. Religious traditionalists cheered but liberals jeered when he withdrew American support from international health programs

that sanctioned abortion, advocated federally financed faith-based social-welfare initiatives, and sharply limited government-sponsored research on embryonic stem cells, which many scientists believed held the key to conquering diseases such as Parkinson's and Alzheimer's. He pleased corporate chieftains but angered environmentalists by challenging scientific findings on groundwater contamination and global warming, repudiating the **Kyoto Treaty** limiting greenhouse gas emissions (negotiated by the Clinton administration but never ratified by the Senate), advocating new oil exploration in the Arctic National Wildlife Refuge on Alaska's ecologically fragile north coast, and allowing Vice President Cheney to hammer out his administration's energy policy in behind-closed-doors meetings with representatives of several giant oil companies. Even many fiscal

FIGURE 41.1 Deficits into Surpluses and Back Again In 1998 the U.S. budget deficit became a surplus for the first time in decades. But by 2002 the government was back in deficit, due to President Bush's tax cuts, a weak economy, and mushrooming defense spending on the Iraq War. Following the onset of the "Great Recession" in 2008, deficits ballooned to historic highs. (Source: Office of Management and Budget, *Historical Tables: Budget of the United States Government, Fiscal Year 2009*.)

conservatives thought him reckless when he pressed ahead with a whopping $1.3 trillion tax cut. Together with a softening economy and the increasing costs of war in Iraq, the tax cut turned the federal budget surpluses of the late 1990s into yawning deficits, reaching more than $400 billion in 2004 (see Figure 41.1).

✶ Terrorism Comes to America

On September 11, 2001, the long era of America's impregnable national security violently ended. On a balmy late-summer morning, suicidal terrorists slammed two hijacked airliners, loaded with passengers and jet fuel, into the twin towers of New York City's World Trade Center. They flew a third plane into the military nerve center of the Pentagon, near Washington, D.C., killing 189 people. Heroic passengers forced a fourth hijacked aircraft to crash in rural Pennsylvania, killing all 44 aboard but depriving the terrorists of an additional weapon of mass destruction. As the two giant New York skyscrapers thunderously collapsed, some three thousand innocent victims perished, including people of many races and faiths from more than sixty countries, as well as hundreds of New York's police- and fire-department rescue workers. A stunned nation blossomed with flags, as grieving and outraged Americans struggled to express their sorrow and solidarity in the face of the catastrophic terrorism of **9/11**.

President Bush responded with a sober and stirring address to Congress nine days later. His solemn demeanor and the gravity of the situation helped to

The Toll of Terror Grief overcame this exhausted firefighter during the search for survivors in the wreckage of New York City's World Trade Center.

© David Turnley/Corbis

dissipate the cloud of illegitimacy that had shadowed his presidency since the disputed election of 2000. While emphasizing his respect for the Islamic religion and Muslim people, he identified the principal enemy as Osama bin Laden, head of a shadowy terrorist network known as **Al Qaeda** ("the base" in Arabic). A wealthy extremist exiled from his native Saudi Arabia, bin Laden was associated with earlier attacks on American embassies in East Africa and on the USS *Cole* in Yemen. He had taken refuge in landlocked Afghanistan, ruled by Islamic fundamentalists called the Taliban. (Ironically, the United States had indirectly helped bring the Taliban to power by supporting religious rebels resisting the Soviet invasion of Afghanistan in the 1980s.) Bin Laden was known to harbor venomous resentment toward the United States for its growing military presence in the Middle East (especially on the sacred soil of the Arabian Peninsula) and its unyielding support for Israel in the face of intensifying Palestinian nationalism. Bin Laden also fed on worldwide resentment of America's enormous economic, military, and cultural power. Ironically, America's most conspicuous strengths had made it a conspicuous target.

When the Taliban refused to hand over bin Laden, Bush ordered a massive military campaign against Afghanistan. Within three months American and Afghan rebel forces had overthrown the Taliban but failed to find bin Laden, and Americans continued to live in fear of future attacks. Confronted with this unconventional, diffuse menace, antiterrorism experts called for a new kind of "asymmetrical warfare," employing not just traditional military muscle but also counter-insurgency tactics like innovative intelligence gathering, training of local police forces, economic reprisals, infiltration of suspected organizations, and even assassinations.

The terrorists' blows diabolically coincided with the onset of a recession. The already gathering economic downturn worsened as edgy Americans shunned air travel and the tourist industry withered. In this anxious atmosphere, Congress in October 2001 rammed through the **USA Patriot Act.*** The act permitted extensive telephone and e-mail surveillance and authorized the detention and deportation of immigrants suspected of terrorism. Just over a year later, Congress created the new cabinet-level **Department of Homeland Security** to protect the nation's borders and ferret out potential attackers. The Justice Department meanwhile rounded up hundreds of immigrants and held them without habeas corpus (formal charges in an open court). The Bush administration further called for trying suspected terrorists before military tribunals, where the usual rules of evidence and procedure did not apply. As hundreds of Taliban fighters captured in Afghanistan languished in legal limbo and demoralizing isolation in the **Guantánamo Detention Camp** on the American military base at Guantánamo, Cuba, public-opinion polls showed Americans sharply divided on whether the terrorist threat fully warranted such drastic encroachments on America's venerable tradition of protecting civil liberties.

---

*The act's official name is Uniting and Strengthening America by Providing Appropriate Tools Required to Intercept and Obstruct Terrorism.

© Bettmann/Corbis

The Attacks Seen Around the World   The attacks of September 11, 2001, became events of international, not just American, significance, as revealed in the newspapers on display in Sofia, Bulgaria.

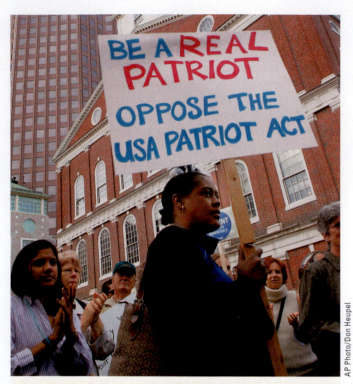

AP Photo/Don Heupel

Liberty or Death Critics of the USA Patriot Act feared the extinction of cherished civil liberties, including the right to protest against the government's policies.

Now, in the context of the new terrorist threat, the Bush administration focused on Iraq with a vengeance.

In January 2002, just weeks after the September 11 attacks, Bush claimed that Iraq, along with Iran and North Korea, constituted an "axis of evil" that gravely menaced American security. Iran and North Korea were both known to be pursuing nuclear weapons programs, and Iran had long supported terrorist operations in the Middle East. But Iraqi tyrant Saddam Hussein, defeated but not destroyed by Bush's father in 1991, became the principal object of the new president's wrath. The elder Bush had carefully assembled a broad international coalition to fight the 1991 Persian Gulf War. He had also spoken so often of "prudence" that late-night television comedians had mocked him for it. In contrast, his son was brashly determined to break with long-standing American traditions and wage a preemptive war against Iraq—and to go it alone if necessary. The younger Bush thus cast off his appeal for America to be a "humble nation" and stood revealed as a plunger, a daring risk-taker willing to embrace bold, dramatic policies, foreign as well as fiscal. In that spirit Bush began laying plans for a war against Iraq.

Itching for a fight, and egged on by hawkish Vice President Cheney and other "neoconservative" advisers, Bush accused the Iraqi regime of all manner of wrongdoing: oppressing its own people; frustrating the weapons inspectors; developing nuclear, chemical, and

Catastrophic terrorism posed an unprecedented challenge to the United States. The events of that murderous September morning reanimated American patriotism, but they also brought a long chapter in American history to a dramatic climax. All but unique among modern peoples, Americans for nearly two centuries had been spared from foreign attack on their homeland. That unusual degree of virtually cost-free national security had undergirded the values of openness and individual freedom that defined the distinctive character of American society. Now American security and American liberty alike were dangerously imperiled.

✷ Bush Takes the Offensive Against Iraq

On only its second day in office, the Bush administration warned that it would not tolerate Iraq's continued defiance of United Nations weapons inspections, mandated after Iraq's defeat in the 1991 Persian Gulf War. Iraqi dictator Saddam Hussein, after playing hide-and-seek with the inspectors for years, expelled them from his country in 1998, inducing President Clinton, with congressional approval, to declare that Saddam's removal ("regime change") was an official goal of U.S. policy. But no sustained military action against Iraq had followed.

In his 2002 state of the union address, President George W. Bush (b. 1946) declared:

❝Iraq continues to flaunt its hostility toward America and to support terror. The Iraqi regime has plotted to develop anthrax, and nerve gas, and nuclear weapons for over a decade. This is a regime that has already used poison gas to murder thousands of its own citizens—leaving the bodies of mothers huddled over their dead children. This is a regime that agreed to international inspections—then kicked out the inspectors. This is a regime that has something to hide from the civilized world.

"States like these, and their terrorist allies, constitute an axis of evil, arming to threaten the peace of the world. By seeking weapons of mass destruction, these regimes pose a grave and growing danger. They could provide these arms to terrorists, giving them the means to match their hatred. They could attack our allies or attempt to blackmail the United States. In any of these cases, the price of indifference would be catastrophic.❞

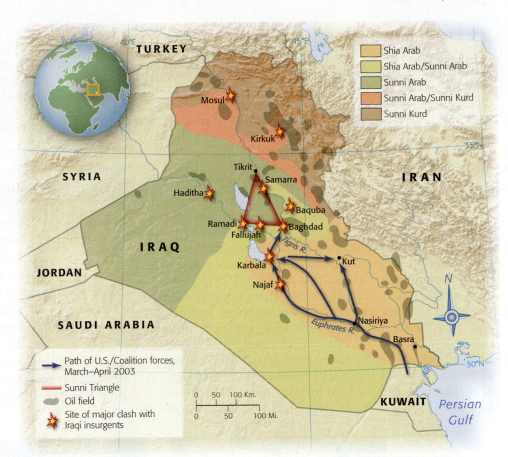

MAP 41.5 Iraq in Transition Carved out of the old Ottoman Empire after World War I, Iraq has long been a combustible compound of rivalrous ethnic and religious groups. Saddam Hussein's dictatorial regime imposed a brutal peace on the country for twenty-four years following his ascent to power in 1979, but after the American invasion in 2003, old feuds resumed, exacerbated by stinging resentment against the occupying forces. © Cengage Learning

Ethnic and religious groups by percent of total population (c. 25,000,000)

biological weapons of mass destruction referred to as "WMD"; and supporting terrorist organizations like Al Qaeda. Perhaps most controversially, he also suggested that a liberated, democratized Iraq might provide a beacon of hope to the Islamic world and thereby begin to improve the political equation in the volatile Middle East. To skeptical observers, including America's usually reliable European allies, the very multiplicity of Bush's reasons for war cast doubt on his case, and his ambition to create a democracy in long-suffering Iraq, burdened with centuries of internecine conflict, seemed naively utopian. Secretary of State Colin Powell urged caution, warning about the long-term consequences for the United States of invading and occupying an unstable, religiously and culturally divided nation of 25 million people. "You break it, you own it," he told the president.

Heavy majorities in both houses of Congress nevertheless passed a resolution in October 2002 authorizing the president to employ armed force to defend against Iraqi threats to America's national security and to enforce United Nations resolutions regarding Iraq. A month later the U.N. Security Council voted unanimously to give Iraq "a final opportunity to comply with its disarmament obligations." There followed a months-long cat-and-mouse game. U.N. weapons inspectors returned to Iraq. Saddam once again harassed and blocked them. No weapons of mass destruction were found. The inspectors

asked for more time. The United Nations declined to authorize the use of force to compel compliance.

In this tense and confusing atmosphere, Bush, with Britain his only major ally, launched the long-anticipated invasion of Iraq on March 19, 2003. Saddam Hussein's vaunted military machine collapsed almost immediately. In less than a month, Baghdad had fallen and Saddam had been driven from power and hounded into hiding. (He was found and arrested some nine months later and executed in 2006.) From the deck of a U.S. aircraft carrier off the California coast, speaking beneath a banner declaring "Mission Accomplished," Bush triumphantly announced on May 1, 2003, that "major combat operations in Iraq have ended" (see Map 41.5).

✴ Owning Iraq

President Bush's words soon came back to haunt him. "Neoconservative" pundits in Washington had predicted that American soldiers would be greeted as liberators and that Saddam's ouster would lead to flowering democracy across the Middle East. In reality post-Saddam Iraq quickly devolved into a seething cauldron of violence. The country's largest ethnic groups, Sunni and Shia Muslims, clashed violently, especially in the capital city of Baghdad. Both groups attacked American forces, especially after the U.S. decision to disband the Iraqi army, which deprived Iraq of an effective indigenous police force. A locally grown insurgency quickly spread, and occupying Iraq became ever more perilous for American troops. Hatred for Americans only worsened with revelations in April 2004 that Iraqi prisoners in Baghdad's **Abu Ghraib prison** had been tortured and humiliated by their American captors. Amid this chaos, jihadist terrorists from around the region flooded into Iraq, often fueling the intra-Iraqi conflicts to further their own radical Islamist vision. Although Al Qaeda had had no link to Iraq under Saddam, as Bush had falsely alleged, the organization certainly

In his 1998 book, A World Transformed, *former president George H. W. Bush (b. 1924) explained his rationale for not driving Saddam Hussein from power during the 1991 Persian Gulf War. His words made sobering reading in the context of his son's subsequent invasion of Iraq:*

❝Trying to eliminate Saddam . . . would have incurred incalculable human and political costs. . . . The coalition would instantly have collapsed, the Arabs deserting it in anger and other allies pulling out as well. Under the circumstances, there was no viable 'exit strategy' we could see, violating another of our principles. Furthermore, we had been self-consciously trying to set a pattern for handling aggression in the post–Cold War world. Going in and occupying Iraq, thus unilaterally exceeding the United Nations' mandate, would have destroyed the precedent of international response to aggression that we hoped to establish.❞

© Bettmann/Corbis

On the Fiery Ground in Basra, Iraq, 2004 These British soldiers are running from a gasoline bomb detonated during a protest by Iraqi job seekers who claimed that they had been promised employment in the security services. The British, who had invaded Iraq alongside the United States, oversaw the southern Iraq city of Basra, a role that proved so unpopular with British voters that Prime Minister Tony Blair was eventually forced to resign.

moved in afterward. These three battles—Shia-Sunni ethnic violence, counter-occupation insurgency, and jihadist terrorism—fed a spiraling maelstrom of bloodshed. By the end of 2006, more Americans had died in Iraq than in the attacks of September 11 (see "Thinking Globally: America Through Foreign Eyes: Hyperpower or Hapless Power?" pp. 980–981).

Almost from the outset of the intervention, American forces began preparing to withdraw. In the summer of 2004, the American military ceded political power and limited sovereignty to an interim Iraqi government. National elections followed in early 2005, and millions of Iraqis voted for a national assembly to draft a constitution. After a referendum vote on the constitution in October 2005, another round of elections chose parliamentary representatives, a prime minister, and a president. But under the seeming stability of Iraq's new democratic government lay deep, violent tensions. Sunni Muslims, the minority that had held power under Saddam Hussein, one of their own, feared reprisals and repressions under a majority Shia government. Sunnis largely boycotted the first election and tried unsuccessfully to block the ratification of the constitution. Unsuccessful at the ballot box, many Sunnis turned to bombings and political assassinations.

✯ Reelecting George W. Bush

Americans had rarely been as divided as they were in the first years of the twenty-first century. Civil libertarians worried that the government was trampling on personal freedoms in the name of fighting terrorism. Revelations in 2002 about flagrant corporate fraud fed rampant popular disillusion with the business community. Cultural tensions brewed over the rights of gay and lesbian Americans when leaders in San Francisco and Massachusetts permitted same-sex couples to marry in 2004. Affirmative action continued to spark sharp debate, as the Supreme Court permitted some preferential treatment in admitting minority undergraduate and law students to the University of Michigan in 2003.

Amid this division George W. Bush positioned himself to run for reelection. He proclaimed that his tax cuts had spurred economic growth. Targeting what he called "the soft bigotry of low expectations," he championed the **No Child Left Behind Act** of 2002, which mandated sanctions against schools that failed to meet federal performance standards. He played to cultural conservatives in opposing stem cell research (see p. xxxx) and called for a constitutional amendment to ban gay marriage. But most of all, he promoted himself as a stalwart leader in wartime, warning the country not to "change horses midstream."

After a bruising round of primary elections, the embattled Democrats chose lanky and long-jawed Massachusetts senator John Kerry to represent their ticket. Kerry pushed progressive visions of government and counted on his Vietnam War record to counter charges that he would be weak in the face of terrorism. But that plan backfired as Kerry fell under attack for his very public opposition to Vietnam once he had returned from battle in the early 1970s. In spite of increased public misgivings about the war in Iraq, Bush nailed down a decisive victory in November 2004. He received the first popular vote majority by a presidential candidate in more than a decade—60,639,281 to 57,355,978—and won the Electoral College, 286 to 252, if by only one state (this time Ohio). This time his victory was clear, constitutional, and uncontested.

✯ Bush's Second Term

Reelection, George W. Bush announced, gave him "political capital," which he intended to spend on an aggressive domestic agenda. The appointment of two new conservative Supreme Court justices (John G. Roberts and Samuel A. Alito, Jr.) upon the retirement of Sandra Day O'Connor and the death of Chief Justice William Rehnquist seemed to bode well for his ambitions. But Bush soon overplayed his hand. Attacking the core of New Deal liberalism, he proposed a radical program to privatize much of Social Security. A massive outcry led by the American Association of Retired Persons (AARP) and other liberal groups reminded Americans how much they loved Social Security, warts and all. Bush's proposal faded away within six months of his reelection. The same fate befell a proposed constitutional amendment to ban same-sex marriage, which had been a major "values" issue in the 2004 campaign.

The president also took (faulty) aim at the contentious issue of immigration reform. Here he parted company with the conservative wing of his party, many of whom wanted to deport the nearly 12 million undocumented people in the United States. His compromise plan to establish a guest-worker program and a "path to citizenship" for the undocumented ended up pleasing no one. Congress rejected it in the summer of 2007, and the issue was dead for the rest of Bush's term (see p. 1000).

Every second-term president since the 1960s had seen scandal mar his later years in office. Nixon had Watergate, Reagan had Iran-contra, and Clinton had Lewinsky. The Bush White House was no exception, but this time the accusations were political, not personal. In the fall of 2005, Vice President Dick Cheney's chief of staff was convicted of perjury in an investigation into the source of a leak that had exposed the identity of an undercover CIA agent as political retaliation against her antiwar husband. Then in December of that year, journalists discovered that the government was

America Through Foreign Eyes: Hyperpower or Hapless Power?

When the Soviet Union disintegrated in 1991, the Cold War concluded at last. So did an era in the history of American foreign policy, and in the history of the international order. For nearly half a century following World War II, the confrontation with the Soviets had deeply shaped Americans' conception of themselves—their national identity—as well as their role and reputation in the wider world. In the long twilight struggle against Soviet communism, they had accumulated unprecedented economic, military, and cultural might, and had taken virtuous pride in themselves as the global champions of democracy, justice, and human rights. Now, as the sole surviving "superpower," they faced no counterbalancing regime and, apparently, no check on their national ambitions. The United States seemed to wield all but limitless power to mold the international environment as it wished. Not since the days of ancient Rome did any people bestride the world so unopposed.

Not everyone welcomed the emergence of this international colossus. Australians grumbled that the United States was a "tall poppy" that needed to be cut down to size. French foreign minister Hubert Védrine coined a new term when he described the United States in 1999 not merely as a superpower but as a "hyper power," one "that is dominant or predominant in all categories," including not only the traditional domains of politics, economics, and the military, but even including "attitudes, concepts, languages, and modes of life." He called upon Europeans to create an alternative to the American "steamroller," to "work in favor of real multilateralism against unilateralism, for balanced multipolarism against unipolarism, for cultural diversity against uniformity." In the parlance of international relations, Védrine was promoting a "balancing" strategy to cope with U.S. power, rather than the "bandwagon" strategy of simply submitting to American hegemony and making the most of it. Notably, he was not proposing outright opposition.

As the last days of the twentieth century slipped through the hourglass, American power surely looked formidable. The United States was the world's third most populous nation (after China and India), enjoyed the world's largest economy (more than three times larger than second-ranked Japan), was the acknowledged global leader in high-tech information and biomedical innovations, and spent more on its armed forces than the rest of the world *combined*. Yet the realities of American power were somewhat less imposing. Uncle Sam struggled to find solid footing in the post–Cold War international arena. Washington in the 1990s badly botched a peacekeeping mission in lawless Somalia; stood by helplessly as genocidal militias murdered nearly a million Rwandans; dithered over how to stabilize chaotic Haiti; fumbled indecisively as nationalist and sectarian violence convulsed the former Balkan nation of Yugoslavia; found

Torture at Abu Ghraib Prison, Baghdad, 2003   Revelations that American soldiers had brutally tortured Iraqi prisoners contributed to condemnation of the nation's disregard for human rights and growing disquiet about America's unilateral policing of the world.

no effective response to terrorist attacks on New York City's World Trade Center, the destroyer USS *Cole*, and American embassies in Kenya and Tanzania; and notoriously failed to bring any conclusion to the decades-old confrontation between Israelis and Palestinians, who erupted in a bloody intifada (rebellion) against the Jewish state in 2000.

The barbarous Al Qaeda assault that finally toppled the twin towers of the World Trade Center on September 11, 2001, momentarily brought an outpouring of sympathy from an astonished and outraged world—and also brought a dramatic shift in American foreign policy. Even *Le Monde*, France's leading newspaper, declared that in this dangerous hour "Nous sommes tous Américains" (We are all Americans). For the first time in history, the North Atlantic Treaty Organization (NATO) invoked the treaty's Article Five, confirming that an attack on one member was an attack on all members.

But such sentiments proved short-lived. When President George W. Bush in 2002 asserted a new right of preemptive war and then proceeded to invade Iraq for what looked to many observers like the most dubious of reasons, anti-American sentiment swelled the world over. In February 2002 some 10 million people in sixty countries demonstrated against the impending U.S. invasion of Iraq. Exacerbated by Washington's rejection of the Kyoto Treaty dealing with global warming, and by several American states' continuing embrace of the death penalty (which had largely disappeared in Europe and elsewhere), America's standing deteriorated even among its traditional allies and sank to rock-bottom lows in Islamic countries. Simmering resentment over the detention of hundreds of captured Afghans at the U.S. military base in Guantánamo, Cuba; revelations about human rights abuses inflicted by American troops on Iraqi prisoners at Baghdad's Abu Ghraib prison; and "rendition" by American

agents of suspected terrorists to the notoriously cruel security services of other countries further drained the depleted reservoirs of America's moral and political capital. The election of Barack Obama in 2008 briefly burnished the American image once more, but in the eyes of many global citizens, America was no longer a "City on a Hill" to be admired and emulated.

Once a moral beacon and political inspiration to a suffering world, the United States in the early twenty-first century had come to be regarded by millions of people the world over as a moral scourge and a political and military danger (see Table 41.1). Recapturing its stature as a legitimate world leader, rebuilding its alliances, restructuring the myriad multilateral institutions it had worked so hard to build in the Cold War era, and recapturing a sense of itself as a just and humane society were tasks that urgently confronted the Republic as the new century advanced.

TABLE 41.1 World Public Opinion of the United States

Question: Do you have a very favorable, somewhat favorable, somewhat unfavorable, or very unfavorable opinion of the United States? (percent favorable)

	2000	2002	2003	2004	2005	2006	2007	2008	2009	2010
Britain	83%	75%	70	58%	55%	56%	51%	53%	69%	65%
France	62	63	43	37	43	39	39	42	75	73
Germany	78	61	45	38	41	37	30	31	64	63
Spain	50	—	38	—	41	23	34	33	58	61
Russia	37	61	36	47	52	43	41	46	44	57
Indonesia	75	61	15	—	38	30	29	37	63	59
Pakistan	23	10	13	21	23	27	15	19	16	17
Jordan	—	25	1	5	21	15	20	19	25	21
Turkey	52	30	15	30	23	12	9	12	14	17
Nigeria	46	—	61	—	—	62	70	64	79	81
Japan	77	72	—	—	—	63	61	50	59	66
India	—	54	—	—	71	56	59	66	76	66
China	—	—	—	—	42	47	34	41	47	58

(Source: From Pew Global Attitudes Report 2010, "Obama More Popular Abroad Than at Home, Global Image of U.S. Continues to Benefit." Reprinted by permission of Pew Research Center.)

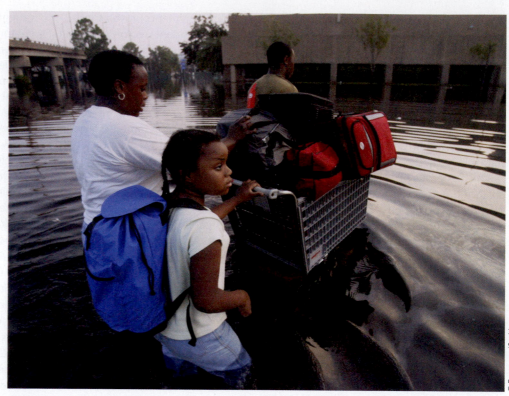

After the Levees Broke in New Orleans, August 2005 When ferocious Hurricane Katrina hammered the Gulf Coast, it overtaxed a deficient levee system and unleashed floodwaters into New Orleans, submerging 80 percent of the city and destroying more than a quarter-million of its homes. Many families unable or unwilling to flee the city sought refuge in the Superdome, where water, food, and other supplies were soon in very short supply. Experts predicted that it would be years before the city fully recovered, if ever.

© Bettmann/Corbis

conducting illegal wiretap surveillance on American citizens inside the United States in violation of federal law. Perhaps the most tragic and avoidable of Bush's missteps came in the botched response to the deadly **Hurricane Katrina**, which devastated New Orleans and much of the Gulf Coast in late August 2005, flooding 80 percent of the historic city and causing over 1,300 deaths and $150 billion in damages. The Federal Emergency Management Agency (FEMA) proved pathetically inept in New Orleans, and Bush came in for still more criticism. A consensus began to build that Bush was a genial personality but an impetuous, unreflective, and frequently feckless leader, a president in over his head in a sea of complex problems that he seemed incapable of mastering.

⭐ Midterm Elections of 2006

As charges of dictatorial power-grabbing, cronyism, and incompetence mounted during Bush's second term, Republicans fell victim in the midterm elections of 2006 to the same anti-incumbency sentiment they had ridden to power twelve years earlier. Democrats narrowly regained control of both houses of Congress for the first time since they had lost them to the Gingrich revolution in 1994 (see p. 968). California Democrat Nancy Pelosi became the first woman to serve as Speaker of the House.

The biggest factor in the Democratic sweep was the perceived mishandling of the war in Iraq. Prewar claims about WMD and Iraq's connections to Al Qaeda and 9/11 had all proved false. By late 2005 polls revealed that a majority of Americans considered the war a mistake. Even more felt that the Bush administration, particularly the Defense Department under Secretary Donald Rumsfeld, had badly mismanaged events on the ground. Rumsfeld resigned after the Republicans' "thumping" in the 2006 midterm elections. But Iraq still knew no peace, and the death toll, Iraqi and

Pismestrovic, Klene Zeitung, Cartoon Arts International, Inc.

European Disapproval of the Iraq War, 2007

American alike, continued to rise. The Bush administration attempted to assert greater control in early 2007 with a "surge" of twenty thousand additional troops. The surge brought a modest measure of stability to Iraq, but as the 2008 election cycle got under way, public opinion nevertheless solidified even more strongly against the war. President Bush's approval ratings sank below 30 percent. Candidate Barack Obama's promise to conclude the war in timely fashion gave him a powerful lift in the upcoming presidential election.

✷ The Presidential Election of 2008

With neither the sitting president nor vice president running, the 2008 election was truly "open" for the first time in eighty years. The Democratic race soon tightened into a fiercely fought contest between the forty-six-year-old, first-term Illinois senator Barack Obama and the precampaign favorite, former First Lady and sitting New York senator Hillary Rodham Clinton. Obama narrowly prevailed, surviving Clinton's attacks on his inexperience. Son of a black Kenyan father and a white Kansan mother and raised in Hawaii and Indonesia, Obama had a cosmopolitan background well suited to the age of globalization. He promised gridlock-weary voters a "postpartisan" politics that would end the divisive battles of the Bush years. To strengthen his national security credentials, he picked foreign-policy-savvy Delaware senator Joseph Biden as his running mate.

In keeping with the country's anti-Bush mood, Republicans nominated long-time Arizona senator John McCain, aged seventy-two, a self-styled "maverick" and a Vietnam War hero who had endured years of torture as a prisoner of war. He had a record of supporting bipartisan legislation on such issues as normalizing relations with North Vietnam, campaign finance, and immigration reform. McCain picked Sarah Palin as his running mate. The former beauty queen, small-town mayor, self-proclaimed "hockey-mom," and staunch abortion rights opponent had served only twenty-one months as Alaska's governor. As McCain hoped, the telegenic Palin galvanized the conservative Republican base. But when interview gaffes exposed her weak grasp of the issues, Palin became fodder for late-night television comedians and, polls showed, at least as much a liability as an asset to the Republican ticket.

Armed with an unprecedented war chest of nearly $700 million, mostly raised from small donors via the Internet, Obama seized the advantage in both the "air war" (television) and the "ground war" (door-to-door campaigning by his legions of volunteers). His poise and gravitas in televised debates favorably impressed many voters, and his campaign slogan, "Yes we can," excited widespread hope and enthusiasm. Then, just six weeks before election day, a sudden economic maelstrom gave his campaign a buoyant boost.

The American housing price bubble, fed by years of the Federal Reserve System's easy-money policies and the private banking system's lax lending practices,

The New First Family President-elect Barack Obama, wife Michelle, and daughters Sacha and Malia, on election night 2008 in Chicago's Grant Park.

©JIM BOURG /Reuters/Corbis

FIGURE 41.2 The Great Recession Takes Hold The financial turmoil that rocked the world in 2008 sent stock market values plummeting. (Source: Data from *http://www.nyse.tv/dow-jones-industrial-average-history-djia.htm.*)

burst at last. The long era of cheap and abundant credit, when bankers had stuffed their balance sheets with complex and highly risky loans, shivered to an alarmingly abrupt halt. By 2008 the collapse in real estate values was generating a tsunami of mortgage defaults, especially among "subprime" borrowers whose escalating mortgage payments stretched them to the breaking point. Bankers and other lenders watched in horror as countless homeowners defaulted and the worth of mortgage-backed securities sank precipitously. Aggressive "**deleveraging**" set in worldwide, as financial institutions from Tokyo to New York to London scrambled to reduce their debt loads by selling assets (at ever-declining prices). But some debts could not be unloaded at any price, and credit markets soon froze everywhere. Following the collapse of the venerable Wall Street firm of Lehman Brothers in September 2008, stocks fell into a deep swoon. The gravest financial hurricane since the Great Depression of the 1930s was gathering ever-increasing force (see Figure 41.2).

In contrast to the infamous 1929 crash that heralded the onset of the Great Depression, it took days, not years, for a terrified Bush administration to intervene on a gigantic scale. The federal government nationalized the country's two biggest mortgage companies, the

Federal National Mortgage Association ("Fannie Mae") and the Federal Home Mortgage Corporation ("Freddie Mac"), and effectively took over the world's biggest insurance company, the American International Group (AIG). Treasury secretary Henry Paulson next persuaded Congress to create the Troubled Assets Relief Program (TARP), authorizing a whopping $700 billion to buy "toxic" assets and inject cash directly into the nation's biggest banks and corporations. (Despite public outrage over TARP's original cost, estimates are that after loans are repaid it will have cost taxpayers about $30 billion—arguably a bargain price to pay for rescuing the nation's financial and business system and staving off a repeat of the Great Depression.)

Candidate Obama seized the political opportunity presented by the mounting economic crisis and declared that electing McCain would amount to a "third Bush term" and lead to further financial turmoil. Obama called for reviving the faltering economy with bold public investments in alternative energy and infrastructure repair. McCain derided such ideas as "socialism."

Unsettled by the galloping economic calamity, voters delivered a historic victory to Barack Obama. He garnered 53 percent of the popular vote, prevailing even in such traditional Republican strongholds as Virginia,

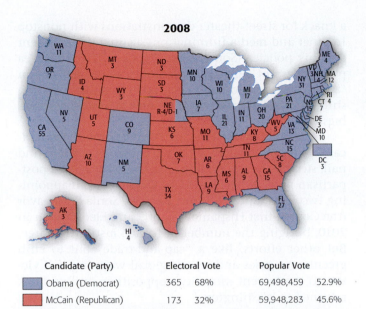

2008

Candidate (Party)	Electoral Vote		Popular Vote	
Obama (Democrat)	365	68%	69,498,459	52.9%
McCain (Republican)	173	32%	59,948,283	45.6%

MAP 41.6 Presidential Election of 2008 A record voter turnout, swelled by millions of young new voters, African Americans, and Latinos, gave Senator Barack Obama an Electoral College landslide and the Democratic party solid control of both houses of Congress. Obama redrew the electoral map by taking nine states won by George W. Bush in 2004.
© Cengage Learning

Nevada, and Colorado, and won the Electoral College 365 to 173 (see Map 41.6). Democrats also enlarged their majorities in the House and the Senate. In further contrast with the famously rocky transition from depression-era president Herbert Hoover to Franklin Roosevelt, the outgoing Bush and incoming Obama administrations conspicuously cooperated to ensure continuity and consistency in combating the economic crisis.

Obama's election opened a new chapter in the long-vexed history of American race relations. It also confronted the nation's first African American president with the daunting challenge of governing a country embroiled in two wars even as it sank into the deepest economic abyss since the 1930s. "Black Man Given Nation's Worst Job," jibed the satirical magazine, *The Onion*.

✴ Obama in the White House

Inspired by Barack Obama's vision of "hope," a vast and exuberant crowd gathered in Washington, D.C., to celebrate his inauguration. Youthful energy was in the air, though in his inaugural address Obama struck a sober note by calling on Americans to "put away childish things" and embrace "a new era of responsibility."

Obama's solemn tone was fitting. Even as he spoke, home construction was grinding to a halt, mortgage

Asked by an interviewer in February 2009, just one month into his presidency, if he felt "burdened" by the welter of problems he faced, President Obama (b. 1961) replied:

❝I think that we are at an extraordinary moment that is full of peril but full of possibility and I think that's the time you want to be president. . . . [T]here's something about this country where hard times, big challenges bring out the best in us. This is when the political system starts to move effectively. This is when people start getting out of the petty and the trivial debates. This is when the public starts paying attention. . . . [W]hen things are going well . . . they've got better things to do than to think about public policy. . . .❞

foreclosures were soaring, and countless businesses were shutting their doors. Most alarmingly, the economy was shedding a sickening 700,000 jobs a month. The unemployment rate climbed above 10 percent—the highest level since the early 1980s and perhaps heralding a return to the catastrophic joblessness of the Great Depression of the 1930s.

Obama strongly counterpunched against the deepening crisis. In his first hundred days he pushed through a series of major initiatives that included a new round of help for troubled banks, tax and mortgage relief, and a huge "stimulus" bill—the **American Relief and Recovery Act**—that contained nearly a trillion dollars of tax cuts, as well as new spending for jobs, infrastructure projects, and relief to state and local governments. The government also shored up bankrupt automakers General Motors and Chrysler, as well as threatened banks and insurance companies. The nonpartisan Congressional Budget Office later estimated that those measures saved up to 3 million jobs, helping substantially to arrest the economy's freefall.

By the summer of 2009, the worst of the panic was over and the economy began to expand once more. Economists tempered their comparisons with the Great Depression and gave the less frightening label "Great Recession" to the turmoil. But the economy had been badly wounded and continued to suffer. Hopes for a rapid recovery proved false, and the first steps toward growth were feeble and faltering. The unemployment rate stayed stuck above 9 percent. As millions of Americans lost jobs and homes, and many more succumbed to anxiety and fear, the effects of the Great Recession wormed their way deeply into the American psyche, and would not be quickly dislodged. Psychology and economics intersected, as newly anxious consumers cut back on spending, further burdening an already sluggish recovery.

Even while pursuing economic recovery, President Obama also sought to achieve the long-sought liberal goal of health-care reform. When attempts to enlist Republican support bogged down in congressional haggling, he had to rely on Democrats alone to pass a landmark health bill, the **Patient Protection and Affordable Care Act**, in March 2010. The new health-care law (derided by critics as "Obamacare") mandated all Americans to purchase health insurance starting in 2014, required states to establish "exchanges" whereby individuals and small businesses could purchase health-care insurance at competitive rates, prohibited insurers from denying coverage to anyone with a preexisting medical condition, and allowed children up to the age of twenty-six to remain covered by their parent's health plans. The price of the bill was estimated at $940 billion over ten years, but experts also predicted that the bill's cost-cutting measures would reduce the federal deficit by more than $1 trillion over twenty years.

Scarcely pausing, Obama soon followed his health-care success with the 2010 **Wall Street Reform and Consumer Protection Act**, which pointed the way to a major overhaul of the nation's financial regulatory system. The act aimed to curb the risky, high-flying practices that had contributed to the debacle of 2008 with new controls on banks, investment houses, and stock markets, and with new truth-in-lending rules to protect consumers.

✴ A Sea of Troubles

Yet Obama had unusual difficulty reaping the political rewards of these legislative achievements. He seemed caught between an anvil and a boulder. Because his measures only halted, but did not reverse, the economy's decline, critics on the left condemned him as too timid. Because federal budget deficits ballooned dramatically on his watch (thanks not only to his own initiatives but also to the Bush-era tax cuts combined with declining tax revenues in the midst of the downturn), critics on the right excoriated him as a big-government spendthrift. The conjunction of expanding federal programs and mounting deficits tapped into a deep vein of American wariness of "big government." Starting with vehement attacks on the health-care bill in the summer of 2009, angry protesters accused the Obama administration of promoting "socialism" and "unconstitutional" controls over individual lives. Calling themselves the "Tea party" after the American Revolutionary Patriots, these noisy citizens combined

a knack for street-theater demonstrations with nonstop Internet and media fulminations against the president and his policies. Some critics groused that the "Tea party" was not a genuine grassroots movement but an "astro-turf" phenomenon—a fake populist uprising shrewdly manipulated by the usual behind-the-scenes bigshots.

Heartened by the Tea party's mobilization, Republicans determined to fight the administration tooth and nail, steadfastly repudiating Obama's promise of a post-partisan politics. The president did succeed in appointing two new Supreme Court Justices, Sonia Sotomayor (the Court's first Hispanic) in 2009 and Elena Kagan in 2010, bringing the number of female justices to three. But other efforts, like a "cap-and-trade" bill to curb greenhouse gases and reduce global warming, fell victim to the fervent minority's opposition, and gridlock returned to Washington.

As the Great Recession continued to weigh heavily upon the land, Obama's approval ratings steadily slipped, and his party slid downhill with him. In the midterm elections of 2010, Republicans gained six seats in the Senate and a whopping sixty-three seats in the House, enough to give them majority control of the lower chamber when the new Congress convened in 2011. President Obama glumly acknowledged his party's "shellacking," but then surprisingly proceeded to wring several major accomplishments out of the postelection "lame-duck" session in December 2010, including an $858 billion package that extended unemployment benefits as well as the Bush-era tax cuts, the repeal of "Don't Ask Don't Tell," and a renewed nuclear arms reduction treaty (New START, or Strategic Arms Reduction Treaty) with Russia. But he fell short of passing the DREAM Act (Development, Relief and Education for Alien Minors Act), which would have created a path to citizenship for undocumented youths who either graduated from college or served in the U.S. armed forces. The vexed issue of immigration reform, especially with respect to the nation's 12 million "illegals," also waited for resolution another day.

✴ Wars, Oil Spills, and Political Backlash

Along with economic problems, Obama also inherited America's wars in Iraq and Afghanistan, as well as a raft of other headaches. The new president sought to wind down the Iraq War while leaving behind a reasonably stable country. Shortly after taking office, Obama announced that American combat operations in Iraq would end in summer 2010 and that all American combat troops would be withdrawn by 2011. Despite

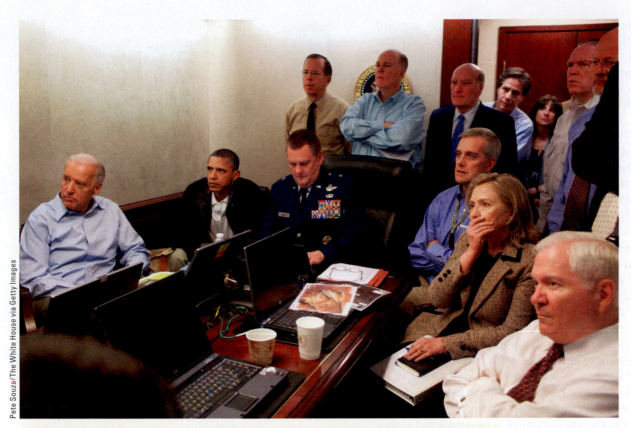

The End of Osama bin Laden   President Barack Obama and his national security team huddle in the White House Situation Room to watch live updates on the mission to kill Osama bin Laden, May 2, 2011. Nearly ten years after the murderous attacks of September 11, 2001, rough justice was meted out to the terrorist mastermind. Much commentary on this photograph has focused on the presence of women in the room and on the President's lack of macho swagger, even as American forces closed in on the nation's most hated foe.

continuing violence and the agonizingly slow birth of a viable Iraqi government, the deadline for ending American-led operations was met. Still, about 50,000 American troops remained in the country to protect U.S. bases and support Iraqi security efforts.

Afghanistan was a thornier nettle to grasp. Obama had declared the Afghan war necessary to defeat Al Qaeda and prevent future terrorism. But Afghan *jihadi* (militant Islamic) fighters grew stronger against an Afghan government plagued by incompetence and corruption. More ominously, the Taliban and Al Qaeda found refuge across the border in unstable but nuclear-armed Pakistan, posing the danger of an expanded conflict there as well.

Pressed by some to deepen the American commitment, and by others to seek a way out of the increasingly costly conflict, Obama chose to do both. In December 2009 he declared that American troops would begin withdrawing by 2011—but that in order to achieve that goal he was deploying an additional thirty thousand U.S. soldiers to combat the insurgency. He

ordered changes in strategy and appointed a new U.S. commander, General David Petraeus. But casualties increased and frustration with the nearly decade-long conflict grew, with no satisfactory exit in sight.

Obama soon faced an unprecedented environmental calamity as well. On April 20, 2010, the BP (formerly British Petroleum) energy corporation's Deepwater Horizon oil platform in the Gulf of Mexico exploded, killing seventeen workers and spewing oil from its deep well nearly two miles below the ocean floor. Over the next four months the American public watched helplessly as nearly 5 billion gallons of oil poured into the Gulf of Mexico, fouling beaches and killing wildlife from Louisiana to Florida. For four months BP futilely attempted to stop the gusher of oil, as anger mounted against both the oil giant's and the federal government's inability to contain the disaster. By the time the well was finally capped in August 2010, it had become the worst oil disaster in U.S. history.

When American forces dramatically concluded a ten-year manhunt and killed Osama bin Laden in May

2011, the president's poll ratings got a brief upward bump. But the lift proved vanishingly brief. As the accumulated federal debt approached its legal limit of $14.3 trillion in the summer of 2011, the Republican Tea Party faction seized the occasion to play a game of fiscal "chicken" with the White House. Raising the debt ceiling had historically been a routine matter, but led by the eighty-five freshmen elected in 2010, House Republicans stubbornly refused to lift the debt limit until the president agreed to a long-term deficit-reduction plan that called for huge spending cuts and few if any tax increases. Heartened by their triumph, Republicans looked to the upcoming 2012 presidential election with increasing hope for victory—though the spectacle of protracted wrangling and partisan intransigence while the nation's credit rating, and the health of the global economy, hung in the balance deeply disillusioned many Americans of both parties. Some critics began to question the soundness of the American political system itself.

Meanwhile, dramatic demographic changes were altering the political landscape, with consequences that both parties struggled to understand (see Map. 41.7). And as so often in the past, economic anxieties stoked anti-immigrant sentiment. In April 2010 Arizona enacted a harsh statute requiring state and local police to help enforce federal immigration laws. Although a federal judge put the statute on hold, Arizona's action was applauded in many other places, especially those with substantial Latino immigrant populations. As Latinos replaced African Americans as the country's largest minority, much of the nation's political future hinged on their sense of belonging and their stake in the future of the republic.

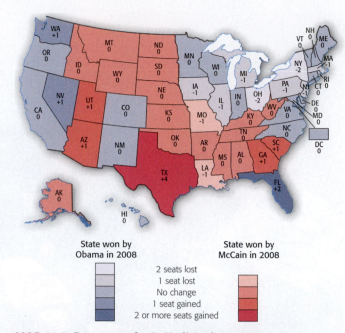

State won by Obama in 2008

State won by McCain in 2008

2 seats lost
1 seat lost
No change
1 seat gained
2 or more seats gained

MAP 41.7 Demography Is (Political) Destiny The United States is one of the few nations with a constitutionally mandated census, a provision reflecting the Founders' expectation that the country's population would grow and spread out, and their commitment to maintaining fair and proportional representation in the federal electoral system. Thus, every ten years congressional districts are redrawn; some states gain and some states lose representation in the House and the Electoral College. This map, showing the reapportionment resulting from the 2010 census, clearly shows the continuing shift of the nation's population and political center of gravity southward and westward. Note that Texas is the biggest gainer from the 2010 census, and that for the first time since becoming a state in 1850, California will gain no congressional seats or electoral college votes. © Cengage Learning

Chapter Review

KEY TERMS

weapons of mass destruction (WMD) (965)

Democratic Leadership Council (965)

"Don't Ask, Don't Tell" (966)

Oklahoma City bombing (967)

Contract with America (968)

Welfare Reform Bill (968)

North American Free Trade Agreement (NAFTA) (969)

World Trade Organization (WTO) (969)

Whitewater (970)

Lewinsky affair (970)

Kyoto Treaty (973)

9/11 (974)

Al Qaeda (975)

USA Patriot Act (975)

Department of Homeland Security (975)

Guantánamo Detention Camp (975)

Abu Ghraib prison (978)

No Child Left Behind Act (979)

Hurricane Katrina (982)

deleveraging (984)

American Relief and Recovery Act (985)

Patient Protection and Affordable Care Act (986)

Wall Street Reform and Consumer Protection Act (986)

PEOPLE TO KNOW

William Jefferson ("Bill") Clinton

H. Ross Perot

Hillary Rodham Clinton

Newt Gingrich

Robert Dole

John McCain

Sarah Palin

Monica Lewinsky

George W. Bush

Richard Cheney

John Kerry

Nancy Pelosi

Barack Obama

Joseph R. ("Joe") Biden

CHRONOLOGY

1992 Clinton defeats Bush and Perot for presidency

1993 NAFTA signed

1994 Republicans win majorities in both houses of Congress

1996 Welfare Reform Bill becomes law
Clinton defeats Dole for presidency

1998 Clinton-Lewinsky scandal
U.S. and Britain launch military strikes against Iraq
House of Representatives impeaches Clinton

1999 Senate acquits Clinton on impeachment charges
Kosovo crisis; NATO warfare with Serbia
Protest in Seattle against World Trade Organization

2000 U.S. normalizes trade relations with China
George W. Bush wins presidency in Electoral College; Albert Gore takes popular vote

2001 Terrorists attack New York City and Washington, D.C., on September 11
U.S. invades Afghanistan
Congress passes USA Patriot Act

2002 Congress passes No Child Left Behind Act
Bush labels Iraq, Iran, and North Korea "axis of evil"
Congress authorizes use of force against Iraq

2002 U.N. Security Council demands that Iraq comply with weapons inspections
Republicans regain Senate

2003 U.S. invades Iraq
Saddam Hussein captured in Iraq
Supreme Court narrowly approves affirmative action

2004 Gay marriage controversy erupts
Iraqi interim government installed
Bush defeats Kerry for presidency

2005 Iraq elects permanent government but quickly descends into sectarian conflict

2006 Saddam Hussein executed

2007 U.S. troop surge in Iraq

2008 Barack Obama elected 44th president of the United States

2009 American Relief and Recovery Act passed

2010 BP Deepwater Horizon oil platform explodes in Gulf of Mexico
Patient Protection and Affordable Care Act passed
Wall Street Reform and Consumer Protection Act passed
"Don't Ask, Don't Tell" policy repealed
New START treaty approved

TO LEARN MORE

John Cassidy, *How Markets Fail: The Logic of Economic Calamities* (2009)

Alan Dershowitz, *Supreme Injustice: How the High Court Hijacked Election 2000* (2001)

Elizabeth Drew, *Showdown: The Struggle Between the Gingrich Congress and the Clinton White House* (1997)

Dave Eggers, *Zeitoun* (2009)

Lloyd C. Gardner, *The Long Road to Baghdad: A History of U.S. Foreign Policy from the 1970s to the Present* (2010)

Joe Klein, *The Natural* (2002)

George Packer, *The Assassins' Gate: America in Iraq* (2005)

Richard Posner, *An Affair of State: The Investigation, Impeachment, and Trial of President Clinton* (1999)

Jack Rakove, *The Unfinished Election of 2000* (2001)

Thomas Ricks, *Fiasco: The American Military Adventure in Iraq* (2006)

James Stewart, *Blood Sport* (1996)

Bob Woodward, *Bush at War* (2002); *Plan of Attack* (2004); *State of Denial: Bush at War, Part III* (2006)

———, *The Choice* (1996)

▶ CourseMate

Go to the CourseMate website at **www.cengagebrain.com** for additional study tools and review materials—including audio and video clips—for this chapter.

A complete, annotated bibliography for this chapter—along with brief descriptions of the People to Know—may be found on the American Pageant website. The Key Terms are defined in a Glossary at the end of the text.

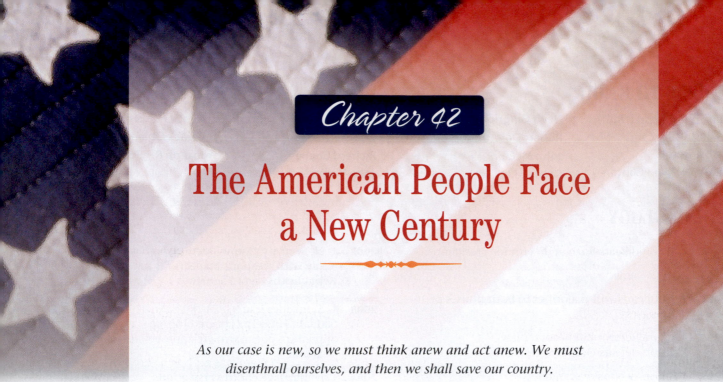

Chapter 42

The American People Face a New Century

As our case is new, so we must think anew and act anew. We must disenthrall ourselves, and then we shall save our country.

ABRAHAM LINCOLN, 1862

Well beyond its two-hundredth birthday as the twenty-first century entered its second decade, the United States was both an old and a new nation. It boasted one of the longest uninterrupted traditions of democratic government of any country on earth. Indeed, it had pioneered the techniques of mass democracy and was, in that sense, the oldest modern polity. As one of the earliest countries to industrialize, America had also dwelt in the modern economic era longer than most nations. But the Republic was in many ways still youthful as well. Innovation, entrepreneurship, and risk-taking—all characteristics of youth—were honored national values.

America's twenty-first century began much like the twentieth, as society continued to be rejuvenated by fresh waves of immigrants, full of energy and ambition. The U.S. economy, despite the impact of the "Great Recession," remained an important engine of world economic growth. American inventions—especially computer and communications technologies—continued to transform the face of global society. Consumers from Berlin to Beijing seemed to worship the icons of American culture—downing soft drinks and donning blue jeans, watching Hollywood films and television series, listening to rock or country music, even adopting indigenous American sports like baseball and basketball. In the realm of consumerism, American products appeared to have Coca-Colonized the globe.

The history of American society also seemed to have increased global significance as the third millennium of the Christian era opened. Americans were a pluralistic people who had struggled for centuries to offer opportunity, tolerance, and justice to many different religious, ethnic, and racial groups. Their historical trials and triumphs could offer valuable lessons to the rapidly internationalizing planetary society that was emerging at the dawn of the twenty-first century.

Much history remained to be made as the country entered its third century of nationhood. The great social experiment of American democracy was far from completed as the United States faced its future. Astonishing breakthroughs in science and technology, especially in genetics, bioengineering, and communications, presented Americans with stunning opportunities as well as wrenching ethical choices. Global climate change made the responsible stewardship of a fragile planet more urgent than ever. Inequality and prejudice continued to challenge Americans to close the gap between their most hallowed values and the stark realities of modern life. The terrorist attacks of September 11, 2001, violently heralded a new era of fear and anxiety. And the severe economic crisis that convulsed the nation and the world in 2008 demonstrated that free-market capitalism could still produce abundant misery as well as material abundance.

But men and women make history only within the framework bequeathed to them by earlier generations. For better or worse, they march forward along time's path bearing the burdens of the past. Knowing when they have come to a truly new turn in the road, when they can lay part of their burden down and when they cannot, or should not—all this constitutes the sort of wisdom that only historical study can engender.

✦ Economic Revolutions

When the twentieth century opened, United States Steel Corporation was the flagship business of America's booming industrial revolution. A generation later, General Motors, annually producing millions of automobiles, became the characteristic American corporation, signaling the historic shift to a mass consumer economy that began in the 1920s and flowered fully in the 1950s. Following World War II, the rise of International Business Machines (IBM) and, later, Microsoft Corporation symbolized yet another momentous transformation, to the fast-paced "information age," when the storing, organizing, and processing of data became an industry in its own right.

The pace of the information age soon accelerated. As the twenty-first century opened, the phenomenal growth of the Internet heralded an explosive communications revolution. New corporate giants like Google redefined the ways that people knew about the world, while social networking services like Facebook and Twitter redefined the ways they knew each other. Businesspeople could now instantaneously girdle the planet with transactions of prodigious scope and serpentine complexity. Japanese bankers might sell wheat contracts in Chicago and simultaneously direct the profits to buying oil shipments from the Persian Gulf offered by a broker in Amsterdam. Peoples from all corners of the planet were rocketing down the "information superhighway" toward the uncharted terrain of an electronic global village, where traditional geographic,

social, and political boundaries could be vaulted with the tap of a keypad.

But the very speed and efficiency of the new communications tools threatened to wipe out entire occupational categories, and even ways of life. Postal carriers, travel agents, store clerks, bank tellers, stockbrokers, and all kinds of other workers whose business it was to mediate between product and client were in danger of becoming road kill on the information superhighway. White-collar jobs in financial services and high-tech engineering, once thought securely anchored in places like Chicago, Los Angeles, and New York, could now be "outsourced" to countries such as Ireland and India, where employees could help keep a company's global circuits firing twenty-four hours a day.

Increasingly, scientific research was the motor that propelled the economy, and new scientific knowledge raised new moral dilemmas and provoked new political arguments. When scientists first unlocked the secrets of molecular genetic structure in the 1950s, the road lay open to breeding new strains of high-yield, pest- and weather-resistant crops; to curing hereditary diseases; and also, unfortunately, to unleashing genetic mutations that might threaten the complex balance of the wondrous biosphere in which humankind was delicately suspended. As the curtain rose on the new century, scientists stood at the threshold of a revolution in biological engineering. The Human Genome Project established the DNA sequencing of the thirty thousand human genes, pointing the way to radical new medical therapies—and to mouthwatering profits

© Bettmann/Corbis

Outsourcing Jobs to India Sophisticated computer technology has allowed developing countries like India to attract Western employers seeking lower labor costs. India's educated and English-speaking work force has made it particularly suitable for international call centers and computer programming.

for bioengineering firms. Startling breakthroughs in the cloning of animals raised thorny questions about the legitimacy of applying cloning technology to human reproduction. Research into human stem cells held out the promise of cures for afflictions like Parkinson's disease and Alzheimer's. But some religious groups protested that harvesting stem cells involved the destruction of human life in embryonic form—just one example of the many ways that Americans continued to struggle with the ethical implications of their vast new technological powers.

Other unprecedented ethical questions also clamored for resolution. What principles should govern the allocation of human organs for lifesaving transplants? Was it wise in the first place to spend money on such costly procedures rather than devote society's resources to improved sanitation, maternal and infant care, and nutritional and health education? How, if at all, should society regulate the increasingly lengthy and often painful process of dying? (See "Makers of America: Scientists and Engineers," pp. 994–995.)

✳ Affluence and Inequality

Americans were still an affluent people at the beginning of the twenty-first century. Median household income reached $49,400 in 2011. Even those Americans with incomes below the government's official poverty level (defined in 2010 as $22,314 for a family of four) enjoyed a standard of living higher than that of two-thirds of the rest of humankind.

Americans were no longer the world's wealthiest people, as they had been in the quarter-century

TABLE 42.1 Widening Income Inequality

Share of Aggregate Income	1980	1990	2000	2008
Lowest fifth	4.2	3.8	3.6	3.4
Second fifth	10.2	9.6	8.9	8.6
Third fifth	16.8	15.9	14.8	14.7
Fourth fifth	24.7	24.0	23.0	23.2
Highest fifth	44.1	46.6	49.8	50.3
Top 5%	16.5	18.5	22.1	21.7

During the last two decades of the twentieth century, the top fifth of the country's households made significant gains in income, while everyone else lost ground.

(Source: *Statistical Abstract of the United States*, 2010; U.S. Census Bureau *Current Population Reports*.)

after World War II. Citizens of several other countries enjoyed higher average per capita incomes, and many nations boasted more equitable distributions of wealth. In an unsettling reversal of long-term trends in American society, during the last two decades of the twentieth century, the rich got fabulously richer, while the poor got an ever-shrinking share of the pie. The richest 20 percent of Americans in 2009 raked in half the nation's income, while the poorest 20 percent received a little over 3 percent (see Table 42.1). The gap between rich and poor began to widen in the 1980s and widened further thereafter. That trend was evident in many industrial societies, but it was most pronounced in the United States. Between 1968 and 2009, the share of the

Two Nations? While decaying neighborhoods and legions of the homeless blighted American cities in the early twenty-first century, affluent Americans lived the good life in booming suburbs and in the more suburbanized cities of the Sunbelt, such as this development of million-dollar homes around a country club in Las Vegas, Nevada.

Tony Savino/The Image Works

© Bettmann/Corbis

	U.S.	CANADA	GERMANY	JAPAN	SWEDEN	HONG KONG	UK	KOREA	ITALY	FRANCE	CZECH	SPAIN
Income Inequality (Gini Index)	45.0	32.1	27.0	37.6	23.0	53.3	34.0	31.4	32.0	32.7	26.0	32.0
Unemployment Rate	9.7	8.0	7.4	5.1	8.3	4.3	7.9	3.3	8.4	9.5	7.1	20.0
Level of Democracy	8.18	9.08	8.38	8.08	9.50	5.92	8.16	8.11	7.83	7.77	8.19	8.16
Life Expectancy at Birth	78.37	81.38	80.07	82.25	81.07	82.04	80.05	79.05	81.77	81.19	77.19	81.17
Food Insecurity	16	8	4	9	6	6	9	11	15	10	14	14
Prison Population Rate	743	117	85	59	78	141	154	98	113	96	214	159
Student Math Scores	487	527	513	529	494	555	492	546	483	497	493	483
Student Science Scores	502	529	520	539	495	549	514	538	489	498	500	488

■ Best ■ Worse ■ Worst

FIGURE 42.1 How the United States Measures Up   Once the undisputed world leader in countless areas of human endeavor, the United States looked to be falling behind on several crucial counts in the early twenty-first century.

nation's income that flowed to the top 20 percent of its households swelled from 40 percent to 50.3 percent. Even more striking, in the same period the top 5 percent of income earners saw their share of the national income grow from about 15 percent to a remarkable 21.7 percent. The Welfare Reform Bill of 1996, restricting access to social services and requiring able-bodied welfare recipients to find work, weakened the financial footing of many impoverished families still further, and the Great Recession added to their ranks.

Widening inequality could be measured in other ways as well. In the 1970s chief executives typically earned forty-one times as much as the average worker in their corporations; by the early 2000s, they earned 245 times as much. Prior to the passage of the Obama health-care bill in 2010, 50 million people had no medical insurance. At the same time, some 46.2 million people remained mired in poverty in 2011 (the largest number in more than 50 years). They represented 15.1 percent of all Americans (approximately 12.3 percent of whites, 25.8 percent of African Americans, 25.3 percent of Latinos, and 12.5 percent of Asians), a depressing indictment of the inequities afflicting an affluent and allegedly egalitarian republic (for comparative data, see Figure 42.1).

What caused the widening income gap? Some critics pointed to the tax and fiscal policies of the Reagan and both Bush (father and son) presidencies, which favored the wealthy (see Table 42.2). But deeper-running historical currents probably played a more powerful role, as suggested by the similar experiences of other industrialized societies. Among the most conspicuous causes were intensifying global economic competition; the shrinkage in high-paying manufacturing jobs for semiskilled and unskilled workers; the greater economic rewards commanded by educated workers in high-tech industries; the decline of unions; the growth of part-time and temporary work; the rising tide of relatively low-skill immigrants; and the increasing tendency of

TABLE 42.2 Who Pays Federal Income Taxes? (share of U.S. income tax, by income percentile)

Income Group (base income shown as of 2007)	1994	2007
Top 1% (above $410,096)	28.7%	40.4%
Top 5% (above $160,041)	47.4	60.6
Top 10% (above $113,018)	59.1	71.2
Top 25% (above $66,532)	79.5	86.6
Top 50% (above $32,879)	95.2	97.1
Bottom 50% (below $32,879)	4.8	2.9

Because the United States has long had a "progressive" income tax system, in which tax obligations are distributed according to ability to pay, widening income inequality was reflected in a redistribution of tax burdens. In the booming 1990s, the rich did indeed get richer—but they also paid an increasing fraction of the total federal tax take. These figures help explain why tax cuts benefit the wealthy more than middle-income earners and the poor.

(Source: Internal Revenue Service data, Tax Foundation; http://www.taxfoundation.org/news/show/250.html.)

Subatomic particles and space-bound satellites do not respect political boundaries. Disease-carrying viruses spread across the globe. Radio waves and Internet communications reach every corner of planet Earth. At first glance science, technology, and medicine appear to be quintessentially international phenomena. Scientists often pride themselves on the universal validity of scientific knowledge and the transnational character of scientific networks. In a world marked by political divisions, science evidently knows no bounds.

But a closer look reveals that national context does influence the character of scientific enterprise. American scientists have repeatedly made significant contributions to the life of the nation. They, in turn, have been shaped by its unique historical circumstances—especially America's intensifying concerns about national security in the twentieth century. Once marginal players in global intellectual life, American scientists now stand at the forefront of worldwide scientific advancement. In many ways the rise of American science has kept pace with the arrival of the United States as a world power.

Nowhere was this trend more evident than in the story of "Big Science." The unusual demands of America's national security state during World War II and the Cold War required vast scientific investments. The result was Big Science, or multidisciplinary research enterprises of unparalleled size, scope, and cost. Big Science and Big Technology meant big bucks, big machines, and big teams of scientists and engineers. The close link between government and science was not new—precedents stretched as far back as the founding of the National Academy of Sciences during the Civil War. But the depression-era Tennessee Valley Authority (TVA) and the wartime Manhattan Project ushered in ventures of colossal scale and ambition. As the head of the TVA wrote in 1944, "There is almost nothing, however fantastic, that (given competent organization) a team of engineers, scientists, and administrators cannot do today."

Cold War competition with the Soviets translated into huge government investments in physics, chemistry, and aerospace. The equation was simple: national security depended on technological superiority, which entailed costly facilities for scientific research and ambitious efforts to recruit and train scientists. In the 1950s defense projects employed two-thirds of the nation's scientists and engineers. Laboratories, reactors, accelerators, and observatories proliferated. After the Soviets launched the world's first artificial satellite (*Sputnik I*) in 1957, the international space race became America's top

Launching *Apollo 11*   NASA flight directors monitor the launch of the *Apollo 11* lunar landing mission from the Manned Spacecraft Center in Houston, Texas, in July 1969.

NASA/Johnson Space Center

scientific priority. To land astronauts on the moon, the National Aeronautics and Space Administration (NASA) spent a whopping $25.4 billion over eleven years on Project Apollo. Another massive aerospace mission, President Reagan's controversial Strategic Defense Initiative (or "Star Wars"), consumed somewhere between $32 billion and $71 billion between 1984 and 1994.

In America's burgeoning "research universities," the federal government found willing partners in the promotion of the scientific enterprise. University-employed scientists, largely paid by government grants, concentrated on basic research, accounting for over 75 percent of the estimated $51.9 billion spent on basic science in 2008. Meanwhile, private industry spent additional billions on applied research and product development.

For consumers of air bags, smart phones, and other high-tech gadgets, these investments yielded rich rewards as innovative technologies dramatically improved the quality of life. Over the course of the twentieth century, American corporations spearheaded a global revolution in communications and information technology. American Telephone and Telegraph (AT&T) and Radio Corporation of America (RCA) attended the birth of telephones, radio, and television. Apple, International Business Machines (IBM), and Microsoft introduced personal computers. Government and industry scientists together invented the Internet.

Twentieth-century advances in medical science and technology have also revolutionized American lives. Thanks to new drugs, devices, and methods of treatment, the average life expectancy in the United States leapt from 47.3 years in 1900 to 77.9 years in 2007. In the first half of the twentieth century, physicians discovered hormones and vitamins, introduced penicillin and other antibiotics, and experimented with insulin therapy for diabetes and radiation therapy for cancer. More recently, cutting-edge medical science has nurtured in-vitro fertilization; developed respirators, artificial hearts, and other medical devices; and largely contained the AIDS epidemic.

Much of the optimism for future medical breakthroughs centers on the $3 billion Human Genome Project, which completed its mapping and sequencing of all the genetic material in the human body in 2003. Deemed the "holy grail" of genomics research, the project promised countless benefits, including new diagnoses for genetic defects, innovative therapies, and untold commercial applications. Coordinated by the Department of Energy and the National Institutes of Health, the project engaged thousands of scientists in universities and laboratories across the nation and around the globe.

To achieve such innovation, Big Science typically demands complex teams of scientists, engineers, and technicians. When traditional channels of recruitment came up short, scientific institutions increasingly recruited foreigners, women, and minorities (see Figure 42.2). Immigrants and exiles played key roles in the development of the atomic bomb and Cold War weaponry. Long relegated to junior positions as assistants and technicians, women and minorities have recently made significant gains in the "white man's world" of science. In 2007 women represented 27 percent of

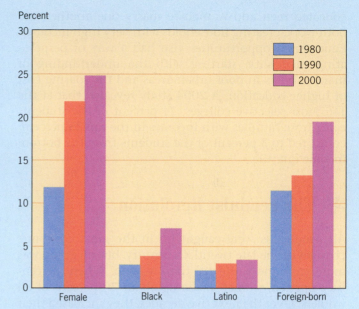

FIGURE 42.2 Demographic Profile of Women, Minorities, and the Foreign-Born in Nonacademic Science and Engineering Occupations, 1980–2000 (Source: *Science and Engineering Indicators, 2002*, http://www.nsf.gov/statistics/seind02/c3/fig03-13.htm.)

employed doctoral scientists and engineers in the United States, African Americans 5 percent, and Hispanics 4 percent, while the foreign-born accounted for 24 percent.

Despite these stunning achievements, evidence suggests that the United States might be losing its preeminence in science. After dominating the intellectual world from the 1960s through the 1990s, American scientists are now winning fewer prizes and patents and publishing fewer scientific papers than their peers in Europe and Asia. Experts predict that current school-age Americans will not be able to meet the rising demand for scientific expertise. Moreover, fewer foreigners will arrive to fill the gap, as international competition for their labor heats up in places like Brazil, China, and India. For the United States to retain preeminence in science in the twenty-first century, it must continue to welcome all talent to the field. That means attracting both foreign-born scientists and young American students whose brainpower has long helped make the nation a scientific power.

© Bettmann/Corbis

A Scientist Working in Her Lab This medical school professor researching pancreatic regeneration was part of the surge of women pursuing scientific careers, particularly in the biological sciences. By 2004 as many women as men enrolled in medical schools, and minority enrollment climbed as well. In that year 7 percent of entering medical students were Latino, and 6.5 percent were African American.

educated men and women to marry one another and both work, creating households with very high incomes. Educational opportunities also had a way of perpetuating inequality, starting with the underfunding of many schools in poor urban areas and the soaring cost of higher education. A 2004 study revealed that at the 146 most selective colleges, 74 percent of the students came from families with incomes in the top 25 percent, compared to 3 percent of the students from the bottom income quartile.

✪ The Feminist Revolution

All Americans were caught up in the great economic changes of the late twentieth century, but no group was more profoundly affected than women. When the century opened, women made up about 20 percent of all workers. Over the next five decades, they increased their presence in the labor force at a fairly steady rate, except for a temporary spurt during World War II. Then, beginning in the 1950s, women's entry into the workplace accelerated dramatically. By the 1990s nearly half of all workers were women, and the majority of working-age women held jobs outside the home. Most astonishing was the upsurge in employment among mothers. In 1950 nearly 90 percent of mothers with children under the age of six did not work for pay. But half a century later, a majority of women with children as young as one year old were wage earners (see Table 42.3). Women now brought home the bacon and then cooked it, too. By 2008 American women participated in the work force in higher numbers than in almost all industrialized countries except Russia and China (see Figure 42.3).

Beginning in the 1960s, many all-male strongholds, including Yale, Princeton, West Point, and even,

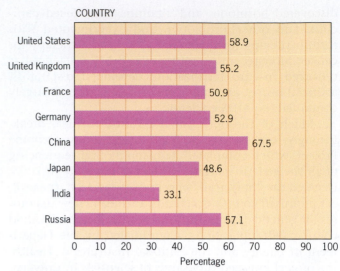

FIGURE 42.3 Women in the Work Force Globally, 2008
(Source: The World Bank, *World Development Indicators*.)

belatedly, southern military academies like the Citadel and Virginia Military Institute, opened their doors to women. By the twenty-first century, women were piloting airliners, orbiting the earth, governing states and cities, and writing Supreme Court decisions.

Yet despite these gains, many feminists remained frustrated. Women continued to receive lower wages—80 cents on the dollar in 2009—compared with men doing the same full-time work. They also tended to concentrate in a few low-prestige, low-paying occupations (the "pink-collar ghetto"). Although they made up more than half the population, women in 2009 accounted for just 32 percent of lawyers and judges (up from 5 percent in 1970) and 32 percent of physicians (up from 10 percent in 1970). Overt sexual discrimination explained some of this occupational segregation, but most of it seemed attributable to the greater burdens of parenthood on women than on men. Women were far more likely than men to interrupt their careers to bear and raise children, and even to choose less demanding career paths to allow for fulfilling those traditional roles. Discrimination and a focus on children also helped account for the persistence of a "gender gap" in voting behavior. Women continued to vote in greater numbers than men for Democratic candidates, who were often perceived as being more willing to favor government support for health and child care, education, and job equality, as well as being more vigilant to protect abortion rights.

As the revolution in women's status rolled on in the 2000s, men's lives changed as well. Some employers provided paternity leave in addition to maternity leave, in recognition of the shared obligations of the two-worker household. More men assumed traditional female responsibilities such as cooking, laundry, and

TABLE 42.3	Working Women: Labor Force Participation Rates for Wives and Mothers, 1950–2007*			
Year	Married	Married, with Children	Married, with Children Ages 6–17	Married, with Children Under Age 6
1950	23.8%	NA	28.3%	11.9%
1960	30.5	NA	39.0	18.6
1970	40.8	39.7	49.2	30.3
1980	50.1	54.1	61.7	45.1
1990	58.2	66.3	73.6	58.9
2000	62.0	70.6	77.2	62.8
2007	61.6	69.3	76.2	61.5

*Percent of women in each specific category in the labor force.

(Source: *Statistical Abstract of the United States*, relevant years.)

Photo by Baerbel Schmidt

© Bettmann/Corbis

A New World for Women Revolutionary changes in the economy and in social values opened new career opportunities for women, even as many of them continued to perform their traditional duties as mothers and homemakers. Here U.S. Air Force Major General Margaret H. Woodward (top left) is shown at her desk as Joint Force Air Component Commander. Drew Gilpin Faust (bottom right) became the first woman to serve as president of Harvard University in 2007. Women athletes also came into their own in the wake of the feminist revolution. Venus and Serena Williams (top right) enthralled the tennis world as individual champions and as a doubles team beginning in the late 1990s.

Boston Globe/Dina Rudick/Landov

child care. Recognizing the new realities of the modern American household, Congress passed a Family Leave Bill in 1993, mandating job protection for working fathers as well as mothers who needed to take time off from work for family-related reasons.

✵ New Families and Old

The traditional nuclear family, once prized as the foundation of society and the nursery of the Republic, suffered heavy blows in modern America. By the 1990s one out of every two marriages ended in divorce. Seven times more children were affected by divorce than at the beginning of the twentieth century. Kids who commuted between separated parents were commonplace. The old ideal of a family with two parents, only one of whom worked, was now a virtually useless way to picture the typical American household.

Traditional families were not only falling apart at an alarming rate but were also increasingly slow to form in the first place. The proportion of adults living alone tripled in the four decades after 1950, and by the 1990s nearly one-third of women aged twenty-five to twenty-nine had never married. In the 1960s, 5 percent of all births were to unmarried women, but three decades later one out of four white babies, one out of three Latino babies, and two out of three African American babies were born to single mothers. Every fourth child in America was growing up in a household that lacked two parents. The collapse of the traditional family contributed heavily to the pauperization of many women and children, as single parents (usually mothers) struggled to keep their households economically

The Modern Family Tree High divorce rates and the increasing number of "blended families" in modern American society could make for confusing "family trees." Reproduced with permission of Punch Ltd., www.punch.co.uk

afloat. Single parenthood outstripped race and ethnicity as the most telling predictor of poverty in America.

Child-rearing, the family's foremost function, was being increasingly assigned to "parent-substitutes" at day-care centers or schools—or to television and DVD players, the modern age's "electronic baby-sitters." Estimates were that the average child by age sixteen had watched up to fifteen thousand hours of TV—more time than was spent in the classroom. Parental anxieties multiplied with the advent of the Internet—an electronic cornucopia where youngsters could "surf" through poetry and problem sets as well as pornography.

But if the *traditional* family was increasingly rare, the family itself remained a bedrock of American society in the early twenty-first century, as viable families now assumed a variety of forms. Children in households led by a single parent, stepparent, or grandparent, as well as children with gay or lesbian parents, encountered a degree of acceptance that would have been unimaginable a generation earlier. Even the notion of gay marriage, which emerged as a major public controversy when the Massachusetts Supreme Judicial Court ruled it legal in 2003, signaled that the idea of marriage retained its luster. Teenage pregnancy, a key source of single parenthood, was also on the decline after the mid-1990s. Even divorce rates appeared to ebb a bit, with 3.4 divorces per thousand people in 2008, down from 5.3 per thousand in 1981. The family was not evaporating, but evolving into multiple forms.

The Aging of America

Old age was more and more likely to be a lengthy experience for Americans, who were living longer than ever before. A person born at the dawn of the century could expect to survive less than fifty years, whereas someone born in 2000 could anticipate a life span of seventy-seven years. (The figures were slightly lower for nonwhites, reflecting differences in living standards, especially diet and health care.) The census of 1950 recorded that women for the first time made up a majority of Americans, thanks largely to greater female longevity. Miraculous medical advances lengthened and strengthened lives. Noteworthy were the development of antibiotics after 1940 and Dr. Jonas Salk's discovery in 1953 of a vaccine against a dreaded crippler, polio.

Longer lives spelled more elderly people. One American in eight was over sixty-five years of age in 2009, and projections were that one of every five people would be in the "sunset years" by 2050, as the median age rose toward forty. This aging of the population raised a host of political, social, and economic questions. Older Americans formed a potent electoral bloc that aggressively lobbied for government favors and achieved real gains for senior citizens. The share of GNP spent on health care for people over sixty-five more than doubled in the three decades after the enactment of Medicare in 1965. This growth in medical payments for the old far outstripped the growth of educational expenditures for the young, with corresponding consequences for the social and economic status of both populations. As late as the 1960s, nearly a quarter of Americans over the age of sixty-five lived in poverty; three decades later only about one in ten did. The figures for young people moved in the reverse direction: whereas 15 percent of children were living in poverty in the 1970s, nearly 21 percent were impoverished in 2008.

These triumphs for senior citizens also brought fiscal strains, especially on the Social Security and Medicare systems. Social Security was established in 1935 to provide income for retired workers. Before that time, most workers continued to toil after age sixty-five. By century's end only a small minority did (about 15 percent of men and 8 percent of women), and a majority of the elderly population relied primarily on Social Security checks for their living expenses. Contrary to popular mythology, Social Security payments to retirees did not represent reimbursement for contributions that the elderly had made during their working lives. In fact, the payments of current workers into the Social Security system funded the benefits to the current generation of retirees. By the time the new century opened, those benefits had risen

so high, and the ratio of active workers to retirees had dropped so low, that drastic adjustments were necessary. The problem intensified as the soaring rise of health-care costs, especially prescription drugs and long-term nursing care, threatened to bankrupt the Medicare system on which most senior citizens relied.

At the beginning of the new century, as the huge wave of post–World War II baby boomers approached retirement age, it seemed that the "unfunded liability"— the difference between what the government had promised to pay to the elderly and the taxes it expected to take in—might rise above $7 trillion, a sum that threatened to inflict fiscal ruin on the Republic unless fundamental reforms were adopted. Yet because of the electoral power of older Americans, Social Security and Medicare reform remained the "third rail" of American politics, which politicians touched only at their peril (see Figure 42.4).

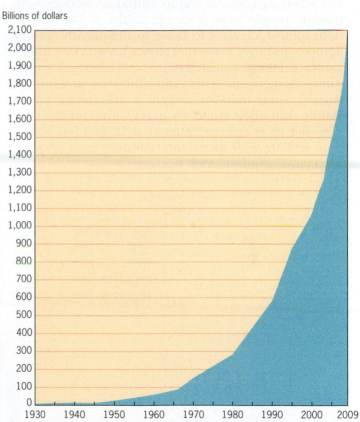

Billions of dollars

FIGURE 42.4 **Government Expenditures for Social Welfare, 1930–2009** "Social welfare" includes unemployment and old-age insurance, health care, and veterans' benefits. The skyrocketing costs from the mid-1960s onward reflect new commitments made through Great Society programs and the increasing size (and political clout) of the elderly population, who were the main beneficiaries of expensive programs like Medicare. The steep rise after 1970 is also explained by the galloping inflation of the 1970s. (Sources: *Statistical Abstract of the United States*, 2010; Office of Management and Budget, Historical Tables http://www.whitehouse.gov/omb/budget/Historicals/.)

Courtesy of the Honolulu Marathon

Senior Power Living longer and living healthier, older Americans coalesced into one of America's most politically powerful interest groups in the early twenty-first century.

✵ The New Immigration

Newcomers continued to come ashore in waves that numbered nearly 1 million persons per year from the 1980s into the early twenty-first century—the largest inflow of immigrants in America's experience. In striking contrast to the historic pattern of immigration, Europe contributed far fewer people than did Asia and Latin America (see Figure 42.5). And unlike their predecessors, many of the new immigrants settled not only in traditional ethnic enclaves in cities and towns but also in the sprawling suburbs of places like Los Angeles, Dallas, and Atlanta, where many of the new jobs were to be found.

What prompted this new migration to America? The truth is that the newest immigrants came for many of the same reasons as the old. They typically left countries where populations were growing rapidly and where agricultural and industrial revolutions were shaking people loose from old habits of life—conditions almost identical to those in nineteenth-century Europe. And they came to America, as previous immigrants had done, in search of jobs and economic opportunity. Some came with skills and even professional degrees, from India or Taiwan or the former Soviet Union, and they found their way into middle-class jobs. But most came with fewer skills and less education, seeking work as janitors, nannies, farm laborers, lawn cutters, or restaurant workers.

The Southwest, from Texas to California, felt the immigrant impact especially sharply, as Mexican migrants—by far the largest contingent of modern immigrants—concentrated heavily in that region. By the turn of the century, Latinos made up nearly one-third of the population in Texas, Arizona, and California and 40 percent in New Mexico—amounting to a demographic *reconquista* of the lands lost by Mexico in the war of 1846–1848 (see "Makers of America: The Latinos," pp. 1002–1003).

The size and geographic concentration of the Latino population in the Southwest had few precedents in the history of American immigration. Most previous groups had been so thinly scattered across the land that they had little choice but to learn English and make their way in the larger American society, however much they might have longed to preserve their native language and customs. But it seemed possible that Mexican Americans might succeed in creating a truly bicultural zone in the booming southwestern states, especially since their mother culture lay accessible just next door. Some old-stock Americans worried about the capacity of the modern United States to absorb these new immigrants. The Immigration Reform and Control Act of 1986 attempted to choke off illegal entry by penalizing employers of undocumented aliens and by granting amnesty to many of those already here. But immigrants just kept coming, legal and illegal alike, as political leaders struggled in vain to devise an

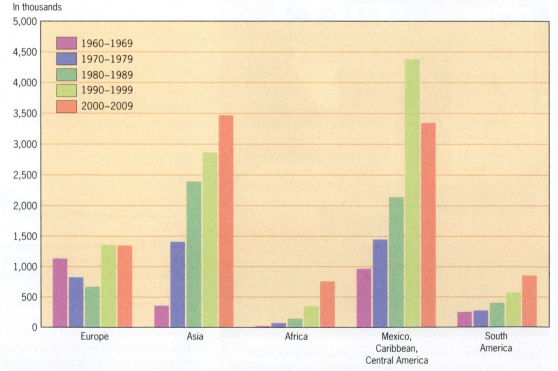

FIGURE 42.5 Recent Legal Immigration by Area of Origin, 1961–2009   (Source: *Yearbook of Immigration Statistics*, 2009, Department of Homeland Security.)

"I CAN TELL BY THE COLOR OF YOUR SKIN YOU'RE NOT FROM AROUND HERE, ARE YOU?"

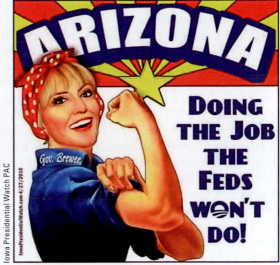

Immigration Confrontation   When Arizona Governor Jan Brewer signed a tough new bill in 2010 authorizing local police to crack down on illegal immigrants, the national debate over immigration policy grew still more bitterly divisive. Champions of the bill hailed Arizona for taking a stand in the void left by federal inaction. Critics denounced it as an invitation to the harassment of all Hispanics—indeed, all people of color—regardless of their citizenship status.

immigration system that was fair, realistic, and true to the nation's traditions.

Yet the fact was that foreign-born people accounted for only about 13 percent of the American population in 2007, a far smaller proportion than the historical high point of nearly 15 percent recorded in the census of 1910, but evidence nonetheless that American society continued to welcome—and need—newcomers. Somewhat inconsistently, critics charged both that immigrants robbed citizens of jobs and that they dumped themselves on the welfare rolls at the taxpayers' expense. But studies showed that immigrants took jobs scorned by Americans and that they paid more dollars in federal taxes (withholding and Social Security taxes, as well as excise taxes) than they claimed for welfare payments. The story was different at the state level, where expenditures for immigrant education and health care often exceeded the net tax contribution of the immigrants themselves. Yet the infusion of young immigrants and their offspring was just what the country needed when faced with the challenges of an aging population. A more urgent worry was that unscrupulous employers might take cruel advantage of alien workers, who often had scant knowledge of their legal rights.

Debates over immigration were complicated by the problem of illegal immigrants. The intensity mounted in 2006, when xenophobic pundits and politicians fanned the old flames of anxiety that millions of undocumented workers were usurping American tax dollars and privileges. Immigrant sympathizers argued that unlawful aliens had to be legalized so that they could receive the same protections as other workers. Amid this chaos President George W. Bush and a bipartisan group of legislators proposed a law to establish a guest-worker program for undocumented workers and create a path to citizenship, albeit after paying a fine. Anti-immigrant forces condemned the plan as "amnesty." Business interests protested that it put too great a burden on employers to verify the right to work. And immigrant rights advocates claimed that it would create "second-class citizens." In the end, the compromise bill pleased no one and fell into the dustbin. But the debate over immigration only grew more bitter. Legislators in Arizona, provoked by continuing immigrant flows over the state's long desert border with Mexico, passed a harsh anti-immigrant law in 2010 requiring local police to detain people if there was "reasonable suspicion" that they were illegal. Critics complained that the law amounted to unfair "racial profiling," and that the state was unconstitutionally usurping federal responsibility for controlling immigration. The matter seemed destined for eventual adjudication by the United States Supreme Court. Later in that same year, Congress rejected the DREAM Act (Development, Relief and Education for Alien Minors), which would have provided a path to citizenship for undocumented youth who either finished college or served in the U.S. military.

*T*oday Mexican food is handed through fast-food drive-up windows in all fifty states, Spanish-language broadcasts fill the airwaves, and the Latino community has its own telephone book, the *Spanish Yellow Pages*. Latinos send representatives to Congress and mayors to city halls, record hit songs, paint murals, and teach history. Latinos, among the fastest-growing segments of the U.S. population, include Puerto Ricans, frequent voyagers between their native island and northeastern cities; Cubans, many of them refugees from the communist dictatorship of Fidel Castro, concentrated in Miami and southern Florida; and Central Americans, fleeing the ravages of civil war in Nicaragua and El Salvador.

But the most populous group of Latinos derives from Mexico (see Figure 42.6). The first significant numbers of Mexicans began heading for *El Norte* ("the North") around 1910, when the upheavals of the Mexican Revolution stirred and shuffled the Mexican population into more or less constant flux. Their northward passage was briefly interrupted during the Great Depression, when thousands of Mexican nationals were deported. But immigration resumed during World War II, and since then a steady flow of legal immigrants has passed through border checkpoints, joined by countless millions of their undocumented countrymen and countrywomen stealing across the southwestern frontier on moonless nights.

For the most part, these Mexicans came to work in the fields, following the ripening crops northward to Canada through the summer and autumn months. In winter many headed back to Mexico, but some gathered instead in the cities of the Southwest—El Paso, Los Angeles, Houston, and San Bernardino. There they found regular work, even if lack of skills and racial discrimination often confined them to manual labor. City jobs might pay less than farm labor, but the work was steady and offered the prospect of a stable home. Houses may have been shabby in the barrios, but these Mexican neighborhoods provided a sense of togetherness, a place to raise a family, and the chance to join a mutual aid society. Such societies, or *mutualistas*, sponsored baseball leagues, helped the sick and disabled, and defended their members against discrimination.

Mexican immigrants lived so close to the border that their native country acted like a powerful magnet, drawing them back time and time again. Until tighter border controls were put in place after the terrorist attacks of September 2001, Mexicans frequently returned to see relatives or visit the homes of their youth, and relatively few became U.S. citizens. Indeed, in many Mexican American communities, it was a badge of dishonor to apply for U.S. citizenship.

The Mexican government, likewise influenced by the proximity of the two countries, intervened in the daily lives of its nationals in America, sometimes discouraging them from becoming citizens of their adopted country. As Anglo reformers attempted to Americanize the immigrants in the 1910s and 1920s, the Mexican consulate in Los Angeles launched a Mexicanization

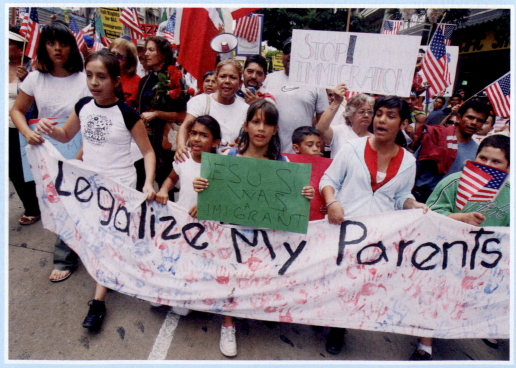

Demonstrating for Immigrant Rights, Los Angeles, 2007 Latinos march in downtown Los Angeles in support of legalizing undocumented parents who have children born in the United States. U.S. law gives the right of citizenship to anyone born on American soil ("jus soli"), but not necessarily to the parents of that child.

© Bettmann/Corbis

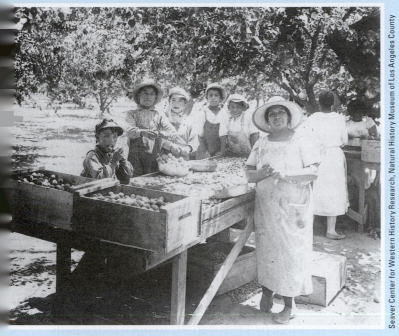

Seaver Center for Western History Research, Natural History Museum of Los Angeles County

Mexican American Farmworkers Pitting Apricots in Fruit Groves near Los Angeles, 1924

Cuban
3.5%
(1.6 million)

Puerto Rican
8.9%
(4.2 million)

Central/South
American or
other Latino
21.9%
(10.3 million)

Mexican
65.7%
(30.7 million)

FIGURE 42.6 **Sources of Latino Population in the United States, 2008** (Source: U.S. Census Bureau; Pew Hispanic Center, *Statistical Portrait of Hispanics in the United States, 2008*.)

program. The consulate sponsored parades on Cinco de Mayo ("Fifth of May"), celebrating Mexico's defeat of a French army at the Battle of Puebla in 1862, and opened special Spanish-language schools for children. Since World War II, the American-born generation has carried on the fight for political representation, economic opportunity, and cultural preservation.

Fresh arrivals from Mexico and from the other Latin American nations daily swell Latino communities across America. The census of 2000 revealed that Latinos had become the largest minority group in the United States, surpassing African Americans. As the United States moves through the twenty-first century, it is taking on a pronounced Spanish accent, and increasingly Latinos are making themselves a force to be reckoned with in American politics, culture, and the economy.

Michael Dwyer/AP Images

Young Latina Activists in East Boston, 2004
Latinos have become increasingly influential voters, courted by Democratic and Republican candidates alike.

✦ Beyond the Melting Pot

Thanks both to continued immigration and to their own high birthrate, Latinos were becoming an increasingly important minority. The United States by 2008 was home to about 47 million of them. They included some 31 million Chicanos, or Mexican Americans, mostly in the Southwest, as well as 4 million Puerto Ricans, chiefly in the Northeast, and more than 1 million Cubans in Florida (where it was jokingly said that Miami had become the most "Anglo" city in Latin America).

Flexing their political muscles, Latinos elected mayors of Miami, Denver, San Antonio, and Los Angeles. After years of struggle, the United Farm Workers Organizing Committee (UFWOC), headed by the soft-spoken and charismatic César Chávez, succeeded in improving working conditions for the mostly Chicano "stoop laborers" who followed the cycle of planting and harvesting across the American West. Latino influence was destined to grow, as suggested by the increasing presence of Spanish-language ballots and television broadcasts. Latinos, newly confident and organized, became the nation's largest ethnic minority, outnumbering even African Americans, in 2003. Indeed by the early twenty-first century, the Chicano population of America's largest state, California, led the Anglo population, making the state a patchwork of minorities with no single ethnic majority. In 2003 most newborns in California were Latino, a powerful harbinger of the state's demographic future—and the nation's. By 2010, the Census Bureau counted four "majority-minority" states (all of them in the booming West), where no ethnic group commanded a majority: Texas, New Mexico, California, and Hawaii. Nationwide, the birthrate for nonwhites in 2010 was poised to eclipse the white birthrate for the first time in history.

Asian Americans also made great strides. By the 1980s they were America's fastest-growing minority, numbering nearly 15 million by 2008. Once feared and hated as the "yellow peril" and consigned to the most menial and degrading jobs, citizens of Asian ancestry were now counted among the most prosperous Americans. Their rising political influence was heralded in the 1998 election of Oregon's Taiwan-born David Wu as the first Chinese American to serve in the House of Representatives.

Indians, the original Americans, numbered more than 2.5 million in the 2010 census. Half of them had left their reservations to live in cities. Meanwhile, unemployment and alcoholism had blighted reservation life. Many tribes took advantage of their special legal status as independent nations to open bingo halls and gambling casinos for the general public on reservation lands, but the cycle of discrimination and poverty proved hard to break.

✦ Cities and Suburbs

America's "alabaster cities" of song and story grew more sooty and less safe in the closing decades of the twentieth century. Crime was the great scourge of urban life. The rate of violent crimes committed in cities

The Oldest Americans
Members of the Cheyenne River Sioux Tribe celebrate the opening of the Smithsonian Institution's National Museum of the American Indian in Washington, D.C., 2004.

AP Photo/Pablo Martinez Monsivais

reached an all-time high in the drug-infested 1980s and then leveled off in the early 1990s. The number of violent crimes even began to decline substantially in many areas after 1995. Nevertheless, murders, robberies, and rapes remained shockingly common not only in cities but also in suburbs and rural areas. America imprisoned a larger fraction of its citizens than almost any other country in the world, and some desperate citizens resorted to armed vigilante tactics to protect themselves.

The migration from cities to the suburbs was so swift and massive that by the mid-1990s a majority of Americans were suburban dwellers (see Figure 42.7). Jobs, too, became suburbanized. The nation's rather brief "urban age" lasted little more than seven decades after 1920, and with its passing many observers saw a new fragmentation and isolation in American life. Some affluent suburban neighborhoods walled themselves off behind elaborate security systems in "gated communities," making it harder, perhaps, to sustain a sense of a larger and inclusive national community. By the first decade of the twenty-first century, the suburban rings around big cities such as New York, Chicago, Houston, and Washington, D.C., were becoming more racially and ethnically diverse, though individual schools and towns were often homogeneous.

Suburbs grew fastest in the West and Southwest. In the outer orbits of Los Angeles, San Diego, Las Vegas, and Phoenix, builders of roads, water mains, and schools could barely keep up with the new towns sprouting across the hardscrabble landscapes. Newcomers came not only from nearby cities but from other regions of the United States as well. A momentous shift of the American population was under way, as inhabitants from the Northeast and the Rustbelt Midwest moved southward and westward to job opportunities and the sun. The Great Plains, where 60 percent of all counties were losing population as the twentieth century ended, faced the sharpest decline, hollowing out the traditional American heartland. By the early twenty-first century, the Great Plains contained fewer people than the Los Angeles basin, despite being five times the size of the entire state of California.

Some major cities exhibited signs of renewal. Commercial redevelopment gained ground in cities such as New York, Boston, Chicago, San Francisco, and even the classic "city without a center," Los Angeles. Well-to-do residents reclaimed once-fashionable neighborhoods and sent real estate values soaring. But these latter-day urban homesteaders struggled to make their cities genuine centers of residential integration. Cities stubbornly remained as divided by wealth and race as the suburban social landscape surrounding them.

✸ Minority America

Racial and ethnic tensions also exacerbated the problems of American cities. These stresses were especially evident in Los Angeles, which, like New York a century earlier, was a magnet for minorities, especially immigrants from Asia and Latin America. When in 1992 a mostly white jury exonerated white Los Angeles police officers who had been videotaped ferociously beating a black suspect, the minority neighborhoods of South Central Los Angeles erupted in rage. Arson and looting

FIGURE 42.7 Percent of Total Population Living in Metropolitan Areas and in Their Central Cities and Suburbs, 1910–2000 (Source: U.S. Census Bureau, Decennial Census of Population, 1910 to 2000, compiled in *Demographic Trends in the 20th Century*, no. 2002.)

laid waste entire city blocks, and scores of people were killed. In a sobering demonstration of the complexity of modern American racial rivalries, many black rioters vented their anger at the white police and the judicial system by attacking Asian shopkeepers, who in turn formed armed patrols to protect their property. A decade later many a burned-out lot remained abandoned and weed-choked in neighborhoods still plagued by gang violence and the demoralizing effects of grinding poverty.

The Los Angeles riots vividly testified to black skepticism about the American system of justice. Just three years later, again in Los Angeles, the televised spectacle of former football "hero" O. J. Simpson's murder trial fed white disillusionment with the state of race relations. After months of testimony that seemed to point to Simpson's guilt, the jury acquitted him, presumably because certain Los Angeles police officers involved in the case had been shown to harbor racist sentiments. In a later civil trial, another jury unanimously found Simpson liable for the "wrongful deaths" of his former wife and another victim. (In 2008 Simpson was sentenced to thirty-three years in jail for unrelated felony convictions.) The reaction to the Simpson verdicts revealed the yawning chasm that separated white and black America, as most whites continued to believe Simpson guilty, while a majority of African Americans told pollsters that the original not-guilty verdict was justified. Similarly, complaints by African Americans that they had been unlawfully kept from the polls during the 2000 presidential election in Florida reflected the conviction of many blacks that they were still facing a Jim Crow South of systematic racial disfranchisement.

American cities have always held an astonishing variety of ethnic and racial groups, but by the late twentieth century, minorities made up a majority of the population of many American cities, as whites fled to the suburbs. In 2002, 52 percent of all blacks lived in central cities within metropolitan areas, compared with only 21 percent of whites. The most desperate black ghettos, housing a hapless "underclass" in the inner core of the old industrial cities, were especially problematic. Successful blacks who had benefited from the civil rights revolution of the 1950s and 1960s followed whites to the suburbs, leaving a residue of the poorest poor in the old ghettos. Without a middle class to sustain community institutions like schools and small businesses, the inner cities, plagued by unemployment and drug addiction, seemed bereft of leadership, cohesion, resources, and hope.

Single women headed about 45 percent of black families in 2009, more than three times the rate for whites. Many African American women, husbandless and jobless, struggled to feed their children. As social scientists increasingly emphasized the importance of the home environment for success in school, it became clear that many fatherless, impoverished African American children seemed consigned to suffer from educational handicaps that were difficult to overcome.

Some segments of the African American community did prosper in the wake of the civil rights gains of the 1950s and 1960s, although they still had a long hill to climb before reaching full equality. By 2009, 43 percent of all black families (compared to 68 percent of all white families) had incomes of at least $50,000, qualifying them (barely) as middle class. Blacks continued

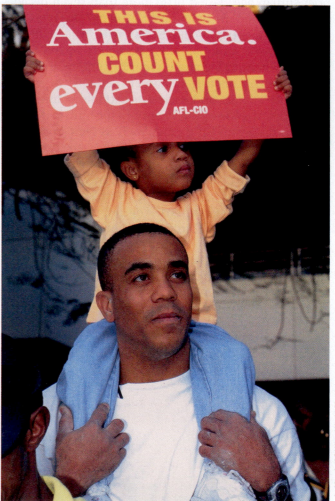

Luis Alvariz/AP Wide World Photos

Still Fighting to Vote An African American father and daughter participate in a rally in downtown Miami several weeks after the November 2000 election to demand a recount of dismissed presidential election ballots. Many Florida blacks complained that election officials had disproportionately disqualified their votes and unfairly turned them away from the polls, resurrecting the kind of obstacles that long had kept blacks from voting in the South.

to make headway in political life. The number of black elected officials had risen above the nine thousand mark, including more than three dozen members of Congress and the mayors of several large cities, not to mention President Barack Obama.

By the early twenty-first century, blacks had also dramatically advanced into higher education, though the educational gap between blacks and whites stubbornly persisted. In 2009, 12.7 percent of blacks over age twenty-five had a bachelor's degree, compared to 19.3 percent of whites and 21 percent of non-Hispanic whites. The political assault against affirmative action in California and elsewhere in the 1990s only compounded the obstacles to advanced training for many young African Americans. But defenders of affirmative action chalked up a major victory in 2003 when the Supreme Court in a key case involving the University of Michigan affirmed that achieving racial diversity on college campuses was a legitimate means to secure a more equitable society. The Court preserved affirmative action in university admissions as long as schools avoided using quotas, point systems, or other mechanistic ways of diversifying their student bodies, though it remained uneasy about letting such programs endure indefinitely. Justice Sandra Day O'Connor said, "We expect that twenty-five years from now, the use of racial preferences will no longer be necessary."

✶ E Pluribus Plures

Controversial issues of color and culture also pervaded the realm of ideas in the late twentieth century. Echoing early-twentieth-century "cultural pluralists" like Horace Kallen and Randolph Bourne, many intellectuals after 1970 embraced the creed of "multiculturalism." The new mantra celebrated diversity for its own sake and stressed the need to preserve and promote, rather than squash, a variety of distinct ethnic and racial cultures in the United States.

The nation's classrooms became battlegrounds for the debate over America's commitment to pluralism. Multiculturalists attacked the traditional curriculum as "Eurocentric" and advocated greater focus on the achievements of African Americans, Latinos, Asian Americans, and Native Americans. In response, critics charged that too much stress on ethnic difference would come at the expense of national cohesion and an appreciation of common American values.

The Census Bureau further enlivened the debate when in 2000 it allowed respondents to identify themselves with more than one of the six standard racial categories (black, white, Latino, American Indian, Asian, and Native Hawaiian or other Pacific Islander). Signifying a mounting revolution in attitudes toward

In 1990 the African American intellectual Shelby Steele (b. 1946) declared in his provocative book, The Content of Our Character,

❝What is needed now is a new spirit of pragmatism in racial matters where blacks are seen simply as American citizens who deserve complete fairness and in some cases developmental assistance, but in no case special entitlements based on color. We need deracinated social policies that attack poverty rather than black poverty and that instill those values that make for self-reliance.❞

race, nearly 7 million Americans chose to describe themselves as biracial or multiracial. As recently as the 1960s, interracial marriage was still illegal in sixteen states. But by the early twenty-first century, many Americans, including such celebrities as golfer Tiger Woods and actress Rosario Dawson, were proclaiming their mixed heritage as a point of pride.

✶ The Postmodern Mind

Despite the mind-sapping chatter of the "boob tube" and the distractions of the Internet, Americans in the early twenty-first century read more, listened to more music, and were better educated than ever before. Colleges awarded some 3 million degrees annually, and more than one person in five in the twenty-five- to thirty-four-year-old age group boasted a college bachelor's degree in 2009. (Nearly one in three had an associate's degree.) The swelling ranks of educated people lifted the economy to more advanced levels while creating more consumers of "high culture." Each year millions of Americans visited museums and patronized hundreds of opera companies and symphony orchestras—as well as countless popular music groups.

Commentators often described these contemporary Americans as living in a "postmodern" age, though few could agree on precisely what that term meant. But whatever else it denotes, *postmodernism* generally refers to a distrust of rational, scientific descriptions of the self or the world, and the insistence that human beliefs and realities are socially "constructed." In place of modernism's faith in certainty, objectivity, and unity, postmodernism stresses skepticism, relativity, and multiplicity. Postmodernism has enormously influenced contemporary philosophy, social theory, art, architecture, and literature, among other fields.

Postmodern architecture made the most visible footprint on the American cultural landscape. Rejecting

Architect Frank Gehry's Walt Disney Concert Hall, Los Angeles, California, Completed in 2003

the austere functionalism that had dominated architecture for much of the last century, postmodernists such as Robert Venturi and Michael Graves revived the decorative details of earlier historical styles. Modernists had valued minimalism and an absence of ornament—"Less is more," the renowned German architect Ludwig Mies van der Rohe proclaimed. But postmodernists celebrated a playful eclecticism of architectural elements—"Less is a bore," as Venturi put it. The flight from stark modernism took especially fanciful forms in Frank Gehry's use of luminous, undulating sheets of metallic skin in the widely hailed Guggenheim Museum (1997) in Bilbao, Spain, and the Walt Disney Concert Hall (2003) in Los Angeles.

The postmodern sensibility carried over into other art forms. Classical music composers like John Adams and John Zorn broke down boundaries between "high"

and "low" styles and blended diverse musical genres and traditions in an experimental mix. Choreographers such as Steve Paxton and Twyla Tharp paired everyday movements with classical techniques and gave contemporary dancers license to improvise. Hip-hop artists from Biz Markie to Jay-Z "sampled" beats from other sound recordings, and lyrical MCs overlaid them with complex "rapping" schemes. Born in America's urban ghettos in the 1970s, hip-hop blossomed into a mainstream cultural phenomenon, both nationally and internationally. "Mash-up" artists also gained popularity, cleverly fusing fragments from songs of different musical genres or remixing one song's vocal track over another song's instrumentals.

Visual artists also felt the eclectic urge. Cindy Sherman, Jenny Holzer, and Kara Walker combined old and new media to confront, confound, and even offend the viewer. Jeff Koons and Shepard Fairey borrowed industrial materials and pop culture imagery to blur the hidebound distinction between highbrow and lowbrow cultures. Their pastiches of disparate fragments, often presented in ironic fashion, came to symbolize postmodern art.

Postmodern literature, like art, had deep roots in the second half of the twentieth century. After World War II, authors like William S. Burroughs, Kurt Vonnegut, and Thomas Pynchon pioneered the use of nonlinear narratives, pastiche forms, parody, and paradox in their fiction. A newer generation of writers, including

The term postmodernism *often means different things to different people. Choreographer Twyla Tharp (b. 1941) captured some of the trouble in defining a term that resists easy definition:*

❝ There's this expression called postmodernism, which is kind of silly, and destroys a perfectly good word called modern, which now no longer means anything.❞

Jason Kempin/Getty Images

Kara Walker Stands Before her Painting, Gone, An Historical of a Civil War as it Occurred Between the Dusky Thighs of One Young Negress and Her Heart, 1994 Walker has daringly adapted the venerable technique of cut-paper silhouettes to explore modern themes of racial identity and historical revisionism. Here she contrasts the romantic image of the antebellum South captured in Margaret Mitchell's celebrated novel and film *Gone with the Wind* with the perspective of an enslaved black woman.

Michael Chabon, Jeffrey Eugenides, and Zadie Smith, adapted these techniques for contemporary audiences. Among these "post-postmodernists," David Foster Wallace playfully lampooned North America's dystopian future in *Infinite Jest* (1996), complete with calendar years named after corporate sponsors. Colson Whitehead ruminated on modern racial uplift among rival schools of elevator operators in *The Intuitionist* (1999). Jonathan Franzen satirized dysfunctional midwestern families to great critical acclaim in *The Corrections* (2001) and *Freedom* (2010).

Other major works of contemporary fiction, especially from the pens of female and minority authors, complemented postmodernism's ethos of pluralism and cultural diversity. Toni Morrison wove a bewitching portrait of maternal affection in *Beloved* (1987) and in 1993 became the first African American woman to win the Nobel Prize for literature. E. Annie Proulx won widespread acclaim with her comical yet tender portrayal of a struggling family in *The Shipping News* (1993). Her moving tale of homoerotic love between two cowboys in "Brokeback Mountain" (1997) reached

Nick Onken/Getty Images

Latinos Breaking in Los Angeles Breakdancing emerged among African Americans in New York in the late twentieth century to become an integral part of hip-hop culture.

In her touching novel The Joy Luck Club *(1989), Amy Tan (b. 1952) explored the complex dilemmas of growing up as a Chinese American:*

"'A girl is like a young tree,' [my mother] said. 'You must stand tall and listen to your mother standing next to you. That is the only way to grow strong and straight. But if you bend to listen to other people, you will grow crooked and weak. . . .' Over the years I learned to choose from the best opinions. Chinese people had Chinese opinions. American people had American opinions. And in almost every case, the American version was much better. It was only later that I discovered there was a serious flaw with the American version. There were too many choices, so it was easy to get confused and pick the wrong thing.**"**

a mass audience in 2005 as an award-winning motion picture. James Welch, Leslie Marmon Silko, Joy Harjo, and Sherman Alexie contributed to a Native American literary renaissance that sought to recover the tribal past while reimagining its present.

Immigration in the new century also began to yield its own rich cultural harvest. Asian American authors flourished, among them playwright David Hwang, novelist Amy Tan, and Chinese-born Ha Jin, who wrote evocatively about his country of origin in novels like *Waiting* (1999) and *War Trash* (2004). Jhumpa Lahiri's *Interpreter of Maladies* (1999) and *Unaccustomed Earth* (2008) explored the sometimes painful relationship between immigrant Indian parents and their American-born children. Latino writers made their mark as well. Junot Diaz's Pulitzer Prize–winning *The Brief Wondrous Life of Oscar Wao* (2007) brilliantly bridged the worlds of the Dominican Republic and New Jersey in a dazzling concoction of street-smart Spanglish.

On the stage, contemporary political themes and social commentary predominated. The AIDS epidemic inspired Tony Kushner's sensationally inventive *Angels in America* (1991), as well as Jonathan Larson's Tony Award–winning musical *Rent* (1996). Eve Ensler espoused feminist empowerment (and an end to violence against women) with comic intimacy in her *Vagina Monologues* (1996). Cuban American Nilo Cruz won a Pulitzer Prize in 2003 for *Anna in the Tropics*, about immigrant cigar makers confronting the tide of mechanization in 1929 Tampa. Tracy Letts peeled back the hypocrisies of middle-American family life in *August: Osage County* (2007). Lynn Nottage's deeply moving *Ruined* (2008), about a young African rape

victim, found hope and redemption even amidst the brutal chaos of the Congo's eternal wars.

Film, the most characteristic American art form, continued to flourish, as pioneering directors such as George Lucas, Steven Spielberg, James Cameron, and Spike Lee were followed by a wave of even bolder young iconoclasts, including Quentin Tarantino, the Coen brothers, and Kathryn Bigelow. Tarantino's *Pulp Fiction* (1994) and David Lynch's *Mulholland Drive* (2001), notable for their unconventional storylines, cinematic allusions, and dark comedic stylings, were prime examples of postmodern film. On the television screen, documentaries thrived, as innovative filmmakers such as Ken Burns chronicled great American themes like the history of baseball, jazz, the national parks, the Civil War, and World War II. Cable television entered a golden era, as high-quality dramas such as *The Sopranos* (1999–2007) and *The Wire* (2002–2008) enjoyed commercial and critical success.

✦ The New Media

By the early twenty-first century, the Internet had dramatically transformed daily life for most Americans. First created by the government for Cold War intelligence sharing, the World Wide Web spread like wildfire through American homes, schools, and offices during the mid-1990s. The percentage of households with Internet access skyrocketed from 18 percent in 1997 to about 70 percent in 2009. In rapidly increasing numbers, Americans turned to the Internet to communicate, shop, work, and electronically bond with family, friends, and lovers. The "dot-com" explosion of Internet-based high-tech companies drove the tremendous economic boom of the late 1990s.

Even as the "dot-com bubble" began to deflate, the Internet demonstrated its staying power. Many online start-up companies failed, but those that survived often became giants in retail (Amazon.com), information gathering (Google), and even finance (E*Trade). The Internet reshaped the traditional corporate world as well, as almost every business, group, or organization—from used-car dealers to sports teams to college arts groups—had its own Web site.

Fulfilling the promises of its early boosters, the Internet seemed to have a democratizing effect, spreading power and information among more and more Americans. Young people in particular flocked to social-networking sites like Facebook and Twitter to make connections, often with people in foreign countries. YouTube allowed everyday users to post home videos online for the whole world to see. And millions of people around the globe started a media revolution with their "Weblogs," or "blogs." "Bloggers" lent their

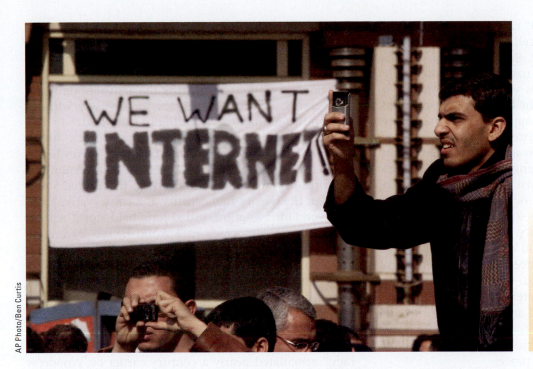

AP Photo/Ben Curtis

Tahrir (Liberation) Square, Cairo, Egypt, January 31, 2011 A man takes pictures with his cell phone amid the uprisings that ousted Egypt's president. Social media fueled the "Arab Spring" protests that swept across the Middle East in early 2011.

voices to issues from foreign policy to college life, offering their beliefs and opinions without fear (and often without research). As the "blogosphere" grew, it posed a major challenge to the traditional media—newspapers especially—that had shaped Americans' understanding of the news for hundreds of years. Supporters argued that this "new Media" added fresh voices and new perspectives, but opponents questioned bloggers' expertise and accused them of spreading misinformation.

Blogs were not the only threat the Internet posed to the "mainstream media." Americans became ever less willing to read the morning paper or watch the evening network news shows when they could access a welter of information on their computer screens. Cable news had challenged the old system since the 1980s, but the spread of the Internet made the twenty-four-hour news cycle a reality. Consumer demand pushed daily newspapers to offer their reporting online, often for free. Subscription rates plummeted, and ad sales—the engine that drives print journalism—fell off markedly. As with railroads and the telegraph in the nineteenth century, and radio and television in the twentieth century, computers and the Internet drove major readjustments in modern American economic, social, and cultural life.

✪ The American Prospect

The American spirit pulsed with vitality in the early twenty-first century, but grave problems continued to plague the Republic. Women still fell short of first-class economic citizenship, and American society groped for ways to adapt the traditional family to the new realities of women's work outside the home. A generation after the civil rights triumphs of the 1960s, full equality remained an elusive dream for countless Americans of color. Powerful foreign competitors challenged America's premier economic status. As manufacturing jobs disappeared, and as corporate giants like Enron and Lehman Brothers collapsed, many Americans began to fear their economy as a treacherous landscape, even as it offered some of them astounding prosperity. The alarmingly unequal distribution of wealth and income threatened to turn America into a society of haves and have-nots, mocking the ideals of democracy and breeding seething resentments along the economic frontier that divided rich from poor.

Environmental worries also clouded the country's future. Coal-fired electrical-generating plants helped form acid rain and measurably contributed to the greenhouse effect, an ominous warming in the planet's temperature. The unsolved problem of radioactive waste disposal hampered the development of nuclear power plants. The planet was being drained of oil. Disastrous accidents like the explosion of BP's Deepwater Horizon oil-drilling rig off the Louisiana coast in 2010, which spilled millions of barrels of oil into nearby coastal waters and threatened the Gulf of Mexico's rich but fragile ecosystem, dramatically underscored the risks of mankind's increasingly desperate quest for fossil fuels.

By the early twenty-first century, the once-lonely cries for alternative fuel sources had given way to public fascination with solar power and windmills, methane fuel, electric "hybrid" cars, and the pursuit of an affordable hydrogen fuel cell. Energy conservation remained another crucial but elusive strategy—much-heralded at the politician's rostrum, but too rarely embodied in public policy, as witnessed in the Bush administration's rejection of the Kyoto Treaty on global warming in 2001 and the disappointing failure of the Copenhagen Climate Conference in 2009.

As the human family grew at an alarming rate on a shrinking globe, new challenges still faced America and its historical beliefs. The task of cleansing the earth of its abundant pollutants—including nuclear weapons—was one urgent mission confronting the American people in the new century. Another was seeking ways to resolve the ethnic and cultural conflicts that erupted with renewed virulence around the globe in the wake of the Cold War's end. At the same time, new opportunities beckoned in outer space and on inner-city streets, at the artist's easel and in the concert hall, at the inventor's bench and in the scientist's laboratory, and in the unending quest for social justice, individual fulfillment, and international peace.

The terrorist attack on America on September 11, 2001, posed yet another challenge to the United States. Shielded for nearly two centuries against assaults on its soil, it would now have to preserve its security in a world made smaller by global communication and transportation, without altering its fundamental democratic values and way of life. The great danger posed by terrorism was not that Al Qaeda or other foreign enemies would seize control of the country or any portion of its territory. It was, rather, that in fighting terrorism, Americans would so compromise their freedoms at home and so isolate the country internationally that it would lose touch with its own guiding principles. Wars in Afghanistan and Iraq made these difficulties clear. The challenge was to enhance national security without eroding democratic liberties, to protect the country's borders without preventing the arrival of desirable immigrants, and to use military force wisely without undermining America's standing in the world.

In facing those challenges, the world's oldest republic had an extraordinary tradition of resilience and resourcefulness to draw on. Born as a revolutionary force in a world of conservatism, the United States stood in the twenty-first century as a conservative force in a world of revolution. It had long held aloft the banner of liberal democracy in a world racked by revolutions of the right and left, including fascism, Nazism, and communism. Yet through it all, much that was truly revolutionary also remained a part of America's liberal democratic heritage, as its people pioneered in revolutions against colonialism, racism, sexism, ignorance, and poverty.

The dream of "making the world safe for democracy," articulated nearly a century earlier by Woodrow Wilson at the end of the First World War, gained a new poignancy after September 11, 2001, when Americans expressed a yearning for greater equality, opportunity, and democracy in the Middle East—all in the hope of diminishing the root causes of international terrorism. The capacity to nurture progress abroad, however, depended on the ability of Americans to improve their own country, and to do so in the midst of new threats to their own security. As Wilson wrote in 1893, long before he became president, "Democratic institutions are never done; they are like living tissue, always a-making. It is a strenuous thing, this of living the life of a free people."

TO LEARN MORE

Nancy Altman, *The Battle for Social Security: From FDR's Vision to Bush's Gamble* (2005)

Margot Canaday, *The Straight State: Sexuality and Citizenship in Twentieth-Century America* (2009)

John Cassidy, *How Markets Fail: The Logic of Economic Calamities* (2009)

Gail Collins, *When Everything Changed: The Amazing Journey of American Women from 1960 to the Present* (2009)

Steven Connor, ed., *The Cambridge Companion to Postmodernism* (2004)

David Dent, *In Search of Black America: Discovering the African American Dream* (2000)

Barbara Ehrenreich, *Nickel and Dimed: On (Not) Getting By in America* (2001)

Bill Ong Hing, *Defining America Through Immigration Policy* (2004)

David A. Hollinger, *Postethnic America: Beyond Multiculturalism*, rev. ed. (2005)

Paul Krugman, *The Great Unraveling: Losing Our Way in the New Century* (2003)

Michael Lewis, *The Big Short: Inside the Doomsday Machine* (2010)

Katherine Newman, *A Different Shade of Gray: Midlife and Beyond in the Inner City* (2003)

George Sanchez, *Becoming Mexican American* (1989)

Go to the CourseMate website at **www.cengagebrain.com** for additional study tools and review materials—including audio and video clips—for this chapter.

A complete, annotated bibliography for this chapter—along with brief descriptions of the People to Know—may be found on the American Pageant website. The Key Terms are defined in a Glossary at the end of the text.

DOCUMENTS

Declaration of Independence

In Congress, July 4, 1776

The Unanimous Declaration of the Thirteen United States of America

[Bracketed material in color has been inserted by the authors. For adoption background see pp. 137–139.]

When, in the course of human events, it becomes necessary for one people to dissolve the political bonds which have connected them with another, and to assume, among the powers of the earth, the separate and equal station to which the laws of nature and of nature's God entitle them, a decent respect to the opinions of mankind requires that they should declare the causes which impel them to the separation.

We hold these truths to be self-evident: That all men are created equal; that they are endowed by their Creator with certain unalienable rights; that among these are life, liberty, and the pursuit of happiness; that, to secure these rights, governments are instituted among men, deriving their just powers from the consent of the governed; that whenever any form of government becomes destructive of these ends, it is the right of the people to alter or to abolish it, and to institute new government, laying its foundation on such principles, and organizing its powers in such form, as to them shall seem most likely to effect their safety and happiness. Prudence, indeed, will dictate that governments long established should not be changed for light and transient causes; and accordingly all experience hath shown that mankind are more disposed to suffer, while evils are sufferable, than to right themselves by abolishing the forms to which they are accustomed. But when a long train of abuses and usurpations, pursuing invariably the same object, evinces a design to reduce them under absolute despotism, it is their right, it is their duty, to throw off such government, and to provide new guards for their future security. Such has been the patient sufferance of these colonies; and such is now the necessity which constrains them to alter their former systems of government. The history of the present King of Great Britain is a history of repeated injuries and usurpations, all having in direct object the establishment of an absolute tyranny over these states. To prove this, let facts be submitted to a candid world.

He has refused his assent to laws, the most wholesome and necessary for the public good. [See royal veto, p. 115.]

He has forbidden his governors to pass laws of immediate and pressing importance, unless suspended in their operation till his assent should be obtained; and, when so suspended, he has utterly neglected to attend to them.

He has refused to pass other laws for the accommodation of large districts of people [by establishing new countries], unless those people would relinquish the right of representation in the legislature, a right inestimable to them, and formidable to tyrants only.

He has called together legislative bodies at places unusual, uncomfortable, and distant from the depository of their public records, for the sole purpose of fatiguing them into compliance with his measures. [e.g., removal of Massachusetts Assembly to Salem, 1774.]

He has dissolved representative houses repeatedly, for opposing, with manly firmness, his invasions on the rights of the people. [e.g., Virginia Assembly, 1765.]

He has refused for a long time, after such dissolutions, to cause others to be elected; whereby the legislative powers, incapable of annihilation, have returned to the people at large for their exercise; the state remaining, in the mean time, exposed to all the dangers of invasions from without and convulsions within.

He has endeavored to prevent the population [populating] of these states; for that purpose obstructing the laws for naturalization of foreigners; refusing to pass others to encourage their migration hither, and raising the conditions of new appropriations of lands. [e.g., Proclamation of 1763, p. 111.]

He has obstructed the administration of justice, by refusing his assent to laws for establishing judiciary powers.

He has made judges dependent on his will alone, for the tenure of their offices, and the amount and payment of their salaries. [See Townshend Acts, p. 118.]

He has erected a multitude of new offices, and sent hither swarms of officers to harass our people and eat out their substance. [See enforcement of Navigation Laws, p. 121.]

He has kept among us, in times of peace, standing armies, without the consent of our legislatures. [See pp. 116, 119.]

He has affected to render the military independent of, and superior to, the civil power.

He has combined with others to subject us to a jurisdiction foreign to our constitution, and unacknowledged by our laws, giving his assent to their acts of pretended legislation:

For quartering large bodies of armed troops among us [See Boston Massacre, p. 119];

For protecting them, by a mock trial, from punishment for any murders which they should commit on the inhabitants of these states [See 1774 Acts, p. 122];

For cutting off our trade with all parts of the world [See Boston Port Act, p. 122];

For imposing taxes on us without our consent [See Stamp Act, pp. 115–117];

For depriving us, in many cases, of the benefits of trial by jury;

For transporting us beyond seas, to be tried for pretended offenses;

For abolishing the free system of English laws in a neighboring province [Quebec], establishing therein an arbitrary government, and enlarging its boundaries, so as to render it at once an example and fit instrument for introducing the same absolute rule into these colonies [Quebec Act, p. 122];

For taking away our charters, abolishing our most valuable laws, and altering fundamentally the forms of our governments [e.g., in Massachusetts, p. 122];

For suspending our own legislatures, and declaring themselves invested with power to legislate for us in all cases whatsoever [See Stamp Act repeal, pp. 117–118.]

He has abdicated government here, by declaring us out of his protection and waging war against us. [Proclamation, pp. 133.]

He has plundered our seas, ravaged our coasts, burned our towns, and destroyed the lives of our people. [e.g., the burning of Falmouth (Portland), p. 133.]

He is at this time transporting large armies of foreign mercenaries [Hessians, p. 133] to complete the works of death, desolation, and tyranny already begun with circumstances of cruelty and perfidy scarcely paralleled in the most barbarous ages, and totally unworthy the head of a civilized nation.

He has constrained our fellow-citizens, taken captive on the high seas [by impressment], to bear arms against their country, to become the executioners of their friends and brethren, or to fall themselves by their hands.

He has excited domestic insurrection among us [i.e., among slaves], and has endeavored to bring on the inhabitants of our frontiers the merciless Indian savages, whose known rule of warfare is an undistinguished destruction of all ages, sexes, and conditions.

In every stage of these oppressions we have petitioned for redress in the most humble terms; our repeated petitions have been answered only by repeated injury. [e.g., pp. 132–134.] A prince, whose character is thus marked by every act which may define a tyrant, is unfit to be the ruler of a free people.

Nor have we been wanting in our attentions to our British brethren. We have warned them, from time to time, of attempts by their legislature to extend an unwarrantable jurisdiction over us. We have reminded them of the circumstances of our emigration and settlement here. We have appealed to their native justice and magnanimity; and we have conjured them, by the ties of our common kindred, to disavow these usurpations, which would inevitably interrupt our connections and correspondence. They, too, have been deaf to the voice of justice and of consanguinity [blood relationship]. We must, therefore, acquiesce in the necessity which denounces [announces] our separation, and hold them, as we hold the rest of mankind, enemies in war, in peace friends.

We, therefore, the representatives of the United States of America, in General Congress assembled, appealing to the Supreme Judge of the world for the rectitude of our intentions, do, in the name and by the authority of the good people of these colonies, solemnly publish and declare, That these United Colonies are, and of right ought to be, FREE AND INDEPENDENT STATES; that they are absolved from all allegiance to the British crown, and that all political connection between them and the state of Great Britain is, and ought to be, totally dissolved; and that, as free and independent states, they have full power to levy war, conclude peace, contract alliances, establish commerce, and do all other acts and things which independent states may of right do. And for the support of this declaration, with a firm reliance on the protection of Divine Providence, we mutually pledge to each other our lives, our fortunes, and our sacred honor.

[Signed by]

JOHN HANCOCK [President]
[and fifty-five others]

Constitution of the United States of America

[Boldface headings and bracketed explanatory matter and marginal comments (both in color) have been inserted for the reader's convenience. Passages that are no longer operative are printed in italic type.]

Article I. **PREAMBLE**

Section I. We the people of the United States, in order to form a more perfect union, establish justice, insure domestic tranquility, provide for the common defense, promote the general welfare, and secure the blessings of liberty to ourselves and our posterity, do ordain and establish this CONSTITUTION for the United States of America.

Section II. *Legislative Department*

Congress

Legislative power vested in a two-house Congress. All legislative powers herein granted shall be vested in a Congress of the United States, which shall consist of a Senate and a House of Representatives.

House of Representatives

1. The people elect representatives biennially. The House of Representatives shall be composed of members chosen every second year by the people of the several States, and the electors [voters] in each State shall have the qualifications requisite for electors of the most numerous branch of the State Legislature.

2. Who may be representatives. No person shall be a Representative who shall not have attained the age of twenty-five years, and been seven years a citizen of the United States, and who shall not, when elected, be an inhabitant of that State in which he shall be chosen.

See 1787 compromise, pp. 170–172.

See 1787 compromise, pp. 170–172.

3. Representation in the House based on population; census. Representatives and direct taxes[1] shall be apportioned among the several States which may be included within this Union, according to their respective numbers, *which shall be determined by adding to the whole number of free persons, including those bound to service for a term of years* [apprentices and indentured servants], *and excluding Indians not taxed, three-fifths of all other persons* [slaves].[2] The actual enumeration [census] shall be made within three years after the first meeting of the Congress of the United States, and within every subsequent term of ten years, in such manner as they shall by law direct. The number of Representatives shall not exceed one for every thirty thousand, but each State shall have at least one Representative; *and until such enumeration shall be made, the State of New Hampshire shall be entitled to choose three, Massachusetts eight, Rhode Island and Providence Plantations one, Connecticut five, New York six, New Jersey four, Pennsylvania eight, Delaware one, Maryland six, Virginia ten, North Carolina five, South Carolina five, and Georgia three.*

---

[1]Modified in 1913 by the Sixteenth Amendment re income taxes (see p. 665).

[2]The word *slave* appears nowhere in the original, unamended Constitution. The three-fifths rule ceased to be in force when the Thirteenth Amendment was adopted in 1865 (see p. 66 and amendments below).

4. Vacancies in the House are filled by election. When vacancies happen in the representation from any State, the Executive authority [governor] therefore shall issue writs of election [call a special election] to fill such vacancies.

See Chase and Johnson trials, pp. 210, 481; Nixon trial preliminaries, pp. 925–928; and discussion of Clinton's impeachment, pp. 970–971.

5. The House selects its Speaker; has sole power to vote impeachment charges (i.e., indictments). The House of Representatives shall choose their Speaker and other officers; and shall have the sole power of impeachment.

Section III. Senate

1. Senators represent the states. The Senate of the United States shall be composed of two Senators from each State, *chosen by the legislature thereof,*[1] for six Years; and each Senator shall have one vote.

2. One-third of senators chosen every two years; vacancies. *Immediately after they shall be assembled in consequence of the first election, they shall be divided as equally as may be into three classes. The seats of the Senators of the first class shall be vacated at the expiration of the second year, of the second class at the expiration of the fourth year, and of the third class at the expiration of the sixth year,* so that one-third may be chosen every second year; *and if vacancies happen by resignation or otherwise, during the recess of the legislature of any State, the Executive* [governor] *thereof may make temporary appointments until the next meeting of the legislature, which shall then fill such vacancies.*[2]

3. Who may be senators. No person shall be a Senator who shall not have attained to the age of thirty years, and been nine years a citizen of the United States, and who shall not, when elected, be an inhabitant of that State for which he shall be chosen.

4. The vice president presides over the Senate. The Vice President of the United States shall be President of the Senate, but shall have no vote, unless they be equally divided [tied].

5. The Senate chooses its other officers. The Senate shall choose their other officers, and also a President *pro tempore,* in the absence of the Vice President, or when he shall exercise the office of the President of the United States.

See Chase and Johnson trials, pp. 210, 481; and discussion of Clinton's impeachment, pp. 970–971.

6. The Senate has sole power to try impeachments. The Senate shall have the sole power to try all impeachments. When sitting for that purpose, they shall be on oath or affirmation. When the President of the United States is tried, the Chief Justice shall preside[3]: and no person shall be convicted without the concurrence of two-thirds of the members present.

7. Penalties for impeachment conviction. Judgment in cases of impeachment shall not extend further than to removal from office, and disqualification to hold and enjoy any office of honor, trust or profit under the United States: but the party convicted shall nevertheless be liable and subject to indictment, trial, judgment and punishment, according to law.

Section IV. Election and Meetings of Congress

1. Regulation of elections. The times, places and manner of holding elections for Senators and Representatives shall be prescribed in each State by the legislature thereof; but the Congress may at any time by law make or alter such regulations, except as to the places of choosing Senators.

2. Congress must meet once a year. The Congress shall assemble at least once in every year, and such meeting *shall be on the first Monday in December, unless they shall by law appoint a different day.*[4]

---

[1]Repealed in favor of popular election in 1913 by the Seventeenth Amendment.
[2]Changed in 1913 by the Seventeenth Amendment.
[3]The vice president, as next in line, would be an interested party.
[4]Changed in 1933 to January 3 by the Twentieth Amendment (see p. 770 and below).

Section V.   Organization and Rules of the Houses

1. Each house may reject members; quorums. Each house shall be the judge of the elections, returns and qualifications of its own members, and a majority of each shall constitute a quorum to do business; but a smaller number may adjourn from day to day, and may be authorized to compel the attendance of absent members, in such manner, and under such penalties, as each house may provide.

See "Bully" Brooks case, pp. 400–401.

2. Each house makes its own rules. Each house may determine the rules of its proceedings, punish its members for disorderly behavior, and with the concurrence of two-thirds, expel a member.

3. Each house must keep and publish a record of its proceedings. Each house shall keep a journal of its proceedings, and from time to time publish the same, excepting such parts as may in their judgment require secrecy; and the yeas and nays of the members of either house on any question shall, at the desire of one-fifth of those present, be entered on the journal.

4. Both houses must agree on adjournment. Neither house, during the session of Congress, shall, without the consent of the other, adjourn for more than three days, nor to any other place than that in which the two houses shall be sitting.

Section VI.   Privileges of and Prohibitions upon Congressmen

1. Congressional salaries; immunities. The Senators and Representatives shall receive a compensation for their services, to be ascertained by law and paid out of the treasury of the United States. They shall in all cases except treason, felony and breach of the peace, be privileged from arrest during their attendance at the session of their respective houses, and in going to and returning from the same; and for any speech or debate in either house, they shall not be questioned in any other place [i.e., they shall be immune from libel suits].

2. A congressman may not hold any other federal civil office. No Senator or Representative shall, during the time for which he was elected, be appointed to any civil office under the authority of the United States, which shall have been created, or the emoluments whereof shall have been increased, during such time; and no person holding any office under the United States shall be a member of either house during his continuance in office.

Section VII.   Method of Making Laws

See 1787 compromise, pp. 171–172.

1. Money bills must originate in the House. All bills for raising revenue shall originate in the House of Representatives; but the Senate may propose or concur with amendments as on other bills.

Nixon, more than any predecessors, "impounded" billions of dollars voted by Congress for specific purposes, because he disapproved of them. The courts generally failed to sustain him, and his impeachment foes regarded wholesale impoundment as a violation of his oath to "faithfully execute" the laws.

2. The president's veto power; Congress may override. Every bill which shall have passed the House of Representatives and the Senate, shall, before it become a law, be presented to the President of the United States; if he approve he shall sign it, but if not he shall return it with his objections to that house in which it shall have originated, who shall enter the objections at large on their journal, and proceed to reconsider it. If after such reconsideration two-thirds of that house shall agree to pass the bill, it shall be sent, together with the objections, to the other house, by which it shall likewise be reconsidered, and, if approved by two-thirds of that house, it shall become a law. But in all such cases the votes of both houses shall be determined by yeas and nays, and the names of the persons voting for and against the bill shall be entered on the journal of each house respectively. If any bill shall not be returned by the President within ten days (Sundays excepted) after it shall have been presented to him, the same shall be a law, in like manner as if he had signed it, unless the Congress by their adjournment prevent its return, in which case it shall not be a law [this is the so-called pocket veto].

3. All measures requiring the agreement of both houses go to president for approval. Every order, resolution, or vote to which the concurrence of the Senate and House of Representatives may be necessary (except on a question of adjournment) shall be presented to the President of the United States; and before the same shall take effect, shall be approved by him, or being disapproved by him, shall be repassed by two-thirds of the Senate and House of Representatives, according to the rules and limitations prescribed in the case of a bill.

Section VIII. **Powers Granted to Congress**

Congress has certain enumerated powers:

1. It may lay and collect taxes. The Congress shall have power to lay and collect taxes, duties, imposts, and excises, to pay the debts and provide for the common defense and general welfare of the United States; but all duties, imposts and excises shall be uniform throughout the United States;

2. It may borrow money. To borrow money on the credit of the United States;

3. It may regulate foreign and interstate trade. To regulate commerce with foreign nations, and among the several States, and with the Indian tribes;

For 1798 naturalization see p. 196. **4. It may pass naturalization and bankruptcy laws.** To establish an uniform rule of naturalization, and uniform laws on the subject of bankruptcies throughout the United States;

5. It may coin money. To coin money, regulate the value thereof, and of foreign coin, and fix the standard of weights and measures;

6. It may punish counterfeiters. To provide for the punishment of counterfeiting the securities and current coin of the United States;

7. It may establish a postal service. To establish post offices and post roads;

8. It may issue patents and copyrights. To promote the progress of science and useful arts by securing for limited times to authors and inventors the exclusive right to their respective writings and discoveries;

9. It may establish inferior courts. To constitute tribunals inferior to the Supreme Court;

See Judiciary Act of 1789, p. 182. **10. It may punish crimes committed on the high seas.** To define and punish piracies and felonies committed on the high seas [i.e., outside the three-mile limit] and offenses against the law of nations [international law];

11. It may declare war; authorize privateers. To declare war,[1] grant letters of marque and reprisal,[2] and make rules concerning captures on land and water;

12. It may maintain an army. To raise and support armies, but no appropriation of money to that use shall be for a longer term than two years;[3]

13. It may maintain a navy. To provide and maintain a navy;

14. It may regulate the army and navy. To make rules for the government and regulation of the land and naval forces;

15. It may call out the state militia. To provide for calling forth the militia to execute the laws of the Union, suppress insurrections, and repel invasions;

See Whiskey Rebellion, pp. 185–186. **16. It shares with the states control of militia.** To provide for organizing, arming, and disciplining the militia, and for governing such part of them as may be employed in the service of the United States, reserving to the States respectively the appointment of the officers, and the authority of training the militia according to the discipline prescribed by Congress;

17. It makes laws for the District of Columbia and other federal areas. To exercise exclusive legislation in all cases whatsoever, over such district (not exceeding ten miles square) as may, by cession of particular States, and the acceptance of Congress, become the seat of government of the United States,[1] and to exercise like

---

[1]Note that presidents, though they can provoke war (see the case of Polk, pp. 369–370) or wage it after it is declared, cannot declare it.

[2]Papers issued private citizens in wartime authorizing them to capture enemy ships.

[3]A reflection of fear of standing armies earlier expressed in the Declaration of Independence.

authority over all places purchased by the consent of the legislature of the State, in which the same shall be, for the erection of forts, magazines, arsenals, dock-yards, and other needful buildings;—and

Congress has certain implied powers:

This is the famous "elastic clause"; See p. 185.

18. It may make laws necessary for carrying out the enumerated powers. To make all laws which shall be necessary and proper for carrying into execution the foregoing powers, and all other powers vested by this Constitution in the government of the United States, or in any departure or officer thereof.

Section IX. Powers Denied to the Federal Government

See 1787 slave compromise, p. 172.

1. Congressional control of slave trade postponed until 1808. *The migration or importation of such persons as any of the States now existing shall think proper to admit shall not be prohibited by the Congress prior to the year 1808; but a tax or duty may be imposed on such importation, not exceeding $10 for each person.*

See Lincoln's unlawful suspension, p. 429.

2. The writ of habeas corpus[2] may be suspended only in cases of rebellion or invasion. The privilege of the writ of habeas corpus shall not be suspended, unless when in cases of rebellion or invasion the public safety may require it.

3. Attainders[3] and ex post facto laws[4] forbidden. No bill of attainder or ex post facto law shall be passed.

4. Direct taxes must be apportioned according to population. No capitation [head or poll tax] or other direct, tax shall be laid, unless in proportion to the census or enumeration herein before directed to be taken.[5]

5. Export taxes forbidden. No tax or duty shall be laid on articles exported from any State.

6. Congress must not discriminate among states in regulating commerce. No preference shall be given by any regulation of commerce or revenue to the ports of one State over those of another; nor shall vessels bound to, or from, one State, be obliged to enter, clear, or pay duties in another.

See Lincoln's unlawful infraction, p. 429.

7. Public money may not be spent without congressional appropriation; accounting. No money shall be drawn from the treasury, but in consequence of appropriations made by law; and a regular statement and account of the receipts and expenditures of all public money shall be published from time to time.

8. Titles of nobility prohibited; foreign gifts. No title of nobility shall be granted by the United States; and no person holding office of profit or trust under them, shall, without the consent of Congress, accept of any present, emolument, office, or title, of any kind whatever, from any king, prince, or foreign state.

Section X. Powers Denied to the States

Absolute prohibitions on the states:

On contracts see Fletcher v. Peck, *p. 238.*

1. The states are forbidden to do certain things. No State shall enter into any treaty, alliance, or confederation; grant letters of marque and reprisal [i.e., authorize privateers]; coin money; emit bills of credit [issue paper money]; make anything but

---

[1]The District of Columbia, ten miles square, was established in 1791 with a cession from Virginia (see p. 183).

[2]A writ of habeas corpus is a document that enables a person under arrest to obtain an immediate examination in court to ascertain whether he or she is being legally held.

[3]A bill of attainder is a special legislative act condemning and punishing an individual without a judicial trial.

[4]An ex post facto law is one that fixes punishments for acts committed before the law was passed.

[5]Modified in 1913 by the Sixteenth Amendment (see p. 742 and amendments below).

gold and silver coin a [legal] tender in payment of debts; pass any bill of attainder,[1] ex post facto,[1] or law impairing the obligation of contracts, or grant any title of nobility.

Conditional prohibitions on the states:

Cf. Confederation chaos, pp. 164–165.

2. The states may not levy duties without the consent of Congress. No State shall, without the consent of Congress, lay any imposts or duties on imports or exports, except what may be absolutely necessary for executing its inspection laws: and the net produce of all duties and imposts, laid by any State on imports or exports, shall be for the use of the treasury of the United States; and all such laws shall be subject to the revision and control of the Congress.

3. Certain other federal powers are forbidden the states except with the consent of Congress. No State shall, without the consent of Congress, lay any duty of tonnage [i.e., duty on ship tonnage], keep [nonmilitia] troops or ships of war in time of peace, enter into any agreement or compact with another State, or with a foreign power, or engage in war, unless actually invaded, or in such imminent danger as will not admit of delay.

Article II.   *Executive Department*

Section I.   President and Vice President

1. The president is the chief executive; term of office. The executive power shall be vested in a President of the United States of America. He shall hold his office during the term of four years,[2] and, together with the Vice President, chosen for the same term, be elected as follows:

See 1787 compromise, pp. 171–172.

See 1876 Oregon case, p. 494.

2. The president is chosen by electors. Each State shall appoint, in such manner as the legislature thereof may direct, a number of electors, equal to the whole number of Senators and Representatives to which the State may be entitled in the Congress; but no Senator or Representative, or person holding an office of trust or profit under the United States, shall be appointed an elector.

A majority of the electoral votes needed to elect a president. *The electors shall meet in their respective States, and vote by ballot for two persons, of whom one at least shall not be an inhabitant of the same State with themselves. And they shall make a list of all the persons voted for, and of the number of votes for each; which list they shall sign and certify, and transmit sealed to the seat of government of the United States, directed to the President of the Senate. The President of the Senate shall, in the presence of the Senate and House of Representatives, open all the certificates, and the votes shall be counted. The person having the greatest number of votes shall be the President, if such number be a majority of the whole number of electors appointed; and if there be more than one who have such major-*

See Burr-Jefferson disputed election of 1800, pp. 203–204.

ity, and have an equal number of votes, then the House of Representatives shall immediately choose by ballot one of them for President; and if no person have a majority, then from the five highest on the list the said house shall in like manner choose the President. But in choosing the President the votes shall be taken by States, the representation from each State having one vote; a quorum for this purpose shall consist of a member or members from two-thirds of the States, and a majority of all the States shall be necessary to a choice. In every case, after the choice of the President, the person having the greatest number of votes of the electors shall

See Jefferson as vice president in 1796, p. 194.

be the Vice President. But if there should remain two or more who have equal votes, the Senate shall choose from them by ballot the Vice President.[3]

---

[1]For definitions see footnotes 3 and 4 on preceding page.
[2]No reference to reelection; for anti–third term Twenty-second Amendment, see below.
[3]Repealed in 1804 by the Twelfth Amendment (for text see below).

3. Congress decides time of meeting of Electoral College. The Congress may determine the time of choosing the electors and the day on which they shall give their votes; which day shall be the same throughout the United States.

To provide for foreign-born people, like Alexander Hamilton, born in the British West Indies.

4. Who may be president. No person except a natural-born citizen, *or a citizen of the United States at the time of the adoption of this Constitution,* shall be eligible to the office of President; neither shall any person be eligible to that office who shall not have attained to the age of thirty-five years, and been fourteen years a resident within the United States [i.e., a legal resident].

Modified by Twentieth and Twenty-fifth Amendments below.

5. Replacements for president. In case of the removal of the President from office or of his death, resignation, or inability to discharge the powers and duties of said office, the same shall devolve on the Vice President, and the Congress may by law provide for the case of removal, death, resignation, or inability, both of the President and Vice President, declaring what officer shall then act as President, and such officer shall act accordingly, until the disability be removed, or a President shall be elected.

6. The president's salary. The President shall, at stated times, receive for his services a compensation, which shall neither be increased or diminished during the period for which he shall have been elected, and he shall not receive within that period any other emolument from the United States, or any of them.

7. The president's oath of office. Before he enter on the execution of his office, he shall take the following oath or affirmation:—"I do solemnly swear (or affirm) that I will faithfully execute the office of the President of the United States, and will to the best of my ability preserve, protect and defend the Constitution of the United States."

Section II.   Powers of the President

See cabinet evolution, p. 182.

1. The president has important military and civil powers. The President shall be commander in chief of the army and navy of the United States, and of the militia of the several States, when called into the actual service of the United States; he may require the opinion, in writing, of the principal officer in each of the executive departments, upon any subject relating to the duties of their respective offices, and he shall have power to grant reprieves and pardons for offenses against the United States, except in cases of impeachment.[1]

For president's removal power, see pp. 480–481.

2. The president may negotiate treaties and nominate federal officials. He shall have power, by and with the advice and consent of the Senate, to make treaties, provided two-thirds of the Senators present concur; and he shall nominate, and by and with the advice and consent of the Senate, shall appoint ambassadors, other public ministers and consuls, judges of the Supreme Court, and all other officers of the United States, whose appointments are not herein otherwise provided for, and which shall be established by law: but the Congress may by law vest the appointment of such inferior officers, as they think proper, in the President alone, in the courts of law, or in the heads of departments.

3. The president may fill vacancies during Senate recess. The President shall have power to fill up all vacancies that may happen during the recess of the Senate, by granting commissions which shall expire at the end of their next session.

Section III.   Other Powers and Duties of the President

For president's personal appearances, see p. 665.

Messages; extra sessions; receiving ambassadors; execution of the laws. He shall from time to time give to the Congress information of the state of the Union, and recommend to their consideration such measures as he shall judge necessary and expedient; he may, on extraordinary occasions, convene both houses, or either of

---

[1] To prevent the president's pardoning himself or his close associates, as was feared in the case of Richard Nixon. See p. 928.

them, and in case of disagreement between them, with respect to the time of adjournment, he may adjourn them to such time as he shall think proper; he shall receive ambassadors and other public ministers; he shall take care that the laws be faithfully executed, and shall commission all the officers of the United States.

Section IV.	Impeachment

See discussion of Presidents Johnson, pp. 480–481; Nixon, pp. 925–928; and Clinton, pp. 970–971.

Civil officers may be removed by impeachment. The President, Vice President and all civil officers[1] of the United States shall be removed from office on impeachment for, and on conviction of, treason, bribery, and other high crimes and misdemeanors.

Article III.	*Judicial Department*

Section I.	The Federal Courts

See Judiciary Act of 1789, p. 182.

The judicial power belongs to the federal courts. The judicial power of the United States shall be vested in one Supreme Court, and in such inferior courts as the Congress may from time to time ordain and establish. The judges, both of the Supreme and inferior courts, shall hold their offices during good behavior, and shall, at stated times, receive for their services a compensation which shall not be diminished[2] during their continuance in office.

Section II.	Jurisdiction of Federal Courts

1. Kinds of cases that may be heard. The judicial power shall extend to all cases, in law and equity, arising under this Constitution, the laws of the United States, and treaties made, or which shall be made, under their authority;—to all cases affecting ambassadors, other public ministers and consuls;—to all cases of admiralty and maritime jurisdiction;—to controversies to which the United States shall be a party;—to controversies between two or more States;—*between a State and citizens of another State*[3];—between citizens of different States;—between citizens of the same State claiming lands under grants of different States, and between a State, or the citizens thereof, and foreign states, citizens or subjects.

2. Jurisdiction of the Supreme Court. In all cases affecting ambassadors, other public ministers and consuls, and those in which a State shall be a party, the Supreme Court shall have original jurisdiction.[4] In all the other cases before mentioned, the Supreme Court shall have appellate jurisdiction,[5] both as to law and fact, with such exceptions, and under such regulations, as the Congress shall make.

3. Trial for federal crime is by jury. The trial of all crimes, except in cases of impeachment, shall be by jury; and such trial shall be held in the State where the said crimes shall have been committed; but when not committed within any State, the trial shall be at such place or places as the Congress may by law have directed.

---

[1] i.e., all federal executive and judicial officers, but not members of Congress or military personnel.

[2] In 1978, in a case involving federal judges, the Supreme Court ruled that diminution of salaries by inflation was irrelevant.

[3] The Eleventh Amendment (see below) restricts this to suits by a state against citizens of another state.

[4] i.e., such cases must originate in the Supreme Court.

[5] i.e., it hears other cases only when they are appealed to it from a lower federal court or a state court.

Section III.   **Treason**

See Burr trial, p. 215.

1. Treason defined. Treason against the United States shall consist only in levying war against them, or in adhering to their enemies, giving them aid and comfort. No person shall be convicted of treason unless on the testimony of two witnesses to the same overt act, or on confession in open court.

2. Congress fixes punishment for treason. The Congress shall have power to declare the punishment of treason, but no attainder of treason shall work corruption of blood, or forfeiture except during the life of the person attained.[1]

Article IV.   *Relations of the States to One Another*

Section I.   Credit to Acts, Records, and Court Proceedings

Each state must respect the public acts of the others. Full faith and credit shall be given in each State to the public acts, records, and judicial proceedings of every other State.[2] And the Congress may by general laws prescribe the manner in which such acts, records, and proceedings shall be proved [attested], and the effect thereof.

Section II.   Duties of States to States

1. Citizenship in one state is valid in all. The citizens of each State shall be entitled to all privileges and immunities of citizens in the several States.

This stipulation is sometimes openly flouted. In 1978 Governor Jerry Brown of California, acting on humanitarian grounds, refused to surrender to South Dakota an American Indian, Dennis Banks, who was charged with murder in an armed uprising.

2. Fugitives from justice must be surrendered by the state to which they have fled. A person charged in any State with treason, felony, or other crime, who shall flee from justice, and be found in another State, shall on demand of the executive authority [governor] of the State from which he fled, be delivered up, to be removed to the State having jurisdiction of the crime.

Basis of fugitive-slave laws; see pp. 385–386.

3. Slaves and apprentices must be returned. *No person held to service or labor in one State, under the laws thereof, escaping into another, shall, in consequence of any law or regulation therein, be discharged from such service or labor, but shall be delivered up on claim of the party to whom such service or labor may be due.*[3]

Section III.   New States and Territories

e.g., Maine (1820); see p. 234.

1. Congress may admit new states. New States may be admitted by the Congress into this Union; but no new State shall be formed or erected within the jurisdiction of any other State; nor any State be formed by the junction of two or more States, or parts of States, without the consent of the legislatures of the States concerned as well as of the Congress.[4]

2. Congress regulates federal territory and property. The Congress shall have power to dispose of and make all needful rules and regulations respecting the territory or other property belonging to the United States; and nothing in this Constitution shall be so construed as to prejudice any claims of the United States, or of any particular State.

Section IV.   Protection to the States

See Cleveland and the Pullman strike, p. 599.

United States guarantees to states representative government and protection against invasion and rebellion. The United States shall guarantee to every

---

[1]i.e., punishment only for the offender; none for his or her heirs.

[2]e.g., a marriage in one is valid in all.

[3]Invalidated in 1865 by the Thirteenth Amendment (for text see below).

[4]Loyal West Virginia was formed by Lincoln in 1862 from seceded Virginia. This act was of dubious constitutionality and was justified in part by the wartime powers of the president. See pp. 420–421.

State in this Union a republican form of government, and shall protect each of them against invasion; and on application of the legislature, or of the executive [governor] (when the legislature cannot be convened), against domestic violence.

Article V. *The Process of Amendment*

The Constitution may be amended in four ways. The Congress, whenever two-thirds of both houses shall deem it necessary, shall propose amendments to this Constitution, or, on the application of the legislature of two-thirds of the several States, shall call a convention for proposing amendments, which, in either case, shall be valid to all intents and purposes, as part of this Constitution, when ratified by the legislatures of three-fourths of the several States, or by conventions in three-fourths thereof, as the one or the other mode of ratification may be proposed by the Congress; provided *that no amendments which may be made prior to the year one thousand eight hundred and eight shall in any manner affect the first and fourth clauses in the ninth section of the first article;*[1] and that no State, without its consent, shall be deprived of its equal suffrage in the Senate.

Article VI. *General Provisions*

This pledge honored by Hamilton, pp. 182–183.

1. The debts of the Confederation are taken over. All debts contracted and engagements entered into, before the adoption of this Constitution, shall be as valid against the United States under this Constitution, as under the Confederation.

2. The Constitution, federal laws, and treaties are the supreme law of the land. This Constitution, and the laws of the United States which shall be made in pursuance thereof; and all treaties made, or which shall be made, under the authority of the United States, shall be the supreme law of the land; and the judges in every State shall be bound thereby, anything in the Constitution or laws of any State to the contrary notwithstanding.

3. Federal and state officers bound by oath to support the Constitution. The Senators and Representatives before mentioned, and the members of the several State legislatures, and all executive and judicial officers, both of the United States and of the several States, shall be bound by oath or affirmation to support this Constitution; but no religious test shall ever be required as a qualification to any office or public trust under the United States.

Article VII. *Ratification of the Constitution*

See 1787 irregularity, pp. 172–174.

The Constitution effective when ratified by conventions in nine states. The ratification of the conventions of nine States shall be sufficient for the establishment of this Constitution between the States so ratifying the same.

Done in Convention by the unanimous consent of the States present, the seventeenth day of September in the year of our Lord one thousand seven hundred and eighty-seven and of the Independence of the United States of America the twelfth. In witness whereof we have hereunto subscribed our names.

[Signed by]

G° WASHINGTON
Presidt and Deputy from Virginia
[and thirty-eight others]

---

[1]This clause, regarding slave trade and direct taxes, became inoperative in 1808.

AMENDMENTS TO THE CONSTITUTION

Amendment I. *Religious and Political Freedom*

For background of Bill of Rights, see pp. 181–182.

Congress must not interfere with freedom of religion, speech or press, assembly, and petition. Congress shall make no law respecting an establishment of religion,[1] or prohibiting the free exercise thereof; or abridging the freedom of speech, or of the press; or the right of the people peaceably to assemble, and to petition the government for a redress of grievances.

Amendment II. *Right to Bear Arms*

The people may bear arms. A well-regulated militia being necessary to the security of a free State, the right of the people to keep and bear arms [i.e., for military purposes] shall not be infringed.[2]

Amendment III. *Quartering of Troops*

See Declaration of Independence and British quartering above.

Soldiers may not be arbitrarily quartered on the people. No soldier shall, in time of peace, be quartered in any house without the consent of the owner, nor in time of war, but in a manner to be prescribed by law.

Amendment IV. *Searches and Seizures*

A reflection of colonial grievances against the crown.

Unreasonable searches are forbidden. The right of the people to be secure in their persons, houses, papers, and effects, against unreasonable searches and seizures, shall not be violated, and no [search] warrants shall issue but upon probable cause, supported by oath or affirmation, and particularly describing the place to be searched, and the persons or things to be seized.

Amendment V. *Right to Life, Liberty, and Property*

When witnesses refuse to answer questions in court, they routinely "take the Fifth Amendment."

The individual is guaranteed certain rights when on trial and the right to life, liberty, and property. No person shall be held to answer for a capital, or otherwise infamous crime, unless on a presentment [formal charge] or indictment of a grand jury, except in cases arising in the naval forces, or in the militia, when in actual service in time of war or public danger; nor shall any person be subject for the same offense to be twice put in jeopardy of life or limb; nor shall be compelled in any criminal case to be a witness against himself, nor be deprived of life, liberty, or property, without due process of law; nor shall private property be taken for public use [i.e., by eminent domain] without just compensation.

Amendment VI. *Protection in Criminal Trials*

See Declaration of Independence above.

An accused person has important rights. In all criminal prosecutions, the accused shall enjoy the right to a speedy and public trial, by an impartial jury of the State and district wherein the crime shall have been committed, which district shall

---

[1] In 1787 "an establishment of religion" referred to an "established church," or one supported by all taxpayers, whether members or not. But the courts have often acted under this article to keep religion, including prayers, out of the public schools.

[2] The courts long held that the right to bear arms was a limited right linked to the maintenance of militias. But in the case of *District of Columbia v. Heller* in 2008, the Supreme Court defined the right to bear arms as an individual right, not contingent on "participation in some corporate body." Yet the Court still left the door open to some kinds of gun-control legislation.

have been previously ascertained by law, and to be informed of the nature and cause of the accusation; to be confronted with the witnesses against him; to have compulsory process [subpoena] for obtaining witnesses in his favor, and to have the assistance of counsel for his defense.

Amendment VII.   *Suits at Common Law*

The rules of common law are recognized. In suits at common law, where the value in controversy shall exceed twenty dollars, the right of trial by jury shall be preserved, and no fact tried by a jury shall be otherwise re-examined in any court of the United States, than according to the rules of the common law.

Amendment VIII.   *Bail and Punishments*

Excessive fines and unusual punishments are forbidden. Excessive bail shall not be required, nor excessive fines imposed, nor cruel and unusual punishment inflicted.

Amendment IX.   *Concerning Rights Not Enumerated*

The Ninth and Tenth Amendments were bulwarks of southern states' rights before the Civil War.

The people retain rights not here enumerated. The enumeration in the Constitution, of certain rights, shall not be construed to deny or disparage others retained by the people.

Amendment X.   *Powers Reserved to the States and to the People*

A concession to states' rights, p. 183.

Powers not delegated to the federal government are reserved to the states and the people. The powers not delegated to the United States by the Constitution, nor prohibited by it to the States, are reserved to the States respectively, or to the people.

Amendment XI.   *Suits Against a State*

The federal courts have no authority in suits by citizens against a state. The judicial power of the United States shall not be construed to extend to any suit in law or equity, commenced or prosecuted against one of the United States by citizens of another State, or by citizens or subjects of any foreign state. [Adopted 1798.]

Amendment XII.   *Election of President and Vice President*

Forestalls repetition of 1800 electoral dispute, pp. 203–204.

See 1876 disputed election. pp. 494–496.

See 1824 election, pp. 246–248.

1. Changes in manner of electing president and vice president; procedure when no presidential candidate receives electoral majority. The electors shall meet in their respective States, and vote by ballot for President and Vice President, one of whom, at least, shall not be an inhabitant of the same state with themselves; they shall name in their ballots the person voted for as President, and in distinct ballots the person voted for as Vice President, and they shall make distinct lists of all persons voted for as President, and of all persons voted for as Vice President, and of the number of votes for each, which lists they shall sign and certify, and transmit sealed to the seat of government of the United States, directed to the President of the Senate;—the President of the Senate shall, in the presence of the Senate and House of Representatives, open all the certificates and the votes shall be counted;—the person having the greatest number of votes for President shall be the President, if such number be a majority of the whole number of electors appointed; and if no person have such majority, then from the persons having the highest numbers not exceeding three on the list of those voted for as President, the House of

Representatives shall choose immediately, by ballot, the President. But in choosing the President, the votes shall be taken by States, the representation from each State having one vote; a quorum for this purpose shall consist of a member or members from two-thirds of the States, and a majority of all the States shall be necessary to a choice. And if the House of Representatives shall not choose a President whenever the right of choice shall devolve upon them, before *the fourth day of March*[1] next following, then the Vice President shall act as President, as in the case of the death or other constitutional disability of the President.

2. Procedure when no vice presidential candidate receives electoral majority. The person having the greatest number of votes as Vice President, shall be the Vice President, if such number be a majority of the whole number of electors appointed; and if no person have a majority, then from the two highest numbers on the list the Senate shall choose the Vice President; a quorum for the purpose shall consist of two-thirds of the whole number of Senators, and a majority of the whole number shall be necessary to a choice. But no person constitutionally ineligible to the office of President shall be eligible to that of Vice President of the United States. [Adopted 1804.]

Amendment XIII. *Slavery Prohibited*

For background see pp. 441–443.

Slavery forbidden. 1. Neither slavery[2] nor involuntary servitude, except as a punishment for crime whereof the party shall have been duly convicted, shall exist within the United States, or any place subject to their jurisdiction.

2. Congress shall have power to enforce this article by appropriate legislation. [Adopted 1865.]

Amendment XIV. *Civil Rights for Ex-slaves,[3] etc.*

For background see pp. 473–474.

For corporations as "persons," see p. 525.

Abolishes three-fifths rule for slaves, Art. I., Sec. II, para. 3.

1. Ex-slaves made citizens; U.S. citizenship primary. All persons born or naturalized in the United States, and subject to the jurisdiction thereof, are citizens of the United States and of the State wherein they reside. No State shall make or enforce any law which shall abridge the privileges or immunities of citizens of the United States; nor shall any State deprive any person of life, liberty, or property, without due process of law; nor deny to any person within its jurisdiction the equal protection of the laws.

2. When a state denies citizens the vote, its representation shall be reduced. Representatives shall be apportioned among the several States according to their respective numbers, counting the whole number of persons in each State, excluding Indians not taxed. But when the right to vote at any election for the choice of Electors for President and Vice President of the United States, Representatives in Congress, the executive and judicial officers of a State, or the members of the legislature thereof, is denied to any of the male inhabitants of such State, being twenty-one years of age and citizens of the United States, or in any way abridged, except for participation in rebellion, or other crime, the basis of representation therein shall be reduced in the proportion which the number of such make citizens shall bear to the whole number of male citizens twenty-one years of age in such State.[4]

Leading ex-Confederates denied office. See p. 474.

3. Certain persons who have been in rebellion are ineligible for federal and state office. No person shall be a Senator or Representative in Congress, or Elector of President and Vice President, or hold any office, civil or military, under the

---

[1]Changed to January 20 by the Twentieth Amendment (for text see below).

[2]The only explicit mention of slavery in the Constitution.

[3]Occasionally an offender is prosecuted under the Thirteenth Amendment for keeping an employee or other person under conditions approximating slavery.

[4]The provisions concerning "male" inhabitants were modified by the Nineteenth Amendment, which enfranchised women. The legal voting age was changed from twenty-one to eighteen by the Twenty-sixth Amendment.

United States, or under any State, who, having previously taken an oath, as a member of Congress, or as an officer of the United States, or as a member of any State legislature, or as an executive or judicial officer of any State, to support the Constitution of the United States, shall have engaged in insurrection or rebellion against the same, or given aid or comfort to the enemies thereof. But Congress may, by a vote of two-thirds of each house, remove such disability.

The ex-Confederates were thus forced to repudiate their debts and pay pensions to their own veterans, plus taxes for the pensions of Union veterans, their conquerors.

4. Debts incurred in aid of rebellion are void. The validity of the public debt of the United States, authorizing by law, including debts incurred for payment of pensions and bounties for services in suppressing insurrection or rebellion, shall not be questioned. But neither the United States nor any State shall assume or pay any debt or obligation incurred in aid of insurrection or rebellion against the United States, or any claim for the loss or emancipation of any slave; but all such debts, obligations, and claims shall be held illegal and void.

5. Enforcement. The Congress shall have power to enforce, by appropriate legislation, the provisions of this article. [Adopted 1868.]

Amendment XV. *Suffrage for Blacks*

For background see p. 475.

Black males are made voters. 1. The right of the citizens of the United States to vote shall not be denied or abridged by the United States or by any State on account of race, color, or previous condition of servitude.

2. The Congress shall have power to enforce this article by appropriate legislation. [Adopted 1870.]

Amendment XVI. *Income Taxes*

For background see p. 665.

Congress has power to lay and collect income taxes. The Congress shall have power to lay and collect taxes on incomes, from whatever source derived, without apportionment among the several States, and without regard to any census or enumeration. [Adopted 1913.]

Amendment XVII. *Direct Election of Senators*

Senators shall be elected by popular vote. 1. The Senate of the United States shall be composed of two Senators from each State, elected by the people thereof, for six years; and each Senator shall have one vote. The electors in each State shall have the qualifications requisite for electors of [voters for] the most numerous branch of the State legislatures.

2. When vacancies happen in the representation of any State in the Senate, the executive authority of such State shall issue writs of election to fill such vacancies: Provided, that the Legislature of any State may empower the executive thereof to make temporary appointments until the people fill the vacancies by election as the Legislature may direct.

3. This amendment shall not be so construed as to affect the election or term of any Senator chosen before it becomes valid as part of the Constitution. [Adopted 1913.]

Amendment XVIII. *National Prohibition*

For background see pp. 704–705.

The sale or manufacture of intoxicating liquors is forbidden. 1. *After one year from the ratification of this article the manufacture, sale, or transportation of intoxicating liquors within, the importation thereof into, or the exportation thereof from the United States and all territory subject to the jurisdiction thereof, for beverage purposes, is hereby prohibited.*

2. *The Congress and the several States shall have concurrent power to enforce this article by appropriate legislation.*

3. *This article shall be inoperative unless it shall have been ratified as an amendment to the Constitution by the legislatures of the several States, as provided by the Constitution, within seven years from the date of the submission thereof to the States by the Congress.* [Adopted 1919; repealed 1933 by Twenty-first Amendment.]

Amendment XIX. Woman Suffrage

For background see pp. 683–684.

Women guaranteed the right to vote. 1. The right of citizens of the United States to vote shall not be denied or abridged by the United States or by any State on account of sex.

2. Congress shall have power to enforce this article by appropriate legislation. [Adopted 1920.]

Amendment XX. *Presidential and Congressional Terms*

Shortens lame duck periods by modifying Art. I, Sec. IV, para. 2.

1. Presidential, vice presidential, and congressional terms of office begin in January. The terms of the President and Vice President shall end at noon on the 20th day of January, and the terms of Senators and Representatives at noon on the 3d day of January, of the years in which such terms would have ended if this article had not been ratified; and the terms of their successors shall then begin.

2. New meeting date for Congress. The Congress shall assemble at least once in every year, and such meeting shall begin at noon on the 3d day of January, unless they shall by law appoint a different day.

3. Emergency presidential and vice presidential succession. If, at the time fixed for the beginning of the term of the President, the President-elect shall have died, the Vice President–elect shall become President. If a President shall not have been chosen before the time fixed for the beginning of his term, or if the President-elect shall have failed to qualify, then the Vice President–elect shall act as President until a President shall have qualified; and the Congress may by law provide for the case wherein neither a President-elect nor a Vice President–elect shall have qualified, declaring who shall then act as President, or the manner in which one who is to act shall be selected, and such persons shall act accordingly until a President or Vice President shall have qualified.

4. The Congress may by law provide for the case of the death of any of the persons from whom the House of Representatives may choose a President whenever the right of choice shall have devolved upon them, and for the case of the death of any of the persons from whom the Senate may choose a Vice President whenever the right of choice shall have devolved upon them.

5. Sections 1 and 2 shall take effect on the 15th day of October following the ratification of this article.

6. This article shall be inoperative unless it shall have been ratified as an amendment to the Constitution by the Legislatures of three-fourths of the several States within seven years from the date of its submission. [Adopted 1933.]

Amendment XXI. *Prohibition Repealed*

For background see pp. 762–763.

1. Eighteenth Amendment repealed. The eighteenth article of amendment to the Constitution of the United States is hereby repealed.

2. Local laws honored. The transportation or importation into any State, Territory, or Possession of the United States for delivery or use therein of intoxicating liquors, in violation of the laws thereof, is hereby prohibited.

3. This article shall be inoperative unless it shall have been ratified as an amendment to the Constitution by conventions in the several States, as provided in the Constitution, within seven years from the date of the submission thereof to the States by the Congress. [Adopted 1933.]

Amendment XXII.

Sometimes referred to as the anti–Franklin Roosevelt amendment.

Anti–Third Term Amendment

1. Presidential term is limited. No person shall be elected to the office of President more than twice, and no person who has held the office of President, or acted as President, for more than two years of a term to which some other person was elected President shall be elected to the office of President more than once. But this article shall not apply to any person holding the office of President when this article was proposed by the Congress [i.e., Truman], and shall not prevent any person who may be holding the office of President, during the term within which this article becomes operative [i.e., Truman] from holding the office of President or acting as President during the remainder of such term.

2. This article shall be inoperative unless it shall have been ratified as an amendment to the Constitution by the legislatures of three-fourths of the several States within seven years from the date of its submission to the States by the Congress. [Adopted 1951.]

Amendment XXIII.

Designed to give the District of Columbia three electoral votes and to quiet the century-old cry of "No taxation without representation." Yet the District of Columbia still has only one nonvoting member of Congress.

District of Columbia Vote

1. Presidential electors for the District of Columbia. The District, constituting the seat of government of the United States, shall appoint in such manner as the Congress shall direct:

A number of electors of President and Vice President equal to the whole number of Senators and Representatives in Congress to which the District would be entitled if it were a State, but in no event more than the least populous State; they shall be in addition to those appointed by the States, but they shall be considered for the purposes of the election of President and Vice President, to be electors appointed by a State; and they shall meet in the District and perform such duties as provided by the twelfth article of amendment.

2. Enforcement. The Congress shall have the power to enforce this article by appropriate legislation. [Adopted 1961.]

Amendment XXIV.

Designed to end discrimination against poor people, including southern blacks who were often denied the vote through inability to pay poll taxes. See p. 903.

Poll Tax

1. Payment of poll tax or other taxes not to be prerequisite for voting in federal elections. The right of citizens of the United States to vote in any primary or other election for President or Vice President, for electors for President or Vice President, or for Senator or Representative in Congress, shall not be denied or abridged by the United States or any State by reason of failure to pay any poll tax or other tax.

2. Enforcement. The Congress shall have the power to enforce this article by appropriate legislation. [Adopted 1964.]

Amendment XXV.

Gerald Ford was the first "appointed president." See pp. 926, 928.

Presidential Succession and Disability

1. Vice president to become president. In case of the removal of the President from office or of his death or resignation, the Vice President shall become President.[1]

2. Successor to vice president provided. Whenever there is a vacancy in the office of the Vice President, the President shall nominate a Vice President who shall take office upon confirmation by a majority vote of both Houses of Congress.

---

[1]The original Constitution (Art. II, Sec. I, para. 5) was vague on this point, stipulating that "the powers and duties" of the president, but not necessarily the title, should "devolve" on the vice president. President Tyler, the first "accidental president," assumed not only the powers and duties but the title as well.

3. Vice president to serve for disabled president. Whenever the President transmits to the President pro tempore of the Senate and the Speaker of the House of Representatives his written declaration that he is unable to discharge the powers and duties of his office, and until he transmits to them a written declaration to the contrary, such powers and duties shall be discharged by the Vice President as Acting President.

4. Procedure for disqualifying or requalifying president. Whenever the Vice President and a majority of either the principal officers of the executive departments or of such other body as Congress may by law provide, transmit to the President pro tempore of the Senate and the Speaker of the House of Representatives their written declaration that the President is unable to discharge the powers and duties of his office, the Vice President shall immediately assume the powers and duties of the office as Acting President.

Thereafter, when the President transmits to the President pro tempore of the Senate and the Speaker of the House of Representatives his written declaration that no inability exists, he shall resume the powers and duties of his office unless the Vice President and a majority of either the principal officers of the executive department[s] or of such other body as Congress may by law provide, transmit within four days to the President pro tempore of the Senate and the Speaker of the House of Representatives their written declaration that the President is unable to discharge the powers and duties of his office. Thereupon Congress shall decide the issue, assembling within forty-eight hours for that purpose if not in session. If the Congress, within twenty-one days after receipt of the latter written declaration, or, if Congress is not in session, within twenty-one days after Congress is required to assemble, determines by two-thirds vote of both Houses that the President is unable to discharge the powers and duties of his office, the Vice President shall continue to discharge the same as Acting President; otherwise, the President shall resume the powers and duties of his office. [Adopted 1967.]

Amendment XXVI.

Lowering Voting Age

A response to the current revolt of youth. See p. 919.

1. Ballot for eighteen-year-olds. The right of citizens of the United States, who are eighteen years of age or older, to vote shall not be denied or abridged by the United States or any state on account of age.

2. Enforcement. The Congress shall have the power to enforce this article by appropriate legislation. [Adopted 1971.]

Amendment XXVII.

Restricting Congressional Pay Raises

Reflects anti-incumbent sentiment of early 1990s. First proposed by James Madison in 1789; took 203 years to be ratified.

Congress not allowed to increase its current pay. No law varying the compensation for the services of the Senators and Representatives shall take effect, until an election of Representatives shall have intervened. [Adopted 1992.]

TABLES

Table A.1 Presidential Elections*

Election	Candidates	Parties	Popular Vote	Electoral Vote
1789	GEORGE WASHINGTON	No party designation		69
	JOHN ADAMS			34
	MINOR CANDIDATES			35
1792	GEORGE WASHINGTON	No party designation		132
	JOHN ADAMS			77
	GEORGE CLINTON			50
	MINOR CANDIDATES			5
1796	JOHN ADAMS	Federalist		71
	THOMAS JEFFERSON	Democratic-Republican		68
	THOMAS PINCKNEY	Federalist		59
	AARON BURR	Democratic-Republican		30
	MINOR CANDIDATES			48
1800	THOMAS JEFFERSON	Democratic-Republican		73
	AARON BURR	Democratic-Republican		73
	JOHN ADAMS	Federalist		65
	CHARLES C. PINCKNEY	Federalist		64
	JOHN JAY	Federalist		1
1804	THOMAS JEFFERSON	Democratic-Republican		162
	CHARLES C. PINCKNEY	Federalist		14
1808	JAMES MADISON	Democratic-Republican		122
	CHARLES C. PINCKNEY	Federalist		47
	GEORGE CLINTON	Democratic-Republican		6
1812	JAMES MADISON	Democratic-Republican		128
	DEWITT CLINTON	Federalist		89
1816	JAMES MONROE	Democratic-Republican		183
	RUFUS KING	Federalist		34
1820	JAMES MONROE	Democratic-Republican		231
	JOHN Q. ADAMS	Independent Republican		1
1824	JOHN Q. ADAMS (Min.)†	Democratic-Republican	108,740	84
	ANDREW JACKSON	Democratic-Republican	153,544	99
	WILLIAM H. CRAWFORD	Democratic-Republican	46,618	41
	HENRY CLAY	Democratic-Republican	47,136	37
1828	ANDREW JACKSON	Democratic	647,286	178
	JOHN Q. ADAMS	National Republican	508,064	83
1832	ANDREW JACKSON	Democratic	687,502	219
	HENRY CLAY	National Republican	530,189	49
	WILLIAM WIRT	Anti-Masonic	33,108	7
	JOHN FLOYD	National Republican		11
1836	MARTIN VAN BUREN	Democratic	765,483	170
	WILLIAM H. HARRISON	Whig		73
	HUGH L. WHITE	Whig	739,795	26
	DANIEL WEBSTER	Whig		14
	W. P. MANGUM	Whig		11

* Candidates receiving less than 1 percent of the popular vote are omitted. Before the Twelfth Amendment (1804), the Electoral College voted for two presidential candidates, and the runner-up became vice president. Basic figures are taken primarily from *Historical Statistics of the United States, Colonial Times to 1970* (1975), pp. 1073–1074, and *Statistical Abstract of the United States,* relevant years.
† "Min." indicates minority president—one receiving less than 50 percent of all popular votes.

Presidential Elections (continued)

Election	Candidates	Parties	Popular Vote	Electoral Vote
1840	WILLIAM H. HARRISON	Whig	1,274,624	234
	MARTIN VAN BUREN	Democratic	1,127,781	60
1844	JAMES K. POLK (Min.)†	Democratic	1,338,464	170
	HENRY CLAY	Whig	1,300,097	105
	JAMES G. BIRNEY	Liberty	62,300	0
1848	ZACHARY TAYLOR	Whig	1,360,967	163
	LEWIS CASS	Democratic	1,222,342	127
	MARTIN VAN BUREN	Free Soil	291,263	0
1852	FRANKLIN PIERCE	Democratic	1,601,117	254
	WINFIELD SCOTT	Whig	1,385,453	42
	JOHN P. HALE	Free Soil	155,825	0
1856	JAMES BUCHANAN (Min.)*	Democratic	1,832,955	174
	JOHN C. FRÉMONT	Republican	1,339,932	114
	MILLARD FILLMORE	American	871,731	8
1860	ABRAHAM LINCOLN (Min.)*	Republican	1,865,593	180
	STEPHEN A. DOUGLAS	Democratic	1,382,713	12
	JOHN C. BRECKINRIDGE	Democratic	848,356	72
	JOHN BELL	Constitutional Union	592,906	39
1864	ABRAHAM LINCOLN	Union	2,206,938	212
	GEORGE B. MC CLELLAN	Democratic	1,803,787	21
1868	ULYSSES S. GRANT	Republican	3,013,421	214
	HORATIO SEYMOUR	Democratic	2,706,829	80
1872	ULYSSES S. GRANT	Republican	3,596,745	286
	HORACE GREELEY	Democratic Liberal Republican	2,843,446	66
1876	RUTHERFORD B. HAYES (Min.)*	Republican	4,036,572	185
	SAMUEL J. TILDEN	Democratic	4,284,020	184
1880	JAMES A. GARFIELD (Min.)*	Republican	4,453,295	214
	WINFIELD S. HANCOCK	Democratic	4,414,082	155
	JAMES B. WEAVER	Greenback-Labor	308,578	0
1884	GROVER CLEVELAND (Min.)*	Democratic	4,879,507	219
	JAMES G. BLAINE	Republican	4,850,293	182
	BENJAMIN F. BUTLER	Greenback-Labor	175,370	0
	JOHN P. ST. JOHN	Prohibition	150,369	0
1888	BENJAMIN HARRISON (Min.)*	Republican	5,447,129	233
	GROVER CLEVELAND	Democratic	5,537,857	168
	CLINTON B. FISK	Prohibition	249,506	0
	ANSON J. STREETER	Union Labor	146,935	0
1892	GROVER CLEVELAND (Min.)*	Democratic	5,555,426	277
	BENJAMIN HARRISON	Republican	5,182,690	145
	JAMES B. WEAVER	People's	1,029,846	22
	JOHN BIDWELL	Prohibition	264,133	0
1896	WILLIAM MC KINLEY	Republican	7,102,246	271
	WILLIAM J. BRYAN	Democratic	6,492,559	176
1900	WILLIAM MC KINLEY	Republican	7,218,491	292
	WILLIAM J. BRYAN	Democratic; Populist	6,356,734	155
	JOHN C. WOOLLEY	Prohibition	208,914	0
1904	THEODORE ROOSEVELT	Republican	7,628,461	336
	ALTON B. PARKER	Democratic	5,084,223	140
	EUGENE V. DEBS	Socialist	402,283	0
	SILAS C. SWALLOW	Prohibition	258,536	0

* "Min." indicates minority president—one receiving less than 50 percent of all popular votes.

Presidential Elections (continued)

Election	Candidates	Parties	Popular Vote	Electoral Vote
1908	WILLIAM H. TAFT	Republican	7,675,320	321
	WILLIAM J. BRYAN	Democratic	6,412,294	162
	EUGENE V. DEBS	Socialist	420,793	0
	EUGENE W. CHAFIN	Prohibition	253,840	0
1912	WOODROW WILSON (Min.)*	Democratic	6,296,547	435
	THEODORE ROOSEVELT	Progressive	4,118,571	88
	WILLIAM H. TAFT	Republican	3,486,720	8
	EUGENE V. DEBS	Socialist	900,672	0
	EUGENE W. CHAFIN	Prohibition	206,275	0
1916	WOODROW WILSON (Min.)*	Democratic	9,127,695	277
	CHARLES E. HUGHES	Republican	8,533,507	254
	A. L. BENSON	Socialist	585,113	0
	J. F. HANLY	Prohibition	220,506	0
1920	WARREN G. HARDING	Republican	16,143,407	404
	JAMES M. COX	Democratic	9,130,328	127
	EUGENE V. DEBS	Socialist	919,799	0
	P. P. CHRISTENSEN	Farmer-Labor	265,411	0
1924	CALVIN COOLIDGE	Republican	15,718,211	382
	JOHN W. DAVIS	Democratic	8,385,283	136
	ROBERT M. LA FOLLETTE	Progressive	4,831,289	13
1928	HERBERT C. HOOVER	Republican	21,391,993	444
	ALFRED E. SMITH	Democratic	15,016,169	87
1932	FRANKLIN D. ROOSEVELT	Democratic	22,809,638	472
	HERBERT C. HOOVER	Republican	15,758,901	59
	NORMAN THOMAS	Socialist	881,951	0
1936	FRANKLIN D. ROOSEVELT	Democratic	27,752,869	523
	ALFRED M. LANDON	Republican	16,674,665	8
	WILLIAM LEMKE	Union	882,479	0
1940	FRANKLIN D. ROOSEVELT	Democratic	27,307,819	449
	WENDELL L. WILLKIE	Republican	22,321,018	82
1944	FRANKLIN D. ROOSEVELT	Democratic	25,606,585	432
	THOMAS E. DEWEY	Republican	22,014,745	99
1948	HARRY S TRUMAN (Min.)*	Democratic	24,179,345	303
	THOMAS E. DEWEY	Republican	21,991,291	189
	J. STROM THURMOND	States' Rights Democratic	1,176,125	39
	HENRY A. WALLACE	Progressive	1,157,326	0
1952	DWIGHT D. EISENHOWER	Republican	33,936,234	442
	ADLAI E. STEVENSON	Democratic	27,314,992	89
1956	DWIGHT D. EISENHOWER	Republican	35,590,472	457
	ADLAI E. STEVENSON	Democratic	26,022,752	73
1960	JOHN F. KENNEDY (Min.)*†	Democratic	34,226,731	303
	RICHARD M. NIXON	Republican	34,108,157	219
1964	LYNDON B. JOHNSON	Democratic	43,129,566	486
	BARRY M. GOLDWATER	Republican	27,178,188	52
1968	RICHARD M. NIXON (Min.)*	Republican	31,785,480	301
	HUBERT H. HUMPHREY, JR.	Democratic	31,275,166	191
	GEORGE C. WALLACE	American Independent	9,906,473	46
1972	RICHARD M. NIXON	Republican	47,169,911	520
	GEORGE S. MC GOVERN	Democratic	29,170,383	17

* "Min." indicates minority president—one receiving less than 50 percent of all popular votes.
† Six Democratic electors in Alabama, all eight unpledged Democratic electors in Mississippi, and one Republican elector in Oklahoma voted for Senator Harry F. Byrd.

Presidential Elections (continued)

Election	Candidates	Parties	Popular Vote	Electoral Vote
1976	JIMMY CARTER	Democratic	40,828,657	297
	GERALD R. FORD	Republican	39,145,520	240
1980	RONALD W. REAGAN	Republican	43,899,248	489
	JIMMY CARTER	Democratic	35,481,435	49
	JOHN B. ANDERSON	Independent	5,719,437	0
1984	RONALD W. REAGAN	Republican	52,609,797	525
	WALTER MONDALE	Democratic	36,450,613	13
1988	GEORGE BUSH	Republican	47,946,422	426
	MICHAEL DUKAKIS	Democratic	41,016,429	111
1992	WILLIAM CLINTON (Min.)*	Democratic	44,909,889	370
	GEORGE BUSH	Republican	39,104,545	168
	H. ROSS PEROT	Independent	19,742,267	0
1996	WILLIAM CLINTON (Min.)*	Democratic	47,401,898	379
	ROBERT DOLE	Republican	39,198,482	159
	H. ROSS PEROT	Reform	7,874,283	0
2000	GEORGE W. BUSH (Min.)*	Republican	50,456,002	271
	ALBERT GORE, JR.	Democratic	50,999,897	266
	RALPH NADER	Green	2,783,728	0
2004	GEORGE W. BUSH	Republican	60,693,281	286
	JOHN KERRY	Democratic	57,355,978	252
	RALPH NADER	Green	405,623	0
2008	BARACK OBAMA	Democratic	65,980,131	364
	JOHN MC CAIN	Republican	57,779,170	174

* "Min." indicates minority president—one receiving less than 50 percent of all popular votes.

Table A.2 Presidents and Vice Presidents

Term	President	Vice President
1789–1793	George Washington	John Adams
1793–1797	George Washington	John Adams
1797–1801	John Adams	Thomas Jefferson
1801–1805	Thomas Jefferson	Aaron Burr
1805–1809	Thomas Jefferson	George Clinton
1809–1813	James Madison	George Clinton (d. 1812)
1813–1817	James Madison	Elbridge Gerry (d. 1814)
1817–1821	James Monroe	Daniel D. Tompkins
1821–1825	James Monroe	Daniel D. Tompkins
1825–1829	John Quincy Adams	John C. Calhoun
1829–1833	Andrew Jackson	John C. Calhoun (resigned 1832)
1833–1837	Andrew Jackson	Martin Van Buren
1837–1841	Martin Van Buren	Richard M. Johnson
1841–1845	William H. Harrison (d. 1841) John Tyler	John Tyler
1845–1849	James K. Polk	George M. Dallas
1849–1853	Zachary Taylor (d. 1850) Millard Fillmore	Millard Fillmore
1853–1857	Franklin Pierce	William R. D. King (d. 1853)

Presidents and Vice Presidents (continued)

Term	President	Vice President
1857–1861	James Buchanan	John C. Breckinridge
1861–1865	Abraham Lincoln	Hannibal Hamlin
1865–1869	Abraham Lincoln (d. 1865) Andrew Johnson	Andrew Johnson
1869–1873	Ulysses S. Grant	Schuyler Colfax
1873–1877	Ulysses S. Grant	Henry Wilson (d. 1875)
1877–1881	Rutherford B. Hayes	William A. Wheeler
1881–1885	James A. Garfield (d. 1881) Chester A. Arthur	Chester A. Arthur
1885–1889	Grover Cleveland	Thomas A. Hendricks (d. 1885)
1889–1893	Benjamin Harrison	Levi P. Morton
1893–1897	Grover Cleveland	Adlai E. Stevenson
1897–1901	William McKinley	Garret A. Hobart (d. 1899)
1901–1905	William McKinley (d. 1901) Theodore Roosevelt	Theodore Roosevelt
1905–1909	Theodore Roosevelt	Charles W. Fairbanks
1909–1913	William H. Taft	James S. Sherman (d. 1912)
1913–1917	Woodrow Wilson	Thomas R. Marshall
1917–1921	Woodrow Wilson	Thomas R. Marshall
1921–1925	Warren G. Harding (d. 1923) Calvin Coolidge	Calvin Coolidge
1925–1929	Calvin Coolidge	Charles G. Dawes
1929–1933	Herbert Hoover	Charles Curtis
1933–1937	Franklin D. Roosevelt	John N. Garner
1937–1941	Franklin D. Roosevelt	John N. Garner
1941–1945	Franklin D. Roosevelt	Henry A. Wallace
1945–1949	Franklin D. Roosevelt (d. 1945) Harry S Truman	Harry S Truman
1949–1953	Harry S Truman	Alben W. Barkley
1953–1957	Dwight D. Eisenhower	Richard M. Nixon
1957–1961	Dwight D. Eisenhower	Richard M. Nixon
1961–1965	John F. Kennedy (d. 1963) Lyndon B. Johnson	Lyndon B. Johnson
1965–1969	Lyndon B. Johnson	Hubert H. Humphrey, Jr.
1969–1974	Richard M. Nixon	Spiro T. Agnew (resigned 1973); Gerald R. Ford
1974–1977	Gerald R. Ford	Nelson A. Rockefeller
1977–1981	Jimmy Carter	Walter F. Mondale
1981–1985	Ronald Reagan	George Bush
1985–1989	Ronald Reagan	George Bush
1989–1993	George Bush	J. Danforth Quayle III
1993–1997	William Clinton	Albert Gore, Jr.
1997–2001	William Clinton	Albert Gore, Jr.
2001–2005	George W. Bush	Richard Cheney
2005–2009	George W. Bush	Richard Cheney
2009–	Barack Obama	Joseph Biden

Table A.3 Admission of States (See Table 9.3 on p. 193 for order in which the original thirteen entered the Union.)

Order of Admission	State	Date of Admission	Order of Admission	State	Date of Admission
14	Vermont	Mar. 4, 1791	33	Oregon	Feb. 14, 1859
15	Kentucky	June 1, 1792	34	Kansas	Jan. 29, 1861
16	Tennessee	June 1, 1796	35	W. Virginia	June 20, 1863
17	Ohio	Mar. 1, 1803	36	Nevada	Oct. 31, 1864
18	Louisiana	April 30, 1812	37	Nebraska	Mar. 1, 1867
19	Indiana	Dec. 11, 1816	38	Colorado	Aug. 1, 1876
20	Mississippi	Dec. 10, 1817	39	N. Dakota	Nov. 2, 1889
21	Illinois	Dec. 3, 1818	40	S. Dakota	Nov. 2, 1889
22	Alabama	Dec. 14, 1819	41	Montana	Nov. 8, 1889
23	Maine	Mar. 15, 1820	42	Washington	Nov. 11, 1889
24	Missouri	Aug. 10, 1821	43	Idaho	July 3, 1890
25	Arkansas	June 15, 1836	44	Wyoming	July 10, 1890
26	Michigan	Jan. 26, 1837	45	Utah	Jan. 4, 1896
27	Florida	Mar. 3, 1845	46	Oklahoma	Nov. 16, 1907
28	Texas	Dec. 29, 1845	47	New Mexico	Jan. 6, 1912
29	Iowa	Dec. 28, 1846	48	Arizona	Feb. 14, 1912
30	Wisconsin	May 29, 1848	49	Alaska	Jan. 3, 1959
31	California	Sept. 9, 1850	50	Hawaii	Aug. 21, 1959
32	Minnesota	May 11, 1858			

Table A.4 Estimates of Total Costs and Number of Battle Deaths of Major U.S. Wars[1]

War	Total Costs[2] (millions of dollars)	Original Costs (millions of dollars)	Number of Battle Deaths
Iraq War (2003–)	N/A	$806,000[3]	3,489[4]
Afghan War (2001–)	N/A	$444,000[5]	1,419[6]
Vietnam Conflict	$352,000	140,600	47,355[7]
Korean Conflict	164,000	54,000	33,629
World War II	664,000	288,000	291,557
World War I	112,000	26,000	53,402
Spanish-American War	6,460	400	385
Civil War { Union only	12,952	3,200	140,414
Civil War { Confederacy (est.)	N.A.	1,000	94,000
Mexican War	147	73	1,733
War of 1812	158	93	2,260
American Revolution	190	100	6,824

[1]Deaths from disease and other causes are not shown. In earlier wars especially, owing to poor medical and sanitary practices, nonbattle deaths substantially exceeded combat casualties.

[2]The difference between total costs and original costs is attributable to continuing postwar payments for items such as veterans' benefits, interest on war debts, and so on.

[3]Through 2011

[4]Through October 6, 2011

[5]Through 2011

[6]Through October 6, 2011

[7]1957–1990

(Sources: *Historical Statistics of the United States, Statistical Abstract of the United States,* relevant years, *The World Almanac and Book of Facts, 1986, Congressional Research Service,* Department of Defense, and Congressional Research Service Reports.)

GLOSSARY OF KEY TERMS

9/11 (2001): Common shorthand for the terrorist attacks that occurred on September 11, 2001, in which 19 militant Islamist men hijacked and crashed four commercial aircraft. Two planes hit the Twin Towers of the World Trade Center in New York City, causing them to collapse. One plane crashed into the Pentagon in Washington, D.C., and the fourth, overtaken by passengers, crashed into a field in rural Pennsylvania. Nearly 3000 people were killed in the worst case of domestic terrorism in American history. (974)

"10 percent" Reconstruction plan (1863): Introduced by President Lincoln, it proposed that a state be readmitted to the Union once 10 percent of its voters had pledged loyalty to the United States and promised to honor emancipation. (470)

ABC-1 agreement (1941): An agreement between Britain and the United States developed at a conference in Washington, D.C., between January 29–March 27, 1941, that should the United States enter World War II, the two nations and their allies would coordinate their military planning, making a priority of protecting the British Commonwealth. That would mean "getting Germany first" in the Atlantic and the European theater and fighting more defensively on other military fronts. (791)

Abraham Lincoln Brigade: Idealistic American volunteers who served in the Spanish Civil War, defending Spanish republican forces from the fascist General Francisco Franco's nationalist coup. Some 3,000 Americans served alongside volunteers from other countries. (783)

abstract expressionism: An experimental style of mid-twentieth-century modern art exemplified by Jackson Pollock's spontaneous "action paintings," created by flinging paint on canvases stretched across the studio floor. (880)

Abu Ghraib prison: A detention facility near Baghdad, Iraq. Under Saddam Hussein, the prison was the site of infamous torturing and execution of political dissidents. In 2004, during the U.S. occupation of Iraq, the prison became the focal point of a prisoner-abuse and torture scandal after photographs surfaced of American soldiers mistreating, torturing, and degrading Iraqi war prisoners and suspected terrorists. The scandal was one of several dark spots on the public image of the Iraq War and led to increased criticism of Secretary of Defense Donald Rumsfeld. (978)

Adamson Act (1916): This law established an eight-hour day for all employees on trains involved in interstate commerce, with extra pay for overtime. It was the first federal law regulating the hours of workers in private companies, and was upheld by the Supreme Court in *Wilson* v. *New* (1917). (666)

***Adkins* v. *Children's Hospital* (1923):** A landmark Supreme Court decision reversing the ruling in *Muller* v. *Oregan,* which had declared women to be deserving of special protection in the workplace. (729)

affirmative action: Program designed to redress historic racial and gender imbalances in jobs and education. The term grew from an executive order issued by John F. Kennedy in 1961 mandating that projects paid for with federal funds could not discriminate based on race in their hiring practices. In the late 1960s, President Nixon's Philadelphia Plan changed the meaning of affirmative action to require attention to certain groups, rather than protect individuals against discrimination. (900)

Agricultural Adjustment Administration (AAA) (1933): A New Deal program designed to raise agricultural prices by paying farmers not to farm. It was based on the assumption that higher prices would increase farmers' purchasing power and thereby help alleviate the Great Depression. (763)

Agricultural Marketing Act (1929): This act established the Federal Farm Board, a lending bureau for hard-pressed farmers. The act also aimed to help farmers help themselves through new producers' cooperatives. As the depression worsened in 1930, the Board tried to bolster falling prices by buying up surpluses, but it was unable to cope with the flood of farm produce to market. (740)

Al Qaeda: Arabic for "The Base," an international alliance of anti-Western Islamic fundamentalist terrorist organizations founded in the late 1980s. Founded by veterans of the Afghan struggle against the Soviet Union, the group was headed by Osama Bin Laden and has taken responsibility for numerous terrorist attacks, especially after the late 1990s. Al Qaeda organized the attacks of September 11, 2001, in the United States, from its headquarters in Taliban-controlled Afghanistan. Since the U.S-led invasion of Afghanistan in 2001 and the launch of the "Global War on Terror," the group has been weakened, but still poses significant threats around the world. (975)

Allies: Great Britain, Russia, and France, later joined by Italy, Japan, and the United States, formed this alliance against the Central Powers in World War I. (670)

American Federation of Labor: A national federation of trade unions that included only skilled workers, founded in 1886. Led by Samuel Gompers for nearly four decades, the AFL sought to negotiate with employers for a better kind of capitalism that rewarded workers fairly with better wages, hours, and conditions. The AFL's membership was almost entirely white and male until the middle of the twentieth century. (536)

American plan: A business-oriented approach to worker relations popular among firms in the 1920s to defeat unionization. Managers sought to strengthen their communication with workers and to offer benefits like pensions and insurance. They insisted on an "open shop" in contrast to the mandatory union membership through the "closed shop" that many labor activists had demanded in the strike wave after World War I. (701)

American Relief and Recovery Act: Among the earliest initiatives of the Obama Administration to combat the Great Recession. It was based on the economic theories of John Maynard Keynes that called for increased government spending to offset decreased private spending in times of economic downturn. The Act was controversial from the outset, passing with no Republican votes in the House, and only three in the Senate, and helping to foster the "Tea Party" movement to curb government deficits, even while critics on the Left argued that the Act's $787 Billion appropriation was not enough to turn the economy around. **(985)**

Americans with Disabilities Act (ADA, 1990): Landmark law signed by President George H. W. Bush that prohibited discrimination against people with physical or mental handicaps. It represented a legislative triumph for champions of equal protections to all. (961)

Anti-Imperialist League (1898–1921): A diverse group formed in order to protest American colonial oversight in the Philippines. It included university presidents, industrialists, clergymen, and labor leaders. Strongest in the Northeast, the Anti-imperialist League was the largest lobbying organization on a U.S. foreign-policy issue until the end of the nineteenth century. It declined in strength after the United States signed the Treaty of Paris (which approved the annexation of the Philippines), and especially after hostilities broke out between Filipino nationalists and American forces. (620)

Apollo (1961–1975): Program of manned space flights run by America's National Aeronautics and Space Administration (NASA). The project's highest achievement was the landing of Apollo 11 on the moon on July 20, 1969. (891)

Appeasement (1938): The policy followed by leaders of Britain and France at the 1938 conference in Munich. Their purpose was to avoid war, but they allowed Germany to take the Sudetenland from Czechoslovakia. (784)

Army-McCarthy Hearings (1954): Congressional hearings called by Senator Joseph McCarthy to accuse members of the army of communist ties. In this widely televised spectacle, McCarthy finally went too far for public approval. The hearings exposed the Senator's extremism and led to his eventual disgrace. (867)

Atlantic Charter (1941): Meeting on a warship off the coast of Newfoundland in August 1941, Franklin Roosevelt and British Prime Minister Winston Churchill signed this covenant outlining the future path toward disarmament, peace, and a permanent system of general security. Its spirit would animate the founding of the United Nations and raise awareness of the human rights of individuals after World War II. (793)

Australian ballot: A system that allows voters privacy in marking their ballot choices. Developed in Australia in the 1850s, it was introduced to the United States during the progressive era to help counteract boss rule. (641)

baby boom (1946–1964): Demographic explosion from births to returning soldiers and others who had put off starting families during the war. This large generation of new Americans forced the expansion of many institutions such as schools and universities. (838)

Bay of Pigs invasion (1961): CIA plot in 1961 to overthrow Fidel Castro by training Cuban exiles to invade and supporting them with American air power. The mission failed and became a public relations disaster early in John F. Kennedy's presidency. (893)

Beat Generation: A small coterie of mid-twentieth-century bohemian writers and personalities, including Jack Kerouac, Allen Ginsberg, and William S. Burroughs, who bemoaned bourgeois conformity and advocated free-form experimentation in life and literature. (884)

Berlin airlift (1948): Year-long mission of flying food and supplies to blockaded West Berliners, whom the Soviet Union cut off from access to the West in the first major crisis of the Cold War. (846)

Berlin Wall: Fortified and guarded barrier between East and West Berlin erected on orders from Soviet Premier Nikita Khrushchev in 1961 to stop the flow of people to the West. Until its destruction in 1989, the wall was a vivid symbol of the divide between the communist and capitalist worlds. (891)

Bible Belt: The region of the American South, extending roughly from North Carolina west to Oklahoma and Texas, where Protestant Fundamentalism and belief in literal interpretation of the Bible were traditionally strongest. (702)

Big Sister policy (1880s): A foreign policy of Secretary of State James G. Blaine aimed at rallying Latin American nations behind American leadership and opening Latin American markets to Yankee traders. The policy bore fruit in 1889, when Blaine presided over the First International Conference of American States. (609)

Black Codes (1865–1866): Laws passed throughout the South to restrict the rights of emancipated blacks, particularly with respect to negotiating labor contracts. Increased Northerners' criticisms of President Andrew Johnson's lenient Reconstruction policies. (471)

Black Monday: October 19, 1987. Date of the largest single-day decline in the Dow Jones Industrial Average until September 2001. The downturn indicated instability in the booming business culture of the 1980s but did not lead to a serious economic recession. (955)

Black Panther party: Organization of armed black militants formed in Oakland, California, in 1966 to protect black rights. The Panthers represented a growing dissatisfaction with the non-violent wing of the civil rights movement, and signaled a new direction to that movement after the legislative victories of 1964 and 1965. (905)

Black Power: Doctrine of militancy and separatism that rose in prominence after 1965. Black Power activists rejected Martin Luther King's pacifism and desire for integration. Rather, they promoted pride in African heritage and an often militant position in defense of their rights. (905)

Black Tuesday (1929): The dark, panicky day of October 29, 1929 when over 16,410,000 shares of stock were sold on Wall Street. It was a trigger that helped bring on the Great Depression. (740)

boll weevils: Term for conservative southern Democrats who voted increasingly for Republican issues during the Carter and Reagan administrations. (945)

Bolshevik Revolution (1917): The second stage of the Russian Revolution in November 1917 when Vladimir Lenin and his Bolshevik party seized power and established a communist state. The first stage had occurred the previous February when more moderate revolutionaries overthrew the Russian Czar. (700)

Bonus Army (1932): Officially known as the Bonus Expeditionary Force (BEF), this rag-tag group of 20,000 veterans marched on Washington to demand immediate payment of bonuses earned during World War I. General Douglas MacArthur dispersed the veterans with tear gas and bayonets. (746)

Boxer Rebellion (1900): An uprising in China directed against foreign influence. It was suppressed by an international force of some eighteen thousand soldiers, including several thousand Americans. The Boxer Rebellion paved the way for the revolution of 1911, which led to the establishment of the Republic of China in 1912. (623)

***Bracero* program (1942):** Program established by agreement with the Mexican government to recruit temporary Mexican agricultural workers to the United States to make up for wartime labor shortages in the Far West. The program persisted until 1964, by when it had sponsored 4.5 million border crossings. (803)

Brain Trust: Specialists in law, economics, and welfare, many of them young university professors, who advised President Franklin D. Roosevelt and helped develop the policies of the New Deal. (752)

Bretton Woods Conference (1944): Meeting of Western allies to establish a postwar international economic order to avoid crises like the one that spawned World War II. Led to the creation of the International Monetary Fund (IMF) and the World Bank, designed to regulate currency levels and provide aid to underdeveloped countries. (841)

***Brown v. Board of Education of Topeka, Kansas* (1954):** Landmark Supreme Court decision that overturned *Plessy v. Ferguson* (1896) and abolished racial segregation in public schools. The Court reasoned that "separate" was inherently "unequal," rejecting the foundation of the Jim Crow system of racial segregation in the South. This decision was the first major step toward the legal end of racial discrimination and a major accomplishment for the Civil Rights Movement. (868)

carpetbaggers: Pejorative used by Southern whites to describe Northern businessmen and politicians who came to the South after the Civil War to work on Reconstruction projects or invest in Southern infrastructure. (478)

Central Powers: Germany and Austria-Hungary, later joined by Turkey and Bulgaria, made up this alliance against the Allies in World War I. (670)

Château Thierry, Battle of (1918): The first significant engagement of American troops in World War I—and, indeed, in any European war. To weary French soldiers, the American doughboys were an image of fresh and gleaming youth. (690)

Checkers Speech (1952): Nationally televised address by vice-presidential candidate Richard Nixon. Using the new mass medium of television shortly before the 1952 election, the vice presidential candidate saved his place on the ticket by defending himself against accusations of corruption. (864)

Chinese Exclusion Act (1882): Federal legislation that prohibited most further Chinese immigration to the United States. This was the first major legal restriction on immigration in U.S. history. (498)

City Beautiful movement: A turn-of-the-century movement among progressive architects and city planners, who aimed to promote order, harmony, and virtue while beautifying the nation's new urban spaces with grand boulevards, welcoming parks, and monumental public buildings. (569)

Civil Rights Act of 1875: The last piece of federal civil rights legislation until the 1950s, the law promised blacks equal access to public accommodations and banned racism in jury selection, but the Act provided no means of enforcement and was therefore ineffective. In 1883, the Supreme Court declared most of the Act unconstitutional. (495)

Civil Rights Act of 1964: Federal law that banned racial discrimination in public facilities and strengthened the federal government's power to fight segregation in schools. Title VII of the act prohibited employers from discriminating based on race in their hiring practices, and empowered the Equal Employment Opportunity Commission (EEOC) to regulate fair employment. (898)

Civilian Conservation Corps (CCC) (1933): A government program created by Congress to hire young unemployed men to improve the rural, out-of-doors environment with such work as planting trees, fighting fires, draining swamps, and maintaining National Parks. The CCC proved to be an important foundation for the post-World War II environmental movement. (757)

Clayton Anti-Trust Act (1914): Law extending the antitrust protections of the Sherman Anti-Trust Act and exempting labor unions and agricultural organizations from antimonopoly constraints. The act conferred long-overdue benefits on labor. (666)

closed shop: A union-organizing term that refers to the practice of allowing only unionized employees to work for a particular company. The AFL became known for negotiating closed-shop agreements with employers, in which the employer would agree not to hire non-union members. (536)

Cold War (1946–1991): The 45-year-long diplomatic tension between the United States and the Soviet Union that divided much of the world into polarized camps, capitalist against communist. Most of the international conflicts during that period, particularly in the developing world, can be traced to the competition between the United States and the Soviet Union. (841)

Committee on Public Information (1917): A government office during World War I known popularly as the Creel Committee for its chairman George Creel, it was dedicated to winning everyday Americans' support for the war effort. It regularly distributed prowar propaganda and sent out an army of "four-minute men" to rally crowds and deliver "patriotic pep." (680)

Commonwealth of Independent States (CIS): Organization formed from the former republics of the Soviet Union in 1991. (957)

Compromise of 1877: The agreement that finally resolved the 1876 election and officially ended Reconstruction. In exchange for the Republican candidate, Rutherford B. Hayes, winning the presidency, Hayes agreed to withdraw the last of the federal troops from the former Confederate states. This deal effectively completed the southern return to white-only, Democratic-dominated electoral politics. (494)

Congress of Industrial Organizations (CIO): A New Deal-era labor organization that broke away from the American Federation of Labor (AFL) in order to organize unskilled industrial workers regardless of their particular economic sector or craft. The CIO gave a great boost to labor organizing in the midst of the Great Depression and during World War II. In 1955, the CIO merged with the AFL. (769)

Congress of Racial Equality (CORE) (1942): Nonviolent civil rights organization founded in 1942 and committed to the "Double V"—victory over fascism abroad and racism at home. After World War II, CORE would become a major force in the civil rights movement. (806)

containment doctrine: America's strategy against the Soviet Union based on ideas of George Kennan. The doctrine declared that the Soviet Union and communism were inherently expansionist and had to be stopped from spreading through both military and political pressure. Containment guided American foreign policy throughout most of the Cold War. (846)

Contract with America (1994): Multi-point program offered by Republican candidates and sitting politicians in the 1994 midterm election. The platform proposed smaller government, Congressional ethics reform, term limits, great emphasis on personal responsibility, and a general repudiation of the Democratic party. This articulation of dissent was a significant blow to the Clinton Administration and led to the Republican party's takeover of both houses of Congress for the first time in half a century. (968)

contras: Anti-Sandinista fighters in the Nicaraguan civil war. The Contras were secretly supplied with American military aid, paid for with money the United States clandestinely made selling arms to Iran. (947)

Court-packing plan (1937): Franklin Roosevelt's politically motivated and ill-fated scheme to add a new justice to the Supreme Court for every member over seventy who would not retire. His objective was to overcome the Court's objections to New Deal reforms. (771)

Crédit Mobilier scandal (1872): A construction company was formed by owners of the Union Pacific Railroad for the purpose of receiving government contracts to build the railroad at highly inflated prices—and profits. In 1872 a scandal erupted when journalists discovered that the Crédit Mobilier Company had bribed congressmen and even the Vice President in order to allow the ruse to continue. (490)

criminal syndicalism laws (1919–1920): Passed by many states during the Red Scare of 1919–1920, these nefarious laws outlawed the mere advocacy of violence to secure social change. Stump speakers for the International Workers of the World, or IWW, were special targets. (701)

Cuban missile crisis (1962): Standoff between John F. Kennedy and Soviet Premier Nikita Khrushchev in October 1962 over Soviet plans to install nuclear weapons in Cuba. Although the crisis was ultimately settled in America's favor and represented a foreign policy triumph for Kennedy, it brought the world's superpowers perilously close to the brink of nuclear confrontation. (895)

Dawes Plan (1924): An arrangement negotiated in 1924 to reschedule German reparations payments. It stabilized the German currency and opened the way for further American private loans to Germany. (737)

Dawes Severalty Act (1887): An act that broke up Indian reservations and distributed land to individual households. Leftover land was sold for money to fund U.S. government efforts to "civilize" Native Americans. Of 130 million acres held in Native American reservations before the Act, 90 million were sold to non-Native buyers. (581)

D-Day (1944): A massive military operation led by American forces in Normandy beginning on June 6, 1944. The pivotal battle led to the liberation of France and brought on the final phases of World War II in Europe. (813)

deleveraging: The inverse of "leveraging," whereby businesses increase their financial power by borrowing money (debt) in addition to their own assets (equity). In times of uncertainty or credit tightening, the same businesses seek to improve their debt-to-equity ratios by shedding debt through the sale of assets purchased with borrowed money. (984)

Democratic Leadership Council: Non-profit organization of centrist Democrats founded in the mid-1980s. The group attempted to push the Democratic party toward pro-growth, strong defense, and anticrime policies. Among its most influential early members was Bill Clinton, whom it held up as an example of "third way" politics. (965)

Department of Homeland Security: Cabinet-level agency created in 2003 to unify and coordinate public safety and anti-terrorism operations within the federal government. (975)

détente: From the French for "reduced tension," the period of Cold War thawing when the United States and the Soviet Union negotiated reduced armament treaties under Presidents Nixon, Ford, and Carter. As a policy prescription, détente marked a departure from the policies of proportional response, mutually assured destruction, and containment that had defined the earlier years of the Cold War. (920)

Dien Bien Phu, Battle of (1954): Military engagement in French colonial Vietnam in which French forces were defeated by Viet Minh nationalists loyal to Ho Chi Minh. With this loss, the French ended their colonial involvement in Indochina, paving the way for America's entry. (875)

dollar diplomacy: Name applied by President Taft's critics to the policy of supporting U.S. investments and political interests abroad. First applied to the financing of railways in China after 1909, the policy then spread to Haiti, Honduras, and Nicaragua. President Woodrow Wilson disavowed the practice, but his administration undertook comparable acts of intervention in support of U.S. business interests, especially in Latin America. (657)

Don't Ask, Don't Tell: From 1993 to 2010, the policy affecting homosexuals in the military. It emerged as a compromise between the standing prohibition against homosexuals in the armed forces and President Clinton's push to allow all citizens to serve regardless of sexual orientation. Military authorities were forbidden to ask about a service member's orientation, and gay service personnel could be discharged if they publicly revealed their homosexuality. At President Obama's urging, Congress repealed DADT in 2010, permitting gays to serve openly in uniform. (966)

Dust Bowl: Grim nickname for the Great Plains region devastated by drought and dust storms during the 1930s. The disaster led to the migration into California of thousands of displaced "Okies" and "Arkies." (764)

Earth Day (1970): International day of celebration and awareness of global environmental issues launched by conservationists on April 22, 1970. (922)

Eighteenth Amendment (1919): Ratified in 1919, this Constitutional amendment prohibited the manufacture, sale, and transportation of alcoholic beverages. It ushered in the era known as Prohibition. (704)

Elkins Act (1903): Law passed by Congress to impose penalties on railroads that offered rebates and customers who accepted them. The law strengthened the Interstate Commerce Act of 1887. The Hepburn Act of 1906 added free passes to the list of railroad no-no's. (649)

Employment Act of 1946: Legislation declaring that the government's economic policy should aim to promote maximum employment, production, and purchasing power, as well as to keep inflation low. A general commitment that was much shorter on specific targets and rules than its liberal creators had wished. The Act created the Council of Economic Advisers to provide the president with data and recommendations to make economic policy. (831)

Environmental Protection Agency (EPA): A governmental organization signed into law by Richard Nixon in 1970 designed to regulate pollution, emissions, and other factors that negatively influence the natural environment. The creation of the EPA marked a newfound commitment by the federal government to actively combat environmental risks and was a significant triumph for the environmentalist movement. (922)

Equal Rights Amendment (ERA): Equal Rights Amendment, which declared full constitutional equality for women. Although it passed both houses of Congress in 1972, a concerted grassroots campaign by anti-feminists led by Phyllis Schlafly persuaded enough state legislatures to vote against ratification. The amendment failed to become part of the Constitution. (931)

Espionage Act (1917): A law prohibiting interference with the draft and other acts of national "disloyalty." Together with the Sedition Act of 1918, which added penalties for abusing the government in writing, it created a climate that was unfriendly to civil liberties. (681)

European Economic Community (EEC): Free trade zone in Western Europe created by Treaty of Rome in 1957. Often referred to as the "Common Market," this collection of countries originally included France, West Germany, Italy, Belgium, the Netherlands, and Luxembourg. The body eventually expanded to become the European Union, which by 2005 included 27 member states. (891)

***Ex parte Milligan* (1866):** Civil War Era case in which the Supreme Court ruled that military tribunals could not be used to try civilians if civil courts were open. (475)

Executive Order No. 9066 (1942): Order of President Franklin D. Roosevelt authorizing the War Department to remove Japanese "enemy aliens" to isolated internment camps. Immigrants and citizens alike were sent away from their homes, neighbors, schools, and businesses. The Japanese internment policy was held to be constitutional by the United States Supreme Court in *Korematsu* v. *U.S.* (1944). (792)

Fair Deal: President Truman's extensive social program introduced in his 1949 message to Congress. Republicans and Southern Democrats kept much of his vision from being enacted, except for raising the minimum wage, providing for more public housing, and extending old-age insurance to many more beneficiaries under the Social Security Act. (854)

Fair Employment Practices Commission (FEPC) (1941): Threatened with a massive "Negro March on Washington" to demand equal job opportunities in war jobs and in the military, Franklin D. Roosevelt's administration issued an executive order forbidding racial discrimination in all defense plants operating under contract with the federal government. The FEPC was intended to monitor compliance with the Executive Order. (805)

Fair Labor Standards Act (1938): Important New Deal labor legislation that regulated minimum wages and maximum hours for workers involved in interstate commerce. The law also outlawed labor by children under sixteen. The exclusion of agricultural, service, and domestic workers meant that many blacks, Mexican Americans, and women—who were concentrated in these sectors—did not benefit from the act's protection. (768)

Federal Highway Act of 1956: Federal legislation signed by Dwight D. Eisenhower to construct thousands of miles of modern highways in the name of national defense. Officially called the National Interstate and Defense Highways Act, this bill dramatically increased the move to the suburbs, as white middle-class people could more easily commute to urban jobs. (873)

Federal Reserve Act (1913): An act establishing twelve regional Federal Reserve Banks and a Federal Reserve Board, appointed by the president, to regulate banking and create stability on a national scale in the volatile banking sector. The law carried the nation through the financial crises of the First World War of 1914–1918. (665)

Federal Trade Commission Act (1914): A banner accomplishment of Woodrow Wilson's administration, this law empowered a standing, presidentially appointed commission to investigate illegal business practices in interstate commerce like unlawful competition, false advertising, and mislabeling of goods. (666)

***The Feminine Mystique* (1963):** Best-selling book by feminist thinker Betty Friedan. This work challenged women to move beyond the drudgery of suburban housewifery and helped launch what would become second-wave feminism. (861)

Fifteenth Amendment (ratified 1870): Prohibited states from denying citizens the franchise on account of race. It disappointed feminists who wanted the Amendment to include guarantees for women's suffrage. (475)

Foraker Act (1900): Sponsored by Senator Joseph B. Foraker, a Republican from Ohio, this accorded Puerto Ricans a limited degree of popular government. It was the first comprehensive congressional effort to provide for governance of territories acquired after the Spanish American War, and served as a model for a similar act adopted for the Philippines in 1902. (620)

Force Acts (1870–1871): Passed by Congress following a wave of Ku Klux Klan violence, the acts banned clan membership, prohibited the use of intimidation to prevent blacks from voting, and gave the U.S. military the authority to enforce the acts. (480)

Force Bill (1833): Passed by Congress alongside the Compromise Tariff, it authorized the president to use the military to collect federal tariff duties. (256)

Fordism: A system of assembly-line manufacturing and mass production named after Henry Ford, founder of the Ford Motor Company and developer of the Model T car. (711)

Fordney-McCumber Tariff Law (1922): A comprehensive bill passed to protect domestic production from foreign competitors. As a direct result, many European nations were spurred to increase their own trade barriers. (732)

Fourteen Points (1918): Woodrow Wilson's proposal to ensure peace after World War I, calling for an end to secret treaties, widespread arms reduction, national self-determination, and a new league of nations. (680)

Fourteenth Amendment (ratified 1868): Constitutional amendment that extended civil rights to freedmen and prohibited states from taking away such rights without due process. (473)

fourth party system (1896–1932): A term scholars have used to describe national politics from 1896–1932, when Republicans had a tight grip on the White House and issues such as industrial regulation and labor concerns became paramount, replacing older concerns such as civil service reform and monetary policy. (604)

Freedmen's Bureau (1865–1872): Created to aid newly emancipated slaves by providing food, clothing, medical care, education, and legal support. Its achievements were uneven and depended largely on the quality of local administrators. (469)

Freedom Riders (1961): Organized mixed-race groups who rode interstate buses deep into the South to draw attention to and protest racial segregation, beginning in 1961. This effort by northern young people to challenge racism proved a political and public relations success for the Civil Rights Movement. (903)

Freedom Summer (1964): A voter registration drive in Mississippi spearheaded by a coalition of civil rights groups. The campaign drew the activism of thousands of black and white civil rights workers, many of whom were students from the north, and was marred by the abduction and murder of three such workers at the hands of white racists. (903)

Fundamentalism: A Protestant Christian movement emphasizing the literal truth of the Bible and opposing religious modernism, which sought to reconcile religion and science. It was especially strong in the Baptist Church and the Church of Christ, first organized in 1906. (710)

GI Bill (1944): Known officially as the Servicemen's Readjustment Act and more informally as the GI Bill of Rights, this law helped returning World War II soldiers reintegrate into civilian life by securing loans to buy homes and farms and set up small businesses and by making tuition and stipends available for them to attend college and job training programs. The Act was also intended to cushion the blow of 15 million returning servicemen on the employment market and to nurture the postwar economy. (831)

Gilded Age (1877–1896): A term given to the period 1865–1896 by Mark Twain, indicating both the fabulous wealth and the widespread corruption of the era. (492)

***Glasnost*:** Meaning "openness," a cornerstone along with *Perestroika* of Soviet president Mikhail Gorbachev's reform movement in the USSR in the 1980s. These policies resulted in greater market liberalization, access to the West, and ultimately the end of communist rule. (949)

Glass-Steagall Banking Reform Act (1933): A law creating the Federal Deposit Insurance Corporation, which insured individual bank deposits and ended a century-long tradition of unstable banking that had reached a crisis in the Great Depression. (756)

Gold Standard Act (1900): An act that guaranteed that paper currency would be redeemed freely in gold, putting an end to the already dying "free silver" campaign. (605)

Good Neighbor policy: A departure from the Roosevelt Corollary to the Monroe Doctrine, the Good Neighbor Policy stressed nonintervention in Latin America. It was begun by Herbert Hoover but associated with Franklin D. Roosevelt. (780)

grandfather clause: A regulation established in many southern states in the 1890s that exempted from voting requirements (such as literacy tests and poll taxes) anyone who could prove that their ancestors ("grandfathers") had been able to vote in 1860. Since slaves could not vote before the Civil War, these clauses guaranteed the right to vote to many whites while denying it to blacks. (508)

Great Rapprochement: After decades of occasionally "twisting the lion's tail," American diplomats began to cultivate close, cordial relations with Great Britain at the end of the nineteenth century—a relationship that would intensify further during World War I. (610)

Great Society (1964–1968): President Lyndon Johnson's term for his domestic policy agenda. Billed as a successor to the New Deal, the Great Society aimed to extend the postwar prosperity to all people in American society by promoting civil rights and fighting poverty. Great Society programs included the War on Poverty, which expanded the Social Security system by creating Medicare and Medicaid to provide health care for the aged and the poor. Johnson also signed laws protecting consumers and empowering community organizations to combat poverty at grassroots levels. (900)

Guantánamo Detention Camp: Controversial prison facility constructed after the U.S.-led invasion of Afghanistan in 2001. Located on territory occupied by the U.S. military, but not technically part of the United States, the facility serves as an extra-legal holding area for suspected terrorists. (975)

Harlem Renaissance: A creative outpouring among African-American writers, jazz musicians, and social thinkers, centered around Harlem in the 1920s, that celebrated black culture and advocated for a "New Negro" in American social, political, and intellectual life. (724)

Hawley-Smoot Tariff (1930): The highest protective tariff in the peacetime history of the United States, passed as a result of good old-fashioned horse trading. To the outside world, it smacked of ugly economic warfare. (740)

Haymarket Square (1886): A May Day rally that turned violent when someone threw a bomb into the middle of the meeting, killing several dozen people. Eight anarchists were arrested for conspiracy contributing to the disorder, although evidence linking them to the bombing was thin. Four were executed, one committed suicide, and three were pardoned in 1893. (533)

Hay-Pauncefote Treaty (1901): A treated signed between the United States and Great Britain, giving Americans a free hand to build a canal in Central America. The treaty nullified the Clayton-Bulwer Treaty of 1850, which prohibited the British or U.S. from acquiring territory in Central America. (628)

Hetch Hetchy Valley: The federal government allowed the city of San Francisco to build a dam here in 1913. This was a blow to preservationists, who wished to protect the Yosemite National Park, where the dam was located. (654)

Hitler-Stalin pact (1939): Treaty signed on August 23, 1939 in which Germany and the Soviet Union agreed not to fight each other. The fateful agreement paved the way for German aggression against Poland and the Western democracies. (784)

holding companies: A company that owns part or all of the other companies' stock in order to extend monopoly control. Often, a holding company does not produce goods or services of its own but only exists to control other companies. The Clayton Anti-Trust Act of 1914 sought to clamp down on these companies when they obstructed competition. (666)

Homestead Act (1862): A federal law that gave settlers 160 acres of land for about $30 if they lived on it for five years and improved it by, for instance, building a house on it. The act helped make land accessible to hundreds of thousands of westward-moving settlers, but many people also found disappointment when their land was infertile or they saw speculators grabbing up the best land. (586)

Homestead Strike (1892): A strike at a Carnegie steel plant in Homestead, P.A., that ended in an armed battle between the strikers, three hundred armed "Pinkerton" detectives hired by Carnegie, and federal troops, which killed ten people and wounded more than sixty. The strike was part of a nationwide wave of labor unrest in the summer of 1892 that helped the Populists gain some support from industrial workers. (506)

Hoovervilles: Grim shantytowns where impoverished victims of the Great Depression slept under newspapers and in makeshift tents. Their visibility (and sarcastic name) tarnished the reputation of the Hoover administration. (743)

horizontal integration: The practice perfected by John D. Rockefeller of dominating a particular phase of the production process in order to monopolize a market, often by forming trusts and alliances with competitors. (521)

House Un-American Activities Committee (HUAC): Investigatory body established in 1938 to root out "subversion." Sought to expose communist influence in American government and society, in particular through the trial of Alger Hiss. (852)

Hundred Days (1933): The first hundred days of Franklin D. Roosevelt's administration, stretching from March 9 to June 16, 1933, when an unprecedented number of reform bills were passed by a Democratic Congress to launch the New Deal. (754)

Hungarian uprising (1956): Series of demonstrations in Hungary against the Soviet Union. Soviet Premier Nikita Khrushchev violently suppressed this pro-Western uprising, highlighting the limitations of America's power in Eastern Europe. (874)

Hurricane Katrina (2005): The costliest and one of the deadliest hurricanes in the history of the United States, killing nearly 2000 Americans. The storm ravaged the Gulf Coast, especially the city of New Orleans, in late August of 2005. In New Orleans, high winds and rain caused the city's levees to break, leading to catastrophic flooding, particularly centered on the city's most impoverished wards. A tardy and feeble response by local and federal authorities exacerbated the damage and led to widespread criticism of the Federal Emergency Management Agency (FEMA). (982)

Immigration Act of 1924: Also known as the "National Origins Act," this law established quotas for immigration to the United States. Immigrants from Southern and Eastern Europe were sharply curtailed, while immigrants from Asia were shut out altogether. (703)

Industrial Workers of the World (1905): The IWW, also known as the "Wobblies," was a radical organization that sought to build "one big union" and advocated industrial sabotage in defense of that goal. At its peak in 1923, it could claim 100,000 members and could gain the support of 300,000. The IWW particularly appealed to migratory workers in agriculture and lumbering and to miners, all of whom suffered from horrific working conditions. (683)

initiative: A progressive reform measure allowing voters to petition to have a law placed on the general ballot. Like the referendum and recall, it brought democracy directly "to the people," and helped foster a shift toward interest-group politics and away from old political "machines." (641)

***Insular Cases* (1901–1904):** Beginning in 1901, a badly divided Supreme Court decreed in these cases that the Constitution did not follow the flag. In other words, Puerto Ricans and Filipinos would not necessarily enjoy all American rights. (621)

***insurrectos*:** Cuban insurgents who sought freedom from colonial Spanish rule. Their destructive tactics threatened American economic interests in Cuban plantations and railroads. (612)

interlocking directorates: The practice of having executives or directors from one company serve on the Board of Directors of another company. J. P. Morgan introduced this practice to eliminate banking competition in the 1890s. (522)

Intermediate-Range Nuclear Forces (INF) Treaty (1987): Arms limitation agreement settled by Ronald Reagan and Mikhail Gorbachev after several attempts. The treaty banned all intermediate-range nuclear missiles from Europe and marked a significant thaw in the Cold War. (949)

International Style: Archetypal, post-World War II modernist architectural style, best known for its "curtain-wall" designs of steel-and-glass corporate high-rises. (882)

Interstate Commerce Act (1887): Congressional legislation that established the Interstate Commerce Commission, compelled railroads to publish standard rates, and prohibited rebates and pools. Railroads quickly became adept at using the Act to achieve their own ends, but the Act gave the government an important means to regulate big business. (519)

Iran-Contra Affair (1987): Major political scandal of Ronald Reagan's second term. An illicit arrangement of selling "arms for hostages" with Iran and using money to support the contras in Nicaragua, the scandal deeply damaged Reagan's credibility. (951)

Iranian hostage crisis: The 444 days, from November 1979 to January 1981, in which American embassy workers were held captive by Iranian revolutionaries. The Iranian Revolution began in January 1979 when young Muslim fundamentalists overthrew the oppressive regime of the American-backed shah, forcing him into exile. Deeming the United States "the Great Satan," these revolutionaries triggered an energy crisis by cutting off Iranian oil. The hostage crisis began when revolutionaries stormed the American embassy, demanding that the United States return the shah to Iran for trial. The episode was marked by botched diplomacy and failed rescue attempts by the Carter Administration. After permanently damaging relations between the two countries, the crisis ended with the hostages' release the day Ronald Reagan became president, January 20, 1981. (939)

irreconcilables: Led by Senators William Borah of Idaho and Hiram Johnson of California, this was a hard-core group of militant isolationists who opposed the Wilsonian dream of international cooperation in the League of Nations after World War I. Their efforts played an important part in preventing American participation in the international organization. (693)

Jim Crow: System of racial segregation in the American South from the end of Reconstruction until the mid-twentieth century. Based on the concept of "separate but equal" facilities for blacks and whites, the Jim Crow system sought to prevent racial mixing in public, including restaurants, movie theaters, and public transportation. An informal system, it was generally perpetuated by custom, violence, and intimidation. (496, 867)

Johnson Debt Default Act (1934): Steeped in ugly memories of World War I, this spiteful act prevented debt-ridden nations from borrowing further from the United States. (782)

Jones Act (1916): Law according territorial status to the Philippines and promising independence as soon as a "stable government" could be established. The United States did not grant the Philippines independence until July 4, 1946. (667)

Kellogg-Briand Pact (1928): A sentimental triumph of the 1920s peace movement, this 1928 pact linked sixty-two nations in the supposed "outlawry of war." (732)

Kent State University (shooting 1970): Massacre of four college students by National Guardsmen on May 4, 1970, in Ohio. In response to Nixon's announcement that he had expanded the Vietnam War into Cambodia, college campuses across the country exploded in violence. On May 14 and 15, students at historically black Jackson State College in Mississippi were protesting the war as well as the Kent State shooting when highway patrolmen fired into a student dormitory, killing two students. (919)

Keynesianism: An economic theory based on the thoughts of British economist John Maynard Keynes, holding that central banks should adjust interest rates and governments should use deficit spending and tax policies to increase purchasing power and hence prosperity. (772)

kitchen debate (1959): Televised exchange in 1959 between Soviet Premier Nikita Khrushchev and American Vice President Richard Nixon. Meeting at the American National Exhibition in Moscow, the two leaders sparred over the relative merits of capitalist consumer culture versus Soviet state planning. Nixon won applause for his staunch defense of American capitalism, helping lead him to the Republican nomination for president in 1960. (878)

Knights of Labor: The second national labor organization, organized in 1869 as a secret society and opened for public membership in 1881. The Knights were known for their efforts to organize all workers, regardless of skill level, gender, or race. After the mid-1880s their membership declined for a variety of reasons, including the Knights' participation in violent strikes and discord between skilled and unskilled members. (533)

Korean War (1950–1953): First "hot war" of the Cold War. The Korean War began in 1950 when the Soviet-backed North Koreans invaded South Korea before meeting a counter-offensive by UN Forces, dominated by the United States. The war ended in stalemate in 1953. (855)

Kristallnacht: German for "night of broken glass," it refers to the murderous pogrom that destroyed Jewish businesses and synagogues and sent thousands to concentration camps on the night of November 9, 1938. Thousands more attempted to find refuge in the United States, but were ultimately turned away due to restrictive immigration laws. (788)

Ku Klux Klan: An extremist, paramilitary, right-wing secret society founded in the mid-nineteenth century and revived during the 1920s. It was anti-foreign, anti-black, anti-Jewish, anti-pacifist, anti-communist, anti-internationalist, anti-evolutionist, and anti-bootlegger, but pro-Anglo-Saxon and pro-Protestant. Its members, cloaked in sheets to conceal their identities, terrorized freedmen and sympathetic whites throughout the South after the Civil War. By the 1890s, Klan-style violence and Democratic legislation succeeded in virtually disenfranchising all Southern blacks. (479, 701)

land-grant colleges: Colleges and universities created from allocations of public land through the Morrell Act of 1862 and the Hatch Act of 1887. These grants helped fuel the boom in higher education in the late nineteenth century, and many of the today's public universities derive from these grants. (555)

League of Nations (1919): A world organization of national governments proposed by President Woodrow Wilson and established by the Treaty of Versailles in 1919. It worked to facilitate peaceful international cooperation. Despite emotional appeals by Wilson, isolationists' objections to the League created the major obstacle to American signing of the Treaty of Versailles. (693)

Lend-Lease Bill (1941): Based on the motto, "Send guns, not sons," this law abandoned former pretenses of neutrality by allowing Americans to sell unlimited supplies of arms to any nation defending itself against the Axis Powers. Patriotically numbered 1776, the bill was praised as a device for keeping the nation out of World War II. (791)

Levittown: Suburban communities with mass-produced tract houses built in the New York and Philadelphia metropolitan areas in the 1950s by William Levitt and Sons. Typically inhabited by white middle-class people who fled the cities in search of homes to buy for their growing families. (838)

Lewinsky affair (1998–1999): Political sex scandal that resulted in Bill Clinton's impeachment and trial by Congress. In 1998, Clinton gave sworn testimony in a sexual harassment case that he had never engaged in sexual activity with a White House intern named Monica Lewinsky. When prosecutors discovered evidence that the President had lied under oath about the affair, to which Clinton admitted, Republicans in Congress began impeachment proceedings. Although Clinton was ultimately not convicted by the Senate, the scandal put a lasting blemish on his presidential legacy. (970)

Liberal Protestants: Members of a branch of Protestantism that flourished from 1875 to 1925 and encouraged followers to use the Bible as a moral compass rather than to believe that the Bible represented scientific or historical truth. Many Liberal Protestants became active in the "social gospel" and other reform movements of the era. (552)

Little Bighorn, Battle of (1876): A particularly violent example of the warfare between whites and Native Americans in the late nineteenth century, also known as "Custer's Last Stand." In two days, June 25 and 26, 1876, the combined forces of over 2,000 Sioux, Cheyenne, and Arapaho Indians defeated and killed more than 250 U.S. soldiers, including Colonel George Custer. The battle came as the U.S. government tried to compel Native Americans to remain on the reservations and Native Americans tried to defend territory from white gold-seekers. This Indian advantage did not last long, however, as the union of these Indian fighters proved tenuous and the United States Army soon exacted retribution. (578)

Lochner v. *New York* (1905): A setback for labor reformers, this 1905 Supreme Court decision invalidated a state law establishing a ten-hour day for bakers. It held that the "right to free contract" was implicit in the due process clause of the Fourteenth Amendment. (645)

London Economic Conference (1933): A sixty-nation economic conference organized to stabilize international currency rates. Franklin Roosevelt's decision to revoke American participation contributed to a deepening world economic crisis. (778)

"Lost Generation": A creative circle of expatriate American artists and writers, including Ernest Hemingway, F. Scott Fitzgerald, and Gertrude Stein, who found shelter and inspiration in post-World War I Europe. (721)

Lusitania: British passenger liner torpedoed and sank by Germany on May 7, 1915. It ended the lives of 1,198 people, including 128 Americans, and pushed the United States closer to war. (672)

Maine (1898): American battleship dispatched to keep a "friendly" watch over Cuba in early 1898. It mysteriously blew up in Havana harbor on February 15, 1898, with a loss of 260 sailors. Later evidence confirmed that the explosion was accidental, resulting from combustion in one of the ship's internal coal bunkers. But many Americans, eager for war, insisted that it was the fault of a Spanish submarine mine. (612)

malaise speech (1979): National address by Jimmy Carter in July 1979 in which the President chided American materialism and urged a communal spirit in the face of economic hardships. Although Carter intended the speech to improve both public morale and his standings as a leader, it had the opposite effect and was widely perceived as a political disaster for the embattled president. (938)

Manhattan Project (1942): Code name for the American commission established in 1942 to develop the atomic bomb. The first experimental bomb was detonated on July 16, 1945, in the desert of New Mexico. Atomic bombs were then dropped on two cities in Japan in hopes of bringing the war to an end: Hiroshima on August 6, 1945, and Nagasaki on August 9, 1945. (820)

March on Washington (1963): Massive civil rights demonstration in August 1963 in support of Kennedy-backed legislation to secure legal protections for American blacks. One of the most visually impressive manifestations of the Civil Rights Movement, the march was the occasion of Martin Luther King's famous "I Have a Dream" speech. (897)

Marshall Plan (1948): Massive transfer of aid money to help rebuild postwar Western Europe, intended to bolster capitalist and democratic governments and prevent domestic communist groups from riding poverty and misery to power. The plan was first announced by Secretary of State George Marshall at Harvard's commencement in June 1947. (847)

McCarthyism: A brand of vitriolic, fear-mongering anti-communism associated with the career of Senator Joseph McCarthy. In the early 1950s, Senator McCarthy used his position in Congress to baselessly accuse high-ranking government officials and other Americans of conspiracy with communism. The term named after him refers to the dangerous forces of unfairness and fear wrought by anti-communist paranoia. (866)

McKinley Tariff (1890): Shepherded through Congress by President William McKinley, this tariff raised duties on Hawaiian sugar and set off renewed efforts to secure the annexation of Hawaii to the United States. (611)

McNary-Haugen Bill (1924–1928): A farm-relief bill that was championed throughout the 1920s and aimed to keep agricultural prices high by authorizing the government to buy up surpluses and sell them abroad. Congress twice passed the bill, but President Calvin Coolidge vetoed it in 1927 and 1928. (735)

Meat Inspection Act (1906): A law passed by Congress to subject meat shipped over state lines to federal inspection. The publication of Upton Sinclair's novel, *The Jungle*, earlier that year so disgusted American consumers with its description of conditions in slaughterhouses and meat-packing plants that it mobilized public support for government action. (650)

mechanization of agriculture: The development of engine-driven machines, like the combine, which helped to dramatically increase the productivity of land in the 1870s and 1880s. This process contributed to the consolidation of agricultural business that drove many family farms out of existence. (594)

Merrimack and _Monitor_ (1862): Confederate and Union ironclads, respectively, whose successes against wooden ships signaled an end to wooden warships. They fought an historic, though inconsequential battle in 1862. (439)

Meuse-Argonne offensive (1918): General John J. "Black Jack" Pershing led American troops in this effort to cut the German railroad lines supplying the western front. It was one of the few major battles that Americans participated in during the entire war, and was still underway when the war ended. (690)

Midway, Battle of (1942): A pivotal naval battle fought near the island of Midway on June 3–6, 1942. The victory halted Japanese advances in the Pacific. (809)

mining industry: After gold and silver strikes in Colorado, Nevada, and other western territories in the second half of the nineteenth century, fortune seekers by the thousands rushed to the West to dig. These metals were essential to U.S. industrial growth and were also sold into world markets. After surface metals were removed, people sought ways to extract ore from underground, leading to the development of heavy mining machinery. This, in turn, led to the consolidation of the mining industry, because only big companies could afford to buy and build the necessary machines. (584)

Miranda warning: A statement of an arrested person's constitutional rights, which police officers must read during an arrest. The warning came out of the Supreme Court's decision in *Miranda* v. *Arizona* in 1966 that accused people have the right to remain silent, consult an attorney, and enjoy other protections. The Court declared that law enforcement officers must make sure suspects understand their constitutional rights, thus creating a safeguard against forced confessions and self-implication. (921)

Mississippi Freedom Democratic party (1964): Political party organized by civil rights activists to challenge Mississippi's delegation to the Democratic National Convention, who opposed the civil rights planks in the party's platform. Claiming a mandate to represent the true voice of Mississippi, where almost no black citizens could vote, the MFDP demanded to be seated at the convention but were denied by party bosses. The effort was both a setback to civil rights activism in the south and a motivation to continue to struggle for black voting rights. (903)

modernism: In response to the demanding conditions of modern life, this artistic and cultural movement revolted against comfortable Victorian standards and accepted chance, change, contingency, uncertainty, and fragmentation. Originating among avant-garde artists and intellectuals around the turn of the twentieth century, modernism blossomed into a full-fledged cultural movement in art, music, literature, and architecture. (720)

Montgomery bus boycott (1955): Protest, sparked by Rosa Parks's defiant refusal to move to the back of the bus, by black Alabamians against segregated seating on city buses. The bus boycott lasted from December 1, 1955, until December 26, 1956, and became one of the foundational moments of the Civil Rights Movement. It led to the rise of Martin Luther King, Jr., and ultimately to a Supreme Court decision opposing segregated busing. (868)

Moral Majority: Political action committee founded by evangelical Reverend Jerry Falwell in 1979 to promote traditional Christian values and oppose feminism, abortion, and gay rights. The group was a major linchpin in the resurgent religious right of the 1980s. (951)

muckrakers: Bright young reporters at the turn of the twentieth century who won this unfavorable moniker from Theodore Roosevelt, but boosted the circulations of their magazines by writing exposés of widespread corruption in American society. Their subjects included business manipulation of government, white slavers, child labor, and the illegal deeds of the trusts, and helped spur the passage of reform legislation. (639)

Muller v. _Oregon_ (1908): A landmark Supreme Court case in which crusading attorney (and future Supreme Court Justice) Louis D. Brandeis persuaded the Supreme Court to accept the constitutionality of limiting the hours of women workers. Coming on the heels of *Lochner* v. *New York*, it established a different standard for male and female workers. (645)

My Lai Massacre (1968): Military assault in a small Vietnamese village on March 16, 1968, in which American soldiers under the command of 2nd Lieutenant William Calley murdered hundreds of unarmed Vietnamese civilians, mostly women and children. The atrocity produced outrage and reduced support for the war in America and around the world when details of the massacre and an attempted cover-up were revealed in 1971. (918)

National American Woman Suffrage Association (NAWSA): An organization founded in 1890 to demand the vote for women. NAWSA argued that women should be allowed to vote because their responsibilities in the home and family made them indispensable in the public decision-making process. During World War I, NAWSA supported the war effort and lauded women's role in the Allied victory, which helped to finally achieve nationwide woman suffrage in the Nineteenth Amendment (1920). (562)

National Labor Union (1866–1872): This first national labor organization in U.S. history was founded in 1866 and gained 600,000 members from many parts of the workforce, although it limited the participation of Chinese, women, and blacks. The organization devoted much of its energy to fighting for an eight-hour workday before it dissolved in 1872. (532)

National Recovery Administration (NRA) (1933): Known by its critics as the "National Run Around," the NRA was an early New Deal program designed to assist industry, labor, and the unemployed through centralized planning mechanisms that monitored workers' earnings and working hours to distribute work and established codes for "fair competition" to ensure that similar procedures were followed by all firms in any particular industrial sector. (761)

National Security Council Memorandum Number 68 (NSC-68) (1950): National Security Council recommendation to quadruple defense spending and rapidly expand peace-time armed forces to address Cold War tensions. It reflected a new militarization of American foreign policy but the huge costs of rearmament were not expected to interfere with what seemed like the limitless possibilities of postwar prosperity. (855)

National War Labor Board (1918): This wartime agency was chaired by former President Taft and aimed to prevent labor disputes by encouraging high wages and an eight-hour day. While granting some concessions to labor, it stopped short of supporting labor's most important demand: a government guarantee of the right to organize into unions. (682)

National War Labor Board (NWLB): Established by President Franklin D. Roosevelt to act as an arbitration tribunal and mediate disputes between labor and management that might have led to war stoppages and thereby undermined the war effort. The NWLB was also charged with adjusting wages with an eye to controlling inflation. (802)

naturalism: An offshoot of mainstream realism, this late-nineteenth-century literary movement purported to apply detached scientific objectivity to the study of human characters shaped by degenerate heredity and extreme or sordid social environments. (567)

Code talkers: Native American men who served in the military by transmitting radio messages in their native languages, which were undecipherable by German and Japanese spies. (806)

Neutrality Act of 1939: This act stipulated that European democracies might buy American munitions, but only if they could pay in cash and transport them in their own ships. The terms were known as "Cash-and-Carry." It represented an effort to avoid war debts and protect American arms-carriers from torpedo attacks. (785)

Neutrality Acts of 1935, 1936, and 1937: Short-sighted acts passed in 1935, 1936, and 1937 to prevent American participation in a European War. Among other restrictions, they prevented Americans from selling munitions to foreign belligerents. (782)

New Deal: The economic and political policies of Franklin Roosevelt's administration in the 1930s, which aimed to solve the problems of the Great Depression by providing relief for the unemployed and launching efforts to stimulate economic recovery. The New Deal built on reforms of the progressive era to expand greatly an American-style welfare state. (753)

New Freedom (1912): Platform of reforms advocated by Woodrow Wilson in his first presidential campaign, including stronger antitrust legislation to protect small business enterprises from monopolies, banking reform, and tariff reductions. Wilson's strategy involved taking action to increase opportunities for capitalist competition rather than increasing government regulation of large trusts. (661)

New Frontier (1961–1963): President Kennedy's nickname for his domestic policy agenda. Buoyed by youthful optimism, the program included proposals for the Peace Corps and efforts to improve education and health care. (889)

New Immigrants: Immigrants from southern and eastern Europe who formed a recognizable wave of immigration from the 1880s until 1924, in contrast to the immigrants from western Europe who had come before them. These new immigrants congregated in ethnic urban neighborhoods, where they worried many native-born Americans, some of whom responded with nativist anti-immigrant campaigns and others of whom introduced urban reforms to help the immigrants assimilate. (543)

New Nationalism (1912): State-interventionist reform program devised by journalist Herbert Croly and advocated by Theodore Roosevelt during his Bull Moose presidential campaign. Roosevelt did not object to continued consolidation of trusts and labor unions. Rather, he sought to create stronger regulatory agencies to insure that they operated to serve the public interest, not just private gain. (662)

Nine-Power Treaty (1922): Agreement coming out of the Washington "Disarmament" Conference of 1921–1922 that pledged Britain, France, Italy, Japan, the United States, China, the Netherlands, Portugal, and Belgium to abide by the Open Door Policy in China. The Five-Power Naval Treaty on ship ratios and the Four-Power Treaty to preserve the status quo in the Pacific also came out of the conference. (731)

Nineteenth Amendment (1920): This Constitutional amendment, finally passed by Congress in 1919 and ratified in 1920, gave women the right to vote over seventy years after the first organized calls for woman's suffrage in Seneca Falls, New York. (684)

Nixon Doctrine: President Nixon's plan for "peace with honor" in Vietnam. The doctrine stated that the United States would honor its existing defense commitments but, in the future, countries would have to fight their own wars. (917)

No Child Left Behind Act (2001): An education bill created and signed by the George W. Bush administration. Designed to increase accountability standards for primary and secondary schools, the law authorized several federal programs to monitor those standards and increased choices for parents in selecting schools for their children. The program was highly controversial, in large part because it linked results on standardized to federal funding for schools and school districts. (979)

Norris-La Guardia Anti-Injunction Act (1932): This law banned "yellow-dog," or anti-union, work contracts and forbade federal courts from issuing injunctions to quash strikes and boycotts. It was an early piece of labor-friendly federal legislation. (746)

North American Free Trade Agreement (NAFTA) (1993): Free trade zone encompassing Mexico, Canada, and the United States. A symbol of the increased reality of a globalized market place, the treaty passed despite opposition from protectionists and labor leaders. (969)

North Atlantic Treaty Organization (NATO): Military alliance of Western European powers and the United States and Canada established in 1949 to defend against the common threat from the Soviet Union, marking a giant stride forward for European unity and American internationalism. (849)

Nuremberg war crimes trial (1946): Highly publicized proceedings against former Nazi leaders for war crimes and crimes against humanity as part of the Allies denazification program in postwar Germany. The trials led to several executions and long prison sentences. (845)

Office of Price Administration (OPA) (1941–1947): A critically important wartime agency charged with regulating the consumer economy through rationing scarce supplies, such as automobiles, tires, fuel, nylon, and sugar, and by curbing inflation by setting ceilings on the price of goods. Rents were controlled as well in parts of the country overwhelmed by war workers. The OPA was extended after World War II ended to continue the fight against inflation, but was abolished in 1947. (802)

Oklahoma City bombing (1995): Truck-bomb explosion that killed 168 people in a federal office building on April 19, 1995. The attack was perpetrated by right-wing and anti-government militant Timothy McVeigh, later executed by the U.S. government for the crime. (967)

Open Door note (1899–1900): A set of diplomatic letters in which Secretary of State John Hay urged the great powers to respect Chinese rights and free and open competition within their spheres of influence. The notes established the "Open Door Policy," which sought to ensure access to the Chinese market for the United States, despite the fact that the U.S. did not have a formal sphere of influence in China. (623)

Operation Desert Storm (1991): U.S.-led multi-country military engagement in January and February of 1991 that drove Saddam Hussein's Iraqi army out of neighboring Kuwait. In addition to presaging the longer and more protracted Iraq War of the 2000s, the 1991 war helped undo what some called the "Vietnam Syndrome," a feeling of military uncertainty that plagued many Americans. (959)

Operation Dixie (1948): Failed effort by the CIO after World War II to unionize southern workers, especially in textile factories. (830)

Operation Wetback (1954): A government program to roundup and deport as many as one million illegal Mexican migrant workers in the United States. The program was promoted in part by the Mexican government and reflected burgeoning concerns about non-European immigration to America. (873)

Organization of Petroleum Exporting Countries (OPEC): Cartel comprising Middle Eastern states and Venezuela first organized in 1960. OPEC aimed to control access to and prices of oil, wresting power from Western oil companies and investors. In the process, it gradually strengthened the hand of non-Western powers on the world stage. (876)

Pacific Railroad Act (1862): Helped fund the construction of the Union Pacific transcontinental railroad with the use of land grants and government bonds. (473)

panic of 1873: A world-wide depression that began in the United States when one of the nation's largest banks abruptly declared bankruptcy, leading to the collapse of thousands of banks and businesses. The crisis intensified debtors' calls for inflationary measures such as the printing of more paper money and the unlimited coinage of silver. Conflicts over monetary policy greatly influenced politics in the last quarter of the nineteenth century. (491)

Patient Protection and Affordable Care Act (2010): Also known, somewhat derisively, as "Obamacare," the Act extended health care insurance to some 30 million Americans, marking a major step toward achieving the century-old goal of universal health care coverage for all citizens. **(986)**

patronage: Practice of rewarding political support with special favors, often in the form of public office. Upon assuming office, Thomas Jefferson dismissed few Federalist employees, leaving scant openings to fill with political appointees. (493)

Payne-Aldrich Bill (1909): While intended to lower tariff rates, this bill was eventually revised beyond all recognition, retaining high rates on most imports. President Taft angered the progressive wing of his party when he declared it "the best bill that the Republican party ever passed." (658)

Peace Corps: A federal agency created by President Kennedy in 1961 to promote voluntary service by Americans in foreign countries. The Peace Corps provides labor power to help developing countries improve their infrastructure, health care, educational systems, and other aspects of their societies. Part of Kennedy's New Frontier vision, the organization represented an effort by postwar liberals to promote American values and influence through productive exchanges across the world. (889)

Pearl Harbor (1941): An American naval base in Hawaii where Japanese warplanes destroyed numerous ships and caused 3,000 casualties on December 7, 1941—a day that, in President Roosevelt's words, was to "live in infamy." The attack brought the United States into World War II. (794)

Pendleton Act (1883): Congressional legislation that established the Civil Service Commission, which granted federal government jobs on the basis of examinations instead of political patronage, thus reigning in the spoils system. (499)

Pentagon Papers: Secret U.S. government report detailing early planning and policy decisions regarding the Vietnam War under Presidents Kennedy and Johnson. Leaked to the *New York Times* in 1971, it revealed instances of governmental secrecy, lies, and incompetence in the prosecution of the war. (919)

Perestroika: Meaning "restructuring," a cornerstone along with *Glasnost* of Soviet president Mikhail Gorbachev's reform movement in the USSR in the 1980s. These policies resulted in greater market liberalization, access to the West, and ultimately the end of communist rule. (949)

Philadelphia Plan (1969): Program established by Richard Nixon to require construction trade unions to work toward hiring more black apprentices. The plan altered Lyndon Johnson's concept of "affirmative action" to focus on groups rather than individuals. (921)

Platt Amendment (1901): Following its military occupation, the United States successfully pressured the Cuban government to write this amendment into its constitution. It limited Cuba's treaty-making abilities, controlled its debt, and stipulated that the United States could intervene militarily to restore order when it saw fit. (621)

Plessy v. *Ferguson* (1896): An 1896 Supreme Court case that upheld the constitutionality of segregation laws, saying that as long as blacks were provided with "separate but equal" facilities, these laws did not violate the Fourteenth Amendment. This decision provided legal justification for the Jim Crow system until the 1950s. (496)

policy of boldness (1954): Foreign policy objective of Dwight Eisenhower's Secretary of State John Foster Dulles, who believed in changing the containment strategy to one that more directly engaged the Soviet Union and attempted to roll back communist influence around the world. This policy led to a build-up of America's nuclear arsenal to threaten "massive retaliation" against communist enemies, launching the Cold War's arms race. (874)

Populists: Officially known as the People's party, the Populists represented Westerners and Southerners who believed that U.S. economic policy inappropriately favored Eastern businessmen instead of the nation's farmers. Their proposals included nationalizing the railroads, creating a graduated income tax, and most significantly the unlimited coinage of silver. (598)

Potsdam conference (1945): From July 17 to August 2, 1945, President Harry S Truman met with Soviet leader Joseph Stalin and British leaders Winston Churchill and later Clement Attlee (when the Labour party defeated Churchill's Conservative party) near Berlin to deliver an ultimatum to Japan: surrender or be destroyed. (820)

pragmatism: A distinctive American philosophy that emerged in the late nineteenth century around the theory that the true value of an idea lay in its ability to solve problems. The pragmatists thus embraced the provisional, uncertain nature of experimental knowledge. Among the most well-known purveyors of pragmatism were John Dewey, Oliver Wendell Holmes, Jr., and William James. (557)

Proposition 13 (1978): A successful California state ballot initiative that capped the state's real estate tax at 1 percent of assessed value. The proposition radically reduced average property tax levels, decreasing revenue for the state government and signaling the political power of the "tax revolt," increasingly aligned with conservative politics. (945)

Pullman strike (1894): An 1894 strike by railroad workers upset by drastic wage cuts. The strike was led by socialist Eugene Debs but not supported by the American Federation of Labor. Eventually President Grover Cleveland intervened and federal troops forced an end to the strike. The strike highlighted both divisions within labor and the government's new willingness to use armed force to combat work stoppages. (599)

Pure Food and Drug Act (1906): A law passed by Congress to inspect and regulate the labeling of all foods and pharmaceuticals intended for human consumption. This legislation, and additional provisions passed in 1911 to strengthen it, aimed particularly at the patent medicine industry. The more comprehensive Food, Drug, and Cosmetic Act of 1938 largely replaced this legislation. (650)

Quarantine Speech (1937): An important speech delivered by Franklin Roosevelt in which he called for "positive endeavors" to "quarantine" land-hungry dictators, presumably through economic embargos. The speech flew in the face of isolationist politicians. (784)

racketeers: People who obtain money illegally by fraud, bootlegging, gambling, or threats of violence. Racketeers invaded the ranks of labor during the 1920s, a decade when gambling and gangsterism were prevalent in American life. (708)

Reaganomics: Informal term for Ronald Reagan's economic policies, which focused on reducing taxes, social spending, and government regulation, while increasing outlays for defense. (946)

realism: Mid-nineteenth-century movement in European and American literature and the arts that sought to depict contemporary life and society as it actually was, in all its unvarnished detail. Adherents eschewed the idealism and nostalgia of the earlier romantic sensibility. (566)

recall: A progressive ballot procedure allowing voters to remove elected officials from office. (641)

Reciprocal Trade Agreements Act (1934): This act reversed traditional high-protective-tariff policies by allowing the president to negotiate lower tariffs with trade partners, without Senate approval. Its chief architect was Secretary of State Cordell Hull, who believed that tariff barriers choked off foreign trade. (780)

Reconstruction Act (1867): Passed by the newly elected Republican Congress, it divided the South into five military districts, disenfranchised former confederates, and required that Southern states both ratify the Fourteenth

Amendment and write state constitutions guaranteeing freedmen the franchise before gaining readmission to the Union. (475)

Reconstruction Finance Corporation (RFC) (1932): A government lending agency established under the Hoover administration in order to assist insurance companies, banks, agricultural organizations, railroads, and local governments. It was a precursor to later agencies that grew out of the New Deal and symbolized a recognition by the Republicans that some federal action was required to address the Great Depression. (746)

red scare (1919–1920): A period of intense anti-communism lasting from 1919 to 1920. The "Palmer raids" of Attorney General A. Mitchell Palmer resulted in about six thousand deportations of people suspected of "subversive" activities. (700)

Redeemers: Southern Democratic politicians who sought to wrest control from Republican regimes in the South after Reconstruction. (476)

referendum: A progressive reform procedure allowing voters to place a bill on the ballot for final approval, even after being passed by the legislature. (641)

regionalism: A recurring artistic movement that, in the context of the late nineteenth century, aspired to capture the peculiarities, or "local color," of America's various regions in the face of modernization and national standardization. (567)

reservation system: The system that allotted land with designated boundaries to Native American tribes in the West, beginning in the 1850s and ending with the Dawes Severalty Act of 1887. Within these reservations, most land was used communally, rather than owned individually. The U.S. government encouraged and sometimes violently coerced Native Americans to stay on the reservations at all times. (576)

rock 'n' roll: "Crossover" musical style that rose to dominance in the 1950s, merging black rhythm and blues with white bluegrass and country. Featuring a heavy beat and driving rhythm, rock 'n' roll music became a defining feature of the 1950s youth culture. (863)

Roe v. Wade (1973): Landmark Supreme Court decision that forbade states from barring abortion by citing a woman's constitutional right to privacy. Seen as a victory for feminism and civil liberties by some, the decision provoked a strong counter-reaction by opponents to abortion, galvanizing the Pro-Life movement. (932)

Rome-Berlin Axis (1936): Nazi Germany, under Adolf Hitler, and Fascist Italy, led by Benito Mussolini, allied themselves together under this nefarious treaty. The pact was signed after both countries had intervened on behalf of the fascist leader Francisco Franco during the Spanish Civil War. (781)

Roosevelt Corollary (1904): A brazen policy of "preventive intervention" advocated by Theodore Roosevelt in his Annual Message to Congress in 1904. Adding ballast to the Monroe Doctrine, his corollary stipulated that the United States would retain a right to intervene in the domestic affairs of Latin American nations in order to restore military and financial order. (630)

Root-Takahira agreement (1908): Signed on November 30, 1908, the United States and Japan agreed to respect each other's territorial possessions in the Pacific and to uphold the Open Door in China. The Agreement was credited with easing tensions between the two nations, but it also resulted in a weakened American influence over further Japanese hegemony in China. (631)

Rough Riders (1898): Organized by Theodore Roosevelt, this was a colorful, motley regiment of Cuban war volunteers consisting of western cowboys, ex-convicts, and effete Ivy Leaguers. Roosevelt emphasized his experience with the regiment in subsequent campaigns for Governor of New York and Vice-President under William McKinley. (615)

SALT II: Strategic Arms Limitation Treaty agreement between Soviet leader Leonid Brezhnev and American president Jimmy Carter. Despite an accord to limit weapons between the two leaders, the agreement was ultimately scuttled in the U.S. Senate following the Soviet invasion of Afghanistan in 1979. (938)

Sandinistas: Leftwing anti-American revolutionaries in Nicaragua who launched a civil war in 1979. (947)

scalawags: Derogatory term for pro-Union Southerners whom Southern Democrats accused of plundering the resources of the South in collusion with Republican governments after the Civil War. (478)

Schenck v. United States (1919): A Supreme Court decision that upheld the Espionage and Sedition Acts, reasoning that freedom of speech could be curtailed when it posed a "clear and present danger" to the nation. (681)

Scientific Management: A system of industrial management created and promoted in the early twentieth century by Frederick W. Taylor, emphasizing stopwatch efficiency to improve factory performance. The system gained immense popularity across the United States and Europe. (711)

settlement houses: Mostly run by middle-class native-born women, settlement houses in immigrant neighborhoods provided housing, food, education, child care, cultural activities, and social connections for new arrivals to the United States. Many women, both native-born and immigrant, developed life-long passions for social activism in the settlement houses. Jane Addams's Hull House in Chicago and Lillian Wald's Henry Street Settlement in New York City were two of the most prominent. (549)

Seward's Folly (1867): Popular term for Secretary of State William Seward's purchase of Alaska from Russia. The derisive term reflected the anti-expansionist sentiments of most Americans immediately after the Civil War. (482)

sharecropping: An agricultural system that emerged after the Civil War in which black and white farmers rented land and residences from a plantation owner in exchange for giving him a certain "share" of each year's crop. Sharecropping was the dominant form of southern agriculture after the Civil War, and landowners manipulated this system to keep tenants in perpetual debt and unable to leave their plantations. (496)

Sheppard-Towner Maternity Act (1921): Designed to appeal to new women voters, this act provided federally financed instruction in maternal and infant health care and expanded the role of government in family welfare. (684)

Sherman Anti-Trust Act (1890): A law that forbade trusts or combinations in business, this was landmark legislation because it was one of the first Congressional attempts to regulate big business for the public good. At first the law was mostly used to restrain trade unions as the courts tended to side with companies in legal cases. In 1914 the Act was revised so it could more effectively be used against monopolistic corporations. (525)

silent majority: Nixon Administration's term to describe generally content, law-abiding middle-class Americans who supported both the Vietnam War and America's institutions. As a political tool, the concept attempted to make a subtle distinction between believers in "traditional" values and the vocal minority of civil rights agitators, student protesters, counter-culturalists, and other seeming disruptors of the social fabric. (918)

Six-Day War (1967): Military conflict between Israel and its Arab neighbors, including Syria, Egypt, and Jordan. The war ended with an Israeli victory and territorial expansion into the Sinai Peninsula, the Golan Heights, the Gaza Strip, and the West Bank. The 1967 war was a humiliation for several Arab states, and the territorial disputes it created formed the basis for continued conflict in the region. (907)

Smith-Connally Anti-Strike Act (1943): Passed amidst worries about the effects that labor strikes would have on war production, this law allowed the federal government to seize and operate plants threatened by labor disputes. It also criminalized strike action against government-run companies. (803)

"smoking gun" tape: Recording made in the Oval Office in June 1972 that proved conclusively that Nixon knew about the Watergate break-in and endeavored to cover it up. Led to complete break-down in Congressional support for Nixon after the Supreme Court ordered he hand the tape to investigators. (926)

Social Darwinists: Believers in the idea, popular in the late nineteenth century, that people gained wealth by "survival of the fittest." Therefore, the wealthy had simply won a natural competition and owed nothing to the poor, and indeed service to the poor would interfere with this organic process. Some social Darwinists also applied this theory to whole nations and races, explaining that powerful peoples were naturally endowed with gifts that allowed them to gain superiority over others. This theory provided one of the popular justifications for U.S. imperial ventures like the Spanish-American war. (525)

social gospel: A reform movement led by Protestant ministers who used religious doctrine to demand better housing and living conditions for the urban poor. Popular at the turn of the twentieth century, it was closely linked to the settlement house movement, which brought middle-class, Anglo-American service volunteers into contact with immigrants and working people. (639)

Social Security Act (1935): A flagship accomplishment of the New Deal, this law provided for unemployment and old-age insurance financed by a payroll tax on employers

and employees. It has long remained a pillar of the "New Deal Order." (767)

Southern Renaissance: A literary outpouring among mid-twentieth-century southern writers, begun by William Faulkner and marked by a new critical appreciation of the region's burdens of history, racism, and conservatism. (886)

southern strategy (1972): Nixon reelection campaign strategy designed to appeal to conservative whites in the historically Democratic south. The President stressed law and order issues and remained noncommittal on civil rights. This strategy typified the regional split between the two parties as white Southerners became increasingly attracted to the Republican party in the aftermath of the Civil Rights Movement. (922)

SPARs (U.S. Coast Guard Women's Reserve): See **WAACs (Women's Auxiliary Army Corps).** (803)

Sputnik (1957): Soviet satellite first launched into Earth orbit on October 4, 1957. This scientific achievement marked the first time human beings had put a man-made object into orbit and pushed the USSR noticeably ahead of the United States in the Space Race. A month later, the Soviet Union sent a larger satellite, *Sputnik II*, into space, prompting the United States to redouble its space exploration efforts and raising American fears of Soviet superiority. (877)

Standard Oil Company (1870–1911): John D. Rockefeller's company, formed in 1870, which came to symbolize the trusts and monopolies of the Gilded Age. By 1877 Standard Oil controlled 95% of the oil refineries in the U.S. It was also one of the first multinational corporations, and at times distributed more than half of the company's kerosene production outside the U.S. By the turn of the century it had become a target for trust-busting reformers, and in 1911 the Supreme Court ordered it to break up into several dozen smaller companies. (524)

Stonewall Rebellion (1969): Uprising in support of equal rights for gay people sparked by an assault by off-duty police officers at a gay bar in New York. The rebellion led to a rise in activism and militancy within the gay community and furthered the sexual revolution of the late 1960s. (913)

Strategic Defense Initiative (SDI): Reagan administration plan announced in 1983 to create a missile-defense system over American territory to block a nuclear attack. Derided as "Star Wars" by critics, the plan typified Reagan's commitment to vigorous defense spending even as he sought to limit the size of government in domestic matters. (946)

Student Nonviolent Coordinating Committee (SNCC): Youth organization founded by southern black students in 1960 to promote civil rights. Drawing on its members' youthful energies, SNCC in its early years coordinated demonstrations, sit-ins, and voter registration drives. (872)

Students for a Democratic Society (SDS): A campus-based political organization founded in 1961 by Tom Hayden that became an iconic representation of the New Left. Originally geared toward the intellectual promise of "participatory democracy," SDS emerged at the forefront of the civil rights, antipoverty, and antiwar movements during the 1960s. (913)

Suez crisis (1956): International crisis launched when Egyptian president Gamal Abdel Nasser nationalized the Suez Canal, which had been owned mostly by French and British stockholders. The crisis led to a British and French attack on Egypt, which failed without aid from the United States. The Suez crisis marked an important turning point in the post-colonial Middle East and highlighted the rising importance of oil in world affairs. (875)

Sunbelt: The fifteen-state crescent through the American South and Southwest that experienced terrific population and productivity expansion during World War II and particularly in the decades after the war, eclipsing the old industrial Northeast (the "Frostbelt"). (835)

supply-side economics: Economic theory that underlay Ronald Reagan's tax and spending cuts. Contrary to Keynesianism, supply-side theory declared that government policy should aim to increase the supply of goods and services, rather than the demand for them. It held that lower taxes and decreased regulation would increase productivity by providing increased incentives to work, thus increasing productivity and the tax base. (945)

Taft-Hartley Act (1947): Republican-promoted, anti-union legislation passed over President Truman's vigorous veto that weakened many of labor's New Deal gains by banning the closed shop and other strategies that helped unions organize. It also required union leaders to take a noncommunist oath, which purged the union movement of many of its most committed and active organizers. (830)

Tampico Incident (1914): An arrest of American sailors by the Mexican government that spurred Woodrow Wilson to dispatch the American navy to seize the port of Veracruz in April 1914. Although war was avoided, tensions grew between the United States and Mexico. (669)

Teapot Dome scandal (1921): A tawdry affair involving the illegal lease of priceless naval oil reserves in Teapot Dome, Wyoming and Elk Hills, California. The scandal, which implicated President Harding's Secretary of the Interior, was one of several that gave his administration a reputation for corruption. (733)

Teller Amendment (1898): A proviso to President William McKinley's war plans that proclaimed to the world that when the United States had overthrown Spanish misrule, it would give Cuba its freedom. The amendment testified to the ostensibly "anti-imperialist" designs of the initial war plans. (614)

Tennessee Valley Authority (TVA) (1933): One of the most revolutionary of the New Deal public works projects, the TVA brought cheap electric power, full employment, low-cost housing, and environmental improvements to Americans in the Tennessee Valley. (766)

Tenure of Office Act (1867): Required the President to seek approval from the Senate before removing appointees. When Andrew Johnson removed his secretary of war in violation of the act, he was impeached by the house but remained in office when the Senate fell one vote short of removing him. (480)

Truman Doctrine (1947): President Truman's universal pledge of support for any people fighting any communist or communist-inspired threat. Truman presented the doctrine to Congress in 1947 in support of his request for $400 million to defend Greece and Turkey against Soviet-backed insurgencies. (846)

trust: A mechanism by which one company grants control over its operations, through ownership of its stock, to another company. The Standard Oil Company became known for this practice in the 1870s as it eliminated its competition by taking control of smaller oil companies. (521)

Tuskegee Institute: A normal and industrial school led by Booker T. Washington in Tuskegee, Alabama. It focused on training young black students in agriculture and the trades to help them achieve economic independence. Washington justified segregated, vocational training as a necessary first step on the road to racial equality, although critics accused him of being too "accomodationist." (555)

Tweed Ring: A symbol of Gilded Age corruption, "Boss" Tweed and his deputies ran the New York City Democratic party in the 1860s and swindled $200 million from the city through bribery, graft, and vote-buying. Boss Tweed was eventually jailed for his crimes and died behind bars. (490)

U-boats: German submarines, named for the German *Unterseeboot,* or "undersea boat," proved deadly for Allied ships in the war zone. U-boat attacks played an important role in drawing the United States into the First World War. (672)

Underwood Tariff (1913): This tariff provided for a substantial reduction of rates and enacted an unprecedented, graduated federal income tax. By 1917, revenue from the income tax surpassed receipts from the tariff, a gap that has since been vastly widened. (664)

Union League: Reconstruction-Era African American organization that worked to educate Southern blacks about civic life, built black schools and churches, and represented African American interests before government and employers. It also campaigned on behalf of Republican candidates and recruited local militias to protect blacks from white intimidation. (478)

United Nations (U.N.): International body formed in 1945 to bring nations into dialogue in hopes of preventing further world wars. Much like the former League of Nations in ambition, the UN was more realistic in recognizing the authority of the Big Five Powers in keeping peace in the world. Thus, it guaranteed veto power to all permanent members of its Security Council—Britain, China, France, the Soviet Union, and the United States. (844)

United Negro Improvement Association (UNIA): A black nationalist organization founded in 1914 by the Jamaican-born Marcus Garvey in order to promote resettlement of African Americans to their "African homeland" and to stimulate a vigorous separate black economy within the United States. (720)

USA Patriot Act (2001): Legislation passed shortly after the terrorist attacks of September 11, 2001, that granted broad surveillance and detention authority to the government. (975)

V-E (Victory in Europe) Day: The source of frenzied rejoicing, May 8, 1945 marked the official end to the war in Europe, following the unconditional surrender of what remained of the German government. (818)

Versailles, Treaty of (1919): World War I concluded with this vengeful document, which secured peace but imposed sharp terms on Germany and created a territorial mandate system to manage former colonies of the world powers. To Woodrow Wilson's chagrin, it incorporated very few of his original Fourteen Points, although it did include the League of Nations that Wilson had long sought. Isolationists in the United States, deeply opposed to the League, led the opposition to the Treaty, which was never ratified by the Senate. (694)

vertical integration: The practice perfected by Andrew Carnegie of controlling every step of the industrial production process in order to increase efficiency and limit competition. (521)

Vietnamization: Military strategy launched by Richard Nixon in 1969. The plan reduced the number of American combat troops in Vietnam and left more of the fighting to the South Vietnamese, who were supplied with American armor, tanks, and weaponry. (917)

V-J (Victory in Japan) Day: August 15, 1945 heralded the surrender of Japan and the final end to World War II. (821)

Volstead Act (1919): A federal act enforcing the Eighteenth Amendment, which prohibited the manufacture, sale, and transportation of alcoholic beverages. (704)

Voter Education Project (1962–1968): Effort by SNCC and other civil rights groups to register the South's historically disenfranchised black population. The project typified a common strategy of the civil rights movement, which sought to counter racial discrimination by empowering people at grassroots levels to exercise their civic rights through voting. (896)

Voting Rights Act of 1965: Legislation pushed through Congress by President Johnson that prohibited ballot-denying tactics, such as literary tests and intimidation. The Voting Rights Act was a successor to the Civil Rights Act of 1964 and sought to make racial disenfranchisement explicitly illegal. (903)

WACs (Women's Army Corps), WAVES (Women Accepted for Volunteer Emergency Service), and SPARs (U.S. Coast Guard Women's Reserve: The women's branches of the U.S. Army, Navy, and Coast Guard, established during World War II to employ women in non-combatant jobs. Women now participated in the armed services in ways that went beyond their traditional roles as nurses. (803)

Wabash, St. Louis & Pacific Railroad Company* v. *Illinois (1886): A Supreme Court decision that prohibited states from regulating the railroads because the Constitution grants Congress the power to regulate interstate commerce. As a result, reformers turned their attention to the federal government, which now held sole power to regulate the railroad industry. (519)

Wade-Davis Bill: Passed by Congressional Republicans in response to Abraham Lincoln's "10 percent plan," it required that 50 percent of a state's voters pledge allegiance to the Union, and set stronger safeguards for emancipation. Reflected divisions between Congress and the President, and between radical and moderate Republicans, over the treatment of the defeated South. (470)

Wagner Act (1935): Also known as the National Labor Relations Act, this law protected the right of labor to organize in unions and bargain collectively with employers, and established the National Labor Relations Board to monitor unfair labor practices on the part of employers. Its passage marked the culmination of decades of labor protest. (767)

Wall Street Reform and Consumer Protection Act (2010): Also known as the Dodd-Frank Act, after its Democratic sponsors, Connecticut Senator Christopher Dodd and Massachusetts Representative Barney Frank. In an effort to avoid another financial crisis like the Great Recession, the Act updated many federal regulations affecting the financial and banking systems, and created some new agencies such as the Bureau of Consumer Financial Protection. (986)

War Industries Board (1917): Headed by Bernard Baruch, this federal agency coordinated industrial production during World War I, setting production quotas, allocating raw materials, and pushing companies to increase efficiency and eliminate waste. Under the economic mobilization of the War Industries Board, industrial production in the United States increased 20 percent during the war. (682)

War Powers Act (1973): Law passed by Congress in 1973 limiting the President's ability to wage war without Congressional approval. The act required the President to notify Congress within 48 hours of committing troops to a foreign conflict. An important consequence of the Vietnam War, this piece of legislation sought to reduce the President's unilateral authority in military matters. (924)

War Production Board (WPB): Established in 1942 by executive order to direct all war production, including procuring and allocating raw materials, to maximize the nation's war machine. The WPB had sweeping powers over the U.S. economy and was abolished in November 1945 soon after Japan's defeat. (802)

War Refugee Board (1944): A United States agency formed to help rescue Jews from German-occupied territories and to provide relief to inmates of Nazi concentration camps. The agency performed noble work, but it did not begin operations until very late in the war, after millions had already been murdered. (788)

Watergate: Series of scandals that resulted in President Richard Nixon's resignation in August 1974 amid calls for his impeachment. The episode sprang from a failed burglary attempt at Democratic party headquarters in Washington's Watergate Hotel during the 1972 election. (925)

WAVES (Women Accepted for Volunteer Emergency Service): See WAACs (Women's Auxiliary Army Corps).

"Waving the bloody shirt": The use of Civil War imagery by political candidates and parties to draw votes to their side of the ticket. (489)

Weapons of mass destruction (WMD): Refers to weapons—nuclear, biological, and chemical—that can kill large numbers of people and do great damage to the built and natural environment. The term was used to refer to nuclear weapons during the Cold War. The Bush administration's claim that Saddam Hussein had developed WMD provided the rationale for the United States's invasion of

Iraq in 2003. These weapons were never found after the invasion. (965)

Welfare Reform Bill (1996): Legislation that made deep cuts in welfare grants and required able-bodied welfare recipients to find employment. Part of Bill Clinton's campaign platform in 1992, the reforms were widely seen by liberals as an abandonment of key New Deal/Great Society provisions to care for the impoverished. (968)

Whitewater: A series of scandals during the Clinton Administration that stemmed from a failed real estate investment from which the Clintons were alleged to have illicitly profited. The accusations prompted the appointment of a special federal prosecutor, though no indictments. (970)

Woman's Loyal League (1863–1865): Women's organization formed to help bring about an end to the Civil War and encourage Congress to pass a constitutional amendment prohibiting slavery. (477)

Women's Christian Temperance Union (WCTU): Founded in Ohio in the 1870s to combat the evils of excessive alcohol consumption, the WCTU went on to embrace a broad reform agenda, including campaigns to abolish prostitution and gain the right to vote for women. (646, 564)

Workingmen's Compensation Act: Passed under Woodrow Wilson, this law granted assistance to federal civil-service employees during periods of disability. It was a precursor to labor-friendly legislation passed during the New Deal. (666)

World Trade Organization (WTO) (1995): An international body to promote and supervise liberal trade among nations. The successor to the General Agreement on Tariffs and Trade, it marked a key world trade policy achievement of the Clinton Administration. (969)

World's Columbian Exposition (1893): Held in Chicago, Americans saw this World's Fair as their opportunity to claim a place among the world's most "civilized" societies, by which they meant the countries of western Europe. The Fair honored art, architecture, and science, and its promoters built a mini-city in which to host the fair that reflected all the ideals of city planning popular at the time. For many, this was the high point of the "City Beautiful" movement. (569)

Wounded Knee, Battle of (1890): A battle between the U.S. Army and the Dakota Sioux, in which several hundred Native Americans and 29 U.S. soldiers died. Tensions erupted violently over two major issues: the Sioux practice of the "Ghost Dance," which the U.S. government had outlawed, and the dispute over whether Sioux reservation land would be broken up because of the Dawes Act. (581)

Yalta conference (1945): Meeting of Franklin Roosevelt, Winston Churchill, and Joseph Stalin, in February 1945 at an old Tsarist resort on the Black Sea, where the Big Three leaders laid the foundations for the postwar division of power in Europe, including a divided Germany and territorial concessions to the Soviet Union. (839)

yellow journalism: A scandal-mongering practice of journalism that emerged in New York during the Gilded Age out of the circulation battles between Joseph Pulitzer's *New York World* and William Randolph Hearst's *New York Journal*. The expression has remained a pejorative term referring to sensationalist journalism practiced with unethical, unprofessional standards. (558)

Zimmermann note (1917): German foreign secretary Arthur Zimmerman had secretly proposed a German-Mexican alliance against the United States. When the note was intercepted and published in March 1917, it caused an uproar that made some Americans more willing to enter the war. (678)

INDEX

Aachen, in World War II, 814

"A&P Gypsies," 715

Abbott, Luman, 539

ABC (Anybody but Carter) movement, 943

ABC-1 agreement, 798

Abilene, Kansas, 586

Abolition and abolitionism, feminism and, 934

Abortion rights: Bush, George H. W., and, 961; controversy over, 929; Reagan and, 953; *Roe* v. *Wade* decision and, 921, 932, 954; *Webster* v. *Reproductive Health Services and,* 954

Abraham Lincoln Brigade, 783

Abrams v. *United States,* 561

Absalom, Absalom! (Faulkner), 724

Abstract expressionism, 880–881

Abu Ghraib prison, 978, 980

Abzug, Bella, 935

Acheson, Dean, 850, 855, 864, 866, 908

"Acres of Diamonds" (Conwell), 525

Adams, Charles Francis, 568

Adams, Henry, 488, 568, 720

Adams, John, 568

Adamson Act (1916), 666

Addams, Jane, 549, 639, 641, 704; election of 1912 and, 661; Hull House and, 549, 645; on vote for women, 562

Adjusted Compensation Act (1924), 730

Adkins v. *Children's Hospital,* 729

Adventures of Augie March, The (Bellow), 886, 887

Adventures of Huckleberry Finn, The (Twain), 566, 886

Adventures of Tom Sawyer, The (Twain), 566

Advertising: in 1950s, 833, 862–863; on radio, 715; sexual allure in, 718; after World War I, 710–711

Aerospace industry, 835, 860

Affirmative action, 900, 922, 932, 953–954; Bush and, 961; Clinton and, 968; on college campuses, 1007; Reagan and, 953

Affluence: inequality and, 992–996; in 1950s, 860–862; in 1970s, 917; after World War II, 831–838

Afghanistan, 829, 1012; Obama and, 986, 987; Soviet Union in, 939; Taliban in, 975

AFL. *See* American Federation of Labor

AFL-CIO, 877

Africa: Europeans and, 609; imperialism in, 633; independence in, 933; UNIA and, 720; in World War II, 811, 812. *See also* specific locations

African Americans, 640, 716; in Abraham Lincoln Brigade, 783; in armed forces, 691; Black Codes and, 471–472; Black Power and, 904–906; as Buffalo Soldiers, 577; in cities, 838; Colored Farmers' National Alliance and, 506–507, 598; education for, 554–555; farming by, 596; in FDR's administration, 760; in Great Depression, 770; great migration to North, 637; in Harlem, 719; Harlem Renaissance and, 724; Jim Crow and, 496, 508; Ku Klux Klan and, 479–480; labor unions and, 533, 534, 535;

lynchings of, 496–497; migration by, 467, 683, 806, 838, 870–871; music of, 718–719; panic of 1873 and, 491; Populism and, 506–508; as president, 829, 965; prosperity of, 1006–1007; rights of, 903–904; segregation and, 867–868; sharecropping and tenant farming by, 496; single women as family heads, 1006; in South, 487, 528; in Spanish-American War, 615; as strikebreakers, 683; in suburbs, 837; on Supreme Court, 961; United Negro Improvement Society and, 720; whites and, 1006; women, 478, 563–564; in World War I, 683, 687, 691; in World War II, 805, 806. *See also* Civil rights; Civil rights movement; Obama, Barack

African Methodist Episcopal Church, 469

Afrikaners (Boers), 593

Agassiz, Louis, 553, 560

Age and aging. *See* Elderly

Age of Innocence, The (Wharton), 567

Age of Reform, The (Hofstadter), 510, 675

Agnew, Spiro T., 909, 918, 925–926

Agribusiness, 595, 834

Agricultural Adjustment Act: of 1933, 755, 758; of 1938, 758, 764

Agricultural Adjustment Administration (AAA), 763

Agricultural Marketing Act (1929), 740

Agriculture: crop-lien system in, 496; Dust Bowl and, 764, 765 (map); genetic engineering and, 991; Hoover and, 740; Japanese Americans in, 800–801; labor for, 624; vs. manufacturing, 528; mechanization of, 594–595, 735, 764; railroads and, 518; under Roosevelt, Franklin D., 763–764; in South, 465, 526–527; after World War II, 834. *See also* Farms and farming

Agriculture Department, Forestry Division of, 658

Aguinaldo, Emilio, 614, 615, 622, 623

AIDS (acquired immunodeficiency syndrome), 913, 1010

Aid to Families with Dependent Children (AFDC), 921

Air Force One (airplane), 860

Airlift, in Berlin, 846

Airplanes: Lindbergh flight and, 714–715; in 1950s, 860; in World War I, 692, 714; in World War II, 789, 810, 811; Wright brothers and, 714

Alabama, civil rights movement in, 903, 904

Alamogordo, New Mexico, atomic testing in, 820

Alaska, 658, 880; Arctic National Refuge in, 973; and lower forty-eight states, 482 (map); purchase of, 481–482; in World War II, 809

Albanians, ethnic, 969

Albee, Edward, 886

Albright, Madeleine, 970

"Alcan" Highway, 809

Alcatraz, Indian seizure of, 933

Alcohol: industry, during Great Depression, 762–763; prohibition of, 704–708. *See also* Whiskey

Aldrich, Nelson W., 665

Aldrich-Vreeland Act (1908), 656

Aldrin, Edwin ("Buzz"), 891

Alexie, Sherman, 1010

Algeciras, Spain, conference in, 630

Alger, Horatio, 537, 565

Alito, Samuel A., Jr., 979

Allende, Salvador, 920

Alliance for Progress, 893

Allies (World War I), 670, 678, 686; loans to, 671, 737; at Paris Peace Conference, 694; in Russia, 688; war debt repayment by, 737–738

Allies (World War II), 790, 798, 811, 812, 821–824, 840–841

All the King's Men (Long), 886

Alperovitz, Gar, 825

Altgeld, John Peter, 533, 599, 638

Amazon.com, 1010

America First Committee, 789

American (magazine), 641

American Association of Retired Persons (AARP), 979

American Dilemma, An (Myrdal), 868

American Diplomacy (Kennan), 697

American Federation of Labor (AFL), 503, 533, 535, 536, 683, 768, 769. *See also* AFL-CIO

American Indians. *See* Native Americans

American International Group (AIG), 984

American Legion, 730

American Missionary Association, 469

American Museum of Natural History, 760

American plan, 701

American Populism (McMath), 510

American Protective Association, 551

American Railway Union, 599

American Red Cross, 564–565

American Relief and Recovery Act, 985

American Samoa, 609

American Society for the Prevention of Cruelty to Animals, 564

Americans with Disabilities Act (ADA, 1990), 961

American System (1824), 520

American Tobacco Company, 526

American Tragedy, An (Dreiser), 720

Americas. *See* Central America; Colonies and colonization; Latin America; North America

America's Hidden Success (Schwarz), 913

"Amos 'n' Andy," 715

Anacostia Flats, Battle of, 746

Anarchy and anarchism, 533, 550

Anderson, John, 943, 944 (map)

Anderson, Jourdan, 468

Anderson, Sherwood, 721

Angels in America (Kushner), 1010

Anglo-American alliance, of Reagan-Thatcher, 944–945

Angola, Cuba and, 936

Anna in the Tropics (Cruz), 1010

Annexation: of Hawaii, 611, 611 (map), 614; of Philippines, 611 (map), 617–620, 622
Anthony, Susan B., 476, 477, 563
Anthropology, 760
Anti-abortion movement, 953
Anti-ballistic missile (ABM) treaty, 920
Antibiotics, 995
Antiforeignism, 550–551, 701
Anti-German sentiment, in World War I, 670–671, 673
Antigovernment attitude, in 1980s, 944–945
Anti-immigrant sentiment, 487, 637
Anti-Imperialist League, 620
Antin, Mary, 545
Antipoverty programs, of Johnson, Lyndon B., 902–903
Anti-Saloon League, 564
Antisedition law, Smith Act as, 852
Anti-Semitism, 788; in Nazi Germany, 822. See also Jews and Judaism
Antitrust movement, 525; Harding and, 729; Interstate Commerce Act and, 519–520; Roosevelt, Theodore, and, 649–650; Sherman Anti-Trust Act and, 525–526; under Taft, 658; under Wilson, 666. See also Corporations; Trusts
Antiwar movement: end of, 929; in Sixties, 913; in Vietnam War, 907, 918–919; in World War I, 681, 682, 683–684
Antwerp, 816
Apache Indians, 575, 579
Apollo 11, 891, 994
Appalachian region, textile mills in, 528
Appeasement, 784, 785
Aquino, Corazon, 949
Arabic (ship), sinking of, 673
Arab-Israeli wars, Six-Day War and, 907
Arabs and Arab world: oil embargo in, 924–925; Truman and, 848. See also Middle East
"Arab Spring," in Middle East, 1011
Arafat, Yasir, 907, 970
Araucanian people (Argentina), 593
Archangel, Russia, 688
Architecture: international style, 723; modernism in, 723; postmodern, 1007–1008; post-World War II, 882; Prairie School of, 723; skyscrapers and, 539, 723
Arctic National Wildlife Refuge, 973
Ardennes Forest, in World War II, 816
Argentina, 592, 593; immigrants in, 546
Argonne Forest, World War I in, 690
Ariel (Plath), 883
Arikara Indians, 576
Arizona, 575, 589, 618; illegal immigrants in, 1001; Mexican migrants in, 668
Arkansas, school integration in, 869
Armed forces: African Americans in, 577, 691; great railroad strike and, 497; in Persian Gulf War, 959; in Philippines, 622; unification of, 849; women in, 803, 812; before World War I, 682; in World War I, 686–687, 691; World War II and, 807. See also Military; Soldiers; Wars and warfare
Armistice: in Spanish-American War, 616; in World War I, 682, 691
Armory Show, 722
Armour, Philip, 524, 585
Arms and armaments: after World War II, 849–850. See also Weapons
Arms control: Carter and, 936; Reagan and, 947
Arms embargo, 783, 785
Arms race, H-bomb and, 851–852

Armstrong, Louis, 719, 724
Army. See Armed forces
Army-McCarthy hearings, 866, 867
Arnautoff, Victor, mural by, 760
Arsenal of democracy, U.S. as, 803
Art(s): modernism in, 720–724; naturalism in, 565–566, 567; in 1920s, 720–724; postmodern, 1007–1010; realism in, 565, 566–567; regionalism in, 565, 566, 567–568. See also specific arts and artists
Arthur, Chester A., 499; death of, 502; election of 1880 and, 498; spoils system and, 499
"Aryans," Nazis and, 822
Asia: immigrants from, 498, 630–631; imperialism in, 633; Japanese attacks in, 808; U.S. isolationism and, 779; U.S.-Japan rivalry in, 630; after World War II, 850–852. See also specific locations
Asian Americans, 1004; as authors, 1010; racial attacks on, 1006; in West, 594. See also Chinese Americans; Japanese Americans
As I Lay Dying (Faulkner), 724
Assembly lines, 520, 710, 711–712
Assimilation: immigrants and, 544, 547, 718; of Native Americans, 580, 581–584
Assistant, The (Malamud), 887
Associated Press, 558
AT&T (American Telephone and Telegraph), 994
Atchison, Topeka and Santa Fe Railroad, 516
Athletes, women as, 997
Atkinson, Fort, signing of treaties at, 576
Atlanta Constitution, 526, 527
Atlanta University, 555
Atlantic Charter, 793, 802, 842
Atlantic Community, 891
Atlantic Conference (1941), 793
Atlantic Monthly, 558, 566, 568
Atlantic Ocean region, in World War II, 810
Atomic bombs: Soviet explosion of, 851; in World War II, 820, 825. See also Nuclear weapons
Atomic power, 844. See also Nuclear weapons
Attu, in World War II, 809, 810
Audiotapes, in Nixon White House, 926–928
Audubon Society, 653, 654
August: Osage County (Letts), 1010
Australia, frontier in, 592
Australian ballot, 641
Austria: German takeover of, 784; after World War II, 845
Austria-Hungary, World War I and, 670
Autobiography of Alice B. Toklas, The (Stein), 721
Autobuses, 713
Automobiles and automobile industry: financial support of, 985; Ford and, 711–712; growth of, 710, 711–712; hybrid, 1012; international comparison of number of autos, 712; Model T and, 712; in 1950s, 833; oil industry and, 524; social change and, 712–714; strikes in, 768; suburbs and, 713, 836; unions in, 768
Awakening, The (Chopin), 568
"Axis of evil," Bush, George W., on, 976
Axis powers, in World War II, 792, 812, 813
Ayers, Edward L., 510

Babbitt (Lewis), 721
Baby boom, 653, 838, 999

Bad Heart Bull, Amos, 579
Baer, George F., 647
Baghdad, 960
Bailey, James A., 570
Baker, Josephine, 868
Baker, Ray Stannard, 640, 641
Bakke, Allan, 932
Balanced budget, 772
Baldwin, James, 886
Balkan region, 969, 980
Ballinger, Richard, 658
Baltimore, Maryland, 541
Baltimore Sun, 720
Bank(s) and banking, 487; failures of, 724, 741, 756; housing loans and, 983–984; New Deal and, 765; Roosevelt, Franklin D., and, 755–757; S&L crisis and, 955; Wilson and reforms of, 665–666. See also Economy
Bankruptcy, of railroads, 516
Baptists, 469, 552; Fundamentalism and, 710
Baraka, Imamu Amiri. See Jones, LeRoi
Barbed wire, 586, 588
Barnum, Phineas T., 570
Barton, Bruce, 710–711
Barton, Clara, 565
Baruch, Bernard, 682, 844
Baseball, 570–571, 711, 863, 868
Basketball, 571
Bataan Death March, 808, 809 (map)
Bathtub gin, 708
Batista, Fulgencio, 780
"Battle Hymn of the Republic" (Howe), 689
Battle of Britain, 789
Battle of the Atlantic, in World War II, 810
Battles. See specific battles and wars
Bauhaus architecture, 723
Bay of Pigs invasion (Cuba), 893–895
Beale, Howard K., 483, 634
Beard, Charles, 510, 962
Beard, Mary, 510, 962
Beat Generation, 883, 884–885
Beatles, 863
"Beatniks," 885
Becker, Joseph H., 515
Beecher family: Catharine, 562; Henry Ward, 559. See also Stowe, Harriet Beecher
Beer and Wine Revenue Act (1933), 755
Begin, Menachem, 934, 936
Beijing (Peking), 623
Belgium, 670, 688, 786
Belknap, William, 490
Bell, Alexander Graham, 521
Bell, Daniel, 962
Bell Jar, The (Plath), 883
Bellow, Saul, 886, 887
Beloved (Morrison), 1009
Benedict, Michael, 483
Benedict, Ruth, 760
Ben Hur:... (Wallace), 565
Berger, Victor L., 659
Berkeley, California, Free Speech Movement in, 911
Berlin, airlift to, 846
Berlin Wall, 891, 892, 956–957
Bernstein, Barton J., 775, 825
Bernstein, Leonard, 619
Bessemer process, 522
Bethune, Mary McLeod, 760, 762
Beveridge, Albert J., 620
Beyond Entitlements (Meade), 913
Bias, in newspaper articles, 899
Bible Belt, 702, 709–710, 879
Bible reading, in schools, 921

Bicentennial celebration, 933
Bicycles, 571, 572
Biden, Joseph, election of 2008 and, 983
Bierstadt, Albert, 594
Big business, 487, 497; agriculture as, 595; cattle ranching as, 586; Kennedy, John F., and, 890; mining industry as, 584–585; New Deal and, 765; political contributions and, 499, 504; railroads as, 517; sports as, 711. *See also* Business; Commerce
Bigelow, Kathryn, 1010
Big Five, 844
Big Four legislative achievements, 902
Big government: Obama and, 986; Reagan on, 942
Bighorn Mountains, 578
Big Science, 994
Big Sister policy, 609
Big Stick policy, of Theodore Roosevelt, 629, 630, 631, 667
Big Technology, 994
Big Three, at Yalta, 839–840
Big Two, in World War II, 812, 813
Bikini Atoll, H-bomb test at, 851
Billion-Dollar Congress, 504–505
Billy the Kid, 592
Bin Laden, Osama, 975, 987–988
Biological engineering, 991–992
Biosphere, balance of, 991
Biracial Americans, 1007
"Birds of passage," 545, 546
Birmingham, Alabama, 527; church bombing in, 898; desegregation of, 896–897
Birth control, 559, 562; movement, 716–718; pill for, 912; Supreme Court on, 920–921
Birth of a Nation (film), 716
Birthrate: baby boom and, 838; decline in, 562, 741; Latino population and, 1004; of New Immigrants, 550; for nonwhites, 1004; to single parents, 997–998
Bismarck, Otto von, 610
Bison. *See* Buffalo
Bitter Cry of the Children, The (Spargo), 640
Black Boy (Wright), 886
Black Cabinet, 762
Black Codes, 471–472, 474
Black Elk (Oglala Sioux), 583
Blackface performance, 718
Black Friday (September 24, 1869), 490
Black Hills, gold in, 578–579
Black list, 532
Black Monday (October 19, 1987), 955
Black Panther party, 905
Black Power movement, 904–906, 913
Blacks. *See* African Americans
Black Star Line Steamship Company, 720
Black Tuesday, 740
Blaine, James G., 494, 498, 502–503, 504, 609
Blair, Tony, 978
Blake, Eubie, 724
Blended families, 998
Blessed Among Nations (Rauchway), 510
Blockade: in Korean War, 856; in World War I, 671–672; in World War II, 785
Block signal, 517
Blogs, 1010–1011
Blue-collar jobs, 547, 860
Bly, Oregon, Japanese firebomb and, 823, 824
Boas, Franz, 760
Boat people, from Vietnam, 931
Bodmer, Karl, 584
Boeing Company, 860

Boers, 593
Boer War, 628
Bohlen, Charles, 817
Boldness policy, of Dulles, 874, 875
Boll weevils, southern Democrats as, 945
Bolshevik Revolution (1917), 700, 840
Bolsheviks, 687, 688
Bombs and bombings: atomic, 820, 821; of Cambodia, 924; Haymarket, 533; of Japan, 818; of North Vietnam, 923; of Oklahoma City Federal Building, 967; during red scare, 700, 701; of Vietnam, 894 (map), 907; in World War II, 811, 816
Bonds, for World War I, 686
Bonus Army, 746, 747
Bonus bill (1922), 730
Bonus Expeditionary Force (BEF), 746
Books: in 1880s, 557. *See also* Literature
Boom and bust cycles, 734
Boomtowns, 584
Bootlegging, 705, 708
Borah, William, 693
Borders, 1002. *See also* Boundaries
Border States, 739
Bosnia, 958, 969
Boss (political), 490, 546–547
Boston, Massachusetts, 569
Bostonians, The (James), 567
Boundaries: British Guiana-Venezuela dispute over, 609–610; eastern of West, 575. *See also* Borders
Bourgeois, protests against (1960s), 911–912
Bourgeoisie, Marx on, 642
Bourne, Randolph, 704
Boxer Rebellion (China), 623–626
Boxing, 571, 711
Boycotts, of segregated buses, 868
Boy Scouts of America, 654
Bozeman Trail, 578
Bracero program, 803
Brain Trust, 752–753
Branch Davidians, 967
Brandeis, Louis D., 645–646, 665, 704
Breakdancing, 1009
Breaker boys, 530
Bretton Woods Conference (1944), 841
Bretton Woods system, 922
Brewer, David J., 648
Brezhnev, Leonid, 707, 938
Bricker, John, 866
Brief Wondrous Life of Oscar Wao, The (Diaz), 1010
Brinkley, Alan, 776, 962
Britain: Battle of, 789. *See also* England (Britain)
British Broadcasting Corporation (BBC), 739
British Guiana, Venezuela and, 609–610
British Military Area (1914), 672 (map)
British Petroleum (BP), oil spill by (2010), 987, 1011
"Brokeback Mountain" (Proulx), 1009–1010
Brooklyn Bridge, 541
Brooklyn Dodgers, in Los Angeles, 863
Brotherhood of Sleeping Car Porters, 805
Brown v. *Board of Education of Topeka, Kansas*, 868–869
Bruce, Blanche K., 478
Bryan, William Jennings, 638, 720; Cross of Gold speech of, 597, 601–602, 604; election of 1896 and, 510, 601–604, 603 (map); election of 1900 and, 626–627; election of 1908 and, 656; election of 1912 and, 661; free silver and, 509; in Scopes trial, 710; as Secretary of State, 667, 673
Buchenwald, in World War II, 818

Buck, Pearl S., 760–761
Budget, balanced, 772
Budget, Bureau of the, 725
Budget deficits: under Bush, George H. W., 962; Clinton's reduction of, 967; in 1890s, 508; under Reagan, 946, 951. *See also* Federal budget
Buenos Aires, 539
Buffalo (bison): Native Americans and, 576, 582; near annihilation of, 580
Buffalo Soldiers, 577
Buford ("Soviet Ark"), 701
Building trades, padrone system in, 547
Bulgaria, 670, 839
Bulge, Battle of the, 816, 816 (map)
Bullitt, William, 785
Bull moose Progressives, 667, 674; election of 1912 and, 662; election of 1920 and, 696
Buna beach, New Guinea, 809
Bunau-Varilla, Philippe, 628
Bundy, McGeorge, 825
Bunyan, John, 639
Bureaucracy, segregation of federal, 666
Burger, Warren E., as Chief Justice, 921
Burlingame, Anson, 500
Burlingame Treaty (1880), 500, 501
Burma, 633, 808
Burnham, Daniel, 569
Burroughs, William S., 885, 1008
Bus boycott, in Montgomery, 868
Bush, George Herbert Walker, 829, 955–962; Cold War and, 955–959; domestic policies of, 961–962; election of 1988 and, 955; election of 1992 and, 965–966, 966 (map); national debt and, 952; Persian Gulf crisis and, 959–960, 978
Bush, George Walker, 829, 965; on "axis of evil," 976; domestic policy under, 972; economy and, 984; election of 2000 and, 972, 972 (map), 973 (map); election of 2004 and, 979; guest-worker program of, 1001; Hurricane Katrina and, 982; Kyoto Treaty and, 1012; September 11, 2001, terrorist attacks and, 965, 974–975; state of the union address (2002), 976; Supreme Court and, 979
Business: agri-, 595; computers and, 860; Coolidge and, 734; depression of 1893 and, 508; Harding and, 729–730; Internet and, 1010; inventions for, 521; Kennedy, John F., and, 890; New Deal and, 774; in 1950s, 862–864; in 1970s, 917; panic of 1873 and, 491; in 21st century, 991. *See also* Corporations
Business (social) class, 537
Business organization: horizontal integration, 521–522; vertical integration, 521
Butler, Benjamin F., 481, 489n
Butow, R. J. C., 825

Cabinet (presidential): women in, 760, 762. *See also* specific presidents
Cable television, 1010
Caen, Herb, 885
California, 644; agriculture as big business in, 595; in census of 2010, 988 (map); Chicano population of, 1004; Chinese immigrants in, 498; Dust Bowl migrants in, 764; Japanese in, 630–631, 667; Mexican migrants in, 668; progressive reforms in, 645; after World War II, 835
California gold rush, 500
Call of the Wild, The (London), 567, 654
Calvinism, 552

Cambodia: secret bombing of, 924; Vietnam War and, 918–919

Cameron, James, 1010

Camp, Walter C., 571

Campaigns (political): contributions from federal employees, 499; finance reform and, 773; negative, 900. *See also* Elections

Camp David, Maryland, Eisenhower-Khrushchev meeting at, 878

Camp David Agreement (1978), 934–935, 936

Canada, 708; bank failures in, 756*n*; immigrants from, 703; sealhunting dispute and, 609; westward movement in, 592–593

Canals, Panama, 627–629

Cape Colony, 593

Capital. *See* District of Columbia; Washington, D.C.

Capital investment, tax policies and, 710

Capitalism: communism and, 840; Marx and, 642; Roosevelt, Franklin D., and, 774–775; spread of, 862

Capone, "Scarface" Al, 708

Capper-Volstead Act (1921), 735

Careers, for women, 997

Carey Act (1894), 651

Caribbean region: Central America and, 947 (map); dollar diplomacy in, 658; Roosevelt Corollary and, 630; Spanish-American War in, 614–616, 616 (map); U.S. dominance in, 947; U.S. intervention in, 668, 668 (map), 736. *See also* specific locations

Carlisle Indian School, 581

Carmichael, Stokely, 905, 913, 935

Carnaval (Carnival), 619

Carnegie, Andrew, 486, 505, 557, 620, 664; "Gospel of Wealth" of, 525; Morgan and, 523; in steel industry, 522–523; vertical integration and, 521

Caroline Islands, 694*n*

Carpenter, Mrs. Herbert, 636

Carpentier, Georges, 711

Carpetbaggers, 478

Carranza, Venustiano, 669, 670

Cars. *See* Automobiles and automobile industry

Carson, Rachel, 653, 922

Carter, James Earl, Jr. ("Jimmy"), 829, 933–939; diplomacy of, 933–936; economy, energy, and, 936–938; election of 1976 and, 933; election of 1980 and, 943–944, 944 (map); Farewell Address of, 944; foreign policy of, 938–939; human rights under, 933–936; Iran hostage crisis and, 938–939; "malaise speech" of, 938; and Nicaragua, 947

Carver, George Washington, 555

Casablanca, in World War II, 812, 813

Cash-and-carry policy, 785

Cash registers, 521

Cassady, Neal, 884, 885

Cassatt, Mary, 568

Castro, Fidel, 878, 893

Casualties: in Homestead Strike, 506; in Philippine insurrection, 622, 623; in railroad strike (1877), 497. *See also* specific wars

Catch-22 (Heller), 883

Catcher in the Rye (Salinger), 886

Cather, Willa, 720

Cathode ray tubes, 860

Catholic Church: immigrants and, 545; Kennedy and, 879; New Immigrants and, 552; in 1960s, 911; in Philippines, 617*n*; Polish in, 706; Smith, Alfred E., and, 739

Catlin, George, 582, 594

Cat on a Hot Tin Roof (Williams), 883

Catt, Carrie Chapman, 563, 684

Cattle, long-horned, 585, 586

Cattle drives, railroads and, 586

Cattle trails, 586 (map)

Cease-fire, in Vietnam, 923, 924

Censorship, 716; World War I and, 681

Census: of 1870, 488, 539; of 1890, 548, 589; of 1900, 548; of 1910, 671; of 1920, 716; of Latino Americans, 1003; racial categories in, 1007; U.S. demography and, 988. *See also* Population

Central America: canal across, 627; Caribbean region and, 949 (map); Reagan and, 947; U.S. intervention in, 736. *See also* Latin America; specific locations

Central government. *See* Government (U.S.)

Central Intelligence Agency (CIA): Chile and, 920; Cuba and, 893; Iran and, 875; Latin America and, 878; Vietnam and, 907

Central Pacific Railroad, 515, 517, 556

Central Park (New York City), 569

Central Powers (World War I), 670; Allies-U.S. trade and, 671

Century of Dishonor, A (Jackson), 580

Cermak, Anton J., 753

Chabon, Michael, 1009

Chan-Chä-Uiá-Teüin, Teton Sioux Woman (Bodmer), 583

Chappaquiddick Island, Kennedy, Edward, and, 943

Charleston, South Carolina, after Civil War, 466

Château-Thierry, Battle of, 690, 814

Chautauqua movement, 554

Chávez, César, 1004

Chechnya, 958

Checkers Speech, 864

Cheever, John, 883

Cheney, Richard, 972, 973, 976, 979

Chesnutt, Charles W., 568

Cheyenne, Wyoming, 586

Cheyenne Indians, 576; cradleboard of, 583

Cheyenne River Sioux Tribe, 1004

Chiang Kai-shek. *See* Jiang Jieshi

Chicago, Illinois, 784; Dearborn Street in (c. 1900), 487; Democratic National Convention (1968), 909; fire in (1871), 542; gangsters in, 708; Haymarket Square episode in, 533; Hull House in, 549; immigrants in, 544; meatpacking industry in, 650; Poles in, 706, 707; population in, 539; Pullman strike in, 599; race riot in (1919), 683; redesign of, 569; skyscrapers in, 539; stockyards in, 586; World's Columbian Exposition in, 569–570. *See also* Illinois

Chicago Daily News, 558

Chicanos, in California, 1004

Chief Joseph (Nez Perce), 578 (map), 579

Child care, women and, 996

Child labor, 527, 528, 530, 531, 640; laws restricting, 666, 761, 768

Child-rearing, 835, 998

Children: of freed slaves, 467; of immigrants, 545, 546, 547, 639

Children's Bureau, 645

Chile, 609; Allende in, 920

China, 609, 633, 667; Boxer Rebellion in, 623–626; Clinton and, 969; communism in, 840, 850–851; diplomatic relations with, 935; Japan and, 694, 747–748, 784; after Korean War, 865; MacArthur and, 855–856; Nine-Power Treaty and, 731–732; Nixon in, 920; Open Door policy toward, 623, 626, 658; Southeast Asia and, 892; Soviet Union and, 919–920; Tiananmen Square protest in, 955–956; in United Nations, 844; after World War II, 850–851; in World War II, 808

Chinatowns, 500

Chinese, as migrant farm labor, 595

Chinese Americans: citizenship and, 498; labor unions and, 533, 534; in population (1850–2008), 501; as railroad labor, 515; Tan on, 1010

Chinese Exclusion Act (1882), 498, 501, 534, 542, 551

Chinese immigrants, 500–501, 542; in California, 498; in Hawaii, 611

Chippewa Indians, 576

Chivington, J. M., 577, 578

Cholera, 576

Chopin, Kate, 568

Christianity: conservative, 952, 953; after World War II, 847. *See also* Catholic Church; Missions and missionaries; Religion

Christian Science, 552–553

Christian socialism, 549

Church and state, separation of, 902, 921

Churches: black, 467–469; Fundamentalists vs. Modernists, 718; in 1960s, 911; urban population and, 551–553

Churches of Christ, 710

Churchill, Winston: at Atlantic Conference, 793; on atomic bomb, 825; at Casablanca, 812, 813; at Potsdam, 820; at Tehran Conference, 813; in World War II, 786, 792 (map), 810; at Yalta conference, 839–840

Church of Christ, Scientist (Christian Science), 552–553

Church of Jesus Christ of Latter-Day Saints. *See* Mormons

CIO (Congress of Industrial Organizations), 535, 769, 770, 815; Operation Dixie of, 830–831. *See also* Committee for Industrial Organization (CIO)

Circus, 570

Cities and towns: African Americans in, 806; architecture in, 539; boomtowns, 584; in Civil War, 465, 466; company, 532; crime in, 541; department stores in, 540–541; families in, 562; gangsters in, 708; ghost towns, 584; growth of, 486, 539–542; immigrants in, 547; minorities in, 1006; modernist architecture in, 723; movement from rural areas to, 486, 539–540; Native Americans in, 1004; population of, 486, 539, 636, 716; presidential politics and, 603; progressive movement in, 644–645; railroads and, 518; religion and, 551–553; renewal in, 1005; residential segregation in, 838; sanitation in, 541; settlement houses in, 549; shift of population to, 540; size of world cities (1850–1900), 540 (map); slums in, 542; transportation to, 539; in 21st century, 992; in 2000s, 1004–1005; walking city, 539; women in, 562–564; in World War

II, 804–805; World War II migration to, 806. *See also* Urbanization
Citizenship: blacks and, 473, 477–478; doctrine of birthright and, 498; for Filipinos, 625; Fourteenth Amendment and, 474; for Hawaiians, 614; for Native Americans, 581; for Puerto Ricans, 618
City Beautiful movement, 569
City Lights Bookstore, 885
City-manager system of government, 645
City planning, 569
"City upon a hill," 981
Civilian Conservation Corps (CCC), 755, 757, 764, 802
Civil liberties: FBI and, 829; in 21st century, 979; World War I and, 681
Civil rights: of Chinese immigrants, 500; Fourteenth Amendment and, 474; as Sixties issue, 913
Civil Rights Act: of 1875, 479, 495–496; of 1957, 869; of 1964, 898–899, 903
Civil Rights Bill (1866), 473, 474
Civil Rights Cases (1883), 495–496
Civil Rights Commission, 869
Civil rights movement, 807, 868–872, 897–898; Black Power and, 904–906; under Eisenhower, 868–872; feminism and, 934–935; Freedom Riders in, 896; Freedom Summer in, 903; under Johnson, 898–900; under Kennedy, 895–898; March on Washington (1963) in, 897; Native Americans, 933; under Roosevelt, Franklin D., 762; school desegregation and, 868–869; as second Reconstruction, 484; in Selma, 903, 904. *See also* Voting and voting rights
Civil Service Commission, 499
Civil service reform, 499, 503
Civil war(s), in Spain, 783
Civil War (U.S., 1861–1865), financing of, 585
Civil Works Administration (CWA), 758–759
Claflin, Tennessee, 559
Class(es): industrial age and divisions in, 529; urban life and, 540
Class conflict: election of 1936 and, 770; in Gilded Age, 497–498; Marx and, 642
Class consciousness, 535, 642
Clayton Anti-Trust Act (1914), 666
Clayton-Bulwer Treaty (1850), 627
Clean Air Act (1970), 922
Clemenceau, Georges, at Paris Peace Conference, 692, 693, 694
Clemens, Samuel Langhorne. *See* Twain, Mark
Cleveland, Grover, 502, 503n, 512–513; cabinet of, 503; civil service reform and, 503; depression of 1893 and, 508–509; election of 1884 and, 502–503; election of 1888 and, 504; election of 1892 and, 507, 508; election of 1896 and, 601, 602; Hawaii and, 611; interstate commerce and, 519; military pensions and, 503–504; Pullman strike and, 599; tariff issue and, 503, 504; Venezuelan boundary dispute and, 610
Climate, of Great Plains, 588
Clinton, Hillary Rodham, 967; election of 2008 and, 983; heath care reform and, 967; as secretary of state, 967
Clinton, William Jefferson ("Bill"), 829; budget under, 967; economy and, 967, 968–969; election of 1992 and, 965–966, 966 (map); election of 1996 and, 968–969, 968 (m); foreign policy

of, 969–970; legacy of, 971–972; Middle East policy of, 969–970; scandal and impeachment of, 970–971
Cloning, 992
Closed shop, 536, 830
Clothing: flapper, 718; ready-made, 541; women's bathing suits, 718
Coal and coal industry, 706; strikes against, 647–648. *See also* Mines and mining
Coaling stations, 614, 621
Coast Guard, women in, 803
"Code talkers" (World War II), 806
Cody, William F. ("Buffalo Bill"), 570, 571, 580
Coeur d'Alene strike, 506
Cohan, George M., 681
Cohen, Lizabeth, 776
Coin's Financial School (Harvey), 598
Cointelpro, 907
Cold War, 561, 829, 841, 846–853; atomic bombs in World War II and, 825; Carter and, 936; containment doctrine in, 846, 855, 857; Eisenhower and, 877–878; end of, 955–959, 965; Europe after, 957 (map); in Europe and Middle East, 875–876; Gorbachev and, 949; Korean War and, 854–856; militarization of, 849–850; under Reagan, 946–947; responsibility for, 857; scientific research during, 994; U.S. national identity after, 980–981
Cole, USS (ship), attack on, 975
Collective bargaining, 767
Collective security, 748
Colleges. *See* Education; Universities and colleges
Collier, John, 764–765
Collier's, 639, 640
Cologne, bombing of, 811
Colombia, Panama Canal and, 628
Colonialism: imperialism and, 632; World War I and, 693
Colonies and colonization: of Great Powers (1913), 633 (map); in Indochina, 874–875; of U.S., 617; after World War I, 693; World War II and, 787–788
Color. *See* Skin color
Colorado, 588–589; gold in, 584; woman suffrage in, 585
Color barrier, in baseball, 868
Colored Farmers' National Alliance, 506–507, 598
Colored National Labor Union, 533
Columbia, South Carolina, in Civil War, 465
Columbia Basin Project, 763
Columbian Exposition. *See* World's Columbian Exposition
Columbia River region, 762
Columbia University, 709, 911
Columbus, Christopher, 618
Columbus, New Mexico, Villa in, 669
Comanche Indians, 575, 582
Combinations, 649; in oil industry, 524; in railroad industry, 519; Sherman Anti-Trust Act and, 525
Coming Apart (O'Neill), 914
Commentary (magazine), 942
Commerce: in cities, 1005; interstate, 519–520, 525
Commerce, Department of, 648–649
Commission form, of government, 645
Committee for Industrial Organization (CIO), 768. *See also* CIO
Committee on Public Information, 680

Committee to Defend America by Aiding the Allies, 789
Common Market, 891
Common Sense Book of Baby and Child Care, The (Spock), 835
Commonwealth of Independent States (CIS), 957
Communications: global revolution in, 994; radio in, 715; sign language, 582; in 21st century, 991
Communism: capitalism and, 840; collapse in Eastern Europe, 956–958; in Cuba, 878; in France, 632; immigrants and, 550; Johnson, Lyndon B., and, 906; in Korea, 865; McCarthy and, 866–867; Nixon and, 920; red scare and, 852–853; threat of, 841 (map); Truman and, 847, 852–853, 854; in U.S., 700; in Western Europe, 847. *See also* China; Soviet Union; specific locations
Company town, 532
Competition, 521, 522, 730; global, 993–996; international system, imperialism, and, 632–633; railroads and, 519
Compromise of 1877, 494–495
Computers, 861; in 1950s, 860. *See also* Electronic media
Comstock, Anthony, 559
Comstock Law, 559
Comstock Lode, 584
Concentration camps, in World War II, 816–818
Condon, Edward, 851
Confessions of Nat Turner, The (Styron), 887
Congress (U.S.): Billion-Dollar, 504–505; census and, 988 (map); Eisenhower and, 877; ex-Confederates in, 472–473; Great Society legislation and, 901–903; Hundred Days, 754, 755, 756, 757, 761, 762, 764, 765; interstate commerce and, 525; Johnson, Andrew, and, 474, 480–481; Joint Committee on Reconstruction of, 474; Kennedy, John F., and, 890; in New Deal, 822; railroad development and, 512; readmittance of states and, 470; southern blacks in, 478; Vietnam War and, 907; Wilson address to, 664. *See also* House of Representatives (U.S.); Senate (U.S.)
Congressional Budget Office, 985
Congressional elections. *See* Elections
Congressional Reconstruction, 472–473
Congress of Industrial Organizations. *See* AFL-CIO; CIO
Congress of Racial Equality (CORE), 806
Congress of the Socialist Party (Tours, France), 632
Conjure Women, The (Dunbar), 568
Conkling, Roscoe ("Lord Roscoe"), 494, 498
Conquistadores, 583, 618
Conscientious objectors, in World War I, 687
Conscription. *See* Military draft
Conservation, 757; of energy, 1012; movement for, 922; New Deal programs and, 763–764; Roosevelt, Theodore, and, 651–655; Taft and, 658. *See also* Environment
Conservatism: of Coolidge, 734; under Eisenhower, 872–874; "movement conservatives" and, 951–952; in 1980s, 942–962; origins of modern, 962; of Reagan, 944–946; of Supreme Court, 953–954
Conservatives, on New Deal, 773–774

Consolidation, 524, 730
Constitution(s): Cuban, 621; state, in Reconstruction, 475
Constitution (U.S.): census and, 548; due process and, 525; impeachment in, 971; three-fifths clause in, 473
Constitutional conventions, in Reconstruction, 478
Constraints school, 776
Construction industry: Italian workers in, 547; New Deal and, 767
Consumer culture, in 1950s, 862–864
Consumer price index, 917, 937
Consumer Product Safety Commission (CPSC), 922
Consumers and consumerism: department stores and, 540; protecting, 986; Roosevelt, Theodore and, 650; in 21st century, 990
Consumption, mass-, 710–711
Containment doctrine, 846, 855, 857
Content of Our Character, The (Steele), 1007
Continental Army, Poles in, 706
Continental Illinois Bank, failure of, 955
Contraception. *See* Birth control
Contraction policy, 492
Contract Labor Law (1885), 534
Contracts, employer set-asides and, 922
Contract with America, 968
Contras, 947, 950
Conwell, Russell, 525
Coolidge, Calvin, 637, 725, 730, 733–734, 738; debt cancellation and, 737; election of 1920 and, 696; election of 1924 and, 735–736; foreign policy under, 736–737; tariff policies under, 732
Cooper, John Milton, Jr., 698
Cooperatives: farmer, 597; producers', 597
Cooperativism, Powderly and, 534
Copenhagen Climate Conference (2009), 1012
Coral Sea, Battle of, 808–809
Corbett, "Gentleman Jim," 571
CORE. *See* Congress of Racial Equality
Cornell University, 556
Corporations: billion-dollar, 523; Harding and, 729–730; Hoover and, 746; horizontal integration in, 521–522; incorporation laws and, 525; political contributions and, 499; vertical integration in, 521; worker rights and, 531–532; in World War II, 807. *See also* Antitrust movement; Business
Corrections, The (Franzen), 1009
Corregidor: Fortress, 667; in World War II, 808, 809 (map)
Corruption, 487; Crédit Mobilier, 490, 514, 518; election of 1876 and, 494–495; election of 1884 and, 502; of federal Indian agents, 577; under Grant, 489–490; under Harding, 728, 729, 732–733; Homestead Act and, 587; Plunkitt on, 489; progressive attack on, 638–639, 641; in railroads, 518–519; in Reconstruction governments, 479; Tweed Ring and, 490
Corrupt-practices acts, in states, 641
Cosmopolitan, 639, 640
Cosmopolitanism, 704
Cost of living, in 1970s, 917
Cotton and cotton industry: mechanical picker for, 806; post Civil War, 465; world production (1903), 528. *See also* Textile industry
Cotton Stabilization Corporation, 740
Coughlin, Charles, 759, 962
Council of Economic Advisers, 831

Council of National Defense, 682
Counterculture, 885, 913
Couples (Updike), 883
Coups: in Czechoslovakia, 848; against Diem (Vietnam), 893
Court-packing plan, of Roosevelt, Franklin, 770–771
Courts: records of, 648; reform bill for, 771
Cowboys, 586, 592
Cox, James M., election of 1920 and, 696
Coxey, Jacob S., 599
Coxey's Army, 599
Craft unions, 533
Crane, Stephen, 567
Crash, of 1929, 637, 740–742
Crazy Horse, 579
Credit: American, abroad, 508; buying on, 711; in crop-lien system, 496; for farmers, 666; panic of 1873 and, 491; real estate collapse of 2008 and, 984
Crédit Mobilier scandal, 490, 514, 518
Creditor nation, U.S. as, 736–737
Creditors, vs. hard-money advocates, 492
Creel, George, 680, 681
CREEP (Committee to Re-Elect the President), 925
Creole Jazz Band, 719
Crime: automobiles as factor in, 713–714; in cities, 541, 708, 1004–1005; hate, 497; Lindbergh kidnapping as, 709; prohibition and, 708. *See also* Gangsters
Criminal syndicalism laws, 701
Croats, 543
Croly, Herbert, 662
Crop-lien system, 496
Crops: genetic engineering and, 991; in West, 588
Croquet, 571
Cross of Gold speech (Bryan), 597, 601–602
Crow Indians, 576, 583
Crucible, The (Miller), 886
Cruz, Nilo, 1010
Cuba: Bay of Pigs invasion of, 893–895; Castro in, 878, 893; Guantánamo Detention Camp in, 975; Kennedy, John F., and, 893–895; Platt Amendment and, 621, 780; revolt of, 612; Soviet Union and, 878, 895; in Spanish-American War, 614–616, 616 (map); U.S. embargo on, 878; U.S. intervention in, 630, 658
Cuban Americans: literature of, 1010. *See also* Hispanics; Latinos
Cuban missile crisis, 895
Culebra Cut, 628–629
Cult of domesticity, 862
Cultural anthropology, 760
Cultural pluralism, 704, 1007
Cultural wars, under Reagan, 953
Culture(s): African American, 719–720, 724; consumer, in 1950s, 862–864; "high culture" and, 1007; Native American, 581; in 1920s, 720–724; in 1960s, 910–914; of Plains Indians, 577; popular, 572; Protestants and, 552; Puerto Rican, 619; renaissance of, 880–887; skin color and, 1007; youth, 838
Culture wars, Monkey Trial and, 709, 710
Currency: coinage of silver dollars, 492; deflation of, 595; emergency, 656; gold standard and, 922; inelasticity of, 665; managed under Roosevelt, Franklin D., 756–757; panic of 1873 and, 491–492; Resumption Act (1875) and, 492. *See also* Economy; Greenbacks

Curriculum: classical, 557; influences on university, 557; at Tuskegee Institute, 554
Custer, George Armstrong, 578–579
Czechoslovakia, 688, 784, 848, 912, 956
Czech Republic, in NATO, 969

Dakotas: Native Americans in, 577. *See also* North Dakota; South Dakota
Dakota Sioux Indians, 580
Daley, Richard M., 909
Dams, 652, 653; Hetch Hetchy Valley and, 654–655; Hoover, 744–746; irrigation and, 588, 651; on Tennessee River, 766, 766 (map)
Dance: in 1920s, 718; breakdancing, 1009; postmodernism in, 1008
Dancig, Edward, 824
Darrow, Charles, in Scopes trial, 710
Darwin, Charles, 525, 553, 560
Darwinism, 553; interpretation of, 525; Social Darwinism and, 525
Daugherty, Harry M., 729, 730, 732
Daughters of the American Revolution, 549
David Copperfield, 557
Davis, Jefferson: citizenship restored to, 465; imprisonment of, 465
Davis, John W., 735, 736 (map)
Dawes, Charles, 737
Dawes Plan (1924), 737
Dawes-Severalty Act (1887), 581–584, 584 (map), 765, 873
Dawson, Rosario, 1007
D-Day (June 6, 1944), 813–814, 817
Dean, James, 911
Dean, John, III, 926
Death of a Salesman (Miller), 886
Debates. *See* Presidential debates
Debs, Eugene V.: election of 1908 and, 656; election of 1912 and, 642, 663, 663 (map); election of 1920 and, 682, 696; Espionage Act and conviction of, 681, 682; imprisonment of, 599–600; Pullman strike and, 599; Socialist party and, 600, 642
Debt(s): Confederate, 474; credit buying and, 711; of farmers, 496, 506, 595; federal, 474; of sharecroppers, 472, 496; of workers, 532. *See also* International debt; National debt
Debtors: panic of 1873 and, 491–492; U.S. as, 736
"Declaration of Constitutional Principles" (1956), against desegregation, 869
Declaration of Sentiments, 934
Decolonization, 633
Defense Department, 849, 889
Defense industries: ban on segregation in, 871; in World War II, 804, 807
Defense spending: in 1980s, 945, 946–947; after World War II, 832
Deficit. *See* Budget deficit
Deficit spending, planned, 772
Deflation, 492, 595
De Gaulle, Charles, 891; NATO and, 907
Degler, Carl, 775
De Kooning, Willem, 880
Deleveraging, 984
De Lôme, Enrique Dupuy. *See* Dupuy de Lôme, Enrique
Demagogues, in Great Depression, 759
Demilitarized zone (DMZ), 923
Democracy: in Japan, 850; in 21st century, 990
Democratic Leadership Council, 965–966

Democratic National Convention (Chicago, 1968), 909
Democratic party: in Gilded Age, 492–494; Mississippi Freedom, 903; after World War I, 828. *See also* Elections
Democratic Promise: The Populist Moment in America (Goodwyn), 510
Demography, U.S. census and, 988 (map)
Dempsey, Jack, 711
Denmark, 668, 786
Dennis v. United States, 852
Dent family, 490
Department stores: growth of, 540–541; in World War II, 807
Deportation, of aliens, 701
Depressions: of 1870s, 492, 497, 519, 533; of 1893, 508–509, 605. *See also* Great Depression; Panics
Desegregation: of education, 868–869; in 1950s, 867–868; of schools, 905–906, 932; southern resistance to, 869; white flight and, 932. *See also* Civil rights movement
"Desert Fox" (Rommel), 811
Desert Land Act (1877), 651
Desktop computers, 861
Détente policy, 895, 920, 928, 936
Detroit, Michigan: automobile industry in, 711; race riots in, 806, 871, 905
Developing countries, 653, 843
Devries, Martin, 743
Dewey, George, 614, 614 (map)
Dewey, John, 560, 561, 704, 709, 722
Dewey, Thomas E.: election of 1940 and, 790–791, 791 (map); election of 1944 and, 814, 815–816; election of 1948 and, 853–854
Diaz, Junot, 1010
Diaz, Porfirio, 669
Dictaphone, 521
Dictators: Hitler as, 780–781; in Latin America, 878
Diem, Ngo Dinh, 875, 893
Dien Bien Phu, Battle of, 875
Dime novels, 565
Dingley Tariff Bill (1897), 605
Diplomacy: dollar, 657–658, 667, 669; in 1880s and 1890s, 609–610; in Mexico, 668–670; in progressive era, 637; in World War I, 673–674. *See also* Foreign policy
Direct election, of senators, 641–644
Direct primary elections, 641
Direct tax clause, 509*n*
Disabled people, ADA and, 961
Disarmament, after World War I, 731, 781
Discrimination: against Asian students, 630–631; against Chinese, 501; Civil Rights Act (1964) and, 900; in employment, 922; in public accommodations, 479; reverse, 922, 932; sexual, 930–931, 996. *See also* Race and racism
Disease: bioengineering and, 992; impact on Native Americans, 576, 579, 580; influenza pandemic (1918–1919), 691; Panama Canal construction and, 629; in Spanish-American War, 616; in World War I, 688. *See also* specific conditions
Disfranchisement: of blacks, 480, 508; of ex-Confederates, 471, 475
Disneyland, 862
District of Columbia: electoral votes for, 923. *See also* Washington, D.C.
Diversity: on college campuses, 1007; racial, 1007

Divorce, 997, 998; divorce revolution and, 562; increase in, 559; rate to marriages, 562
Dixiecrats, in 1948, 853
Doctors. *See* Medicine
Documentary films, 1010
Documentary photography, 531
Dodge City, 586
Doenitz, Karl, 844
Dogs, Indian use of, 582
Doheny, Edward L., 733
Dole, Robert, 968, 968 (map)
Dollar (U.S.), devaluation of, 922
Dollar diplomacy, 657–658, 667, 669
Domesticity, 862
Dominican Republic, 630, 658, 668, 736, 906
Domino theory, Vietnam War and, 857
Donlin, Bob, 885
Donnelly, Ignatius, 598
"Don't Ask, Don't Tell" policy, 966, 986
Dos Passos, John, 686
Dot-com explosion, 1010
Double-tracking, 517
Doughboys, 688, 692, 730
Douglas, Stephen A., 474
Douglass, Frederick, 477, 483
"Doves" (Vietnam War), 907, 910, 918, 919
Draft. *See* Military draft
"Drake's Folly," 523
Drama, post-World War II, 883–884
DREAM Act (Development, Relief and Education for Alien Minors Act), 986, 1001
Dreiser, Theodore, 540–541, 567, 639, 720
Drinking and drunkenness. *See* Alcohol; Temperance movement
Drought: in Great Plains, 588; in Mississippi Valley (1930), 742–743; in trans-Mississippi West, 596
Dry farming, 588, 764
"Dry" laws, 647
Du Bois, W. E. B., 483, 484, 555
Duchamp, Marcel, 722–723
Due process clause, 525
Dukakis, Michael, election of 1988 and, 955
Duke, James Buchanan, 526–527
Duke University, 527
Dulles, John Foster, 874, 875
Dumbbell tenements, 542
Dunbar, Paul Laurence, 568
Dunkirk, evacuation of, 786
Dunne, Finley Peter, 615, 630
Dunning, William A., 483
Dupuy de Lôme, Enrique, 612
Dust Bowl, 588, 764, 765 (map)
Dutch East Indies, in World War II, 808
Dutchman (Baraka), 886
Dysentery, 616

Eagleton, Thomas, 923
Eakins, Thomas, 568
Earth Day, 653, 922
Earthquake, in San Francisco (1906), 630
Eastern Asia (1955–1956), 875 (map)
Eastern Europe: after Cold War, 965; collapse of communism in, 956–958; immigrants from, 543, 706–707; Soviets and, 840, 846; after World War II, 839–840. *See also* specific locations
East Germany, 845 (map), 846–847; Berlin Wall and, 891, 892; communist collapse in, 956. *See also* Germany; West Germany
East Indies. *See* Dutch East Indies

East of Eden (Steinbeck), 882
East St. Louis, Missouri, 683
Eckford, Elizabeth, 869
Ecological science, 652–653
Economic aid, after World War II, 847–848, 848 (map)
Economic competition, global, 993–996
Economic imperialism, 748
Economics, supply-side, 945–946
Economy: bull market and, 725, 726; Bush, George H. W., and, 962; Bush, George W., and, 972, 984; Carter and, 936–938; after Civil War, 465; Clinton and, 967, 968–969; consumer, 711; depression of 1893 and, 508–509; in early 21st century, 1011; energy and, 834; Gilded Age and, 492–493; Great Depression and, 772; Great Recession (2008–) and, 808, 965, 974, 985–986, 990; growth of, 512; industrialization and, 486; Keynes' theories of, 772; mass-consumption, 710–711; Nixon and, 916–917, 922; Obama and, 983, 984–985, 986; railroads and, 512, 517–518; Reagan and, 945–946, 951; in South, 805; in 21st century, 990, 991–992; after World War I, 730; World War I and, 682, 685–686; after World War II, 828–829, 830–835; in World War II, 802–803, 807. *See also* Currency; Depressions; Inflation; Panics; Tariff(s)
Ecosystems, in Gulf of Mexico, 1011
Eddy, Mary Baker, 552–553
Edison, Thomas Alva, 520, 521, 523, 568, 715
Edsall, Thomas, 962
Education, 1007; blacks in, 1007; Bush, George W., and, 979; Chautauqua movement and, 554; compulsory, 554; equality in, 868; evolution and, 557; expenditures on, 998–999; for freedmen, 468, 469; Fundamentalism and, 709–710; GI Bill and, 830; for immigrants, 547, 1001; income inequalities and, 996; industrialization and, 557; levels of (1870–2010), 556; in 1920s, 709; progressive, 709; after World War II, 834. *See also* Higher education; Schools; Universities and colleges
Education Amendments, Title IX of, 930
Education of Henry Adams, The (Adams), 488, 568
EEC. *See* European Economic Community
Egypt, 865–876, 924, 934–935, 1011
Eighteenth Amendment, 647, 685, 704
Eight-hour day, 533, 666
Einstein, Albert, 789, 820, 851
Eisenhower, Dwight D., 828, 877, 879–880; civil rights movement and, 868–872; election of 1948 and, 853; election of 1952, 864–865, 865 (map); election of 1956 and, 876–877; Farewell Address of, 880; foreign policy under, 874; labor and, 877; McCarthy and, 866; Native Americans and, 873; presidency of, 860, 872–874; racial issues and, 868, 869; Vietnam and, 866, 874–875; in World War II, 812, 813, 816, 824
Eisenhower Doctrine, 878
El Alamein, 811
El Caney, battle at, 615
Elderly: aging of population and, 998–999; extended lifespan and, 998–999; as interest group, 999; Medicare and, 902, 903, 998; in 2000s, 998–999. *See also* Social Security

Elections: of 1848, 877; of 1864, 469–470; of 1866, 474; of 1868, 488–489; of 1872, 490–491; of 1874, 492; of 1876, 494–495, 494 (map); of 1878, 492; of 1880, 498, 598; of 1884, 502–503; of 1888, 504; of 1892, 505, 506–508, 507 (map), 598; of 1894, 509; of 1896, 509, 510, 600–604, 603 (map); of 1900, 626–627; of 1904, 655; of 1908, 656; of 1910, 659; of 1912, 642, 659, 661–663, 663 (map); of 1916, 674–675, 675 (map); of 1918, 692; of 1920, 682, 696–697; of 1924, 735–736, 736 (map); of 1928, 738–739, 739 (map), 751; of 1930, 746; of 1932, 752–753; of 1936, 769–770; of 1938, 773, 774; of 1940, 790–791, 791 (map); of 1942, 802; of 1944, 814–815; of 1948, 853–854; of 1952, 864, 865–866, 865 (map); of 1956, 876–877; of 1960, 878–879, 880 (map); of 1964, 900–901; of 1968, 908–910, 910 (map); of 1972, 922–924; of 1976, 933; of 1980, 942–944, 944 (map); of 1984, 947–948; of 1986, 954; of 1988, 955; of 1992, 965–966, 966 (map); of 1996, 968–969, 968 (map); of 2000, 965, 972, 972 (map), 1006; of 2004, 979; of 2006, 982–983; of 2008, 981, 983, 984–985, 985 (map); of 2010, 965, 986; direct primary, 641; in Nicaragua, 959; poll tax eliminated from, 903; of senators, 641–644
Elective system, 557
Electoral College, calls for abolition of, 972
Electoral commission (1877), 494, 495
Electoral Count Act (1877), 494–495
Electric dynamo, 521
Electric industry, TVA and, 765–766, 766 (map)
Electricity, 540, 710; dams and, 762, 763; households with (1900–1960), 767; lighting and, 520, 521, 523–524
Electric railway, 521
Electric trolleys, 539
Electronic media, 1010–1011
Electronics: industry, 835; in 1950s, 860
Elementary schools, 553–554
Eliot, Charles W., 557
Eliot, T. S., 721
Elk Hills (California), 733
Elkins Act (1903), 649
Ellis Island, 546
Ellison, Ralph, 886
El Salvador, 959
Emancipation, freedmen's responses to, 466–467
Embargo: on Cuba, 878; by OPEC, 924; in World War II, 794
Embassies, terrorist attacks on U.S., 975
"Emerald Necklace" (Boston), 569
Emergency Banking Relief Act (1933), 755
Emergency Quota Act (1921), 703
Emerson, Ralph Waldo, 560, 652; on immigrant labor, 520
Emigration: of Filipinos to U.S., 623; of Poles, 706–707
Empey, Arthur Guy, 700
Empire, United States as, 620
Employers: court regulation of discrimination by, 953–954; illegal workers and, 1001; set-asides by, 922
Employment: in auto industry, 712; civil-service, 502; discrimination in, 922; outsourcing of, 991; in suburbs, 836–837; Truman and, 854; in 21st century, 991; white-collar, 860, 861;

in World War II, 807. See also Labor; Unemployment; Workers
Employment Act (1946), 831
Endangered Species Act (1973), 653, 922
Endless-chain operations, 508, 509
Enemy aliens, in World War II, 799
Energy: conservation of, 1012; sources of, 1011; after World War II, 834. See also Atomic power; Oil and oil industry
Energy crisis: Carter and, 936–938; in 1970s, 924–925
Energy Department, 933
Engels, Friedrich, 642
Engel v. Vitale, 921
Engineering: biological, 991–992; hydraulic, 589; in 21st century, 994–995
Engines, gasoline, 711, 714, 734
England (Britain): Battle of Britain and, 789; British Guiana-Venezuela boundary dispute and, 609–610; Common Market and, 891–892; Great Depression and, 772; immigrants from, 542, 703; Iraq War and, 977, 978; lend-lease and, 791–792, 792 (map), 793–794; Reagan and, 944–945; Suez crisis and, 875, 876; in United Nations, 844; women in World War II, 803–804; in World War I, 670, 671–672; in World War II, 785, 786, 789–790, 811, 812. See also Colonies and colonization
Enigma codes, in World War II, 810
Enron, 1011
Ensler, Eve, 1010
Entertainment: in late 1800s, 570–572; in 1950s, 873. See also Movies and movie industry
Entitlement programs, 902, 921, 945
Environment, 1011; BP oil spill and, 987, 1011; Bush, George W., and, 973; Nixon and, 922; of West, 588. See also Conservation
Environmentalists, 652–653, 922
Environmental Protection Agency (EPA), 653, 922
Epidemics. See Disease
Episcopal Church, 552
Equality: for blacks in professional schools, 868; Du Bois on, 555; in early 21st century, 1011; racial, 495
Equal opportunity, Truman and, 868
Equal Rights Amendment (ERA): in 1923, 718; in 1972, 931, 932, 934
Erie Railroad, 518
Erosion, in Dust Bowl (1930s), 765 (map)
Esch-Cummins Transportation Act (1920), 730
Escobedo v. Illinois, 921
Espionage Act (1917), 681, 682
Estancias (ranches), 593
Estate taxes, 726
"Esthete in Harlem" (Hughes), 724
Ethics, medicine and, 992
Ethiopia, 633; Cuba and, 936; Italian attack on, 781
Ethnic Albanians, 969
Ethnic cleansing, 969
Ethnic groups: in Bosnia, 969; in cities, 1005–1007; clashes between working class, 497–498; after Cold War, 1012; communities of, 704; in former Yugoslavia, 958; in Iraq, 977, 978, 979; in Rwanda, 969; in Western United States, 1004. See also Race and racism; specific groups
E*Trade, 1010
Eugenides, Jeffrey, 1009

European Community (EC), 847
Europe and Europeans: Cold War and, 875, 957 (map); expatriates and, 721; financial collapse in, 742; immigrants from, 542–550; imperialism by, 623, 626, 633; Indian contact with, 583; totalitarianism in, 780–782; U.S. tariffs and, 732; welfare programs in, 767. See also specific locations
European Economic Community (EEC), 891
European Union (EU), EEC and, 891
Evans, Hiram Wesley, 702
Evans, Sara, 914
"Eveready Hour," 715
Evers, Medgar, 898
Everybody's magazine, 639, 640
Evolution: Darwinism and, 553; organic, 553; prohibitions on teaching, 709; Scopes trial and, 710
Excess-profits tax, repeal of, 726
Exchange-rate stabilization, 778
Excise taxes, 725
Executive Office, 773
Executive Orders: No. 8802, 870–871; No. 9066, 799
Exodusters, 467
Expansion and expansionism: overseas, 487, 608–610, 634; Plains Indians and westward, 487; Soviet, 841 (map); U.S. (1857–1917), 611 (map). See also Imperialism; Westward movement
Ex parte Milligan, 475–476
Expatriates, in postwar Europe, 721
Exploration. See Space exploration
Exports: to belligerents (1914–1916), 671; Carter and, 939

Fabian socialism, 559
Facebook, 991, 1010
Factories, 486; lend-lease and, 792; reforms of, 645–646; tobacco, 527; women in, 803; in World War I, 681–682; in World War II, 802. See also Manufacturing
Factory system, 537
Fair competition codes (NRA), 761–762
Fair Deal, 854
Fair Employment Practices Commission (FEPC), 805
Fairey, Shepard, 1008
Fair Labor Standards Act (1938), 530, 758, 768–769
Fall, Albert B., 728–729, 732
Falwell, Jerry, 951, 953
Families: in cities, 562; Congress and welfare of, 684; female heads of, 1006; of freedmen, 467; in Great Depression, 741; of Polish immigrants, 706–707; size of, 562; in tenements, 640; traditional, 997–998; in 21st century, 997–999; women in, 1006; after World War II, 836. See also Marriage
Family wage, 529
Fannie Mae. See Federal National Mortgage Association
FAO (Food and Agricultural Organization), 844
Farewell Address: of Carter, 944; of Eisenhower, 880
Farewell to Arms, A (Hemingway), 720
Farm bloc, 734–735
Farmers' Alliance, 505, 598
Farms and farming: automobiles and, 712; bonanza, 595; debt of, 496, 506, 595; depression in (1920s), 734–735; dry, 588, 764; Dust Bowl and, 764, 765 (map);

in Great Depression, 743, 763–764; grievances of, 595–596, 597–598; Homestead Act and, 587; immigrants and, 546–547; Japanese Americans in, 800–801; mechanization of, 594–595, 734, 735; Mexican workers for, 1002; migrant labor for, 595; People's party and, 486–487; post World War I, 740; protest in, 596–598; railroads and, 518, 519; sharecropping in, 472, 496, 526; tariffs and, 505; technology for, 506; tenant, 496, 526, 595, 743; in West, 586–588; after World War I, 734–735; after World War II, 824; in World War II, 802. *See also* Agriculture

Fascism: in Germany, 780–781; in Italy, 780; in Spain, 783

Fathers. *See* Families; Men

Faubus, Orval, 869

Faulkner, William, 721–724, 886

FBI (Federal Bureau of Investigation), civil liberties and, 829

FDR. *See* Roosevelt, Franklin Delano

Federal Art Project, 760

Federal budget, 945–946, 967, 986. *See also* Budget deficits

Federal courts, 531. *See also* Courts; Supreme Court (U.S.)

Federal Deposit Insurance Corporation, 755, 756

Federal Emergency Management Agency (FEMA), 982

Federal Emergency Relief Act (1933), 755, 757–758

Federal Emergency Relief Administration (FERA), 755, 757–758

Federal Farm Board, 740

Federal Farm Loan Act (1916), 666

Federal Highway Act (1956), 873–874

Federal Home Mortgage Corporation ("Freddie Mac"), 984

Federal Housing Administration (FHA), 758, 767, 835

Federal National Mortgage Association ("Fannie Mae"), 984

Federal Reserve: Act (1913), 656, 665; Board, 665, 667, 675, 740; Notes, 665; System, 665, 667, 983–984

Federal Securities Act (1933), 755, 765

Federal spending. *See* Spending

Federal Tariff Commission, 675

Federal Trade Commission, 666, 667

Federal Trade Commission Act (1914), 666

Feminine Mystique, The (Friedan), 861–862, 934

Feminism, 639, 644, 934–935; civil rights movement and, 934, 935; in late 20th and early 21st centuries, 996–998; literature and, 562, 1010; in 1970s, 929–932; social, 676; after World War II, 829

Ferlinghetti, Lawrence, 885

Ferraro, Geraldine, 947

Ferrell, Frank J., 535

Fetterman, William J., 578

Fiction, 1009

Field, Cyrus, 524

Fifteenth Amendment, 475, 478, 480

Fifty-Niners, 584

Filibuster, in Senate, 678

Filipino Americans, 624–625

Filipinos, 614, 622, 624–625

Films. *See* Movies and movie industry

Finance(s): collapse in 2008, 984; World War I and, 686. *See also* Economy

Financial panics. *See* Panics

Financial sector, 991

Financier, The (Dreiser), 639

Finland, in World War II, 786

Fire Next Time, The (Baldwin), 886

Fireside chats, 755–756

First Amendment, 681, 885

First-wave feminism, 934

First World War. *See* World War I

Fiscal reforms, 655–656

Fisk, "Jubilee Jim," 489–490

Fitzgerald, F. Scott, 720, 721, 886

Fitzgerald, Zelda, 721

Fiume, in Treaty of Versailles, 694

Five-Power Naval Treaty (1922), 731

Flappers, 718

Flexible response, doctrine of, 892–893

Flophouses, 542

Florida, 835; Compromise of 1877 and, 494, 495; Cubans in, 878; election of 2000 and, 972, 1006

Flower children, 913

Fluoroscopes, 520

Fluoroscopes, 520

Foch, Ferdinand, 688

Folklore: black, 568; cowboys in, 586; mining frontier and, 585

Following the Color Line (Baker), 640

Foner, Eric, 483

Food: in Great Depression, 763; in World War I, 685, 686

Food Administration, 685

Food Stamps, 921

Football, 571

Foraker Act (1900), 620

Forbes, Charles R., 732–733

Force Acts (1870 and 1871), 480

Ford, Gerald ("Jerry"), 829, 928, 933

Ford, Henry, 520, 705, 710, 711–712, 762

Ford automobile, in 1950s, 833

Fordism, 711–712

Ford Motor Company, 713

Fordney-McCumber Tariff Law (1922), 732, 740

Foreclosures, in Great Depression, 763

Foreign aid, after World War II, 847–848, 848 (map)

Foreign-born Americans, 995, 1001

Foreign policy: of Bush, George H. W., 955–960; of Carter, 933–936, 938–939; of Clinton, 969–970; of Coolidge, 736–737; dollar diplomacy in, 657–658, 667; of Eisenhower, 874, 892; of Harding, 730–732; of Johnson, Andrew, 481–482; of Johnson, Lyndon B., 906–910; of Kennedy, 892–893; Kissinger and, 919–920; of Nixon, 917–920; of Obama, 986–987; Open Door policy and, 623, 626; of Reagan, 946–951; of Roosevelt, Franklin D., 778–780; Roosevelt Corollary and, 629–630; of Truman, 847, 852, 855–856, 857; Wilson and, 667–671, 697–698; after World War II, 828. *See also* Imperialism; Manifest Destiny; Monroe Doctrine

Forest Reserve Act (1891), 651

Forestry Division, 658

Forests, 652, 654

Forest Service, 652, 655

Formosa (Taiwan), 633, 850

For the Union Dead (Robert Lowell), 883

Fort Laramie, Treaty of: in 1851, 576; in 1868, 578

Fortress Corregidor, 667

Fortress Europe, 798

Fossil fuels, 1011

Four Freedoms, The (Rockwell), 803

Four-Power Treaty, 731, 732

Fourteen Points (Wilson), 679–680, 691, 694

Fourteenth Amendment, 473–474, 480, 496; due process clause of, 525; *male* inserted in, 477; women and, 934

Fourth party system, 604

France, 551; communism in, 847, 848; D-Day invasion of, 813–814; Indochina and, 874–875; occupation of Ruhr Valley, 737; protests in, 911; Security Treaty for, 694; Suez crisis and, 875, 876; Treaty of Versailles and, 694; in United Nations, 844; after World War I, 697, 737–738; in World War I, 670, 685, 687–688, 688 (map); in World War II, 786, 811–812

Franco, Francisco, 783

Frankson, Canute, 783

Franzen, Jonathan, 1009

Frazier-Lemke Farm Bankruptcy Act (1934), 758, 764

Freddie Mac. *See* Federal Home Mortgage Corporation

Freedman's Savings and Trust Company, 491

Freedmen: Black Codes and, 471–472; education for, 467, 469; land for, 469; responses to freedom, 466–469; rights for, 475; schools of, 479; Union League and, 478; voting by, 478, 489, 493

Freedmen's Bureau, 469, 473, 474, 483

Freedom (Franzen), 1009

Freedom(s): in Cold War, 852; former slaves and, 466–469; of seas, 782

Freedom Riders, 896

Freedom Summer (1964), 903

Free market, neoconservatives and, 942

Free silver, 508, 509, 598, 602. *See also* Silver

Free speech, clear and present danger and, 681

Free Speech Movement, 911

Free trade, 602, 632, 780, 842; in EEC, 891; imperialism and, 698; NAFTA and, 969

French Canal Company, 628

"Frenzied Finance" (Lawson), 640

Freud, Sigmund, 718, 723

Friedan, Betty, 861–862, 934, 935

From Here to Eternity (Jones), 883

Frontier: boundaries of, 575; "closing" of, 589–594, 605; global, 592–593

Frontiero v. Richardson, 931–932

"Frontier thesis" (Turner), 592, 605–606

Fronts. *See* World War I; World War II

Frost, Robert, 721, 890

Frostbelt, 835

Fuel Administration, 685–686

Fundamentalism, 709; evolutionary theory and, 710; Islamic, 937, 959; Modernists vs., 718

Gaddis, John Lewis, 857, 913

Gaillart Cut, 628–629

Galbraith, John Kenneth, 864

Gallup, George, 787

Galveston, Texas, reforms in, 645

Gambling casinos, Native American, 1004

Gandhi, Mohandas (Mahatma), 868

Gangsters and gangsterism, 708–709, 781, 877

Garfield, James A., 498–499

Garland, Hamlin, 569

Garvey, Marcus, 719–720

Gassed (Sargent), 690

Gas stations, 713

Gauges, railroad, 517
Gays and lesbians: Don't Ask, Don't Tell policy, 966, 986; Gay Pride Parade and (1970), 912; marriage by, 998; as parents, 998; protests for rights, 912–913
Gaza Strip, 907, 970
Gehry, Frank, 1008
Gender and gender issues: Civil Rights Act (1964) and, 900; imperialism and, 634; in 1950s, 861–862; occupational segregation by, 996; sex discrimination and, 930–931; Supreme Court rulings and, 729; in workplace, 830. See also Men; Women
Gender gap, 961, 996
General Agreement on Tariffs and Trade (GATT), 843, 969
General Assembly (U.N.), 844
General Federation of Women's Clubs, 563, 645
General Motors, 768
Generation Divided, A (Klatch), 914
Genetics, breakthroughs in, 991
Geneva: summit conference in (1985), 949; summit meeting in (1955), 875
Geneva Conference: of 1954, 875; of 1962, 892
Genocide, in World War II, 788, 816–818, 822
Gentlemen's Agreement (1907–1908), 631, 801
George, Henry, 512, 558–559, 595
Georgia, Black Codes and, 471
German Americans: internment in World War II, 799; during World War I, 681, 694
German Samoa, 609
Germany: China and, 623; communism in, 847; Great Depression and, 772; hyper-inflation in, 738; in 1970s, 917; occupation zones in, 839, 845–846, 845 (map); reparations and, 736, 737; repentance by (1918), 691; reunification of, 957; Samoan Islands and, 609; Versailles Treaty and, 694; in World War I, 670, 671–674, 678–679, 687–688, 689–691; after World War II, 844–845. See also Nazi Germany
Geronimo (Apache), 579, 580
Gestapo, 822
Ghettos, poor people in, 1006
Ghost Dance cult, 581
Ghost towns, 584
GI: use of term, 803; after World War II, 830
Gibbons, James (Cardinal), 552
GI Bill, 547, 831
Gibson, Charles Dana, 528, 530
Gibson Girl, 528, 530
Gideon v. Wainwright, 921
Gift tax, 725
Gilbert Islands, in World War II, 810
Gilded Age: political parties in, 603 (map); politics in, 488, 492–494, 509; progressive historians and, 510; in South, 484
Gilded Age, The (Warner and Twain), 510, 566
Gilman, Charlotte Perkins, 562
Gilpin, Drew, 997
Gingrich, Newt, 968, 971
Ginsberg, Allen, 884, 885, 911
Ginsburg, Ruth Bader, 966
Gitlin, Todd, 914
Glacier Point, 651
Gladden, Washington, 549
Glasnost, 949, 957

Glass-Steagall Banking Reform Act (1933), 755, 756; bank failures before and after, 756
Glen Canyon, 653
Glidden, Joseph F., 588
Globalization: Clinton and, 969; era of, 842–843; outsourcing and, 991; use of term, 891
Global warming, 653, 973, 1012
Global work force, women in, 996
Gloucester (warship), 618
G-men, prohibition and, 705
Godkin, Edwin L., 558
Goebbels, Joseph, 788
Goering, Hermann, 824, 844, 845
Goethals, George Washington, 629
Golan Heights, 907
Gold: in Black Hills, 578; discoveries of, 584, 605; reserves in Treasury, 508–509; Resumption Act and, 492; Roosevelt, Franklin D., and, 756–757; scandal and price of, 489–490; vs. silver, 600, 605
"Gold Bugs," 602, 605
Golden spike, 515, 517
Gold Reserve Act (1934), 758
Gold rush, in California, 500
Gold standard, 509, 756, 757, 922
Gold Standard Act (1900), 605
"Gold Star Mothers," 691
Goldwater, Barry, 900–901, 901 (map), 962
Gompers, Samuel, 535, 536, 620, 666, 683
Goodbye, Columbus (Roth), 887
Good Earth, The (Buck), 761
Good Neighbor policy, 748, 779–780
Goodwyn, Lawrence, 510
Google, 1010
G.O.P. (Grand Old Party). See Republican Party
Gorbachev, Mikhail, 949; Cold War and, 857; end of Soviet Union and, 957; Reagan and, 948–949, 950
Gordon, Linda, 676, 776
Gore, Albert, 965, 972, 972 (map), 973 (map)
Gorgas, William C., 621, 629
Gospel of wealth, 552
"Gospel of Wealth" (Carnegie), 525
Gotcher, Mrs. E., 648
Gould, Jay, 489–490, 518, 533
Government (U.S.): African Americans in, 1007; Asian Americans in, 1004; civil-service reform and, 499, 502; economic planning and, 682; expansion of, 486, 487, 686; financial collapse of 2008 and, 984; income from tariffs, 504; Latinos in, 1004; social welfare expenditures (1930–2009), 999
Government, ten-percent, 471, 474
Graft. See Corruption
Graham, Billy, 863
Grain Stabilization Corporation, 740
Grand Alliance, in World War II, 840–841
Grand Army of the Republic (GAR), 493, 503–504
Grand Canyon, 588, 655
Grand Canyon National Park, 653
Grand Central Terminal (New York), 569
Grand Coulee Dam, 762, 763
Grandfather clause, 508
Grange, 519, 596–597
Granger Laws, 597
Grant, Ulysses S., 488; cabinet of, 490; corruption under, 489–490; election of 1868 and, 488–489; election of 1872 and, 490–491; election of 1876 and, 494;

panic of 1873 and, 491–492; Supreme Court and, 492n
Grapes of Wrath, The (Steinbeck), 764
Graves, Michael, 1008
Great American Desert, 587, 588
Great Basin, 589 (map)
Great Britain. See England (Britain)
Great Depression (1929–1941), 537, 619, 637, 682, 740–747; African Americans and, 770, 870; causes of, 742–743; Dust Bowl in, 764, 765 (map); economic impact of (1929–1940), 772; Hoover and, 743–746; 1929 crash and, 637, 740–742; tariffs and, 740; unemployment in, 740–741, 754, 757–759, 772; in U.S. and world, 822–823. See also New Deal
Great Gatsby, The (Fitzgerald), 720, 886
Great migration, of blacks to North, 637
Great Northern Railroad, 516
Great Plains: Dust Bowl in, 764, 765 (map); homesteads on, 587; Shelterbelt project on, 652. See also Plains Indians; West
Great powers: colonial possessions of (1913), 633 (map); imperialism and status of, 632–633; after World War II, 840–841, 844. See also World Power
Great railroad strike (1877), 497
Great Rapprochement, 610
Great Recession (2008–), 808, 903, 974, 985–986, 990; Obama and, 965; welfare recipients in, 993
Great Sioux Reservation, 577, 579
Great Society, 828–829, 900, 910, 933; Congress during, 901–903; modern conservatism and, 962
Great Train Robbery, The (film), 716
Great White Fleet, 631
Greece, immigrants from, 543
Greeley, Horace, 491, 558
Greenback Labor party, 492, 597–598, 638
Greenback movement, 596
Greenbacks: Ohio Idea and, 489; panic of 1873 and, 491–492. See also Currency
Green Berets, 892–893
Greening of America, 913
Greensboro, North Carolina, sit-ins, 869
Greenwich Village (New York), 724
Greer (destroyer), 794
Greer County, Oklahoma, 587
Grenada, U.S. invasion of, 947
Griffith, D. W., 716
Griggs v. Duke Power Co., 922
Griswold v. Connecticut, 920–921
Gropius, Walter, 723
Gross national product (GNP), 830, 832; expenditures on elderly and, 998–999; in 1970s, 936; after World War II, 831–832
Guadalcanal, 637, 809, 810
Guam, 616, 808, 810
Guantánamo: imprisonment of Taliban fighters at, 975; naval base at, 621, 780
Guatemala, CIA-directed coup in, 878
Guerrilla warfare: in Philippine insurrection, 622; in Vietnam, 874–875, 906
Guest-worker program, 979, 1001
Guggenheim Museum (Bilbao, Spain), 1008
Guiteau, Charles J., 499
Gulf of California, 588
Gulf of Mexico region: BP oil spill in, 987, 1011; Hurricane Katrina in, 982
Gulf War. See Persian Gulf War
Gunboat diplomacy, 906
Guthrie, Oklahoma, 589
Gutman, Herbert, 537

Hague, The, International Criminal Court in, 969
Hahn, Steven, 484
Haiti: dollar diplomacy in, 658; Marines in, 667, 668, 736, 780
Haldeman, H. R., 928
Half-Breeds, 494
Halsey, Harlan P., 565
Halsey, William F., 818
Hammerstein, Oscar, 724
Hampton Institute, 555
Hancock, Winfield Scott, 498
Handy, W. C., 719
Hanna, Marcus Alonzo, 600–601, 602, 626
Hanoi, 923
Hansberry, Lorraine, 886
Harding, Warren G., 637, 700, 728–729; cabinet of, 728, 729; corruption and, 728, 729, 732–733; death of, 733; election of 1920 and, 696; foreign policy under, 730–732; tariff and, 732
Hard-money advocates, 492, 602
Harjo, Joy, 1010
Harlem, 719
Harlem Renaissance, 724
Harper's (Harper's New Monthly Magazine), 558
Harrington, Michael, 900
Harrison, Benjamin, 504, 611
Harrison, William Henry, 504
Hart, Gary, 955
Harte, Bret, 567–568, 585, 594
Harvard University, 557
Harvester trust, 524
Harvey, William Hope, 598
Hatch Act (1887), 555
Hatch Act (1939), 758, 773
Haussmann, Georges-Eugène, 569
Havana, 612
Havana Conference (1940), 788
Hawaii, 880; acquisition of, 610–611, 611 (map), 614; immigrant workers in, 611, 624; Japanese immigrants in, 800; Pearl Harbor attack in, 798; revolt of whites in, 611
Hawaiian Sugar Planters Association, 624
"Hawks" (Vietnam War), 910, 919
Hawley-Smoot Tariff (1930), 740, 742, 780
Hawthorne, Nathaniel, 560
Hay, John, 621, 623, 626
Hay-Bunau-Varilla Treaty (1902), 628
Hayes, Rutherford B., 496, 498; election of 1876 and, 493, 494–495, 494 (map); railroad strike and, 497
Haymarket Square episode, 533, 599, 642
Hay-Pauncefote Treaty (1901), 628
Hays, Samuel P., 675
Hays Code, 716
Hayslip, Le Ly, 894 (map)
Haywood, William D. ("Big Bill"), 681
H-bomb, 851–852
Head Start, 903
Health care: Clinton and, 967; costs of, 999; Obama policies toward, 986, 993. *See also* Disease
Hearst, William Randolph, 558, 608, 612, 669
Hebrew schools, 545
Hegemony, of United States, 980
Helicopters, Eisenhower and, 877
Heller, Joseph, 883
"Hello girls," 528
Helms-Burton Act (1996), 878
Helsinki accords (1975), 928
Hemingway, Ernest, 566, 720–721, 882
Henretta, James, 537
Henry Street Settlement, 549

Hepburn Act (1906), 649
Herblock (cartoonist), 954
Herzog (Bellow), 887
Hess, Rudolf, 844
Hetch Hetchy Valley, flooding of, 654–655
Hickok, James B., 586
Hicks, John D., 510
"High crimes and misdemeanors," 481
High culture, 1007
Higher education: blacks in, 1007. *See also* Universities and colleges
High-rise buildings, 882
High schools, 554, 709
High-tech industries, 834, 991
Highways. *See* Roads and highways
Hill, Anita, 961
Hill, James J., 516, 649
Hillbillies, 528
Hine, Lewis, photography of, 530, 531
Hip-hop, 1008
Hippies, 885
Hirohito (Japan), 821
Hiroshima, atomic bombing of, 820, 825
Hispanics: in Southwest, 594; on Supreme Court, 986. *See also* Latinos
Hiss, Alger, 852
History and historians: on atomic bomb use, 825; on Cold War, 857; constraints school of, 776; on imperialism, 634; on industrialization, 537; leftist school of, 537, 697–698, 775; on modern conservatism, 962; on New Deal, 775–776; New Left school of, 634, 675; New Western, 605–606; in 1960s, 913–914; organizational school of, 675–676; on Populists, 510; progressive school of, 510; on progressivism, 675–676; "realist," 697; on Reconstruction, 483–484; revisionist school of, 634, 857, 962; on Turner's thesis, 605–606; on U.S. imperialism, 634; on Wilson, 697–698
History of the United States During the Administrations of Jefferson and Madison (Adams), 568
Hitler, Adolf, 694, 697, 740, 781, 786; appeasement of, 784; Great Depression and, 822; Jewish policies of, 784; last days of, 816–818, 792; lend-lease and, 792; Spanish Civil War and, 783; suicide by, 818; in World War II, 811, 824
Hitler-Stalin pact (1939), 784–785
Hoar, George F., 620
Hoboes ("tramps"), 508
Ho Chi Minh, 632, 633, 874
Hoffa, James R. ("Jimmy"), 877
Hofstadter, Richard, 510, 634, 675, 962
Holding companies, 666, 765
Holland. *See* Netherlands
Holloway, Houston H., 467
Hollywood, movie industry in, 716
Holmes, Oliver Wendell, Jr. (son), 560, 561, 729
Holocaust: refugees from, 788; in World War II, 816–818, 822
Holzer, Jenny, 1008
Home brew, 708
Home front: in World War I, 680–686; in World War II, 807, 871
Homeland Security, Department of, 975
Home Loan Bank bill, 745
Home loans, 835
Home Owner's Loan Corporation (HOLC), 755, 758
Home Owner's Refinancing Act (1933), 755
Homer, Winslow, 568, 569
Home Rule regimes, in South, 476

Homestead Act (1862), 473, 586–587, 596
Homesteading, 586–588, 587, 588
Homestead Strike, 505–506, 642
Homosexuals. *See* Gays and lesbians
Honduras, dollar diplomacy in, 658
Hong Kong, 633, 808
Hookworms, eradication of, 709
Hoover, Herbert, 637, 739, 744, 745, 746–747, 767, 770; election of 1928 and, 738–739, 739 (map); election of 1932 and, 753; as Food Administration head, 685; Good Neighbor policy of, 748; Great Depression policies of, 743–746; as Secretary of Commerce, 728, 729
Hoover, J. Edgar, 889, 896
Hoover Dam, construction of, 744–746
Hoovervilles, 743, 746
Hopkins, Harry L., 757, 758n, 759
Hopwood v. *Texas*, 968
Horizontal integration, 521–522
Hormones, 995
Horses, 576, 583
Hostage crisis (Iran, 1979), 938–939, 950
Households: with electric service, 767; income of, 992; men's responsibilities in, 996–997
House of Mirth, The (Wharton), 567
House of Representatives (U.S.): control of (1869–1891), 492; impeachment in, 480–481; Judiciary Committee in, 928; Reed as Speaker of, 505. *See also* Congress (U.S.); Senate (U.S.)
House Un-American Activities Committee (HUAC), 852
Housing: Hoovervilles, 743; lending collapse and, 983–984; New Deal and, 767; in 1950s, 860; slums, 542; sod, 588, 596; wealth gap in, 992
Housing Act (1949), 854
Housing and Urban Development, Department of (HUD), 902
Howard, John Langley, 742
Howard, Oliver O., 469
Howard University, 469, 555
Howe, Julia Ward, 689
Howe, Marie Jenny, 644
Howells, William Dean, 566
"Howl" (Ginsberg), 884, 885
Howl and Other Poems (Ginsberg), 885
How the Other Half Lives (Riis), 638–639
HUAC. *See* House Un-American Activities Committee
Huerta, Victoriano, 668, 669
Hughes, Charles Evans, 645; election of 1916 and, 674–675, 675 (map); as Secretary of State, 728, 731
Hughes, Langston, 719, 724
Hull, Cordell, 778, 780, 788
Hull House, 549, 645
Human Genome Project, 991–992
Human rights: Carter and, 933–936, 944; Helsinki accords and, 928; U.S. and, 980
Humphrey, Hubert H., 909–910, 910 (map)
Hundred Days, in New Deal, 754, 755, 822
Hundred Days (Emergency) Congress, 755, 756, 757, 761, 762, 764, 765
Hungary: communist collapse in, 956; Jewish refugees from, 788; in NATO, 969; uprising of 1956 in, 874, 875
Hunting, by Plains Indians, 582, 583
Huntington, Collis P., 515
Hurricane Katrina, 982
Hurston, Zora Neale, 724
Hwang, David, 1010
Hybrid cars, 1012
Hydraulic mining, 585
Hydroelectric power, 766

Hydrogen bombs. *See* Atomic bombs; H-bomb; Nuclear weapons
Hydrogen fuel cell, 1012
Hyper-inflation, 738
"Hyper power," United States as, 980

IBM (International Business Machines), 860, 991, 994
Ickes, Harold L., 762
Idaho, 584, 585, 589
Identity, preservation of ethnic, 704
Identity politics, of religious right, 952
"I Have a Dream" speech (King), 897, 905
Illegal immigration, 1000–1001; in Arizona, 1001; Obama and, 986
Illinois: railroad regulation in, 597. *See also* Chicago
Illiteracy: of blacks (1900), 554; fall in rate of, 554; of immigrants, 544. *See also* Literacy tests
Immigrants and immigration, 550, 703; antiforeignism and, 487, 550–551; in Arizona, 1001; Bush, George W., and, 979; of Cubans, 878; education for, 547; Filipino, 624–625; Japanese, 800, 801; jobs for female, 550; labor of, 520–521; Latino, 988; legal (1961–2009), 1000; literature and, 1010; national-origins system and, 703; New, 543–550, 703, 1000–1001; Obama and, 986; Old, 542–543, 544; patriotism in World War II, 799; population of, 542, 543 (figure); principal foreign elements in U.S. (1910), 671; railroads and, 518, 587; reasons for, 544–545, 706; reforms of, 902, 986; restrictions on, 498, 551, 703–704; return to country of origin, 545; settlement houses for, 549; to Sunbelt, 834–835; Vietnamese, 928, 930–931. *See also* Illegal immigration; specific groups
Immigration Act: of 1924, 703; of 1929, 703n
Immigration and Nationality Act (1965), 902
Immigration Reform and Control Act (1986), 1000–1001
Impeachment, 971; of Clinton, 970–971; of Johnson, Andrew, 480–481; Nixon and, 928
Imperialism: Anti-Imperialist League and, 620; beginnings of, 608–610; in China, 623–626; in Cuba, 621; economic, 748; 1870–1914, 632–633; election of 1900 and, 626; of free trade, 698; Great Powers and colonial possessions (1913), 633 (map); in Hawaii, 610–611; historians on, 634; Japanese, 747–748; justifications for, 632; mercantilism and, 632; at Paris Peace Conference, 694; in Philippines, 487, 617–620, 622–623; in Puerto Rico, 617, 618; by U.S., 634; Wilson and, 667
Imperialism: The Highest Stage of Capitalism (Lenin), 634
Inauguration: of Lincoln, 465; of Roosevelt, Franklin, 753, 754, 770, 773
Income: family share of (1980–2009), 953; of middle class, 946; 1970–2008, 916; in 21st century, 992; after World War II, 831. *See also* Wages
Income gap, 992–996
Income taxes, 509; payment of, by group, 993; reduction of, 726; Sixteenth Amendment and, 509n, 665
Incorporation laws, 525

India: Clinton and, 970; outsourcing of jobs to, 991. *See also* Gandhi, Mohandas
Indian policy: Dawes Act and, 581–584; Indian New Deal, 765; reservation system, 576–577, 582
Indian Removal Act (1830), 584 (map)
Indian Reorganization Act (1934), 584, 758, 765
Indians. *See* Native Americans
Indian Territory, 575, 577
Indian Wars (1860–1890), 577–580, 578 (map), 582
Indies. *See* Dutch East Indies; West Indies
Indigenous peoples, 592, 593. *See also* Native Americans
Individualism, industrial society and, 486
Indochina, 633; France and, 874–875. *See also* Cambodia; Laos; Vietnam
Indoor plumbing, in cities, 540
Industrial capitalism, 537
Industrialization: education and, 557; historians on, 537; imperialism and, 632; in South, 487, 526–528. *See also* Industry
Industrial Revolution, 487, 523, 632; spread of, 512
Industrial societies, income gap in, 993
Industrial Workers of the World (IWW, Wobblies), 643, 681, 683
Industry: aerospace, 835; in Great Depression, 761–763; growth of, 486; high-tech, 834; in 1900, 529 (map); in 1920s, 710; research and product development by, 994; tariff reduction and, 504; in World War I, 681–682; in World War II, 802, 804, 824. *See also* Industrialization; Manufacturing; specific industries
Infant industries, 601
Infinite Jest (Wallace), 1009
Inflation, 605; under Carter, 944; free silver and, 492, 506, 602; in Germany, 737; managed currency and, 757; in 1970s, 937; under Nixon, 917, 922; panic of 1873 and, 491–492; Vietnam War and, 829; World War I and, 683. *See also* Economy
Influence of Sea Power upon History, 1660–1783, The (Mahan), 609
Influenza pandemic (1918–1919), 691
Information age, 860, 991
Information superhighway, 991
INF Treaty. *See* Intermediate-Range Nuclear Forces Treaty
Initiative, 641
Injunctions, 531, 599; against strikers, 600, 730
Innovations: in industry, 520–521; in transportation, 520. *See also* Inventions
Installment buying, 742
Insular Cases, 621
Insull, Samuel, 765
Insurance, medical, 993
Insurrectos, 612, 615
Integration (racial): Eisenhower and, 869; residential, 1005; of schools, 868–869, 905–906; of University of Mississippi, 896. *See also* Civil rights movement; Segregation
Intellectual thought: "Gospel of Wealth" and, 525; on immigrant role in society, 704; multiculturalism in, 1007; pragmatism and, 557, 560–561; in sciences, 557; Social Darwinism and, 525. *See also* Art(s); Literature; Philosophy
Inter-American Conference (1936), 780

Interchangeable parts, 520
Interlocking directorates, 522, 666
Intermarriage, Asian-Caucasian, 624
Intermediate-Range Nuclear Forces (INF) Treaty (1987), 949
Internal combustion engine, 524
International Bank for Reconstruction and Development. *See* World Bank
International Criminal Court (The Hague), 969
International debt, after World War I, 736–737
International Energy Agency, 925
International Exhibition of Modern Art (Armory Show), 722
International Monetary Fund (IMF), 841, 843
International style, of architecture, 723, 882
International trade. *See* Trade
International Women's Day, 934–935
Internet, 1007, 1010
Internment camps, in World War II, 799–802
Interpreter of Maladies (Lahiri), 1010
Interstate commerce, 519, 525, 666
Interstate Commerce Act (1887), 519–520, 526
Interstate Commerce Commission (ICC), 519, 649, 729, 730
Interstate highways, 837
Intervention: preventive, 630; Roosevelt Corollary and, 630
Intifada, against Israel, 970
Intuitionist, The (Whitehead), 1009
Inventions: by Edison, 520, 521. *See also* Electronic media; specific inventions and inventors
Investment(s): foreign, 510, 512, 520, 567; imperialism and, 632; in railroads, 517
Invisible Man (Ellison), 886
In-vitro fertilization, 995
Iran: in axis of evil, 976; OPEC and, 876; revolution in (1979), 937; shah in, 875, 937; after World War II, 846
Iran-contra affair, 950–951
Iranian hostage crisis, 938–939, 944
Iran-Iraq War, 948 (map)
Iraq, 977 (map); awarded to Great Britain, post World War I, 693; Bush, George W., and, 976–977; OPEC and, 876; in Persian Gulf War, 959–960; post-Saddam government of, 979; Saddam Hussein in, 959; U.S. invasion of, 959–960, 981. *See also* Iraq War
Iraq War (2003–), 829, 977, 982, 1012; Obama and, 986–987; "surge" in (2007), 983
Ireland: immigrants from, 703; outsourcing of jobs to, 991
Irish Americans: Chinese immigrants and, 497–498; League of Nations opposition of, 695; railroad labor of, 514–515
Iron and iron industry, in Midwest, 520
Iron Heel, The (London), 567
Irreconcilables, 693, 695, 696, 730
Irrigation, 588, 651, 762
Islam: Black Islam and, 904–905; fundamentalism of, 937, 959; growth of, 905. *See also* Arabs and Arab world; Muslims
Island hopping strategy, in World War II, 810
Isolationism, 636–637, 678, 698; Roosevelt, Franklin D., and, 778, 779; Vietnam War and, 924; after World War I, 694,

703, 730–731, 736; World War II and, 781–782, 784, 786, 789, 790, 828
Israel: Camp David Agreement and, 934–935, 936; Lebanon invasion by, 947; Palestine intifada against, 970; in Persian Gulf War, 959; PLO and, 970; Six-Day War in, 907, 924; Truman and, 847–849; U.N. and, 844; Yom Kippur War (1973) in, 924
Issei, 801
Isserman, Maurice, 914
Italian Americans: in suburbs, 547; Versailles Treaty and, 694
Italy, 609; communism in, 847l, 848; immigrants from, 543, 546–547; lynching of Italians in New Orleans and, 609; Treaty of Versailles and, 694; in Tripartite Pact, 781; in World War I, 670, 688; in World War II, 812–813
Iwo Jima, in World War II, 819
IWW. See Industrial Workers of the World

Jackson, Helen Hunt, 580, 594
Jackson, Jesse, 955
Jackson, Kenneth, 776
James, Henry, 560, 566–567, 568, 720
James, William, 549, 553, 557, 560–561, 567, 620, 721, 722
Jamestown, Polish people in, 706
Japan: appeasement of, 784; atomic bomb and, 820, 825; bombings in World War II, 810; China and, 623, 658, 747–748, 784; democratic government in, 850; emigration from, 800; Gentlemen's Agreement with, 631, 801; "Hate America" rallies in, 703; Korea and, 855; League of Nations and, 781; MacArthur and, 818, 850; modernization of, 800; in 1970s, 917; Pacific region and, 807–810; Pearl Harbor attack by, 637, 794–795, 798, 799; propaganda against, 802; Root-Takahira agreement with, 631; Russian war with, 630; Treaty of Versailles and, 694; in Tripartite Pact, 781; World War I and, 670, 688; World War II and, 798, 807–810, 818–821; Yalta conference and, 839–840
Japanese Americans: in California, 630–631, 667; discrimination against, 800–801, 802; in Hawaii, 611, 800; immigration to U.S., 703; internment in World War II, 799–802
Jaruzelski, Wojciech (Poland), 707
Jay-Z, 1008
Jazz, 718–719, 885
Jazz Age, 714, 725
Jazz Singer, The (film), 716, 717–718
Jefferson, Thomas, 528
Jews and Judaism: Hitler and, 784, 786, 822; Holocaust and, 786, 816–818, 822; as immigrants, 537, 543, 545; Israel and, 848–849; literature after World War II, 887; Nazi Germany and, 816–818; New Immigrants and, 552; Six-Day War and, 907
Jiang Jieshi (Chiang Kai-shek), 850, 851; Manchuria and, 840; in World War II, 808, 813
Jihadi fighters, in Afghanistan, 987
Jim Crow laws, 496, 508, 867–868, 1006
Jin, Ha, 1010
Jingoism, 621
Jobs: of Chinese immigrants, 498, 500; outsourcing of, 991; in South, 528. See also Employment
Johns Hopkins University, 557

Johnson, Andrew, 469, 470, 483; Black Codes and, 474; Congress and, 474, 480–481; election of 1864 and, 469–470; Fourteenth Amendment and, 474; Freedmen's Bureau and, 474; impeachment of, 480–481, 971; pardons by, 465; Reconstruction plan of, 471; Southern policy of, 474; white supremacy of, 469
Johnson, Hiram W., 645, 693
Johnson, Lyndon Baines, 901–903; African American rights and, 903–904; civil rights movement and, 898–900; in Congress, 898; death of, 910; election of 1960 and, 878; election of 1964 and, 900–901, 901 (map); election of 1968 and, 908; foreign policy of, 906–910; Great Society of, 828–829, 933; Vietnam War and, 906–909
Johnson Debt Default Act (1934), 782
Joint Chiefs of Staff, 817, 875
Joint Committee on Reconstruction, 474
Jolson, Al, 718
Jones, James, 883
Jones, Le Roi (Imamu Amiri Baraka), 886
Jones, Mary Harris ("Mother"), 534
Jones Act (1916), 667
Jordan, 907, 947
Joseph, Chief (Nez Perce), 578 (map), 579
Josephson, Matthew, 537
Journalism: electronic media and, 1011; Hearst and, 558; Pulitzer and, 558. See also Magazines; Newspapers; Press; Yellow journalism
Joy Luck Club, The (Tan), 1010
Judaism. See Jews and Judaism
Judicial deference, 561
Jungle, The (Sinclair), 650
Jus sanguinis, 498
Jus soli, 498
Justice Department, trust prosecutions by, 526
Juvenile delinquency, reforms and, 645

Kagan, Elena, 986
Kahn, Louis, 882
Kaiser, Henry J., 802
Kallen, Horace, 704, 1007
Kaltenbrunner, Ernest, 844
Kamikaze suicide pilots, 819
Kansas: black migration to, 467; Populists in, 507
Kansas City, stockyards in, 586
Kansas Pacific Railroad, 518, 580
Katrina, Hurricane, 982
Katz, Michael, 537
Kazin, Michael, 914
KDKA radio station, 715
Kearney, Denis, 498
Kearny (destroyer), attack on, 794
Keitel, Wilhelm, 844
Kelley, Florence, 549, 645
Kelley, Oliver H., 596
Kellogg, Frank B., 732
Kellogg-Briand Pact (1928), 732
Kelly, Ned, 592
Kelly, William, 522
Kennan, George F., 697, 846, 847
Kennedy, David, 776
Kennedy, Edward, 943
Kennedy, Jacqueline, 879
Kennedy, John F. ("Jack"): assassination of, 898; civil rights under, 895–898; election of 1960 and, 878–879, 880 (map); foreign policy under, 892–893; inauguration of, 889; New Frontier of, 889–891; Soviet Union and, 895;

speaking in shopping mall, 881; Vietnam and, 893
Kennedy, Robert F. ("Bobby"), 889, 896, 908
Kennedy Library, 882
Kennedy Round, 891
Kent State University, shooting at, 919
Kern, Jerome, 724
Kerosene, 523, 530
Kerouac, Jack, 884, 911
Kerry, John F., election of 2004 and, 979
Kessler-Harris, Alice, 776
Kettle Hill, battle at, 615
Keynes, John Maynard, 772
Keynesianism, 772
Khrushchev, Nikita S., 874; Nixon's kitchen debate with, 878; summit meetings and, 878; U.S. trip by, 878
Kidnapping, Lindbergh, 709
Kindergarten, 554
Kinetoscopes, 520
King, Coretta Scott, 872
King, Martin Luther, Jr., 868, 896; arrest of, 872; in Birmingham, 896–897; Black Power and, 904–905; "I Have a Dream" speech of, 897, 905; March on Washington and, 897, 905; Montgomery bus boycott and, 868; voter registration and, 903–904
Kiowa Indians, 576
Kipling, Rudyard, 620, 622
Kiska, in World War II, 809, 810
Kissinger, Henry A., 697, 919–920, 923
Kitchen debate (1959), 878
Kitty Hawk, Wright brothers at, 714
Klatch, Rebecca, 914
Knights of Labor, 533–535, 536, 768
Knock, Thomas J., 697
Knox, Philander C., 658
Koehler, Robert, 532
Kolko, Gabriel, 675, 857
Kolko, Joyce, 857
Koons, Jeff, 1008
Korea, 633; Clinton and, 970; after Korean War, 865; Soviet downing of airliner, 947
Korean War, 854–856, 856 (map), 865; casualties in, 865; Eisenhower and, 865; MacArthur and, 855–856; spending for, 834
Korematsu v. U.S., 799
Kosovo, 969
Kramer, Paul, 634
Kremlin. See Soviet Union
Kristallnacht, 788
Kristol, Irving, 942
Ku Klux Klan (KKK), 716; comeback of, 637; in 1920s, 701–703; during Reconstruction, 479–480
Kushner, Tony, 1010
Kuwait, 876, 959, 960
Kyoto Treaty, 973, 1012

Labor: AFL-CIO and, 877; Chinese immigrants as, 500; for continental railroad, 514–515; for cotton industry, 806; Eisenhower and, 877; of Filipino immigrants, 624; Hoover and, 746; immigrant, 520–521, 547; of Japanese Americans, 631, 800; migrant, 595; NAFTA and, 969; New Deal and, 761–763, 767–769; southern, 528; Square Deal for, 647; after World War II, 804, 830–831; in World War II, 802–803. See also Labor unions; Servants; Slaves and slavery; Workers; Workforce

Laboratory School (University of Chicago), 561

Labor contracts, freedmen and, 469, 471

Labor Day, 537

Labor Department, 645; Women's Bureau in, 684

Labor movement: closed shop in, 536; weakness of, 497. *See also* Labor unions; Strikes

Labor union. *See also* specific unions

Labor unions: for African Americans, 533, 534, 535; antitrust prosecution and, 666; barring of nonproducers from, 533; Civil War and, 532; in coal industry, 648; corporations and, 531–532; craft, 533; election of 1944 and, 815; ethnic differences and, 704; immigrants and, 551; injunctions used against, 600, 730; membership in selected countries, 769; National Labor Union and, 532–533; New Deal and, 767–769; in 1950s, 860–861; prejudice in, 533; racketeers in, 708; red scare and, 701; Sherman Anti-Trust Act and, 525; World War I and, 683; after World War II, 830–831; in World War II, 802–803

Lacambanne family, 715

LaFeber, Walter, 634

La Follette, Robert M. ("Fighting Bob"), 645; election of 1912 and, 659; election of 1924 and, 735–736

La Follette Seaman's Act (1915), 666, 730

Lahiri, Jhumpa, 1010

Laissez-faire philosophy, 503, 638, 729

Lake Powell, Utah, 653

Lakota (Sioux) Indians, 581

Lamarck, Jean-Baptiste, 553

Lame-duck period, 753, 770, 986

Land: conservation and, 651; Dawes Act and Indian, 581–584; for freedmen, 469; Homestead Act and, 586–587; homesteads from public lands, 587; Native American, 577, 584 (map); railroads' impact on, 518

Land-grant colleges, 555

Land grants: to railroads, 512–514, 514 (map), 516; for state universities, 555

Landon, Alfred, 769–770

Landrum-Griffin Act (1959), 877

Landscape architects, 569

Laos, 892

Larson, Jonathan, 1010

Latin America: Big Sister policy toward, 609; CIA interference in, 878; debt defaults in, 629; Good Neighbor policy and, 748, 779–780; immigrants from, 703; Kennedy, John F., and, 893–895; Monroe Doctrine and, 788; Roosevelt Corollary and, 630; World War II and, 787–788. *See also* Central America; Spanish America; specific locations

Latinos, 1002–1003; in California, 1004; immigrant population of, 988; as largest U.S. minority, 1003; literature by, 1010; in Southwest, 1000; U.S. population of, 1004. *See also* Hispanics

LaVinge, Robert, 885

Lawrence, Jacob, 870

Lawson, Thomas W., 640

Lazarus, Emma, 551

League Covenant, 693, 697

League of Nations, 693, 759, 842; Germany and, 781; Italian takeover of Ethiopia and, 781; Japan and, 747, 748, 781; opposition to, 693–694, 695, 696–697; Paris Peace Conference and, 694; U.S.

and, 730–731, 736, 747; Wilson and, 680, 693, 694

League of Women Voters, 752

Learning by doing, 709

Lease, Mary Elizabeth, 598

Leather trust, 524

Lebanon, 878; Israeli invasion of, 947

Le Corbusier, 723

Lee, Harper, 886

Lee, Spike, 1010

Leffler, Melvyn, 857

Leftist school of historians, 537, 697–698, 775

Legal Tender Act, 492*n*

Legislation, of Hundred Days Congress (1933), 755

Legislatures: radical, 479. *See also* Congress (U.S.)

Lehman Brothers, 984, 1011

Leisure: in late 1800s, 570–572. *See also* Entertainment

LeMay, Curtis, 909

Lend-lease, to Soviet Union, 840

Lend-Lease Bill (1940), 791–792, 792 (map), 793

Lenin, Vladimir, 634, 956

Leopold (Belgium), 633

Lesbians. *See* Gays and lesbians

Letts, Tracy, 1010

Leuchtenburg, William, 776

Levittown, 837, 838

Lewinsky, Monica, 970

Lewis, John L., 768, 769

Lewis, Sinclair, 721, 724, 761

Leyte Gulf, battle at, 818

Liberalism: in religion, 552; after World War II, 828, 829

Liberal Protestants, 552

Liberal Republican party, 490–491

Liberia, 633

Liberties. *See* Freedom(s)

Liberty Loan drives, 686

Libraries, public, 523, 557

Library of Congress, 557

Libya, Reagan and, 949

Lichtenstein, Roy, 882

Lieberman, Joseph, 972

Life expectancy, 843; increase in, 557, 709; medical advancements and, 994–995; in 2000s, 998

Life Studies (Robert Lowell), 883

Lifestyle. *See* Culture(s); Society

Lightbulb, 521, 523–524

Lighting: in cities, 645. *See also* Electricity

Liliuokalani (Hawaii), 611, 612

Limerick, Patricia Nelson, 605

Lincoln, Abraham, 488, 990; assassination of, 471; inauguration of, 465; Reconstruction plan of, 470, 471

Lindbergh, Charles A., 709, 714, 789

Lindbergh Law, 709

Lindsay, Vachel, 602

Link, Arthur S., 697

Linotype, 557

Lintheads, 528

Liquor. *See* Alcohol

Literacy tests: for immigrants, 551; for voting, 480, 507–508. *See also* Illiteracy

Literary clubs, 645

Literary Digest, 787

Literature: Asian American, 1010; black dialect and folklore in, 568; dime novels as, 565; feminist, 562; immigrant, 1010; modernism in, 720–724; muckrakers and, 639–641; naturalism in, 567; in 1920s, 720–724; Nobel Prize for, 882; popular fiction, 565; postmodern,

1008–1009; progressive, 638–639; realism in, 566–567, 720; regionalism in, 565, 566, 567–568, 721–724; on religion, 553; Southern Renaissance, 886–887; by women, 567, 568, 760–761; after World War I, 883; after World War II, 882–883. *See also* Novels

Little Bighorn, Battle of the, 578–579

Little Rock, Arkansas, desegregation in, 869

Litwack, Leon, 483

Living standards, for whites and nonwhites, 998

Lloyd, Henry Demarest, 638

Lloyd George, David, 692

Loans: to Allies (World War I), 737; to foreigners, 736–737; for homes, 835, 838; pump-priming, 746

Lobbyists, 499, 665

Lochner v. *New York*, 561, 646

Lockouts, 531

Lodge, Henry Cabot, 609, 612, 620, 692; League of Nations and, 693; Versailles Treaty and, 695–696

Lodge, Henry Cabot, Jr., election of 1960 and, 878

Logging, 654

London, Jack, 567, 654

London, subway in, 539

London Economic Conference (1933), 778

Lonely Crowd, The (Riesman), 864

Long, Huey P., 759, 822, 962

Long, John D., 614

Long Drive, 586

Long-horned cattle, 585

Longshoremen, Italians as, 547

Looking Backward (Bellamy), 559

Los Angeles, California, race riots in, 905, 1005–1006

Losing Ground (Murray), 913

"Lost Cause," 466

"Lost Cause" literature, in South, 886

"Lost Generation," 721

Louisiana: blacks in, 467, 480; Compromise of 1877 and, 494, 495; government graft in, 479

Lowell, Robert, 883

Lowery, Joseph E., 868

Loyalists (Spanish Civil War), 783

Loyalty program, of Truman, 852

Loyalty Review Board, 852

Lucas, George, 1010

"Luck of Roaring Camp, The" (Harte), 568

Lusitania (passenger liner), 672–673

Luzon, Philippines, 819

Lyceums, 554

Lynch, David, 1010

Lynch, John R., 479

Lynchings: of African Americans, 496–497, 867, 868; crusade against, 563, 564; of German American, 681; of Italians, in New Orleans, 609; persons by race (1882–2005), 497

Lynd, Helen, 714

Lynd, Robert, 714

Lyrics of Lowly Life (Dunbar), 568

Macao, 633

MacArthur, Douglas, 759; Bonus Army and, 746; Japan and, 818, 850; Korean War and, 855–856; Truman and, 855–856; in World War II, 808, 810, 824

Machine politics. *See* Political machines

Machinery, for agribusiness, 834

Macy's department store, 540, 807

Magazines: muckrakers and, 639; social reform, 558–559. *See also* Journalism; Press

Maggie: A Girl of the Streets (Crane), 567
Mahan, Alred Thayer, 609, 621–622
Mail: civil-service employment and, 502; transcontinental airmail route, 714
Mailer, Norman, 883
Mail-order houses, 541
Mainc, 770
Maine (ship), 612–613, 784
Main Street (Lewis), 721
Majority-minority states, 1004
Makin Island, 810
"Malaise speech" (Carter), 938
Malamud, Bernard, 887
Malaria, 616
Malaya, in World War II, 808
Malay Peninsula, 633
Malcolm X, 904–905
Male, use of term in Fourteenth Amendment, 477
Managed currency, 756–757
Manchukuo, 748
Manchuria: Japan's takeover of, 626, 747, 748; Russo-Japanese War and, 630; Soviet Union and, 840; Taft and, 658
Mandan Indians, 576
Mandela, Nelson, 958–959
Manela, Erez, 698
Manhattan Project, 820, 994
Manifest Destiny, of Russians and South Africans, 592
Manila, battle at, 614
Man in the Gray Flannel Suit, The (Wilson), 864
Manned Spacecraft Center, Houston, 994
Man Nobody Knows, The (Barton), 710
Manpower, in World War I, 803–804
Manufacturing: in early 21st century, 1011; mechanization and, 520–521; vertical integration and, 521. *See also* Factories; Industrialization; Industry; Tariff(s)
Manzanar, 801
Mao Zedong (Mao Tse-tung), 850
March on Washington (1963), 897, 899, 905
Marconi, Guglielmo, 715
Marcos, Ferdinand, 949
Mariana Islands, 694n, 810, 818
Marine Corps: bombing of barracks in Lebanon, 947; in Cuba, 630; in Haiti, 667, 668; in Nicaragua, 658; in World War I, 687. *See also* Armed forces
Maritime powers, Japan as, 819
Market(s): for farm produce, 595, 596; imperialism and, 632; international, 530; overseas expansion and, 608
Markie, Biz, 1008
Marne, Second Battle of, 690
Marriage: and divorces, 562; of freedmen, 467; by 1990s, 997; polygamy and, 589; same-sex, 979, 998; "slave marriages," 467. *See also* Families; Intermarriage
Marshall, George C., 824, 847, 866
Marshall, Thurgood, 961
Marshall Field's, 540
Marshall Islands, 694n, 810, 851
Marshall Plan, 847–848
Martin v. *Wilks*, 953
Marx, Karl, 642
Marxism, 642, 956
"Mash-up" artists, 1008
Massachusetts, gay marriage in, 998
Mass-consumption economy, 710–711
Massive retaliation doctrine, 874
Mass media, 716; television and, 862–863
Mass production, 520
Mass tourism, 655
Mass transit, 539

Matisse, Henri, 721
Mattachine Society, 912
Matusow, Allen, 913
May Day strikes (1886), 533
McAuliffe, A. C., 816
McCain, John, election of 2008 and, 983
McCarran Internal Security Bill (1950), 852–853
McCarthy, Eugene, 908, 909
McCarthy, Joseph, and McCarthyism, 852–853, 866–867
McClure's, 639, 640
McDonald's, 862, 863
McGirr, Lisa, 914
McGovern, George, 923, 944
McKay, Claude, 724
McKinley, William, 604–605; assassination of, 627; Cuban policy of, 621; election of 1896 and, 600–604; election of 1900 and, 626–627; imperialism and, 620; Philippines and, 617–620, 623; as Representative, 505; Spanish-American War and, 613, 614; trust formation and, 526
McKinley Tariff (1890), 505, 605, 611
McMath, Robert C., 510
McNamara, Robert S., 889, 892, 907
McNary-Haughen Bill, 735
McVeigh, Timothy, 967
Mead, George Herbert, 560
Mead, Margaret, 760
Meade, Lawrence, 913
Meat Inspection Act (1906), 650, 675
Meatpacking industry, 524, 585–586, 650; food safety and, 650
Mechanization: of agriculture, 594–595, 734, 735, 764; industrial growth and, 520–521; in tobacco industry, 526
Media: new media, 1010–1011; social, 991, 1010–1011. *See also* Mass media
Medicaid, 902, 921
Medical insurance, 993
Medical schools, 557, 995
Medicare, 902, 903, 998, 999
Medicine: advances in, 994–995; bioengineering and, 992; patent medicine, 557, 640; polio vaccine and, 872; in World War II, 821–824
Mediterranean region, in World War II, 812
Meiji Restoration (Japan), 800
Mellon, Andrew W., 710, 725–726, 728, 734
Melting pot: ethnic differences and, 704; in schools, 639
Men: household responsibilities of, 996–997; husbandless families and, 1006; immigrant, 546; paternity leave for, 996; after World War II, 836
Mencken, H. L., 720, 759
Merchant marine, 627, 666
Merchant Marine Act (1920), 730
Meredith, James, 896
Mergers, banking and, 955
Merit system, 503
Mesabi Range, 520, 521
Metaphysical Club, 560, 561
Metropolitan areas: population in (1910–2000), 1005. *See also* Cities and towns
Metropolitan Opera House, 568
Mettler, Suzanne, 776
Mexican Americans: bicultural zone of, 1000; *Bracero* program and, 803; Operation Wetback and, 872, 873; zoot suit riots and, 806. *See also* Hispanics; Latinos

Mexican people: as migrant farm labor, 595; migration to U.S., 668
Mexico: foreign investment in, 668; Good Neighbor policy and, 780; immigration from, 1000; intervention in lives of immigrants to U.S., 1002–1003; Latinos from, 1002; moralistic diplomacy in, 668–670; oil resources in, 736; revolution in, 668–669; U.S. intervention in, 669–670; Zimmermann note and, 678
Microsoft, 991
Middle class, 843; income of, 946; progressivism and, 675; strikes and, 532; tax burden of, 726; women in, 528, 645; after World War II, 832
Middle East: "Arab Spring" protest in, 1011; Clinton and, 969–970; Cold War in, 875–876; Harding and, 731; Israeli invasion of Lebanon in, 947; Suez crisis in, 875–876; Truman and, 848–849; after World War II, 948 (map). *See also* Arabs and Arab world
Middletown, 714
Midway, Battle of, 809
Midwest: Grange in, 597; Klan in, 702; wheat belt in, 734
Mies van der Rohe, Ludwig, 723, 1008
Migrant farm workers, 595, 624
Migration: African American, 467, 806, 838, 870–871; of Chinese men, 500; from cities, 542; Mexican, 668; to Sunbelt, 834–835; to West, 588–589, 590; during World War II, 804–805, 805 (map)
"Migration of the Negro, The" (Lawrence), 870
Militancy, of African Americans, 807
Military, 798; under Kennedy, John F., 892–893; spending on, 832–834; in Vietnam, 906, 907–908. *See also* Armed forces; Militia
Military academies, women in, 996
Military districts, in South, 475, 476 (map)
Military draft: Carter and, 939; in Vietnam War, 919; in World War I, 686–687; in World War II, 787
Military pensions, 503–504
Military Reconstruction, 475–476, 476 (map)
Military spending, 783, 832–834, 906, 946; and close of U.S. bases, 958; under Reagan, 946
Military tribunal, Supreme Court on, 475–476
Militia, paramilitary, 967
Miller, Arthur, 883–886
Milliken v. *Bradley*, 932
Millionaires, 520, 525; philanthropy of, 556–557; railroads and, 518
Millionaires' Club, 641
Mills, in South, 528
Milosević, Slobodan, 969
Mimeograph, 521
Mines, Bureau of, 658
Mines and mining: child labor in, 530; hydraulic, 585; railroads and, 518; strikes in, 506; in West, 584–585. *See also* Coal and coal industry
Minorities, 1005–1007; affirmative action and, 922; Asian Americans as, 1004; independence for European, 680; Latinos as, 1003; in medical schools, 995; in nonacademic science and engineering, 995; set-asides for, 922; Versailles Treaty and liberation of, 694. *See also* Race and racism; specific groups

Minstrel shows, 560, 718
Miranda v. *Arizona*, 921
Miranda warning, 921
MIRVs (multiple independently targeted reentry vehicles), 920
Miss America pageant, protest at, 935
Missiles, 877; ABM treaty and, 920; Cuban missile crisis and, 895; INF Treaty and, 949; in Persian Gulf War, 959. *See also* Nuclear weapons; Space exploration
Missions and missionaries: in China, 623; overseas expansion and, 608. *See also* Religion(s)
Mississippi: African Americans voting in, 903; Black Codes in, 471; civil rights workers' deaths in, 903
Mississippi Freedom Democratic party, 903
Mississippi River region, 594
Missouri (ship), Japanese surrender on, 821
Mitchell, Margaret, 1009
Miyatake, Toyo, 801
Mobility: internal migration and, 835; social, 838
Mobilization, for World War I, 680–686
Model T, 520, 711, 712
Modernism, 720–724
Modernists, vs. Fundamentalists in religion, 718
Modernization theory, 893
Mondale, Walter, 947–948
Monetary policy: in 1870s, 491–492; election of 1868 and, 489; gold vs. silver in, 600, 605
Money. *See* Currency; Greenbacks
Money trust, 598, 665
Monkey Trial, 709, 710
Monopoly(ies), 504, 521, 525–526; in oil industry, 524–525; railroads as, 519; Roosevelt, Theodore, and, 649
Monroe, Marilyn, 863
Monroe Doctrine (1823), 694, 748; dollar diplomacy and, 658; Roosevelt Corollary to, 629–630, 779
Montana, 584, 589, 658
Monte Cassino, 812
Montgomery, Alabama, bus boycott in, 868
Montgomery, Bernard, 811
Montgomery, David, 537
Montgomery Ward, 541
Mont-Saint-Michel and Chartres (Adams), 568
Moody, Dwight Lyman, 552
Moon landing, 890–891
Moonshiners, 705
Moralism-legalism, 697
Morality: in 1920s, 718; new, 559
Moral Majority, 914, 951, 953
Morgan, J. P., and Company, 671
Morgan, J. Pierpont (J.P.), 521, 522, 649; Carnegie and, 522–523; competition and, 522; loan to U.S., 509
Morgan, Robin, 935
Mormons, 575; polygamy and, 589
Morrill Land-Grant College Act (1862), 555
Morrill Tariff Act (1861), 473
Morrison, Toni, 1009
Mortgages: on farms, 595, 763, 764; federal help for, 758; real estate market collapse and, 984; after World War II, 836
Morton, Jelly Roll, 719
Moscow, summit conference in (1988), 949
Mothers, in labor force, 996
"Movement conservatives," 951–952
Movies and movie industry, 521, 715–716, 1010; censorship of, 716; drive-in theater, 873; in 1950s, 862; Reagan and,

943; "talkies" in, 716, 718; World War I propaganda and, 680
Muckrakers, 639–641
Mugwumps, 502, 503
Muhammed, Elijah, 905
Muir, John, 651, 652, 654–655
Mulberry Street (New York City), 544
Muller, Curt, 648
Muller v. *Oregon*, 645–646, 648, 729
Mulligan letters, 502
Multiple-use resource management, 655
Multiracial Americans, 1007
Munch, Edward, 722
Muncy, Robyn, 676
Munich Conference (1938), 784
Munitions. *See* Weapons
Murray, Charles, 913
Muscle Shoals, 766; Bill for, 746
Music, 689; African American, 718–719; Beats and, 885; blues, 568; in 1880s and 1890s, 568–569; jazz, 568, 718–719; military marching-band, 621; modernist, 723, 724; in 1920s, 724; in 1950s, 863; in 1960s, 911; postmodernism in, 1008; ragtime, 568; from World War I era, 680–681, 688, 689
Muslims: Black Muslims and, 904–905; fundamentalism and, 937. *See also* Islam
Mussolini, Benito, 780, 781, 783, 786
Mutualistas (mutual aid societies), 1002
Myanmar (Burma), 633
My Lai massacre, 918
Myra Breckinridge (Vidal), 883
Myrdal, Gunnar, 868

NAACP. *See* National Association for the Advancement of Colored People
Nader, Ralph, 972 (map)
NAFTA. *See* North American Free Trade Agreement
Nagasaki, bombing of, 821, 825
Naismith, James, 571
Naked and the Dead, The (Mailer), 883
Naked Lunch (Burroughs), 885
Nasser, Gamal Abdel, 875–876
Nast, Thomas, political cartoons by, 482, 490, 491, 559
Nation, 558
Nation, Carrie, 564
National Academy of Sciences, 994
National Aeronautics and Space Administration (NASA), 877, 994; Kennedy, John F., and, 890–891
National American Woman Suffrage Association, 562–563, 564, 684
National Association for the Advancement of Colored People (NAACP), 483, 555, 805–806, 868, 961
National Association of Colored Women, 564
National Banking Act, 665
National Child Labor Committee, 531
National Consumers League, 549, 645
National debt: Mellon and, 726; 1930–1950, 808; 1930–2009, 952; Roosevelt, Franklin D., and, 774; Wilson and, 725; in World War II, 807
National Defense and Education Act (1957), 877
National Endowment for the Arts and Humanities, 902
National forests, 652
National Gallery of Art, 882
National Grange of the Patrons of Husbandry. *See* Grange

National Guard: at Kent State, 919; Pullman strike and, 600
National Housing Act (1934), 758
National identity, after Cold War, 980–981
National Industrial Recovery Act (1933), 755
Nationalism: African Americans and, 905; extreme, 778; imperialism and, 632. *See also* New Nationalism
Nationalist China, collapse of, 850–851
National Labor Relations Act (1935), 758, 767–768, 771
National Labor Relations Board, 767–768
National Labor Union, 532–533
National Organization for Women (NOW), 934, 961
National-origins quota system, 703, 704, 902
National parks, 590, 651
National Progressive Republican League, 659
National Prohibition party, 564
National Recovery Administration (NRA), 755, 761–762
National Security Act (1947), 849
National Security Council (NSC), 849; NSC-68, 855
National Urban League, 807
National War Labor Board (NWLB), 683, 802
National Woman's party, 683–684, 718
National Women's Conference, 935
National Youth Administration, 802; Office of Minority Affairs in, 760, 762
Nation of Islam, 720, 904–905
Nation Under Our Feet, A,:... (Hahn), 484
Native Americans, 1004; in Argentina, 593; assimilation of, 580, 581–584; Black Hills gold discovery and, 579; boarding schools for, 581; buffalo and, 576, 580, 582; Dawes Act and, 581–584; disease and, 576, 579, 580; education for, 581; Eisenhower and, 873; equal rights for, 933; government and society of, 577; horses and, 576, 583; literature of, 1010; migration from reservations, 806; New Deal and, 764–765; Plains Indians, 486, 487, 575–584; population of, 575, 584, 1004; railroads and, 579–580; religion of, 580–581; reservations for, 576–577, 579, 582; Sand Creek massacre against, 577; transcontinental railroad and, 515; in trans-Mississippi West, 594; treaties with, 576, 578; wars with, 577–580, 578 (map)
Native Son (Wright), 886
Nativism, 544, 550–551, 703
NATO (North Atlantic Treaty Organization), 849–850, 875, 907, 969
Natural, The (Malamud), 887
Naturalism, in arts, 565–566, 567
Natural resources, 520; conservation of, 650–655; multiple-use resource management policy and, 655; rational use philosophy and, 652
Natural selection, 525, 553
Navajo Code Talkers, 806
Naval stations (bases), in Cuba, 621, 780
Navy: British, 731; disarmament and, 731–732; German, 789, 792; Japanese, 781
Navy (U.S.), 627; disarmament and, 731; Great White Fleet and, 631; imperialism and, 621–622; overseas expansion and, 609; in Spanish American War, 614, 614 (map), 615, 616 (map); Veracruz seizure by, 669; in Vietnam, 901; women in,

803; in World War I, 686, 687; in World War II, 810, 819. *See also* Armed forces

Nazi Germany, 637; concentration camps and, 816–818; Great Depression and, 822; Hitler in, 780–781; Jews in, 788; League of Nations and, 781; nonaggression pact with Soviet Union, 784–785; in Rome-Berlin Axis, 781; Soviet Union invasion by, 792–793; in Tripartite Pact, 781; after World War II, 844–846; in World War II, 785, 789, 792–793, 798, 812, 816–818. *See also* Germany; Hitler, Adolf; World War II

Nazi-Soviet pact. *See* Hitler-Stalin pact

Nebraska, Stevenson, Robert Louis, on, 591

Negative campaigning, 900

Neighborhoods, 539

Neoconservatism, 942, 976, 978

Netherlands: World War II in, 786

Neutrality: legislation in 1930s, 738, 782–783; lend-lease, 792; in 1940, 789; Wilson and, 670–671, 672–673

Neutrality Acts: of 1935, 1936, 1937, 782–783; of 1939, 785, 794

Nevada, 584

Newark, New Jersey, race riots in, 905

New Day in Babylon: The Black Power Movement and American Culture, 1965–1975 (Van Deburg), 913, 1000

New Deal, 510, 596, 637, 656, 752, 772–774; African Americans and, 762; agriculture in, 763–764; banking and, 755–757; conservation and, 652; historians on, 775–776; housing and, 767; Hundred Days in, 822; industry and, 761–763; labor and, 761–763, 767–769; legislation, 753, 755, 758; modern conservatism and, 962; Native Americans and, 764–765; Social Security and, 767; Supreme Court and, 762, 771; unemployment and, 757–759. *See also* Great Depression; Roosevelt, Franklin Delano

New Deal coalition, 776

Newfoundland, 793

New Freedom, 661, 662, 676

New Frontier, 878, 889–891

New Guinea, 633; in World War II, 809, 810, 818

New Immigration, 543–550, 552, 703, 770, 1000–1001

"New isolationism," 924

New Jersey, 618; incorporation laws in, 525

Newlands Act (1902), 651

New Left, 962

New Left school, of historians, 634, 675

"New look," in foreign policy, 874

New media, 1010–1011

New Mexico, 575, 589; Mexican migrants in, 668

New Nationalism, 658, 662, 676

New Orleans, Louisiana: Hurricane Katrina in, 982; lynching of Italians in, 609

New Panama Canal Company, 628

New Right, 942, 944, 952–953

Newspapers: bias in, 899; decline of print journalism and, 1011; foreign-language, 545; Hearst and, 558; Linotype and, 557; Pulitzer and, 558; yellow journalism and, 557. *See also* Journalism; Press

New START treaty, 986

New Western historians, 605–606

New York (city): African Americans in, 719; Armory Show in, 722; Central Park in, 569; Greenwich Village in, 724; Harlem Renaissance in, 724; Henry Street Settlement in, 549; immigrants in, 544, 545, 546; in panic of 1873, 491; population of, 539; Puerto Ricans in, 619; September 11, 2001, terrorist attack on, 974–975; slums in, 542; Tammany machine in, 489, 641; tenements in, 640; Tweed Ring in, 490

New York Central Railroad, 516–517, 522

New York Evening Post, 598

New York Giants, in San Francisco, 863

New York Sun, 638

New York Times, Tweed Ring and, 490

New York World, 558

New Zealand, woman suffrage in, 563

Nez Perce Indians, 578 (map), 579

Nicaragua: free elections in, 959; Reagan and, 947; Sandinistas in, 947, 950; U.S. troops in, 658, 736

Nickelodeons, 716

Nicotine. *See* Tobacco and tobacco industry

Niebuhr, Reinhold, 847

Nimitz, Chester W., 809, 810, 824

Nine-Power Treaty (1922), 626, 731–732

Nineteenth Amendment, 563 (map), 636, 684, 729, 760, 934

Nissei, 801

Nixon, Richard M., 829, 916; Cambodia and, 924; Checkers speech of, 864; in China, 920; communism and, 920; diplomacy of, 923; domestic policy of, 920–924; economy and, 916–917, 922; election of 1952, 864; election of 1952 and, 864; election of 1956 and, 876; election of 1960, 878–879, 880 (map); election of 1968, 909–910, 910 (map); election of 1972 and, 922–924; foreign policy of, 917–920; Khrushchev and, 878; pardon of, 928; as red-hunter, 852; resignation by, 928; Supreme Court and, 921; as vice president, 875; Vietnam War and, 923–924; Watergate and, 925–928, 926

Nixon Doctrine, 917–918

Nobel Peace Prize: for Addams, Jane, 540; to Carter (2002), 944; for Kellogg, 732; for Roosevelt, Theodore, 630

Nobel Prize for literature, 882, 886, 887, 1009; to Buck, 761; to Hemingway, 721; to Lewis, Sinclair, 724; to O'Neill, 724

No Child Left Behind Act (2004), 979

Nonintervention policy, toward Latin America, 779–780

Nonviolent resistance, 868

Nonwhites: birthrate for, 1004; living standards for, 998

Noriega, Manuel, 959

Normalcy, 637

Normal schools, 554

Normandy landing, 813–814, 817

Norris, Frank, 567

Norris, George W., 766

Norris-La Guardia Anti-Injunction Act (1932), 746

North (region): African American migration to, 683, 806, 870; Spanish-American War and, 622

North Africa, 630, 812

North American Free Trade Agreement (NAFTA), 969

North Atlantic Treaty Organization. *See* NATO

North Dakota, 589. *See also* Dakotas

Northern Ireland, 970

Northern Pacific Railroad, 516, 587

Northern Securities Company, 649

Northern Securities decision, 649

North Korea, 855, 976. *See also* Korea; Korean War

North Vietnam, 875, 901, 918–919, 923; bombing of, 923; Nixon and, 923–924. *See also* Vietnam War

North-West Mounted Police (Mounties), 592, 593

Northwest Territories (Canada), 592

Norway, World War II in, 786

Nottage, Lynn, 1010

Novels, 886. *See also* Literature

No-Yong Park, 754

NSC. *See* National Security Council

Nuclear weapons, 844, 851, 874, 1012; Nixon and, 920; "open skies" program and, 874; Soviet, 957–958; testing of, 877–878. *See also* Atomic bombs

Nude Descending a Staircase No. 2 (Duchamp), 722–723

Nuremberg war crimes trial, 844, 845

Nursing: Filipinos in, 625; in World War I, 685

Nye, Gerald, 782

Oakley, Annie, 570

Oath of allegiance: in Lincoln's Reconstruction plan, 470; in Wade-Davis Bill, 470

Obama, Barack, 829, 965, 984–986, 1007; election of 2008 and, 981, 983, 984–985, 985 (map); family of, 983; foreign policy of, 986–987; Supreme Court and, 986

Occupation (military): of Cambodia, 924; in Germany, 839, 845–846; of South, 475, 476 (map)

Occupational Safety and Health Administration (OSHA), 922

Occupations (jobs): segregation, by gender, 996; for women, 861. *See also* Employment; Jobs

Occupation zones, in Germany, 839, 845–846, 845 (map)

O'Connor, Flannery, 887

O'Connor, Sandra Day, 953, 954, 979, 1007

Octopus, The (Norris), 567

Officeholders: blacks as, 478, 479; ex-Confederates as, 472–473, 474

Office of Price Administration (OPA), 802

Office of Scientific Research and Development, 807

Ogallala, Nebraska, 586

Ogden, Utah, transcontinental railroad in, 515

Oglala Sioux Indians, 579, 583

Ohio Gang, 729

"Ohio Idea," 489

Ohio River region, Rustbelt in, 835

Ohio State University, 555

Oil and oil industry: Arab oil embargo and (1970s), 924–925; Carter and, 937–938; economy and, 834; growth of, 524, 712; in Mexico, 736, 780; in Middle East, 731, 848–849, 876; in 1970s, 917; OPEC and, 924–925; Rockefeller in, 521–522, 524; Teapot Dome scandal and, 733. *See also* Energy crisis

Oil shocks, 925, 936

Oil spill, by British Petroleum (2010), 987

Okies, 764

Okinawa, 633, 819

Oklahoma, 575, 589

Oklahoma City Federal Building, bombing of, 967

Old-age insurance, 854

Old-age pensions, 767

Oldenburg, Claes, 882

Older Americans. *See* Elderly

Old Immigrants, 542–543, 544

Old Right, 942
Olds, Ransom E., 711
O'Leary, J. A., 675
Oligarchs, in Soviet Union, 947
Oligarchy, of money, 529
Oliver, Joseph "King," 719
Olmsted, Frederick Law, 569
Olney, Richard, 519, 599, 610
Olympic Games, boycotts of, 939, 947
Omaha, Nebraska, Populists in, 505
"One-China" policy, 920
101st Airborne Division, 816
O'Neill, Eugene, 723, 724, 761
O'Neill, William, 914
Online companies, 1010
On the Road (Kerouac), 884–885
Open Door note, 623
Open Door policy, toward China, 623,
    626, 631, 658
"Open skies" inspection program, 874
Opera, 568
Operation Desert Storm, 959, 960 (map)
Operation Dixie, 830–831
Operation Rolling Thunder, 906
Operation Wetback, 872, 873
Oppenheimer, J. Robert, 820, 851
Opportunity, Truman and, 868
Oregon (battleship), 627
Oregon Country, 644; progressive reforms
    in, 645
Organizational school of historians,
    675–676
Organization Man, The (Whyte), 864
Organization of Petroleum Exporting
    Countries (OPEC), 924–925
Organized crime, 708–709. See also
    Gangsters and gangsterism
Oriental View of American Civilization, An
    (No-Yong Park), 754
Orlando, Vittorio, 692
Osbourne, Frances, 591
OSHA. See Occupational Safety and Health
    Administration
Oswald, Lee Harvey, 898
Other America, The (Harrington), 900
Other People's Money and How the Bankers
    Use It (Brandeis), 665
Our Country: Its Possible Future and Its
    Present Crisis (Strong), 608
"Outcasts of Poker Flat, The" (Harte), 568
Outsourcing, 991
Overland Monthly, 558
OVERLORD, in World War II, 817

Pacific Ocean region: Four Power Treaty
    and, 731; Spanish-American War in,
    614; U.S. and Japan in, 631; World War
    II in, 637, 798, 807–810, 811 (map)
Pacific Railroad Act, 473
Pacifism: of Addams, Jane, 549, 644; of
    progressive-era feminists, 683–684
Pact of Paris (1928), 732
Padrone system, 547
Pahlevi, Mohammed Reza (Shah), 875, 937
Painting: abstract expressionism and,
    880–881; modernism in, 722–723;
    realism and regionalism in, 568
Pakistan: Clinton and, 970; Taliban and Al
    Qaeda in, 987
Palestine: fighting over, 947; intifada
    against Israel, 970; refugees from, 907.
    See also Middle East
Palestine Liberation Organization (PLO),
    907, 970
Palin, Sarah, 983
Palmer, A. Mitchell, 700

Panama, 780; revolt in, 628; U.S. troops
    in, 959
Panama Canal, 612, 668; building of,
    627–629, 628–629; dollar diplomacy
    and, 657; return to Panamanians, 935,
    936
Panama Canal Tolls Act (1912), 667
Panama Canal Zone, 628
Pan-American Conference: of 1889, 609;
    of 1933, 779–780
Panay, Japanese bombing of, 784
Pandemics, influenza (1918–1919), 691
Panics: of 1873, 491–492, 497; of 1893,
    508, 536, 599; of 1907, 655–656, 665; of
    2008–, 985–986
Paper money, 508, 509
Paramilitary militias, 967
Paranoid Style in American Politics, The
    (Hofstadter), 962
Pardons: of Debs, 681; by Johnson,
    Andrew, 465, 471; of Nixon, 928
Paris: Hitler in, 786; rebuilding of, 569;
    World War II liberation of, 813
Paris, Treaties of: of 1898, 616–620; of
    1973, 923
Paris Peace Conference (1919), 692–694
Parkman, Francis, 594
Parks, Rosa, 868
Parochial schools, 545, 554
Partitions, of Germany, 845 (map)
Patent medicines, 557, 640
Patents, 521
Paternity leave, 996
Patient Protection and Affordable Care Act
    (2010), 986
Patriot Act (2001), 975, 976
Patriotism, of immigrants, 799
Patronage, 493–494
Patrons of Husbandry. See Grange
Patterns of Culture (Benedict), 760
Patterson, James, 776
Paul, Alice, 683, 718
Paulson, Henry, 984
Pawnee Indians, 576, 577
Paxton, Steve, 1008
Payne-Aldrich Bill (1909), 658, 732
Payroll tax, 767
Peace Corps, 889, 907
Peaceful coexistence, with Soviet Union,
    895
Peacekeeping: in Lebanon, 947; in
    Somalia, 969
Pearl Harbor: Japanese attack on, 637,
    794–795, 798, 799; U.S. interests in, 610
Peirce, Charles Sanders, 560
Pelosi, Nancy, 982
Pendleton Act (1883), 499
Penicillin, 824, 995
Pennsylvania, 647; abortion rights in, 954;
    petroleum industry in, 523; September
    11, 2001, plane crash in, 974
Penny press, 558
Pensions: military, 503–504, 505; old-age,
    767
Pentagon, terrorist attack on, 974
Pentagon Papers, 919, 925
People's Party: origin of, 598. See also
    Populists
Per capita income, in 21st century, 992
Percy, Walker, 886
Perestroika, 949, 957
Perkins, Francis, 760, 761
Perot, Ross, 910, 966, 968, 968 (map)
Perry, Matthew C., 800
Pershing, John J ("Black Jack"): Villa and,
    670; World War I and, 690, 692
Persian Gulf, Carter on, 939

Persian Gulf War, 959–960, 976, 978
Personal Politics (Evans), 914
Pesticides, 653
Petroleum. See Oil and oil industry
Philadelphia, Pennsylvania, population
    of, 539
Philadelphia Eagles (football), 761–762
Philadelphia Plan (1969), 921–922
Philanthropy, 487, 523, 554–556, 557
Philippines, 487, 731; annexation of, 611
    (map), 617–620, 633; Dewey in, 614;
    freedom for, 623, 779; insurrection
    in, 615, 622–623; Jones Act and, 667;
    Marcos and, 949; in World War II, 808,
    810, 818
Philippine Sea, Battle of the, 810
Phillips, David G., 640
Phillips, Kevin, 962
Phillips, Wendell, 477
Philosophy, pragmatism and, 560
Phonographs, 520, 521, 568–569, 715
Phony war, 785–786
Photography: documentary, 531; of Lewis
    Hine, 530, 531
Picasso, Pablo, 721, 722
Picture brides, Japanese women as, 800
Piedmont region, textile mills in, 528
Pilgrim's Progress (Bunyan), 638
Pill, the, 912
Pinchot, Gifford, 651, 652, 655, 658
"Pink-collar ghetto," 861, 996
Pinkerton's Detective Agency, 506
Pinochet, Augusto, 920
Pit, The (Norris), 567
Pittsburgh, Pennsylvania, steel strike in
    (1919), 682
Plains Indians, 486, 487, 575–584; era of
    the horse, 583; European invasion and,
    583; in sixteenth century, 582
Planned deficit spending, 772
Planned Parenthood v. Casey, 954
Planters and plantations: absentee
    landownership in, 526; after Civil War,
    465–466, 472; before and after the Civil
    War, 497 (map); in Hawaii, 624
Plath, Sylvia, 883
Platt Amendment (1901), 621, 780
Plattism, 621
Playboy (magazine), 863–864
Playwrights, 724, 883–884. See also Drama
Plenty Coups (Indian spokesman), 581
Plessy v. Ferguson, 496, 868–869
Plows, iron, 587
Plunkitt, George Washington, 489
Pluralism, 990; cultural, 704
Plutocracy, Constitution and, 525
Pocket vetoes, 470
Podhoretz, Norman, 942
Poets and poetry: in 1920s, 721; post-
    World War II, 883, 884–885. See also
    Literature
Poland: Germany and, 785; immigrants
    from, 543, 706–707; in NATO, 969;
    partition of, 706; Solidarity movement
    in, 707, 947, 956; Stalin and, 785; after
    World War I, 707; after World War II,
    839
Polio vaccine, 872, 998
Polish Americans, 706–707
Political machines, 645
Political parties: in Gilded Age, 492–494.
    See also specific parties
Politics: African Americans in, 478,
    1007; Asian Americans in, 1004; civil
    rights and, 896; demography and, 988
    (map); in Gilded Age, 488, 492–494;
    government and business in, 512;

Grangers and, 597; international economy and, 510; Latinos in, 1004; in 1990s, 968; progressivism and, 641–644; public opinion polls and, 787; radio and, 715; in shopping malls, 881; after World War II, 828–829

Pollock, Jackson, 880, 882

Poll tax, abolition of, 903

Pol Pot, 924

Polygamy, 589

Pools (railroad), 519

Poor people: in cities, 1006; wealthy on, 525. See also Poverty

Pop art, 882

Popular culture, 572

Popular fiction, in post-Civil War era, 565

Popular music, in 1950s, 863

Population: aging of, 998–999; baby boom and, 838; of Chinese ancestry (1850–2008), 501; in cities, 486, 539; in 1870, 488; of farmers, 596; foreign-born percentage of, 1001; increase in (1950–2008), 835 (map); Latino, 988, 1002–1003; median age by 2050, 998; in metropolitan areas, 1005; Mexican, 1002; Native American, 575, 584; Puerto Ricans in, 619; shift to cities, 540; in Sunbelt, 834–835, 835 (map); of United States, 980. See also Census

Populist Revolt, The (Hicks), 510

Populists, 598–599, 638; African American vote and, 507–508; election of 1892 and, 505, 506–508, 507 (map), 598; election of 1896 and, 602–604, 603 (map); platform of, 505, 525; subtreasury plan of, 598. See also People's party

"Pork-barrel" bills, 504

Port Arthur, 630, 633, 840

Portnoy's Complaint (Roth), 887

Portrait of a Lady, The (James), 567

Portsmouth, New Hampshire, Russo-Japanese peace conference at, 630

Postal Reorganization Act (1971), 502

Postal system. See Mail

Postmodernism, 885, 1007–1010

Postrevisionist historians, on Cold War, 857

Potsdam conference (1945), 820

Pound, Ezra, 721, 883

Poverty: in cities, 1006; of elderly, 999; of immigrants, 544; Johnson, Lyndon B., programs and, 902–903; of Puerto Ricans in U.S., 619; rate of, 903; in South, 466; in 21st century, 992, 993; of young people, 999

Poverty line, 906

Powderly, Terence V., 533, 534–535

Powell, Colin, 977

Powell, John Wesley, 588, 653

Power (political), of United States, 980–981

Pragmatism, 557, 560–561

Pragmatism (James), 557

Prague Spring, in Czechoslovakia, 912

Prairie School of architecture, 723

Pratt, Julius, 634

Pregnancy, teen, 998

Preservationists, 652, 653; Hetch Hetchy Valley and, 654–655. See also Conservation

Presidency: "forgettable presidents" and, 509; in progressive era, 636–637; Roosevelt, Theodore, and, 627, 656; two-term tradition in, 494, 659, 790

President(s): after World War II, 828. See also specific presidents

Presidential debates: Clinton-Bush-Perot, 966; Kennedy-Nixon, 879

Presidential elections. See Elections

Presidential Reconstruction, 470–471

Presley, Elvis, 863, 864

Press: advances in, 557; penny, 558; Roosevelt, Franklin D., and, 756. See also Journalism; Newspapers

Preventive intervention, 630

Price controls, in World War II, 807

Prime rate, 937

Princeton University, 996

Principles of Psychology (James), 557

Printed circuits, 860

Prisoner exchange, with Korea, 856

Privacy rights, 921

Privatization, of Social Security, 979

Pro-choice organizations, 954

Prodemocracy movement, in China, 955–956

Producers, 535

Producers' cooperatives, 740

Production, assembly-line, 520, 710, 711–712

Productivity: in 1970s, 916; after World War II, 834

Professional schools, 557

Profiteers, in Civil War, 520

Profits, in World War II, 807

Progress and Poverty (George), 558–559

Progressive education, 709

Progressive historians, 510

Progressive party: election of 1912 and, 661–663, 663 (map); election of 1916 and, 674; election of 1948 and, 853

Progressivism, 549, 636–637; in cities, 644–645; conservation movement and, 652; Harding and, 729, 730; historians on, 675–676; muckrackers and, 640–641; political, 641–644; roots of, 638–639; in states, 645; under Wilson, 666–667; women in, 639, 645–647, 676

Prohibition, 564, 685, 704–708; repeal of, 762–763

Project Head Start, 903

Pro-life voters, 952

Promised Land, The (Antin), 545

Promise of American Life, The (Croly), 662

Promise of the New South (Ayers), 510

Promontory Point, Utah, 517

Propaganda: against Japan, 802; temperance, 647; in World War I, 680–681, 690; in World War II, 789

Property rights, for women, 479

Proposition 13 (California), 945

Proposition 209 (California), 968

Prosperity: of African Americans, 1006–1007; after 1896 election, 605; in 1920s, 710–711, 740; after WWII, 831–838

Prostitution, 500, 585, 645

Protective tariffs, 658

Protectorate, Haiti as, 668

Protest(s): in Arab Spring, 1011; Beat writers and, 885; civil rights, 896–897; in 1960s, 911; against Vietnam War, 907, 918. See also Revolts and rebellions; Revolution(s)

Protestantism, 911; liberal, 552; shift to city and, 552

Proulx, E. Annie, 1009

Prussian Poles, 706

Psychology: behavioral, 557; World War I use of, 681

Public health programs, 709

Public Interest, The (magazine), 942

Public lands, Ballinger-Pinchot quarrel over, 658

Public opinion, of United States, 981

Public-opinion polling, in 1930s, 787

Public schools: in South, 479; tax-supported schools and, 553–553

Public utilities, 645

Public Utility Holding Company Act (1935), 758, 765

Public works: Hoover and, 744–746; in South, 479

Public Works Administration (PWA), 755, 762, 763

Pueblo, Colorado, 695

Pueblo Indians, 765

Puerto Ricans: immigration of, 616, 618–619; U.S. citizenship for, 618. See also Hispanics; Latinos

Puerto Rico: Foraker Act and, 620; poverty in, 619; Spanish-American War and, 616, 618; U.S. acquisition of, 611 (map), 616, 620, 633

Pugilism, 571

Pujo, Arsene, 665

Pulitzer, Joseph, 558, 608, 612

Pullman Palace Car Company, strike at, 599–600, 642

Pullman Palace Cars, 517

Pump priming, 746, 772

Pure Food and Drug Act (1906), 650

Puritans and Puritanism, 720

Pynchon, Thomas, 1008

Quarantine Speech (Roosevelt), 778, 784

Quayle, J. Danforth, 965–966

Quotas: in college admissions, 1007; on immigrants, 703–704, 902

Rabbit, Run (Updike), 883

Rabin, Yitzhak, 969–970

Race and racism, 1005–1007; in armed forces, 687; in Black Codes, 472; census categories and, 1007; Executive Order 8802 against, 870–871; Filipinos and, 622, 624–625; immigration restrictions and, 703–704; imperialism and, 634; labor unions and, 533; in 1970s, 932–933; Populist party and, 508; against Puerto Ricans, 619; segregation and, 867–868; Simpson, O. J., murder trial and, 1006; suburbs and, 837, 838; Wilson and, 666, 667; in workplace, 830–831; in World War II, 799–802, 805–807, 871. See also African Americans; Civil rights; Civil rights movement

Race riots: in Chicago, 683; in Detroit, Michigan, 806, 871, 905; in Los Angeles, 904, 905, 1005–1006; in Newark, New Jersey (1967), 905; in 1919, 637; during Reconstruction, 475; during World War I, 683; after World War II, 871

Racial discrimination: Civil Rights Act (1964) and, 900; in hiring, 953–954

Racketeers, 708

Radical Islam, 978

Radicalism, 544, 637, 700, 701; machine age and, 529

Radical Reconstruction, 477–479

Radical Republicans, 471, 474–475, 483; Johnson, Andrew and, 480–481

Radical Right, The (Bell), 962

Radio, 715; fireside chats on, 755–756; in presidential campaigns, 738; Voice of America and, 849

Radioactive waste, 1011

Radiotelephones, 715
Raeder, Erich, 844
Railroad(s): buffalo and, 580; Chinese workers on, 500, 515; combination in, 519; consolidation and, 730; corruption and, 518–519; depression of 1893 and, 508; economic growth and, 517–518; farming and, 518, 596; gauges of, 517; growth of, 512–514; immigration and, 518, 587; Irish workers on, 514–515; iron use by, 522; land grants to, 512–514, 514 (map); Native Americans and, 579–580; ranching and, 585–586, 586 (map); rate-setting systems of, 527; rebates of, 519, 524; refrigerator cars and, 521, 586, 595; regulation of, 519–520, 597, 645, 649; in Russia, 593; safety and, 517; in South, 465, 527; steel rail and, 517, 522; strikes against, 497, 533, 730; time zones and, 514 (map), 518; transcontinental, 486, 500, 512, 514–516, 517; in West, 515, 518, 587; worldwide (1889), 513
Railway Labor Board, 730
"Rainbow coalition," 955
Rainfall, 589 (map)
Raisin in the Sun, A (Hansberry), 886
Ramona (Jackson), 580
Ranching, in West, 585–586, 586 (map)
Randolph, A. Philip, 805
Rapid Deployment Force, 939
Rap music, 1008
Rate wars, of railroads, 519
Rational use philosophy, 652
Rauchway, Eric, 510
Rauschenbusch, Walter, 549
RCA (Radio Corporation of America), 994
Reading, 1007
Reagan, Ronald Wilson, 829, 944–946; assassination attempt against, 945; budget and, 945–946; as California governor, 943; Cold War and, 857, 946–947, 948–949; conservatism of, 962; economy under, 945–946, 951; election of 1976 and, 933; election of 1980 and, 942–944, 944 (map); election of 1984 and, 947–948; election of 1988 and, 954–955; foreign policy of, 946–951; Gorbachev and, 948–949, 950; inauguration of, 942; Iran-contra and, 950–951; national debt and, 952; Nicaragua and, 947; Panama Canal and, 935; SDI and, 946–947; Supreme Court and, 953–954
Reaganomics, 946, 951
"Reagan recession" (1981–1982), 946
Reagan Revolution, 944–947
Real estate: collapse of, 984; values in cities and towns, 1005
Realism: in arts, 565, 566–567, 720; in literature, 886
"Realist" historians, 697
Real wages, in unionized sectors, 683
Rearmament: NSC-68 and, 855; after World War II, 849–850
Rebates, railroad, 519, 524, 649
Rebellions. See Revolts and rebellion
Rebel Without a Cause (movie), 911
Recall, 641
Recession: business (1914), 671; of 1920–1921, 710; "Reagan," 946; Roosevelt, 772; in 2008, 808
Reciprocal Trade Agreements Act (1934), 758, 780
Reclamation, 654
Reclamation, Bureau of, 655
Reclamation Service, 652

Reconcentration camps: in Cuba, 612; in Philippines, 622
Reconstruction, 465–484; Black Codes during, 471–472, 474; Congressional, 472–473; end of, 476, 482, 495, 496; freedmen during, 466–469; Johnson, Andrew, and, 474; Ku Klux Klan during, 479–480; legacy of, 482–483; Lincoln's plan for, 470; military, 475–476, 476 (map); presidential, 470–471; proposals and plans for, 471; radical, 477–479; scalawags and carpetbaggers in, 478–479; second, 484, 495; by state, 477
Reconstruction Act (1867), 475
Reconstruction Finance Corporation (RFC), 746
Red Badge of Courage, The (Crane), 567
Redeemers, 476, 479
Redemption Day (1879), 492
Red-light districts, reforms and, 645
Red scare (1919–1920), 700–701
Reed, Thomas B., 505, 605
Reed, Walter, 621
Reed v. Reed, 931
Referendum, 641
Reform(s), 487; civil service, 499, 503; under Clinton, 966–967, 968–969; in education, 557; fiscal, 655–656; of health care, 967, 986; of immigration, 704, 979; by Johnson, Lyndon B., 828–829; labor unions and, 533; muckrakers and, 639–641; for Native Americans, 580; New Deal, 755; progressive, 636, 638–639, 641–647; settlement houses and, 549; social, 549; of Social Security and Medicare, 999; in Soviet bloc (1960s), 912; of spoils system, 499
Refrigeration, in railroad cars, 521, 586, 595
Refugees: Bosnian, 958; from Dust Bowl, 764; from Holocaust, 788; Palestinian, 907; Vietnamese, 928, 930–931
Regionalism, in arts, 565, 566, 567–568, 721–724
Regulation, 486; Hoover on, 730; of immigration, 498; of interstate commerce, 519–520, 597; of railroads, 519–520, 597, 645, 649; of trusts, 525–526, 649–650
Religion(s): cities and, 551–553; Darwinism and, 553; evolution and, 709–710; Fundamentalist vs. Modernist, 718; of immigrants, 544; in Iraq, 977; of Native Americans, 580–581; in 1950s, 863; in 1960s, 910–911; in presidential campaigns, 739; revival of, 914; social gospel and, 549, 552, 639; Supreme Court on, 921. See also Catholic Church
Religious right, 951–953
Relocation centers, for Japanese Americans, 801
Remington, Frederic, 576, 594, 612
Renaissance, cultural, 880–887
Rent (Larson), 1010
Reorganization Act (1939), 758, 773
Reparations (German), 736, 737
Representation, census and, 988 (map)
Republican party: ex-Confederates in Congress and, 472–473; in Gilded Age, 490–491, 492–494; Half-Breed faction of, 494; hard-money policy of, 492; moderates in, 474–475, 483; in 1960s and 1970s, 829; Old Guard of, 658, 659; radical faction in, 471, 474, 480–481, 483; Reconstruction and, 476, 482–483; reformist wing of, 658; in South, 476,

493; Stalwart faction of, 494; Taft and split of, 658; Tea Party faction in, 986, 988. See also Elections
Republic Steel Company, massacre at, 768
Requiem for a Nun (Faulkner), 721
Research and development (R&D), 834, 991–992, 994
Reservations (Indian), 576–577, 579, 582, 806, 1004
Resettlement Administration, 758, 764
Residential segregation, 838
Restraint of trade, 658
Resumption Act (1875), 492
Retirement age, extensions of, 999
Reuben James (destroyer), attack on, 794
Reunification, of Germany, 957
Revels, Hiram, 478
Reverse discrimination, 922, 932
Revisionist school of historians, 634, 962
Revolts and rebellions: Boxer Rebellion, 623–626; in Cuba, 612; in Hawaii, 611; Hungarian uprising and (1956), 874, 875; in Panama, 628; against U.S. in Philippines, 615, 622–623
Revolution(s): Bolshevik, 840; in Cuba (1959), 878; in Iran (1979), 937; in Mexico, 668–669; Russian, 678, 687, 700
Reykjavik, summit conference in (1986), 949
Rhineland: Hitler's occupation of, 784; post-WWI, 694
Rhine River region, in World War II, 816
Rhodes, Cecil, 633
Rhodesia (Zimbabwe), 933
Ribak, Louis, 744
Ribbentrop, Joachim von, 844
Ribuffo, Leo, 962
Rickover, H. G., 613
Riesman, David, 864
Rights: of African Americans, 903–904; for freedmen, 475; of illegal workers, 1001; of Native Americans, 933; of suspects, 921. See also Civil rights; Civil rights movement; Women
Right-to-life movement, 953, 954
Right wing (political): New Right and, 942; in 1980s, 945; religious right and, 950–951
Riis, Jacob A., 638–639, 640
Riots: at Democratic National Convention (1968), 909; against Freedom Riders, 896. See also Race riots
Rise of American Civilization, The (Beard and Beard), 510
Rise of Silas Lapham, The (Howells), 566
Rite of Spring (Stravinsky), 723
Rivers, hydroelectric power and, 766
Roads and highways: auto-use growth and, 712; Federal Highway Act (1956) and, 873–874; interstate, 837; after World War II, 834
Robber Barons, 518, 523, 524, 537
Robert Gould Shaw Memorial, 568
Roberts, Grace, 623
Roberts, John G., 979
Roberts, Oral, 863
Roberts, Owen J., 771
Robeson, Paul, 868
Robin Moor (merchant ship), 792
Robinson, Jackie, 868
Roca, Julio (Argentina), 593
Rockefeller, John D., 486, 557; as Baptist, 552; horizontal integration and, 521–522; wealth of, 523, 525
Rockefeller Foundation, 709
Rockets: in World War II, 798. See also Space exploration

Rock 'n' roll music, 838, 863, 911
Rockwell, Norman, 803
Rocky Mountains, 584
Rodgers, Daniel T., 676
Roe v. *Wade*, 921, 932
Roebling family: Emily Warren, 541; John Augustus, 541; Washington, 541
Röhm, Ernst, 822
Roman Catholic Church. *See* Catholic Church
Romania, 839, 956
Rome-Berlin Axis, 781
Rommel, Erwin, 811
Roosevelt, Eleanor, 751–752, 760
Roosevelt, Franklin Delano, 751, 752, 822; assassination attempt against, 753; at Atlantic Conference, 793; banking and, 755–757; cabinet of, 760, 762; at Casablanca, 812, 813; death of, 818, 841; defense of, 774–775; election of 1920 and, 696; election of 1932 and, 752–753; election of 1936 and, 769–770; election of 1940 and, 790–791, 791 (map); election of 1944 and, 814–815; Executive Order 8802 and, 871; fireside chats of, 755–756; foreign policy of, 778–780; globalization and, 842; gold buying and, 756–757; Great Depression and, 822; inauguration of, 753, 754, 770, 773; on isolationists, 786; labor relations under, 767–769; legislation of Hundred Days Congress and, 754–755; lend-lease and, 791–792, 793; at London Economic Conference, 778; neutrality and, 785; New Deal and, 802; Quarantine Speech of, 778, 784; on South, 804; Spanish Civil War and, 783; Supreme Court and, 770–771; at Tehran Conference, 813, 817; unemployment and, 757–759; war message to Congress by, 794; World War II and, 786–787, 789–790; at Yalta Conference, 839–840. *See also* Great Depression; New Deal; World War II
Roosevelt, Theodore ("Teddy"), 620, 637, 639, 751; American Legion and, 730; as Assistant Secretary of the Navy, 614; assumption of presidency, 627; Big Stick Policy of, 629; conservation and, 651–655; consumer protection and, 650; contributions of, 656–657; death of, 696; election of 1900 and, 626; election of 1904 and, 655; election of 1908 and, 656; election of 1912 and, 659, 661–663, 663 (map); election of 1916 and, 674–675; expansionism and, 609; foreign policy under, 627–630; Gentlemen's Agreement and, 631, 801; imperialism of, 634; labor relations and, 647–649; muckraker speech of, 639, 640; as New York governor, 626; Nobel Peace Prize to, 630; Panama Canal and, 628–629; Panic of 1907 and, 655–656; on patronage system, 499; as progressive, 641, 656; as Rough Rider, 615, 616; Russo-Japanese War and, 630; Square Deal of, 638, 647, 656–657; Taft and, 656, 657, 658, 659; trust busting and, 649–650; as war hawk, 674; World War I and, 673
Roosevelt Corollary, to Monroe Doctrine, 629–630, 668, 779
Roosevelt Dam, 651
Roosevelt recession, 772
Root, Elihu, 622
Root-Takahira agreement (1908), 631
Roper, Elmo, 787
"Rosie the Riveter" (character), 803

Rostow, Walt Whitman, 893
Roth, Philip, 887
Rothko, Mark, 880–881
Rouge River Ford plant, 710
Roughing It (Twain), 566
Rough Riders, 615, 616
Royal Air Force, 789
Royal Canadian Mounted Police, 592
Royal Navy. *See* Navy, British
Rubber, 802
Ruby, Jack, 898
Ruhr Valley, French in, 737
Ruined (Nottage), 1010
Rule of reason, 658
Rumsfeld, Donald, 982
Rural areas: movement to cities from, 486, 539–540, 716; in South, 527, 528
Rural Electrification Agency, 767
Russia: Alaska sale by, 481–482; China and, 623, 658; Civil War and, 482; frontier in, 593; Jewish immigrants from, 545; New START treaty with, 986; peasants from, 593; in World War I, 670, 687, 688. *See also* Soviet Union
Russian Republic, after Soviet Union, 957
Russian Revolution (1917), 678, 687, 700
Russo-Japanese War, 630
Rustbelt, 835
Ruth, George H. ("Babe"), 710, 711
Rwanda, 969, 980

Saarinen, Eero, 882
Saar Valley, after World War I, 694
SAC. *See* Strategic Air Command
Sacco, Nicola, 701
Sadat, Anwar, 933–934, 936
Saddam Hussein, 950, 959, 976, 977
Safety-valve theory, 590
Sage, Russell, 524
Saigon, 875, 893, 930, 931. *See also* Vietnam
Saint-Gaudens, Augustus, 568
St. Lawrence River region, St. Lawrence waterway in, 880
St. Louis (ship), Jewish refugees on, 788
"St. Louis Blues," 719
St. Louis Post-Dispatch, 558
St. Mihiel, battle at, 688 (map), 690, 692
St. Valentine's Day massacre (1929), 708
Saipan, 810, 818
Sakhalin Island, 630, 840
Salinger, J. D., 886
Salk, Jonas, polio vaccine and, 872, 998
Salk Institute, 882
Saloons, 646, 647
SALT (Strategic Arms Limitation Talks), 920; SALT II, 938, 939
Salvation Army, 552
Same-sex marriage, 979, 998
Samoan Islands, U.S.-German conflict over, 609
Sandburg, Carl, 721
Sand Creek, Colorado, massacre at, 577
Sandinistas, 947, 950, 959
San Francisco, California, 654; Chinese immigrants in, 498; general strike in, 767; segregation in, 630–631
San Francisco Examiner, 558
Sanger, Margaret, 716–718
Sanitation: in cities, 541; in meatpacking industry, 650
Santiago, Cuba, Spanish-American War in, 615
Sarajevo, 670
Sargent, John Singer, 568, 690
Satellites, 877. *See also* Space exploration
Saturday Club, 560

Saturday Night Massacre, by Nixon, 926
Sauckel, Fritz, 844
Saudi Arabia, in Persian Gulf War, 959
Savings and loan (S&L) crisis, 954–955
Scabs, 533
Scalawags, 478
Scandals. *See* Corruption
Schechter case, 762
Schenck v. *United States*, 681
Schermann, Anton, 706
Schirach, Baldur von, 844
Schlafly, Phyllis, 932
Schlesinger, Arthur M., Jr., 775
School District of Abington Township v. *Schempp*, 921
School prayer, Reagan on, 943
Schools: baby boom and, 838; Bush, George W., and, 979; desegregation and, 932; elementary, 553–554; federal funding of, 902; Hebrew, 545; high schools, 554, 709; integration of, 868–869, 905–906; melting pot in, 639; for Native Americans, 581; parochial, 545, 554; professional and technical, 557; public, 479, 553–554; segregation in, 630–631; teacher-training (normal), 554. *See also* Education; Higher education; Universities and colleges
Schwarz, John, 913
Schwarzkopf, Norman ("Stormin' Norman"), 959
Science: advances in, 709; Darwinism and, 553; medical, 557; national context of, 994; in 1950s, 860; teaching of, 877; in 21st century, 994–995
Science and Health with Key to the Scriptures (Eddy), 552–553
Scientific Management, 711
Scientific research, 991–992
Scopes, John T., 710
Screen Actors Guild, Reagan and, 943
Scribner's Monthly, 558
"Scud" missiles, 959
Sculpture, 568
SDI. *See* Strategic Defense Initiative
Seagram Building, 882
Seal hunting, Canadian-U.S. dispute over, 609
Seaports, immigrants in, 545
Sears, 541
Sears Tower (Chicago), 882
Seattle, Washington, general strike in, 700
Second Agricultural Adjustment Act (1934), 758
Second Battle of the Marne, 690
Second front, in World War II, 811–813, 840
Second Reconstruction, 484, 495
Second-wave feminism, 934–935
Second World War. *See* World War II
Securities and Exchange Commission (SEC), 758, 765
Security Council (U.N.), 844, 959
Security Treaty (France), 694, 697
Sedition Act, of 1918, 681
Segregation: in armed forces, 687, 691; in cities, 539, 838; Civil Rights Act (1964) and, 898–900; of Mexican migrants, 668; in 1950s, 867–868; residential, 837, 838; in San Francisco schools, 630–631; in South, 487, 496; Wilson and, 666; in workplace, 830–831; in World War II, 805, 806
Selective Service System, 849
Self-determination: in Atlantic Charter, 842; principle of, 620, 664, 680, 693, 694

Selma, Alabama, civil rights movement in, 903, 904
Senate (U.S.): African Americans in, 478; direct election of senators to, 641–644; impeachment in, 481; Republican, 943–944; Versailles Treaty and, 694, 695–696; Watergate hearings in, 926. *See also* Congress(U.S.); House of Representatives (U.S.)
Seneca Falls Convention, for women's rights, 934
Senior citizens. *See* Elderly
Sensationalism, in newspapers, 558
Separate but equal philosophy, 496, 868–869
Separate spheres, 645
Separation of church and state, 921; Johnson, Lyndon B., and, 902
September 11, 2001, terrorist attacks, 829, 965, 974–976; lifestyle after, 990
Sequoia National Park, 590
Serbia, 670, 969
Servants: African American women as, 550; Filipinos as, 624
Service sector, growth of, 862
Set-asides, by employers, 922
Settlement houses, 549, 645
Seventeenth Amendment, 644
Seward, William H., purchase of Alaska and, 482
Seward's Folly, 482
Sex and sexuality: new morality and, 559; in 1920s, 718; in World War I, 688. *See also* Gender and gender issues
Sex discrimination, 930–931, 996
Sexton, Anne, 883
Sexual harassment, Thomas, Clarence, and, 961
Sexually transmitted diseases, 913
Sexual revolution, in 1960s, 912–913
Seymour, Horatio, 489
Shafter, William R., 615
"Shame of the Cities, The" (Steffens), 640, 641
Shandong Peninsula, in Treaty of Versailles, 694
Shanghai, Japanese bombing of, 748
Sharecropping, 472, 496, 526
Share Our Wealth program, 759
Shaw, Robert Gould, 568
Sheen, Fulton J., 863
Sheep: in Australia, 592; in West, 586
Shelterbelt project, 652
Sheppard-Towner Maternity Act (1921), 684
Sheridan, Philip, 581
Sherman, Cindy, 1008
Sherman Anti-Trust Act (1890), 525–526, 658, 666
Sherman Silver Purchase Act (1890), repeal of, 509
Sherwin, Martin J., 825
Shia Muslims, in Iraq, 977, 978, 979
Shipping Board, 730
Shipping News, The (Proulx), 1009
Ships and shipping: Japanese, 818; of natural resources, 520; after World War I, 730; in World War I, 671–672, 678, 687; in World War II, 802, 819. *See also* Navy (U.S.)
Shogun (Japan), 800
Shopping malls, 881
Show Boat (musical), 724
Siberia, 593, 688
Sicily, in World War II, 812

Sierra Club, 653, 654
Sierra Nevada Mountains, transcontinental railroad in, 515
"Significance of the Frontier in American History, The" (Turner), 590, 605
Silent majority, 918
Silent Spring (Carson), 653, 922
Silko, Leslie Marmon, 1010
Silver: coinage of, 492, 508, 598; discoveries of, 492, 584; free silver, 508, 509, 585, 598, 602; government purchases of, 505; mining of, 585; as Populist issue, 598. *See also* Currency
Silver Senators, 585
Simpson, O. J., 1006
Sinai Peninsula, 907
Sinclair, Harry F., 733
Sinclair, Upton, 650
Single parenthood, 997–998
Single-tax plan, 559
Sioux Indians, 576, 577, 578, 579, 581, 583; carving of, 583
Sister Carrie (Dreiser), 540–541, 567
Sit-in movement, 869
Sitkoff, Harvard, 776
Sitting Bull, 579
Six-Day War (1967), 907
Sixteenth Amendment, 509n
Sixth Nation, of Iroquois Confederacy, 665
Sixties, evaluation of, 913–914
Sixties: Years of Hope, Days of Rage, The (Gitlin), 914
Skid road, 654
Skilled workers, 520, 533, 768
Skin color, culture and, 1007
Skocpol, Theda, 676
Skyscrapers, 539, 723
Slaughterhouse Five (Vonnegut), 883
Slaveholders (slaveowners), freed slaves and, 466
"Slave marriages," 467
Slaves and slavery: end of, 465; marriage of, 467; three-fifths clause and, 473. *See also* African Americans; Freedmen
Slovaks, 543
Slumlords, urban reform and, 645
Slums, 542
Smallpox, 576
Smith, Alfred E., 738, 739 (map), 752
Smith, Gerald L. K., 759
Smith, Zadie, 1009
Smith Act (1940), 852
Smith-Connally Anti-Strike Act (1943), 803
Smog, 714
"Smoking gun" tape, of Nixon, 926–928
SNCC. *See* Student Nonviolent Coordinating Committee
Social Darwinists, 525
Social Democratic party (Germany), 642
Social engineering, 902
Social evils, muckrakers attacks on, 640
Social feminism, 676
Social gospel movement, 549, 552, 639
Socialism, 642–643, 659; Christian, 549; Debs and, 600, 642; Eisenhower on, 872; Fabian, 559; Gompers and, 536; immigrants and, 550; machine age and, 529; New Deal and, 774; Powderly on, 534; progressive movement and, 639; red scare and, 701; World War I and, 681
Socialist party, election of 1912 and, 663, 663 (map)
Social media, 1010–1011
Social mobility: by baby boomers, 838; class tensions and, 537; nature and extent of, 537

Social networking, 991
Social sciences, women in, 760
Social Security, 767; Bush, George W., and, 979; dependence upon, 999; under Nixon, 921
Social Security Act: of 1935, 758, 767, 771, 822; of 1950, 854
Social services, restricted access to, 993
Social welfare. *See* Medicare; Social Security; Welfare programs
Social work (profession), 549, 676
Societies, for freedmen, 469
Society: affluence and inequality in, 992–996; airplane travel and, 715; automobile's impact on, 712–714; industrial, 486; industrialization and, 528–530; McCarthyism in, 866–867; Native American, 577; in 1920s, 716–720; in 1950s, 864; in 1960s, 910–914; segregation in, 867–868; suburban, 836–837; in 21st century, 990–1012; wealth gap in, 1011
Sodbusters, 587
Sod houses, 588, 596
Soft money, 509
Soil Conservation and Domestic Allotment Act (1936), 758, 763–764
Soil Conservation Service, 652
Solar power, 1011
Soldiers: in Afghanistan, 987; in World War I, 688; in World War II, 805, 806, 816, 819. *See also* Armed forces; Military
Solidarity movement (Poland), 707, 947, 956
Solomon Islands, in World War II, 637, 809–810
Somalia, peacekeeping in, 969, 980
Sombart, Weiner, 642–643
Sone, Monica, 799
Sooners, Oklahoma land rush and, 589
Sorghum, 588
Sotomayor, Sonia, 986
Souls of Black Folk, The (Du Bois), 555
Sound and the Fury, The (Faulkner), 724
Sousa, John Philip, 621
South (region): African Americans in, 487, 496–497, 506–508; agriculture in, 465, 526–527; Black Codes in, 471, 474; black migration from, 683; civil rights movement and, 869–872; after Civil War, 465–466; cotton in, 806; Democratic party in, 493; economy in, 465, 805; education in, 479, 554; Grange in, 597; Home Rule regimes in, 476; industrialization in, 487, 526–528; Jim Crow in, 496, 508, 1006; Kennedy, John F., and, 879; Ku Klux Klan in, 479–480, 701; literature on, 568; military districts in, 475, 476 (map); population of, 835 (map); Populists in, 506–507, 598; prohibition in, 704–705; radical regimes in, 479; railroads in, 465, 527; Reconstruction and, 477–479, 482; Redeemers in, 476, 479; Republican regimes in, 476; segregation in, 487, 496; Spanish-American War and, 622; sports in, 863; tenant farming in, 595; textile industry in, 527–528; after World War II, 835; in World War II, 804. *See also* Sunbelt
South Africa, 933, 958–959
South America. *See* Latin America; specific locations
South Carolina: Compromise of 1877 and, 494, 495; government graft in, 479
South Dakota, 589

Southeast Asia: Laos and, 892; from 1954–1975, 894 (map); in 1955–1956, 875 (map); Vietnam and, 874–875, 906–909

Southern Africa, frontier and Boers in, 593

Southern Christian Leadership Conference (SCLC), 956

Southern Europe, immigrants from, 543, 544–545, 703

Southern Pacific Railroad, 516, 525, 645

Southern Renaissance writers, 886–887

Southern strategy (Nixon), 922–924

South Korea, 855–856. See also Korea; Korean War

South Vietnam, 875, 901, 928, 930; Cambodia and, 919; Nixon and, 917, 923–924; U.S. support for, 893. See also Vietnam War

Southwest: Hispanics in, 594; immigration to, 1000; Mexican workers in, 1002; Spanish Mexican settlements in, 575; after World War II, 835. See also West

Soviet bloc, protests in (1960s), 912

Soviet Union: in Afghanistan, 939; atomic bomb of, 851; Bolshevik government in, 731; Carter and, 936; China and, 919–920; collapse of, 956–958; Cuba and, 878, 895; Eastern Europe and, 840, 846; at Geneva (1955), 875; German attack on, 792–793; Hungarian uprising and, 874, 875; Kennedy, John F., and, 879, 895; lend-lease to, 793; Nazi-Soviet nonaggression pact, 784; nuclear testing by, 877–878; Reagan and, 946–947; Spanish Civil War and, 783; Stalin and, 780; as superpower, 840; Truman and, 846; in United Nations, 844; U.S. and, 779, 840–841; women in World War II, 803–804; in World War II, 786, 792–793, 811, 816, 821, 823; Yalta conference and, 839–840. See also Cold War; Russia

Soyer, Isaac, 773

Space exploration: Apollo 11 and, 891; in Cold War, 994; under Kennedy, 890–891; Soviet, 877

Spain: conquistadores from, 583; Cuba and, 612; Maine explosion and, 613; Puerto Rico and, 618; Treaty of Paris (1898) and, 616–620. See also Spanish America

Spanglish, 1010

Spanish America: Chinese in, 500. See also Latin America

Spanish-American War, 486, 613–616, 621, 627; casualties in, 615, 616; in Cuba, 614–616, 616 (map); disease in, 616; in Philippines, 614, 614 (map); in Puerto Rico, 616, 618; Rough Riders in, 615, 616; Treaty of Paris (1898) and, 616–620; yellow journalism and, 613

Spanish Civil War (1936–1939), 783

Spanish-language schools, 1003

Spare-the-rich policies of taxation, 726

Spargo, John, 640

SPARs (U.S. Coast Guard Women's Reserve), 803

Speakeasies, 708

Special creations, dogma of, 553

Special Forces (Green Berets), 892–893

Specie payments, 585

Spectator sports, 571

Speculation: Hoover and, 740; in land, 724; stock, 518, 725

Speech, freedom of. See Free speech

Spencer, Herbert, 525

Spending: military, 832–834, 906, 946; in 1950s, 864; in Sunbelt, 835; on Vietnam War, 929; after World War II, 807

Sphere of influence: economic, in China, 623; Soviet, 840

Spielberg, Steven, 1010

Spies and spying, industrial, 524

Spirit of St. Louis (plane), 714

Spock, Benjamin, 835

Spoils system, 499

Sports: in 1800s, 570–571; in 1920s, 711, 715

Spruance, Raymond A., 809, 824

Sputnik I and II, 877, 994

Square Deal, 638, 647, 656–657

Stages of Economic Growth, The (Rostow), 893

"Stagger Lee," 689

Stalin, Joseph, 780; death of, 874; pact with Hitler, 784–785; at Potsdam conference, 820; at Tehran Conference, 813, 817; in World War II, 811, 821; at Yalta conference, 839–840

Stalwart faction, of Republican party, 494, 499

Stampp, Kenneth, 483

Standardization, 572; Ford and, 711–712; of railroads, 517; of time zones, 518

Standard Oil Company, 521–522, 524, 530; dissolution of, 658; Lloyd's attack on, 638; Tarbell's attack on, 640, 641

Standing Rock Reservation, 581

Stanford, Leland, 515, 517

Stanford University, 517, 556

Stanton, Edwin M., 480, 481

Stanton, Elizabeth Cady, 476, 477, 562–563, 934

START (Strategic Arms Reduction Treaty): New START and, 986; START II accord, 958

Star Wars (SDI), 946–947

State(s): abortion rights and, 954; constitutions of, 478; criminal syndicalism laws in, 701; election of 2000 and, 973 (map); Hawaii and Alaska as, 880; majority-minority, 1004; progressive movement in, 645; readmittance of, 470, 473, 475, 477

State Department, Jim Crow, communism, and, 868

States Rights party, election of 1948 and, 853

Statue of Liberty, 551, 703

Steele, Shelby, 1007

Steel industry, 520; Bessemer process in, 522; Carnegie in, 521, 522–523; Kennedy, John F., and, 890; Morgan and, 522–523; Pittsburgh plus pricing system in, 527; railroads and, 517, 522; strikes in, 505–506, 682, 683, 730, 768

Steffens, Lincoln, 640, 641

Stein, Gertrude, 721, 723

Steinbeck, John, 760, 764

Stem cell research, 973

Stenographers, 528

Stephens, Alexander, 472–473

Stevens, Thaddeus, 474, 475, 481, 483

Stevens, Wallace, 883

Stevenson, Adlai E. (grandfather), as vice president, 509

Stevenson, Adlai E. (grandson), election of 1952 and, 864, 865 (map)

Stimson, Henry L., 747, 807

Stimson doctrine, 747

Stock(s): index of prices (1921–1937), 741; railroad, 518–519

Stock market: bull market in, 725, 726; New Deal legislation and, 765; 1929 collapse of, 637, 740–742; plunge in 1987, 955

Stock ticker, 521

Stock watering, 518–519

Stonewall Rebellion, 912, 913

"STOP ERA" campaign, 932

Stowe, Harriet Beecher, 562

Strange Case of Dr. Jekyll and Mr. Hyde, The (Stevenson), 591

Strange Interlude (O'Neill), 724

Strategic Air Command (SAC), 860, 874

Strategic Defense Initiative (SDI, Star Wars), 946–947, 994

Strategies of Containment (Gaddis), 913

Stravinsky, Igor, 723

Strikebreakers, 533, 683

Strikes: in auto industry, 768; in coal industry, 647–648; in Coeur d'Alene, 506; between 1881 and 1900, 537; in Great Depression, 767; great railroad strike (1877), 497, 533; by hatmakers, 666; Homestead, 505–506; May Day (1886), 533; middle class and, 532; Pullman, 599–600; against railroads, 497, 533, 730; in steel industry, 505–506, 682, 683, 730, 768; by women in needle trades, 646; World War I and, 682–683, 700; in World War II, 803

Strong, Josiah, 608–609

Student Nonviolent Coordinating Committee (SNCC), 872, 905

Students: income status of, 996; 1960s protests by, 911–912

Students for a Democratic Society (SDS), 913

Styron, William, 887

Submarines: in World War I, 672–674, 672 (map), 678; in World War II, 789, 792, 793–794, 810

Subsidies, to railroads, 512, 514, 515

Subsidized scarcity, 763

Substitutes, in Civil War, 503n

Subtreasury plan, 598

Suburban Warriors (McGirr), 914

Suburbs, 537, 836–837; African Americans in, 837; appearance of, 838; automobiles and, 713, 833; migration from cities to, 542; in 21st century, 992; in 2000s, 1004–1005; whites in, 838, 932, 1006; after World War II, 835–838

Subways, 539

Sudetenland, Hitler and, 784

Suez Canal, 530

Suez crisis, 875–876

Suffrage: black, 475, 507–508; universal male, 478; woman, 562–563, 636, 644, 683–684, 685. See also Voting and voting rights; Woman suffrage

Suffragists, 562, 563, 684

Sugar and sugar industry, 524; in Cuba, 612, 878; in Hawaii, 610, 611; in Puerto Rico, 618

Sugrue, Thomas, 962

Suicide bombers, in U.S. Marine barracks (Lebanon), 947

Sullivan, John L., 571

Sullivan, Louis, 539, 723

Summit conference: Eisenhower-Khrushchev, 878; in Geneva (1955), 875; in Geneva (1985), 949; in Moscow (1988), 949; Reagan-Gorbachev, 949; in Reykjavik (1986), 949

Sumner, Charles, 474

Sumner, William Graham, 525

Sun Also Rises, The (Hemingway), 720

Sunbelt, 804–805, 834–835, 835 (map)

Sun Dance, 581

Sunday, Billy, 700

Sunni Muslims, in Iraq, 977, 978 979

Superpowers, 840

Supplemental Security Income (SSI), 921

Supply-side economics, 945–946

Supreme Court (U.S.): on AAA, 763; on affirmative action in colleges, 1007; on antitrust regulation, 649; under Brandeis, 666; Bush, George H. W., and, 961; Bush, George W., and, 979; child labor and, 666; on civil rights violations, 496; on congressional delegation of legislative powers to executive, 762; conservatism in, 953–954; Court-packing plan (F. Roosevelt), 770–771; on free speech and clear and present danger, 681; under Grant, 492*n*; Harding's appointments to, 729; on income tax, 509; on military tribunals, 475–476; on monopolies, 649; Native Americans and, 933; Nixon and, 920, 921; Obama and, 986; progressive legislation and, 729; on protection of women workers, 645–646, 648; railroad regulation and, 519, 597; Reagan and, 953–954; on rights in American possessions, 621; rule of reason and, 658; on "separate but equal" facilities, 496; on suspension of mortgage foreclosures, 764; on ten-hour work day, 646; on term-limit laws, 967; on trusts, 658; under Warren, 868–869, 920, 921

Surplus: agricultural, 740; in federal budget, 967, 974; from tariffs, 504

Surtax, 726

Surveillance, illegal, by government, 982

Survival of the fittest, 525

Sussex, sinking of, 673–674

Sussex pledge (1916), 674

Sweatshops: women workers in, 545; working conditions in, 645, 646

Sweatt v. Painter, 868

Swift, Gustavus F., 524, 585

"Swimmer, The" (Cheever), 883

Symphony orchestras, 568

Syria, 693, 924

Taft, Robert A., election of 1940 and, 790

Taft, William Howard, 637, 657; cabinet of, 657; as Chief Justice, 663, 729; dollar diplomacy of, 657–658; election of 1908 and, 656; election of 1912 and, 659, 662–663, 663 (map); National War Labor Board and, 683; and Philippines, 623; Roosevelt, Theodore, and, 656, 658, 659; trusts and, 650, 658

Taft-Hartley Act (1947), 830, 853, 877

Tahrir Square, Cairo, revolution in, 1011

Taino Indians, 618

Taiwan. *See* Formosa

Taliban: in Afghanistan, 975; in Pakistan, 975

Tammany Hall, 489, 641

Tampico Incident (1914), 669

Tan, Amy, 1010

Tanks, in World War II, 811

Tarantino, Quentin, 1010

Tarawa, 810

Tarbell, Ida M., 641; Standard Oil exposé by, 640

Tariff(s), 528; in 1880s, 503, 504, 505; Cleveland and, 503, 504; Dingley (1897), 605; Fordney-McCumber (1922), 732, 740; Hawley-Smoot (1930), 740, 742, 780; Kennedy Round and, 891; McKinley (1890), 505, 605, 611; Morrill (1861), 473; Payne-Aldrich (1909), 658, 732; Reciprocal Trade Agreements Act and, 780; Taft and, 658; Underwood (1913), 664–665, 732; Wilson-Gorman (1894), 509, 605, 612. *See also* Trade

Tariff Commission, 732

TARP. *See* Troubled Assets Relief Program

Taxation: Bush, George H. W., and, 962; Bush, George W., and, 972; capital investment and, 710; Carter and, 933; excess-profits tax, 726; of farmers, 596; gasoline, 712; immigrant payments of, 1001; Nixon and, 917; Obama and, 986; for rich, 726; single-tax plan, 559; for Social Security, 767, 772; in South, 479; for World War I, 686, 725. *See also* Excise taxes; Income taxes

Tax revolt, Proposition 13 as, 945

Taylor, Frederick W., 711

Taylor, Zachary, 877

Teachers, women as, 469

Teacher-training schools, 554

Teamsters Union, 877, 969

Tea Party, 986, 988

Teapot Dome scandal, 733, 734

Technical schools, 557

Technology: atomic power and, 844; bioengineering and, 991–992; lifestyle and, 994; in 1950s, 860; in 21st century, 994–995. *See also* Innovations; Inventions

Teenagers: baby boomers as, 838; pregnancy of, 998

Tehran, Iran, hostage crisis in, 938–939

Tehran Conference (1943), 813, 817

Telegraph, 517, 520, 530

Telephone, 520, 521, 528, 540

Telephone operators, 521

Televangelists, 951

Television, 715, 1007; election of 1952 and, 864; in Kennedy-Nixon debates, 879; in 1950s, 861, 862

Teller Amendment (1898), 614, 620

Temperance movement, 564, 565, 646–647

10 percent governments, 471, 474

10 percent Reconstruction plan, 470

Tenant farming, 496, 526, 595, 743, 870

Tender Buttons (Stein), 721

Tenements, 548, 640; dumbbell, 542

Ten-hour day, 646, 648

Tennessee: Ku Klux Klan (KKK) in, 479; Scopes trial in, 710

Tennessee Coal and Iron Company, 650

Tennessee Valley Authority (TVA), 652, 746, 755, 762, 765–766, 766 (map), 767, 872, 994

Tenure of Office Act (1867), 480–481

Termination policy, for Native Americans, 873

Term-limit laws, 967

Terrorism: by Klan, 479–480; September 11, 2001, attacks and, 829, 965, 974–975, 974–976, 990, 1012. *See also* Violence

Tet offensive, 908

Texas, 835; cattle ranching in, 586; in census of 2010, 988 (map); Mexican migrants in, 668

Texas (ship), 615

Texas A&M, 518, 555

Texas and Pacific Railroad, 495, 518

Textile industry: children in, 531; in South, 527–528, 769

Tharp, Twyla, 1008

Thatcher, Margaret, 944–945

Theater. *See* Drama

Theory of the Leisure Class, The (Veblen), 638

Therapies, medical, 995

Thermonuclear weapons, 851, 877–878

Thernstrom, Stephan, 537

Third parties, 604; in 1968, 910, 910 (map); in 1992, 966

Third World, 527, 955

Thirteenth Amendment, 471, 477

This Side of Paradise (Fitzgerald), 720

Thomas, Clarence, 961

Thoreau, Henry David, 652

"Three Boys at Manzanar" (Miyatake), 801

Three-fifths clause, 473

369th Colored Infantry Regiment, 691

Three Lives (Stein), 721

Thurmond, J. Strom, 853, 854

Tiananmen Square protest, 955, 956

Ticket splitting, 493

Tilden, Samuel J., 490, 494, 494 (map)

Till, Emmett, 867

Tilton, Theodore, 477

Time: changing concept of, 528; standardization of, 518

Time zones, 514 (map), 518

Titan, The (Dreiser), 639

Title VII, of Civil Rights Act, 900

Title IX, of Education Amendments, 930

Tlingit people, 757

Tobacco and tobacco industry, 524; Duke in, 526–527

To Bedlam and Part Way Back (Sexton), 883

Tocqueville, Alexis de, 537, 642, 643

To Kill a Mockingbird (Lee), 886

Tokyo, bombings of, 818

Tongs, 500

Tonkin Gulf Resolution, 901, 919

Torture, at Abu Ghraib prison, 980

"To Secure These Rights" (report), 868

Totalitarianism, in Europe, 780–782

Tourism, mass, 655

Towns. *See* Cities and towns

Townsend, Francis E., 759

Trade: with China, 969; free, 842; international, 530, 742, 843; under Kennedy, 891; reciprocal trade policy and, 780; restraint of, 658; World War I and, 671–672. *See also* Commerce; Tariff(s)

Trade agreement, 536

Trade associations, 730

Trade Expansion Act (1962), 891

Trade unions, 666

Trails, cattle, 586 (map)

Transatlantic telegraph, 530

Transcontinental railroads, 486, 500, 512, 514–515, 585; completion of, 515–516, 517

Transistors, 860

Trans-Mississippi West, 590–594

Transnationality, 704

Transportation: innovations in, 520; mass transit, 539. *See also* Railroad(s)

Transportation Department, 902

Travel: transcontinental, 591. *See also* Transportation

Travels with Charley (Steinbeck), 882

Travois, 582

"Treason of the Senate, The" (Phillips), 640

Treasure Island (Stevenson), 591

Treasury Department: contraction policy of, 492; endless-chain operations and, 508, 509; Fisk-Gould scandal and, 489–490; gold reserve in, 508–509, 756; Liberty Loan drives by, 686; loans to Allies (World War I), 737; surplus of, 504

Treaties: disarmament, 731–732; with Native Americans, 576, 578. *See also* specific treaties

Trench warfare, in World War I, 686, 690
Trials, of Nazis, 844, 845
Triangle Shirtwaist Company, 646
Tribes (Native American), dissolving of, 581
Trickle-down philosophy, of Hoover, 744
Trilling, Lionel, 962
Trinity College, 526–527
Tripartite Pact (1935), 781
Troops. See Armed forces; Military; Soldiers
Troubled Assets Relief Program (TARP), 984
Truman, Harry S, 838–839; assumption of presidency, 818; civil rights movement and, 868; and communism, 847, 852–853, 854; election of 1944 and, 815; election of 1948 and, 853–854; Fair Deal under, 854; foreign policy under, 847, 852, 855–856, 857; on German attack on Soviet Union, 793; H-bomb and, 851; Iran and, 846; Korean War and, 855–856, 857; loyalty program of, 852; MacArthur and, 855–856; Middle East and, 848–849; on nuclear weapons, 844; at Potsdam, 820; Soviet view of, 849
Truman Doctrine, 846–847
Trusteeship Council (U.N.), 844
Trusts, 524–525, 638; farmers and, 597; Fourteenth Amendment and, 525; money, 598; muckrakers attacks on, 640; in oil industry, 521–522, 524; Roosevelt, Theodore, and, 649–650; Taft and, 658; use of term, 522; Wilson and, 666. See also Antitrust movement; Corporations
Truth-in-lending rules, 986
Truth in Securities Act (1933), 765
Tunisia, in World War II, 812
Turkey, in World War I, 670
Turner, Frederick Jackson, 575, 590, 592, 605–606
Tuskegee Airmen, 806
Tuskegee Institute, 554–555
TVA. See Tennessee Valley Authority
Twain, Mark, 492, 510, 566, 585, 594, 620, 886, 955
Tweed, William Marcy ("Boss"), 479, 489, 490, 494
Tweed Ring, 490
Twentieth Amendment, 770
Twenty-fifth Amendment, 926
Twenty-first Amendment, 763
Twenty-fourth Amendment, 903
Twenty-sixth Amendment, 919
Twenty-third Amendment, 923
Twitter, 991, 1010
Tydings-McDuffie Act (1934), 779
Typewriters (machine), 521, 528
Typhoid, 576; in Spanish-American War, 616

U-boats, 672, 678, 679. See also Submarines
U-2 spy plane incident, 878
Unaccustomed Earth (Lahiri), 1010
Unconditional surrender, in World War II, 812, 819–821
Underclass, in black ghettos, 1006
Underwood Tariff (1913), 664–665
Unemployment: Bush, George H. W., and, 962; in Great Depression, 740–741, 754, 757–759, 772; Obama and, 985; in panic of 1873, 491; in panic of 1893, 599. See also Employment
Unemployment Relief Act (1933), 755
UNESCO (United Nations Educational, Scientific, and Cultural Organization), 844

UNIA. See United Negro Improvement Association
Union League, 478
Union of Soviet Socialist Republics. See Soviet Union
Union Pacific Railroad, 516, 518; scandal and, 490; transcontinental railroad and, 514–515
Union party, 469–470
Unions. See Labor unions
Unitarians, 552
United Farm Workers Organizing Committee (UFWOC), 1004
United Mine Workers, 768
United Nations (U.N.), 843, 844; Charter of, 841; headquarters of, 882; Iraq and, 977; Korean War and, 855; Persian Gulf crisis and, 959
United Nations Conference (1945), 841
United Nations Relief and Rehabilitation Administration (UNRRA), 848
United Negro Improvement Association, 719, 720
United States: comparative conditions in, 993; as empire, 611 (map); Great Depression in, 822–823; as "hyper power," 980; national identity of, 980–981; public opinion of, 981; Soviet Union and, 840–841; as superpower, 840; in United Nations, 844
U.S. Geological Survey, 588
United States Housing Authority (USHA), 758, 767
U.S. Steel, 523, 650, 658, 768
United States v. Wheeler, 933
Universal suffrage, male, 478
Universities and colleges: affirmative action in admissions, 1007; for African Americans, 555; in antebellum period, 557; after Civil War, 555–557; land-grant, 555; 1960s protests in, 911–912; philanthropy for, 554–556; student backgrounds and, 996; women in, 555, 996
University of California, 555; Free Speech Movement in, 911
University of Chicago, 557, 561
University of Michigan, racial diversity in, 1007
University of Mississippi, integration of, 896
Unraveling of America, The (Matusow), 913
Unskilled workers, 520–521, 531; in labor unions, 533, 768
Updike, John, 883
Up from Slavery (Booker T. Washington), 554
Urban areas. See Cities and towns; Metropolitan areas; Suburbs
Urbanization, 521, 539–542. See also Cities and towns
Urban League, 807
USA Patriot Act (2001), 975, 976
USSR. See Soviet Union
Utah, 575, 618; woman suffrage in, 585
Utilities, public ownership of, 645

Vacations, 713
Vaccine, polio, 872
Vagina Monologues (Ensler), 1010
Values, in 1960s, 910–911
Van Buren, Martin, 504
Van Deburg, William L., 913
Vanderbilt family: "Commodore" Cornelius, 516–517, 519, 522, 524; William H., 518, 519
Van Dyck, Henry, 719

Van Gogh, Vincent, 722
Vanguard missile, 877
Vanzetti, Bartomeo, 701
Vaudeville, 570
Veblen, Thorstein, 638
V-E (Victory in Europe) Day (1945), 818
Védrine, Hubert, 980
Venereal disease, in World War I, 688
Venezuela: boundary dispute with British Guiana, 609–610; debt default by, 629; OPEC and, 876
Venturi, Robert, 1008
Veracruz, 669
Versailles, Treaty of (1919), 693–694; collapse of, 697; U.S. rejection of, 694, 695–696, 730
Vertical integration, 521
Veterans: antiwar protests by, 918; of Civil War, 493, 505; GI Bill and, 831; murder of African American, 867; pensions for, 503–504, 505; after World War I, 730
Veterans Administration (VA), 831, 835, 836
Veterans Bureau, 730, 732
Veterans of Future Wars, 782
Vetoes: of Cleveland, 503, 504, 744; of Coolidge, 730; of Grant, 492; of Harding, 730; of Hoover, 746; of Johnson, Andrew, 473, 474, 480; of literacy tests for immigrants, 551; pocket, 470; in United Nations, 840
Victory gardens, 685
Victory Loan campaign (1919), 686
Vidal, Gore, 883
Viet Cong, 906, 908, 918–919
Viet Minh, 874–875
Vietnam, 633; American evacuation from, 930; Cold War policies and, 874–875; Eisenhower and, 866, 874–875; immigrants from, 928, 930–931; Johnson, Lyndon B., and, 901, 906–909; Kennedy, John F., and, 893; 1954–1975, 894 (map)
Vietnamization, 917–918
Vietnam War, 829, 913–914; Cambodianizing, 918–919; casualties in, 907, 918; Eisenhower and, 866, 874–875; escalation of, 906; European attacks on, 923; impact on status of U.S., 929; Johnson and, 906–909; Kennedy and, 893; in 1970s, 917–918; Nixon and, 917–918, 923–924; origins of, 857; as Sixties issue, 913; Tonkin Gulf Resolution and, 901; Treaty of Paris in, 923; U.S. defeat in, 928–929
Vigilante justice, 584
Villa, Francisco ("Pancho"), 669, 670
Villages: railroads and, 514. See also Cities and towns
Violence: against African Americans, 496–497; by Central Powers agents, 670–671; Chinese immigrants, 498; global ethnic and cultural, 1012; by Ku Klux Klan, 479–480; labor, 486, 497, 642. See also Terrorism
Virginia City, Nevada, 584
Virginia Military Institute, women in, 996
Virgin Islands, purchase from Denmark, 668
Visual arts, postmodern, 1008
Vitamins, 994
V-J (Victory in Japan) Day (1945), 821, 824
"Voice of America," 849
Volstead Act (1919), 704
Vonnegut, Kurt, Jr., 883, 1008
Voter Education Project, 896

Voting and voting rights: African American, 475, 478, 507–508, 903–904, 1006; Australian ballot and, 641; corruption in, 504; by freedmen, 478; grandfather clause and, 508; immigrants and, 546–547; literacy tests for, 480, 507–508; progressives and, 641–644; Twenty-sixth Amendment and, 919; voter turnout and, 493, 604; for women, 476–477, 562–563, 563 (map), 585, 644, 683–684, 685, 934, 996. See also Elections
Voting Rights Act (1965), 903–904
Voting rights bill, Johnson, Lyndon B., and, 902

WAAC (Women's Army Auxiliary Corps), 812
Wabash, St. Louis & Pacific Railroad Company v. Illinois, 519, 597
Wabash Railroad, 533
WACs (Women's Army Corps), 803
Wade, Benjamin, 481
Wade-Davis Bill, 470
Wage earners, industrialization and, 530, 531
Wages, 758; family wage, 529; Great Depression and, 742; minimum wage for women, 771; in unionized sectors, 683; for women, 996. See also Income
Wages and Hours Bill (1938), 758, 768–769
Wage slaves, 534
Wagner, Robert F., 767
Wagner Act (1935), 758, 767–768, 771
Waiting (Ha Jin), 1010
Wake Island, in World War II, 808
Wald, Lillian, 549, 639
Walker, Kara, 1008, 1009
Walker, Mary Richardson, 587
Walking city, 539
Walkouts, labor, 767
Wallace, David Foster, 1009
Wallace, George C., 909, 910 (map)
Wallace, Henry A., 814–815, 853
Wallace, Lewis (Lew), 565
Wall Street: bombing on, 701; in 1920s, 725, 726; power of, 487
Wall Street Reform and Consumer Protection Act (2010), 986
Walt Disney Concert Hall, Los Angeles, 1008
Wanghia, Treaty of (1844), 626
Wapshot Chronicle, The (Cheever), 883
War criminals, in Japan, 850
Ward, Aaron Montgomery, 594
War Democrats, 470
War Department, "work or fight" rule (1918), 682–683
Ward's Cove Packing v. Antonia, 953
Warehouse Act (1916), 666
Warfare-welfare state, 807
War hawks, Roosevelt, Theodore, as, 674
Warhol, Andy, 882
War Industries Board, 682, 686, 730
Warner, Charles Dudley, 510, 566
War on Poverty, 900, 902, 910, 913
War Powers Act (1973), 924
War Production Board (WPB), 802
War Refugee Board, 788
Warren, Earl: as Chief Justice, 868–869, 920, 921; Kennedy assassination and, 898
Warren, Robert Penn, 886
Wars and warfare: mechanized, 906; of Plains Indians, 576. See also specific battles and wars

War Trash (Ha Jin), 1010
Washakie (Shoshone Indian), 575
Washington (state), 589, 644, 654
Washington, Booker T., 554–555
Washington, D.C.: Bonus Army in, 746, 747; labor demonstration in, 536; redesign of, 569; summit conference in (1987), 949. See also District of Columbia; March on Washington
Washington Daily News, 745
Washington "Disarmament" Conference (1921–1922), 731, 736
Washington Naval Treaty, termination of, 781
Washington Post, 608
WASP (white Anglo-Saxon Protestant) elite, 883
Waste disposal, 541; radioactive, 1011
Waste Land, The (Eliot), 721
Water: in cities, 541, 645; in West, 961
"Water cure," 622
Watergate, 925–928
Waterways. See Canals; specific river regions
Watson, Thomas Edward ("Tom"), 506, 508
Watts (Los Angeles), race riot in, 904
WAVES (Women Accepted for Volunteer Emergency Service), 803
"Waving the bloody shirt," 489, 498
Wealth: industrialization and, 528; industry and, 487, 524; in 1980s, 946; in post-Civil War South, 466; religion and, 552; Social Darwinism and, 525; in 21st century, 992; Veblen on, 638
Wealth Against Commonwealth (Lloyd), 638
Wealth gap, 526, 529, 992–996, 1011
Weapons: lend-lease and, 792; in Persian Gulf War, 959; sales to Iran, 950; U.N. inspectors of, 977; in World War I, 692; in World War II, 798, 820. See also Bombs and bombings; Nuclear weapons
Weapons of mass destruction (WMD), 965, 977
Weary Blues, The (Hughes), 719
Weaver, James B., 598; election of 1892 and, 505, 507 (map), 598
Weaver, Robert C., 902
Weber, David J., 605
Webster v. Reproductive Health Services, 954
Welch, James, 1010
Welch, Joseph, 866
Welfare programs: expenditures on (1930–2009), 999; Reagan and, 945; after World War II, 828
Welfare Reform Bill (1996), 968, 993
Welfare state: Europe models of, 676; female activism and, 646, 676; Progressives and, 662
Wells, David A., 492
Wells, H. G., 692
Wells, Ida B., 563, 564
Welty, Eudora, 886–887
"We Shall Overcome" (song), 903
West (region): Chinese immigrants in, 500; conservation and, 655; farming in, 586–588, 594–596; federal government and, 594; frontier and, 589–594, 605–606; homesteading in, 586–588; Latinos in, 1004; legends of, 567–568; majority-minority states in, 1004; mining in, 584–585; Native Americans in, 575–584; Populists in, 598; prohibition in, 704–705; railroads and, 515, 518, 587; ranching in, 585–586, 586 (map); sports in, 863; states in, 588–589;

woman suffrage in, 563, 563 (map), 585, 644; after World War II, 835. See also Southwest; Westward movement
West Bank, 907, 947, 970
Western Europe: communism and, 847; immigrants from, 542; NATO and, 850
Western front, in World War II, 816
West Germany, 845 (map), 846–847; Berlin Wall and, 891, 892; in NATO, 875. See also East Germany; Germany
West Indies, 668
Westinghouse air brake, 517
West Point, women in, 996
West Side Story (musical), 619
West Virginia (battleship), destruction of, 795
Westward movement, of sports, 863
Weyler y Nicolau, Valeriano ("Butcher"), 612, 622
Whaling, 523
Wharton, Edith, 567, 568, 720
Wheat, 588, 594, 734
Wheeler, Burton, 792
Wheeler, Joseph, 622
When Heaven and Earth Changed Places (Le Ly Hayslip), 894 (map)
Whiskey Ring, 490
Whistler, James, 568
Whistle-stop campaigns, 739
White, Richard, 605
White, William Allen, 641, 647, 662, 663
White citizens councils, 869
White-collar jobs, 550, 860, 991
White flight, 838; to suburbs, 932
Whitehead, Colson, 1009
Whiteman, Paul, 719
White man's burden, 620, 622
Whites: blacks and, 1006; freedmen and, 472; living standards for, 998; Plains Indians and, 576; resistance to black empowerment, 480; in South, 528; in suburbs, 1006
White supremacy: black political power and, 480; Johnson, Andrew, and, 469
Whitewater affair, 970
WHO (World Health Organization), 844
Who's Afraid of Virginia Woolf? (Albee), 886
Why Is There No Socialism in the United States? (Sombart), 642–643
Whyte, William H., Jr., 864
Wiebe, Robert H., 675
"Wild West" shows, 570, 571
Wiley, Harvey W., 640
Will, George, 962
Willard, Frances E., 646–647
Williams, Tennessee, 883
Williams, Venus and Serena, 997
Williams, William Appleman, 634, 697–698
Williams, William Carlos, 883
Wilson, Woodrow, 637, 661, 693; banking and, 665; on democracy, 1012; education of, 557; election of 1912 and, 661–663, 663 (map); election of 1916 and, 674–675, 675 (map); election of 1920 and, 696; foreign policy under, 667–671; Fourteen Points of, 679–680; globalization and, 842–843; as governor of New Jersey, 661; historians on, 697–698; idealism of, 679, 692, 697; neutrality and, 670–671, 672–673; at Paris Peace Conference, 692–693, 694; at Princeton, 664; progressivism under, 666–667; segregation and, 666; southern background of, 663–664; stroke of, 695; tariffs and, 664–665;

trusts and, 666; war message of (1917), 678, 679; women's suffrage and, 684
Wilson-Gorman Tariff (1894), 509, 605
Wilsonianism, 697–698
Windmills, 1011
Winesburg, Ohio (Anderson), 721
Wings of the Dove, The (James), 567
Wiretaps, illegal, 982
Wisconsin, progressive reforms in, 645
WITCH (Women's International Terrorist Conspiracy from Hell), 935
Witch hunt, red hunt as, 852–853
Wives, in labor force, 996
Wobblies. *See* Industrial Workers of the World
"Wolf packs," in World War II, 810
Woman's Christian Temperance Union (WCTU), 564, 646–647
Woman's Loyal League, 477
Woman's Rights Convention (Seneca Falls), 934
Woman suffrage: before Nineteenth Amendment, 563 (map); progressives and, 644; in selected nations, 684; during World War I, 683–684, 685
Woman suffrage movement, 562–563
Women: African American, 760, 762; in armed forces, 687; automobiles and, 713; bicycling and, 571, 572; black emancipation and, 476–477; in cities, 562–564; Civil Rights Act (1964) and, 900; in early 21st century, 1011; in factories, 803; as family heads, 1006; as flappers, 718; Gibson Girl image for, 528, 530; Grange and, 596–597; immigrant, 545, 547; Japanese, 800, 850; in Ku Klux Klan, 702; labor unions and, 533, 534, 535; in late 20th and early 21st centuries, 996–998; literary contributions of, 567, 568; marriage by, 995, 997; on mining frontier, 585; as missionaries, 623; in muckraking movement, 640, 641; Native American, 582; New Deal and, 776; in new industrial age, 528–529; new morality and, 559; in 1960s, 911; opportunities for, 922; in presidential race, 559; in progressive movement, 639, 645–647, 676; rights of, 929–932; in Roosevelt, Franklin, administration, 760, 762; in rural areas, 541; in sciences, 995; settlement house movement and, 549, 645; as Speaker of the House, 982; on Supreme Court, 953, 986; in sweatshops, 545; as telephone operators, 521; unequal wages for, 996; as vice presidential candidate, 947; voting and, 476–477, 562–563, 563 (map), 585, 685, 696, 996; in white-collar work, 861; in workforce, 527, 528, 549–550, 862; in workplace (1900–2000), 861; in World War I, 683–684, 687; after World War II, 829, 832, 836; in World War II, 803–804
Women and Economics (Gilman), 562
Women's Army Corps, 812
Women's Bureau, 645, 684
Women's club movement, 645
Women's movement, World War I and, 683–684
Women's organizations, 563; black women and, 563–564
Women's Peace Party, 644
Women's rights, march for, 935
Women's rights movement, Reconstruction and, 476–477

Women's Stride for Equality, 930
Women's Trade Union League, 645, 752
Wood, Leonard, 615, 620
Woodhull, Victoria, 559
Woodhull and Claflin's Weekly, 559
Woods, Tiger, 1007
Woodward, C. Vann, 510
Woodward, Margaret H., 997
Woolf, Virginia, 722, 723
Woolworth's, lunch counter sit-ins at, 869
Work day: eight-hour day, 533, 666; ten-hour day, 646, 648
Workers: in age of big business, 530–531; factory, 486; Mexican *braceros* as, 803; Mexicans as, 1002; in 1970s, 916; NRA and, 761; productivity of, 834; retirement age for, 999; skilled, 520, 533, 768; during World War I, 682–683; after World War II, 836; in World War II, 802–803, 804
Workers' compensation laws, 646
Workforce: characteristics of women in, 996; children in, 527, 528, 530, 531; ex-farmers in, 594–595; families in, 562; immigrants in, 547; in 1950s, 860–861; women in, 528–529, 545, 549–550, 645–646
Working class, 497, 537; in cities, 540–541; job and wage protection for, 530; women in, 528–529
Working conditions: in factory system, 645; industrialization and changes in, 530–531
Workingmen's Compensation Act (1916), 666
Workplace: employers' total control over, 646; safety in, 646; segregation in, 830–831; women in (1900–2000), 861
Works Progress Administration (WPA), 758, 759–760, 802
World Anti-Slavery Convention, 934
World Bank, 841, 842–843
World Court, 736, 759
World Power, U.S. as, 634
World's Columbian Exposition, 569–570
World Trade Center, terrorist attack on, 829, 974–975
World Trade Organization (WTO), 969
World War I (1914–1918), 637, 678–692; African Americans in, 683, 687; armistice in, 682, 691; casualties in, 688, 690, 691; civil liberties during, 681; draft in, 686–687; eastern front in, 687; economy in, 682, 685–686; events leading to, 670; exports to belligerents during (U.S.), 671; home front in, 680–686; literature after, 883; peace conference after, 692–694; propaganda in, 680–681; submarine warfare during, 672–674, 678; trade during, 671–672; U.S. entry into, 678–679; U.S. neutrality and, 670–671, 672; weapons purchases in, 692; western front in, 687–688, 688–691, 688 (map); women in, 683–684, 687
World War II (1939–1945), 798; African American migration during, 870; African Americans soldiers in, 805, 806; Allies in, 798, 811, 812; appeasement and, 784; Atlantic Charter in, 802; atomic bombings in, 820; cash-and-carry policy in, 785; casualties in, 788, 794, 810, 823; costs of (comparative), 823; D-Day in, 813–814; draft in, 787; economy in, 802–803, 807; end of,

821–824; events leading to, 780–785; fall of Japan in, 818–821; industry in, 802, 824; internal migration during, 804–805, 805 (map); Italian Americans in, 547; labor unions in, 802–803; lend-lease and, 791–792; medicine in, 821–824; military leadership in, 824; Nazi concentration camps in, 816–818; in Pacific region, 807–810, 811 (map); Pearl Harbor attack in, 637; phony war in, 785–786; second front in, 811–813; Soviet Union and, 811, 841; strikes in, 803; submarines in, 789, 792, 793–794; U.S. mainland in, 823, 824; U.S. entry into, 795; wartime conferences during, 793; workers in, 802–804
World Wide Web, 1010
Worster, Donald, 605
Wounded Knee, South Dakota: Battle of, 581; Indian seizure of, 933
Wright, Chauncey, 560
Wright, Frank Lloyd, 723, 882
Wright, Orville, 714
Wright, Richard, 886
Wright, Wilbur, 714
Writers. *See* Literature
Wu, David, 1004
Wyoming, 589, 658; Teapot Dome in, 732; woman suffrage in, 563, 563 (map), 585
Wyoming Stock-Growers Association, 586

Yale University, 663; women in, 996
Yalta Conference (1945), 839–840, 839 (i)
"Yankee Doodle Dandy," 689
Yankee Stadium, 711
Yellow-dog contracts, 531, 746, 761
Yellow fever, 616, 621
Yellow journalism, 558, 608, 612, 613; segregation of San Francisco schools and, 631
Yellow peril, 630, 1004
Yellowstone National Park, 590
Yeltsin, Boris, 957
Yiddish literature, after World War II, 887
Yom Kippur War, 924
York, Alvin C., 690
Yosemite Falls, 651
Yosemite National Park, 590, 654
Young, Andrew, 767, 933
Young Men's Christian Association (YMCA), 553
Young people: automobiles and, 713; movement to cities, 540; in 1920s, 718; poverty of, 999; pregnancy of, 998
Young Women's Christian Association (YWCA), 553
Youth culture, 889
YouTube, 1010
Yugoslavia: end of, 958; in Treaty of Versailles, 694; violence in former, 958, 980. *See also* Bosnia
Yuppies, 946

Zangwill, Israel, 550
Zen Buddhism, Beats and, 885
Zimbabwe. *See* Rhodesia
Zimmermann note, 678
Zola, Émile, 567
Zones, in Germany, 839, 845 (map)
Zoot suits, 806
Zulus, 593

Territorial Growth of the United States

1820 Date of states admission to the Union

● Geographic center of population by decade

CANADA

Lake Superior
Lake Michigan
Lake Huron
Lake Ontario
Lake Erie

St. Lawrence R.

MAINE 1820
VT. 1791
N.H.
MASS.
CONN.
R.I.

WISCONSIN 1848
MINNESOTA 1858
MICHIGAN 1837

NEW YORK

IOWA 1846

ILLINOIS 1818
INDIANA 1816
OHIO 1803

PENNSYLVANIA

MASON-DIXON LINE

THIRTEEN COLONIES

NEW JERSEY
DELAWARE 1790
MARYLAND

MISSOURI 1821
2010
36°30'N MISSOURI COMPROMISE LINE
ARKANSAS 1836

KENTUCKY 1792
WEST VIRGINIA 1863
VIRGINIA

THE ORIGINAL

THE ORIGINAL UNITED STATES
(By Treaty with Britain, 1783)

NORTH CAROLINA

TENNESSEE 1796

SOUTH CAROLINA

MISSISSIPPI 1817
ALABAMA 1819
GEORGIA

LOUISIANA 1812

(Seized from Spain, 1810, 1813)

ATLANTIC OCEAN

Mississippi R.

Gulf of Mexico

FLORIDA
(By Treaty with Spain, 1819)

FLORIDA 1845

BAHAMAS

CUBA

DOMINICAN REPUBLIC
HAITI

0   150   300 Km.
0   150   300 Mi.

PUERTO RICO
(Acquired from Spain, 1898)

VIRGIN IS.
(Acquired from Denmark, 1916–1917)

19°N
68°W
PUERTO RICO
VIRGIN ISLANDS
18°N
67°W
66°W
65°W

0   25   50 Km.
0   25   50 Mi.

GREENLAND
(DENMARK)

ICELAND

ALASKA
(U.S.)

CANADA

IRELAN

UNITED STATES

PORTUGAL

Azores
(Port.)

ATLANTIC OCEAN

Bermuda
(U.K.)

MO

WESTERN
SAHARA
(MOROCCO)

Midway Is.
(U.S.)

BAHAMAS

DOMINICAN REP.

MEXICO

CUBA

Virgin Is.
(U.S.)

ST. KITTS AND NEVIS
ANTIGUA AND BARBUDA
DOMINICA
BARBADOS

MAURITAN

Hawaiian Is.
(U.S.)

JAMAICA
BELIZE
HONDURAS

HAITI

Puerto Rico
(U.S.)

CAPE
VERDE

SENEGAL

PACIFIC OCEAN

GUATEMALA
EL SALVADOR

NICARAGUA

ST. LUCIA
GRENADA

ST. VINCENT AND
THE GRENADINES

GAMBIA

GUINEA-BISSAU

GUINEA

COSTA RICA

TRINIDAD AND TOBAGO

SIERRA
LEONE

I

C

PANAMA

VENEZUELA

GUYANA

LIBERIA

C
EQU

COLOMBIA

FR. GUIANA
(FRANCE)

Galapagos Is.
(Ecuador)

ECUADOR

SURINAM

SÃO TOMÉ

Equator

PERU

BRAZIL

SAMOA

French Polynesia
(France)

BOLIVIA

TONGA

PARAGUAY

20°S

Easter Is.
(Chile)

CHILE

URUGUAY

ARGENTINA

40°S

Falkland Is.
(U.K.)

60°S

| 0 | 1,000 | 2,000 Km. |
| 0 | 1,000 | 2,000 Mi. |

80°S

160°W   140°W   120°W   100°W   80°W   60°W   40°W   20°W

80°N   60°N   40°N   20°N   0°   20°S

C OCEAN

PACIFIC OCEAN

INDIAN OCEAN

RUSSIA

RWAY
FINLAND
SWEDEN
ESTONIA
LATVIA
LITHUANIA
BELARUS
RMANY POLAND
CZ.
SLK.
UKRAINE
AUS.
HUNG.
MOLDOVA
SLN. CR.
ROMANIA
ITALY
B. H.
SE.
MO.
K.
BULGARIA
ALBANIA
MAC.
GREECE
TURKEY
CYPRUS
ARMENIA
MALTA
LEBANON
SYRIA
TUNISIA
ISRAEL
IRAQ
JORDAN
KUWAIT

KAZAKHSTAN

MONGOLIA

N. KOREA
S. KOREA
JAPAN

UZBEKISTAN
KYRGYZSTAN
GEORGIA
TURKMENISTAN
TAJIKISTAN
AZERBAIJAN
AFGHANISTAN
PEOPLE'S REPUBLIC OF CHINA
IRAN
BAHRAIN
QATAR
PAKISTAN
BHUTAN
NEPAL
TAIWAN
LIBYA
EGYPT
SAUDI
ARABIA
UNITED
ARAB EMIRATES
OMAN
BANGLADESH
INDIA
MYANMAR
(BURMA)
LAOS
NIGER
CHAD
SUDAN
ERITREA
YEMEN
THAILAND
VIETNAM
CAMBODIA
(KAMPUCHEA)
PHILIPPINES
NIN
GERIA
DJIBOUTI
CENTRAL
AFRICAN REP.
SOUTH
SUDAN
ETHIOPIA
SRI LANKA
BRUNEI
DARUSSALAM
PALAU
CAMEROON
SOMALIA
MALDIVES
MALAYSIA
GABON
UGANDA
KENYA
SINGAPORE
NGO
RWANDA
DEM. REP.
OF CONGO
BURUNDI
TANZANIA
SEYCHELLES
ANGOLA
COMOROS
ZAMBIA
MALAWI
MADAGASCAR
NAMIBIA
ZIMBABWE
BOTSWANA
MAURITIUS
MOZAMBIQUE
SWAZILAND
SOUTH
AFRICA
LESOTHO

Mariana
Islands
(U.S.)
Guam
(U.S.)
Wake I.
(U.S.)
MARSHALL
ISLANDS

FEDERATED STATES
OF MICRONESIA

KIRIBATI

NAURU

INDONESIA
TIMOR LESTE
PAPUA
NEW
GUINEA
SOLOMON IS.

TUVALU

VANUATU

FIJI

New Caledonia
(France)

AUSTRALIA

NEW
ZEALAND

ABBREVIATIONS

AUS.	AUSTRIA
BEL.	BELGIUM
B. H.	BOSNIA AND HERZEGOVINA
CR.	CROATIA
CZ.	CZECH REPUBLIC
DEN.	DENMARK
HUNG.	HUNGARY
K.	KOSOVO
LUX.	LUXEMBOURG
MAC.	MACEDONIA
MO.	MONTENEGRO
NETH.	NETHERLANDS
SE.	SERBIA
SLK.	SLOVAKIA
SLN.	SLOVENIA
SWITZ.	SWITZERLAND

20°E   40°E   60°E   80°E   100°E   120°E   140°E   160°E